SUCCEEDING
IN THE WORLD OF WORK

Teachers

Log on to the **Online Learning Center** *through* **glencoe.com!**

Integrated Academics

- Academic Skills in the Workplace: English Language Arts, Mathematics, Science, Social Studies, World Languages
- Math in Action and Science in Action
- Math Appendix
- Academic Vocabulary Glossary

New Student Edition Features

- Reading Strategies and Assessments
- 21st Century Workplace
- Everyday Ethics
- Hot Jobs!
- Real-World Connection
- Tech Savvy
- Career Spotlight
- Unit Thematic Project with *BusinessWeek* Connection

Technology

- TeacherWorks™ Plus
- *ExamView® Assessment Suite*
- Interactive Chalkboard
- Interactive Student Edition
- Online Student Edition

D1174002

Online Learning Center

- Career Clusters Information
- Outside Reading Suggestions
- Chapter Practice Tests
- Chapter Games and Links
- Section Review Answers
- WebQuest Links
- Podcasts
- Standardized Test Practice

GAYLE CARMODY
MEREDITH PRESS

Teacher Wraparound Edition

Teacher Manual

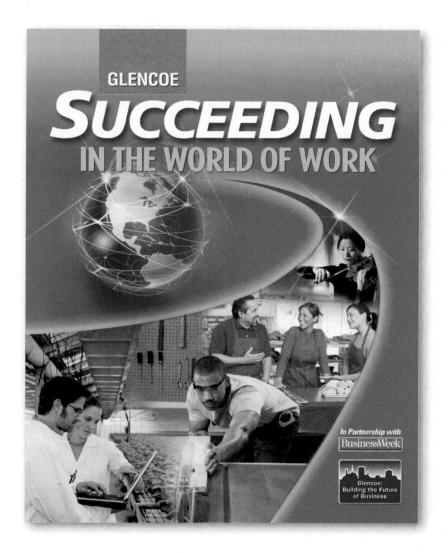

Grady Kimbrell
Educational Consultant
Santa Barbara, California

Ben S. Vineyard
Professor and Chairman Emeritus
Vocational and Technical Education
Pittsburg State University
Pittsburg, Kansas

Glencoe

New York, New York   Columbus, Ohio   Chicago, Illinois   Woodland Hills, California

CARLYLE CAMPBELL LIBRARY
MEREDITH COLLEGE

CC
64
G48K
2008

Our Partner at McGraw-Hill

BusinessWeek

BusinessWeek is the leading global resource for ground-breaking business news and news analysis that offers essential insight into the real world of business. *BusinessWeek* is the world's most widely read business magazine, with more than eight million readers each week, including online and television viewers.

Notice: Information on featured companies, organizations, and their products and services is included for educational purposes only and does not present or imply endorsement of the *Succeeding in the World of Work* program.

 Glencoe

The *McGraw·Hill* Companies

Copyright © 2008 by The McGraw-Hill Companies, Inc. All rights reserved. Except as permitted under the United States Copyright Act, no part of this publication may be reproduced or distributed in any form or by any means, or stored in a database or retrieval system, without prior written permission of the publisher.

Printed in the United States of America.

Send all inquiries to:
Glencoe/McGraw-Hill
21600 Oxnard Street, Suite 500
Woodland Hills, CA 91367

ISBN: 978-0-07-874828-8   (Student Edition)
MHID: 0-07-874828-3   (Student Edition)
ISBN: 978-0-07-877167-5   (Teacher Wraparound Edition)
MHID: 0-07-877167-6   (Teacher Wraparound Edition)

2 3 4 5 6 7 8 9   027/043   12 11 10 09 08

CARL FILE CAMPBELL LIBRARY
MEREDITH COLLEGE

Contributing Writers, Reviewers, and Industry Advisory Board

Contributing Writers

Brian Bachtel
Career Based Intervention Coordinator
Lake Shore Compact-Mentor Schools
Mentor, OH

Betty Jo Wimmer, Ed.D., NCC
Career Development Coordinator
Middle Creek High School
Apex, NC

Educational Reviewers

We wish to acknowledge the contributions of the following reviewers:

Patrick L. Atchley
Business Education Teacher and
    Cooperative Education Coordinator
Urbana High School
Urbana, IL

Teresa Beatty
Department Head, Business, Medical
    and Accounting
ECPI College of Technology
Newport News, VA

Dr. Shirl A. Barker
Purdue University
West Lafayette, IN

Annie Hunter Clasen
Program Manager/Instructor
Learey Technical Center
Tampa, FL

Cheryl I. Cooper
Instructor
Southeast Career Center
Columbus, OH

Arlene Dupree
Career Technology Instructor
Southern Oklahoma Technology Center/
    Ardmore High School
Ardmore, OK

Karen Ann Altfilisch Ellis
Career & Technology Education Director
Denver Public Schools
Lakewood, CO

Barbara Martin Greene
Business and Marketing Teacher
Briggs High School
Columbus, OH

Penny D. Guthrie
Business and Information Technology
    Instructor
High Plains Technology Center
Woodward, OK

Debbie Hartley-Fischer
Student Educational Opportunities
    Coordinator
Northeast Career Center
Columbus, OH

Terri Huddleston
Business Instructor
Sapulpa High School
Sapulpa, OK

Margaret Kaste, MS
Guidance Director
Alternative Education–Riverview L.C.
Volusia County School Board
Daytona Beach, FL

Gary L. Schepf
SITE Coordinator/Advanced & Applied
    Technology
The Academy of Irving ISD
Irving, TX

Sheila E. Scott
Supervisor, Curriculum Development &
    Instructional Support
Columbus Public Schools
Columbus, OH

Business and Career Education Industry Advisory Board

Peggy Bradfield
Vons, A Safeway Co.
Burbank, CA

Andy Chaves
Marriott International Inc.
Washington, DC

Mike De Fabio
Otis Spunkmeyer
Torrance, CA

Brian Dunn
J.D. Power and Associates
Westlake Village, CA

Donna Farrugia
Carrie Nebens
Robert Half International
Westlake Village, CA

Mark Hatch
Ohio Association of Public School
    Employees
Columbus, OH

Mike Kulis
The Sherwin-Williams Co.
Cleveland, OH

Dr. David M. Mitchell
Johnson & Wales University
Providence, RI

Debbie Moreton
J.C. Penney Co., Inc.
Dallas, TX

Joyce Winterton
USA Today
McLean, VA

Succeeding in the World of Work contains a wealth of information. The trick is to know where to look to access all the information in the book. Guide students through the Treasure Hunt, located on page iv of the Student Edition, to preview the text and help them understand its organization.

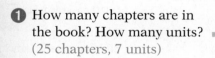

Treasure Hunt

Succeeding in the World of Work contains a wealth of information. The trick is to know where to look to access all the information in the book. If you go on the Treasure Hunt with your teacher, you will discover how the textbook is organized, and how to get the most out of your reading and study time. Let's go!

❶ How many chapters are in the book? How many units? (25 chapters, 7 units)

❷ What part of the textbook will show you where homeowners insurance is taught? (Index)

❸ Where do you find the WebQuest Internet Project? (on a unit opener page)

❹ What business is featured in the Unit 1 Creative Business Practices? Where do you first find the business name? (the Table of Contents or the unit itself)

❺ If you need help with one of the math applications, where would you look? (Math Appendix)

❻ Where can you find the definitions of **globalization, résumé,** and **economics**? (Key Terms Glossary)

❼ What skill do you practice in Chapter 13, Section 13.1, After You Read? (Mathematics)

❽ Where do you find a Unit Thematic Project? (at the end of a unit)

❾ What is the URL that takes you to the *Succeeding in the World of Work* Online Learning Center? (glencoe.com)

Teacher Manual Contents

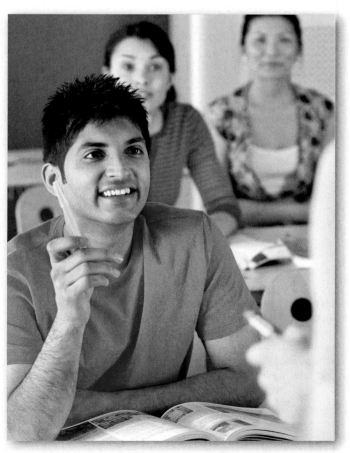

Connect Students to the Community

Units

The twenty-five chapters in *Succeeding in the World of Work* are organized in seven units, each with its own theme. Unit activities show you the "big picture," by providing activities and interviews that bring life to the world of work. The unit opener introduces the Unit Thematic Project.

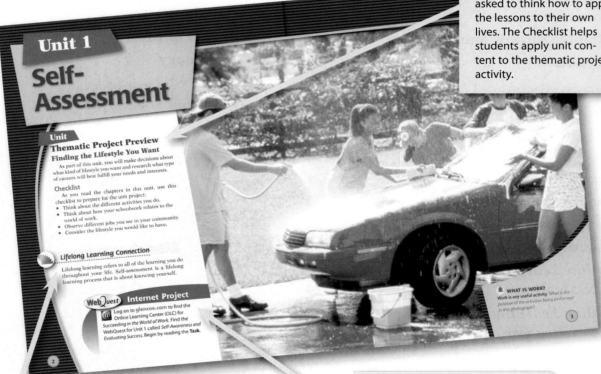

Thematic Project Preview
This unit activity will introduce students to an issue or situation they will face as they prepare to enter the world of work. They will be asked to think how to apply the lessons to their own lives. The Checklist helps students apply unit content to the thematic project activity.

Lifelong Learning Connection
This feature connects the content of the unit with lifelong learning strategies and concepts: self-assessment; setting goals and making decisions; your career plan and career path; academics, school, and other formal training; community and civic involvement; technology skills; interpersonal communication skills; and life skills (the skills you need to cope with everyday life).

WebQuest Internet Project
In this activity, students will use their technology skills to investigate and produce a project related to topics in the unit. Their starting point is found on the Online Learning Center through **glencoe.com**.

and to **Real-World Careers**

Thematic Project

Each Unit concludes with a Thematic Project that explores an important issue in the world of work. To complete each project, students will evaluate their resources, conduct research, preview a real-world company profile, and report their findings.

Six Steps
There are six steps in each Thematic Project. Step 1 sends students to the *Succeeding in the World of Work* OLC through **glencoe.com** for a graphic organizer to use to list the skills and resources they will need to complete the activity.

Real-World Company Profile
Step 2 features an interview with an employee of a real-world company. The profile provides practical answers on how the company manages all aspects of industry. (See page TM57.)

Research, Connect, Report
Steps 3, 4, and 5 guide students through researching procedures, connecting to the community, and reporting their findings.

Self Evaluation
Students can go to the *Succeeding in the World of Work* OLC to download a printable Rubric for self-evaluation. You can also use the rubric for teacher evaluation or student-peer evaluation.

BusinessWeek Connection
BusinessWeek is the world's most widely read business magazine. Go to the OLC through **glencoe.com** to access a *BusinessWeek* article related to the aspect of industry described in this feature.

Chapters

The chapters of *Succeeding in the World of Work* are organized around issues and strategies that relate to the world of work and lifelong learning. They are divided logically into two sections, and offer numerous learning strategies that will help your students get the most from their studies.

Chapter Objectives
The Chapter Objectives preview the content students will learn.

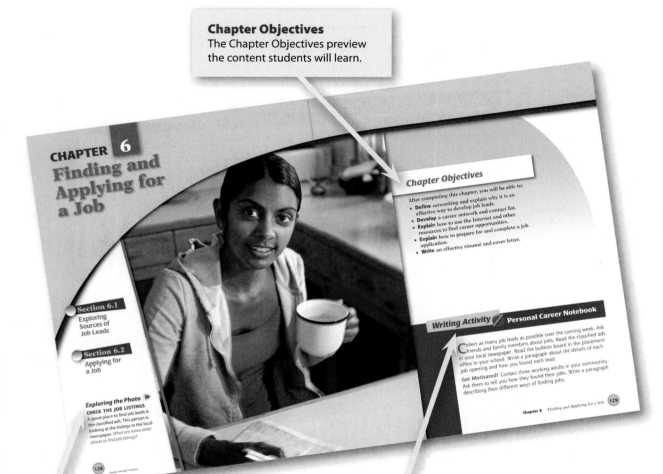

Exploring the Photo
The chapters begin with a photo that visually illustrates chapter content and a caption that asks students a question designed to help them to start thinking about what they will read.

Writing Activity
The Personal Career Notebook asks students to relate to their own background knowledge of chapter subject, make predictions, and record other thoughts related to the chapter subject. Get Motivated! asks students to interact with or research a person or organization in their community regarding the chapter subject.

Chapter Review & Activities

The Chapter Review & Activities allow your students to practice their skills and reinforce understanding of key concepts in the chapter.

Review
Section Summaries, Key Terms and Academic Vocabulary Review, Review Key Concepts, and Critical Thinking provide comprehension review and assessment.

Real-World Skills and Applications
Helps students to develop strong workplace, communication, and technology skills as well as lifelong learning skills such as financial literacy. Students can also participate in role plays and "learn by doing."

Writing Skills Practice
Students will practice and apply different types of writing.

Academic Skills in the Workplace
Opportunities are provided for students to apply content to academics.

Standardized Test Practice
The Standardized Practice and Test-Taking Tip are designed to provide practice and address the practical aspects of taking standardized tests.

Net Connection
Students are given an opportunity to practice their Internet and other technology application skills.

Personal Academic and Career Portfolio
Helps students develop and maintain a portfolio that they can use to keep track of academic and career growth.

Sections

Each chapter section begins with a Reading Guide to preview section content.

Reading Guide
The section objectives, main idea, key concepts, and vocabulary are previewed here.

Before You Read
A pre-reading question or statement will help students make a personal connection to content.

Academic Standards
Academic standards are integrated into text content.

Graphic Organizer
A graphic organizer gives a visual tool to help students organize and remember new content. You and your students can download printable graphic organizers from the *Succeeding in the World of Work* OLC through **glencoe.com**.

Reading Strategies

Structured *before, during,* and *after* reading strategies, designed to enrich your students' reading skills.

Organize the Work Area

You have learned strategies for using your time effectively. What else can you do to work faster and better? You can organize the things in your work area. No matter how skilled you are at your job, you can work more efficiently if you can find the tools or materials you need quickly.

Put Everything in Its Place

One rule for organizing a work area is the *near-far rule*. This means that you should place the things you use most often near you and those you use seldom farther away. For example, plumbers often carry a toolbox. The toolbox contains the tools of the trade they use most frequently. The tools they seldom use they keep in the truck.

A second guideline is to put similar things together. Keep files, supplies, and tools used for one type of job together.

Decide how you are going to store the items you use. You might use boxes, drawers, or files. Be sure to label your storage containers. If you have lots of boxes or files, alphabetize them, group them by content, or organize them in some other way. Doing this will enable you to find things easily.

Neatness Counts

Neatness can also save you time. Take time occasionally to put your work area back in order. Return tools to their correct places. Tidy and reorganize your desk. This way, you will not have to spend time searching for things.

✓ Reading Check IDENTIFY What are some strategies for organizing your work space?

As You Read
Explain What are the advantages of organizing your work space?

As You Read
As You Read provides a cue to connect students' background knowledge to what students are reading.

Reading Check
Reading Check allows students to make a quick comprehension self-check.

Section 1.1 After You Read

Review Key Concepts
1. Give one example each of a job, an occupation, and a career.
2. Give an example of a skill that might be used in a specific job.
3. Describe a situation that might cause a person to change his or her main reason for working.

Practice Academic Skills
Mathematics
4. Most Americans spend more than 30% of their yearly income on housing expenses. If you earn $27,000 per year, how much money will you need to spend on housing?

THEORY Multiply Decimals by Whole Numbers A percent is a ratio that compares a number to 100. To multiply with percentages:
Step 1: You can rewrite the percent (30%) as a fraction with a denominator of 100. Convert the fraction to a decimal.
Step 2: Multiply this decimal by the number ($27,000). Remember to put the decimal point in the correct place in your answer.

Math For math help, go to the Math Appendix located at the back of this book.

After You Read
Review Key Concepts helps students organize and process their understanding of what you have read. Practice Academic Skills connects content to academics.

Features

The features in each chapter help students see the relevance between the classroom and the world of work.

The 21st Century Workplace
This feature introduces students to a concept or gives students expanded information about today's global 21st century workplace, including information about languages across cultures, diversity, and other modern workplace practices.

The 21st Century Workplace

¿Cómo se dice esto en español?
(How do you say that in Spanish?)

In today's global workplace, there are opportunities in many jobs and industries to work with people who speak Spanish. The Spanish language ranks third in the world in number of speakers, after Chinese and English. It is the official language of Spain, Mexico, Cuba, Puerto Rico, the countries of Central America, and the majority of countries in South America. In addition, according to the U.S. Department of Labor, by 2050, one quarter of all Americans will be of Hispanic origin.

CRITICAL THINKING
In what ways might the changing American population affect consumer goods and services?

In Your Community
If there is another population in your community that speaks a language other than English, identify some common phrases you think would ... with your class in ...

COMMON SPANISH WORDS AND PHRASES

hello	hola
good day	buenos días
goodbye	adiós/que vaya bien
yes	sí
no	no
please	por favór
How are you?	¿Cómo está usted?
good	bien
thank you	muchas gracias
you're welcome	De nada

Extend Your Learning Spanish dialects can vary according to country, region, or even city. For Web links about dialects, go to this book's OLC through glencoe.com.

Everyday Ethics
The ethics feature gives students an opportunity to explore ethical challenges and choices that relate to the workplace. Students are given a real-world scenario and asked to make a decision about what action they would take. Students are then encouraged to discuss the scenario and their decision with others.

Everyday ETHICS

CALLING IN SICK

Is it ever okay to tell a lie?

VACATION DAYS You recently started a new job at an office supply store. You can't take vacation days until you have been there for three months, but you can take sick days whenever you need them. Before you got your job, you and your friends had planned to go to the beach tomorrow. You really want to go since you have not been able to hang out with your friends much since you started your job.

What Would You Do? Will you lie to your boss and say you are sick so you can go to the beach?

Will the lie hurt anyone? If it does not hurt anyone, is it okay to lie? Write a half-page journal entry explaining your decision.

DISCUSS IT Lying often has consequences you cannot predict. For instance, what if the store is suddenly busy? Is it fair for the store manager to do all the work herself when she is paying you to help her? What if she finds out you went to the beach? How does that affect your reputation? Brainstorm the possible consequences of calling in sick and going to work and share them with the class.

Creative Business Practices
These business profiles offer examples of real-world businesses that demonstrate innovative workplace, community, and leadership trends.

Creative Business Practices

PATAGONIA   Exploring Opportunities

Patagonia, Inc., a company that makes outdoor and adventure sports gear, encourages employees to have adventures of their own. The company provides endangered paid leave for employees who want to work as interns with nonprofit groups, such wilderness projects that help save endangered species. During internships, Patagonia employees receive their regular salary and benefits for up to 60 days. Patagonia employees have worked on projects such as the Chumbe Island Project, which encourages coral reef protection, and the Mist Preservation Society, which helps preserve the subtropical forests of New Zealand.

The Patagonia internship program benefits everyone involved. Nonprofit groups benefit from the experience of talented volunteers, employees get time away from the office to make a difference in the world, and Patagonia gets to support worthy efforts.

CRITICAL THINKING If you had the opportunity to take part in Patagonia's internship program, which programs would interest you? Why?

 Connect to the Real World To read more about Patagonia, visit the company's Web site via the link on this book's Online Learning Center through glencoe.com.

Math In Action

Calculate Pay

Esteban is deciding between two job offers. One pays $13.00 an hour for 50 hours a week; the other pays $15.50 an hour for 40 hours a week. Esteban wants to spend more time with his family, so he will probably choose the second job. If he does, how much less will he make each year?

Starting Hint: Calculate how much he will make in each job per year before you calculate the difference in pay.

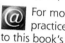 For more math practice go to this book's OLC through **glencoe.com**.

Science In Action

Temperature

Many scientific processes use the Celsius scale to measure temperature, while the general U.S. public uses the Fahrenheit scale. Convert 68° Fahrenheit to degrees Celsius. Round to the closest whole number. The conversion formula is $°C = \frac{5}{9}[(°F)-(32°F)]$.

Starting Hint: Start the conversion by filling in the variables you know in the formula, degrees Fahrenheit (°F): $°C = \quad [(°68)-(32°F)]$.

 For more science practice, go to this book's OLC through **glencoe.com**.

Math in Action
This brief practical math activity includes a Starting Hint and a directive to the OLC.

Science in Action
This brief practical science activity includes a Starting Hint and a directive to the OLC.

Career Checklist
This simple checklist contains general tips related to the chapter topic.

Career ✓ Checklist

When Entering the Workplace:

✓ Define your goals.
✓ Stay informed of changes in the workplace.
✓ Expect the best from yourself and others.
✓ Maintain a positive attitude.
✓ Learn from your mistakes.
✓ Take advantage of every opportunity to learn.

Hot Jobs!
A brief introduction to an interesting job in one of the 16 career clusters. Exploring careers can help students set goals that can lead them to career success.

HOT JOBS!

Speech Therapist

Speech therapists work with people who have difficulty with speech, language, communication, swallowing, and fluency. For example, a speech therapist might work with someone who has a stutter or someone who wishes to eliminate an accent. This job requires attention to detail, good communication skills, and knowledge of speech-related disorders.

Real-World Connection
A real-world anecdote or passage that deals with issues regarding school, the workplace, or other aspects of life-long learning.

Real-World Connection

Career Mentors

You love the outdoors and want a career that will let you work outside. Your school counselor recently announced that you are a finalist for a scholarship in computer science, based on your high test scores in a programming class. You do not see how a technology major will be compatible with your goal to work outdoors.

Critical Thinking How can you pursue a technology major and still remain true to your lifestyle goals?

Do Your Own Research Find an adult who works outdoors and has agreed to mentor students. Talk with your school counselor, career development coordinator, or work-based learning coordinator if you need help locating someone appropriate. Conduct an informational interview with the mentor, and include questions about the role of technology in his or her job.

Tech Savvy
Helps students build their technological literacy, outlining technology, Internet, and e-commerce trends, products, or issues related to both academics and career. Students are directed to the OLC to expand and apply their knowledge of the trend.

TechSavvy

Evaluating Web Sites

Imagine that you are thinking of pursuing several different careers and you want to use the Internet to research the future demand for a job that interests you. How can you determine which Web sites have good and reliable information?

Government sites are often a good source of information, but you should always evaluate any information you read. To evaluate a Web site, ask: Who is giving you the information? Is the information accurate, thorough, free from bias, and up-to-date? A librarian may be able to help you find the answers to these questions.

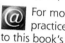 Visit this book's OLC through **glencoe.com** and find a link to the U.S. Bureau of Labor Statistics Web site. Research the current five-year career outlook for three jobs that interest you. Write a half-page summary of each job outlook, and explain whether you think it would be worthwhile to pursue these careers.

Career Spotlight

This feature offers a profile of a real-world worker. The jobs are aligned across the U.S. Department of Education's 16 career clusters. Career clusters are groups of similar occupations and industries. The career clusters were developed as a way to help individuals identify their career interest areas and to help them develop career plans. By studying and becoming familiar with career clusters, students can learn about the range of jobs and careers available in today's 21ˢᵗ century global workplace.

Career Facts

This part of the Career Spotlight offers more detailed information about the career profiled in the Career Spotlight Interview, including information on education and training, academic skills required, technology needed, workplace safety, and possible career paths for that job or other jobs within that career cluster. A **career path** is like a road map that includes all of the jobs and experiences that are needed in order to work toward a specific career goal.

Career Spotlight Interview

The interview gives the student a picture of the responsibilities of and requirements for the person's job.

Academic Skills

This table details the academic skills needed to perform the specific tasks required for the job featured in the interview.

Personal Academic and Career Portfolio

A personal academic and career portfolio is a collection of information about a person, including documents, projects, and work samples that show a person's skills, talents, and qualifications. It includes information about interests, goals, and accomplishments, as well as information needed for a job search. Students can use their portfolios throughout their careers to keep track of their goals and accomplishments.

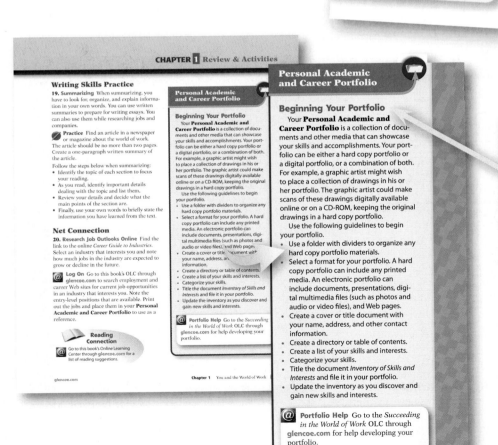

The **Personal Academic and Career Portfolio** margin callout points out activities or information in chapter text that students may wish to add to their portfolios. This information can help them develop and maintain a personal academic and career portfolio that they can use to keep track of their academic and career growth.

Personal Academic and Career Portfolio

Go to the chapter review to find guidelines for creating your own **Personal Academic and Career Portfolio.**

Preparing a R

A **résumé** is a brief summ mation, education, skills, we ests. When you are applying f employer by regular mail, e-m an interview. A poorly written hand, may ruin your chance make yourself look good to a

A good first step is to choos you will emphasize, and how your résumé. Avoid any negati experience, focus on the skil Include awards, hobbies, or a indicate that you will provide tion in a folder in your **Person** Refer to this folder when crea

The **Personal Academic and Career Portfolio** activity in each chapter review gives students guidelines that can help them create, develop, and maintain specific parts of their portfolios. A directive to the Online Learning center provides extra guidance.

Assessment

Succeeding in the World of Work features end-of-section and end-of-chapter review and activities. The varied assessments enable you and your students to evaluate understanding.

Section Assessment

Each section ends with a review and academic questions.

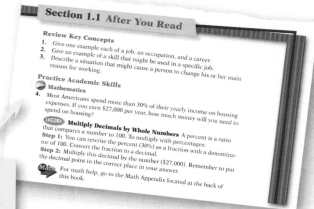

Section 1.1 After You Read

Review Key Concepts
1. Give one example each of a job, an occupation, and a career.
2. Give an example of a skill that might be used in a specific job.
3. Describe a situation that might cause a person to change his or her main reason for working.

Practice Academic Skills
Mathematics
4. Most Americans spend more than 30% of their yearly income on housing expenses. If you earn $27,000 per year, how much money will you need to spend on housing?

THEORY Multiply Decimals by Whole Numbers A percent is a ratio that compares a number to 100. To multiply with percentages:
Step 1: You can rewrite the percent (30%) as a fraction with a denominator of 100.
Step 2: Convert the fraction to a decimal. Multiply this decimal by the number ($27,000). Remember to put the decimal point in the correct place in your answer.

Math For math help, go to the Math Appendix located at the back of this book.

After You Read
Assess comprehension with Review Key Concepts questions. Connect content to academics with the Academic Skills questions.

Chapter Review & Activities
The Chapter Review & Activities contains a variety of assessments.

Real-World Skills and Applications
These activities help students develop strong workplace, communication, and technology skills as well as lifelong learning skills such as financial literacy.

Section Summaries
Restate the main concepts of each section.

Key Terms and Academic Vocabulary Review
Includes Key Terms taught in the text. Academic Vocabulary helps students learn words that they will see in their reading and on tests.

CHAPTER 1 Review & Activities

CHAPTER SUMMARY
Section 1.1
You should consider your interests and skills when planning your career. A job is work that people do for pay, an occupation is the type of work you do, and a career is a series of related jobs built on a person's interests, knowledge, training, and experience. Your lifestyle is the way you use your time, energy, and resources. Your work affects your lifestyle. Four important reasons people work are to earn money, to fulfill wants and needs, to be around other people, to contribute to society, and for self-fulfillment.

Section 1.2
The global economy refers to the ways in which the world's economies are linked. It affects what kinds of jobs will be available. You will need basic skills, thinking skills, personal qualities, and adaptability to meet the demands of the global job market. Other workplace trends include the use of technology, diversity, the use of teams, outsourcing, and telecommuting. In the United States, most new jobs are predicted to be in the service-producing industries. When looking for careers, you need to be aware of economic, technological, and workplace trends, job outlook, and personal job satisfaction.

Key Terms and Academic Vocabulary Review
1. Use each of these key terms and academic vocabulary words in a sentence.

Key Terms
▶ interests (p. 7)
▶ skills (p. 7)
▶ transferable skills (p. 7)
▶ job (p. 9)
▶ occupation (p. 9)
▶ career (p. 9)
▶ lifestyle (p. 10)

▶ economy (p. 15)
▶ global economy (p. 15)
▶ job market (p. 15)
▶ outsourcing (p. 17)
▶ telecommute (p. 17)
▶ team (p. 17)
▶ lifelong learning (p. 21)

Academic Vocabulary
▶ specific (p. 7)
▶ determine (p. 10)
▶ environment (p. 10)
▶ economic (p. 15)

Review Key Concepts
2. **Define** a job, an occupation, and a career. Give an example of each.
3. **Describe** how skills, interests, and desired lifestyle may shape career plans.
4. **Explain** how work life affects lifestyle.
5. **List** some of the reasons that people work.
6. **List** factors that affect today's workplace.
7. **Explain** why it is important to evaluate job outlooks when making career plans.

Critical Thinking
8. **Compare and Contrast** In what ways might a decrease or increase in income affect aspects of your lifestyle?
9. **Evaluate** What is the value of observing changes in the world of work, even when you may not be working full-time for a while?

24 Unit 1 Self-Assess

Real-World Skills and Applications

Interpersonal and Collaborative Skills
10. **Working in Teams** Team up with one or more classmates. Identify a number of jobs in the Arts, Audio/Video Technology, and Communications career cluster. Choose one of these jobs and create a five-minute presentation that features some of the skills, training, and technology that is needed to perform this job. Your presentation might use software, visual aids, or brief skits.

Technology Applications
11. **Creating a Spreadsheet** You are in charge of the equipment for a 16-member soccer team. You must record the type of equipment the team purchases, such as balls, shoes, towels, and uniforms, as well as when each piece of equipment was ordered and received. Use spreadsheet software to create a document that can list and categorize all the equipment.

Financial Literacy Skills
12. **Determining Your Financial Situation** To figure out your personal financial situation, start by making a list of items that relate to your finances: savings, monthly income (job earnings, allowance), monthly expenses (money you spend), and debts (money you owe to others). Use a notebook, a spreadsheet, or another document to categorize your expenses over a set period of time, such as a week or a month.
Log On Go to this book's Online Learning Center through glencoe.com for help with financial literacy.

13. **ACTIVE LEARNING Brainstorming and Sharing Information** Take one minute to brainstorm skills you might use in the classroom that you might also use at a service job, such as a checker at a grocery store. Team up with a classmate and share your answers verbally for two to three minutes. Volunteer to share both of your answers with the class. Take notes on all the skills that are mentioned.

14. **ROLE PLAY Career Counseling Visit**
Situation You have been employed by the U.S. Department of Labor to help students understand the importance of transferable skills. For your job, you are required to visit high school classrooms across the country to deliver presentations and answer questions. You hope to encourage students to broaden their horizons by developing their transferable skills.
Activity Make a five- to ten-minute presentation about transferable skills within a career that interests you. Use presentation software or other visual aids to describe different transferable skills. Be prepared to answer questions that other students pose about your presentation.
Evaluation You will be evaluated on how well you meet the following performance indicators:
■ Explain a variety of transferable skills.
■ Provide specific and comprehensive information about skills.
■ Effectively handle a question-and-answer session.

25

Review Key Concepts
These questions review student comprehension.

Critical Thinking
These questions ask you to think more deeply to relate text to real situations.

Active Learning
Here students have an opportunity to "learn by doing," either on their own or as part of a team.

Role Play
Role-play scenarios provide practice for real-world situations as well as competitive events. Performance evaluation information is included.

Academic Skills in the Workplace
These activities provide students with practice applying English Language Arts, Mathematics, Science, Social Studies, and World Languages skills to workplace-related content.

Writing Skills Practice
Here students will practice different types of writing and writing skills.

Personal Academic and Career Portfolio
Each chapter portfolio activity gives guidelines on developing and maintaining sections of and documents for students' **Personal Academic and Career Portfolios**.

Standardized Test Practice
These activities provide students with an opportunity to sharpen their test-taking skills. The activities also includes a valuable Test-Taking Tip.

Net Connection
This activity gives students the opportunity to practice their Internet and other technology application skills.

Choose Proven Teaching Solutions

Units

Units begin with well-organized, easy-to-reference pages preceding each unit of the student edition.

Overview
Chapter Titles and Chapter Objectives give you a preview of unit content.

Resources
A key is provided for coded teaching strategies, leveled instruction, and print and digital resources.

Unit Overview
Introduce the unit with chapter summaries. Out of Time? helps you adjust to varied class schedules.

TeacherWorks Resources
A list of print resources offered on the TeacherWorks software is included.

Build Background
Questions are suggested to activate students' prior knowledge of the main chapter themes.

Unit Thematic Project Preview
Introduces the topic of the project students will complete at the end of the unit and prompts students to think more deeply about the project.

Extend the Photo
Provides an answer to the question posed in the Student Edition as well as providing prompts for discussion.

for Effective Results

FOCUS: Six Steps
This lesson features a four-step teaching plan with teaching strategies for each step of the project.

Spotlight on Technology
Explores how technology is integrated into today's workplace.

TEACH: Research, Connect, Report
Steps 3, 4, and 5 guide students through researching procedures, connecting to the community, and reporting their findings.

TEACH: Real-World Company Profile
Step 2 provides practical answers on how a real-world company manages all aspects of industry.

Developing Industry Partners
Suggestions on how to integrate industry and business partners into the Career Education classroom.

ASSESS and CLOSE
Students are directed to evaluate their projects. A culminating activity is also provided.

BusinessWeek Connection
BusinessWeek is the world's most widely read business magazine. Students are directed to the OLC to access a *BusinessWeek* article related to the aspect of industry described in this feature.

Chapters

Chapters in *Succeeding in the World of Work* are organized around the major topics that relate to today's workplace as well as to future workers and lifelong learners. Each chapter has two sections.

Planning Guide
A list of features and follow-up activities in the chapter, including the Before You Read, As You Read, and After You Read reading strategies.

Correlations
A list of all the No Child Left Behind correlations in the chapter.

Review the Objectives
Chapter Objectives tell how students will be able to demonstrate newly acquired knowledge.

Chapter Overview
Here you will find Introduce the Chapter, a short summary of chapter content and main ideas, as well as Build Background, with suggestions for accessing prior knowledge.

Exploring the Photo
Answer and discussion ideas will enable you to lead students to visually connect their own experiences to the chapter content. A follow-up prompt is given to elicit further discussion.

Classroom Resources
All chapter print and technology resources are listed here to help you plan your lessons.

Writing Activity
Guidelines on how to evaluate and facilitate this activity.

Answer Key
Answers and answer suggestions for the Chapter Review & Activities begin here.

Standardized Test Practice
Here you will find talking points on strategies for Standardized Test success.

Personal Academic and Career Portfolio
Suggestions, tips, and examples for portfolio content are featured here, as well as a guideline for assessing student portfolios.

WorkKeys™
WorkKeys is a job skills assessment program. This directs you to the Teacher Center at the Online Learning Center to find links to information on leveled assessment for Communication Skills, Problem-Solving Skills, and Interpersonal Skills.

Sections

Each chapter has two sections, each with a six-part **Glencoe Classroom Management Plan.** Each lesson features teaching suggestions, both guided practice and independent practice activities, background information, point-of-use teaching strategies, leveled activities for differentiated instruction, and answer keys. Bracketed letters on the reduced student edition pages correspond to teaching strategies in the Teacher Wraparound Edition, showing you exactly where to use the teaching strategies and activities.

FOCUS

A Bell Ringer Activity begins the lesson, then **Preteaching** activities assure that all students have the same background and preparation.

D Coded strategies such as the Develop Concepts activity connect learning activities to content. The bracketed annotation on the student page shows you the related text. Develop Concepts activities use various strategies to help you gauge and plan for students' concept development.

TEACH

This part of the lesson provides suggestions for discussion, reading activities, answers to questions on each page, guided skills practice, and resource suggestions.

R Reading Strategy activities help you teach reading skills and vocabulary.

U Universal Access activities provide strategies to reach all types of learners in the classroom. These activities may or may not have brackets.

S Skill Practice activities provide guided and independent practice and leveled instruction to reach students at all ability levels.

W Writing Support provides independent and guided writing practice to help students understand the text.

ASSESS

Review opportunities enable you to evaluate your students' needs.

RETEACH

Different activities are provided to reinforce lesson content. The variety of activities provided in RETEACH allows your students to assimilate knowledge using their varied learning styles. Questions are designed to help students apply and extend what they learned.

ASSESS

Re-evaluate student comprehension with varied assignments. Answers for the After You Read section review are provided.

CLOSE

Provides a Culminating Activity designed to use new knowledge in an independent assignment. The CLOSE activity helps students make the connection between what they read and its meaning and application to the real world.

Explore Teaching Solutions

Print Resources

Student Activity Workbook with Academic Integration

The *Student Activity Workbook with Academic Integration* includes a variety of activities for each chapter in the text. Completed activities that students may wish to add to their **Personal Academic and Career Portfolios** are labeled, as are activities that correspond to skills and competencies.

- Note Taking
- Academics
  - English Language Arts, including content vocabulary and academic vocabulary
  - Mathematics
  - Science
  - Social Studies
- Study Skills
- Test Prep
- Test Taking
- Real-World Application

The Teacher Annotated Edition of the Student Activity Workbook includes cyan annotated answers to all of the student activities.

Fast File Unit Resources

These booklets provide teaching materials and student activities to reinforce content.

Teacher Materials
- Lesson Plans
- Chapter Resources
- Answer Keys

- **Personal and Academic Career Portfolio Project** Student Rubrics

Student Materials
- Graphic Organizers
- Chapter Summaries with Key Terms and Academic Vocabulary (English and Spanish)
- Reading Activities

- Chapter Self-Checks (English and Spanish)
- Internet Activities
- School-to-Career Connections
- Work-Based Learning Project
- Unit Tests
- Unit Thematic Project Rubrics

for Planning & Instructional Support

Technology Solutions

TeacherWorks™ Plus

TeacherWorks Plus gives you instant access to a variety of useful program resources in one easy-to-use CD. The software provides a calendar format for you to plan lessons, manage daily activities, access textbook materials, and utilize Internet resources. TeacherWorks Plus includes built-in lesson plans that can be customized to meet your individual classroom needs. It also includes links to printable program resources:

Printable Program Resources

Student Materials

- Graphic Organizers
- Chapter Summaries with Key Terms and Academic Vocabulary (English and Spanish)
- Reading Activities
- Chapter Self-Checks (English and Spanish)
- Internet Activities
- School-to-Career Connections
- Work-Based Learning Project
- Unit Tests
- Unit Thematic Project Rubrics
- *Career Plan Project Workbook*

Career Plan Project Workbook

The *Career Plan Project Workbook* in TeacherWorks Plus gives students templates and instruction for the essential elements of a career plan. It provides simple step-by-step directions for students to create their own career plans. The Workbook also includes teaching and assessment suggestions where applicable.

Teacher Materials

- Teacher Wraparound Edition
- Lesson Plans
- Chapter Resources
- Answer Keys
- Personal and Academic Career Portfolio Project Student Rubrics
- Student Activity Workbook with Academic Integration, Teacher Annotated Edition
- Strategies for Students with Special Needs

Interactive Student Edition

The Interactive Student Edition CD includes the complete text of the student edition, formatted like the hardbound book, in a .pdf on CD, viewable through Adobe® Acrobat Reader®. With Glencoe's Interactive Student Edition, you can search through a multitude of materials quickly, and click on the hotlinks to locate documents correlated to the Student Edition.

ExamView® Assessment Suite

Streamline assessment from start to finish with the ***ExamView*® *Assessment Suite*** CD. The ***ExamView Assessment Suite*** (including the Test Generator and Test Manager) is a comprehensive solution for creating, administering, and scoring tests. It provides an accurate and exhaustive source of test items for a wide variety of examination styles. It contains thousands of test questions organized by chapter and unit. This easy-to-use software will help you to quickly create customized chapter, unit, midterm, or final assessments.

Use the ExamView Test Generator to:
- Create a paper test in fewer than five minutes.
- Print multiple versions of the same test.
- Use bimodal questions to alternate between multiple choice and short answer.
- Enter your own questions.
- Develop tests using state standards.
- Prepare an online test, study guide, and worksheet.
- Upload tests to WebCT and Blackboard.

Use the ExamView Test Manager to:
- Create a class roster.
- Automatically score a paper test using a scanner.
- Administer and score an online test.
- Prepare a variety of useful class and student reports.

Interactive Chalkboard

The *Succeeding in the World of Work* Interactive Chalkboard CD provides visually motivating presentations that enable teachers to present dynamic lessons for every section of *Succeeding in the World of Work*. The PowerPoint® presentations, which can be edited and customized, include text highlights, graphic organizers, charts, graphs, figures, and original quick quizzes. It also includes interactive games and chapter assessment presentations that can be used with TurningPoint® student response systems.

Technology Resources
How to Access the Online Learning Center

Follow these steps to access the textbook resources at the *Succeeding in the World of Work* Online Learning Center.

Step 1
Go to **glencoe.com**.

Step 2
Select your state from the pull-down menu.

Step 3
Select Teacher.

Step 4
Scroll through the subject menu to select Career Education.

Step 5
Click ENTER.

Step 6
Select *Succeeding in the World of Work* © 2008.

Step 7
Click Teacher Center to access a wide variety of classroom resources.

Digital Resources
Online Learning Center Student Site

The *Succeeding in the World of Work* Online Learning Center provides resources to enrich and enhance learning.

Glencoe's Study-to-Go is online content that students can download onto their PDAs, giving them a portable version of their textbook-related materials.

Glencoe's Teaching Today Web site provides teaching tips, free downloadable materials, in-depth articles, and a host of other features.

Online Student Edition

The Online Student Edition is an interactive version of the textbook. It offers the same content as the printed text, as well as multimedia-enhanced content.

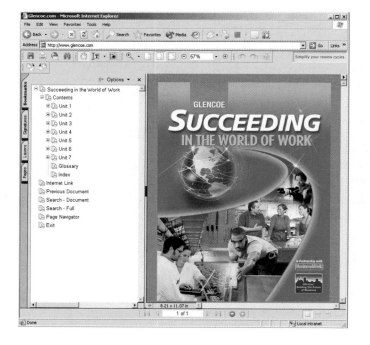

Teach Career Education and Academics at the Same Time

Scope and Sequence

These charts provide an overview of the academic standards covered in *Succeeding in the World of Work*.

National Council of Teachers of Mathematics Standards for Grades 9-12	
Number and Operation	
Understand numbers, ways of representing numbers, relationships among numbers, and number systems	pp. 12, 48, 430, 396, 430
Understand the meanings of operations and how they relate to one another	pp. 139, 145, 220, 233, 255, 268, 301, 306, 326, 339, 372, 467, 480, 488, 500, 519, 524, 537, 539, 559
Compute fluently and make reasonable estimates	pp. 11, 12, 34, 38, 270, 275, 311, 314, 446–448, 449, 519, 538, 559
Algebra	
Understand patterns, relations, and functions	pp. 550
Represent and analyze mathematical situations and structures using algebraic symbols	pp. 26, 93, 115, 150, 367, 405
Use mathematical models to represent and understand quantitative relationships	pp. 26, 120
Analyze change in various contexts	pp. 161, 450
Geometry	
Analyze characteristics of two- and three-dimensional geometric shapes and develop mathematical arguments about geometric relationships	pp. 98, 200
Use visualization, spatial reasoning, and geometric modeling to solve problems	pp. 189, 352, 450
Measurement	
Understand measurable attributes of objects and the units, systems, and processes of measurement	pp. 174, 238, 280, 306
Apply appropriate techniques, tools, and formulas to determine measurements	pp. 247, 280, 317

Data Analysis and Probability	
Formulate questions that can be addressed with data and collect, organize, and display relevant data to answer them.	pp. 78, 352, 391, 414, 440
Select and use appropriate statistical methods to analyze data	pp. 73, 209, 480
Develop and evaluate inferences and predictions that are based on data	pp. 326
Understand and apply basic concepts of probability	pp. 326, 460
Problem Solving	
Apply and adapt a variety of appropriate strategies to solve problems	pp. 38, 401, 539
Solve problems that arise in mathematics and in other contexts	pp. 38, 92, 139, 192, 227, 361, 401, 492
Build new mathematical knowledge through problem solving	pp. 260, 571
Monitor and reflect on the process of problem solving	pp. 98, 189, 200

National Science Education Standards	
Content Standard 1 Students should develop an understanding of science unifying concepts and processes: systems, order, and organization; evidence, models, and explanation; change, constancy, and measurement; evolution and equilibrium; and form and function.	pp. 16, 247, 301, 469, 508
Content Standard A Students should develop abilities necessary to do scientific inquiry, understandings about scientific inquiry	pp. 16, 26, 78, 156, 220, 247, 301, 389, 414, 396, 440, 480, 508
Content Standard B Students should develop an understanding of the structure of atoms, structure and properties of matter, chemical reactions, motions and forces, conservation of energy and increase in disorder, and interactions of energy and matter	pp. 65, 113, 120, 200, 208, 346, 372, 460, 469, 564
Content Standard C Students should develop understanding of the cell; molecular basis of heredity; biological evolution; interdependence of organisms; matter, energy, and organization in living systems; and behavior of organisms	pp. 48, 150, 174, 238, 280,326, 352, 433, 550
Content Standard D Students should develop an understanding of energy in the earth system, geochemical cycles, origin and evolution of the earth system, origin and evolution of the universe	pp. 306, 524
Content Standard E Students should develop abilities of technological design, understandings about science and technology	All Tech Savvy features: pp. 17, 68,111, 158, 206, 250, 342. 391, 430, 472, 513, 558
Content Standard F Students should develop understanding of personal and community health; population growth; natural resources; environmental quality; natural and human-induced hazards; science and technology in local, national, and global challenges	pp. 174, 240–261, 280, 314, 396
Content Standard G Students should develop understanding of science as a human endeavor, nature of scientific knowledge, historical perspectives	pp. 26

National Council of Teachers of English Standards for English Language Arts

NCTE 1 Students read a wide range of print and non-print texts to build an understanding of texts, of themselves, and of the cultures of the United States and the world; to acquire new information; to respond to the needs and demands of society and the workplace; and for personal fulfillment. Among these texts are fiction and nonfiction, classic and contemporary works.	pp. 2–656
NCTE 2 Students read a wide range of literature from many periods in many genres to build an understanding of the many dimensions (e.g., philosophical, ethical, aesthetic) of human experience.	pp. 247; all Reading Connection lists (through the Online Learning Center at **glencoe.com**)
NCTE 3 3 Students apply a wide range of strategies to comprehend, interpret, evaluate, and appreciate texts. They draw on their prior experience, their interactions with other readers and writers, their knowledge of word meaning and of other texts, their word identification strategies, and their understanding of textual features (e.g., sound-letter correspondence, sentence structure, context, graphics).	pp. 63, 64, 66, 85, 230, 232, 506, 508, 513, 508, 513, 515, 518
NCTE 4 Students adjust their use of spoken, written, and visual language (e.g., conventions, style, vocabulary) to communicate effectively with a variety of audiences and for different purposes.	pp. 9, 17, 21, 26, 27, 43, 48, 49, 78, 79, 98, 99, 120,121, 135, 141, 151, 158, 164, 169, 173, 194, 195, 200, 201, 206, 215. 221 228, 239, 247, 261, 275, 280, 281, 295, 298, 306, 307, 327, 334, 336, 347, 373, 383, 397, 424, 430, 435, 441, 538, 545, 551, 554, 558, 567
NCTE 5 Students employ a wide range of strategies as they write and use different writing process elements appropriately to communicate with different audiences for a variety of purposes.	pp. 26, 27, 49, 79, 99, 121, 151, 173, 201, 221, 239, 273, 275, 281, 327, 352, 353, 373, 397, 415, 430, 434, 441, 461, 480, 481, 500, 501,525, 531, 538, 549–551, 573
NCTE 6 Students apply knowledge of language structure, language conventions (e.g., spelling and punctuation), media techniques, figurative language, and genre to create, critique, and discuss print and non-print texts.	pp. 340–353, 365
NCTE 7 Students conduct research on issues and interests by generating ideas and questions, and by posing problems. They gather, evaluate, and synthesize data from a variety of sources (e.g., print and non-print texts, artifacts, people) to communicate their discoveries in ways that suit their purpose and audience.	pp. 70, 109, 187, 228, 238, 252, 365, 385, 448, 472, 474, 487
NCTE 8 Students use a variety of technological and information resources (e.g., libraries, databases, computer networks, video) to gather and synthesize information and to create and communicate knowledge.	pp. 61, 90, 108, 111, 158, 174, 188, 212, 214, 215, 221, 244, 266, 275, 292, 359, 383, 391, 514, 518, 563
NCTE 9 Students develop an understanding of and respect for diversity in language use, patterns, and dialects across cultures, ethnic groups, geographic regions, and social roles.	pp. 14, 41, 92, 138, 165, 212, 214, 226, 293, 332, 380, 404, 453, 471, 479, 492, 566
NCTE 10 Students whose first language is not English make use of their first language to develop competency in the English language arts and to develop understanding of content across the curriculum.	Spanish Glosario (pp. 624–637); All Universal Access English Language Learner activities in TWE wrap
NCTE 11 Students participate as knowledgeable, reflective, creative, and critical members of a variety of literacy communities.	pp. 2–656
NCTE 12 Students use spoken, written, and visual language to accomplish their own purposes (e.g., for learning, enjoyment, persuasion, and the exchange of information).	pp. 159, 164, 169, 220, 260, 312, 313, 321, 334, 345, 361, 409 , 455, 461, 466, 481, 487, 494, 495, 541

Make Your Teaching Flexible

90 Day

and **Adaptable** to **Any** Schedule

180 Day

Integrate Academic and Workplace Skills

Standards-Based Lesson Planning

Skills and Competencies
Each chapter interleaf includes a chart of the 21st Century Skills, Foundation Skills, and Workplace Competencies that students will develop as they study the chapter.

Academic Standards Correlations
Each chapter interleaf includes a table of English Language Arts, Mathematics, and Science standards correlations that show the locations of features and activities that will help your students achieve academic proficiency.

into the Career Education Classroom

NCLB

Brackets on the reduced student pages correspond to activities that help students practice and improve their abilities in Mathematics, English Language Arts, and Science.

Science in Action
Many Science in Action features and Science questions in the Chapter Review are correlated to national Science standards.

Academic Standards
Academics Standards listed in the Reading Guide at the beginning of each section correlate to features and section content.

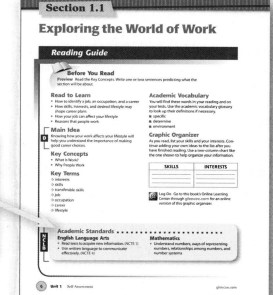

Science In Action

Temperature
Many scientific processes use the Celsius scale to measure temperature, while the general U.S. public uses the Fahrenheit scale. Convert 68° Fahrenheit to degrees Celsius. Round to the closest whole number. The conversion formula is $°C = \frac{5}{9}[(°F)-(32°F)]$.

Starting Hint: Start the conversion by filling in the variables you know in the formula, degrees Fahrenheit (°F): $°C = \frac{5}{9}[(°68)-(32°F)]$.

@ For more science practice, go to this book's OLC through glencoe.com.

Math In Action

Calculate Pay
Esteban is deciding between two job offers. One pays $13.00 an hour for 50 hours a week; the other pays $15.50 an hour for 40 hours a week. Esteban wants to spend more time with his family, so he will probably choose the second job. If he does, how much less will he make each year?

Starting Hint: Calculate how much he will make in each job per year before you calculate the difference in pay.

@ For more math practice, go to this book's OLC through glencoe.com.

Math in Action
Math in Action features and Mathematics questions in the Chapter Review are correlated to national Math standards.

Section 1.1
Exploring the World of Work

Reading Guide

Before You Read
Preview Read the Key Concepts. Write one or two sentences predicting what the section will be about.

Read to Learn
- How to identify a job, an occupation, and a career
- How skills, interests, and desired lifestyle may shape career plans
- How your job can affect your lifestyle
- Reasons that people work

Main Idea
Knowing how your work affects your lifestyle will help you understand the importance of making good career choices.

Key Concepts
- What Is Work?
- Why People Work

Key Terms
- interests
- skills
- transferable skills
- job
- occupation
- career
- lifestyle

Academic Vocabulary
You will find these words in your reading and on your tests. Use the academic vocabulary glossary to look up their definitions if necessary.
- specific
- determine
- environment

Graphic Organizer
As you read, list your skills and your interests. Continue adding your own ideas to the list after you have finished reading. Use a two-column chart like the one shown to help organize your information.

SKILLS	INTERESTS

@ Log On Go to this book's Online Learning Center through glencoe.com for an online version of this graphic organizer.

Academic Standards
English Language Arts
- Read texts to acquire new information. (NCTE 1)
- Use written language to communicate effectively. (NCTE 4)

Mathematics
- Understand numbers, ways of representing numbers, relationships among numbers, and number systems

6   Unit 1   Self-Assessment   glencoe.com

CHAPTER 1 Review & Activities

Academic Skills in the Workplace

English Language Arts
15. Practice Expository Writing Changes in the world affect what kinds of jobs are available. Knowing about these changes can help you make good decisions about your career. Write a one-page journal entry citing an example of a change in your community that might affect the local job market.

Mathematics
16. Calculate Average Work Time Three restaurant workers spend a total of four hours working together to prepare vegetables for the salad bar. What is the average number of minutes each worker spends to keep it filled?

Use Variables and Operations Translating words into algebraic expressions requires knowledge of the meaning of the verbal descriptions. In algebra, a variable is a symbol used to represent a number. Arithmetic operations include addition, subtraction, multiplication, and division.

Starting Hint If x = the average number of hours each worker spends to keep the bar filled, the algebraic expression for this problem is $3x ÷ (4 × 60)$. Solve for x.

Science
17. Form a Hypothesis The scientific method is a way to consider scientific questions. It involves collecting data, forming a hypothesis that explains the data, testing the hypothesis, interpreting the results, and stating a conclusion that can be evaluated by others. One hypothesis might read: *Manufacturing jobs are decreasing in the United States because more manufacturing work is being done overseas.* Create your own hypothesis about the world of work. Then, brainstorm ways you would find data to prove your hypothesis. Create a two-paragraph summary of your proposed research project.

Social Studies
18. Research International Job Outlook Imagine that you are interested in living and working in Mexico. Use the library and other resources to research the current job outlook in Mexico. Which industries and

Academic Activities
Academic Activities in the After You Read section reviews and Chapter Review & Activities are correlated to Mathematics, English Language Arts, Science, Social Studies, and World Languages standards.

Section 1.1 After You Read

Review Key Concepts
1. Give one example each of a job, an occupation, and a career.
2. Give an example of a skill that might be used in a specific job.
3. Describe a situation that might cause a person to change his or her main reason for working.

Practice Academic Skills
Mathematics
4. Most Americans spend more than 30% of their yearly income on housing expenses. If you earn $27,000 per year, how much money will you need to spend on housing?

Multiply Decimals by Whole Numbers A percent is a ratio that compares a number to 100. To multiply with percentages:
Step 1: You can rewrite the percent (30%) as a fraction with a denominator of 100. Convert the fraction to a decimal.
Step 2: Multiply this decimal by the number ($27,000). Remember to put the decimal point in the correct place in your answer.

For math help, go to the Math Appendix located at the back of this book.

12   Unit 1   Self-Assessment

Raise the Bar and Help Students Clear It

Academic Integration

Academic skills are crucial for success both inside and outside the classroom. In addition to traditional academic skills, your students will need communication skills, interpersonal skills, and strong technology skills in order to compete in the workplace. Basic skills will support your students in completing the tasks that their jobs and lives will demand.

The No Child Left Behind Act

The No Child Left Behind Act of 2001 emphasizes student achievement in basic academic subjects. It introduces strict accountability measures for schools in the form of standardized testing. Traditionally, core academic subjects have been defined as language arts, science, and mathematics. No Child Left Behind names the following academic subjects:

- English
- Reading/Language Arts
- Mathematics
- Science
- World Languages
- Civics and Government
- Economics
- Art
- History
- Geography

The Importance of Integrating Academics

In a recent survey of high school graduates—many of whom had gone directly to work rather than into postsecondary education—more than half the respondents said their high schools should have placed more emphasis on basic academic skills.

Unfortunately, these students—like so many others—were not able to recognize the relevance of their course work while they were in high school.

By explicitly integrating academic skills into the business curriculum, you can make students more aware of the connections between schoolwork and the real world.

Integrated learning offers the following additional benefits to students:

- It provides real-world learning and thus establishes patterns of lifelong learning.
- It improves the academic achievement of all students—including those who will begin their careers directly after high school, those who will go on to postsecondary education or training, and those who will obtain four-year college degrees and beyond.
- It helps students make realistic plans for their own careers and education.

Academics in the Career Education Curriculum

Integrate academic skills into the classroom as a regular part of your classroom activities. For example, by having students read class assignments and texts, write letters and reports, give presentations, and perform mathematics exercises, you are helping them improve their academic skills. Make expectations clear. For example, if you ask your students to prepare a written report, explain that grammar, spelling, and presentation will be evaluated along with subject content. Stress that clear writing, accuracy, and attention to detail are skills that students will need for success in school and at work.

To integrate academics into your career education course, you must incorporate principles from other subjects in a way that students can understand either on a concrete level or on metaphoric terms. This type of teaching will help those students who learn best when they are exposed to a variety of examples.

Deliver Efficient Instruction to All Students

Accountability

A consequential result of the No Child Left Behind Act, and the reauthorization of the Perkins Act through 2012, is that more states require testing for graduation at the secondary level. Accountability measures new to the Perkins reauthorization bill include:

- Academic proficiency as measured by the state criteria developed under NCLB;
- Graduation rates, also as defined by NCLB;
- Number of students to continue to postsecondary education;
- Number of students to complete state or industry certification or licensure; and
- Student achievement on assignments aligned with industry standards.

Connection to Relevance

With the mandatory requirements for proven test scores and graduation numbers, how can we assure that our students are learning? Most educators agree it is by connecting the relevance of education to life.

ACTE president Bob Scarborough says the Perkins reauthorization "ensures we are providing all students with an education that will help them succeed in the workplace and in life." William Daggett writes in *Achieving Academic Excellence through Rigor and Relevance:*

> What is important is that students enter the global economy with the ability to apply what they learned in school to a variety of ever-changing situations that they may not have been able to foresee before graduating.

The Rigor/Relevance Framework, developed at the International Center for Leadership in Education, illustrates leveled learning processes that enable students to perform high-level thinking. The learning process defines student performance in four sequential categories: acquisition, application, assimilation and adaptation.

As educators, our goal is to teach students to adapt their acquired knowledge and skills in complex ways to any situations, known and unknown. As educators, we are committed to provide the connectivity between classroom learning and real-world application.

Applications

Studies show that students understand and retain knowledge when they experience or apply it to relevant situations. The *Succeeding in the World of Work* program is dedicated to meet the challenge. Every chapter in *Succeeding in the World of Work* is filled with ways to engage students in experiential learning and applying their knowledge to their lives.

Features designed to help students find the relevance in content include:

- Real-World Connection
- WebQuest
- Unit Thematic Project (featuring skills self-assessment, Lifelong Learning Connection, career exploration, connection to the community, and the *BusinessWeek* Connection)
- The 21st Century Workplace
- Everyday Ethics
- Tech Savvy
- Career Spotlight
- Science in Action and Math in Action
- Hot Jobs!
- Chapter Review & Activities, including Real-World Skills and Applications, Academic Skills in the Workplace, Net Connection, Writing Practice, and Role Play (competitive event practice)

The content and teaching strategies in *Succeeding in the World of Work* are designed to help applied learning students acclimate into the real world and to prepare them for high-skill, high-wage, and high-demand professions.

Gather the Tools You'll Need

Universal Access
by Douglas Fisher, Ph.D.

Today's classroom includes students from many backgrounds with a variety of learning styles, strengths, and challenges. As teachers, we face the challenge of helping all of our students reach their educational potential. With careful planning, you can address the needs of all students in your classroom. The basis for this planning is universal access. When classrooms are planned with universal access in mind, fewer students require specific accommodations.

Universal Design

Universal design was first conceived as an architectural design concept when business people, engineers, and architects began making adjustments to allow for physical access to buildings. The idea was to plan the environment in advance to ensure that everyone had access. As a result, the environment would not have to be changed later for people with physical disabilities, people pushing strollers, workers who had injuries, or others for whom the environment would be difficult to negotiate. The Center for Universal Design **www.design.ncsu.edu/cud** defines universal design as: The design of products and environments to be usable by all people, to the greatest extent possible, without the need for adaptation or specialized design.

Universal Design and Access in Education

Researchers, teachers, and parents have expanded the development of built-in adaptations and inclusive accommodations from architectural space to the educational experience, especially in the area of curriculum.

In 1998, the National Center to Improve the Tools of Educators, with the partnership of the Center for Applied Special Technology, proposed an expanded definition of universal design focused on education: In terms of learning, universal design means the design of instructional materials and activities that allows learning goals to be achievable by individuals with wide differences in their abilities to see, hear, speak, move, read, write, understand English, attend, organize, engage, and remember.

Universal design and access in education suggests the following:

- **Inclusive Classroom Participation**—Curricula should be designed with all students and their needs in mind. The Glencoe/McGraw-Hill texts and materials are designed to accommodate a wide range of students. For example, understanding that English learners and students who struggle with reading will be using this textbook, vocabulary is specifically taught and reinforced. Teacher-support materials provide multiple instructional methods to meet the needs of the students in the class. The text is written to identify the main idea for all learners. Activating prior knowledge an identifying connections between what students know and think about are made within the text.

- **Maximum Text Readability**—In universally designed classrooms that provide access for all students, texts use direct language, clear noun-verb agreements, and clear construct-based wording. In addition to these factors, *Succeeding in the World of Work* uses embedded definitions for key terms and academic vocabulary, provides for specific instruction in reading skills, uses a number of visual representations, and includes note-taking guides.

to Reach Every Student

- **Adaptable and Accommodating**—The content in this textbook can be easily translated, read aloud, or otherwise changed to meet the needs of students in the classroom. The section and end-of-chapter assessments provide students with multiple ways to demonstrate their content knowledge and activities to help them see the connection between course study and the real world.

Differentiated Instruction

To differentiate instruction, teachers must appreciate student differences in background knowledge and current reading, writing, and English language skills. They must also consider student learning styles and preferences, interests, and needs, so they can react accordingly. There are a number of general guidelines for differentiating instruction in the classroom to reach all students, including:

- **Link Assessment with Instruction**—Assessments should occur before, during, and after instruction to ensure that the curriculum is aligned with what students do and do not know. Using assessments in this way allows you to plan instruction for whole groups, small groups, and individual students. Backward planning, where you establish the assessment before you begin instruction is also important.
- **Clarify Key Concepts and Generalizations**—Students need to know what concepts are essential and how this information can be used in their future learning. In addition, students need to develop a sense of the Big Ideas—ideas that transcend time and place.
- **Emphasize Critical and Creative Thinking**—The content, process and classroom should require students to think about what they are learning. While some students may require

support, additional motivation, varied tasks, materials, or equipment, the overall focus on critical and creative thinking allows all students to participate in the lesson.
- **Include Teacher- and Student-Selected Tasks**—A differentiated classroom includes both teacher- and student-selected tasks and activities. At some points in the day or lesson, the teacher must provide instruction and assign learning activities. In other parts of the lesson, students should be provided with choices in how they engage with the content. A balance of guided and chosen activities increases motivation, engagement, and learning.

Support for Individual Students

The vast majority of students will thrive in a universal access classroom that is focused on differentiated instruction. However, wise teachers recognize that no single option will work for all students and that there may be students who require unique systems of support to be successful.

Tips for Instruction

The following tips for instruction can support your efforts to help all students reach their maximum potential:

- Survey students to discover their individual differences. Use interest inventories to learn their unique talents so you can encourage contributions in the classroom.
- Be a model for respecting others. Adolescents crave social acceptance. Students with learning differences are especially sensitive to correction and criticism, particularly when it comes from a teacher. Your behavior will set the tone for how students treat one another.
- Expand opportunities for success. Provide a variety of instructional activities that reinforce skills and concepts.

- Establish measurable objectives and decide how you can best help students who meet them.
- Celebrate successes and make note of and praise "work in progress."
- Keep it simple. Point out problem areas if doing so can help a student effect change. Avoid overwhelming students with too many goals at one time.
- Assign cooperative group projects that challenge all students to contribute in solving a problem or creating a product.

Students with Learning Disabilities

- Provide support and structure. Clearly specify rules, assignments, and responsibilities.
- Practice skills frequently. Use games and drills to help maintain student interest.
- Incorporate many modalities into the learning process. Provide opportunities to hear, speak, write, read, and act out important concepts and information.
- Link new skills and concepts to those that have already been mastered.
- If possible, allow students to record answers on audiotape.
- Allow extra time to complete assessments and assignments.
- Let students demonstrate proficiency with alternative presentations, including oral reports, role plays, art projects, and musical presentations.
- Provide outlines, notes, or tape recordings of lecture materials.
- Pair students with peer helpers, and provide class time for pair interaction.

Students with Behavioral Challenges

- Provide a structured environment with clear-cut schedules, rules, seat assignments, and safety procedures.
- Reinforce appropriate behavior and model it for students.
- Cue distracted students back to the task using verbal signals as well as teacher supervision.

- Set goals that can be achieved in the short term. Work for long-term improvement in the big areas.

Students with Physical Challenges

- Openly discuss any uncertainties you have about when to offer aid with the student.
- Ask family members or therapists and students what special devices or procedures are needed and whether any special safety precautions need to be taken.
- Welcome students with physical challenges into all activities, including field trips, special events, and projects.
- Provide information about needed support to class members and adults.

Students with Visual Impairments

- Facilitate independence. Modify assignments as needed.
- Teach classmates how and when to serve as visual guides.
- Limit unnecessary noise in the classroom if it distracts students with visual impairments.
- Provide tactile models whenever it is possible.
- Foster a spirit of inclusion. Describe people and events as they occur in the classroom. Remind classmates that students with visual impairments cannot interpret gestures and other forms of nonverbal communication.
- Provide taped lectures and reading assignments for use outside the classroom.
- Team students with a sighted peer for written work.

Students with Hearing Impairments

- Seat students where they can see your lip movements easily and where they can avoid any visual distractions.
- Avoid standing with your back to the window or to a light source.
- Use an overhead projector so you can maintain eye contact while writing notes for students.

- Write all assignments on the board, or hand out written instructions.
- If the student has a manual interpreter, allow both the student and interpreter to select the most favorable seating arrangements.
- Teach students to look directly at each other when they speak.

English Language Learners

- Remember, a student's ability to speak English does not reflect his or her academic abilities.
- Try to incorporate the student's cultural experience into your instruction. The help of a bilingual aid may be effective.
- Avoid any references in your instruction that could be construed as cultural stereotypes.
- Preteach important vocabulary and concepts.
- Encourage students to preview text before they begin reading, noting headings.
- Remind students to use graphic organizers, photographs, and maps take advantage of the information contained in these visuals.
- Use realia and photographs whenever possible to build background knowledge and understanding.

Gifted Students

- Make arrangements for students to take selected subjects early and to work on independent projects.
- Ask "what if" questions to develop high-level thinking skills. Establish an environment safe for risk-taking in your classroom.
- Emphasize concepts, theories, ideas, relationships, and generalizations about the content.
- Promote interest in the past by inviting students to make connections to the present.
- Let students express themselves in alternate ways such as through creative writing, acting, debates, simulations, drawing, or music.
- Provide students with a catalog of helpful resources, listing such things as agencies that provide free and inexpensive materials, appropriate community services and programs, and community experts who might be called upon to speak to your students.
- Assign extension projects that allow students to solve real-life problems related to their communities.

Empower Your Students with the Reading Skills

How Can I Motivate Students to Read?

As a teacher, your role is to help students make personal connections in order to understand "Why do I need to learn this?" Emphasize that reading is not only a necessity for work and for life; it can also bring enjoyment and enlightenment.

Ask your students, "What role does reading play in your life?" You can open this discussion by modeling examples: I love historical biographies; I read menus and order meals in Spanish; I read magazines and the Internet to stay up-to-date on my favorite sports teams.

Improving or Fine-Tuning Reading Skills Will Help Your Students:

- ◆ Improve grades
- ◆ Read faster and more efficiently
- ◆ Improve their study skills
- ◆ Remember more information accurately
- ◆ Improve their writing

The Reading Process

Good reading skills build on one another, overlap, and spiral in much the same way that a winding staircase goes around and around while leading readers to a higher place. The Reading Skills Handbook is designed to help your students find and use the tools to use before, during, and after reading.

Reading Strategies

- ◆ Identify, understand, and learn new words
- ◆ Understand why you read
- ◆ Take a quick look at the whole text
- ◆ Try to predict what you are about to read
- ◆ Take breaks during reading and ask questions about the text
- ◆ Take notes
- ◆ Keep thinking about what will come next
- ◆ Summarize

Vocabulary Development

Word identification and vocabulary skills are the building blocks of reading and writing. By learning to use a variety of strategies to build word skills and vocabulary, your students will become stronger readers.

Use Context to Determine Meaning

The best way for your students to expand and extend vocabulary is to read widely, listen carefully, and participate in a rich variety of discussions. When reading independently, students can often figure out the meanings of new words by looking at their context, the other words and sentences that surround them.

They Will Use in the Real World

Predict a Possible Meaning

Another way to determine the meaning of a word is to take the word apart. If a reader understands the meaning of the **base,** or **root,** part of a word, and knows the meanings of key syllables added either to the beginning or end of the base word, it becomes easy to figure out what the word means.

Word Origins Since Latin, Greek, and Anglo-Saxon roots are the basis for much of our English vocabulary, having some background in one of these languages can be a useful vocabulary tool. For example, *astronomy* comes from the Greek root *astro,* which means "relating to the stars." *Stellar* also has a meaning referring to stars, but its origin is Latin. Knowing root words in other languages can help readers determine meanings, derivations, and spellings in English.

Prefixes and Suffixes A prefix is a word part that can be added to the beginning of a word. For example, the prefix *semi* means "half" or "partial," so *semicircle* means "half a circle." A suffix is a word part that can be added to the end of a word. Adding a suffix often changes a word from one part of speech to another.

Using Dictionaries A dictionary provides the meaning or meanings of a word. Look at the sample dictionary entry in the student edition Reading Skills Handbook to see what other information it provides.

Thesauruses and Specialized Reference Books A thesaurus provides synonyms and often antonyms. It is a useful tool to use to expand vocabulary. Remind students to check the exact definition of the listed words in a dictionary before using a thesaurus. Specialized dictionaries such the *Barron's Dictionary of Business Terms* or *Black's Law Dictionary* list terms and expressions not commonly included in a general dictionary.

Glossaries Many textbooks and technical works contain condensed dictionaries that provide an alphabetical listing of words used in the text and their specific definitions.

Recognize Word Meanings Across Subjects Words often have different meanings when used for different purposes. The word product may mean one thing in math and another in science. For example:

Math After you multiply the two numbers, explain how you arrived at the **product.**

Science One **product** of photosynthesis is oxygen.

Economics The Gross National **Product** is the total dollar value of goods and services produced by a nation.

Help Students Understand What They Read

Reading comprehension means understanding—deriving meaning from—what has been read. Using a variety of strategies can help improve comprehension and make reading more interesting and more fun.

Read for a Reason

To get the greatest benefit from reading, teach students to **establish a purpose for their reading.** In school, some of the reasons for reading are to:

- learn and understand new information
- find specific information
- review before a test
- complete an assignment
- prepare (research) before you write

As reading skills improve, you will notice that your students apply different strategies to fit the different purposes for reading. For example, a person reading for entertainment may read quickly, but reading to gather information or follow directions might require reading more slowly, taking notes, constructing a graphic organizer, or rereading sections of text.

Draw on Personal Background

Drawing on personal background, or activating prior knowledge, helps students connect their culture and experiences to their reading. Before introducing a new topic, you may want to encourage students to ask:

- What have I heard or read about this topic?
- Do I have any personal experience relating to this topic?

You can also set common background knowledge with discussion before reading. For example, to prepare students to read the novel *A Farewell to Arms*, you might lead a discussion about these common background themes:

- World War I
- Italy (You might ask a student to show Italy on a map)
- Other Ernest Hemingway titles
- The Nobel Prize in literature

Having this historical background will help to set the scene for students as they read.

Using a KWL Chart A KWL chart is a good device for organizing information gathered before, during, and after reading. In the first column, students list what they already know, then list what they want to know in the middle column. They use the third column to review and assess what they learned. You or your students can add more columns to record places where they found information and places where they can look for more information.

K (What I already know)	W (What I want to know)	L (What I have learned)

Adjust Your Reading Speed Reading speed is a key factor in how well students understand what they read. Reading speed can vary depending on the purpose for reading.

Scanning means running one's eyes quickly over the material to look for words or phrases. Readers scan to find a specific piece of information.

Skimming means reading a passage quickly to find its main idea or get an overview. Skim a passage as a preview to determine what the material is about.

Reading for detail involves careful reading while paying attention to text structure and monitoring understanding. Readers read for detail to learn concepts, follow complicated directions, or prepare to analyze a text.

Techniques to Help Students Understand and Remember What They Read

Preview

Previewing strategies help students begin at a visual level, then drill down to evaluate, predict, draw conclusions, and use contextual clues about what they will read.

Previewing Strategies

Read the title, headings, and subheadings of the selection.

Look at the illustrations and notice how the text is organized.

Skim the selection: Take a glance at the whole thing.

Decide what the main idea might be.

Predict what a selection will be about.

Predict

As students read, they take educated guesses about story events and outcomes. They make predictions before and during reading. This helps them focus their attention on the text and that focus improves understanding.

Determine the Main Idea

When students look for the main idea, they are looking for the most important statement in a text. Depending on what kind of text they read, the main idea can be located at the very beginning (news stories in newspaper or a magazine) or at the end (scientific research document).

Encourage students to ask these questions to determine the main idea:
● What is each sentence about?
● Is there one sentence that is more important than all the others?
● What idea do the details support or point out?

Keep track of the text's structure (see below). Looking at headers and content structure will give students important clues about the main idea.

Taking Notes

Cornell Note-Taking system: There are many methods for note taking. The **Cornell Note-Taking System** is a well-known method that can help students organize what they read. To the right is a note-taking activity based on the Cornell Note-Taking System.

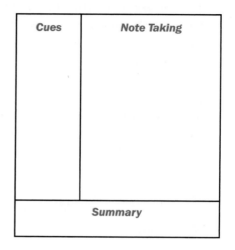

Graphic organizers: Using a graphic organizer to retell content in a visual representation will help students remember and retain content. Encourage students to make charts or diagrams to organize what they have read. Some good examples are:

Venn diagrams: A Venn diagram is a good way to organize information in a compare-and-contrast text structure. The outer portions of the circles show how two characters, ideas, or items contrast, or are different, and the overlapping part compares two things, or shows how they are similar.

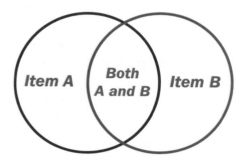

Flow charts: Students can a track sequence of events or cause and effect on a flow chart. Demonstrate how to arrange ideas or events in their logical, sequential order. Then draw arrows between ideas to indicate how one idea or event flows into another.

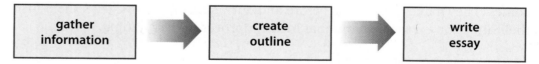

Go to **glencoe.com** for more information about note taking and additional study tools.

Visualize

Encourage students to try to form a mental picture of scenes, characters, and events as they read. This helps them to use the details and descriptions the author gives readers. If students can **visualize** what they read, they will become more interested and will remember the information better.

Question

Tell students to ask questions about the text while they read. Encourage them to ask about the importance of the sentences they read, how the sentences relate to one another, whether they understand what they just read, and what they think is going to come next.

Clarify

Encourage students to try these techniques when they don't understand meaning (through questioning):

What to Do When You Do Not Understand

- ◆ **Reread confusing parts of the text.**
- ◆ **Diagram (chart) relationships between chunks of text, ideas, and sentences.**
- ◆ **Look up unfamiliar words.**
- ◆ **Separate the text out of oneself. Pretend to tell it to someone else.**
- ◆ **Read the passage once more.**

Review

Make sure students take time to stop and review what they have read. Use note-taking outlines or any other graphic organizers, charts or visual aids.

Monitor Comprehension

Teach students to continue to check their understanding using the following two strategies:

Summarize Pause and state the main ideas of the text and the key supporting details. Try to answer the following questions: Who? What? When? Where? Why? and How?

Paraphrase Pause, close the book, and try to retell what they have just read in their own words. It helps students to retell or paraphrase reading into their own words.

Understanding Text Structure

Good writers do not just put together sentences and paragraphs; they organize their writing with a specific purpose in mind. That organization is called text structure. When students understand and follow the structure of a text, it is easier to remember the information they read. There are many ways text may be structured. Each type of structure usually makes use of some specific words. Teach students to watch for these **signal words.** They will help them follow the text's organization (remind them to use these techniques as they write).

Comparison and Contrast

This structure shows similarities and differences between people, things, and ideas. This is often used to demonstrate that things that seem alike are really different, or vice versa.

Signal words: similarly, more, less, on the one hand/on the other hand, in contrast, but, however

Cause and Effect

Writers use the cause and effect structure to explore the reasons for something happening and to examine the results or consequences of events.

Signal words: so, because, as a result, therefore, for the following reasons

Problem and Solution

When writers organize text around the question how, they state a problem and suggest solutions.

Signal words: how, help, problem, obstruction, overcome, difficulty, need, attempt, have to, must

Sequence

Sequencing tells readers in which order to consider thoughts or facts. Examples of sequencing are:

Chronological order refers to the order in which events take place.

Signal words: first, next, then, finally

Spatial order describes the organization of things in space (to describe the placement of objects in a room, for example).

Signal words: above, below, behind, next to

Order of importance lists things or thoughts from the most important to the least important (or the other way around).

Signal words: principal, central, main, important, fundamental

Thinking about Reading

It is important for students to think about what they are reading to get the most information from a text, to understand the consequences of what the text says, to remember the content, and to form their own opinions about what they read.

Interpret

Interpreting involves asking, "What is the writer really saying?" and then using what students already know to answer the question.

Infer

Writers do not always state exactly everything they want readers to understand. They sometimes imply certain information by providing clues and details. An inference involves using reasoning and experience to develop the idea, based on what an author implies or suggests. What is most important when drawing inferences is to be sure that readers have accurately based their guesses on supporting details from the text. If students cannot point to a place in the selection to help back up an inference, encourage them to rethink that guess.

Draw Conclusions

A conclusion is a general statement a reader can make and explain using reasoning or supporting details from a text.

Analyze

To understand persuasive nonfiction (a text that lists facts and opinions to arrive at a conclusion), readers must analyze statements and examples to see if they support the main idea. To understand an informational text, students need to keep track of how the ideas are organized to find the main points.

Hint: Have students use graphic organizers and note-taking charts.

Distinguish Facts from Opinions

This is one of the most important reading skills students can learn. A fact is a statement that can be proven. An opinion is what the writer believes. A writer may support opinions with facts, but an opinion cannot be proven. For example:

Fact: California produces fruit and other agricultural products.

Opinion: California produces the best fruit and agricultural products.

Evaluate

Remind students that to rely on accurate information, they will need to consider who wrote it and why. Where did the writer get information? Is the information one-sided? Can readers verify the information?

Reading for Research

To guide students in reading actively to research a topic, encourage them to follow these directions:
- Generate an interesting, relevant, and researchable question.
- Categorize that information.
- Evaluate the information.
- Organize information in a new way for a specific audience.
- Draw conclusions about the original research question.

What Is Academic English?

by Robin Scarcella, Ph.D.

Academic English is the language commonly used in business and education. It is the language used in academics, business, and courts of law. It is the type of English used in professional books, including textbooks, and it contains specific linguistic features that are associated with all disciplines. Proficiency in reading and using academic English is strongly related to long-term success in all parts of life.

What Is Academic Vocabulary?

By the time children have completed elementary school, they must have acquired the knowledge needed to understand academic vocabulary. How many words should they acquire to be able to access their textbooks? A basic 2,000-word vocabulary of high-frequency words makes up 87% of the words. Three percent of the remaining words are technical words. The remaining 2% are low-frequency words. There may be as many as 123,000 low-frequency words in academic texts.

Why Should Students Learn Academic Vocabulary?

English language learners who have mastered a basic 2,000-word vocabulary are ready to acquire the majority of general words found in their texts and on standardized tests.

Knowledge of academic words, combined with continued acquisition of general words, can significantly boost an English learner's comprehension level of academic texts. English learners who learn and practice these words before they graduate from high school are likely to be able to master academic material with more confidence and speed. They waste less time and effort in guessing words than those students who know only the basic 2,000 words that characterize general conversation.

Academic Vocabulary and Academic English in the Career Education Classroom

Teachers can provide their students with rich samples of academic vocabulary and help students understand the academic English of their text. To develop academic English, students must have already acquired a large amount of basic proficiency in the grammar of everyday English.

Academic English should be taught within contexts that make sense. Academic English arises not only from a knowledge of linguistic code and cognition but also

to Career & Real-World Content

from social practices in which academic English is used to accomplish communicative goals. The acquisition of academic vocabulary and grammar is necessary to advance the development of academic English.

Tips for Teaching Academic Vocabulary:

- **Expose Students to Academic Vocabulary**—Students learn academic vocabulary through use and in reading content. You do not need to call attention to all academic words students are learning because they will acquire them subconsciously.
- **Do Not Correct Students' Mistakes When Using Academic Vocabulary**—All vocabulary understanding and spelling errors are developmental and will disappear once the student reads more.
- **Help Students Decode the Words Themselves**—Once they learn the alphabet, they should be able to decode words. Decoding each word they do not recognize will help them more than trying to focus on sentence structure. Once they can recognize words, they can read "authentic" texts.
- **Do Not Ignore the English Learner in This Process**—They can learn academic vocabulary before they are completely fluent in spoken English.
- **Helping Students Build Academic Vocabulary Leads to Broader Learning**—Students who have mastered the basic academic vocabulary are ready to continue acquiring words from the rest of the vocabulary groups. Use the Internet to find lists of appropriate vocabulary word lists.

There are a number of guidelines that teachers can follow when teaching academic English and vocabulary:

Guidelines for Teaching Academic Vocabulary

1. Use direct and planned instruction.
2. Employ models that have increasingly difficult language.
3. Focus attention to form by pointing out linguistic features of words.
4. Provide practice opportunities.
5. Motivate student interest and self-confidence.
6. Provide instructional feedback.
7. Use assessment tools on a regular basis.

Generate the Best Performance

Assessment

In response to the growing demand for accountability in the classroom, educators must use multiple assessment measures to accurately gauge student performance. In addition to quizzes, tests, essay exams, and standardized tests, assessment today incorporates a variety of performance-based measurements and portfolio opportunities.

Performance assessment activities provide hands-on approaches to learning concepts. Through activities students are able to actually experience these concepts rather than just reading and listening about them. These types of activities also help students become aware of diverse audiences for their work. Performance assessment tasks are based on what is most essential in the curriculum and what is interesting to the student.

Performance-Based Assessments

One good way to present a performance assessment is in the form of an open-ended question.

- Journals—Students write from the perspective of a businessperson or a consumer of a particular historical era.
- Letters—Students write a letter from one businessperson to another or from a businessperson to another audience.
- Position Paper or Editorial—Students explain a controversial issue and present their own opinions and recommendations, supported with strong evidence and convincing reasons.
- Newspaper—Students write stories from the perspective of a business reporter. This could also involve the writing of editorials or letters to the editor.
- Biographies and Autobiographies—Students write about business leaders either from the third person point of view (biography) or from the first person (autobiography).
- Creative Stories—Students integrate business events into a piece of fiction.
- Poems and Songs—Students follow the conventions of a particular type of song or poem as they tell about a business event or person.
- Research Reports—Students synthesize information from a variety of sources into a well-developed research report.

Oral Presentations

Oral presentations allow students to demonstrate their business literacy in front of an audience. Oral presentations are often group efforts, although this need not be the case.

- Simulations—Students hold simulations of actual events, such as a role play in a business scenario.
- Debates—Students debate two or more sides of a business policy or issue.
- Interview—Students conduct a mock interview of a business leader or worker.
- Oral Reports—Students present the results of research efforts in a lively oral report. This report may be accompanied by visuals.
- Skits and Plays—Students use business events as the basis for a play or skit.

Visual Presentations

Visual presentations allow students to demonstrate their understanding in a variety of visual formats. Visual presentations can be either group or individual projects.

- Model—Students make a model to demonstrate or represent a business process.
- Museum Exhibit—Students create a rich display of materials around a topic. Typical displays might include models, illustrations,

photographs, videos, writings, and presentation software.

- Graph or Chart—Students analyze and represent data in a line graph, bar graph, table, or other chart format.
- Drawing—Students represent a business event or period through illustration, including cartoons.
- Posters and Murals—Posters and murals may include maps, time lines, diagrams, illustrations, photographs, and written explanations that reflect students' understanding of business information.
- Quilt—Students sew or draw a design for a patchwork quilt that shows a variety of perspectives, events, or issues related to a key topic.
- Videotapes—Students film a video to show a simulation of a business event.
- Multimedia Presentation—Students create a computer-generated presentation or slide show containing business information and analysis.

How Are Performance Assessments Scored?

There are a variety of means used to evaluate performance tasks. Some or all of the following methods may be used.

- Scoring Rubrics—A scoring rubric is a set of guidelines for assessing the quality of a process and/or product. It sets out criteria used to distinguish acceptable responses from unacceptable ones, generally on a scale from excellent to poor. Rubrics may be used as guidelines as the students prepare their products. They are also commonly used for peer-to-peer assessment and self-assessment.

- Models of Excellent Work—Teacher-selected models of excellent work concretely illustrate expectations and help students set goals for their own projects.
- Student Self-Assessment—Common methods of self-assessment include ranking work in relation to the model, using a scoring rubric, and writing their own goals and then evaluating how well they have met the goals they set for themselves. Regardless of which method or methods students use, they should be encouraged to evaluate their behaviors and processes, as well as the finished product.
- Peer or Audience Assessment—Many of the performance tasks target an audience other than the classroom teacher. If possible, the audience of peers should give feedback. Have the class create rubrics for specific projects together.
- Observation—As students carry out their performance tasks, you may want to formally observe them at work. Start by developing a checklist, identifying all the specific behaviors and understandings you expect students to demonstrate. Then observe students as they carry out performance tasks and check off behaviors as you observe them.
- Interviews—As a form of ongoing assessment, you may want to conduct interviews with students, asking them to analyze, explain, and assess their participation in performance tasks. When projects take place over an extended period of time, you can hold periodic interviews as well as exit interviews. In this way the interview process allows you to gauge the status of the project and to guide the students' efforts along the way.

Prepare Your Students Well

Test-Prep Strategies

Students can follow the steps below to prepare for the standardized assessments they are required to take.

- Read About the Test—Students can familiarize themselves with the format, the types of questions, and the amount of time they will have to complete the test. Emphasize that it is very important for students to budget their time during test-taking.
- Review the Content—Consistent study will help students build knowledge and understanding. If there are specific objectives or standards that are tested on the exam, help students review facts or skills.
- Practice—Provide practice, ideally with real tests, to build students' familiarity with the content, format, and timing of the real exam. Students should practice all the types of questions they will encounter on the test.
- Pace—Students should pace themselves differently depending on how the test is administered. As students practice, they should try to increase the number of questions they can answer correctly. If students have trouble with an item, they should mark it and come back to it later.
- Analyze Practice Results—Help students improve test-taking performance by analyzing their test-taking strengths and weaknesses. Help students identify what kinds of questions they found most difficult. Look for patterns in errors and tailor instruction to review the appropriate test-taking skills or content.

Test-Taking Strategies

It's not enough for students to learn facts and concepts—they must be able to show what they know in a variety of test-taking situations.

Objective Tests

Apply the following strategies to help students do their best on objective tests.

Multiple-Choice Questions

- Students should read the directions carefully to learn what answer the test requires—the best answer or the right answer. This is especially important when answer choices include "all of the above" or "none of the above."
- Advise students to watch for negative words in the questions, such as not, except, unless, never, and so forth.
- Students should try to mentally answer the question before reading the answer choices.
- Students should read all the answer choices and eliminate those that are obviously wrong.

True/False Questions

- It is important that students read the entire question before answering. For an answer to be true, the entire statement must be true. If one part of a statement is false, the answer should be marked false.
- Remind students to watch for words such as all, never, every, and always. Statements containing these words are often false.

Matching Questions

- Students should read through both lists before they mark any answers.
- Unless an answer can be used more than once, students should cross out each choice as they use it.
- Using what they know about grammar can help students find the right answer. For instance, when matching a word with its definition, the definition is often the same part of speech (noun, verb, adjective, and so forth) as the word.

and You'll Improve Their *Performance*

Essay Tests

Essay tests require students to provide thorough and well-organized written responses, in addition to telling what they know. Help students use these strategies on essay tests.

Read the Question

The key to writing successful essay responses lies in reading and interpreting questions correctly. Teach students to identify and underline key words to guide them in understanding what the question asks.

Plan and Write the Essay

Students should follow the writing process to develop their answer. Encourage students to follow these steps to plan and write their essays.

1. Map out an answer. Make lists, webs, or an outline to plan the response.
2. Decide on an order in which to present the main points.
3. Write an opening statement that directly responds to the essay question.
4. Write the essay. Expand on the opening statement. Support key points with specific facts, details, and reasons.
5. Write a closing statement that brings the main points together.
6. Proofread to check for spelling, grammar, and punctuation.

The table below defines purposes for different writing strategies.

Writing Strategies	
Analyze	To analyze means to systematically and critically examine all parts of an issue or event.
Classify or Categorize	To classify or categorize means to put people, things, or ideas into groups, based on a common set of characteristics.
Compare and Contrast	To compare is to show how things are similar, or alike. To contrast is to show how things are different.
Describe	To describe means to present a sketch or impression. Rich details, especially details that appeal to the senses, flesh out a description.
Discuss	To discuss means to systematically write about all sides of an issue or event.
Evaluate	To evaluate means to make a judgment and support it with evidence.
Explain	To explain means to clarify or make plain.
Illustrate	To illustrate means to provide examples or to show with a picture or other graphic.
Infer	To infer means to read between the lines or to use knowledge and experience to draw conclusions, make a generalization, or form a prediction.
Justify	To justify means to prove or to support a position with specific facts and reasons.
Predict	To predict means to tell what will happen in the future, based on an understanding of prior events and behaviors.
State	To state means to briefly and concisely present information.
Summarize	To summarize means to give a brief overview of the main points of an issue or event.
Trace	To trace means to present the steps or stages in a process or event in sequential or chronological order.

Base Your Teaching on Best Practices

Critical Thinking

One of the factors that determines workplace success is a person's ability to deal with the varied demands of the fast-paced business world. This requires insightful decision making, creative problem solving, and interactions with diverse groups: employees, management, investors, customers, or clients. Thus, teaching critical thinking equips your students with the skills necessary to achieve success.

The Value of Critical Thinking

Critical thinking is the process of reasonably or logically deciding what to do or believe. It involves the ability to:
- Compare and contrast
- Solve problems
- Make decisions
- Analyze and evaluate
- Synthesize and transfer knowledge
- Engage in metacognition

Critical thinking skills are important for these reasons:
- They help students investigate their own problem-solving mechanisms.
- They help students find creative resolutions.
- They lead students to compare and contrast what they know with unknowns.
- They allow students to make decisions about their own learning while making them aware of their learning processes.

Cognitive Development

All learning requires thinking. Benjamin Bloom's Taxonomy of the Cognitive Domain is probably the most widely recognized schema of levels of thinking. Each of Bloom's six cognitive categories lists various thinking skills and indi–cates the types of behavior students are expected to perform to fulfill specific learning goals. See chart below.

CATEGORY	GOAL	EXPECTED STUDENT RESPONSE	APPROPRIATE QUESTIONS/PROMPTS
Knowledge	Identify and recall of information	Define, recognize, recall, identify, label, show, collect, understand, examine	Who…? What…? When…? Where…? How…? Describe….
Comprehension	Organize and select facts and ideas	Translate, interpret, explain, describe, summarize, extrapolate	Retell in your own words…. What is the main idea of…?
Application	Use facts, rules, and principles	Apply, solve, show, experiment, predict	How is…an example of…? How is…related to…?
Analysis	Separate a whole into component parts	Connect, relate, differentiate, classify, arrange, check, group, distinguish, organize, categorize, detect, compare, infer	Classify…according to…. How does… compare/contrast with…?
Synthesis	Combine ideas to form a new whole	Produce, propose, design, construct, combine, formulate, compose, plan, hypothesize	What would you predict/infer from…? What might happen if you combined…with…?
Evaluation	Develop opinions, judgments, or decisions	Appraise, judge, criticize, decide	What do you think about…? Prioritize….

and Your Students Will Benefit

Cooperative Learning

Studies show that students learn faster and retain more information when they are actively involved in the learning process. Cooperative learning is one method that gets students actively involved in learning and at the same time allows for peer teaching.

Using Cooperative Learning

Your business course provides many opportunities for students to learn and apply the skills necessary for positive interpersonal relationships. Through the use of cooperative learning, you can offer a structured method of teaching team-building, collaborative social skills, and team decision making while teaching basic concepts— essential skills for the workplace.

Cooperative Learning in This Text

In *Succeeding in the World of Work,* students and teachers have a variety of materials to assist with cooperative learning activities. Many of the features and section and chapter assessment activities can be completed in a cooperative learning environment.

The Benefits of Cooperative Learning

- Cooperative learning emphasizes working toward group goals rather than the traditional emphasis on individual competition and achievement.
- Students discover that not only must they learn the material themselves, but they are also responsible for helping everyone in the group learn the material.
- Cooperative learning increases academic achievement and develops essential social skills.
- Students learn valuable problem-solving, team-building, and creativity skills that transfer to real-world occupations and work environments.
- People who help each other and work together toward a common goal generally begin to feel more positive about themselves and each other.
- Students have the opportunity to perceive other students as colleagues rather than competitors. As a result, they recognize the value of helping others rather than working competitively.

School-to-Career

A major goal set by the No Child Left Behind Act and the Perkins Act, reauthorized through 2012, is to prepare students to succeed in the constantly changing work world. *Succeeding in the World of Work* successfully integrates work skills preparation with course content and academics. Each chapter in this Teacher Wraparound Edition is preceded by a 21st Century Skills, Foundation Skills, and Workplace Competencies correlations chart that previews the essential skills to be developed in chapter content and activities. Using the charts as guidelines, you can target the needs of your class and the needs of students as individuals to prepare them all for high skill, high wage, and high demand professions.

School-to-career programs are important developments in providing students a sense of relevance in their learning. These programs assume different forms in order to meet the needs of different communities, schools, and students.

Benefits of School-to-Career Programs

All school-to-career programs provide these benefits to students:

- An improved understanding of self,
- An appreciation of the relevance of school learning to "real life," and
- A clearer vision of a productive future and how to make that vision a reality,
- Familiarity with a wide range of career options,
- Increased motivation to stay in and to succeed in school.

An effective school-to-career program involves a close relationship between schools and local businesses. This relationship can result in benefits to schools and to businesses alike, as well as to parents and the community.

PURPOSES OF SCHOOL-TO-CAREER PROGRAMS
• To facilitate the creation of a universal, high-quality school-to-career transition system to enable students to identify and pursue paths to progressively more rewarding roles in the workplace;
• To utilize workplaces as learning environments in the educational process by making employers and educators joint partners in providing opportunities for students to participate in high-quality, work-based learning;
• To promote the formation of partnerships dedicated to linking the worlds of school and work among secondary schools and private and public employers, labor organizations, government, community-based organizations, parents, students, state and local educational agencies, and training and human services agencies;
• To increase knowledge and improve student skills by integrating academic and occupational learning and building links between secondary and postsecondary educational institutions;
• To motivate all students to stay in or return to school and strive to continue their education in postsecondary institutions;
• To expose students to a broad array of career opportunities and facilitate the selection of major areas of study, based on individual interests, goals, and abilities.

Aspects of Industry

Today's workplace requires employees to be independent and competent decision makers and team players. This includes having the ability to think critically about how their workplace decisions impact a business or organization as a whole. Components of all aspects of industry include planning; management; finance; technical and production skills; underlying principles of technology; labor issues; health, safety and environmental issues; and community issues.

Benefits of Teaching All Aspects of Industry

Teaching all aspects of industry in the career education classroom results in tangible benefits to both students and their future employers.

Benefits for Students

Students who consider employment and careers in terms of all aspects of an industry are better prepared to contribute effectively to both their career plans and their work environments. These students tend to learn more quickly, work well with others, and adapt to both anticipated and unexpected changes in today's rapidly changing workplace. They learn to see their role as a worker as part of the "big picture" instead of as an isolated component. Because they have learned "how to learn," they move fluidly from one set of responsibilities to another and are able to acquire and maintain transferable skills.

Students' basic awareness of how industries work, combined with their adaptability and flexibility, results in more career opportunities. Because these students understand industries holistically, their career choices are more informed and less likely to lead to disappointment.

Benefits for Employers

Employers benefit when workers are fully aware of all aspects of their industry. The adaptability and flexibility of their employees may enable technological and procedural changes to be implemented quickly and with less resistance. In addition, cross-training or rotation through different positions

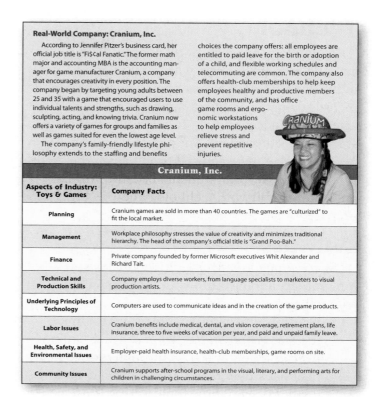

Real-World Company: Cranium, Inc.

According to Jennifer Pitzer's business card, her official job title is "Fi$cal Fanatic." The former math major and accounting MBA is the accounting manager for game manufacturer Cranium, a company that encourages creativity in every position. The company began by targeting young adults between 25 and 35 with a game that encouraged users to use individual talents and strengths, such as drawing, sculpting, acting, and knowing trivia. Cranium now offers a variety of games for groups and families as well as games suited for even the lowest age level.

The company's family-friendly lifestyle philosophy extends to the staffing and benefits choices the company offers: all employees are entitled to paid leave for the birth or adoption of a child, and flexible working schedules and telecommuting are common. The company also offers health-club memberships to help keep employees healthy and productive members of the community, and has office game rooms and ergonomic workstations to help employees relieve stress and prevent repetitive injuries.

Cranium, Inc.

Aspects of Industry: Toys & Games	Company Facts
Planning	Cranium games are sold in more than 40 countries. The games are "culturized" to fit the local market.
Management	Workplace philosophy stresses the value of creativity and minimizes traditional hierarchy. The head of the company's official title is "Grand Poo-Bah."
Finance	Private company founded by former Microsoft executives Whit Alexander and Richard Tait.
Technical and Production Skills	Company employs diverse workers, from language specialists to marketers to visual production artists.
Underlying Principles of Technology	Computers are used to communicate ideas and in the creation of the game products.
Labor Issues	Cranium benefits include medical, dental, and vision coverage, retirement plans, life insurance, three to five weeks of vacation per year, and paid and unpaid family leave.
Health, Safety, and Environmental Issues	Employer-paid health insurance, health-club memberships, game rooms on site.
Community Issues	Cranium supports after-school programs in the visual, literary, and performing arts for children in challenging circumstances.

throughout an industry has greater success rates when workers already value each aspect of industry.

Teaching All Aspects of Industry

To teach all aspects of an industry, it is important to involve real-world employers, industry experts, and mentors as well as counselors and educators, because students need to become actively engaged in all aspects of their chosen industry. These goals can be met through job shadowing, workplace mentoring, informational interviews, paid or unpaid work experience, and classroom programs in both academic and applied coursework.

Information on the U.S. Department of Education's 16 Career Clusters is given throughout *Succeeding in the World of Work* and on the Online Learning Center through **glencoe.com**. This information is designed to introduce students to all aspects of the specific industry or industries and help students develop transferable skills that offer them preparation to succeed in any career.

Technology

Technology affects how all people work, interact, and live. Technology will affect your students in the work world. For example, they may keep records using a computer, apply for a job over the Internet, or telecommute. It will also affect your students as consumers. An increasing number of people market, buy, and sell products on the Web. It is critical that your students become familiar and comfortable with technology now in order to prepare for successful careers.

Activities

Succeeding in the World of Work helps you integrate technology into your teaching with technology-based activities:

- Features and assessments provide a link the *Succeeding in the World of Work* Online Learning Center (OLC) through **glencoe.com** to assist students in finding answers and to further research the topic or find a project.
- The section opening **Reading Guide** provides a link to the OLC for students to download the printable graphic organizer for each section.

- Each section **After You Read** review sends students to the OLC to check their answers.
- The Unit Thematic Project Preview in the Unit Opener provides a **WebQuest** research activity through the OLC at **glencoe.com**.
- The in-chapter features **Creative Business Practices, Tech Savvy, The 21st Century Workplace,** and **Career Spotlight** feature students to the OLC for helpful links or an extension activity. Math in Action and Science in Action send the student to the OLC for more math or science practice.
- Each **Real-World Skills and Applications** section in the Chapter Review and Activities assessment contains at least one Technology Application. Each Financial Literacy and Net Connection assessment activity sends students to the OLC for helpful links or an extension activity.
- Each *BusinessWeek* **Connection** in the Unit Thematic Project sends students to the OLC for an outside article to summarize and analyze.
- The OLC provides outside reading suggestions for each chapter.
- Students can use assessment rubrics on the OLC to self-evaluate their thematic projects.

Using the Internet Effectively

There are steps you can take to use the Internet effectively in the classroom:

- Look for sites that are created by the government or universities (their URLs typically end in .gov or .edu). These are reliable sites with factual integrity and stability.
- Find out who created the site. If the purpose and creator of the Web site are unclear, its content may be unreliable.
- Use multiple search engines when you are looking for information on a topic. This will help you find as many of the pertinent sites as possible.
- Combine your Internet research with traditional research methods. Ask librarians and experts for information and sources. Use books and magazines.

Ethics

Helping students learn about ethical behavior and how to consider the effects of a decision before it is made are important life skills for your students preparing for the business world.

The Benefits of Integrating Ethics

The goal of teaching ethical decision-making skills is not to teach values. It is to help students clarify their ethical beliefs and learn how to evaluate ethical situations. Make your classroom a risk-free environment in which students can discuss issues and make ethical decisions. Students need to learn how to evaluate their actions and to ask questions such as, "Will I be proud of myself if I take this action?" and "Would I want others to know about my actions?"

The Ethical Decision Model

Your students will learn to analyze ethical situations better if they have a model to use in deliberating the issues that helps them to understand how a decision can affect others. Several decision models exist, but the basic steps for an ethical decision model are as follows:

1. Determine the ethical issue.
2. Identify the actions for handling the situation.
3. Identify the people affected by the situation.
4. Analyze how the situation affects the people involved.
5. Decide which of the actions to take.

Classroom Strategies

Everyday Ethics features and some Real-World Connection features provide real-world situations posing ethical conundrums. Both features can be catalysts for lively classroom discussion. In addition, you might lead discussion about topical ethics issues or have students bring in newspaper or magazine articles that suggest ethical dilemmas. Have students analyze the situations in class and, perhaps, write short reports on their analyses and conclusions. Some formats, such as learning groups, role-plays, and debates, are particularly well suited to teaching students about ethics.

Cooperative Learning Groups

Small groups of students are especially well suited to discuss cases and share their ideas about ethical issues. Divide students into groups of four or five. Observe groups and encourage all students to participate. Allow each group to reach its own conclusions, and then ask a member of each group to share their ideas with the class.

Role Plays and Debates

Have your students role-play ethical situations, using their own ideas about how to respond to a given situation. Discuss class responses to the role-play, guiding students in using the ethical decision model. Set up debate teams to present different sides of an ethical issue.

Everyday ETHICS

CALLING IN SICK

Is it ever okay to tell a lie?

VACATION DAYS You recently started a new job at an office supply store. You can't take vacation days until you have been there for three months, but you can take sick days whenever you need them. Before you got your job, you and your friends had planned to go to the beach tomorrow. You really want to go since you have not been able to hang out with your friends much since you started your job.

What Would You Do? Will you lie to your boss and say you are sick so you can go to the beach?

Will the lie hurt anyone? If it does not hurt anyone, is it okay to lie? Write a half-page journal entry explaining your decision.

DISCUSS IT Lying often has consequences you cannot predict. For instance, what if the store is suddenly busy? Is it fair for the store manager to do all the work herself when she is paying you to help her? What if she finds out you went to the beach? How does that affect your reputation? Brainstorm the possible consequences of calling in sick and going to work and share them with the class.

Diversity

Succeeding in the World of Work is designed to help students recognize and discuss issues of cultural diversity. During class activities, you may also find it appropriate to integrate questions related to cultural diversity. For example, you might expand a class discussion by asking:

- Would your response change if the customer or coworker did not speak the same native language as you speak? If so, how?
- Would you direct your employee differently if his or her ethnic background were different from yours?
- Would your decision change if your coworker were a male or female? From your own ethnic background? From a different background? Why?

Integrating Cultural Diversity

As future employees and employers, your students will be faced with a diverse world in which people of many different cultures are both workers and consumers. Cultural knowledge may be the difference between success and failure in conducting business in the global economy. For students to become productive workers and responsible citizens, they must be open to cultural differences.

As students learn about skills needed to be successful, they should keep in mind the wide diversity of the people they are likely to encounter in every aspect of their working and personal lives. In the classroom and in one-on-one conferences, you can help your students consider the diversity of the U.S. population, not only in terms of ethnicity, but also in terms of customs, attitudes, religious beliefs, language backgrounds, and physical capabilities. High school students need to understand that ability and success are not related to skin color or gender.

Multicultural Education

Multicultural education incorporates the idea that all students—regardless of their gender and social class, and their ethnic, racial, or cultural characteristics—should have an equal opportunity to learn in school. Learning about other cultures concurrently with their own culture helps students recognize similarities and appreciate differences, without perceiving inferiority or superiority of one or the other. To foster cultural awareness:

- Recognize that all students are unique, having special talents and abilities.
- Promote uniqueness and diversity as positive traits.
- Know, appreciate, and respect the cultural backgrounds of your students.
- Use authentic situations to provide cultural learning and understanding.
- Make sure people of all cultures are represented fairly and accurately.
- Make sure that historical information is accurate and nondiscriminatory.
- Make sure that materials do not include stereotypical roles.
- Make sure there is gender equity.
- Welcome family and community involvement.
- Use current news stories, advertisements, or other forms of media to call students' attention to cultural differences that influence businesses, communities, and the world of work.

Table of Contents

Table of Contents

Table of Contents

Table of Contents

Table of Contents

Table of Contents

Table of Contents

Table of Contents

Table of Contents

Table of Contents

To the Student

Succeeding in the World of Work Organization

Succeeding in the World of Work includes seven units that are logically organized into 25 chapters. Each chapter contains two sections. This structure presents your lessons clearly and simply. Your book also contains a wide variety of features to clarify the lessons and tie them to real-world situations.

Units

The units serve as an introduction to major themes of the world of work. They show you "the big picture." Activities are included to bring the real world of work to life.

Thematic Project Preview

This unit activity will introduce you to an issue you will face as you enter the world of work. You will begin to think about the decisions you will need to make to apply the lesson to your own life. The Checklist helps you prepare for the thematic project at the end of the unit.

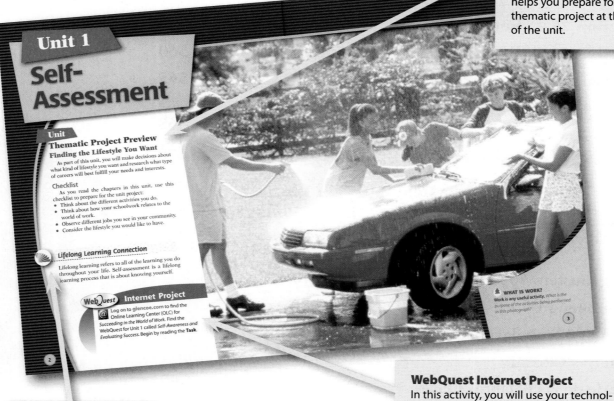

Lifelong Learning

This feature connects the content of the unit with lifelong learning strategies and concepts.

WebQuest Internet Project

In this activity, you will use your technology skills to help you investigate some of the topics in the unit. Your starting point is the *Succeeding in the World of Work* Online Learning Center (OLC), which you can access through **glencoe.com**.

Thematic Project

Each Unit concludes with a Thematic Project that explores an important issue in the world of work. To complete each project, you will evaluate your resources, conduct research, preview a real-world company profile, and report your findings.

Real-World Company Profile

Step 2 features an interview with an employee of a real-world company. The profile provides practical answers on how the company manages all aspects of industry.

Six Steps

There are six steps in each Thematic Project. Step 1 sends you to the *Succeeding in the World of Work* OLC through **glencoe.com** for a graphic organizer to use to list the skills and resources you will need to complete the activity.

Research, Connect, Report

Steps 3, 4, and 5 guide you through researching procedures, connecting to the community, and reporting your findings.

Self Evaluation

Go to the OLC to download a rubric that you can use to evaluate your Thematic Project.

BusinessWeek Connection

BusinessWeek is the world's most widely read business magazine. Go to the OLC to access a *BusinessWeek* article related to the aspect of industry described in this feature.

To the Student

Chapters

The chapters of *Succeeding in the World of Work* are organized around subjects that prepare you for today's global workplace. The chapters are divided logically into two sections and offer numerous learning strategies that will help you get the most from your studies.

Chapter Objectives
The Chapter Objectives preview the content you will learn.

CHAPTER 6
Finding and Applying for a Job

Section 6.1
Exploring Sources of Job Leads

Section 6.2
Applying for a Job

Exploring the Photo
CHECK THE JOB LISTINGS
A good place to find job leads is the classified ads. This person is looking at the listings in the local newspaper. *What are some other places to find job listings?*

Chapter Objectives
After completing this chapter, you will be able to:
- **Define** *networking* and explain why it is an effective way to develop job leads.
- **Develop** a career network and contact list.
- **Explain** how to use the Internet and other resources to find career opportunities.
- **Explain** how to prepare for and complete a job application.
- **Write** an effective résumé and cover letter.

Writing Activity **Personal Career Notebook**
Collect as many job leads as possible over the coming week. Ask friends and family members about jobs. Read the classified ads in your local newspaper. Read the bulletin board in the placement office in your school. Write a paragraph about the details of each job opening and how you found each lead.

Get Motivated! Contact three working adults in your community. Ask them to tell you how they found their jobs. Write a paragraph describing their different ways of finding jobs.

Chapter 6   Finding and Applying for a Job   129

Exploring the Photo
The chapters begin with a photo that visually illustrates chapter content and a caption that asks you a question designed to help you to start thinking about what you will read.

Writing Activity
The Personal Career Notebook asks you to relate your own background knowledge of the chapter subject, make predictions, and record other thoughts related to the chapter subject. Get Motivated! asks you to interact with or research a person or organization in your community regarding the chapter subject.

Sections

Each chapter section begins with a Reading Guide to give you a preview of section content.

Reading Guide
The section objectives, main idea, key concepts, and vocabulary are previewed here.

Before You Read
A pre-reading question or statement will help you connect to what you read.

Graphic Organizer
A graphic organizer gives you a visual tool to help you organize and remember new content.

Academic Standards
Succeeding in the World of Work helps you gain proficiency in English Language Arts, Mathematics, and Science. The section openers list the academic standards that the section will help you develop.

Section 1.1

Exploring the World of Work

Reading Guide

Before You Read
Preview Read the Key Concepts. Write one or two sentences predicting what the section will be about.

Read to Learn
- How to identify a job, an occupation, and a career
- How skills, interests, and desired lifestyle may shape career plans
- How your job can affect your lifestyle
- Reasons that people work

Main Idea
Knowing how your work affects your lifestyle will help you understand the importance of making good career choices.

Key Concepts
- What Is Work?
- Why People Work

Key Terms
- interests
- skills
- transferable skills
- job
- occupation
- career
- lifestyle

Academic Vocabulary
You will find these words in your reading and on your tests. Use the academic vocabulary glossary to look up their definitions if necessary.
- specific
- determine
- environment

Graphic Organizer
As you read, list your skills and your interests. Continue adding your own ideas to the list after you have finished reading. Use a two-column chart like the one shown to help organize your information.

SKILLS	INTERESTS

@ Log On Go to this book's Online Learning Center through glencoe.com for an online version of this graphic organizer.

Academic Standards . . . .
English Language Arts
- Read texts to acquire new information. (NCTE 1)
- Use written language to communicate effectively. (NCTE 4)

Mathematics
- Understand numbers, ways of representing numbers, relationships among numbers, and number systems

6 **Unit 1** Self-Assessment

glencoe.com

What Is Work?

Think about your world. What do you do each day? How do you spend your time? Right now, you probably spend most of your time in school. Do you wonder what you are going to do after high school? Will you continue to go to school? Will you learn a trade? Perhaps it is time to think about your options and to prepare for them. Some day, work will be a big part of your life.

What is work? Work is any useful activity. For example, cleaning your room is work. One of the main reasons people work is to make money to pay for things they need or want. You probably will not be surprised to learn that most people prefer to do work that uses their interests. After all, work takes up a lot of time. With a full-time job, you could spend more than 2,000 hours a year at work.

What kind of job would be right for you? Think about your interests and your skills. Your **interests** are the things you like to do. You may like to listen to music, dance, play basketball, or work with computers. Knowing your interests will help you plan different parts of your life.

Skills are things you know how to do. They are the result of knowledge combined with experience. Skills can also include things you are good at, or even ways of behaving. Some skills are **specific** to certain tasks. For example, knowing how to drive a car, how to water a plant, or how to calculate change, are skills you use for certain tasks. Skills that you can use in many different situations are called **transferable skills**. Writing, getting along with people, being organized, and making decisions are all transferable skills. For example, you can use your writing skills to write an essay for a language arts class or to send an e-mail to a coworker or friend.

✎ Vocabulary
You can find definitions in the **Key Terms** glossary and Academic Vocabulary glossary at the back of this book.

▶ REWARDING WORK
Mark chose to teach martial arts because he was good with children and interested in martial arts. *What other skills and interests might be helpful for a teacher?*

7

To the Student

Reading Strategies

Glencoe is committed to your reading success. Every section of *Succeeding in the World of Work* includes a number of reading strategies that will help you master this crucial skill.

Reading Check
Reading Checks allow you to make a quick comprehension self-check.

As You Read
As You Read provides a cue to connect you to what you are reading.

After You Read
Reviewing your reading is a powerful study skill. Review Key Concepts will help you organize and process your understanding of what you have read. Practice Academic Skills will connect content to academics.

Section 1.1 After You Read

Review Key Concepts
1. Give one example each of a job, an occupation, and a career.
2. Give an example of a skill that might be used in a specific job.
3. Describe a situation that might cause a person to change his or her main reason for working.

Practice Academic Skills
Mathematics
4. Most Americans spend more than 30% of their yearly income on housing expenses. If you earn $27,000 per year, how much money will you need to spend on housing?

THEORY Multiply Decimals by Whole Numbers A percent is a ratio that compares a number to 100. To multiply with percentages:
Step 1: You can rewrite the percent (30%) as a fraction with a denominator of 100. Convert the fraction to a decimal.
Step 2: Multiply this decimal by the number ($27,000). Remember to put the decimal point in the correct place in your answer.

Math For math help, go to the Math Appendix located at the back of this book.

Features

The features in each chapter help you see the relevance between what you read and the real world.

The 21st Century Workplace
Expanded information about today's global 21st century workplace, including information about languages across cultures, diversity, and other modern workplace practices.

The 21st Century Workplace

¿Cómo se dice esto en español?
(How do you say that in Spanish?)

In today's global workplace, there are opportunities in many jobs and industries to work with people who speak Spanish. The Spanish language ranks third in the world in number of speakers, after Chinese and English. It is the official language of Spain, Mexico, Cuba, Puerto Rico, the countries of Central America, and the majority of countries in South America. In addition, according to the U.S. Department of Labor, by 2050, one quarter of all Americans will be of Hispanic origin.

CRITICAL THINKING
In what ways might the changing American population affect consumer goods and services?

In Your Community
If there is another population in your community that speaks a language other than English, identify some common phrases you think would ... with your class in

COMMON SPANISH WORDS AND PHRASES	
hello	hola
good day	buenos días
goodbye	adiós/que vaya bien
yes	sí
no	no
please	por favór
How are you?	¿Cómo está usted?
good	bien
thank you	muchas gracias
you're welcome	De nada

 Extend Your Learning Spanish dialects can vary according to country, region, or even city. For Web links about dialects, go to this book's OLC through **glencoe.com**.

Everyday Ethics
This feature lets you look at the ethical challenges and choices related to the workplace.

Everyday ETHICS

CALLING IN SICK

Is it ever okay to tell a lie?

VACATION DAYS You recently started a new job at an office supply store. You can't take vacation days until you have been there for three months, but you can take sick days whenever you need them. Before you got your job, you and your friends had planned to go to the beach tomorrow. You really want to go since you have not been able to hang out with your friends much since you started your job.

What Would You Do? Will you lie to your boss and say you are sick so you can go to the beach?

Will the lie hurt anyone? If it does not hurt anyone, is it okay to lie? Write a half-page journal entry explaining your decision.

DISCUSS IT Lying often has consequences you cannot predict. For instance, what if the store is suddenly busy? Is it fair for the store manager to do all the work herself when she is paying you to help her? What if she finds out you went to the beach? How does that affect your reputation? Brainstorm the possible consequences of calling in sick and going to work and share them with the class.

Creative Business Practices
Profiles of businesses that demonstrate innovative workplace, community, or leadership trends.

Creative Business Practices

PATAGONIA Exploring Opportunities

Patagonia, Inc., a company that makes outdoor and adventure sports gear, encourages employees to have adventures of their own. The company provides endangered paid leave for employees who want to work as interns with nonprofit groups, such wilderness projects that help save endangered species. During internships, Patagonia employees receive their regular salary and benefits for up to 60 days. Patagonia employees have worked on projects such as the Chumbe Island Project, which encourages coral reef protection, and the Mist Preservation Society, which helps preserve the subtropical forests of New Zealand.

The Patagonia internship program benefits everyone involved. Nonprofit groups benefit from the experience of talented volunteers, employees get time away from the office to make a difference in the world, and Patagonia gets to support worthy efforts.

CRITICAL THINKING If you had the opportunity to take part in Patagonia's internship program, which programs would interest you? Why?

 Connect to the Real World To read more about Patagonia, visit the company's Web site via the link on this book's Online Learning Center through **glencoe.com**.

To the Student

Tech Savvy
This feature includes technology trends, products, or issues related to the workplace.

TechSavvy

Evaluating Web Sites

Imagine that you are thinking of pursuing several different careers and you want to use the Internet to research the future demand for a job that interests you. How can you determine which Web sites have good and reliable information?

Government sites are often a good source of information, but you should always evaluate any information you read. To evaluate a Web site, ask: Who is giving you the information? Is the information accurate, thorough, free from bias, and up-to-date? A librarian may be able to help you find the answers to these questions.

@ Visit this book's OLC through **glencoe.com** and find a link to the U.S. Bureau of Labor Statistics Web site. Research the current five-year career outlook for three jobs that interest you. Write a half-page summary of each job outlook and explain whether you think it would be worthwhile to pursue these careers.

Real-World Connection

Career Mentors

You love the outdoors and want a career that will let you work outside. Your school counselor recently announced that you are a finalist for a scholarship in computer science, based on your high test scores in a programming class. You do not see how a technology major will be compatible with your goal to work outdoors.

Critical Thinking How can you pursue a technology major and still remain true to your lifestyle goals?

Do Your Own Research Find an adult who works outdoors and has agreed to mentor students. Talk with your school counselor, career development coordinator, or work-based learning coordinator if you need help locating someone appropriate. Conduct an informational interview with the mentor, and include questions about the role of technology in his or her job.

Math in Action
This brief practical mathematics activity includes a Starting Hint.

Math In Action

Calculate Pay

Esteban is deciding between two job offers. One pays $13.00 an hour for 50 hours a week; the other pays $15.50 an hour for 40 hours a week. Esteban wants to spend more time with his family, so he will probably choose the second job. If he does, how much less will he make each year?

Starting Hint: Calculate how much he will make in each job per year before you calculate the difference in pay.

@ For more math practice go to this book's OLC through **glencoe.com**.

Science In Action

Temperature

Many scientific processes use the Celsius scale to measure temperature, while the general U.S. public uses the Fahrenheit scale. Convert 68° Fahrenheit to degrees Celsius. Round to the closest whole number. The conversion formula is $°C = \frac{5}{9}[(°F)-(32°F)]$.

Starting Hint: Start the conversion by filling in the variables you know in the formula, degrees Fahrenheit (°F): $°C = \frac{5}{9}[(°68)-(32°F)]$.

@ For more science practice, go to this book's OLC through **glencoe.com**.

Real-World Connection
This feature gives you a real-world anecdote or passage that deals with issues regarding work or school.

Science in Action
This brief practical science activity includes a Starting Hint.

Career Checklist

A simple checklist that contains general tips related to the chapter topic.

Career ✓ Checklist

When Entering the Workplace:

- ✓ Define your goals.
- ✓ Stay informed of changes in the workplace.
- ✓ Expect the best from yourself and others.
- ✓ Maintain a positive attitude.
- ✓ Learn from your mistakes.
- ✓ Take advantage of every opportunity to learn.

HOT JOBS!

Speech Therapist

Speech therapists work with people who have difficulty with speech, language, communication, swallowing, and fluency. For example, a speech therapist might work with someone who has a stutter or someone who wishes to eliminate an accent. This job requires attention to detail, good communication skills, and knowledge of speech-related disorders.

Hot Jobs!

A brief introduction to an interesting job. Exploring careers can help you set goals that can lead you to career success.

Career Spotlight

This feature offers an interview with a real-world individual about their job.

Academic Skills

This table details the academic skills needed to perform the specific tasks required for the job featured in the interview.

Career Facts

Detailed information about the featured career, and possible career paths for that jobs or other jobs in that career cluster. A **career path** is like a road map that includes all of the jobs and experiences needed to work toward a specific career goal.

To the Student

Assessment

Assessment is an important part of the learning process. Knowing what you have learned is a good way to find out what you need to study further.

Section Assessment

Each section ends with a review and academic questions.

Section 1.1 After You Read

Review Key Concepts
1. Give one example each of a job, an occupation, and a career.
2. Give an example of a skill that might be used in a specific job.
3. Describe a situation that might cause a person to change his or her main reason for working.

Practice Academic Skills
Mathematics
4. Most Americans spend more than 30% of their yearly income on housing expenses. If you earn $27,000 per year, how much money will you need to spend on housing?

Multiply Decimals by Whole Numbers A percent is a ratio that compares a number to 100. To multiply with percentages:
Step 1: You can rewrite the percent (30%) as a fraction with a denominator of 100. Convert the fraction to a decimal.
Step 2: Multiply this decimal by the number ($27,000). Remember to put the decimal point in the correct place in your answer.

For math help, go to the Math Appendix located at the back of this book.

After You Read
Assess your own comprehension with Review Key Concepts questions. Connect content to academics with the Practice Academic Skills questions.

Real-World Skills and Applications
These activities help you to develop strong workplace, communication, and technology skills, as well as lifelong learning skills such as financial literacy.

Chapter Review & Activities

The Chapter Review & Activities contains a variety of review questions and activities.

Section Summaries
The Section Summaries quickly restate the main concepts of the section.

Key Terms and Academic Vocabulary Review
This section lists words you will see on your tests.

Review Key Concepts
These questions will review your comprehension.

Critical Thinking
These questions ask you to think more deeply to relate text to real situations.

CHAPTER 1 Review & Activities

CHAPTER SUMMARY

Section 1.1
You should consider your interests and skills when planning your career. A job is work that people do for pay, an occupation is the type of work you do, and a career is a series of related jobs built on a person's interests, knowledge, training, and experience. Your lifestyle is the way you use your time, energy, and resources. Your work affects your lifestyle. Four important reasons people work are to earn money, to fulfill wants and needs, to be around other people, to contribute to society, and for self-fulfillment.

Section 1.2
The global economy refers to the ways in which the world's economies are linked. It affects what kinds of jobs will be available. You will need basic skills, thinking skills, personal qualities, and adaptability to meet the demands of the global job market. Other workplace trends include the use of technology, diversity, the use of teams, outsourcing, and telecommuting. In the United States, most new jobs are predicted to be in the service-producing industries. When looking for careers, you need to be aware of economic, technological and workplace trends, job outlook, and personal job satisfaction.

Key Terms and Academic Vocabulary Review

1. Use each of these key terms and academic vocabulary words in a sentence.

Key Terms
- interests (p. 7)
- skills (p. 7)
- transferable skills (p. 7)
- job (p. 9)
- occupation (p. 9)
- career (p. 9)
- lifestyle (p. 10)
- economy (p. 15)
- global economy (p. 15)
- job market (p. 15)
- outsourcing (p. 17)
- telecommute (p. 17)
- team (p. 17)
- lifelong learning (p. 21)

Academic Vocabulary
- specific (p. 7)
- determine (p. 10)
- environment (p. 10)
- economic (p. 15)

Review Key Concepts

2. **Define** a job, an occupation, and a career. Give an example of each.
3. **Describe** how skills, interests, and desired lifestyle may shape career plans.
4. **Explain** how work life affects lifestyle.
5. **List** some of the reasons that people work.
6. **List** factors that affect today's workplace.
7. **Explain** why it is important to evaluate job outlooks when making career plans.

Critical Thinking

8. **Compare and Contrast** In what ways might a decrease or increase in income affect aspects of your lifestyle?
9. **Evaluate** What is the value of observing changes in the world of work, even when you may not be working full-time for a while?

CHAPTER 1 Review & Activities

Real-World Skills and Applications

Interpersonal and Collaborative Skills
10. **Working in Teams** Team up with one or more classmates. Identify a number of jobs in the Arts, Audio/Video Technology, and Communications career cluster. Choose one of these jobs and create a five-minute presentation that features some of the skills, training, and technology that is needed to perform this job. Your presentation might use software, visual aids, or brief skits.

Technology Applications
11. **Creating a Spreadsheet** You are in charge of the equipment for a 16-member soccer team. You must record the type of equipment the team purchases, such as balls, shoes, towels, and uniforms, as well as when each piece of equipment was ordered and received. Use spreadsheet software to create a document that can list and categorize all the equipment.

Financial Literacy Skills
12. **Determining Your Financial Situation** To figure out your personal financial situation, start by making a list of items that relate to your finances: savings, monthly income (job earnings, allowance), monthly expenses (money you spend), and debts (money you owe to others). Use a notebook, a spreadsheet, or another document to categorize your expenses over a set period of time, such as a week or a month.

Log On Go to this book's Online Learning Center through glencoe.com for help with financial literacy.

13. **ACTIVE LEARNING** **Brainstorming and Sharing Information** Take one minute to brainstorm skills you might use in the classroom that you might also use at a service job, such as a checker at a grocery store. Team up with a classmate and share your answers verbally for two to three minutes. Volunteer to share both of your answers with the class. Take notes on all the skills that are mentioned.

14. **ROLE PLAY** **Career Counseling Visit**
Situation You have been employed by the U.S. Department of Labor to help students understand the importance of transferable skills. For your job, you are required to visit high school classrooms across the country to deliver presentations and answer questions. You hope to encourage students to broaden their horizons by developing their transferable skills.
Activity Make a five- to ten-minute presentation about transferable skills within a career that interests you. Use presentation software or other visual aids to describe different transferable skills. Be prepared to answer questions that other students pose about your presentation.
Evaluation You will be evaluated on how well you meet the following performance indicators:
- Explain a variety of transferable skills.
- Provide specific and comprehensive information about skills.
- Effectively handle a question-and-answer session.

24 **Unit 1** Self-Assessment

Real-World Skills and Applications
These activities help you to develop strong workplace, communication, and technology skills, as well as lifelong learning skills such as financial literacy.

Active Learning
Here you have an opportunity to "learn by doing," either on your own or as part of a team.

Role Play
Role-play scenarios give you an opportunity to imagine and perform your actions in a real-world situation. You will also learn how your performance will be evaluated during a role-play for a competitive event.

Academic Skills in the Workplace
These activities give you practice applying your English Language Arts, Mathematics, Social Studies, Science, and World Languages academic skills to workplace-related content.

Writing Skills Practice
Here you will practice different types of writing.

Net Connection
This activity gives you the opportunity to practice your Internet and other technology application skills.

Standardized Test Practice
Here you have an opportunity to sharpen your test-taking skills. The activity also includes a valuable Test-Taking Tip.

Personal Academic and Career Portfolio

A personal academic and career portfolio is a collection of information about a person, including documents, projects, and work samples that show a person's skills, talents, and qualifications. It includes information about interests, goals, and accomplishments, as well as information needed for a job search. You can use your portfolio throughout your career to keep track of your accomplishments.

The **Personal Academic and Career Portfolio** activity in each chapter review and callouts to the portfolio in the text will help you develop and maintain a personal academic and career portfolio that you can use to keep track of academic and career growth.

Personal Academic and Career Portfolio

Beginning Your Portfolio

Your **Personal Academic and Career Portfolio** is a collection of documents and other media that can showcase your skills and accomplishments. Your portfolio can be either a hard copy portfolio or a digital portfolio, or a combination of both. For example, a graphic artist might wish to place a collection of drawings in his or her portfolio. The graphic artist could make scans of these drawings digitally available online or on a CD-ROM, keeping the original drawings in a hard copy portfolio.

Use the following guidelines to begin your portfolio.

- Use a folder with dividers to organize any hard copy portfolio materials.
- Select a format for your portfolio. A hard copy portfolio can include any printed media. An electronic portfolio can include documents, presentations, digital multimedia files (such as photos and audio or video files), and Web pages.
- Create a cover or title document with your name, address, and other contact information.
- Create a directory or table of contents.
- Create a list of your skills and interests.
- Categorize your skills.
- Title the document *Inventory of Skills and Interests* and file it in your portfolio.
- Update the inventory as you discover and gain new skills and interests.

@ **Portfolio Help** Go to the *Succeeding in the World of Work* OLC through **glencoe.com** for help developing your portfolio.

To the Student

Online Learning Center

Follow these steps to access the textbook resources at the *Succeeding in the World of Work* Online Learning Center.

Step 1
Go to glencoe.com.

Step 2
Select your state from the pull-down menu.

Step 3
Select Student/Parent.

Step 4
Select Career Education.

Step 5
Click ENTER.

Step 6
Select *Succeeding in the World of Work* © 2008.

Step 7
Click Student Center to access student resources.

Step 8
Select a Chapter from the Chapter Activities pull-down menu to access resources for each chapter.

Reading Skills Handbook

▶ Reading: What's in It for You?

What role does reading play in your life? The possibilities are countless. Are you on a sports team? Perhaps you like to read about the latest news and statistics in your sports or find out about new training techniques. Are you looking for a part-time job? You might be looking for advice about résumé writing, interview techniques, or information about a company. Are you enrolled in an English class, an algebra class, or a business class? Then your assignments require a lot of reading.

> **Improving or Fine-Tuning Your Reading Skills Will:**
>
> ◆ Improve your grades
> ◆ Allow you to read faster and more efficiently
> ◆ Improve your study skills
> ◆ Help you remember more information accurately
> ◆ Improve your writing

▶ The Reading Process

Good reading skills build on one another, overlap, and spiral around in much the same way that a winding staircase goes around and around while leading you to a higher place. This handbook is designed to help you find and use the tools you'll need **before, during,** and **after** reading.

> **Strategies You Can Use**
>
> ◆ Identify, understand, and learn new words
> ◆ Understand why you read
> ◆ Take a quick look at the whole text
> ◆ Try to predict what you are about to read
> ◆ Take breaks while you read and ask yourself questions about the text
> ◆ Take notes
> ◆ Keep thinking about what will come next
> ◆ Summarize

▶ Vocabulary Development

Word identification and vocabulary skills are the building blocks of the reading and the writing process. By learning to use a variety of strategies to build your word skills and vocabulary, you will become a stronger reader.

Use Context to Determine Meaning

The best way to expand and extend your vocabulary is to read widely, listen carefully, and participate in a rich variety of discussions. When reading on your own, though, you can often figure out the meanings of new words by looking at their **context,** the other words and sentences that surround them.

Tips for Using Context

Look for clues such as:

A synonym or an explanation of the unknown word in the sentence:
*Elise's shop specialized in **millinery**, or **hats for women**.*

A reference to what the word is or is not like:
*An **archaeologist**, like a historian, deals with the past.*

A general topic associated with the word:
*The **cooking** teacher discussed the best way to braise meat.*

A description or action associated with the word:
*He used the **shovel** to **dig up** the garden.*

Predict a Possible Meaning

Another way to determine the meaning of a word is to take the word apart. If you understand the meaning of the **base,** or **root,** part of a word, and also know the meanings of key syllables added either to the beginning or end of the base word, you can usually figure out what the word means.

Word Origins Since Latin, Greek, and Anglo-Saxon roots are the basis for much of our English vocabulary, having some background in languages can be a useful vocabulary tool. For example, *astronomy* comes from the Greek root *astro,* which means "relating to the stars." *Stellar* also has a meaning referring to stars, but its origin is Latin. Knowing root words in other languages can help you determine meanings, derivations, and spellings in English.

Prefixes and Suffixes A prefix is a word part that can be added to the beginning of a word. For example, the prefix *semi* means "half" or "partial," so *semicircle* means "half a circle." A suffix is a word part that can be added to the end of a word. Adding a suffix often changes a word from one part of speech to another.

Using Dictionaries A dictionary provides the meaning or meanings of a word. Look at the sample dictionary entry on the next page to see what other information it provides.

Thesauruses and Specialized Reference Books A thesaurus provides synonyms and often antonyms. It is a useful tool to expand your vocabulary. Remember to check the exact definition of the listed words in a dictionary before you use a thesaurus. Specialized dictionaries such as *Barron's Dictionary of Business Terms* or *Black's Law Dictionary* list terms and expressions that are not commonly included in a general dictionary. You can also use online dictionaries.

Glossaries Many textbooks and technical works contain condensed dictionaries that provide an alphabetical listing of words used in the text and their specific definitions.

Dictionary Entry

Forms of the word

Numbered definitions

Usage label

Part of speech

Example of use

help (help) **helped** or *(archaic)* **holp**, **helped** or *(archaic)* **hol-pen**, **help-ing**. *v.t.* **1.** to provide with support, as in the performance of a task; be of service to: *He helped his brother paint the room.* ▲ also used elliptically with a preposition or adverb: *He helped the old woman up the stairs.* **2.** to enable (someone or something) to accomplish a goal or achieve a desired effect: *The coach's advice helped the team to win.* **3.** to provide with sustenance or relief, as in time of need or distress; succor: *The Red Cross helped the flood victims.* **4.** to promote or contribute to; further. *The medication helped his recovery.* **5.** to be useful or profitable to; be of advantage to: *It might help you if you read the book.* **6.** to improve or remedy: *Nothing really helped his sinus condition.* **7.** to prevent; stop: *I can't help his rudeness.* **8.** to refrain from; avoid: *I couldn't help smiling when I heard the story.* **9.** to wait on or serve (often with to): *The clerk helped us. The hostess helped him to the dessert.* **10. cannot help but.** *Informal* cannot but. **11. so help me (God).** oath of affirmation. **12. to help oneself to.** to take or appropriate: *The thief helped himself to all the jewels.—v.i.* to provide support, as in the performance of a task; be of service. *—n.* **1.** act of providing support, service, or sustenance. **2.** source of support, service, or sustenance. **3.** person or group of persons hired to work for another or others. **4.** means of improving, remedying, or preventing. [Old English *helpan* to aid, succor, benefit.] **Syn.** *v.t.* **1. Help, aid, assist** mean to support in a useful way. Help is the most common word and means to give support in response to a known or expressed need or for a definite purpose: *Everyone helped to make the school fair a success.* **Aid** means to give relief in times of distress or difficulty: *It is the duty of rich nations to aid the poor.* **Assist** means to serve another person in the performance of his task in a secondary capacity: *The secretary assists the officer by taking care of his corresponding.*

Idioms

Origin (etymology)

Synonyms

Recognize Word Meanings Across Subjects Have you learned a new word in one class and then noticed it in your reading for other subjects? The word might not mean exactly the same thing in each class, but you can use the meaning you already know to help you understand what it means in another subject area. For example:

Math After you multiply the two numbers, explain how you arrived at the **product.**

Science One **product** of photosynthesis is oxygen.

Economics The Gross National **Product** is the total dollar value of goods and services produced by a nation.

▶ Understanding What You Read

Reading comprehension means understanding—deriving meaning from—what you have read. Using a variety of strategies can help you improve your comprehension and make reading more interesting and more fun.

Read for a Reason

To get the greatest benefit from what you read, you should **establish a purpose for reading.** In school, you have many reasons for reading. Some of them are:

- To learn and understand new information
- To find specific information
- To review before a test
- To complete an assignment
- To prepare (research) before you write

As your reading skills improve, you will notice that you apply different strategies to fit the different purposes for reading. For example, if you are reading for entertainment, you might read quickly, but if you read to gather information or follow directions, you might read more slowly, take notes, construct a graphic organizer, or reread sections of text.

Draw on Personal Background

Drawing on personal background may also be called activating prior knowledge. Before you start reading a text, ask yourself questions like these:

- What have I heard or read about this topic?
- Do I have any personal experience relating to this topic?

Using a KWL Chart A KWL chart is a good device for organizing information you gather before, during, and after reading. In the first column, list what you already **know,** then list what you **want** to know in the middle column. Use the third column when you review and you assess what you **learned.** You can also add more columns to record places where you found information and places where you can look for more information.

K (What I already know)	W (What I want to know)	L (What I have learned)

Adjust Your Reading Speed Your reading speed is a key factor in how well you understand what you are reading. You will need to adjust your speed depending on your reading purpose.

Scanning means running your eyes quickly over the material to look for words or phrases. Scan when you need a specific piece of information.

Skimming means reading a passage quickly to find its main idea or to get an overview. Skim a text when you preview to determine what the material is about.

Reading for detail involves careful reading while paying attention to text structure and monitoring your understanding. Read for detail when you are learning concepts, following complicated directions, or preparing to analyze a text.

▶ Techniques to Understand and Remember What You Read

Preview

Before beginning a selection, it is helpful to **preview** what you are about to read.

> **Previewing Strategies**
>
> Read the title, headings, and subheadings of the selection.
>
> Look at the illustrations and notice how the text is organized.
>
> Skim the selection: Take a glance at the whole thing.
>
> Decide what the main idea might be.
>
> Predict what a selection will be about.

Predict

Have you ever read a mystery, decided who committed the crime, and then changed your mind as more clues were revealed? You were adjusting your predictions. Did you smile when you found out you guessed the murderer? You were verifying your predictions.

As you read, take educated guesses about story events and outcomes; that is, **make predictions** before and during reading. This will help you focus your attention on the text and it will improve your understanding.

Determine the Main Idea

When you look for the **main idea**, you are looking for the most important statement in a text. Depending on what kind of text you are reading, the main idea can be located at the very beginning (news stories in newspaper or a magazine) or at the end (scientific research document). Ask yourself:

- What is each sentence about?
- Is there one sentence that is more important than all the others?
- What idea do details support or point out?

Taking Notes

Cornell Note-Taking System: There are many methods for note taking. The **Cornell Note-Taking System** is a well-known method that can help you organize what you read. To the right is a note-taking activity based on the Cornell Note-Taking System.

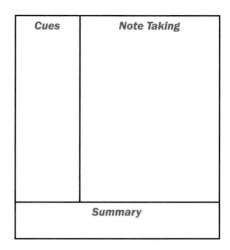

Graphic organizers: Using a graphic organizer to retell content in a visual representation will help you remember and retain content. You might make a **chart** or **diagram,** organizing what you have read. Here are some examples of graphic organizers:

Venn diagrams: When mapping out a comparison-and-contrast text structure, you can use a Venn diagram. The outer portions of the circles will show how two characters, ideas, or items contrast, or are different, and the overlapping part will compare two things, or show how they are similar.

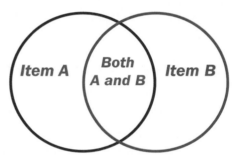

Flow charts: To help you track the sequence of events, or cause and effect, use a flow chart. Arrange ideas or events in their logical, sequential order. Then draw arrows between your ideas to indicate how one idea or event flows into another.

Visualize

Try to form a mental picture of scenes, characters, and events as you read. Use the details and descriptions the author gives you. If you can **visualize** what you read, it will be more interesting and you will remember it better.

Question

Ask yourself questions about the text while you read. Ask yourself about the importance of the sentences, how they relate to one another, if you understand what you just read, and what you think is going to come next.

Clarify

If you feel you do not understand meaning (through questioning), try these techniques:

> **What to Do When You Do Not Understand**
>
> ◆ Reread confusing parts of the text.
> ◆ Diagram (chart) relationships between chunks of text, ideas, and sentences.
> ◆ Look up unfamiliar words.
> ◆ Talk out the text to yourself.
> ◆ Read the passage once more.

Review

Take time to stop and review what you have read. Use your note-taking tools (graphic organizers or Cornell notes charts). Also, review and consider your KWL chart.

Monitor Your Comprehension

Continue to check your understanding by using the following two strategies:

Summarize Pause and tell yourself the main ideas of the text and the key supporting details. Try to answer the following questions: Who? What? When? Where? Why? How?

Paraphrase Pause, close the book, and try to retell what you have just read in your own words. It might help to pretend you are explaining the text to someone who has not read it and does not know the material.

▶ Understanding Text Structure

Good writers do not just put together sentences and paragraphs, they organize their writing with a specific purpose in mind. That organization is called text structure. When you understand and follow the structure of a text, it is easier to remember the information you are reading. There are many ways text may be structured. Watch for **signal words**. They will help you follow the text's organization (also, remember to use these techniques when you write).

Compare and Contrast

This structure shows similarities and differences between people, things, and ideas. This is often used to demonstrate that things that seem alike are really different, or vice versa.

> **Signal words:** similarly, more, less, on the one hand / on the other hand, in contrast, but, however

Cause and Effect

Writers used the cause and effect structure to explore the reasons for something happening and to examine the results or consequences of events.

Signal words: so, because, as a result, therefore, for the following reasons

Problem and Solution

When they organize text around the question "how?" writers state a problem and suggest solutions.

Signal words: how, help, problem, obstruction, overcome, difficulty, need, attempt, have to, must

Sequence

Sequencing tells you in which order to consider thoughts or facts. Examples of sequencing are:

Chronological order refers to the order in which events take place.

Signal words: first, next, then, finally

Spatial order describes the organization of things in space (to describe a room, for example).

Signal words: above, below, behind, next to

Order of importance lists things or thoughts from the most important to the least important (or the other way around).

Signal words: principal, central, main, important, fundamental

▶ Reading for Meaning

It is important to think about what you are reading to get the most infor–mation out of a text, to understand the consequences of what the text says, to remember the content, and to form your own opinion about what the content means.

Interpret

Interpreting is asking yourself, "What is the writer really saying?" and then using what you already know to answer that question.

Infer

Writers do not always state exactly everything they want you to understand. By providing clues and details, they sometimes imply certain information. An **inference** involves using your reason and experience to develop the idea on your own, based on what an author implies or suggests. What is most important when drawing inferences is to be sure that you have accurately based your guesses on supporting details from the text. If you cannot point to a place in the selection to help back up your inference, you may need to rethink your guess.

Draw Conclusions

A conclusion is a general statement you can make and explain with reasoning, or with supporting details from a text. If you read a story describing a sport where five players bounce a ball and throw it through a high hoop, you may conclude that the sport is basketball.

Analyze

To understand persuasive nonfiction (a text that discusses facts and opinions to arrive at a conclusion), you need to analyze statements and examples to see if they support the main idea. To understand an informational text (a text, such as a textbook, that gives you information, not opinions), you need to keep track of how the ideas are organized to find the main points.

Hint: Use your graphic organizers and notes charts.

Distinguish Facts and Opinions

This is one of the most important reading skills you can learn. A fact is a statement that can be proven. An opinion is what the writer believes. A writer may support opinions with facts, but an opinion cannot be proven. For example:

Fact: California produces fruit and other agricultural products.

Opinion: California produces the best fruit and other agricultural products.

Evaluate

Would you take seriously an article on nuclear fission if you knew it was written by a comedic actor? If you need to rely on accurate information, you need to find out who wrote what you are reading and why. Where did the writer get information? Is the information one-sided? Can you verify the information?

▶ Reading for Research

You will need to **read actively** in order to research a topic. You might also need to generate an interesting, relevant, and researchable **question** on your own and locate appropriate print and nonprint information from a wide variety of sources. Then you will need to **categorize** that information, evaluate it, and **organize** it in a new way in order to produce a research project for a specific audience. Finally, **draw conclusions** about your original research question. These conclusions may lead you to other areas for further inquiry.

Locate Appropriate Print and Nonprint Information

In your research, try to use a variety of sources. Because different sources present information in different ways, your research project will be more interesting and balanced when you read a variety of sources.

Literature and Textbooks These texts include any book used as a basis for instruction or a source of information.

Book Indices A book index, or a bibliography, is an alphabetical listing of books. Some book indices list books on specific subjects; others are more general. Other indices list a variety of topics or resources.

Periodicals Magazines and journals are issued at regular intervals, such as weekly or monthly. One way to locate information in magazines is to use the *Readers' Guide to Periodical Literature.* This guide is available in print form in most libraries.

Technical Manuals A manual is a guide or handbook intended to give instruction on how to perform a task or operate something. A vehicle owner's manual might give information on how to operate and service a car.

Reference Books Reference books include encyclopedias and almanacs, and are used to locate specific pieces of information.

Electronic Encyclopedias, Databases, and the Internet There are many ways to locate extensive information using your computer. Infotrac, for instance, acts as an online readers guide. CD encyclopedias can provide easy access to all subjects.

Organize and Convert Information

As you gather information from different sources, taking careful notes, you will need to think about how to **synthesize** the information, that is, convert it into a unified whole, as well as how to change it into a form your audience will easily understand and that will meet your assignment guidelines.

1. First, ask yourself what you want your audience to know.
2. Then, think about a pattern of organization, a structure that will best show your main ideas. You might ask yourself the following questions:
   - When comparing items or ideas, what graphic aids can I use?
   - When showing the reasons something happened and the effects of certain actions, what text structure would be best?
   - How can I briefly and clearly show important information to my audience?
   - Would an illustration or even a cartoon help to make a certain point?

Chapter	Chapter Objectives
CHAPTER 1 You and the World of Work	• **Define** a job, an occupation, and a career. • **Describe** how skills, interests, and desired lifestyle may shape career plans. • **Explain** how work life affects lifestyle. • **List** reasons that people work. • **Identify** workplace trends such as the global economy, changing technology, diversity, and teamwork. • **Evaluate** job outlooks when making career plans.
CHAPTER 2 Getting to Know Yourself	• **Name** the seven steps in the decision-making process. • **Explain** how to use the decision-making process to choose a career. • **Determine** your values, interests, aptitudes, and abilities. • **Explain** the importance of a good self-concept in choosing a career. • **Identify** your personality and learning styles and match them to career choices.

Understanding Brackets, Letters, and Ability Levels in the Teacher Wraparound Edition

Brackets Brackets on the reduced student edition page correspond to teaching strategies and activities in the Teacher Wraparound Edition. As you teach the lesson, the brackets show you exactly where to use the teaching strategies and activities.

Letters The letters on the reduced student edition page identify the type of strategy or activity. See the key below to learn about the different types of strategies and activities.

Ability Levels Teaching Strategies that appear throughout the chapters have been identified by one of three codes to give you an idea of their suitability for students of varying learning styles and abilities.

Resources Key program resources are listed in each chapter. Icons indicate the format of resources.

KEY TO LETTERS

R **Reading Strategy** activities help you teach reading skills and vocabulary.

C *Critical Thinking* strategies help students apply and extend what they have learned.

S **Skill Practice** strategies help students practice historical analysis and geographical skills.

W **Writing Support** activities provide writing opportunities to help students comprehend the text.

D **Develop Concepts** activities use various strategies to help teachers gauge and plan for students' concept development.

U **Universal Access** activities provide differentiated instruction for English language learners, and suggestions for teaching various types of learners. *These activities may or may not have brackets.*

NCLB **No Child Left Behind** activities help students practice and improve their abilities in academic subjects.

KEY TO ABILITY LEVELS

L1 Strategies should be within the ability range of all students. Often full class participation is required.

L2 Strategies are for average to above-average students or for small groups. Some teacher direction is necessary.

L3 Strategies are designed for students able and willing to work independently. Minimal teacher direction is necessary.

KEY TO RESOURCE ICONS

📁 Print Material

💿 CD-ROM

🌐 Internet

TeacherWorks™
All-In-One Planner and Resource Center

Teacher Wraparound Edition

For the Unit:
Unit Thematic Project Student Rubrics
Unit Test
Unit Connecting Activities Projects

For the Chapter:
Chapter Resources
Program Resources
Additional Print and Media Resources
Lesson Plans
Chapter Summaries, Key Terms, and
 Academic Vocabulary *(English and Spanish)*

Graphic Organizers
Reading Activities
Chapter Self-Checks *(English and Spanish)*
Internet Activities
School-to-Career Connections
Work-Based Learning Projects
Personal and Academic Career Portfolio Student Rubrics

Student Activity Workbook with Academic Integration

Strategies for Students with Special Needs

Career Plan Project Workbook

 Link to the *Succeeding in the World of Work* Online **Learning Center with Podcasts** through **glencoe.com**.

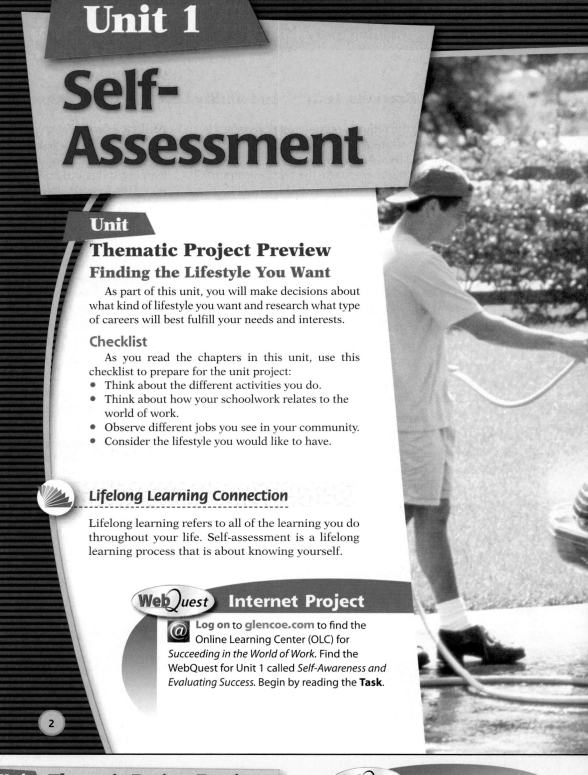

Unit Overview
Introduce the Unit
Introduce the unit by describing the main concepts of each chapter in the unit.

Unit 1 introduces students to the world of work by explaining how personal, global, and technological factors all influence career decisions and the types of careers available.

Chapter 1 describes how career choices affect lifestyle. Students will also learn how the global economy and technology will affect their career plans.

Chapter 2 explains the decision-making process and informs students how they can learn about themselves and match their personal interests with career options.

⬛⬛:⬛⬛ OUT OF TIME?

If class time is too short to cover all of the chapters in this unit, have students:
- Write down the key terms and their definitions.
- Read the chapter summaries at the beginning of each chapter review.
- Go to the *Succeeding in the World of Work* Online Learning Center (OLC) through **glencoe.com** to download Study-to-Go content to their PDAs or cell phones.

Self-Assessment

Unit

Thematic Project Preview
Finding the Lifestyle You Want
As part of this unit, you will make decisions about what kind of lifestyle you want and research what type of careers will best fulfill your needs and interests.

Checklist
As you read the chapters in this unit, use this checklist to prepare for the unit project:
- Think about the different activities you do.
- Think about how your schoolwork relates to the world of work.
- Observe different jobs you see in your community.
- Consider the lifestyle you would like to have.

Lifelong Learning Connection
Lifelong learning refers to all of the learning you do throughout your life. Self-assessment is a lifelong learning process that is about knowing yourself.

WebQuest Internet Project
@ **Log on** to **glencoe.com** to find the Online Learning Center (OLC) for *Succeeding in the World of Work*. Find the WebQuest for Unit 1 called *Self-Awareness and Evaluating Success*. Begin by reading the **Task**.

2

Unit Thematic Project Preview
Tell students that as part of this unit, they will assess themselves and careers that correspond with their interests, abilities, and skills. They will also conduct career research using a variety of resources, and use the decision-making process to evaluate possible career choices by making career profiles. Then they will choose a career that aligns to their lifestyle goals.

WebQuest
For WebQuest teaching suggestions and rubrics, go to the Teacher Center of this book's Online Learning Center (OLC) through **glencoe.com**.

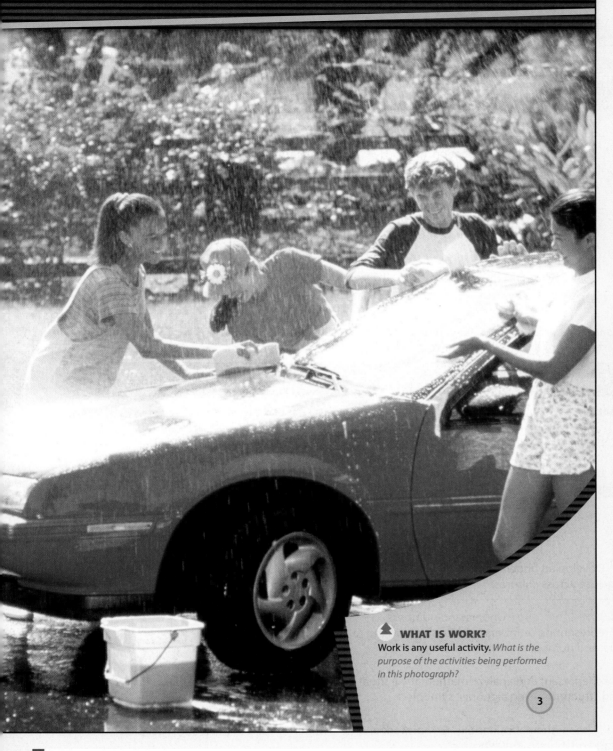

WHAT IS WORK?
Work is any useful activity. *What is the purpose of the activities being performed in this photograph?*

3

Ask students these questions to activate prior knowledge:

Chapter 1
What are some reasons people work? (Answers may vary. Encourage students to identify reasons other than making money, such as to be around other people, to learn new skills, or to have a feeling of accomplishment.)

What is diversity? (Encourage students to understand that diversity means including people from many different backgrounds, including ethnicity, gender, age, nationality, and those with disabilities.)

What are some forms of technology used in the workplace? (Encourage students to identify the different forms of technology used in many workplaces, such as telephones and computers, as well as technology that is specific to certain tasks, such as construction equipment.)

Chapter 2
Is there a connection between your talents (what you do well) and the subjects you have studied in school or the activities you have chosen to do? (Answers may vary. Encourage students to realize that just as aptitudes and abilities influence what you study in school or do for fun, they also influence the career you may choose.)

What are values? (Values are beliefs and principles to live by.)

Extend the Photo

Caption Answer The purpose of the activities being performed in the photograph is to wash the car.

Discussion Ask students to name the different activities involved in washing a car. Have students brainstorm reasons the people in the photo might be engaging in these activities. If students mention fundraising, have them brainstorm other activities for fundraising and identify the ones they feel qualify as "work."

Chapter Resources Planning Guide with Activities and Features

Section	Features	Activities
Section 1.1 **Exploring the World of Work**	Creative Business Practices (p. 8) Real-World Connection (p. 9) Hot Jobs! (p. 12)	Before You Read (p. 6) Graphic Organizer (p. 6) As You Read (pp. 8, 11) After You Read (p. 12)
Section 1.2 **The Changing Workplace**	21st Century Workplace (p. 14) Science in Action (p. 16) Tech Savvy (p. 17) Career Checklist (p. 19) Everyday Ethics (p. 20)	Before You Read (p. 13) Graphic Organizer (p. 13) As You Read pp. (14, 17) After You Read (p. 21)

NCLB Activities, information, and skills practice will help your students attain No Child Left Behind proficiency. Students will improve their abilities in the following academic standards areas:

Academic Standards Correlations

Discipline	Standard	Feature/Activity
English Language Arts	**NCTE 1** Read texts to acquire new information.	Creative Business Practices (p. 8)
	NCTE 4 Use written language to communicate effectively.	Real-World Connection (p. 9) Tech Savvy (p. 17) After You Read (p. 21) Academic Skills in the Workplace (p. 26) Writing Skills Practice (p. 27)
	NCTE 9 Develop an understanding of diversity in language use across cultures.	21st Century Workplace (p. 14)
Mathematics	**Number and Operation:** Understand numbers, ways of representing numbers, relationships among numbers, and number systems	After You Read (p. 12)
	Algebra: Represent and analyze mathematical situations and structures using algebraic symbols	Academic Skills in the Workplace (p. 26)
	Algebra: Use mathematical models to represent and understand quantitative relationships	Academic Skills in the Workplace (p. 26)
Science	**Unifying Concepts and Processes:** Change, constancy, and measurement	Science in Action (p. 16)
	History and Nature of Science: Nature of scientific knowledge	Academic Skills in the Workplace (p. 26)

CORRELATIONS This chart shows the 21st Century Skills, foundation skills, and workplace competencies that students develop as they work in this chapter.

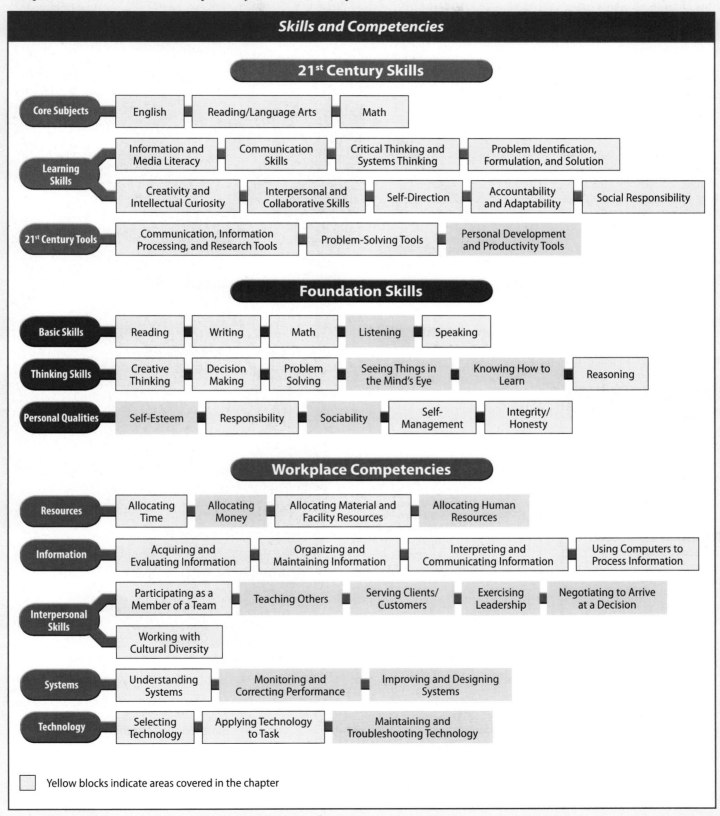

Skills and Competencies

21st Century Skills

Core Subjects
- English
- Reading/Language Arts
- Math

Learning Skills
- Information and Media Literacy
- Communication Skills
- Critical Thinking and Systems Thinking
- Problem Identification, Formulation, and Solution
- Creativity and Intellectual Curiosity
- Interpersonal and Collaborative Skills
- Self-Direction
- Accountability and Adaptability
- Social Responsibility

21st Century Tools
- Communication, Information Processing, and Research Tools
- Problem-Solving Tools
- Personal Development and Productivity Tools

Foundation Skills

Basic Skills
- Reading
- Writing
- Math
- Listening
- Speaking

Thinking Skills
- Creative Thinking
- Decision Making
- Problem Solving
- Seeing Things in the Mind's Eye
- Knowing How to Learn
- Reasoning

Personal Qualities
- Self-Esteem
- Responsibility
- Sociability
- Self-Management
- Integrity/Honesty

Workplace Competencies

Resources
- Allocating Time
- Allocating Money
- Allocating Material and Facility Resources
- Allocating Human Resources

Information
- Acquiring and Evaluating Information
- Organizing and Maintaining Information
- Interpreting and Communicating Information
- Using Computers to Process Information

Interpersonal Skills
- Participating as a Member of a Team
- Teaching Others
- Serving Clients/Customers
- Exercising Leadership
- Negotiating to Arrive at a Decision
- Working with Cultural Diversity

Systems
- Understanding Systems
- Monitoring and Correcting Performance
- Improving and Designing Systems

Technology
- Selecting Technology
- Applying Technology to Task
- Maintaining and Troubleshooting Technology

☐ Yellow blocks indicate areas covered in the chapter

CHAPTER 1

Chapter Overview
Introduce the Chapter

In this chapter, students learn that personal and economic factors influence career choice decisions.

Section 1.1 focuses on the difference between a job and a career, and examines how lifestyle and personal motivation steer people to different careers.

Section 1.2 explains how the rapidly changing global economy and technology affect career opportunities and the skills workers will need to succeed in future jobs.

Build Background

Ask students to brainstorm ten different jobs or careers that they have seen in real life or in the media. Then ask volunteers to describe characteristics for each job, such as the skills you would use or the tasks you would perform.

 Exploring the Photo

Caption Answer Classes you might take in school that would prepare you for working with technology include computer application classes or specific vocational or technical classes.

Discussion Ask students to discuss what kinds of technology a music producer might use. (Answers will vary but may include a headset, a microphone, a sound board, or digital editing equipment.)

You and the World of Work

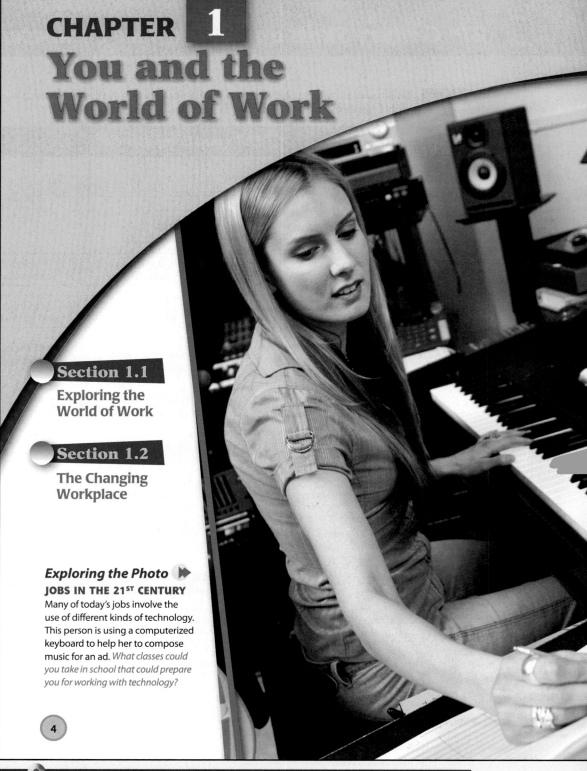

Section 1.1
Exploring the World of Work

Section 1.2
The Changing Workplace

Exploring the Photo ▶
JOBS IN THE 21ST CENTURY
Many of today's jobs involve the use of different kinds of technology. This person is using a computerized keyboard to help her to compose music for an ad. *What classes could you take in school that could prepare you for working with technology?*

4

Classroom Resources

- Student Edition
- Teacher Wraparound Edition
- Student Activity Workbook with Academic Integration
- Student Activity Workbook with Academic Integration TAE
- *Fast File,* Unit 1 Resources

- Inclusion in the Career Education Classroom
- TeacherWorks™ Plus
- *ExamView Assessment Suite*
- Interactive Chalkboard
- Interactive Student Edition
- Online Student Edition
- Online Learning Center (OLC) with Podcasts

Chapter Objectives

After completing this chapter, you will be able to:

- **Define** a job, an occupation, and a career.
- **Describe** how skills, interests, and desired lifestyle may shape career plans.
- **Explain** how work life affects lifestyle.
- **List** reasons that people work.
- **Identify** workplace trends such as the global economy, changing technology, diversity, and teamwork.
- **Evaluate** job outlooks when making career plans.

Writing Activity — Personal Career Notebook

Think about your interests. What do you like to do? What classes do you like? What activities do you enjoy? Now imagine yourself ten years from now. What will you be doing? Will you be working? Write your answers in a one-page journal entry. You can use this journal to record other thoughts related to your future and your career.

Get Motivated! Contact a working adult in your community. Ask that person to tell you his or her personal reasons for working. Summarize your interview in a one-page report.

Writing Activity — Personal Career Notebook Answer Guide

The personal career notebook is an active learning activity that prompts the student to reflect on the subjects addressed in the chapter. After students have completed their journal activity, encourage them to share some of their responses in class if they feel comfortable doing so. Student responses can be used to prompt classroom discussions.

Get Motivated! Reports will vary but should show an understanding of the information given by the interviewed working adults in the community. Evaluate reports for clarity, length, and content.

Review the Objectives

Introduce the chapter by reviewing the chapter objectives:

Section 1.1 Objectives

Define a job, an occupation, and a career. (A job is work that you do for pay, an occupation is the type of work you do, and a career is a series of related jobs or occupations.)

Describe how skills, interests, and desired lifestyle may shape career plans. (Your skills, interests, and desired lifestyle may influence you to chose a career in which you can use those skills and interests or achieve that lifestyle.)

Explain how work life affects lifestyle. (Your work affects how much time, energy, and resources you have for other parts of your lifestyle.)

List reasons that people work. (Reasons may include to pay for wants and needs, to be around other people, to contribute to society, or for positive self-fulfillment.)

Section 1.2 Objectives

Identify workplace trends such as the global economy, changing technology, diversity, and teamwork. (The global economy refers to the ways in which the world's economies are linked. Technology advances create jobs and new ways of doing existing jobs. Diversity includes people of different cultures and backgrounds. Teamwork is work that is done by an organized group that has a common goal.)

Evaluate job outlooks when making career plans. (Being aware of trends can enable you to make good career decisions.)

FOCUS

Exploring the World of Work

FOCUS

Bell Ringer Activity

Exploring the World of Work

Ask students to spend three to four minutes making a list of ten jobs or careers they would like to know more about. Have students volunteer to share their lists and write examples on the board.

Resources

Interactive Chalkboard
The Interactive Chalkboard CD provides visual teaching aids for this section.

@ Online Learning Center
The Online Learning Center (OLC) through **glencoe.com** features chapter vocabulary, chapter summaries, and other study materials.

Preteaching
Read the definitions of the key terms aloud. As you read each definition, ask students to write a sentence using each key term.

Graphic Organizer
Tell students to go to the OLC through **glencoe.com** for a printable graphic organizer. (Graphic organizers will vary but should properly classify skills and interests.)

NCLB connects academic correlations to book content.

Reading Guide

Before You Read

Preview Read the Key Concepts. Write one or two sentences predicting what the section will be about.

Read to Learn
- How to identify a job, an occupation, and a career
- How skills, interests, and desired lifestyle may shape career plans
- How your job can affect your lifestyle
- Reasons that people work

Main Idea
D Knowing how your work affects your lifestyle will help you understand the importance of making good career choices.

Key Concepts
- What Is Work?
- Why People Work

Key Terms
- interests
- skills
- transferable skills
- job
- occupation
- career
- lifestyle

Academic Vocabulary
You will find these words in your reading and on your tests. Use the academic vocabulary glossary to look up their definitions if necessary.
- specific
- determine
- environment

Graphic Organizer
As you read, list your skills and your interests. Continue adding your own ideas to the list after you have finished reading. Use a two-column chart like the one shown to help organize your information.

SKILLS	INTERESTS
————	————
————	————
————	————

@ Log On Go to this book's Online Learning Center through **glencoe.com** for an online version of this graphic organizer.

NCLB

Academic Standards . . . .

English Language Arts
- Read texts to acquire new information. (NCTE 1)
- Use written language to communicate effectively. (NCTE 4)

Mathematics
- Understand numbers, ways of representing numbers, relationships among numbers, and number systems

Reading Guide

Before You Read
Point out to the class that the concept of work means different things to different people, and that similarly, different individuals have different reasons for working or for choosing the jobs that they do.

D Develop Concepts
Main Idea Discuss the main idea with students. Ask: What do you think "good career choices" are? (Answers will vary. Good career choices may include choices that involve training, education, or job skills that allow you to get the job you want.)

What Is Work?

Think about your world. What do you do each day? How do you spend your time? Right now, you probably spend most of your time in school. Do you wonder what you are going to do after high school? Will you continue to go to school? Will you learn a trade? Perhaps it is time to think about your options and to prepare for them. Some day, work will be a big part of your life.

What is work? Work is any useful activity. For example, cleaning your room is work. One of the main reasons people work is to make money to pay for things they need or want. You probably will not be surprised to learn that most people prefer to do work that uses their interests. After all, work takes up a lot of time. With a full-time job, you could spend more than 2,000 hours a year at work.

What kind of job would be right for you? Think about your interests and your skills. Your **interests** are the things you like to do. You may like to listen to music, dance, play basketball, or work with computers. Knowing your interests will help you plan different parts of your life.

Skills are things you know how to do. They are the result of knowledge combined with experience. Skills can also include things you are good at, or even ways of behaving. Some skills are **specific** to certain tasks. For example, knowing how to drive a car, how to water a plant, or how to calculate change, are skills you use for certain tasks. Skills that you can use in many different situations are called **transferable skills**. Writing, getting along with people, being organized, and making decisions are all transferable skills. For example, you can use your writing skills to write an essay for a language arts class or to send an e-mail to a coworker or friend.

R

◀ **Vocabulary**
You can find definitions in the **Key Terms** glossary and **Academic Vocabulary** glossary at the back of this book.

▶ **REWARDING WORK**
Mark chose to teach martial arts because he was good with children and interested in martial arts. *What other skills and interests might be helpful for a teacher?*

TEACH

Discussion Starter
What Is Work? Ask students to list tasks that they do every day that they would categorize as work. (Examples of work may include doing homework, taking tests, taking notes in class, doing chores, or tasks they might do at a volunteer or paid job.)

R Reading Strategy
Creating a List Ask students to create a list of skills and to categorize those skills as task-specific skills or transferable skills. (Examples of task-specific skills may include driving a car, calculating change, painting walls, teaching a foreign language, or assembling a machine. Examples of transferable skills may include writing, reading, or public speaking.)

Resources

TeacherWorks™ Plus The TeacherWorks software includes customizable built-in lesson plans and links to printable program resources.

▶ *Extend the Photo*

Caption Answer Answers may include that teachers need training in the subject they teach and good communication and organizational skills.

Discussion Ask students to discuss what kinds of materials a martial arts teacher might use.

Encourage students to think about technology and other materials that might be used to organize class information and individual student progress as well as specific equipment such as a first-aid kit for emergencies.

TEACH *(cont.)*

S Skill Practice
Guided Practice

List Ask students to compile a list of their skills and interests using a graphic organizer like the one in the Section 1.1 Reading Guide. (Student lists will vary but should show an understanding of the concepts of skills and interests.) **L1**

Explain Have students write a 250-word paragraph about how their skills have led them to success in school, at work, or at home. Encourage students to think of success as both external (such as good grades or an award for citizenship) and internal (achieving a personal goal). (Paragraphs will vary but should show evidence that students understand the connection between skills, interests, and levels of success.) **L2**

Classify Ask students to write a 300-word paragraph that explains why some activities could be classified as both skills and interests, but that the two do not always correspond. For example, one skilled welder may be interested in construction, but another skilled welder may be uninterested in construction. (Paragraphs will vary but should show that students understand that the relationship between specific skills and interests is not always evident.) **L3**

As You Read

Identifying your interests can influence you as the type of things you like to do can influence the training, education, and employment you wish to pursue.

As You Read

Connect How can identifying your interests help you to succeed at school and at work?

Your Skills and Interests

People who have similar skills and interests are often good at the same types of activities. They therefore tend to enjoy and excel at similar careers. It is important to consider your personality, skills, and interests as you plan your career. When you are using your skills and following your interests, you feel more satisfied with your life.

Knowing and evaluating your skills and interests can help you make good choices about the world of work. To get an idea of what **S** work you would like to do, compile a list of your interests and a list of your skills. If you list playing in a band as an interest, think of all the different things that you have to be able to do in order to play in a band. Do you have to read or understand music? Do you have to be good with your hands? Do you have to be able to listen and to work well with others? Being good with your hands, being able to listen, and working well with others are all skills.

Analyze your activities and think about what you have done to be successful in your interests. You may find you have skills that you never thought of or paid much attention to before.

Creative Business Practices

PEPSICO   **Taking Advantage of Diversity**

PepsiCo is the corporation that owns products such as Pepsi-Cola, Tropicana, and Gatorade beverages, and Quaker cereals. The company sells its products in more than 170 countries. That means that it must appeal to a wide range of customers in diverse markets throughout the world.

An important part of PepsiCo's strategy is to buy goods and services from suppliers that represent its employees, consumers, retailers, and communities. This commitment to diversity and inclusion provides a competitive advantage for PepsiCo. By doing business with people in communities where it sells its products, PepsiCo builds customer loyalty and brand recognition.

PepsiCo's commitment to diversity is reflected within the company, too. According to Paula A. Banks, Senior Vice President of Diversity and Inclusion and Organizational Partnerships, the company believes high performance begins with the ability to value different points of view. PepsiCo's President and Chief Financial Officer, Indra Nooyi, is one of the highest-ranking Indian-born businesswomen in the United States.

CRITICAL THINKING How does PepsiCo benefit from a commitment to diversity?

@ Connect to the Real World To read more about PepsiCo and its commitment to diversity, visit the company's Web site via the link on this book's Online Learning Center through **glencoe.com**.

Creative Business Practices

CRITICAL THINKING ANSWER Answers will vary. Companies like PepsiCo benefit from a commitment to diversity because diversity promotes greater innovation, sharing of ideas, and creative thinking. Fostering diversity also helps global companies keep in touch with its diverse customer base and recruit local employees. Some students may say that companies that value diversity do better in the marketplace because they are able to reach more potential customers or maintain existing customers.

When you have finished your lists, brainstorm a corresponding list of possible career options that might match your interests and skills. You can later place your lists in a **Personal Academic and Career Portfolio**. This portfolio is a collection of documents and projects that can help you achieve the career and lifestyle you want. A portfolio can help you organize and keep track of your achievements in school and in the world of work.

Roberta Zhan, a graphic designer, enrolled in art, design, and computer classes while she was in school. She also learned about photography on her own. Roberta always enjoyed visualizing something in her mind's eye and then finding a way to create her vision on paper, in a photograph, or by using a computer. Here is what she has to say about the meaning of work: "I've found that work can be an enjoyable experience, not just the thing you do to make money. If you have a job you like, work means much more than just paying your bills or buying new things. It means using your talents, being with people who have similar interests, making a contribution, and getting a real sense of satisfaction from doing a good job."

Roberta uses desktop publishing software to arrange the words, photographs, and artwork in magazines, books, and print advertisements. She finds her work satisfying because it allows her to use her interests and her skills.

Jobs, Occupations, and Careers

Work includes jobs, occupations, and careers. A **job** is work that you do for pay. The work usually consists of certain tasks. For example, Roberta's current job title is Production Artist. Often a job is a specific position with a company.

An **occupation** is the type of work you do. People can change jobs and still have the same occupation. For example, though Roberta may have had different jobs with different companies, her occupation is *graphic designer*. She may have performed a different range of tasks at each job or even had different job titles.

A **career** is a series of related jobs or occupations built on a foundation of interest, knowledge, training, and experience. Roberta developed her career in graphic design by working at different jobs. As she gained experience, she found more challenging work with each new job. Like Roberta, many people work at several jobs during their careers. Still others may change occupations. The average American will have more than eight different jobs by the age of 32. Experience working at different jobs can help you find the employment opportunities that best suit your lifestyle.

Money, Lifestyle, and Happiness

You know that you need money for things like food, shelter, medicine, and transportation. Money can help you reach your goals, such as going to college, buying a car, or saving for the future. It can help you get the lifestyle you might want. Money can also give us a lot of things that we might want, but do not need.

Critical Thinking Are people who have a lot of money always happier than people who do not?

Do Your Own Research Talk to two adults you know about the value of money. Ask them if they believe that money can make a person happy. Write down their responses and record them in a journal entry.

TEACH (cont.)

W Writing Support
Guided Practice

Drawing Conclusions Tell students that talents that can be displayed publicly, such as musical ability or exceptional physical agility, often guide a person's career choice, for example, in becoming a musician or a professional basketball player. Ask students to write a two-paragraph journal entry on how people whose skills are less obvious can match their abilities with possible careers.

C Critical Thinking

Drawing Conclusions The text notes that careers and jobs are not the same. Ask students to share other thoughts on how jobs and careers may differ. (Answers will vary but may include that a career is pursued as a life work and a culminating process, whereas a job has the connotation of performing an activity or task for pay to provide income.)

Discussion Starter

Work and Lifestyle Lead a discussion by asking students to name individuals in different areas, such as activism, politics, sports, business, or entertainment. Ask students to brainstorm what skills and talents each of these individuals has and how each of their careers might affect aspects of their lifestyles. (Answers should demonstrate that students understand the basic components of lifestyle.)

Real-World Connection

Critical Thinking Answer Answers will vary but most students should recognize that money does not automatically bring happiness. It can also bring more pressure and more responsibility.

Do Your Own Research Encourage students to share the results of their interviews about the value of money.

Go to the chapter review to find guidelines for creating your own **Personal Academic and Career Portfolio**.

Personal Academic and Career Portfolio

TEACH *(cont.)*

U Universal Access

Visual Impairments

Students with visual impairments are constantly challenged because a large part of traditional learning is visual. Plan for these challenges by giving detailed verbal descriptions of illustrations, photographs, charts, and procedures. Have course outlines prepared in an alternative format such as Braille, enlarged print, or audio recording.

✓ Reading Check

EXPLAIN Your career choice can affect your lifestyle by influencing the amount of time, resources, and energy you have for other aspects of your lifestyle.

ASSESS

Review Key Terms

Have students write sentences using each key term.

Online Study Tools

Have students go to the OLC through **glencoe.com** to:

- Download **Podcast** study tools.
- Download free **Study-to-Go** content to their PDAs or cell phones.

Resources

ExamView Assessment Suite CD allows you to print out ready-made unit and chapter tests complete with answer keys. You can also create customized tests.

U ▲ **A JOB TAKES TIME AND ENERGY** Maria's part-time job allows her to earn money to pay for school. Her job schedule also allows her to spend time with her family. *How can your job affect the other parts of your life?*

Work and Lifestyle

Your **lifestyle** is the way you use your time, energy, and resources. Many people use much of their time and energy and many of their resources at work. The work you do affects other parts of your life. It can determine how much time you have to spend with friends and family and how much money and energy you have to pursue your favorite activities.

To see how work affects lifestyle, read about Carlo. Carlo Russo's goal is to be a teacher, but for now, he works at a day-care center in the afternoons and takes classes in childhood education in the morning. Carlo's schedule does not leave him much time for friends, but he is happy to spend most of his energy pursing his future career and lifestyle goals.

S₁

What kind of lifestyle do you want in the future? What changes are you willing to make in your current life to achieve your future goals? Would you be able to spend less on entertainment if you needed to save money for college or a training program? Would you be okay with adjusting the time you spend with family and friends if it meant that you would be able to follow a particular career path? Make a list of how you would like to spend your time, resources, and energy. Look back at the lists you made earlier about your skills and interests. These lists can help you find out the kind of work you would like to do and the kind of lifestyle you would like to have.

✓ Reading Check EXPLAIN How can your career choice affect your lifestyle?

Why People Work

Why do people work? Why do your family members or friends work? If you have an after-school job or a part-time job, why do you work? You know that people work to earn money. Can you think of other reasons? Here are some common reasons why people work:

- **To Pay for Wants and Needs** People work to earn money to pay for housing, transportation, food, clothes, and other expenses, such as health care, insurance, education, taxes, and recreation. Look at **Figure 1.1** to **determine** how American consumers spend their money.

- **To Be Around Others** People also work because they want to be with other people. They may enjoy being in an **environment** with people who have similar interests. For example, a person who designs costumes for films may like being around and sharing ideas with other people who work with movies. A person who enjoys working in teams might choose to work in an office rather than to start his or her own business.

▶ Extend the Photo

Caption Answer A job is one factor that can determine the amount of time, energy, and other resources you have for other parts of your lifestyle. For example, a part-time job can allow you more financial resources to further your education but still allow you to spend time on social activities or schoolwork.

Discussion Reiterate to students that for many people, the jobs they have are the most important factor that determines how much time, energy, and resources they have left for other parts of their lives. Ask students to brainstorm situations in which something other than a job affects the other parts of a person's lifestyle.

- **To Make a Contribution** Making a positive contribution to society is another reason why people may choose to work in a particular field. You may choose to be a marine biologist because you care about the natural world. You may choose to become a teacher because you care about giving people an education. Knowing you are positively affecting the world around you can inspire you to continue working.
- **Self-Fulfillment** Self-fulfillment is another reason people work. They feel good about themselves when they do a job well. Working at a job that suits them gives them a feeling of accomplishment and self-respect. They feel valued when others depend on them and respect them for their work. Being good at what you do can help you build confidence in who you are.

As You Read

Summarize What are some reasons why people work?

Figure 1.1 **AMERICAN CONSUMER SPENDING**

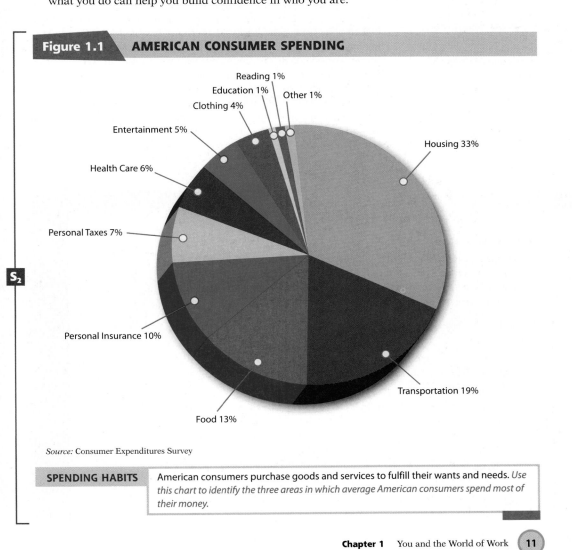

Reading 1%
Education 1%
Other 1%
Clothing 4%
Entertainment 5%
Health Care 6%
Personal Taxes 7%
Personal Insurance 10%
Food 13%
Transportation 19%
Housing 33%

Source: Consumer Expenditures Survey

SPENDING HABITS American consumers purchase goods and services to fulfill their wants and needs. *Use this chart to identify the three areas in which average American consumers spend most of their money.*

As You Read

Reasons people work include to pay for wants and needs, to be around others, to make a contribution, and for self-fulfillment.

EXTEND THE FIGURE **Figure 1.1**

Caption Answer According to the pie chart in **Figure 1.1**, American consumers spend most of their money on housing, transportation, and food.

Discussion Ask students to discuss which of these percentages listed in the chart surprise them and which percentages did not surprise them. Why or why not?

RETEACH

S₁ Skill Practice Independent Practice

Research Have students use the library and other resources, such as the school guidance counselor, to locate print career research resources. Ask students to list at least three resources, including title, type of media (such as book or Web site), location, and copyright year if applicable. **L1**

Teamwork Have students who have similar career interests work together to create a chart showing career progression (from entry-level to top-level titles) for three different jobs within a particular career. **L2**

Apply Technology If your school has access to the Internet or computer databases, have students learn how to use these services to conduct career research. **L3**

S₂ Skill Practice Guided Practice

Using Charts Give students the local minimum wage and have them calculate the monthly salary for a full-time worker (40 hours/week for four weeks) at this wage. Have students use the percentages in **Figure 1.1** to calculate how much the worker would spend in each category. (Answers will vary according to local minimum wage.)

Resources

📂 **Student Activity Workbook** Assign the Chapter 1 activities in the Student Activity Workbook.

After You Read

Have students complete the Section 1.1 After You Read section review.

Online Study Tools

Have students go to the OLC through **glencoe.com** to:

- Take the Section 1.1 **Practice Test**.
- Download **Podcast** study tools.
- Download free **Study-to-Go** content to their PDAs or cell phones.

CLOSE

Culminating Activity

Lifestyle and Work Have students draw a chart that represents the lifestyle of an individual they know. Then have students create a 200-word summary describing how this person's work has influenced his or her lifestyle. Tell students that many individuals and countries consider volunteer work and domestic work (such as managing a household or caring for family members) when determining the percentage of people in certain jobs or careers.

N C L B Activity correlated to Mathematics standards.

HOT JOBS!

Music Band Manager

A manager can help a band manage its time and resources. Band managers use communication skills, sales skills, and business math skills. Job duties can include negotiating recording contracts, planning tours, creating marketing materials and merchandise, and maintaining industry contacts. Managers of very successful artists take about 10 percent of their clients' earnings.

Job Satisfaction

People can find satisfaction in their jobs for many reasons. Eli Fernandez, a video game programmer, loves to create video games. He gets a real sense of satisfaction when he writes computer programs that help artists, writers, and other programmers assemble all the parts that go into a successful video game.

Think about the different activities you do. You can include your activities at home, at school, and in the community. You can also include your volunteer experiences and your work experiences. How do you feel during these experiences? Do you feel proud or happy about what you have accomplished?

What task or job have you done recently that gave you a feeling of accomplishment? Perhaps it was illustrating a poster for a school project or volunteering to coach basketball to younger children in your neighborhood. Perhaps it was a good grade you received on a mathematics test. Perhaps it was a goal that you set for yourself, such as exercising every day for a month. Write a brief journal entry describing the task or job and how you felt after completing it. What else could you do that might give you that feeling again? Finding self-fulfillment, or being satisfied with what you do, has lasting effects. You feel good about yourself and about what you do.

Section 1.1 After You Read

Review Key Concepts

1. Give one example each of a job, an occupation, and a career.
2. Give an example of a skill that might be used in a specific job.
3. Describe a situation that might cause a person to change his or her main reason for working.

Practice Academic Skills

 Mathematics

4. Most Americans spend more than 30% of their yearly income on housing expenses. If you earn $27,000 per year, how much money will you need to spend on housing?

N C L B

 Multiply Decimals by Whole Numbers A percent is a ratio that compares a number to 100. To multiply with percentages:

Step 1: You can rewrite the percent (30%) as a fraction with a denominator of 100. Convert the fraction to a decimal.

Step 2: Multiply this decimal by the number ($27,000). Remember to put the decimal point in the correct place in your answer.

 For math help, go to the Math Appendix located at the back of this book.

 12 **Unit 1** Self-Assessment

Section 1.1 After You Read

Review Key Concepts

1. Student answers should demonstrate an understanding of the concepts of job, occupation, and career.
2. Examples will vary. A sample answer might be that a professional musician must possess the skill of reading music and the skill of being able to play an instrument or to sing.
3. A person who works at a lucrative job but feels isolated may change to a less lucrative job that allows that person to interact with others.

Practice Academic Skills

4. You will spend $8,100 if you earn $27,000 per year (0.30 × $27,000 = $8,100).

The Changing Workplace

Reading Guide

Before You Read

Preview Understanding causes and effects can help clarify connections. A cause is an event or action that makes something happen. An effect is a result of a cause. Ask yourself, "Why does this happen?" to help you recognize cause-and-effect relationships in this section.

Read to Learn
- How the workplace is affected by forces such as changing technology and the global economy
- How to evaluate job outlooks when making career plans

D Main Idea
Familiarity with changes in the workplace will help you in your search for a job.

Key Concepts
- The World of Work Is Changing
- Job Outlook
- Work, Change, and Lifelong Learning

Key Terms
◇ economy
◇ global economy
◇ job market
◇ outsourcing
◇ telecommute
◇ team
◇ lifelong learning

Academic Vocabulary
You will find this word in your reading and on your tests. Use the academic vocabulary glossary to look up its definition if necessary.
- economic

Graphic Organizer
As you read, list causes of change in the workplace and in your career outlook. Continue adding your own ideas to the list after reading. Use a chart like the one shown to help organize your information.

CHANGES
1 _____
2 _____

 Log On Go to this book's Online Learning Center through **glencoe.com** for an online version of this graphic organizer.

NCLB

Academic Standards •

English Language Arts
- Read texts to acquire new information. (NCTE 1)
- Use written language to communicate effectively. (NCTE 4)
- Develop an understanding of diversity in language use across cultures. (NCTE 9)

Science
- Unifying Concepts and Processes: Change, constancy, and measurement

---

Reading Guide

Before You Read

Model cause and effect for the class. For example, the statement *I was late to school because I overslept* is an example of a cause and effect relationship. Explain that just because one event follows another does not necessarily mean that the second event was caused by the first event.

For example, if you sneezed and then it rained, the fact that it rained was not necessarily caused by the fact that you sneezed.

D Develop Concepts
Main Idea Ask students to share where they receive information about the workplace.

 FOCUS

Bell Ringer Activity

The Changing Workplace

Ask students to revisit the lists of careers they made for Section 1.1. Ask if they would revise their lists at this point, based on what they have learned. Lead a discussion about ways that acquiring new knowledge can affect the decision-making process.

Resources

Interactive Chalkboard
The Interactive Chalkboard CD provides visual teaching aids for this section.

@ Online Learning Center
The OLC through **glencoe.com** features chapter vocabulary, chapter summaries, and other study materials.

Preteaching
Read the definitions of the key terms aloud. Ask students to write a sentence using each key term.

Graphic Organizer
Tell students to go to the OLC through **glencoe.com** for a printable graphic organizer. (Graphic organizers will vary but should properly list causes of change.)

 NCLB connects academic correlations to book content.

Discussion Starter

The Changing Workplace
Ask students to take five minutes to brainstorm some of the recent changes they have seen in the world of work. Encourage students to name trends specific to a job or industry as well as general workplace changes.

As You Read

Some ways students may keep up with trends may include through media such as magazines, television, radio, and Web sites.

R Reading Strategy

Use Reference Materials
Ask volunteers to list trends they like to follow and the specific resources they use to keep up with those trends. (Examples will vary but may include Web sites, magazines, newspapers, and other sources of information.)

Resources

☉ Interactive Chalkboard
The Interactive Chalkboard CD provides visual teaching aids for every section.

N C L B
Activity correlated to English Language Arts standards.

As You Read

Connect What are some ways in which you can keep up with trends?

The World of Work Is Changing

Your place in the world of work will influence every aspect of your life. This is why choosing the kind of work you will do is one of the most important decisions you will ever make. So far, you have been thinking about the kind of work that might fit your interests and skills. You have also been thinking about the kind of lifestyle you would like to have and how your work will affect it. What else might be important to consider when thinking about the work you would like to do?

The workplace is constantly changing. Changes in the world affect what work is available for people to do and the way in which they do it. Knowing about these changes can help you make sound decisions about your job, your career, and your future. How can you keep up with all these changes?

R You can follow trends in the world of work the same way you keep up with what is happening in music, fashion, sports, and entertainment. Which are the up-and-coming industries and occupations? Which ones are on the way out? To find out, read newspapers, magazines, and Web sites, and watch or listen to the news on television or on the radio. Talk to people who work in a field that interests you and ask them questions about the changes and opportunities in their workplaces.

The 21ˢᵗ Century Workplace

¿Cómo se dice esto en español? (How do you say that in Spanish?)

N C L B In today's global workplace, there are opportunities in many jobs and industries to work with people who speak Spanish. The Spanish language ranks third in the world in number of speakers, after Chinese and English. It is the official language of Spain, Mexico, Cuba, Puerto Rico, the countries of Central America, and the majority of countries in South America. In addition, according to the U.S. Department of Labor, by 2050, one quarter of all Americans will be of Hispanic origin.

CRITICAL THINKING _____

In what ways might the changing American population affect consumer goods and services?

In Your Community

If there is another population in your community that speaks a language other than English, identify some common phrases you think would be useful in communicating with members of this population. Share these phrases with your class in a two-minute oral presentation.

COMMON SPANISH WORDS AND PHRASES	
hello	hola
good day	buenos días
goodbye	adiós/que vaya bien
yes	sí
no	no
please	por favór
How are you?	¿Cómo está usted?
good	bien
thank you	muchas gracias
you're welcome	de nada

@ Extend Your Learning Spanish dialects can vary according to country, region, or even city. For Web links about dialects, go to this book's OLC through **glencoe.com**.

The 21ˢᵗ Century Workplace

CRITICAL THINKING ANSWER Answers may vary but may include changes in consumer product packaging labeling, and the types of products and services added. Encourage students to volunteer specific examples of changes (such as media products becoming fully bilingual).

In Your Community Encourage students to verify phrases with more than one individual in the community from which they have obtained phrases.

ECONOMIC TRENDS As a part of the global economy, consumers can buy products from other parts of the world. *What are other advantages of the global economy?*

C Critical Thinking

Evaluate Information Ask students what they think when they see merchandise stamped "Made in Spain" (or any other country). Ask students why they think goods are labeled with their country of manufacture. (Answers will vary but may include that goods are labeled so that consumers can choose to buy products that are constructed according to safety or fair labor laws in a particular country.)

U Universal Access

English Language Learners If any of your students can speak other languages, ask them to develop scenarios such as greetings and farewells, asking for directions, or ordering food from a menu. Then have those students role-play the scenarios with you or with another student. Ask students if they can identify the cultural situation being role-played.

S Skill Practice
Independent Practice

Research Have students work in teams of three to five to research the countries to which the United States exports the most goods (by dollar amount). Have them find out the countries from which the United States imports the most goods, also by dollar amount. Finally, have students create a table of imports and exports, ranked by country from largest to smallest dollar amount. Students can use between five and ten countries to complete this activity.

The Global Workplace

C Look at a few of the things you own—a pair of pants, a CD, a bicycle—and check their labels or packaging. Where were they made? At least some of your possessions were probably made in other countries. When you buy goods and services from other countries, you are participating in the global economy. An **economy** refers to the ways in which a group produces, distributes, and consumes its goods and services. *Goods* are the items that people buy. *Services* are activities done for others for a fee. The **global economy** refers to the ways in which the world's economies are linked.

U The global economy impacts the **job market**, or the demand for particular jobs, in each country. How does the global economy affect the job market in the United States?

Some believe that trade with foreign countries can lead to American workers losing their jobs to workers in other countries. For instance, some American computer software companies hire software programmers in other countries whose labor and production costs may be lower than those of the United States. Many customer service jobs that require information to be shared over the phone or over e-mail are also being performed overseas.

S On the other hand, many American businesses export goods, or sell goods to other countries, and these exports create jobs. Some feel that the use of overseas workers may help the economy by holding down costs. U.S.-based offices of foreign firms also provide jobs for many Americans.

Keeping informed about global **economic** changes can help you learn more about the international job market. For example, which jobs will be sent abroad? Which jobs will be created because of the changing economy? Which jobs will involve international trade?

◀ Vocabulary

You can find definitions in the **Key Terms** glossary and **Academic Vocabulary** glossary at the back of this book.

Chapter 1 You and the World of Work **15**

 Extend the Photo

Caption Answer Answers may include lower prices and a greater variety of products for American consumers, and less expensive labor and production costs for some American businesses.

Discussion Have students share examples of products they consume that are fabricated in or imported from countries outside of the United States.

TEACH *(cont.)*

W Writing Support
Independent Practice

Global Skills Ask students to write a one-page expository response explaining what skills or knowledge they might need to work for a global company that practices diversity. (Responses will vary but may include the following: good basic and transferable skills, the ability to adapt, the ability to communicate clearly and use communication technology, the desire and ability to learn another language, being aware of cultural differences, and understanding different business practices.)

C Critical Thinking

Making Connections Ask students what kinds of tasks or activities you can do as a student that could help you become familiar with workplace skills. (Answers will vary; examples include that academic coursework can help you develop basic skills such as reading, math, and critical thinking skills; working on independent projects can help you develop personal responsibility.)

N C L B Activity correlated to Science standards.

Science In Action

68° Fahrenheit is equal to 20° Celsius: $°C = [\frac{5}{9}(68°F - 32°F)]$; $68 - 32 = 36$; $\frac{5}{9}(36) = 20°C$. The brackets and parentheses in this equation indicate the order of operations. The calculation within the parentheses must be made first.

Science In Action

N C L B

Temperature
Many scientific processes use the Celsius scale to measure temperature, while the general U.S. public uses the Fahrenheit scale. Convert 68° Fahrenheit to degrees Celsius. Round to the closest whole number. The conversion formula is $°C = \frac{5}{9}[(°F)-(32°F)]$.

Starting Hint: Start the conversion by filling in the variables you know in the formula, degrees Fahrenheit (°F): $°C = \frac{5}{9}[(°68)-(32°F)]$.

@ For more science practice, go to this book's OLC through **glencoe.com**.

Skills for the Global Economy

The global economy creates competition by increasing the number of workers who can do different jobs, as well as increasing the number of businesses that can produce goods or perform services. As a result, employers need workers who can do a variety of tasks and who possess a variety of skills.

How can you meet the demands of the global economy? You can familiarize yourself with the diverse economies and cultures of the world. You can develop transferable skills—many of which you are already learning—and apply them in your job. Certain fundamental skills, necessary for employment in all industries, will help you achieve success on the job: **W**

Basic Skills Basic skills include communication skills such as reading, writing, and language arts, as well as mathematical skills and scientific literacy.

Thinking Skills Thinking skills include creative thinking, critical thinking, decision making, problem solving, seeing things in the mind's eye (picturing things in your mind), curiosity, knowing how to learn, and reasoning. **C**

Personal Qualities Personal qualities include personal responsibility, social and civic responsibility, self-direction and self-management, self-esteem, adaptability, integrity, and honesty.

Adaptable Workers

Employers want workers who can complete tasks quickly and effectively, whether the task is writing an article by a deadline, building a wall, or developing a new video game. They want workers who can think critically and work well within the environment of that particular workplace. They value workers who are motivated, who can work well with others, and who can use the tools of the workplace. Knowing what your skills are and how to use them in different situations will allow you to explore job opportunities in a variety of industries.

◀◀ LEARN TO LISTEN
Communication skills, such as speaking and listening, are valuable on any job. *Why is listening an important aspect of communicating?*

16 Unit 1 Self-Assessment

glencoe.com

▶ Extend the Photo

Caption Answer Answers may include that communication involves both speaking (conveying a message) and listening (the process of receiving and interpreting a spoken message). This skill is important when receiving instruction and feedback, sharing ideas, and problem solving.

Discussion Ask students to brainstorm types of communication other than spoken communication, which involves both a speaker and a listener. Encourage students to think of both one-way communication strategies, such as the posting of a bulletin with no contact information.

Technology in the Workplace

Not long ago, very few people had cell phones or access to the Internet. Laptops and desktop computers were just coming into common use in businesses and households. Today, advances in technology are constantly—and rapidly—changing how people work. People working in very different fields use a wide range of technology to help them do their work effectively. As companies increase their use of technology, the number and types of jobs will change.

Technology Trends

Just as global competition affects the types of jobs and salaries available, modern technology allows workers to perform many jobs from anywhere in the world. Technology affects not only what work you do but also how and where you do it. Trends that are affected by technology include outsourcing and telecommuting.

Outsourcing is when businesses hire other companies or individuals to produce their services or goods. For example, airline companies often contract with other companies to provide baggage handling and meals for their customers. The term outsourcing also refers to the hiring of workers in other countries.

Technology also allows workers to have flexibility in how, where, and when they do their jobs. Millions of workers do not work exclusively at a company's work site. Instead, they **telecommute**, or work from home or in an office center, using technology such as computers, faxes, cell phones, and telephones to perform their jobs. Telecommuting is becoming popular in some industries, as it allows workers to balance their job with other parts of their lives.

Other Workplace Trends

Workplace trends are changing every day. Today's workers need to be able to work well in teams and with different kinds of people. **Figure 1.2** on page 18 shows examples of some of these trends.

Working in Teams

Many workers work in teams. A **team** is an organized group that has a common goal. Team members collaborate, or work together, to set goals, make decisions, and implement actions. Teams allow people to share their skills and ideas. Today's employers expect workers to be able to work well together. Good team members do their share of the work, have good communication skills, and have a positive attitude.

As You Read

Question Why do employers want workers who can use technology?

TechSavvy

Evaluating Web Sites

Imagine that you are thinking of pursuing several different careers and you want to use the Internet to research the future demand for a job that interests you. How can you determine which Web sites have good and reliable information?

Government sites are often a good source of information, but you should always evaluate any information you read. To evaluate a Web site, ask: Who is giving you the information? Is the information accurate, thorough, free from bias, and up-to-date? A librarian may be able to help you find the answers to these questions.

 Visit this book's OLC through **glencoe.com** and find a link to the U.S. Bureau of Labor Statistics Web site. Research the current five-year career outlook for three jobs that interest you. Write a half-page summary of each job outlook, and explain whether you think it would be worthwhile to pursue these careers.

S Skill Practice
Guided Practice

List Strategies Ask students to think of the ways they use technology in their daily lives. Have students brainstorm ways they can learn about technology and keep up with future changes. Emphasize that students will need to develop a habit of lifelong learning if they are to maintain job skills. (Possible ways to keep up with technology are to take computer courses, participate in work-training programs, and use the Internet.) **L1**

Apply Teamwork Organize students into teams of five to six members. Have students choose one technological trend and predict how that trend will affect, or describe how that trend has already affected, the global workplace. (Answers should show an understanding of how technology can affect the global workplace.) **L2**

Practice Self-Management Have students choose a software application that they want to learn, and make a list of the things they want to be able to do with it. Then have them develop a list of goals for learning the application. (Goals should reflect an understanding of the chosen software's potential.) **L3**

N C L B Activity correlated to English Language Arts standards.

As You Read

Answers may include that employers want workers who can use technology because technology can allow jobs to be done more quickly and easily and that it allows workers to be flexible about how, when, and where they do their jobs.

TechSavvy

Evaluating Web Sites

Answer Summaries should show evidence of student understanding of job outlooks. Evaluate summaries for the clarity and type of information provided about the career outlook, the source named for the information, and the reasoning students provided.

TEACH (cont.)

R Reading Strategy

Understanding Words in Context Have students read an article in a business magazine (such as *BusinessWeek*) about contemporary business practices that emphasize diversity in the workplace. Encourage students to look up the meaning of any words in the article that are unfamiliar to them. Have students share what they learned from the article in a five-minute oral presentation. (Presentations will vary according to the business and the article. All presentations should demonstrate an understanding of the concept of diversity).

U Universal Access

Physical Impairments Students with physical impairments may have uncontrollable body movements, the loss of use of one or more limbs, or other severe symptoms. Have students with physical disabilities that affect their dexterity prepare assignments electronically, if possible. If computers are available, consider having students use software and other assistive technology to take notes in class.

Cooperative Learning
Enrichment

Preparing for Guest Speakers Organize students into small groups of three to five. Have groups create a list of five questions they may have about the challenges of diversity. Review the groups' questions before the speakers arrive. A suggested question may be about the special challenges the individual speakers face in the workplace.

Figure 1.2   WORKPLACE TRENDS

CHANGES IN THE WORLD OF WORK Technology, teamwork, and diversity are all global workplace trends. *List examples of trends you have observed in the world of work.*

▶ **TECHNOLOGY** Technology includes the knowledge and tools that make it possible to do new things or to do things differently. Technology can help you create, calculate, change, and organize information or things.

◀◀ **TEAMWORK** Members of a team work together towards a common goal. Good communication skills help a team function.

▶ **DIVERSITY** The workplace can benefit from the ideas and perspectives of many different individuals. Respecting differences aids communication at home, at school, and at work.

18   **Unit 1**   Self-Assessment

EXTEND THE FIGURE   Figure 1.2

Caption Answer Student observations may include specific examples relating to technology, diversity, and teamwork, or other general observations such as the decreasing number of manufacturing jobs, the increasing number of jobs in the service industry, and the need for workers to continue to learn new skills.

Discussion Ask students to connect trends in the world of work to trends they may have noticed in the classroom. Encourage students to provide specific examples.

Diversity in the Workplace

Today's workforce is becoming more diverse. As you work, you will encounter people who come from different countries, cultures, backgrounds, and generations. They may act differently from you or speak different languages. It is important to respect these differences. Part of respecting diversity means valuing the contribution of every individual. In the United States, everyone has equal opportunity to pursue most jobs. Being able to work well with a variety of people is a valuable skill.

✓ **Reading Check** **SUMMARIZE** Describe some workplace trends and skills workers need in the global economy.

The Job Outlook

What job market can you expect when you graduate from high school? Most new jobs will be in the service-producing industries. *Service-producing industries* provide services for a fee. These services might include medical care, travel accommodations, and education. Fewer jobs are expected in the *goods-producing industries*, which provide goods such as stereo systems and cars.

The graph in **Figure 1.3** identifies these different industries and shows expectations for their growth or decline over a sample ten-year period. Think about your skills and interests. Which industries do you think would be appropriate for you?

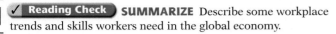

Career ✓ Checklist

When Entering the Workplace:

✓ Define your goals.
✓ Stay informed of changes in the workplace.
✓ Expect the best from yourself and others.
✓ Maintain a positive attitude.
✓ Learn from your mistakes.
✓ Take advantage of every opportunity to learn.

Figure 1.3 **JOB GROWTH CHANGE FOR SERVICES AND GOODS INDUSTRIES**

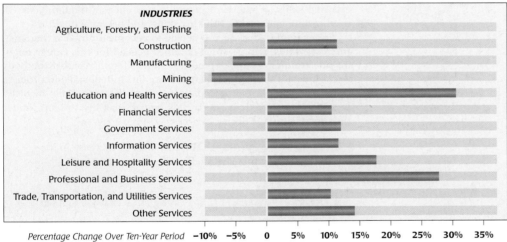

SERVICES GROWTH This graph shows by what percentages jobs in these industries might increase or decrease over a ten-year period. You will find graphs like these when researching the job outlook for a particular time period. *According to this graph, which industries are declining in this ten-year period?*

Chapter 1 You and the World of Work **19**

✓ **Reading Check**

SUMMARIZE Workplace trends in the global economy include technology, teamwork, and diversity. Skills workers need in the global economy include skills relating to workplace trends as well as transferable skills such as basic skills, thinking skills, and personal qualities. Encourage students to be specific when identifying aspects of these skills.

EXTEND THE FIGURE **Figure 1.3**

Caption Answer According to this chart, the industries in which jobs are declining in the ten-year period featured in **Figure 1.3** include manufacturing; agriculture, forestry, and fishing; and mining.

Discussion Ask students to speculate about which industries are currently adding to or reducing the number of jobs available.

W Writing Support

Job Skills Have students locate a lengthy or confusing job description in the paper or on the Internet. Model a clear and concise job ad for students. Ask students to rewrite the job description so it is clear what tasks the job entails and what skills and interests are required for any job applicant.

S Skill Practice

Guided Practice

Estimating After students have reviewed the information in **Figure 1.3,** have them work in groups of three to five to estimate the percentage by which jobs in each of the industries in the figure have increased or decreased. (Answers will vary but should provide a reasonable estimate according to the chart). Direct students to the Web site of the U.S. Bureau of Labor Statistics to find the most current job outlook information for specific industries and have volunteers report the information back to the class.

ASSESS

Review Key Terms

Have students write sentences using the key terms they have read so far in the text.

Online Study Tools

Have students go to the OLC through **glencoe.com** to:

- Download **Podcast** study tools.
- Download free **Study-to-Go** content to their PDAs or cell phones.

RETEACH

C Critical Thinking

Making Inferences The text tells you that you do not have to choose a career just because it has a good job outlook or because you will earn the most money. Ask students what they can infer about the dangers of choosing a career for these reasons alone. (Answers will vary but may include that choosing a career that matches your interests and skills will be more fulfilling and enjoyable.)

✓ Reading Check

ANALYZE An increase in the service-producing industries increases the number of jobs available in those industries.

Resources

📂 **Student Activity Workbook** Assign the Chapter 1 activities in the Student Activity Workbook.

ASSESS

After You Read
Have students complete the Section 1.2 After You Read section review.

Online Study Tools
Have students go to the OLC through **glencoe.com** to:

- Take the Section 1.2 **Practice Test**.
- Download **Podcast** study tools.
- Download free **Study-to-Go** content to their PDAs or cell phones.

Everyday ETHICS

MAKING DECISIONS

When you make decisions, do you think about whether your choices are right or wrong?

SUMMER JOB It's almost the end of the school year, and you haven't started looking for a summer job yet. Your guidance counselor has told you about a summer job opening at the local newspaper. He has told you that you can tell other people about the opening as well. Your friend Mandy wants to be a journalist and you know she would be interested in the job. You are not interested in journalism, but you want a job in order to save money for a car, so you are thinking about just applying for the job yourself and not telling Mandy about it.

What Would You Do? Will you tell your friend about the position at the newspaper? Why or why not? Write a brief journal entry explaining your decision.

DISCUSS IT Decisions that involve others are often ethical decisions. What does it mean to be ethical? Where do you get your sense of right and wrong? In teams, discuss the possible actions you could take in the summer job situation. Brainstorm the consequences of the different decisions and share them with the class.

Impact on Today's Workers

You do not have to choose a career just because it seems to offer the best job outlook or because you will earn the most money in it. Even though you are learning to follow trends in the job market, you still want to find work that fulfills you and that matches your interests and skills. Whatever occupation you choose, though, you will need certain basic skills, thinking skills, and personal qualities.

For example, suppose you decide to become a physical therapist. Interests, skills, and personal qualities needed for this career might include training to understand how the different parts of the body work, a desire to help people, good organizational skills in order to be able to handle multiple patients, good listening skills in order to understand your patients' needs, and the ability to work under the supervision of a doctor at times.

✓ Reading Check **ANALYZE** How does an increase in the service-producing industries affect the job market?

Work, Change, and Lifelong Learning

Many of today's workers have grown up using technology at home, at school, and at work. They are familiar with different languages and cultures. New ways of working are being created to help workers in every industry communicate and do their jobs. Tomorrow's workers will have to adjust to even more changes.

Everyday ETHICS

What Would You Do? Answer Student responses will vary. One ethical response might be to tell your friend about the position at the newspaper because you were encouraged to do so specifically by the person who gave you that information.

DISCUSS IT Encourage students to envision other ethical considerations that might play a role in their decision. For example, ask: How might your decision change if the reason you suddenly needed a car was to be able to care for an ill family member?

You will probably continue learning for as long as you work. While changes in technology and society offer you many different opportunities for work, it also means that you will need training and education to keep up with the changes. You will benefit from practicing lifelong learning. **Lifelong learning** means continuing to learn more about new technologies, new practices, and new ideas throughout your life. Staying on top of new developments through reading, online forums, classes, and workshops can help keep your skills up-to-date and give you an edge when you are searching for the next job or promotion.

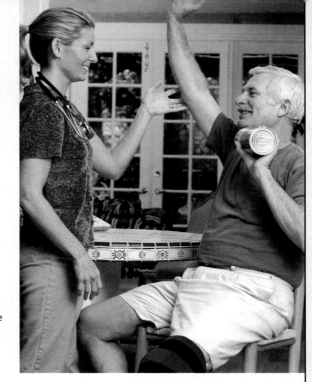

▶ **PERSONAL QUALITIES**
A physical therapist helps people recover their strength after an injury or surgery. *Why might a physical therapist need to have a sense of compassion?*

Resources

🌐 *ExamView Assessment Suite* **CD** allows you to print out ready-made unit and chapter tests complete with answer keys. You can also create customized tests.

CLOSE

Culminating Activity
Work, Change, and Lifelong Learning Ask students to write a one-paragraph description about how their study of this section has changed or informed their ideas about the kinds of skills needed in the current and future world of work. (Descriptions should reflect section content.)

Section 1.2 After You Read

Review Key Concepts
1. Describe different forms of technology used in telecommuting.
2. List some advantages and disadvantages of the global economy.
3. Explain why it is important to evaluate job outlooks when making career plans.

Practice Academic Skills
🌐 **English Language Arts**
4. Choose a career that interests you and research how various technologies may affect it. Use at least two sources in your research. Write a two-paragraph description of what technology is used in this career.
5. Which of the following do you consider more important in choosing a career—finding a career that matches your interests, or finding a career with a positive job outlook? Write a one-page response, giving reasons for your answers.

@ Check your answers at this book's OLC through **glencoe.com**.

NCLB

▶ **Extend the Photo**

Caption Answer A sense of compassion may help a physical therapist relate to patients and encourage them through what can be a challenging process of therapy, recovery, or rehabilitation.

Discussion Ask students to discuss what other traits might be useful for a physical therapist. Answers may include physical strength, responsibility, and patience.

NCLB Activity correlated to English Language Arts standards.

Section 1.2 After You Read

Review Key Concepts
1. Computers, fax machines, mobile devices, and telephones; other answers are possible
2. Advantages may include lower costs of labor and production for businesses, increased variety of imported goods for consumers, and possible job opportunities abroad. Disadvantages may include the loss of jobs to foreign workers and increasing competition for goods.
3. Being aware of job outlooks can enable you to make good career decisions.

Practice Academic Skills
4. Descriptions should demonstrate research into a career of interest and an understanding of the technology used in that career.
5. Essays should demonstrate an understanding of the importance of considering both interests and job outlook when choosing a career.

CAREER SPOTLIGHT

Career Cluster: Arts, Audio/Video Technology, and Communications

Discussion Starter

Arts, Audio/Video Technology, and Communications Lead a discussion about the different types of careers that can be found in this career cluster. Have students brainstorm different careers and jobs within the career cluster. (Answers will vary but students should show an understanding of the many types of careers that fall within the career cluster.)

W Writing Support
Independent Practice

Conduct an Interview Have students use the questions in the Career Spotlight to conduct and record an interview with an individual in the featured career cluster. (Answers will vary but should follow the interview format of the Career Spotlight).

C Critical Thinking

Physical Impairments and the Fine Arts Have students list the mechanical, technical, spatial, or motor skills they might need for a fine arts career. Then ask them to brainstorm any aids or technology that could be used to assist a person with physical disabilities to fulfill the necessary tasks of that career. (Answers will vary. For example, an interior designer would need spatial skills to envision the interior of a building, and motor skills to create a visual plan. Assistive technology could be used to create the visual plan.)

Liz Wong
Fine Artist/Craftsperson

Q: Describe your job.
A: Creating and selling artwork and functional items, such as paintings, handbags, and greeting cards.

Q: Describe a typical workday.
A: First I would work on filling any orders that have come in from my Web site, preparing those items for shipping and corresponding via e-mail with customers who have ordered items. Then I might work on creating new items to send to galleries that carry our work, or creating items to sell at craft fairs. Other tasks would include updating my Web site, keeping business records, and developing advertising strategies.

Q: What skills are most important to you in your job?
A: Artistic skill, customer service, and language skills. Although I never thought I would need math skills as an artist, I use my math skills almost every day to figure out materials, pricing, and budgets.

Q: What academic skills and lifelong learning skills are helpful in preparing for your career?
A: Communication skills, math, and in-depth knowledge of whatever your subject is. For example, if I am creating a series of paintings about Rome, I may want to study Roman history, geography, and culture. The more that you read and learn about our world, the more interest and depth you can bring to your artwork.

Q: What is your key to success?
A: Constantly creating new work and making connections with other artists. The more work you create, the better your art becomes. In addition, you must promote yourself constantly. No one can buy your art if they don't know it exists.

Q: What training and preparation do you recommend for students?
A: Although a fine arts degree is not necessary, it is useful for the focused time that you get to concentrate on your art, the skills that you gain, and the relationships that you build with professors and other students. If you intend to approach galleries, it may be useful to have a degree on your résumé. Regardless of what your focus is, I recommend learning as many different art processes as possible, which you can do in a school setting or by taking classes independently. In addition, a few art history classes are recommended.

Q: What are some ways you recommend students prepare for this career?
A: Practice: spend a few minutes every day working on art. Talent helps, but you would be amazed how much you can improve by just drawing a little bit every day. Don't worry about making a masterpiece every time. Look at other artists' work. Find an artist who inspires you, and ask yourself what appeals to you about their work. Make a reproduction of their work—this will help.

Q: What do you like most about your work?
A: Creating artwork can be very fun and fulfilling. I love to see finished products that I have made myself.

 For more about Career Clusters, go to this book's OLC through **glencoe.com**.

Teaching Tip

The goals of the NCLB Act include a strong emphasis on reading skills. The use of modeling in your classroom will help students become better at identifying information. For example, ask a question that can be answered by reading the chart on page 23. Verbally identify the elements of the chart that might help the student identify the answer: the stars and the academic skills labels.

Sample Question How many of the tasks on this chart require three or more academic skills to complete? (Three tasks require three or more academic skills to complete: create artwork, develop new products, and advertising/self-promotion.)

- **Education or Training** A bachelor's or master's degree in fine arts is useful but not entirely necessary. Lots of practice is key. A well-rounded education is helpful for finding subjects and developing concepts for artwork. Entrepreneurial skills are necessary for artists who wish to make a living selling their work.

- **Academic Skills Required** English, Language Arts, Mathematics, Social Studies, Science.

- **Technology Needed** Computers, digital camera, scanner; photo, graphics, and web editing software; accounting software. Artists will also use technology that is specific to the materials they are working with. For example, a jeweler or metalsmith may use welding devices, while a handbag designer may use a sewing machine.

- **Aptitudes, Abilities, and Skills** Creativity, customer service, organizational skills, entrepreneurship, basic accounting skills, Web site design, and computer image production and editing skills.

- **Workplace Safety** Some traditional art supplies can be toxic, and technology can be dangerous if improperly used. Some tasks and tools will involve repetitive motion and detailed handiwork, which can cause muscle strain.

- **Career Outlook** Jobs in this sector, especially jobs that involve computer-related art, will be increasing over the next ten years.

- **Career Path** Artists may work as fine artists, illustrators, or craftspeople. Related jobs are also available as educators and in arts organizations.

Academic Skills Required to Complete Tasks

Tasks	English Language Arts	Mathematics	Science	Social Studies
Create artwork	★	★	★	★
Accounting and maintaining business records	★	★		
Develop Web site	★		★	
Customer service	★			★
Develop new products	★	★		★
Advertising/self-promotion	★	★		★
Contact stores and galleries	★			

N C L B

Critical Thinking

What are some informal things that students who are interested in art can do to develop their skills?

N C L B This chart relates academic skills such as English Language Arts, Mathematics, Science, Social Studies, and World Languages to specific tasks that are performed for the job featured in the Career Spotlight feature.

Critical Thinking

Answers may vary. Some informal things that students can do to develop their skills include spending a few minutes every day working on art, looking at the work of other artists, and making reproductions of the work of other artists.

CAREER SPOTLIGHT

ASSESS

Make Connections

Ask students to list specific correlations between academic subjects and workplace tasks. For example, a jeweler might benefit by studying geology, mineralogy, and chemistry because a jeweler's tasks might include heating and mixing liquid metal. An architect must study geometry and physics in order to design structures that balance various forces such as pressure, weight, and gravity. (Answers will vary but students should show an understanding of how academic skills relate directly to workplace tasks.)

CLOSE

Culminating Activity

Lifelong Learning and Career Clusters Encourage students to come up with informal ways that an artist might develop skills that would apply to a particular career in the Arts, Audio/Video Technology, and Communications career cluster. For example, digital animators, who create moving images using computer software, take their inspiration from "concept artists" who create drawings or pictures of art using traditional media such as oils, charcoal, and sculpture. Another example would be that broadcast journalists might keep an online blog to practice their writing skills. Have students volunteer to share their ideas in class. (Answers should show evidence of understanding the career as profiled in the Career Spotlight.)

Key Terms and Academic Vocabulary Review

1. Students should write complete sentences using each term correctly. A sample answer might read: "Examples of *transferable skills* include writing, getting along with people, and making decisions."

Review Key Concepts

2. A job is work you do for pay. An occupation is the type of work you do. A career is a series of related jobs or occupations built on a foundation of interest, knowledge, training, and experience. Student examples will differ; one example is a job as a teacher's aide, an occupation of teaching, and a career in education.

3. Skills may lead you to a career doing something you can do well, interests may lead you to a career that engages you, and desired lifestyle may draw you to a career that allows you to live the kind of lifestyle you want.

4. Your lifestyle is how you spend your time and energy. Work affects your lifestyle because it uses some of your time, energy, and resources, leaving the rest for other parts of your lifestyle, such as responsibilities and interests.

5. Reasons people work include: to pay for wants and needs, to be with other people, to contribute to society, and for self-fulfillment.

6. Factors that affect today's workplace include the global economy, changing technology, the increasing use of teams, and a diverse workforce.

7. It is a good idea to evaluate job outlooks when making career plans because the availability of certain jobs may be declining while the availability of other jobs may

---

CHAPTER SUMMARY

Section 1.1

You should consider your interests and skills when planning your career. A job is work that people do for pay, an occupation is the type of work you do, and a career is a series of related jobs built on a person's interests, knowledge, training, and experience. Your lifestyle is the way you use your time, energy, and resources. Your work affects your lifestyle. Four important reasons people work are to earn money, to fulfill wants and needs, to be around other people, to contribute to society, and for self-fulfillment.

Section 1.2

The global economy refers to the ways in which the world's economies are linked. It affects what kinds of jobs will be available. You will need basic skills, thinking skills, personal qualities, and adaptability to meet the demands of the global job market. Other workplace trends include the use of technology, diversity, the use of teams, outsourcing, and telecommuting. In the United States, most new jobs are predicted to be in the service-producing industries. When looking for careers, you need to be aware of economic, technological and workplace trends, job outlook, and personal job satisfaction.

Key Terms and Academic Vocabulary Review

1. Use each of these key terms and academic vocabulary words in a sentence.

Key Terms
- interests (p. 7)
- skills (p. 7)
- transferable skills (p. 7)
- job (p. 9)
- occupation (p. 9)
- career (p. 9)
- lifestyle (p. 10)
- economy (p. 15)
- global economy (p. 15)
- job market (p. 15)
- outsourcing (p. 17)
- telecommute (p. 17)
- team (p. 17)
- lifelong learning (p. 21)

Academic Vocabulary
- specific (p. 7)
- determine (p. 10)
- environment (p. 10)
- economic (p. 15)

Review Key Concepts

2. **Define** a job, an occupation, and a career. Give an example of each.
3. **Describe** how skills, interests, and desired lifestyle may shape career plans.
4. **Explain** how work life affects lifestyle.
5. **List** some of the reasons that people work.
6. **List** factors that affect today's workplace.
7. **Explain** why it is important to evaluate job outlooks when making career plans.

Critical Thinking

8. **Compare and Contrast** In what ways might a decrease or increase in income affect aspects of your lifestyle?
9. **Evaluate** What is the value of observing changes in the world of work, even when you may not be working full-time for a while?

---

be increasing. It is important to match your skills and interests to a career that will allow you to have the future lifestyle you want. Being aware of expectations of growth or decline in a particular industry or job, as well as trends that affect that job, such as salary and career growth, can enable you to make good career decisions such as choosing academic coursework, career training, or further education.

Critical Thinking

8. Answers will vary but should show an understanding of how income affects some elements of lifestyle. For example, an increase in income will allow you to pursue aspects of your lifestyle such as how you spend your free time or upgrading your living arrangements, but the increase in income may also mean that you have to work more hours or you may have to do tasks you might not enjoy. A decrease in

Real-World Skills and Applications

Interpersonal and Collaborative Skills

10. Working in Teams Team up with one or more classmates. Identify a number of jobs in the Arts, Audio/Video Technology, and Communications career cluster. Choose one of these jobs and create a five-minute presentation that features some of the skills, training, and technology that is needed to perform this job. Your presentation might use software, visual aids, or brief skits.

Technology Applications

11. Creating a Spreadsheet You are in charge of the equipment for a 16-member soccer team. You must record the type of equipment the team purchases, such as balls, shoes, towels, and uniforms, as well as when each piece of equipment was ordered and received. Use spreadsheet software to create a document that can list and categorize all the equipment.

Financial Literacy Skills

12. Determining Your Financial Situation To figure out your personal financial situation, start by making a list of items that relate to your finances: savings, monthly income (job earnings, allowance), monthly expenses (money you spend), and debts (money you owe to others). Use a notebook, a spreadsheet, or another document to categorize your expenses over a set period of time, such as a week or a month.

 Log On Go to this book's Online Learning Center through **glencoe.com** for help with financial literacy.

---

13. **Brainstorming and Sharing Information** Take one minute to brainstorm skills you might use in the classroom that you might also use at a service job, such as a checker at a grocery store. Team up with a classmate and share your answers verbally for two to three minutes. Volunteer to share both of your answers with the class. Take notes on all the skills that are mentioned.

---

14. **Career Counseling Visit**

Situation You have been employed by the U.S. Department of Labor to help students understand the importance of transferable skills. For your job, you are required to visit high school classrooms across the country to deliver presentations and answer questions. You hope to encourage students to broaden their horizons by developing their transferable skills.

Activity Make a five- to ten-minute presentation about transferable skills within a career that interests you. Use presentation software or other visual aids to describe different transferable skills. Be prepared to answer questions that other students pose about your presentation.

Evaluation You will be evaluated on how well you meet the following performance indicators:
- Explain a variety of transferable skills.
- Provide specific and comprehensive information about skills.
- Effectively handle a question-and-answer session.

---

11. Spreadsheets will vary but should demonstrate that students are able to accurately construct a spreadsheet using computer applications. All spreadsheets should include the type of equipment the team uses and also include columns for the dates each piece of equipment was ordered and received.

12. Student methods of organizing and presenting their personal financial situation may vary. Encourage students who may be uncomfortable sharing real-life financial information with you to create documents using hypothetical savings, monthly income, monthly expenses, and debts. Tell students that it is important to keep much of your personal financial information private and in a safe place. Encourage students to double-check any mathematical calculations they have made.

13. Answers will depend on the job chosen, but encourage students to recognize that jobs in the service industry will often involve mathematics skills, organization skills, and communication skills.

14. Effective presenters should demonstrate an understanding of transferable skills. They should also be able to respond to questions about transferable skills.

---

income may mean that you may have to restrict some aspects of your lifestyle, such as how you spend your free time or what kind of living arrangements you have.

9. Students may answer that observing changes in the world of work now will help you connect your current activities to activities in the world of work. Observing the world of work can also help you plan and prepare for a career that is right for you.

Real-World Skills and Applications

10. Answers will vary but students should demonstrate an understanding of the Arts, Audio/Video Technology, and Communications career cluster as well as an understanding of what skills, training, and technology are required for the particular position. Presentations can include visual aids, software, or brief skits to enhance the content.

Academic Skills in the Workplace

15. Journal entries will vary but should be limited to one page and demonstrate understanding of how changes in a community can affect the local job market. For example, the arrival of a new corporation branch in a job market could increase the number of jobs available or create new opportunities for businesses that relate to employees of the corporation.

16. The average number of minutes each worker spends to keep it filled is 80 minutes (One hour contains 60 minutes; $4 \times 60 = 240$; $240 \div 3 = 80$). Let students know that when writing out an algebraic expression based on the wording of a problem, they should read the problem carefully, pick out key words and phrases and determine their equivalent mathematical meaning, replace any unknowns with a variable, and put them all together in an algebraic expression.

17. Summaries should demonstrate that students have an understanding of the scientific method. A sample hypothesis might be: Technology allows an increasing number of people to work from home in the United States. Ways to find data might include personal surveys, human resources data from public or private organizations, or city, state, or national tax records that show if a person is operating from a home office.

18. Oral reports should reflect that students are able to use various resources, such as online or print newspapers, magazines, interviews, library information specialists, and other sources to acquire information about job outlooks in Mexico.

Academic Skills in the Workplace

English Language Arts

15. Practice Expository Writing Changes in the world affect what kinds of jobs are available. Knowing about these changes can help you make good decisions about your career. Write a one-page journal entry citing an example of a change in your community that might affect the local job market.

Mathematics

16. Calculate Average Work Time Three restaurant workers spend a total of four hours working together to prepare vegetables for the salad bar. What is the average number of minutes each worker spends to keep it filled?

CONCEPT Use Variables and Operations
Translating words into algebraic expressions requires knowledge of the meaning of the verbal descriptions. In algebra, a variable is a symbol used to represent a number. Arithmetic operations include addition, subtraction, multiplication, and division.

Starting Hint If x = the average number of hours each worker spends to keep the bar filled, the algebraic expression for the problem is $3x = (4 \times 60)$. Solve for x.

Science

17. Form a Hypothesis The scientific method is a way to consider scientific questions. It involves collecting data, forming a hypothesis that explains the data, testing the hypothesis, interpreting the results, and stating a conclusion that can be evaluated by others. One hypothesis might read: *Manufacturing jobs are decreasing in the United States because more manufacturing work is being done overseas.* Create your own hypothesis about the world of work. Then, brainstorm ways you would find data to prove your hypothesis. Create a two-paragraph summary of your proposed research project.

Social Studies

18. Research International Job Outlook Imagine that you are interested in living and working in Mexico. Use the library and other resources to research the current job outlook in Mexico. Which industries and occupations are growing and which are declining? Use presentation software or other visual aids to create a five-minute oral report featuring the results of your research.

STANDARDIZED TEST PRACTICE

MULTIPLE CHOICE

Directions Read the following sentence. Then read the question below the sentence. Read the answer choices below each sentence and choose the best answer to fill in the blank.

Test-Taking Tip In a multiple-choice test, the answers should be specific and precise. Read the question first, then read all the answer choices. Eliminate answers that you know are incorrect.

1. People also work because they may enjoy being in an environment with people who have similar interests.

In this sentence, the word *environment* means _____.
a. one's surroundings
b. an apartment or house
c. ecology and temperature
d. envelopment

For more Standardized Test Practice, go to the OLC @ glencoe.com.

 ## STANDARDIZED TEST PRACTICE

Answer
1. a. one's surroundings

Test-Taking Strategies
Whether your students have a standardized test coming up in a few days or a few weeks, these last-minute test-prep tips and strategies will help students relax and do their best.

Test Format Help your students become familiar with the format of the specific test they are going to take by practicing with test items that imitate the actual test items as closely as possible.

Test Timing Have your students take one or more timed practice tests so that they become comfortable with the test format.

Writing Skills Practice

19. Summarizing When summarizing, you have to look for, organize, and explain information in your own words. You can use written summaries to prepare for writing essays. You can also use them while researching jobs and companies.

 Practice Find an article in a newspaper or magazine about the world of work. The article should be no more than two pages. Create a one-paragraph written summary of the article.

Follow the steps below when summarizing:
- Identify the topic of each section to focus your reading.
- As you read, identify important details dealing with the topic and list them.
- Review your details and decide what the main points of the section are.
- Finally, use your own words to briefly state the information you have learned from the text.

Net Connection

20. Research Job Outlooks Online Find the link to the online *Career Guide to Industries*. Select an industry that interests you and note how much jobs in the industry are expected to grow or decline in the future.

@ Log On Go to this book's OLC through **glencoe.com** to search employment and career Web sites for current job opportunities in an industry that interests you. Note the entry-level positions that are available. Print out the jobs and place them in your **Personal Academic and Career Portfolio** to use as a reference.

Reading Connection
@ Go to this book's Online Learning Center through **glencoe.com** for a list of reading suggestions.

Personal Academic and Career Portfolio

Beginning Your Portfolio

Your **Personal Academic and Career Portfolio** is a collection of documents and other media that can showcase your skills and accomplishments. Your portfolio can be either a hard copy portfolio or a digital portfolio, or a combination of both. For example, a graphic artist might wish to place a collection of drawings in his or her portfolio. The graphic artist could make scans of these drawings digitally available online or on a CD-ROM, keeping the original drawings in a hard copy portfolio.

Use the following guidelines to begin your portfolio.
- Use a folder with dividers to organize any hard copy portfolio materials.
- Select a format for your portfolio. A hard copy portfolio can include any printed media. An electronic portfolio can include documents, presentations, digital multimedia files (such as photos and audio or video files), and Web pages.
- Create a cover or title document with your name, address, and other contact information.
- Create a directory or table of contents.
- Create a list of your skills and interests.
- Categorize your skills.
- Title the document *Inventory of Skills and Interests* and file it in your portfolio.
- Update the inventory as you discover and gain new skills and interests.

@ Portfolio Help Go to the *Succeeding in the World of Work* OLC through **glencoe.com** for help developing your portfolio.

Personal Academic and Career Portfolio

Maintaining a Portfolio

Tell students that their **Personal Academic and Career Portfolios** will always be works in progress. As their circumstances, skills, interests, and lifestyles change, the content of their portfolios should be updated. The structure of their portfolio may also change. For example, a hard copy portfolio may be appropriate for some jobs, but an online or portable digital portfolio may be appropriate for other jobs. Individuals may wish to remove or add information or categories to the folders in their portfolios. Encourage students to review their portfolios regularly to ensure that they remain current.

Writing Skills Practice

19. Article summaries will vary but should briefly and accurately convey the meaning of the selected article in one paragraph. Encourage students to attach a copy of the article or provide a URL link to the source of the article.

Net Connection

20. Answers should demonstrate that students are able to navigate the online *Career Guide to Industries*. Students should research job outlook trends in their chosen industry for the next few years. They then should locate a number of entry-level positions in their chosen industry via the Internet. Students should be able to identify detailed information about salary, hours, and benefits for each position.

Resources

ExamView Assessment Suite CD allows you to print out ready-made unit and chapter tests complete with answer keys. You can also create customized tests.

WorkKeys

WorkKeys® is a job skills assessment program. For information on leveled assessment for Communication Skills (Business Writing; Listening; Reading for Information; and Writing), go to the WorkKeys link on this book's OLC through **glencoe.com**.

Chapter Resources Planning Guide with Activities and Features

Section	Features	Activities
Section 2.1 **Decision Making**	Creative Business Practices (p. 33) Hot Jobs! (p. 34)	Before You Read (p. 30) Graphic Organizer (p. 30) As You Read (pp. 31, 32, 33) After You Read (p. 34)
Section 2.2 **Setting Lifestyle Goals**	Real-World Connection (p. 37) Math in Action (p. 38) Everyday Ethics (p. 39) 21st Century Workplace (p. 41) Career Checklist (p. 43)	Before You Read (p. 35) Graphic Organizer (p. 35) As You Read (p. 37) After You Read (p. 43)

NCLB Activities, information, and skills practice will help your students attain No Child Left Behind proficiency. Students will improve their abilities in the following academic standards areas:

Academic Standards Correlations

Discipline	Standard	Feature/Activity
English Language Arts	**NCTE 1** Read texts to acquire new information.	Creative Business Practices (p. 33) Hot Jobs! (p. 34)
	NCTE 4 Use written language to communicate effectively.	After You Read (p. 43) Academic Skills in the Workplace (p. 48) Writing Skills Practice (p. 49) Real-World Connection (p. 37)
	NCTE 9 Develop an understanding of diversity in language use across cultures.	21st Century Workplace (p. 41)
Mathematics	**Number and Operation:** Compute fluently and make reasonable estimates	After You Read (p. 34)
	Problem Solving: Solve problems that arise in mathematics and in other contexts	Math in Action (p. 38)
	Number and Operation: Understand numbers, ways of representing numbers, relationships among numbers, and number systems	Academic Skills in the Workplace (p. 48)
Science	**Life Science:** Interdependence of organisms	Academic Skills in the Workplace (p. 48)

21st Century Skills and Workplace Competencies Correlations

CORRELATIONS The charts show the 21st Century Skills, foundation skills, and workplace competencies that students develop as they work in this chapter.

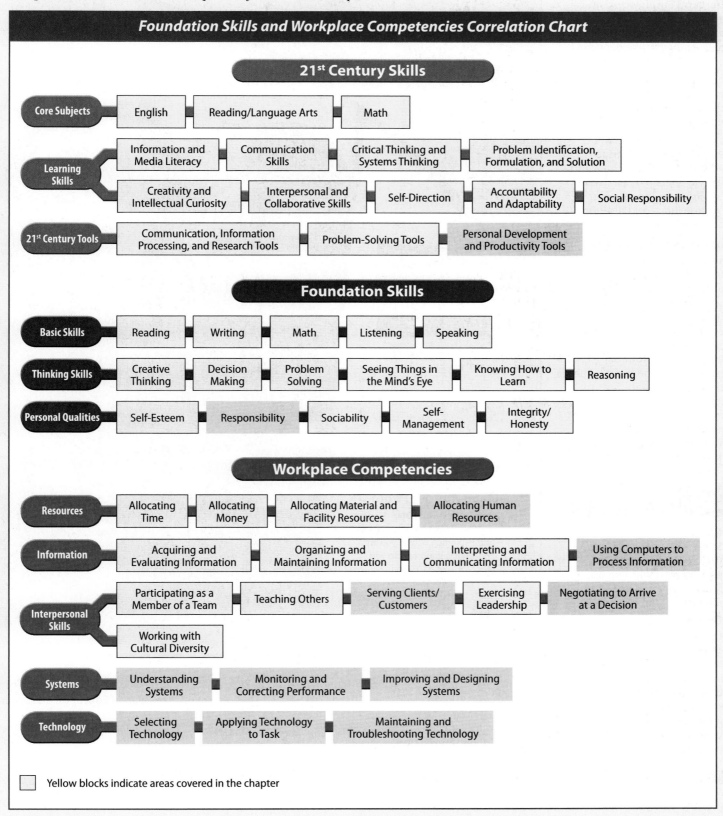

Foundation Skills and Workplace Competencies Correlation Chart

21st Century Skills

Core Subjects
- English
- Reading/Language Arts
- Math

Learning Skills
- Information and Media Literacy
- Communication Skills
- Critical Thinking and Systems Thinking
- Problem Identification, Formulation, and Solution
- Creativity and Intellectual Curiosity
- Interpersonal and Collaborative Skills
- Self-Direction
- Accountability and Adaptability
- Social Responsibility

21st Century Tools
- Communication, Information Processing, and Research Tools
- Problem-Solving Tools
- Personal Development and Productivity Tools

Foundation Skills

Basic Skills
- Reading
- Writing
- Math
- Listening
- Speaking

Thinking Skills
- Creative Thinking
- Decision Making
- Problem Solving
- Seeing Things in the Mind's Eye
- Knowing How to Learn
- Reasoning

Personal Qualities
- Self-Esteem
- Responsibility
- Sociability
- Self-Management
- Integrity/Honesty

Workplace Competencies

Resources
- Allocating Time
- Allocating Money
- Allocating Material and Facility Resources
- Allocating Human Resources

Information
- Acquiring and Evaluating Information
- Organizing and Maintaining Information
- Interpreting and Communicating Information
- Using Computers to Process Information

Interpersonal Skills
- Participating as a Member of a Team
- Teaching Others
- Serving Clients/Customers
- Exercising Leadership
- Negotiating to Arrive at a Decision
- Working with Cultural Diversity

Systems
- Understanding Systems
- Monitoring and Correcting Performance
- Improving and Designing Systems

Technology
- Selecting Technology
- Applying Technology to Task
- Maintaining and Troubleshooting Technology

☐ Yellow blocks indicate areas covered in the chapter

Chapter Overview
Introduce the Chapter

Chapter 2 emphasizes students' need to reflect on personal values and lifestyle goals as they make decisions about potential careers.

Section 2.1 presents a decision-making activity for self-evaluation and career selection.

Section 2.2 helps students identify individual values and the roles that values and lifestyle goals play in career decisions; and focuses on how aptitudes and abilities affect career choices.

Build Background

Ask students to brainstorm the kinds of decisions that they make, from daily ones such as what to wear to school or work, to larger decisions like where to live and what kinds of jobs to pursue. Write students' responses on the board. Then ask students what kinds of factors affect these decisions. For instance, a student might respond that a dress code would affect decisions about what to wear to school.

 Exploring the Photo

Caption Answer
Students should recognize that knowing their values and interests will help them find a career they will find fulfilling.

Discussion Ask students to think of adults whose careers they admire, and then ask what values and interests might have led to those careers. (An example might be a hair stylist who is interested in fashion and beauty, and who values working with customers.)

CHAPTER **2**
Getting to Know Yourself

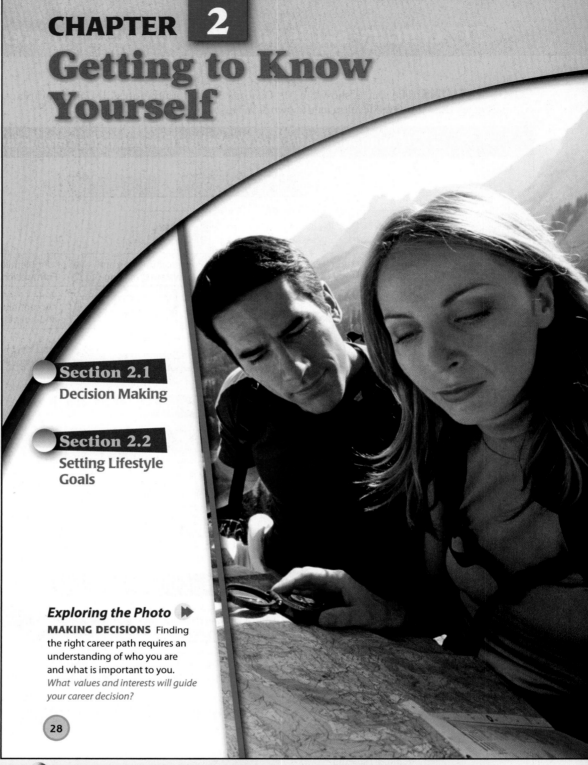

Section 2.1
Decision Making

Section 2.2
Setting Lifestyle Goals

Exploring the Photo ▶▶
MAKING DECISIONS Finding the right career path requires an understanding of who you are and what is important to you. *What values and interests will guide your career decision?*

28

Classroom Resources

- 📁 Student Edition
- 📁 Teacher Wraparound Edition
- 📁 Student Activity Workbook with Academic Integration
- 📁 Student Activity Workbook with Academic Integration TAE
- 📁 *Fast File,* Unit 1 Resources

- 📁 Inclusion in the Career Education Classroom
- ⚙ TeacherWorks™ Plus
- ⚙ *ExamView Assessment Suite*
- ⚙ Interactive Chalkboard
- ⚙ Interactive Student Edition
- 💾 Online Student Edition
- 💾 Online Learning Center (OLC) with Podcasts

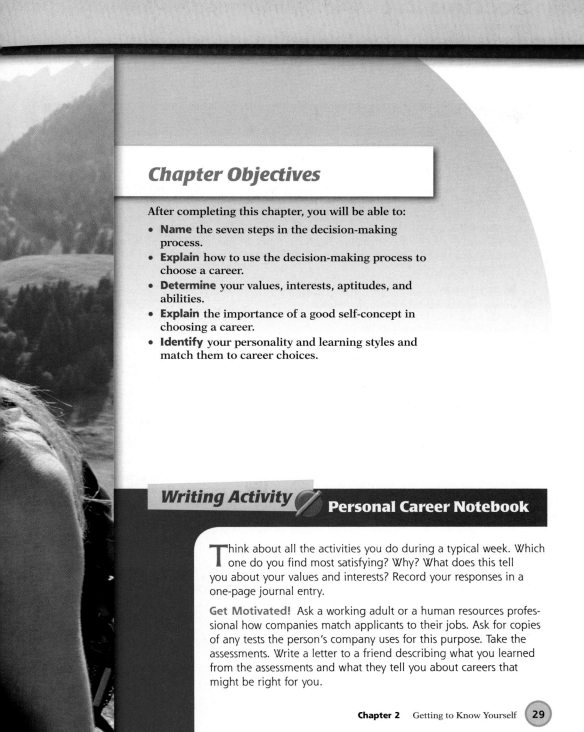

Chapter Objectives

After completing this chapter, you will be able to:

- **Name** the seven steps in the decision-making process.
- **Explain** how to use the decision-making process to choose a career.
- **Determine** your values, interests, aptitudes, and abilities.
- **Explain** the importance of a good self-concept in choosing a career.
- **Identify** your personality and learning styles and match them to career choices.

Writing Activity

Personal Career Notebook

Think about all the activities you do during a typical week. Which one do you find most satisfying? Why? What does this tell you about your values and interests? Record your responses in a one-page journal entry.

Get Motivated! Ask a working adult or a human resources professional how companies match applicants to their jobs. Ask for copies of any tests the person's company uses for this purpose. Take the assessments. Write a letter to a friend describing what you learned from the assessments and what they tell you about careers that might be right for you.

Chapter 2 Getting to Know Yourself **29**

Review the Objectives

Introduce the chapter by reviewing the chapter objectives:

Section 2.1 Objectives

Name the seven steps in the decision-making process. (The seven basic steps of the decision-making process are define your needs and wants; analyze your resources; identify your choices; gather information; evaluate your choices; make a decision; and plan how to reach your goal.)

Explain how to use the decision-making process to choose a career. (You can use the seven decision-making steps to analyze how your lifestyle goals fit your career goals.)

Section 2.2 Objectives

Determine your values, interests, aptitudes, and abilities. (Your values are your beliefs and principles; your interests are what you enjoy doing; an aptitude is your potential for learning a new skill; and your abilities are the skills you already have.)

Explain the importance of a good self-concept in choosing a career. (Knowing the way you see yourself will help you determine the right career for you.)

Identify your personality and learning styles and match them to career choices. (Your personality is your unique combination of attitudes, behaviors, and characteristics. Learning styles are the different ways in which people think and learn.)

Writing Activity

Personal Career Notebook Answer Guide

Student activities might include going to school, playing sports, being part of an after-school club, shopping, and preparing meals at home. Activities that students find satisfying might help them learn what they want to pursue as a career. For instance, students who enjoy shopping might enjoy a career in retail or marketing.

Get Motivated! Letters should show an understanding of what students have learned from speaking with human resources professionals, and from taking any tests the company uses to screen applicants. Evaluate letters for clarity, length, and content.

FOCUS

Bell Ringer Activity

Decision Making

Ask students to list three situations in which they have made a decision or will soon need to make a decision. Ask volunteers to read items on their lists.

Resources

⚙ Interactive Chalkboard
The Interactive Chalkboard CD provides visual teaching aids for this section.

@ Online Learning Center
The Online Learning Center (OLC) through **glencoe.com** features chapter vocabulary, chapter summaries, and other study materials.

Preteaching

Assign key terms to student pairs. Have the pairs find the words in context, define them, and then present their words and definitions to the class.

Graphic Organizer

Tell students to go to the OLC through **glencoe.com** for a printable graphic organizer. (Students should be able to list the seven decision-making steps from this section. Summaries should properly explain the main idea of each step.)

NCLB connects academic correlations to book content.

Decision Making

Reading Guide

Before You Read

Preview Look at the photo and figure in this section and read their captions. Write one or two sentences predicting what the section will be about.

Read to Learn
- The seven steps of the decision-making process
- How to use the decision-making process to choose a career

D | Main Idea
Using a consistent decision-making process will enable you to make sound career decisions and other decisions throughout your life.

Key Concept
- Making Decisions

Key Term
◆ decision-making process

Academic Vocabulary
You will find these words in your reading and on your tests. Use the academic vocabulary glossary to look up their definitions if necessary.
- affect
- sequence

Graphic Organizer
As you read, list the steps in the decision-making process, then summarize the steps in your own words. Use a chart like the one below to help organize your information.

Decision-Making Steps	Summary
1.	
2.	
3.	
4.	
5.	
6.	
7.	

 Log On Go to this book's Online Learning Center through **glencoe.com** for an online version of this graphic organizer.

N C L B | Academic Standards •

English Language Arts
- Read texts to acquire new information. (NCTE 1)

Mathematics
- Compute fluently and make reasonable estimates

Reading Guide

Before You Read
Point out to the class that decision making often involves more than a *yes* or *no* answer. Explain to students that they will face complex decisions in their lives and will need strategies for making good decisions.

D Develop Concepts
Main Idea Discuss the main idea with students. Ask: How do you think a "decision-making process" would help when deciding on a career? (Students may point out that a step-by-step process would help them organize their thoughts and weigh complex options.)

Making Decisions

How do you make decisions? Do you flip a coin? Talk to friends? Make a list of pros and cons? Decisions are not always easy to make, especially when it comes to something as important as career choice. If you are the kind of person who waits for someone else to make decisions for you, remember that you may not be happy with the outcome.

You might be surprised to know that half of all employed people simply fall into their jobs out of laziness or luck, or because they are unaware of their options. You do not have to be one of these people. You can choose a career that is right for you. Maybe you have been putting off deciding what to do after graduation. Maybe you do not know where to start. A good place to start is by learning how to make good decisions.

The Decision-Making Process

If you have ever made an important decision, you know that good decision making does not just happen. The longer a decision will **affect** your life, the more time you need to think about it. One of the biggest decisions in your life—your career choice—will require serious planning. This will be easier if you follow a **decision-making process**, which is a series of steps that can help you identify and evaluate possibilities and make a good choice.

Vocabulary
You can find definitions in the **Key Terms** glossary and **Academic Vocabulary** glossary at the back of this book.

As You Read
Analyze What are some life decisions to which you might apply the decision-making process?

HELP WITH DECISIONS The decision-making process can help you make big decisions. *How might knowing his resources help this person decide which car to buy?*

Getting to Know Yourself 31

TEACH

Discussion Starter
Making Decisions Ask students to list everyday decisions they make. Encourage students to include in their lists even the smallest decisions they make, such as what to wear to school. (Lists might include when to leave home for school, what to eat for lunch, and how to spend free time after school.)

R Reading Strategy
Give Examples Ask students to give examples of major decisions and to brainstorm reasons why these decisions require more time to think about than everyday decisions. (Major decisions might include large purchases, such as cars or houses, or decisions that involve a longer time commitment, such as joining the armed forces or enrolling in college. Major decisions often require more thought because they will have more lasting effects than minor decisions.)

As You Read
Life decisions might include where to buy a house or rent an apartment; what kind of car to buy; and when to change jobs.

Resources
TeacherWorks™ Plus The TeacherWorks software includes customizable built-in lesson plans and links to printable program resources.

Extend the Photo

Caption Answer By knowing his resources, this person will know how much money he can spend on car payments and insurance. He might also make a decision based on whether he has the ability or the time to learn how to drive a car with a manual transmission.

Discussion Ask students what personal resources are needed to buy a car. Encourage students to think of resources besides money, such as the ability to drive a car with a manual transmission versus the need to buy a car with an automatic transmission, or whether they live in a region where they would need a car that could handle driving in difficult weather, such as snow.

TEACH *(cont.)*

C Critical Thinking

Connect to the Community Have students apply the decision-making process to choosing an apartment. Collect rental ads from the local newspaper or have students bring ads to class. Set an amount students can spend, then have them follow the process to make a decision.

U Universal Access

Students with Learning Disabilities Students with learning disabilities may require additional guidelines or study aids to get the most out of text material. You may wish to make audio recordings for students who find written text difficult to use. Establish a relaxed reading pace, and use a bell or clicker to signal page turns. Elicit the help of classmates who have clear voices.

As You Read

By following the seven steps, you can organize your thoughts and feel more confident about the decisions you make.

 ASSESS

Review Key Terms

Have students write sentences using the key terms they have read so far in the text.

Online Study Tools

Have students go to the OLC through **glencoe.com** to:

- Download **Podcast** study tools.
- Download free **Study-to-Go** content to their PDAs or cell phones.

32

Figure 2.1 **THE DECISION-MAKING PROCESS**

STEP	1	Define your needs and wants.
STEP	2	Analyze your resources.
STEP	3	Identify your choices.
STEP	4	Gather information.
STEP	5	Evaluate your choices.
STEP	6	Make a decision.
STEP	7	Plan how to reach your goal.

SEVEN STEPS TO A DECISION Following this process will help you gather and organize the information you need to make an important decision, such as a career choice. *What steps should you take before you make your decision?*

The Seven Steps

Following a decision-making process may feel awkward at first as you work through the basic steps. Think of it as learning a new dance or how to play a new game. Once you know the steps, it is easier. You can even add variations to make the process fit different situations. These are the seven basic steps of the decision-making process:

1. Define your needs and wants.
2. Analyze your resources.
3. Identify your choices.
4. Gather information.
5. Evaluate your choices.
6. Make a decision.
7. Plan how to reach your goal.

Figure 2.1 shows these steps in **sequence**. The decision-making process can be used to help you make any kind of decision. However, the process is especially helpful for making important or difficult decisions.

As You Read

Explain How does the decision-making process help you to make decisions?

Using the Decision-Making Process to Choose a Career

You can use the seven-step decision-making process to choose a career that is right for you. As you continue through this and the next three chapters, you will use these seven steps to create a written career plan.

32 Unit 1 Self-Assessment

EXTEND THE FIGURE **Figure 2.1**

Caption Answer The steps you must take are: Define your needs and wants; analyze your resources; identify your choices; gather information; and evaluate your choices.

Discussion Ask students to discuss the role feelings or intuition play in decision making. (Some decisions just "feel" right, perhaps because the decision maker has studied the issues and weighed the alternatives)

Step 1: Define Your Needs and Wants

The path to a career starts with thinking about your goals, hopes, and dreams, as well as thinking about the lifestyle you want. Where do you want to live? Do you want to work full-time? How much money will you need to earn in order to have the lifestyle you want? In Section 2.2, you will examine your personal goals and learn why knowing your goals can help you make effective career decisions.

Step 2: Analyze Your Personal Resources

In choosing a career, your personal resources are who you are and what you have to offer an employer. Your personal resources include your values, interests, aptitudes and abilities, talents, personality traits, and learning styles. Being aware of who you are and what you have to offer will help you make good career choices. You will explore your personal resources in Section 2.2.

Step 3: Identify Your Career Choices

In this step, you will select several possible careers and match them to your personal needs and resources. You may not know which career you want yet. Like many young people, you may choose a career and then change your mind. That is part of the learning process. Just keep your mind open to life's changes and possibilities. Chapters 3 and 4 in this book can help you research and discover your career options.

As You Read

Connect How has exploring your options affected a decision you have made in the past?

Creative Business Practices

PATAGONIA Exploring Opportunities

Patagonia, Inc., a company that makes outdoor and adventure sports gear, encourages employees to have adventures of their own. The company provides paid leave for employees who want to work as interns with non-profit groups, such wilderness projects that help save endangered species. During internships, Patagonia employees receive their regular salary and benefits for up to 60 days. Patagonia employees have worked on projects such as the Chumbe Island Project, which encourages coral reef protection, and the Mist Preservation Society, which helps preserve the subtropical forests of New Zealand.

The Patagonia internship program benefits everyone involved. Nonprofit groups benefit from the experience of talented volunteers, employees get time away from the office to make a difference in the world, and Patagonia gets to support worthy efforts.

CRITICAL THINKING If you had the opportunity to take part in Patagonia's internship program, which programs would interest you? Why?

@ **Connect to the Real World** To read more about Patagonia, visit the company's Web site via the link on this book's Online Learning Center through **glencoe.com**.

Creative Business Practices

CRITICAL THINKING ANSWER Students should give reasons for their choice of programs. Point out to students that because Patagonia employees continue to receive salary and benefits while they are volunteering, they are likely to be highly motivated and more willing to volunteer.

RETEACH

S **Skill Practice**

Independent Practice

Calculate Anna wants to buy a car from a friend for $6,000. Anna earns $115 a week and has $2,500 as a down payment. The owner will let her pay the remainder over 18 months without interest. Calculate the amount of the payments and decide whether you would buy the car if you were Anna. (The monthly payment would be $194. Students would probably buy the car because the payments are affordable and no interest is being charged.) **L1**

Gather Information One step in the decision-making process is gathering information. Tell students they are to buy camping equipment. What resources would they use to decide what type of equipment they need? (Possible answers include books, trade shows, magazines, advertisements, and the Internet.) **L2**

Apply Have students create a career plan using the seven-step decision-making process. Students should list each step, then write answers. (Answers should reflect an understanding of the decision-making process.) **L3**

As You Read

Students should recognize that even simple decisions, such as what to eat for lunch, involve weighing options and evaluating choices.

Resources

📁 **Student Activity Workbook** Assign the Chapter 2 activities in the Student Activity Workbook.

Section 2.1

ASSESS

After You Read

Have students complete the Section 2.1 After You Read section review.

Online Study Tools

Have students go to the OLC through **glencoe.com** to:

- Take the Section 2.1 **Practice Test**.
- Download **Podcast** study tools.
- Download free **Study-to-Go** content to their PDAs or cell phones.

CLOSE

Culminating Activity

Applying the Decision-Making Process Have students draw a graph with two columns and seven rows. The left column should list the seven decision-making steps. In the right column, ask students to think of a decision they need to make, and to write responses to the seven steps in the corresponding rows. Then ask students to write a 200-word paragraph that summarizes their results.

Activity correlated to Mathematics standards.

HOT JOBS!

Speech Therapist

Speech therapists work with people who have difficulty with speech, language, communication, swallowing, and fluency. For example, a speech therapist might work with someone who has a stutter or someone who wishes to eliminate an accent. This job requires attention to detail, good communication skills, and knowledge of speech-related disorders.

Step 4: Research Your Career Choices

After you identify possible careers, you will want to learn more about them before making a choice. In Chapter 3 you will learn how to research careers. In Chapter 4, you will explore the option of opening your own business. How well have you explored your options so far?

Step 5: Evaluate Your Career Choices

By the time you reach this step, you will have a lot of information about yourself and different career possibilities. Evaluating your career choices means looking at each career choice and thinking about whether it matches your personal needs and resources. In Chapter 5, you will learn a helpful strategy for evaluating career choices.

Steps 6 and 7: Make Your Decision and Plan How to Reach Your Goal

Though your career goal may change, it is still important for you to make a career decision and a career plan. You may discover at some point that your career goal is unrealistic or undesirable. You may have to compromise or adapt your original plan. You can then repeat the decision-making process to arrive at a new goal.

Chapter 5 in this book can also help you with these last two steps in the career decision-making process.

Section 2.1 After You Read

Review Key Concepts

1. List the seven steps in the decision-making process.
2. Explain how you would use the seven-step decision-making process to decide how to spend $1,000.
3. Describe how to identify your career choices.

Practice Academic Skills

 Mathematics

4. Some people decide where to live based on living costs, such as rent. If a one-bedroom apartment that rents for $450 in Detroit rents for 250% of that price in Manhattan, what is the rent in Manhattan?

   CONCEPT **Multiply by Percents Greater than 100** Percents greater than 100 represent values greater than one. They can be converted to mixed numbers or decimals greater than one.
   Step 1: Change the percent (250%) to a decimal greater than one.
   Step 2: Multiply this decimal by the number ($450). Be sure the decimal point is in the right place in your answer.

    For math help, go to the Math Appendix located at the back of this book.

Section 2.1 After You Read

Review Key Concepts

1. The seven steps are: define your needs and wants; analyze your personal resources; identify your choices; gather information; evaluate your choices; make your decision; and plan how to reach your goal.

2. Answers should demonstrate, through relevant and concrete examples, students' understanding of the seven steps in the decision-making model.

3. You can identify your career choices by considering several possible careers that match your personal goals and resources.

Practice Academic Skills

4. The rent in Manhattan is $1,125 ($2.5 × $450 = $1,125).

Setting Lifestyle Goals

Reading Guide

Before You Read

Preview Choose a Key Term or Academic Vocabulary word that is new to you. When you find it in the text, write down the definition.

Read to Learn

- How to determine your values, interests, aptitudes, and abilities
- The importance of a good self-concept in choosing a career
- How to identify your personality and learning styles and match them to career choices

Main Idea

D Developing a good self-concept and using it to guide your career decisions will help you lead a rewarding, enjoyable life.

Key Concepts

- Your Lifestyle Goals
- Your Values
- Your Interests
- Your Aptitudes and Abilities
- Your Personality and Learning Styles

Key Terms

◇ lifestyle goals
◇ values
◇ data
◇ aptitude
◇ ability
◇ personality
◇ self-concept
◇ learning styles

Academic Vocabulary

You will find this word in your reading and on your tests. Use the academic vocabulary glossary to look up its definition if necessary.

■ examine

Graphic Organizer

As you read, list your values, aptitudes and abilities, and personality traits. Continue adding to your list after you have finished reading. Use a three-column chart like the one shown to help you organize your information.

Values	Aptitudes and Abilities	Personality Traits

Log On Go to this book's Online Learning Center through **glencoe.com** for an online version of this graphic organizer.

Academic Standards ● ● ● ● ● ● ● ● ● ● ● ● ● ● ● ● ● ●

N C L B

English Language Arts
- Read texts to acquire new information. (NCTE 1)
- Develop an understanding of diversity in language across cultures. (NCTE 9)

Mathematics
- Compute fluently and make reasonable estimates

glencoe.com

Chapter 2 Getting to Know Yourself **35**

Bell Ringer Activity

Setting Lifestyle Goals

Have students write a list of five jobs. For each job, have them describe a basic personality type that might be good at the job (for example, an outgoing person in a sales job). Ask them to list other character traits a person doing each job should have.

Resources

Interactive Chalkboard
The Interactive Chalkboard CD provides visual teaching aids for this section.

@ Online Learning Center
The OLC through **glencoe.com** features chapter vocabulary, chapter summaries, and other study materials.

Preteaching

Read each term aloud and then work with students to scan the section to find each term in context. Have a volunteer read the definition while everyone in class records it.

Graphic Organizer

Tell students to go to the OLC through **glencoe.com** for a printable graphic organizer. (Graphic organizers should reflect an understanding of values, aptitudes and abilities, and personality traits.)

N C L B NCLB connects academic correlations to book content.

Reading Guide

Before You Read

Ask a volunteer to choose a career and then write it on the board. Then have the class brainstorm what personality traits they envision a person would need to be successful in the chosen career.

D Develop Concepts

Main Idea Ask students to brainstorm the meaning of *self-concept* and what factors contribute to a person's self-concept.

TEACH

Discussion Starter

Your Lifestyle Goals Ask students to take five minutes to brainstorm goals they want to achieve during the next five years. Encourage students to be specific about the time periods in which they want to achieve their goals, whether it be some-time today or by next year. Ask how long-term goals might be similar to or different from short-term goals.

✓ Reading Check

EXPLAIN Knowing your lifestyle goals can help you determine how to spend your time, energy, and resources.

R Reading Strategy

Expand the Concept Ask volunteers to share their answers to the lifestyle goal questions on this page. List their responses on the board. Then ask the class to brainstorm possible careers that match these goals. (Answers will vary but students should reflect an understanding of lifestyle goals.)

Resources

⊙ Interactive Chalkboard
The Interactive Chalkboard CD provides visual teaching aids for this section.

◀ Vocabulary
You can find definitions in the **Key Terms** glossary and **Academic Vocabulary** glossary at the back of this book.

Your Lifestyle Goals

By getting to know yourself, you can plan your future and choose a career you will want to pursue. You can begin this inward exploration by considering your lifestyle goals.

Your **lifestyle goals** are the ways you want to spend your time, energy, and resources in the future. Consider the lifestyle you would like to have someday. Ask yourself a few questions:

- What do you want to accomplish in life?
- Where would you like to live? For example, would you like to live in a house or an apartment? In the city or the country?
- How do you want to spend your free time?
- Do you want a lot of money or just enough to be comfortable?
- Do you plan to have a family?

Now imagine your life five or ten years from today. Write about or sketch the life you want. What career or careers would make this life-style possible? To determine if these careers are realistic choices for you, you need to **examine** yourself and what you want from life.

✓ Reading Check **EXPLAIN** How can knowing your lifestyle goals help you decide on a career?

▶▶ LIFESTYLE GOALS
Some people choose a career that will allow them to spend time with their family and friends. *What are your lifestyle goals?*

▶▶ Extend the Photo

Caption Answer Answers should reflect an understanding of the lifestyle goals questions, such as "Where would you like to live?" or "Do you want to have a lot of money?"

Discussion Ask students to discuss what kinds of lifestyle goals a person would need to be an automobile designer. Encourage students to consider how each of the lifestyle goals questions given in the text might be answered by a person who wanted to be an automobile designer.

Your Values

Becoming aware of your values is an important part of getting to know yourself. Your **values** are your beliefs and principles. They define who you are, shape your attitudes and choices, and help you set priorities.

You can determine your values by thinking about what is really important to you. For example, if you spend a lot of time playing guitar and listening to music, one of your values may be artistic expression. If you like activities such as volunteering at a local nursing home, you probably value helping others. Choosing a career that matches your values can help ensure that you will enjoy your work. It will also give you a sense of self-fulfillment. As you think about a future career, you should consider how well that career suits your values.

Six General Values

Values may change as you go through life. However, you may keep a core set of values that you learned early in your life from people who were important to you. These people may include family, teachers, and friends. Values are also influenced by spiritual beliefs, society, and personal experiences. To help determine your current values, consider the following list of six general values. Which ones are important to you? Which ones concern you less? Can you think of careers suited to each value? Do any of these careers appeal to you?

- **Responsibility** Being responsible means fulfilling obligations in a dependable and trustworthy way.
- **Relationships** If you value relationships, your family and friends are important to you. You may make career decisions that allow you to work with people you like or to live near your family.
- **Compassion** Compassion is caring deeply about people and their well-being. You may also feel compassion for other creatures, such as lost or endangered animals.
- **Courage** Courage is the ability to overcome difficulties or to conquer fear or despair. You use courage, for example, when you speak up for an unpopular cause.
- **Achievement** Valuing achievement means you want to succeed in whatever you do, whether you are an artist or an auto mechanic.
- **Recognition** If you value recognition, you want other people to appreciate and respect your accomplishments. You want to be rewarded for your work.

S₁

S₂

Real-World Connection

Career Mentors

You love the outdoors and want a career that will let you work outside. Your school counselor recently announced that you are a finalist for a scholarship in computer science, based on your high test scores in a programming class. You do not see how a technology major will be compatible with your goal to work outdoors.

Critical Thinking How can you pursue a technology major and still remain true to your lifestyle goals?

Do Your Own Research Find an adult who works outdoors and has agreed to mentor students. Talk with your school counselor, career development coordinator, or work-based learning coordinator if you need help locating someone appropriate. Conduct an informational interview with the mentor, and include questions about the role of technology in his or her job.

As You Read

Connect What are some of your values?

S₁ Skill Practice
Independent Practice
Cooperative Learning Assign students to groups of four or five. Each group is to list the six general values and additional values to the list (up to a total of ten). Have teams rank their list of values from most important to least important. *(Encourage teams to provide reasons for how they rank their values.)*

S₂ Skill Practice
Guided Practice
Cooperative Learning Write each of the six general values on the board. Have students give examples of each value. Discuss how people's values affect the choices they make. *(For example, a person who values academic achievement might pass up a movie to study for a test.)* Next, ask students to add other values to the list. *(Examples might include art, music, physical fitness, and punctuality.)*

As You Read

Answers will vary but should reflect an understanding of the six general values.

Real-World Connection

Critical Thinking Answer Students may discover a number of outdoor careers that rely heavily on technology, such as land surveying, soil and water conservation, and agricultural research.

Do Your Own Research Encourage students to share the results of their interviews about the roles of technology in the workplace.

S TEACH (cont.)

S Skill Practice
Independent Practice

Writing Have students picture themselves in a career. Ask them to write a one-page description of what they see in their imagination. What are they doing on a typical workday? Are they working in a city or a suburb? How do they feel about the work they are doing? **L1**

Organizing and Maintaining Information Have students create a chart of their personal values and interests. Encourage students to use these charts as they research careers. **L2**

Working with Cultural Diversity Tell students to imagine they are working in a large city hospital admissions office. Many of the patients speak little or no English. What special values and interests might students need to work in this career? (Values might include compassion, patience, and interest in helping others. Special interests might include health care, clerical work, and learning other languages.) **L3**

✓ Reading Check

EVALUATE Answers should reflect students' beliefs and principles.

N C L B Activity correlated to Mathematics standards.

Math In Action

Calculate Pay

Esteban is deciding between two job offers. One pays $13.00 an hour for 50 hours a week; the other pays $15.50 an hour for 40 hours a week. Esteban wants to spend more time with his family, so he will probably choose the second job. If he does, how much less will he make each year?

Starting Hint: Calculate how much he will make in each job per year before you calculate the difference in pay.

@ For more math practice, go to this book's OLC through **glencoe.com**.

N C L B

Now make your own list, and rank your values in order of importance. You may include some or all of the six general values, and you may add as many others as you wish. Keep this list for later use. Can you imagine a career that would satisfy your particular mix of values?

S

Putting Your Values into Practice

While many people may share the same value—for example, the value of helping others—each person may put that value into practice in a different way. In trying to match a career to your set of values, you will probably find that you have many choices. For instance, you may decide helping others is one of your values. Jobs that match that value include librarian, teacher, and nurse's aide. Which one should you pursue? To narrow your choices, consider your interests.

✓ Reading Check

EVALUATE What are three values that are most important to you?

R₁

Your Interests

In addition to considering your values, you should pay attention to your interests when choosing a career. Your interests are the things you enjoy doing. For example, you may like singing in a choir or collecting rocks. If you are not sure what your interests are, one way to find out is to try new activities. Take a karate class, for example, or volunteer at an animal shelter or a senior center.

▶ **ACTING ON VALUES**
Some people choose jobs that allow them to put their values into practice. *What might this computer programmer's choice to work with seniors at a community center say about her values?*

Math In Action

Esteban will make $1,560 less if he takes the job that pays $15.50 an hour. (50 × $13.00 × 52 = $33,800.00; 40 × $15.50 × 52 = $32,240).

▶ **Extend the Photo**

Caption Answer Values mentioned might include a goal to work with older people and to help others.

Discussion Ask students to brainstorm types of jobs that involve helping others in the community. Encourage students to consider jobs in community centers and hospitals, as well as donation centers and fund-raising activities.

Everyday ETHICS

CALLING IN SICK

Is it ever okay to tell a lie?

VACATION DAYS You recently started a new job at an office supply store. You can't take vacation days until you have been there for three months, but you can take sick days whenever you need them. Before you got your job, you and your friends had planned to go to the beach tomorrow. You really want to go since you have not been able to hang out with your friends much since you started your job.

What Would You Do? Will you lie to your boss and say you are sick so you can go to the beach?

Will the lie hurt anyone? If it does not hurt anyone, is it okay to lie? Write a half-page journal entry explaining your decision.

DISCUSS IT Lying often has consequences you cannot predict. For instance, what if the store is suddenly busy? Is it fair for the store manager to do all the work herself when she is paying you to help her? What if she finds out you went to the beach? How does that affect your reputation? Brainstorm the possible consequences of calling in sick and going to work and share them with the class.

Favorite Activities

You probably already enjoy a variety of activities, so make a list of your ten favorite activities and rank them in order of preference. Think of activities you like to do with friends or by yourself—at school, at home, at work, or outdoors. You can add this list to your **Personal Academic and Career Portfolio**.

Data, People, or Things?

Identifying your interests can help you recognize whether you would prefer to work with data, people, or things.

Data refer to information, knowledge, ideas, facts, words, symbols, figures, and statistics. Accountants, librarians, physicists, and proofreaders are examples of people who work with data.

Those individuals who prefer to work with people may enjoy careers that involve working with others, such as teaching, counseling, or training rescue dogs and their handlers.

Working with things may involve handling physical objects of any size, such as instruments, tools, plants, machinery, equipment, raw materials, and vehicles. Because many careers involve combinations of data, people, and things, think about which area you would like to be your main focus. For example, a technical support representative for a computer company may work with *data*, in creating codes and logging calls; *people*, in answering calls and helping customers with technical problems; and *things*, in determining how to fix malfunctioning equipment.

Personal Academic and Career Portfolio

Go to the chapter review to find guidelines for creating your own **Personal Academic and Career Portfolio**.

R₁ Reading Strategy

Researching Jobs Have students read the classified section of your local newspaper to find three intriguing jobs. Have students make a list of three values and three interests a person would need to succeed in the jobs.

**W Writing Support
Guided Practice**

Explore Interests Have students make a list of ten activities they like to do, and indicate whether each involves primarily data, people, or things. Have each student then write a paragraph that summarizes their results. (Paragraphs will vary but should show an understanding of the people, data, and things concept.)

R₂ Reading Strategy

Explain Ask a volunteer to choose a career, and then ask the class how the data, people, and things categories might overlap for a person working in that career. (An example might be a sales representative who works mainly with people, but also uses computers and data.)

Chapter 2 Getting to Know Yourself **39**

Everyday ETHICS

What Would You Do? Answer Students should take into account their obligations to their new employer, to themselves, and to their friends, as well as their employer's obligation to respect their outside lives. A solution might be to mention previous plans at the time of hiring.

DISCUSS IT Encourage students to role-play as employee and manager and explore possible outcomes if the employee's lying is discovered by the employer.

TEACH (cont.)

 Skill Practice

Guided Practice

Present Have students present their special abilities and aptitudes to the class with a poster, flyer, picture, or other medium. (Student projects should reflect an understanding of the concepts of abilities and aptitudes.) **L1**

Identify Ask students to make a list of aptitudes they feel they have. Then ask them to explain in a 250-word paragraph which of these aptitudes they could develop into a career-related skill and why. (Answers will vary, but students should recognize that not all aptitudes can be developed into career-related skills.) **L2**

Evaluate Ask students to write a 300-word paragraph that first describes an aptitude they feel they already have, and then suggests ways they can develop this aptitude into a career-related skill. (Answers will vary but should describe the relationship between aptitudes and abilities.) **L3**

✓ **Reading Check**

EXPLAIN You can determine your interests by making a list of favorite activities or by taking a formal or informal career interest and aptitude test.

▶ **WHO ARE YOU?**
Knowing your values, interests, aptitudes and abilities, personality, and learning styles will help you choose a career. *What do you think are this person's interests?*

Interest and Aptitude Assessment

Another way to identify your interests is to take a formal career interest and aptitude assessment, which is like a test that has no right or wrong answers. You choose from a long list of activities and aptitudes to determine which ones you have. Then you match your interests and aptitudes to possible careers. Ask your teacher or guidance counselor for help in locating and completing such a survey.

✓ **Reading Check** **EXPLAIN** How can you determine what your interests are?

S Your Aptitudes and Abilities

Now that you have identified some of your values and interests, you should consider your aptitudes and abilities. An **aptitude** is a potential for learning a certain skill. An **ability** is a skill you have already developed. Think of them as the "before" and "after" of learning a skill. Suppose you discover that you have the knack for training your new dog. If you study and work to become a professional dog trainer, your aptitude will become your ability.

How do you discover your aptitudes and abilities? First, you need to realize that there are many kinds of skills. Thinking creatively, making decisions, knowing how to learn, and seeing things in the mind's eye are all skills important to your success. Other skills, such as running and welding, involve physical abilities. What other skills can you name?

▶ **Extend the Photo**

Caption Answer Students may respond that this person likes working with animals or is interested in farming and agriculture.

Discussion Lead a class discussion asking students what kinds of careers might be possible for someone who has the same interests as those mentioned as caption answers.

Identifying Your Aptitudes and Abilities

To get a clear picture of your aptitudes and abilities, list as many of your skills as you can. Need help? Try these techniques:

- Make a three-column chart with the headings *Mental*, *Physical*, and *Social*. List aptitudes and abilities in each column.
- Ask friends or family members what they think your aptitudes and abilities are. What ideas do they have?

Matching Your Aptitudes and Abilities to Careers

Review your list of aptitudes and abilities, and try to think of at least one career that requires each of your skills. For example, if one of your aptitudes is caring for children, you might choose a career as a teacher. Finding a realistic career match for your aptitudes and abilities will help you find work you enjoy.

✓ **Reading Check** **CONTRAST** What is the difference between an aptitude and an ability?

The 21ˢᵗ Century Workplace

Language Reflects Culture

Japanese contains many words that express specifically Japanese ideas and customs. The majority of these words do not have corresponding words in other languages. For example, the Japanese concept *wabi-sabi* represents an approach to things that celebrates beauty that is natural or subtle.

The Japanese language also features an honorific system called *keigo*, which allows the speaker to express various levels of politeness and formality. Understanding these and other language subtleties can benefit workers and others who interact with Japanese speakers.

CRITICAL THINKING _____

Why might visitors to Japan benefit from an understanding of keigo?

In Your Community

Language is often closely linked to culture. Identify some examples of how language and culture are linked in your community or another community that interests you. Share your findings with the class in a two- to five-minute oral presentation.

COMMON JAPANESE WORDS AND PHRASES	
good day	kon-nichi wa
goodbye	sayonara
yes	hai
no	iie
please	onegaishimasu
good	ii desu
thank you	dômo arigatô/ gozaimasu
you're welcome	douitashimashite
sorry/excuse me	sumimasen

@ Extend Your Learning The Japanese use three different writing systems: *hiragana*, *katakana*, and *kanji*. For links to Web sites about the Japanese writing systems, go to this book's OLC through **glencoe.com**.

The 21ˢᵗ Century Workplace

CRITICAL THINKING ANSWER Visitors might be able to communicate more clearly and respectfully, and they might also be better able to determine social relationships between others.

In Your Community Ask students to choose a common phrase from above and compare how it is written in the three different writing styles: *hiragana*, *katakana*, and *kanji*.

TEACH *(cont.)*

U Universal Access
Students with Visual Impairments One of the ways students with visual impairments cope with classroom printed material is by listening to taped classroom lectures. Keeping that in mind, think carefully about what you say in class. When writing on the board or while presenting information visually, be clear and specific.

✓ **Reading Check**

CONTRAST An aptitude is a potential for learning a skill, and an ability is a skill you have already developed.

N C L B Activity correlated to English Language Arts standards.

ASSESS

Review Key Terms
Have students write sentences using the key terms they have read so far in this section.

Online Study Tools
Have students go to the OLC through **glencoe.com** to:

- Download **Podcast** study tools.
- Download free **Study-to-Go** content to their PDAs or cell phones.

RETEACH

C **Critical Thinking**

Drawing Conclusions Have students interview five people regarding their learning styles. Do most people identify one particular style, or do they use different styles depending on what they need to learn? (Answers will vary but encourage students to provide examples from their interviews to support their findings.)

Resources

📁 **Student Activity Workbook** Assign the Chapter 2 activities in the Student Activity Workbook.

Your Personality and Learning Styles

Your personality should also influence your career choice. Your **personality** is your unique combination of attitudes, behaviors, and characteristics. These qualities and characteristics define who you are as an individual. To explore your personality, you need to examine your self-concept and styles of learning.

Your Self-Concept

The way you see yourself is your **self-concept**. When you think of yourself, do you think of someone who is confident, curious, dependable, or funny? Some of your personality traits may seem to contradict one another. For example, you may feel shy in new situations but outgoing in familiar surroundings. However, you probably have a fairly consistent self-concept. Your self-concept is the kind of person you think you are.

Figure 2.2 **EIGHT LEARNING STYLES**

Type of Learner	Likes	Best Ways to Learn
Verbal/Linguistic	Likes to read, write, and tell stories	Saying, hearing, and seeing words
Logical/Mathematical	Likes to experiment, work with numbers, and explore patterns and relationships	Making categories, classifying, and working with patterns
Visual/Spatial	Likes to draw, build, design, and create things	Using the mind's eye and working with colors and pictures
Rhythmic/Musical	Likes to sing, hum, play an instrument, and listen to music	Through rhythm and melody
Bodily/Kinesthetic	Likes to touch and move around	Interacting with people and objects
Interpersonal	Likes having lots of friends, talking to people, and joining groups	Sharing, comparing, and cooperating
Intrapersonal	Likes to work alone and pursue interests at own pace	Through independent study
Naturalistic	Likes to spend time outdoors and work with plants, animals, and other parts of the natural world	Recognizing patterns, sorting, and classifying

HOW DO YOU LEARN? While most people may have a preferred learning style, many people use more than one, depending on the situation. *How can knowing your learning styles help you decide on a career?*

EXTEND THE FIGURE **Figure 2.2**

Caption Answer It can help you choose a job and a work environment that suit you and your learning styles.

Discussion Find out how many students have made decisions only to later change their minds or wish they could reverse their decisions. Ask how they could avoid such situations in the future.

Different Learning Styles

The different ways in which people naturally think and learn are called **learning styles**. Being aware of your own learning styles helps you to determine the best way to learn something. It will also help you choose a career. You will do well in a career that suits your strongest learning style. Look at the learning styles listed in **Figure 2.2** on page 42. Which styles apply to you?

Knowing what makes you who you are gives you a great advantage as you explore career choices. In this chapter, you have learned about values and interests, aptitudes and abilities, personality, and learning styles. Do you know yourself better? Write a description of yourself that includes your values, interests, aptitudes and abilities, and personality traits and learning styles. Use art materials or computer software to add a photo or drawing if you wish.

Determining Your Personality Type

Psychologists, counselors, and human resources professionals use many tests to determine an individual's personality type. Knowing your personality type can help you understand your natural abilities and which careers would suit you best. No personality is better than another, but some personality characteristics may help you succeed in a certain profession. For example, a sociable person might do better in a career in sales than a person who is reserved. A curious, independent person might do well as a scientist. Personality characteristics such as self-discipline, persistence, and self-motivation are useful in any career.

Personality tests can also help you understand how you behave in social situations. Perhaps you enjoy helping others or you are good at motivating people. Maybe you prefer to work alone. Understanding your personality can help you communicate with others in both life and work.

Career ✓ Checklist

To Learn More About Yourself:

✓ Identify what is important to you.

✓ Keep an open mind.

✓ Document your experiences and things that you learn about yourself.

✓ Try new things, and don't be afraid of failure.

✓ View criticism as an opportunity to learn.

ASSESS

After You Read

Have students complete the Section 2.2 After You Read section review.

Online Study Tools

Have students go to the OLC through **glencoe.com** to:

- Take the Section 2.2 **Practice Test**.
- Download **Podcast** study tools.
- Download free **Study-to-Go** content to their PDAs or cell phones.

Resources

ExamView Assessment Suite CD allows you to print out ready-made unit and chapter tests complete with answer keys. You can also create customized tests.

Section 2.2 After You Read

Review Key Concepts

1. List the differences between an aptitude and an ability.
2. Explain how your values can influence the career choice you might make.
3. Explain how knowing your learning style can help you select a career.

Practice Academic Skills

 English Language Arts

N C L B

4. Choose a career that interests you. Describe how the career involves data, people, or things in a three-paragraph summary.
5. Research careers that would fit someone with a naturalistic learning style. Choose one and prepare a three-minute oral report describing the career.

@ Check your answers at this book's OLC through **glencoe.com**.

CLOSE

Culminating Activity

Define Dislikes Ask students to decide which of these careers suits them least: accountant, park ranger, social worker, plumber, salesperson, poet, astronomer, and athletic coach. Have students write a 200-word paragraph explaining why the career does not suit them. (Paragraphs should show an understanding of how aptitudes and abilities, values, personality, self-concept, and learning styles affect career choices.)

 N C L B Activity correlated to English Language Arts standards.

Section 2.2 After You Read

Review Key Concepts

1. An aptitude is a potential for learning a certain skill; an ability is a skill that has already been developed.
2. Knowing your values can help you select a career that is fulfilling, with goals that are important to you.
3. Knowing your learning style can help you select a career that suits your strongest learning style.

Practice Academic Skills

4. In their summaries, students should demonstrate an understanding of how their interests in working with data, people, and things can affect their career choices.
5. Oral reports should demonstrate research into a career that might appeal to a person who enjoys outdoor work with plants, animals, and other parts of the natural world, and who tends to learn by recognizing patterns, sorting, and classifying.

43

FOCUS

Discussion Starter

Human Services Lead a discussion about the different types of careers that can be found in this career cluster. Have students brainstorm different careers and jobs within the career cluster. (Answers will vary but students should show an understanding of the many types of careers that fall within the career cluster.)

TEACH

W **Writing Support**
Independent Practice

Conduct an Interview Have students use the questions in the Career Spotlight to conduct and make a written record of an interview with an individual in the featured career cluster. (Answers will vary but should follow the interview format of the Career Spotlight.)

C **Critical Thinking**

Assess Values and Interests Have students list the values and interests they might need for a career in middle school counseling. (Values might include wanting to help others. Interests might include education and child development.)

CAREER SPOTLIGHT

Career Cluster: Human Services

Donita Jackson
Middle School Counselor

Q: Describe your job.
A: My primary role is to be an advocate for the intellectual, social, mental, and emotional health of students in our building.

Q: Describe a typical workday.
A: Each day begins with greeting students. I check messages and meet with teachers, parents, and administrators. I am available to listen to students who are experiencing various issues from bullying to family problems to relationship changes. I encourage students to make social connections. I guide students and parents to resource materials such as tutors to workshops. I help families to schedule classes and make sure students are appropriately placed in courses that will be challenging, and I also serve as testing coordinator for state and national standardized tests.

W **Q: What skills are most important to you in your job?**
A: My job focuses upon the emotional and social needs of people—primarily students. It is most important to be able to make connections with people, from students to staff, from parents to administrators. The most important skill in my job is to use empathy and try to see from everyone's point of view. It helps to stay in touch with the feelings that students may experience during adolescence and to be aware of their culture.

Q: What academic skills and lifelong learning skills are helpful in preparing for your career?
A: Communication skills are most important. A strong academic base will assist you in helping students through their academia. However, your emotional quotient and ability to work with other people is very important as a guidance counselor. Be goal-oriented, dedicated, and realistic.

Q: What is your key to success?
A: I love working with people and enjoy helping them solve problems.

Q: What training and preparation do you recommend for students?
A: Upon completion of an undergraduate degree, you must complete a master's program in school counseling. In addition, you must take public speaking and communications courses. You also need to enhance your written and oral communication skills.

Q: What are some ways you recommend students prepare for this career?
A: Spend time engaging with other people. Always look for the positive in situations. Listen to others with your eyes. Hear what is said but pay close attention to nonverbal behaviors.

Q: What do you like most about your work?
A: I really enjoy connecting with other people. Working with students is rewarding. Adolescence can be a very difficult time for many students. Being a part of their lives as they progress from childhood into adulthood is extremely rewarding.

C

 For more about Career Clusters, go to this book's OLC through **glencoe.com**.

N C L B   NO CHILD LEFT BEHIND

Teaching Tip

To help students meet the NCLB Act's goal of mastering computer technologies, enhance research concepts with technology skills:

• Ask students to search the Internet for topics through search engines.

• Encourage adding computer-presentation elements to reports.

Sample Question Visit the American School Counselor Association Web site and research the education and certification requirements for guidance counselors in your state. Document what you find. (Student documentation should show evidence of research.)

- **Education or Training** All states require school counselors to hold state school counseling certification and to have completed at least some graduate course work. Most require the completion of a master's degree.

- **Academic Skills Required** English Language Arts, Mathematics, Science, Social Studies

- **Technology Needed** Computer knowledge for record keeping and communicating with students, parents, and administrators

- **Aptitudes, Abilities, and Skills** Communication and other interpersonal skills, creativity, critical thinking, listening and problem-solving skills

- **Workplace Safety** Counselors must possess high levels of physical and emotional energy to handle the array of problems they address. Dealing daily with these problems can cause stress. Occasionally, counselors must cope with unruly behavior and violence in the schools.

- **Career Outlook** Jobs as counselors are expected to grow faster than average over the next ten years.

- **Career Path** With additional preparation, school counselors may move into positions as school administrators including principal, instructional coordinator, and superintendent. Other counselors move into careers in labor relations, human resources, psychology, or social work.

Academic Skills Required to Complete Tasks

Tasks	English Language Arts	Mathematics	Science	Social Studies
Help a student solve a problem with friends	★			★
Help students schedule classes	★	★	★	★
Introduce new families to the school	★			★
Meet with parents regarding an issue with their child	★		★	★
Conduct standardized testing with students	★	★	★	★

NCLB

Critical Thinking

What classes and extracurricular activities might help you prepare for a career in counseling?

NCLB This chart relates academic skills such as English Language Arts, Mathematics, Science, Social Studies, and World Languages to specific tasks that are performed for the job featured in the Career Spotlight feature.

Critical Thinking

Students who want to pursue a career in counseling might take courses in psychology, volunteer at a community center, and improve their communication skills by participating on a debate team.

CAREER SPOTLIGHT

ASSESS

Make Connections

Ask students to list specific correlations between academic subjects and the workplace tasks for this career. (Answers will vary but students should show an understanding of how academic skills relate directly to workplace tasks.)

CLOSE

Culminating Activity

Values and Career Clusters Have students write each of the six general values and then explain in a 200-word paragraph if and how these values apply to a career in school counseling. For example, a counselor would need to value forming relationships with all kinds of students from diverse backgrounds. Also encourage students to think of two additional values a counselor might have. (Answers should reflect an understanding of the concept of values.)

Key Terms and Academic Vocabulary Review

1. Students should write complete sentences using each term correctly. A sample answer might read: "Gathering information is the third step in the *decision-making process*."

Review Key Concepts

2. The decision-making process will help you identify and evaluate career choices that will help you decide the right career to pursue.

3. Your lifestyle goals—the way you want to spend your time, money, and energy—will help you determine a career that will allow you to achieve these goals.

4. Answers will vary. One possible answer: Knowing my interests help me choose a career that I will can find satisfying.

5. Data refers to information, ideas, facts, symbols, figures, or statistics. People are human beings. Things are physical objects of any size, such as instruments, tools, plants, machinery, equipment, raw materials, and vehicles.

6. An example might be a person who has a knack for learning foreign languages studying to become a foreign-language teacher. In this example, learning foreign languages is the aptitude and teaching foreign languages to students is the ability.

7. Answers should include three of the following: verbal/linguistic—likes to read, write, and tell stories; logical/mathematical—likes to do experiments, work with numbers, and explore patterns and relationships; visual/spatial—likes to draw,

CHAPTER SUMMARY

Section 2.1

Good decisions take careful thought and planning, especially if they are important decisions such as making a career choice. Making decisions is easier if you follow a decision-making process, which is a series of steps that can help you identify and evaluate possibilities and make a good choice. There are seven steps in the decision-making process: define your needs and wants, analyze your resources, identify your choices, gather information, evaluate your choices, make a decision, and plan how to reach your goal.

Section 2.2

Getting to know yourself will help you to choose a career that is right for you. You can begin to explore who you are by defining your lifestyle goals, and your values, which are your beliefs and principles. You should also consider your interests, the things you enjoy doing, when choosing a career. Your interests can help you determine whether you prefer to work with data, people, or things. Another factor to consider when deciding on a career is your aptitudes and abilities. An aptitude is your potential for learning a skill. An ability is a skill you have developed. Your personality and your learning styles should also influence your career choice.

Key Terms and Academic Vocabulary Review

1. Use each of these key terms and academic vocabulary words in a sentence.

Key Terms
- decision-making process (p. 31)
- lifestyle goals (p. 36)
- values (p. 37)
- data (p. 39)
- aptitude (p. 40)
- ability (p. 40)
- personality (p. 42)
- self-concept (p. 42)
- learning styles (p. 43)

Academic Vocabulary
- affect (p. 31)
- sequence (p. 32)
- examine (p. 36)

Review Key Concepts

2. Explain how the decision-making process can help you make a good career choice.
3. Explain how lifestyle goals affect career choice.
4. Describe how values, interests, skills, personality, and learning styles may shape career plans.
5. Define data, people, and things. Give an example of each.
6. Explain how an aptitude becomes an ability. Give an example.
7. Describe three different learning styles.

Critical Thinking

8. Analyze Why might your career choice change as you age?
9. Evaluate How might changes in your life, such as marriage and health, affect your lifestyle goals?

design, and create things; rhythmic/musical—likes to sing, hum, play an instrument, and listen to music; bodily/kinesthetic—likes to touch and move around; interpersonal—likes having lots of friends, talking to people, and joining groups; intrapersonal—likes to work alone and pursue interests at own pace; naturalistic—likes to spend time outdoors and work with plants, animals, and other parts of the natural environment.

Critical Thinking

8. Answers should show an understanding that values and lifestyle goals change as you get older and develop new skills and aptitudes.

9. An example of health affecting a person's lifestyle goals might be if an individual who works in a job that is physically demanding, such as firefighting, becomes injured. This individual may have to change or modify his or her career path or lifestyle to accommodate the injury.

Real-World Skills and Applications

Interpersonal and Collaborative Skills

10. Speaking Imagine that you have been offered a promotion. The new job will pay better, but it involves a lot of travel that will take you away from your family and friends. Prepare a five-minute oral report describing how you will use the decision-making process to decide whether to accept the promotion. List specific factors you will consider. Practice your oral report at home before presenting it to the class.

Technology Applications

11. Making a Graph Conduct a study of the learning styles in your class. Ask each student to identify his or her main learning style. Use a spreadsheet or word-processing program to create a bar graph showing the number of students with each learning style.

Information Literacy Skills

12. Organizing and Maintaining Information Create a chart to help you keep track of what you have learned about yourself. Use these seven column headings:

- Lifestyle Goals
- Values
- Interests
- Aptitudes
- Abilities
- Personality Traits
- Learning Styles

Fill in the chart and add to it throughout the year. You can add this chart to your **Personal Academic and Career Portfolio**.

13. **Working as a Team** Working with three other classmates, make a list of job-related skills or abilities. Share your list with another group, and then combine the two lists into one. As the larger group, meet with another group and continue the process until all student groups have participated in creating one list of job-related skills.

14. **ROLE PLAY**

Demonstrating Skills and Abilities at Work

Situation Your employer, Eric, thinks a group of new employees lacks basic skills. Eric has asked you and a coworker to perform three skits for the new employees as part of a new training program. The skits should show work-related scenarios that demonstrate essential skills such as decision making, communication, and knowing how to learn.

Activity Create three brief skits that show how skills and abilities can be used in everyday work experiences. Perform your skits for the class. Provide brief introductory and closing statements to explain your skits.

Evaluation You will be evaluated on how well you meet the following performance indicators:

- Demonstrate preparation and creativity in enacting skits.
- Accurately convey skills and abilities.
- Provide meaningful background and closing comments.

ACTIVE LEARNING

13. Lists should demonstrate an understanding of skills and abilities. Students should be able to explain how the skills and abilities on this list are job-related. This activity may benefit from teacher guidance; instruct students to delete or combine similar entries to avoid duplication.

ROLE PLAY

14. Skits should clearly demonstrate the practical application of three skills in a place of work. Supplementary explanation should extrapolate from the broader application of each skill.

Real-World Skills and Applications

10. Students' reports should indicate an understanding of the decision-making process as well as an understanding of the concepts of promotion and responsibility.

11. Bar graphs will vary but should demonstrate that students are able to accurately construct a bar graph in a spreadsheet or word-processing program. Bar graphs should include the eight learning styles from **Figure 2.2** organized to show the number of students who use each style.

12. Answers will vary, but students should list one or more entries under each column heading and display an understanding of each column heading.

Academic Skills in the Workplace

15. Students' paragraphs will vary but should include information about each partner's aptitudes, abilities, interests, and values.

16. The ratio of volunteer work time to paid work time is 1:5 (400 ÷ 2,000 = 1/5).

17. Students should display an understanding of the term *biome* and should also provide support for the kind of biome in which they would want to live.

18. Research will vary depending on the culture the students chose to research. Reports must list three values, such as religious observance, close family ties, or education is valued.

Academic Skills in the Workplace

 English Language Arts

15. Conduct an Interview Pair up with a partner. Take turns interviewing one another about your aptitudes, abilities, interests, and values. Take notes on your partner's responses. Create a one-paragraph summary of what you learned about that person.

 Mathematics

16. Calculate Ratios Volunteer work is important to Tekla. Of the 2,400 hours she works each year, she spends 400 hours doing volunteer work. The rest of that time is spent doing paid work. What is the ratio of her volunteer work time to her paid work time?

CONCEPT **Represent Ratios** Ratios are comparisons of numbers that can be represented in different forms. Usually, ratios are represented in simplest form. The ratio *1:2* can also be expressed as *1 out of 2, 1 to 2,* or *½*.

Starting Hint Set this ratio up as a fraction, with 400 as the numerator and 2,000 as the denominator. Your answer should be a fraction in lowest terms.

 Science

17. Describe a Biome Biologists study the features of different areas around the earth called *biomes*. A biome is an area of the earth that has related geographic features, temperature, moisture, plants, and animals. For instance, the desert is a biome found in many parts of the earth. Can you describe what the geographic features are in a desert? How about the temperature and moisture level? Research what kind of plants and animals live in a desert biome. Is this similar to or different from the biome where you live? In which kind of biome would you like to live and work? Explain your answers in a one-page report.

 Social Studies

18. Research Values Research another culture's system of values. If possible, interview someone who grew up in that culture. Name and describe three values in that culture. Explain how those values affect the world of work in that culture. Share your findings with the class in a five-minute oral report.

STANDARDIZED TEST PRACTICE

MULTIPLE CHOICE

Directions Read the following sentence. Then read the question below the sentence. Read the answer choices below each question and choose the best answer to fill in the blank.

Test-Taking Tip In a multiple choice test, read the question before you read the answer choices. Try to answer the question before you read the answer choices. This way, the answer choices will not throw you off.

1. Lena's interpersonal learning style made her biased towards working in an office.

In this sentence, the word *biased* means _____.

  a. running diagonally across the weave of a fabric
  b. a distortion of a set of statistical data
  c. voltage applied across an electronic device
  d. having a preference

 ## STANDARDIZED TEST PRACTICE

Answer
1. d. having a preference

Test-Taking Strategies
Whether your students have a standardized test coming up in a few days or a few weeks, this last-minute test-prep tip will help them relax and do their best.

Multiple-Choice Tests Tell students to read directions to multiple-choice tests carefully. Usually only one answer is required; however, sometimes more than one answer may be possible or necessary.

Writing Skills Practice

19. Writing Research Reports When writing a research report, you must research, organize, and interpret factual information. You then use your own words and cite facts from your research. You can use research reports for longer essays or term papers. You may also use reports in many careers, such as marketing, financial, and technological careers.

 Practice Write a one-page research report on learning styles.

Follow the steps below when researching and writing your report:

- Write a draft of your research report. Include a list of learning styles, a definition of each learning style, and the factual information you gained from your research.
- Edit and proofread your draft.
- Add any visual aids that may enhance your report.
- Write the final one-page research report.

Net Connection

20. Match Interests to Careers Visit this book's OLC through **glencoe.com** to find the link to the *Occupational Outlook Handbook*. Create a list of at least ten career opportunities that match your interests and aptitudes.

 Log On Search career and employment Web sites to research and gather information about five of the jobs that you listed. Decide which positions you are interested in investigating further and create a one-sentence description of each.

 Reading Connection

Go to this book's Online Learning Center through **glencoe.com** for a list of reading suggestions.

Personal Academic and Career Portfolio

Create a Self-Profile

You have learned a lot about yourself in this chapter. And the information you have gathered will help you choose a career that is right for you. To keep a record of what you have learned, create a self-profile and add it to your **Personal Academic and Career Portfolio**. As you make a career decision and begin to follow a career, it will be a good idea to look at this information periodically, to be sure the path you are taking fits who you are. You can also update your profile of yourself as your goals and values change.

Follow the following guidelines to create a self-profile for your portfolio:

- Using spreadsheet or word-processing software, or paper and pencil, create a chart with the following headings: *Lifestyle Goals*, *Values*, *Interests*, *Aptitudes* and *Abilities*, *Personality Traits*, and *Learning Styles*.
- Fill in the chart, listing as many items as you can. The more you write, the more complete your self-profile will be.
- Create a new section in your portfolio and label it *Self-Profile*, or add your self-profile to the section you created in Chapter 1.
- Use the chart as you pursue your career to be sure you are on the right path.
- Update the chart as necessary.

 Portfolio Help Go to the *Succeeding in the World of Work* OLC through **glencoe.com** for help developing your portfolio.

Writing Skills Practice

19. Reports should reflect the results of their research. The eight learning styles should be listed, with explanations of each, and how the styles are spread out among the students.

Net Connection

20. Students should use a variety of resources, including people and the Internet, to conduct in-depth research about opportunities in their chosen area and to create a list of positions in which they may be interested.

Resources

ExamView Assessment Suite **CD** allows you to print out ready-made unit and chapter tests complete with answer keys. You can also create customized tests.

WorkKeys

WorkKeys® is a job skills assessment program. For information on leveled assessment for Problem-Solving Skills (Applied Mathematics; Applied Technology; Locating Information; and Observation), go to the WorkKeys link on this book's OLC through **glencoe.com**.

Personal Academic and Career Portfolio

Evaluating Hobbies

Students who need additional direction in choosing a career might create a document for their **Personal Academic and Career Portfolio** that examines their hobbies for career potential. Have students answer these questions about a favorite hobby: What values do you express through this hobby? What interests help you enjoy it? What skills with people, data, or things does it demand? What aptitudes or abilities do you bring to it? How does it fit your personality? Have students summarize their findings in a one-page report that they can include in their portfolio.

Unit 1 Thematic Project

Finding the Lifestyle You Want

You know that choosing a career is a very important decision. You have learned how the decision-making process can help you make some preliminary choices about your future. You know that your career can affect the lifestyle you have. Based on your personal needs, values, and interests, you have identified careers that appeal to you. Now you will perform the research and contemplation necessary to make some decisions about the lifestyle you want and how your career can help you achieve that lifestyle.

FOCUS

Discussion Starter

Ask students what potential careers seem most popular among their friends and acquaintances. Encourage students to keep in mind how technology and globalization affect their lifestyle and career choices. Ask students to brainstorm why certain careers are popular, then ask if they think it is a good idea for many people to enter a popular career.

STEP 1

Evaluate Your Skills and Resources

Have students go to the OLC through **glencoe.com** for a graphic organizer they can use to organize the skills, tools, and resources they will need to complete the project.

TEACH

C Critical Thinking

Ask students to write a list of the different types of jobs that might be involved in producing educational materials such as this textbook program, including the book itself and any online or technology materials. Compile the lists to give students an idea of the variety of jobs available within a specific industry.

Project Assignment

- Research three careers that seem compatible with your interests, aptitudes, values, and abilities. Access career information using a variety of resources, including the Internet, trade journals, and personal interviews.
- Next, write a career profile for each career and decide which career is the best option for your desired lifestyle.
- Create a detailed career profile for that career and write a two-page essay explaining your choice. In your essay, state the steps you plan to take now to prepare for this career. Be sure to include a basic education and training plan that you will use to achieve your career and lifestyle goals.

Lifelong Learning Connection

Lifelong learning concepts found in this project include:
- self-assessment
- setting goals and making decisions
- your career plan and career path

STEP 1 Evaluate Your Skills and Resources

To complete this project, you must have access to the Internet as well as books, magazines, and other media. You may also interview people in the careers that interest you, taking notes throughout the interviews. During interviews, you will need an audio or video recorder, a writing instrument and notepad, or a writing device. You will also need a word-processing program, presentation software, or visual display materials to prepare your career profiles.

Skills you may need to complete the Unit Thematic Project include:

Academic Skills reading, writing, mathematics, social studies

Transferable Skills communication, research, problem-solving, and decision-making skills

Technology Skills presentation, telecommunication, word-processing, and Internet skills

@ Resources Organizer To find a graphic organizer you can use to determine the skills, tools, and resources you will need for this project, go to this book's Online Learning Center through **glencoe.com**.

SPOTLIGHT ON TECHNOLOGY

Technology in the Workplace

Ask students if they can think of any jobs that do not involve working with technology. Let them know that most people think of computers when they think of technology, but a lot of highly technical careers fall outside the information technology industry. People who are interested in technology may work in the fields of agriculture, design, and manufacturing. Have students brainstorm a list of careers that involve working closely with technology, both with computers and with technology other than computers. (Answers will vary. Students may point out that many software programs allow you to do more creative work using computers.)

STEP 2 Preview a Real-World Company Profile

When researching careers, it may help you to interview and profile a person who works for a particular company. The company featured below is known for its attention to employee lifestyle. A company profile can help you identify aspects of the company that suit the career and lifestyle you want.

Real-World Company: Cranium, Inc.

According to Jennifer Pitzer's business card, her official job title is "Fi$¢al Fanatic." The former math major and accounting MBA is the accounting manager for game manufacturer Cranium, a company that encourages creativity in every position. The company began by targeting young adults between 25 and 35 with a game that encouraged users to use individual talents and strengths, such as drawing, sculpting, acting, and knowing trivia. Cranium now offers a variety of games for groups and families, as well as games suited for even the lowest age level.

The company's family-friendly lifestyle philosophy extends to the staffing and benefits choices the company offers: all employees are entitled to paid leave for the birth or adoption of a child, and flexible working schedules and telecommuting are common. The company also offers health-club memberships to help keep employees healthy and productive members of the community. The Cranium office features game rooms and ergonomic workstations to help employees relieve stress and prevent injuries.

Cranium, Inc.

Aspects of Industry	Company Facts
Planning	Cranium games are sold in more than 40 countries. The games are "culturized" to fit the local market.
Management	Workplace philosophy stresses the value of creativity and minimizes traditional hierarchy. The head of the company's official title is "Grand Poo-Bah."
Finance	Private company founded by former Microsoft executives Whit Alexander and Richard Tait.
Technical and Production Skills	Company employs diverse workers, from language specialists to marketers to visual production artists.
Underlying Principles of Technology	Computers are used to communicate ideas and in the creation of the game products.
Labor Issues	Cranium benefits include medical, dental, and vision coverage, retirement plans, life insurance, three to five weeks of vacation per year, and paid and unpaid family leave.
Health, Safety, and Environmental Issues	Employer-paid health insurance, health-club memberships, game rooms on site.
Community Issues	Cranium supports after-school programs in the visual, literary, and performing arts for children in challenging circumstances.

51

Developing Industry Partners

Establish School-Business Partnerships

As you begin to establish school-business partnerships, you may focus on direct contact with local business leaders. You can also ask your students for suggestions. Family members and other working adults can be important allies in the career education classroom. By using letters, notes, or conferences, share your career education ideas and goals with students' families. Encourage their responses and input and be prepared for some excellent ideas and leads.

TEACH (cont.)

STEP 2
Preview a Real-World Company Profile

Ask students to share what they like about the business that is featured in the Real-World Company profile in Step 2. (Answers will vary. Students may say that they like the fun product ideas and the casual corporate culture. Others may mention the benefits that impact worker health and safety.)

R Reading Strategy
Guided Practice
Aspects of Industry

Tell students that understanding aspects of industry can aid their transition to employment in the rapidly changing global workplace and help them connect their academic coursework to the world of work. In class, restate the aspects of industry for the toys and games industry in the Real-World Company profile in Step 2. Locate a written real-world company profile in an online or print magazine and ask the class to read the profile and identify any of the following aspects of industry for that company: planning; management; finance; technical and production skills; underlying principles of technology; labor issues; health, safety, and environmental issues; and community issues.

TEACH (cont.)

STEP 3

Research Procedures

Have students go to the OLC through **glencoe.com** for a graphic organizer they can use to organize the results of their research.

STEP 4

Connect to Community

Ask students to describe what the word *community* means to them. Write their ideas on the board. (A community is a group of people who have something in common.) Ask students to list ways they have gotten involved in their communities. (Students might suggest community service or working or volunteering at a local business or organization. Students might also detail how they are active in online communities, such as a Web site that is used to connect people with similar goals or interests.)

STEP 5

Report Your Findings

Give students these tips on report writing:

- Know your audience.
- Organize your report by developing an outline.
- Write concisely (briefly but completely).
- Write in readable, simple language.

STEP 3 Research Procedures

Keeping in mind the suggestions offered in Chapters 1 and 2, identify three careers that interest you and follow the steps listed below:

1. Perform research using a variety of electronic, written, and in-person resources.
2. Take notes on your three career choices, organizing your notes according to the suggestions offered in the Helpful Hints section in Step 5.
3. When you have accumulated enough research, create your career profiles and decide which career suits you best. If your research indicates that your career choices do not fit well with the lifestyle you desire, research more careers until you find one that is compatible with your needs, interests, aptitudes, values, and abilities.

@ Resources Organizer To find a graphic organizer you can use to organize your research, go to this book's OLC through **glencoe.com**.

STEP 4 Connect to Community

Get Local Survey a number of individuals in your community who are part of the workforce to understand how the work you do is connected to your lifestyle. You could talk to friends, family, or working adults. Try to identify what kind of lifestyles each of these individuals wants and ask how the jobs they are doing affect their current lifestyles and the future lifestyles they plan to have.

Take the Next Step If possible, contact an individual who already works in the same industry as the career which you have selected to profile. Ask this person specific questions about how his or her career fulfills his or her needs and interests. You could also ask this person what skills are used in his or her job, and what education and training that person has had.

STEP 5 Report Your Findings

Your final products for the Unit Thematic Project should include a detailed career profile and a two-page essay explaining why the career you have profiled fits the lifestyle you want.

- Create a comprehensive career profile of the career you have selected, using visual aids or word-processing, presentation, or graphic design software.
- Use word-processing software to write a two-page essay explaining why this career is a good choice for the lifestyle you want and the steps you would need to take if you decide to pursue this career.

Helpful Hints To create accurate and complete career profiles, you will need to perform thorough research about the careers you have identified. Each profile should include the following information about your career:

- advantages
- disadvantages
- job outlook
- education requirements

Developing Community Involvement

Contribute to the Community

Have students brainstorm ways they could contribute to the community in a class-wide project. Ideas might include collecting items for a charity, tutoring younger students, cleaning up a public area, or removing graffiti from school or other public property. The class can vote on three ideas, research what would be needed for the project (such as identifying permissions or permits required), and document their work with charts, photographs, or journal entries.

- training requirements
- salary
- benefits
- work schedule
- travel requirements
- work conditions, including physical and safety concerns
- opportunities for advancement
- opportunities for innovation
- personal qualities needed
- how the job fits your values
- how well the job fits your lifestyle

STEP 6 **Presentation and Evaluation**

Your career profile will be evaluated based on:
- organization of research
- comprehensiveness, relevance, and currentness of data
- evidence of thorough research
- mechanics—neatness and presentation

Personal Academic and Career Portfolio

Print out a copy of your career profile and your essay to include in your **Personal Academic and Career Portfolio**. You can use this career profile as a model for future careers which may interest you. You can use the completed report as a model for future career plans you may develop.

Your two-page essay will be evaluated based on:
- content and thoughtfulness
- identification of a desired lifestyle
- identification of a career education and training plan
- mechanics—neatness and presentation

@ Evaluation Rubric To find a rubric you can use to evaluate your project, go to this book's OLC through **glencoe.com**.

BusinessWeek — *Connection*

Understanding All Aspects of Industry: Labor Issues and Community Issues

Understanding all aspects of industry can help you prepare to succeed in a career in that industry. You can learn a lot about a business by understanding how it interacts both with its employees and with the community around it. Businesses can affect local, worldwide, and virtual communities by providing jobs, income, and services, and through involvement in civic activities such as job training and donations. They can also contribute to employees' lifestyles at and outside of

work by providing benefits and opportunities for lifelong learning growth, such as community involvement.

@ Go to this book's Online Learning Center through **glencoe.com** to find *BusinessWeek* articles titled "The Best Small Companies to Work for in America" and "The Corporate Springboard to Community Service." Read the articles and use a word-processing program to create a one-page summary of each article. Add the summaries to your **Personal Academic and Career Portfolio**.

STEP 6

Presentation and Evaluation

Rubric Encourage students to go to the OLC through **glencoe.com** for a rubric they can use to evaluate their project. Encourage students to use the rubric as a content checklist when researching careers for their project.

CLOSE

Culminating Activity

Career Interviews In this activity, students applied the thematic unit topic to their own lives by researching their own lifestyle goals as well as career paths that can help them achieve those goals. Have students form pairs and interview one another about the careers they researched and how their perceptions of the career and their lifestyle goals may have changed during the course of the Unit project. Have students summarize the main points of their interviews using note-taking skills. (Interviews should show evidence of career research and critical thinking.)

BusinessWeek — *Connection*

All Aspects of Industry: Labor Issues and Community Issues

Tell students that one function of a community is to prepare its members for the world of work. One way organizations can do this is by creating opportunities for community service, which can help develop workplace skills. Have students brainstorm opportunities for community service in their communities. (Answers may include

service on behalf of schools, volunteer organizations, and cultural institutions such as museums or parks.) Tell students that understanding the current labor issues in a particular industry can help them absorb and process economic concepts they will encounter in school and in the real world. For example, local history and social studies courses might cover the relationship between labor unions and management in your community.

Chapter	Chapter Objectives
CHAPTER 3 Researching Careers	• **Describe** formal and informal methods of researching careers. • **Evaluate** sources of career information. • **Identify** work experiences that can help you explore careers. • **Develop** key questions to ask when researching and assessing careers. • **Identify** the characteristics used to develop a career profile. • **Determine** the education and training needed for different careers.
CHAPTER 4 Entrepreneurship	• **Define** *entrepreneur* and name the traits that most successful entrepreneurs share. • **Summarize** the advantages and disadvantages of entrepreneurship. • **Identify** the four main ways to become a business owner and explain the advantages and disadvantages of each. • **Identify** the different forms of legal business ownership. • **Explain** how to prepare to finance a new business. • **Identify** factors that can affect business success.
CHAPTER 5 Developing a Career Plan	• **Evaluate** different career possibilities. • **Choose** a career that seems right for you. • **Develop** a career plan and set intermediate career goals. • **Determine** the education and training you need to reach your career goals.

Understanding Brackets, Letters, and Ability Levels in the Teacher Wraparound Edition

Brackets Brackets on the reduced student edition page correspond to teaching strategies and activities in the Teacher Wraparound Edition. As you teach the lesson, the brackets show you exactly where to use the teaching strategies and activities.

Letters The letters on the reduced student edition page identify the type of strategy or activity. See the key below to learn about the different types of strategies and activities.

Ability Levels Teaching Strategies that appear throughout the chapters have been identified by one of three codes to give you an idea of their suitability for students of varying learning styles and abilities.

Resources Key program resources are listed in each chapter. Icons indicate the format of resources.

KEY TO LETTERS

R **Reading Strategy** activities help you teach reading skills and vocabulary.

C **Critical Thinking** strategies help students apply and extend what they have learned.

S **Skill Practice** strategies help students practice historical analysis and geographical skills.

W **Writing Support** activities provide writing opportunities to help students comprehend the text.

D **Develop Concepts** activities use various strategies to help teachers gauge and plan for students' concept development.

U **Universal Access** activities provide differentiated instruction for English language learners, and suggestions for teaching various types of learners. *These activities may or may not have brackets.*

N C L B **No Child Left Behind** activities help students practice and improve their abilities in academic subjects.

KEY TO ABILITY LEVELS

L1 Strategies should be within the ability range of all students. Often full class participation is required.

L2 Strategies are for average to above-average students or for small groups. Some teacher direction is necessary.

L3 Strategies are designed for students able and willing to work independently. Minimal teacher direction is necessary.

KEY TO RESOURCE ICONS

📁 Print Material

💿 CD-ROM

🖱 Internet

TeacherWorks™
All-In-One Planner and Resource Center

Teacher Wraparound Edition

For the Unit:
Unit Thematic Project Student Rubrics
Unit Test
Unit Connecting Activities Projects

For the Chapter:
Chapter Resources
Program Resources
Additional Print and Media Resources
Lesson Plans
Chapter Summaries, Key Terms, and
　　Academic Vocabulary *(English and Spanish)*

Graphic Organizers
Reading Activities
Chapter Self-Checks *(English and Spanish)*
Internet Activities
School-to-Career Connections
Work-Based Learning Projects
Personal and Academic Career Portfolio Student Rubrics

Student Activity Workbook with Academic Integration

Strategies for Students with Special Needs

Career Plan Project Workbook

 Link to the *Succeeding in the World of Work* **Online Learning Center with Podcasts** through **glencoe.com**.

Unit 2

Exploring Careers

Unit Overview
Introduce the Unit

Introduce the unit by describing the main concepts of each chapter in the unit.

Unit 2 discusses how to identify, research, and evaluate career and employment options and how to use this information to draw up a career plan.

Chapter 3 identifies a wide range of methods for performing career research and outlines what aspects of a career, such as values, work environment, and required education and training, students should explore in their research.

Chapter 4 introduces students to the risks and rewards of entrepreneurship and outlines various ways to become a business owner. It also helps students understand the planning required to start a business.

Chapter 5 shows students how to evaluate careers using relevant personal criteria and how to transform their tentative career decision into a career plan that lists their short-, medium-, and long-term goals.

OUT OF TIME?

If class time is too short to cover all of the chapters in this unit, have students:
- Write down the key terms and their definitions.
- Read the chapter summaries at the beginning of each chapter review.
- Go to the *Succeeding in the World of Work* Online Learning Center (OLC) through **glencoe.com** to download free Study-to-Go content to their PDAs or cellphones.

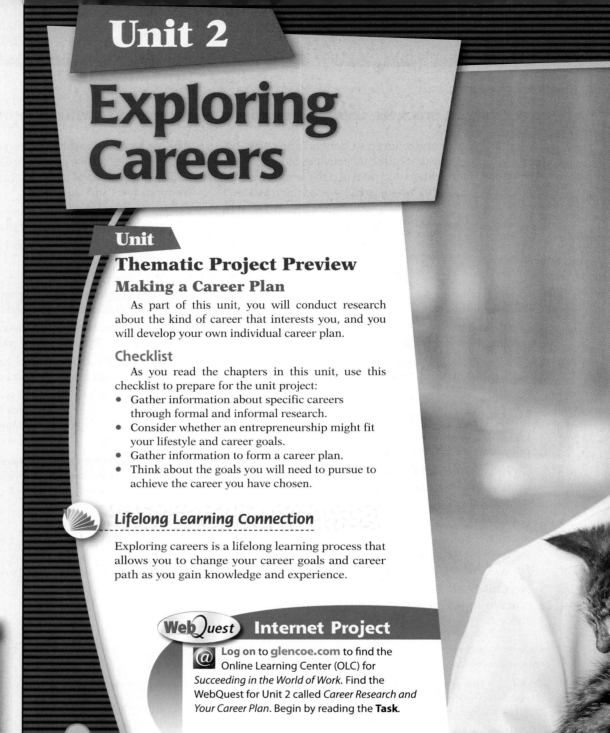

Unit
Thematic Project Preview
Making a Career Plan

As part of this unit, you will conduct research about the kind of career that interests you, and you will develop your own individual career plan.

Checklist

As you read the chapters in this unit, use this checklist to prepare for the unit project:
- Gather information about specific careers through formal and informal research.
- Consider whether an entrepreneurship might fit your lifestyle and career goals.
- Gather information to form a career plan.
- Think about the goals you will need to pursue to achieve the career you have chosen.

Lifelong Learning Connection

Exploring careers is a lifelong learning process that allows you to change your career goals and career path as you gain knowledge and experience.

Web Quest — Internet Project

@ **Log on** to **glencoe.com** to find the Online Learning Center (OLC) for *Succeeding in the World of Work*. Find the WebQuest for Unit 2 called *Career Research and Your Career Plan*. Begin by reading the **Task**.

54

Unit Thematic Project Preview

Tell students that as part of this unit, they will create a career plan that describes their ultimate career goal as well as short- and medium-term goals they will need to accomplish to reach that career goal. They will conduct interviews with an entrepreneur and an employee in order to investigate which employment option best fits their career goals and to learn more about the career field that interests them.

Web Quest

For WebQuest teaching suggestions and rubrics, go to the Teacher Center of this book's Online Learning Center (OLC) through **glencoe.com**.

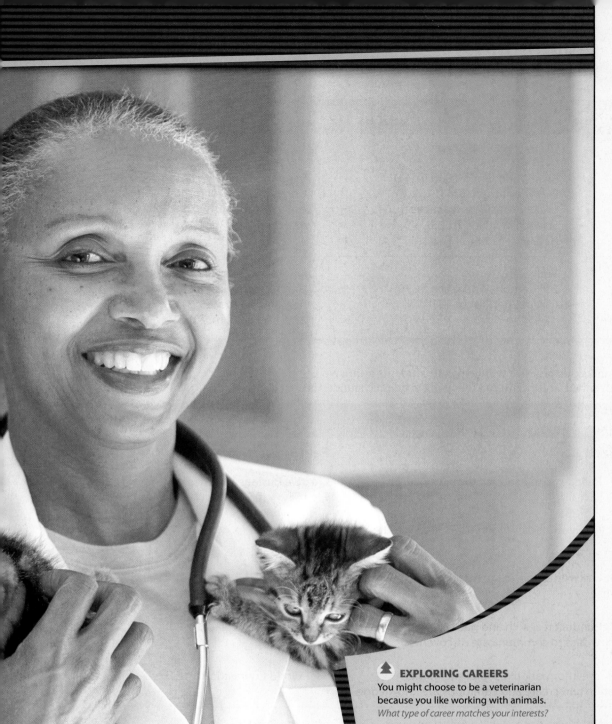

EXPLORING CAREERS
You might choose to be a veterinarian because you like working with animals. *What type of career matches your interests?*

55

Chapter 3
What are some ways to learn about the different careers that are available? (Students may mention research using print or online resources or conversations with teachers, counselors, and other working adults.)

What are some important facts to find out about the careers that interest you? (Students may mention factors such as job tasks and responsibilities, pay, working hours, level of skill and education required, and potential for growth and advancement.)

Chapter 4
What are some pros and cons of running your own business? (Pros include being in charge, enjoying a sense of accomplishment, and possibly making a good income; cons include risk, long hours, and many responsibilities.)

What is a business plan? (A business plan is specific information about all key aspects of a business, including products and services, location, financing, marketing, competition, and so on.)

Chapter 5
How can you tell whether a specific career is right for you? (Answers will vary, but students should understand that they need to compare key facts about a career, such as tasks and responsibilities and required education, with key information about themselves, such as their values, aptitudes, and interests.)

How can you obtain the education and training you need for your future career? (Students may mention on-the-job training, apprenticeships and internships, postsecondary education at a college, university, or trade school, or military service.)

▶ Extend the Photo

Caption Answer Answers will vary depending on students' interests but may include scientist, teacher, writer, athlete, artist, musician, or businessperson.

Discussion Ask students to think of as many different careers as they can that all relate in some way to a specific interest, such as music or sports. For example, what careers would satisfy an interest in animals besides that of veterinarian? (Students may mention veterinary assistant, dog trainer, zookeeper, animal protection officer, farmer, and so on.)

Chapter Resources Planning Guide with Activities and Features

Section	Features	Activities
Section 3.1 **Exploring Careers**	Real-World Connection (p. 61) Everyday Ethics (p. 63) Creative Business Practices (p. 64) Science in Action (p. 65) Hot Jobs! (p. 66)	Before You Read (p. 58) Graphic Organizer (p. 58) As You Read (pp. 60, 63) After You Read (p. 66)
Section 3.2 **What to Research**	Tech Savvy (p. 68) 21st Century Workplace (p. 70) Career Checklist (p. 71)	Before You Read (p. 67) Graphic Organizer (p. 67) As You Read (pp. 68, 71) After You Read (p. 73)

NCLB Activities, information, and skills practice will help your students attain No Child Left Behind proficiency. Students will improve their abilities in the following academic standards areas:

Academic Standards Correlations

Discipline	Standard	Feature/Activity
English Language Arts	**NCTE 1** Read texts to acquire new information.	Creative Business Practices (p. 64) Tech Savvy (p. 68)
	NCTE 3 Apply strategies to interpret and evaluate texts.	After You Read (p. 66)
	NCTE 4 Use written language to communicate effectively.	Academic Skills in the Workplace (p. 78) Writing Skills Practice (p. 79)
	NCTE 7 Conduct research and gather, evaluate, and synthesize data to communicate discoveries.	21st Century Workplace (p. 70)
	NCTE 8 Use information resources to gather information and create and communicate knowledge.	Real-World Connection (p. 61)
Mathematics	**Data Analysis and Probability:** Select and use appropriate statistical methods to analyze data	After You Read (p. 73)
	Data Analysis and Probability: Formulate questions that can be addressed with data and collect, organize, and display relevant data to answer them	Academic Skills in the Workplace (p. 78)
Science	**Physical Science:** Motions and forces	Science in Action (p. 65)
	Science as Inquiry: Abilities necessary to do scientific inquiry	Academic Skills in the Workplace (p. 78)

CORRELATIONS The charts show the 21st Century Skills, foundation skills, and workplace competencies that students develop as they work in this chapter.

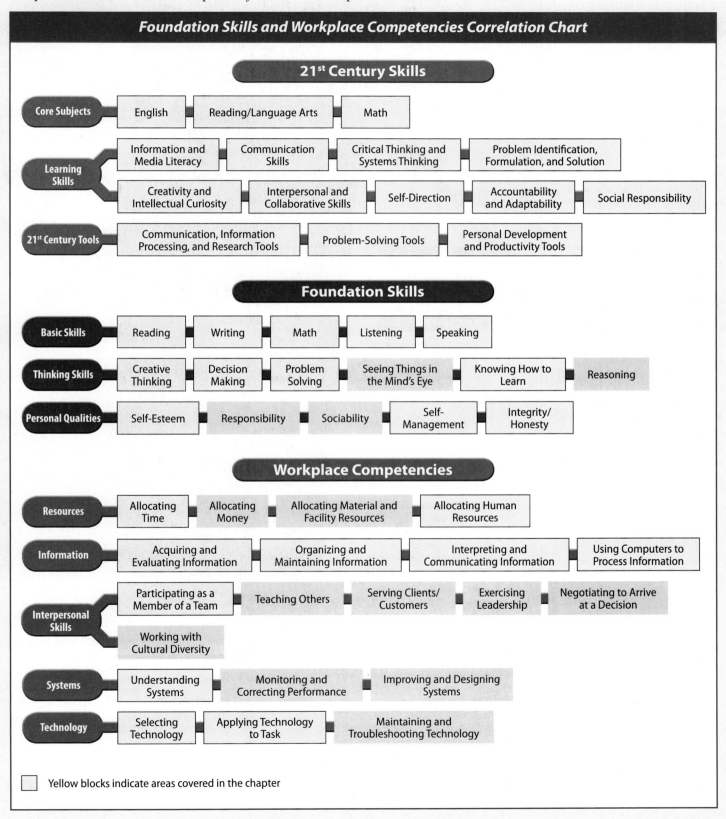

Foundation Skills and Workplace Competencies Correlation Chart

21st Century Skills

Core Subjects
- English
- Reading/Language Arts
- Math

Learning Skills
- Information and Media Literacy
- Communication Skills
- Critical Thinking and Systems Thinking
- Problem Identification, Formulation, and Solution
- Creativity and Intellectual Curiosity
- Interpersonal and Collaborative Skills
- Self-Direction
- Accountability and Adaptability
- Social Responsibility

21st Century Tools
- Communication, Information Processing, and Research Tools
- Problem-Solving Tools
- Personal Development and Productivity Tools

Foundation Skills

Basic Skills
- Reading
- Writing
- Math
- Listening
- Speaking

Thinking Skills
- Creative Thinking
- Decision Making
- Problem Solving
- Seeing Things in the Mind's Eye
- Knowing How to Learn
- Reasoning

Personal Qualities
- Self-Esteem
- Responsibility
- Sociability
- Self-Management
- Integrity/Honesty

Workplace Competencies

Resources
- Allocating Time
- Allocating Money
- Allocating Material and Facility Resources
- Allocating Human Resources

Information
- Acquiring and Evaluating Information
- Organizing and Maintaining Information
- Interpreting and Communicating Information
- Using Computers to Process Information

Interpersonal Skills
- Participating as a Member of a Team
- Teaching Others
- Serving Clients/Customers
- Exercising Leadership
- Negotiating to Arrive at a Decision
- Working with Cultural Diversity

Systems
- Understanding Systems
- Monitoring and Correcting Performance
- Improving and Designing Systems

Technology
- Selecting Technology
- Applying Technology to Task
- Maintaining and Troubleshooting Technology

☐ Yellow blocks indicate areas covered in the chapter

Chapter Overview
Introduce the Chapter

In this chapter, students explore ways to research careers.

Section 3.1 presents methods of conducting career research and discusses the value of part-time work as a means of exploring a career.

Section 3.2 looks at ten factors that can affect career decisions.

Build Background

Tell students to think about what they enjoy doing and whether they would want to turn an interest into a career. Then ask volunteers how they would go about finding information on careers.

 Exploring the Photo

Caption Answer
Developing skills in an area that interests you could help you get a jump start on obtaining the education and experience needed for the area of interest.

Discussion Ask students to discuss what kinds of skills a photographer might need. (Answers might include technology skills, computer skills, and creative skills.)

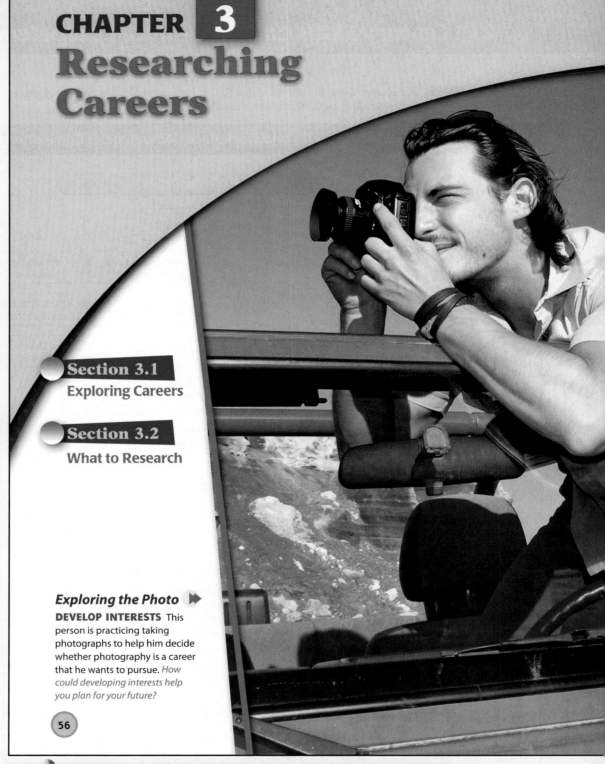

Section 3.1
Exploring Careers

Section 3.2
What to Research

Exploring the Photo ▶▶
DEVELOP INTERESTS This person is practicing taking photographs to help him decide whether photography is a career that he wants to pursue. *How could developing interests help you plan for your future?*

56

Classroom Resources

- 📁 Student Edition
- 📁 Teacher Wraparound Edition
- 📁 Student Activity Workbook with Academic Integration
- 📁 Student Activity Workbook with Academic Integration TAE
- 📁 *Fast File,* Unit 2 Resources

- 📁 Inclusion in the Career Education Classroom
- 💿 TeacherWorks™ Plus
- 💿 *ExamView Assessment Suite*
- 💿 Interactive Chalkboard
- 💿 Interactive Student Edition
- 💻 Online Student Edition
- 💻 Online Learning Center (OLC) with Podcasts

Chapter Objectives

After completing this chapter, you will be able to:

- **Describe** formal and informal methods of researching careers.
- **Evaluate** sources of career information.
- **Identify** work experiences that can help you explore careers.
- **Develop** key questions to ask when researching and assessing careers.
- **Identify** the characteristics used to develop a career profile.
- **Determine** the education and training needed for different careers.

Writing Activity — Personal Career Notebook

Every day you observe people in many different careers: teachers, salespeople, doctors, and administrators. Sometimes you observe only the products of a person's work. You hear the work of musicians on the radio. You see the work of television producers when you watch your favorite shows. You view the work of marketing professionals on billboards or in magazines. Have you ever wondered how individuals get these positions? Brainstorm different careers that seem interesting to you. In a one-page journal entry, begin a list of questions you have about one of these careers. Add to this list as you continue your research.

Get Motivated! Contact a person in a field you are interested in and interview the person using the questions from your journal entry. Summarize your findings in a one-page report.

Chapter 3 Researching Careers **57**

Writing Activity — Personal Career Notebook Answer Guide

Journal entries will vary. Questions might include: What is your typical day like? What are your daily responsibilities? With how many people do you work? Students should also consider questions specific to the career in which they are interested.

Get Motivated! Summaries should show an understanding of interviewing and the ability to summarize notes in a report.

Review the Objectives

Introduce the chapter by reviewing the chapter objectives:

Section 3.1 Objectives

Describe formal and informal methods of researching careers. (Informal information comes from everyday conversations, reading magazines, and watching TV shows; formal research focuses on information found at the library, Internet job services, interviews, and part-time work.)

Evaluate sources of career information. (Useful career information needs to come from reliable sources, and it needs to be up-to-date.)

Identify work experiences that can help you explore careers. (Job shadowing, volunteering, interning, and working part-time all allow you to learn about a career.)

Section 3.2 Objectives

Develop key questions to ask when researching and assessing careers. (You will need to ask questions to find out what a career is like and whether it is right for you.)

Identify the characteristics used to develop a career profile. (The ten career characteristics are values; tasks and responsibilities; working with data-people-things; work environment, working hours; aptitudes and abilities; education and training; salary and benefits; career outlook; and international career outlook.)

Determine the education and training needed for various careers. (You need to be aware of the kinds and levels of education required to pursue the career of your choice.)

Exploring Careers

Bell Ringer Activity

Exploring Careers

Ask students to respond in writing to this question: "If money was not an issue and you could work at anything you wanted, what would you do?" Allow students five minutes to write their responses.

Resources

⚙ Interactive Chalkboard
The Interactive Chalkboard CD provides visual teaching aids for this section.

@ Online Learning Center
The Online Learning Center (OLC) through **glencoe.com** features chapter vocabulary, chapter summaries, and other study materials.

Preteaching
Read the definitions of the key terms aloud. As you read each definition, ask students to write a sentence using each key term.

Graphic Organizer
Tell students to go to the OLC through **glencoe.com** for a printable graphic organizer. (Graphic organizers will vary but should show types of information sources and examples of each.)

NCLB connects academic correlations to book content.

Reading Guide

Before You Read
Preview Write a list of what you want to know about researching careers. As you read, write down the heads in this section that provide that information.

Read to Learn
- How to use formal and informal methods to research careers
- How to evaluate sources of career information
- How to identify work experiences that can help you explore careers

D Main Idea
Exploring careers will help you find the employment possibilities that best match your interests, values, and personal needs.

Key Concepts
- Researching Career Options
- Learning from Experience

Key Terms
- ◆ career clusters
- ◆ exploratory interview
- ◆ temp work
- ◆ cooperative program
- ◆ job shadowing
- ◆ internship
- ◆ service learning

Academic Vocabulary
You will find these words in your reading and on your tests. Use the academic vocabulary glossary to look up their definitions if necessary.
- ■ source
- ■ index

Graphic Organizer
As you read, list the different types of information sources discussed and give an example of each. Add your own ideas for sources of information. Use a chart like the one shown to help organize the information.

Types of Sources	Examples of Sources	Primary or Secondary?

 Log On Go to this book's Online Learning Center through **glencoe.com** for an online version of this graphic organizer.

NCLB Academic Standards ....

English Language Arts
- Apply strategies to interpret and evaluate texts. (NCTE 3)
- Use information resources to gather information and create and communicate knowledge. (NCTE 8)

Science
- Physical Science: motions and forces

Reading Guide

Before You Read
Help students understand that research can be a part of everyday life by asking them for information about a favorite musical group or television show. Ask how they learned the information.

D Develop Concepts
Main Idea Discuss the main idea with students. Ask: How do you go about exploring careers? (Answers will vary but may include talking to family members and friends, attending job fairs, and reading job listings in newspapers and online.)

Researching Career Options

Think of your skills and interests. What kinds of activities do you like to do? What kind of work do you enjoy? Have you wondered what kinds of jobs would fit your skills and interests? Knowing what you like to do and what you are good at is important when searching for a career. Now you need to know what kinds of careers match your skills and interests.

The U.S. Department of Education has organized careers into 16 different career clusters. **Career clusters** are groups of related occupations. Look at **Figure 3.1** on page 60. Which career cluster—or career clusters—might fit the kind of person you are? Narrow your search by choosing one. Then start exploring related careers that might be right for you.

To explore any topic, you need to know how to find sources of information. A **source** can be a book, a Web site, a person, or anything that supplies information on the topic you are exploring. A primary source is original. It is a person, event, or document from which you get information directly. For example, if you interview an engineer about her experiences on the job, she is a primary source. A secondary source contains information that other people have gathered and commented on, such as Web sites, documentaries, or magazine articles. As you read, note possible sources of information for your research.

 CHECK OUT THE LIBRARY Local and school libraries have a broad range of career materials—plus help if you need it. *What kinds of career materials do you think you might find at the local library?*

Informal Research

You can discover some of what the world of work has to offer simply by keeping your eyes and ears open. Look around as you go through your day. During the next week, list all the careers that you notice. This kind of informal research can be very helpful in generating ideas.

You can also interview people you know about their career experiences. Use the list of questions you created in your personal career notebook or ask a few of the following questions:
- What was your favorite job?
- What was your least favorite job?
- What was your most unusual job?
- How do you like your current job?

Vocabulary

You can find definitions in the **Key Terms** glossary and **Academic Vocabulary** glossary at the back of this book.

TEACH

Discussion Starter

Researching Career Options Ask students what kinds of research they conduct when they are assigned to write research papers. (Examples of research might include the use of encyclopedias, dictionaries, libraries, newspapers, and the Internet.)

R Reading Strategy

Modeling Explain to students that Web sites can be either primary or secondary sources. For example, a company's own official Web site would be a primary source of information, while an online newspaper article written about the same company would be an example of a secondary source.

Resources

⊙ **TeacherWorks™ Plus** The TeacherWorks software includes customizable built-in lesson plans and links to printable program resources.

 Extend the Photo

Caption Answer Items that can be found in the library include computer stations for accessing the Internet, business magazines and other periodicals and newspapers, and books on résumé writing.

Discussion Reiterate to students that the library can be a useful place to find up-to-date career data, and that most libraries have computer stations that can be used to access the Internet.

TEACH (cont.)

R **Reading Strategy**

Identifying Ask students to imagine they have career interests in physical performance (sports, dance, or gymnastics, for example). What career clusters include these types of jobs? (Arts; education and training; hospitality and tourism)

C **Critical Thinking**

Evaluating Ask: How does researching a career cluster help you identify a possible career? (You can use the career cluster to match your areas of interest to job examples, including opportunities about which you may not have known.)

U **Universal Access**

English Language Learners Students who are English language learners will benefit from a preview of the vocabulary used in the chapter. Focus not only on the new terms introduced in the chapter but also on other complex words that may be unfamiliar to these students. Define concepts and terms in more than one way. Also, have students define the concepts and terms in their own words.

As You Read

By conducting informal research, you can find various sources that reflect a range of experiences about the career in which you are interested.

As You Read

Analyze How can informal research help you to explore careers?

Put your listening skills to work as you gather firsthand information from these primary, or original, sources. Summarize the interview afterward or write notes as you listen, noting important points.

Finding Career Inspiration

You can find career inspiration by observing and interacting with individuals, but you can also find inspiration through characters or people portrayed in visual, print, and digital media. Think about the movies, TV shows, magazines, video games, and other forms of media that you know. Can you think of any characters or people you have read about or seen who are doing jobs that you would like to do?

Figure 3.1 | **THE U.S. DEPARTMENT OF EDUCATION CAREER CLUSTERS**

Career Cluster	Job Examples
❖ **Agriculture, Food, and Natural Resources**	farmer, ecologist, veterinarian, biochemist
❖ **Architecture and Construction**	contractor, architect, plumber, building inspector
❖ **Arts, Audio/Video Technology, and Communications**	graphic designer, musician, actor, journalist, filmmaker
❖ **Business, Management, and Administration**	executive assistant, receptionist, bookkeeper, business owner
❖ **Education and Training**	teacher, trainer, principal, counselor, librarian
❖ **Finance**	bank teller, tax preparer, stockbroker, financial planner
❖ **Government and Public Administration**	soldier, postal worker, city manager, nonprofit director
❖ **Health Science**	pediatrician, registered nurse, dentist, physical therapist
❖ **Hospitality and Tourism**	chef, hotel manager, translator, tour guide
❖ **Human Services**	social worker, psychologist, child care worker
❖ **Information Technology**	Web designer, software engineer, technical writer
❖ **Law, Public Safety, Corrections, and Security**	attorney, police officer, firefighter, paralegal
❖ **Manufacturing**	production supervisor, manufacturing engineer, welding technician, quality technician
❖ **Marketing, Sales, and Service**	sales associate, retail buyer, customer service representative
❖ **Science, Technology, Engineering, and Mathematics**	lab technician, marine biologist, electrical engineer, cryptanalyst
❖ **Transportation, Distribution, and Logistics**	pilot, railroad conductor, truck driver, automotive mechanic

CAREER CLUSTERS The U.S. Department of Education groups careers into 16 career clusters based on similar job characteristics. *How might career clusters help you explore careers?*

EXTEND THE FIGURE | **Figure 3.1**

Caption Answer Answers will vary but students should be able to give reasons for their answers.

Discussion Read the title of each career cluster and ask for a show of hands from students interested in that cluster. Tally responses and identify the most popular career cluster. Discuss why that may be the case.

If so, research more about those jobs. That is how Mala Khan found her career. She never missed her favorite TV program—real-life rescues of people in medical emergencies. When she thought about it, she realized that emergency rescue work was exactly what she wanted to do. She decided to research how to become an emergency medical technician.

Formal Research

While informal research is initial research that gives you ideas, it usually does not yield enough information. Formal research is fully developed, formally presented, and gives you enough information to act on your ideas. Written reports, prepared speeches, and multimedia presentations are examples of what you might find doing formal research.

As you research, keep a log, or notebook, of what you find. When you find a source, write the author or name of the organization that put the information together. This is the source of the information. Also write down where you found the information and a brief summary of what you found. This log will help you track your research and remember what information you found and where you found it.

As you find information, you will need to determine how credible, or believable, the sources are. Find out how current the information is. Check it against other sources you have found. Is the information complete and accurate? Does it express a particular bias or point of view? Keep these questions in mind as you research.

Libraries

Many school and public libraries have career information centers. You can search the catalog or database to find reference books, magazines, CDs, DVDs, and other media sources of career information.

One of a library's best resources is the librarian. The librarian can help you locate information and give suggestions on how to use different search tools, such as the library's catalog, databases, and Internet search engines.

Books

Look for these useful books published by the U.S. Department of Labor:
- The *Occupational Outlook Handbook,* updated every two years, describes the type of work, the training and education required, and the future outlook for many careers.
- The *Guide for Occupational Exploration* groups careers into categories, such as careers that involve working with food, and describes many occupations within each category.

Chapter 3   Researching Careers   **61**

Real-World Connection

Time Management

This semester, you are going to do an internship at a local lawn care service. To receive credit, you must work 180 hours on the job and keep a record of your hours worked. Your supervisor will have to sign the time sheet when it is completed. You want to be sure that you will have enough time in your schedule to complete the required hours.

Critical Thinking How can you ensure that you will work the required hours and meet the course requirements?

Do Your Own Research Think of the tools people use to schedule activities. You may ask adults you know how they plan their time. Choose one method of time management and create a schedule showing how you will meet the course requirements. Include the number of days and the number of hours each day you will work.

TEACH (cont.)

S Skill Practice
Guided Practice

List Have students make a list of all the careers they hear about during the course of a designated day—while attending classes, watching television, listening to the radio, and reading books and magazines. Have students share their lists with the class. **L1**

Report Have students research a career of interest to them and give three-to five-minute talks on the job skills and training needed for the career. Tell students to include information about the wide range of jobs within a career area. **L2**

Research Have students choose an unusual job or career area. Some examples might include a personal shopper, a golf pro, an animal trainer, a movie stunt person, or an agribusiness technician. Have students research the career and create a profile of a person working in that career. The profile should include education required, special skills, prior job experience, and personal traits that would help a person succeed. Ask students to share their research in a class discussion. **L3**

Real-World Connection

Critical Thinking Answer Students will need to determine the days and hours that they could work on the internship. They would also need to decide on one way to keep up with their hours and use that format for the whole project. They will need to establish the routine of writing their hours down at the end of each shift of work. Submitting a completed time sheet to the supervisor will show responsibility.

Do Your Own Research Have students research internship opportunities in newspapers, trade journals, or online. Have them scan the ads and highlight those that specify the amount of time employers expects from the interns per week. Have students share their findings.

W Writing Support
Guided Practice

Researching Careers Have students start a notebook of career information. Have students research the Dictionary of Occupational Titles (or a similar reference) and choose three career areas that interest them. Tell students to write descriptions of each career area in their notebooks. They should include data about potential openings in the field, career outlook, and training needed to work in the field.

C Critical Thinking

Drawing Conclusions Why is it important to consider several career options, even if you are sure of your career choice? (It is important to consider several options because you may develop new interests and change significantly as you mature.)

Looking at categories of careers may help you find new career options. Discovering the tasks and activities of particular careers will help you plan for your future. When you look at these books, take notes on the descriptions, tasks, and education required for careers of interest. Do your findings match your expectations?

Additional Resources

Libraries and bookstores also contain other print media resources, including newspapers, magazines, and government reports. Job listings in local publications show what employment is available in your local job market.

The *Reader's Guide to Periodical Literature* is an **index**, or categorized list, of magazine articles. Use it to find stories about specific industries and career trends. Business magazines such as *BusinessWeek* and *Wired* cover the major issues and inside news of many industries. The *Occupational Outlook Quarterly*, published by the U.S. Department of Labor, provides up-to-date information on employment trends.

Many labor organizations and industry service groups produce video or audio resources of workers in action.

Internet Career Resources

The Internet offers a wide range of career resources, such as employment or job skills Web sites and online bulletin boards created by trade organizations, companies, and individuals— all designed for job recruitment and career research. There are many local, national, and international job posting sites. You can also search on a specific company or organization Web site to find information on careers at that company or organization.

Online government career services include O*NET, a database of worker attributes and job characteristics. O*NET offers up-to-date information on thousands of careers and career outlooks.

◀◀ **USE THE WEB** When searching for job or career information online, use specific search terms that identify the job or career. *What search terms would you use if you were looking for a job as a dental assistant?*

▶ Extend the Photo

Caption Answer Possible search terms include *dentist*, *dental assistant*, and *orthodontics*.

Discussion Have students discuss various online job search methods. Have them compare and contrast the benefits of using a search engine versus a job placement Web site. For example, a search engine will bring up career information in addition to job listings, but you might have to search through inappropriate search results, whereas a job placement site will focus mostly on specific job listings, but will provide more focused information.

Everyday ETHICS

YOUR WORK ETHIC

Why do you work?

VOLUNTEER JOB You and two classmates volunteer at a local nursing home as a service learning activity. You arrive on time and spend time with the residents. Your classmates, however, often arrive late and leave early, and take frequent breaks to make cell phone calls. They tell you that since they are not getting paid, they do not need to work hard.

What Would You Do? What is your response to your classmates' work ethic?

DISCUSS IT A service learning project is often done for academic credit. A frequent requirement of a service learning project is to keep a log of how your time is spent. What must your classmates do to fulfill the service learning requirements? What do their actions reveal about their commitment to the project and their attitude toward work? Share your responses with the class.

Most career Web sites list job opportunities according to industry title, key duties, location, and other criteria. Once you find a career that interests you, you can use an Internet search engine to get a list of career-related Web sites. As you search for a job online, choose specific search terms, such as *research assistant* or *marketing,* to help you find jobs that match your interests. Many Web sites will e-mail you when jobs in your desired field become available.

The Internet provides fast and easy access to information from a variety of sources. And many people post information on a variety of topics. However, searching the Internet can be frustrating when your search terms lead you to unrelated information or when you follow a path of links that do not lead you to your goal. Also, since anyone can post information on the Internet, you need to make sure that the information you use is from a credible source.

Exploratory Interviews

Ask your family, friends, neighbors, teachers, and counselors to help you build a list of people who work in careers that you find interesting. After doing some initial research into a career, call someone on the list and arrange an exploratory interview. An **exploratory interview** is a short, informal talk with someone who works in a career that appeals to you. Prepare for the interview by reviewing your research. Think about what you want to know about this career and develop some questions. You may ask questions such as these:

- How did you start your career?
- What education and training did it require?
- What do you like about your job?
- What do you do during a typical workday?

As You Read

Analyze What are some advantages and disadvantages of using the Internet to do research?

Everyday ETHICS

What Would You Do? Answer Answers will vary but students should recognize that the behavior described is both irresponsible and dishonest.

DISCUSS IT Class responses will vary but students should point out that classmates must work the required amount of hours to receive academic credit. These actions show a dishonest work ethic and a lack of commitment to the job.

TEACH (cont.)

C Critical Thinking

Connect to Technology The text notes that students should make sure the information they find online is from a credible source. Ask: How can you determine which Web sites are credible and up-to-date? (You should look for *official* sites that are maintained by the company or organization, as opposed to *unofficial* sites that can be maintained by anybody. You should also look for copyright dates or dates that specify when information was put on the site.)

As You Read

The Internet offers fast and easy access to a wide range of information; however, you need to make sure the information comes from a reliable source, since anyone can post material on the Internet.

W Writing Support
Guided Practice

Writing Interview Questions Have students choose a career they want to learn more about by conducting an exploratory interview. Tell them to write a list of at least ten questions they would ask in such an interview. (Questions will vary. Encourage students to think of open-ended questions, using words such as "What," "How," and "Why," that will result in more than *yes* or *no* answers. For example, instead of asking "Did you like your first marketing job?" ask "What aspects did you like and dislike about your first marketing job?")

TEACH *(cont.)*

Discussion Starter
Learning from Experience
Have students discuss the possible benefits of learning about a career through experience. (Learning through experience helps students get firsthand experience about a career field, including what a typical day is like and what activities a worker in that field does.)

✓ Reading Check

CONTRAST Informal research consists of personal observations and conversations with friends, family, and acquaintances. Formal research is more fully developed and formally presented.

ASSESS

Review Key Terms
Have students write sentences using each key term in this section.

Online Study Tools
Have students go to the OLC through **glencoe.com** to:
• Download **Podcast** study tools.
• Download free **Study-to-Go** content to their PDAs or cell phones.

Resources

 ***ExamView Assessment Suite* CD** allows you to print out ready-made unit and chapter tests complete with answer keys. You can also create customized tests.

Personal Academic and Career Portfolio

Go to the chapter review to find guidelines for creating your own **Personal Academic and Career Portfolio**.

Do not be afraid to ask people for interviews. They may have received someone else's help starting out and may be happy to pass along the favor. Take notes during or ask permission to record each interview. Afterward, write down your reflections on the experience in a folder labeled *Career Resource File*. You can place this file in your **Personal Academic and Career Portfolio**.

When John Liu was researching careers, he interviewed a friend's aunt who worked as a retail department store buyer. "I learned more about buying and selling in an hour with her than I could have imagined. She was smart and creative, and she loved her work." The interview paid off. John went on to become a well-known retail consultant. "Knowing how she started her career helped me figure out what kind of education and experience I needed to have on my résumé."

✓ Reading Check **CONTRAST** What is the difference between informal and formal research?

Learning from Experience

The most direct way to learn about a career is to work. If your schedule allows it, working part-time will enable you to observe a career from the inside. To explore this option, talk to employers in your area to find out what they are looking for in part-time employees and how to get part-time work. You will gain experience, make personal contacts, and put some money in your pocket at the same time.

Creative Business Practices

STARBUCKS **Putting People First**

Putting people before products is a practice that has paid off for Starbucks Coffee Company. Since opening in Seattle in 1971, the company has grown to 8,000 locations in 36 countries worldwide.

The company's commitment to putting people first begins with Starbucks' Make Your Mark program, which matches employee volunteer hours with cash contributions for designated nonprofit organizations. The company matches every volunteer hour with a $10 donation, up to $1,000 per project.

Both local and global communities benefit from Starbucks' community involvement. Local involvement includes improving public parks, sponsoring violence prevention and literacy programs, and supporting the Seattle arts. Global involvement includes improving social and economic conditions for coffee farmers and taking measures to protect the environment.

CRITICAL THINKING How do businesses like Starbucks benefit from community involvement?

 Connect to the Real World For more information about Starbucks' community service, visit their Web site via the link on this book's Online Learning Center through **glencoe.com**.

64 **Unit 2** Exploring Careers

glencoe.com

Creative Business Practices

CRITICAL THINKING ANSWER By committing time and resources to the community, companies such as Starbucks gain community trust and respect, which results in increased patronage and better profits for the business.

◀ **LEARN BY DOING**
You can learn about careers through volunteer work. *What job skills might volunteering help you develop?*

People also gain job experience as temp workers. **Temp work**, or temporary work, is short-term employment. Temporary employment agencies specialize in placing employees who have the skills companies need for a short time period. Temp jobs can last from a few days to indefinitely. Though temp work does not always offer benefits or job security, it does give an opportunity to develop job skills, learn about different work environments, and develop contacts that may help you find a permanent job.

Work Experience Programs

You may find a part-time job through a vocational education program. Such programs are designed to give you a chance to learn job skills while you are still in high school. As a bonus, the work also earns you class credit and a grade. A **cooperative program** is an arrangement in which local businesses team up with schools, hiring students to perform jobs that use knowledge and skills taught in their school classes. One high school's cooperative program used math and science classes to prepare students for work at a local environmental services company. Another high school created a school-based business. Students learned marketing and retailing in classes and then applied their knowledge working at the store.

Job Shadowing

[S] **Job shadowing** involves following a worker on the job for a few days. By watching and listening to the worker, students can learn firsthand what it would be like to work in a particular field.

Science In Action

Kinetic Energy

Things that move have kinetic energy. When an apple falls from a tree, its potential energy is converted to kinetic energy. Energy is measured in Joules. What is the kinetic energy of a 10 kg bike that is moving at a velocity of 20.0 meters per second?

Starting Hint: The formula for determining kinetic energy is $KE = \frac{1}{2} mv^2$, where m = mass and v = velocity.

@ For more science practice, go to this book's OLC through **glencoe.com**.

RETEACH

[S] **Skill Practice**
Independent Practice
Write a Letter Have students write a letter to a company in which they would like to have a job-shadowing experience. Encourage students to specify the type of work they are interested in knowing more about. (Letters will vary but should conform to business letter formatting.)

[N C L B] Activity correlated to Science standards.

Science In Action

The kinetic energy is 2,000 joules ($\frac{1}{2} \times 10 \times 2,000 = 2,000$).

Resources

📁 **Student Activity Workbook** Assign the Chapter 3 activities in the Student Activity Workbook.

 Extend the Photo

Caption Answer Volunteers often gain experience working with others, serving customers, practicing time management skills, and other job-specific skills.

Discussion Tell students that volunteer work allows them to give back to the community. Ask students to brainstorm volunteer opportunities.

ASSESS

After You Read

Have students complete the Section 3.1 After You Read section review.

Online Study Tools

Have students go to the OLC through **glencoe.com** to:

- Take the Section 3.1 **Practice Test.**
- Download **Podcast** study tools.
- Download free **Study-to-Go** content to their PDAs or cell phones.

CLOSE

Culminating Activity

Positive Versus Negative
For one week, have students take notes on the positive and negative things they hear people say about their own careers. Have them draw conclusions about the information they have gained. Then ask them how one can decide if the negatives outweigh the positives. Have students report their conclusions in a three-paragraph report. (Reports will vary, but students should provide support for their conclusions.)

 Activity correlated to English Standards.

HOT JOBS!

Occupational Therapist

Occupational therapists help people with mental, physical, emotional, or developmental difficulties handle everyday life and work. Most occupational therapists specialize in work with certain types of individuals, such as children or the elderly. Many work on a freelance basis at a school, hospital, or other such facility.

Job shadowing helped television camera operator Elena Sanchez choose her career path. When she was a student, she did not know anyone in the entertainment industry. As she tells it, "I was always hanging around our local TV studio, and one day I just asked the camera operator if I could talk to her about her job. She offered to let me shadow her. I stuck to her like glue for a week. TV production has been my life ever since."

Volunteering, Internships, and Community Work

Volunteer work is work you do without receiving pay. Volunteers gain valuable experience that can help them make career decisions. Hospitals, parks, and museums are just a few workplaces that use volunteers.

An **internship** is a short-term job or work project that usually requires formal commitment. Like volunteers, interns are often unpaid, but they learn vital job skills. Interns can sometimes move on to full-time, paying positions.

Many communities and schools offer service learning programs as a way to explore careers. **Service learning** programs connect academic work with community service, allowing students to explore issues discussed in the classroom through personal experiences and community work. For example, students in a service learning program might remove litter from a park as they study environmental issues, or work with preschool children as they study child development.

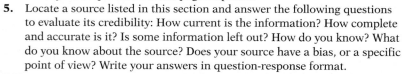

Section 3.1 After You Read

Review Key Concepts

1. Describe one informal method of researching careers.
2. Distinguish between the types of information you would find using the O*NET and the *Guide for Occupational Exploration.*
3. Explain how unpaid volunteer work might help you choose a career.

Practice Academic Skills

English Language Arts

4. List the skills you might develop though volunteer work, part-time employment, and educational programs. How are these skills similar or different? How could each type of experience affect your career options? Write your responses in a one-page response.
5. Locate a source listed in this section and answer the following questions to evaluate its credibility: How current is the information? How complete and accurate is it? Is some information left out? How do you know? What do you know about the source? Does your source have a bias, or a specific point of view? Write your answers in question-response format.

@ Check your answers at this book's OLC through **glencoe.com**.

Section 3.1 After You Read

Review Key Concepts

1. Talking to people and using media resources can be seen as informal methods of research when they are used simply to generate ideas rather than gather specific information for a report.
2. Though they are both government resources, the O*Net provides worker attributes and job characteristics, while the Guide for Occupational Exploration groups careers by category and describes occupations within each category.
3. Possible answers include being able to observe a career from the inside, gaining experience, developing contacts, and learning what employers want.

Practice Academic Skills

4. Possible responses may include ability to cooperate and collaborate on projects, ability to listen, and ability to take charge of a situation.
5. Answers will vary. Students should evaluate each source using all questions.

What to Research

Reading Guide

Before You Read

Preview Read the Key Concepts. Write one or two sentences predicting what the section will be about.

Read to Learn

- How to develop key questions to ask when researching and assessing careers
- How to identify the characteristics used to develop a career profile
- How to determine the education and training needed for different careers

D

The Main Idea

Asking the right questions about jobs that interest you will make your career search more productive.

Key Concepts

- Your Career Expectations
- Career Outlook

Key Terms

- work environment
- flextime
- career pathways
- benefits

Academic Vocabulary

You will find these words in your reading and on your tests. Use the academic vocabulary glossary to look up their definitions if necessary.

- visualize
- decline
- potential

Graphic Organizer

As you read, list the characteristics of a career profile and your response or expectations for each characteristic. Continue adding and changing the list as you research and discover more about what you want for your future. Use a two-column chart like the one shown to help organize your information.

Characteristics	My Response/ Expectations

 Log On Go to this book's Online Learning Center through **glencoe.com** for an online version of this graphic organizer.

N C L B

Academic Standards •

English Language Arts
- Read texts to acquire new information. (NCTE 1)
- Conduct research and gather, evaluate, and synthesize data to communicate discoveries. (NCTE 7)

Mathematics
- Select and use appropriate statistical methods to analyze data

glencoe.com

Reading Guide

Before You Read

Point out to students that career preparation means more than receiving the required education for a career. It also means researching how careers are expected to change over the next ten years.

D Develop Concepts

Main Idea Discuss the main idea with students. Ask: What are the "right" questions to ask when researching careers? (The best questions vary according to career, but are generally those that are open-ended and those that relate as specifically as possible to the students' interests.)

FOCUS

🔔 Bell Ringer Activity

What to Research

Have students assume that they love to buy clothes and enjoy wearing the latest styles. Would they enjoy a career in retailing? How could they decide whether a retailing career would be satisfying? (Research the career, take a part-time retailing job, shadow one or more retail workers.)

Resources

Interactive Chalkboard
The Interactive Chalkboard CD provides visual teaching aids for this section.

@ Online Learning Center
The OLC through **glencoe.com** features chapter vocabulary, chapter summaries, and other study materials.

Preteaching

Read the definitions of the key terms aloud. As you read each definition, ask students to write a sentence using each key term.

Graphic Organizer

Tell students to go to the OLC through **glencoe.com** for a printable graphic organizer. (Graphic organizers will vary but should show an understanding of the ten career characteristics and how they relate to the student's chosen career.)

Discussion Starter

Your Career Expectations
For five minutes, have students write a list of all the things they would want to know about a job that interests them. Write students' answers on the board. If students have not mentioned all ten characteristics from this page, add the missing items to the list and discuss how each relates to career choice.

As You Read

Answers will vary, but students should demonstrate an understanding of the ten career characteristics by effectively explaining those that are most important.

R Reading Strategy

Assess Priorities Ask: Which of these characteristics are most important to you? Which are least important? List the characteristics in order of importance, from the most to the least important.

Resources

Interactive Chalkboard
The Interactive Chalkboard CD provides visual teaching aids for this section.

As You Read

Evaluate Which of these ten characteristics is most important to you? Why?

Your Career Expectations

Once you know where to get career information, the next question is what information you should get. You will want to know what the career is like and whether it is right for you. Review the information you have already collected. What more would you need to know before investing your time, money, or other resources in any of your career choices? What questions has your research left unanswered? You can find out more by examining careers in terms of these ten characteristics:

1. values
2. tasks and responsibilities
3. working with data-people-things
4. work environment
5. working hours
6. aptitudes and abilities
7. education and training
8. salary and benefits
9. career outlook
10. international career outlook

R

Reflect on your own ideas and expectations for your career and lifestyle. Keep this in mind as you gather information on each of these characteristics. In doing this you will lay the groundwork for a personal career profile, a document that compares what is important to you with what you have learned about different careers. You will learn more about personal career profiles in Chapter 5.

TechSavvy

Résumé Software

For a first-time job hunter, the task of creating a résumé may seem overwhelming. Résumé software can help job seekers create a résumé that looks and sounds professional.

The most basic résumé software walks you through the process of creating a résumé, prompting you to enter information in fields such as work experience, education, and contact information. You can then choose a set format to organize your information. A *format* refers to the layout and style of a document, such as the size and shape of the letters, the size of the text area, or the width of the margins. These standardized formats are sometimes called *templates*.

@ Visit this book's Online Learning Center through **glencoe.com** to learn more about résumé software. Create a spreadsheet table that lists five features of two kinds of résumé software.

Values

When you look into a career, ask yourself if your values match the values that will help you in that career. What do you really care about? What do people in that career really care about? For example, do people in that career care about being creative? Do they care about society? Justice? Art? Money? Health? Fame?

Tasks and Responsibilities

When you go to work each day, what will you actually be doing? Use the common question words—who, what, where, when, why, and how—to develop questions important to your search. Specific questions you could ask include:

- What specific tasks do workers in this career perform?
- How are the workdays structured? Are they repetitive or full of new experiences?
- How easy is the pace? Is the job a high-pressure job?
- Is the work primarily physical or mental?
- What specific challenges does this job offer?

TechSavvy

Résumé Software

Answer Spreadsheets should show evidence of research into two different kinds of résumé software. Evaluate spreadsheets for the clarity of information provided about the software. Also evaluate the five features that have been provided under each program name in the spreadsheet.

◀◀ **DATA-PEOPLE-THINGS**
The construction worker in this photo is doing work that focuses on data and things. *In which area or areas would you like to focus most of your time and energy?*

Working with Data-People-Things

Careers involve working with data, people, and things. Some careers involve working with all three. However, in most careers, one area tends to dominate. Statisticians, for example, work mainly with data, home nurse aides work primarily with people, and technicians usually work with things. Would you prefer to work with data, people, or things? What are some examples of how you work with all three now?

Work Environment

Because you will be spending a lot of time at work, you should consider your work environment when making career choices. Your **work environment** is your physical and social surroundings at work. Do you want to work indoors or outdoors? Would you rather work alone or with other people? Take a few minutes to **visualize** your ideal work environment. Then create a picture or write a paragraph describing what you envisioned. As you research careers, try to find those that match that image.

Working Hours

When you think about work, do you assume you will be starting at 9:00 A.M. and stopping at 5:00 P.M.? Many careers are not 9–5. Restaurant owner Andrew Barros starts work at 3:00 P.M. and leaves after the last guest does—at about 11:00 P.M. Andrew's restaurant buys produce from Ahmi Ko, who works from 4:00 A.M. to noon. When are you at your best? Are you a night owl or a morning person?

Some careers allow flexible scheduling. With **flextime**, workers construct their work schedules to suit their lives. Some people work four ten-hour days and enjoy three-day weekends. Some work early

▶ Vocabulary

You can find definitions in the **Key Terms** glossary and **Academic Vocabulary** glossary at the back of this book.

TEACH *(cont.)*

Discussion Starter

Work Environment Ask students who have part-time jobs to share their thoughts about their work environment. How does it affect their attitudes toward their jobs? (Answers will vary, but students who participate should be able to explain how their work environment affects their overall attitude at work.)

C Critical Thinking

Synthesize Have students take an informal survey of their friends and relatives, asking whether they work with people, data, or things. Tally the responses in class. Do most people work with one more than the other? (Students' answers will vary but should demonstrate an understanding of data-people-things.)

R Reading Strategy

Evaluate Ask: How does the employer benefit by offering flextime? (Possible answers include more satisfied, productive workers; and fewer commuting problems as workers can choose less busy times to travel to and from work.)

▶ Extend the Photo

Caption Answer Answers will vary but students should be able to identify a specific area—data, people, or things—that they would like to pursue.

Discussion Ask students to brainstorm various jobs and classify them as being in the areas of data, people, or things. (Data jobs include computer programmer, Web designer, and financial planner. People jobs include sales associate, politician, and firefighter. Things jobs include welding technician, architect, and novelist.)

TEACH (cont.)

C Critical Thinking

Making Inferences Ask students to think about the role that talent plays in a career decision. Use an example of a famous athlete. Is that person naturally gifted or did he or she develop talent through great effort and sacrifice? (Students might mention devoting a great deal of time to practicing, studying for many years, giving up entertainment and time with friends and family, and observing healthy habits to maintain strength.)

U Universal Access

Students with Behavior Disorders Students who have attention difficulties may find it easier to stay on target if they are actively involved in learning. Have students select one section of this chapter to teach to another student. Afterward, discuss with the students whether they learn better when they are the teacher or the student.

NCLB Activity correlated to English Language Arts standards.

shifts to make more time for other activities. Some people telecommute, or use technology to communicate with clients and colleagues away from the office.

Aptitudes and Abilities

As you know, skills for any kind of work are more easily learned if you have an aptitude for learning them. In Chapter 2, you analyzed your own aptitudes and abilities. As you do your research, find out which aptitudes and abilities are needed for each career. You can then match your natural talents with careers that require those same abilities. Anton Cabet was a high school student who loved to talk. He had the ability to get people to open up to him. When he realized that talking was what he was really good at, his career started to take shape, and today he hosts his own radio talk show.

Career Preparation

When preparing for a career, you need to know what employers in that career will expect from you as well as what your job will be like. Learn the **career pathways**, which are routes that lead to a particular career. Career pathways include the types of education, training, and work experiences that will help you achieve your career goal. Discover how the careers you are interested in are expected to change over the next ten years. Preparing yourself now will help ensure success later.

The 21st Century Workplace

Employee Wellness

A healthy workforce is good for business. Employee absenteeism due to sickness costs companies billions of dollars in lost productivity each year. Healthy employees take fewer sick days, live longer, and cost less to insure than employees with poor health. For these reasons, business has embraced the idea of employee wellness.

Many companies now encourage employees to develop healthy habits by stocking vending machines with healthy snacks and offering company-sponsored walks and yoga classes. Some even provide on-site gyms or offer gym memberships as a benefit. Businesses are also redesigning the workplace to prevent muscle fatigue and unnecessary risk. Some new company headquarters are designed to encourage workers to walk between meetings. Seasonal offerings may include flu shots and advice about weather changes or allergies.

In addition to increasing productivity, company wellness programs build company loyalty and make the company attractive to new employees.

CRITICAL THINKING
How can companies encourage employees to take part in wellness programs?

In Your Community
Research local resources for developing a healthier lifestyle. As a class, classify these resources under categories such as nutrition, stress management, and exercise, and compile them in a single directory.

 Extend Your Learning Wellness can also be practiced at school and at home. For links related to wellness, go to this book's OLC through **glencoe.com**.

The 21st Century Workplace

CRITICAL THINKING ANSWER Companies can encourage employees to participate in wellness programs by sending e-mails and putting up posters around the office that illustrate the benefits of taking advantage of such programs.

In Your Community Resources for nutrition would include health food stores and vitamin stores; resources for stress management would include yoga studios; and exercise resources would include gyms and fitness centers.

Education and Training

Careers demand different kinds and levels of education and training. You may need a two-year associate degree, a four-year bachelor's degree, or a technical or business school license or certificate. As you research, note how much time, money, and effort it will take to attain the necessary education and training for various careers.

Look at the different levels of education needed for careers in the same field. If you know you are interested in health care, for example, what education and training do you need to become a physician's assistant or a physician?

Your high school classes can provide you with certain skills or background information that will start you on your career path. As you discover the education and training requirements of different careers, look at the courses offered at your school. Which ones would help you as you plan for your future career?

Salary and Benefits

Occupational directories and Internet salary sites often include general information on what jobs pay. They list an hourly rate or a weekly or annual salary, as well as salary ranges based on national averages.

Of course, many company employees receive more than their paychecks. **Benefits** are employment extras, which may include health insurance, paid vacation and holiday time, and retirement plans. Other benefits may include regular bonuses, product or service discounts, low-interest loans, or gym memberships. Many employees feel benefits are necessary as they experience changes in their lives. Family members often rely on personal days to take care of an ill family member. Employees often rely on paid vacation to spend time with family, reconnect with friends, or simply have time for themselves.

Salaries and benefits can vary depending on the field you are in, your position, and your level of education. Compare the salaries of three careers you are interested in and the kind of training or education you would need to be competitive in those careers. Knowing your **potential** salary and what you have to do to prepare yourself will help you plan for your financial future.

✓ Reading Check **ANALYZE** How can knowing job salaries affect your career decision?

Career Outlook

What will careers in the industry or career area you are interested in be like in ten years? Many of the research materials described in Section 3.1 can tell you about industry prospects and help you make career decisions. **Figure 3.2** on page 72 shows the career outlook for those careers requiring at least a bachelor's degree.

As You Read

Explain Why should you consider levels of training needed for a career?

Career ✓ Checklist

To Identify a Career Path:

✓ Imagine yourself in a variety of different careers.

✓ Be realistic about job requirements and skills.

✓ Have confidence in your own abilities.

✓ Research careers that require a lot of education or training.

✓ Base career decisions on your interests.

As You Read

You should know what kinds of training you need in order to plan your education and to stay competitive with other people in your field.

Section 3.2

TEACH (cont.)

C Critical Thinking
Conducting Research Have students choose a career in which they are interested and research the education requirements for the career. Encourage students to research online or at the library to determine whether the careers they choose require a high school diploma, an associate degree, a bachelor's degree, or a business school certificate or license. (Answers will vary depending on the career chosen.)

S Skill Practice
Guided Practice
Calculate Ramon is considering two jobs. The first pays $22,500 per year plus a health benefits package worth $95 per month. The second pays $22,200 per year plus a health benefits package of $115 a month. Which job has a higher total yearly value? (first job: $22,500 + ($95 × 12) = $23,640; second job: $22,200 + ($115 × 12) = $23,580)

✓ Reading Check

ANALYZE Knowing salaries will help you determine which jobs will pay enough to meet your lifestyle goals.

ASSESS

Review Key Terms
Have students write sentences using the key terms they have read so far in the text.

Online Study Tools
Have students go to the OLC through **glencoe.com** to:

• Download **Podcast** study tools.

• Download free **Study-to-Go** content to their PDAs or cell phones.

71

RETEACH

C Critical Thinking

Career Outlook Give students this scenario: Suppose you decide to become an elementary school teacher. After four years of college, you discover that the outlook for this career is not promising because your local area is small and few teaching jobs become available. What could you have done before deciding on this career? What compromises might you have to make now? (Possible answers include researching the local market for openings and also learning about the jobs that are available in the area. Compromises might include taking a non-teaching job for a while or moving to an area where a teaching job is available.)

Resources

📂 **Student Activity Workbook** Assign the Chapter 3 activities in the Student Activity Workbook.

ASSESS

After You Read

Have students complete the Section 3.2 After You Read section review.

Online Study Tools

Have students go to the OLC through **glencoe.com** to:

- Take the Section 3.2 **Practice Test.**
- Download **Podcast** study tools.
- Download free **Study-to-Go** content to their PDAs or cell phones.

Knowing whether the demand for workers in your chosen career area is growing or declining will help you make wise career choices. Knowing where that growth or **decline** is occurring may affect where you choose to live. If demand for architects is falling, will you look for a similar career, such as construction, that is expected to grow? Or will you concentrate on gaining more educational and work experience to become more competitive? If the demand for health-care workers rises, will salaries rise as well?

Kathy Silno's research helped her. Kathy liked to work with machines, and she considered a career in manufacturing. Her research, however, pointed to an upcoming increase in service jobs. Kathy decided on automotive repair and found a service job with a good future.

International Career Outlook

With the growth in the global economy and the availability of communication technology, more and more of today's careers involve working internationally. Brainstorm with your friends and family. Do they know someone who has lived worked in one or more different countries? Do they know someone who has traveled to another country for work? Do they know someone whose career involves working with people other countries? Pool your responses with those of other students and make a list of international career

Figure 3.2 **TOP TEN JOBS REQUIRING A BACHELOR'S DEGREE OR HIGHER**

Occupation	Average Annual Openings
❖ Postsecondary teachers	52,400
❖ General and operations managers	30,800
❖ Elementary school teachers, except special education	26,500
❖ Accountants and auditors	26,400
❖ Computer software engineers, applications	22,200
❖ Computer systems analysts	15,300
❖ Secondary school teachers, except vocational education	14,800
❖ Computer software engineers, systems software	14,600
❖ Physicians and surgeons	13,600
❖ Network systems and data communications analysts	12,600

JOB OPPORTUNITIES This chart displays the ten careers that are projected to have the most job openings in the near future. *Why do you think the job outlook is favorable for these careers?*

EXTEND THE FIGURE **Figure 3.2**

Caption Answer Students may answer that the numbers of jobs increase when there is an increasing demand for certain kinds of work. For example, because of our increasing use of technology, there will be a growing need for computer systems analysts.

Discussion Ask students how many of them are interested in the jobs above. Ask if their interest is affected by the average annual openings. Would they reconsider if openings were comparatively low? Have students explain their answers.

possibilities, such as an English teacher, a civil engineer, or a health-care worker. You can find plenty of information about international careers by using library and Internet resources. Good communication skills and excellent interpersonal skills, such as the ability to get along with many types of different people, are valuable qualities for a person who wishes to work internationally. Are you interested in an international career? If so, what kind of experience do you think would you need to pursue these careers?

GLOBAL OPPORTUNITIES
In today's global economy, many jobs are available in other countries. *What do you think would be the advantages and disadvantages of working in another country?*

Section 3.2 After You Read

Review Key Concepts

1. Develop two questions that would help you decide if a career is right for you.
2. List the ten characteristics of a career profile and enumerate them in order of their importance to you, with the first (1) being the most important.
3. Name one thing you can do now to help prepare yourself for a career that interests you.

Practice Academic Skills

 Mathematics

4. Hyung-Jin did an analysis of starting salaries of elementary school teachers in his area. He called three schools and was quoted the following salaries: $28,300, $27,000, and $23,000. What is the average salary in his area?

CONCEPT **Measures of Central Tendency** The mean, median, and mode are all measures of central tendency because they provide a summary of numerical data in one number. The mean is the same as the average.
Step 1: To find the mean, first add all of the values ($28,300, $27,000, and $23,000) together.
Step 2: Divide the total of the values by the number of values in the set of data (3).

Math For math help, go to the Math Appendix located at the back of this book.

Chapter 3   Researching Careers   **73**
Royalty-free/Age FotoStock

Section 3.2 After You Read

Review Key Concepts

1. Answers may vary. Responses may include: whether you are working indoors or outdoors, the number of hours and time of day that you would be working, whether you are working with people or on your own.
2. Lists will vary depending on the student's ideas and expectations for their career and lifestyle.

3. Students might mention developing key questions to ask about jobs that interest them; identifying characteristics used to develop a career profile; and determining the education and training needed for different careers.

Practice Academic Skills

4. The average salary is $26,100 (28,300 + $27,000 + $23,000 = $78,300; $78,300 ÷ 3 = $26,100).

 ASSESS *(cont.)*

Resources

ExamView Assessment Suite CD allows you to print out ready-made unit and chapter tests complete with answer keys. You can also create customized tests.

CLOSE

Culminating Activity

Values and Careers Tell students to think of a career that would be unsuitable to them because of their personal values. Have them write a 250-word paragraph explaining what about the career conflicts with their values. (Paragraphs will vary but should provide specific reasons why the career would not be suitable.)

Extend the Photo

Caption Answer Advantages might include adventure, advancement, and a good salary; disadvantages might include living far from loved ones and needing to learn a new language quickly.

Discussion Ask students to name U.S. companies in other countries that might be a source of a job abroad. (Examples include McDonald's, KFC, Coca-Cola, and the Disney Company.)

NCLB Activity correlated to Mathematics standards.

CAREER SPOTLIGHT

Career Cluster: Health Science

FOCUS

Discussion Starter

Health Science Lead a discussion about the various types of careers that can be found in this career cluster. Have students brainstorm various careers and jobs within the career cluster. (Answers will vary but students should show an understanding of the many types of careers that fall within the career cluster.)

TEACH

W Writing Support
Independent Practice

Use Research Materials A clinical research associate needs to know Food and Drug Administration regulations. Have students visit the FDA's Web site and write a 250-word paragraph that explains which types of products the FDA regulates. (Answers include food, drugs, medical devices, biologics (vaccines), cosmetics, radiation-emitting products, and combination products.)

C Critical Thinking

Stay Organized A clinical research associate needs to be organized in order to keep up with multiple medical studies. Brainstorm with students on methods of maintaining efficient organization. (Organizational methods include keeping a calendar, date book, or online scheduler, keeping a tidy workstation, and responding promptly to e-mails and phone calls.)

**Michael Shah
Clinical Research Associate**

Q: Describe your job.
A: Before a pharmaceutical company can sell a new medication, it has to do extensive testing on patients to make sure that it works and that there are not any harmful side effects. My job is to go to different hospitals and doctors' offices that are recruiting these patients and to make sure the studies are being performed according to the clinical trial protocol and the Food and Drug Administration (FDA) requirements.

Q: Describe a typical workday.
A: It varies. Some days I work from my home; I have a home office. Other days I have to get up early and travel to a hospital or doctor's office in another city, state, or country. When I am at the hospital or doctor's office, I spend the day reviewing the subjects' medical records and the doctor's notes.

Q: What skills are most important to you in your job?
A: To do this job well, you have to be detail-oriented, have a good memory, and be organized. Since you could be working on a diabetes study one day and an asthma study the next day, you have to be able to juggle your thinking between several studies.

Q: What academic skills and lifelong learning skills are helpful in preparing for your career?
A: Most people in the development of clinical trials have a background in medicine or science. My background is in chemistry and biology. You also have to learn to be organized and to be able to meet timelines that are given to you.

Q: What is your key to success?
A: Always be professional and do the best work that you can do. The

pharmaceutical industry is not that big, especially when it comes to clinical trials, so people remember when you do a good job. I am self-employed and depend on referrals for additional business.

Q: What are some disadvantages to your career?
A: The job requires travel and sometimes you have to be away from your home and family. Sometimes I am away for an entire week.

Q: What training and preparation do you recommend for students?
A: This position requires a four-year bachelor's degree in a science such as chemistry, biology, or nursing.

Q: What are some ways you recommend students prepare for this career?
A: Working or interning at a doctor's office where they do clinical studies. That way you can see what it is like and have some exposure to it.

Q: What do you like most about your work?
A: I currently am self-employed and therefore can set my own schedule. I take time off when I want to. There is also a lot of demand for clinical research associates, and that results in good pay. It feels good knowing that I am helping in getting new medications approved and that these medications are helping ill people.

 For more about Career Clusters, go to this book's OLC through **glencoe.com**.

NO CHILD LEFT BEHIND

Teaching Tip

The goals of the NCLB Act include a strong emphasis on writing skills. When you incorporate writing activities in your classroom, students will improve their skills in gathering information and organizing their thoughts on paper. For example, the Writing Support activity on this page encourages students to conduct basic research and summarize their findings in a brief paragraph.

Sample Question Based on the interview above and the career facts on the next page, what are the education and training requirements for a clinical research assistant? Write your answer in a short paragraph. (Answer: This position requires a four-year bachelor's degree in chemistry, biology, or nursing, as well as lab experience and an internship in a doctor's office.)

- **Education or Training** A bachelor's degree in a science such as chemistry, biology, or nursing. Laboratory experience is helpful.

- **Academic Skills Required** English Language Arts, Mathematics, Science, Social Studies

- **Technology Needed** Home office material, including computer and fax machine, as well as mobile technology for working on the road.

- **Aptitudes, Abilities, and Skills** Attention to detail is essential, because small differences or changes in test substances or numerical readouts can be crucial for patient care. A self-employed associate should possess strong business and communication skills and be familiar with regulatory issues and marketing and management techniques.

Workplace Safety Medical offices may contain hazardous materials as well as patients with various diseases. Travel hazards may occur in jobs which require a large amount of travel.

Career Outlook Employment in clinical research is projected to grow about as fast as average for all occupations over the next ten years, as biotechnological research and development continues to drive job growth. Expected expansion of research related to health issues such as HIV, cancer, and Alzheimer's disease also should create more jobs.

Career Path Clinical research associates may work for themselves or find employment with a pharmaceutical business or the government.

Academic Skills Required to Complete Tasks

Tasks	English Language Arts	Mathematics	Science	Social Studies
Assemble and run home office		★		
Accounting and maintaining business records	★	★		
Customer service	★			★
Prepare travel itinerary	★	★		
Analyze doctor's notes		★	★	
Prepare reports	★	★	★	★
Get referrals for jobs	★			★

NCLB

Critical Thinking

Why would a doctor allow a clinical research associate to go through his or her confidential paperwork?

NCLB This chart relates academic skills, such as English Language Arts, Mathematics, Science, Social Studies, and World Languages to specific tasks that are performed for the job featured in the Career Spotlight feature.

Critical Thinking

A doctor would most likely be confident that a clinical research associate would have the science skills needed to read and understand the paperwork.

CAREER SPOTLIGHT

ASSESS

Make Connections

Ask students to research career opportunities in the local area, using the Internet, library, newspaper, and any other resources available. Encourage them also to research the career outlook for clinical research in the area, and predict whether a career in clinical research would be available to them locally if they received the necessary training. Have students write a 250-word paragraph with their findings. (Reports should reflect research in the field of clinical research.)

CLOSE

Culminating Activity

Lifelong Learning and Career Clusters In addition to a four-year bachelor's degree in a science, a career in clinical research also requires academic skills to perform tasks such as providing customer service and running a home office. Ask students to brainstorm ways they can develop the academic skills needed to perform the tasks in the table on this page. (Students might mention that a part-time job in a retail store would help them develop the English Language Arts skills necessary to provide customer service.)

Key Terms and Academic Vocabulary Review

1. Students should write complete sentences using each term correctly.

Review Key Concepts

2. Informal methods of research include talking to people, observing your environment, and using media resources. Formal methods of research include conducting formal interviews, using library resources or the Internet to gather information, or contacting professional organizations for information. Informal research is used to generate ideas while formal research is fully and carefully developed using credible sources and formally presented through multimedia presentations, written reports, or speeches.

3. A primary source is an original source that you have observed or spoken to personally. A secondary source contains information that has been collected and/or analyzed by other people.

4. Part-time or temporary work may give you an idea of what a particular job might be like, help you discover what employers want, and help you develop particular skills.

5. Answers may include questions regarding salary, educational or work experience, job tasks, personal traits or characteristics, on-the-job training opportunities, etc.

6. A career profile includes values (what you find important), tasks and responsibilities (what you will have to do on a daily basis at a job), working with data, people or things (what you will be working with), work environment (what your workplace will be like), work hours

CHAPTER SUMMARY

Section 3.1

The U.S. Department of Education's 16 career clusters can help you explore careers. You can use primary and secondary sources to research careers. Informal career research can include observing the world around you and talking to people. Formal research can include libraries, print and Internet resources, exploratory interviews, and also work experience, which includes temp work, cooperative programs, job shadowing, volunteering, internships, and community service.

Section 3.2

Determining what you need to know about a career will make your research more productive and help you make good career decisions. Start by researching and defining a career in terms of characteristics such as values, tasks and responsibilities, work environment, and education and training required. Then compare the characteristics of the career with your own expectations to determine if the career is right for you. Awareness of different career outlooks can help you plan for the future.

Key Terms and Academic Vocabulary Review

1. Use each of these key terms and academic vocabulary words in a sentence.

Key Terms
- career clusters (p. 59)
- exploratory interview (p. 63)
- temp work (p. 65)
- cooperative program (p. 65)
- job shadowing (p. 65)

- internship (p. 66)
- service learning (p. 66)
- work environment (p. 69)
- flextime (p. 69)
- career pathways (p. 70)
- benefits (p. 71)

Academic Vocabulary
- source (p. 59)
- index (p. 62)
- visualize (p. 69)
- potential (p. 71)
- decline (p. 72)

Review Key Concepts

2. Describe formal and informal methods of researching careers.
3. Evaluate a primary and a secondary source of information.
4. Explain how part-time work or temporary work can help you explore career choices.
5. List key questions you would ask in researching careers.
6. Define the characteristics of a career profile, giving examples of each.
7. Describe the education and training needed for a career that interests you.

Critical Thinking

8. Analyze What are some advantages of doing formal career research?
9. Predict How might work experience in a foreign country help you in your career if you chose to return to work in the United States?

(what time of the day and days of the week you will work), aptitudes and abilities (what you are good at), education and training (what you will need to show you have learned in a formal program), salary and benefits (how you will be compensated), career outlook (what will happen in your field in the next ten years or so), international career outlook (what will happen in your field internationally in the next ten years or so). Examples will vary.

7. Answers will vary but students should understand the educational requirements of the careers they choose.

Critical Thinking

8. Answers may include collecting credible information that will help you make informed decisions about a career, discovering career options that you had not thought of before.

Real-World Skills and Applications

Time-Management Skills

10. Prioritizing Your Activities Imagine that you have the opportunity to intern with a company that interests you. The program will give you valuable experience in your chosen career. However, you also have a part-time job, which pays for going out to the movies on the weekends, and you are on the swim team. Evaluate each of your current activities. Why is each important to you? Estimate how many hours per week you would need to devote to each activity. If you had to give up an activity, which would you choose and why? Summarize your answers in a few written paragraphs.

Technology Applications

11. Self-Management Contact your counselor or your school information office and get a copy of your transcript. Compare the courses you have taken and the credits you have earned to your high school's graduation requirements and course listings. Determine which courses you need to take to fulfill graduation requirements and which courses would help you as you prepare for your career. Use a spreadsheet to create a chart showing the courses you have successfully completed and the courses you would like to take to fulfill graduation requirements and prepare for your future.

Information Literacy Skills

12. Comparing Sources Compare two secondary sources of career information, one print and one online. Prepare a three-minute presentation for your classmates describing the kind of information available in the sources. In your presentation, describe how easy the source was to use, what questions the source helped you answer, and whether you would recommend the source and why.

13.   **Arrange a Job-Shadowing Experience** Find someone who will agree to allow you to job shadow. Make notes on the career in terms of the ten characteristics listed on page 68. Find Web sites that are related to this career and research the same ten characteristics. Compare this information to the notes that you have from your job shadowing experience. Report your findings to your class.

14. **Exploratory Interview**

Situation You are to assume the role of a real estate agent from a large city. A student from a local high school has asked you to visit his classroom to discuss your career. He is hoping that an exploratory interview will give him a better idea of what is involved in a career in real estate.

Activity Your task is to research a career as a real estate agent, paying particular attention to the ten characteristics listed on page 68. You must be prepared to answer questions that might be asked in an exploratory interview.

Evaluation You will be evaluated on how well you meet the following performance indicators:

- Explain the nature of the work.
- Address the necessary skills and education or training.
- Give an overview of realistic expectations in this career.

Chapter 3 Researching Careers **77**

---

12. Answers will vary. Presentations should include clear points about the sources that classmates can write down and where the source can be found.

ACTIVE LEARNING

13. Answers will depend on the person whose job is shadowed, but students should demonstrate an understanding of how the ten characteristics can be applied to the job. Students should also be able to make effective comparisons between career information found on the Internet and the person whose job is shadowed.

ROLE PLAY

14. Effective presenters should demonstrate their research findings about a career in real estate. They should be able to determine which of the characteristics on page 68 apply to this career. Students should be also able to respond to questions about the skills and education or training required for a career in real estate.

---

9. Possible answers: Having learned to adapt to new situations, been exposed to other cultures and ways of doing things, developed contacts in other countries, or even having learned a new language would show that you are willing to try new things and are able to deal with new situations. Many employers want people who are problem solvers and are willing to jump into new situations and make them work.

Real-World Skills and Applications

10. Answers will vary. Use the activity to illustrate how every experience can contribute to work-readiness.

11. Spreadsheets should accurately show courses taken and courses students plan to take.

Academic Skills in the Workplace

15. Answers will vary. Students should concentrate on gathering accurate information and formatting the information into bibliographic entries. The three entries should be correctly alphabetized by the author's last name.

16. Answers may vary but should resemble the example below:

Salaries of Three Frontier Company Employees

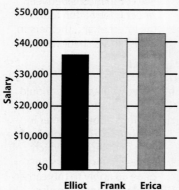

17. Visual aids should show how the four organisms they chose relate on the food chain. An example might show a shark eating a trout, which in turn has eaten a minnow that feeds on algae.

Academic Skills in the Workplace

 English Language Arts

15. Create a Bibliography A bibliography credits your sources and can help you find them again if necessary. Choose three sources and record the following information for each. Write down (1) the author(s) first and last name or the name of the group that compiled the information; (2) the title of the book or article; (3) the title of the publication; (4) the name and location of the publisher; (5) the date the information was published or posted; (6) the pages where you found the information; (7) the date you found the information; (8) and the URL. Alphabetize the information by the authors' last names.

 Mathematics

16. Compare Salaries Three Frontier Company employees each make between $35,000 and $45,000 a year. Frank makes more than Elliot, but less than Erica. Draw a hypothetical bar graph of what their salaries could be.

CONCEPT Representing Data in a Graph A bar graph represents data using shaded bars to show each value. The graph's axes should always be labeled, and the graph should have a title and a legend stating what the different shades represent.

Starting Hint Be sure to give the graph labeled axes and a title.

 Science

17. Interdependence of Organisms A network is like an ecosystem. An ecosystem is made up of biological organisms interacting with one another and with their environment. A food chain is one collection of relationships between organisms that shows the transfer of energy between them in an ecosystem—in other words, who eats whom. For instance, at the bottom of one food chain might be plants like algae, which harvest energy from the sun to make their own food. Organisms such as shrimp may eat the algae for energy, and larger organisms like fish may then eat the shrimp. A food web is made up of all the different possible transfers of energy within an ecosystem. Create a visual aid that shows the relationship between at least four organisms in an ecosystem.

STANDARDIZED TEST PRACTICE

MULTIPLE CHOICE

Directions Read the following question. Then read the answer choices and choose the best possible answer.

> **Test-Taking Tip** In a multiple choice test, be sure to read the directions to see if you need to look for the *best* answer or the *correct* answer. If you are looking for the best answer, there may be more than one correct answer to choose from.

1. According to this chapter, what is the best way to find out what a day in a particular career would be like?
 a. Read a description of the career, its tasks, and educational requirements in *The Occupational Outlook Handbook*.
 b. Talk to your friends.
 c. Read the job listings in your local paper.
 d. Shadow a person working in that field for a week.

For more Standardized Test Practice, go to the OLC @ glencoe.com.

STANDARDIZED TEST PRACTICE

Answer
1. d. Shadow a person working in that field for a week.

Test-Taking Strategies
Whether your students have a standardized test coming up in a few days or a few weeks, these last-minute test-prep tips and strategies will help them to relax and do their best.

True/False Questions Read each statement slowly and carefully. If any part of the statement is not accurate, then the entire statement is false. For the statement to be true, every part must be true.

Multiple Choice Questions Read the statement and try to complete it before you look at the choices. If your answer is among the choices, mark it.

Writing Skills Practice

18. Paraphrasing Paraphrasing is restating information in your own words. When you are researching a particular topic, paraphrasing the information you are reading can help you keep track of important points without rewriting or copying entire documents.

 Practice Find the most recent *Occupational Outlook Quarterly* online. Choose an article and follow the directions below to paraphrase a portion of your article.

- Skim the article for overall meaning. Note headings, subheadings, and any figures.
- Read the article carefully. Look up any words that you do not understand and note where you have questions.
- Write your paraphrase. Stick to main ideas and the important points that support those ideas. Do not use every detail; you want to restate the general meaning not the whole article. State each idea as clearly as possible. Be sure to arrange your ideas in a logical way.

Net Connection

19. Research Educational Programs Visit this book's OLC through **glencoe.com** and find the link to the 16 U.S. Department of Education career clusters. Find out what kind of education is required for a career that interests you.

@ **Log On** Go online to research schools that offer programs on your selected career. Choose one school that has a strong program and use software or art materials to prepare a brochure highlighting the career benefits of the program. Add this brochure to your **Personal Academic and Career Portfolio**.

Reading Connection

@ Go to this book's Online Learning Center through **glencoe.com** for a list of reading suggestions.

Personal Academic and Career Portfolio

Career Research Results

It is a good idea to add the information you gathered researching careers to your portfolio. As you develop further questions about jobs and careers, you may want to refer to the sources you discovered in this chapter. You may decide that you are still interested in the same career cluster but wish to consider another job within that career cluster, or your values or needs may change and you may want to find another career that better matches your new goals.

The following guidelines will help you organize and add the results of your research to your portfolio:

- Create a new section for your portfolio, using a divider for hard copy material and a computer folder for electronic files.
- Label the section *Career Research*.
- You may wish to create subsections or subfolders with names such as *Career Clusters* and *Sources of Information*.
- Add the section and subsections to your table of contents.
- Add the following: information about career clusters that interest you, sources of information you found helpful, information you found through those resources, any career interviews, and your career evaluations.
- Update your research results as you continue to explore your career options.

 Portfolio Help Go to the *Succeeding in the World of Work* OLC through **glencoe.com** for help developing your portfolio.

Writing Skills Practice

18. Answers will vary but should reflect the student's ability to understand informational texts, identify main points, and retell information.

Net Connection

19. Students should research and locate specific, accurate information about the training/education programs available for the careers they have chosen. Brochures should be creative, neat, and organized, and they should also offer evidence that students have contemplated the advantages and disadvantages of educational programs relevant to their career interests.

Resources

⊙ ***ExamView Assessment Suite* CD** allows you to print out ready-made unit and chapter tests complete with answer keys. You can also create customized tests.

WorkKeys

WorkKeys® is a job skills assessment program. For information on leveled assessment for Problem-Solving Skills (Applied Mathematics; Applied Technology; Locating Information; and Observation), go to the WorkKeys link on this book's OLC through **glencoe.com**.

Personal Academic and Career Portfolio

Maintaining a Portfolio

As students refine their career options, they may rule out certain jobs and careers that no longer interest them or which will not work for other reasons. Students might be tempted to discard materials with information about these careers.

Encourage students to keep this information for future reference as they might want to refer back to it later. They can create a new section for outdated or otherwise unnecessary materials. The more items students have to choose from, the better their portfolios are likely to be.

Chapter Resources Planning Guide with Activities and Features

Section	Features	Activities
Section 4.1 **What is Entrepreneurship?**	Everyday Ethics (p. 83) Hot Jobs! (p. 85)	Before You Read (p. 82) Graphic Organizer (p. 82) As You Read (pp. 83, 84) After You Read (p. 85)
Section 4.2 **Being a Business Owner**	Creative Business Practices (p. 88) Real-World Connection (p. 90) Math in Action (p. 92) 21st Century Workplace (p. 92) Career Checklist (p. 93)	Before You Read (p. 86) Graphic Organizer (p. 86) As You Read (p. 88) After You Read (p. 93)

NCLB Activities, information, and skills practice will help your students attain No Child Left Behind proficiency. Students will improve their abilities in the following academic standards areas:

Academic Standards Correlations

Discipline	Standard	Feature/Activity
English Language Arts	**NCTE 1** Read texts to acquire new information.	Creative Business Practices (p. 88)
	NCTE 4 Use written language to communicate effectively.	Academic Skills in the Workplace (p. 98) Writing Skills Practice (p. 99)
	NCTE 3 Apply strategies to interpret and evaluate texts.	After You Read (p. 85)
	NCTE 8 Use information resources to gather information and create and communicate knowledge.	Real-World Connection (p. 90)
	NCTE 9 Develop an understanding of diversity in language across cultures.	21st Century Workplace (p. 92)
Mathematics	**Problem Solving:** Solve problems that arise in mathematics and other contexts	Math in Action (p. 92)
	Algebra: Represent and analyze mathematical situations and structures using algebraic symbols	After You Read (p. 93)
	Geometry: Specify locations and describe special relationships using coordinate geometry and other representational systems	Academic Skills in the Workplace (p. 98)
Science	**Life Science:** Matter, energy, and organization in living systems	Academic Skills in the Workplace (p. 98)

21st Century Skills and Workplace Competencies Correlations

CORRELATIONS The charts show the 21st Century Skills, foundation skills, and workplace competencies that students develop as they work in this chapter.

Foundation Skills and Workplace Competencies Correlation Chart

21st Century Skills

Core Subjects
- English
- Reading/Language Arts
- Math

Learning Skills
- Information and Media Literacy
- Communication Skills
- Critical Thinking and Systems Thinking
- Problem Identification, Formulation, and Solution
- Creativity and Intellectual Curiosity
- Interpersonal and Collaborative Skills
- Self-Direction
- Accountability and Adaptability
- Social Responsibility

21st Century Tools
- Communication, Information Processing, and Research Tools
- Problem-Solving Tools
- Personal Development and Productivity Tools

Foundation Skills

Basic Skills
- Reading
- Writing
- Math
- Listening
- Speaking

Thinking Skills
- Creative Thinking
- Decision Making
- Problem Solving
- Seeing Things in the Mind's Eye
- Knowing How to Learn
- Reasoning

Personal Qualities
- Self-Esteem
- Responsibility
- Sociability
- Self-Management
- Integrity/Honesty

Workplace Competencies

Resources
- Allocating Time
- Allocating Money
- Allocating Material and Facility Resources
- Allocating Human Resources

Information
- Acquiring and Evaluating Information
- Organizing and Maintaining Information
- Interpreting and Communicating Information
- Using Computers to Process Information

Interpersonal Skills
- Participating as a Member of a Team
- Teaching Others
- Serving Clients/Customers
- Exercising Leadership
- Negotiating to Arrive at a Decision
- Working with Cultural Diversity

Systems
- Understanding Systems
- Monitoring and Correcting Performance
- Improving and Designing Systems

Technology
- Selecting Technology
- Applying Technology to Task
- Maintaining and Troubleshooting Technology

Yellow blocks indicate areas covered in the chapter

Chapter Overview
Introduce the Chapter
Chapter 4 explores the personal characteristics of entrepreneurs and the elements involved in starting and maintaining a business.

Section 4.1 describes entrepreneurship and highlights the traits entrepreneurs need to be successful.

Section 4.2 looks at different ways to enter business other than starting from scratch.

Build Background
Explain to students that the U.S. has a free enterprise system where people have the right to make their own decisions about what products to buy, whether to own private property, and whether to start a business and compete with other businesses.

▶ *Exploring the Photo*

Caption Answer
Attributes might include ambition, organization, and self-management skills.

Discussion Lead students in a class discussion about why a person might choose to be an entrepreneur.

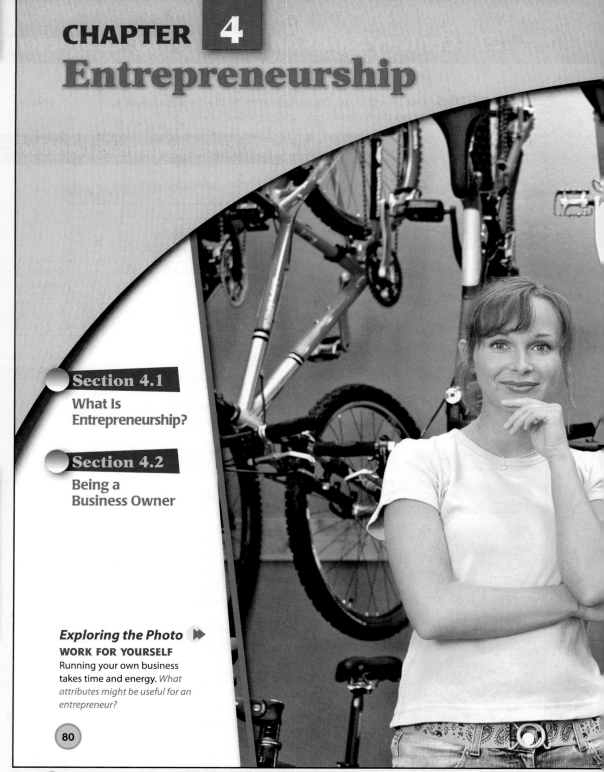

CHAPTER **4**
Entrepreneurship

Section 4.1
What Is Entrepreneurship?

Section 4.2
Being a Business Owner

Exploring the Photo ▶▶
WORK FOR YOURSELF
Running your own business takes time and energy. *What attributes might be useful for an entrepreneur?*

80

Classroom Resources

- Student Edition
- Teacher Wraparound Edition
- Student Activity Workbook with Academic Integration
- Student Activity Workbook with Academic Integration TAE
- *Fast File,* Unit 2 Resources

- Inclusion in the Career Education Classroom
- TeacherWorks™ Plus
- *ExamView Assessment Suite*
- Interactive Chalkboard
- Interactive Student Edition
- Online Student Edition
- Online Learning Center (OLC) with Podcasts

Chapter Objectives

After completing this chapter, you will be able to:

- **Define** *entrepreneur* and name the traits that most successful entrepreneurs share.
- **Summarize** the advantages and disadvantages of entrepreneurship.
- **Identify** the four main ways to become a business owner and explain the advantages and disadvantages of each.
- **Identify** the different forms of legal business ownership.
- **Explain** how to prepare to finance a new business.
- **Identify** factors that can affect business success.

Writing Activity — Personal Career Notebook

Entrepreneurship is an exciting and challenging undertaking—but it is not for everyone. How well does entrepreneurship fit your values, interests, and abilities? In a one-page journal entry, list the skills and personality traits you think an entrepreneur should have. Add to this list as you read the chapter.

Get Motivated! Think of a business you would like to open. Research the skills and experience you would need. Create a chart listing those skills and types of experiences. Next to each, indicate whether it is a skill or type of experience you already have or one you need.

Chapter 4   Entrepreneurship   **81**

Writing Activity — Personal Career Notebook Answer Guide

Journal entries should reflect students' thoughts about entrepreneurship and the skills and traits they think are necessary to start a business.

Get Motivated! Charts will vary. Encourage students to think of skills related to opening a business as well as those skills related to a particular type of business. For instance, students may be interested in opening a skate shop because they are interested in and know about skateboarding. Remind students that opening a business requires more than experience with the product or service; it also requires solid business and entrepreneurial skills.

Section 4.1 Objectives
Define *entrepreneur* and name the traits that most successful entrepreneurs share. (An entrepreneur is a person who organizes and then runs a business. Most successful entrepreneurs have motivation, sight and foresight, and good decision-making skills.)

Summarize the advantages and disadvantages of entrepreneurship. (Advantages of an entrepreneurship are that you are in charge; there is great job satisfaction; and entrepreneurship can lead to good income. Disadvantages are the financial risk; entrepreneurs work long hours; competition can be difficult to overcome; and there are no guarantees of success.)

Section 4.2 Objectives
Identify the four main ways to become a business owner and explain the advantages and disadvantages of each. (The four main ways are to start a new business; buy an existing business; buy a franchise; or join a family business.)

Identify the different forms of legal business ownership. (The forms of legal business ownership are sole proprietorship, partnership, and corporation.)

Explain how to prepare to finance a new business. (To apply for a business loan, you must first create a business plan with specific information about your business. You also need a financial plan that spells out your start-up costs, operating expenses, and other costs for the first few months.)

Identify factors that can affect business success. (Factors include location, competition, and management.)

Section 4.1

What Is Entrepreneurship?

What Is Entrepreneurship?

Write this ad on the board: *Business opportunity. Discount store in popular shopping mall. 65K purchase price.* Have students write answers to these questions: Would you buy this business? Why or why not? What else would you want to know about the business? (Student responses should recognize the risks involved in buying a business.)

Reading Guide

Before You Read

Preview Look at the photo in this section and read its caption. Write one or two sentences predicting what the section will be about.

Read to Learn
- What *entrepreneur* means and the traits that most successful entrepreneurs share
- What the advantages and disadvantages of entrepreneurship are

Main Idea

D Gaining knowledge about entrepreneurship and its advantages and disadvantages will help you decide if this is a good career option for you.

Key Concept
- What Is an Entrepreneur?

Key Term
◇ entrepreneur

Academic Vocabulary

You will find these words in your reading and on your tests. Use the academic vocabulary glossary to look up their definitions if necessary.
- enterprise
- trait

Graphic Organizer

As you read, list the advantages and disadvantages of entrepreneurship. Use a two-column chart like the one shown to help organize your information.

ENTREPRENEURSHIP	
Advantages	**Disadvantages**

 Log On Go to this book's Online Learning Center through **glencoe.com** for an online version of this graphic organizer.

Academic Standards •

English Language Arts
- Apply strategies to interpret and evaluate texts. (NCTE 3)
- Use different writing process elements to communicate effectively. (NCTE 5)

Resources

🔵 Interactive Chalkboard
The Interactive Chalkboard CD provides visual teaching aids for this section.

@ Online Learning Center
The Online Learning Center (OLC) through **glencoe.com** features chapter vocabulary, chapter summaries, and other study materials.

Preteaching
Ask students to predict the meaning of the word *entrepreneur*. Tell students they can check their prediction as they read the section.

Graphic Organizer
Tell students to go to the OLC through **glencoe.com** for a printable graphic organizer. (Organizers should list the advantages and disadvantages of entrepreneurship.)

NCLB NCLB connects academic correlations to book content.

Reading Guide

Before You Read
Point out to students that entrepreneurship can mean more than just opening a store that sells goods. Entrepreneurs can also start businesses that provide services such as dry cleaning, catering, or event planning.

D Develop Concepts
Main Idea Discuss the main idea with students. Ask: Why is gaining knowledge about entrepreneurship helpful when researching careers? (Students should recognize that entrepreneurship is an option when deciding on a career.)

What Is an Entrepreneur?

Think of the businesses you know. You may have a favorite ice cream shop, video store, or music store. Who makes the shoes you wear and the backpack you use to carry your books? Have you ever thought about who started those businesses?

Chances are that each of those businesses was started as a small business with a handful of employees, or maybe just one or two. Small businesses, usually those with fewer than 500 employees, represent more than 99 percent of American businesses. They employ more than 50 percent of the nonmilitary workforce. A person who organizes and then runs a business is called an **entrepreneur**.

An entrepreneur's life is challenging. Planning a new business **enterprise** and then working to make it succeed is not easy. Entrepreneurs must make good decisions and find inventive solutions to their problems. The risks are high, but if the business succeeds the rewards can be great.

Does this challenge appeal to you? Are you willing to take on the risks of starting a new business? Then maybe your career path leads to entrepreneurship.

Advantages of Entrepreneurship

If you think entrepreneurship would demand a great deal from you, you are right. Why take on the challenge? What are the advantages?
- You are in charge. Entrepreneurs decide when and how hard to work and how their businesses will operate.
- There is great job satisfaction.
- Entrepreneurship can lead to a good income.

Vocabulary
You can find definitions in the **Key Terms** glossary and **Academic Vocabulary** glossary at the back of this book.

As You Read
Summarize What are the advantages of entrepreneurship?

Everyday ETHICS

COMPETING FAIRLY

Is it fair to compete with a former employer?
GOING OUT ON YOUR OWN You have been the assistant manager of a coffee house for the past five years and have made friends with many of the customers. You are thinking about opening up a coffee house of your own. There is an ideal space available in a shopping center around the corner from your current place of work, and you think many of the customers that you have befriended would follow you there.

What Would You Do? Is it fair to open up a shop in direct competition with your current employer? Why or why not?

DISCUSS IT Business owners must deal with competition, but they might not think it is fair for a former employee to compete with them. Do you think it is fair? How can you open your own business but stay on good terms with your past employer? Share your response with the class.

TEACH

Discussion Starter
What Is an Entrepreneur? Ask students whether the idea of working on their own appeals to them. Use this question to lead into a discussion of the advantages and disadvantages of being an entrepreneur.

R Reading Strategy
Conduct a Survey Have students conduct an informal survey of businesses at a local mall and write a brief report of their findings. Students should count the number owned by corporations (such as department store chains) and the number owned and operated by independent entrepreneurs. Have students create a graph or spreadsheet summarizing their findings. (Graphs and spreadsheets should reflect an understanding of businesses owned by corporations and those owned by entrepreneurs.)

As You Read
The advantages of entrepreneurship are being in charge; great job satisfaction; and the possibility of good income.

Resources

TeacherWorks™ Plus The TeacherWorks software includes customizable built-in lesson plans and links to printable program resources.

Everyday ETHICS

What Would You Do? Answer Students should be aware that while this may be a common business practice, it disregards certain values such as integrity, honor, and fairness. Other responses may state that this type of competition is fair as long as all actions are done openly.

DISCUSS IT Suggestions might include opening a business that offers a different service or proposing to enter into a partnership with the owner of the coffee house.

Review Key Terms
Have students write sentences using each key term.

Online Study Tools
Have students go to the OLC through **glencoe.com** to:
- Download **Podcast** study tools.
- Download free **Study-to-Go** content to their PDAs or cell phones.

Resources

ExamView Assessment Suite CD allows you to print out ready-made unit and chapter tests complete with answer keys. You can also create customized tests.

RETEACH

S Skill Practice

Independent Practice

Predict Have students write their own two-page autobiographies as entrepreneurs from the perspective of ten years in the future. Have them include the type of business they started, how successful it has been, and future plans. (Answers will vary but students should explain what traits and skills they will have used to run a successful business.)

As You Read
Answers should reflect an understanding of entrepreneurs.

▶▶ **HEAVY WORKLOAD**
New business owners often work seven days a week.
Why do many entrepreneurs work long hours?

As You Read
Connect Can you name any entrepreneurs in your community?

Disadvantages of Entrepreneurship

While entrepreneurship can be exciting and rewarding, there are also potential drawbacks:
- There is financial risk. You can lose your investment and sometimes more.
- Entrepreneurs often work long hours.
- Competition can be difficult to overcome.
- There are no guarantees of success. Almost half of new businesses fail within their first four years.

Traits of Entrepreneurs

Most successful entrepreneurs have the following personality traits. Do you share these traits?

Motivation

Entrepreneurs have the **trait** of self-motivation. They know what they want and believe in their ability to achieve it. They stay motivated by setting short- and long-term goals. Then they plan how to achieve those goals.

Sight and Foresight

Entrepreneurs are perceptive. They see opportunities where others do not. They look at problems and see opportunities.

Take Thuy Nguyen, for example. When he was 17, Thuy noticed that large companies used logos to promote their products, but small companies did not. He thought logos would help small companies

---

 Extend the Photo

Caption Answer Entrepreneurs often work long hours because they are ultimately responsible for getting all of the work done to ensure the success of their businesses.

Discussion Ask students what skills an entrepreneur would need to hire and manage employees. (management skills, organizational skills, interpersonal skills, and time-management skills.)

too. So he started a business creating logos for small companies. Eventually, his business succeeded. Thuy felt proud, not only because he had succeeded, but because he had helped his clients too.

Seeing opportunities is part of the process of starting a new business. Once an entrepreneur sees a need, he or she must research it, evaluate the risks and rewards, and decide whether to accept the challenge and start a business.

As a college student, Karin thought she could make extra money by selling digital podcasts of class lectures to other students. She researched the idea by talking with other people who had started campus businesses and with students who might use the service. They thought it was a great idea, so she decided to go for it. She took out a loan to buy equipment. Then she began recording class lectures and selling the podcasts. Before she knew it, she had enough money to pay her living expenses. Her research did not end when the business started, though. Like all successful entrepreneurs, she continued to follow business trends and talk to her customers to evaluate their needs.

Decision Making

Entrepreneurs are decisive. They make business decisions every day, and the decisions must be good ones. Refer back to Section 2.1 in Chapter 2 of this book for a review of the decision-making process.

HOT JOBS!

Brand Manager

Companies and their advertising agencies employ brand managers to create, implement, enforce, and maintain the "brand"—a collection of standards and marketing plans designed to promote their products. For example, the Nike® "brand" might be represented by particular images, colors, and words. A brand manager needs good business and communication skills and the ability to analyze market research.

ASSESS

After You Read

Have students complete the Section 4.1 After You Read section review.

Online Study Tools

Have students go to the OLC through **glencoe.com** to:

- Take the Section 4.1 **Practice Test**.
- Download **Podcast** study tools.
- Download free **Study-to-Go** content to their PDAs or cell phones.

Resources

📁 **Student Activity Workbook** Assign the Chapter 4 activities in the Student Activity Workbook.

CLOSE

Culminating Activity

Cooperative Learning
Divide your class into teams of three to four students and tell them to imagine they are forming business partnerships. Have each partnership decide on a type of business, a location, and the start-up costs they might incur. Ask them to put this information in an outline that could be used to create a business plan. Have groups present their outlines to the class. (Business plan outlines should include the type of business, location, and estimated start-up costs.)

NCLB Activity correlated to English Language Arts standards.

Section 4.1 After You Read

Review Key Concepts

1. Name one trait common to most entrepreneurs. Explain why you think that trait helps people begin and run successful businesses.
2. Choose one disadvantage of entrepreneurship. Explain how you might overcome that disadvantage if you ran your own business.
3. Does entrepreneurship appeal to you? Explain why or why not.

Practice Academic Skills

🌐 **English Language Arts**

4. Identify your talents, skills, and abilities. How would they help you deal with the challenges of entrepreneurship? How do they compare with the traits of entrepreneurs listed in this section? Write your answers in a one-page response.
5. Review the challenges involved in one way to enter business. Which challenges do you think you are particularly capable of handling? Which challenges would be more difficult for you to handle? Why? Write your answers in a one-page response.

 Check your answers at this book's OLC through **glencoe.com**.

glencoe.com   **Chapter 4**   Entrepreneurship   **85**

Section 4.1 After You Read

Review Key Concepts

1. Traits common to entrepreneurs include motivation, sight, foresight, and the ability to make effective decisions. Explanations should reflect an understanding of the common traits.
2. Disadvantages might include competition, long hours, financial risk, and no guarantee of success.
3. Possible answer: Entrepreneurship appeals to me because the idea of creating

a business from your own ideas, talents or goals would be really satisfying.

Practice Academic Skills

4. Students should address each question and support their answers with detailed explanations that demonstrate their understanding of entrepreneurial traits.
5. Answers should reflect an understanding of the challenges of entrepreneurship.

Bell Ringer Activity

Being a Business Owner

Tell students to imagine that they have decided to start a business. Ask: Would you prefer to start a business on your own, with one partner, or with several partners? Encourage students to give reasons for their preferences.

Resources

Interactive Chalkboard
The Interactive Chalkboard CD provides visual teaching aids for this section.

Online Learning Center
The OLC through **glencoe.com** features chapter vocabulary, chapter summaries, and other study materials.

Preteaching

Read the definitions of the key terms aloud. As you read each definition, ask students to write a sentence using each key term.

Graphic Organizer

Tell students to go to the OLC through **glencoe.com** for a printable graphic organizer. (Graphic organizers should correctly identify the four ways to go into a business as discussed in this section.)

 NCLB connects academic correlations to book content.

Being a Business Owner

Reading Guide

Before You Read

Preview Choose a Key Concept that is new to you and write it down. When you find it in the text, write one or two sentences explaining the concept.

Read to Learn
- The four main ways to become a business owner and the advantages and disadvantages of each
- The different forms of legal business ownership
- How to prepare to finance a new business
- Factors that can affect business success

D Main Idea
Knowing the factors that affect a business's success will help you to launch a successful business.

Key Concepts
- Going into Business
- Owning a Business
- Operating Your Business

Key Terms
- start-up costs
- lease
- goodwill
- market outlook
- franchise
- sole proprietorship
- partnership
- corporation
- operating expenses
- income statement
- revenue
- gross profit
- net profit

Academic Vocabulary
You will find this word in your reading and on your tests. Use the academic vocabulary glossary to look up its definition if necessary.
- proprietor

Graphic Organizer
As you read, list the four ways to go into business and their advantages and disadvantages. Use a chart like the one shown to organize your information.

Ways to Go into Business	Advantages	Disadvantages
1.		
2.		
3.		
4.		

 Log On Go to this book's Online Learning Center through **glencoe.com** for an online version of this graphic organizer.

Academic Standards • • • • • • • • • • • • • • • • • • •
Mathematics
- Represent and analyze mathematical situations and structures using algebraic symbols
- Apply appropriate techniques, tools, and formulas to determine measurements

Reading Guide

Before You Read
Share this anecdote with students: Paul Orfalea was in college when he borrowed $5,000 to open a copy shop called Kinko's near campus. Today FedEx Kinko's stores are located throughout the country.

D Develop Concepts
Main Idea Discuss with students how entrepreneurs find ideas for businesses. (Possibilities might include looking for services that are not being provided, and thinking about ways to improve people's lives.)

Going into Business

There are four main ways to go into business: start a new business, buy an existing business, buy a franchise, or join a family business.

Starting a New Business

Starting a new business is a dream many people share. It is a chance to work hard and put your business ideas to the test.

Rewards

Building a business from scratch is hard work, but it has many rewards: For example, you do not inherit a previous owner's mistakes or poor reputation. You can develop your own reputation and can build your business your way, using your experiences and the information you have gained from studying other businesses. You also get personal satisfaction from knowing you built the business.

Challenges

No matter how you go into business, you will face challenges. If you start a new business, you will face a few additional challenges: (1) Starting a new business requires more time and effort than buying an established business. (2) Start-up costs are often high. **Start-up costs** are the expenses involved in going into business. Examples include renting or buying space; and buying equipment, office supplies, and insurance. (3) To borrow money, you will have to convince lenders that your business idea is sound. (4) It is risky. There are no guarantees that your business will succeed.

Buying an Existing Business

If you do not want to start a new business, you might buy an existing one. A successful business may be for sale because the owners are retiring or starting a new business. An unsuccessful business might be for sale for many reasons. One reason might be that the business is losing money. Before buying, determine whether the problems of the business can be fixed, and at what cost.

 CHOOSING A BUSINESS Your interests and hobbies can help you choose an entrepreneurial pursuit. *What small businesses might be related to this young man's interest in music?*

TEACH

Discussion Starter

Going into Business Ask students to think of a new business that may have opened recently in the local area. Ask students how the challenges and rewards faced by a new business owner compare to the challenges and rewards faced by someone who chooses to enter a new career field as an employee.

R Reading Strategy

Make a List According to some estimates, 700,000-800,000 new businesses are started each year. Many of these new businesses fail. Ask students to brainstorm ideas to improve the chances of business success. (Answers may include doing research to make sure a market need exists; having enough capital to get through the start-up period; avoiding high expenses; and analyzing the overall economy to make sure the timing for starting a business is right.)

Resources

 Interactive Chalkboard The Interactive Chalkboard CD provides visual teaching aids for this section.

▶ Extend the Photo

Caption Answer Businesses mentioned might include a musical instrument store, an instrument repair service, or a talent agency for musicians. Other answers are possible.

Discussion Ask students who play musical instruments if they have considered a career in music. Would they want to play in a professional band or in a different instrument-related job?

Section 4.2

TEACH (cont.)

U **Universal Access**

Interpersonal and Intrapersonal Learners
Divide students into groups and ask each group what kind of business it could open by pooling its members' skills. Try to see that the groups are balanced, containing both outgoing, interpersonal learners as well as reflective, intrapersonal learners.

C **Critical Thinking**

Connect Have students think about their loyalty to local businesses. Ask what might attract them to or make them think well of particular stores or restaurants. Conversely, ask what would keep them away. (Answers will vary. Students may say that good products, services, and selection might earn some businesses repeat customers, while bad products, services, and selection might keep customers away.)

As You Read

By starting a new business, you do not inherit a previous owner's mistakes or poor reputation. By buying an existing business, you can save on start-up costs and take advantage of the previous owner's business agreements.

As You Read

Compare How do the advantages of starting a new business compare with those of buying an existing business?

Advantages

Buying an existing business can put you several steps ahead. You can save on start-up costs by taking advantage of the previous owner's business agreements, such as a lease signed when prices were lower. A **lease** is a contract to use something for a specified period of time. You may be able to purchase the existing office furniture or equipment.

If the business was successful, you can build on that success. The **goodwill**, or loyalty, of existing customers is one of a business's most valuable assets. You also may benefit from an existing positive reputation and a trained staff.

Disadvantages

An existing business may come with existing problems:
1. The location may be poor.
2. The competition may be taking business away.
3. The **market outlook**, or potential for future sales, may be poor.
4. The building or equipment may need expensive repairs or replacement.
5. The business may have a poor reputation.

Buying a Franchise

One way to enter into an existing business that offers specific advantages is the franchise. A **franchise** is the legal right to sell a company's goods and services in a particular area. Many restaurants and real estate offices offer franchises.

Creative Business Practices

WENDY'S **Wendy's Works for Adoption**

In 1992, Wendy's International, Inc. founder Dave Thomas created the Foundation for Adoption. Thomas, who himself was adopted at an early age, founded the organization to support the "vision that every child deserves a permanent home and a loving family." The foundation works to raise public awareness of adoption and to make adoption more affordable.

The foundation also has a program called Wendy's Wonderful Kids, which pays the expenses of an employee at local adoption agencies. That employee's full-time job is to find permanent adoptive families for children. In the first year of the program, 47 percent of the children in the program were placed with permanent families. That is success!

CRITICAL THINKING **How does this passage affect what you think about this company?**

@ **Connect to the Real World** To read more about Wendy's International, visit the company's Web site via the link on this book's Online Learning Center through **glencoe.com**.

88 **Unit 2** Exploring Careers

glencoe.com

Creative Business Practices

CRITICAL THINKING ANSWER Answers will vary but some students may be more likely to think well of and be customers of businesses whose practices they respect or admire.

88

When you buy a franchise, you actually buy the right to sell another company's products. In addition to paying for the franchise, you agree to pay a percentage of your profits to the parent company.

Advantages

A franchise may be a wise choice for people with limited business experience. Here are some other benefits:
1. a recognized product name,
2. established procedures and management systems,
3. a business reputation and customer goodwill,
4. training and support services,
5. advertising, and
6. financing.

Disadvantages

A franchise is not the right choice for everyone. Because you pay a portion of your profits to the parent company, a franchise may be less profitable. You must follow the parent company's guidelines. Also, since you did not build the company from scratch, there may be less satisfaction.

Joining a Family Business

Does a member of your family own a business? If so, this might give you a shortcut to entrepreneurship.

Advantages

Taking over a family business can offer the advantages of the franchise without the fees:
1. Your relatives might help you finance the business.
2. Family members tend to be loyal and to trust each other.
3. Family members working as a team can achieve more than individuals.
4. Relatives can teach you the business.
5. Customers are likely to give the same trust and goodwill to a new owner who is part of the previous owner's family.

Potential Disadvantages

A family business can present special issues in addition to the usual hazards of business ownership. Some families work well together, others do not. Difficulties at work can affect family relationships.

 ✓ Reading Check **IDENTIFY** What are four ways to become a business owner?

▲ **THE FAMILY BUSINESS** Joining a family business can be a quick entry into the business world. *What are some possible disadvantages of joining a family business?*

TEACH *(cont.)*

S Skill Practice
Independent Practice
Communicate Have students assume they want to join the family eco-friendly dry-cleaning business. Have them write letters to a relative who owns the business and explain why they want to join the business and what they have to offer. (Student letters should highlight their entrepreneurial traits and interest in contributing to the business.) **L1**

Research Have students interview a bank loan officer and ask about small business loans and services. Which services might they use if they went into business? **L2**

Research Have students visit the local Chamber of Commerce or log on to the Chamber's Web site to find out about programs for entrepreneurs and small business owners. Have students organize the information into categories and share their information in class. **L3**

✓ Reading Check

IDENTIFY You can become a business owner by starting a new business, buying an existing business, buying a franchise, or joining a family business.

▶ **Extend the Photo**

Caption Answer Mixing personal relationships with business relationships can jeopardize both. Some people also have trouble leaving work behind when they go home.

Discussion Lead a discussion brainstorming ways family members who own a business together could keep their work lives and personal lives separate.

TEACH *(cont.)*

W Writing Practice
Independent Practice

Create a Checklist Have students create a checklist to use when seeking partners with whom to start a business. Students should first consider their own strengths and weaknesses, then list traits they think are necessary for a business partner to have. (Checklists should reflect students' understanding of partnerships.)

Discussion Starter

Financing Ask: How much do you feel would be an acceptable amount of money to borrow from friends and family to open a new business? (Answers will vary but smaller amounts would probably be more acceptable.)

NCLB Activity correlated to English Language Arts standards.

Real-World *Connection*

Create a Product

You have developed a new product for your science fair project, and one of the fair judges is interested in talking to you about marketing your product. The judge is currently a successful entrepreneur in your community, but you know that she has also been involved in two failed business ventures.

Critical Thinking Should you take the advice of someone who has had a business failure? Why or why not?

Do Your Own Research Using the local Chamber of Commerce directory or a business journal, locate a business in your community that is run by one or two employees. Arrange to visit or talk to the owners, and write a one-page report detailing how long they have been in business and how they got their start, whether they have had any setbacks, what makes their product(s) unique, and who their competitors are.

NCLB

Vocabulary

You can find definitions in the **Key Terms** glossary and **Academic Vocabulary** glossary at the back of this book.

Owning a Business

As a business owner, one of the first questions you will have to answer is how to organize your business. Will you own the business by yourself, or will you share the work and the risks?

Forms of Legal Ownership

There are three basic choices for legal form of business ownership: sole proprietorship, partnership, and corporation. **Figure 4.1** on page 91 compares the advantages and disadvantages of each form.

Sole Proprietorship

Most businesses begin as a sole proprietorship. In a **sole proprietorship**, the business is completely owned by one person. The owner, or **proprietor**, owns all the business's assets and is responsible for all its debts.

Partnership

A **partnership** is a legal arrangement in which two or more people share ownership. Control and profits are divided among the partners according to a partnership agreement. In a partnership, all partners are *liable*, or legally responsible, for the debts of the business. **W**

Corporation

A **corporation** is a business chartered by a state that legally operates apart from the owner(s). The owners buy shares, or parts, of the company. They are called shareholders and earn a profit based on the number of shares they own.

Corporations are more complex than other forms of ownership and are required to keep more records. Shareholders have only limited responsibility for the debts of a corporation.

Operating Your Business

Whatever type of business you launch, you will need money to finance it.

Financing

Where will you get the money to start your business? You might draw on your savings or get a loan from friends. More likely, you will need to borrow money from a commercial lender. To apply for a loan, you will need a business plan and a financial plan.

A *business plan* gives specific information about your business. It describes your product and states where your business will be located. It specifies how many employees you will hire and what their salaries

---

Real-World *Connection*

Critical Thinking Answer Successful entrepreneurs often learn from previous failures. You should always listen to advice; then you can decide if you want to follow it.

Do Your Own Research Reports should show that students spoke with local business owners and summarized the interviews in an informative way.

will be. It describes your competitors and points out their strengths and weaknesses. It also describes your marketing plan and your timetable for starting the business.

A *financial plan* spells out your start-up costs, operating expenses, and other costs for the first few months. **Operating expenses** are the costs of doing business, such as the costs of manufacturing and selling the product.

Ongoing Operations

Once you start a business, you will have to keep accurate financial records. These records are needed for tax purposes and for seeking additional financing. They will also tell you how your business is doing.

One essential business record is the **income statement**, which is a summary of a business's income and expenses during a specific period, such as a month, a quarter, or a year. The first item in an income statement is **revenue**, which is the income from sales. Another item is **gross profit**, which is the difference between the cost of goods and their selling price. **Net profit** is the amount left after operating expenses are subtracted from the gross profit.

Figure 4.1   FORMS OF BUSINESS OWNERSHIP

Forms of Business Ownership	Advantages	Disadvantages
Sole Proprietorship	• Owner makes all decisions • Easiest form of business to set up • Least regulated form	• Limited by the skills, abilities, and financial resources of one person • Difficult to raise funds to finance business • Owner has sole financial responsibility for company; personal assets may be at risk
Partnership	• Can draw on the skills, abilities, and financial resources of more than one person • Easier to raise funds than in sole proprietorship	• More complicated than sole proprietorship • Tensions may develop among partners • Owners liable for all business losses; personal property may be at risk
Corporation	• Easier to finance than other forms of business • Financial liability of shareholders limited (usually they can lose only what have have invested)	• Expensive to set up • Record keeping can be time-consuming and costly • Can pay more taxes than other forms

OWNERSHIP   Every form of business ownership has its advantages and disadvantages. *What business do you know that is a sole proprietorship? A partnership? A corporation?*

Chapter 4   Entrepreneurship   **91**

TEACH *(cont.)*

R **Reading Strategy**
Assess the Competition Ask students how they would learn about their competition and assess the competition's strengths and weaknesses when putting together a business plan. (Answers might include visiting the competitors' Web sites and physical locations, conducting online research, making telephone calls, consulting experts, reading trade journals, and surveying customers and suppliers.)

C **Critical Thinking**
Identify Ask: What part of the income statement would indicate whether you are charging enough for the goods you are selling in your business? (By reading the gross profits on the income statement, you can calculate the cost of the goods versus how much you are making from selling them. If the cost of the goods exceeds the price for which you are selling them, you will not make money.)

ASSESS

Review Key Terms
Have students write sentences using each key term.

Online Study Tools
Have students go to the OLC through **glencoe.com** to:
• Download **Podcast** study tools.
• Download free **Study-to-Go** content to their PDAs or cell phones.

EXTEND THE FIGURE   **Figure 4.1**

Caption Answer Answers should reflect an understanding of sole proprietorships, partnerships, and corporations.

Discussion Ask students which form of business they find most appealing. Encourage them to explain their answers.

RETEACH

R Reading Strategy

Connect Ask students to give examples of personal assets and liabilities. (Personal assets may include cars or money in a bank account. Liabilities may include credit and debt loans.)

NCLB Activity correlated to Mathematics standards.

Math In Action

The gross profit for each item sold is $19.49 ($29.99 × 0.35 = $10.4965, round to $10.50; $29.99 − $10.50 = $19.49).

Resources

📂 **Student Activity Workbook** Assign the Chapter 4 activities in the Student Activity Workbook.

Math In Action

NCLB

Gross Profit

The retail price for a new item is $29.99. If the production costs are 35% of retail, what is the gross profit on each item sold?

Starting Hint Multiply the retail price by the percentage that is production costs and subtract that number from the total retail price: $29.99 × 0.35 = **?**

@ For more math practice, go to this book's OLC through **glencoe.com**.

Another important business record is a *balance sheet*, which summarizes a business's assets, liabilities, and owner equity. *Assets* are anything of monetary value that you own. Money in the bank and inventory are current assets. Fixed assets include land, equipment, furniture, and fixtures. *Liabilities* are debts a business owes. Current liabilities must be paid during the current year. Long-term liabilities are not due in the next 12 months. *Net worth* is the difference between assets and liabilities. The savings you invest in your business are your *equity*, or ownership interest, in the business.

R

A *cash flow statement* is another essential business record. This statement is a monthly plan that shows when you anticipate cash coming into the business and when you expect to pay out cash. A cash flow statement helps you see if you will have enough money to pay your bills.

Succeeding in Business

Knowing the factors that affect business success will improve your chances of success. These factors include financing, location, competition, and management.

Location

Location can be very important to some businesses. For example, a restaurant must be physically near potential customers. With an online business, however, you may be able to process orders and ship goods from anywhere. In this case, location is not as important.

When location is important, consider these factors: the type of businesses in the area, the condition of streets and buildings, the cost of property, the location of the competition, and the location of your customers.

The 21st Century Workplace

English Goes Global

About 300 million people speak English as their native language. About the same number of people speak English as a second or foreign language. English is an official language in more than 100 countries and is common in many fields, particularly science.

Because so many people around the world speak English, it is often the language of choice in the global workplace. In your career, you may encounter and communicate with many colleagues or customers who speak English as a foreign language, or speak a different kind of English than you do. Building your English skills will help you communicate clearly.

CRITICAL THINKING _____
What are the advantages of being skilled at speaking, reading, and writing English in the global workplace?

In Your Community
Locate a person in your community who speaks English as a second language. Ask this person how he or she learned English. Share your findings with the class.

@ **Extend Your Learning** For links to Web sites about English in the global workplace, go to this book's OLC through **glencoe.com**.

The 21st Century Workplace

CRITICAL THINKING ANSWER Since English is often the language of choice in the global marketplace, you are more likely to be able to communicate with others, regardless of their nationality, if you are able to speak, read, and write English.

In Your Community Answers will vary but students should get feedback from those who speak English as a second language.

If your business allows for it, you might consider working at home. It can be less costly than renting or leasing a location and more convenient. You will also enjoy more flexibility. Be aware, though, that some communities restrict the kinds of businesses that can operate in residential areas. Also, many business owners feel isolated working at home.

Competition
Running a successful business means competing successfully. To do that, you must be familiar with your competitor's product or service—and produce a better one.

Management
Businesses that are successful are usually managed well. Poor management is one of the main reasons for business failure. To manage their businesses, entrepreneurs need a variety of skills and competencies, including reading, writing, listening, and speaking. For example, math skills are needed for almost every aspect of business, from setting prices to calculating payroll. If you open a business, how will you use your reading, writing, listening, speaking, and math skills?

Career ✓ Checklist

When Starting Your Own Business:

✓ Research the business needs of your own community.
✓ Talk to entrepreneurs in your area of interest.
✓ Create a business plan.
✓ Be creative—unique ideas can become successful.
✓ Be persistent! It may take time for your business to become successful.

Section 4.2 After You Read

Review Key Concepts
1. Name the four ways to become a business owner. Which one would you choose? Why?
2. Explain the differences between a partnership and a corporation.
3. Describe one of the documents you would need to prepare to apply for a business loan.

Practice Academic Skills

Mathematics
4. Jun and Lisa just started a landscaping business. Their first job is to put sod in a park. There are two areas that need grass, one measuring 32 feet by 15 feet and another measuring 20 feet by 14 feet. How many square feet of sod will they need?

> **CONCEPT** **Calculating Area** The formula for area is length times width. Area is always measured in square units, such as square feet.
> **Step 1:** Calculate the area of each of the two parts of the park by multiplying the lengths (32 feet and 20 feet) by their respective widths (15 feet and 14 feet). Remember to label with square units.
> **Step 2:** Add the two areas together to get the total area. Again, remember to label.

 For math help, go to the Math Appendix located at the back of this book.

After You Read
Have students complete the Section 4.2 After You Read section review.

Online Study Tools
Have students go to the OLC through **glencoe.com** to:
- Take the Section 4.2 **Practice Test**.
- Download **Podcast** study tools.
- Download free **Study-to-Go** content to their PDAs or cell phones.

Resources
ExamView Assessment Suite CD allows you to print out ready-made unit and chapter tests complete with answer keys. You can also create customized tests.

CLOSE

Culminating Activity
Research Have students imagine that they want to open a business in the local area. Tell them to select a location and determine how much it would cost to lease the space. Have students make a list of information they would need to provide when applying for a loan for start-up costs. (Information needed would include monthly rent, maintenance costs, typical selling/marketing expenses, employees' salaries, and projections for earnings with data supporting the projections.)

NCLB Activity correlated to Mathematics standards.

Section 4.2 After You Read

Review Key Concepts
1. Buy an existing business, start your own business, buy a franchise, or take over a family business.
2. A partnership is a legal arrangement in which two or more people share direct ownership, while a corporation is a business that legally operates apart from the owners.
3. You would need to provide a business plan and a financial plan.

Practice Academic Skills
4. Jun and Lisa will need 760 square feet of sod (32 × 15 = 480; 20 × 14 = 280; 480 + 280 = 760).

FOCUS

Discussion Starter

Career Clusters: Marketing, Sales, and Service Lead a discussion about the various types of careers that can be found in this career cluster. Have students brainstorm various careers and jobs within the career cluster. (Answers will vary but students should show an understanding of the many types of careers that fall within the career cluster.)

TEACH

W Writing Support
Independent Practice

Create an Advertisement Ask students to choose an upcoming school event, such as a play, a dance, or a sports event, and write an advertisement for the event. Remind students to include all necessary information, including the event's time and location, in addition to anything else visitors would need to know if they plan to attend. Encourage students to be creative with their writing and to "think outside the box" to make the event sound exciting.

C Critical Thinking

Conduct Research Have students search print and online job ads for public relations positions. What education, skills, and aptitudes do the job ads emphasize? Have students write a 200-word paragraph summarizing their findings. (Answers will vary but should reflect an understanding of career research skills.)

CAREER SPOTLIGHT

Career Cluster: Marketing, Sales, and Service

Vanessa Perry
Public Relations Specialist

Q: Describe your job.

A: I am a public relations specialist for a hospital system.

Q: Describe a typical workday.

A: I start my day by checking e-mail and phone messages, then I proceed to daily tasks. This could involve organizing a special event; working with our advertising agency and design firm; and writing newsletter and magazine articles, advertisements, and direct mail pieces. I might schedule photo shoots for a magazine or brainstorm ideas for a special promotion. My work involves lots of meetings where I check on the status of projects and start new ones.

Q: What skills are most important to you in your job?

A: Writing, language, project management, and customer service skills are extremely important.

W

Q: What academic skills and lifelong learning skills are helpful in preparing for your career?

A: You need to have good writing and communication skills. Being able to interact well with others also is a plus in this field because you will constantly deal with people to obtain information to get the job done. In addition, being creative with your writing can turn a dull subject into an exciting story. The expression "thinking outside the box" comes to mind.

Q: What is your key to success?

A: Understanding my customers, multitasking and managing projects well, and paying attention to detail. I need to understand what my customers want in order to provide them with quality work. When I am faced with several projects,

being able to multitask and prioritize well is essential to getting my work done. Finally, paying attention to details enables me to write accurately and catch any errors.

Q: What training and preparation do you recommend for students?

A: A degree in communications or public relations will help. Also, internships give you the opportunity to work in your field and learn simultaneously. My internship helped me tremendously for these reasons and because it enabled me to see if I really liked the work.

Q: What are some ways you recommend students prepare for this career?

A: Find ways to improve your writing skills by reading books specifically on the topic, taking courses, and practicing. Volunteer to help with public relations efforts on a local project in your area or even a nonprofit organization. It will allow you to gain experience and materials for your portfolio.

Q: What do you like most about your work?

A: My work gives me a sense of fulfillment because I typically work on projects from start to finish. Also, I've always enjoyed writing, so being able to tell a story well is satisfying for me.

 For more about Career Clusters, go to this book's OLC through **glencoe.com**.

NCLB NO CHILD LEFT BEHIND

Teaching Tip

The goals of the NCLB Act include a strong emphasis on reading skills. The use of modeling in your classroom will help students become better at identifying information. For example, ask a question that can be answered by reading the interview on this page.

Sample Question What two recommendations does Vanessa Perry suggest for students who want to prepare for a career in public relations? (Answer: Improve writing skills and volunteer on a local project or for a nonprofit organization.)

C

- **Education or Training** A bachelor's degree in marketing, public relations, communications or journalism is necessary to advance beyond entry level. Internships provide a broad range of experience. Involvement in college and community organizations is helpful, especially those organizations that include making sales and marketing presentations and/or public speaking.

- **Academic Skills Required** English Language Arts, Mathematics, Social Studies

- **Technology Needed** Computer skills for writing, editing, and designing printed content and Web content

- **Aptitudes, Abilities, and Skills** Creativity, customer service skills, organization skills, photography, design skills, business administration

skills, writing and editing skills, public speaking, and sales marketing skills.

- **Workplace Safety** Because the work can involve long periods in front of a computer terminal typing on a keyboard, carpal tunnel syndrome and other hand and wrist injuries can occur.

- **Career Outlook** Employment of public relations specialists is expected to grow faster than average for all occupations over the next ten years.

- **Career Path** Public relations specialists are advocates for businesses, nonprofit organizations, universities, hospitals, and other organizations. Higher-level positions involve managing others and public speaking.

N C L B

Academic Skills Required to Complete Tasks

Tasks	English Language Arts	Mathematics	Social Studies
Plan special events	★	★	★
Write advertisements, articles, and scripts	★		★
Coordinate and attend photo shoots		★	★
Write and edit newsletters, magazine articles, Web content, and mailings	★	★	★

Critical Thinking

Why are communication skills important for workers in the public relations field?

N C L B This chart relates academic skills such as English Language Arts, Mathematics, Science, Social Studies, and World Languages to specific tasks that are performed for the job featured in the Career Spotlight feature.

Critical Thinking

Communication skills are important because people in this line of work must be able to obtain information and then relay it to others effectively.

ASSESS

Make Connections

The text states that carpal tunnel and hand and wrist injuries can occur for employees who spend long periods of time in front of a computer. Have students research *ergonomics* and ask: What is the goal of ergonomics and how does it benefit workers? (Ergonomics is the study of creating and adjusting work equipment and practices to make workplaces more comfortable and safer. Workers benefit from ergonomically correct counters, desks, cash registers, and shipping lines that are set at the correct height so that workers maintain a healthy and appropriate stance and posture and do not overextend themselves.)

CLOSE

Culminating Activity

Job Shadowing and Career Clusters Have students write a draft of a letter to Vanessa Perry, asking for a job shadowing experience with her. Encourage students to detail their aptitudes and the abilities and skills they are learning that would relate to a position in public relations. Have students put the letters in their **Personal Academic and Career Portfolios**. (Letters should reflect an understanding of job shadowing, and of aptitudes, abilities, and skills; and should be correctly formatted and phrased.)

Key Terms and Academic Vocabulary Review

1. Students should write complete sentences using each term correctly. An example might be: "I plan to start a *sole proprietorship* because I have always dreamt of going into business for myself."

Review Key Concepts

2. An entrepreneur is someone who organizes and then runs a business. Entrepreneurs should be motivated, have sight and foresight, and be able to make good decisions.

3. The advantages of entrepreneurship include being able to decide when and where to work and doing work that is satisfying and may lead to a good income. Disadvantages include the financial risk of owning your own business, working long hours, dealing with competition, and no guarantee of being successful.

4. The four main ways to become a business owner are to start a business, buy a business, buy a franchise, or take over a family business. When starting your own business, you do not inherit anyone's mistakes, you can build the business your way, but it requires more time, effort, money and risk. When buying a business, you also inherit the previous owner's business agreements, customer base, reputation, location, the existing competition, and the equipment, which could be in good condition or bad condition. Buying a franchise can be easier because you do not have to create the products, but you have to follow the parent company's guidelines and there may be less job satisfaction. When taking over a family business, your relatives may help out with

CHAPTER SUMMARY

Section 4.1

An entrepreneur organizes and then operates a business. Advantages of entrepreneurship include a chance to be in charge, job satisfaction, and to earn a high income. Disadvantages of entrepreneurship include financial risk, long hours, competition, and no guarantee of success. Entrepreneurs are decisive and self-motivated, and they see opportunities around them.

Section 4.2

You can become a business owner by starting a business, buying an existing business, buying a franchise, or Joining a family business. The three legal forms of business ownership are sole proprietorship, partnership, and corporation. Applications to finance businesses require a business plan and a financial plan. Factors that affect business success include financing, location, competition, and management.

Key Terms and Academic Vocabulary Review

1. Use each of these key terms and academic vocabulary words in a sentence.

Key Terms
- entrepreneur (p. 83)
- start-up costs (p. 87)
- lease (p. 88)
- goodwill (p. 88)
- market outlook (p. 88)
- franchise (p. 88)
- sole proprietorship (p. 90)
- partnership (p. 90)
- corporation (p. 90)
- operating expenses (p. 91)
- income statement (p. 91)
- revenue (p. 91)
- gross profit (p. 91)
- net profit (p. 91)

Academic Vocabulary
- enterprise (p. 83)
- trait (p. 84)
- proprietor (p. 90)

Review Key Concepts

2. **Define** *entrepreneur* and name the traits that most successful entrepreneurs share.
3. **Summarize** the advantages and disadvantages of entrepreneurship.
4. **Identify** the four main ways to become a business owner and explain the advantages and disadvantages of each.
5. **Identify** the different forms of legal business ownership.
6. **Explain** how to prepare to finance a new business.
7. **Identify** factors that can affect business success.

Critical Thinking

8. **Compare and Contrast** Is a family business more like a franchise or more like a new business? Explain your answer.
9. **Evaluate** An entrepreneur prepares an income statement. It shows that, while the business has had strong sales and high revenue, instead of a gross profit, it has a gross loss. What should the entrepreneur understand about the cost of the goods being sold?

advice or finances, or may teach you the basics of running a business, but family dynamics and issues can cause problems at the workplace.

5. A sole proprietorship is a business completely owned by one person, while a partnership is a business legally owned by two or more people and the control and profits are divided between them. A corporation is a business that legally

operates apart from the owners, and the owners buy shares in the company.

6. A business plan or financial plan requires a business owner to research what kinds of resources are available and affordable, the legal requirements in the area their business will operate, how much it will cost to start-up and maintain the business, and what it will take in manpower and money to provide the product or service that the owner wants to sell.

Real-World Skills and Applications

Problem-Solving Skills

10. Serving Clients and Customers Alicia owns a bakery. During busy hours, the customers become upset when they are waited on out of order or have to wait too long. Alicia cannot afford to pay another employee, but she is concerned about losing customers. Other than hiring more employees, what might Alicia do to keep her customers happy?

Technology Applications

11. Creating a Presentation With one or more classmates, brainstorm different businesses that you could start at your school or in your community. Develop a business plan that includes your service or product, possible locations, how you plan to finance the business, the number of employees and their salaries, resources, and your potential business competitors. Use presentation software to present your business plan to the class.

Financial Literacy Skills

12. Identifying Resources You have decided to start your own auto shop. You need money for tools, materials, rent, and a business license. Identify ways to finance your start-up. For example, you could enter into an equipment leasing agreement for tools. Explain the details of your research in a one-page report.

 Log On Go to this book's OLC through **glencoe.com** for help with business financing.

 13. **Interviewing a Business Owner** Find a business owner in your community who is willing to share his or her experiences as a business owner. Ask the owner questions about planning, financing, and challenges and successes. Present your findings to your class in a five-minute oral report.

 14. **Retaining Employees**
Situation Lately, your employer, a small catering company, has lost a lot of key employees. Customers have begun to notice the high turnover and have complained about the service. The business owner cannot afford to give employees a raise, so she has asked you to come up with a comprehensive plan to improve employee retention that does not involve raising wages.
Activity Research how major corporations and small businesses keep good employees from resigning. Then develop an employee retention plan. Present your plan to the company's owner, using visual aids and statistics to enhance your presentation.
Evaluation You will be evaluated based on how well you meet the following performance indicators:
- Demonstrate thorough research.
- Propose practical, yet innovative solutions.
- Enhance the presentation with effective visual aids.

Real-World Skills and Applications

10. Answers will vary. Alicia might have customers take numbers when they come in. She could also have common orders already prepared or partially prepared.

11. Presentations should provide information about what service will be offered, the number of employees and their salaries, resources, and potential competitors.

12. Students should demonstrate an understanding of business financing as discussed in this chapter.

 ACTIVE LEARNING

13. Oral reports should summarize students' interviews with business owners and should focus on how the businesses plan, finance, and respond to challenges and successes.

ROLE PLAY

14. Employee retention plans should include presentations and visual aids that reflect the students' research on how businesses keep employees.

7. Financing, location, competition, and management can all affect the success of a new business.

Critical Thinking

8. Answers will vary. Students might say it is more like a franchise because the business and product already exist and the family may expect it to remain the same. Others may say that a family business is more like a start-up because you have the opportunity to take and remake a business by modifying the services or products or changing the way the business operates on a daily basis.

9. The cost of the goods may be higher than what the entrepreneur is selling them for. The entrepreneur may need to find cheaper supplies or raise prices. Either choice could affect the customer base. However, continuing to operate at a loss will affect the financial success of the business.

Academic Skills in the Workplace

15. Flyers should include the restaurant's location and phone number, hours of operation, and information on the new menu and any other new improvements that might attract new customers.

16. Answers should look similar to the figure below. After 4 years he will have made back his initial investment.

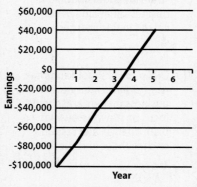

Alex's Earnings over a Five-Year Period

17. The speed would be 2,283 miles per hour (Mach 3 = 761 miles per hour × 3 = 2,283).

18. Summaries should show students' research into local laws that affect home businesses.

Academic Skills in the Workplace

English Language Arts

15. Design a Flyer You recently bought a neighborhood restaurant. The restaurant had been in the neighborhood for a long time and had been losing customers for a few years. The restaurant has been closed for two months while you remodeled it and designed a new menu. Design a flyer that will let the neighborhood know the restaurant will reopen under new management.

Mathematics

16. Calculate Return on Investment Alex wants to open a hair salon. He expects to make an initial investment of $100,000, and figures he will be able to make a salary of $28,000 yearly. Use the Cartesian coordinate system to graph Alex's earnings. How many years will it take him to make back the money he invested?

CONCEPT Cartesian Coordinates In the Cartesian coordinate system, the x-axis extends to the right and left of the origin, and the y-axis extends above and below the origin. The origin is the point (0, 0) at which the two axes intersect. Both positive and negative numbers can be represented in this graph.

Starting Hint The first point on the graph will be (–$100,000, 0), because Alex initially did not take a salary. At the end of the first year he kept $28,000, reducing his loss to $72,000, so draw the next point at 1 on the x-axis and –$72,000 on the y-axis.

Science

17. Calculate Speed Ever think of becoming a pilot and flying faster than the speed of sound? The speed of sound in air is about 761 miles per hour, Mach 1. *Mach* is the ratio of an object's speed to the speed of sound. If a plane is going twice the speed of sound, then it is moving at Mach 2. Calculate the speed of a pilot flying at Mach 3.

Social Studies

18. Research Your Community Ken wants to operate a landscaping business out of his garage. In your neighborhood, would it be legal to run such a business at home? Research your community's guidelines for home businesses. Write a two-paragraph summary of your findings.

 STANDARDIZED TEST PRACTICE

MULTIPLE CHOICE:

Directions Read the following question. Then read the answer choices and choose the best possible answer.

Test-Taking Tip Be sure to read all of the question and all of the answers. To be true, all parts of a statement must be true.

1. Which of these statements is true?
   a. Entrepreneurs who work out of their homes can feel isolated.
   b. A sole proprietor directly owns his business and is not liable for the business debts.
   c. Corporations are chartered by the state and owned directly by an individual.
   d. In a partnership, the owners can never lose their personal property if their business fails.

For more Standardized Test Practice, go to the OLC *glencoe.com.*

 STANDARDIZED TEST PRACTICE

Answer

1. a. Entrepreneurs who work out of their home can feel isolated.

Test-Taking Strategies

Whether your students have a standardized test coming up in a few days or a few weeks, these last-minute test-prep tips and strategies will help students relax and do their best.

Test Preparation Have students double check that they know all of the supplies they will need for the test.

Test Timing Have students mark those questions they cannot answer immediately and move on to other questions before returning to those they have marked.

Writing Skills Practice

19. Persuading Persuasive writing expresses an opinion and then tries to convince others that the opinion is valid using supporting details. Many forms of writing include elements of persuasion, including letters to convince a bank to grant a loan to start a business.

Practice Write a persuasive letter to a bank explaining why you would be a good candidate for a business loan.

- Gather details about yourself, including relevant skills and talents.
- Form an opinion statement. Clearly state why you would be a good candidate for a loan.
- Organize your details. Decide in which order you will present the details you have gathered. Be sure each detail supports your opinion statement.
- Write your letter, including your details.
- Review your letter to make sure all the details support your opinion statement.

Net Connection

20. Write a Financial Plan Visit this book's OLC through **glencoe.com** to find links to help you write a financial plan.

Log On Go online to research how to write a financial plan for a business you would like to start. Assume you need financing from a commercial lender. Write a financial plan for your business. Be sure to include start-up costs, operating expenses, and other costs for the first few months. Add this financial plan to your **Personal Academic and Career Portfolio**.

Reading Connection

 Go to this book's Online Learning Center through **glencoe.com** for a list of reading suggestions.

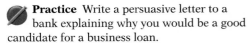

Personal Academic and Career Portfolio

Starting a Business

You can add the information you have gathered about entrepreneurship to your **Personal Academic and Career Portfolio**. Perhaps you are ready to start a business now. Perhaps you may have an idea for a business but are not ready to launch it yet. At a later point in your life, you may want to refer back to your idea and what you learned about starting a business. That will be easier if you create a written record of your ideas.

The following guidelines will help you gather and record the information you need to be an entrepreneur:

- Create a new section for your portfolio. Label the section *My Own Business*.
- Create a business plan. Describe yourself, your skills, your company, your company goals, your product, and the features and benefits of your product.
- Add the proposed business plan to your table of contents.
- Add the following: your ideas for a business, a list of the traits of entrepreneurs and your personality traits, the four ways to become a business owner, the forms of business ownership, financial documents needed, and factors that affect business success.
- Update this information as you develop your ideas for a business.
- Use this same checklist to organize any new business ideas you may have.

 Portfolio Help Go to the *Succeeding in the World of Work* OLC through **glencoe.com** for help developing your portfolio.

Writing Skills Practice

19. Letters should include detailed points that support a clear opinion statement.

Net Connection

20. Answers will vary. Each plan should include projections for how much it will cost to start up the business and potential operating costs, including rent, supplies, and salaries.

Resources

ExamView Assessment Suite CD allows you to print out ready-made unit and chapter tests complete with answer keys. You can also create customized tests.

WorkKeys

WorkKeys® is a job skills assessment program. For information on leveled assessment for Problem-Solving Skills (Applied Mathematics; Applied Technology; Locating Information; and Observation), go to the WorkKeys link on this book's OLC through **glencoe.com**.

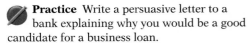

Personal Academic and Career Portfolio

Developing Portfolios for Entrepreneurs

When organizing their **Personal Academic and Career Portfolios**, students may want to focus on entrepreneurial goals. Students who want to develop an entrepreneur section of their portfolio should also consider creating subsections or subfolders with names such as *Business* *Ideas* and *Financing*. Encourage them to also add information they gathered from this chapter, such as ideas for businesses, a list of traits of entrepreneurs, the four ways to become a business owner, the forms of business ownership, financial documents they might need, and factors that affect business success.

Chapter Resources Planning Guide with Activities and Features

Section	Features	Activities
Section 5.1 **Evaluating Career Choices**	Hot Jobs! (p. 105)	Before You Read (p. 102) Graphic Organizer (p. 102) As You Read (p. 104) After You Read (p. 105)
Section 5.2 **Your Career Plan**	21st Century Workplace (p. 108) Real-World Connection (p. 109) Tech Savvy (p. 111) Creative Business Practices (p. 112) Science in Action (p. 113) Everyday Ethics (p. 114) Career Checklist (p. 115)	Before You Read (p. 106) Graphic Organizer (p. 106) As You Read (pp. 108, 113) After You Read (p. 115)

NCLB Activities, information, and skills practice will help your students attain No Child Left Behind proficiency. Students will improve their abilities in the following academic standards areas:

Academic Standards Correlations

Discipline	Standard	Feature/Activity
English Language Arts	**NCTE 1** Read texts to acquire new information.	Hot Jobs (p. 105) Creative Business Practices (p. 112)
	NCTE 4 Use written language to communicate effectively.	After You Read (p. 105) Academic Skills in the Workplace (p. 120) Writing Skills Practice (p. 121)
	NCTE 7 Conduct research and gather, evaluate, and synthesize data to communicate discoveries.	Real-World Connection (p. 109)
	NCTE 8 Use information resources to gather information and create and communicate knowledge.	21st Century Workplace (p. 108) Tech Savvy (p. 111)
Mathematics	**Algebra:** Represent and analyze mathematical situations and structures using algebraic symbols	After You Read (p. 115)
	Algebra: Use mathematical models to represent and understand quantitative relationships	Academic Skills in the Workplace (p. 120)
Science	**Physical Science:** Motions and forces	Science in Action (p. 113) Academic Skills in the Workplace (p. 120)

CORRELATIONS The charts show the 21st Century Skills, foundation skills, and workplace competencies that students develop as they work in this chapter.

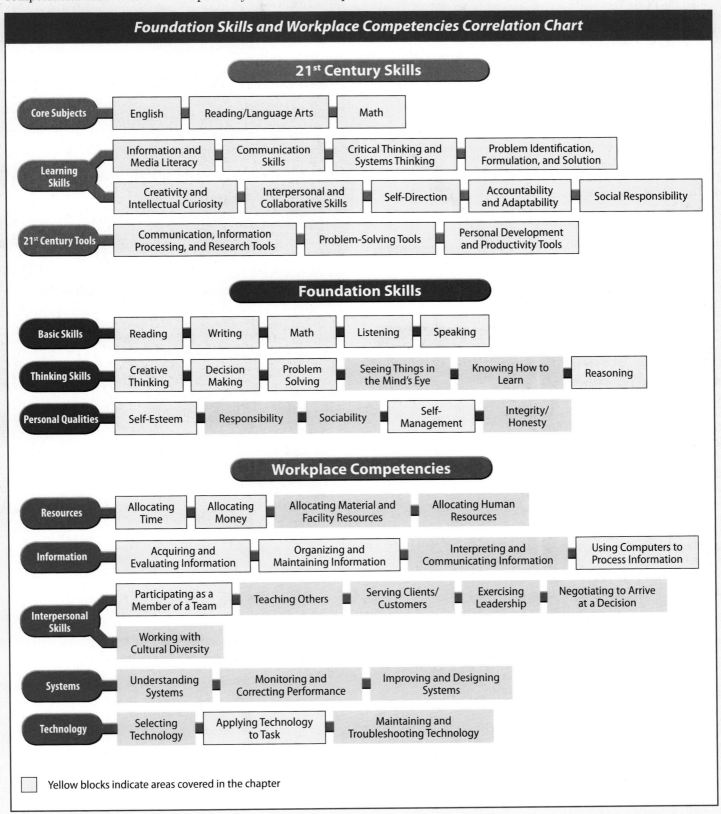

Foundation Skills and Workplace Competencies Correlation Chart

21st Century Skills

Core Subjects
- English
- Reading/Language Arts
- Math

Learning Skills
- Information and Media Literacy
- Communication Skills
- Critical Thinking and Systems Thinking
- Problem Identification, Formulation, and Solution
- Creativity and Intellectual Curiosity
- Interpersonal and Collaborative Skills
- Self-Direction
- Accountability and Adaptability
- Social Responsibility

21st Century Tools
- Communication, Information Processing, and Research Tools
- Problem-Solving Tools
- Personal Development and Productivity Tools

Foundation Skills

Basic Skills
- Reading
- Writing
- Math
- Listening
- Speaking

Thinking Skills
- Creative Thinking
- Decision Making
- Problem Solving
- Seeing Things in the Mind's Eye
- Knowing How to Learn
- Reasoning

Personal Qualities
- Self-Esteem
- Responsibility
- Sociability
- Self-Management
- Integrity/Honesty

Workplace Competencies

Resources
- Allocating Time
- Allocating Money
- Allocating Material and Facility Resources
- Allocating Human Resources

Information
- Acquiring and Evaluating Information
- Organizing and Maintaining Information
- Interpreting and Communicating Information
- Using Computers to Process Information

Interpersonal Skills
- Participating as a Member of a Team
- Teaching Others
- Serving Clients/Customers
- Exercising Leadership
- Negotiating to Arrive at a Decision
- Working with Cultural Diversity

Systems
- Understanding Systems
- Monitoring and Correcting Performance
- Improving and Designing Systems

Technology
- Selecting Technology
- Applying Technology to Task
- Maintaining and Troubleshooting Technology

☐ Yellow blocks indicate areas covered in the chapter

CHAPTER 5
Developing a Career Plan

Chapter Overview
Introduce the Chapter
Chapter 5 guides students through the process of evaluating career choices, deciding on a career, and then developing an individual career plan.

Section 5.1 helps students learn how to evaluate career choices by analyzing their personal values; personality; preferences for working with people, data, or things; skills and aptitudes; and education.

Section 5.2 teaches students how to set goals and meet their goals.

Build Background
Have students write the term "future career choices" in the center of a piece of paper and then create a word web around this term with words that describe their goals and aspirations.

▶ Exploring the Photo

Caption Answer Encourage students to think of "dream" jobs that fit their lifestyle goals, interests, and values.

Discussion Ask students what kinds of courses, training, and experience this woman might have needed to achieve her goal of working with dolphins. (Answers might include zoology, marine biology, and veterinary courses, and working or volunteering at an aquarium.)

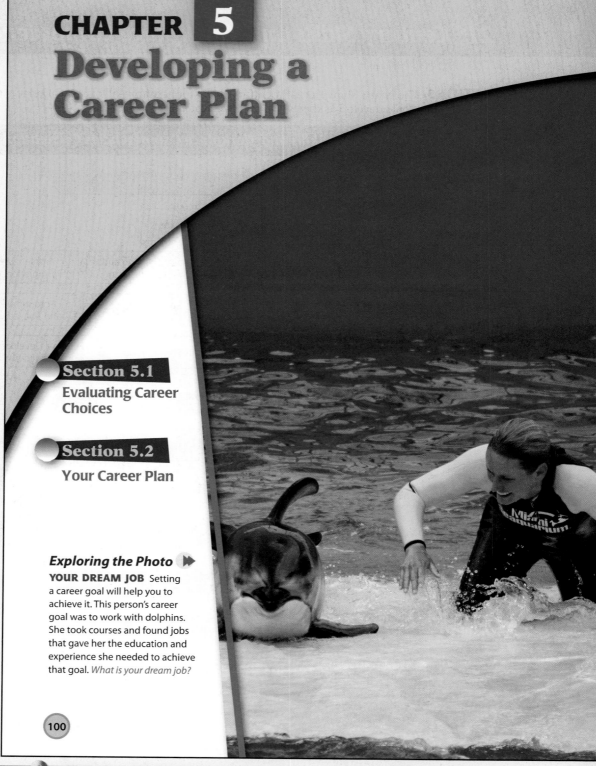

● **Section 5.1**
Evaluating Career Choices

● **Section 5.2**
Your Career Plan

Exploring the Photo ▶▶
YOUR DREAM JOB Setting a career goal will help you to achieve it. This person's career goal was to work with dolphins. She took courses and found jobs that gave her the education and experience she needed to achieve that goal. *What is your dream job?*

100

📖 **Classroom Resources**

- 📁 Student Edition
- 📁 Teacher Wraparound Edition
- 📁 Student Activity Workbook with Academic Integration
- 📁 Student Activity Workbook with Academic Integration TAE
- 📁 *Fast File,* Unit 2 Resources

- 📁 Inclusion in the Career Education Classroom
- 💿 TeacherWorks™ Plus
- 💿 *ExamView Assessment Suite*
- 💿 Interactive Chalkboard
- 💿 Interactive Student Edition
- 💿 Online Student Edition
- 💿 Online Learning Center (OLC) with Podcasts

Chapter Objectives

After completing this chapter, you will be able to:

- **Evaluate** different career possibilities.
- **Choose** a career that seems right for you.
- **Develop** a career plan and set intermediate career goals.
- **Determine** the education and training you need to reach your career goals.

Writing Activity
Personal Career Notebook

Think of a goal you have set for yourself. How did you decide on this particular goal? How does it reflect your values or interests? What steps are you taking toward achieving that goal? What progress have you made? Which of your personal characteristics are important in achieving this goal? Record your answers in a one-page response.

Get Motivated! Contact an adult in your community who works in a career that interests you. Ask this person how he or she decided on a career. What were his or her career goals? What steps did he or she take to achieve them? Take notes during the interview and create a one-page summary.

Chapter 5 Developing a Career Plan **101**

Review the Objectives

Introduce the chapter by reviewing the chapter objectives:

Section 5.1 Objectives
Evaluate different career possibilities. (You can evaluate possible career choices by matching the career information you have gathered to your personal interests and resources.)

Choose a career that seems right for you. (By creating a career profile for each career that interests you, you can review your information systematically and analyze which career choice will work best for you.)

Section 5.2 Objectives
Develop a career plan and set intermediate career goals. (A career plan breaks down a long-term career goal into more manageable, intermediate steps. Setting short-, medium-, and long-term goals will enable you to evaluate your career path as you progress.)

Determine the education and training you need to reach your career goals. (Acquiring more education and training will increase your employment opportunities in your chosen career.)

Writing Activity
Personal Career Notebook Answer Guide

Responses will vary but students should address each of the above questions as a way of understanding how they choose goals and work toward achieving various goals.

Get Motivated! Summaries will vary but should reflect interviewing, note taking, and summarizing skills.

Section 5.1

FOCUS

Bell Ringer Activity

Evaluating Career Choices

Have students brainstorm various activities that are more successful when they are carefully planned. Ask volunteers to share their responses and make a list on the board. (Answers might include travel vacations and sports, such as football, that involve careful strategizing.)

Resources

Interactive Chalkboard
The Interactive Chalkboard CD provides visual teaching aids for this section.

@ Online Learning Center
The Online Learning Center (OLC) through **glencoe.com** features chapter vocabulary, chapter summaries, and other study materials.

Preteaching

Write the key terms from Section 5.1 on the board and have students speculate on how the terms relate to making a career decision.

Graphic Organizer

Tell students to go to the OLC through **glencoe.com** for a printable graphic organizer. (Graphic organizers should show the six factors as listed in this section.)

NCLB connects academic correlations to book content.

Evaluating Career Choices

Reading Guide

Before You Read

Preview Read the Key Concepts. Write one or two sentences predicting what the section will be about.

Read to Learn
• How to evaluate different career possibilities
• How to choose a career that seems right for you

D Main Idea
Once you choose a career that seems right for you, you can begin planning the steps to take to achieve your goal.

Key Concepts
• Evaluate Your Choices
• Make Your Decision

Key Terms
◆ resources
◆ evaluation
◆ personal career profile

Academic Vocabulary
You will find these words in your reading and on your tests. Use the academic vocabulary glossary to look up their definitions if necessary.
■ factors
■ pursue

Graphic Organizer
As you read, list the factors to consider when evaluating career choices. Use a chart like the one shown to help organize your information.

Factors to Consider When Evaluating Careers
1 _____
2 _____
3 _____
4 _____
5 _____
6 _____

@ Log On Go to this book's Online Learning Center through **glencoe.com** for an online version of this graphic organizer.

NCLB **Academic Standards** •
English Language Arts
• Read texts to acquire new information. (NCTE 1)

Reading Guide

Before You Read
Point out to students that deciding on a career is essential in order to plan the steps to achieve it.

D Develop Concepts
Key Concepts Discuss the key concepts with students. Ask: How will you know if you have chosen the right career? (Answers will vary. Some students may be more certain than others, but point out that a career is a long-term goal that can be revised as students gain training and work experience.)

Evaluate Your Choices

Chapters 2, 3, and 4 of this book show you how to complete the first four steps in the decision-making process by exploring career possibilities. Chapter 2 shows you how to take a close look at your own personal needs and resources. **Resources** are things that can be used for help and support. You then identified your options and began gathering information as part of your career research.

If you do your research well, you will probably find many career choices—more than you have time to pursue. Now you are ready to evaluate these choices and narrow them down to a few. This step needs to be done with special care.

The fifth step of the decision-making process is evaluation. **Evaluation** involves comparing and contrasting sets of data to rank them and determine the best choice. When you evaluate career choices, you will compare your personal data with the career information you have gathered. This will help you determine the best possible match between yourself and a career.

You can evaluate your career choices using a number of **factors** or characteristics. One of these factors is the possible outcome of each career. Ask yourself: If I take this course of action, what will happen? Visualizing or imagining the outcome of different career choices can help you make career decisions. Imagine how different careers will affect your time with your family and friends, your finances, and other important parts of your lifestyle.

You can also evaluate career choices based on how well they fit your values. Ask yourself: If I make this choice, will I be living according to my beliefs? Will I be doing something I find meaningful or important?

Vocabulary

You can find definitions in the **Key Terms** glossary and **Academic Vocabulary** glossary at the back of this book.

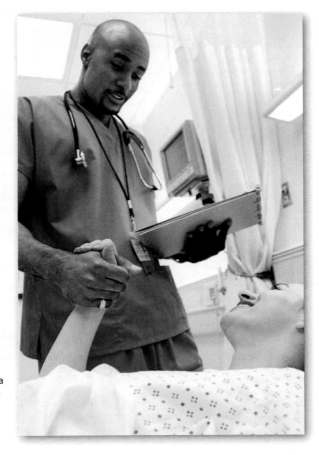

▶▶ THE RIGHT FIT
The career you choose should be a good match for your values, interests, and personality. *What other factors should you consider when making a career decision?*

Chapter 5   Developing a Career Plan   **103**

Section 5.1

TEACH

Discussion Starter
Evaluate Your Choices
Have students write a 50-word paragraph explaining the problems that could result from not analyzing career choices and making a decision to pursue a specific career. List on the board some of the problems students identify. Stress the importance of making career decisions early so that students will have time to find out what training they will need and how they can get it. Remind students that they always have the option of later changing their minds and pursuing a different career.

R Reading Strategy
Identify Personal Data Ask students to list five things they know about themselves. Ask them to categorize each thing as a value, interest, personality, data-people-things preference, skill or aptitude, or training and education preference. Have them suggest a label for anything that does not fit one of the categories mentioned. (Answers will vary, but for example, a student who likes to help others would categorize helping as a value.)

Resources

TeacherWorks™ Plus
The TeacherWorks software includes customizable built-in lesson plans and links to printable program resources.

Extend the Photo

Caption Answer Other factors to consider would be data-people-things preferences, skills and aptitudes, and education and training.

Discussion Ask students why it is important to evaluate and determine the most suitable careers for them. (Students who find a career that matches their strengths and interests are more likely to enjoy it.)

103

ASSESS

Review Key Terms
Have students write sentences using each key term.

Online Study Tools
Have students go to the OLC through **glencoe.com** to:
- Download **Podcast** study tools.
- Download free **Study-to-Go** content to their PDAs or cell phones.

Resources
ExamView Assessment Suite CD allows you to print out ready-made unit and chapter tests complete with answer keys. You can also create customized tests.

RETEACH

Cooperative Learning
Enrichment

Evaluate Career Profiles
Have all students complete personal career profiles for each career that interests them. Divide students into groups of three or four. Have them present their career profiles to each other and evaluate their choices by answering the questions on pages 104–105 aloud. Encourage group members to offer constructive feedback regarding each other's career plans.

As You Read
The personal career profile helps you determine how well your personal information and the characteristics of a career match.

As You Read
Infer How can a personal career profile help you choose a career?

A good tool to use in evaluating career choices is the personal career profile shown in **Figure 5.1**. A **personal career profile** is a chart in which you compare what you have learned about yourself and what you have learned about a particular career possibility.

In the third column of this form, you use a 1-to-10 rating system to indicate how well your personal information and the characteristics of the career match. A perfect ten (or close to a ten) in all categories shows a good match.

The following questions will help you assign a score for each category of the personal career profile:
- **Values** How well does this career match my values?
- **Interests and Responsibilities** How well do the day-to-day job responsibilities reflect my interests?

Figure 5.1   PERSONAL CAREER PROFILE

Name: *Gloria Perry*   **Career:** *Fashion Industry Publicist*

Personal Information	Career Information	Match (1–10)
❖ **Your Values** I believe in equal opportunities for all people! I like to do creative things, too. I also like to work with others.	❖ **Career Values** All kinds of people work in fashion. As a publicist, I would be able to use my creativity, as well as work with other people.	9
❖ **Your Interests** My hobbies include reading and socializing. I love fashion and keep up with the new styles.	❖ **Career Duties and Responsibilities** As a fashion publicist, I would make contacts with stores and buyers, arrange fashion shows and launch parties, and send out press releases.	8
❖ **Your Personality** I'm very outgoing and enjoy having lots of friends. I get bored in class unless there are open discussions. I have a good imagination.	❖ **Personality Type Needed** A publicist must be outgoing and friendly. She must also be responsible and stay on top of things. Communication skills are important.	6
❖ **Data-People-Things Preferences** I like being with people best of all. I find people fascinating. Sometimes facts interest me, too, but I prefer spending time with people.	❖ **Data-People-Things Relationships** Publicists work mostly with people. In the fashion industry, you must be on top of style trends, which are constantly changing.	9
❖ **Skills and Aptitudes** I'm average at drawing. My teacher says I'm "excellent" at speaking and reading comprehension, but I don't do well at grammar.	❖ **Skills and Aptitudes Requirements** Good verbal and writing skills are essential for a publicist. You also must be a good "people person."	7
❖ **Education/Training Acceptable** I would love to go to fashion school in New York City. I need some business training as well.	❖ **Education/Training Required** A four-year fashion school would be best— one that has a good business department.	9

LOOKING FOR A MATCH   Gloria Perry completed this personal career profile form to determine whether this career is a good career choice for her. *Do you think Gloria should pursue a career as a fashion industry publicist? Why or why not?*

EXTEND THE FIGURE   Figure 5.1

Caption Answer Gloria may well be on the right track because the ratings in most of the categories are high.

Discussion Ask students what other possible careers might appeal to someone with this type of personal profile. (Someone who is interested in fashion and who would like to pursue an education at a fashion school might also enjoy a career as a personal shopper or wardrobe stylist. A person who has these interests and likes to be around people might also research a career in retail marketing or management.)

- **Personality** How happy will I be with the work environment and hours?
- **Data-People-Things** How well do the data-people-things requirements of this career match my own preferences?
- **Skills and Aptitudes** How well do my skills and aptitudes match those required for this career?
- **Education/Training** How willing am I to get the education and training needed for this career?

Complete a personal career profile form for each of your career choices. Then tally the scores on all the forms and see which career choice ranks the highest. You are now ready for the next step.

✓ **Reading Check** **SUMMARIZE** What are some factors to consider when evaluating a career?

Make Your Decision

Now it is time to make a choice. Which career will you **pursue**? Have confidence in your research, evaluations, and goals. Remember, unless you define a goal, you are not likely to reach it. Also, remember that your career choice is flexible and it will probably change as your life develops. Making a choice will give you a place to start planning.

In the next section, you will work on the final step in the decision-making process: You will draw up your plan of action.

HOT JOBS!

Conservation Scientist

Conservation scientists manage, improve, and protect natural resources for recreational and economic purposes. Typical jobs include supervising the harvesting and planting of trees, developing plans to restore farmland where soil has been eroded, and ensuring that a population is provided with enough clean water.

Section 5.1 After You Read

Review Key Concepts

1. Give two examples of careers that interest you. Explain how you would evaluate these two career possibilities to see which one would be better for you.
2. Suppose the personal career profile forms you complete for two careers result in the same rating. Identify the criteria you would use to choose between them (for instance, one may offer a bigger salary or better match your values).
3. Explain the importance of making a career decision now.

Practice Academic Skills

 English Language Arts

N C L B
4. Explain how you made your career choice. How did your evaluation affect your choice? What key factors affected your choice? Write your response in a one-page essay.
5. Now that you have made a career decision, predict what your next steps should be. What does your career goal require you to do? What experiences could you seek out now that may help you achieve your career goal? What skills or individual characteristics should you develop? Record your thoughts in a one-page response.

@ Check your answers at this book's OLC through **glencoe.com**.

ASSESS

After You Read
Have students complete the Section 5.1 After You Read section review.

Online Study Tools
Have students go to the OLC through **glencoe.com** to:
- Take the Section 5.1 **Practice Test**.
- Download **Podcast** study tools.
- Download free **Study-to-Go** content to their PDAs or cell phones.

Resources

📁 **Student Activity Workbook** Assign the Chapter 5 activities in the Student Activity Workbook.

CLOSE

Culminating Activity
Weigh Pros and Cons Have students identify the pros and cons of any or all of the career choices they made for their personal career profiles. Have them write a paragraph evaluating a career choice by balancing the pros and cons.

✓ **Reading Check**

SUMMARIZE Factors to consider are values, interests and responsibilities, personality, data-people-things preferences, skills and aptitudes, and education/training.

 N C L B Activity correlated to English Language Arts standards.

Section 5.1 After You Read

Review Key Concepts
1. Answers will vary. Students should include comments comparing and contrasting the two career possibilities.
2. Answers should reflect students' understanding of the career profile.
3. Possible answer: "The sooner I make a career decision, the sooner I can begin preparing myself through classes,

volunteer opportunities, or internships. The more prepared I am after high school, the more opportunities I will have."

Practice Academic Skills
4. Essays should reflect students' knowledge and application of the career profile.
5. Answers will vary but students should use the questions to predict the next steps.

Section 5.2

Your Career Plan

Bell Ringer Activity

Your Career Plan
Have students write their ultimate career goal and then list the steps they plan to take to achieve that goal.

Resources

Interactive Chalkboard
The Interactive Chalkboard CD provides visual teaching aids for this section.

@ Online Learning Center
The OLC through **glencoe.com** features chapter vocabulary, chapter summaries, and other study materials.

Preteaching
Have students skim the section to preview each of the key terms.

Graphic Organizer
Tell students to go to the OLC through **glencoe.com** for a printable graphic organizer. (Graphic organizers should reflect an understanding of career short-term, medium-term, and long-term goals.)

N C L B
NCLB connects academic correlations to book content.

Reading Guide

Before You Read
Preview Look at the photos and figure in this section and read their captions. Write one or two sentences predicting what the section will be about.

Read to Learn
- How to develop a career plan and set intermediate career goals
- How to determine the education and training you need to reach your career goals

D Main Idea
Making a career plan will help you achieve your career goals.

Key Concepts
- Plan How to Reach Your Goal
- Steps Along the Way
- Education and Training
- Commit Yourself in Writing

Key Terms
- ◈ individual career plan
- ◈ online learning
- ◈ on-the-job training
- ◈ apprentice
- ◈ vocational-technical center
- ◈ trade school
- ◈ continuing education

Academic Vocabulary
You will find these words in your reading and on your tests. Use the academic vocabulary glossary to look up their definitions if necessary.
- ■ intermediate
- ■ vocation

Graphic Organizer
As you read, create a chart of the short-term, medium-term, and long-term goals you will need to achieve to reach your career goal. List your career goal first as a long-term goal. Use a two-column chart like the one shown to organize this information.

Goal	Type of Goal
1. *Become a marine biologist*	*long-term*
2. *Take biology and chemistry in high school*	*medium-term*

 Log On Go to this book's Online Learning Center through **glencoe.com** for an online version of this graphic organizer.

Academic Standards ●

N C L B

English Language Arts
- Conduct research and gather, evaluate, and synthesize data to communicate discoveries. (NCTE 7)
- Use information resources to gather information and create and communicate knowledge. (NCTE 8)

Mathematics
- Represent and analyze mathematical situations and structures using algebraic symbols

Science
- Physical Science: Motions and forces

Reading Guide

Before You Read
Ask students what goals they have set for themselves lately. Examples might include higher grades, completing a school project, getting on a sports team, or saving money.

D Develop Concepts
Main Idea Ask students to share any plans they may have already made for job-related training or education. Encourage students who have already received training or extracurricular education to share the experiences they have had with part-time jobs or extracurricular classes.

Plan How to Reach Your Goal

Making your career goals a reality means planning a course of action for your career, which is called an **individual career plan**. This is the seventh and final step in the career decision-making process. There is no substitute for planning if you want to be successful in reaching your goal. Having a plan does not guarantee success, but it greatly improves your chances of success. You may get help from many sources, but the most workable plan will probably be one you design yourself. How will you begin?

Steps Along the Way

To reach your ultimate career goal, you first need to establish some **intermediate** planning goals. These are the steps you will take to get from where you are now to where you want to be. If your career goal is to become a real estate agent, for example, one intermediate goal might be to find out the training you need to qualify for a real estate license. The next goal might be to find schools that offer that training.

Intermediate planning goals are important because they break your career plan into manageable steps. Then the prospect of reaching a particular career goal does not seem so overwhelming. Intermediate goals can also help you feel focused and confident.

Since where you are now is high school, a good first intermediate goal might be to identify high school courses related to your career choice or career interest area. A career interest area is a general area of interest that can lead to a career, such as biology, business, or art. You can develop a graduation plan that includes high school courses and experiences that can lead you to choose a particular career.

 EQUAL OPPORTUNITY
Today's employers must choose workers for their skills and include workers with diverse backgrounds. *How do you think this policy affects an individual's career options?*

Chapter 5 Developing a Career Plan **107**

Vocabulary
You can find definitions in the **Key Terms** glossary and **Academic Vocabulary** glossary at the back of this book.

Section 5.2

TEACH

Discussion Starter
Plan How to Reach Your Goal Ask students to name some well-known people who overcame great odds to pursue their career choices. (For example, mention former U.S. Senator Max Cleland, who was severely wounded in Vietnam in 1968.) Students may also know someone in the local community who fits this description. Query students on the role that setting goals played in that person's achievements.

R Reading Strategy
Set Intermediate Goals Explain to students that intermediate goals often involve the training and education required to achieve long-term career goals. Have students write three intermediate goals they could include in their individual career plan. (Responses might include getting a part-time job, taking classes at a community college, or volunteering in a field of interest.)

Resources

TeacherWorks™ Plus The TeacherWorks software includes customizable built-in lesson plans and links to printable program resources.

Extend the Photo

Caption Answer Students might point out that individuals need to research the skills necessary to pursue a career in order to make sure that they will have the proper education and training to be competitive in the field.

Discussion Ask: Are you surprised to see women firefighters in this photograph? If so, why? What are some other occupations that were once viewed as being mainly for men or for women?

107

R **Reading Strategy**

Draw Conclusions Ask students to explain how Daniel's short-term goals will help him reach his long-term goal of being a chef and owning his own business. (Students might point out that Daniel's high school courses taught him basic business skills; and his experience in the restaurant is giving him hands-on experience that he will be able to apply to his long-term goal of owning a restaurant.)

C **Critical Thinking**

Analyze Ask: Why might it be a good idea to re-examine your career decisions every so often? (Students might mention that re-examining decisions is necessary to make sure their careers are still on track. As their careers develop, students will most likely adjust their medium- and long-term goals.)

As You Read

Medium-term goals usually take about one to five years to complete, whereas long-term goals, such as career goals, go further into the future.

N C L B Activity correlated to English Language Arts standards.

R

That is what Daniel Porter of Chelsea, Massachusetts, did. Daniel wants to be a chef and own his own restaurant. While he was in high school, he took courses in business, food science, and math. Since graduating from high school, Daniel has worked five nights a week as a waiter at a French restaurant. During the day, he attends a culinary arts institute, where he is learning to become a chef. This is how he describes his job:

"It's a little hectic most of the time, but when things slow down, I can watch how the kitchen is run and how various dishes are prepared. I'm earning tips, which is helping me pay for school. I wouldn't want to have this job forever, but the restaurant experience I'm getting—not to mention the cash—is helping me prepare for the career I really want."

As You Read

Compare What is the difference between a medium-term and a long-term career goal?

Short-Term, Medium-Term, and Long-Term Goals

C

It is a good idea to give your goals a timeframe, which is a period of time in which the goals will be accomplished. What do you need to do now? Next year? Five years from now? Goals you can start on now and may accomplish quickly are short-term goals. Those goals that will take longer to reach, maybe one to five years, are medium-term goals. Those goals that are further in the future, such as your career goal, are long-term goals.

The 21ˢᵗ Century Workplace

N C L B

Government Jobs Makeover

While the world of business is known as the private sector, the government is known as the public sector. Working for the government as a civilian—sometimes called being a civil servant—is not for everyone. Governments everywhere have reputations for having slow-moving hiring processes, and since many of these jobs are not marketed extensively to civilians, it's no wonder the U.S. government has difficulty attracting qualified applicants.

But the U.S. government needs workers. Projections suggest that more than half of civil servants may need to be replaced in the next decade. To better recruit, government agencies are changing their hiring strategies. They now stress the positive elements of working for the government, such as patriotism, good citizenship, social responsibility, and the making a difference. As rising insurance costs force many private sector

businesses to decrease benefits, government jobs may appeal more if they offer better benefits than private businesses.

CRITICAL THINKING _____

What are some benefits of working for the government?

In Your Community

Look up local government job listings and review at least four of them. For each, create a new recruiting strategy that includes who the job listing will target and how to approach them.

 Extend Your Learning Some civil servants are expected to be politically neutral. For links to Web sites about civil service and politics, go to this book's OLC through **glencoe.com**.

The 21ˢᵗ Century Workplace

CRITICAL THINKING ANSWER Reasons for working for the government include a sense of patriotism, good citizenship, social responsibility, and the feeling of making a difference.

In Your Community Answers will vary but encourage students to use visual aids such as brochures and posters as part of their recruiting strategy.

SET SPECIFIC GOALS
Making goals specific can help you achieve them. *Why might a person who wished to become a veterinary surgeon have a specific intermediate goal of getting emergency animal care certification?*

TEACH *(cont.)*

U Universal Access
Hearing Impairments
Arrange for a reliable class-mate to take notes for a student with hearing impairments, so that he or she can concentrate on lip reading or following an interpreter.

W Writing Support
Guided Practice
Create a List Have students write down a career they may like to pursue, and then list three intermediate goals that might help them achieve the long-term career goal. For instance, someone who wants to be a graphic designer might decide to take art classes while in high school, research four-year colleges that offer degrees in graphic design, and find local businesses that might hire graphic design interns. (Lists should include specific intermediate goals that can lead to a career.)

Think of Daniel Porter's career plan, for example. While his ultimate long-term career goal is to be the chef and owner of a restaurant, he is currently working on a short-term goal: to get practical restaurant experience serving as a waiter. He is also working on a medium-term goal: to earn a certificate within a few years from a culinary institute. One long-term goal he has is to study with a master chef in Italy or France. **Figure 5.2** on page 110 shows examples of short-term, medium-term, and long-term career goals within a career plan.

Having short-, medium-, and long-term goals will allow you to change course if you decide your ultimate goal is not right for you. On the basis of his experience as a waiter, Daniel might decide he would prefer to own and operate a restaurant. He could then revise his medium-term goals to include taking business courses.

Be Specific

W As you develop your intermediate goals, make them as specific as possible. The more specific these intermediate goals, the more likely you are to achieve them. For example, if your ultimate career goal is to become a veterinary surgeon, it is not enough to say your intermediate goal is "to get a job working in a veterinarian's office." That is like throwing a dart in the general direction of the dartboard. Instead, your immediate goal might be "to enroll in a program that will train me to be a veterinary emergency room medical technician."

To practice, write down a few intermediate goals for your career choice. Then try to make each one more specific. Try linking each goal to an activity or behavior.

 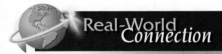**Real-World** *Connection*

Volunteering

Tamara enjoys volunteering at the local animal shelter and is beginning to think about a career working with animals. She spends most of her free time after school at the shelter, but the time she spends there has started to cut into her homework and study time.

Critical Thinking How can you balance volunteer work with schoolwork?

Do Your Own Research Contact an organization in your community that offers volunteer opportunities for high school students. What kind of work do they offer? How much time would you have to commit? How might this help you choose a career? Record your findings in a one-page response.

Chapter 5 Developing a Career Plan **109**
LWA-Dann Tardif/Corbis

▶ Extend the Photo

Caption Answer By knowing the specific certifications that are required, this person would be able to set specific intermediate goals to get the training needed to meet these requirements.

Discussion Ask: What other specific intermediate goals might an aspiring animal surgeon consider? (Other goals might include attending veterinary school and interning at an animal hospital.)

Real-World *Connection*

Critical Thinking Answer Keeping a detailed schedule or planner can help students stay organized and plan how much time needs to be spent on schoolwork while maintaining a volunteer commitment.

Do Your Own Research Responses should reflect research into a specific volunteer opportunity.

TEACH *(cont.)*

C₁ Critical Thinking

Set Personal Goals Model for students the need to set personal goals along with their career goals. Some students may need to improve communication skills or their attitudes. Some may want to become more aware of how others perceive them. Discuss how students can set personal goals and work toward achieving them. (For example, someone who wants to improve communication skills might ask parents or friends to remind them when they are not communicating effectively.)

C₂ Critical Thinking

Long and Short-term Training Tell students that on-the-job training can be formal or informal. Training can last any period of time, from a week to several years. Jobs that require long-term training often pay more than jobs that require short-term training. Ask: Why do you think this is true? (Short-term training involves basic tasks that can be learned quickly. Many people can do these jobs. Long-term training involves complex tasks that take time and commitment to learn. Fewer people are available for jobs that involve long-term training, so the pay is often higher than for jobs that involve short-term training.)

Figure 5.2   TYPES OF GOALS

ONE STEP AT A TIME Using short-term, medium-term, and long-term goals can help you meet your ultimate career goal. *What planning goals will help you achieve your career goal?* C₁

▶ **SHORT-TERM GOALS**
A short-term goal might include taking a class on how to use a computers in the workplace, a transferable skill.

◀ **MEDIUM-TERM GOALS** A medium-term goal might be to volunteer or intern at a company or organization. This is a good way to develop ideas and skills particular to an industry that interests you. C₂

▶ **LONG-TERM GOALS**
A long-term goal might include getting a job at or creating your own company in the industry that interests you.

110   **Unit 2**   Exploring Careers

EXTEND THE FIGURE   Figure 5.2

Caption Answer Students should consider education, training, and work experience when planning goals to achieve a career goal.

Discussion Ask students whether they think their goals will remain the same for the next five years. Then ask about the next ten years. (Goals change as life circumstances change; students' goals will likely change as well.)

Be Realistic

Besides being specific, planning goals should be realistic. To plan realistic goals, you must think about who you are and what you know about your career choice. It would be impossible to hit a target if you did not know where you were standing in relation to the target. It is just as difficult to reach a career goal if you are not honest with yourself about your skills, interests, and personality traits.

For example, if you dislike science and mathematics, you may not be happy as an engineer. However, you may strongly believe that you would enjoy being an engineer. Therefore, a realistic—and necessary—intermediate goal would be to strengthen your science and math skills.

Be careful not to confuse the words *realistic* and *traditional*. For example, in the past, women or men may have been considered inappropriate for certain jobs. Today, however, it is realistic for both men and women to consider all jobs. Also, since you will be developing your career in the future, do not limit yourself to the current reality of the world. Allow yourself to imagine and think creatively.

✓ **Reading Check** **ANALYZE** How can you be sure your intermediate goals are realistic?

Education and Training

One of your first intermediate goals should be receiving the education and training you need to achieve your ultimate career goal. Many careers require specific degrees or certificates. Even if your chosen career does not, taking related courses will give you an advantage over other job candidates and give you the knowledge you need to succeed.

Make a list of several careers in your career interest area. You may use the research information you gathered in Chapter 3 and the career profiles you created in Section 5.1. Then develop a chart identifying employment opportunities for each career and the educational and training requirements for each employment opportunity. Use this to inform your decisions about education and training.

Many options are available for getting the education and training you will need, including online learning, apprenticeships, and schools.

Online Learning

One of the newest ways to receive education and training is online, or e-learning. **Online learning** is computer-based training that uses interactive technologies, such as computers, CD-ROMs, and digital television. Although it is relatively new, online education is gaining

TechSavvy

Pay by Print

A customer at a retail store who is registered to use a *biometric payment system* can place a finger on an electronic screen that records a digital image. This image, coded to protect the consumer, is then electronically linked to the customer's credit or debit card. A picture ID confirms the customer's identity.

Biometric payment systems are being used in stores and at ATM machines. Consumers can pay for goods and services without having to carry cash, a credit card or a checkbook. The system can also help businesses by cutting down on credit card fraud.

@ Visit this book's OLC through **glencoe.com** to find out about biometric payment systems. Use a word-processing program to create a fact sheet about the technology.

TechSavvy

Pay By Print
Answer Fact sheets will vary but should reflect students' basic understanding of biometric payment systems.

TEACH *(cont.)*

C Critical Thinking
Allocating Time Have students choose a career that they have been considering and determine the training or education they will need to get an entry-level job. Tell students to imagine they will need to work part-time (about 20 hours a week) during their training. Have students write a 200-word paragraph detailing how they would allocate their time and determine how long it will take them to complete their training. (In their responses, students should be able to estimate how long their training will take and suggest ideas about how they will balance training with a work schedule).

R Reading Strategy
Conduct Research Divide students into groups and have each group research a type of training program offered in your area, such as an on-the-job training program, apprenticeship, or vocational training program. Students should be able to get information through the local Chamber of Commerce or other business organization, the local public library, the school guidance counselor, or the Internet. Have students evaluate whether the program would be valuable for them, given their interests and abilities.

✓ **Reading Check**

ANALYZE In order to make sure your intermediate goals are realistic, you should make sure they are compatible with your skills, interests, and personality traits.

S **Skill Practice**
Guided Practice

Using Computers to Process Information Have students use a database program to create a file of career references. For each career choice, have them collect the following information: schools/training programs; names and addresses of companies offering jobs, and names and telephone numbers of human resources personnel; career counseling contacts, such as teachers, school counselors, friends, relatives, or businesspeople; Internet addresses for helpful sites; and job search references, including books, magazines, and databases. Have students print out their databases and discuss how to combine them into a single database.

in popularity. Many people are attracted by the convenience and flexibility of online classes, which allow them to work when and where they want and at their own pace.

Before opting for an online education, however, remember that interaction with a teacher, discussion, and the stimulation of class participation are strong motivators and among the most powerful educational tools. Some interaction can be achieved online in classroom chat rooms or bulletin boards.

On-the-Job Training: Learning by Doing

On-the-job training is on-site instruction in how to perform a particular job. Many companies offer this type of training. It may consist of a few days of orientation for new employees or more formal long-term instruction. Where safety is a concern, workers receive training on safety measures. Workers at nuclear power plants, for example, undergo continual training in technical and safety procedures.

The need to be on the cutting edge of new trends leads many companies to offer ongoing employee training. For instance, many companies offer courses on the latest software and computer technology.

Creative Business Practices

WHOLE FOODS **Environmental Solutions**

Whole Foods Market is not your average grocery store. Shelves are filled with foods from around the world, and many products are organically grown. This means the food is grown without the use of pesticides. Pesticides are chemicals used to kill insects and can be harmful to the environment and to living creatures.

The company's motto is "Whole Foods, Whole People, Whole Planet." The company puts action behind their motto. One day a year, all stores worldwide contribute 5 percent of their sales to the Animal Compassion Foundation™. The foundation is a nonprofit organization that works to improve the lives of farm animals worldwide. In addition, employees work with farmers to grow food that saves the soil. The company is also committed to recycling programs, reducing and reusing packaging, and water and energy conservation.

The commitment to find solutions for global problems is paying off. Whole Foods Market is the world's leading natural and organic foods supermarket.

CRITICAL THINKING Why might Whole Foods Market be a good place to work?

 Connect to the Real World For more information about Whole Foods Market, visit their Web site via the link on this book's Online Learning Center through **glencoe.com**.

Creative Business Practices

CRITICAL THINKING ANSWER A company like Whole Foods, which gives back to the environment, might also be committed to fostering good employee relations.

Apprenticeships

An **apprentice** is someone who learns how to do a job through hands-on experience under the guidance of a skilled worker. Apprenticeships are still fairly common for some types of work, especially in construction and manufacturing.

Anna Yu of Raleigh, North Carolina found her apprenticeship as a sheet-metal worker through a state apprenticeship agency. Although she does not make much money now, she feels lucky to be getting paid to learn a trade that will eventually earn her a better position.

Vocational-Technical Centers

A **vocation** is another word for an occupation or career. You can prepare for many careers by attending a **vocational-technical center**, a school that offers a variety of skills-oriented programs, such as courses in automotive or computer technology. Some *vo-techs,* as they are called, offer a high school diploma and a certificate for a particular career. Most vocational-technical centers have evening classes and are relatively inexpensive.

Trade Schools

The culinary arts institute that Daniel Porter attends in Massachusetts is an example of a trade school. A **trade school** is a privately run institution that trains students for a particular profession. Trade schools are usually more expensive than vocational-technical centers. However, they sometimes offer specialized programs that vocational-technical centers do not.

Community and Technical Colleges

Community colleges and technical colleges offer two-year and certificate programs in many occupational areas, such as accounting, tourism, paralegal work, and desktop publishing. These colleges usually offer night and weekend classes as well as classes during the day and tuition and fees are often less than those of trade schools or four-year colleges. A graduate from a community or technical college with an associate degree can usually transfer his or her credits to a college or university to pursue further study.

Four-Year Colleges and Universities

Many jobs require a bachelor's degree from a four-year college or university. Other careers—such as those in law, architecture, and medicine—may require even more advanced degrees. In choosing a college, you should consider such factors as location, size, cost, the quality of your particular program, entrance requirements, and the availability of financial aid.

Science In Action

Motions and Forces

Newton's Third Law of Motion states that for every action, there is an equal and opposite reaction. For instance, when a baseball batter hits an incoming baseball, the baseball changes direction and quickly flies away in another direction. Can you think of some other instances where you notice a roughly equal and opposite reaction to some applied force?

Starting Hint: Think of actions you perform or see every day, such as riding a bike.

@ For more science practice, go to this book's OLC through **glencoe.com**.

NCLB

As You Read

Compare How does a community college differ from a four-year college?

TEACH *(cont.)*

R Reading Strategy
Identify Ask students what businesses would be most likely to provide apprenticeship training. (Businesses could include electrical, construction, plumbing, and manufacturing companies.)

As You Read

Community colleges offer two-year and certificate programs; four-year colleges offer bachelor's degree programs.

NCLB Activity correlated to Science standards.

ASSESS

Review Key Terms
Have students write sentences using each key term.

Online Study Tools
Have students go to the OLC through **glencoe.com** to:
- Download **Podcast** study tools.
- Download free **Study-to-Go** content to their PDAs or cell phones.

STUDY TO GO

Science In Action

Answers will vary but might include a basketball bouncing (ball vs. ground), a car crashing into a wall (car vs. wall), or walking across a floor (foot vs. floor).

Critical Thinking

Conduct Research Have students work in small groups to research adult education courses offered in their community's high schools. Ask the groups to report the names, descriptions, and schedules of the courses that are offered.

C Critical Thinking

Discuss Ask: Why might the armed forces be a good career choice for some and not for others? (Students might point out that some people may not be suited for the rigors and discipline of military life.)

Resources

📁 **Student Activity Workbook** Assign the Chapter 5 activities in the Student Activity Workbook.

Everyday ETHICS

CHANGE OF PLANS

Does your career decision affect only you?

FAMILY BUSINESS Your parents own a sandwich shop. Because you are an only child, they assume that you will take over the family business. They have offered to pay for your college tuition so that you can earn a business management degree that will help you run the shop. You have decided that you are not interested in business and have been taking courses in early childhood education so that you can one day be a teacher.

What Would You Do? How will you tell your parents about your future plans? Do you think you should offer to help pay your tuition now that you have decided to major in education?

DISCUSS IT If you decide to tell your parents about your change in career plans, should you tell them right away, or wait until you have completed several education courses? Share your ideas with the class.

Continuing Education

R Many adults return to school at some point in their lives to complete their education, improve their skills, or change careers. Many high schools, vo-techs, colleges, and universities offer **continuing education**—formal courses of study designed for adult students. Many of these institutions offer continuing education through online and correspondence courses. Some of these programs can lead to academic degrees.

Military Service

C Did you know that the military is the largest employer in the United States? If you think you might be interested in military service, you may receive training in one of more than 200 different occupations, including health technician and air traffic controller. Depending on your career choice, you must enlist for up to six years of active duty. Sometimes you can attend school before or during your service. In other instances, the military will pay for your education after you serve.

Personal Academic and Career Portfolio

Go to the chapter review to find guidelines for creating your own **Personal Academic and Career Portfolio**.

Commit Yourself in Writing

Do you feel overwhelmed by the future? That is only natural when faced with so many career options, but do not waste time worrying. Instead, take out a notebook or turn on your computer and begin to write your individual career plan. You can add this plan to your **Personal Academic Career Portfolio**.

114 **Unit 2** Exploring Careers

Everyday ETHICS

What Would You Do? Answer Students should consider having an honest discussion with their parents, explaining why they think their course of action is valid and realizing that their parents may not agree. If students offer to pay some of their tuition, they should consider how they would pay and how much.

DISCUSS IT Answers will vary. If you wait until you have taken education courses before talking to your parents, they are likely to feel deceived when they discover that they have been paying for classes not related to running a business.

Questions and Answers

You can start by creating a list of questions about your career goals, education, and training. You might use some of these:

- What is my ultimate career goal?
- What is my first step, or my first short-term goal?
- How much time is needed to accomplish this first step?
- What is one of my medium-term goals?
- Which educational programs offer the training I need?
- How much money will I need to pay for my education and training? Where will this money come from?

Remember that your decisions, choices, and plans are all flexible. Expect them to change as your interests and abilities develop. The advantage of having an educational and career plan is that it will encourage you to move forward until you find the right career.

Career ✓ Checklist

When Choosing a Career:

✓ Explore careers in different fields.

✓ Talk to people in your field of interest.

✓ Look for jobs and classes that will help you advance on your chosen career path.

✓ Volunteer, intern, or apply for a job at an organization that interests you.

✓ Set realistic career goals.

Section 5.2 After You Read

Review Key Concepts

1. Explain why establishing intermediate steps or goals can help you reach your ultimate career goal.
2. Identify the characteristics of good intermediate planning goals.
3. Identify two education and training options for a career that interests you.

Practice Academic Skills

 Mathematics

4. Last year, Paul earned $27,000 in his primary job, $18,000 at his second job, and $4,200 on investments. This year he expects to make about $4,500 on investments, and he quit his second job. How much will he have to make in his primary job for his income this year to be greater than or equal to his income last year?

   CONCEPT Solving Inequalities Solving an inequality means finding the values of a variable that make the inequality true. Just as with equations, when you add or subtract the same number from each side of an inequality, you do not change the value of the inequality.
   Step 1: Write an inequality using the appropriate symbol ($<$, $>$, $\leq$, or $\geq$) with the earnings for last year ($27,000, $18,000, and $4,200) on one side and those for this year on the other side ($4,500). Use a variable ($x$) to represent this year's earnings in the primary job.
   Step 2: Solve the inequality. Your answer should also be an inequality.

    For math help, go to the Math Appendix located at the back of this book.

Section 5.2

ASSESS

After You Read
Have students complete the Section 5.2 After You Read section review.

Online Study Tools
Have students go to OLC through **glencoe.com** to:
- Take the Section 5.2 **Practice Test**.
- Dowload **Podcast** study tools.
- Download free **Study-to-Go** content to their PDAs or cell phones.

Resources

ExamView Assessment Suite CD allows you to print out ready-made unit and chapter tests complete with answer keys. You can also create customized tests.

CLOSE

Culminating Activity
Goals and Careers Have students complete personal career profiles. Have them write their goals for gaining the education or training needed and the steps they plan to take to achieve their goals. (Personal career profiles should reflect an understanding of short-, medium-, and long-term goals and the education necessary to achieve students' individual career goals.)

N C L B Activity correlated to Mathematics standards.

Section 5.2 After You Read

Review Key Concepts

1. Having intermediate goals allows you to break your career goal down into manageable steps and keeps your ultimate goal from seeming overwhelming. Intermediate goals can help you feel confident and focused and prepare you for being successful.
2. Good intermediate planning goals are specific and realistic.
3. Answers will vary but may include four-year colleges, military training, trade schools, or apprenticeships.

Practice Academic Skills

4. Paul will need to earn $44,700 ($27,000 + $18,000 + $4,200 $\leq$ x + $4,500; $49,200 $\leq$ x + $4,500; $44,700 $\leq$ x).

Discussion Starter

Government and Public Administration Lead a discussion about the different types of careers that can be found in this career cluster. Have students brainstorm different careers and jobs within the career cluster. (Answers will vary but students should show an understanding of the many types of careers that fall within the career cluster.)

TEACH

W Writing Support

Independent Practice

Create a Personal Career Profile Have students create a Personal Career Profile for a career as a quality of working life coordinator. Using Figure 5.1 on page 104 as a model, students should use this Career Spotlight to fill in the Career Information column, and then add what they have learned about themselves in the Personal Information column. After they have filled in the ratings for each category, ask: Is this a career that you would want to pursue? Why or why not? Have students summarize their findings in a 200-word report.

C Critical Thinking

Communication Skills and Government and Public Administration Ask: Why are good communication skills important to a quality of working life coordinator? (A quality of working life coordinator needs to be able to communicate and problem-solve in order to be an effective go-between for management and workers.)

116

CAREER SPOTLIGHT

Career Cluster: Government and Public Administration

Jeffrey Friend
Quality of Working Life
Coordinator/Postal Worker

Q: Describe your job.

A: I work for the United States Postal Service (USPS). I started off as a mail carrier and then became a mail sorter. Now I attend to the quality of working life at our facility. I act as a go-between for management and workers. I research and develop programs to improve conditions and increase productivity. I also coach and train workers.

Q: Describe a typical workday.

A: I'm usually doing clerical work or preparing proposals. If not, I'm conducting meetings with troubleshooting committees and other groups.

Q: What skills are most important to you in your job?

A: Organization is very important because I always have multiple projects on my desk and a number of tasks on my to-do list. Brainstorming with coworkers is another important skill that I have developed. Because the USPS is such a big institution, making everyone happy is a real art form.

Q: What academic skills and lifelong learning skills are helpful in preparing for your career?

A: Critical thinking and quantifying skills are crucial for systematic problem solving. Also, basic computer skills, public speaking, and communication in general are essential for making presentations. I have become quite an expert at PowerPoint®, and now I'm trying to make instructional videos. It's like I'm learning indie filmmaking on the job!

Q: What is your key to success?

A: When working with such a large and diverse workforce, focusing on common ground is key. You have to determine mutual interests and take it from there.

Q: What training and preparation do you recommend for students?

A: Work on time management, learn basic computer skills, and practice methodical problem solving. At my job, we always use a scientific 12-step process to approach each problem. By using the same system every time, we make sure every angle and outcome is considered, and we can back up our conclusions.

Q: What are some ways you recommend students prepare for this career?

A: To work for the USPS, you have to take a three-part examination. In each segment, you demonstrate that you can follow instructions, handle multiple tasks, and use the English language. If you can handle those things, you'll probably pass. Then you wait for an opening.

Q: What do you like most about your work?

A: I enjoy working with a diverse group of people, developing my skills and résumé, and not having to do the same thing everyday. I face different challenges in different fields. In a week, I might learn about the mechanics of forklifts, figure out issues with air conditioning, create a democratic awards program, or do something totally different. I'm learning something new all the time.

 For more about Career Clusters, go to this book's OLC through **glencoe.com**.

NO CHILD LEFT BEHIND

Teaching Tip

The goals of the NCLB Act include a strong emphasis on reading skills. The use of modeling in your classroom will help students become better at identifying information. For example, ask a question that can be answered by reading the chart on page 117. Verbally identify the elements of the chart that will help the student identify the answer: the stars and the academic skills.

Sample Question How many of the tasks on this chart require three academic skills to complete? (Answer: Three tasks require three academic skills to complete: conduct research, write proposals, and create instructional videos.)

- **Education or Training** Initial qualification is based on a three-part examination.

- **Academic Skills Required** English Language Arts, Mathematics, Social Studies

- **Technology Needed** Computer skills for clerical work and presentations.

- **Aptitudes, Abilities, and Skills** Organizational skills, attention to detail, and the physical ability to carry and deliver heavy loads.

- **Workplace Safety** Workers may have to move heavy loads or objects. They are usually on their feet, and processing mail can be tiring. Many sorters, processors, and machine operators work at night or on weekends, because most large post offices process mail around the clock, and the largest volume of mail is sorted during the evening and night shifts. Workers can experience stress as they process mail under tight production deadlines and quotas.

Career Outlook Postal Service employment is expected to decline over the next ten years. However, new workers will be required to replace those who retire or leave. The number of applicants typically exceeds the number of job openings because of the occupation's low entry requirements and attractive wages and benefits.

Career Path Carriers and sorters can move to administrative and management positions.

N C L B

Academic Skills Required to Complete Tasks

Tasks	English Language Arts	Mathematics	Social Studies
Clerical work	★	★	
Conduct research	★	★	★
Write proposals	★	★	★
Run meetings	★		★
Conduct training	★		★
Make presentations	★		★
Create instructional videos	★	★	★

Critical Thinking

Why would the USPS hire a person with carrying and sorting experience to tend to the quality of life in the workplace?

N C L B This chart relates academic skills such as English Language Arts, Mathematics, Science, Social Studies, and World Languages to specific tasks that are performed for the job featured in the Career Spotlight feature.

Critical Thinking

Jeffrey Friend's carrying and sorting experience would be valuable in his position as a quality of working life coordinator, because his experience has given him firsthand knowledge of the quality of life issues that affect postal workers.

CAREER SPOTLIGHT

ASSESS

Make Connections

Ask students to imagine themselves working as an entry-level postal worker. Ask: What do you think you would like about the working conditions in this job? What do you think you would not like? (Students might mention that they enjoy working with a diverse group of people. They might dislike working on their feet for long hours or dealing with customers.)

CLOSE

Culminating Activity

Applying the Individual Career Plan Have students create an individual career plan that they could use if they decided to pursue a career as a quality of working life coordinator. Ask students to consider the short-term, medium-term, and long-term goals they would need to achieve this career. (A short-term goal might be to ask for an informational interview to learn more about postal work. A medium-term goal would be to get an entry-level job with the postal service. The long-term goal would be to become a quality of working life coordinator.)

CHAPTER **5** Review & Activities

Key Terms and Academic Vocabulary Review

1. Students should write complete sentences using each term correctly. A sample answer might read: "I need to complete my *individual career plan* in order to set goals to achieve my long-term career goal."

Review Key Concepts

2. Students should identify two careers that they might like to pursue. Their answers should explain how the two careers fit their values, interests, personality, data-people-things preferences, skills and aptitudes, and education/training. Students may use the rating system from the personal career profile to contrast the two careers they have chosen with less suitable careers.

3. One characteristic students might mention is to imagine the possible outcome of pursuing the career they evaluated. Students might also use the characteristics listed on the personal career profile—the personal information and the career information—to assess the careers they are considering.

4. Students should identify intermediate goals that will help them get the education and training they will need to achieve their long-term career goals. Intermediate goals might include education, training, and part-time jobs or internships.

5. Student responses should reflect an understanding of the educational requirements needed to achieve their career goals.

CHAPTER SUMMARY

Section 5.1

After you have explored career possibilities, the next step in the career planning process is to evaluate your choices before you make a decision. In evaluating possible careers, you should match the career information you have gathered to your personal interests and resources. Creating a career profile for each career that interests you allows you to review your information systematically and analyze which career choice will work best for you.

Section 5.2

A career plan breaks down a long-term career goal into more manageable, intermediate steps. Setting short-, medium-, and long-term goals will enable you to evaluate your career path as you progress and determine whether you are on the right path. Acquiring more education and training will increase your employment opportunities in your chosen career. Committing to your plan of action in writing will help you develop and revise specific career plans while you continue to move ahead toward a career that will be right for you.

Key Terms and Academic Vocabulary Review

1. Use each of these key terms and academic vocabulary words in a sentence.

Key Terms
- resources (p. 103)
- evaluation (p. 103)
- personal career profile (p. 104)
- individual career plan (p. 107)
- online learning (p. 111)
- on-the-job training (p. 112)
- apprentice (p. 113)
- vocational-technical center (p. 113)
- trade school (p. 113)
- continuing education (p. 114)

Academic Vocabulary
- factors (p. 103)
- pursue (p. 105)
- intermediate (p. 107)
- vocation (p. 113)

Review Key Concepts

2. **Evaluate** two careers as potential careers for you. Why do these careers fit you better than your other possibilities?
3. **Describe** the different characteristics you considered as you made your career choices.
4. **Develop** three intermediate career goals. Explain how these intermediate goals will help you achieve your long-term career goals.
5. **Describe** the kind of education or training you would need to reach one possible career goal.

Critical Thinking

6. **Predict** What consequences might result from settling on a career that conflicts with your personal values?
7. **Evaluate** When evaluating your hopes and dreams, it helps to visualize, or picture, your future. How might good visualization skills help you in your job or career?

Critical Thinking

6. Possible answers: If a career conflicts with your personal values, you may be dissatisfied or unhappy with your job. You also may not perform very well, which could affect your career success.

7. Possible answers: Visualizing your future can help you anticipate potential problems and make decisions to avoid those problems. Visualizing can help you decide whether a career would fit into the kind of lifestyle you picture for yourself. It can also help you decide whether or not the tasks of a particular career are really something that you would want to do and do well.

Real-World Skills and Applications

Critical Thinking Skills

8. Decision Making Andreas just graduated from high school. He plans to build a career in the communications industry. He has just been offered an excellent job as publicity coordinator for a local radio station. However, it is a full-time job with irregular hours, and Andreas has been planning to attend college full-time. Use word-processing software to write Andreas a letter offering advice that will help him decide what to do.

Interpersonal Skills

9. Working in Teams Work in teams to research and compile a list of the names and addresses of various vocational-technical centers, trade schools, community and technical colleges, and four-year colleges and universities. Then select one of these educational institutions. As a team, write a letter requesting information from the institution you have selected. Send your letter to the institution. When you receive the materials, read through them and write a summary of the institution's highlights. Create a class display with the materials you received, your original letter, and your team's summary.

Technology Applications

10. Information Literacy Paying for education or training programs can be difficult. However, there are a number of different ways to fund your education. Using library and Internet resources, find various sources of money for your educational needs. Be sure to check out scholarships, loans, and work-study programs. Ask your school librarian, teachers, or counselors to suggest resources such as Web sites and books. Use spreadsheet software to organize your findings and report your findings to the class.

11. **Sharing Information** Take a few moments to list the ways in which your career goals reflect your work values and needs. How do your goals reflect who you are and what is important to you? Team up with a classmate and exchange your answers verbally for two to three minutes. Then share both of your answers with the class.

12. **Securing an Internship**
Situation You would like to be a graphic artist and want to spend your summer vacation working at a business that will allow you to gain relevant experience. You know of an ideal local business that produces brochures, business cards, and advertisements.
Activity Prepare a brief presentation and a design portfolio that will enable you to convince the business owner of your commitment to secure an internship. Choose specific skills and talents to highlight, and explain how your internship will benefit the company.
Evaluation You will be evaluated based on how well you meet the following performance indicators:
- Demonstrate preparation while presenting personal qualifications.
- Create and use a professional portfolio to enhance your presentation.
- Convey maturity and enthusiasm throughout your presentation.

Chapter 5 Developing a Career Plan 119

ACTIVE LEARNING

11. Students should make clear connections between values and needs and how these affect their career choices.

ROLE PLAY

12. Students should include concrete examples of their strengths and demonstrate planning skills and speaking skills. Portfolios should be neat and organized in a clear and logical way that supports their main points.

Real-World Skills and Applications

8. In their letters to Andreas, students might point out that careers in communications generally require a four-year bachelor's degree. Letters might suggest that Andreas visualize his career in communications and determine whether he needs to adjust his intermediate goals to include a college education, or if he should stick with his goal of getting on-the-job experience with the radio station.

9. Displays should include the letter that was written to the college; material the students received back from the college; and a summary of what the college offers its students.

10. Spreadsheets should reflect research about financial aid and funding for education and training programs.

Academic Skills in the Workplace

13. Answers will vary. Students should include details that support their main point. Students may want to develop a timeline or brainstorm everything they remember about the event before beginning the writing process.

14. Drawing should resemble figure below. It would take 40 hours for the second job to compensate for the lack of bonus.

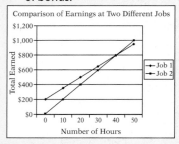

Comparison of Earnings at Two Different Jobs

15. You can collect data by interviewing people, photographing things, recording video, drawing pictures, counting things, and comparing and contrasting things.

16. Answers should include pricing of programs as well as the academic classes, possible internship or job placement opportunities. Compare and contrast skills should be applied.

Academic Skills in the Workplace

English Language Arts

13. Practice Expository Writing Linking your skills and interests to what you have learned from a specific experience or event will help you stand out from other college or job applicants. Think of an event or an experience in which you learned more about yourself and your abilities, such as being a volunteer. In a one-page response, describe how this experience is related to what you learned.

Mathematics

14. Multiple Equations Dienyih is trying to decide between two job offers. One job pays $15 per hour plus a $200 starting bonus, and the other pays $20 an hour with no bonus. After how many hours would the higher salary at the second job compensate for the lack of a bonus? Graph both earnings to determine how many hours it would take.

CONCEPT **Solving Systems of Equations** Two or more equations together are called a system of equations. One method of solving them is by graphing both equations on the same coordinate plane. The point of intersection is the solution.

Starting Hint Draw a coordinate plane and label the axes. Draw lines for both equations by plugging in numbers. Remember, in this case, you only need two points to draw each line. Find where the two lines intersect. This is the answer.

Science

15. Collecting Data The scientific method is what scientists use to study the universe and understand how it works. One important part of the scientific method is collecting data and studying it to see what it reveals about phenomena. This is a key method involved in any type of research. What are some ways in which you can collect data to learn about the world and different careers?

Social Studies

16. Performing and Presenting Research Mina recently graduated from high school. Her career goal is to become a computer programmer. Using the library, the Internet, or the telephone, research the costs of training programs in your area. Determine which program offers the best training for the lowest cost. Organize your findings in a one-page presentation.

STANDARDIZED TEST PRACTICE

MULTIPLE CHOICE

Directions Read the question below. Read each answer choice and choose the best answer to fill in the blank.

Test-Taking Tip In a multiple choice test, read the questions carefully. Look for negative words (*not, never, except, unless*) and positive words such as *always* or *sometimes,* which can affect how you answer the problem.

1. Opportunities for gaining education and training to pursue career goals do not include _____.

   a. online learning
   b. four-year colleges
   c. apprenticeships
   d. a career plan

For more Standardized Test Practice, go to the OLC @ glencoe.com.

STANDARDIZED TEST PRACTICE

Answer
1. d. a career plan

Test-Taking Strategies
Whether your students have a standardized test coming up in a few days or a few weeks, these last minute test-prep tips and strategies will help students relax and do their best.

Test Format Remind students that there is no penalty for guessing on tests.

Test Timing Suggest that students bring a watch to time themselves as there may not be a clock in the testing room.

Writing Skills Practice

17. Using Details Including details when making an argument in a paper or in a conversation with friends strengthens that argument.

 Practice Imagine you are writing a letter introducing yourself to a potential employer. The one-page letter needs to give the employer reasons why she should meet with you and potentially offer you a job. Follow the steps below as you prepare your letter:

- List your personal characteristics and aptitudes that best match what the employer might need.
- List support, examples, facts, or details, demonstrating why you would be a good choice.
- Draft your letter. Make sure each of your arguments is supported by an example, fact, or detail.
- Review your draft. Underline all of your arguments. Highlight all of your support.
- Write your final draft.

Net Connection

18. Gender and the Workplace Interview a woman who has been successful in her career. Ask her whether her gender has affected her career in any way. Present your findings to the class in a brief oral summary.

 Log On Visit this book's OLC through **glencoe.com** to find links to the U.S. Bureau of Labor Statistics. Find statistics that compare average male and female salaries. Summarize your findings and present them to your class.

Reading Connection
Go to this book's Online Learning Center through **glencoe.com** for a list of reading suggestions.

Personal Academic and Career Portfolio

Preparing a Career Plan

After you have used the decision-making process to make a career decision, you can make a career plan. Your first step in making this plan is to set a career goal. Then you can set the short-term goals, medium-term goals, and long-term goals that will lead you to your career goal.

Reviewing your career plan will help motivate you to keep moving toward your career goal and can help you decide whether a particular career goal is right for you.

The following guidelines will help you organize your career plans:

- Create a separate folder for each career that interests you.
- Research career information using print and online resources.
- Prepare an educational or training plan for each career.
- List the goals you would need to achieve this career goal and the time it would take to achieve each goal.
- Categorize the goals as short-term goals, medium-term goals, or long-term goals.
- Put a check box next to each goal. Check off each goal as you reach it.
- Add sources of information about the career or career cluster.
- Review, update, or create new career plans as you continue to explore your career options.

 Portfolio Help Go to the *Succeeding in the World of Work* OLC through **glencoe.com** for help developing your portfolio.

Writing Skills Practice

17. Answers will vary. Have students review their own skills, talents, and aptitudes. They should brainstorm activities or hobbies that they enjoy and that demonstrate what they want to highlight in their letters. Have them read classmates' letters and make suggestions for additional details or information.

Net Connection

18. Summaries should reflect what students learn from speaking with a successful career woman.

Resources

 ExamView Assessment Suite CD allows you to print out ready-made unit and chapter tests complete with answer keys. You can also create customized tests.

WorkKeys

WorkKeys® is a job skills assessment program. For information on leveled assessment for Problem-Solving Skills (Applied Mathematics; Applied Technology; Locating Information; and Observation), go to the WorkKeys link on this book's OLC through **glencoe.com**.

Personal Academic and Career Portfolio

Career Planning with Portfolios

Have students create a career plan for each possible career they add to their **Personal Academic and Career Portfolio**. Career plans can help students keep their career and life goals in mind and help motivate them to take certain classes or participate in certain activities. As students narrow down their career choices, they should create a separate section in their portfolio to file plans for careers they have decided not to pursue.

Unit 2 Thematic Project

Making a Career Plan

You have learned that a successful career starts with research and planning. You have also learned that you have two basic employment options in the world of work: You can work for yourself as an entrepreneur, or you can work for an existing organization or business as an employee. In this project, you will conduct interviews with both an entrepreneur and an employee and use what you learn to create a career plan that shows your ultimate career goal and your related short-term, medium-term, and long-term goals.

FOCUS

Discussion Starter

Ask students if any of them has worked as an entrepreneur. Cite some examples of entrepreneurial work, such as providing child care, mowing lawns, or providing computer repair. Ask about the rewards and drawbacks of working for themselves. (Students may say that they liked the freedom and flexible schedule of self-employment and that they enjoyed the feeling of taking the initiative. They may also point out that income was sporadic or that they had to provide all their own resources and supplies.)

STEP 1

Evaluate Your Skills and Resources

Have students go to the *Succeeding in the World of Work* OLC through **glencoe.com** for a graphic organizer they can use to organize the skills, tools, and resources they will use to complete the project.

TEACH

C Critical Thinking

Ask students to discuss whether certain career interest areas lend themselves to entrepreneurship more than others. For example, does it make more sense for someone with an interest in art or technology to start his or her own business than for someone with an interest in medicine or the environment? Why or why not? (Students should understand the broad range of entrepreneurship options—from opening a retail store to providing specialized freelance services or even starting an independent medicine practice.)

122

Project Assignment

- Choose the career field that most interests you and identify a successful entrepreneur and a successful employee in that field.
- Brainstorm a list of questions to ask these individuals about their long-term and stepping-stone goals, the educational requirements for the career field, the pros and cons of being an entrepreneur and an employee, and any other topics that will help you create your own career plan.
- Arrange, record, and transcribe interviews with both of your candidates.
- Do research and use what you have learned in the interviews and to create a career plan listing your ultimate career goal and your related short-, medium-, and long-term goals.

Lifelong Learning Connection

Lifelong learning concepts found in this project include:
- self-assessment
- setting goals and making decisions
- your career plan and career path
- interpersonal communication skills

STEP 1 Evaluate Your Skills and Resources

To complete this project, you must first research businesses in your area to identify two interview candidates in the field that interests you. During your interviews, you will need a voice or film recorder. To conduct further research for your career plan, you will need access to the Internet as well as to print resources such as books and magazines. To create your career plan, you will also need access to a word-processing program.

Skills you may need to complete the Unit Thematic Project include:

Academic Skills reading, writing, social studies

Transferable Skills communication, research, problem-solving, and decision-making skills

Technology Skills transcribing and word-processing skills

@ Resources Organizer To find a graphic organizer you can use to determine the skills, tools, and resources you will need for this project, go to this book's Online Learning Center through **glencoe.com**.

glencoe.com

SPOTLIGHT ON TECHNOLOGY

Technology Skills

Ask students to brainstorm a list of technology skills that entrepreneurs need in order to plan and run a successful business. Then ask them to research the classes and other learning opportunities available at their school, at local community colleges, night schools, and vocational-technical centers, and through online learning, to build these skills. (Answers should include skills at using computer programs such as word-processing and spreadsheet software, as well as skills at selecting and understanding technology and technology trends in the specific field. Encourage students to be creative in finding educational opportunities.)

STEP 2 Preview a Real-World Company Profile

When researching careers, it may help you to interview and profile individuals who work in careers or at companies that interest you. A good way to learn about the risks and rewards of entrepreneurship is talk to people who have started their own businesses.

Real-World Company: Better World Club

Kelly Ward found out about Better World Club through a friend. Although she did not know much about automobiles, her experience as an environmental activist and organizer made her an ideal job candidate for the company, a roadside assistance provider with a green perspective. She appreciates that the company offers hybrid car rentals, environmentally-friendly tour packages, and roadside assistance for bicyclists in addition to traditional services.

As director of sales and service for The Better World Club, Ward not only believes in the company's services, but also uses them herself.

All company employees are provided with membership benefits.

Better World Club is growing as more and more consumers look for environmentally sustainable alternatives to existing products and services. By offering competitive prices and equal or extra roadside services and appealing to a growing market niche, it thrives in a field that is dominated by large companies.

Better World Club

Aspects of Industry	Company Facts
Planning	Better World Club began with a business plan to capture 1 percent of the roadside assistance market.
Management	Managers share an assistant and meet once a week to discuss issues and keep lines of communication open.
Finance	The founders launched the company with their own money and with capital from investors who believed in their idea.
Technical and Production Skills	Dispatchers, roadside assistance providers, and travel agents all need strong communication and technology skills.
Underlying Principles of Technology	Better World boosts efficiency with a Web-based "hotel engine" that connects to the reservations systems of hotels worldwide.
Labor Issues	Employees receive free membership benefits such as auto service and travel help. They also receive bus passes and health care.
Health, Safety, and Environmental Issues	Better World offers environmental services such as carbon offsets, which enable travelers to make up for the greenhouse gases they generate.
Community Issues	Better World Club donates 1 percent of revenue to environmental cleanup. It also participates in bike fairs, sustainability events, and other community gatherings.

123

Developing Industry Partners

Establish School-Business Partnerships

When first establishing contact with local businesses, it is essential to emphasize how a school-business partnership can benefit not only students, but also the management and workers at the business. Find out what individual business leaders want to gain from the partnership, then use this information to craft a program and specific activities that work toward mutual goals.

TEACH (cont.)

STEP 2
Preview a Real-World Company Profile
Ask students how a company like Better World Club, whose business plan involves capturing a small but targeted segment of the overall roadside assistance market, could do research ahead of time in order to project whether their service will appeal to their target market. (Students may mention online or in-person surveys, talking to competitors' customers, holding focus groups, and testing services in chosen localities before going national.)

R Reading Strategy
Guided Practice
Aspects of Industry
Tell students that understanding aspects of industry can aid their transition to employment in the rapidly changing global workplace and help them connect their academic coursework to the world of work. Ask students to work in pairs to research and define the eight aspects of industry listed in this chart and then to profile a local company using this Real-World Company Profile as a model. (Definitions should reflect an understanding of the importance of each aspect to the success of a business. Profiles should be grounded in solid research and in-person interviews with the leaders of the relevant company.)

TEACH (cont.)

STEP 3

Research Procedures
Have students go to the *Succeeding in the World of Work* OLC through **glencoe.com** for a graphic organizer they can use to organize the results of their research.

STEP 4

Connect to Community
Ask students whether they think businesses have a responsibility to connect to and assist in their communities. Why or why not? (Some students may feel that businesses have an obligation to be of service to the community in some way, while others may feel that businesses only have an obligation to provide products or services at a fair price.)

Ask students why they think many companies give money to local nonprofit organizations, sponsor art and community events, organize volunteer drives among their employees, and sponsor other community programs. What do businesses gain from such community involvement?

STEP 5

Report Your Findings
Give students these tips on drawing up their career plans:

- Clearly label your ultimate career goal.
- Make sure that your short- and medium-term goals relate to your long-term goals.
- Be realistic about the time required to accomplish each goal. Some work experience is usually required to become an entrepreneur.

STEP 3 Research Procedures
Keeping in mind the guidelines for creating a career plan in Chapter 5, identify a career that most interests you and follow these steps:

1. Identify an entrepreneur and an employee in the career field that interests you.
2. Contact the two individuals and set up an interview.
3. Before the interview, create a list of thoughtful questions to pose, such as:
- Why did you choose to become an entrepreneur or an employee?
- What do you like and dislike about being self-employed or an employee?
- What is your ultimate career goal? What are your medium-term goals?
- How do you keep yourself on track toward your goals?
- How does your current employment relate to your ultimate career goal?
- Did you create a career plan when you first started out? Why or why not?

- What education or training is required to enter this career field?
- What skills, qualities, and personal traits are helpful for a person in this line of work?
- What advice would you give to a student who is creating a first career plan?
- What are your keys to success?

4. During your interviews, record responses and take notes.
5. Transcribe the interviews and reflect on how you can use the interviewees' responses and advice to help you create your own career plan.
6. Do further research to gather all the information you need to know in order to create your career plan. For example, you may need to research specific education requirements for your desired career

@ Resources Organizer To find a graphic organizer you can use to organize your research, go to this book's OLC through **glencoe.com**.

STEP 4 Connect to Community
Get Local Ask your interview subjects about how their businesses are related to the community. Do they benefit from local customers, culture, or where they are located?
Take the Next Step Ask interviewees how they give back to their communities. Develop a list of ways that businesses and employees can contribute to their social and physical environments.

STEP 5 Report Your Findings
Your final products for this project should include a transcript of your interviews and a career plan that incorporates what you learned from the interviews, as well as original research.

Developing Community Involvement

Fund-Raising for Nonprofit Organizations
Host a pancake breakfast, car wash, or cookout to raise money for a local charitable organization chosen by the class. Get permission to use a recreation hall or park, and arrange to have food or other supplies donated or sold at reduced cost. Have

students divide into teams to take on tasks such as planning, advertising, recruiting volunteers, and cooking, serving, or washing. Afterward, have the class send thank-you notes to those who donated time and supplies. Also have the class evaluate the event to see what they could improve next time.

- Use word-processing software to transcribe your interviews. Be sure to use correct spelling and grammar.
- Use word-processing software to create a comprehensive career plan that lists your ultimate career goal as well as all the short-term and medium-term goals you will need to accomplish along the way. Make sure to include specifics about your education and training goals and to explain whether you prefer to be an entrepreneur or an employee, and why.
- Format your career plan as a timeline as in the sample career plan in Chapter 5.

Helpful Hints Here are interview tips:
- Always ask for permission to record a person during an interview.
- Show up at the interview prepared; have your questions and other materials ready.
- Do not ask only yes or no questions.
- After the interview, send your subject a brief thank-you note.

Personal Academic and Career Portfolio

Print out a copy of your transcribed interview and your career plan to include in your **Personal Academic and Career Portfolio**. You can use the transcript as a model for future interview-based career research. You can use the career plan as a roadmap to accomplish your short-term, medium-term, and long-term goals.

STEP 6 Presentation and Evaluation

Your report will be evaluated based on:
- depth of interviews and questions
- content of your career plan and timeline
- mechanics—presentation and neatness

@ Evaluation Rubric To find a rubric you can use to evaluate your project, go to this book's OLC through **glencoe.com**.

ASSESS

STEP 6
Presentation and Evaluation
Rubric Encourage students go to the *Succeeding in the World of Work* OLC through **glencoe.com** for a rubric they can use to evaluate their project. Encourage students to use the rubric as a checklist to make sure that their career plans are complete and based on solid research.

CLOSE

Culminating Activity
Career Plan Feedback In this project, students applied the Unit topic to their own lives by talking to successful workers and drawing up their own career plan based on research and self-reflection. Have students work in pairs to present and discuss their career plans and to elicit feedback on whether the plans seem complete and realistic. Encourage students to share the reasoning and decision-making process behind their plans. Have each student list at least two useful observations made by their partners. (Discussions and observations may vary, but encourage students to be open to feedback, as well as tactful and noncritical in their observations. Encourage students to use this activity as a reality check to verify whether their career plans are realistic.)

BusinessWeek Connection

Understanding All Aspects of Industry: Planning

Understanding all aspects of industry can help you prepare to succeed in a career in that industry. Planning is how a business sets its goals, decides what products and services to offer to consumers, and assesses its performance with consumers and in the marketplace. For example, a food company must consider what new products and services will appeal to its customers, what new scientific and dietary breakthroughs will affect product and service demand, and what products and services that company's competitors are developing.

@ Go to this book's Online Learning Center through **glencoe.com** to find a *BusinessWeek* article titled "Nestlé: Fattening Up On Skinnier Foods." Read the article and identify the how this particular company is modifying its planning strategies to meet customers' demands. Use a word-processing program to create a one-page summary of the article. Add this summary to your **Personal Academic and Career Portfolio**.

BusinessWeek Connection

All Aspects of Industry: Planning
Tell students that the planning process does not end once a business opens its doors. To stay successful, companies must constantly monitor their customers' changing needs and their competitors' innovations. Ask students to brainstorm ways that companies in various industries make changes and how they can anticipate coming changes before they happen. (Examples of innovations might include auto manufacturers creating more hybrid vehicles, clothing designers producing new fashions, movie theater chains upgrading their seating and sound systems, or Web sites offering the latest graphics or encryption services. Ways to keep current may include studying sales trends, holding focus groups, and researching the competition.)

Chapter	Chapter Objectives
CHAPTER 6 **Finding and Applying for a Job**	• **Define** *networking* and explain why it is an effective way to develop job leads. • **Develop** a career network and contact list. • **Explain** how to use the Internet and other resources to find career opportunities. • **Explain** how to prepare for and complete a job application. • **Write** an effective résumé and cover letter.
CHAPTER 7 **Interviewing**	• **List** ways to prepare for a job interview. • **Develop** answers to typical and tough interview questions. • **Identify** the importance of body language in creating a good impression. • **Explain** how to project a positive attitude and use good communication skills. • **Describe** how to follow up after a job interview. • **Summarize** best methods for accepting and rejecting employment offers and handling rejection.

Understanding Brackets, Letters, and Ability Levels in the Teacher Wraparound Edition

Brackets Brackets on the reduced student edition page correspond to teaching strategies and activities in the Teacher Wraparound Edition. As you teach the lesson, the brackets show you exactly where to use the teaching strategies and activities.

Letters The letters on the reduced student edition page identify the type of strategy or activity. See the key below to learn about the different types of strategies and activities.

Ability Levels Teaching Strategies that appear throughout the chapters have been identified by one of three codes to give you an idea of their suitability for students of varying learning styles and abilities.

Resources Key program resources are listed in each chapter. Icons indicate the format of resources.

KEY TO LETTERS

R **Reading Strategy** activities help you teach reading skills and vocabulary.

C **Critical Thinking** strategies help students apply and extend what they have learned.

S **Skill Practice** strategies help students practice historical analysis and geographical skills.

W **Writing Support** activities provide writing opportunities to help students comprehend the text.

D **Develop Concepts** activities use various strategies to help teachers gauge and plan for students' concept development.

U **Universal Access** activities provide differentiated instruction for English language learners, and suggestions for teaching various types of learners. *These activities may or may not have brackets.*

NCLB **No Child Left Behind** activities help students practice and improve their abilities in academic subjects.

KEY TO ABILITY LEVELS

L1 Strategies should be within the ability range of all students. Often full class participation is required.

L2 Strategies are for average to above-average students or for small groups. Some teacher direction is necessary.

L3 Strategies are designed for students able and willing to work independently. Minimal teacher direction is necessary.

KEY TO RESOURCE ICONS

Print Material

CD-ROM

Internet

TeacherWorks™
All-In-One Planner and Resource Center

Teacher Wraparound Edition

For the Unit:
Unit Thematic Project Student Rubrics
Unit Test
Unit Connecting Activities Projects

For the Chapter:
Chapter Resources
Program Resources
Additional Print and Media Resources
Lesson Plans
Chapter Summaries, Key Terms, and
   Academic Vocabulary *(English and Spanish)*

Graphic Organizers
Reading Activities
Chapter Self-Checks *(English and Spanish)*
Internet Activities
School-to-Career Connections
Work-Based Learning Projects
Personal and Academic Career Portfolio Student Rubrics

Student Activity Workbook with Academic Integration

Strategies for Students with Special Needs

Career Plan Project Workbook

 Link to the ***Succeeding in the World of Work*** **Online Learning Center with Podcasts** through **glencoe.com**.

Unit Overview
Introduce the Unit
Introduce the unit by describing the main concepts of each chapter in the unit.

Unit 3 introduces students to the steps and skills involved in finding, applying for, and interviewing for a job.

Chapter 6 explores sources of job leads, with an emphasis on creative networking skills. Students learn about the many different ways to find job openings and discover how to fill out a job application form accurately and professionally.

Chapter 7 covers all aspects of the job interview—how to do company research and practice interview techniques, how to make a good first impression and handle typical and tough questions, and how to follow up after the interview.

OUT OF TIME?

If class time is too short to cover all of the chapters in this unit, have students:
- Write down the key terms and their definitions.
- Read the chapter summaries at the beginning of each chapter review.
- Go to the *Succeeding in the World of Work* Online Learning Center (OLC) through **glencoe.com** to download free Study-to-Go content to their PDAs or cell phones.

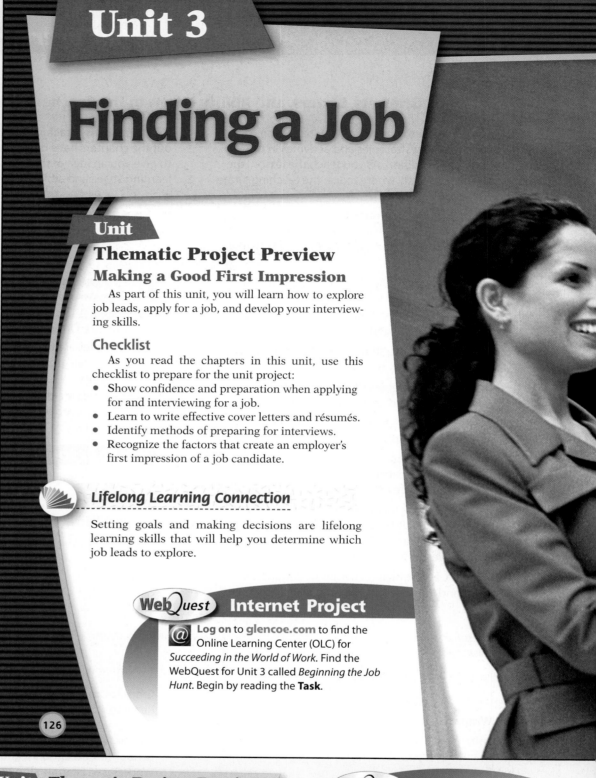

Unit 3
Finding a Job

Unit
Thematic Project Preview
Making a Good First Impression
As part of this unit, you will learn how to explore job leads, apply for a job, and develop your interviewing skills.

Checklist
As you read the chapters in this unit, use this checklist to prepare for the unit project:
- Show confidence and preparation when applying for and interviewing for a job.
- Learn to write effective cover letters and résumés.
- Identify methods of preparing for interviews.
- Recognize the factors that create an employer's first impression of a job candidate.

Lifelong Learning Connection
Setting goals and making decisions are lifelong learning skills that will help you determine which job leads to explore.

WebQuest Internet Project
@ **Log on** to **glencoe.com** to find the Online Learning Center (OLC) for *Succeeding in the World of Work*. Find the WebQuest for Unit 3 called *Beginning the Job Hunt*. Begin by reading the **Task**.

126

Unit Thematic Project Preview
Tell students that as part of this unit, they will work on improving their communication and presentation skills by role-playing and recording two interviews. They will work in pairs to devise realistic interview scenarios and to practice and record two job interviews. Then they will analyze their recordings in order to find specific ways to improve their interview skills in the future.

WebQuest
For WebQuest teaching suggestions and rubrics, go to the Teacher Center of this book's Online Learning Center (OLC) through **glencoe.com**.

FIRST IMPRESSIONS
A smile can give a positive impression.
Why are first impressions important in an interview?

(127)

Build Background
Ask students these questions to activate prior knowledge:

Chapter 6
What are some ways to find job openings, or jobs that need to be filled? (Students may mention speaking to friends, relatives, teachers, counselors, and other working adults, using career Web sites, or looking for help wanted ads or signs.)

What is networking? (Networking is communicating with people you know or can get to know to share information and advice.)

What information do most job application forms require? (Most job application forms require basic personal and contact information as well as information about employment and education history, job and job tasks desired, references, and days and hours available to work.)

What is a résumé? (A résumé is a brief summary of your personal information, education, skills, work experience, activities, and interests.)

Chapter 7
How can you prepare for a job interview? (Do research on the company or organization in order to ask intelligent questions, prepare answers to typical and tough interview questions, plan one's clothing, transportation, and other logistical details, and conduct practice interviews.)

What are some typical interview questions? (Students may guess some of the following: What are your goals? What are your strengths and weaknesses? Why do you want this job? Why should I hire you?)

What should you do after the interview is over? (Send a thank-you note restating your interest in the job and specifying when you will contact the interviewer for a hiring decision.)

▶ Extend the Photo

Caption Answer Students may mention that appearance, poise, open body language (smiling, upright posture, welcoming gestures), eye contact, and other signs of self-confidence and enthusiasm are important in an interview.

Discussion Ask students to describe the differences between making a good first impression on a new friend or classmate and making a good first impression on an interviewer. (Students should understand that interviewers use different criteria in assessing interviewees than they use in assessing potential friends. They are likely to be impressed by an interviewee who is well-spoken and well-dressed and has a professional, respectful demeanor.)

Chapter Resources Planning Guide with Activities and Features

Section	Features	Activities
Section 6.1 Exploring Sources of Job Leads	Creative Business Practices (p. 134) Hot Jobs! (p. 135)	Before You Read (p. 130) Graphic Organizer (p. 130) As You Read (p. 133) After You Read (p. 135)
Section 6.2 Applying for a Job	21st Century Workplace (p. 138) Math in Action (p. 139) Everyday Ethics (p. 140) Real-World Connection (p. 141) Career Checklist (p. 145)	Before You Read (p. 136) Graphic Organizer (p. 136) As You Read (p. 138) After You Read (p. 145)

NCLB Activities, information, and skills practice will help your students attain No Child Left Behind proficiency. Students will improve their abilities in the following academic standards areas:

Academic Standards Correlations

Discipline	Standard	Feature/Activity
English Language Arts	**NCTE 1** Read texts to acquire new information	Creative Business Practices (p. 134) Hot Jobs! (p. 135)
	NCTE 4 Use written language to communicate effectively	After You Read (p. 135) Real-World Connection (p. 141) Writing Skills Practice (p. 151)
	NCTE 9 Develop an understanding of diversity in language use across cultures	21st Century Workplace (p. 138)
Mathematics	**Problem Solving:** Solve problems that arise in mathematics and in other contexts	Math in Action (p. 139)
	Number and Operation: Understand meanings of operations and how they relate to one another	After You Read (p. 145)
	Algebra: Represent and analyze mathematical situations and structures using algebraic symbols	Academic Skills in the Workplace (p. 150)
Science	**Life Science:** Molecular basis of heredity	Academic Skills in the Workplace (p. 150)

21st Century Skills and Workplace Competencies Correlations

CORRELATIONS The charts show the 21st Century Skills, foundation skills, and workplace competencies that students develop as they work in this chapter.

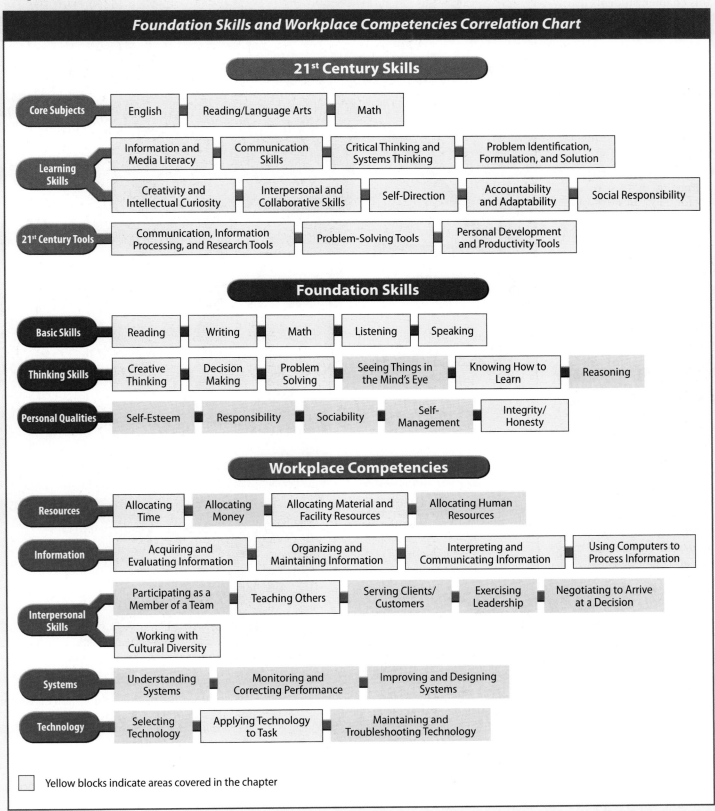

Foundation Skills and Workplace Competencies Correlation Chart

21st Century Skills

Core Subjects
- English
- Reading/Language Arts
- Math

Learning Skills
- Information and Media Literacy
- Communication Skills
- Critical Thinking and Systems Thinking
- Problem Identification, Formulation, and Solution
- Creativity and Intellectual Curiosity
- Interpersonal and Collaborative Skills
- Self-Direction
- Accountability and Adaptability
- Social Responsibility

21st Century Tools
- Communication, Information Processing, and Research Tools
- Problem-Solving Tools
- Personal Development and Productivity Tools

Foundation Skills

Basic Skills
- Reading
- Writing
- Math
- Listening
- Speaking

Thinking Skills
- Creative Thinking
- Decision Making
- Problem Solving
- Seeing Things in the Mind's Eye
- Knowing How to Learn
- Reasoning

Personal Qualities
- Self-Esteem
- Responsibility
- Sociability
- Self-Management
- Integrity/Honesty

Workplace Competencies

Resources
- Allocating Time
- Allocating Money
- Allocating Material and Facility Resources
- Allocating Human Resources

Information
- Acquiring and Evaluating Information
- Organizing and Maintaining Information
- Interpreting and Communicating Information
- Using Computers to Process Information

Interpersonal Skills
- Participating as a Member of a Team
- Teaching Others
- Serving Clients/Customers
- Exercising Leadership
- Negotiating to Arrive at a Decision
- Working with Cultural Diversity

Systems
- Understanding Systems
- Monitoring and Correcting Performance
- Improving and Designing Systems

Technology
- Selecting Technology
- Applying Technology to Task
- Maintaining and Troubleshooting Technology

Yellow blocks indicate areas covered in the chapter

Chapter Overview
Introduce the Chapter
In this chapter, students learn effective methods for finding and applying for jobs.

Section 6.1 explains where to find job openings and how to use networking to find unadvertised jobs.

Section 6.2 guides students through filling out a job application and preparing a résumé and cover letter.

Build Background
Ask: Imagine that you're ready for a job. Besides looking for "Help Wanted" signs, how can you find a good job? Ask students to brainstorm ideas on how they might find job openings. Encourage them to think not only about *where* and *how* they might find openings, but also *who* might be able to tell them about possible jobs.

Exploring the Photo

Caption Answer Career Web sites are excellent sources of job listings. School counselors, friends and relatives, employment agencies and career centers, and professional organizations are other good sources.

Discussion Explain that more and more classified advertisements, including job leads, are found online. Ask: Does this make job listings easier to find, or harder? Why? (Students should understand that online job listings are extremely convenient to search by location and keyword, and often provide more information than short-format print job listings. However, those without easy computer access may find print listings easier to find and use.)

128

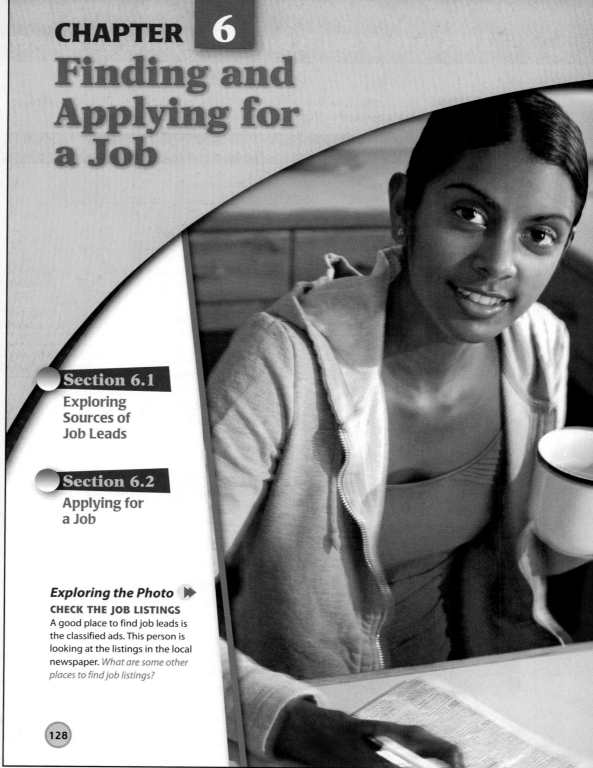

CHAPTER **6**
Finding and Applying for a Job

● **Section 6.1**
Exploring Sources of Job Leads

● **Section 6.2**
Applying for a Job

Exploring the Photo ▶▶
CHECK THE JOB LISTINGS
A good place to find job leads is the classified ads. This person is looking at the listings in the local newspaper. *What are some other places to find job listings?*

(128)

Classroom Resources

- 📁 Student Edition
- 📁 Teacher Wraparound Edition
- 📁 Student Activity Workbook with Academic Integration
- 📁 Student Activity Workbook with Academic Integration TAE
- 📁 *Fast File,* Unit 3 Resources

- 📁 Inclusion in the Career Education Classroom
- ⊙ TeacherWorks™ Plus
- ⊙ *ExamView Assessment Suite*
- ⊙ Interactive Chalkboard
- ⊙ Interactive Student Edition
- 📁 Online Student Edition
- 📁 Online Learning Center (OLC) with Podcasts

Review the Objectives
Introduce the chapter
by reviewing the chapter
objectives:

Chapter Objectives

After completing this chapter, you will be able to:

- **Define** *networking* and explain why it is an effective way to develop job leads.
- **Develop** a career network and contact list.
- **Explain** how to use the Internet and other resources to find career opportunities.
- **Explain** how to prepare for and complete a job application.
- **Write** an effective résumé and cover letter.

Section 6.1 Objectives
Define *networking* and explain why it is an effective way to develop job leads. (Networking is communicating with people to share information about jobs. It is the source of 60 to 80 percent of all jobs.)

Develop a career network and contact list. (Students can find contacts through personal, professional, organizational, opportunistic, and online associations.)

Explain how to use the Internet and other resources to find career opportunities. (Students should demonstrate basic Internet search skills to find job postings on career and corporate Web sites.)

Section 6.2 Objectives
Explain how to prepare for and complete a job application. (Answer every question in standard English, making sure all answers are accurate, neat, and positive.)

Write an effective résumé and cover letter. (An effective résumé is concise, well organized, error-free, and skill-focused. An effective cover letter makes a convincing case for why the employee is a good choice for the job.)

Writing Activity — Personal Career Notebook

Collect as many job leads as possible over the coming week. Ask friends and family members about jobs. Read the classified ads in your local newspaper. Read the bulletin board in the placement office in your school. Write a paragraph about the details of each job opening and how you found each lead.

Get Motivated! Contact three working adults in your community. Ask them to tell you how they found their jobs. Write a paragraph describing their different ways of finding jobs.

Chapter 6   Finding and Applying for a Job   **129**

Writing Activity — Personal Career Notebook Answer Guide

Student entries should reflect initiative and effort and should cover as many sources of job leads as possible. Encourage students to be creative in finding job leads. For example, they might visit a store or business that interests them and simply ask if any jobs are available or might be available in the future.

Get Motivated! Student answers will vary based on the experiences of their interviewees. Many people find jobs through someone they know or through a print or online job advertisement. Once students have completed their research, take an in-class poll to tally the results. Discuss what the results show about where most people find jobs.

FOCUS

Bell Ringer Activity

Exploring Sources of Job Leads

Ask students to list jobs that interest them. Then ask them to think of creative ways they could find out whether such jobs are available in their community.

Resources

⊙ Interactive Chalkboard

The Interactive Chalkboard CD provides visual teaching aids for this section.

@ Online Learning Center

The Online Learning Center (OLC) through **glencoe.com** features chapter vocabulary, chapter summaries, and other study materials.

Preteaching

Divide the class into eight small groups and assign one key term to each group. Ask them to find the definition of the key term in the text and explain how the term relates to finding and applying for a job.

Graphic Organizer

Tell students to go to the OLC through **glencoe.com** for a printable graphic organizer. (Graphic organizers may list friends, relatives, organizations, job ads, employment agencies, or cold calling.)

NCLB connects academic correlations to book content.

Exploring Sources of Job Leads

Reading Guide

📖 Before You Read

Preview Read the Key Terms and Academic Vocabulary words below. In one or two sentences, predict what you think the section will be about.

Read to Learn

- What *networking* means and why this is an effective way to develop job leads
- How to develop a career network and contact list
- How to use the Internet and other resources to find career opportunities

D Main Idea

The best way to find career opportunities is by using a variety of strategies, including networking and research using media resources.

Key Concept

- Finding Job Leads

Key Terms

- ◈ job lead
- ◈ networking
- ◈ contact list
- ◈ referral
- ◈ school-to-work programs
- ◈ temp job
- ◈ temp-to-hire job
- ◈ Internet

Academic Vocabulary

You will find this word in your reading and on your tests. Use the academic vocabulary glossary to look up its definition if necessary.

- ■ qualifications

Graphic Organizer

As you read, list the different ways to find job leads and add notes about each way. Use a two-column chart like the one shown to help you organize your information.

Ways to Find Job Leads	Notes
1.	
2.	
3.	
4.	
5.	

 Log On Go to this book's Online Learning Center through **glencoe.com** for an online version of this graphic organizer.

NCLB Academic Standards •

English Language Arts
- Read texts to acquire new information. (NCTE 1)
- Use written language to communicate effectively. (NCTE 4)

Reading Guide

Before You Read

Ask students how they think most workers find jobs. Ask: Is it through classified ads? "Help Wanted" signs? Friends or relatives? Explain that 60 to 80 percent of all jobs are found through networking, and that employers often like to hire people who come recommended to them.

D Develop Concepts

Main Idea Discuss the main idea with students. Ask: Why is it a good idea to use as many strategies as possible to find job leads? (Students should understand that the more job openings they find, the better chance they have of finding an interesting, well-paying job.)

Finding Job Leads

Getting a job is the beginning of a new lifestyle. You will meet new people, be in new surroundings, and have new challenges and your own income. To get started on this adventure, you need to find a job that you will enjoy and that will start you on a career path.

Finding the right job usually begins with a job lead. A **job lead** is information about a job that is available. It can be a tip from someone you know, an ad in the newspaper or on the Internet, or information from organizations.

Networking

One of the most effective ways to find job leads is by networking. **Networking** is communicating with people you know or meet to share information and advice about jobs. Between 60 to 80 percent of all jobs are found by networking.

Your networking contacts may work at or know about a company that is hiring. These contacts can tell you what types of jobs are available and what the company is looking for in employees. They can also recommend you for a job and even help you get an interview.

You can start networking by making a contact list. A **contact list** is a list of people you know who might be helpful in your job search.

Think of all the people you know, such as your family, your friends, or people you may have worked with in the past. Can any of those people help you find a job? Have any of your friends started new jobs recently? Ask them if they have any leads to share with you. Do you know people who own and manage their own businesses? They may need someone with your **qualifications** or may know someone who is looking for an employee.

Vocabulary
You can find definitions in the **Key Terms** glossary and **Academic Vocabulary** glossary at the back of this book.

 JOIN A CLUB A club or professional organization can be a good place to start a network. *What club can you join now to start building your network of contacts?*

TEACH

Discussion Starter
Finding Job Leads Tell students that it is often said that looking for a job is a full-time job in itself. Ask: Why should you work hard at finding a job? Why not just look for "Help Wanted" signs? (Students should understand that finding a good job can take time. A person may network and research for days, weeks, or even months before finding just the right job. The financial and career rewards of finding a good job, however, are more than worth the time spent.)

R Reading Strategy
Activating Prior Knowledge Ask: Where have you heard the word *network* before? What image does it bring to mind? (Students probably know the phrase "television network," so the word should call to mind a system of interconnected people or things. Point out that a job information network is a group of people who are related to your job search.)

Resources
● **TeacherWorks™ Plus** The TeacherWorks software includes customizable built-in lesson plans and links to printable program resources.

 Extend the Photo

Caption Answer Answers may include school and community groups such as scouting groups, drama club, DECA, engineering societies, or chess club.

Discussion Ask: How could joining a club organized around an interest, such as chess, benefit you in finding job openings?

(Students should understand that clubs of all sorts are a great way to meet people in peer groups who share interests. These people are likely to know about job openings, and they can serve as references to your character and skills.)

S **Skill Practice**
Guided Practice

Find Contacts Ask a volunteer to share the name of a job or career field of interest. Ask whether anyone in the class knows a worker in that job or field. Have the class brainstorm how the student could expand his or her network to meet more people in that job or field. (Students should learn from this exercise that they can find contacts in almost any field by asking everyone they know for help and referrals.) **L1**

Build Contacts Students often underestimate the number of resources available to them to find a job. Have each student make a list of contacts, then share it with a classmate. After sharing the lists, have students revise their own lists to add other resources resulting from their discussions. (Students should work together to generate creative ways to build their contact lists.) **L2**

Write a Letter Have students write letters to a local company to ask how the company fills its job openings. Students should ask whether openings are first posted for current employees and whether the company provides incentives for employees to refer qualified acquaintances. Have students write 200 words summarizing what they learned. (Students' reports will vary, but most companies encourage employees to refer qualified applicants.) **L3**

Figure 6.1 **TYPES OF ASSOCIATIONS**

ASSOCIATIONS IN SUCCESSFUL NETWORKS

Association	Description	Examples
Personal	All the people you know personally	Classmates, neighbors, family, friends
Professional	The people you know through their business, your business, or a professional organization	Your doctor or plumber, coworkers, supervisors, customers, colleagues
Organizational	People you know because of organizations or clubs to which you belong	Members of your Sierra Club chapter, computer club, softball team, church, temple
Opportunistic	People you meet by chance	The clerk at the music store, the person sitting next to you on the bus, the contractor repairing a neighbor's house
Online	People you communicate with over the Internet	People you talk to in a chat room or on an online bulletin board

BUILDING A NETWORK You can build a network by finding contacts through five different types of associations: personal, professional, organizational, opportunistic, and online. *Why should you try to use all five types of associations?*

S List people you know who work for or are connected with companies where you would like to work. Most business owners or managers welcome applications from friends of their employees because they trust the opinions of current employees. Valued company employees make good recommendations because they understand the skills, values, and work ethic of their company. **Figure 6.1** shows different types of associations through which you can build the contact list for your network.

If you have established a good relationship with people in your network, they may provide you with referrals for jobs. A **referral** is a recommendation from a contact who is part of your network.

Organizations

Professional and community organizations provide good opportunities for networking. By joining these groups, you can meet people who may know of job openings. Electronic mailing lists, which are e-mail networks that link professionals working in specific industries, often provide useful job leads and contacts. Although some memberships can cost money, the opportunities that they provide may make the fee worthwhile.

EXTEND THE FIGURE **Figure 6.1**

Caption Answer Using all five types of associations provides more opportunities to find job leads by bringing you into contact with people of many different backgrounds and career fields.

Discussion Ask students how they might start a conversation about jobs with a person they bump into by chance. (Student ideas will vary. A student might ask a person where he or she works and then say, "Oh, you work at JonesCorp? I've been looking for a job in computers, too. Do you know of anything open right now?")

School Resources

Be sure to use the career search resources that are available through your school. A counselor, teacher, or a school placement office can help you set up interviews with employers or identify and follow up on job leads in specific career areas.

They may also be able to get you into a school-to-work program or a school-to-career program. **School-to-work programs** are programs that bring schools and local businesses together to give students the opportunity to get valuable training and work experience. When students in these programs graduate, they may be given preference for jobs where they worked while in the program.

Print Job Advertisements

Sources of print advertisements include newspapers, magazines, and publications that are designed for a particular group of individuals or for a particular industry. Classified ads in newspapers and magazines can be part of your job search, but they should not be the only part. Only around 20 percent of job seekers find their jobs through the classified ads. Classified ads are usually brief and contain job title, job tasks, pay, location, skills required, and how to apply.

Using the Telephone

You can use the telephone to make calls to aid you in your job search. A *hot call* is a call to a specific person or to get specific job information, such as a call to follow up a referral or job lead. A *cold call* is a phone call to a prospective employer with whom you have had no prior contact. If you make cold calls, follow these guidelines to get the information you need:

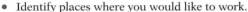

- Identify places where you would like to work.
- Write an introductory script to use. Begin by introducing yourself and saying why you are calling.
- Write questions you would like answered, such as "Are there available job openings?"
- Request referrals.
- Thank the person for speaking with you.
- Now make your call. Ask for the personnel director or the supervisor of a department.
- After each call, record important information and evaluate how helpful the call was.

As You Read

Explain What information does a classified ad usually contain?

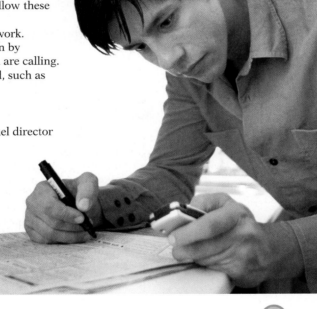

▶▶ **COLD CALLING** Before making a cold call, prepare for what you are going to say. *What else might you do to prepare for cold calling?*

TEACH *(cont.)*

W Writing Support
Independent Practice

Writing Concisely Have students write succinct introductory scripts to use when cold calling. Students should give their full name, briefly summarize their background, and say why they are calling in 10 second or less. (Scripts should be polite and concise.)

As You Read

A classified ad usually contains the job title, job tasks, pay, location, skills required, and how to apply.

ASSESS

Review Key Terms
Have students write sentences using each key term.

Online Study Tools
Have students go to the OLC through **glencoe.com** to:
- Download **Podcast** study tools.
- Download free **Study-to-Go** content to their PDAs or cell phones.

 Resources

● *ExamView Assessment Suite* **CD** allows you to print out ready-made unit and chapter tests complete with answer keys. You can also create customized tests.

▶ Extend the Photo

Caption Answer Students can prepare for cold calling by researching the company, checking its Web site for current job openings, and finding the name of the person to whom they should speak.

Discussion Explain to students that, to be effective, cold calling should be targeted—that is, students should target places they would like to work and then call those companies. Ask: How can you find companies in the field that interests you? (Students may mention asking their contacts or consulting the print or online yellow pages, which group companies by industry.)

RETEACH

S Skill Practice

Independent Practice

Research Local Agencies
Ask students to contact or visit a local public employment agency in their community and to summarize the services it offers. (Lists will vary but should include common services such as providing job leads, reviewing résumés, matching job seekers with jobs, and interview coaching.)

C₁ Critical Thinking

Connecting to Financial Literacy Ask students to contact or visit a local private employment agency in their community, to summarize its services and fees, and to explain whether they believe the fees are worth the services. (Fees may vary dramatically. Students' opinions may vary but should be based on a realistic assessment of the quality and breadth of services offered.)

C₂ Critical Thinking

Drawing Inferences Ask students to speculate about the impact of the Internet on the ease of finding job leads and career information. (The Internet has provided easier access to more information than ever before, has in some cases reduced the expense of publishing job listings, and has centralized access to job leads for job seekers.)

Resources

Student Activity Workbook Assign the Chapter 6 activities in the Student Activity Workbook.

Creative Business Practices

HBO **Encouraging Employees to Mentor**

Cable television network Home Box Office Inc. (HBO) sponsors a mentoring program for young people in which HBO employees mentor underprivileged children. The program encourages long-term relationships with the hope that mentor pairs will be together for several years. The children visit their mentors at the HBO offices each week.

The mentor program gives HBO employees a chance to give back to the community. It offers young people hope for the future and gets them interested in finding a career.

HBO recruits mentors with posters, e-mails, and a promotional video. HBO supports the program by paying for transportation, food, and special activities, such as bowling, softball games, picnics, holiday gifts, and other special presents throughout the year.

CRITICAL THINKING Would you ever consider becoming a mentor? Why or why not?

 Connect to the Real World To read more about HBO, visit the company Web site via the link on this book's Online Learning Center through **glencoe.com**.

A telephone call may be the first contact that you have with a potential employer. Make your call effective. Practice your speaking and listening skills before making both hot calls and cold calls. Keep a record of your contacts and all the information you received from each conversation. Be sure to ask how to spell and pronounce the names of each person with whom you spoke.

Employment Agencies

An employment agency matches job seekers with job openings. Job seekers provide information to the agency by filling out applications and providing résumés. Businesses notify the agency when they have openings. The employment agency then brings the business and qualified job seekers together.

There are two kinds of employment agencies—public and private. Public agencies provide free placement services. Private agencies charge a fee, which may be paid by the job seeker, the employer, or both. Private agencies may give more personal service and list jobs not on file with a public agency.

Private agencies often specialize in temp jobs or temp-to-hire jobs. A **temp job** is a temporary job. It can last for one day or for many months. It is common for people to do temp work while they look for a permanent job. A **temp-to-hire job** is a temporary job that becomes a permanent job after a period of evaluation by the potential employer.

 Creative Business Practices

CRITICAL THINKING ANSWER Answers will vary. Students who have had mentors may be more likely to want to become mentors themselves. Some students may say that they would be more likely to mentor if their employer encouraged it and paid for the associated costs, as does HBO.

Using the Internet

C₂

The **Internet**, a worldwide public system of computer networks, is a good source of job leads. Job listings on the Internet are often called job postings.

Finding the Right Web Sites

Many Web sites connect job seekers with employers. Some sites list all types of jobs, while other sites might list jobs in a particular industry. Sites such as Monster.com and local newspaper Web sites are popular among job searchers and employers alike. At such sites, you can search for jobs according to job title, location, and other criteria. You can also search by keyword. A *keyword* is a word that is used to find related information. For example, if you want a job as a graphic designer, you might type *graphic designer* in the search area. Once you find a job, you can e-mail your résumé and cover letter directly to the company.

Most career Web sites provide more than job listings. Some sites permit you to post your résumé online so that recruiters can access it while searching for qualified applicants. Other sites provide support services such as personal job search agents, career counseling, career networks, bulletin boards, and free newsletters.

Some companies post job openings on their own Web sites. If you are interested in working for a specific company, you may want to visit that company's official Web site. To find a company Web site, type the name of the company into the search bar of an Internet search engine.

Section 6.1 After You Read

Review Key Concepts

1. Explain why networking is an effective strategy for finding jobs.
2. Name two people you would include on your contact list. Why do you think they would be good contacts?
3. Identify two ways, other than networking, that you would use to help you search for job opportunities. Explain your choices.

Practice Academic Skills

English Language Arts

N C L B

4. The saying "it's not *what* you know, but *who* you know" often applies to finding a job. Write a one-page essay about why you agree or disagree with this statement. Give examples.
5. List five jobs that interest you. For each job, write a list of questions you would ask in a cold call.

@ Check your answers at this book's OLC through **glencoe.com**.

HOT JOBS!

Cryptanalyst

Cryptanalysis is the study and practice of encryption—code making and code breaking. Cryptanalysts use advanced math and logic skills to create and understand systems used to protect and distribute sensitive information. Banks, the government, and the military are the biggest employers of cryptanalysts.

Section 6.1

ASSESS

After You Read

Have students complete the Section 6.1 After You Read section review.

Online Study Tools

Have students go to the OLC through **glencoe.com** to:

- Take the Section 6.1 **Practice Test**.
- Download **Podcast** study tools.
- Download free **Study-to-Go** content to their PDAs or cell phones.

CLOSE

Culminating Activity

Getting Ready to Network Have students create a chart of their contacts with the following column headings: Name, Job Title, Company, Contact Information, and Met Through/Referred By. Have students double the length of the list by calling each contact and asking for one referral.

N C L B

Activity correlated to English Language Arts standards.

Section 6.1 After You Read

Review Key Concepts

1. Networking is effective because it uncovers unlisted jobs and because employers like to hire people they know and who come recommended by a friend or colleague.
2. Students should initially focus on people who are successful in their chosen career and who themselves have a wide network of contacts.
3. Students may mention searching print ads or online job postings, making cold calls, getting help from a school counselor, or signing up with a public or private employment agency.

Practice Academic Skills

4. Students should understand that who you know is often the most important factor in landing a job. However, getting a job is not the same thing as succeeding at a job. Being an excellent worker ("what you know") will not only net positive referrals and recommendations, but will also help you build your contact list.
5. Student lists will vary, but questions to ask in a cold call may include, "Are there any entry-level openings in this career field?," "Do you have any advice on getting into this career?," or "Can you tell me what skills and qualifications you are looking for?"

Bell Ringer Activity

Applying for a Job

Ask students to imagine that they are an employer in charge of hiring for an open position. What will they want to know about the job applicants in order to decide whom to hire? Have students take four minutes to write a list of criteria.

Resources

Interactive Chalkboard
The Interactive Chalkboard CD provides visual teaching aids for this section.

@ Online Learning Center
The OLC through **glencoe.com** features chapter vocabulary, chapter summaries, and other study materials.

Preteaching

Assign key terms to student pairs or small groups. Ask each group to define the term and then complete the sentence, "This relates to applying for a job because. . . ."

Graphic Organizer

Tell students to go to the OLC through **glencoe.com** for a printable graphic organizer. (Graphic organizers should list neatness, completeness, standard English, and a positive attitude.)

NCLB connects academic correlations to book content.

Applying for a Job

Reading Guide

Before You Read

Preview Choose a Key Term or Academic Vocabulary word that is new to you. Write it on a piece of paper. When you find it in the text, write down the definition.

Read to Learn
- How to prepare for and complete a job application
- How to write an effective résumé and cover letter

D Main Idea
Making a good first impression on potential employers is essential to securing a job.

Key Concepts
- Preparing to Apply
- Job Applications
- Preparing a Résumé
- Writing Cover Letters

Key Terms
◇ Social Security number
◇ work permit
◇ standard English
◇ job application
◇ personal fact sheet
◇ references
◇ résumé
◇ cover letter

Academic Vocabulary
You will find these words in your reading and on your tests. Use the academic vocabulary glossary to look up their definitions if necessary.
- relates
- accurate

Graphic Organizer
As you read, make a list of guidelines for completing a job application. Add your own ideas to the list. Use a table like the one shown to help organize your information.

Guidelines for Completing a Job Application
1.
2.
3.
4.

 Log On Go to this book's Online Learning Center through **glencoe.com** for an online version of this graphic organizer.

Academic Standards • • • • • • • • • • • • • •

NCLB

English Language Arts
- Read texts to acquire new information. (NCTE 1)
- Develop an understanding of diversity in language use across cultures. (NCTE 9)

Mathematics
- Understand meanings of operations and how they relate to one another
- Solve problems that arise in mathematics and in other contexts

---

Reading Guide

Before You Read

Explain to students that there are several ways to apply for a job. For some jobs, an applicant may just fill out a short form, have an on-the-spot interview, and start work. For other jobs, an applicant may send a résumé, cover letter, and portfolio, and have several lengthy job interviews.

D Develop Concepts

Main Idea Ask: What do you think makes a good first impression on an employer? How is this different from the impression on someone you meet at a party? (Students might point out that a neat, professional appearance makes a good first impression on an employer.)

A JOB APPLICATION
A job application helps a prospective employer learn more about you. *What might an employer learn from your handwriting?*

Preparing to Apply

Employers are looking for the best person to fill the job. They want to know whether or not you have the ability to do the work. They will be influenced by the way you present yourself. They will also notice the way you dress and how well you communicate. They will want to know everything about you that **relates** to the job.

Be Confident

You may feel anxious and insecure when applying for a job. This is natural. Do your best to project confidence and a positive, professional image. Display this image every time you communicate with an employer over the phone, in writing, or in person.

Be Prepared

To apply for a job, you will need certain documents and information. If you have them when you apply for a job, it will show an employer that you are prepared.

First, you will need a **Social Security number**, a unique nine-digit number issued by the federal government that is required for all workers. If you do not already have a number, you can get an application for one at the post office or local Social Security office, or complete an online application at the Social Security Administration Web site.

 Vocabulary
You can find definitions in the **Key Terms** glossary and **Academic Vocabulary** glossary at the back of this book.

Section 6.2

TEACH

Discussion Starter
Preparing to Apply Ask students what they should bring with them when they go to fill out a job application at a business. (Students should mention all relevant personal information; names, addresses, and contact numbers of past schools and employers; Social Security number and work permit [if needed]; names and contact information of references; and a dictionary and a pen and pencil.)

W Writing Support
Guided Practice
Perfecting Handwriting and Spelling Have students obtain an official job application, either by asking a local business for one or by downloading and printing one from the Web. Have them fill out the application and then work in pairs to review one another's work. Students should correct any misspelled words and make suggestions to improve the legibility of the handwriting.

Resources

TeacherWorks™ Plus
The TeacherWorks software includes customizable built-in lesson plans and links to printable program resources.

Extend the Photo

Caption Answer An employer might learn whether you are careful or careless, neat or sloppy. He or she might also learn something about your personality from the style of your handwriting.

Discussion Tell students that *how* they write their job applications can tell employers as much about them as *what* they write. Ask: What are some common mistakes to avoid when filling out a job application? (Students may mention messy handwriting, crumpled or stained paper, misspellings, crossed out entries, or answers that are incomplete, show lack of thought or interest, or are too short or too long.)

TEACH *(cont.)*

S Skill Practice

Research Work Permits
Have students conduct research online to determine local state regulations regarding work permits. Who must have one, and how do they apply? (Answers will vary depending on the state.)

W Writing Support

Guided Practice

Mastering Formal English Explain to students that different levels of formality are appropriate in different situations. For example, a student might use informal language to chat with a friend and formal language to discuss a job with a potential employer. Have students work together to list examples of specific differences between formal English and informal English. (Examples could include slang words and phrases and nonstandard pronunciations and grammatical elements.)

As You Read

Work permits for young people help ensure that their parents and school know and approve of their work plans, that they do not skip school for work, and that they are not exploited by employers.

✓ Reading Check

RECALL To legally work, you need your Social Security number (or card) and a work permit if your state requires it.

N C L B Activity correlated to English Language Arts standards.

The 21st Century Workplace

Italian: Many Dialects, One Language

Italian is spoken in many countries besides Italy, including Switzerland, Croatia, and Vatican City. Like many languages, Italian is really a group of dialects. *Dialects* are forms of a language that differ from one another in vocabulary, pronunciation, and grammar. In school, Italian speakers learn modern standard Italian, the form of the language used in government and business. Standard Italian is really a dialect, too. It comes from the Italian spoken in the city of Florence. You will learn modern standard Italian if you take a course in Italian. If you encounter Italian speakers, though, you will discover many words and pronunciations that differ from the ones in your textbook.

CRITICAL THINKING

Why would it benefit a language learner to know that most languages have dialects?

In Your Community

Italian words are used frequently in the fields of cooking, art, and music. Ask a chef, artist, or musician which Italian words are used in his or her profession. Compile a list of these words as a class.

COMMON ITALIAN WORDS AND PHRASES	
hello (formal)	buon giorno
goodbye (formal)	arrivederci
hello/goodbye (informal)	ciao
welcome	benvenuto
yes	sí
no	no
please	per favore
thank you	grazie
I'm sorry	mi dispiace

@ Extend Your Learning In italian, the spelling reflects pronunciation almost exactly. For links to Web sites about Italian, go to this book's OLC through **glencoe.com**.

As You Read

Analyze Why do you think some states require work permits for workers under 18?

If you are not a U.S. citizen or permanent resident, you may also need a work permit. A **work permit** is a document that shows you are allowed to work in the United States. In addition, some states require work permits if you are under age 16 or 18, as there are laws restricting the hours young people can work and the kinds of jobs they can hold. You can check your state's requirements and get an application for a work permit at your school's guidance office.

An employer may also request your résumé. A résumé is a great way to list your experience, education, and skills. You will learn more about résumés on page 140.

Communicate Effectively

The way you speak and write is one of the first and strongest impressions you will make on an employer, so it is important to use standard English. **Standard English** is the form of English you are taught in school. It is the form used in newspapers. Avoid slang and the use of filler words such as *um*, *like*, and *you know*. You may want to prepare by practicing answering typical interview questions with a friend.

✓ Reading Check **RECALL** What documents must you have in order to be able to work?

The 21st Century Workplace

CRITICAL THINKING ANSWER Even if a person is fluent in standard Italian or another standard language, he or she might not be able to communicate well with all speakers in a country, as some speak a dialect that differs greatly from the standard.

In Your Community Italian words used in cooking include *al dente*, *spaghetti*, and *antipasto*. Italian words used in art include *fresco* and *chiaroscuro*. Italian words used in music include *opera* and *concerto*.

Job Applications

One way employers screen job applicants is by using job applications. A **job application** is a form that asks questions about a job applicant's skills, work experience, education, and interests. You can request job applications in person, over the phone, and through the Internet.

You can make sure your application is **accurate** by creating a **personal fact sheet**, or a list of all the information about yourself that you will need for a job application form. A fact sheet will include your name, phone number, and address, your Social Security number (sometimes abbreviated as SSN), the date you can start work, the days and hours you can work, and the pay you want.

You may also include schools you have attended, places you have lived, and awards or accomplishments. For any jobs you may have had, include the contact information for the place you worked, your title, the tasks you did, when you worked there and for how long, your pay rate, and your reason for leaving the job.

Always fill out a job application completely, neatly, and accurately. On every job application, be sure to:

- Read and follow directions exactly.
- Use standard English and check your spelling with a dictionary.
- Answer every question. If a question does not apply to you, draw a short line in the space to show that you did not skip it unintentionally.
- Make your statements positive. If you believe that answering a question might disqualify you, write "Will explain in interview."
- Keep your options open. For example, if you are asked whether you will work nights, you can write "Will consider."

Know that employers do not have a right to ask about your age, disability status, race, national origin, religion, or gender on a job application. You do not have to tell them if you have been arrested, although you are required to disclose whether you have been convicted of a felony.

To get practice completing job applications, obtain a real-world application from a local company or find one online. Fill out an application for an employment opportunity in a career that interests you, then prepare a list of the information that you needed to complete the form.

References

Applications often request references. **References** are people who will recommend you to an employer. Choose references carefully and be prepared to list them on the application. Teachers, counselors, and former employers make good references. Make sure you ask permission to use people as references.

Math In Action

Salary Increase

Ty was offered a salary of $28,000/year with a 4% increase the second year. What will his salary be the second year?

Starting Hint: Calculate how much Ty would make the second year by multiplying by 100% plus the increased percentage stated in decimal form: (100% + 4% = 104% = 1.04; $28,000 × 1.04 = **?**)

@ For more math practice, go to this book's OLC through **glencoe.com.**

Math In Action

Ty's salary would be $29,120 ($28,000 × 1.04 = $29,120).

TEACH (cont.)

S Skill Practice
Independent Practice
Write a Personal Fact Sheet Have students draw up personal fact sheets for use in filling out employment applications. Have them include the names, addresses, and phone numbers of schools they have attended and places they have lived and worked, as well as date ranges for each. (Fact sheets should be as comprehensive as possible. Encourage students to check all spellings and phone numbers to make sure they are accurate.)

U Universal Access
Students with Learning Disabilities For students who have trouble with sequential tasks involving numbers and with following step-by-step instructions, break tasks into smaller parts or give them a list of steps to follow. Advise such students to ask to take employment applications home to complete.

C Critical Thinking
Reasoning Ask students why it is essential to ask your references for permission to give their names and contact information to potential employers. Also ask: What else must you ask each of your references? (Asking permission shows courtesy and alerts the references that they might receive a call. Students must also ask whether the reference feels comfortable giving a positive recommendation.)

NCLB Activity correlated to Mathematics standards.

TEACH *(cont.)*

S Skill Practice
Independent Practice

Research Tests Have students contact an employer or employment agency that administers tests to job applicants. Tell students to ask questions such as: What tests do you administer? What do the tests measure? What do test scores reveal? How are scores used? If an applicant does poorly on a test, can the test be retaken?

R Reading Strategy
Compare and Contrast
Ask students to compare and contrast the definitions of *job application* and *résumé*. Describe differences in their format, appearance, and content. (A job application is a form printed by a company, usually with blank lines, that asks for answers to fixed questions. A résumé is a word-processed document prepared by a job applicant that lists skills and accomplishments.)

Cooperative Learning
Enrichment

List Skills and Experience Have students work in pairs to decide what to include— and what not to include—on their résumés. Students should help each other pick their strongest skills and educational experiences, and then make lists for use in writing their résumés. (Student lists will vary, but should focus on skills and accomplishments that are relevant to the jobs they want.)

✓ Reading Check

IDENTIFY You should bring a personal fact sheet, your Social Security number (or card), a work permit if your state requires it, your résumé, and a list of references.

140

Everyday ETHICS

MIXED MESSAGES

Is it wrong to withhold information?

FAMILY CONNECTION Your uncle's friend owns a music store in the mall, and he needs a part-time sales clerk. Your uncle left a message on your family's answering machine to tell your sister about the job, and to let her know that his friend would be at the store this afternoon to interview her. You are also looking for a job, and you know that your sister is out with her friends and will not be home until tonight.

What Would You Do? Would you go to see your uncle's friend about the job? Would you try to get in touch with your sister first? Why or why not?

DISCUSS IT How can you express your interest in the job while still leaving the opportunity open to your sister? In pairs, discuss possible ways to handle the situation and the consequences of each. Share your ideas with the class.

Taking Tests

When you apply for a job, you may have to take one or more tests.

S
- A performance test or a skills test evaluates how well you can do a particular task. An example is a keyboarding test.
- A drug test is a blood, hair, or urine test for illegal drugs.
- A polygraph test is a lie detector test. It may be required if you are applying for a job in law enforcement or government.

✓ Reading Check IDENTIFY
What documents should you bring with you when you apply for a job?

Preparing a Résumé

A **résumé** is a brief summary of a job applicant's personal information, education, skills, work experience, activities, and interests. When you are applying for a job, you send your résumé to an employer by regular mail, e-mail, or fax. A good résumé may get you an interview. A poorly written and disorganized résumé, on the other hand, may ruin your chance of getting an interview. How can you make yourself look good to a potential employer on your résumé?

R

A good first step is to choose carefully what you will include, what you will emphasize, and how you will describe your experiences on your résumé. Avoid any negative information. If you do not have work experience, focus on the skills, education, and training you have. Include awards, hobbies, or activities. You can list your references or indicate that you will provide them on request. Place all this information in a folder in your **Personal Academic and Career Portfolio**. Refer to this folder when creating your résumés.

Personal Academic and Career Portfolio

Go to the chapter review to find guidelines for creating your own **Personal Academic and Career Portfolio**.

Everyday ETHICS

What Would You Do? Answer Answers will vary, but students should understand that, because the message was meant for the sister, she should be given the message first. She may not even want the job, leaving the sibling free to pursue it. In addition, showing up at the store uninvited might make a negative impression on the uncle's friend.

DISCUSS IT You might tell your sister that you overheard the message and would be interested in the job if she decides not to accept it. You might also ask your sister to tell your uncle's friend that you would be interested in the next job that becomes available.

The best résumés are brief. Limit the length of your résumé to one page. It should be word-processed or typed. It should also be neat and free from errors in spelling, grammar, or usage. Before you send your résumé, evaluate it as though it belonged to someone else. Ask yourself: Would I hire this person? If the answer is no, keep working on your résumé.

Employers will see your résumé as a reflection of you, so make sure the document is well-written and organized.

Organizing Your Résumé

You must also decide how to organize the information on your résumé. There are two basic résumé formats, a chronological résumé and a skills résumé.

A *chronological résumé* presents your experiences in reverse time order. You list your most recent job first, then your previous job, and so on. You organize your education and other information in the same reverse time order. **Figure 6.2** on page 142 shows an example of a chronological résumé.

The advantage of a chronological résumé is that it shows your growth in experience. It works best for a person with continuous work experience.

A *skills résumé* is organized around skills or strengths, such as attention to detail or interpersonal skills. This type of résumé highlights your skills and accomplishments. The advantage of the skills résumé is that you can emphasize your strengths. It is a good choice if you have limited work experience. **Figure 6.3** on page 143 shows one way to organize a skills résumé.

Scannable and Electronic Résumés

Many companies use only e-mailed or electronically submitted résumés. Others scan paper résumés, copying and storing them electronically in their computers. When the companies need to hire someone, they do an electronic search of the résumés. They look for keywords that describe skills or job experiences they are seeking. Online job sites also store electronic résumés and use keywords to match job applicants with job openings.

Here are some tips for making your résumé easy to scan:
- Keep the résumé clean.
- Use crisp, dark type.
- Avoid italics, underscores, and other formatted type.
- Use white paper.
- Use keywords in describing your experience.

✓ **Reading Check** **CONTRAST** How does an electronic résumé differ from a printed résumé?

Real-World Connection

Writing the Right Résumé

Frank has an assignment in English class to write a résumé. He was told that his résumé can be used to help references write letters of recommendation for him, aid in his scholarship applications, and help him when he applies for a job. He knows that a résumé needs to be brief, accurate, and truthful. Since he has never had a full-time job, he is not sure what to list for work experience.

Critical Thinking Other than full- and part-time jobs, what kinds of work experience could you include in your résumé?

Do Your Own Research Look at several Internet sites that show examples of résumés. Pay close attention to the formatting, including how information is organized and formatted. Write a résumé that includes your own work experiences.

TEACH (cont.)

S Skill Practice
Guided Practice

Gather Résumés Have students collect sample résumés from the school counselor, from people they know, or from résumé books or Web sites. Ask students to choose one or two résumés as models for their own résumé and explain their choices. **L1**

Write an Outline Have students write an outline for a one-page chronological or skills résumé using **Figure 6.2** or **Figure 6.3** as a guide. The outline should include an objective, specific headers, and brief descriptions of each entry. **L2**

Research Résumé Guidelines Have students use the Internet to find reputable information on writing effective résumés. Have students make a list of things to do in crafting an excellent résumé and five things not to do. As a class, compile results into a master list. **L3**

✓ **Reading Check**

CONTRAST An electronic résumé is a résumé stored as a computer file. Unlike a printed résumé, which must be mailed or submitted in person, an electronic résumé can be e-mailed or posted on the Web.

Real-World Connection

Critical Thinking Answer Students should list any relevant experience they have accrued. Examples of unpaid work include volunteer work and the after-school care of a younger sibling.

Do Your Own Research Different Web sites offer different résumé models, but most recommend a bulleted format using action verbs to describe accomplishments. Students' résumés should be error-free and concise and should focus on accomplishments and achievements rather than just summarizing activities.

TEACH *(cont.)*

C Critical Thinking

Evaluate Ask students whether this person seems qualified for the job she is seeking. Would they hire her? Why or why not? (Students will have different opinions, but they should note that the author of this résumé has a history of increasingly responsible work experience.)

W Writing Strategy
Independent Practice

Write a Chronological Résumé Have students create a chronological résumé based on the one in this figure. Encourage them to substitute school activities and coursework for work experience (under the general header "Experience") if they lack job experience. (Experiences should be listed in reverse chronological order and should show a progression toward greater skill and experience.)

S Skill Practice
Independent Practice

Critique Design Job applicants can use a whole range of fonts, colors, type sizes, even photos and graphics, to design their résumés. Have students consult a human resources representative or career counselor about best practices in résumé design and summarize their findings in 200 words. (Résumé design is generally conservative. Most experts recommend using one, or at most two, typefaces and type sizes. Black type on light paper is usually best, with at most one graphic or photo.)

142

Figure 6.2 CHRONOLOGICAL RÉSUMÉ

Name and Contact Information
Write your name, full address, e-mail address, and telephone number (with area code) at the top of your résumé.

Job Objective
State the job you are applying for. Be sure to change this item if you are using the same résumé when applying for different jobs.

Work Experience
List your work experience, beginning with your most recent job. Include volunteer work if it relates to the job for which you are applying.

Skills Summary
Identify any business or other skills and abilities that you have gained in school, on a job, or in other situations.

Education
List the schools you have attended and diplomas or degrees you have received, beginning with your most recent education or training. You may also include any special subjects or programs.

Jennifer Reynolds
6400 Old Harford Rd.
Baltimore, MD 21214
(410) 555-0135
jreynolds@emails.com

Job Objective Full-time administrative assistant position in a law office.

Work Experience Nov. 2010–present
Jenkins Law Firm, Roswell, MD
Administrative Assistant (part-time)
- Perform essential administrative tasks such as scheduling, filing, managing correspondence, and answering busy phones.
- Transcribe case files and notes.

Feb. 2010–Oct. 2010
Sykes Assisted Living Facility, Sykes, MD
Staff Assistant (part-time)
- Performed administrative and managerial duties such as handling phone calls, keeping patient logs, filing, and answering questions from prospective residents and family members.
- Coordinated activities for senior citizens.

Skills Summary
- Dependable, responsible, and hardworking.
- Strong interpersonal and communication skills.
- Able to maintain confidentiality working with legal documents.
- Knowledge of word-processing and database software, including Microsoft Excel and Microsoft Word.
- Bilingual and bicultural English/Spanish.
- Type 65 wpm.

Education 2010
Liberty High School, Liberty Heights, MD
High School Diploma
- Course work in criminal justice and introduction to law.
- Participant in statewide Law Honors Project.
- Three semesters of computer applications courses.

EMPHASIZING EXPERIENCE A chronological résumé organizes information in reverse time order, beginning with work experience. You can use titles and spacing to identify major categories of information. *When would this type of résumé be a good choice?*

EXTEND THE FIGURE **Figure 6.2**

Caption Answer A chronological résumé is a good choice for a job applicant who has a continuous record of work experience.

Discussion Explain that many employers prefer chronological résumés over skills résumés. Why might that be? (Chronological résumés allow employers to track an applicant's career arc and to see whether there are any unexplained gaps in work experience that might indicate a problem.)

Figure 6.3 SKILLS RÉSUMÉ

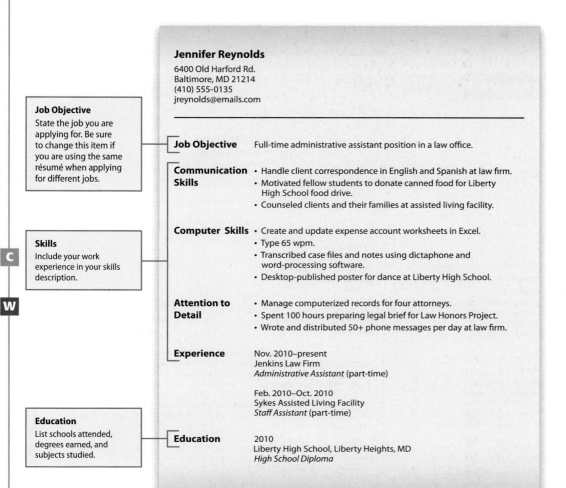

Job Objective
State the job you are applying for. Be sure to change this item if you are using the same résumé when applying for different jobs.

Skills
Include your work experience in your skills description.

Education
List schools attended, degrees earned, and subjects studied.

Jennifer Reynolds
6400 Old Harford Rd.
Baltimore, MD 21214
(410) 555-0135
jreynolds@emails.com

Job Objective   Full-time administrative assistant position in a law office.

Communication Skills
• Handle client correspondence in English and Spanish at law firm.
• Motivated fellow students to donate canned food for Liberty High School food drive.
• Counseled clients and their families at assisted living facility.

Computer Skills
• Create and update expense account worksheets in Excel.
• Type 65 wpm.
• Transcribed case files and notes using dictaphone and word-processing software.
• Desktop-published poster for dance at Liberty High School.

Attention to Detail
• Manage computerized records for four attorneys.
• Spent 100 hours preparing legal brief for Law Honors Project.
• Wrote and distributed 50+ phone messages per day at law firm.

Experience
Nov. 2010–present
Jenkins Law Firm
Administrative Assistant (part-time)

Feb. 2010–Oct. 2010
Sykes Assisted Living Facility
Staff Assistant (part-time)

Education
2010
Liberty High School, Liberty Heights, MD
High School Diploma

EMPHASIZING SKILLS   A skills résumé contains the same information as a chronological résumé but is organized to highlight job-related skills and abilities. *When would this type of résumé be a good choice?*

EXTEND THE FIGURE   **Figure 6.3**

Caption Answer   A skills résumé is a good choice when you have limited work experience, such as when you are looking for your first job, or when you have experience in a lot of different areas that does not show a progression toward a specific goal.

Discussion   Explain to students that skills résumés are often used by engineers, computer programmers, and others in technical fields. Ask why a skills résumé might be a good choice for a worker in a technical career. (Technical employers may be less interested in an applicant's job history than in his or her specific skills. A programmer, for example, might list programming languages, project management experience, and so on.)

TEACH   (cont.)

C **Critical Thinking**
Compare and Contrast
Ask students to compare the skills résumé shown here to the chronological résumé in **Figure 6.2**. Which do they think would impress a potential employer more? Why? (Opinions will vary, but students should back up their opinions with specific facts. Some students may prefer the skills résumé because it calls the employer's attention to specific strengths, while other students may prefer the easy scannability of the chronological résumé.)

W **Writing Strategy**
Independent Practice
Write a Skills Résumé Have students create a skills résumé based on the one in this figure. Encourage them to devise their own skills headers rather than simply repeating the ones shown here. (Students should pick skills that correlate to the job they are seeking. Computer skills, communication skills, and interpersonal skills are helpful for any job.)

ASSESS

Review Key Terms
Have students write sentences using each key term.

Online Study Tools
Have students go to the OLC through **glencoe.com** to:
• Download **Podcast** study tools.
• Download free **Study-to-Go** content to their PDAs or cell phones.

C₁ Critical Thinking

Making Inferences Tell students that many job applicants tailor their résumés and cover letters to every job for which they apply. Is this a good idea? Why or why not? (You should always tailor your cover letter to the specific job. It may also be advisable to edit your résumé to highlight job-relevant skills.)

S Skill Practice

Write a Cover Letter Have students find a job in their local community that interests them and write a cover letter saying where they found the opening and why they are qualified. (Letters should follow the format shown in **Figure 6.4** and should be impeccable in grammar, spelling, and punctuation.)

C₂ Critical Thinking

Reasoning Creatively Tell students that a cover letter helps an employer decide whether to consider the employee further or to go on to the next applicant. Ask: What can you say in the first two sentences to grab the reader's attention and get him or her to read on? (Ideas will vary. Students could lead with a strong description of their skills, mention a person who referred them, use a creative turn of phrase, or highlight some other fact that would demonstrate that they are a good fit for the job.)

Resources

Student Activity Workbook Assign the Chapter 6 activities in the Student Activity Workbook.

Writing Cover Letters

C₁ When you send your résumé, you should always include a cover letter. A **cover letter** is a brief letter that introduces you to the employer and explains why you are sending your résumé. The letter reflects your understanding of the company and how you may be able to meet its needs. When writing a cover letter, emphasize facts that make you especially well qualified for the job. Your cover letter should be divided into three parts, as shown in **Figure 6.4**.

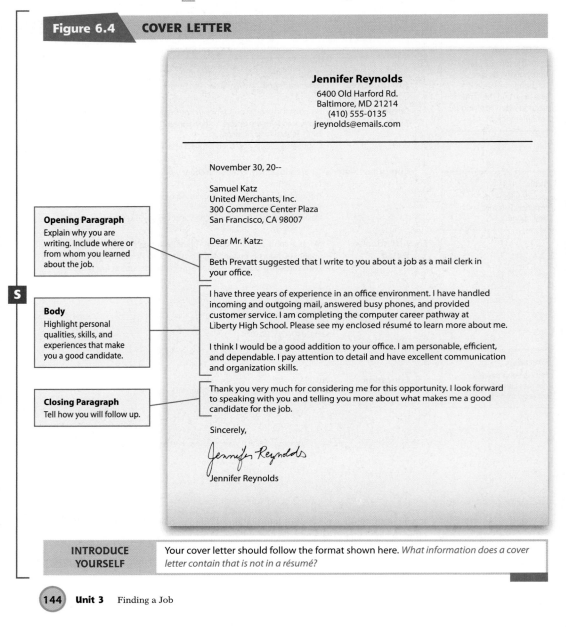

Figure 6.4   COVER LETTER

Jennifer Reynolds
6400 Old Harford Rd.
Baltimore, MD 21214
(410) 555-0135
jreynolds@emails.com

November 30, 20--

Samuel Katz
United Merchants, Inc.
300 Commerce Center Plaza
San Francisco, CA 98007

Dear Mr. Katz:

Opening Paragraph
Explain why you are writing. Include where or from whom you learned about the job.

Beth Prevatt suggested that I write to you about a job as a mail clerk in your office.

Body
Highlight personal qualities, skills, and experiences that make you a good candidate.

I have three years of experience in an office environment. I have handled incoming and outgoing mail, answered busy phones, and provided customer service. I am completing the computer career pathway at Liberty High School. Please see my enclosed résumé to learn more about me.

I think I would be a good addition to your office. I am personable, efficient, and dependable. I pay attention to detail and have excellent communication and organization skills.

Closing Paragraph
Tell how you will follow up.

Thank you very much for considering me for this opportunity. I look forward to speaking with you and telling you more about what makes me a good candidate for the job.

Sincerely,

Jennifer Reynolds

Jennifer Reynolds

INTRODUCE YOURSELF   Your cover letter should follow the format shown here. *What information does a cover letter contain that is not in a résumé?*

EXTEND THE FIGURE   Figure 6.4

Caption Answer The cover letter contains personal information and information that relates the job seeker's experiences to the specific job for which he or she is applying. The letter should convince the employer to give the job seeker an interview and should contain information on how the job seeker will follow up for a decision.

Discussion Explain that many companies now prefer to receive résumés and job applications by e-mail or via an online form. Ask: Do you still need to send a cover letter if you are e-mailing your résumé? If so, should it be different than a printed cover letter? (A cover letter is always advisable, no matter how you submit your résumé. An e-mail cover letter should generally be slightly shorter than a printed cover letter, but should contain the same information.)

The opening paragraph of a cover letter explains why you are writing. Give the title of the job you are interested in and say where, or from whom, you learned about the job.

The body of your cover letter should persuade someone to hire you. In this section, highlight personal qualities, skills, and experiences that make you a good candidate for the job opening.

The closing paragraph tells how you will follow up. Always include your telephone number and e-mail address, if you have one, in this paragraph so that the employer can contact you.

Put time and effort into producing your cover letter. Like your résumé, your letter should be free of errors in grammar, spelling, and punctuation. If possible, ask someone else to proofread your cover letter before sending it to a prospective employer.

It is also a good idea to personalize your letter. For instance, when Andrea was a child, she loved Playskool® toys. When she applied for a job with the company, she mentioned this fact in her cover letter, and it helped her to get the job.

Remember that a business will not hire you just because you need a job. Each job will have many applicants. Your cover letter should convince the employer that you have the necessary skills and abilities to do the job.

Career ✓ Checklist

When Looking for a Job:

✓ Search community, school, and media resources for available jobs in your field of interest.

✓ Create a résumé that highlights your skills.

✓ Write effective cover letters.

✓ Utilize all of your networking contacts.

✓ Prepare for the interview.

✓ Have confidence in yourself.

Section 6.2 After You Read

Review Key Concepts

1. Name three documents you may need when you apply for a job.
2. Explain why it is important to use standard English on a job application.
3. Distinguish between a skills résumé and a chronological résumé, and explain when it is best to use each format.

Practice Academic Skills

Mathematics

4. Anna wants to know how much she is likely to spend preparing her résumé. She does some research and finds that stationery will cost $23.45, envelopes will cost $18.63, stamps will be $7.80, and a new pen will be $3.99. What will her total expenditures be?

   CONCEPT Adding Decimals To add decimals, simply list the numbers vertically, being sure to line up the decimal points. Add normally from right to left, carrying when necessary. Be sure to bring the decimal point down into the answer.

   Step 1: List the numbers ($23.45, $18.63, $7.80, and $3.99) in a vertical line, with the decimal points lined up.

   Step 2: Add, starting with the hundredths place. Be sure to place the decimal point correctly in the answer, and label the answer.

    For math help, go to the Math Appendix located at the back of this book.

---

result

ASSESS

After You Read
Have students complete the Section 6.2 After You Read section review.

Online Study Tools
Have students go to the OLC through **glencoe.com** to:

- Take the Section 6.2 **Practice Test**.
- Download **Podcast** study tools.
- Download free **Study-to-Go** content to their PDAs or cell phones.

Resources

ExamView Assessment Suite CD allows you to print out ready-made unit and chapter tests complete with answer keys. You can also create customized tests.

CLOSE

Culminating Activity
Making a Positive Impression Ask students to write a paragraph describing how their study of this section has changed or expanded their idea of how to make a positive impression on a potential employer during this process. (Paragraphs will vary, but students may mention that they learned the importance of mastering written forms such as the résumé and cover letter.)

Activity correlated to Mathematics standards.

Section 6.2 After You Read

Review Key Concepts

1. Documents often legally required to apply for a job include a Social Security card, a work permit, and photo identification. You may also need to submit a list of references, a completed job application, a résumé, and a cover letter.
2. Using standard English shows your writing skills, and standard English is the language of the professional workplace.

3. In a skills résumé, achievements and experience are grouped by skill (such as communication skills, computer skills, etc.). In a chronological résumé, achievements and experience are listed in reverse order (most recent first) and job titles, company names, and date ranges are specified.

Practice Academic Skills

4. Anna's expenditures would be $53.87 ($23.45 + $18.63 + $7.80 + $3.99 = $53.87).

CAREER SPOTLIGHT

FOCUS

Discussion Starter

Science, Technology, Engineering, and Mathematics Discuss the wide range of jobs in the science, technology, engineering, and mathematics career cluster. Ask students to make a list of products and services that workers in this career cluster help develop. (Lists might include vehicles, chemicals, computer hardware and software, buildings, medical equipment, vaccines, rockets, military equipment, even food.)

TEACH

W Writing Support
Independent Practice

Analyze Presentation Skills Have students use print or online resources or interviews with working professionals to research and summarize the skills involved in giving effective presentations. (Students may cite command of standard English, organizational skills, storytelling ability, self-confidence, positive body language, ability to connect emotionally with an audience, knowledge of presentation software, and other related skills.)

C Critical Thinking

People Skills and Science Explain that some jobs involve being around people more than others. Have students brainstorm types of jobs in which they would work mostly with others and jobs in which they would work mostly alone. (Examples may include politics, teaching, or retail [work with others], or research, writing, or computer programming [work alone].)

146

CAREER SPOTLIGHT

Career Cluster: Science, Technology, Engineering, and Mathematics

Valerie Abati
Television Meteorologist

Q: Describe your job.
A: I forecast, produce, and present daily weather segments for the news.

Q: Describe a typical workday.
A: I look at satellite imagery, radar, weather computer models, and maps so I can make my forecast for the next seven days. Once I've made the forecast, I make all of the weather graphics that you see behind me during the weather presentation. I typically do a weather segment at the beginning of the newscast, followed by a longer weather segment in the middle. I also create and record weather forecasts for local radio stations, and return phone calls and e-mails from viewers.

Q: What skills are most important to you in your job?
A: I use communication, teamwork, computer, and time-management skills daily. In college, math was my most important tool.

Q: What academic skills and lifelong learning skills are helpful in preparing for your career?
A: The biggest help academically for me was math. I used mathematics in just about every one of my college courses. Geography is a big help. When you know names of areas, mountain ranges, and river valleys, it helps your presentation. Computer skills will also help you immensely. Good communication skills are a must.

Q: What is your key to success?
A: To become a successful meteorologist you need to be a good communicator with a good personality. You must be authoritative in cases of severe weather yet be fun and personal in most other situations.

Q: What training and preparation do you recommend for students?
A: Going to college and getting your meteorology degree is a must. When you're in college, it's also best to get involved with your local college television station and do an internship. In both of these cases, you'll be able to practice being in front of a camera and giving presentations. Your internship will also help you prepare for making your own forecasts. Other meteorologists can give you a lot of insight into forecasting and all of the current and developing technology.

Q: What are some ways you recommend students prepare for this career?
A: A good way to prepare is to get involved in many different activities. Theatre, athletics, and student council will all help you be comfortable with people and in front of them. Public speaking is the biggest part of the job, so the more you are in front of large audiences, the more comfortable you'll be in front of the camera.

Q: What do you like most about your work?
A: Being responsible for my own show gives me flexibility and creativity in my job. I love being around people, and with this career I am constantly around the public.

 For more about Career Clusters, go to this book's OLC through **glencoe.com**.

N C L B | NO CHILD LEFT BEHIND

Teaching Tip

The goals of the NCLB Act include a strong emphasis on reading skills. The use of modeling in your classroom will help students become better at identifying information. For example, ask a question that can be answered by reading the interview on this page.

Sample Question What are the four skills most important to television meteorology, according to Valerie Abati? (Answer: Communication, teamwork, computer, and time-management skills are most important.)

CAREER FACTS

- **Education or Training** A bachelor's degree in meteorology is required and a master's degree is preferred. Getting involved in broadcasting at your college radio or television station provides great training, as do internships. Any opportunity to speak in public is good training.

- **Academic Skills Required** English Language Arts, Mathematics, Science, Social Studies

- **Technology Needed** Computers, digital cameras, atmospheric monitoring equipment including Doppler radar and satellite equipment, TV and radio broadcast equipment

- **Aptitudes, Abilities, and Skills** Creativity, research skills, advanced design and computer skills, organizational skills, public speaking, and the ability to react quickly to changing situations

Workplace Safety TV meteorologists usually have a fixed schedule, but most weather stations operate around the clock. Jobs in such facilities usually involve night, weekend, and holiday work, so stamina is required. During weather emergencies, such as hurricanes, operational meteorologists may work overtime.

Career Outlook Jobs in this sector are expected to increase at an average pace over the next ten years.

Career Path The federal government is the largest single employer of civilian meteorologists. Meteorologists also may work for professional, scientific, and technical services firms, including weather consulting services, radio and television broadcasting, air carriers, and state government.

NCLB

Academic Skills Required to Complete Tasks

Tasks	English Language Arts	Mathematics	Science	Social Studies
Research satellite imagery, radar, maps, and computer models		★	★	★
Create forecast	★	★	★	
Create weather graphics	★		★	
Present forecast on TV and radio	★			★
Respond to viewer calls and e-mails	★			★

Critical Thinking

How are mathematical skills important in meteorology?

NCLB This chart relates academic skills such as English Language Arts, Mathematics, Science, Social Studies, and World Languages to specific tasks that are performed for the job featured in the Career Spotlight feature.

Critical Thinking

Meteorologists need math skills to calculate temperatures, determine averages, and use complex three-dimensional weather forecasting models.

ASSESS

Make Connections

Ask students to list careers in science, technology, engineering, and mathematics that would require strong English Language Arts skills. For example, why might a mechanical engineer need strong writing skills? Why might a pharmacist need strong reading skills? (Examples will vary, but students should understand that all careers in this career cluster require the ability to read and absorb large amounts of information as well as the ability to communicate complex information about one's work clearly to colleagues, managers, and the public.)

CLOSE

Culminating Activity

Résumés and Career Clusters Ask students to pick a specific career in science, technology, engineering, or mathematics. Besides a résumé and cover letter, what else might someone in that career send to a potential employer to convince him or her that they have the skills needed for the job? Why? (Students should mention supporting materials that prove that they have key technical skills. For example: patents they have registered, math problems they have solved, research papers they have published, and so on. The meteorologist in this feature would likely send a DVD of clips.)

147

Key Terms and Academic Vocabulary Review

1. Students should write complete sentences using each term correctly. A sample answer might read: "A *cover letter* accompanies a *résumé* and gives me a chance to introduce myself and say why I would be right for the job."

Review Key Concepts

2. Networking is effective because it uncovers unlisted jobs, and because employers like to hire people they know and who come recommended by a friend or colleague. In fact, networking is the source of 60 to 80 percent of all jobs.

3. Students should strive to find contacts through personal, professional, organizational, opportunistic, and online associations. Students' contact lists should also list referrals, or recommendations from contacts.

4. Students should demonstrate knowledge of basic Internet search skills, including the use of keywords to look for desired information. Students can find job postings on three different types of Web sites: sites that list all types of jobs; sites that list jobs in a certain field or industry; and company Web sites that list jobs open in their organization.

5. Students should answer every question on a job application in standard English, making sure all answers are accurate and are written, typed, or word-processed neatly. Students should make only positive statements and should keep their options open about possibilities such as part-time work, evening hours, overtime, and so on.

CHAPTER SUMMARY

Section 6.1

Sources of job leads can include networking, employment agencies, school placement centers, classified ads, and the Internet. A good way to start networking is to make a list of contacts who can help you in your job search. Placement centers can help you identify and apply for jobs. You can find classified ads for job listings in print and online publications. Employment agencies match job seekers with employers. You can find job listings and online career centers on the Internet.

Section 6.2

Before you apply for a job, you should get a Social Security number, and you may need a work permit. You may also need a list of references and a résumé. Use standard English to complete a job application. A chronological résumé presents your experiences in reverse time order. A skills résumé highlights abilities and is used when you have few work experiences. A cover letter introduces you to an employer.

Key Terms and Academic Vocabulary Review

1. Use each of these key terms and academic vocabulary words in a sentence.

Key Terms
- job lead (p. 131)
- networking (p. 131)
- contact list (p. 131)
- referral (p. 132)
- school-to-work programs (p. 133)
- temp job (p. 134)
- temp-to-hire job (p. 134)
- Internet (p. 135)

- Social Security number (p. 137)
- work permit (p. 138)
- standard English (p. 138)
- job application (p. 139)
- personal fact sheet (p. 139)
- references (p. 139)

- résumé (p. 140)
- cover letter (p. 144)

Academic Vocabulary
- qualifications (p. 131)
- relates (p. 137)
- accurate (p. 139)

Review Key Concepts

2. **Explain** how networking helps you develop job leads.
3. **Identify** at least two places you could find contacts to add to your contact list.
4. **Summarize** the advantages of using the Internet to search for job openings.
5. **Identify** three guidelines for completing a job application.
6. **Explain** the difference between a skills résumé and a chronological résumé.
7. **Explain** the purpose of a cover letter.

Critical Thinking

8. **Analyze** Why might prospective employers reject a résumé with only minor mistakes?
9. **Evaluate** What you would look for in an applicant's cover letter if you were an employer?

6. A skills résumé is organized around skills or strengths, and a chronological résumé presents your work experience in reverse order, beginning with your most recent job.

7. An effective cover letter makes a convincing case for why the employee is a good choice for the job.

Critical Thinking

8. A résumé with mistakes, even minor ones, might suggest to an employer that the job applicant either does not have the skills to write an error-free document or is not interested enough in the job to proofread carefully.

9. Answers will vary but should cite excellent writing skills, an impressive summary of skills, and a strong argument about why the applicant is a good fit for the job. Some employers may also be impressed if a job applicant mentions a mutual acquaintance who recommended him or her for the job.

Real-World Skills and Applications

Thinking Skills

10. Knowing How to Learn Ask someone from your school placement office to give a presentation to your class on how the placement office can help you find job leads. If you do not have a placement office, invite someone from a local employment office to address the class. Write a one-page summary of what you learned from the lecture. Also write a half-page thank-you note to the speaker.

Interpersonal and Collaborative Skills

11. Giving Feedback Team up with three other classmates. One of you will play an employer. Another will play a person who is cold calling to ask information about a company. The other two will observe and

take notes. The observers should note what kind of questions the cold caller asks and whether he or she uses standard English. Change roles until everyone has had a turn cold calling.

Technology Applications

12. Creating a Spreadsheet Schedule You attend school, play on a soccer team, and practice with the school band. You need to describe to a prospective employer how much time you spend on each activity. Use spreadsheet software to prepare a weekly schedule. Assume that you have the following weekly time commitments for each activitiy: 30 hours of school, 10 hours of homework, 4 hours of soccer, and 5 hours of band practice.

13. **Team Brainstorming** Use the Internet, newspaper and classified ads, networking, and other job lead resources to make a list of three jobs that you find interesting. Add your list to that of another student, combining duplicates, so that you have one longer list. Brainstorm how it would be best to apply for each job. Use the skills you learned in this chapter.

14. **Offering Advice**

Situation Your friend Tracey wants to apply for a summer internship. She was absent from school on the days that your class discussed how to write a résumé, and she would like you to teach her how to write it.

Activity Teach Tracey how to prepare a résumé. Explain the importance and purpose of the résumé, then outline the key steps involved in writing a résumé. Present an example of a good résumé so that Tracey will understand exactly what she needs to do to prepare her own.

Evaluation You will be evaluated based on how well you meet the following performance indicators:

- Explain the essential steps relevant to résumé writing.
- Provide and explain the parts of a sample résumé.
- Organize your points in a coherent outline.

12. Spreadsheets should show accurate time figures as given in the assignment and should be clearly labeled and organized. If desired, ask students to use the chart-making function of the spreadsheet program to make a pie chart of their schedule showing the percentages devoted to each activity.

ACTIVE LEARNING

13. Encourage students to use sources other than online or print job ads to compile their lists of jobs. The best way to apply for each job is to follow the specific guidelines given in the job ad (such as visiting a store to complete a job application, e-mailing a résumé and cover letter, etc.) Encourage students to think of what supplementary materials, such as a portfolio or writing sample, they might send with their application to showcase their skills.

ROLE PLAY

14. This exercise should demonstrate that students have mastered the key steps involved in creating an impressive résumé: selecting relevant information to include, organizing it in the most appropriate format, writing the résumé with action verbs to highlight accomplishments, and proofreading the résumé to check for errors. Another good step is to show the résumé to at least one trusted friend or working professional for advice and suggestions. Students should also demonstrate that they are able to explain a procedure to another person in a clear and coherent manner.

Real-World Skills and Applications

10. Summaries will vary but should cite many of the ideas for finding job leads contained in the chapter: networking, combing through print and online job advertisements, using school resources, consulting an employment agency, joining a club or professional association, and so on. Students' thank-you letters should follow the business letter format shown in the cover letter example in **Figure 6.4** on page 144.

11. Students should follow the steps described on page 133, including introducing themselves with a short script that gives their name and summarizes their skills, asking for available job openings and requesting referrals, and thanking the person for his or her time and help. Cold callers should speak fluently and should be gracious and appreciative at all times. Observers should offer constructive feedback.

Academic Skills in the Workplace

15. Letters will vary depending on the company chosen and the information learned through research. However, all cover letters should be impeccably written and should contain strong skills summaries and a persuasive argument about why Laura is a good fit for a job at the corporation.

16. Marc spent $295 ($140.00 − $35.00) + ($232.00 × 0.75) + (2 x $8.00) = $105.00 + $174.00 + $16.00 = $295).

17. The second strand of DNA would be TCGATG.

18. Answers will vary, but students should consult either general career Web sites or specific online job boards focusing on nursing (some may be offered by nursing organizations and require login or membership). Advice will vary but might include doing research on hospitals where jobs are available, to find out about working conditions and management, looking for jobs that offer a signing bonus, and/or information comparing and contrasting work at a hospital with work at a clinic, doctor's office, or nursing agency.

Academic Skills in the Workplace

 English Language Arts

15. Write a Cover Letter Laura is interested in sending a résumé to a corporation. Choose a corporation she might apply to and research it. Then write a cover letter she might send to the corporation. Use your research in your letter.

 Mathematics

16. Write Equations Marc bought new clothes on sale for a job interview. He bought the following: a $140 suit at $35 off, a $232 briefcase at 25% off, and two pairs of socks that are $8 each. How much did Marc spend?

CONCEPT Order of Operations To solve an equation you must use the correct order of operations. First, simplify within the parentheses, and then evaluate any exponents. Multiply and divide from left to right, then add and subtract from left to right.

Starting Hint Before solving this problem, write an expression, using the correct symbols (remember that 25% off means that he paid 75% of the price (0.75): ($140 − $35) + ($232 × 0.75) + (2 × $8). Solve using the correct order of operations.

 Science

17. DNA Careers in biology involve working with DNA. DNA is made up of 4 molecules: Adenine (A), Guanine (G), Cytosine (C), and Thymine (T). These molecules line up across from each other, much like a zipper. A always lines up across from T, and G always lines up across from C. For example:

Strand 1: ACGTCAGGT
          | | | | | | | | |
Strand 2: TGCAGTCCA

You are given the following strand of DNA. Can you figure out the second strand?

Strand 1: AGCTAC
          | | | | | |
Strand 2: ??????

Social Studies

18. Research Online Job Boards Sheila wants to find out about opportunities in nursing in Texas. Use the Internet to find some online job bulletin boards. Find some jobs for Sheila. Research and explore an online career service to get some advice for her. Write a one-page summary of your findings.

STANDARDIZED TEST PRACTICE

SHORT ANSWER

Directions Answer the following questions in one to three sentences.

> **Test-Taking Tip** In a short answer question, write as neatly as possible. Double-check your grammar, spelling, and punctuation. Neatly written answers often get higher marks.

1. Explain the difference between a résumé and a cover letter.

2. List and describe the components of a skills résumé.

STANDARDIZED TEST PRACTICE

Answer

1. A résumé is a concise summary of a job applicant's skills, work experience, and education. A cover letter accompanies a résumé and is a business letter in which a job applicant introduces him- or herself to a possible employer and explains why he or she would be a good fit for a job.

2. A skills résumé contains: name and contact information; job objective; skills and abilities, grouped by specific skill with supporting information for each; education, and often other information such as activities and awards.

Test Timing Short answer test questions are usually timed. Have students practice writing to the clock by giving them timed sentence-writing assignments at the beginning or end of class.

Writing Skills Practice

19. Preparing a Résumé Before preparing a résumé, research sample résumés to use as models.

 Practice Use a word-processing program to create a résumé for an employment opportunity in a career that interests you. Follow these steps to create your résumé:

- Write a draft of your résumé. Include your contact information, education and work experience, and any other relevant information.
- Have an adult help you edit and proofread your résumé. Ask the adult if the résumé accurately describes your abilities.
- Put your résumé away for a few days, then read it over to see if you want to make any changes.
- Add your résumé to your **Personal Academic and Career Portfolio**.
- Keep an electronic copy of your résumé. Update it as you gain experience.

Net Connection

20. Find Jobs Online Find a Web site that allows you to look for job leads and post résumés online.

 Log On Go to this book's OLC through **glencoe.com** to find a link to a Web site that posts job openings or allows you to post your résumé online. Look for any job openings that match your interests. Print out the jobs and place them in your **Personal Academic and Career Portfolio**. Then create a one-paragraph document describing how to post your résumé to the Web site.

Reading Connection

Go to this book's Online Learning Center through **glencoe.com** for a list of reading suggestions.

Personal Academic and Career Portfolio

Job Leads, Your Résumé, and a Cover Letter

Your **Personal Academic and Career Portfolio** is a good place to put information on job leads that you find interesting. You should also have a copy of your résumé and a sample cover letter in your portfolio to use when following up job leads.

Research to find a job opening that interests you. Note the qualifications required for the job. Contact the company to find the name of the person in charge of hiring for this job. Create a cover letter and résumé that are tailored to the specific job. Be sure to relate the skills you have to the skills required for the job.

Use the following guidelines to help you:

- Brainstorm to decide what skills you have that match the skills listed in the job opening.
- Make a list of your skills, awards, and any organizations that you belong to that match the job opening.
- Use the guidelines in this chapter to create a draft of your résumé.
- Use the guidelines in this chapter to create a draft of your cover letter.
- Edit and proofread your résumé and cover letter.
- Rewrite your résumé and cover letter, if necessary, to fix any errors you found while editing.

Portfolio Help Go to the *Succeeding in the World of Work* OLC through **glencoe.com** for help developing your portfolio.

Writing Skills Practice

19. Assess students' résumés based on choice of information, clarity of organization, and quality of writing (no errors in grammar, spelling, or punctuation). Skills and work experience should be written in such a way as to support the stated job objective.

Net Connection

20. Many career Web sites, such as Monster.com, Yahoo! Jobs, and even Craigslist allow job seekers to post their résumés online, free or for a nominal fee. Many also allow job seekers to post their résumés anonymously, to protect their privacy. Students' paragraphs should clearly describe all the steps involved in posting a résumé online. These steps typically include registering (setting up an account) with the site, formatting the résumé, and transmitting it electronically. As part of the registration process, job seekers may have an opportunity to indicate their career interests, geographical location, experience level, desired pay, and so on.

 Resources

ExamView Assessment Suite CD allows you to print out ready-made unit and chapter tests complete with answer keys. You can also create customized tests.

Personal Academic and Career Portfolio

Maintaining a Portfolio

Tell students that they can use their **Personal Academic and Career Portfolios** to store documents they will need for the job hunt, including their personal fact sheet, résumé, and cover letter(s). Students should also store relevant job listings or printed job postings in their portfolios; these provide valuable information about necessary qualifications for jobs in the student's career interest area. Emphasize to students that their résumés will evolve as they gain education and job experience. Students should update their résumés each time they complete a new achievement, develop a new skill, or change jobs.

WorkKeys

WorkKeys® is a job skills assessment program. For information on leveled assessment for Interpersonal Skills (Teamwork), go to the WorkKeys link on this book's OLC through **glencoe.com**.

151

Chapter Resources Planning Guide with Activities and Features

Section	Features	Activities
Section 7.1 **Preparing for the Interview**	Science in Action (p. 156) Creative Business Practices (p. 157) Tech Savvy (p. 158) Everyday Ethics (p. 159) Hot Jobs! (p. 161)	Before You Read (p. 154) Graphic Organizer (p. 154) As You Read (p. 157) After You Read (p. 161)
Section 7.2 **Succeeding in the Interview**	Real-World Connection (p. 164) 21st Century Workplace (p. 165) Career Checklist (p. 169)	Before You Read (p. 162) Graphic Organizer (p. 162) As You Read (pp. 163, 166) After You Read (p. 169)

NCLB Activities, information, and skills practice will help your students attain No Child Left Behind proficiency. Students will improve their abilities in the following academic standards areas:

Academic Standards Correlations

Discipline	Standard	Feature/Activity
English Language Arts	**NCTE 1** Read texts to acquire new information.	Creative Business Practices (p. 157)
	NCTE 4 Use written language to communicate effectively.	Tech Savvy (p. 158) After You Read (p. 169) Writing Skills Practice (p. 175)
	NCTE 8 Use information resources to gather information and create and communicate knowledge.	Academic Skills in the Workplace (p. 174)
	NCTE 9 Develop an understanding of diversity in language use.	21st Century Workplace (p. 165)
	NCTE 12 Use language to accomplish individual purposes.	Real-World Connection (p. 164)
Mathematics	**Algebra:** Analyze change in various contexts	After You Read (p. 161)
	Measurement: Understand measurable attributes of objects and the units, systems, and processes of measurement	Academic Skills in the Workplace (p. 174)
Science	**Science as Inquiry:** Abilities necessary to do scientific inquiry	Science in Action (p. 156)
	Life Science: Behavior of organisms **Science in Personal and Social Perspectives:** Personal and community health	Academic Skills in the Workplace (p. 174)

CORRELATIONS The charts show the 21st Century Skills, foundation skills, and workplace competencies that students develop as they work in this chapter.

Foundation Skills and Workplace Competencies Correlation Chart

21st Century Skills

Core Subjects
- English
- Reading/Language Arts
- Math

Learning Skills
- Information and Media Literacy
- Communication Skills
- Critical Thinking and Systems Thinking
- Problem Identification, Formulation, and Solution
- Creativity and Intellectual Curiosity
- Interpersonal and Collaborative Skills
- Self-Direction
- Accountability and Adaptability
- Social Responsibility

21st Century Tools
- Communication, Information Processing, and Research Tools
- Problem-Solving Tools
- Personal Development and Productivity Tools

Foundation Skills

Basic Skills
- Reading
- Writing
- Math
- Listening
- Speaking

Thinking Skills
- Creative Thinking
- Decision Making
- Problem Solving
- Seeing Things in the Mind's Eye
- Knowing How to Learn
- Reasoning

Personal Qualities
- Self-Esteem
- Responsibility
- Sociability
- Self-Management
- Integrity/Honesty

Workplace Competencies

Resources
- Allocating Time
- Allocating Money
- Allocating Material and Facility Resources
- Allocating Human Resources

Information
- Acquiring and Evaluating Information
- Organizing and Maintaining Information
- Interpreting and Communicating Information
- Using Computers to Process Information

Interpersonal Skills
- Participating as a Member of a Team
- Teaching Others
- Serving Clients/Customers
- Exercising Leadership
- Negotiating to Arrive at a Decision
- Working with Cultural Diversity

Systems
- Understanding Systems
- Monitoring and Correcting Performance
- Improving and Designing Systems

Technology
- Selecting Technology
- Applying Technology to Task
- Maintaining and Troubleshooting Technology

☐ Yellow blocks indicate areas covered in the chapter

Chapter Overview
Introduce the Chapter

In this chapter, students learn how to prepare for and succeed in a job interview.

Section 7.1 focuses on preparing for the interview by doing company research, preparing answers to likely interview questions, and practicing interview skills and positive body language.

Section 7.2 discusses how to demonstrate a positive attitude and other employability skills during the interview and how to follow up after the interview.

Build Background

Write the words "job interview" on the board and define the term. Ask students to share what they know or believe about job interviews. What happens during a job interview? Why is a job interview important? Collect students' ideas to revisit later.

▶ Exploring the Photo

Caption Answer Good steps to take to prepare for an interview include researching the job, company, and industry, preparing an appropriate outfit, and practicing answers to typical interview questions.

Discussion Ask students why employers conduct interviews. What could a company learn about you in an interview that they might not know from your résumé? (Interviewers can learn who you are as a person, can assess your attitude and motivation, and can see how you respond under pressure.)

Interviewing

Section 7.1
Preparing for the Interview

Section 7.2
Succeeding in the Interview

Exploring the Photo ▶
GET THE JOB YOU WANT The interview is your chance to make your case for the job you want. *What can you do to prepare for your interview?*

152

Classroom Resources

- 📂 Student Edition
- 📂 Teacher Wraparound Edition
- 📂 Student Activity Workbook with Academic Integration
- 📂 Student Activity Workbook with Academic Integration TAE
- 📂 *Fast File,* Unit 3 Resources

- 📂 Inclusion in the Career Education Classroom
- ⚙ TeacherWorks™ Plus
- ⚙ *ExamView Assessment Suite*
- ⚙ Interactive Chalkboard
- ⚙ Interactive Student Edition
- 🖥 Online Student Edition
- 🖥 Online Learning Center (OLC) with Podcasts

Chapter Objectives

After completing this chapter, you will be able to:

- **List** ways to prepare for a job interview.
- **Develop** answers to typical and tough interview questions.
- **Identify** the importance of body language in creating a good impression.
- **Explain** how to project a positive attitude and use good communication skills.
- **Describe** how to follow up after a job interview.
- **Summarize** the best methods for accepting and rejecting employment offers and handling rejection.

Writing Activity — Personal Career Notebook

In a one-page journal entry, write four questions that you might be asked in a job interview. Think of questions that might help the interviewer understand you as a person, beyond your job skills. Record answers to the four questions as well.

Get Motivated! Talk to a manager who has interviewed job applicants. Ask him or her about common mistakes people make during job interviews. What advice would this person give every applicant? Record the key points of your interview in a one-page journal entry.

Chapter 7 Interviewing **153**

Writing Activity — Personal Career Notebook Answer Guide

Students might include questions about current and past employment such as, "Tell me what activities you like best at school," questions about personal traits such as, "What are your strengths and weaknesses?" or questions designed to test thinking skills, such as, "What would you do if a customer angrily demanded a refund but the store policy was 'exchanges only'?"

Get Motivated! Students' notes will vary but should include common interviewee mistakes such as arriving late or unprepared, not knowing answers to common questions, dressing inappropriately for the workplace, and possibly even major blunders such as lying or exaggerating.

Review the Objectives

Introduce the chapter by reviewing the chapter objectives:

Section 7.1 Objectives

List ways to prepare for a job interview. (Find out the time, place, and other important details about the interview. Research the company and the industry. Prepare answers to typical and tough interview questions. Practice interviewing techniques.)

Develop answers to typical and tough interview questions. (Good answers to typical and tough interview questions are honest, highlight the positive, and demonstrate thinking skills and desirable personal qualities.)

Identify the importance of body language in creating a good impression. (Body language can help create a positive impression because it is one of the first things an interviewer notices, and because it communicates interest, alertness, openness, and relaxed self-confidence.)

Section 7.2 Objectives

Explain how to project a positive attitude and use good communication skills. (A positive attitude is projected through positive body language, by accenting the positive and avoiding the negative in comments and responses, and by showing interest in the job and company.)

Describe how to follow up after a job interview. (Send a thank-you note to the interviewer(s) and follow up with the interviewer about a hiring decision.)

Summarize the best methods for accepting and rejecting employment offers and handling rejection. (If offered the job, take time to think about it and possibly to negotiate a better offer. If rejected, accept the decision gracefully and ask for feedback to help you next time.)

Section 7.1

Bell Ringer Activity

Preparing for the Interview

Ask students to imagine that they've just been offered a job interview—tomorrow. Have students work in pairs to make a list of ten things they should do to get ready.

 Resources

Interactive Chalkboard
The Interactive Chalkboard CD provides visual teaching aids for this section.

@ Online Learning Center
The Online Learning Center (OLC) through **glencoe.com** features chapter vocabulary, chapter summaries, and other study materials.

Preteaching

Read the definitions of the key terms aloud. Ask students to look up and share the definitions of the three components of body language—gestures, posture, and eye contact.

Graphic Organizer

Tell students to go to the OLC through **glencoe.com** for a printable graphic organizer. (Graphic organizers will vary but should include company research, preparing answers to interview questions, creating a personal "commercial," and practicing interviewing techniques, including good body language.)

N C L B NCLB connects academic correlations to book content.

Preparing for the Interview

Reading Guide

 Before You Read

Preview Look at the photos and the figure in this section and read the captions. Write one or two sentences predicting what you will learn.

Read to Learn
- Ways to prepare for a job interview
- Answers to typical and tough interview questions
- The importance of body language in creating a good impression

Main Idea
Preparing for a job interview involves research and practice.

Key Concepts
- What Is an Interview?
- Do Your Research
- Prepare Your Answers
- Practice Interviewing Techniques

Key Terms
◇ interview
◇ body language

Academic Vocabulary
You will find these words in your reading and on your tests. Use the academic vocabulary glossary to look up their definitions if necessary.
- minimize
- anticipate

Graphic Organizer
As you read, create a list of specific actions you can take to prepare for a job interview. Use a chart like the one shown to help organize the information.

To Do Before a Job Interview

- Check date, time, and address of company
- _____
- _____

@ Log On Go to this book's Online Learning Center through **glencoe.com** for an online version of this graphic organizer.

Academic Standards •

N C L B

English Language Arts
- Read texts to acquire new information. (NCTE 1)
- Use information resources to gather information and create and communicate knowledge. (NCTE 8)
- Use language to accomplish individual purposes. (NCTE 12)

Mathematics
- Analyze change in various contexts

Science
- Science as Inquiry: Abilities necessary to do scientific inquiry

Reading Guide

 Before You Read

Explain to the class that having an interview means that an employer is interested in you, but does not mean that the employer has already decided to hire you. In fact, employers often interview many candidates for the same job. Usually, it is the best-prepared and most self-assured interviewee who ultimately lands the job.

D Develop Concepts

Main Idea Discuss the main idea with students. Ask: Why does it matter whether you prepare for an interview or not? (Students should understand that employers look for candidates who are organized, prepared, and hard working, and who really want the job—and that means candidates who take time to think ahead about the interview.)

What Is an Interview?

An **interview** is a meeting between an employer and a job applicant to discuss possible employment. An interview can be formal or informal, long or short. An interview can even take place over the phone. You may meet a single interviewer or several interviewers together or separately.

An interview is the employer's chance to meet you as a person, not just as a name on a résumé. It is also your chance to learn more about the job and decide whether it is a good fit for you. The interview is the most exciting part of the job hunt. It can also be the most stressful. Preparing ahead of time will **minimize** your anxiety and help you make a great impression.

✓ Reading Check **SUMMARIZE** Describe the various forms and types of job interviews.

Do Your Research

R A manager may interview dozens of candidates for a single job. Many of these candidates will be qualified and competent. You can stand out by preparing thoroughly in the days before the interview.

Get All the Facts

Confirm the exact time and location of the interview. Plan how you will get to the interview and how long the trip will take. Make sure you know the interviewer's job title and how to pronounce his or her full name. If you are not sure, call the company's main number and ask the person who answers the phone.

▶ **Vocabulary**
You can find definitions in the **Key Terms** glossary and **Academic Vocabulary** glossary at the back of this book.

 DO YOUR HOMEWORK
Before an interview, you should find out information about the company or organization. *What are some sources of information?*

TEACH

Discussion Starter
What Is an Interview? Tell students that an interview is like a "tryout" for a job. Ask students to brainstorm other areas in life where they might have to "try out" in person for what they want. (Students may mention school activities such as drama, band, sports, and government. Some postsecondary schools also conduct interviews. Students may even mention dating as a kind of "tryout" for a relationship.)

R Reading Strategy
Activating Prior Knowledge Students have learned that there are many points in the career development process that require research. Ask: What other steps in the job hunt require research? (Students may mention various types of research, such as researching possible careers, looking for suitable job openings, and researching how to write a résumé and cover letter.)

✓ Reading Check

SUMMARIZE An interview can be one-on-one with a potential employer, or a panel interview with several interviewers, or even take place over the phone. These are different from the exploratory interview, covered in Chapter 3.

Resources

⚙ **TeacherWorks™ Plus**
The TeacherWorks software includes customizable built-in lesson plans and links to printable program resources.

▶ Extend the Photo

Caption Answer Sources of company information include the company's Web site, business information Web sites, business and industry magazines and newspapers, and company literature.

Discussion Remind students that research can help them decide whether a certain company is a right fit for them. For example, some job applicants may only want to work at a company that allows flexible hours to take care of family responsibilities; others may want a company that promotes strongly from within. Ask students to share some of the things they would look for in an ideal company.

TEACH *(cont.)*

S Skill Practice
Independent Practice

Research Have students find and read an article about a local company and explain how the information in the article might help them in a job interview with that company. (Learning more about a company will help students ask intelligent questions during the interview and show that they have spent time and effort preparing for the interview.)

C Critical Thinking

Drawing Conclusions Tell students that talking to people who work at a company is a great way to get an insider's view. Ask students how they might be able to tell whether the information an employee gives them is fair and objective. (Students can gain solid information by asking for concrete facts with questions such as, "What is the rate of employee turnover in your division?," or "Does the company offer educational assistance?")

W Writing Support
Guided Practice

Writing Persuasively Tell students that the process of writing can help them clarify their thoughts. Writing answers to interview questions can not only help students practice their interview techniques, but can also help them refine their language and ideas and answer questions in a concise, confident, persuasive way. Ask students to write a two-sentence answer to each of the six questions on this page, then have students work in pairs to help refine and perfect their answers.

NCLB Activity correlated to science standards.

156

Science In Action

Chemical Solutions

You are making a solution that calls for 100g of Tris-HCl powder in 1 Liter of water, or 100g/L. How many grams of Tris-HCl powder would you add if you wanted 2L of this Tris-HCl solution?

Starting Hint: Solve for ? in the following equation:

$$\frac{100g}{1L} \times 2L = ?g$$

@ For more science practice, go to this book's OLC through **glencoe.com**.

Plan what to wear to the interview as well. Match your clothes to the job. If you can, visit the workplace to see what other workers are wearing. Plan to dress a little more formally than they do. Your clothes do not need to be expensive, just neat and clean.

Research the Company

Another way to stand out is to learn all you can about the organization where you want a job. Doing research helps you ask intelligent questions about the company and the industry. This will also show your interviewer that you are resourceful, thorough, and willing to work. Here are some smart ways to do company research:

- Find books, magazines, and newspaper articles about the company, its competitors, and its industry.
- Ask the public relations department for the company's annual report or press kit. Read about the company's history, accomplishments, financial situation, and leaders.
- Visit the company's Web site to find out what is new. What takes up the most space on the home page? This tells you what is important to the organization right now.
- Talk to people who work for the company or who have worked there in the past.

Many candidates do not bother to learn about a company before the interview. Taking the time to prepare will make you stand out among the competition.

Research Protects You

Researching a company can also protect you. For instance, you might learn that the company does not really fit with your career goals. The company may be in financial trouble or have high employee turnover, which suggests that workers are not happy there.

✓ Reading Check **ANALYZE** Why is doing company research before an interview worth your time and effort?

Prepare Your Answers

The next step is to prepare answers to typical questions. The interviewer will ask questions to find out who you are and what you can do for the company. Try to **anticipate** questions he or she might ask. Think about how you would answer standard interview questions such as:

- What are your career goals?
- What are your greatest strengths? Your greatest weaknesses?
- Why do you want this job?
- Why do you think you are right for this job?
- Why did you leave your last job?
- Where do you see yourself in five or ten years?

Write down sample answers to these questions and review them with a trusted adult. Concentrate on your positive skills in your answers. To answer a question about your weaknesses, for example,

---

Science In Action

You would need to add 200g of Tris-HCl powder.

✓ Reading Check

ANALYZE Doing company research helps you make a good impression at the interview. It gives you ideas for questions to ask and ideas to offer. Company research also helps you decide whether a certain company would be a good fit for you and offer career advancement opportunities.

you can talk about ways you are working on a certain area that may be a challenge for you. For example, you might say, "Time management is always a challenge. I have improved my time management skills by using a day planner, which has really helped me stay on track."

Create Job-Specific Answers

Make sure your answers to possible interview questions relate to the job you want. Imagine that you are applying for a sales job at a music store. When asked about your career goals, you might say, "I'm interested in a career in the music industry. A sales job is a good way to get to know what kind of music customers are looking for."

Create a Commercial for Yourself

Interviewers frequently ask open-ended questions, such as "What can you tell me about yourself?" One good strategy to prepare for these kinds of questions is to prepare a 30-second "commercial" to highlight your unique talents and skills and market yourself.

Amelia Abad, an aspiring journalist, wrote this commercial for herself: "I work hard, I meet deadlines, and I enjoy learning new things. Coworkers have told me that they love working with me because I am easy to get along with and have a sense of humor. My journalism teacher says I'm a talented writer who can make anything sound interesting."

As You Read

Explain On what should you focus when you answer interview questions?

Creative Business Practices

MACY'S — Keeping Good Employees

The turnover rate for retail salespeople is one of the highest in any industry. That's why Macy's created a retention program to keep good employees at its department stores.

Designers of the retention program realized that store managers had a heavy schedule and a full workload. The retention program restructured all management positions so managers now have more time to get to know the people who work for them. This practice encourages managers to meet employee needs whenever possible, such as with flexible work schedules. Macy's also promotes a family atmosphere among the staff.

Sales associates are also part of the retention program. To keep them interested in their work, Macy's provides opportunities for training and advancement. Associates can work with a mentor, attend career development seminars, receive monthly and yearly awards, and volunteer with other community groups to help the community.

CRITICAL THINKING If you owned your own business, what would you do to keep employees happy with their jobs?

@ Connect to the Real World For more information about Macy's retention program, visit the company's Web site via the link on this book's Online Learning Center through **glencoe.com**.

glencoe.com

C Critical Thinking

Analyzing Ask students to imagine that an interviewer asks them a personal question such as, "What do you like to do on weekends?" Ask students how they could answer such a question in a way that relates to the job they want—and why it would be wise for them to do so. (Students could relate such a question to the job by highlighting activities that build relevant skills, such as reading, volunteering, and team sports.)

U Universal Access

English Language Learners Students who are learning English as a second language may find the prospect of a job interview stressful. For these students, creating and rehearsing a positive "commercial" is an especially wise idea. Ask the class to brainstorm specific ways in which an interviewee who speaks English as a second language could feature his or her background in a "commercial." (The interviewee could mention his knowledge of the relevant culture and how that could benefit the company in a global economy.)

As You Read

When answering interview questions, focus on the skills and personal qualities that are relevant to your ability to excel at the job. Always focus on the positive.

Creative Business Practices

CRITICAL THINKING ANSWER Answers will vary but might include offering fair pay and generous benefits, recognizing employees' accomplishments, sharing profits, providing training and staff development, implementing an "open-door" policy with management, or eliciting employee feedback on how to make the company better.

TEACH *(cont.)*

S Skill Practice
Guided Practice

Problem Solving Have students imagine that they are being interviewed for a position as assistant to an executive who travels a lot. The interviewer asks, "Your boss is traveling and cannot be reached. You receive an urgent message for your boss to contact the CEO of the company. What do you do?" (Most interviewers would expect an answer such as, "I would contact the CEO or her assistant right away and explain the situation, then ask if there is anything I could do to solve the problem.") **L1**

Answering Questions Have students work in small groups to list four difficult questions (besides those listed here) that an interviewer might ask a job applicant. Ask them to write a sample answer for each question and to briefly explain why an interviewer might ask that question. (Questions will vary but should be relevant to the job candidate's job skills, personal traits, or thinking skills.) **L2**

Research Have students use the Internet or the school or public library to find books or articles on successful interviewing and make a list of 20 questions that are typically asked in an interview. Tell students to write answers to each question using the guidelines in the book or article. (Questions should be realistic and should reflect an understanding of the purpose of a job interview. Answers should focus on the positive and on students' skills.) **L3**

Prepare for Difficult Questions

You should also prepare for more challenging questions, such as:

- What qualities do you have that make up for your lack of experience?
- We are a very competitive company. Why should we hire you?
- Imagine you made a major mistake on the job. What would you do to fix it?
- Do you feel a little too inexperienced for this position?
- Have you ever been fired?
- What makes you different from all the other candidates I have interviewed?
- What do you see yourself doing in five years?

Focus on the Positive

Interviewers often ask difficult questions to see how you respond or how you think under pressure. There is no one right answer. Be honest and show confidence in yourself.

When asked what makes you different, you might say, "Every candidate has a different combination of strengths. Mine are intelligence, curiosity, organizational skills, and the flexibility to handle new situations." Some interviewers may ask you what your weaknesses are. Be honest, but focus on the positive. Show how you are working to improve yourself. For example, you may respond, "In the past, I have taken on too many tasks without planning for them. Now I use a PDA and a to-do list, which allows me to keep track of my tasks and manage my time better."

✓ **Reading Check** SUMMARIZE List at least two actions you should take to prepare for a job interview.

Practice Interviewing Techniques

Now that you have created and written down your answers, it's time to practice! Practice boosts your communication skills and your self-confidence. Team up with friends, classmates, family members, and teachers or counselors for practice interviews. Have them ask you a range of questions so you can practice your answers. Keep your answers brief and to the point. Remain businesslike—do not get too casual. Dressing in business clothing and meeting in a business setting will help you pretend that this is a real interview.

S

TechSavvy

Video Glasses Training

Have you ever been trained for a task at home, at school, or at work? How did you learn the task? Did someone instruct you in person? Or did you watch a video or read a book? You can put on a pair of video glasses instead and watch a virtual instructor show you how to do something new.

Video glasses operate using batteries. Sound is built into the glasses. Users can hook up the video glasses to an MP3 player, a computer, a portable DVD player, a video cell phone, a computer, or a video game console. The glasses weigh only a few ounces and fit close to your face, so it appears as though you are looking at a screen from several feet away.

@ Visit this book's OLC through **glencoe.com** and find the link to a description of video glasses technology. Write a two-paragraph description of how you could use video glasses to practice for a job interview.

TechSavvy

Video Glasses Training

Answer Answers will vary but should reflect an understanding of the value of multimedia training in learning new skills. Video glasses could be useful in preparing for a job interview because they allow you to see and hear the performance of model job applicants.

✓ **Reading Check**

SUMMARIZE To prepare for an interview, do the following: find out all the logistical details about the interview; research the company and the industry; prepare answers to typical and tough interview questions and create a "commercial" for yourself; practice interviewing techniques, including positive body language; and use feedback from others (and yourself!) on your interview performance to help you improve.

◀◀ **STAY RELAXED**
Be relaxed but attentive
during the interview.
*What might body lan-
guage such as fidgeting
convey to an interviewer?*

Watch Your Body Language

As you practice your answers, practice your body language, too. **Body language** is the gestures, posture, and eye contact you use to send messages. We are often unaware of our body language. Positive body language is key to making a good impression. Eye contact, good posture, and a firm handshake signal self-confidence. Nodding and leaning forward show that you are paying attention. Keeping your hands relaxed and still shows you are calm. All these things create a positive image.

Biting your nails, playing with pens or jewelry, or crossing and uncrossing your legs frequently may suggest that you are nervous. Crossing your arms over your chest can indicate that you would rather be somewhere else. **Figure 7.1** on page 160 shows examples of body language.

Everyday ETHICS

CLARIFYING DUTIES

How do you know if you are prepared to do a task?

VETERINARY TECHNICIAN You have just been offered a job as a veterinary technician. Because your last position was at an animal hospital, the veterinarian assumes you have performed various procedures on animals, such as taking a pet's temperature and administering shots. During your interview, there was no opportunity to clarify the duties of the job. At your last job, you did not handle the animals, but you have seen enough of the procedures to feel comfortable doing them on your own.

What Would You Do? Do you tell the vet that you did not handle the animals at your last job and refuse to perform the procedures until you are trained, or do you see how your first procedure goes? Explain.

> *DISCUSS IT* Is it safe to perform procedures you have not done before? In teams, discuss the possible ways you, the veterinarian, and animals might be affected if you made a mistake during a procedure. Share your answers with the class.

Everyday ETHICS

What Would You Do? Answer Students should understand that it is important to clear up the misunderstanding with the veterinarian. Even though the situation arose from a misunderstanding and not a lie, it is not ethical to allow the veterinarian to extend a job offer based on faulty information.

DISCUSS IT Performing medical or veterinary procedures without proper training is irresponsible. An animal could get hurt or even die. The veterinarian could lose business or even be sued. The person who misrepresented his or her skills could be fired and have trouble finding another job in the same field.

TEACH (cont.)

 C **Critical Thinking**
Differentiating Explain to students that it is normal to be slightly nervous during a job interview. Why, then, might an interviewer dislike body language that shows nervousness, such as biting nails or playing with jewelry? (Students should understand that, while feeling nervous is normal, having nervous habits or body language can distract from what they are saying and may also suggest that they are not able to handle the responsibilities of the job, or deal with clients and customers in a professional manner.)

U **Universal Access**
Students with Orthopaedic or Visual Impairments Students with orthopaedic or visual impairments may be limited in their use of body language, such as eye contact or hand gestures. Encourage such students to ask for necessary accommodations when the interview is being arranged and to find alternative ways of signaling self-confidence and interest in the interview.

▶ *Extend the Photo*

Caption Answer Restless body language, such a fidgeting, could convey nervousness, boredom, or (worse) that the interviewer might have something to hide.

Discussion Ask students, "How can you become more aware of your body language, to make sure you don't have any bad habits?" (Practice your interviewing techniques with a partner who will give you honest feedback.)

159

Section 7.1

ASSESS

Review Key Terms
Have students write sentences using each key term.

Online Study Tools
Have students go to the OLC through **glencoe.com** to:
- Download **Podcast** study tools.
- Download free **Study-to-Go** content to their PDAs or cell phones.

Resources

ExamView Assessment Suite CD allows you to print out ready-made unit and chapter tests complete with answer keys. You can also create customized tests.

RETEACH

C Critical Thinking
Drawing Inferences Ask students, "Does smiling make a person seem more likeable and trustworthy? Why or why not?" (Answers will vary, but students should recognize that, in our culture, smiling is seen not only as an indication of happiness but as a reflection of openness and enthusiasm.)

Resources

Student Activity Workbook Assign the Chapter 7 activities in the Student Activity Workbook.

160

Figure 7.1   BODY LANGUAGE

POSITIVE BODY LANGUAGE You can use good body language to show that you are a positive, confident person. *What are some examples of good body language?*

▶ **GIVE A FIRM HANDSHAKE** Hold out your hand to shake hands with your interviewer. Smile and make eye contact.

◀ **AVOID NEGATIVE BODY LANGUAGE** Slouching, fidgeting, and avoiding eye contact may be interpreted as boredom or disrespect.

▶ **SHOW INTEREST** Lean forward slightly in your chair. Make eye contact with the interviewer and nod your head to show that you are paying attention.

160   **Unit 3**   Finding a Job

EXTEND THE FIGURE   Figure 7.1

Caption Answer Positive body language includes making sustained eye contact, smiling, having an upright but slightly relaxed posture, leaning forward slightly to indicate interest, and keeping your hands relaxed.

Discussion Some people "talk with their hands" more than others. Ask students whether animated hand gestures while speaking are positive or negative body language. (Answers will vary. Most people use some hand gestures while speaking. Using constant hand gestures may strike some people as distracting, while using no gestures at all may strike others as overly reserved.)

Use the following techniques in your practice interviews. They can help you become aware of your body language.

- **Use a mirror.** Make sure you are sitting up straight and making eye contact with the interviewer. Are you calm or fidgeting? Is your facial expression pleasant or anxious?
- **Record the interview.** Listen to it when you are done. Are your words clear? Do you sound confident, or do you use a lot of filler words, such as *like* and *um*?
- **Practice interviewing by phone.** You may have an interview on the phone or talk to the employer by phone after the interview. Practice speaking clearly and at a moderate pace. Try smiling as you talk—it actually makes you sound more positive.

Get Feedback
After you practice, ask for feedback, which is a detailed response. Was your body language positive? Were you confident and well-spoken? What did the practice interviewer like or dislike about your behavior or your responses? You can use this feedback to improve your performance in future interviews.

Section 7.1 After You Read

Review Key Concepts
1. Name three ways to research a company before a job interview.
2. Choose one typical question and one tough question from those listed in the text and write answers you can use during an interview.
3. Give three examples of body language.

Practice Academic Skills
 Mathematics
4. Before going to an interview for a new job, you decide to research the company. The company made $150,000 the first year, $200,000 the second year, and $250,000 the third year. Use slope-intercept form to create a graph that shows these earnings and estimates the company's earnings for the next year if the company continues to grow at the same rate.

CONCEPT **Slope-Intercept Form** An equation in slope-intercept form is written $y = mx + b$ where m is the slope and b is the y-intercept, or the point where the line crosses the y-axis.
Step 1: Draw a coordinate plane, labeling the axes. Plot the three points that you already know: $150,000; $200,000; and $250,000. Connect the points.
Step 2: Calculate the slope by dividing rise over run or the change in y divided by the change in x between two points. Find the y-intercept by finding where the line crosses the y-axis. Write an equation for the line.

Math For math help, go to the Math Appendix located at the back of this book.

HOT JOBS!

Art Handler
How do fragile works of art end up in museums? Art handlers transport, assemble, and install art in museums and galleries. Especially complex or valuable pieces may require the expertise of a certain individual or team of handlers who install these pieces wherever they are exhibited. Required skills include construction and conservation skills.

Section 7.1

ASSESS

After You Read
Have students complete the Section 7.1 After You Read section review.

Online Study Tools
Have students go to the OLC through **glencoe.com** to:
- Take the section 7.1 **Practice Test**.
- Download **Podcast** study tools.
- Download free **Study-to-Go** content to their PDAs or cell phones.

CLOSE

Culminating Activity
Preparing for the Interview Have students create interview tip sheets listing five specific actions that job seekers can take to prepare for an interview and five tips on answering typical and tough interview questions. Have students switch lists with one another and amend or add to one another's lists. As a class, compile a master tip sheet that contains the best of all students' tips.

NCLB Activity correlated to Mathematics standards.

Section 7.1 After You Read

Review Key Concepts
1. Answers should include three of the following: look up printed resources; consult online resources; request materials from the company's press office; talk to people who work at the company or who have worked there in the past.
2. Students' answers should focus on the positive and show reasoning skills, self-confidence, and correct use of standard English.
3. Answers should include examples of gestures, posture, and/or eye contact. Students should understand that absence of gestures or eye contact is body language that sends a message.

Practice Academic Skills
4. Graph should resemble this figure.
Slope = ($200,000 − $150,000)/1 = $50,000
y-intercept = $100,000
Equation for line: $y = \$50,000x + \$100,000$

Section 7.2

FOCUS

🔔 Bell Ringer Activity

Hiring the Best Job Candidate

Ask students to imagine that they are a business owner looking to hire a new computer repair technician. What personal qualities or personality traits would they look for in interviewees, and why? What if they were hiring a college teacher or a graphic designer?

Resources

⚙ **Interactive Chalkboard**
The Interactive Chalkboard CD provides visual teaching aids for this section.

@ **Online Learning Center**
The OLC through **glencoe.com** features chapter vocabulary, chapter summaries, and other study materials.

Preteaching

Ask: What do *role-playing*, *problem solving*, and *stress* have to do with succeeding in a job interview? Ask students to make guesses, then scan the chapter for the key terms and revise their answers based on what they find.

Graphic Organizer

Tell students to go to the OLC through **glencoe.com** for a printable graphic organizer. (Graphic organizers should include information on answering questions confidently, showing positive body language and a positive attitude, and following up after the interview.)

Succeeding in the Interview

Reading Guide

📖 Before You Read

Preview Choose a Key Concept that is new to you. Write it on a piece of paper. When you find it in the text, write one or two sentences explaining the concept.

Read to Learn
- How to project a positive attitude and use good communication skills
- How to follow up after a job interview
- The best methods for accepting and rejecting employment offers and handling rejection

Main Idea
Projecting a good first impression and properly following up after an interview are essential to succeeding in your career.

Key Concepts
- Arrive on Time and Prepared
- Have a Good Attitude
- Speak for Success
- Follow Up after the Interview

Key Terms
◈ role-playing
◈ problem solving
◈ stress

Academic Vocabulary
You will find these words in your reading and on your tests. Use the academic vocabulary glossary to look up their definitions if necessary.
- simultaneously
- establish

Graphic Organizer
As you read, write notes about what to do before, during, and after the interview. Use a chart like the one shown to help organize the information.

Before Interview	During Interview	After Interview

 Log On Go to this book's Online Learning Center through **glencoe.com** for an online version of this graphic organizer.

N C L B

Academic Standards •
English Language Arts
- Read texts to acquire new information. (NCTE 1)
- Use written language to communicate effectively. (NCTE 4)
- Develop an understanding of diversity in language use across cultures. (NCTE 9)
- Use language to accomplish individual purposes. (NCTE 12)

Reading Guide

Before You Read
Tell students that a positive attitude is key to succeeding at a job interview. Ask students what they think a "positive attitude" means and to describe people they know who are positive. What do these people do—and *not* do—to show that they have a positive attitude?

D Develop Concepts
Main Idea Ask students how they form a first impression of a person when meeting him or her for the first time. List all the factors that might contribute to a positive or negative impression, including appearance, grooming, voice, body language, etc.

Arrive on Time and Prepared

Start the interview right by arriving on time, alone, and prepared. Arrive a few minutes early to give yourself time to fill out any paperwork. Be sure that you have your Social Security number and any relevant contact information.

Bring a pen, something to write on, and two or more copies of your résumé. Your interviewer may ask you for it. Employers often ask questions about your résumé, so reread it at least once right before the interview. Bring any notes you have about the company, as well as the answers you have created for typical interview questions. You can rely on your prepared notes in the interview if you feel nervous.

Dress for Success

The first thing an employer sees is not your great personality or your list of accomplishments—it's your appearance. Make sure you are well-groomed, with trimmed nails, clean teeth, and neat hair. If you are male and do not wear a beard, shave before your interview. If you wear makeup, wear very little. Be sure to bathe before you dress for an interview. Use deodorant if necessary. Wear very little cologne, perfume, or aftershave. Many people are sensitive to or allergic to fragrance.

Your shoes should be clean and unscuffed, and your clothing should be clean and unwrinkled. Remember to dress conservatively. Let your skills stand out, not your flashy suit or jewelry.

✓ **Reading Check** **EXPLAIN** Why is correct dress so important in a job interview?

Have a Good Attitude

Attitude is very important, especially for first-time job seekers. When James Coblin of Nucor Steel interviews applicants for a mill in South Carolina, he does not focus on job skills. Coblin knows that he can teach workers how to make steel. What he looks for is the right attitude. He wants people who are enthusiastic, who want to do a good job, and who pitch in to solve problems together.

LOOK THE PART You can say you are right for the job by wearing the right clothes to the interview. *Is this person more appropriately dressed for an interview at a sporting goods store or for a professional office?*

TEACH

Discussion Starter
Arrive on Time and Prepared Ask students, "What can clothing say about a person?" Ask students to list different types of dress and the messages that each might convey to an interviewer. Why is it a good idea to choose a conservative style of dress for a job interview?

 Reading Strategy
Making a List Ask students to create a list of things to bring with them to the interview and to classify these things as for their own personal use or for possible use by the interviewer. (Encourage students to elaborate on the items listed in the text. For example, students might want to bring a notepad to take notes, a planner or calendar in case a follow-up interview is scheduled, articles on the industry, and a printout of information from the company's Web site.)

As You Read
Bring a résumé to a job interview both so you can refer to it yourself during the interview and so you can give a copy to the interviewer(s), if asked. Bringing your résumé with you also shows that you are organized and that you think ahead.

Extend the Photo

Caption Answer This person is dressed perfectly for a job in a professional office.

Discussion Ask students how they can find out ahead of time what style of dress might be appropriate for a particular workplace. (Students might call the company's main number and ask the receptionist for dress guidelines.)

✓ **Reading Check**

EXPLAIN Correct dress shows that you are a professional who understands the norms and expectations of the company where you would like to work. It also shows self-respect, as well as respect for the interviewer.

Resources

Interactive Chalkboard
The Interactive Chalkboard CD provides visual teaching aids for this section.

TEACH (cont.)

R Reading Strategy

Finding Details Remind students that interacting positively with others is a big part of showing a positive attitude. Ask students to find in this passage four examples of how to show a positive attitude by relating respectfully to others. (The text mentions greeting an interviewer by name, smiling and making eye contact, waiting to be seated until asked, and not placing belongings on the interviewer's desk.)

S Skill Practice
Guided Practice

Define Ask students to look up and define "standard English." Have them explain the concept to the class and describe the difference between standard English and slang, giving specific examples. (Standard English is the form of writing and speaking most students learn in school. Slang is an informal, everyday form of language.)

✓ Reading Check

EXPLAIN You can communicate a positive attitude through a combination of words and body language. Focus on the positive in your answers, and do not make negative comments about past jobs, employers, coworkers, or yourself. Be honest, courteous, and respectful. Show that you are willing to work hard and learn.

Be Positive

Go into the interview with a positive attitude. Enthusiasm is a big part of a positive attitude. It shows that you are eager to work and willing to learn.

Be courteous to everyone you meet. When you meet the interviewer, greet him or her by name and say, "Hello, it's nice to meet you" in a clear, confident voice. Give a firm handshake, smile, and make eye contact. Show good manners. Wait until the interviewer asks you to be seated before you sit. Do not place your belongings on the interviewer's desk.

✓ Reading Check EXPLAIN How can you show a positive attitude in a job interview?

Speak for Success

Good communication skills will help you make a good impression. Use these guidelines for good oral communication:
- Speak clearly in standard English.
- Speak at a moderate pace and loudly enough to be heard.
- Make only positive, honest comments about your teachers.
- Listen attentively and give concise, honest answers. If you do not understand a question, ask the interviewer to explain it.

Be specific and precise when you speak. This shows that you think clearly. Compare these answers:

Question: "Do you enjoy working with others or on your own?"

Answer 1: "I enjoy working with others."

Answer 2: "It depends. Some tasks demand team work. Our soccer team, for example, won the city tournament because we worked together to put our strategy into action. But I also enjoy being able to work by myself so I can devote my full concentration to a task."

Which answer do you think an interviewer would prefer? Why?

Stay Calm and Focused

No matter what questions the interviewer asks, stay calm and do not get defensive. Keep the emphasis on your skills. For example, if an employer asks about your lack of experience, you might say: "You're right. I only have one year of full-time job experience. But my work on the Fernandez project proves that I'm a great organizer."

Real-World Connection

Punctuality Planning

You have been granted an interview for a job that you want very much. On the day of the interview, you wake up late because your sibling, with whom you share a room, turned off the alarm clock. You will not be able to make it to the interview on time.

Critical Thinking How can you ensure you will be on time for your interviews?

Do Your Own Research Use an Internet mapping tool to create directions from your school to the address of a company in your community. Note the miles and estimated travel time. In a small group, discuss the Internet directions and examine local maps to pinpoint time hazards such as railroad crossings, school zones, and fire departments. Plan an alternate route around possible barriers. Brainstorm with your group ways to be sure that you wake up on time.

 ### Real-World Connection

Critical Thinking Answer Being on time requires planning. You need to know how long you need to get ready and how long it will take to get there, with or without traffic. If something goes wrong and an interviewee must be more than a couple of minutes late, he or she should call ahead to the interview site with a brief explanation of the problem and an apology. It may be necessary to reschedule the interview. Accidents do happen, and interviewers will usually accept an honest apology.

Do Your Own Research Maps will vary, but students should understand that estimated driving times are just that—estimates. They often do not take into account construction, traffic jams, and other delays.

The 21st Century Workplace

Talk Like a Mandarin

China has become a major producer, potential market, and center for business in Asia and around the world. Knowing one of its languages can be a valuable asset in the global workplace, especially in the manufacturing and retail industries. Which Chinese language should one learn for commerce? That depends on with what part of China you do business. Although Mandarin Chinese is the official Chinese language that is spoken in the capital of Beijing, the southern portion of China and Hong Kong traditionally speak Cantonese. Meanwhile, large cities such as Shanghai have their own dialects as well.

CRITICAL THINKING

What might be some reasons to learn a Chinese dialect other than Mandarin?

In Your Community

Identify a strategy for learning Mandarin Chinese, or, if you already speak Mandarin Chinese, create a strategy for learning another language

that is new to you. Research local schools and other local organizations that might help you learn a second language.

COMMON MANDARIN WORDS AND PHRASES

hello	ni hao
goodbye	zai jian
How are you?	ni hao ma?
thank you	xie xie
you're welcome	bu ke qi

@ Extend Your Learning Research different Chinese dialects. For links to Web sites about the Chinese dialects, go to this book's OLC through **glencoe.com.**

S₁ If several people interview you **simultaneously**, address one question at a time. Make eye contact with each of your interviewers, one by one. You may also face questions designed to challenge you. Remember: There is often no one right answer. It is how you react that counts. Use positive communication skills and refer to your notes to help keep yourself on track.

Ask Your Own Questions

Be prepared to ask your own questions. Asking questions of the interviewer demonstrates genuine interest. It also shows that you value your skills and want to make sure this job is the right fit for you. Important questions to ask include:

S₂
- What is the company culture?
- What is the potential for growth in this company? (Growth refers to promotions and more job responsibilities over time.)
- What are the employee benefits?
- Does the company pay for training?

Also ask questions that show how much you learned when you did your company research. For example, you might ask:

- The company has an important new client in China. Would learning Chinese be an asset for this job?
- Many companies in your industry advertise online. Do you plan to do the same?

The 21st Century Workplace

CRITICAL THINKING ANSWER Answers will vary, but students may suggest geography, such as the need to communicate or work with people in Hong Kong or Taiwan, or a specialized need, such as communicating or working with individuals who speak Cantonese rather than Mandarin.

In Your Community There is an almost unlimited array of methods to learn another language, from traditional group classes to immersion trips overseas to online tutorials and podcasts. Local interest groups may also meet to speak and learn Chinese together.

TEACH (cont.)

W Writing Support
Guided Practice

Writing Clearly Ask students to imagine that they interview a young applicant who uses slang, gives vague answers, and blames others for his or her mistakes. Have students write a letter to the applicant explaining how to communicate effectively in an interview. (Letters will vary but should mention the principles of effective communication outlined here.)

S₁ Skill Practice
Guided Practice

Eye Contact Assign students to groups of three or four. Have one student play the interviewee while the others act as a panel of interviewers. Students' task is to answer questions while making eye contact with each interviewer for five to ten seconds at a time. (Students may find this challenging or uncomfortable. Suggest to students that they try to relax and focus on one person at a time.)

S₂ Skill Practice
Guided Practice

Write Questions Ask students to write the top three questions they would ask an interviewer and the reasons. As a class, discuss the pros and cons of various groups' questions. (Questions will vary but should ask for information job seekers need in order to make a wise choice, such as specifics about work environment, work schedules, and potential for career advancement.)

NCLB Activity correlated to English Language Arts standards.

TEACH *(cont.)*

C₁ Critical Thinking

Solving Problems Give students this sample interview question, which involves problem solving: "Imagine that a coworker is having a personal problem and you are taking on more and more of his work every week. What do you do?" Have students work in teams to draft responses. Compare the solutions as a class. (Responses will vary but should show assertiveness and initiative. Most interviewers would want to hear a plan to take action by talking to the coworker and the relevant manager.)

C₂ Critical Thinking

Evaluating The text states that informal interviews with open-ended questions can be difficult. Ask students whether they agree. Why might open-ended questions be harder to answer well than specific questions? (Open-ended questions require the interviewee to structure coherent responses with little guidance. Well-prepared interviewees will find these questions less difficult, however.)

S Skill Practice
Guided Practice

Assertiveness Explain to students that questions about marital status, age, health, felony record, disabilities, or children or child care are illegal. Have students work in pairs to practice "turning around" illegal questions to focus on skills. Have students share their best ideas for what to say in these situations. (Responses should show poise and tact while focusing on job skills.)

◄ Vocabulary
You can find definitions in the **Key Terms** glossary and **Academic Vocabulary** glossary at the back of this book.

As You Read
Analyze Why do you think questions about citizenship, race, or age are not legal for an interviewer to ask?

Think on Your Feet

Some interviews require you to think on your feet. For example, some interviews focus on **role-playing**, a situation in which you are asked to play a role in an invented situation and are evaluated on the skills you display. For example, job candidates for Iowa company MicroTraining must play the role of teachers and make a presentation to show that they are able to get up in front of strangers and present material.

You also may face a question that requires **problem solving**, or using thinking skills to suggest a solution. For example, you may be asked, "What would you do if you could not meet a deadline?" Remember that the interviewer is evaluating your resourcefulness, creativity, and attitude, not looking for one right answer.

Expect the Unexpected

Some interviewers ask few questions and expect you to do all of the talking. They may not be prepared with specific questions, or they may simply prefer a less formal interview. Such an interviewer may pose vague questions such as "Tell me about yourself." This type of interview sounds casual, but it can prove very difficult.

Establish your qualifications for the job by citing relevant skills, experience, and personal qualities. Use the "commercial" you created about yourself. Be sure to mention why you would like to work for the company.

Know Your Rights

The law prohibits interviewers from asking you about certain matters. For example, you do not have to answer questions about age, disabilities, citizenship, lawsuits, marital status, or if you have children.

If an interviewer asks you a question that is not job-related, turn it around to focus on your skills. A good response is, "I assure you that this area is not a problem. Let me tell you about the skills I have that fit this job."

Expect Stress

During an interview, you may experience stress. **Stress** is mental or physical tension that is the body's natural response to conflict. Relax and be yourself. Remember that you have solid skills. Keep the experience in perspective. The worst thing that can happen is that you do not get the job. There are other jobs. Besides, if the interviewer does not think you are right for the company, the company may not be right for you.

Make a Graceful Exit

Let the interviewer decide when the interview is over. Thank the interviewer for his or her time and interest. You may be offered the job on the spot. If not, ask when the interviewer hopes to make a decision. You might say, "May I call you next week to hear your decision?" Make sure that you have the interviewer's correct contact

As You Read
Sending a thank-you note shows that you are polite and conscientious, and it gives you another chance to sell yourself.

information. On your way out, thank everyone who helped you that day, such as the receptionist.

✓ **Reading Check** **EVALUATE** How can you establish your qualifications for a job during a job interview?

Follow Up After the Interview

The interview process does not end when you walk out the door. There are three more things to do: evaluate your performance, send a thank-you note, and deal with acceptance or rejection.

Evaluate Your Performance

It is important to evaluate your performance at the interview. What went well? What do you need to improve? Did you speak clearly? Did you show enthusiasm? Can you think of any additional information about yourself that you should have provided? Make notes and use them to improve your next interview.

Send a Thank-You Note

Write a thank-you note or letter to the interviewer as soon as the interview is over. Writing a thank-you note is polite. It shows that you are thoughtful and conscientious. It also gives you another chance to sell yourself.

In the letter, thank the interviewer for his or her time. Briefly summarize the interview in order to jog the interviewer's memory of you. Then explain why your skills would be a good match for the job. Finish by naming a day when you will contact the employer by phone or e-mail to follow up on his or her decision. **Figure 7.2** on page 168 illustrates a typical printed thank-you letter.

Type out your thank-you letter. Be sure to check the spelling of the interviewer's name by referring to his or her business card. Follow up on your commitment to call or e-mail the interviewer about a decision. This shows that you do what you say you will, and it might land you the job.

Deal with Acceptance or Rejection

The most important thing to do after the interview is to deal with being offered the job or not being offered the job.

▼ **FOLLOW UP**
Following up after an interview demonstrates your continued interest in the job. *What should you say in a thank-you note?*

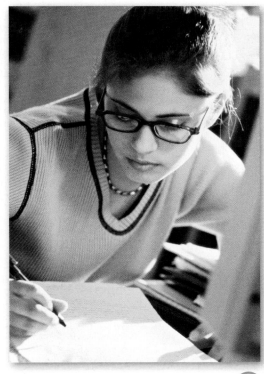

TEACH *(cont.)*

W **Writing Support**
Independent Practice
Writing a Business Letter Have students research the elements of a business letter (return address, date, greeting, close, and so on). Then have students write and word-process their own follow-up letters. If desired, have students share letters and give one another feedback.

U **Universal Access**
Students with Learning Disabilities Students with learning disabilities may find it difficult to compose text by hand or with a computer keyboard. Instead, they may find it easier to use voice-recognition software to dictate letters, essays, and other written materials. More and more software contains voice-recognition features for use with built-in or plug-in computer microphones.

✓ **Reading Check**

EVALUATE Establish your qualifications by focusing on the skills and personal qualities that are most relevant to the job you want. Give specific examples from your past schooling and experience that show that you have these skills and qualities.

ASSESS

Review Key Terms
Have students write sentences using each key term.

Online Study Tools
Have students go to the OLC through **glencoe.com** to:
- Download **Podcast** study tools.
- Download free **Study-to-Go** content to their PDAs or cell phones.

167

▶ **Extend the Photo**

Caption Answer A follow-up letter should thank the interviewer, express enthusiasm for the job, make a case for why you are a good candidate, and name a date when you would like to contact the interviewer for a decision.

Discussion Ask students, "Is it too pushy to contact the interviewer for a decision after the interview? Why or why not?" (Students may feel that it is up to the interviewer to make the next move. However, contacting the interviewer to ask—politely—about a hiring decision shows initiative and strong interest.)

RETEACH

C **Critical Thinking**

Making Inferences The text repeatedly emphasizes the importance of conveying interest in the company and the job, both during the interview and in the thank-you letter that follows. Ask students, "Why is this something an interviewer would like to hear from a job applicant?" (Employees who want the job will have a better attitude, work harder, and be more pleasant to be around than those who take the job grudgingly or because they have no other choice.)

Resources

📂 **Student Activity Workbook** Assign the Chapter 7 activities in the Student Activity Workbook.

ASSESS

After You Read

Have students complete the Section 7.2 After You Read section review.

Online Study Tools

Have students go to the OLC through **glencoe.com** to:

• Take the Section 7.2 **Practice Test**.
• Download **Podcast** study tools.
• Download free **Study-to-Go** content to their PDAs or cell phones.

Accepting an Offer

You hear those magic words: "You're hired." Now what do you do? Believe it or not, you do not have to say yes immediately. If you want time to think about it, ask the employer if you can take some time to decide. List the job's pros and cons before calling back to accept the job. Ask for a formal offer letter for your records. Send an acceptance letter, and keep a copy for yourself.

Figure 7.2 **THANK-YOU LETTER**

1246 Evergreen Drive
Santa Rosa, NM 88434

May 17, 20 – –

Anita Gupta
Fields Educational Technologies
1200 Center Way
Santa Rosa, NM 88435

Dear Ms. Gupta:

Thank you very much for taking the time to speak to me last Wednesday morning about the position of assistant designer at Fields Educational Technologies. I enjoyed learning more about the products you are developing for high school students and appreciated the tips you offered about pursuing a career in Web design.

I am even more confident now that I would enjoy and excel at this job. I believe that my organizational skills and sense of humor would make me a great fit for your company.

As we discussed, I will call or e-mail you next Friday, May 26, to see whether you have made your decision. Thank you once again for your time and consideration.

Sincerely,

Elias Carneros

Elias Carneos

FORMAL THANKS Everyone likes to be thanked, even an interviewer. *What might job candidates mention about their interviews in their thank-you letters?*

EXTEND THE FIGURE **Figure 7.2**

Caption Answer You could mention something you learned or enjoyed, particularly something you learned about the job or company that makes you even more enthusiastic to work there or more confident that you are a good match.

Discussion Reiterate to students that writing a follow-up letter is a great chance to remind the interviewer that you are still available and interested. Tell students that many interviewees neglect to send a follow-up letter. Ask: why do you think relatively few people take this important step? (Students might cite lack of time, effort, knowledge, or interest.)

Declining an Offer

Suppose an employer wants to hire you, but the job is not exactly what you want. Do not immediately say no and decline the offer. Take a day to think about it. You might change your mind, or you might be able to negotiate the things about the job that do not satisfy you.

If you decide to ask for higher pay, make sure you have researched what other people in similar jobs earn. For example, you might say, "The average wage for gardeners in this area is $12.00 an hour. Are you able to bring your offer closer to that figure?" You and the employer may reach a compromise, or the employer may offer to raise your pay after you have worked there for a few months.

If you still decide to reject the job, be polite and give a reason for your answer. Do not say anything negative about the company. For example, you might say, "I really like your company's working environment, but I've decided that a job in technology might better serve my long-term career goals." Make sure to stay on good terms with the company—you may want to work there in the future.

Handling Rejection

If an employer turns you down, consider it a learning experience. Remain polite and positive, and thank the interviewer again for the opportunity. Politely ask why you were not hired. For example, you might say, "Would you be able to share what made you choose another candidate?" You might need more training, or you might not have been prepared enough for the interview. This feedback will help you in future interviews.

Review your notes on how you performed in the interview, and practice so you will be better prepared for the next one.

Career ✓ Checklist

On the Day of the Interview:

✓ Arrive on time and well-rested.

✓ Review the answers that you have prepared for key questions.

✓ Dress appropriately.

✓ Go to the interview alone.

✓ Maintain a positive attitude.

✓ Be confident, and sell yourself!

Section 7.2 After You Read

Review Key Concepts

1. Explain why attitude is important to employers and how you can project a positive attitude during your interview.
2. List one method for accepting a job offer and one method for rejecting a job offer.
3. Describe the process of following up a job interview.

Practice Academic Skills

English Language Arts

N C L B

4. Imagine that you are an employer. List and define six personal qualities that you would look for in new employees, and give an example of how a job candidate could demonstrate those qualities during a job interview.
5. Write down two questions you might ask if you were rejected for a job.

@ Check your answers at this book's OLC through **glencoe.com**.

ASSESS (cont.)

Resources

 ExamView Assessment Suite CD allows you to print out ready-made unit and chapter tests complete with answer keys. You can also create customized tests.

CLOSE

Culminating Activity

Skills for Job Interviews
Ask students to write one paragraph citing five things they learned in this section and how they can apply this knowledge to real-world situations when they have a job interview. (Paragraphs will vary but should mention showing a positive attitude, conveying a strong interest in the job, sending a follow-up letter, taking time to think about a job offer, and asking for feedback upon being rejected.)

N C L B

Activity correlated to English Language Arts standards.

Section 7.2 After You Read

Section 7.2 Review

1. Employees' attitude is the major influence on how hard and how well they work. You can show a positive attitude through body language and by demonstrating enthusiasm.
2. Ask for a formal offer letter for your records, send an acceptance letter, and keep a copy for yourself. Be polite and give a reason for your answer when rejecting an offer.
3. Evaluate your performance and make notes to help you for next time; send a thank-you note to the interviewer(s); handle acceptance or rejection gracefully.

Practice Academic Skills

4. Students should cite qualities that would characterize a hard-working and responsible employee, such as honesty and initiative. A job candidate can demonstrate personal qualities during a job interview through responses to questions, through the questions he or she asks, and the way he or she behaves toward others.
5. Questions should be polite and should reflect a genuine desire to learn how to be a better job candidate at the next interview.

169

CAREER SPOTLIGHT

Career Cluster: Arts, Audio/Video Technology, and Communications

FOCUS

Discussion Starter

Arts, Audio/Video Technology, and Communications
Tell students that this career cluster includes not only jobs in the fine arts, but also in film, television, radio, cable TV, Internet, and other jobs relating to communications. Have students brainstorm jobs in their local community in these career areas. (Jobs might include cable TV technician, radio news producer, theater usher, graphic designer, newspaper reporter, television repairperson, and so on.)

TEACH

C Critical Thinking

Skills for Work and Life
Ask students to scan the text for the six skills Carter sites as crucial to success and to cite them. Ask: Why would you need these skills to succeed in life, not just on the job? Elicit specific examples of how these skills could be useful. (Answers and examples will vary but should focus on the importance of having control of your own life.)

W Writing Support

Guided Practice

Write a Plan Ask students to follow Carter's example by writing down one goal they want to achieve over the next year and creating a detailed plan to achieve it, with stepping-stone goals described in time order. If desired, have students share their plans and give each other feedback. (Goals will vary but should include all important details and be listed in logical order.)

Bobby K. Carter
Film Editor/Filmmaker

Q: Describe your job.

A: I am a freelance film editor, filmmaker, and entrepreneur. I edit television programs and run my own business, *Diversion Video Magazine,* which covers freestyle bike riding around the world.

Q: Describe a typical workday.

A: I wake up in the morning and edit TV programs for clients. After taking a lunch break, I go ride flatland BMX. Later in the afternoon, I take steps that will inch *Diversion* toward its goals. That includes corresponding with riders and working on mail orders and distribution. In the evening, I edit more TV programming for clients. Then I take more time to work on my own videos or relax and come up with more steps I can take to make my dreams reality.

Q: What skills are most important to you in your job?

A: Self-motivation, time management, money management, the ability to stay focused, communication, and being able to dream—the same skills you need to succeed in life and be happy!

Q: What academic skills and lifelong learning skills are helpful in preparing for your career?

A: In my business, filmmaking and computer skills are a must. As part of a team of workers, writing skills are also needed to communicate ideas to others in a clear manner. As an entrepreneur, money management is necessary, too. Problem-solving skills are also very useful, and learning how to operate efficiently and on a budget, if you're going to take your own projects to the next level.

Q: What is your key to success?

A: I write down my dreams and create detailed plans to achieve them. Writing everything down is very important

because it forces you to consider details and makes you accountable. Also, I make sure I enjoy every day and focus on the positive aspects of life.

Q: What training and preparation do you recommend for students?

A: Take math and science classes to learn problem solving along with art and filmmaking classes to think abstractly. Also, learn as much as you can about using computers, navigating the Internet, and managing money. That will help you execute your ideas when you come up with projects to do on your own.

Q: What are some ways you recommend students prepare for this career?

A: Look around and come up with ways to solve problems around you. Take as many classes as you can about various subjects. Take part in various programs after school and outside of school. This will help you find your passion. When you know what you want, start making plans.

Q: What do you like most about your work?

A: I get to live the life I want while making a positive contribution to the community. I hope my videos change the way people look at the landscape in a different way and empower people to do their own thing.

 For more about Career Clusters, go to this book's OLC through **glencoe.com.**

NCLB NO CHILD LEFT BEHIND

Teaching Tip

NCLB puts a strong emphasis on mathematics skills. Students should understand that skills in calculating and mathematical reasoning are necessary not only for jobs in science and engineering, but also for careers in the arts and other fields. Encourage students to become comfortable with numbers by modeling the performance of mental calculations

and by calling on them to perform impromptu calculations.

Sample Question Chapter 7 begins on page 152 and ends on page 175. How many pages does it contain? (Answer: 24. Because the chapter begins on 152 and runs through 175, inclusive, it contains 24 pages rather than 23, which is the difference between 152 and 175.)

Education or Training Film editors usually acquire their skills through on-the-job training or formal postsecondary training at vocational schools, colleges, universities, or photographic institutes. Bachelor's degree programs, especially those including business courses, provide a well-rounded education.

Academic Skills Required English Language Arts, Mathematics, Science, Social Studies

Technology Needed Computers, editing software, audio and video equipment, lighting and sound gear, home office.

Aptitudes, Abilities, and Skills The ability to use equipment to edit soundtracks, film, and video. Visual and communication skills. Independent filmmakers must also be able to manage time, money, and staff.

Workplace Safety Film editors can work long hours and should watch out for injuries from repetitive tasks or poor ergonomics.

Career Outlook Employment of video editors is expected to grow about as fast as the average for all occupations over the next ten years. Rapid expansion of the entertainment market, especially motion picture production and distribution, will spur growth of camera operators. In addition, computer and Internet services will provide new outlets for interactive productions.

Career Path Film editors can become directors or producers of TV programming, online content, or commercials. They can also be entrepreneurs who make and distribute their own projects.

Academic Skills Required to Complete Tasks

Tasks	English Language Arts	Mathematics	Science	Social Studies
Accounting and maintaining business records	★	★		
Edit film for clients	★	★	★	★
Make films	★	★		
Handle DVD distribution		★		
Market DVDs	★	★		★
Create and keep a budget		★		
Contact new clients	★			★

NCLB

Critical Thinking

How can writing down career goals help you achieve success?

NCLB This chart relates academic skills such as English Language Arts, Mathematics, Science, Social Studies, and World Languages to specific tasks that are performed for the job featured in the Career Spotlight feature.

Critical Thinking

By writing down career goals, you can organize your thoughts on paper. You can make lists of the pros and cons of possible career choices and ways to achieve smaller, more attainable goals that will help you achieve success.

CAREER SPOTLIGHT

ASSESS

Make Connections

Ask students why they think Carter recommends math and science classes for "problem solving" skills rather than specific math or science knowledge. How do math and science classes teach problem-solving skills that could be useful in any field? (Students should understand that many mathematical and scientific operations, such as solving equations, conducting experiments, or writing proofs, are all about solving specific problems. Science and math also develop creative reasoning and observational skills that are helpful in solving problems in any field.)

CLOSE

Culminating Activity

Career Cluster and Education For some careers, college education is optional. Film editors, for example, can acquire skills either through on-the-job training or through postsecondary education. What could a college education provide that on-the-job experience could not? What does it mean to have a "well-rounded education," and why does this matter? (Students should understand that a college education provides a broad base of knowledge and a foundation of thinking, reading, writing, and speaking skills that apply to any career. Formal education is also useful for mastering theories, ideas, and abstract concepts that are usually not covered in on-the-job training.)

Key Terms and Academic Vocabulary Review

1. Students should write complete sentences using each term correctly. A sample answer might read: "*Anticipating* questions an interviewer will ask can help me prepare and practice specific, concise answers."

Review Key Concepts

2. Find out the time, the place, and other important details about the interview. Research the company and the industry. Prepare answers to typical and tough interview questions. Practice interviewing techniques.

3. Students' answers to the questions listed in the chapter will vary. Good answers to typical and tough interview questions are honest, highlight the positive, and demonstrate thinking skills and desirable personal qualities.

4. Body language can help create a positive impression not only because it is one of the first things an interviewer notices about a job candidate and because it communicates interest, alertness, openness, and relaxed self-confidence.

5. Project a positive attitude by using positive body language, accenting the positive and avoiding the negative in your comments and responses, and by showing interest in the job and company.

6. Follow up after a job interview by sending a thank-you note to the interviewer(s) thanking them for their time and expressing your interest and qualifications for the job. Follow up with the interviewer about a hiring decision.

CHAPTER SUMMARY

Section 7.1

Preparation is essential to interview success. Make sure you know when and where to go for the interview and how to dress. Research the company and current trends in the industry so you can ask intelligent questions. Prepare answers to typical and tough interview questions, as well as questions to ask the interviewer. Practice your interviewing skills with a friend, teacher, or parent, paying attention to your body language and tone of voice. Ask for feedback.

Section 7.2

Arrive for an interview on time and prepared. Dress conservatively and groom well. Be positive, be enthusiastic, and demonstrate good communication skills. Respond to tough questions calmly and with a positive attitude. Be aware that some interviews involve role-playing or problem solving to evaluate your ability to think on your feet. Respond to illegal questions by turning the question around to focus on your skills. After the interview, evaluate your performance and send a thank-you letter.

Key Terms and Academic Vocabulary Review

1. Use each of these key terms and academic vocabulary words in a sentence.

Key Terms
- interview (p. 155)
- body language (p. 159)
- role-playing (p. 166)
- problem solving (p. 166)
- stress (p. 166)

Academic Vocabulary
- minimize (p. 155)
- anticipate (p. 156)
- simultaneously (p. 165)
- establish (p. 166)

Review Key Concepts

2. List ways to prepare for a job interview.
3. Develop answers to typical and tough interview questions.
4. Identify the importance of body language in creating a good impression.
5. Explain how to project a positive attitude and use good communication skills.
6. Describe how to follow up after a job interview.
7. Summarize the best methods for accepting and rejecting employment offers and handling rejection.

Critical Thinking

8. Analyze How would conducting research about a company help you decide whether a job there would be right for you? Give specific examples.
9. Evaluate Imagine that an interviewer asks you, "Are you an American citizen?" Write down an appropriate answer to this question. Explain why you think employers are not allowed to ask such questions.

7. If offered the job, take time to think about it. You may want to negotiate a better offer, if appropriate. If rejected, accept the decision gracefully and ask for feedback to help you next time.

Critical Thinking

8. Conducting research about a company can show you whether the company's industry area, products and services, and company culture and values are a good match for your goals, interests, personality, and values.

9. An appropriate answer might be, "I assure you that I am legally available to work and that my citizenship status will not affect my ability to do this job, either now or in the future." Employers are not allowed to ask such questions because they may reflect discriminatory hiring practices. Such questions are also not

Real-World Skills and Applications

Self-Management Skills

10. Handling Stress Michael is in the middle of a job interview. Suddenly, he feels very stressed and nervous and begins to fidget. Write a paragraph telling Michael how he can keep himself on track during the interview and what he can do to feel calmer and finish the interview successfully.

Interpersonal Skills

11. Showing Self-Confidence Imagine that an interviewer says to you: "Tell me about a mistake you made at work, and how you handled it afterwards." Write four sentences describing how you could answer this question in a way that shows maturity and ability to take charge of a situation.

Technology Applications

12. Creating a Presentation Use presentation software to develop a two-minute "commercial" that summarizes your skills and abilities. Create separate slides for your job skills, personal qualities, career goals, hobbies and interests, and educational achievements, as well as a slide with quotations from your teachers, coworkers, or work supervisors. Present your live "commercial" as if you were presenting it during an interview for an appropriate job.

13. **Reading Body Language** Team up with a classmate. Each of you should spend one day paying attention to the other's body language. List eight specific gestures, postures, or uses of eye contact that you observed in your classmate, and write down what they communicated to you. Swap lists and discuss your observations of each other, then offer suggestions for how to modify your body language to succeed in a job interview.

14. **Conducting an Interview**

Situation You are conducting your first interview for an entry-level sales position at the department store where you work. Your supervisor would like to sit in on the interview. You have reviewed many résumés and have chosen four candidates.

Activity Create a description for your company's job opening and identify the skills it requires. Then role-play interviewing four candidates as your supervisor observes. Decide which person you would like to hire and explain this decision to your supervisor.

Evaluation You will be evaluated on how well you meet the following performance indicators:
- Develop a relevant job description.
- Conduct realistic interviews.
- Evaluate candidates using appropriate criteria.

ACTIVE LEARNING

13. Students should show awareness of the components of body language (gestures, posture, and eye contact) and the different messages they can communicate in different situations.

ROLE PLAY

14. Job descriptions should describe the position and qualities desired in an applicant as well as some information about the company. They should also reflect knowledge of real-world sales jobs. The interviews should be taken seriously, and interview questions should be effective and targeted to requirements stated in the job description. A candidate should be selected based on job-relevant criteria.

---

directly relevant to the candidate's qualifications for the job.

Real-World Skills and Applications

10. Michael should remind himself that he is doing fine and that it is normal to feel stress during a job interview. He should remind himself of his skills and qualifications, and focus on communicating those to the interviewer.

11. An interviewee should approach this question by honestly describing a relatively small mistake he or she made and how he or she used initiative and problem-solving skills to correct the situation.

12. Presentations should be honest and well written, reflect self-knowledge and self-confidence, and be delivered using positive body language.

Academic Skills in the Workplace

15. Trends will vary, but may include: the shift toward Web-based software, the development of open-source software, the use of database-driven Web sites using XML, the increasing attention to accessibility issues, and the importance of Web technologies such as RSS and blogging. Students should understand that they can use this information during an interview to demonstrate their knowledge and ask intelligent questions.

16. Laura should allow at least 50 minutes: 35 minutes of driving time (35 miles at 1 minute per mile), plus 15 minutes extra to arrive early.

17. Good oral hygiene helps prevent bad breath; clean teeth are part of your appearance and should be as clean as your clothing and hair.

18. Answers will vary based on the country selected, but should be factually accurate, demonstrate respect for the culture, and show an understanding of how greatly body language norms differ around the world.

Academic Skills in the Workplace

English Language Arts

15. Research and Analyze Imagine that you have an interview for an entry-level technical support job at a software company. Use library resources, current magazines, newspapers, or the Internet to compile a list of five current trends in business software. Then write four or five sentences describing how you might use this information in your interview.

Mathematics

16. Calculate Driving Time Laura has a job interview that is 20 miles away. However, due to construction, she will have to take a detour of about 15 miles. If she drives at an average of 60 miles per hour and wants to arrive 15 minutes early, how much time should Laura allow for the trip?

CONCEPT **Making Reasonable Estimates** When you estimate, you make your best guess at a solution. You can use estimation when you are not sure of your exact data.

Starting Hint Start by calculating how much time the trip would take Laura if she did not want to arrive early and if there were no delays due to construction.

Science

17. Understand Bacteria Bacteria live all around us: in the ground, in the air, in other animals, and in us. Nitrogen-fixing bacteria use nitrogen to grow. However, bacteria on your teeth eat food that is left on your teeth and secrete acid as a byproduct. This acid eats into your teeth and causes cavities if not controlled with proper dental care. This is why it is important to brush your teeth two to three times a day, floss at least once a day, and see a dentist every six months for a cleaning. Why would good dental care affect your appearance on the job? Explain your answer in one or two sentences.

Social Studies

18. Research Cultural Differences Select a country and research its "rules" about body language. List several gestures, postures, facial expressions, and uses of eye contact that are considered positive and negative in that country. Prepare and give a five-minute oral report and demonstration for the class.

STANDARDIZED TEST PRACTICE

ESSAY

Directions Consider the following statement about tough questions in job interviews:

> **Test-Taking Tip** Read, reread, and think about the essay question first. Then write a short outline with your main points. Make sure your outline addresses all the questions in the essay topic. Include your own original ideas, but support every major statement with specific facts and examples.

"There is often no one right answer. It is how you react that counts." Explain what this statement means. Do you agree or disagree? Why? Write a one-page essay explaining your response.

STANDARDIZED TEST PRACTICE

Answer

This statement means that interviewers are usually not looking for one single answer to interview questions. Instead, they want to see how job candidates present and express themselves and how well they can think on their feet. Students may agree or disagree, but they should offer a clear thesis statement and a convincing argument for their position.

Test-Taking Strategy

Test Timing Essay and short-answer test questions are usually timed. Have your students take one or more timed essay tests or free writing exercises so that they become comfortable with writing for a fixed length of time.

Writing Skills Practice

19. Persuading When you write a cover letter or thank-you note, you are trying to persuade the person who reads your letter that you are a good job candidate.

 Practice Find a job opening that matches your skills. Write a five-paragraph letter that will persuade the employer to consider you for the job.

- Begin your letter by stating that you would make an excellent choice for the job opening. Give three brief reasons.
- Write one short paragraph for each of the listed reasons. Match your job requirements with your skills and experiences.
- Summarize your argument in the final paragraph.

Net Connection

20. Evaluate Your Performance Research standardized scoring systems used by human resources professionals to evaluate job candidates. Choose one scoring system and use it to evaluate how well you have done in your practice interviews.

@ Log On Visit this book's OLC through **glencoe.com** to locate more information about key skills and personal qualities that human resources professionals look for in interviewees. Then create two lists: a list of the skills and personal qualities that you already have, and a list of skills and personal qualities that you would like to develop further. Print out your lists and place them in your **Personal Academic and Career Portfolio**.

Reading Connection
@ Go to this book's Online Learning Center through **glencoe.com** for a list of reading suggestions.

Personal Academic and Career Portfolio

Develop Interviewing Skills

You will discover a lot about yourself as you prepare for and complete your first job interviews. Recording your observations about yourself and the interview process will help you do better and better each time you have a job interview.

Every worker has stories of interviews that went well and interviews that went poorly. Interview several workers about their experiences with job interviews. Ask them to offer tips on what has worked for them. Add these notes to your Portfolio.

The following guidelines will help you organize and add the results of your research to your portfolio:

- Create a new section for your portfolio, using a divider for hard copy material and a computer folder for electronic files.
- Label the section *Job Interviews*.
- Add the section to your table of contents.
- Add the following: a record of interviews you have had and notes on what you learned, any correspondence with a company about job interviews, good sources of information on companies in the career cluster that interests you, tips on body language and strong oral communication, and feedback from friends, teachers, parents, and interviewers on your interview style and skills.
- Update your portfolio as you gain more experience with job interviews.

@ Portfolio Help Go to the *Succeeding in the World of Work* OLC through **glencoe.com** for help developing your portfolio.

Writing Skills Practice

19. Letters should follow the five-paragraph format and should be tailored to the job description chosen. Letters should also show that students understand that they need to effectively market themselves by explaining why they are a good fit for the job and why they would be an asset to the company.

Net Connection

20. Students' lists of desirable employee qualities should reflect research using quality sources and should reflect some of the personal qualities described in Chapter 13. Lists should reflect the student's developing self-awareness, as well as knowledge about the skills required for success in the student's field(s) of interest.

Resources

ExamView Assessment Suite CD allows you to print out ready-made unit and chapter tests complete with answer keys. You can also create customized tests.

WorkKeys

WorkKeys® is a job skills assessment program. For information on leveled assessment for Problem-Solving Skills (Applied Mathematics; Applied Technology; Locating Information; and Observation), go to the WorkKeys link on this book's OLC through **glencoe.com**.

Personal Academic and Career Portfolio

Maintaining a Portfolio

Tell students that their **Personal Academic and Career Portfolios** will continue to evolve as they learn more about themselves, build job skills, and gain work experience. Explain to students that interviews are learning opportunities. Most interviewers are pleased to share information about their company and industry and to offer career advice and constructive feedback about an interviewee's performance. This information can enrich students' portfolios and help them track their progress as they gain experience on the job market.

Unit 3
Thematic Project

Discussion Starter

Ask students to describe any past experiences with job interviews. What questions did the interviewer ask? Which questions were easy, which were more challenging, and why? How would students assess their interview performance? Looking back, what could they have done to make a better impression? (Students should understand that practice and preparation are key to performing well in any interview situation.)

STEP 1

Evaluate Your Skills and Resources

Have students go to the *Succeeding in the World of Work* OLC through **glencoe.com** for a graphic organizer they can use to organize the skills, tools, and resources they will use to complete the project.

S Skill Practice

Ask student pairs to interview two working adults in the community to elicit advice about succeeding in job interviews. Have students first work together to identify interview candidates and to draft a list of questions about various aspects of interview success, including preparation, dress, body language, handling difficult questions, and following up after the interview. Have students conduct the interviews together and then summarize what they learned in a bulleted list.

Making a Good First Impression

You know that creativity, research, and networking are important ways to find possible jobs. You have learned that employers consider many factors when choosing among job candidates, including skills, education, employment history, personal qualities, and enthusiasm for the job. You also know that most employers want to meet job candidates face-to-face before they make a final decision. In this project, you will practice interviewing and assess your own performance in order to make the best possible impression in a job interview.

Project Assignment

- Working with a partner, create two role-play situations in which you interview one another for ten minutes. Together, decide upon two realistic interview scenarios for your interviews. Each partner should serve once as an interviewer and once as an interviewee.
- Arrange to record both of your interviews.
- Watch or listen to the tapes of your interviews together and critique both interviews. Note things that you did well and things that could be improved.
- Compile your notes and create a presentation to share with the class. Play the recordings of your interviews and offer tips that may help other students improve their interviewing skills.

Lifelong Learning Connection

Lifelong learning concepts found in this project include:
- Interpersonal communication skills
- Self-assessment
- Setting goals and making decisions
- Your career plan and career path

STEP 1 Evaluate Your Skills and Resources

To complete this project, you will need to do research about what makes a good interview. Create a list of common and difficult interview questions and positive interview techniques by consulting print and online resources and talking to human resource professionals and working adults who have experience with job interviews. You will also need access to a video camera or an audio recorder to record your interviews.

Skills you will need to complete the Unit Thematic Project include:

Academic Skills reading, writing, social studies

Transferable Skills communication, research, problem-solving, and decision-making skills

Technology Skills audiovisual technology and word-processing skills

@ Resources Organizer To find a graphic organizer you can use to determine the skills, tools, and resources you will need for this project, go to this book's Online Learning Center through **glencoe.com**.

SPOTLIGHT ON TECHNOLOGY

Technology in the Hiring Process

Some companies use computer and Internet technology in every phase of the hiring process—including the interview. Employers search résumés posted by job seekers on career Web sites for keywords related to the job they need to fill. Some companies even offer virtual interviews via videoconferencing or the Web. Ask students how a virtual interview might differ from a personal interview. What aspects of the interview would become more or less important? (In a written online interview, writing skills would be of paramount importance. In a videoconference, a clear, confident voice and eye contact would be important, but other aspects of body language might be less important.)

STEP 2 Preview a Real-World Company Profile

Doing research before the interview is key to making a good first impression. Knowing about the company where you would like to work, and about how different companies handle planning, management, and other key business areas, will help you ask intelligent questions during the interview.

Real-World Company: craigslist.org

As a Web developer, Joshua Thayer is one of less than thirty employees who help craigslist serve more than 15 million people around the world every month. The craigslist Web site consists of local community classifieds and forums. Although the company's staff is small, its versatility, chemistry, and passion allow users in various cities to use its Web sites to advertise for and sell couches, buy concert tickets, find apartments and jobs, and conduct other person-to-person transactions easily and effectively.

While the site is free for most users, businesses are charged fees to post help-wanted ads in a few

of craigslist's city-specific subsites, and housing brokers in certain cities are charged fees for their posts as well. Although these fees are low compared to the fees that are charged by other sites, the revenue they bring in to craigslist is more than enough to keep the small and efficient site going. Overhead is low, efficiency is high, and craigslist successfully handles more than 130 million page views by online users each day.

craigslist.org

Aspects of Industry	Company Facts
Planning	Craigslist is a for-profit corporation but has a mission of community service. The site grows and adds new location-specific subsites based on user requests.
Management	Employees work on a project basis. Although there is a manager for each project, there is little formal hierarchy.
Finance	Initially, funding came out of founder Craig Newmark's pockets. Since the site started charging fees for certain job and housing listings, it has become self-sufficient.
Technical and Production Skills	Because there is a small staff, employees must have a range of skills including teamwork, troubleshooting, and problem solving.
Underlying Principles of Technology	Craigslist's service is based on open-source custom software that automatically posts e-mail messages to the web.
Labor Issues	Employees are paid well with good benefits and vacation time. Hours are flexible and employees are not asked to work the long hours often associated with startups.
Health, Safety, and Environmental Issues	Craigslist empowers users to flag and delete postings that are offensive, dangerous, or illegal. This keeps the online community safe.
Community Issues	The company funds a foundation that works with nonprofit groups. Also, the company will match any donations employees make to nonprofits.

177

Developing Industry Partners

Building Visibility

Making speeches, attending meetings, joining committees, participating in panel discussions and conferences, responding to questionnaires, going to business openings and open houses—these are just some of the things you and other teachers and administrators can do to help

develop school-business partnerships. Reaching out to the community will help you and your program to become visible in the business community. The time you spend establishing friendly, effective relationships will benefit your program and your students.

TEACH (cont.)

STEP 2

Preview a Real-World Company Profile
Tell students that the company featured here, craigslist, is still a relatively young company with a small staff. Ask students what they see as the advantages and disadvantages of working at a small, young company like craigslist, as opposed to a larger, more established company. (Advantages of working at a small start-up company may include room for career advancement, a sense of mission, greater job flexibility and a less rigid decision-making hierarchy. Disadvantages might include the risk that the company may fail, possible need to work longer hours to ensure the company's success, and lack of established management.)

R Reading Strategy
Guided Practice
Aspects of Industry
Remind students that understanding aspects of industry can aid their transition to employment in the rapidly changing global workplace and help them connect their academic coursework to the world of work. Ask students to imagine that they are preparing for a job interview with the company profiled here. Ask them to use the Real-World Company Profile and their own research to draft a list of eight questions, one about each aspect of industry, that they might ask at the interview. (Questions will vary but should demonstrate knowledge of the company and focus on information that can help the student decide whether a job at the company would be a good fit for his or her skills, interests, and personality traits.)

TEACH (cont.)

STEP 3

Research Procedures

Have students go to the *Succeeding in the World of Work* OLC through **glencoe.com** for a graphic organizer they can use to organize the results of their research.

STEP 4

Connect to Community

Ask students to identify and describe a local business that they feel is an asset to their community and to explain why. For example, does the business provide much-needed products or services at a fair price? Does the staff provide excellent service? Does the business have positive environmental or community policies?

Ask students to visit two local businesses and ask how they find and screen potential new employees. How do they advertise job openings? Do they use a job application form? Do they conduct job interviews? If so, approximately what percentage of the interviewed candidates do they decide to hire?

STEP 5

Report Your Findings

Give students these tips on critiquing their interviews:

- Watch the interview at least twice. On the first pass, pay attention to words and tone of voice. On the second pass, pay attention to body language and eye contact.
- Look for areas to improve rather than areas to criticize.
- Show the recording to a successful working adult for feedback.

STEP 3 — Research Procedures

Before you and your partner begin, decide on the scenario for the interview. Choose the type of company, the job, and the interview format. Follow these steps to prepare a thorough and realistic presentation:

- Research the types of questions that would be posed in real-life interviews similar to your role-play exercises.
- As an interviewer, decide which questions you will ask. As an interviewee, formulate answers to likely questions.
- Select suitable clothing for your interviews.
- Before recording your presentation, practice your parts independently.
- Choose an appropriate setting for recording your interviews. If you don't have much experience using a video or tape recorder, ask an experienced person to help you.
- When you are ready, start the recording device and take turns interviewing and being interviewed.
- Watch or listen to your interviews several times to critique them thoroughly. Pay

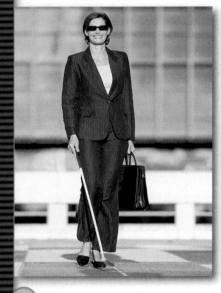

attention to body language, tone of voice, and quality of responses.

- Combine your notes and observations and prepare a presentation for the class. Create an outline to guide your presentation.
- Practice your presentation before delivering it. Make sure that you and your partner deliver equal portions of the presentation.

 Resources Organizer To find a graphic organizer you can use to organize your research, go to this book's OLC through **glencoe.com**.

STEP 4 — Connect to Community

Get Local Choose a local business and ask a manager to share stories about interviewing prospective employees. What makes a good impression? What are some common mistakes made by interviewees? Ask for tips on impressing an interviewer.

Take the Next Step Ask a local business to conduct a mock interview with you. Ask them to treat you as if you were an actual interviewee and give you feedback about your performance. Have the interviewer give you suggestions on how to improve your interviewing skills.

STEP 5 — Report Your Findings

Your final product for this project should include two recorded interviews and a presentation that summarizes and critiques your interviews.

Helpful Hints The interviewer and interviewee can do different things to prepare. Interviewers should do the following:

- Prepare for the interview by generating a list of typical and tough questions.
- Do not share your questions with your partner before your interview.
- Consider asking questions that require the interviewee to demonstrate creativity and problem solving.

Developing Community Involvement

Contribute to a Local Facility

Choose a park, community or senior center, after-school center, nature trail, bike trail, or other community asset in your area that needs grooming or repair. Work with local officials or an existing community or conservation group, such as the Sierra Club or a neighborhood association, to arrange for the

class to take part in an improvement project. Brainstorm individual tasks that are part of the project and divide the class into teams for each task. For example, teams can be in charge of picking up litter, painting, repairing trails or signs, or planting trees. Teams can also be in charge of securing donations of the supplies needed to complete their task.

- Make frequent eye contact throughout the interview.
- Ask for clarifications and examples where relevant.

Interviewees should do the following:

- Pretend that your partner is truly an interviewer. If you treat your interviewer as a friend or classmate, your interview will not be a valid practice exercise.
- Anticipate common interview questions and prepare solid responses.
- Make frequent eye contact throughout the interview.
- Use a confident tone of voice.

STEP 6 Presentation and Evaluation

Your interview will be evaluated based on:
- preparation displayed
- realism
- evidence of thoroughness

Personal Academic and Career Portfolio

Print out a copy of the outline you used for your class presentation and add it to your **Personal Academic and Career Portfolio**. If possible, also add a CD or DVD of the interview you conducted with a fellow student. You can use these resources to review interview tips and techniques as you look for jobs.

Your presentation will be evaluated based on:
- preparation displayed
- content and thoughtfulness
- quality of delivery
- quality of critique and suggestions offered

@ Evaluation Rubric To find a rubric you can use to evaluate your project, go to this book's OLC through **glencoe.com**.

BusinessWeek Connection

Understanding All Aspects of Industry: Finance

Understanding all aspects of industry can help you prepare to succeed in a career in that industry. It can help you determine what subjects you need to study and what training you need to acquire in order to participate in that industry. Finance is managing money. It includes acquiring the capital needed to begin or expand a business, tracking and projecting revenue, income, and expenses, paying employees, and more. All companies need to have a financial strategy as part of their overall business plan. Finance is the aspect of industry that drives many business decisions.

@ Go to this book's Online Learning Center through **glencoe.com** to find the *BusinessWeek* articles titled "They Signed Gnarls Barkley" and "A talk with craigslist's keeper." Read the articles and identify the financial strategies that the companies profiled use to compete with larger companies. Use a word-processing program to create a one-page summary of each article. Add these summaries to your **Personal Academic and Career Portfolio**.

BusinessWeek Connection

All Aspects of Industry: Finance

Explain to students that some companies are privately owned, while others—especially large companies—are publicly owned. This means that their stock, or shares, are bought and sold on a public stock exchange. It also means that stockholders have a say in how the company is run. Ask students to research the difference between private and public ownership, to list the advantages and disadvantages of each, and to specify which form of ownership they would choose if they owned a company. (Taking a company public is an opportunity to raise capital and boost visibility, but it also subjects a company to stricter financial reporting laws and requires that profits and some decision-making power be shared with stockholders.)

ASSESS

STEP 6
Presentation and Evaluation

Rubric Encourage students go to the *Succeeding in the World of Work* OLC through **glencoe.com** for a rubric they can use to evaluate their project. Encourage students to use the rubric as a checklist to use as they watch and critique their recorded interviews.

CLOSE

Culminating Activity

Project Assessment In this activity, students applied the Unit topic to their own lives by trying out their interview skills and assessing their performance in order to improve their future interview performance. Have student teams work together to pool their observations on the success of this Unit Thematic Project. What parts of the interview project felt particularly challenging or stressful, and why? What parts felt realistic or unrealistic, and why? Was it difficult to critique their own performance? Why or why not? Have student groups create a list of tips for making future practice interviews as realistic and productive as possible. (Students should assess their own performance honestly and use their experiences to improve future practice.)

Chapter	Chapter Objectives
CHAPTER 8 **Beginning a New Job**	• **Describe** how to manage the anxieties and challenges of a first day of work. • **Explain** how to dress for work. • **Explain** the purpose of orientation and distinguish among the different types of orientation program. • **Identify** typical forms of payment. • **Describe** common employee benefits. • **Explain** the role of employee performance reviews.
CHAPTER 9 **Workplace Ethics**	• **Identify** the skills and personal qualities employers look for in employees. • **Describe** ways to demonstrate desirable personal qualities on the job. • **Explain** the importance of ethics in the workplace. • **Identify** ethical principles and ways to apply them in a work setting. • **Describe** strategies for handling unethical practices.
CHAPTER 10 **Developing a Positive Attitude**	• **Explain** why a positive attitude, high self-esteem, and enthusiasm contribute to career success. • **Develop** the ability to think positively, overcome doubt, and deal with mistakes. • **Describe** how to assert yourself on the job. • **Develop** effective strategies to handle criticism, pressure, and gossip in the workplace. • **Identify** ways to manage negative feelings.
CHAPTER 11 **Workplace Health and Safety**	• **Explain** the relationship between good health and career success. • **Describe** how a nutritious diet and good sleep hygiene contribute to health. • **Identify** the causes of stress and ways to manage stress. • **Describe** rules and procedures for maintaining a safe workplace. • **Summarize** the role of the employer and the employee in protecting the environment. • **Explain** how to respond effectively to workplace emergencies.
CHAPTER 12 **Workplace Legal Matters**	• **Explain** how labor laws and labor unions affect the workplace. • **Identify** the main antidiscrimination laws and explain their role in protecting workers. • **Describe** effective strategies for handling sexual harassment. • **Distinguish** between civil law and criminal law. • **Give examples** of civil law cases and explain how they are resolved. • **Explain** how to find and evaluate legal services.

Understanding Brackets, Letters, and Ability Levels in the Teacher Wraparound Edition

Brackets Brackets on the reduced student edition page correspond to teaching strategies and activities in the Teacher Wraparound Edition. As you teach the lesson, the brackets show you exactly where to use the teaching strategies and activities.

Letters The letters on the reduced student edition page identify the type of strategy or activity. See the key below to learn about the different types of strategies and activities.

Ability Levels Teaching Strategies that appear throughout the chapters have been identified by one of three codes to give you an idea of their suitability for students of varying learning styles and abilities.

Resources Key program resources are listed in each chapter. Icons indicate the format of resources.

KEY TO LETTERS

R **Reading Strategy** activities help you teach reading skills and vocabulary.

C **Critical Thinking** strategies help students apply and extend what they have learned.

S **Skill Practice** strategies help students practice historical analysis and geographical skills.

W **Writing Support** activities provide writing opportunities to help students comprehend the text.

D **Develop Concepts** activities use various strategies to help teachers gauge and plan for students' concept development.

U **Universal Access** activities provide differentiated instruction for English language learners, and suggestions for teaching various types of learners. *These activities may or may not have brackets.*

NCLB **No Child Left Behind** activities help students practice and improve their abilities in academic subjects.

KEY TO ABILITY LEVELS

L1 Strategies should be within the ability range of all students. Often full class participation is required.

L2 Strategies are for average to above-average students or for small groups. Some teacher direction is necessary.

L3 Strategies are designed for students able and willing to work independently. Minimal teacher direction is necessary.

KEY TO RESOURCE ICONS

📁 Print Material

💿 CD-ROM

🖱 Internet

TeacherWorks™
All-In-One Planner and Resource Center

Teacher Wraparound Edition

For the Unit:
Unit Thematic Project Student Rubrics
Unit Test
Unit Connecting Activities Projects

For the Chapter:
Chapter Resources
Program Resources
Additional Print and Media Resources
Lesson Plans
Chapter Summaries, Key Terms, and
Academic Vocabulary *(English and Spanish)*

Graphic Organizers
Reading Activities
Chapter Self-Checks *(English and Spanish)*
Internet Activities
School-to-Career Connections
Work-Based Learning Projects
Personal and Academic Career Portfolio Student Rubrics

Student Activity Workbook with Academic Integration

Strategies for Students with Special Needs

Career Plan Project Workbook

@ Link to the *Succeeding in the World of Work* Online **Learning Center with Podcasts** through **glencoe.com**.

Unit Overview

Introduce the Unit

Introduce the unit by describing the main concepts of each chapter in the unit.

Unit 4 describes skills and personal qualities that will help new workers succeed in their jobs and careers and minimize safety risks and legal conflicts.

Chapter 8 covers what to expect at a new job.

Chapter 9 identifies the key attributes of a valuable employee and explains how to show ethical behavior on the job.

Chapter 10 emphasizes the importance of attitude and how to handle criticism, pressure, gossip, and anger.

Chapter 11 discusses how to be a healthy worker by getting enough rest, exercising, eating healthfully, and handling stress. Students learn the role of government, employers, and employees in workplace safety and discover how to prepare for and handle workplace emergencies.

Chapter 12 describes employment laws and what happens when employers and employees come into legal conflict.

▦▦:▦ OUT OF TIME?

If class time is too short to cover all of the chapters in this unit, have students:
- Write down the key terms and their definitions.
- Read the chapter summaries at the beginning of each chapter review.
- Go to the *Succeeding in the World of Work* Online Learning Center (OLC) through **glencoe.com** to download free Study-to-Go content to their PDAs or cell phones.

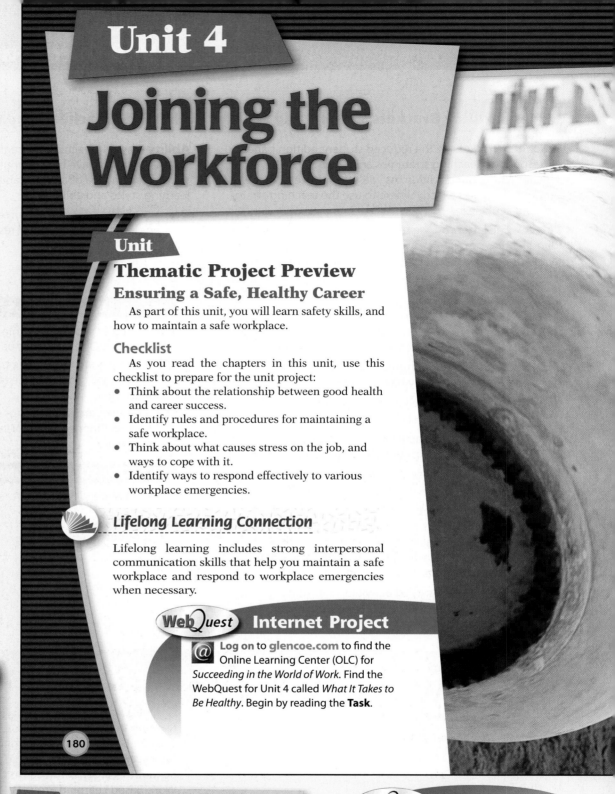

Unit 4
Joining the Workforce

Unit

Thematic Project Preview

Ensuring a Safe, Healthy Career

As part of this unit, you will learn safety skills, and how to maintain a safe workplace.

Checklist

As you read the chapters in this unit, use this checklist to prepare for the unit project:
- Think about the relationship between good health and career success.
- Identify rules and procedures for maintaining a safe workplace.
- Think about what causes stress on the job, and ways to cope with it.
- Identify ways to respond effectively to various workplace emergencies.

Lifelong Learning Connection

Lifelong learning includes strong interpersonal communication skills that help you maintain a safe workplace and respond to workplace emergencies when necessary.

WebQuest Internet Project

@ **Log on to glencoe.com** to find the Online Learning Center (OLC) for *Succeeding in the World of Work*. Find the WebQuest for Unit 4 called *What It Takes to Be Healthy*. Begin by reading the **Task**.

180

Unit Thematic Project Preview

Tell students that as part of this unit, they will investigate safety and health hazards in their chosen career field. They will do research to discover the most common safety and health problems, such as on-the-job illnesses and injuries, and will develop solutions to minimize the risk of such problems. Using presentation software, they will then share their ideas and research with the class.

WebQuest

For WebQuest teaching suggestions and rubrics, go to the Teacher Center of this book's Online Learning Center (OLC) through **glencoe.com**.

ENSURING SAFETY Different workplaces require different safety measures. *What kinds of safety issues would this worker need to be aware of in his job?*

181

Ask students these questions to activate prior knowledge:

Chapter 8
What company policies are important for you to know when you start a job? (payment schedule, rules on sick days, holidays, and coming in late, and the schedule for performance reviews and raises, among others.)

Chapter 9
Why is initiative important to employers? (Employees with initiative solve problems quickly and do not require constant oversight.)

How can you show your employer that you are honest and trustworthy? (Be honest about time worked, about money and expenses, and about your own and others' actions.)

Chapter 10
Why does a positive attitude matter on the job? (Your attitude determines how you react to situations and how others perceive you.)

Chapter 11
What is stress? (Stress is a physical and emotional response to conflict.)

What can workers do to make their workplaces safer? (Learn and follow all safety rules and guidelines, use equipment safely, and report safety hazards.)

Chapter 12
What are some labor laws that affect employers? (Laws mandate that employers pay at least a minimum wage, allow labor unions, and give equal treatment to all workers.)

What is sexual harassment? (any unwelcome behavior of a sexual nature)

▶ *Extend the Photo*

Caption Answer Construction and maintenance workers like the one shown in this photo need to understand how to use all equipment and machinery, how to handle possibly hazardous materials, and how to protect themselves and others against falling and flying objects.

Discussion Ask students whether they would or should consider the health and safety risks involved in various careers as they make their career plans. For example, would they hesitate to enter a career in law enforcement, construction, or another field that has a high rate of on-the-job injuries and illnesses? Why or why not? (Opinions will vary, but students should understand that workplace health and safety risks can have a large impact on workers' quality of life.)

Chapter Resources Planning Guide with Activities and Features

Section	Features	Activities
Section 8.1 Preparing for Your First Day on the Job	Creative Business Practices (p. 186) Real-World Connection (p. 187) 21st Century Workplace (p. 188) Hot Jobs! (p. 189)	Before You Read (p. 184) Graphic Organizer (p. 184) As You Read (pp. 185, 188) After You Read (p. 189)
Section 8.2 What You Can Expect from Your Employer	Math in Action (p. 192) Everyday Ethics (p. 194) Career Checklist (p. 195)	Before You Read (p. 190) Graphic Organizer (p. 190) As You Read (p. 193) After You Read (p. 195)

NCLB Activities, information, and skills practice will help your students attain No Child Left Behind proficiency. Students will improve their abilities in the following academic standards areas:

Academic Standards Correlations

Discipline	Standard	Feature/Activity
English Language Arts	**NCTE 1** Read texts to acquire new information.	Creative Business Practices (p. 186) Hot Jobs! (p. 189) Everyday Ethics (p. 194)
	NCTE 4 Use written language to communicate effectively.	After You Read (p. 195) Academic Skills in the Workplace (p. 200) Writing Skills Practice (p. 201)
	NCTE 7 Conduct research and gather, evaluate, and synthesize data to communicate discoveries.	Real-World Connection (p. 187)
	NCTE 8 Use information resources to gather information and create and communicate knowledge.	21st Century Workplace (p. 188)
Mathematics	**Geometry:** Use visualizations, spatial reasoning, and geometric modeling to solve problems	After You Read (p. 189)
	Problem Solving: Solve problems that arise in mathematics and in other contexts	Math in Action (p. 192)
	Geometry: Analyze characteristics and properties of two- and three-dimensional geometric shapes and develop mathematical arguments about geometric relationships	Academic Skills in the Workplace (p. 200)
Science	**Physical Science:** Motions and forces	Academic Skills in the Workplace (p. 200)

CORRELATIONS The charts show the 21st Century Skills, foundation skills, and workplace competencies that students develop as they work in this chapter.

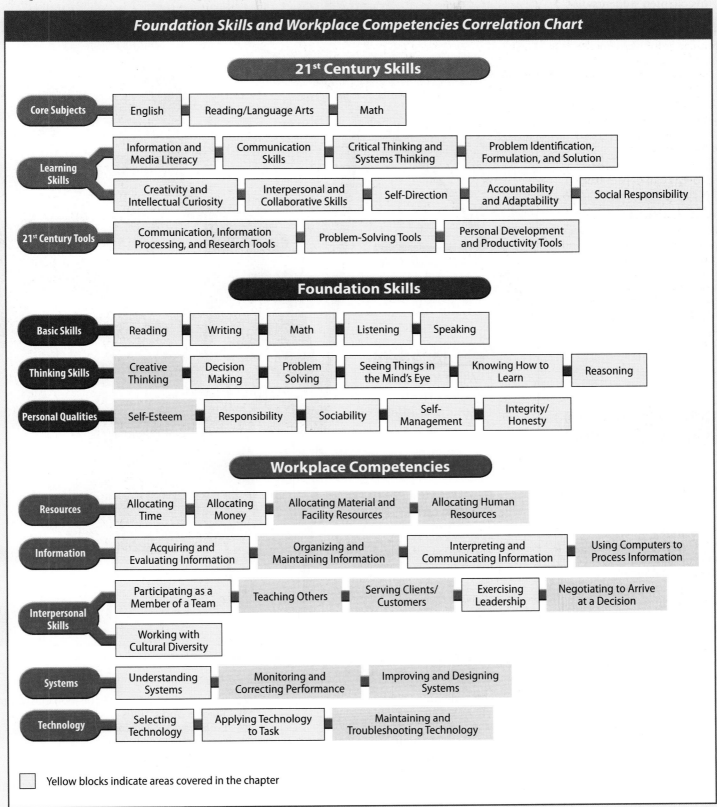

Foundation Skills and Workplace Competencies Correlation Chart

21st Century Skills

Core Subjects
- English
- Reading/Language Arts
- Math

Learning Skills
- Information and Media Literacy
- Communication Skills
- Critical Thinking and Systems Thinking
- Problem Identification, Formulation, and Solution
- Creativity and Intellectual Curiosity
- Interpersonal and Collaborative Skills
- Self-Direction
- Accountability and Adaptability
- Social Responsibility

21st Century Tools
- Communication, Information Processing, and Research Tools
- Problem-Solving Tools
- Personal Development and Productivity Tools

Foundation Skills

Basic Skills
- Reading
- Writing
- Math
- Listening
- Speaking

Thinking Skills
- Creative Thinking
- Decision Making
- Problem Solving
- Seeing Things in the Mind's Eye
- Knowing How to Learn
- Reasoning

Personal Qualities
- Self-Esteem
- Responsibility
- Sociability
- Self-Management
- Integrity/Honesty

Workplace Competencies

Resources
- Allocating Time
- Allocating Money
- Allocating Material and Facility Resources
- Allocating Human Resources

Information
- Acquiring and Evaluating Information
- Organizing and Maintaining Information
- Interpreting and Communicating Information
- Using Computers to Process Information

Interpersonal Skills
- Participating as a Member of a Team
- Teaching Others
- Serving Clients/Customers
- Exercising Leadership
- Negotiating to Arrive at a Decision
- Working with Cultural Diversity

Systems
- Understanding Systems
- Monitoring and Correcting Performance
- Improving and Designing Systems

Technology
- Selecting Technology
- Applying Technology to Task
- Maintaining and Troubleshooting Technology

☐ Yellow blocks indicate areas covered in the chapter

Chapter Overview
Introduce the Chapter
In this chapter, students discover how to start their jobs on the right foot by learning what the employer expects from them and what they, in turn, can expect from the employer.

Section 8.1 examines dressing appropriately, company orientation programs, and company policies.

Section 8.2 covers what employees can expect from their employers.

Build Background
Ask students how they expect work to be different from and similar to school. For example, students must follow a dress code while at school. How might they be expected to dress for work? (Students might point out that they are expected to arrive to class on time, and most employers also require employees to be punctual.)

▶ *Exploring the Photo*

Caption Answer Be well groomed and dressed appropriately (e-mail or call your supervisor or the person with whom you interviewed if you are unsure what to wear); bring paper and pens and any identification or Social Security cards that might be needed to add you to the company's payroll.

Discussion Discuss how students would benefit from preparing for a first day at work. (Being prepared and learning as much as you can about the company before your first day will give you confidence to speak with knowledge about the company and your position.)

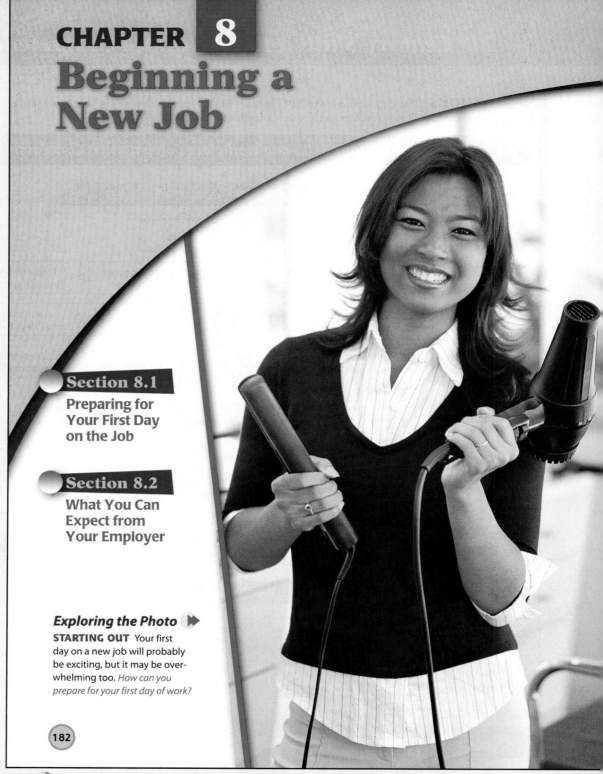

CHAPTER 8
Beginning a New Job

● Section 8.1
Preparing for Your First Day on the Job

● Section 8.2
What You Can Expect from Your Employer

Exploring the Photo ▶▶
STARTING OUT Your first day on a new job will probably be exciting, but it may be overwhelming too. *How can you prepare for your first day of work?*

182

Classroom Resources

- 📁 Student Edition
- 📁 Teacher Wraparound Edition
- 📁 Student Activity Workbook with Academic Integration
- 📁 Student Activity Workbook with Academic Integration TAE
- 📁 *Fast File,* Unit 4 Resources

- 📁 Inclusion in the Career Education Classroom
- ⚙ TeacherWorks™ Plus
- ⚙ *ExamView Assessment Suite*
- ⚙ Interactive Chalkboard
- ⚙ Interactive Student Edition
- 🏊 Online Student Edition
- 🏊 Online Learning Center (OLC) with Podcasts

Chapter Objectives

After completing this chapter, you will be able to:

- **Describe** how to manage the anxieties and challenges of a first day of work.
- **Explain** how to dress for work.
- **Explain** the purpose of orientation and distinguish among the different types of orientation program.
- **Identify** typical forms of payment.
- **Describe** common employee benefits.
- **Explain** the role of employee performance reviews.

Writing Activity Personal Career Notebook

Your first day on a new job can make you feel both excited and anxious. In your notebook, write a list of five or six questions and concerns you might have on your first day. Then list things you could do to answer your questions and address your concerns.

Get Motivated! Talk to a family member, acquaintance, or friend who has a job. Ask this person to tell you about his or her first day on the job. Ask what questions or concerns the person had and what he or she did to prepare for the job. Create a one- or two-page summary or transcript of your interview.

Chapter 8 Beginning a New Job (183)

Writing Activity Personal Career Notebook Answer Guide

Some questions might include: What is the pay schedule? Is there a dress code or what should I wear to work? Will my work schedule be the same or change weekly? How do I record the hours I have worked for payroll? Read any and all orientation materials first; many commonly asked questions will be answered there. Address additional questions to your supervisor or human resources administrator.

Get Motivated! Summaries or transcripts will vary but should adequately reflect a conversation with someone who has shared an experience about a first day on the job.

Review the Objectives

Introduce the chapter by reviewing the chapter objectives:

Section 8.1 Objectives

Describe how to manage the anxieties and challenges of a first day of work. (On your first day, allow extra time to get ready and get to work. When introduced to new coworkers and when given job tasks, repeat the name or task to help you remember it. Ask questions about anything you forget or do not understand.)

Explain how to dress for work. (When interviewing, it is helpful to observe what people are wearing in order to determine how you should dress on your first day. You can also call and ask your human resources representative or supervisor.)

Explain the purpose of orientation and distinguish among the different types of orientation programs. (Orientation introduces you to the company's policies, procedures, values, and benefits. Orientation may be informal—lunch with a supervisor, for example; or formal, which might include an employee manual and an organized presentation.)

Section 8.2 Objectives

Identify typical forms of payment. (Methods of payment include hourly wages, salary, commission, and incentive plans.)

Describe common employee benefits. (The most common employee benefits are health insurance and paid days off for holidays, sickness, and vacation.)

Explain the role of employee performance reviews. (Reviews evaluate how well you are doing in your job.)

FOCUS

Bell Ringer Activity

Exploring Careers
Ask students to write a list of at least five characteristics or traits they think a good employee should have as well as characteristics of a good coworker. Have students share their lists with the class.

Resources

 Interactive Chalkboard
The Interactive Chalkboard CD provides visual teaching aids for this section.

@ Online Learning Center
The Online Learning Center (OLC) through **glencoe.com** features chapter vocabulary, chapter summaries, and other study materials.

Preteaching

Write *company culture, orientation,* and *mentor* on the board. Have students describe how each term relates to what they need to know before starting their first job.

Graphic Organizer

Tell students to go to the OLC through **glencoe.com** for a printable graphic organizer. (Graphic organizers should show what students might expect on their first day at a job.)

NCLB connects academic correlations to book content.

Preparing for Your First Day on the Job

Reading Guide

Before You Read
Preview Choose a Key Term or Academic Vocabulary word that is new to you. Write it on a piece of paper. When you find it in the text, write down the definition.

Read to Learn
- How to manage the anxieties and challenges of a first day of work
- How to dress for work
- The purpose of orientation and the different types of orientation program

D Main Idea
Knowing what to expect your first day at a job can help to make it a good experience.

Key Concepts
- What to Expect Your First Day
- Dressing for the Job
- Orientation

Key Terms
◇ company culture
◇ orientation
◇ mentor

Academic Vocabulary
You will find these words in your reading and on your tests. Use the academic vocabulary glossary to look up their definitions if necessary.
■ strategy　　■ appropriate

Graphic Organizer
As you read, use a concept web like the one shown to help organize your information. In each circle, write one thing you can expect your first day at a new job.

 Log On Go to this book's Online Learning Center through **glencoe.com** for an online version of this graphic organizer.

Academic Standards • • • • • • • • • • • • • • •

N C L B

English Language Arts
- Conduct research and gather, evaluate, and synthesize data to communicate discoveries. (NCTE 7)

Mathematics
- Use visualizations, spatial reasoning, and geometric modeling to solve problems

---

Reading Guide

Before You Read
Point out to students that the first day at a new job might be comparable to the first day of the school year. In both cases, students will learn names of new people, new procedures, and a new environment.

D Develop Concepts
Main Idea Discuss the main idea with students. Ask: Why is it helpful to learn what to expect on the first day at a job? (Knowing what to expect can help you manage your anxieties and arrive prepared, which will help give coworkers and supervisors a good first impression.)

What to Expect Your First Day

Getting a new job is like moving to a different country. You may have an idea of what it will be like, but you will not know for certain until you get there. What can you do to prepare for your first day at a new job?

Dealing with Stress and Anxiety

Your first day on the job can be exciting. You will meet new people and learn new things. It may also be stressful. What will your employer expect of you? Will you be able to meet the challenges of the new job? Learning to handle stress and anxiety will help your first day go more smoothly.

Figure out how long it will take you to get ready and get to work. Then allow extra time. Being late will add to the stress and anxiety you may already feel.

At work, you will be introduced to your new coworkers and supervisors. Do not worry if you cannot remember everyone's name at first. Just ask again. A simple trick that may help you remember a person's name is to say it as you are introduced. Then use that person's name again while talking to him or her.

To remember job tasks, you can use the same **strategy**. Repeat or write down directions, then practice the task. You will learn more about managing stress in Chapter 11.

As You Read

Connect What strategies do you use to remember things?

 A NEW JOB You may meet many new people and learn new tasks when you begin a new job. *What are some ways to help you remember new names and tasks?*

TEACH

Discussion Starter

What to Expect Your First Day Ask students to imagine it is their first day on the job and they have not been given a lot of directions. Ask them to brainstorm what they could do in the situation. (Students might mention asking questions when they do not understand a task.)

R Reading Strategy

Anticipating the First Day Have students write what they imagine their first day of work will be like, including what they will wear, how they will get to work, who their coworkers will be, what will be expected of them, and how they'll feel, particularly at the end of the day. (After students have read this section, have them add to or revise these expectations.)

As You Read

If students do not already have strategies for remembering coworkers' names or job tasks, encourage them to think of ways they remember other things, such as class notes, game rules, or driving directions.

Resources

TeacherWorks™ Plus The TeacherWorks software includes customizable built-in lesson plans and links to printable program resources.

Extend the Photo

Caption Answer Repeating a person's name when you are introduced or repeating instructions that you have been given are helpful ways to remember names and tasks.

Discussion Point out to students that they may encounter coworkers to whom they have not yet been introduced. Ask: What should you do if no one introduces you to your coworkers? (You should introduce yourself, and let them know where you work in the company.)

TEACH *(cont.)*

C₁ Critical Thinking

Analyze Ask students why they might need to be patient during their first days of a new job. (New employees rarely learn everything they need to know on the first day at work. Being patient and maintaining a good attitude will help new workers understand over time why and how things are done.)

C₂ Critical Thinking

Draw Conclusions Ask: Why do you think some employers ask their employees to wear uniforms? (Employees might be required to wear a uniform for safety reasons; so employees look professional and not sloppy; and to promote the company's image.)

✓ Reading Check

EXPLAIN Company culture refers to the behavior, attitudes, values, and habits of the employees and owners of a company. Learn about it by listening to and observing coworkers and supervisors.

◄ Vocabulary

You can find definitions in the **Key Terms** glossary and **Academic Vocabulary** glossary at the back of this book.

The Company Culture

As soon as you become a company employee, you will be immersed in the company culture. **Company culture** is the behavior, attitudes, values, and habits of the employees and owners that are unique to each company. It is also known as *corporate culture*.

You can learn the company culture by listening to and observing your coworkers and supervisors. How do they behave and interact? Does what you see match your values and interests? Learning the company culture takes a while. Until you understand it, take your time trying to fit in. Use your skills of listening, knowing how to learn, and sociability. Soon you will know if the company is a good match for you and if you will fit in.

✓ Reading Check **EXPLAIN** What is company culture and how can you learn about it at a new job?

Dressing for the Job

What is **appropriate** dress for your first day on the job? Should you wear jeans or a business suit? Unless your job requires a uniform, it may be hard to know what to wear on the job. Here are some suggestions that will help you decide.

Creative Business Practices

WALT DISNEY COMPANY

Strong Corporate Culture

For more than 50 years, the Walt Disney Company has built a corporate culture that is reflected in every corner of the Magic Kingdom. The company has a strict code of behavior and dress that helps to reinforce the company's image as a provider of wholesome entertainment for the whole family.

At Disney World, for example, employees, or "cast members," are considered to be the official representatives of the company. They are instructed on how to act and to be friendly to guests. The company believes that its trademark of friendliness is key to attracting repeat customers.

Disney's dress code encompasses an employee's whole appearance. It emphasizes neatness and simplicity: natural-looking hair color and nails, groomed facial hair, minimal jewelry, and no visible tattoos. Employees are regularly rewarded for maintaining the Disney culture through more than 20 employee recognition programs.

CRITICAL THINKING Why is it important for service-oriented companies to have a strong corporate culture?

 Connect to the Real World For more information about Disney, visit the company's Web site via the link on this book's Online Learning Center through **glencoe.com**.

 186 **Unit 4** Joining the Workforce

Jack Sullivan/Alamy

glencoe.com

Creative Business Practices

CRITICAL THINKING ANSWER Companies benefit from having a strong corporate culture to keep employee morale up and to help employees develop a positive self-concept.

First, consider the industry. What you wear to work depends on the kind of work you will be doing. If you are starting a job in a manufacturing plant or on a construction site, for example, jeans and a clean shirt will most likely be appropriate. If you will be working in a restaurant or store, you may be asked to wear clothing provided by the employer.

Appropriate dress for office workers varies. Many retail businesses have uniforms or require workers to wear set colors and articles of clothing, such as black pants and a button-down white shirt. Some businesses require employees to wear suits. Others have moved to *business casual* dress, which allows more relaxed professional clothing, such as khakis, sweaters, and button-down shirts. Some offices allow jeans, while others do not. A good way to learn what to wear your first day is to observe what people are wearing when you go for your interview.

You can also ask. Try to remember to ask about the dress code during your interview. If you forget, you can call your supervisor or a human resources representative before you start your job. You can follow these guidelines for your first day on the job.
- If you are unsure how to dress, dress conservatively.
- Avoid bright or garish colors and trendy outfits.
- Keep jewelry simple and minimal.
- Wear clothes that are clean and not frayed or worn out.
- If you will be meeting the public, wear more traditional business clothing.

✓ Reading Check **EXPLAIN** What are some guidelines for dressing for your first day on a new job?

Orientation

You have a lot to prepare for and to think about before you start a new job. Your employer also has a lot to prepare for you. To help new employees get started, companies often provide orientation. **Orientation** is a program that introduces you to the company's policies, procedures, values, and benefits.

Orientation may be informal. You may simply meet with the office manager to talk about benefits, have lunch with your supervisor, and tour the workplace. Some companies have more formal orientation programs. In addition to meeting your supervisors and coworkers and touring the workplace, you may receive a company manual or attend an orientation presentation with other new employees. These orientations may last anywhere from a few hours to a couple of days and may include interactive or online activities.

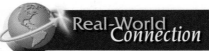

Real-World Connection

Non-Compete Agreement

You just started a job at a small computer company. During orientation, you learned that company policy requires that new employees sign a document called a "non-compete agreement" before they are given access to the company's computers. You were told that this is standard industry procedure. You are not sure you want to sign this document. Does it mean you will not be able to take a job with another computer company in a year or two?

Critical Thinking Should you sign the document? Why or why not?

Do Your Own Research Investigate what a non-compete agreement involves, including how long it may be in effect after a person leaves a particular company. Learn what some of the consequences of signing or not signing such an agreement are. Use the Internet and search for "non-compete agreement" or "non-competition agreement" to find details. Record your findings in a one-page report.

TEACH *(cont.)*

S Skill Practice Guided Practice

Work In Teams Have students work in small groups to create an orientation program for new students at your school. Ask: What activities or information would you include? (Students might include visual aids such as a map of the school and the location of a new student's locker and homeroom. They might also include dress code information and a pamphlet of school rules and regulations.)

U Universal Access

Students with Learning Disabilities Many teachers find that students with special needs understand visually presented materials more readily than isolated numbers. For example, if student progress is presented in graph form, as opposed to numerical grades, the students are better able to understand how they are doing.

ASSESS

Review Key Terms
Have students write sentences using each key term.

Online Study Tools
Have students go to the OLC through **glencoe.com** to:
- Download **Podcast** study tools.
- Download free **Study-to-Go** content to their PDAs or cell phones.

✓ Reading Check

EXPLAIN Guidelines include dressing conservatively, avoiding bright colors and trendy outfits, keeping jewelry minimal, and wearing clothes that are clean and in good condition.

Real-World Connection

Critical Thinking Answer Answers will vary, but students should keep in mind that signing a non-compete agreement might be a condition of employment in a given job.

Do Your Own Research Reports should show an understanding of non-compete agreements.

RETEACH

C Critical Thinking

Make Connections Ask: Why should you learn about your responsibilities and company goals as soon as possible? (Knowing your responsibilities and the company's goals will help you avoid misunderstandings about what is expected of you and what you can expect from the company.)

As You Read

Mentors coach new employees on the skills and procedures needed to do their jobs and help them learn the company culture and company policies.

Resources

📂 **Student Activity Workbook** Assign the Chapter 8 activities in the Student Activity Workbook.

N C L B Activity correlated to English Language Arts standards.

188

The 21st Century Workplace

Workplace Diversity and Disabilities

In the workplace, many people use the word *diversity* to refer to differences in gender, culture, and ethnicity. Diversity includes more than this, however. It includes all the ways people vary, including age, economic and family background, and abilities and disabilities.

About one in five Americans has a disability of some kind, from poor vision to difficulty reading fluently. Disabilities can be physical, emotional, or cognitive (mental). Today, assistive technology is helping more and more people with disabilities to participate fully in the workforce. *Assistive technology* refers to tools that help people with disabilities perform tasks. These tools can be as simple as a handrail to help people who use wheelchairs maneuver down a hallway, or as complex as software that responds to spoken commands.

CRITICAL THINKING

Who might benefit from using software that responds to voice commands?

In Your Community

Many everyday tools, such as eyeglasses and pencil grips, are examples of assistive technology. Write down examples of assistive technology that you see at your school or workplace. Share your examples with the class.

@ **Extend Your Learning** Some hearing-impaired workers use a sign language interpreter in the workplace. For links to Web sites about using sign language in the workplace, go to this book's OLC through **glencoe.com**.

As a new employee, you will benefit from orientation by learning about the company and your job. The employer benefits by having employees who are well trained and informed.

As You Read

Explain How does a mentor help new employees?

Mentors

At some companies, a new employee is paired with a senior co-worker who acts as a mentor. A **mentor** is an informal teacher or guide who helps new employees adjust to their new workplace. If there is no formal mentoring process at your company, you may seek out a more experienced worker to act as a mentor. Mentors coach new employees in the skills and procedures needed to do their jobs and help them learn the company culture and company policies. A mentor can also provide guidance that may help you in your career.

Your Responsibilities and Company Goals

Whatever type of orientation you receive, it should give you a clear idea of your responsibilities and the company goals. It should answer the following questions:

C
- What is the company's mission, or purpose? How do your job and your department fit into the mission?
- What are your exact job responsibilities?
- Who should you go to when you have questions?
- How and when will your performance be evaluated?
- What benefits will you receive and when will you receive them?

The 21st Century Workplace

CRITICAL THINKING ANSWER People who are vision-impaired or who have limited use of their hands would benefit from technology that uses voice commands.

In Your Community Other examples of assistive technology might include hand or wrist braces to prevent or help correct musculoskeletal disorders resulting from repetitive stress. Wheelchair ramps and elevators are legally required in many public spaces to accommodate people with disabilities.

188

Company Policies

During orientation, you will also be introduced to company policies and procedures. Every company has specific policies that spell out what the company expects of you and what you can expect of the company. You may be given a company manual or other written statement of official policies. Read these policies right away. By learning the company's policies, you can protect yourself from breaking a company rule and ensure that you live up to your employer's expectations. These are just a few questions answered by company policies:

- When will you be paid?
- How many sick days are you allotted each year?
- How many vacation days are you allotted and how do you request them?
- What paid holidays does the company allow?
- When will you receive a raise? What is required for a raise?
- What health and safety procedures are in place?

HOT JOBS!

Vet Tech

Veterinary technicians assist veterinarians, the doctors who care for pets, wild animals, and livestock. Using their studies in biology, science, and math, *vet techs* often work in a team environment. Their duties include working with and caring for the animals, administering medication and treatment, performing tests, and assisting during surgery.

Section 8.1 After You Read

Review Key Concepts

1. List two things you can do to help make your first day at a new job go smoothly.
2. Describe how to determine what to wear on your first day at a new job.
3. Explain the purpose of a company orientation program.

Practice Academic Skills

Mathematics

4. On your first day of work at a furniture design firm, your boss asks you to draw a storage trunk that the company is designing. Draw two different two-dimensional representations of a rectangular prism. First make a traditional drawing of the object, then "unfold" the object by drawing a net. Label the dimensions as follows: length = 4 feet, width = 1.5 feet, and height = 2 feet.

CONCEPT **Two-Dimensional Representations of Three-Dimensional Objects** Three-dimensional objects are represented in two dimensions to more easily determine properties such as area and volume.
Step 1: Draw a traditional representation of a three-dimensional object in two dimensions. Label the length, width, and height.
Step 2: Draw an unfolded version, or net, of the object by imagining cutting it along 7 of its vertices, laying it flat, and outlining it.

Math For math help, go to the Math Appendix located at the back of this book.

N C L B

Chapter 8 Beginning a New Job **189**

Section 8.1 After You Read

Review Key Concepts

1. Answers might include planning extra time to get ready and get to work, and dressing appropriately.
2. At the time of your interview, observe what other workers are wearing, or ask a human resources representative or your supervisor before arriving for work on your first day.

3. Orientation programs introduce you to the company's policies, procedures, values, and benefits.

Practice Academic Skills

4. Drawings should resemble these figures.

Section 8.1

ASSESS

After You Read
Have students complete the Section 8.1 After You Read section review.

Online Study Tools
Have students go to the OLC through **glencoe.com** to:
- Take the Section 8.1 **Practice Test**.
- Download **Podcast** study tools.
- Download free **Study-to-Go** content to their PDAs or cell phones.

STUDY TO GO

Resources

ExamView Assessment Suite CD allows you to print out ready-made unit and chapter tests complete with answer keys. You can also create customized tests.

CLOSE

Culminating Activity
What to Expect Divide students into groups of three or four. Have each group prepare and perform a skit demonstrating help offered by two or three friends to another friend who has just taken a new job. Skits should include what the new employee should expect on the job, how to dress, what will take place during orientation, and suggestions for making a good impression.

N C L B Activity correlated to Mathematics standards.

189

Section 8.2

FOCUS

Bell Ringer Activity

What You Can Expect from Your Employer

Have students list three things an employee should expect from an employer. Write students' responses on the board. (Lists will likely include payment. Use this discussion to introduce various forms of payment.)

Resources

Interactive Chalkboard

The Interactive Chalkboard CD provides visual teaching aids for this section.

@ Online Learning Center

The Online Learning Center (OLC) through **glencoe.com** features chapter vocabulary, chapter summaries, and other study materials.

Preteaching

Have students choose three key terms from this section and use them in complete sentences.

Graphic Organizer

Tell students to go to the OLC through **glencoe.com** for a printable graphic organizer. (Graphic organizers will vary but should reflect an understanding of payment, benefits, and performance reviews.)

 NCLB connects academic correlations to book content.

190

What You Can Expect from Your Employer

Reading Guide

Before You Read

Preview Read the Key Concepts. Write one or two sentences predicting what the section will be about.

Read to Learn
- Typical forms of payment
- Common employee benefits
- The role of employee performance reviews

D Main Idea
Understanding company policies and procedures will help you to know what to expect from your employer and how to protect your rights.

Key Concepts
- The Relationship Between Employer and Employee
- Payment
- Benefits
- Performance Reviews
- Preparing for Job Loss

Key Terms
- ◇ wage
- ◇ overtime
- ◇ nonexempt employees
- ◇ exempt employees
- ◇ salary
- ◇ commission
- ◇ profit-sharing plan
- ◇ performance bonuses
- ◇ pension plan
- ◇ performance review
- ◇ probation
- ◇ layoff

Academic Vocabulary
You will find these words in your reading and on your tests. Use the academic vocabulary glossary to look up their definitions if necessary.
- ■ incentive
- ■ terminate

Graphic Organizer
As you read, list details about the things that you can expect from your employer. Use a graphic organizer like the one shown to help organize your information.

PAYMENTS	BENEFITS	PERFORMANCE REVIEWS

 Log On Go to this book's Online Learning Center through **glencoe.com** for a larger version of this graphic organizer.

N C L B
Academic Standards • • • • • • • • • • • • • • • • • •
English Language Arts
- Read texts to acquire new information. (NCTE 1)
- Use written language to communicate effectively. (NCTE 4)

Mathematics
- Solve problems that arise in mathematics and in other contexts

190 **Unit 4** Joining the Workforce

glencoe.com

Reading Guide

Before You Read
Point out to students that money is not the only form of payment that should concern employees. They should also consider benefits, such as medical coverage and paid time off.

D Develop Concepts
 Main Idea Discuss the main idea with students. Ask: Why is it important to know the policies that protect your rights in the workplace?

The Relationship Between Employer and Employee

Every employee works for one or more reasons, such as salary, health insurance, stability, or a pension. These are some of the things you may want and expect from your employer.

What your employer is likely to provide changes over time. The factors affecting business that you learned about in Chapter 1, such as globalization and outsourcing, influence what a business can provide for its employees. These factors affect the relationship between employer and employee. For instance, globalization has forced companies to be more efficient to stay competitive. One way to be efficient is to operate with fewer employees. As a result, workers have less job security than they once had. **Figure 8.1** shows other ways the employer-employee relationship is changing.

✓ **Reading Check** IDENTIFY What are some reasons the relationship between employers and employees is changing?

Figure 8.1	CHANGES IN THE EMPLOYER-EMPLOYEE RELATIONSHIP	
Aspects of a Job	**In the Past**	**Today**
Job Security	• Experience or length of time with a company guaranteed job security. • Workforce consisted mainly of full-time employees. • Company was responsible for worker's security.	• Continued training provides job security. • Increasing numbers of temporary workers and independent contractors • Freedom from company ties
Salary	• Based on experience • Based on number of years with company	• Based on current value of work • Based on knowledge and skill level
Benefits	• Companies paid premiums for employees. • Health insurance stopped when employment ended. • Retirement package was assured after years of employment; included lifetime health insurance. • Benefits were not considered one of the main ways to attract good employees.	• Employees pay part of premium or have reduced benefits. • COBRA keeps workers insured for a period of time if they lose their jobs. • Retirement benefits are less; often health insurance is reduced or ends with retirement. • Benefits are a large part of the employee package.
Corporate Culture	• Employees stayed with a company for years and were treated like family. • Employees were promoted based on years of service.	• To benefit their personal goals, employees move to companies that offer the best opportunities. • Employees must perform to keep their jobs.
CHANGING EXPECTATIONS	The competitive global economy is changing what American workers can expect from their employers. *What are the advantages and disadvantages of these changes for today's worker?*	

TEACH

Discussion Starter
The Relationship Between Employer and Employee Ask students what they believe is the most important aspect of the relationship between the employee and the employer at a job.

R Reading Strategy
Make a List Based on the information in **Figure 8.1,** ask students to make a list of strategies they should consider to stay competitive in the workplace. (Students might mention the need to stay abreast of new technology, continue their training, and regularly assess the quality of their work to make sure they maintain high performance levels.)

✓ **Reading Check**

IDENTIFY Globalization and outsourcing have forced companies to be more efficient and to stay competitive, which has resulted in companies operating with fewer employees. Consequently, workers have less job security.

Resources

● **TeacherWorks™ Plus** The TeacherWorks software includes customizable built-in lesson plans and links to printable program resources.

EXTEND THE FIGURE   **Figure 8.1**

Caption Answer Advantages: Today's workers have greater independence and more control over their future. They can improve their income by improving their skills. Disadvantages: There are no guarantees of job security.

Discussion Almost all workers need technology skills. Ask students how they can begin gaining these skills while they are still in school. (Students can take computer courses, spend study period in the computer lab, and learn software at home.)

S **Skill Practice**

Independent Practice

Calculate Wages Rosanna delivers packages for a delivery service. She earns $7.50 an hour. Last week she worked 44 hours. The normal work week is 40 hours. Assuming Rosanna earns time-and-a-half for overtime, how much did Rosanna earn last week? (She earned $345: $7.50 × 40 = $300 + ($7.50 × 1.5) × 4 = $45 + $300 = $345.)

C **Critical Thinking**

Compare Payment Methods Tell students to imagine they work in a sales job. Ask them to discuss the pros and cons of working for a straight salary versus working for a reduced salary plus commission. (Pros of commission-based salary might include being motivated to increase sales in order to make a higher commission; cons might include reduced pay during a slow sales period. A pro for straight salary would be a steady income; a con might be less opportunity to earn extra money as a result of outstanding performance.)

✓ **Reading Check**

COMPARE Nonexempt employees are normally paid an hourly wage and earn overtime pay when they work more than 40 hours a week. Exempt employees earn a salary, which is a fixed amount paid over a certain period of time.

Activity correlated to Mathematics standards.

Math In Action

Inflation

Fabian just got a new job. This year he will make $56,000. He was promised a 3.25% pay increase next year and a 1.25% increase to compensate for inflation. What will his total salary be next year?

Starting Hint: Add the percents to figure the total percent increase. Then multiply to find the total salary:
0.0325 + 0.0125 = **?**

 For more math practice, go to this book's OLC through **glencoe.com**.

Vocabulary

You can find definitions in the **Key Terms** glossary and **Academic Vocabulary** glossary at the back of this book.

Payment

Workers expect to be paid for the work they do. Pay may be calculated in a number of ways.

Basic Payment Methods

Most entry-level employees receive hourly wages. A **wage** is a fixed amount of money paid to a worker for a set amount of time spent working. The most common type of wage is an hourly wage. At the end of each pay period, pay is calculated by multiplying the number of hours worked by the hourly wage rate.

Hourly wages are affected by whether or not workers are paid overtime. **Overtime** is pay received for working more than 40 hours in a week. Usually workers on overtime are paid one and one-half times their normal hourly wage for each hour in excess of 40 hours. For example, if workers are normally paid $10 per hour, they get $15 per hour to work overtime.

A federal law requires that nonexempt employees be paid overtime. **Nonexempt employees** are workers who are normally paid an hourly wage and are entitled to earn overtime. Exempt employees do not have to be paid overtime. **Exempt employees** are workers who earn a salary. A **salary** is a fixed amount of pay for a certain period of time, usually a month or a year.

Workers in some kinds of jobs—such as sales or telemarketing—may be paid a **commission**, or earnings based on how much a person sells. They might, for example, earn 2 percent of the value of the merchandise they sell. By basing pay directly on performance, this system aims to motivate people to work harder.

Incentive Plans

Another way workers are paid is through **incentive** plans. These plans reward workers for achievement and help to keep them motivated. Incentive plans help employees know that their efforts are appreciated. Types of incentive plans include profit-sharing plans and performance bonuses.

In a **profit-sharing plan**, workers receive a share of the company's profits. The better the company performs, the more each worker receives. One example of this is the rewarding of stock options to qualifying employees. A stock option is the right to buy or sell a stock at a specified price within a stated period of time.

Performance bonuses reward workers for high levels of performance. Some companies pay bonuses to workers who increase the quantity or quality of their work. For example, factory workers who have relatively low salaries may receive a bonus nearly equal to their salaries if they reach their productivity goal.

✓ **Reading Check** **COMPARE** What is the difference between an exempt employee and a nonexempt employee?

Math In Action

Fabian's total salary next year will be $58,520 (0.0325 + 0.0125 = 0.0450; $56,000 × 0.0450 = $2,520; $2,520 + $56,000 = $58,520).

Benefits

Many jobs come with benefits. Benefits are extras that a company provides in addition to pay. They can include anything from insurance to product discounts. The most common benefits are paid health insurance and paid days off for holidays, sickness, and vacation. There may be a waiting period before employees are eligible for some kinds of benefits.

Because the cost of employee benefits is rising, some companies are limiting the benefits they offer. A recent study shows that benefits average nearly 30 percent of employers' payrolls. A good benefits package is now a way for employers to attract qualified employees in a competitive job market. Benefits are an important factor you should consider as you search for a job.

Health Benefits

Health insurance is probably the most valuable benefit. Because of the high cost of healthcare, many employers have cut back coverage or asked employees to pay part of their premiums. To ensure broader access to health care, some states now require companies to provide minimum health coverage for their employees.

Pension Plans

A **pension plan** is a savings plan for retirement. Retirement is when you stop working because of age or disability. The different types of retirement plans will be discussed in Chapter 21 of this book. The types of plans and the amounts employers and employess can contribute to these plans varies from company to company. These plans can consist of voluntary contributions by employees, contributions for each worker, matching contributions, and other options.

Convenience Benefits

Some employers also provide convenience benefits, which are services that make workers' lives easier. These benefits can include anything from public transportation refunds to gym memberships. Many companies offer services that help employees handle personal issues, such as legal matters, child care, and financial planning. Such benefits are designed to reduce stress, improve the employees' health, and make employees more productive and loyal.

▲ **HEALTH CARE** The rising cost of health insurance has caused many employers to limit employee health benefits. *Would you accept a job that did not offer health benefits?*

As You Read
Evaluate Which job benefits would you most like to have?

TEACH *(cont.)*

C **Critical Thinking**
Drawing Conclusions Ask: Even though you will not be retiring for many years from now, why is a pension a good benefit to have now? *(Pension plans build funds over a long stretch of time, so the earlier you start, the more money you can accrue for retirement. Pension plans are also important for workers who become disabled and can no longer work.)*

As You Read
Answers should reflect an understanding of the different types of job benefits.

ASSESS

Review Key Terms
Have students write sentences using each key term.

Online Study Tools
Have students go to the OLC through **glencoe.com** to:
- Download **Podcast** study tools.
- Download free **Study-to-Go** content to their PDAs or cell phones.

Extend the Photo

Caption Answer Students may respond "yes" or "no" but should provide support for their reasoning. For example, a student who would accept a job with no health benefits should point out other benefits of working for the job that make up for the lack of health coverage.

Discussion Ask: Should companies be required to provide medical coverage to all their employees? Why or why not?

RETEACH

C Critical Thinking

Take Steps to Improve Ask: What steps would you take if you received a negative performance review? (Workers should examine why they received a negative review. They could approach their supervisor about ways to improve their performance.)

✓ Reading Check

EXPLAIN Students should consider job benefits because they are part of a worker's payment, in addition to monetary compensation.

Resources

📂 **Student Activity Workbook** Assign the Chapter 8 activities in the Student Activity Workbook.

ASSESS

After You Read

Have students complete the Section 8.2 After You Read section review.

Online Study Tools

Have students go to the OLC through **glencoe.com** to:

- Take the Section 8.2 **Practice Test**.
- Download **Podcast** study tools.
- Download free **Study-to-Go** content to their PDAs or cell phones.

Everyday ETHICS

CHANGING PLACES

Should you falsify test results?

DRUG TESTING You and your friend recently started working at a large corporation. The human resources department conducts random drug testing, and your friend was picked but you were not. Your friend tells you that she has been taking pain pills for her bad back and asks you to take the test for her. She says that because the company is so big, no one will ever know the difference.

What Would You Do? Will you take the drug test for your friend? Why or why not?

DISCUSS IT In teams, discuss the reasons companies might conduct drug testing. Could the workplace be unsafe if an employee worked while under the influence of drugs? If your friend has a doctor's prescription for her pills, should the company take this under consideration? What would happen if your friend had an accident on the job related to the pills? What might happen if your friend had an accident and your boss discovered you took the drug test for her? Share your ideas with the class.

Cafeteria Plan

A cafeteria plan is a benefits policy that allows employees to choose only the benefits they need or want. For example, a company may offer the benefits of health insurance, a flexible spending account for healthcare, vision insurance, disability insurance, and day care reimbursement. Out of these, one employee may elect to have the benefit of disability insurance but not the benefit of vision insurance, while another employee may elect to have the benefit of a flexible spending account only.

Employees must estimate the costs they will have during the plan's upcoming year and then elect to contribute different amounts of their salaries into the appropriate benefits. These employee contributions are often pre-tax, which means that they are excluded from taxable income on the federal level and in many states.

✓ Reading Check EXPLAIN Why should you consider job benefits when you are looking for work?

Performance Reviews

C How will you know if you are succeeding at work? Many companies have formal performance reviews. A **performance review** is a meeting between you and your supervisor to evaluate how well you are doing your job.

Performance reviews are important to you and to your supervisor. Promotions, pay increases, new responsibilities, and your future with the company may be based on these evaluations. If your company

---

Everyday ETHICS

What Would You Do? Answer When answering, students should consider their personal convictions, the value of loyalty and friendship, and the potential consequences of taking the drug test for their friend.

DISCUSS IT Encourage students to take the perspective of the employer or supervisor who is responsible for the safety of the employees and the workplace. For example, if a worker causes an accident while under the influence of drugs, the employer might be held liable for any damages or injuries. How might this change students' opinions?

does not provide regular evaluations, ask for one. The feedback you receive will help you improve your performance.

In some companies, new employees have a probationary period after they are first hired. In the workplace, **probation** is the initial period of employment during which your employer will monitor you closely to evaluate whether you are suited to the job. When you are hired, ask if your company has a probation policy. If it does, ask what guidelines will be used for the evaluation.

✓ **Reading Check** EXPLAIN How can employees benefit from a performance review?

Preparing for Job Loss

A company can **terminate** an employee's employment for any of several reasons. Some employees may lose their jobs for poor job performance and some may lose their jobs because of business decisions that are unrelated to an employee's performance. These kinds of business decisions may include relocation or a need to cut costs or reduce the workforce because business or the economy has slowed.

A job loss that results from a business decision is called a **layoff**. Workers who are laid off may be rehired once a company's business improves.

You should always be prepared for job loss. Be aware of changes in the economy. Keep your job-hunting network active and your skills up-to-date. Put aside money that can help you through a time of unemployment.

Career ✓ Checklist

When Preparing to Start a New Job...

✓ Research the company's corporate culture.

✓ Carefully review any material that you receive from your new employer.

✓ Be sure that you understand job expectations.

✓ Be attentive during any training.

✓ Ask questions about your responsibilities.

Section 8.2 After You Read

Review Key Concepts

1. Explain the difference between nonexempt employees and exempt employees and how this difference affects pay.
2. Name two benefits you would like to receive with your job. Give reasons for your choices.
3. Explain why performance reviews are important to employees.

Practice Academic Skills

 English Language Arts

[NCLB]

4. Which do you think offers more financial security—a salary or commission? Write a one-page response, giving reasons for your answer.
5. Contact a company you would like to work for to learn about their benefits package. Write a summary of the benefits offered, then explain which of the benefits you would like to have as an employee and why.

@ Check your answers at this book's OLC through **glencoe.com**.

Resources

● **ExamView Assessment Suite CD** allows you to print out ready-made unit and chapter tests complete with answer keys. You can also create customized tests.

CLOSE

Culminating Activity

Conduct a Survey Have students survey five local businesses and determine whether they complete annual reviews of their employees' job performance. Tell students to ask for general categories on which employees are evaluated (for example, reliability, quality of work, attitude, teamwork, etc.) Have students create a chart that compares the five businesses' review policies. (Charts should show whether the businesses mentioned conduct reviews, and how the reviews are categorized.)

✓ **Reading Check**

EXPLAIN During performance reviews, employees can receive valuable feedback about what they are doing well and how they can improve in other areas.

[NCLB] Activity correlated to English Language Arts standards.

Section 8.2 After You Read

Review Key Concepts

1. Nonexempt employees are normally paid an hourly wage and earn overtime pay when they work more than 40 hours a week. Exempt employees earn a salary, which is a fixed amount paid over a certain period of time.
2. Responses should reflect an understanding of job benefits.
3. Reviews help workers determine how well they are performing and identify where their performance can be improved.

Practice Academic Skills

4. Students who choose salary should point out that a salary gives a fixed income that offers more security. Responses in favor of commission might point out that a commission would give workers an incentive to work hard to earn commission, which in turn would make them valuable to the company.
5. Summaries should reflect an understanding of the benefits the company has to offer, and which of these the student would most like to have.

Discussion Starter

Agriculture, Food, and Natural Resources Lead a discussion about the various types of careers that can be found in this career cluster. Have students brainstorm various careers and jobs within the career cluster. (Answers will vary but students should show an understanding of the many types of careers that fall within the career cluster.)

TEACH

W Writing Support Independent Practice

Creative Writing Have students research a particular flower, tree, or other kind of plant and write a 50-word description that might make a customer want to buy it. Encourage students to be creative in their descriptions, and include details about what the plant looks like, in which season it grows, and the kind of care it needs.

C Critical Thinking

Business Plans and Agriculture Ask: What do you think is more important in starting an agricultural and natural resources business—a good idea or a solid business plan? Why? (Some students may feel that a strong product or service idea can compensate for weaknesses in a company's business plan. Other students may feel that the success of a business is more dependent on good planning than on imaginative ideas.)

CAREER SPOTLIGHT

Career Cluster: Agriculture, Food, and Natural Resources

Susan O'Connell
Flower Farmer

Q: Describe your job.

A: I grow potted plants to sell to gardeners and flowers to cut for bouquets and dried flower arrangements in the fall.

Q: Describe a typical workday.

A: As the seasons change, my work changes. In early spring, I am busy in the greenhouse starting seeds and growing my seedlings. My work moves outside to the field as the snow melts, where I plow and prepare my soil and plan out my plants. I spend almost every waking moment at the height of summer harvesting flowers and making bouquets, or selling them at farmers' markets. Late in the year, I turn to harvesting greens and making holiday wreaths.

Q: What skills are most important to you in your job?

A: Writing good descriptions of my plants turns an idle passerby into a customer. Basic math skills also are essential for me. I am constantly figuring how many plants per row, how many seedlings per tray, how many stems per bouquet, or how many bouquets can be made in an hour.

Q: What academic skills and lifelong learning skills are helpful in preparing for your career?

A: Basic science, math, and research skills are all helpful. Creating a good business plan makes a big difference, and learning when you need to ask for outside help is crucial. You can't be good at everything!

Q: What is your key to success?

A: My passion for what I do. I love my work, and I love each new season and the new chores it brings. My plants are like old friends to me. This helps me to put the extra effort into growing them well, and my enthusiasm inspires my customers.

Q: What are some disadvantages of your career?

A: I am at the mercy of the weather. I can grow perfect seedlings, but if a strong hailstorm comes along, they will be killed.

Q: What training and preparation do you recommend for students?

A: There are excellent agricultural and horticultural programs available, and you can learn a lot from those. Most important I think for any small business person is to be a creative thinker, always considering what will work better and finding ways to improve your business.

Q: What are some ways you recommend students prepare for this career?

A: Before making the decision to farm, try it first. Many farmers accept interns or hire help, especially in the summer. Each farm is different, but I think it is important to get a feel for the work before you make any serious plans.

Q: What do you like most about your work?

A: I love being able to share my passion for flowers and for growing with my customers, especially young children.

 For more about Career Clusters, go to this book's OLC through **glencoe.com**.

NCLB

NO CHILD LEFT BEHIND

Teaching Tip

To help achieve some of the goals of the NCLB Act, you might try a shared writing exercise in which you act as the scribe while students dictate their answers. Have students look over the Career Spotlight to answer your questions.

Sample Questions What are two disadvantages of this career? What kinds of technology do you need to know? What academic skills are required to complete the tasks mentioned in the table? (Record students' answers on the board. Encourage students to modify their answers as they see their words in writing.)

Education or Training An associate or bachelor's degree in business or farm management with a concentration in agriculture or horticulture is important. Those new to farming may need to spend time working with an experienced farmer to learn how to apply their skills. Some farms offer formal apprenticeships to help young people acquire practical skills.

Academic Skills Required English Language Arts, Mathematics, Science, Social Studies

Technology Needed Different kinds of farming requires specialized equipment, such as tractors, harvesters, and irrigation equipment. In addition, computers are used for record-keeping, business analysis, planning, marketing, and weather tracking.

Aptitudes, Abilities, and Skills Creativity, stamina, mechanical aptitude, ability to work with tools, research skills, customer service, organizational skills, personnel management, accounting skills

Workplace Safety Farm work can be hazardous. Tractors and other farm machinery can cause serious injury, and workers must be careful when handling chemicals to protect themselves and their environment.

Career Outlook Jobs as self-employed farmers are expected to decline over the next ten years.

Career Path Farmers, ranchers, and agricultural managers strive to improve the quality of agricultural products and the efficiency of farms. Their work can lead to jobs as agricultural engineers, agricultural and food scientists, purchasing agents, and buyers of farm products.

NCLB

Academic Skills Required to Complete Tasks

Tasks	English Language Arts	Mathematics	Science	Social Studies
Plant seedlings in greenhouse		★	★	
Plow and prepare soil		★	★	
Harvest flowers		★	★	
Create bouquets		★	★	
Sell flowers and promote business	★	★		★

Critical Thinking

What other industries depend on the weather for success?

ASSESS

Make Connections

Ask: If you wanted to pursue a career as a self-employed farmer, how would the projected decline in available jobs over the next ten years affect your individual career plan? (Those who want to pursue this career should get as much education and work experience as they can, in order to stay competitive in a crowded line of work. Self-employed farmers might also need to be willing to move to areas where there are more job opportunities.)

CLOSE

Culminating Activity

Lifelong Learning and Career Clusters Ask students to write an advertisement for Susan O'Connell's business. Encourage students to select the most important information from the text and highlight the ways that Susan can attract customers' attention with her services and experience.

NCLB This chart relates academic skills such as English Language Arts, Mathematics, Science, Social Studies, and World Languages to specific tasks that are performed for the job featured in the Career Spotlight feature.

Critical Thinking

Other industries that depend on the weather include forestry, conservation, logging, and fishing.

197

Key Terms and Academic Vocabulary Review

1. Students should write complete sentences using each term correctly. A sample answer might read: "I enjoy working *overtime*, especially since I earn time-and-a-half for the hours I work over 40."

Review Key Concepts

2. Allow time to get to work; do not worry if you forget coworkers' names, ask them their names again.

3. If there is no uniform, ask about the dress code and observe what others are wearing when you go for the interview.

4. Orientation is a program that will introduce you to the company's policies, procedures, values, and benefits. Orientation may be informal at a small company. At a large company, orientation may be with other new employees and last up to a week.

5. A wage is a fixed amount of money paid to a worker in exchange for work performed on an hourly basis. A salary is a fixed amount of pay for a certain period of time. Commission is pay based on sales.

6. Benefits may include health insurance; retirement plan, such as a pension plan; and convenience benefits, or services that make employees' lives easier, such as flexible work hours.

CHAPTER SUMMARY

Section 8.1

You can prepare for a new job by managing stress and anxiety and learning the company culture. The company culture is the behavior, attitudes, values, and habits of a company's employees and owners. You can learn the company culture by listening to and observing your coworkers. Some companies help new employees learn policies and procedures through orientation programs. Company policies explain what the company expects of new employees and what employees can expect from the company.

Section 8.2

What you can expect from your employer changes over time. Methods of payment include hourly wages, salary, and commission. Workers often also receive benefits, such as health insurance or convenience benefits. Employee performance reviews may influence raises and promotions. Some employers have probation periods for new employees. Employee termination may result from poor worker performance or slow business. You should always be prepared for possible job loss.

Key Terms and Academic Vocabulary Review

1. Use each of these key terms and academic vocabulary words in a sentence.

Key Terms
- company culture (p. 186)
- orientation (p. 187)
- mentor (p. 188)
- wage (p. 192)
- overtime (p. 192)
- nonexempt employees (p. 192)
- exempt employees (p. 192)
- salary (p. 192)
- commission (p. 192)
- profit-sharing plan (p. 192)
- performance bonuses (p. 192)
- pension plan (p. 193)
- performance review (p. 194)
- probation (p. 195)
- layoff (p. 195)

Academic Vocabulary
- strategy (p. 185)
- appropriate (p. 187)
- incentive (p. 192)
- terminate (p. 195)

Review Key Concepts

2. **Explain** how you might manage the stress, anxieties, and challenges of a first day at work. Give examples.
3. **Describe** ways you could figure out how to dress for your first day of work.
4. **Explain** the purpose of orientation, and identify the different types of orientation.
5. **List** three typical methods of payment and explain each.
6. **List** two common employee benefits and explain each.
7. **Explain** the role of employee performance reviews.

Critical Thinking

8. **Explain** How can watching other employees help a worker succeed on the job?
9. **Analyze** If you were the employer, would you devote time to orientation? Why or why not?

7. Promotions, pay increases, new responsibilities, and your future with the company are determined by your performance. Employee performance reviews let you know where you are doing well and where you need to improve.

Critical Thinking

8. By seeing how others behave, a new employee can learn the company culture.

9. Answers will vary, but students should show an understanding of the importance of orientation and realize that orientation helps new employees understand the company and their job.

Real-World Skills and Applications

Critical Thinking Skills

10. Obtaining Information Imagine that your new employer has called to offer you a job as a grocery store checker. List five questions you will ask your new employer about what you can expect your first day of work. Then list at least one possible answer to each question.

Interpersonal and Collaborative Skills

11. Developing Social Skills In teams of three to five, develop a list of suggestions that coworkers can use to get to know one another. You may use the ideas given in the chapter and then try to add a few of your own ideas. Choose one idea and develop a team presentation or poster that describes the idea or technique. Share your presentation or poster with the class.

Technology Applications

12. Selecting Technology Research the kind of technology you might need to use if you planned on becoming an organic farmer. Select a crop or the crops you will be growing and use spreadsheet software to create a one-page chart that details the types of equipment, materials, and technology you could use to manage and run your farm. Present your spreadsheet to the class.

13. **Collaborating with Others** Partner with a classmate to make a list of information you need to do a job you just started. Write a company manual that provides that information. Take turns asking each other questions about the company and the job, based on the information in the manual. Count one point for each correct answer. Provide the correct answers to any missed questions.

14. **ROLE PLAY** **Orientation Program**

Situation You are part of a four-person human resources team for a large company. You need to develop an orientation program for new employees.

Activity Design a presentation about the company to welcome new employees to their jobs. You can choose to invent a company or choose an existing one. Present the company to the class using an overhead transparency, poster, or PowerPoint presentation. Be prepared to answer questions that would typically be asked by a new employee.

Evaluation Your group will be evaluated on how well it meets the following performance indicators:
- Give an overview of the company's values and mission.
- Describe the company's policies and procedures.
- Explain the various benefits offered to employees.

 ACTIVE LEARNING

13. Company manuals should include information discussed in this chapter, including the company's dress code, mission statement, policies, procedures, values, benefits, and performance evaluations. Encourage partners to give each other feedback about any additional information that might be helpful after they share their manuals.

ROLE PLAY

14. Orientation programs should include information about the company's culture, values, and mission statement. Programs should also include policies and procedures, including job responsibilities, to whom questions should be addressed, how and when performance will be evaluated, and benefits information including when they will become active. Policies such as how employees will be paid, and information about sick days, vacation days, and holidays might also be included.

Real-World Skills and Applications

10. Questions might include: What are my hours? To whom will I report? What is my salary? Does this job offer benefits? What is the dress code? Students' questions and answers will vary; encourage students to envision a specific job for which they can generate focused questions and answers.

11. Presentations will vary but an example might be a poster that shows a mentor introducing a new employee to his or her coworkers, giving a tour of the workspace, and giving career guidance.

12. Charts will vary but should reflect research into a specific crop or crops, and the equipment, materials, and technology that would be needed to manage a farm with these crops.

Academic Skills in the Workplace

15. Questionnaires should ask questions such as these: How tall are you? How much do you weigh? How often do you exercise? What kind of exercise do you prefer? Are you a smoker?

16. The width of the boxes should be 12 inches ($1,800 = 15 \times w \times 10$; $1,800 = 150w$; $w = 12$).

17. The current running through the wires would be 2 amperes (20 volts/10 ohms = 2 amperes).

18. Students may say they would demonstrate the steps in completing each of the tasks.

Academic Skills in the Workplace

 English Language Arts

15. Write a Survey As a new benefit for employees, your employer has decided to create a company wellness program to improve employee health and fitness. Write a one-page questionnaire for workers to complete that will inform your employer about the habits that affect their health and well-being.

 Mathematics

16. Calculate Dimensions At her new job, Tina has been asked to calculate the dimensions of the boxes for the new line of kitchenware. The volume of the boxes can be no more than 1,800 cubic inches. To accommodate the products, the length must be 15 inches and the height 10 inches. What should the width of the boxes be?

CONCEPT Dimensions and Volume To calculate the volume of a three-dimensional figure use the formula: $V = l \times w \times h$.

Starting Hint Use the information that you have to create an equation for the volume of the box. Use w to represent the width: $V = 15 \times w \times 10$, solve for w.

 Science

17. Electrical Current Electrical engineers must often calculate the amount of electrical current flowing through the wires of machines they design. They can calculate this with the following equation, called Ohm's Law: $V = IR$, where V = voltage (measured in volts), I = current (measured in amperes), and R = resistance (measured in ohms). Let's say you designed a machine that had 20 volts across a wire. The resistance of the wire is 10 ohms. What would be the current in amperes running through the wire?

World Languages

18. Give Instructions You work in a company's shipping room. Your supervisor has assigned you as a mentor for a new employee whose native language is not English. The new employee's tasks include copying order forms, filling out address labels, and wrapping packages. Write a paragraph explaining how you would explain these tasks to the new employee.

STANDARDIZED TEST PRACTICE

TRUE/FALSE

Directions Carefully read each question. Pay attention to any key words. Also look for words like *always* or *never*. These mean the statement must be true all the time or none of the time.

Decide if the following statement is true or false. Circle the T or F.

Test-Taking Tip Usually, most of the statements are true on a true/false test. You have a 50 percent chance of getting the correct answer, even if you are guessing. If you leave the question blank, you have no chance of getting it right.

1. Health insurance is an example of a benefit that employers always offer to employees.
  T F

For more Standardized Test Practice, go to the OLC **glencoe.com.**

STANDARDIZED TEST PRACTICE

Answer
1. F

Test-Taking Strategies
Whether your students have a standardized test coming up in a few days or a few weeks, these last-minute test-prep tips and strategies will help students relax and do their best.

Study Tip Encourage students to use any useful class notes when studying for a test.

Study Tip Suggest to students that they join a study group if they find studying with others effective.

Writing Skills Practice

19. Write a Report When writing a report, you need to research facts and then organize and explain those facts. You can use reports to present information to others and to summarize the results of your research.

 Practice Write a one-page report on a federal, state, or other law created to ensure safe and fair treatment of employees.

Follow the steps below when researching and writing your report:

- Research information from government agencies such as the U.S. Department of Labor.
- After completing your research, organize your notes under two or three main topics.
- Write a draft of your report.
- Add any additional information.
- Edit your draft to produce a one-page report.
- Proofread your report for any mistakes.
- Produce a final report.

Net Connection

20. Research Job Salaries Online Find the salaries of at least three career choices in your career interest area with different education requirements.

Log On Go to this book's OLC through **glencoe.com** to search employment and career Web sites for current information about benefits packages and salary payment methods for these careers. Use a spreadsheet program to make a chart of this information. Use this chart to determine which career choice matches your salary preferences most closely.

Reading Connection
Go to this book's Online Learning Center through **glencoe.com** for a list of reading suggestions.

Personal Academic and Career Portfolio

Job Benefits

Job benefits differ from company to company. They may even change during the year. Being familiar with the different types of benefits that may be offered and determining the types of benefits that are important to you will help as you search for a job.

To begin to familiarize yourself with types of workplace benefits, research the benefits offered by different companies. Identify the benefits by the following categories: health benefits, retirement plans, convenience benefits, and other kinds of benefits. You can then create a chart to organize the information you find and place it in your **Personal Academic and Career Portfolio**.

The following guidelines will help you develop your chart:

- Use print, online, and in-person resources to identify three companies or organizations offering jobs in your career interest area.
- Use the companies' Web sites or contact their human resources departments to determine the benefits the companies offer.
- Use spreadsheet software or other means to create a chart to organize the information you find.
- Add a tab or file to your **Personal Academic and Career Portfolio**, label it *Benefits Information*, and place the chart in the file.

 Portfolio Help Go to the *Succeeding in the World of Work* OLC through **glencoe.com** for help developing your portfolio.

Writing Skills Practice

19. Reports should demonstrate research on federal and state laws that protect employee rights.

Net Connection

20. Spreadsheets should show three jobs with education requirements and salaries.

Resources

ExamView Assessment Suite CD allows you to print out ready-made unit and chapter tests complete with answer keys. You can also create customized tests.

WorkKeys

WorkKeys® is a job skills assessment program. For information on leveled assessment for Interpersonal Skills (Teamwork), go to the WorkKeys link on this book's OLC through **glencoe.com**.

Personal Academic and Career Portfolio

Maintaining a Portfolio

Tell students that job benefits are an important part of a job offer. Encourage students to identify three or four companies that offer jobs in their area of career interest. Then have them research the benefits offered by each company, by searching the company Web site or by calling the company's human resources department.

Chapter Resources Planning Guide with Activities and Features

Section	Features	Activities
Section 9.1 Desirable Employee Qualities	Tech Savvy (p. 206) Creative Business Practices (p. 207) Science in Action (p. 208) Hot Jobs! (p. 209)	Before You Read (p. 204) Graphic Organizer (p. 204) As You Read (p. 207) After You Read (p. 209)
Section 9.2 Ethical Behavior	Real-World Connection (p. 212) Career Checklist (p. 213) Everyday Ethics (p. 213) 21st Century Workplace (p. 214)	Before You Read (p. 210) Graphic Organizer (p. 210) As You Read (p. 213) After You Read (p. 215)

NCLB Activities, information, and skills practice will help your students attain No Child Left Behind proficiency. Students will improve their abilities in the following academic standards areas:

Academic Standards Correlations

Discipline	Standard	Feature/Activity
English Language Arts	**NCTE 1** Read texts to acquire new information.	Creative Business Practices (p. 207) Hot Jobs! (p. 209)
	NCTE 4 Use written language to communicate effectively.	Tech Savvy (p. 206) After You Read (p. 215) Writing Skills Practice (p. 221)
	NCTE 8 Use information resources to gather information and create and communicate knowledge.	Real-World Connection (p. 212) 21st Century Workplace (p. 214)
	NCTE 12 Use language to accomplish individual purposes.	Academic Skills in the Workplace (p. 220)
Mathematics	**Data Analysis and Probability:** Select and use appropriate statistical methods to analyze data	After You Read (p. 209)
	Number and Operation: Understand meanings of operations and how they relate to one another	Academic Skills in the Workplace (p. 220)
Science	**Physical Science:** Interactions of energy and matter	Science in Action (p. 208)
	Science as Inquiry: Understandings about scientific inquiry	Academic Skills in the Workplace (p. 220)

CORRELATIONS The charts show the 21st Century Skills, foundation skills, and workplace competencies that students develop as they work in this chapter.

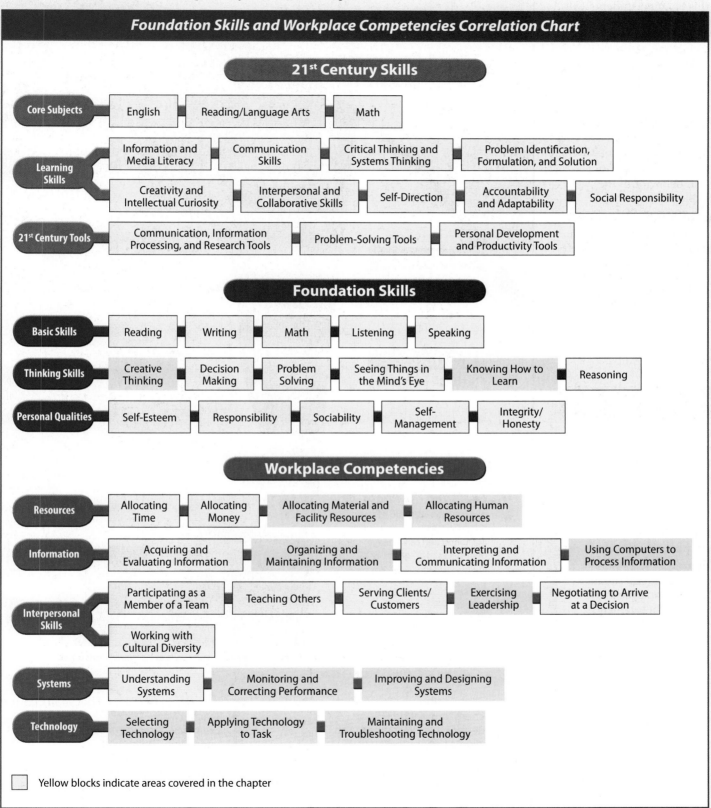

Foundation Skills and Workplace Competencies Correlation Chart

21st Century Skills

Core Subjects
- English
- Reading/Language Arts
- Math

Learning Skills
- Information and Media Literacy
- Communication Skills
- Critical Thinking and Systems Thinking
- Problem Identification, Formulation, and Solution
- Creativity and Intellectual Curiosity
- Interpersonal and Collaborative Skills
- Self-Direction
- Accountability and Adaptability
- Social Responsibility

21st Century Tools
- Communication, Information Processing, and Research Tools
- Problem-Solving Tools
- Personal Development and Productivity Tools

Foundation Skills

Basic Skills
- Reading
- Writing
- Math
- Listening
- Speaking

Thinking Skills
- Creative Thinking
- Decision Making
- Problem Solving
- Seeing Things in the Mind's Eye
- Knowing How to Learn
- Reasoning

Personal Qualities
- Self-Esteem
- Responsibility
- Sociability
- Self-Management
- Integrity/Honesty

Workplace Competencies

Resources
- Allocating Time
- Allocating Money
- Allocating Material and Facility Resources
- Allocating Human Resources

Information
- Acquiring and Evaluating Information
- Organizing and Maintaining Information
- Interpreting and Communicating Information
- Using Computers to Process Information

Interpersonal Skills
- Participating as a Member of a Team
- Teaching Others
- Serving Clients/Customers
- Exercising Leadership
- Negotiating to Arrive at a Decision
- Working with Cultural Diversity

Systems
- Understanding Systems
- Monitoring and Correcting Performance
- Improving and Designing Systems

Technology
- Selecting Technology
- Applying Technology to Task
- Maintaining and Troubleshooting Technology

Yellow blocks indicate areas covered in the chapter

CHAPTER 9

Chapter Overview
Introduce the Chapter

In this chapter, students will learn that being an effective employee involves more than knowing how to do a certain job. Students will learn about personal skills that also contribute to career success.

Section 9.1 presents the skills and qualities employers look for in employees and helps students develop them.

Section 9.2 focuses on ethical behavior in the workplace.

Build Background

Have students talk about the role of ethics between a business and its customers as well as between a business and its competition. Then have them discuss the role of ethics between coworkers in a business. How does its importance compare to the former relationships?

▶ Exploring the Photo

Caption Answer Reasons for honesty in the workplace include ensuring fairness toward employers, fostering a supportive working environment for employees, and ensuring that customers have the best possible experience.

Discussion Ask students to discuss ethical situations that the employee in the photo might experience. (Answers will vary, but may include handling customers' personal information in a confidential manner and opportunities to do favors for friends.)

CHAPTER 9
Workplace Ethics

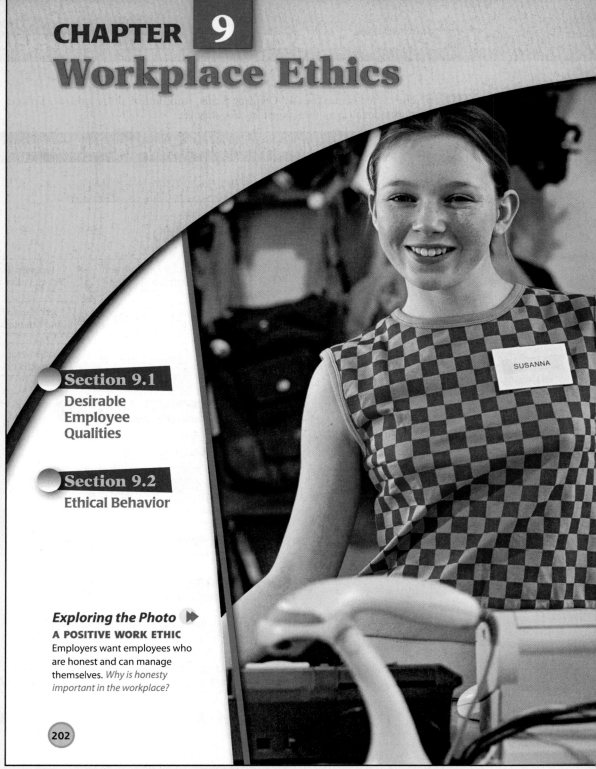

● **Section 9.1**
Desirable Employee Qualities

● **Section 9.2**
Ethical Behavior

Exploring the Photo ▶▶
A POSITIVE WORK ETHIC
Employers want employees who are honest and can manage themselves. *Why is honesty important in the workplace?*

202

Classroom Resources

- Student Edition
- Teacher Wraparound Edition
- Student Activity Workbook with Academic Integration
- Student Activity Workbook with Academic Integration TAE
- *Fast File,* Unit 4 Resources

- Inclusion in the Career Education Classroom
- TeacherWorks™ Plus
- *ExamView Assessment Suite*
- Interactive Chalkboard
- Interactive Student Edition
- Online Student Edition
- Online Learning Center (OLC) with Podcasts

Chapter Objectives

After completing this chapter, you will be able to:

- **Identify** the skills and personal qualities employers look for in employees.
- **Describe** ways to demonstrate desirable personal qualities on the job.
- **Explain** the importance of ethics in the workplace.
- **Identify** ethical principles and ways to apply them in a work setting.
- **Describe** strategies for handling unethical practices.

Writing Activity Personal Career Notebook

What basic ethics should guide the behavior of a well-known business leader? In what ways—if any—should that leader's ethics differ from those of a part-time worker in the leader's company? How do the leader and the part-time worker affect each other's work ethics? Write a one-page notebook entry discussing your ideas.

Get Motivated! Pick a negative or unethical trait that you sometimes see in yourself. For one week, concentrate on acting in the opposite manner. At the end of the week, write a half-page report describing the negative trait and how successful you were in changing it.

Chapter 9 Workplace Ethics **203**

Review the Objectives
Introduce the chapter by reviewing the chapter objectives:

Section 9.1 Objectives
Identify the skills and personal qualities employers look for in employees. (Skills and qualities include cooperativeness, willingness to follow directions, willingness to learn, initiative, and willingness to take responsibility.)

Describe ways to demonstrate desirable personal qualities on the job. (An employee can demonstrate desirable qualities through self-management and loyalty.)

Section 9.2 Objectives
Explain the importance of ethics in the workplace. (Ethics help workers do what is right and help a business act responsibly toward customers, the community, and the environment.)

Identify ethical principles and ways to apply them in a work setting. (Ways to apply ethical principles in the workplace include practicing honesty, showing respect toward others, maintaining confidentiality, and treating people with fairness.)

Describe strategies for handling unethical practices. (Strategies include keeping a written record, checking your observations with others, getting advice, checking your motives, collecting evidence, deciding whether to remain anonymous or speak openly, and reporting only the facts.)

Writing Activity Personal Career Notebook Answer Guide

Students might point out that, although a business leader and part-time employee should exercise the same level of ethical behavior, the business leader has the additional responsibility of setting a high standard that employees will follow. The leader's influence can affect the part-time worker's ethics, but the part-time worker's ethics can also have a great impact on the success or failure of the business leader's company.

Get Motivated! Reports should show the student's awareness of a negative or unethical trait and a specific approach to correcting the trait. Students should then assess how successful they were in changing the behavior.

Section 9.1

Bell Ringer Activity

Desirable Employee Qualities

Ask students to list at least five positive traits or characteristics of employees with which they would want to work. As a class, discuss students' lists and decide whether these traits and characteristics are equally valued in various workplace environments.

Resources

Interactive Chalkboard
The Interactive Chalkboard CD provides visual teaching aids for this section.

@ Online Learning Center
The Online Learning Center (OLC) through **glencoe.com** features chapter vocabulary, chapter summaries, and other study materials.

Preteaching

Read the definitions of the key terms aloud. As you read each definition, ask students to rephrase it in their own words.

Graphic Organizer

Tell students to go to the OLC through **glencoe.com** for a printable graphic organizer. (Graphic organizers should properly identify desirable employee qualities and those the student plans to develop.)

NCLB connects academic correlations to book content.

Desirable Employee Qualities

Reading Guide

Before You Read

Preview Look at the photos in this section and read their captions. Write one or two sentences predicting what the section will be about.

Read to Learn
- The skills and personal qualities employers look for in employees
- Ways to demonstrate desirable personal qualities on the job

D Main Idea
The ability to demonstrate the skills and personal qualities employers want will help you to succeed in the workplace.

Key Concepts
- What Do Employers Want?
- Self-Management
- Loyalty

Key Terms
- cooperativeness
- initiative
- responsibility
- self-management

Academic Vocabulary
You will find this word in your reading and on your tests. Use the academic vocabulary glossary to look up its definitions if necessary.
- structure

Graphic Organizer
As you read the desirable qualities employers want in employees, think about which of these qualities you have and what qualities you need to develop. Use the graphic organizer like the one below to help you organize your thoughts.

@ Log On Go to this book's Online Learning Center through **glencoe.com** for an online version of this graphic organizer.

Academic Standards •

N C L B

English Language Arts
- Read texts to acquire new information. (NCTE 1)
- Use written language to communicate effectively. (NCTE 4)

Mathematics
- Select and use appropriate statistical methods to analyze data

Science
- Physical Science: Interactions of energy and matter

Reading Guide

Before You Read
Point out to students that although every job requires different skills and aptitudes, the personal qualities employers look for are the same in every profession.

D Develop Concepts
Main Idea Discuss the main idea with students. Ask: What does "success in the workplace" mean to you? (Answers will vary, but may include financial security and personal satisfaction.)

What Do Employers Want?

Raymond Brixley, director of human resources for the Quaker Oats Company, explains what employers want in new employees. "We look for someone capable of doing lots of things well," he says, "and more importantly, someone who fits into the organization's **structure**."

To prepare for doing lots of things well and fitting in, you should master a wide range of personal and academic skills. Solid thinking skills, math skills, communication skills, and strong personal qualities will help you adapt to and succeed in today's workplace.

Cooperativeness

One of an employee's most valued qualities is cooperativeness. **Cooperativeness** is a willingness to work well with others to reach a common goal. Cooperativeness is closely linked to other important personal qualities and skills, including listening skills, responsibility, and self-management.

How can you be cooperative?

- Do tasks you do not like without complaining or trying to avoid them.
- Do your fair share of a job when working with others.
- Volunteer to help coworkers meet deadlines or reach goals.

Vocabulary

You can find definitions in the **Key Terms** glossary and **Academic Vocabulary** glossary at the back of this book.

 DO YOUR SHARE Doing tasks with a positive attitude shows that you are willing to cooperate to get a job done. *Why do you think employers promote cooperative workers?*

TEACH

Discussion Starter

What Do Employers Want? Ask students what personal qualities they think an employer looks for in an employee. (Answers may include fairness, honesty, trust, and loyalty—traits that are similar to what an employee might want from an employer.)

R Reading Strategy

Create a List Have students make a list of personal and academic skills that can help them in the workplace as they read the chapter. After they have finished the chapter, ask them to write examples of how they see each skill in businesses that they frequent. (Lists may include thinking skills, math skills, communication skills, and strong personal qualities such as cooperativeness, willingness to follow directions, willingness to learn, initiative, and willingness to take responsibility.)

Resources

TeacherWorks™ Plus The TeacherWorks software includes customizable built-in lesson plans and links to printable program resources.

Extend the Photo

Caption Answer Answers may include that cooperative workers with a positive attitude are better able to accomplish work and are better able to handle management tasks.

Discussion Have students list at least three other ways workers can show cooperation. Examples may include listening carefully to work assignments, volunteering to help others, and learning about the company so as to be more productive workers.

S **Skill Practice**
Guided Practice

List Ask students to compile a list of learning experiences. Examples can range from physical items such as riding a bicycle to intellectual challenges such as learning a new language. (Lists may include swimming, mastering a video game, or using new technology.) **L1**

Explain Have students write a 250-word paragraph describing a learning experience and how their attitude affected their learning process. Encourage them to compare and contrast how their mental approach affects different types of activities. (Paragraphs will vary, but students should agree that willingness to learn is beneficial in every scenario.) **L2**

Classify Ask students to write a 300-word paragraph that explains steps to learning how to learn. Suggest that willingness is the first step, and ask how else a person can approach learning more effectively. (Paragraphs will vary, but students may suggest that getting enough rest, eating well, and considering ergonomics and environment can help one who is learning.) **L3**

N C L B
Activity correlated to English Language Arts standards.

Willingness to Follow Directions

On the job, you will be asked to complete many tasks. To complete a task, you must follow directions.

Following directions requires many skills. Listening is one of the most important. These suggestions may help you:

- Stop whatever you are doing, and listen to the directions being given.
- Listen carefully, even if you think you already know the procedure. Some details might surprise you.
- Take notes, if possible.
- Identify the goal, or purpose, of the task. Then try to visualize the steps leading to the goal.
- If you do not understand the directions, ask questions rather than guessing.

Willingness to Learn

Imagine your life in a few years' time. You have graduated and started your first full-time job. You may think you are done with learning. You are not. You still have a lot to learn, even if your job is one for which you have been trained. You will have to learn the company's system.

Because you are a new employee, your employer will not expect you to know everything. Do not pretend to know something. Ask questions. Be willing to learn any task or procedure, no matter how small, or even if it is not part of your job. For example, when the copier gets jammed, watch how to fix it. Next time, you can take care of it yourself. Look for opportunities to get more training. Many companies will pay for their employees to attend workshops or training programs. Take advantage of every opportunity to learn.

S

Initiative

You may get by just through doing what you are told. Many employers expect more from you, however. They want employees to show initiative. Taking **initiative** means doing what needs to be done without being told.

Disney World deliberately seeks out employees who have initiative. Robert Sias, a trainer for Disney, gives an example of what the company wants. A family had just bought a box of popcorn and given it to a young boy. The child stumbled and dropped the popcorn, spilling it everywhere. The boy burst into tears. Just at that moment, a costumed employee on his way

C

TechSavvy

Text Messaging Language

Text messaging consists of sending brief messages to a handheld device such as a cell phone or PDA. Acronyms like "BRB" stand for "Be Right Back."

In addition to text messaging for personal use, you may need to use text messaging on the job. More and more businesses are using text messaging as a form of communication. Text messaging takes less time than phone calls, and managers can send text messages to several employees at once.

@ Visit this book's Online Learning Center through **glencoe.com** and find the link to learn more text messaging. List types of acronyms that might be appropriate for the workplace.

N C L B

TechSavvy

Text Messaging Language

Answer Appropriate acronyms may include *ASAP* (As Soon as Possible) and *TBA* (To Be Announced). Inappropriate ones may include *LOL* (Laugh Out Loud) and *IMHO* (In My Humble Opinion). Explain to students that acronyms are not suggested for memos or e-mail correspondence.

to another part of the park walked by. Without a pause, he scooped up the empty popcorn box, asked the popcorn vendor for another box of popcorn, and handed the full box to the little boy.

The Disney employee showed initiative. He saw a problem and fixed it. This is what employers want.

Willingness to Take Responsibility

Employers want employees who are willing to take responsibility. **Responsibility** is the willingness to accept an obligation and to be accountable for an action or situation.

Marriott Hotels encourages its employees to act responsibly. One of its employees is Tony Prsyszlak. If he worked for another hotel, he might be called a doorman. At Marriott, he is called a "guest service associate." The title is not the only difference, and Prsyszlak's responsibilities include more than just greeting guests at the hotel entrance. He can also take the initiative and check in a guest, take a guest's luggage to the room, reserve a table at a restaurant for the guest, or provide other services for the guest.

As You Read

Connect Why does Marriott Hotels use the job title "guest service associate" rather than "doorman?"

Creative Business Practices

BEN & JERRY'S

Environmental Commitment

The Burlington, Vermont-based ice cream, frozen yogurt, and sorbet company Ben & Jerry's Homemade, Inc. is as well known for its commitment to making the world a better place as it is for its innovative product flavor names, such as Chunky Monkey and Cherry Garcia.

One Ben & Jerry's initiative has to do with the containers the company uses for packaging. Bleached paper is one of the biggest causes of toxic water pollution in the United States. Toxic water poisons water and plant life and can harm humans as well. To help protect the waterways, the company manufactures and uses containers made of unbleached paper.

Environmental commitment is reflected in every aspect of the company, from production to handling waste. Everything from printer ink to notepads to production-size fiber drums are made from recyclable products, and the company sends their whey and other byproducts to be composted. Ben & Jerry's commitment to the environment makes life a little sweeter for everyone.

CRITICAL THINKING Why should companies be concerned with the impact on the environment? If you owned a successful company, what would you do to make the world a better place?

@ Connect to the Real World For more information about Ben & Jerry's community and environmental programs, visit the company's Web site via the link on this book's Online Learning Center through **glencoe.com**.

TEACH *(cont.)*

C Critical Thinking
Making Connections Ask students why some workers might be unwilling to show initiative. (Answers may include the reluctance to create more work, to overstep boundaries, or to do unfamiliar work. Help students realize that showing initiative requires thought and moderation.)

As You Read
Students should point out that a Marriott guest service associate's duties extend beyond the entry area of a hotel.

ASSESS

Review Key Terms
Have students write sentences using each key term.

Online Study Tools
Have students go to the OLC through **glencoe.com** to:
- Download **Podcast** study tools.
- Download free **Study-to-Go** content to their PDAs or cell phones.

Resources
ExamView Assessment Suite CD allows you to print out ready-made unit and chapter tests complete with answer keys. You can also create customized tests.

Creative Business Practices

CRITICAL THINKING ANSWER Student responses should recognize that a responsible business should give back to the communities in which it thrives. It should not harm the environment that allows it to profit as an act of goodwill as well as a survival technique. Ways to do this might include conserving energy in the workplace, encouraging workers to carpool or use public transportation, and donating money to charities that concern the environment, as well as sponsoring neighborhood tree planting, trash pickups, and recycling programs.

RETEACH

S Skill Practice
Independent Practice

Assess Self-Management Skills Have students rate themselves on a scale from one to ten on their self-management skills. Then have students write a paragraph identifying ways they could improve these skills. *(Paragraphs should reflect students' understanding of their own self-management skills and how they can improve these skills.)*

✓ Reading Check

SUMMARIZE Learning can extend beyond high school through taking initiative and accepting more responsibility.

✓ Reading Check

ANALYZE Employers look for workers who exercise self-management because these workers are efficient, work independently, and do not need extra supervision.

Resources

📂 **Student Activity Workbook** Assign the Chapter 9 activities in the Student Activity Workbook.

Activity correlated to Science standards.

Science In Action

The average speed is 15 m/s (12 + 15 + 16 + 17 = 60; 60 m/s ÷ 4 = 15 m/s)

N C L B

Science In Action

Average Speed
The higher the average speed of particles in a substance, such as air, the higher the temperature. Calculate the average speed for the following particles:
a: 12 m/s, **b:** 15 m/s, **c:** 16 m/s, **d:** 17 m/s.

Starting Hint: You can measure the average speed of particles by adding up the speeds of all the particles and dividing by the number of particles.

@ For more science practice, go to this book's OLC through **glencoe.com**.

What do you get out of taking on more responsibility? Your job becomes more interesting. You gain experience and a chance for promotion. You increase your value to the company and earn job security.

Prove to your employer that you can accept greater responsibility. Show that you are not afraid of change. Volunteer for new jobs. Think about where the added responsibility will get you in a year's time.

✓ Reading Check **SUMMARIZE** Explain how learning can continue beyond high school.

Self-Management

Who do you think is going to get you a job, a promotion, a raise? Only you. You have to take responsibility for the work you do and the results you want. **Self-management** means being able to manage your own behavior to get the career you want. Some self-management tips include:

- Set career goals, and develop a plan for reaching them. As you achieve goals, or as your situation changes, set new goals.
- Monitor your work habits and performance. For example, you might keep a diary to track how you spend your time. Then you can identify ways to be more time-efficient.
- Ask your supervisors for feedback. Act on what you learn to improve your work habits and skills.

S

✓ Reading Check **ANALYZE** Explain why an employer would find self-management a desirable quality in an employee.

▶▶ **MANAGE YOURSELF**
Self-management is a valued employee quality. *How can you become a self-manager?*

Jolanda Cats & Hans/Corbis

glencoe.com

▶ **Extend the Photo**

Caption Answer You can become a self-manager by setting goals, monitoring your work habits, and asking your supervisor for feedback.

Discussion Ask students to discuss how they can practice self-management in school. What are the benefits as a student and as a future worker?

Loyalty

You may know what it means to be loyal to your country and your school. It is also important to be loyal to your company. After all, you, your coworkers, your supervisors, and the owners are a team working toward a common goal.

How do you show loyalty at work? Be positive. Look for solutions. If you have critical comments, express them only to your direct manager in private.

When a situation comes up at work that takes extra effort, pitch in and help your company and your coworkers through the difficult period. This may involve some sacrifices, such as doing overtime, learning and doing new or different tasks, or staying late without pay if you are a salaried employee.

Remember that responding to and overcoming challenges can help you build new transferable skills and can help you build a positive reputation at work. Loyalty to your company and your coworkers is a trait that most employers appreciate.

HOT JOBS!

Digital Services Librarian

A digital services librarian works to design, develop, and maintain a library's digital catalog. He or she works in conjunction with administrators and other librarians to develop a functioning system. Such jobs require a balance of library science and computer skills, and can be found in public library settings as well as private libraries, such as those of law firms.

Section 9.1

ASSESS

After You Read
Have students complete the Section 9.1 After You Read section review.

Online Study Tools
Have students go to the OLC through **glencoe.com** to:
- Take the Section 9.1 **Practice Test**.
- Download **Podcast** study tools.
- Download free **Study-to-Go** content to their PDAs or cell phones.

CLOSE

Culminating Activity
Building Traits Have students debate whether traits are developed or people are born with them. Have them list examples of people they know, how they act, and whether traits are developed. Then ask students to write a 200-word essay explaining their opinion on the subject. (Answers will vary but most students should agree that traits are developed by individuals and influenced by the people around them.)

Activity correlated to Mathematics standards.

Section 9.1 After You Read

Review Key Concepts

1. Name three personal qualities employers look for in employees. Explain why each quality is important to employers.
2. Give an example of how you might demonstrate initiative in a work setting.
3. Explain why the skill of self-management is valuable to both an employee and his or her employer.

Practice Academic Skills

 Mathematics

4. Your boss is submitting a report to an organization that ensures employees in your industry are paid fairly. He has asked you to calculate some summary statistics of salaries including the range and the mean. The salaries are as follows: $48,000, $41,000, $29,000, $48,000, $32,000. Provide the statistics for your boss.

CONCEPT **Summary Statistics** Summary statistics provide important information about a data set without listing the entire data set. The range is simply the highest number in a data set minus the lowest number. The mean is the average of all of the numbers in a data set.
Step 1: Calculate the range by subtracting the lowest number ($29,000) from the highest number ($48,000).
Step 2: To calculate the mean, add all of the salaries together and divide by the total number of salaries (5).

 For math help, go to the Math Appendix located at the back of this book.

Section 9.1 After You Read

Review Key Concepts

1. Answers may include cooperativeness, willingness to follow directions, willingness to learn, initiative, and willingness to take responsibility. Examples will vary, but should be specific and pertinent to the workplace.
2. Examples of how to demonstrate initiative in a work setting will vary, but should be specific and pertinent to the workplace.
3. Answers will vary, but may include quality of work and ability to be promoted.

Practice Academic Skills

4. The range of salaries is $19,000 ($48,000 − $29,000 = $19,000) The mean is $39,600. ($48,000 + $41,000 + $29,000 + $48,000 + $32,000 = $198,000; $198,000 / 5 = $39,600).

Section 9.2

FOCUS

Bell Ringer Activity

Ethical Behavior

Have students imagine they are entrepreneurs starting their own business. Ask what personal traits they would look for when they begin hiring employees. (Answers will vary, but may include ethical behavior such as honesty, integrity, and fairness.)

Resources

 Interactive Chalkboard

The Interactive Chalkboard CD provides visual teaching aids for this section.

@ Online Learning Center

The Online Learning Center (OLC) through **glencoe.com** features chapter vocabulary, chapter summaries, and other study materials.

Preteaching

Read the definitions of the key terms aloud. As you read each definition, ask students to rephrase it in their own words.

Graphic Organizer

Tell students to go to the OLC through **glencoe.com** for a printable graphic organizer. (Graphic organizers will vary but should list ways to act ethically on the job.)

 NCLB connects academic correlations to book content.

Reading Guide

Before You Read

Preview Choose a Key Term that is new to you. Write it on a piece of paper. When you find it in the text, write down the definition.

Read to Learn

- The importance of ethics in the workplace
- How to apply ethical principles in the workplace
- Strategies for handling unethical practices

D Main Idea

Behaving ethically in the workplace will earn you the trust and respect of both your employers and your coworkers.

Key Concepts

- What Are Ethics?
- Honesty
- Interacting with Others
- Handling Unethical Practices

Key Terms

◈ ethics
◈ confidentiality
◈ prejudice

Academic Vocabulary

You will find these words in your reading and on your tests. Use the academic vocabulary glossary to look up their definitions if necessary.

- conduct
- cultures
- community

Graphic Organizer

As you read, list ways you can act ethically. Continue adding to your list after you have finished reading. Use a two-column chart like the one shown. In the left column the five important areas of acting ethically are listed. In the right column, you should list ways you do, or can, act ethically in each area.

Ethics on the Job	Ways I Can Act Ethically
With customers	
With coworkers	
With company property	
With the community	
With the environment	

 Log On Go to this book's Online Learning Center through **glencoe.com** for an online version of this graphic organizer.

N C L B

Academic Standards •

English Language Arts
- Read texts to acquire new information. (NCTE 1)
- Use information resources to gather information and create and communicate knowledge. (NCTE 8)

Reading Guide

Before You Read

Have students explain what they think this statement means: "The best job security is your good reputation."

D Develop Concepts

Main Idea Discuss the main idea with students. Ask: What does "ethics in the workplace" mean to you? (Answers will vary, but may include treating the employer, fellow employees, and customers with respect.)

What Are Ethics?

Ethics are the principles of **conduct** that govern a group or society. How crucial are ethics in the workplace? Is it important for employees to behave ethically toward one another? Toward their company?

Many business people think ethical behavior is critically important to success, and have created programs to promote ethics. Do you think this is a good idea? Write down your answer to this question and list reasons for your opinion. As you read this section, add other reasons you discover to your list.

R Having a code of ethics and a personal sense of what is right and wrong will help you choose the right course of action at work. You can serve as a role model for others by acting ethically with customers, coworkers, the company, company property, your **community**, and the environment.

✓ **Reading Check** **EXTEND** How can you serve as an ethical role model for others in the workplace?

Honesty

Employers expect their employees to be honest. Dishonesty is at the root of most ethics problems in the workplace. **Figure 9.1** shows that lying is one of the most commonly observed types of unethical behavior.

What is the penalty for dishonesty? On a personal level, it can be devastating. One lie can destroy your reputation. How much does your reputation matter? If you were an employer, would you hire someone with a reputation for dishonesty? Be honest with your employer and your company. As an honest worker you will have a much better chance of being successful in a career.

▶ Vocabulary
You can find definitions in the **Key Terms** glossary and **Academic Vocabulary** glossary at the back of this book.

Figure 9.1	COMMONLY OBSERVED UNETHICAL BEHAVIOR

Types of Unethical Workplace Behavior

❖ Lying	❖ Misreporting actual time or hours worked
❖ Withholding needed information	❖ Discrimination
❖ Abusive or intimidating behavior toward employees	❖ Misuse of Internet and e-mail privileges

Source: Ethics Resource Center (ERC)

BEHAVIOR AT WORK	This chart shows common types of unethical workplace behavior. *Does the information in the chart surprise you? Why or why not?*

Chapter 9 Workplace Ethics **211**

Section 9.2

TEACH

Discussion Starter
What Are Ethics? Ask students to share their list of traits from the Bell Ringer activity. Write the traits on the board. Students will likely mention resourcefulness, cooperation, willingness to share, and honesty as key traits. Tell students that in a work situation, employees who work together cooperatively and honestly have a better chance of succeeding than those who go their own way or treat others poorly.

R **Reading Strategy**
Understanding Words in Context Have students look up the word *community* in the dictionary and discuss its different definitions. Ask them to consider in what communities a business might belong. (Examples may include being part of a neighborhood, part of a trade, or part of a chamber of commerce.)

Resources

⚙ **TeacherWorks™ Plus**
The TeacherWorks software includes customizable built-in lesson plans and links to printable program resources.

EXTEND THE FIGURE	Figure 9.1

Caption Answer Answers will vary, but students should agree that there are many opportunities to act unethically in the workplace.

Discussion Ask students whether they think it is acceptable for employees to perpetrate "minor" unethical infractions, such as checking personal e-mail or instant messaging with friends. (Answers will vary, but students may agree that any unethical behavior can lead to other infractions.)

TEACH *(cont.)*

C **Critical Thinking**

Making Connections In any organization, peer pressure can encourage people to be dishonest with matters such as money. Have students discuss how peer pressure in school affects their behavior. Then ask: How might the attitude of a worker like Jane Benes encourage someone to behave dishonestly? How could students avoid such situations when they are employed? (Answers may include having a positive self-image and following their own beliefs when making choices.)

U **Universal Access**

Visual Learning With the students, compile a list of property that an employee might access in the workplace. Categorize them in lists such as physical property (pens, paper clips), technology (software, Internet access), and intellectual property (business ideas or lists of clients or contacts). As a class, discuss the value of each.

✓ **Reading Check**

SUMMARIZE Answers may include dishonesty about work hours, dishonesty about money, and disrespect for an employer's property (including technology and time).

Stretching the Truth

You have worked at a restaurant for four years. A month ago you were promoted from head waiter to assistant manager. The restaurant is now going out of business. You apply for a job as the manager of a café, and the owner wants someone with experience in management. You had only one month of management experience before the restaurant closed. You are tempted to stretch the truth on your application.

Critical Thinking How would the owner benefit from hiring a manager with more experience? How would he benefit from hiring one with less experience?

Do Your Own Research Interview a small-business owner who employs a small staff. Ask what qualifications he or she looks for when hiring. Do some positions require more experience than others? Is the owner willing to train new employees, or does he or she expect new employees to bring the necessary experience with them? Write a one-page journal entry that summarizes your findings.

Honesty About Work Hours

One of the most common ways in which employees can demonstrate honesty concerns their work hours. This is especially true for employees whose work takes them away from the company, who work at home, or who work on flextime, or flexible schedules. In each case, employees are trusted to work the hours they say they will. What might be the consequence if employees are dishonest about the time they work?

Honesty About Money

Taking money out of the cash drawer is clearly dishonest. In many instances, however, determining what is honest and what is dishonest can be more difficult. Consider the following case.

Jane Benes is a salesperson. On a business trip, she spent more for meals than her expense account allowed. She thought she would have to pay the difference out of her own pocket. On the other hand, she thought she could make up the difference by adding the amount to two blank taxi receipts, since she had chosen to walk to some locations during her trip. Would this be dishonest?

Benes at first reasoned that it was only a technicality. Other employees probably did the same thing. Then she thought about telling her children what she had done. She realized that in their eyes, her behavior would be dishonest.

Often you may think there is a thin line between honesty and dishonesty. As you reason through such cases in your career, think how your action might appear to others. Also remember that, like everything else, dishonesty becomes easier with practice. Once you lie about one small matter, it will be that much easier to lie in future situations.

Respecting Employers' Property

Another way to risk your reputation and job is to be careless with or misuse company property. Do not illegally copy company software for your personal use. Do not take office supplies home for your own use. Do not use company property, such as telephones, for personal use without permission. These items may seem small, but the costs for small items can add up. Using work materials inappropriately can result in being disciplined or fired.

✓ **Reading Check** **SUMMARIZE** What are common types of unethical behavior at work?

Real-World *Connection*

Critical Thinking Answer Reasons for having a more experienced manager might include know-how, awareness of the field, and connections in the trade. Reasons for a less experienced manager might include fresh views and lower salary.

Do Your Own Research Encourage students to share the results of their interviews about the qualifications employers look for.

Interacting with Others

Whatever business you enter, you will be talking and working with others. Occasionally, your interactions may involve ethical issues.

Confidentiality

As an employee, you may have information that would harm the company if you told others. This information might have to do with products, expansion plans, promotions, and so on. Your company will expect you to observe confidentiality. In the world of work, **confidentiality** means not talking about company business with other people.

Confidentiality is behavior your friends, family, and coworkers also expect from you. They do not want their secrets told either. For example, most medical records are confidential. This is so your personal health information cannot be shown to others without your consent.

On the surface, confidentiality seems easy. Sometimes, though, there are conflicting interests. Take the situation involving Sheila Williams. Williams ran into a former coworker and friend at a seminar. They had dinner together. While talking, Williams learned about a new product her friend's company was developing. It was a product similar to one Williams's own company was working on. Not only that, but her friend's company had solved a problem that Williams's company was stuck on. Her friend did not know Williams's company was a rival. Should Williams use the information to help her company compete with the rival? If you were Williams, would you use the information to help your company compete? Why or why not?

Career Checklist

When Faced With Ethical Workplace Decisions:

✓ Do not do things that make you uncomfortable.
✓ Maintain your integrity.
✓ Respect the values of your coworkers and others on the job.
✓ Avoid gossip and rumors.
✓ Remember that you are accountable for your own actions.

As You Read

Explain Why is confidentiality important in the workplace?

Everyday ETHICS

SHARING SECRETS

Is it ever okay to share confidential information?

CONFIDENTIALITY You recently started working at a new software company. Your new supervisor wants you to tell her everything you know about a secret program that you were working on at your old company. You never signed a confidentiality agreement, but you know that the program will be a great accomplishment for your former company once it is released. Your supervisor tells you that you will receive a large bonus and a promotion if you tell her about the program.

What Would You Do? Would you tell your supervisor about the program? Why or why not?

> **DISCUSS IT** Even after you move on to a new job, you may not want to "burn bridges" with your previous employer. How would your previous employer react if he or she found out you revealed confidential information at your new job? Brainstorm with a partner to discuss possible actions you could take.

TEACH (cont.)

S Skill Practice
Independent Practice
Reasoning Shoplifting and other forms of theft cost businesses (such as the Frame Shop) millions of dollars every year. Have students write 100-word paragraphs tracing the effect of these costs on consumers, employers, local government, and business owners. (Consumers pay higher prices, employees earn lower wages or have fewer jobs, local government gets less money from income taxes, and business owners make less money.)

As You Read
In the workplace, confidentiality means not talking about company business with other people.

ASSESS

Review Key Terms
Have students write sentences using each key term.

Online Study Tools
Have students go to the OLC through **glencoe.com** to:

- Download **Podcast** study tools.
- Download free **Study-to-Go** content to their PDAs or cell phones.

Everyday ETHICS

What Would You Do? Answer Students should take into account that an employee's obligations to an employer do not necessarily end when he or she leaves a job. Suggest that employers may identify those who divulge other company's classified information to be security risks.

> **DISCUSS IT** Encourage students to role play their scenarios to see what solution works best for them.

RETEACH

W Writing Support
Independent Practice

Write a Policy Have students imagine they work for a company of their choice, and they have been assigned to write a 250-word company policy manual that discusses how to deal with unethical behavior, including honesty, confidentiality, and prejudice issues. (Students should name the type of company they work for and use clear and concise language to recommend ways of handling unethical behavior.)

✓ Reading Check

EXPLAIN Consequences for making prejudicial comments may include an employee being fired and an employer or company being sued.

Resources

📂 **Student Activity Workbook** Assign the Chapter 9 activities in the Student Activity Workbook.

ASSESS

After You Read

Have students complete the Section 9.2 After You Read section review.

Online Study Tools

Have students go to the OLC through **glencoe.com** to:

- Take the Section 9.2 **Practice Test**.
- Download **Podcast** study tools.
- Download free **Study-to-Go** content to their PDAs or cell phones.

STUDY TO GO

The 21st Century Workplace

Temp Work

Hiring temporary workers instead of full-time employees allows employers to save money by adjusting their staff according to the amount of workload; they don't need to keep paying a full crew of workers when there's a lull in work. It also frees businesses from providing benefits such as health insurance.

Unfortunately for employees, project work can mean less pay and less job security than full employment. Project workers can be relieved of their jobs for any reason. If they find temporary jobs through an agency, it might also mean having to give up some of their pay in fees.

However, there can be benefits for project workers. Project work allows individuals to survey different fields of work, and choose a career more wisely. It also offers variety and lessens the chance of burnout. For a person new to the workplace or unwilling to commit to an industry, temporary employment can be a smart way to go.

CRITICAL THINKING _____

Why might a person accept a temporary or project-based job rather than full-time employment?

In Your Community

Look in a phone book or on the Internet to find temp agency listings. Compare your findings and create a list of qualities to look for in such an agency. Consider issues such as benefits, pay, and whether the agency serves a particular industry.

> @ **Extend Your Learning** What are the tax requirements of temporary employment? For links related to temporary employment, go to this book's OLC through **glencoe.com**.

Treating People with Fairness

Virtually every business includes men and women of different backgrounds and **cultures**. You will interact with people as customers, owners, and coworkers. Treat everyone fairly, openly, and honestly.

Prejudice, which is a negative attitude toward a person or group, is an ethical issue. Prejudice comes in many forms, including racist or sexist comments, stereotyping, name-calling, and generalizations. Prejudice in any form is hurtful, offensive, and unacceptable; it cannot be tolerated in today's workplace. Not only can employees be disciplined or fired for making prejudicial comments, but they and their companies or organizations can face legal action.

✓ Reading Check EXPLAIN What are possible consequences for employees and employers who display prejudice?

Handling Unethical Practices

What should you do if you are the victim of unethical practices? What if you experience prejudice in the workplace? What if you observe unethical business practices?

Consider the incident. Was it one time or is it an ongoing practice? **W** Can the matter be cleared by a calm, open discussion?

If the offense is deliberate, do not ignore it. But, do not act rashly, either. First, consider your options. If you are dealing with a customer, you might simply walk away. You do not have to sell a product to an abusive or dishonest customer. Report the incident to your supervisor.

The 21st Century Workplace

CRITICAL THINKING ANSWER Answers will vary, but reasons for choosing temporary or project-based work include a flexible schedule, ability to choose projects, and reluctance to commit to a long-term job or career.

In Your Community Qualities to look for might include an abundance of jobs, fair and quick payment, health care, and a field in which one is interested.

If you are dealing with a coworker, you might tell him or her you will not tolerate his or her behavior. If that does not work, talk to your supervisor. Look for solutions.

What if your employer is unethical? You can choose to live with the situation. You can keep quiet and find another job. You can report it to the appropriate authority. The choice may not be easy. Remember that in the end other people's opinions of you will largely reflect how ethically you act. If you decide to take action, these pointers may help:

- Keep a written record. Describe each incident. Record the date and time.
- Check your observations with trusted others. They may be able to explain or help.
- Get advice from people you trust.
- Check your motives. Are you acting for the right reasons?
- Collect any evidence you can, such as receipts, invoices, or contracts.
- Decide whether you want to remain anonymous or to speak up openly.
- Report only facts or observations. Do not exaggerate or speculate.

 FAIR TREATMENT
To be sure that you treat everyone fairly, listen to what someone is saying rather than think of who is saying it. *What else can help you to be fair?*

Section 9.2 After You Read

Review Key Concepts

1. Describe ways that employee ethics can affect a company.
2. Give an example of how you might demonstrate fairness to another employee.
3. Summarize the actions you would take if a coworker told a lie about you.

Practice Academic Skills

English Language Arts

4. How important is it that your personal ethics be similar to the ethics of a company for which you work? For example, assume you are an animal lover. A company has offered you a job as a lab technician, but the company performs animal testing. Write a one-page paper that explains why you would or would not take the job.
5. Scan current issues of newspapers or magazines to find one example of unethical behavior on the part of both an employer and an employee. Write a summary that explains the case and the actions taken.

N C L B

@ Check your answers at this book's OLC through **glencoe.com**.

 ASSESS *(cont.)*

Resources

ExamView Assessment Suite CD allows you to print out ready-made unit and chapter tests complete with answer keys. You can also create customized tests.

CLOSE

Culminating Activity

Building Trust Ask students to make a list of people they trust and explain why they have trust in those individuals. Then ask them how lost trust can be regained. (Lists and reasons will vary, but most students will agree that trust is difficult to regain.)

▶ Extend the Photo

Caption Answer
Answers might suggest letting people speak for themselves rather than believing gossip and asking for clarification if you're not sure what someone is saying instead of interpreting the statement yourself.

Discussion Ask students how gossip at school compares to gossip at work.

N C L B Activity correlated to English Language Arts standards.

Section 9.2 After You Read

1. Employee ethics affect the health of relationships between employers and employees, employees and colleagues, and employees and customers.
2. Ways to demonstrate fairness to a fellow employee might include being objective, being a good listener, not gossiping, and not letting personal biases affect your relationship.
3. Actions might include confronting the coworker, clarifying the truth to others, or approaching a supervisor or human resources person (if available).

Practice Academic Skills

4. Answers will vary, but most students should agree that ideal employment would not force a person to do things that seem unethical.
5. Summaries should clearly specify the unethical acts of an employer and an employee as well as the steps taken to remedy them.

215

CAREER SPOTLIGHT

FOCUS

Discussion Starter

Business, Management, and Administration Lead a discussion about the different types of careers that can be found in this career cluster. Have students brainstorm different careers and jobs within the career cluster. (Answers will vary but students should show an understanding of the many types of careers that fall within the career cluster.)

TEACH

W Writing Support

Writing Clearly Ask students to think about the different types of individuals Dan de Vriend might communicate with in a typical day. How might his interactions differ with school administrators, instructors, the maintenance crew, students, and other groups? (Answers will vary, but may include differences in tone and use of professional jargon.)

C Critical Thinking

Learning on the Job A position such as Dan de Vriend's requires him to work in different fields every day. Ask: What do you think is the best way to learn physical tasks such as electrical work, plumbing, or grounds keeping? (Answers will vary, but will probably include the physical act of doing something, rather than reading about it or watching a video.)

Dan de Vriend
Facilities Supervisor

Q: Describe your job.

A: I am the facilities supervisor for a K-12 school. I take care of everything having to do with the facility's building and grounds, including the supervision of the security, maintenance, grounds, and janitorial staffs.

Q: Describe a typical workday.

A: I typically get in at 7 A.M., but I have people on site 24 hours a day, so I may get emergency phone calls at any time, day or night. I begin by putting on my cell phone, walkie-talkie, flashlight, and multi-tool. Then I walk around the campus, looking for safety hazards, burnt-out lights, holes in the walls, and anything else that needs repairing or maintaining. At about 8 A.M., I meet with my crew and we discuss projects for the day. These can vary from simply replacing light bulbs to managing a multi-day project involving wall building. We also discuss any special events happening that day or evening and the rooms where they will be held.

Q: What skills are most important to you in your job?

A: Communication skills are the most important. I take requests and communicate them to my crew. Knowing how to communicate well with non-native speakers is very useful.

Q: What academic skills and lifelong learning skills are helpful in preparing for your career?

A: I use math every day: I calculate square footage and surface coverage, and I also use geometry to figure out angles and shapes. Also, I'm constantly scheduling. I schedule security shifts, figure out when janitorial and grounds staff members can work without disturbing teachers, students, and other staff groups, and determine

when the maintenance crew can gain access to classrooms to perform repairs.

Q: What is your key to success?

A: I have impeccable references from previous jobs, and I have built up a varied skill set. I also have supervisory experience, which is very important. It's important to know how to make the different staff members work as one to benefit the school as a whole.

Q: What training and preparation do you recommend for students?

A: An engineering degree wouldn't hurt, but the best training simply comes from working. Work on a carpentry crew, assist a plumber or electrician, and do whatever you can to learn more skills. Many schools offer courses on these types of trades, but real-world experience is invaluable.

Q: What are some ways you recommend students prepare for this career?

A: Build your résumé with varied experiences to make yourself more skillful, versatile, and valuable to a potential employer.

Q: What do you like most about your work?

A: It's flexible, I do something different every day, and I'm outside a lot. Also, the kids always love the maintenance guys.

 For more about Career Clusters, go to this book's OLC through **glencoe.com**.

NCLB NO CHILD LEFT BEHIND

Teaching Tip

The goals of the NCLB Act include mastering computer technologies. To help students become proficient users of technology, include assignments that use different technologies to expand students' awareness of historical concepts as well as to sharpen technology skills.

Sample Question: Ask students to search the Internet for Facilities Supervisor or related positions. Ask them to print copies of the listings they find and have volunteers share their listings with the class.

Education or Training Most facilities workers learn their skills on the job. As they gain more experience, they are assigned more complicated tasks. In some cities, programs run by unions, government agencies, or employers teach janitorial skills.

Academic Skills Required English Language Arts, Mathematics, Science, World Languages

Technology Needed Students learn how to operate and maintain machines, such as construction, electrical, and industrial tools as well as building systems.

Aptitudes, Abilities, and Skills The ability to coordinate, schedule, and supervise the activities of grounds and facilities staffs as well as perform maintenance duties. Good communication skills to assign tasks. Also, the ability to issue supplies and equipment, and inspect building areas to see that work has been done properly.

Workplace Safety Workers must follow safety and health regulations and be familiar with the dangers of electrical work, plumbing, and other repairs.

Career Outlook Overall employment of facilities managers is expected to grow at an average rate for all occupations over the next ten years, as more office complexes, apartment houses, schools, factories, and hospitals are built to accommodate a growing population and economy.

Career Path School facilities managers can move on to similar positions at private businesses with campus-like settings.

Academic Skills Required to Complete Tasks

Tasks	English Language Arts	Mathematics	Science	World Languages
Maintain facilities and grounds	★	★	★	
Manage staff	★	★		★
Oversee supplies	★	★		
Prepare rooms for events		★		
Receive requests for work	★			
Schedule security and other staff	★	★		
Make repairs and install or create projects		★	★	

NCLB

Critical Thinking

What are some businesses, institutions, or other places that might utilize a facilities manager?

NCLB This chart relates academic skills such as English Language Arts, Mathematics, Science, Social Studies, and World Languages to specific tasks that are performed for the job featured in the Career Spotlight feature.

Critical Thinking

Other places that may utilize a facilities manager include a college campus, industrial park, or shopping mall.

CAREER SPOTLIGHT

ASSESS

Make Connections
Ask students to list specific correlations between academic subjects and workplace tasks. For example, a facilities manager might benefit from mathematics to determine surface area when painting or seeding lawn. He or she would use language arts skills when writing a request to fund certain projects, developing memos, or instructing a crew. The person might also use science when determining gardening supplies or controlling pests. (Answers will vary, but students should show an understanding of how academic skills relate directly to workplace tasks.)

CLOSE

Culminating Activity
Lifelong Learning and Career Clusters Encourage students to suggest ways that a facilities manager might develop skills that would apply to a career in business, management, and administration. For example, one whose employer is constructing a sports stadium might look into pesticides, weed control, and turfs that can withstand cleats. A facilities manager whose employer is renovating its computer system might require extra phone lines or secure power lines. Have students volunteer their ideas to the class.

Key Terms and Academic Vocabulary Review

1. Sentences will vary. All should reflect an understanding of the definition of the word. A sample answer might read: "Because he knew the new position would not be overseen by a supervisor, the head chef looked for a cookie baker with strong *self-management* skills."

Review Key Concepts

2. Employers look for strong thinking skills, math skills, and communication skills. They also look for personal qualities such as cooperativeness, a willingness to follow directions, a willingness to learn, initiative, a willingness to take on more responsibility, and loyalty.

3. Two ways to demonstrate desirable personal qualities would be to do tasks without complaining, and to stop what one is doing and listen to directions.

4. Ethics are essential in the workplace for maintaining the reputation of the company and its employees.

5. One example of an ethical principle is honesty, which should be applied when documenting hours worked and when handling money. Another ethical principle is respect for others, which includes respecting a coworker's property and privacy.

6. Possible answer: If you are dealing with a coworker, tell him or her that you will not tolerate his or her unethical behavior, or tell your supervisor. Look for solutions to ethical problems, not revenge.

CHAPTER SUMMARY

Section 9.1

Employers look for employees who can do many things and who will fit well into the company's structure. Cooperativeness, a willingness to follow directions, initiative, a willingness to take responsibility, and a willingness to learn are key traits that you should strive for in the workplace. Employers also value effective self-management skills and loyalty.

Section 9.2

Ethical behavior is essential in the workplace. As an employee, you should strive to be honest, especially regarding time, money, and your employer's property. Respecting the confidentiality of your employer and coworkers, and acting fairly with everyone are also critical to your success. When you are the victim or observer of unethical behavior, there are several ways to respond. Choosing the correct response can be challenging.

Key Terms and Academic Vocabulary Review

1. Use each of these key terms and academic vocabulary words in a sentence.

Key Terms
- cooperativeness (p. 205)
- initiative (p. 206)
- responsibility (p. 207)
- self-management (p. 208)

- ethics (p. 211)
- confidentiality (p. 213)
- prejudice (p. 214)

Academic Vocabulary
- structure (p. 205)
- conduct (p. 211)
- community (p. 211)
- cultures (p. 214)

Review Key Concepts

2. **Describe** three skills and personal qualities employers look for in employees.
3. **Describe** two ways you can demonstrate desirable personal qualities on the job.
4. **Explain** the importance of ethics in the workplace.
5. **List** two ethical principles and ways to apply them in a work setting.
6. **Describe** a strategy for handling unethical practices.

Critical Thinking

7. **Predict** How might learning tasks that are not part of your regular job make you a more valuable employee?
8. **Analyze** What are some positive and negative consequences that might result from reporting a coworker's unethical behavior?

Critical Thinking

7. Learning tasks that are not part of your regular job will make you better able to handle new situations and more likely to get promoted.

8. Positive consequences for reporting a coworker's unethical behavior include clearing innocent people from blame and making the workplace more sound. Negative consequences may include making enemies of the perpetrator and his or her acquaintances.

Real-World Skills and Applications

9. Reports should demonstrate research was done regarding dishonesty in the workplace, ethics in the workplace, or prejudice in the workplace. Reports should include specific information such as who was involved, what was said, and when the occurrences took place. Make sure that students document their sources.

Real-World Skills and Applications

Information Literacy

9. Performing Research Use library or Internet resources to research one of the following topics: (1) Dishonesty in the workplace; (2) Ethics in the workplace; or (3) Prejudice in the workplace. Use at least two sources and write a one-page report summarizing what you have learned.

Scientific Literacy and Civic Responsibility

10. Investigating Options In most communities, special care must be taken when disposing of toxic materials such as chemical cleaning products, solvents, and paint. Research the local legal requirements for the disposal of such toxic materials, and share your findings with the class in a five-minute oral report.

Technology Applications

11. Creating a Self-Assessment Spreadsheet Use a spreadsheet software program to prepare a personal inventory form that could be used to assess a prospective employee's personal qualities. Select at least five different personal qualities and design an evaluation scale for assessment. For example, a scale of poor to excellent could range from 1 to 5. Use the form to take your own personal inventory.

12. **Investigating a Company** Arrange a field trip with your class to a local business show. Pick up information from booths of the companies that have jobs that interest you. Write down what interests you about the company or the jobs they offer. After the show, highlight what interests you in the brochure. Take the brochures and your written thoughts to class with you. Organize into groups of four to discuss the different companies, the jobs being offered, and each group member's thoughts about the company.

13. **Offering Helpful Advice**

Situation You and your friend Donato are working at an office as administrative assistants for the summer. At first, Donato was very diligent about his job. Lately, though, he has been receiving a lot of personal calls, taking long lunches, and even has left work early twice without permission. You have noticed that your supervisor has been taking note of Donato's behavior.

Activity Role-play a conversation in which you tactfully offer advice to Donato. Plan what you will say in advance and try to avoid making comments that will cause Donato to feel defensive or angry. Offer suggestions as to how Donato can regain his good standing at work.

Evaluation You will be evaluated based on how well you meet the following performance indicators:
- Choose an appropriate approach for making suggestions to Donato.
- Offer helpful, realistic advice.
- Present suggestions and advice in a tactful and caring manner.

Chapter 9 Workplace Ethics **219**

 ACTIVE LEARNING

12. Brochure, booths, and shows will vary. Encourage students to consider the traits determined by the jobs that interest them, as well as whether the ethics of the companies match up with their personal ethical beliefs. For example, would they be willing to work for a marketing company that works with tobacco-related businesses?

ROLE PLAY

13. Students should try to show objectivity in their approach and display concern for Donato's well being and career. They should try to avoid becoming emotional in their delivery or judgmental in their assessment of the situation.

10. Local legal requirements for handling toxic materials will vary, but reports should cite regulations for your city, county, or state, and should explain reasons why special care should be taken when disposing of them.

11. Spreadsheets should include categories for evaluation and a sincere look at personal qualities an employer could assess. Qualities might include self-management, fairness, and willingness to learn.

14.
Essays should include an argument either for or against the company's recall of disposable contact lenses. Arguments for the recall might include looking out for the safety of customers and protecting the company's reputation for selling safe products. Arguments against the recall might include damaging the company's reputation by implying that its products are dangerous and not looking out for stockholders' interests.

15.
Janet's earnings will be $41,300 ($34,000 × 20 percent = $6,800 + $500 = $7,300; $7,300 + $34,000 = $41,300).

16.
Responses might address making manufacturers accountable for how their processes affect the environment, ensuring that utilities companies serve communities without exploiting them, and forcing health care providers to serve all patients at an equally high level without concern for their income. Companies that are ethical would be noted while those that abuse their customers, the community, or the environment would be punished.

17.
Interviews should discuss strategies for promoting ethics in the workplace and coping with unethical behaviors. Encourage students to compare their findings in the two interviews and note differing views or philosophies. As a class, discuss whether everyone acts according to the same ethics or whether ethics are subjective.

Academic Skills in the Workplace

English Language Arts

14. Form a Written Opinion Consider a situation in which a company recalled all of its disposable contact lenses after it discovered that some users were diagnosed with a rare eye disease, even though no concrete link had yet been discovered between the lenses and the occurrences of the disease. Write a one-page essay that states your position on the recall. For example, you could condemn the company for overreacting and losing money, or you could praise the company for customer-sensitive business practices.

Mathematics

15. Calculate Bonuses Janet's boss is so pleased with Janet's ability to work with others and help solve problems between her coworkers that he is going to give her a 20% bonus at the end of the year on top of her $500 holiday bonus. If her salary is $34,000, what will her total earnings for the year be with the two bonuses, before taxes?

CONCEPT Multi-Step Problems When solving problems with more than one step, think through the steps before you start.

Starting Hint To set up this problem, first write an equation for the amount of the end-of-the-year bonus: $34,000 \times 0.20 = x$. Then write an expression for her total earnings: $34,000 + x + 500, and solve.

Science

16. Ethics in Science All reputable scientists follow a guide of ethics and laws when doing their research. For instance, many scientists will not perform experiments that knowingly harm or kill living beings. Scientists who falsify data or lie about research conclusions or who engage in other unethical practices are discredited and lose their authority. How could these same ethical principles benefit other professions? Write a one-page response.

Social Studies

17. Conduct Interviews Conduct interviews with two local employers to determine the importance of work ethics such as fairness, promptness, respect, and honesty. Write a two-page report that details your findings and demonstrates your understanding of productive work habits and attitudes.

STANDARDIZED TEST PRACTICE

MULTIPLE CHOICE

Directions Choose the phrase that best completes the following statement.

> **Test-Taking Tip** In a multiple-choice test, the answers should be specific and precise. Read the questions first, then read all the answer choices. Eliminate answers that you know are incorrect.

1. According to this chapter, *initiative* means
   a. to follow someone else's example.
   b. to do what needs to be done without being told.
   c. to get going.
   d. to prohibit from doing something.

For more Standardized Test Practice, go to the OLC @ glencoe.com.

STANDARDIZED TEST PRACTICE

Answer
1. b. to do what needs to be done without being told

Test-Taking Strategies
Whether your students have a standardized test coming up in a few days or a few weeks, these last-minute test-prep tips and strategies will help students relax and do their best.

Read the Question Ask students to read the question carefully, and make sure they know what the question is asking for. For example, some questions may ask the students which option is incorrect, rather than correct.

Read Every Answer Suggest that students read every answer, even if they think the first, second, or third answer may be right. Often some answers are better than others.

Writing Skills Practice

18. Taking Notes Taking notes can help you follow directions thoroughly and correctly. Notes can be used to prompt you on what you need to do, or you can use your notes to create step-by-step instructions explaining how to complete a more complicated task.

 Practice Ask a teacher or coworker to explain a process you would like to know more about. Take notes on what they tell you and write a step-by-step list on how you would complete the project.

Follow the steps below when taking notes:

- Use note cards or a pad to record important information.
- Ask questions about what you do not understand or when you need more details.
- Organize your notes into a concise list.
- Use your own words to summarize your findings.

Net Connection

19. Select a day at work or school and record all the ethical and unethical behavior you observe. At the end of the day, reflect on the items you have listed. Which type of behavior did you observe most frequently—ethical or unethical? Share your findings with the class.

Log On Many organizations are devoted to fostering ethical standards for specific groups or society in general. Visit the Web site of such an organization and use a word-processing program to write a one-page report about what you discover. For help finding links, go to this book's OLC through **glencoe.com**.

Reading Connection
Go to this book's Online Learning Center through **glencoe.com** for a list of reading suggestions.

Personal Academic and Career Portfolio

Adding Your Ethics Information

Knowing what qualities employers look for in employees and what employee ethics align with your own can help you decide which jobs will be a good fit. The following guidelines will help you organize and add information about desirable employee qualities and ethical behavior to your portfolio:

- Create a new section for your portfolio, using a divider for hard copy material and a computer folder for electronic files.
- Label the section *Ethics*.
- You may wish to create subsections or subfolders with names such as *Ethical Employers* and *My Personal Ethics*.
- Add the section to your table of contents.
- Add the following: information about companies or organizations that have good ethical practices, examples of checklists you can follow if you encounter unethical behavior in the workplace, government or other local sources for information on best business practices and workplace ethics, and information you found through those resources.
- You can also include ethical practices specific to a particular job or industry. For example, if you work in the field of health care, it is useful to be aware of the ethical requirements for licensed health care providers.
- Update your research results as you continue to explore your career options.

 Portfolio Help Go to the *Succeeding in the World of Work* OLC through **glencoe.com** for help developing your portfolio.

Chapter 9 Workplace Ethics **221**

Writing Skills Practice

18. Suggest to students that although the notes they take may never be seen by supervisors or coworkers, it is important to be neat, clear, and detail oriented. If you cannot make sense of them later, they will not be useful to you. Ask students to compare strategies and tips.

Net Connection

19. Answers will vary, but students might agree that although students will have different opinions, interests, and experiences, there are ethics in common that allow them to get along. Ask students the worth of considering these ethics, studying ethics online, and thinking about them, rather than simply acting in accordance with others. (Students' opinions will vary, but most should see the worth of examining one's life.)

 Resources

 ExamView Assessment Suite CD allows you to print out ready-made unit and chapter tests complete with answer keys. You can also create customized tests.

WorkKeys

WorkKeys® is a job skills assessment program. For information on leveled assessment for Interpersonal Skills (Teamwork), go to the WorkKeys link on this book's OLC through **glencoe.com**.

Personal Academic and Career Portfolio

Presenting a Portfolio

Tell students that the effectiveness of their **Personal Academic and Career Portfolio** will be influenced by its appearance. Ask that they file their work in a simple, clean binder and arrange the pages according to theme, chronology, or types of work to make a sensible and attractive presentation. Also emphasize the importance of effective labeling, good spelling, and proper grammar. Suggest making business cards, postcards, brochures, or CD-ROMs for the interviewer's records.

Chapter Resources Planning Guide with Activities and Features

Section	Features	Activities
Section 10.1 **Attitudes for Success**	21st Century Workplace (p. 226) Math in Action (p. 227) Real-World Connection (p. 228)	Before You Read (p. 224) Graphic Organizer (p. 224) As You Read (p. 226) After You Read (p. 228)
Section 10.2 **Acting Like a Professional**	Hot Jobs! (p. 230) Creative Business Practices (p. 230) Career Checklist (p. 231) Everyday Ethics (p. 232)	Before You Read (p. 229) Graphic Organizer (p. 229) After You Read (p. 233)

NCLB Activities, information, and skills practice will help your students attain No Child Left Behind proficiency. Students will improve their abilities in the following academic standards areas:

Academic Standards Correlations

Discipline	Standard	Feature/Activity
English Language Arts	NCTE 1 Read texts to acquire new information.	Creative Business Practices (p. 230) Hot Jobs! (p. 230)
	NCTE 3 Apply strategies to interpret texts.	Everyday Ethics (p. 232)
	NCTE 4 Use written language to communicate effectively.	After You Read (p. 228) Writing Skills Practice (p. 239)
	NCTE 7 Conduct research and gather, evaluate, and synthesize data to communicate discoveries.	Real-World Connection (p. 228) Academic Skills in the Workplace (p. 238)
	NCTE 9 Develop an understanding of diversity in language across cultures.	21st Century Workplace (p. 226)
Mathematics	**Problem Solving:** Solve problems that arise in mathematics and other contexts	Math in Action (p. 227)
	Numbers and Operations: Understand meanings of operations and how they relate to one another	After You Read (p. 233)
	Measurement: Understand measurable attributes of objects and the units, systems, and processes of measurement	Academic Skills in the Workplace (p. 238)
Science	**Life Science:** Behavior of organisms	Academic Skills in the Workplace (p. 238)

21st Century Skills and Workplace Competencies Correlations

CORRELATIONS The charts show the 21st Century Skills, foundation skills, and workplace competencies that students develop as they work in this chapter.

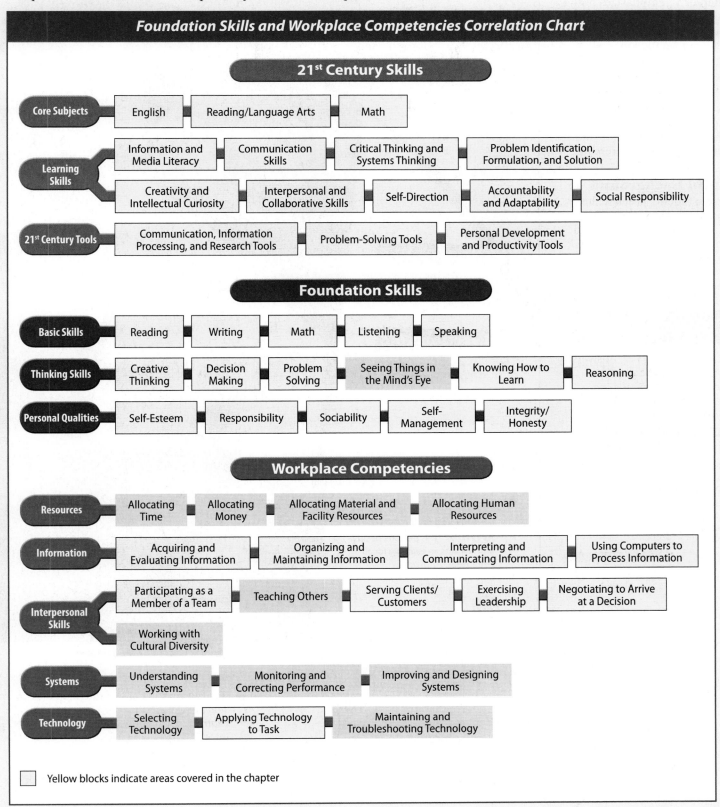

Foundation Skills and Workplace Competencies Correlation Chart

21st Century Skills

Core Subjects
- English
- Reading/Language Arts
- Math

Learning Skills
- Information and Media Literacy
- Communication Skills
- Critical Thinking and Systems Thinking
- Problem Identification, Formulation, and Solution
- Creativity and Intellectual Curiosity
- Interpersonal and Collaborative Skills
- Self-Direction
- Accountability and Adaptability
- Social Responsibility

21st Century Tools
- Communication, Information Processing, and Research Tools
- Problem-Solving Tools
- Personal Development and Productivity Tools

Foundation Skills

Basic Skills
- Reading
- Writing
- Math
- Listening
- Speaking

Thinking Skills
- Creative Thinking
- Decision Making
- Problem Solving
- Seeing Things in the Mind's Eye
- Knowing How to Learn
- Reasoning

Personal Qualities
- Self-Esteem
- Responsibility
- Sociability
- Self-Management
- Integrity/Honesty

Workplace Competencies

Resources
- Allocating Time
- Allocating Money
- Allocating Material and Facility Resources
- Allocating Human Resources

Information
- Acquiring and Evaluating Information
- Organizing and Maintaining Information
- Interpreting and Communicating Information
- Using Computers to Process Information

Interpersonal Skills
- Participating as a Member of a Team
- Teaching Others
- Serving Clients/Customers
- Exercising Leadership
- Negotiating to Arrive at a Decision
- Working with Cultural Diversity

Systems
- Understanding Systems
- Monitoring and Correcting Performance
- Improving and Designing Systems

Technology
- Selecting Technology
- Applying Technology to Task
- Maintaining and Troubleshooting Technology

☐ Yellow blocks indicate areas covered in the chapter

CHAPTER 10
Developing a Positive Attitude

Chapter Overview
Introduce the Chapter

Chapter 10 emphasizes how to develop a positive attitude and demonstrate professional behavior on the job.

Section 10.1 presents strategies for developing positive attitudes and self-esteem.

Section 10.2 explores methods of accepting and responding to criticism and learning to handle pressure and gossip at work.

Build Background

Have students preview the chapter, looking at the pictures, reading captions, and noting content headings. Ask students to describe what they expect to learn in this chapter.

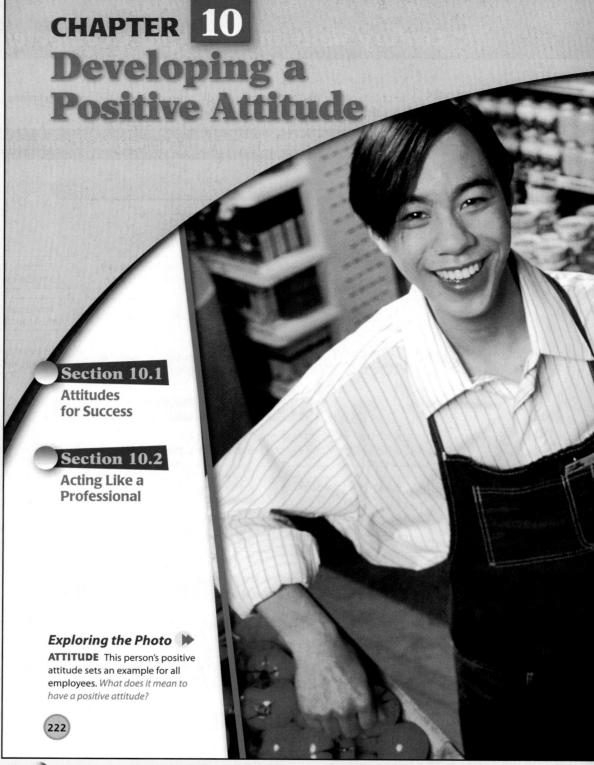

> ▶ **Exploring the Photo**
>
> **Caption Answer** Answers might include accepting challenges, encouraging coworkers, and handling pressure well.
>
> **Discussion** Ask students how a positive attitude can be displayed at school. (Students might mention handling criticism well, encouraging other students, and fostering teamwork in group projects.)

○ **Section 10.1**
Attitudes for Success

○ **Section 10.2**
Acting Like a Professional

Exploring the Photo ▶▶
ATTITUDE This person's positive attitude sets an example for all employees. *What does it mean to have a positive attitude?*

222

Classroom Resources

- 📂 Student Edition
- 📂 Teacher Wraparound Edition
- 📂 Student Activity Workbook with Academic Integration
- 📂 Student Activity Workbook with Academic Integration TAE
- 📂 *Fast File,* Unit 4 Resources

- 📂 Inclusion in the Career Education Classroom
- 💿 TeacherWorks™ Plus
- 💿 *ExamView Assessment Suite*
- 💿 Interactive Chalkboard
- 💿 Interactive Student Edition
- 📶 Online Student Edition
- 📶 Online Learning Center (OLC) with Podcasts

Chapter Objectives

After completing this chapter, you will be able to:

- **Explain** why a positive attitude, high self-esteem, and enthusiasm contribute to career success.
- **Develop** the ability to think positively, overcome doubt, and deal with mistakes.
- **Describe** how to assert yourself on the job.
- **Develop** effective strategies to handle criticism, pressure, and gossip in the workplace.
- **Identify** ways to manage negative feelings.

Writing Activity — Personal Career Notebook

Think about your attitude. Are you a cheerful person? An angry person? A positive person? A negative person? How could your attitude affect your relationships with coworkers and customers? In a two-page response, create at least six job scenarios that illustrate positive and negative employee and customer relations.

Get Motivated! Interview three employers or human resources managers in your community. Choose human resources managers or employers from companies for which you might like to work. Ask them to describe the attitudes they most look for in employees. Write a one-page summary of your interviews.

Chapter 10 Developing a Positive Attitude **223**

Review the Objectives

Introduce the chapter by reviewing the chapter objectives:

Section 10.1 Objectives

Explain why a positive attitude, high self-esteem, and enthusiasm contribute to career success. (Attitude determines how an individual reacts to certain situations and, often, other people's perceptions.)

Develop the ability to think positively, overcome doubt, and deal with mistakes. (Ways to think positively include solving problems instead of complaining, turning negative situations into positive ones, and presenting ideas in a positive manner. Positive self-talk is a way to overcome doubt. Dealing with mistakes entails patience, accepting responsibility, and forgiving oneself.)

Describe how to assert yourself on the job. (Be friendly, outgoing, and respectful. Be a volunteer, make suggestions, and record your accomplishments.)

Section 10.2 Objectives

Develop effective strategies to handle criticism, pressure, and gossip in the workplace. (Handling criticism entails listening, understanding, identifying a solution, and taking action. Handle pressure through prioritizing and practicing self-management. Avoid gossip.)

Identify ways to manage negative feelings. (Count to ten, identify the source of anger, and channel your energy.)

Writing Activity — Personal Career Notebook Answer Guide

After students have written six job scenarios that illustrate positive and negative employee and customer relations, encourage them to share them with the class. Ask students to consider how their attitudes might affect their relationships with customers and coworkers. Ask them if attitudes are something they are born with or whether they can be nurtured.

Get Motivated! Interviews should show an understanding of attitudes that employers look for in potential workers. Evaluate summaries for clarity, length, and content.

FOCUS

🔔 Bell Ringer Activity

Attitudes for Success

Have students identify a person whom they consider to be successful and write at least 10 words that describe the characteristics or traits that help make that person successful.

💿 Resources

⚙ Interactive Chalkboard

The Interactive Chalkboard CD provides visual teaching aids for this section.

@ Online Learning Center

The Online Learning Center (OLC) through **glencoe.com** features chapter vocabulary, chapter summaries, and other study materials.

Preteaching

Assign key terms to student pairs. Have the pairs find the words in context, define them, and then present their words and definitions to the class.

Graphic Organizer

Tell students to go to the OLC through **glencoe.com** for a printable graphic organizer. (Graphic organizers should list ways to show a positive attitude.)

NCLB connects academic correlations to book content.

Attitudes for Success

Reading Guide

Before You Read

Preview Look at the photos in this section and read their captions. Write one or two sentences predicting what the section will be about.

Read to Learn

- Why a positive attitude, high self-esteem, and enthusiasm contribute to career success
- How to think positively, overcome doubt, and deal with mistakes
- How to assert yourself on the job

D Main Idea

Employers value workers who are positive, self-confident, and enthusiastic about their work.

Key Concepts

- Develop a Positive Attitude
- Develop Self-Esteem

Key Terms

- ◈ attitude
- ◈ self-esteem
- ◈ enthusiasm
- ◈ assertive
- ◈ arrogance

Academic Vocabulary

You will find these words in your reading and on your tests. Use the academic vocabulary glossary to look up their definitions if necessary.

- ■ perceive
- ■ receptive

Graphic Organizer

As you read, use a concept map like the one below to record attitudes that will lead to attitude success. In the center circle, write "Attitudes for Success." On the main lines, write major ideas, and then add details about these major ideas on the smaller lines.

@ Log On Go to this book's Online Learning Center through **glencoe.com** for an online version of this graphic organizer.

Academic Standards ●

NCLB

English Language Arts
- Conduct research and gather, evaluate, and synthesize data to communicate discoveries. (NCTE 7)
- Develop an understanding of diversity in language use across cultures. (NCTE 9)

Mathematics
- Solve problems that arise in mathematics and in other contexts

 224 **Unit 4** Joining the Workforce

glencoe.com

Reading Guide

Before You Read

Point out to the class that successful attitudes can be learned. Suggest that a positive attitude can benefit them not only at work, but in other areas of life as well.

D Develop Concepts

Main Idea Discuss the main idea with students. Ask: How do you think an "attitude" can be developed? (Students may suggest practice, help from friends, and examining one's decisions and actions.)

Develop a Positive Attitude

A positive attitude is an important part of succeeding in the world of work. Your **attitude** is your basic outlook on life and your way of looking at people and the world. Your attitude determines how you react to certain situations and, often, how others **perceive** you. While you cannot control everything that happens on the job, a positive attitude can help you control how you react. How well you get along with your employer and your coworkers will depend on your attitude.

Here are some steps to help you develop a positive attitude:

- Take action to solve problems instead of complaining. People with a positive attitude get along well with others, complain rarely, admit mistakes, and like to cooperate.
- Turn a negative situation into a positive one by listing the good aspects of the situation. Seemingly negative situations may have some benefits. For example, working overtime may result in a bigger paycheck or the opportunity to learn new skills.
- Present your ideas in a positive way. Speak clearly and politely.

Positive Thinking

One of the best ways to maintain a positive attitude is to think positively. Positive thinking will help you get along better with others, handle problems more effectively, and reach your goals by motivating you to act. When you think positively, you are more **receptive**, or open, to the people around you.

✓ Reading Check **SUMMARIZE** Explain why employers prefer employees with a positive attitude.

⬛▶ Vocabulary
You can find definitions in the **Key Terms** glossary and **Academic Vocabulary** glossary at the back of this book.

 STAY POSITIVE A positive attitude will help you succeed at work. *How can you develop a positive attitude?*

TEACH

Discussion Starter
Developing a Positive Attitude Ask: If you had to rely on one person to help you get ahead in your career, would you want that person to be a positive thinker or negative thinker? (Most students will agree that positive thinkers will be more beneficial.)

U Universal Access
Verbal Learning Have students go to your local library and obtain recordings that encourage positive thinking on CD, MP3, or cassette. Have them choose a portion to share with the class.

✓ Reading Check

SUMMARIZE Positive thinkers get along better with others, handle problems effectively, and are more likely to reach their goals.

Resources

⊙ TeacherWorks™ Plus
The TeacherWorks software includes customizable built-in lesson plans and links to printable program resources.

▶▶ Extend the Photo

Caption Answer A positive attitude can also be developed by turning negative situations into positive ones and presenting ideas in a positive way.

Discussion As a class, have students brainstorm ways to turn their negative thinking into positive thinking. (Stop and analyze negative assumptions, focus on changing the way you think, create daily reminders to think positively.)

S Skill Practice

Independent Practice

Developing Self-Esteem
Have students survey at least ten people, asking two questions of each person: How have you observed me being positive? Have you observed me being negative? Tell students to record the responses and then develop a plan to improve their negative actions or attitudes.

As You Read
Answers will vary, but students should recognize the effects of positive or negative attitudes on a person's self-esteem.

ASSESS

Review Key Terms
Have students write sentences using each key term.

Online Study Tools
Have students go to the OLC through **glencoe.com** to:
- Download **Podcast** study tools.
- Download free **Study-to-Go** content to their PDAs or cell phones.

STUDY TO GO

Resources

ExamView Assessment Suite CD allows you to print out ready-made unit and chapter tests complete with answer keys. You can also create customized tests.

N C L B Activity correlated to English Language Arts standards.

As You Read
Connect Has someone's positive or negative attitude affected your own self-esteem?

Develop Self-Esteem

When you present your ideas and your thoughts in a positive way, you show **self-esteem**, which is recognition and regard for yourself and your abilities. Self-esteem is essential for a positive attitude. High self-esteem can build confidence. Confidence generates success.

How to Build Self-Esteem

Developing a positive self-concept is one way to build self-esteem. Here are some other techniques:
- Make lists of your abilities and successes. Review them often and remind yourself that you have even more successes ahead.
- Set reachable goals, and work to achieve them.
- Think about a positive impact you have had on others.
- Work on improving your abilities. Accomplishing something that is challenging helps build self-esteem.

Enthusiasm Is Important

It is easy to have **enthusiasm**, or eager interest, when you love your work. However, even your dream job will have frustrating moments. Sometimes you may have to push yourself to act with enthusiasm. While this may not feel natural, it is worth the effort. Having an upbeat attitude in difficult situations will help you develop a good reputation. Employers look for workers who are enthusiastic and who can handle a challenge.

The 21ˢᵗ Century Workplace

Korean: A Unique Language

Almost all languages belong to *language families* and have sister languages that are similar in grammar and vocabulary. Not so Korean. Many linguists believe that Korean is a *language isolate*, which means that it does not belong to any known family. Others say that it is part of a loose-knit Asian language family that includes Japanese, Mongolian, and Turkish.

The Korean language reflects how important respect is in Korean culture. While English speakers conjugate verbs based on the subject (*I, you, they*, etc.), Korean speakers conjugate verbs based on their relationship to the people they are addressing. Koreans use one verb form for equals, such as friends and siblings their own age. They use other forms for people who command more respect, such as parents, teachers, customers, and supervisors. These kinds of grammatical forms based on personal relationships are called *honorifics*.

N C L B

CRITICAL THINKING
Why do you think customers are addressed with honorifics in Korean?

In Your Community
Find a person in your community whose native language is not English. Ask that person if his or her native language has different forms to address people of different social status or relationships to the speaker. If so, gather some examples and share them with your classmates.

@ Extend Your Learning The English language belongs to the Germanic branch of the Indo-European language family. For links to Web sites about language families, go to this book's OLC through **glencoe.com**.

The 21ˢᵗ Century Workplace

CRITICAL THINKING ANSWER Students may suggest that customers are addressed with honorifics to show respect. The employees are providing a service for their customers.

In Your Community Findings will vary, but may include Spanish speakers using the *Usted* tense in formal occasions rather then the informal *tu* tense in casual situations.

◄◄ **SELF-ESTEEM** Doing things you are good at will develop your self-esteem. *What are some areas in which you excel?*

S **Skill Practice**
Independent Practice

Research Have students make lists of positive comments they can make toward classmates or coworkers. **L1**

Teamwork Have students share an example of a mistake they have made at work. Did they admit their mistake? What happened as a result? **L2**

Critical Thinking Have students look at magazines for advertising slogans. Ask them for examples of positive and critical statements toward readers. Which do they find more effective? (Answers will vary, but students might find that ads typically point out deficiencies in the reader and offer ways to help them.) **L3**

NCLB Activity correlated to Mathematics standards.

Overcoming Doubt

Do you have a voice inside your head that sometimes whispers negative messages, such as "You are not smart enough to get that new job"? Many people reduce inner self-doubt through positive self-talk.

Positive self-talk means you "out-talk" your self-doubt. When the voice says, "You can't do it," you answer, "I can and I will!" Making a list of positive statements can help you overcome self-doubt. These statements might include "I am in charge of my life" and "I can achieve whatever I want with hard work." Try repeating these statements to yourself to improve your self-esteem.

Use Your Mistakes to Grow

S Successful people use mistakes as opportunities to learn and grow. Whenever you make a mistake, be patient with yourself. You probably will have the opportunity to correct the mistake. Also, you will have other opportunities to succeed.

Accept that you will make mistakes from time to time, and prepare yourself to act effectively when you do. When you think you have made a mistake, follow these steps:
1. Make sure it is really a mistake. Just because a project did not turn out the way you planned does not mean it is a mistake.
2. Accept responsibility for any mistakes.
3. Offer a way to solve the problem.
4. Find a lesson you can learn from your mistake.
5. Forgive yourself. Do not dwell on your mistake. Learn from it, and move on.

Math **In Action**

Bonuses

For every 250 items you produce at work, you will receive a $75 bonus. If you can produce 150 items in an 8 hour work day, how much bonus money will you make in a 5-day work week?

Starting Hint: Calculate how many items you would make in a week by solving for x: $150 \times 5 = x$

 For more math practice, go to this book's OLC through **glencoe.com**.

Math **In Action**

The bonus money for one week would be $225 ($150 \times 5 = 750$; $750 \div 250 = 3$; $3 \times \$75 = \$225$).

📁 **Student Activity Workbook** Assign the Chapter 10 activities in the Student Activity Workbook.

After You Read
Have students complete the Section 10.1 After You Read section review.

▶▶ *Extend the Photo*

Caption Answer Areas where students excel will vary, but might include academic skills, athletic ability, and creative gifts.

Discussion Ask students why it is important to consider their strengths and weaknesses when choosing a career. (Students should agree that working in a field in which they show aptitude will benefit their attitudes and potential for success.)

ASSESS (cont.)

Online Study Tools

Have students go to the OLC through **glencoe.com** to:

- Take the Section 10.1 **Practice Test**.
- Download **Podcast** study tools.
- Download free **Study-to-Go** content to their PDAs or cell phones.

CLOSE

Culminating Activity

Write a Memo Tell students to imagine that they work as assistant buyers for a local department store. Yesterday they sent out a new sportswear price sheet. Today they noticed an error in the price of sweatshirts. The sweatshirts were marked at a retail price of $59.99; the correct price is $65.99. Have students write a memo addressed to all sales personnel advising them of this error.

Real-World *Connection*

Critical Thinking Answer Answers will vary, but some students will argue that he should withdraw because of the current conflict of interests.

Do Your Own Research Lists should mention the names of the contests and any qualifications, such as whether the contestant needs to be a certain age, or whether the winner needs to participate in any publicity.

N C L B Activity correlated to English Language Arts standards.

228

Real-World *Connection*

Contest Eligibility

Barry works for a food-marketing agency. Before he began to work there, he entered a national recipe contest; and he has been named a finalist for his entry. Since Barry's agency does not represent the sponsor of the contest, he is eligible to win. However, Barry is concerned that his coworkers will see his win as support for the competition.

Critical Thinking Should Barry withdraw from the contest?

Do Your Own Research Select several contests from magazines or the Internet and read the disclaimers. Read the qualifications carefully and develop a list of things that would disqualify a contestant. Learn what kinds of publicity may be required for winners of the contests you selected.

Practice Assertiveness

To get recognition for the job you do, practice being assertive. Being **assertive** means being direct, honest, and polite. When you confidently present yourself and your abilities to those around you, you are showing assertiveness.

Assert Yourself

The first step in practicing assertiveness is to be friendly, outgoing, and respectful. Use positive language and speak with confidence. Volunteer for projects or committees. Making suggestions, asking questions, and asking your supervisor for advice are also excellent ways to let your supervisor know that you care about your job. Keeping a record of your accomplishments will allow you to ask for things you need with confidence.

Avoid Arrogance

Most employers will accept and even admire assertive employees. However, do not confuse assertiveness with **arrogance**, which is overbearing behavior marked by excessive self-importance. Arrogant behavior is considered rude and impolite.

Section 10.1 After You Read

Review Key Concepts

1. Explain how a positive attitude can help you to get a raise or a promotion.
2. Describe how you would react if your boss asked you to reorganize the storage closet, a task you know will involve many hours of tedious work. Explain your response.
3. Jamaica works hard at her job but feels that her more confident coworkers get the praise she also deserves. Identify steps she can take to demonstrate assertiveness on the job.

Practice Academic Skills

 English Language Arts

N C L B

4. Design a poster for a seminar on developing a positive attitude in the workplace. Show at least three points that demonstrate a positive attitude. Present your poster to the class.
5. Imagine that you have worked very hard on a project for which you have been chosen to receive the employee of the month award. How might this success at work affect your self-concept? Explain your answer in a two-paragraph response.

 Check your answers at this book's OLC through **glencoe.com**.

228 **Unit 4** Joining the Workforce

glencoe.com

Section 10.1 After You Read

Review Key Concepts

1. A positive attitude can allow an employee to accomplish more work, cooperate better with coworkers, and encourage teamwork.
2. Answers will vary, but students should recognize that having a positive attitude will impress the boss and make the task easier.
3. Steps include being direct, honest, and polite, as well as being confident and recording accomplishments.

Practice Academic Skills

4. Posters will vary, but points may include positive thinking, being enthusiastic, overcoming doubt, growing from mistakes, and asserting oneself.
5. Paragraphs will vary but might suggest that being recognized and rewarded for work helps boost one's self-esteem and self-concept.

Acting Like a Professional

Reading Guide

 Before You Read

Preview Read the Key Concept and the Key Terms. Write one or two sentences predicting what the section will be about.

Read to Learn
- Effective strategies for handling criticism, pressure, and gossip in the workplace
- Ways to control your anger

Main Idea

D Learning to handle difficult situations in a professional manner is essential to succeeding in the workplace.

Key Concept
- Working Well with Others

Key Terms
- ◇ professionalism
- ◇ constructive criticism
- ◇ defensive
- ◇ gossip

Academic Vocabulary

You will find this word in your reading and on your tests. Use the academic vocabulary glossary to look up its definition if necessary.
- ■ clarity

Graphic Organizer

As you read, list ways that will help you work well with others and demonstrate professional behaviors. Continue to add your own ideas to the list after you finish reading. Use a graphic organizer like the one below to help you organize your information.

TIPS FOR WORKING WITH OTHERS

1. _____
2. _____
3. _____
4. _____

 Log On Go to this book's Online Learning Center through **glencoe.com** for an online version of this graphic organizer.

Academic Standards • • • • • • • • • • • • • • • • • •

English Language Arts
- Read texts to acquire new information. (NCTE 1)
- Apply strategies to interpret texts. (NCTE 3)

Mathematics
- Understand meanings of operations and how they relate to one another

Bell Ringer Activity

Acting Like a Professional

Ask students to think of a situation in which someone criticized them. How did they feel? How did they react? Have them write three or four sentences describing the situation.

Resources

 Interactive Chalkboard
The Interactive Chalkboard CD provides visual teaching aids for this section.

@ Online Learning Center
The Online Learning Center (OLC) through **glencoe.com** features chapter vocabulary, chapter summaries, and other study materials.

Preteaching
Read the definition of the key terms aloud. Ask students to write a sentence using each key term.

Graphic Organizer
Tell students to go to the OLC through **glencoe.com** for a printable graphic organizer. (Graphic organizers should include ways to work well with others and demonstrate professional behaviors.)

NCLB connects academic correlations to book content.

Reading Guide

Before You Read

Explain to students that a professional attitude can be shown in how workers give and take criticism, whether they are open to advice, and how they handle gossip. Ask them if there are any times when they should act unprofessionally.

D **Develop Concepts**

Main Idea Ask students to share examples of people acting professionally. As a class, discuss how each example benefits the workplace.

TEACH

Discussion Starter
Working Well with Others
Ask students to give examples of a "win-win" situation, then a "win-lose" situation (either I win, you lose or you win, I lose) situation. Use the win-lose examples and have students discuss how they could have turned them into win-win situations.

C Critical Thinking
Practicing Professionalism
Some employees criticize workers because they allow their personal lives to spill over to the workplace. Have students write 50-word responses to this comment: "Good employees leave their personal lives at home each morning."

U Universal Access
Musical Learners Ask students to name their favorite upbeat songs or TV jingles. Divide students into groups and have each group write new words to the songs that convey a positive attitude. Ask the most confident students to perform their "attitude" songs.

Resources

⊙ **TeacherWorks™ Plus**
The TeacherWorks software includes customizable built-in lesson plans and links to printable program resources.

HOT JOBS!

Humane Law Enforcement Officer

This law enforcement branch monitors and investigates complaints of cruelty or mistreatment of domestic and agricultural animals. Volunteering at an animal shelter can provide valuable experience for this profession. Customer service skills and a love for animals are important in this growing field.

Working Well with Others

Think about a difficult time at school or work. Perhaps you were so overwhelmed that you felt you would explode if someone told you to do just one more thing.

Now divide a sheet of paper into three columns. In the first column, briefly describe the *situation* you recalled. In the second, list the *feelings* you experienced. In the third, describe the *action* you took. Then turn the paper over and write answers to these questions: Was your reaction a mature response to your problem? Was your answer constructive? What could you have done differently?

In the workplace, ask yourself these same questions before you react to a situation. They will help you think things through and avoid doing something you may regret. At work, you will need to work well with others in a variety of situations. Of all the employees who are fired each year, 70 percent are fired because they cannot work well with others. As workplace diversity increases, it is becoming even more important to develop an attitude that will help you work with others effectively. On the job, you need to show professionalism. **Professionalism** is the ability to handle problems, criticism, and pressure gracefully and maturely.

Creative Business Practices

GENERAL ELECTRIC

Leadership Programs

General Electric (GE) offers leadership programs that allow employees to improve their job skills through a mixture of classroom training and on-the-job experience.

These programs are available to all levels of employees. GE also has a leadership program for students through internships and co-ops. Both the internships and co-ops are full-time positions where students are paid for their work.

Students who are interns or co-ops obtain real-work experience at GE, learn where and how they fit into the company, and begin their careers. Employees in the entry-level leadership program work on many different assignments, which allows them to learn a lot about the company and work on their job skills at the same time. Experienced-level leadership programs allow more advanced employees to work with senior employees in their job areas.

CRITICAL THINKING What would be some professional advantages of working as an intern or co-op student at GE?

 Connect to the Real World For more information about GE's leadership programs, visit the company's Web site via this book's Online Learning Center through **glencoe.com**.

Creative Business Practices

CRITICAL THINKING ANSWER Professional advantages of working as an intern or co-op student at General Electric include the following: getting on-the-job experience, making contacts with professionals, learning more about a prospective employer and field, and gaining job skills.

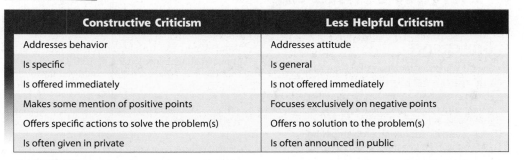

Figure 10.1   WHAT MAKES CRITICISM CONSTRUCTIVE?

Constructive Criticism	Less Helpful Criticism
Addresses behavior	Addresses attitude
Is specific	Is general
Is offered immediately	Is not offered immediately
Makes some mention of positive points	Focuses exclusively on negative points
Offers specific actions to solve the problem(s)	Offers no solution to the problem(s)
Is often given in private	Is often announced in public

CRITICISM   You can learn to give and accept constructive criticism. *Why is it easier to accept constructive criticism than criticism that is not constructive?*

Accepting Criticism

The ability to accept criticism is vital to your survival in any job. Criticism presented in a way that can help you learn and grow is called **constructive criticism**. Your ability to accept and respond to this type of criticism demonstrates your professionalism. It shows you are willing to learn and take advice.

Many supervisors try to offset constructive criticism by offering positive comments along with their suggestions for improvement. By praising employees, supervisors remind the employees of their value. Employees who feel valued are more likely to accept constructive criticism.

Figure 10.1 compares constructive criticism to less helpful criticism. You can use the standards in this figure to evaluate criticism you receive. You can also use them if your job requires you to evaluate employees.

Not all criticism is offered tactfully or constructively. Focus on how the criticism will help you grow. Many employees actually welcome criticism because it teaches them better ways to succeed at their jobs.

Responding to Criticism

Jin overheard her supervisor tell a colleague that if Paolo continued to be late, he would lose his job. After work, Jin told Paolo what she had heard and suggested he try to get to work on time. Paolo snapped back, "But it's not my fault! And who are you to judge me?"

Paulo was being **defensive**, which means being closed to other people's opinions about you or your actions. Examples of defensive reactions include becoming angry and refusing to listen. It is important to be receptive to other people's opinions in the workplace and in your personal life.

Career **Checklist**

To Develop a Positive Work Attitude:

✓ Accept challenges as opportunities.

✓ Always show respect and consideration for others, even if you disagree with them.

✓ Take responsibility for your actions.

✓ Manage workplace stress effectively.

Chapter 10   Developing a Positive Attitude   **231**

TEACH *(cont.)*

S Skill Practice
Guided Practice

Serving Clients/ Customers Have students write how they would respond to a customer who has returned merchandise, complaining that it fell apart with its first use, and criticizing you for being too slow in completing the transaction. **L1**

Interpreting and Communicating Information Tell students to imagine that they are reporters for the local newspaper. The topic of their articles is a survey of local employers on the skills employees need to get ahead. Have students interview at least three employers about the job skills they see as most valuable. Have students write 200-word articles using their interview information. **L2**

Using Computers to Process Information Have students write an essay on dealing with gossip. Then have students use a desktop publishing program to format their essays into newspaper article style, complete with headlines and photos, where appropriate. **L3**

ASSESS

Review Key Terms
Have students write sentences using each key term.

Online Study Tools
Have students go to the OLC through **glencoe.com** to:
- Download **Podcast** study tools.
- Download free **Study-to-Go** content to their PDAs or cell phones.

EXTEND THE FIGURE   Figure 10.1

Caption Answer Answers will vary, but students will probably agree that most people prefer to hear a positive attitude than a negative one.

Discussion Ask students if it is easier to give constructive criticism or criticism that is not constructive. Why? (Most students will agree that it is easier to give criticism that is not constructive because it includes a complaint without a suggestion.)

RETEACH

W Writing Support
Guided Practice

Write Clearly Have students write a brief guide about managing job-related stress. Tell them to arrange their work as if it will be presented to new employees at a business of their choice. Emphasize the importance of organization and clarity. Afterward, ask volunteers to share their work with the class.

Resources

Student Activity Workbook Assign the Chapter 10 activities in the Student Activity Workbook.

ASSESS

After You Read

Have students complete the Section 10.2 After You Read section review.

Online Study Tools

Have students go to the OLC through **glencoe.com** to:

- Take the Section 10.2 **Practice Test**.
- Download **Podcast** study tools.
- Download free **Study-to-Go** content to their PDAs or cell phones.

Everyday ETHICS

DUE CREDIT

Should you cover for a coworker?

COWORKER COMPETITION You and your coworker are both up for a promotion because of a successful project that the two of you recently completed. What your boss does not know is that your coworker was having problems at home and you worked late many nights to cover for her and completed most of the project yourself. Your coworker has not brought this to your boss's attention, and the promotion decision is scheduled to be made next week.

What Would You Do? Would you tell your boss about what happened on the project? Or will you confront your coworker? What could you say to your coworker?

DISCUSS IT One possible tactic is to focus on your own attributes instead of your coworker's deficiencies when speaking to your boss. In teams, discuss possible ways to show your positive attributes to your boss without alienating your coworker.

◤ Vocabulary

You can find definitions in the **Key Terms** glossary and **Academic Vocabulary** glossary at the back of this book.

Here is a four-step process that you can use to help you respond effectively to criticism:

1. Listen to the criticism.
2. Make sure you understand the criticism. If you do not understand, ask the speaker for **clarity**.
3. Identify a solution to the problem.
4. Take action to fix the problem. If the problem is complex, break it down into smaller bits. Then you can take action one step at a time.

In the end, you must use your own judgment. Even if the rest of the world thinks you have made a poor decision, you may know inside that you did the right thing. This is especially true when you are standing up for values that are important to you.

Avoid Gossip

Avoid gossip in the workplace. **Gossip** consists of saying negative things about people behind their backs. Gossip is often untrue and can be hurtful. People often gossip so that they can feel important or to damage someone's reputation.

Manage Job-Related Stress

In today's fast-paced workplace, job-related stress is common. Managers are often under great pressure. That tension can spread down to lower-level employees, putting pressure on employees to produce more without a loss of quality. Adding to the stress is employee awareness that company reorganizations have become routine, and even the best workers can lose their jobs. To cope with or lessen job-related stress, set priorities and practice effective self-management.

Everyday ETHICS

What Would You Do? Answer Answers will vary, but most students will agree that if your coworker is indeed having personal problems, it may not be necessary to bring them up to your supervisor unless the situation affects the coworker's job performance.

DISCUSS IT Ask students to think of ways to bring up their own attributes without alienating their coworker. Have the class discuss each way, and choose the best solution.

Controlling Anger

Controlling your anger is part of getting along with others. Things will not always go the way you want them to go at work. Avoid letting frustration turn to anger.

There are some simple ways to manage anger. One common strategy is to take a deep breath and count to ten. This gives you a chance to calm down before you react.

If you are feeling angry, think about what you are really angry about. Ask yourself: Are you angry about a situation at work or are you angry about another situation in your life?

Try to channel your energy into problem solving instead of into anger. Use this five-step model:

1. Define the problem.
2. Decide on possible solutions.
3. Evaluate those solutions.
4. Make a decision.
5. Take action.

🌲 **MANAGING PRESSURE**
A good way to control your emotions is to count to ten before you react. *Why is it a good idea to stay calm when dealing with conflicts at work?*

Section 10.2 After You Read

Review Key Concepts

1. Sean's supervisor has called him to her office to discuss a problem with a project he just finished. The problem was not his fault, and Sean feels that he did his best. How should Sean behave in this situation?
2. Identify steps you can take to manage feeling overwhelmed by work.
3. List two tips for managing anger.

Practice Academic Skills

 Mathematics

4. Chav has taken her employees out for a team-building lunch. The final bill is $92.50. How much should Chav leave for a 20% tip?

CONCEPT Multiplying Decimals When you multiply one decimal by another, place the decimal point in the answer by counting the number of decimal places in the two factors and placing the decimal point that number of places from the right.
Step 1: Change the percent to a decimal. Multiply the two numbers (0.20 × $92.50).
Step 2: To find the total, add the tip you calculated in Step 1 to the total for the meal.

Math For math help, go to the Math Appendix located at the back of this book.

ASSESS *(cont.)*

Resources

💿 **ExamView Assessment Suite CD** allows you to print out ready-made unit and chapter tests complete with answer keys. You can also create customized tests.

CLOSE

Culminating Activity

Personal Inventory Have students write a 500-word paragraph that begins with this sentence: "The personal traits or attitudes that will help me succeed in my chosen career are…" (Paragraph might discuss a positive attitude, good self-esteem, ability to handle criticism, and being assertive.)

 Extend the Photo

Caption Answer Answers will vary, but students should agree that they make wiser decisions when they are calm.

Discussion Have students think of ways to keep calm in tense situations. Suggest deep breathing, counting to ten, or thinking through a situation before rushing to action.

NCLB Activity correlated to Mathematics standards.

Section 10.2 After You Read

Review Key Concepts

1. Sean should see the occasion as an opportunity to learn more about his profession.
2. Steps to manage pressure include setting priorities and self-managing.
3. Ways to manage anger include counting to ten, analyzing the situation, and channeling energy using the five-step model.

Practice Academic Skills

4. Chav should leave an $18.50 tip ($92.50 × .20 = $18.50).

FOCUS

Discussion Starter

Human Services Lead a discussion about the different types of careers that can be found in this career cluster. Have students brainstorm different careers and jobs within the career cluster. (Answers will vary but students should show an understanding of the many types of careers that fall within the career cluster.)

TEACH

W **Writing Support**
Independent Practice

Conduct an Interview Have students use the questions in the Career Spotlight to conduct and record an interview with an individual in the featured career cluster. (Answers will vary but should follow the interview format of the Career Spotlight.)

C **Critical Thinking**

Traits and Abilities Have students discuss why acting professionally is so important for a person who works in law, public safety, corrections, and security. (Answers might refer to Gilligan's quote that they deal with people on the worst days of their lives. It is important for workers such as firefighters not to get caught up in emotions.)

CAREER SPOTLIGHT

Career Cluster: Law, Public Safety, Corrections, and Security

Jim Gilligan
Firefighter

Q: Describe your job.
A: I'm a firefighter and paramedic. My duties include providing fire prevention and suppression as well as advanced life support during medical emergencies. Downtime tasks include fire inspections, public education, and making sure all equipment is stocked and ready to respond.

Q: Describe a typical workday.
A: Firefighters work a schedule referred to as "24/48," which is a 24-hour shift, followed by 48 hours off. When I arrive at the station, I receive a report that informs me of any issues or problems that may have occurred on the previous shift as well as any other information pertinent to my shift. Next, all crew members check the equipment and check their self-contained breathing apparatus for proper operation. We respond to all Emergency Medical Service (EMS) and fire calls which can happen at any time. In between calls, we train, work out, maintain equipment, and perform fire inspections, public education, and hydrant maintenance. If time allows, our 24-hour shift includes eating, sleeping, and working out.

Q: What skills are most important to you in your job?
A: We deal with people on the worst days of their lives. We must be professional and not get caught up in emotions.

Q: What academic skills and lifelong learning skills are helpful in preparing for your career?
A: Good study habits with retention and good writing skills for report writing. Also, maintain a clean background check.

Q: What is your key to success?
A: Good training and experience get me through my work day. When I'm working, I'll give it everything I have, but when I'm off duty, I'm involved in coaching youth baseball and football.

Q: What do you like most about your work?
A: Helping people in time of need.

Q: What are some disadvantages of your career?
A: The biggest disadvantage is missing important events because I'm working a 24-hour shift. We don't get holidays off! Also, it's tough keeping it together when I have to deliver bad news.

Q: What training and preparation do you recommend for students?
A: Get as much training as you can before you apply for a job. While large cities conduct recruit classes, smaller departments require you to obtain a paramedic card and fire training before you apply.

Q: What are some ways you recommend students prepare for this career?
A: Contact your local fire department and ask for a tour and a ride-along. If you then feel it's what you want to pursue, ask if the department will help you with training or proper direction to that training.

 For more about Career Clusters, go to this book's OLC through **glencoe.com**.

NO CHILD LEFT BEHIND

Teaching Tip

The goals of the NCLB Act include a strong emphasis on reading skills. The use of modeling in your classroom will help students become better at identifying information. For example, ask a question that can be answered by reading the chart on page 235.

Sample Question: Which tasks on this chart require Social Studies academic skills? (Answer: Both responding to fire and EMS calls and preparing written reports of incidents.)

Education or Training Applicants for firefighting jobs generally must pass a written exam and a medical exam as well as tests of strength, physical stamina, coordination, and agility. Classroom instruction and practical training teach firefighting techniques, fire prevention, hazardous materials control, local building codes, and emergency medical procedures, including first aid and CPR (cardiopulmonary resuscitation). Community college courses in fire science may improve an applicant's chances. For promotion to positions higher than battalion chief, many fire departments now require a bachelor's degree, preferably in fire science, public administration, or a related field. An associate degree is required for executive fire officer certification from the National Fire Academy.

Academic Skills Required English Language Arts, Mathematics, Science, Social Studies

Technology Needed Fire hoses, special breathing apparatus, extinguishers and sprinkler systems, and specialty pumps and meters. Fire trucks and other emergency vehicles are equipped with computerized equipment used by firefighters and other first responders.

Aptitudes, Abilities, and Skills Organization and teamwork, physical strength, and stamina.

Workplace Safety Firefighting is a high-risk job that involves the risk of death or injury from collapsing structures, traffic accidents when responding to calls, and exposure to flames and smoke. Firefighters also may come in contact with poisonous, flammable, or explosive gases and chemicals, as well as radioactive or other hazardous materials that may have immediate or long-term effects on their health.

Career Outlook Employment of firefighters is expected to grow faster than average over the next ten years.

Career Path Some firefighters become fire investigators who determine the origin and cause of a fire. Others can move up to various levels of command or serve as inspectors or consultants.

Academic Skills Required to Complete Tasks

Tasks	English Language Arts	Mathematics	Science	Social Studies
Check equipment for proper operation	★	★	★	
Respond to fire and EMS calls	★	★	★	★
Prepare written report of incident	★	★	★	★
Perform fire inspections	★	★	★	
Maintain fire hydrants		★	★	

NCLB

Critical Thinking

Why is it important for firefighters to be in good physical shape?

NCLB This chart relates academic skills such as English Language Arts, Mathematics, Science, Social Studies, and World Languages to specific tasks that are performed for the job featured in the Career Spotlight feature.

Critical Thinking

Students who want to pursue a career in firefighting are required to operate heavy machinery, open stuck doors, climb ladders, and carry people, as well as work long hours.

CAREER SPOTLIGHT

ASSESS

Make Connections

Ask students to choose a career in law, public safety, corrections, or security. Have them develop a list of classes one can take that will benefit a person in that job, as well as explanations of how each course is pertinent. (Lists will vary according to jobs chosen. An example might be that a police officer might take language arts for communication skills and civics for legal awareness, as well as a non-English language class to meet the needs of emerging globalization.)

CLOSE

Culminating Activity

Lifelong Learning and Career Clusters Inform students that positions such as firefighting and law enforcement require physical strength and ability. What steps can such workers take to ensure employment as they grow older? (Answers will vary but may include taking steps to prolong their health such as eating well, exercising, and doing yoga. They might also study administrative, managerial, or training aspects of the job.)

Key Terms and Academic Vocabulary Review

1. Students should write complete sentences using each term correctly. A sample answer might read: "Having positive *self-esteem* helped Jerry overcome unjust criticism from the new supervisor."

Review Key Concepts

2. A positive attitude, high self-esteem, and enthusiasm are all qualities that employers like to see in employees.

3. Surround yourself with positive thinkers; turn negative situations into positive ones by listing the good aspects of the situation; present your ideas in a positive way.

4. Ways to assert yourself on the job include being friendly and outgoing, and confidently indicating your real accomplishments and abilities.

5. Possible strategies: accept the criticism and use it to improve; to relieve stress, set priorities and practice effective self-management tips; think before joining in gossip, ask yourself what your motivation is for gossiping, and ask yourself if your comments could damage someone.

6. Ways to manage negative emotions include counting to ten, considering what you are really angry about, and using the five-step model to control anger.

Critical Thinking.

7. Students may respond that negative self-talk leads to negative thoughts and feelings, while positive self-talk improves self-confidence through positive thinking.

CHAPTER SUMMARY

Section 10.1

A positive attitude helps workers succeed. While employees cannot control everything that happens on the job, they can control how they react. A positive attitude, the ability to overcome doubt, and the ability to learn from your mistakes can contribute to high self-esteem. Employers want employees who act with enthusiasm and who are assertive but not arrogant. Being assertive helps you get the recognition you deserve.

Section 10.2

Good employees work well with others and handle criticism gracefully and maturely. Employees need to show professionalism at work. Professionalism is handling problems, criticism, and pressures effectively. It includes not being defensive when receiving constructive criticism. Employers do not value employees who gossip. Anger has no place at work. Employees must learn to prevent frustration from becoming anger.

Key Terms and Academic Vocabulary Review

1. Use each of these key terms and academic vocabulary words in a sentence.

Key Terms
- attitude (p. 225)
- self-esteem (p. 226)
- enthusiasm (p. 226)
- assertive (p. 228)
- arrogance (p. 228)
- professionalism (p. 230)
- constructive criticism (p. 231)
- defensive (p. 231)
- gossip (p. 232)

Academic Vocabulary
- perceive (p. 225)
- receptive (p. 225)
- clarity (p. 232)

Review Key Concepts

2. Explain why a positive attitude, high self-esteem, and enthusiasm contribute to career success.

3. Describe ways to think positively, overcome doubt, and deal with mistakes.

4. Describe how to assert yourself on the job.

5. List three effective strategies to handle criticism, pressure, and gossip in the workplace.

6. Identify two ways to manage negative emotions.

Critical Thinking

7. Compare and Contrast Talk to yourself in negative self-talk for 30 seconds, and then switch to positive self-talk for another 30 seconds. How does the negative self-talk affect your self esteem? How does the positive self-talk affect your self-confidence?

8. Evaluate When you are angry, counting to ten can help you calm down and think clearly. What other techniques might accomplish the same goal?

---

8. Other techniques for dealing with anger would be to ask yourself what you are really angry about, and channeling your energy into problem solving using the five-step model: define the problem, decide on possible solutions, evaluate those solutions, make a decision, and take action.

Real-World Skills and Applications

9. Possible sentence for writing: Making lists of your abilities and successes is a good way to build your self-esteem. Possible sentence for thinking: When you act enthusiastically about a project, you are likely to think about it more enthusiastically. Possible sentence for listening: Listening to feedback from managers and coworkers is a good way to learn.

Real-World Skills and Applications

Critical Thinking Skills

9. Evaluating Information Write a sentence for each of the following skills explaining how they can help you to develop a better attitude on the job: writing, thinking, listening.

Interpersonal Skills

10. Participating as a Team Member Abigail, Dara, and Thomas work as a team as cashiers and baggers at a supermarket. All of them are being considered for one new managerial position. Though the three are good friends, Thomas and Dara tell Abigail that they think she is playing up too much to their supervisor by always

complimenting him. Write a paragraph explaining how Abigail should respond to this criticism. Should she change her behavior? Why or why not?

Technology Applications

11. Creating a Reference Letter Use a word-processing program to write a personal reference letter for another student in class. In the letter highlight the student's positive traits and behaviors and illustrate the type of worker the student would be for an employer. Discuss your letter with the student and explain what positive work skills you think this student has.

12. **Discussing an Issue** Organize into groups of four to discuss this situation: What is the difference between sharing helpful information with your coworkers and gossiping? Each person in the group is to offer an opinion while the other members listen respectfully. Then open the discussion with each group member contributing to the discussion. After 15 minutes, select one member of the group to summarize the discussion for the class.

13. **Human Resources Seminar**
Situation You are part of a human resources team for your company. Recently, several employees have come to you with problems ranging from not enjoying their work environment to fearing that a supervisor is making a number of mistakes on a project. One employee has complained that he puts in long hours to complete his work, but his supervisor receives the credit. Another employee who was assigned a new, complex assignment wonders if she can manage.
Activity Working with a three-person team, prepare and run a seminar for the office. Address the concerns of the employees, explaining to them why they feel as they do and how they can manage those feelings. In order to avoid office gossip, you must address these concerns without linking any one employee with a particular problem.
Evaluation Your group will be evaluated based on how well it meets the following performance indicators:
- Demonstrate understanding of the problems and their solutions.
- Present a clear, well-organized, and interesting seminar.
- Discuss the problems in a professional and understanding manner.

ACTIVE LEARNING

12. Summaries should reflect an understanding that gossip hurts others while sharing helpful information is useful when doing your job. In the discussions, make sure that students listen to the speakers respectfully.

ROLE PLAY

13. Students should use this as an opportunity to address the challenges of professionalism in the office and to behave in a professional manner themselves. Presentations should address all employee concerns mentioned, provide effective solutions to the problems, be well organized, and be presented in a professional manner.

10. Students should be aware that Thomas and Dara may not be objective critics. They are competing with Abigail for a position, so it might be in Thomas and Dara's interest for Abigail to look bad. Abigail should continue to practice assertiveness while trying to be a good team member.

11. Letters should highlight the student's positive traits and behaviors and illustrate the type of worker the student would be. Encourage letter writers to include specific examples of how the student demonstrates the traits and behaviors that are being highlighted. Reference letters should conform to proper letter formatting.

14. Students' posters should show up-to-date findings and recommendations regarding the long-term effects of negative job attitude and work-related stress and anger on a person's health.

15. Veronica took seven minutes, 50 seconds to run the mile (2:05 + 1:53 + 2:03 + 1:49 = 7:50).

16. About five salmon would return (5,000 x .001 = 5.

17. Charts should include the demographics changes of gender and cultural diversity.

Academic Skills in the Workplace

English Language Arts

14. Define Stress Management Research in the library or on the Internet to find out what long-term effects a negative job attitude and work-related stress and anger can have on a person's health. What do doctors recommend to prevent these health risks? Create a poster reporting your findings.

Mathematics

15. Calculate Time Exercising every day helps Veronica maintain a positive attitude at school and at work. Yesterday, she went to the track near her house and ran one mile. The track is exactly one quarter of a mile in length and her splits for each lap were as follows (in minutes and seconds): 2:05, 1:53, 2:03, and 1:49. How long did Veronica take to run one mile?

CONCEPT **Adding Up Time** When you add time, remember that there are 60 seconds in a minute and 60 minutes in an hour. Carry a number when the ten seconds place or the ten minutes place reaches 6.

Starting Hint Add the times, remembering to carry a one to the minutes place when the ten seconds place reaches 6.

Science

16. Populations and Ecosystems A positive attitude can help you overcome hurdles and achieve your goals. One species that overcomes a lot of hurdles to reach its goal is the salmon. A typical female wild salmon will produce around 5,000 eggs when they spawn in a freshwater river. Salmon migrate out of the river, live in the ocean for a few years, then migrate many miles back up the river they were born in to spawn again. Due to predators, fishing, and other hazards, only about 0.1% of the salmon born in a river actually make it back to spawn. If a female salmon spawned 5,000 eggs, about how many of these would return?

Starting Hint Multiply the number of eggs (5,000) by 0.001 (0.1%) to calculate the number of salmon returning.

Social Studies

17. Research Workplace Diversity Use library or Internet sources to research the changing demographics of the U.S. workplace. Demographics are characteristics of human population. Create a chart that illustrates some change in workplace diversity from the year 2000 to the present.

STANDARDIZED TEST PRACTICE

OPEN-ENDED RESPONSE

Directions Write one or two sentences to answer the following questions.

Test-Taking Tip Open-ended test questions are often looking for a specific response rather than an opinion. These may include definitions, comparisons, or examples.

1. How does assertiveness differ from arrogance?

2. Describe two strategies for managing anger.

3. What is constructive criticism? Give an example.

STANDARDIZED TEST PRACTICE

Answers

1. Assertiveness is being direct; arrogance is being self-important.

2. Strategies for managing anger include counting to ten, considering what you are really angry about, and channeling your energy into problem solving instead of anger.

3. Constructive criticism is criticism presented in a way that helps one learn and grow. For example, instead of blaming someone for answering the wrong question, one can encourage the person to make sure he or she knows which question to answer.

Essay Questions Tell students that organization matters when writing essays. Having an introductory statement and then supporting it with facts is a useful strategy.

Writing Skills Practice

18. Expository Writing In expository writing, your goal is to explain a topic to your reader. You can use steps to explain a process and examples to reinforce your subject.

 Practice Imagine a new employee has started at the company where you work, and this is his or her first job. Write a two-page report detailing the advice you would give the new employee on his or her first day. Use these terms in your report: attitude, self-esteem, enthusiasm, assertiveness, arrogance, professionalism, constructive criticism, defensiveness, and gossip.

- Before you write, make an outline of the topics you would like to write about.
- Remember your own first day on the job. What was helpful for you to learn? What did you not learn that would have been helpful?
- Remember to include important details that would be useful to a new employee.

Net Connection

19. Investigate Your Dream Job Interview someone who holds a job you would like to have. Ask this person if he or she has to cope with any of the attitude difficulties discussed in the chapter. Find out what strategies help this person maintain a positive attitude at work.

@ **Log On** Go to this book's OLC through **glencoe.com** to find a link to the *Occupational Outlook Handbook*. Look up three different jobs you would enjoy. Find out what you would have to do on a typical day at the job. Would you still enjoy the jobs?

 Reading Connection

@ Go to this book's Online Learning Center through **glencoe.com** for a list of reading suggestions.

Personal Academic and Career Portfolio

Observing Attitude

Use your **Personal Academic and Career Portfolio** to document observations on how one person's attitude can affect other people. For the next three days, observe the interaction between students and teachers in two of your classes. Pay attention to the teacher and the class and how the attitude of one person can affect those of another person. Record your observations in a one-page report and include the report in your **Personal Academic and Career Portfolio**. Use the following guidelines to help you:

- Observe how each teacher opens the class. Is the mood upbeat? Does the teacher generate enthusiasm?
- Observe the teacher's mood. Does the teacher appear to be happy? Stressed? Confident?
- Observe how the students react to the teacher. Do the students respond to questions? Do students appear bored? Excited? Respectful?
- Notice how the teacher interacts with the students. Does the teacher walk through the classroom?
- Observe how the teacher treats students. Are students treated with respect and encouraged to interact?
- After class, record key observations in a notebook. Then expand your notes into a draft of your report.

 Portfolio Help Go to the *Succeeding in the World of Work* OLC through **glencoe.com** for help developing your portfolio.

Writing Skills Practice

18. Two-page reports will vary, but students' advice should cover the following topics: attitude, self-esteem, enthusiasm, assertiveness, arrogance, professionalism, constructive criticism, and gossip.

19. Interviews will vary, but the subject matter should include ways to maintain a positive attitude at work. Questions may address anger management, growing with one's work, and ways to foster teamwork.

Resources

 ExamView Assessment Suite CD allows you to print out ready-made unit and chapter tests complete with answer keys. You can also create customized tests.

WorkKeys

WorkKeys® is a job skills assessment program. For information on leveled assessment for Communication Skills (Business Writing; Listening; Reading for Information; and Writing), go to the WorkKeys link on this book's OLC through **glencoe.com**.

Personal Academic and Career Portfolio

Updating a Portfolio

Tell students that their **Personal Academic and Career Portfolios** will always be a work in progress. As their circumstances, skills, interests, and lifestyles change, the content of their portfolios should be updated. Suggest that as new projects overlap with their old projects, they will be able to upgrade the examples of their work. Let them know that they should consider creating a range of work that shows various skills and abilities. They should also consider customizing their portfolio to meet the needs of their interviewers. For example, an Internet company might be more interested in seeing examples of digital design than a magazine publisher would.

Chapter Resources Planning Guide with Activities and Features

Section	Features	Activities
Section 11.1 Becoming a Healthy Worker	Real-World Connection (p. 244) Creative Business Practices (p. 246) Science in Action (p. 247)	Before You Read (p. 242) Graphic Organizer (p. 242) As You Read (p. 244) After You Read (p. 247)
Section 11.2 Safety and Wellness on the Job	Tech Savvy (p. 250) 21st Century Workplace (p. 252) Hot Jobs! (p. 252) Everyday Ethics (p. 254) Career Checklist (p. 255)	Before You Read (p. 248) Graphic Organizer (p. 248) As You Read (p. 253) After You Read (p. 255)

NCLB Activities, information, and skills practice will help your students attain No Child Left Behind proficiency. Students will improve their abilities in the following academic standards areas:

Academic Standards Correlations

Discipline	Standard	Feature/Activity
English Language Arts	**NCTE 1** Read texts to acquire new information.	Creative Business Practices (p. 246) Tech Savvy (p. 250)
	NCTE 4 Use written language to communicate effectively.	After You Read (p. 247) Writing Skills Practice (p. 261)
	NCTE 7 Conduct research and gather, evaluate, and synthesize data to communicate new discoveries.	21st Century Workplace (p. 252)
	NCTE 8 Use information resources to gather information and create and communicate knowledge.	Real-World Connection (p. 244)
	NCTE 12 Use language to accomplish individual purposes.	Academic Skills in the Workplace (p. 260)
Mathematics	**Number and Operation:** Understand meanings of operations and how they relate to one another	After You Read (p. 255)
	Number and Operation: Build mathematical knowledge through problem solving	Academic Skills in the Workplace (p. 260)
Science	**Unifying Concepts and Processes:** Constancy, change, and measurement	Science in Action (p. 247)
	Life Science: Matter, energy, and organization in living systems	Academic Skills in the Workplace (p. 260)
	Science in Personal and Social Perspectives: Personal and community health	entire chapter (pp. 240–261)

21st Century Skills and Workplace Competencies Correlations

CORRELATIONS The charts show the 21st Century Skills, foundation skills, and workplace competencies that students develop as they work in this chapter.

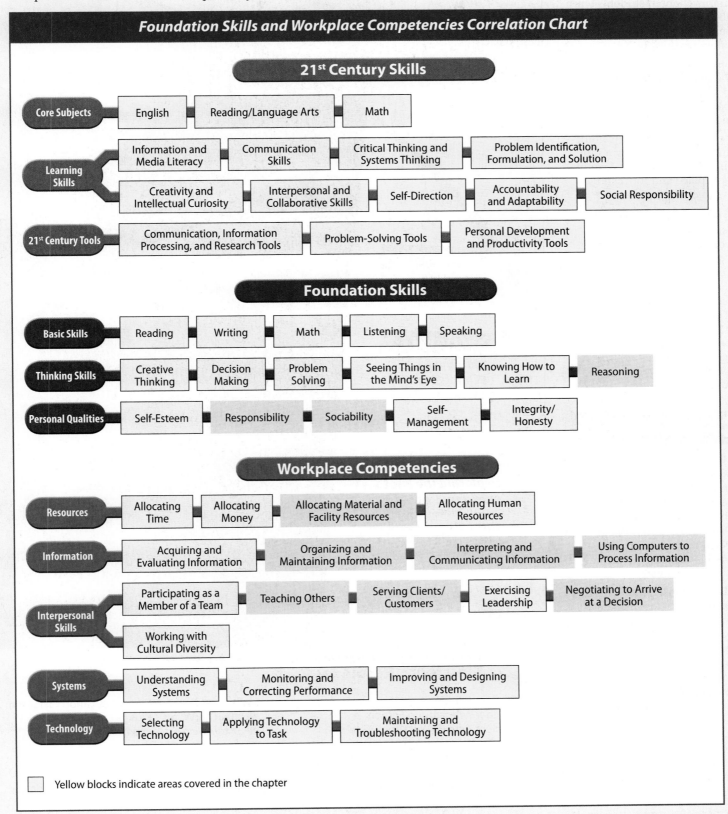

Foundation Skills and Workplace Competencies Correlation Chart

21st Century Skills

Core Subjects: English | Reading/Language Arts | Math

Learning Skills: Information and Media Literacy | Communication Skills | Critical Thinking and Systems Thinking | Problem Identification, Formulation, and Solution | Creativity and Intellectual Curiosity | Interpersonal and Collaborative Skills | Self-Direction | Accountability and Adaptability | Social Responsibility

21st Century Tools: Communication, Information Processing, and Research Tools | Problem-Solving Tools | Personal Development and Productivity Tools

Foundation Skills

Basic Skills: Reading | Writing | Math | Listening | Speaking

Thinking Skills: Creative Thinking | Decision Making | Problem Solving | Seeing Things in the Mind's Eye | Knowing How to Learn | Reasoning

Personal Qualities: Self-Esteem | Responsibility | Sociability | Self-Management | Integrity/Honesty

Workplace Competencies

Resources: Allocating Time | Allocating Money | Allocating Material and Facility Resources | Allocating Human Resources

Information: Acquiring and Evaluating Information | Organizing and Maintaining Information | Interpreting and Communicating Information | Using Computers to Process Information

Interpersonal Skills: Participating as a Member of a Team | Teaching Others | Serving Clients/Customers | Exercising Leadership | Negotiating to Arrive at a Decision | Working with Cultural Diversity

Systems: Understanding Systems | Monitoring and Correcting Performance | Improving and Designing Systems

Technology: Selecting Technology | Applying Technology to Task | Maintaining and Troubleshooting Technology

Yellow blocks indicate areas covered in the chapter

Chapter Overview
Introduce the Chapter

In this chapter, students learn about factors that affect their personal health and their safety on the job.

Section 11.1 focuses on the major components of physical health—diet, exercise, sleep, and stress management.

Section 11.2 presents guidelines for maintaining a safe and environmentally friendly workplace and for responding to emergencies.

Build Background

Tell students to write the words *health* and *work* on a piece of paper. How does work affect a person's health, and how does a person's health affect his or her work? (The demands of work can affect a person's physical and mental health. A person's health, meanwhile, directly contributes to the ability to do a good job at work.)

Exploring the Photo

Caption Answer
Common workplace safety measures include safety equipment such as hard hats and masks, rules on handling and storing chemicals, safety training, and regular equipment maintenance and repair.

Discussion Ask students to name some possible safety hazards that workers at a construction site might face, and discuss how they could prevent them. (Students might mention falling from heights, operating heavy machinery, or being struck by debris. Hardhats and sturdy boots, thorough knowledge of safety practices, and clear hazard communication are ways to prevent injuries.)

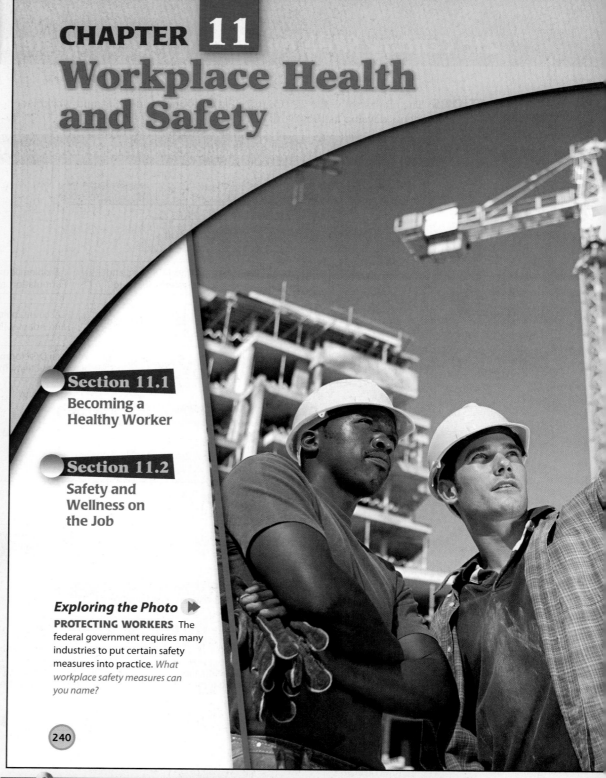

CHAPTER 11
Workplace Health and Safety

Section 11.1
Becoming a Healthy Worker

Section 11.2
Safety and Wellness on the Job

Exploring the Photo ▶▶

PROTECTING WORKERS The federal government requires many industries to put certain safety measures into practice. *What workplace safety measures can you name?*

240

Classroom Resources

- 📁 Student Edition
- 📁 Teacher Wraparound Edition
- 📁 Student Activity Workbook with Academic Integration
- 📁 Student Activity Workbook with Academic Integration TAE
- 📁 *Fast File,* Unit 4 Resources

- 📁 Inclusion in the Career Education Classroom
- 💿 TeacherWorks™ Plus
- 💿 *ExamView Assessment Suite*
- 💿 Interactive Chalkboard
- 💿 Interactive Student Edition
- 📶 Online Student Edition
- 📶 Online Learning Center (OLC) with Podcasts

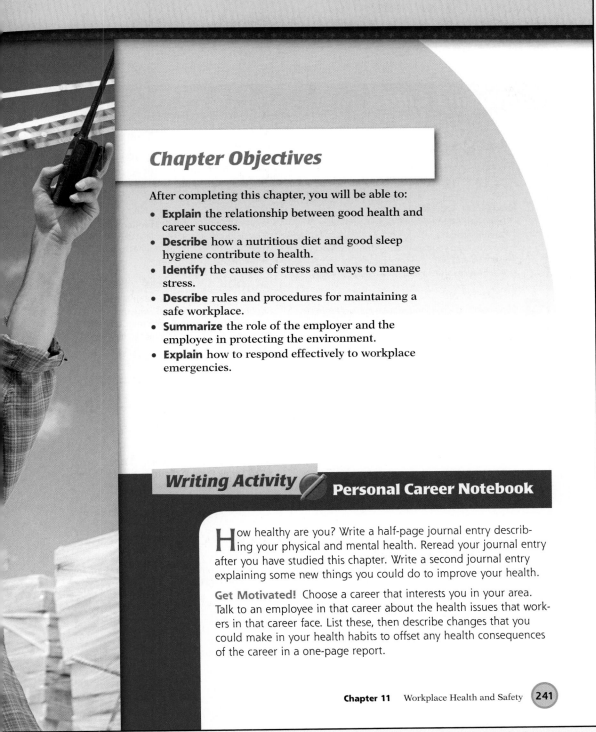

Chapter Objectives

After completing this chapter, you will be able to:

- **Explain** the relationship between good health and career success.
- **Describe** how a nutritious diet and good sleep hygiene contribute to health.
- **Identify** the causes of stress and ways to manage stress.
- **Describe** rules and procedures for maintaining a safe workplace.
- **Summarize** the role of the employer and the employee in protecting the environment.
- **Explain** how to respond effectively to workplace emergencies.

Writing Activity — Personal Career Notebook

How healthy are you? Write a half-page journal entry describing your physical and mental health. Reread your journal entry after you have studied this chapter. Write a second journal entry explaining some new things you could do to improve your health.

Get Motivated! Choose a career that interests you in your area. Talk to an employee in that career about the health issues that workers in that career face. List these, then describe changes that you could make in your health habits to offset any health consequences of the career in a one-page report.

Review the Objectives
Introduce the chapter by reviewing the chapter objectives:

Section 11.1 Objectives
Explain the relationship between good health and career success. (Career success is dependent on good health because good health provides the physical and mental energy you need to give your best at work and pursue your goals.)

Describe how a nutritious diet and good sleep hygiene contribute to health. (A nutritious diet gives you the nutrients necessary for a healthy body. Good sleep hygiene helps you feel alert.)

Identify the causes of stress and ways to manage stress. (Stress is a natural reaction to conflict, which comes in different forms. Managing stress involves dealing with the causes of stress and using stress-management techniques.)

Section 11.2 Objectives
Describe rules and procedures for maintaining a safe workplace. (OSHA, employers, and employees work together to follow laws and regulations that ensure a safe workplace.)

Summarize the role of the employer and the employee in protecting the environment. (Employers and employees can protect the environment by following all laws and reducing pollution and resource use.)

Explain how to respond effectively to workplace emergencies. (Be prepared, learn the steps in the company's emergency action plan, and follow the check-call-care model.)

Writing Activity — Personal Career Notebook Answer Guide

Students should evaluate their health across a variety of factors, including diet, exercise, sleep, and stress (and other mental health issues). Most people could improve their health by reducing fat and salt in their diet, getting more exercise and rest, and finding more and better ways to handle stress.

Get Motivated! Reports will vary depending on the career they choose. Some careers have high rates of on-the-job injuries and illnesses that can be offset by staying healthy and following safety procedures. Other jobs involve sitting for most of the day, which can be offset through regular exercise, breaks, and varying tasks as much as possible.

Section 11.1

FOCUS

Becoming a Healthy Worker

🔔 Bell Ringer Activity

Becoming a Healthy Worker

Ask students to draw a large pie chart containing four pieces with the title "A Healthy Lifestyle." Ask students to label the pieces nutrition, exercise, sleep, and stress management. In each piece, have students write three things they do to lead a healthy life. Discuss students' ideas. (Responses may include eating vegetables, fruits, and whole grains, participating in sports, getting eight hours of sleep each night, and finding time to relax.)

Resources

⊙ Interactive Chalkboard
The Interactive Chalkboard CD provides visual teaching aids for this section.

@ Online Learning Center
The Online Learning Center (OLC) through **glencoe.com** features chapter vocabulary, chapter summaries, and other study materials.

Preteaching

Write the key terms for Section 11.1 on the board. Ask students to find the definitions of the terms in the text.

Graphic Organizer

Tell students to go to the OLC through **glencoe.com** for a printable graphic organizer. (Graphic organizers should include at least one item each relating to diet, exercise, rest, and stress.)

242

Reading Guide

Before You Read

Preview Look at the photo and figure in this section and read their captions. Write one or two sentences predicting what the section will be about.

Read to Learn
- The relationship between good health and career success
- Ways to keep yourself healthy through diet, exercise, and rest
- What causes stress and how to manage stress

D Main Idea
Good health is a solid foundation for success in life and in the workplace.

Key Concepts
- Health and Success
- Care for Your Body
- Manage Your Stress

Key Terms
◇ nutrients
◇ MyPyramid
◇ addiction
◇ sedentary
◇ sleep hygiene
◇ depression

Academic Vocabulary
You will find these words in your reading and on your tests. Use the academic vocabulary glossary to look up their definitions if necessary.
■ mental   ■ genes

Graphic Organizer
Create an idea wheel. Draw a small circle in the center of a piece of paper and write the words "To Do for My Health" inside. As you read, add spokes to your wheel that contain specific things you can do for your health.

Follow MyPyramid Guidelines

To Do for My Health

 Log On Go to this book's Online Learning Center through **glencoe.com** for an online version of this graphic organizer.

Academic Standards •

English Language Arts
- Read texts to acquire new information. (NCTE 1)
- Use written language to communicate effectively. (NCTE 4)
- Use information resources to gather information and create and communicate knowledge. (NCTE 8)

Science
- Unifying Concepts and Processes: Constancy, change, and measurement

N C L B

Reading Guide

Before You Read
Explain to students that their health affects not only the quality of their personal life, but the quality of their work life, too. Why? Being healthy can give them the energy and mental focus they need to be a good employee and can keep them from being sidelined by injury or illness.

D Develop Concepts
Main Idea Discuss the main idea with students. Ask: How do you define being "healthy"? Is health just about physical strength, or is it something more? (Students should recognize that health is a broad concept that includes all aspects of physical and mental well-being, from physical fitness to a positive and resilient mental state.)

Health and Success

R
Good health means having **mental** and physical strength and energy. It also means being free of pain and illness. Good health is a solid foundation for life success. Good health is so important to career success that many employers pay a large portion of their employees' medical, dental, and vision care.

Your **genes** influence your health. Your genes may make you more likely to develop or resist certain illnesses. However, your choices influence your health even more. You can choose to practice good hygiene and to get regular physical and dental checkups. You can also choose to control these three powerful health tools: diet, exercise, and rest.

Eat Wisely and Guard Against Addiction

A healthy diet gives you the energy and stamina you need to succeed in your career. A healthy diet is high in **nutrients**, the substances in food that the body needs to produce energy and stay healthy.

Check for the nutrients you need in **Figure 11.1**. This figure shows **MyPyramid**, a guideline created by the U.S. Department of Health and Human Services to show us the nutrients and other things we

▶ **Vocabulary**
You can find definitions in the **Key Terms** glossary and **Academic Vocabulary** glossary at the back of this book.

Figure 11.1 MYPYRAMID

Grains Make half your grains whole.	Vegetables Vary your veggies.	Fruits Focus on fruits.	Oils	Milk Get your calcium-rich foods.	Meat & Beans Go lean with protein.

Know the limits on fats, sugars, and salt.

Food Groups	Female 14–17 years	Male 14 years	Male 15 years	Male 16–17 years
Grains	6 ounces	8 ounces	9 ounces	10 ounces
Vegetables	2.5 cups	3 cups	3.5 cups	3.5 cups
Fruits	2 cups	2 cups	2 cups	2.5 cups
Milk	3 cups	3 cups	3 cups	3 cups
Meat & Beans	5.5 ounces	6.5 ounces	6.5 ounces	7 ounces

Source: USDA

STAYING HEALTHY The portion amounts shown here are those recommended for 14- to 17-year-olds who exercise 30 to 60 minutes a day. *Why is exercise included in MyPyramid calculations?*

Chapter 11 Workplace Health and Safety **243**

Section 11.1

TEACH

Discussion Starter
Health and Success Ask students: What role does health play in success? Is physical and mental health an important part of being successful? Why or why not? (Opinions will vary, but students should understand that poor physical and mental health can make career and financial success difficult to obtain.)

R **Reading Strategy**
Recognizing Health Factors Ask students what factors they think influence their health. Do inheritance and environment determine their health, or can personal choices make a difference? Ask students to compare their opinions to the information presented in the text. (Students' opinions will vary; the text states that both genes and personal choices influence health, with choices having the larger impact.)

Resources

⊙ **TeacherWorks™ Plus** The TeacherWorks software includes customizable built-in lesson plans and links to printable program resources.

EXTEND THE FIGURE **Figure 11.1**

Caption Answer MyPyramid shows a model for staying healthy, and exercise is a vital part of staying healthy. Exercise also burns calories and therefore affects recommended portions.

Discussion Help students visualize what the measurements in the figure mean. For example, explain that six ounces of grains equals about two modest servings of pasta or four or five slices of sandwich bread. Ask students to estimate how many apples, peaches, or pears add up to two cups (two baseball-sized fruits) and how they could get six ounces of protein (one chicken breast and one bean burrito).

TEACH (cont.)

S Skill Practice
Guided Practice

Survey Your Diet Have students work in groups of three or four to survey one another about what they ate the day before and what they have eaten so far today. Have students compare these foods to the guidelines in MyPyramid to see whether they are getting enough nutrients. **L1**

Assess Your Health Ask students to list ten adjectives that describe their health. Then ask them to complete these statements: "When I wake up in the morning, I generally feel…" and "I would say that my diet is…" Have students look over their responses and write a paragraph describing whether they need to improve their health habits. **L2**

Research Diet and Disease The text states that getting enough nutrients helps ward off disease. Ask students to interview a doctor or nurse or do online research to determine how good nutrition can help strengthen the immune system. **L3**

As You Read

Employers are concerned with employee drug use because it leads to absenteeism, poor productivity, low morale, and possible accidents on the job.

✓ Reading Check

SUMMARIZE You can make sure you are eating a healthy diet by following the guidelines in MyPyramid. Choose fresh unprocessed foods and eat small amounts of fat, sugar, and salt.

244

Real-World Connection

On the Menu

Maria's supervisor has been put in charge of food for the employee retreat next week. Maria has just heard her talking to the caterers and did not hear her mention that some of the employees who will be attending are diabetic, and one is vegetarian.

Critical Thinking Should Maria bring this information to her supervisor's attention, call the caterer herself, or do nothing?

Do Your Own Research Research common foods that a diabetic should avoid. Determine the possible medical consequences of eating these foods. Plan a lunch menu and an afternoon snack that will be acceptable for all employees.

As You Read

Infer Why might employers be concerned about employee drug use?

---

need for good health. MyPyramid also shows foods that we should consume in moderation. Nutrients include carbohydrates, sugars, fats, vitamins, minerals, and fiber, as well as adequate water. A healthy diet is high in vitamins, minerals, and fiber and low in fat, sugar, and salt. Getting enough nutrients boosts your energy, helps prevent disease, and improves your appearance and job performance. Because each person has slightly different needs, the recommendations differ according to a person's age, gender, and activity level. Are you meeting your nutritional needs?

Plan Your Diet

The quality of your diet depends on both internal and external factors. Internal factors include knowledge, planning, and effort. External factors include the price and availability of healthy food in your home and community.

Eating well takes commitment. Shop where you can get healthy food, and plan your meals ahead of time so that you will not be tempted by low-nutrient convenience foods. Learn to read nutrition labels, and always check them before you buy food. Eat moderate portions and choose foods low in salt, sugar, and fat. Eat a wide variety of foods. Check the foods you eat each day against MyPyramid to make sure you are getting all the nutrients you need.

S

Guard Against Addiction

Another important part of nourishing yourself is avoiding substances that can cause addiction. **Addiction** is a physical or psychological need for a substance. Both legal and illegal drugs can be addictive. Addiction can lead to physical and mental health problems, including depression, heart disease, liver disease, and even death.

Addiction does not have to be severe or illegal to cause problems. For example, many people rely on the caffeine in coffee to stay alert at work. The caffeine causes trouble sleeping, so they wake up tired and have to drink more coffee the next day in order to be alert.

At work, addiction can cause injuries, absenteeism, and poor productivity at work. Many companies have established *drug-testing programs* to detect illegal drug use. Some companies might test you when you apply for a job; others have a policy of testing employees periodically. Companies are not likely to hire job applicants who test positive for drugs. Employees who test positive for drugs may lose their jobs or be referred to counseling and treatment.

✓ Reading Check SUMMARIZE How can you make sure you are eating a healthy diet?

Real-World Connection

Critical Thinking Answer Mary might go to the supervisor and ask to discuss the company retreat. Volunteering to follow up with the caterer could be an option. It is also possible that these employees have already made their dietary constraints known to the supervisor and have their own meal plans.

Do Your Own Research In general people with type 2 diabetes should eat diets low in saturated fat and should avoid sugary foods and large servings of simple carbohydrates.

Care for Your Body

You can care for your body with exercise and sleep. Exercise takes energy, but it also gives back energy. Exercise helps you build strength and endurance, feel mentally alert, and be more productive. It increases your lifespan, and reduces tension and anxiety. Exercise is particularly important if you have a sedentary job. **Sedentary** means requiring much sitting or not physically active.

You only need to exercise 30 to 60 minutes a day to get in good shape. Choose any form of exercise: dancing, basketball, yoga, or walking. Try to combine exercise that gets your heart pumping with exercise that builds flexibility and muscle strength.

Recharge Yourself with Sleep

Sleep restores your body and recharges your mind and mood. Almost everyone needs about seven to eight hours of sleep a night. Some people need nine or ten hours.

Many people struggle to find enough time for work, school, home, family, and friends. So they cut back on sleep. Unfortunately, too little sleep can make you irritable and cause difficulty concentrating. It can make you more likely to get sick or cause an accident. Everything seems harder when you do not sleep enough.

Practice Sleep Hygiene

Sleep hygiene is the practice of following good sleep habits to sleep soundly and be alert during the day. To get a good night's sleep, try to go to bed about the same time every night and get up at the same time each day, even on weekends. Try to avoid caffeine-rich foods and drinks, such as chocolate and caffeinated sodas, after noon. Make your bedroom as dark and quiet as possible. Create some quiet time before bed to relax with something calming, such as reading. Making a to-do list for the next day helps many people relax, because then they do not worry about what they have to do.

✓ **Reading Check** **DESCRIBE** How do exercise and sleep help you succeed in your career?

▶ **KEEP MOVING**
Exercising 30 to 60 minutes a day will help to keep you healthy and fit. *How can exercise make you a better worker?*

TEACH *(cont.)*

S **Skill Practice**
Independent Practice
Make an Exercise Plan Ask students to create personal exercise plans that include at least 30 to 60 minutes of exercise each day. Have them use a weekly planner or photocopied page from a monthly calendar to schedule the times they will exercise. (Students' plans will vary. Remind students that they can break up their exercise into small blocks throughout the day.)

✓ **Reading Check**

DESCRIBE Exercise and sleep help you succeed in your career because they give you the mental and physical energy to be alert, think clearly, and focus on your job all day.

ASSESS

Review Key Terms
Have students write sentences using each key term.

Online Study Tools
Have students go to the OLC through **glencoe.com** to:
- Download **Podcast** study tools.
- Download free **Study-to-Go** content to their PDAs or cell phones.

Resources

 ExamView Assessment Suite CD allows you to print out ready-made unit and chapter tests complete with answer keys. You can also create customized tests.

▶ ***Extend the Photo***

Caption Answer Exercise makes you a better worker because it gives you the physical and mental alertness, energy, and stamina to focus throughout the workday.

Discussion Ask students to imagine that they work eight hours a day at a full-time job. Ask:

How can you fit an hour of exercise every day into your busy schedule? (Answers will vary; students may mention walking to work, going to the gym during their lunch hour, or joining a sports team or exercise class.)

RETEACH

S **Skill Practice**
Independent Practice
Plan for Deadlines Ask students to imagine that they have a large writing assignment due in one week. They are feeling stressed. Have students write a paragraph describing what can they do to manage their stress. (Answers will vary, but should mention the importance of making a plan and getting started on the assignment right away.) **L1**

Take a Survey Ask students to survey four working adults about what causes them the most stress, both on the job and in their personal lives, and how they deal with the causes of stress. Have students write and word-process a summary of their findings. (Answers might include financial pressures, balancing work and family, or deadlines and responsibilities at work. Coping strategies will also vary.) **L2**

Harness Positive Stress Ask students to research and describe the difference between positive and negative stress. Have students summarize their findings in two paragraphs, giving examples from their own lives of the benefits of positive stress. (Summaries will vary but should explain that positive stress can enhance performance and alertness.) **L3**

Resources

📁 **Student Activity Workbook** Assign the Chapter 11 activities in the Student Activity Workbook.

Manage Your Stress

To feel well, you need to pay attention to your mental health as well as your physical health. Learning to manage stress helps you stay mentally healthy. Stress is a natural reaction to conflict. During stress, your heart rate and breathing accelerate, your muscles tighten, and your blood pressure climbs. In the short term, these effects can be positive because they help you focus more clearly and act more decisively. When the challenge is over, your body returns to normal.

S Stress becomes negative when your body does not return to normal but stays in an unnecessary state of alertness. This can cause irritability, sleeplessness, chest pain, and headaches. Severe stress can even lead to heart disease, cancer, and depression. **Depression** is severe, ongoing sadness and hopelessness that makes it difficult to go about your daily life. About ten percent of the American population suffers from some form of depression each year.

An estimated one million workers are absent on an average workday due to stress-related complaints. Stress on the job is estimated to cost U.S. industry $300 billion per year in accidents, absenteeism, and diminished productivity.

Beware of Burnout and Depression

When stress goes on for weeks and months, it can cause *burnout*—a state of feeling exhausted, powerless, resentful, and no longer interested in your work.

Creative Business Practices

NORTHWESTERN MUTUAL

Promoting Good Health

Northwestern Mutual Life Insurance Company encourages employees to make healthy lifestyle choices. The company's commitment to employee health started more than 20 years ago, when it began paying employees' health club memberships. Today, the company headquarters in Milwaukee has its own fitness center, complete with exercise machines and weight-training equipment. Almost half of the 4,400 home-office employees work in Milwaukee. Other employees exercise at outside gyms, where memberships are paid for by the company.

Northwestern Mutual regularly offers their employees medical tests to evaluate health, such as tests for high blood pressure. The company also provides programs to help employees lose weight and reduce stress.

CRITICAL THINKING How do you think a healthy worker benefits an employer?

 Connect to the Real World To read more about Northwestern Mutual, visit the company's Web site via the link on this book's Online Learning Center through **glencoe.com**.

Creative Business Practices

CRITICAL THINKING ANSWER Healthy workers benefit employers because they are more productive, miss work less often, get along better with coworkers, and reduce employers' health care costs.

To avoid burnout, you need to take care of yourself mentally and physically. Give yourself good nutrition, regular exercise, and enough sleep. If you notice any symptoms of depression, such as severe sadness or anxiety, see your doctor right away.

Tackle Your Stress

The best way to deal with stress is to identify what causes stress for you and then deal with the causes directly. Overwork and unclear instructions can often cause stress at work. Asking your supervisor to clarify and prioritize your tasks is a good first step. If the problem is a personal conflict, you may consider talking to the person directly to try to work out a solution. Many employers have human resources workers or even counselors who can help you solve a workplace problem.

Here are three widely used stress-management techniques:

- **Deep Breathing** Focusing on your breath has a calming effect. Breathe in and out slowly, both to a count of ten.
- **Visualization** Close your eyes and picture yourself in a calm place—for example, resting on a beach or under a tree.
- **Taking a Time-Out** Get away from a pressure-packed situation for a few minutes—for example, take a walk outside. When you return, you may see solutions you did not see before.

Reducing stress helps you be more productive, feel more satisfied with your job, and enjoy greater well-being. Handling stress is also a leadership skill: Only people who can manage themselves can lead others effectively.

Science In Action

Modes
A wildlife biologist measures the top speed of 8 cheetahs and comes up with the following data set in terms of kilometers per hour: [60, 65, 70, 65, 58, 65, 60, 65]. What is the mode of this data set?

Starting Hint: A mode is the number in set of data that shows up the most often.

 For more science practice, go to this book's OLC through **glencoe.com**.

Section 11.1 After You Read

Review Key Concepts
1. Explain how being healthy can help you succeed in your career.
2. Name three things you can do to keep yourself healthy.
3. Teo is generally a good worker, but whenever he is assigned to work with Sheila, who is extremely critical, he becomes so stressed that he makes a mistake. Identify two strategies that might help Teo cope with this situation.

Practice Academic Skills

English Language Arts

NCLB
4. Your supervisor, Sue, is in charge of instructing you how to do your work. Unfortunately, she often changes her mind and forgets to tell you. This causes stress, because you have to work overtime to redo your work. Prepare for a meeting with Sue by writing a script that describes the current situation and explains how it is affecting your work, giving specific examples. Include suggestions for improving the situation and explain how your suggestions will improve the quality of your work.

@ Check your answers at this book's OLC through **glencoe.com**.

ASSESS

After You Read
Have students complete the Section 11.1 After You Read section review.

Online Study Tools
Have students go to the OLC through **glencoe.com** to:
- Take the Section 11.1 **Practice Test**.
- Download **Podcast** study tools.
- Download free **Study-to-Go** content to their PDAs or cell phones.

CLOSE

Culminating Activity
Being Proactive About Health Explain to students that the best way to stay healthy is to be proactive—to take action before there is a problem. Ask students to create a chart of the four major topics covered in this section (nutrition, exercise, rest, and stress), listing three ways they can be proactive about caring for their health in each area. (Charts will vary but should include some of the nutritional, exercise, sleep hygiene, and stress-management guidelines presented in the text.)

Science In Action

The mode is 65. It shows up four times, more than any other number.

NCLB Activity correlated to English Language Arts standards.

Section 11.1 After You Read

Review Key Concepts
1. Being healthy gives you the physical and mental energy you need to focus on your career.
2. Answers include eating a healthful, balanced diet; exercising regularly; getting enough good-quality rest; and coping effectively with stress and other mental upset.
3. Students should be able to suggest two strategies from this section and explain how they can help Teo.

Practice Academic Skills
4. Scripts should explain the problem clearly, with examples, and offer suggestions for Sue, which will improve your stress level.

Section 11.2

Safety and Wellness on the Job

Bell Ringer Activity

Safety and Wellness on the Job

Ask students to brainstorm all the safety precautions or equipment they have seen at home, school, or work. Give as an example the orange reflective vests worn by highway workers. (Students might mention road cones, hard hats, airbags, fire extinguishers, and storm windows.)

Resources

Interactive Chalkboard
The Interactive Chalkboard CD provides visual teaching aids for this section.

Online Learning Center
The OLC through **glencoe.com** features chapter vocabulary, chapter summaries, and other study materials.

Preteaching
Assign key terms to student pairs. Have them locate the definitions in the text and present the definitions to the class.

Graphic Organizer
Tell students to go to the OLC through **glencoe.com** for a printable graphic organizer. (Graphic organizers should mention knowing safety regulations, wearing PPE, flagging hazards, and following specific safety precautions.)

Reading Guide

Before You Read

Preview Choose a Key Term or Academic Vocabulary word that is new to you. Write it on a piece of paper. When you find it in the text, write down the definition.

Read to Learn
- Rules and procedures for maintaining a safe workplace
- The role of the employer and the employee in protecting the environment
- How to respond effectively to workplace emergencies

Main Idea
Being aware of rules and procedures that promote workplace safety helps you protect yourself and your coworkers.

Key Concepts
- Workplace Safety
- Ergonomics Makes Work Safer
- Protect the Environment
- Prepare for Emergencies

Log On Go to this book's Online Learning Center through **glencoe.com** for an online version of this graphic organizer.

Key Terms
- Occupational Safety and Health Administration (OSHA)
- workers' compensation
- ergonomics
- musculoskeletal disorders (MSDs)
- Environmental Protection Agency (EPA)
- emergency action plan
- first aid

Academic Vocabulary
You will find these words in your reading and on your tests. Use the academic vocabulary glossary to look up their definitions if necessary.
- revising
- violate

Graphic Organizer
As you read, create a list of actions you can take at work to prevent accidents or emergencies. Use a two-column chart like the one shown to help organize your information.

I can...	To prevent...

Academic Standards

English Language Arts
- Read texts to acquire new information. (NCTE 1)
- Conduct research and gather, evaluate, and synthesize data to communicate discoveries. (NCTE 7)

Mathematics
- Understand meanings of operations and how they relate to one another

Science
- Life Science: Regulation and behavior

Reading Guide

Before You Read
Tell students that every job, no matter how sedentary, carries with it the risk of accident and injury. While governments and employers are responsible for minimizing hazards in the workplace, individual workers also have the responsibility to make sure that they and their coworkers stay safe.

D Develop Concepts
Main Idea Discuss the main idea with students. Ask: What kind of "rules and procedures" do you think exist to promote workplace safety? Why? (Answers may include laws about handling chemicals, operating machinery, and reporting hazards.)

Workplace Safety

Learning about workplace safety and maintaining good working conditions helps you avoid injuries at work. Working conditions include the place you work, the tasks you do, and the hours you work.

Cooperate to Improve Workplace Safety

Workplace accidents cost businesses billions of dollars annually in lost wages, medical expenses, and insurance claims. Government, employers, and workers all cooperate to develop rules and procedures that make workplaces safer.

The Government's Role

The federal government protects American workers by setting workplace safety standards and by making sure that injured workers receive care. The **Occupational Safety and Health Administration (OSHA)** is the branch of the U.S. Department of Labor that sets and enforces job safety standards and inspects job sites. If a company fails to meet OSHA standards, it can face fines and other penalties. Workers can also file a complaint with OSHA if they cannot resolve a safety problem at work. OSHA keeps pace with the world of work by **revising** standards when work conditions change or new technologies are developed.

The government also makes sure that workers are compensated, or paid, if they have experienced a workplace or work-related illness or injury that prevents them from working. **Workers' compensation** is an insurance program that provides financial help to cover lost wages and medical expenses for employees who are injured on the job.

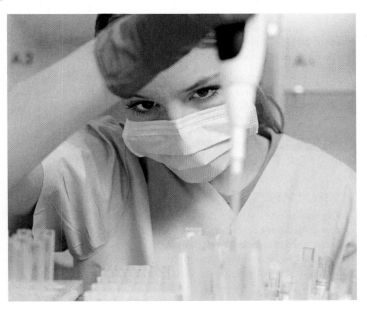

Vocabulary
You can find definitions in the **Key Terms** glossary and **Academic Vocabulary** glossary at the back of this book.

◀◀ WORKPLACE SAFETY
Employers must comply with government safety regulations. *What is this worker doing to ensure her own safety?*

TEACH

Discussion Starter
Workplace Safety Remind students that they are already familiar with one area with many safety laws and regulations—automobile safety. Ask: Who is responsible for automobile safety—the government, automakers, or drivers? (Students should understand that all three parties are responsible for highway safety, although in different ways.)

R Reading Strategy
Make a List Have students read the passage and make a list of five actions OSHA takes to promote workplace safety. (Lists should include setting safety standards, inspecting job sites, fining noncompliant companies, receiving complaints from workers, and revising standards to keep pace with new technologies.)

C Critical Thinking
Drawing Conclusions Tell students that in most states, the workers' compensation system is funded by premiums paid by employers to private and state-run insurance companies. Ask: Do you think it is fair that the law makes employers pay for workers' compensation? Why or why not? (Opinions will vary, but many students may feel that injuries or illnesses caused by workplace conditions should be the employer's financial responsibility.)

Resources

⚙ Interactive Chalkboard
The Interactive Chalkboard CD provides visual teaching aids for this section.

▶▶ Extend the Photo

Caption Answer This person is wearing a safety mask to protect her from inhaling harmful fumes.

Discussion Ask students to share jobs that interest them and have the class brainstorm possible safety risks involved in those jobs. For example, working as a doctor or nurse might involve risks of disease, injury, muscle strain, and so on. (Jobs and risks mentioned will vary, but all jobs carry a risk of accident and injury. Jobs that involve heavy equipment have a particularly high risk.)

TEACH (cont.)

U Universal Access

Logical/Mathematical Learners Have students research the potential health and safety hazards of a career that interests them. Students should list seven hazards and identify specific ways employers can protect employees from each. (Hazards will vary but might include accidents or illnesses. Suggestions will vary but may include safety training and providing proper protective equipment.)

S Skill Practice

Independent Practice
Identify Safety Hazards
Ask students to scrutinize their homes for safety hazards such as loose wires, dull kitchen knives, or uneven floorboards. Have them list the hazards and suggest actions they could take to fix them. (Hazards and suggested actions will vary. Encourage students to think of low- or no-cost ideas, such as keeping exits clear and checking smoke detectors.)
L1

Summarize OSHA Procedures Ask students to contact their regional or area OSHA office to find out how to file a complaint about unsafe conditions. Have them write a paragraph summarizing the complaint process and describing how OSHA follows up on complaints. (OSHA accepts complaints by electronic or paper form. OSHA follows up with an off-site investigation or an on-site inspection.) **L2**

TechSavvy

Low-Tech Ergonomics

Ergonomic tools do not have to be expensive to be effective. Simple adjustments to existing tools can reduce injuries with little cost. Keeping knives sharp, for example, reduces a cook's chances of developing wrist strain. Adding back pillows to chairs can help workers align their spines in a healthy S-curve. Farm workers can reduce their risk of back injury by collecting vegetables in small tubs, which are easy to lift. Janitorial workers can grip and push mops more easily and with less risk of injury by adding an eight-inch push-handle to the end of the tool's shaft.

@ Visit this book's Online Learning Center through **glencoe.com** to learn more about ergonomic tools. Select an existing tool, such as a stapler, keyboard, or broom, and use graphics software to design an improved version of the tool that can help prevent injury.

The Employer's Role

Your employer must make sure your workplace is safe. All employers must:
- Provide a workplace free from known health and accident hazards.
- Provide safety education and training, and communicate safety policies and procedures to workers.
- Provide all necessary *personal protective equipment*, such as helmets and gloves, and teach employees how to use it.
- Inform employees when materials or conditions are hazardous, and post labels or signs to warn employees of potential hazards.
- Keep records of job-related illnesses and injuries.

Your Role

Most accidents and injuries happen through carelessness and occur becuase of human error. For example, a small puddle of water on the floor could cause a fall. Be alert at all times, and follow all of the safety procedures that your employer has explained to you. As a worker, you also must:

- Learn to perform your job safely, and follow all safety instructions.
- Know how to operate, maintain, and troubleshoot tools and equipment safely.
- Wear your personal protective equipment correctly and report any problems with it.
- Report unsafe conditions or practices immediately.
- Read all safety labels and signs, and ask your supervisor if you have any questions or concerns about safety.

If your workplace is not safe, tell your supervisor right away. If your employer does not fix the problem, you have the right to report the problem to OSHA. It is illegal for your employer to take action against you for complaining about a safety issue.

S

✓ **Reading Check** **COMPARE** How does the government's role in work safety differ from the employer's role in work safety?

Ergonomics Makes Work Safer

Ergonomics is the science of designing the workplace to fit the worker. Ergonomic work equipment lets you adjust your workstation and your work movements to your size, your height, and your natural way of moving. Ergonomic equipment also shields you from vibrations and uncomfortable motions, such as twisting and pushing, that can cause injury.

TechSavvy

Low-Tech Ergonomics

Answer Students' redesigned tools will vary but should incorporate design features based on human anatomy and natural movement. For example, a standard stapler could be redesigned to fit the curve of a person's palm and to require less force to operate.

✓ **Reading Check**

COMPARE The government is responsible for creating safety laws and checking workplaces to make sure the laws are followed. The employer, by contrast, is responsible for obeying these laws, providing safety training and equipment, notifying workers of hazards or possible hazards, and keeping safety records.

ERGONOMICS Arranging work tools, including computer keyboards, to minimize stress on muscles helps prevent repetitive stress injury. *Why do you think employers are interested in ergonomic design?*

Ergonomics are helpful in the prevention of both workplace accidents and **musculoskeletal disorders (MSDs)**, which are ailments of the muscles, joints, nerves, tendons, ligaments, or spinal discs caused by forceful or repeated motions. MSDs can cause aching, tingling, numbness, or stiffness in the affected area. MSDs often develop slowly. For example, you could develop tendonitis if your job involves many hours using vibrating hand tools or typing at a computer keyboard. Musculoskeletal disorders are often called *repetitive stress injuries* (RSIs) because they often occur when you repeat the same motion again and again.

Prevent and Treat MSDs

You can minimize your chances of developing MSDs by taking these precautions at work:

- Learn how to use all your work equipment safely to prevent injuries.
- Take frequent short breaks to stretch and walk around.
- Try to maintain a comfortable temperature, ideally between 68° and 72° Fahrenheit, to prevent cramping and stiffness.
- Arrange your workspace so that the tools you use frequently are within easy reach.
- When you work, hold your wrists and neck straight, rather than awkwardly bent or placed.
- If you work at a computer, arrange your monitor at arm's length. Protect your eyes by using a non-glare filter and by tilting the screen so it does not reflect light.

If you experience numbness, swelling, redness or loss of color, or loss of strength or mobility, you may be developing an MSD. Get medical help right away. Conditions may worsen if you ignore the problem and can cause permanent damage to your health. Use a wet ice pack at 38° Fahrenheit or above to reduce the swelling. Your doctor may prescribe rest, stretching, and anti-inflammatory medications to help you recover.

✓ **Reading Check** **EVALUATE** Why would someone who works at a computer be at risk for an MSD?

▶ Extend the Photo

Caption Answer Employers are interested in ergonomic design because it reduces on-the-job injuries and increases productivity.

Discussion Explain to students that frequent or awkward reaching can cause muscle strain.

Ask them how they have their work or study areas arranged. Are they well organized? Are frequently used items within easy reach?

S Skill Practice
Independent Practice
Research PPE Ask students to research and define the term "personal protective equipment" (PPE). Have them use online or print resources to research two types of PPE and then sketch and describe the equipment in a one-page report. (PPE choices and descriptions will vary, but should be based on reliable sources, such as the OSHA Web site.) **L3**

Discussion Starter
Ergonomics Makes Work Safer Explain to students that ergonomically designed tools, chairs, desks, and other equipment makes work more comfortable by conforming to human anatomy and natural motion. Ask students to point out items in the classroom that are ergonomically designed and items that are not. (Common items for analysis might include chairs, tables, pens, scissors, and even doorknobs or window blinds.)

W Writing Support
Independent Practice
Make a Safety Poster Have students use desktop publishing software to design a poster summarizing the recommendations for preventing MSDs. The poster should include a diagram or sketch showing correct posture for computer work.

✓ **Reading Check**

EVALUATE Working at a computer could lead to an MSD because computer work involves repeated motions such as striking keys on a keyboard and using a mouse.

TEACH (cont.)

S Skill Practice
Independent Practice

Understand Environmental Laws Ask students with similar job interests to choose a career cluster and work together to research environmental laws that might affect work in this cluster. For example, laws limiting air and water pollution from factories would apply to the manufacturing career cluster. (Lists will vary, but students should understand that environmental laws, which promote clean air and water, limit toxins, and preserve wildlands, affect most business activity.)

U Universal Access

Gifted Learners Have gifted students work in groups to create a proposal to make their school healthier and more environmentally friendly. Ask them to consider building materials, waste and emissions, energy and water use, and landscaping, and to include cost estimates in their proposal. (Proposals may include suggestions for switching to non-toxic chemicals and building materials, using solar energy, planting shade trees, using compostable packaging in the cafeteria, and so on.)

✓ Reading Check

EXPLAIN Carpooling conserves the resources of gasoline and oil and reduces air and noise pollution. Recycling conserves resources such as steel, paper (from trees), and plastic by returning materials to the production stream to be used again.

N C L B Activity correlated to English Language Arts standards.

252

The 21ˢᵗ Century Workplace

N C L B

A Greener Workplace

Today's businesses realize that using recycled products, encouraging ride shares, and telecommuting are a few easy ways to operate a business that is both profitable and environmentally friendly.

Environmentally-friendly business practices or equipment can actually lower a company's operating costs. Flat-screen computer monitors give out less heat than traditional ones do, and strategic use of air conditioning and fluorescent lighting can cut costs by conserving energy. Using hybrid vehicles for a business may earn that business certain tax breaks and save on fuel costs.

CRITICAL THINKING _____
What are some benefits of operating a "green" business?

In Your Community

Research your local recycling programs. What is done well, and what could be improved? Describe the local programs in a five-minute oral presentation.

@ **Extend Your Learning** What are some environmental workplace trends? For links to Web sites about green business practices, go to this book's OLC through **glencoe.com**.

Protect the Environment

Employers must also follow laws that protect the environment and workers' health. For example, they must dispose of hazardous waste according to strict environmental laws. The **Environmental Protection Agency (EPA)** is the arm of the federal government that enforces environmental laws. If you see any practice that may **violate** an environmental law, you can contact the EPA for advice.

Many employers go beyond what is required by law and design their own workplace programs to make the workplace healthier. For example, some employers use nontoxic building materials, such as zero-emission paint, to make sure that the air workers breathe is healthy. Some manufacturers design cars, computers, and even tennis shoes that can be recycled or reused for parts when they are no longer useful. This reduces the amount of raw materials the company has to buy. It also cuts down on the amount of waste sent to landfills.

Do Your Part to Conserve

What can you do as an employee to protect the environment? Save energy by turning off lights and machines when they are not in use. Know and follow all environmental laws that relate to your work, and let your supervisor know right away if you see a possible violation. Take advantage of any incentives for taking public transportation, or join a ride-share program and carpool to work. Participate in your company's recycling program—or help get one started. Share your ideas for how to make your company's workplace and products healthier.

✓ **Reading Check** **EXPLAIN** How do carpooling and recycling help conserve resources?

HOT JOBS!

Sustainability Specialist

A sustainability specialist helps plan and implement processes that lessen the environmental impact of a business. With a background in engineering or environmental management, the specialist considers such factors as water efficiency, energy use, and indoor environmental quality to research and plan sustainability programs.

The 21ˢᵗ Century Workplace

CRITICAL THINKING ANSWER Benefits of operating a "green" business include good public relations, and in some cases, lower operating costs.

In Your Community Carpooling helps reduce the amount of consumed non-renewable natural resources and recycling helps replenish renewable resource reserves.

Prepare for Emergencies

Your safety and the safety of your coworkers can depend upon your awareness of what to do during an emergency. On your first day of work, learn the location of emergency exits at your workplace and where to assemble once you have reached safety. Give your supervisor and human resources contact the name and phone number of a friend or family member so that they know who to call in an emergency. Sign up for any safety training your company offers.

Have an Emergency Action Plan

An **emergency action plan** describes what you should do to ensure your safety if a workplace emergency occurs. Most emergency action plans discuss common emergencies such as fires, storms, earthquakes, accidents, and medical crises. Look in the plan to find guidelines for the following:

- How to report a safety hazard, fire, chemical spill, or other emergency.
- Where to find emergency supplies, such as a flashlight and first aid kit.
- Who belongs to the emergency response team and where you fit in.
- What escape route to use in an emergency and where to assemble for safety.
- How to evacuate or get help if you have a disability or work with someone who does.
- Who to call for training or if you have questions.

Most companies with ten or more employees are required to have written emergency action plans. Small companies may not have written emergency plans, so you may need to ask your supervisor or human resources about the plan. Write down all the key points and keep your notes handy.

You can also be prepared for an emergency by assembling your own emergency preparedness kit containing first aid supplies, water and nonperishable food, a flashlight, a battery-powered radio, and any medications you may need if you are unable to leave work.

▶ **BE PREPARED** You can ensure your safety and the safety of others by learning safety procedures. *What are some natural disasters that might occur in your area?*

Chapter 11 Workplace Health and Safety **253**

As You Read

Connect How can you find the locations of emergency exits at your workplace?

TEACH *(cont.)*

C Critical Thinking
Clarifying Statements The text states, "Your safety and the safety of your coworkers can depend upon your awareness of what to do during an emergency." Ask students to interpret this statement. Why would their own preparedness affect their coworkers' safety? (In an emergency, prepared workers can help coworkers to safety. Unprepared workers may panic or otherwise hinder their coworkers from responding effectively.)

As You Read

Emergency exits should be clearly marked with exit signs and should be noted on floor plans contained in the company's emergency action plan. Coworkers or managers should also know the location of emergency exits.

ASSESS

Review Key Terms
Have students write sentences using each key term.

Online Study Tools
Have students go to the OLC through **glencoe.com** to:
- Download **Podcast** study tools.
- Download free **Study-to-Go** content to their PDAs or cell phones.

▶▶ *Extend the Photo*

Caption Answer Depending on geographic area, students may mention hurricanes, earthquakes, tornadoes, or other natural disasters. Fires and flooding can occur in any location.

Discussion Ask students to imagine that they start a new job and neither their manager nor their coworkers seems informed about what to do in an emergency. What should they do? (Possibilities include distributing the emergency action plan [or suggesting that one be drawn up] or contacting human resources to ask for training for the department.)

RETEACH

S Skill Practice
Guided Practice

Make a Chart Ask students to make a chart with three columns listing common emergencies and disasters and describing how to prepare for and respond to each. (Lists will vary but should include at minimum the five emergencies listed in the text. Encourage students to add their own ideas.) **L1**

Prevent Fires Ask students to visit or call their local fire station and inquire about the most common causes of fires at workplaces. Have students summarize the top five causes of workplace fires and how they can prevent them. (Students may mention cigarettes, faulty or overloaded wiring, overheated machinery, and arson. Prevention tips include using appliances safely, and being alert to security threats.) **L2**

Apply Technology Ask students to choose a natural disaster that is common in their geographic area and to use print and online resources to research and prepare an action plan for how to deal with such a disaster on the job. Ask students to cite sources. (Plans will vary but should be based on reputable, up-to-date sources.) **L3**

Resources

📁 **Student Activity Workbook** Assign the Chapter 11 activities in the Student Activity Workbook.

Everyday ETHICS

HANDLING STRESS
What is a good way to handle stress?

CUSTOMER SERVICE Lately, a coworker has been rude to other employees and customers at the grocery store where you work. She often leaves early and does not do her share of work. You have been handling the work she leaves behind, and the situation has caused you to have a poor attitude toward your job. When you approach your boss about your coworker's behavior, he says that she is stressed out from problems at home and that she should get better soon.

What Would You Do? How do you respond to your boss's reaction to the situation?

> **DISCUSS IT** In teams, discuss ways to maintain a good attitude while working with a difficult coworker.

Prevent and Respond to Common Emergencies

Find out what kinds of emergencies are most likely to occur in your workplace and how to respond to them. For example, do you work in a geographic area that often experiences floods? Do you work with chemicals that might spill? Being aware and prepared could save your life and the lives of your coworkers and customers.

Floods and Storms Be prepared for floods by learning proper evacuation routes and planning where to find higher ground. The safest place to be during a severe storm, such as a hurricane or tornado, is indoors away from windows.

Earthquakes Prevent injury by bracing heavy equipment and storing bulky or breakable objects on lower shelves. If an earthquake happens when you are inside, stay inside. Move away from windows, brace yourself against an interior wall, and protect your head. If you are outdoors, stand in the open, away from trees, utility poles, and buildings.

Fire Help prevent fires by reporting risky conditions such as overloaded outlets or frayed electrical cords. If a fire breaks out at work, alert your coworkers and leave the building right away via a designated escape route. Report the fire according to your company's emergency management plan—do not fight the flames yourself.

Workplace Violence Violence at work affects more than two million people a year. Help prevent violence by reporting any threats, verbal abuse, intruders, or suspicious behavior right away. Never enter a location if you feel it might be unsafe. If you handle money or work alone or at night, make sure that your workplace is secure.

Hazardous Materials or Chemical Spills If a toxic material spills in your workplace or there is an environmental emergency nearby, alert your coworkers and report the emergency immediately according to your company's emergency action plan. Do not attempt to clean up the spill unless it is your job to handle hazardous materials.

Everyday ETHICS

What Would You Do? Answer Students might suggest talking to the coworker and explaining the consequences of her behavior, citing specific examples. Students might also suggest making a list of specific incidents as they occur, then bringing this list to their manager to convey the seriousness of the situation.

> **DISCUSS IT** Ideas will vary but may include approaching the coworker with specific suggestions for improving the working relationship or turning to a manager or human relations worker for assistance. In serious situations, documenting the coworker's actions may be a good idea.

Master First Aid

Knowing **first aid**, which is emergency care for an injured person, can save lives at work and at home. If you are present when someone has a medical emergency or an accident, follow these emergency action steps developed by the American Red Cross, *Check-Call-Care*:

1. **Check** Calmly survey the scene and make sure that it is safe for you to approach. Figure out what has happened and what may happen next. Check the condition of the victim.
2. **Call** Call out for help. Call 911 or the number listed in your company's emergency action plan. Explain the situation and tell the operator whether the victim has any life-threatening conditions, such as unconsciousness or severe bleeding.
3. **Care** Give basic medical assistance until help arrives. Soothe a burn with cool water, reduce shock by elevating the legs, and control bleeding by covering a wound with a cloth and pressing down firmly. Do not move the victim unless absolutely necessary.

You can be even more prepared for a medical emergency by learning to give rescue breathing and CPR. Businesses or local Red Cross chapters may offer free training.

Career ✓ Checklist

To Ensure Your Health and Safety:

✓ Maintain a clean and clutter-free workspace.
✓ Follow safety equipment and procedures.
✓ Know the safety regulations that apply to the job.
✓ Report any accidents or workplace hazards.
✓ Never place yourself in a position that feels unsafe or uncomfortable.

Section 11.2 After You Read

Review Key Concepts

1. Define OSHA and explain how OSHA benefits workers.
2. Identify ways you can help protect the environment at work.
3. Explain what *Check-Call-Care* means and how it can help you cope in an emergency.

Practice Academic Skills

 Mathematics

4. Two-thirds of an 18-hour safety training program given at your workplace is spent learning about disaster response. How many hours will you spend learning about disaster response?

CONCEPT Multiplying by a Fraction To multiply a whole number by a fraction, multiply the numerator of the fraction by the whole number. Then reduce the fraction if possible, dividing both the new numerator and the denominator by the same number.
Step 1 Set up the problem by writing a multiplication problem with the total number of hours (18) and the fraction of time spent learning about disaster response ($\frac{2}{3}$).
Step 2 Multiply the whole number (18) by the numerator (2). Then divide the numerator and the denominator by three to reduce the fraction to a whole number.

 For math help, go to the Math Appendix located at the back of this book.

NCLB

Review Key Terms
Have students complete the Section 11.2 After You Read section review.

Online Study Tools
Have students go to the OLC through **glencoe.com** to:
- Take the Section 11.2 **Practice Test**.
- Download **Podcast** study tools.
- Download free **Study-to-Go** content to their PDAs or cell phones.

 STUDY TO GO

Resources

ExamView Assessment Suite CD allows you to print out ready-made unit and chapter tests complete with answer keys. You can also create customized tests.

CLOSE

Culminating Activity
Safety, Health, and Responsibility This section emphasizes the individual worker's responsibility for staying healthy and safe on the job. Ask students to create a bulleted list summarizing ten ways they can take action to protect themselves on the job. (Lists should mention many of the topics covered in the section, including following safety rules, asking for and attending training, wearing personal protective equipment, and learning fire safety.)

NCLB Activity correlated to Mathematics standards.

Section 11.2 After You Read

1. OSHA is the Occupational Safety and Health Administration of the U.S. Department of Labor. OSHA protects workers by trying to make workplaces healthy and safe.
2. Recycle and reuse materials, know and follow all relevant environmental laws (such as laws about disposal of hazardous materials), notify management of any environmental hazards or breaches of the law, and share ideas for reducing pollution and resource use.
3. Check-Call-Care is the procedure to follow in a medical emergency or accident. Check the scene and the victim; call for help; and care by giving basic medical assistance until help arrives.

Practice Academic Skills
4. Twelve hours will be spent learning about disaster response ($18 \times \frac{2}{3} = 12$ hours).

CAREER SPOTLIGHT

Career Cluster: Manufacturing

Discussion Starter

Manufacturing Ask students to choose a manufactured product, anything from a pencil to a space shuttle. Then have them brainstorm all the jobs that might be involved in designing and fabricating the item and shipping it to customers. (Jobs may include product designer, materials engineer, assembly line worker, robotics technician, welder, machinist, quality assurance inspector, material mover, shipping clerk, and safety coordinator.)

TEACH

W Writing Support
Independent Practice

Conduct an Interview Have students use the questions in the Career Spotlight to conduct and record an interview with a local business owner. (Answers will vary but should follow the interview format of the Career Spotlight.)

C Critical Thinking

Developing Criteria Manufacturers create products that they hope will sell. Ask students how a manufacturer—in this case, a toy manufacturer—could figure out whether a product might sell and how much people would be willing to pay for it. (Students should mention researching existing similar products, keeping tabs on cultural trends, conducting focus groups and customer surveys, and gathering information from wholesalers, retailers, and individual customers.)

Jim Crawford
Toy Designer and Manufacturer

Q: Describe your job.

A: I am the owner of a collectible toy company in San Francisco, California. We produce original toys designed by artists from the worlds of street art and comics. We also distribute new and original design objects and commission exclusive versions of the best toy designs from around the world. Collaborators and partners come from as far away as Japan, England, and Australia.

Q: Describe a typical workday.

A: I arrive at work at 10 A.M., and spend most of my time on the telephone with our toy designers and the stores that carry our toys. In the late afternoon, I generally correspond and talk with our factory representatives in Asia. The time difference between California and Asia means that when I am ready to stop working, the factories that we work with are just starting their day.

Q: What skills are most important to you in your job?

A: Organization and communication skills are really important because there are so many steps to creating, fabricating, and selling manufactured goods. You have to make sure each step is done properly to make a high-quality product on schedule and on budget.

Q: What academic skills and lifelong learning skills are helpful in preparing for your career?

A: I have a degree in English from a university, which has helped me tremendously with being able to think critically and communicate clearly.

Q: What is your key to success?

A: Keys include time management, hard work, and being flexible enough to "roll with it" when things go wrong.

Q: What training and preparation do you recommend for students?

A: Toy manufacturing involves basic processes of mold making and casting. It would be very helpful to understand how to do this on a small scale beforehand because, for the most part, the same principles apply to what our company does. Spending a lot of time playing with toys and visiting toy stores helps as well! You have to know your market because customers and especially collectors can tell if you're faking it.

Q: What are some ways you recommend students prepare for this career?

A: There are quite a few toy design programs offered by different universities. Internships at toy companies can also be helpful for learning the business end of the trade.

Q: What do you like most about your work?

A: After all the work that goes into designing and making a toy, it's a real kick to hold the final product in my hand! We won't stop until everyone has a designer toy on his or her shelf, computer, kitchen counter, or hi-fi console.

 For more about Career Clusters, go to this book's OLC through **glencoe.com**.

NCLB NO CHILD LEFT BEHIND

Teaching Tip

Improving reading skills is a top priority of NCLB. Help students integrate effective reading strategies—such as monitoring comprehension and stopping to reflect on what they have read—by modeling the strategies in class.

Sample Question Read a passage from the chapter aloud, stopping to monitor your understanding, ponder new words, and verbalize thoughts. Ask students to follow your example with a second passage. Stop students if necessary and ask: Can you summarize what we just heard? What associations are named?

Education or Training A high school diploma or GED is required for many manufacturing production positions. An associate degree in a specific trade or a bachelor's degree in industrial design or engineering is required for some entry-level commercial and industrial design positions. Company-specific training for manufacturing production positions is also common.

Academic Skills Required English Language Arts, Mathematics, Science, Social Studies

Technology Needed In design and manufacturing, employees are expected to work on a variety of standard and proprietary software, machinery, and tools.

Aptitudes, Abilities, and Skills Problem-solving skills and the ability to work independently are important traits. People in the manufacturing

industry need self-discipline to start and finish projects, budget their time, and meet deadlines and production schedules.

Workplace Safety Manufacturing production workers should pay attention to ergonomics and avoid potential strain and injury from repetitive tasks and machinery.

Career Outlook Employment of commercial designers is expected to grow about as fast as average for all occupations over the next ten years, while jobs in manufacturing are expected to decline.

Career Path Manufacturing production employees can move on to supervisory positions or design positions. A manufacturer can expand or create new product lines.

NCLB

Academic Skills Required to Complete Tasks

Tasks	English Language Arts	Mathematics	Science	Social Studies
Work with employees	★	★		★
Collaborate with artists	★			★
Work with manufacturing facilities	★	★	★	
Control quality of products		★	★	
Communicate with customers	★			★

Critical Thinking

What are some other jobs involved in the creation, design, and manufacture of toys?

NCLB

This chart relates academic skills such as English Language Arts, Mathematics, Science, Social Studies, and World Languages to specific tasks that are performed for the job featured in the Career Spotlight feature.

Critical Thinking

Other jobs related to toy manufacturing include toy designer, packaging designer, market research analyst, product safety tester, factory worker, and quality assurance engineer.

CAREER SPOTLIGHT

ASSESS

Make Connections
Ask students to consider why skill in English Language Arts is critical even in a technical or manufacturing field. Have students devise specific workplace scenarios in which skill in oral and written communication would help a manager of a manufacturing company be successful. (Scenarios will vary but could include writing staff memos or e-mails, conducting sales presentations, and answering customer questions.)

CLOSE

Culminating Activity
Safety and Career Clusters Ask students to select four career areas that interest them and consult the Bureau of Labor Statistics (BLS) to obtain data about rates of on-the-job injuries and illnesses in those career areas/industries. Have them use spreadsheet software to create a bar graph comparing the data for the four career areas. (Graphs will vary, but students should realize that while all work carries safety risks, certain industries, such as transportation, construction, and manufacturing, are more hazardous than others.)

Key Terms and Academic Vocabulary Review

1. Students should use each of the key terms and academic vocabulary terms in a sentence. A sample answer might read: "*Ergonomics* helps to prevent injuries by fitting work equipment to workers' physical needs."

Review Key Concepts

2. Career success is dependent on good health because good health provides the physical and mental energy you need to give your best at work and pursue your goals.

3. A nutritious diet gives you the vitamins, minerals, fiber, hydration, and other essentials necessary for a healthy body. Good sleep hygiene ensures that you get enough high-quality rest to feel refreshed each day.

4. Stress is a natural reaction to conflict. Each person faces his or her own personal stressors, or triggers of stress. Managing stress effectively involves a two-pronged approach: first, identify the cause of the stress and try to resolve it. Second, adopt stress-management techniques to cope with and lesson the symptoms of stress.

5. To maintain a safe workplace, employers must provide a hazard-free workplace, give workers safety training and equipment and alert them to hazards, and keep records of job-related illnesses and injuries. Workers must be alert and try to avoid carelessness and human error. They must learn to perform their job safely, follow all safety training and instructions, wear necessary safety equipment, report unsafe conditions, and talk to their supervisors with any questions or concerns right away.

CHAPTER SUMMARY

Section 11.1

Being healthy means having mental and physical strength and energy. Stay physically healthy by eating a diet rich in nutrients and low in fat, sugar, and salt, and by staying on guard against addiction, a physical or emotional dependence on any kind of drug. Follow the guidelines in MyPyramid to achieve a balanced diet. Stay fit by exercising 30 to 60 minutes a day, and practice good sleep hygiene to stay rested and alert. Manage your stress by identifying and addressing the causes of your stress.

Section 11.2

Government, employers, and employees share responsibility for creating and maintaining safe workplaces. Through OSHA, the government sets and enforces safety standards. Employers must provide hazard-free workplaces, safe equipment, and health and safety information. As an employee, you must know and follow safety rules, report hazards, and work with your employer to follow environmental laws. Know your employer's emergency action plan and learn how to prevent and respond to common emergencies. Follow the American Red Cross guideline to check-call-care during a medical emergency.

Key Terms and Academic Vocabulary Review

1. Use each of these key terms and academic vocabulary words in a sentence.

Key Terms
- nutrients (p. 243)
- MyPyramid (p. 243)
- addiction (p. 244)
- sedentary (p. 245)
- sleep hygiene (p. 245)
- depression (p. 246)
- Occupational Safety and Health Administration (OSHA) (p. 249)

- workers' compensation (p. 249)
- ergonomics (p. 250)
- musculoskeletal disorders (MSDs) (p. 251)
- Environmental Protection Agency (EPA) (p. 252)
- emergency action plan (p. 253)
- first aid (p. 255)

Academic Vocabulary
- mental (p. 243)
- genes (p. 243)
- revising (p. 249)
- violate (p. 252)

Review Key Concepts

2. **Explain** the relationship between good health and career success.
3. **Describe** how a nutritious diet and good sleep hygiene contribute to health.
4. **Identify** the causes of stress and ways to manage stress.
5. **Describe** rules and procedures for maintaining a safe workplace.
6. **Summarize** the role of the employer and the employee in protecting the environment.
7. **Explain** how to respond effectively to workplace emergencies.

Critical Thinking

8. **Predict** What materials found in offices, warehouses, or retail stores might affect the quality of the indoor air? Why?
9. **Analyze** Why is it the employee's responsibility to report damaged personal protective equipment and hazards in the workplace?

---

6. Employers can protect the environment by following all health and environmental laws and by setting up programs to reduce pollution and resource use. Employees can help by recycling, conserving energy, following environmental laws, alerting supervisors to possible violations, and sharing ideas for how to make their workplace healthier.

7. The best way to respond to emergencies is to follow the steps laid out in the relevant

emergency action plan and to be ready with your own emergency preparedness kit. Following an accident or medical incident, follow the "check-call-care" guideline. Students should also cite response tips for the emergencies most common in their geographic area.

Critical Thinking

8. Not only chemicals, but also building materials such as carpeting, paint, and particleboard

Real-World Skills and Applications

Organization and Time-Management Skills

10. Planning for a Healthy Diet Eating a healthy diet takes time and planning. List and describe six specific activities you could do to have a healthy diet as shown in MyPyramid. Explain whether these activities would require more time, less time, or the same amount of time and money as you currently spend on your diet.

Technology Applications

11. Creating a Safety Spreadsheet Research the four most common types of workplace injuries using data from the Bureau of Labor Statistics. Create a spreadsheet with three columns. In the first column, name the injury and state how many workers it affected in the past year. In the second column, describe which workers are most at risk for that particular injury and why. In the third column, list ways that workers can help prevent that particular injury.

Information Literacy Skills

12. Comparing Sources of Information Use the Internet to research the amount of and types of exercise you should do each day. Write down the exercise recommendations you find on the Web sites of a nonprofit organization, a government agency, and a for-profit company, such as a fitness center. Nonprofit organization Web site addresses often end in .org, government sites Web sites often end in .gov, and company Web sites often end in .com or .net. Compare and contrast the exercise recommendations you find for accuracy and usefulness in a one-page summary.

13. **Keep a Sleep Journal** A sleep journal is a good way to keep track of how much you sleep. Place a piece of paper or notebook by your bed for a week and use it to record exactly when you go to sleep and when you wake up. Also note whether you have trouble falling or staying asleep and whether you feel drowsy during the day. At the end of the week, write a one-page analysis of your sleep hygiene. Calculate how much you slept each night and analyze whether you felt drowsy on days following nights with less sleep. Figure out how many hours of sleep you need each night to be at maximum alertness. Share your findings with the class.

14. **Emergency Planning**
Situation You are part of your company's emergency planning team. Your group has been asked to make a plan for dealing with a specific weather emergency.
Activity Within your group, select a specific weather emergency. Identify the specific procedures for workers to follow in such an emergency. Present your plan to the class.
Evaluation You will be evaluated on how well you meet the following performance indicators:
- Identify specific emergency preparations.
- Present clear instructions for protection and evacuation.
- Answer any questions that your classmates may have.

Chapter 11 Workplace Health and Safety 259

---

11. Common workplace injuries include sprains, strains, and tears; back injuries; skin diseases and disorders (such as cuts, burns, and bruises), respiratory conditions, poisonings, and hearing loss. Statistics in students' charts will vary based on the year. Ideas for preventing injuries include using protective equipment properly and being vigilant for potential hazards.

12. Most sources recommend a minimum of 30 to 60 minutes a day of moderate exercise—such as walking, dancing, or playing sports. Other sources use other measures, such as number of steps per day (10,000 is a good goal.) The information students find will vary; many experts recommend combining cardiovascular exercise with strength-training moves. No one type of exercise is best for all people, however.

13. Students' sleep journals will vary but should reflect daily observations. Students' analyses should consider both length and quality of sleep, including interruptions caused by noise, anxiety, and so on. Most adults need between seven and nine hours of sleep daily. Adolescents often need more.

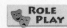

14. Students should choose a specific weather emergency and devise a realistic emergency plan using the information presented in the chapter. The plan should take into account worst-case scenarios such as injuries, blocked exits, downed power lines, and so on.

(which contains formaldehyde) can lower the quality of indoor air. In warehouses, gasoline-powered forklifts and other machinery can create unhealthful fumes.

9. Because employees work most closely with the equipment and notice changes in its condition, fit, or other properties, they are the ones who would notice any damage to equipment first.

Real-World Skills and Applications

10. Activity suggestions could include preparing healthy lunches at home rather than buying fast food; preparing and freezing healthy dinners ahead of time; and cutting down on processed foods with high levels of salt, sugar, and fat.

CHAPTER 11 Review & Activities

Academic Skills in the Workplace

15. Students should base their posters on the MyPyramid in **Figure 11.1** on page 243. Posters should include specific suggestions where to buy and how to cook specific foods that can be prepared quickly.

16. One hour and 35 minutes or 1 $7/12$ hours passes ($1/3 = 4/12$, $3/4 = 9/12$, and $1/2 = 6/12$; $4/12 + 9/12 + 6/12 = 19/12 = 1$ $7/12$).

17. Ideas for mini-workouts might include taking quick brisk walks, climbing stairs, flexing stomach and leg muscles, doing leg lifts (with or without ankle weights), lifting hand weights, and stretching the arms and legs. Office workers can even buy mini exercise bikes that fit under a desk.

18. Reports will vary based on the country chosen. Most countries have industrial safety laws, but many countries, especially in the developing world, have laws and regulations that are less stringent than those in the United States or that are not enforced as vigorously.

Academic Skills in the Workplace

English Language Arts

15. Create a Nutrition Guide Tomás, a teacher's aide at your school, eats fast food every day for lunch. He says he does not have time to do the shopping and cooking it takes to eat better. Create a MyPyramid poster and eating plan for Tomás, including foods that are easy to buy and prepare.

Mathematics

16. Calculate Time Al works out after work. It takes him $1/3$ of an hour to get to the gym, $3/4$ of an hour to work out, and $1/2$ an hour to get home. How much time passes between when Al leaves work and when he gets home?

CONCEPT Adding Unlike Fractions Use the least common multiple of the denominators to rename the fractions with a common denominator before adding unlike fractions. Then, add the numerators. The denominator stays the same.

Starting Hint Use 12 as a common denominator for adding these three fractions. Begin by converting $1/3$ to $4/12$.

Science

17. Plan a Workplace Workout Imagine that you work in a busy office, often sitting at your desk for nine hours a day. You are usually too tired to exercise before or after work and need to develop an exercise program to boost your health and productivity. Research online and print fitness and health publications to find ways you can do mini-workouts throughout the day in a sedentary environment, such as stretches and strength training. Use computer or traditional art materials to create a poster of exercise directions and diagrams for at least one exercise.

Social Studies

18. Research Safety Laws Choose a country that interests you and research its industrial safety and health laws. What laws are in place to protect workers? How do these laws compare to laws in the United States? Does the country have a government agency like OSHA? If not, how does that country's government handle violations of workplace safety laws? Summarize what you learned in a five-minute oral presentation.

STANDARDIZED TEST PRACTICE

ANALOGIES

Directions Select the pair of words that best expresses a relationship similar to that expressed in the capitalized pair.

> **Test-Taking Tip** Analogies are relationships between two words or concepts. Common relationships in analogy questions include cause and effect, part-to-whole, general classification and specific example, and synonym/antonym.

1. NUTRIENTS:HEALTH

a. safety:OSHA
b. stress:deep breathing
c. sleep:alertness
d. emergency:rescue breathing

For more Standardized Test Practice, go to the OLC glencoe.com.

STANDARDIZED TEST PRACTICE

Answer

1. c. sleep:alertness

Test-Taking Strategy

Help students build their logical skills by showing pairs of words and asking students to pinpoint their relationships. (Examples: calories:sugar, headache:stress, carpooling: air pollution.) Help students describe the relationships as precisely as possible, reminding them that they can work backward from the second word to the first. For example, "Headaches are related to stress" is too vague. "Stress causes headache" is more specific and useful.

Writing Skills Practice

19. Taking Notes Notes help you focus on and remember important information. The process of taking notes also helps you pay attention and organize information mentally.

 Practice Practice your note-taking skills at a talk, lecture, or video podcast.

- Focus on central and important points, examples, keywords, and facts. Do not try to write down every word.
- Listen for clues that the speaker is making an important point, such as tone, body language, or repetition.
- Use abbreviations to save time. Write in fragments or very short sentences.
- Note your own questions, ideas, and opinions to think about later.
- Review your notes after the end of the presentation. Fill in blanks while your memory is still fresh.

Net Connection

20. Research Environmental Procedures Interview someone to learn about conservation and environmental practices followed in that person's workplace. Find out what environmental laws apply to that company's business, and what voluntary programs the company has put in place to protect the environment. Describe your findings in a one-page report.

 Log On Conduct research on the Internet to find additional ways that the company could improve its environmental practices. Visit this book's OLC through **glencoe.com** for helpful links. Add those recommendations to your report.

Reading Connection

Go to this book's Online Learning Center through **glencoe.com** for a list of reading suggestions.

Personal Academic and Career Portfolio

Adding Your Health and Safety Information

The information you have learned about health and work safety will be helpful not only in guiding your career choice, but also in helping you stay healthy once you enter the workforce. Research the rate of on-the-job injuries and illnesses in the occupations that interest you. What health and safety risks are you likely to face in the jobs that interest you, and how can your minimize them? Add this information to your portfolio. Knowing the risks of different occupations helps you make an informed choice.

The following guidelines will help you organize and add the results of your research to your portfolio:

- Create a new section for your portfolio, using a divider for hard copy material and a computer folder for electronic files.
- Label the section *Health and Safety*.
- You may wish to create subsections or sub-folders such as *Common Workplace Emergencies* and *Diet and Exercise Guidelines*.
- Add the section to your table of contents.
- Add the following: personalized guidelines on nutrition, exercise, and sleep; information on what you can do to protect the environment in the occupations that interest you; and tips on preventing and handling workplace emergencies.
- Update your research results as you continue to explore your career options.

 Portfolio Help Go to the *Succeeding in the World of Work* OLC through **glencoe.com** for help developing your portfolio.

Writing Skills Practice

19. Notes should be well organized, ideally in a format that mirrors the presenter's outline or organizational principle. They should primarily consist of content words and phrases such as keywords, central points and conclusions, and examples.

20. After learning about the environmental practices of a company, students should further research the topic to see if the company is taking adequate steps in relation to other companies and/or government standards. Students should judge the effectiveness of the company's practices as a whole. Students should come away from this project with a clearer understanding of what companies do (or fail to do) to conserve resources and protect the environment.

 Resources

ExamView Assessment Suite CD allows you to print out ready-made unit and chapter tests complete with answer keys. You can also create customized tests.

WorkKeys

WorkKeys® is a job skills assessment program. For information on leveled assessment for Problem-Solving Skills (Applied Mathematics; Applied Technology; Locating Information; and Observation), go to the WorkKeys link on this book's OLC through **glencoe.com**.

Personal Academic and Career Portfolio

Maintaining a Portfolio

Tell students that their **Personal Academic and Career Portfolios** have at least two roles: first, as personal tools to track progress and compile information and research results, and second, as showcases of their skills to be shown to employers. To employers, a neat, professionally compiled and presented portfolio reflects a organized and prepared job applicant. Explain to students that many workers wait until they experience an on-the-job injury to become conscious of safety. Students who can use their portfolios to show employers that they are knowledgeable and conscious of work safety practices will have an edge in the job market.

CHAPTER 12 *Planning Guide and Correlations*

Chapter Resources Planning Guide with Activities and Features

Section	Features	Activities
Section 12.1 Workplace Rights and Laws	Real-World Connection (p. 266) Everyday Ethics (p. 267) Math in Action (p. 268) Creative Business Practices (p. 268) Career Checklist (p. 270)	Before You Read (p. 264) Graphic Organizer (p. 264) As You Read (p. 267) After You Read (p. 270)
Section 12.2 You and the Legal System	21st Century Workplace (p. 273) Hot Jobs! (p. 275)	Before You Read (p. 271) Graphic Organizer (p. 271) As You Read (p. 273) After You Read (p. 275)

NCLB Activities, information, and skills practice will help your students attain No Child Left Behind proficiency. Students will improve their abilities in the following academic standards areas:

Academic Standards Correlations

Discipline	Standard	Feature/Activity
English Language Arts	**NCTE 1** Read texts to acquire new information.	Creative Business Practices (p. 268) Hot Jobs! (p. 275)
	NCTE 4 Use written language to communicate effectively.	After You Read (p. 275) Academic Skills in the Workplace (p. 280) Writing Skills Practice (p. 281)
	NCTE 5 Use different writing process elements to communicate effectively.	21st Century Workplace (p. 273)
	NCTE 8 Use information resources to gather information and create and communicate knowledge.	Real-World Connection (p. 266)
Mathematics	**Number and Operation:** Understand meanings of operations and how they relate to one another	Math in Action (p. 268)
	Numbers and Operation: Compute fluently and make reasonable estimates	After You Read (p. 275)
	Measurement: Understand measurable attributes of objects and the units, systems, and processes of measurement	Academic Skills in the Workplace (p. 280)
Science	**Life Science:** Matter, energy, and organization in living systems **Science in Personal and Social Perspectives:** Personal and community health	Academic Skills in the Workplace (p. 280)

CORRELATIONS The charts show the 21st Century Skills, foundation skills, and workplace competencies that students develop as they work in this chapter.

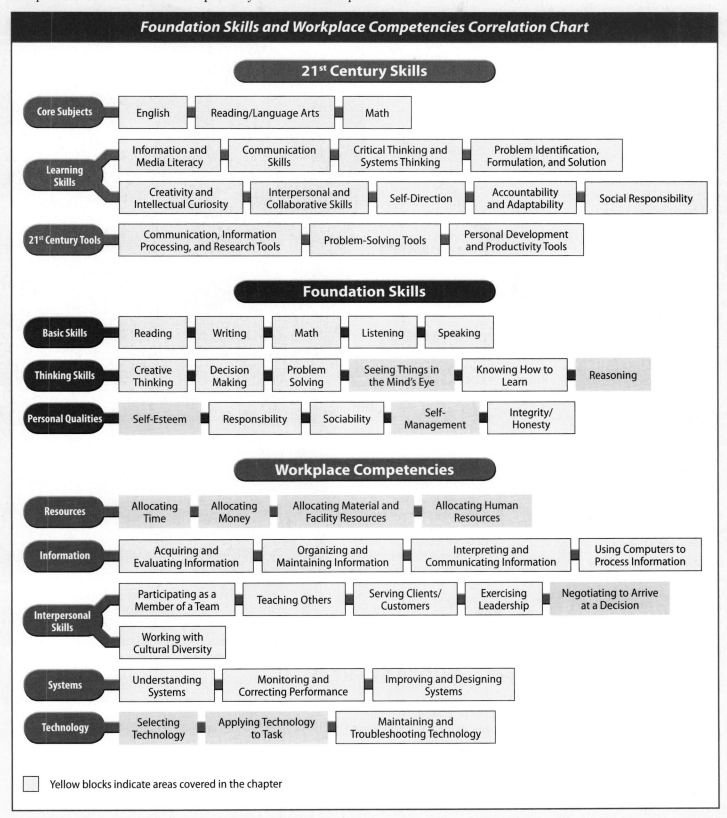

Foundation Skills and Workplace Competencies Correlation Chart

21st Century Skills

Core Subjects
English | Reading/Language Arts | Math

Learning Skills
Information and Media Literacy | Communication Skills | Critical Thinking and Systems Thinking | Problem Identification, Formulation, and Solution
Creativity and Intellectual Curiosity | Interpersonal and Collaborative Skills | Self-Direction | Accountability and Adaptability | Social Responsibility

21st Century Tools
Communication, Information Processing, and Research Tools | Problem-Solving Tools | Personal Development and Productivity Tools

Foundation Skills

Basic Skills
Reading | Writing | Math | Listening | Speaking

Thinking Skills
Creative Thinking | Decision Making | Problem Solving | Seeing Things in the Mind's Eye | Knowing How to Learn | Reasoning

Personal Qualities
Self-Esteem | Responsibility | Sociability | Self-Management | Integrity/Honesty

Workplace Competencies

Resources
Allocating Time | Allocating Money | Allocating Material and Facility Resources | Allocating Human Resources

Information
Acquiring and Evaluating Information | Organizing and Maintaining Information | Interpreting and Communicating Information | Using Computers to Process Information

Interpersonal Skills
Participating as a Member of a Team | Teaching Others | Serving Clients/Customers | Exercising Leadership | Negotiating to Arrive at a Decision
Working with Cultural Diversity

Systems
Understanding Systems | Monitoring and Correcting Performance | Improving and Designing Systems

Technology
Selecting Technology | Applying Technology to Task | Maintaining and Troubleshooting Technology

Yellow blocks indicate areas covered in the chapter

Chapter Overview
Introduce the Chapter

Chapter 12 familiarizes students with laws that affect employment.

Section 12.1 introduces the labor laws that guide work and pay. This section describes the role of labor unions, as well as the laws that protect workers from discrimination and unfair labor practices.

Section 12.2 introduces civil law and guides students through the steps that might be followed to settle a workplace issue in the U.S. legal system.

Build Background

Bring to class an assortment of newspaper articles that feature government regulations of employment or employee rights. Ask students to read one of these articles in class and write a brief summary of the article in their own words.

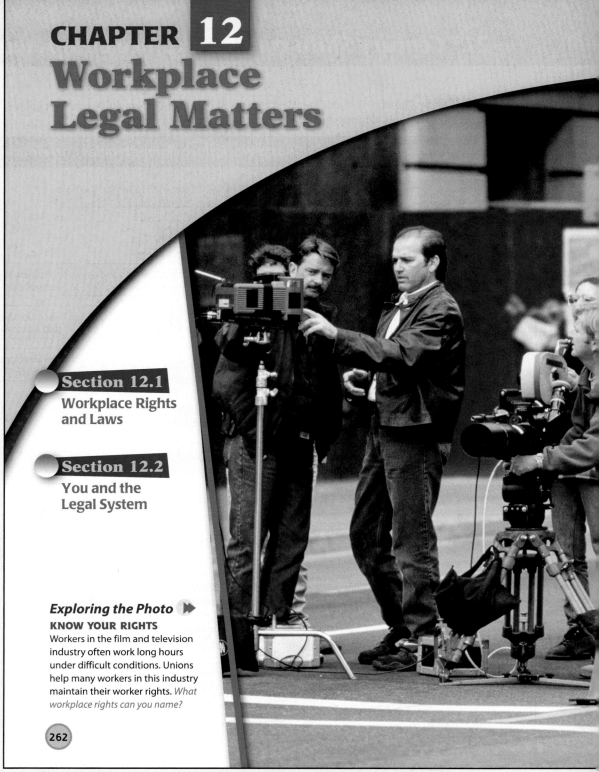

CHAPTER **12**
Workplace Legal Matters

Section 12.1
Workplace Rights and Laws

Section 12.2
You and the Legal System

Exploring the Photo ▶
KNOW YOUR RIGHTS
Workers in the film and television industry often work long hours under difficult conditions. Unions help many workers in this industry maintain their worker rights. *What workplace rights can you name?*

262

▶ Exploring the Photo

Caption Answer
Students might mention rights that will be discussed in this chapter, such as minimum wage, minimum working age, and anti-discrimination laws.

Discussion Lead a discussion about the responsibilities students will likely face as they join the workforce and become managers or entrepreneurs who will be responsible for treating employees fairly.

Classroom Resources

- 📁 Student Edition
- 📁 Teacher Wraparound Edition
- 📁 Student Activity Workbook with Academic Integration
- 📁 Student Activity Workbook with Academic Integration TAE
- 📁 *Fast File,* Unit 4 Resources

- 📁 Inclusion in the Career Education Classroom
- 💿 TeacherWorks™ Plus
- 💿 *ExamView Assessment Suite*
- 💿 Interactive Chalkboard
- 💿 Interactive Student Edition
- 💻 Online Student Edition
- 💻 Online Learning Center (OLC) with Podcasts

Chapter Objectives

After completing this chapter, you will be able to:

- **Explain** how labor laws and labor unions affect the workplace.
- **Identify** the main antidiscrimination laws and explain their role in protecting workers.
- **Describe** effective strategies for handling sexual harassment.
- **Distinguish** between civil law and criminal law.
- **Give examples** of civil law cases and explain how they are resolved.
- **Explain** how to find and evaluate legal services.

Writing Activity Personal Career Notebook

In a notebook or journal, list five words or phrases that come to mind when you hear these terms: police officer, lawyer, judge. What do you think your responses say about your understanding of—and attitude toward—our legal system?

Get Motivated! Contact an adult who works in the legal system—a police officer, a corrections officer, or someone in the court system, such as a lawyer or a court reporter. Ask that person to tell you about the responsibilities of his or her job. Summarize your findings in a one-page report. Include discussion of whether or not you would be interested in that person's job.

Chapter 12 Workplace Legal Matters **263**

Writing Activity Personal Career Notebook Answer Guide

Some students may have an ambivalent attitude about the legal system. Encourage them to consider whether their feelings about the legal system may be affected by the portrayal of the legal system in popular culture, such as television and popular music.

Get Motivated! Reports will vary but should reflect solid interviewing and summarizing skills. Encourage students to provide support for whether or not they are interested in the job they describe.

Review the Objectives

Introduce the chapter by reviewing the chapter objectives:

Section 12.1 Objectives

Explain how labor laws and labor unions affect the workplace. (Labor laws ensure fair treatment for employees by setting a minimum wage, the 40-hour workweek, and child labor laws. Unions negotiate for better working conditions for workers.)

Identify the main antidiscrimination laws and explain their role in protecting workers. (Laws include the Civil Rights Act of 1964, the Age Discrimination Act of 1967, the Rehabilitation Act of 1973, and the Americans with Disabilities Act of 1990.)

Describe effective strategies for handling sexual harassment. (Strategies for dealing with sexual harassment include telling the harasser to stop; writing down what happened; informing a trusted supervisor or human resources person; and getting help from a local human rights office.)

Section 12.2 Objectives

Distinguish between civil law and criminal law. (Civil law applies to conflicts between private parties; under criminal law, the government brings criminal charges against a person or business.)

Give examples of civil law cases and explain how they are resolved. (Civil law cases include workplace disputes, divorce, breach of contract, and personal injury cases. Some legal cases are solved in small claims court; others are settled out of court.)

Explain how to find and evaluate legal services. (Find a lawyer by consulting the phone book, the local bar association, or asking for a recommendation. Evaluate the lawyer's experience by asking questions.

Bell Ringer Activity

Workplace Rights and Laws

Ask students if they think government regulation of employment conditions is necessary. Why or why not? (Answers should convey the idea that government regulations foster fairness and protect employees.)

Resources

Interactive Chalkboard
The Interactive Chalkboard CD provides visual teaching aids for this section.

@ Online Learning Center
The Online Learning Center (OLC) through **glencoe.com** features chapter vocabulary, chapter summaries, and other study materials.

Preteaching
Have students write the key terms from this section, then scan the chapter for the definitions and write them down.

Graphic Organizer
Tell students to go to the OLC through **glencoe.com** for a printable graphic organizer. (Graphic organizers should show the labor laws and their functions as described in this section.)

 NCLB connects academic correlations to book content.

Reading Guide

Before You Read

Preview Choose a Key Term or Academic Vocabulary word that is new to you. Write it on a piece of paper. When you find it in the text, write down the definition.

Read to Learn
- How labor laws and labor unions affect the workplace
- What the main antidiscrimination laws are and how they protect workers
- Effective strategies for handling sexual harassment

Main Idea
D Understanding the laws that affect the workplace will help to ensure that you receive fair treatment on the job.

Key Concept
- Labor Laws Govern the Workplace

Key Terms
◇ minimum wage
◇ compensatory time
◇ collective bargaining
◇ discrimination
◇ affirmative action
◇ sexual harassment

Academic Vocabulary
You will find this word in your reading and on your tests. Use the academic vocabulary glossary to look up its definition if necessary.
■ federal

Graphic Organizer
As you read, list the different labor laws and explain how they protect workers. Use a chart like the one shown to help organize your information.

Labor Laws	How They Protect Workers

 Log On Go to this book's Online Learning Center through **glencoe.com** for an online version of this graphic organizer.

Academic Standards •

NCLB

English Language Arts
- Read texts to acquire new information. (NCTE 1)
- Use information resources to gather information and create and communicate knowledge. (NCTE 8)

Mathematics
- Understand meanings of operations and how they relate to one another
- Compute fluently and make reasonable estimates

Reading Guide

Before You Read
Ask students who are presently employed to give their opinions as to what this section might include.

D Develop Concepts
Main Idea Have students write down all they know (or believe they know) about employment laws. Then, after finishing this section, have students compare what they wrote about employment laws with what they learned from the section.

Labor Laws Govern the Workplace

Laws that govern the workplace are often referred to as labor or employment laws. Labor laws are designed to give employees certain rights and to protect them from unfair treatment on the job. These laws help to ensure that all Americans have an equal opportunity to get and to keep a job, to be paid a just wage, to be considered fairly for promotion, and to be protected in times of personal and economic difficulty. It is important that you understand your rights and responsibilities under labor laws.

Laws About Pay

In 1938, the **federal** government passed the Fair Labor Standards Act (FLSA). This law requires employers to pay a **minimum wage**, which is the lowest hourly wage that an employer can legally pay for a worker's services. The first minimum wage was only $.40 per hour, but it has risen over the years. Lawmakers change the rate periodically to keep up with inflation. Most states also set a minimum wage. When there is a difference between the federal and state minimum wage, employers must pay the higher rate.

The FLSA also set the 40-hour workweek and established overtime pay for hourly workers who work more than 40 hours a week. You learned about overtime in Chapter 8. In some states, employees can receive additional wages or **compensatory time**, which is time off from work rather than money for working overtime. Employees must agree to compensatory time before they work overtime. Compensatory time is against the law in some states or for certain types of employees.

Child labor laws are another result of the FLSA. Less than 100 years ago, many U.S. child factory workers worked 60 hours a week under dangerous conditions. To put an end to such practices, the FLSA set the minimum age for most nonagricultural jobs at 16. There are also restrictions on the hours and types of jobs that children under 18 can do.

◤ Vocabulary
You can find definitions in the **Key Terms** glossary and **Academic Vocabulary** glossary at the back of this book.

CHILD LABOR LAWS
There are legal limits on the hours and types of work those under the age of 18 can do. *Why do you think these laws were created?*

TEACH

Discussion Starter
Labor Laws Govern the Workplace Ask students to give examples of unfair labor practices. Make a list on the board and discuss whether or not all students would agree which are and are not fair labor practices.

R Reading Strategy
Conduct Research Ask: What is the current federal minimum wage? What is the minimum wage in your state? (Answers should reflect the student's ability to gather information online or through other state and federal resources.)

S Skill Practice
Independent Practice
Conduct Research Have students use the Internet, your school's media center, or your local library to research the labor conditions for children during the 1800s. Suggest they use the key words *child labor* in their search, and have them report their findings in a one-page summary.

Resources

TeacherWorks™ Plus
The TeacherWorks software includes customizable built-in lesson plans and links to printable program resources.

▶ Extend the Photo

Caption Answer These laws were created to protect children and young adults from unfair treatment, abuse, and exploitation by parents or employers who may not be looking out for their best interests.

Discussion Ask students why they think the law permits children to work in agriculture as long as the work takes place after school hours. (Answers will vary, but students should demonstrate an understanding that this work does not interfere with the children's schooling.)

TEACH *(cont.)*

S Skill Practice
Independent Practice

Compare Have students read an article about working conditions and the right to organize in another country, preferably a developing country. Ask them to write a one-page paper comparing the conditions and any union activities in that country with those in the United States. *(Reports should mention the specific country and provide specific comparisons between the chosen country and the United States.)*

▶▶ Extend the Photo

Caption Answer Teachers may want to join a union to take advantage of the bargaining power of a union, and its ability to negotiate better wages, benefits, and working conditions for the teacher.

Discussion Lead a discussion with this question: Would it be fair for certain service workers or police officers to go on strike if their contract negotiations were not met? Would there be a danger to the community if police officers went on strike and stopped working?

Real-World Connection

Wage Discrimination

You and your friend Jim were hired by a small manufacturing company at the same time and assigned identical jobs. You work on the same shift and have similar work experience and education. He recently left a pay stub in a stack of papers that he placed on your desk. You discovered that he earns several hundred dollars a month more than you do.

Critical Thinking Is this an example of discrimination? How can you tell? Compare your answer to those of other students. Does your gender, race, or other factor affect your answer?

Do Your Own Research Consult the Wage and Hour Division of the U.S. Department of Labor by phone or online for information about what is and is not wage discrimination. Identify the consequences for employers who discriminate in pay. Write a one-page report summarizing your findings.

The Right to Organize

In another effort to protect people who work, the Wagner Act of 1935 made it legal to organize labor unions and engage in union activities. The Wagner Act established the National Labor Relations Board (NLRB), an independent judicial agency of the U.S. government. The NLRB protects workers who wish to be unionized and investigates charges of unfair labor practices. These unfair practices include interfering with, restraining, or firing employees because they wish to form or join a union.

S

Labor Unions

Labor unions represent workers in their dealings with employers. The workers elect union leaders, who negotiate for job improvements or changes through collective bargaining. **Collective bargaining** is a process through which unions use the power of their numbers (the workers in the union) to negotiate with company management for such things as pensions, wages and salaries, benefits, and working conditions.

If an agreement is not reached, the union may use its most powerful tool—a strike. A *strike* occurs when workers stop working in an effort to force an employer to agree to the union's terms. Most unions maintain *strike funds*, which provide partial salaries to workers on strike.

 UNION REPRESENTATION Police officers, service workers, and public school teachers are just a few professions that have unions. *Why might teachers join a union?*

Real-World Connection

Critical Thinking Answer Student responses will likely vary according to their own gender, race, and nationality. Encourage students to consider how these factors affected their answer.

Do Your Own Research In their reports, students should include information about the factors that constitute wage discrimination, and any penalties employers might incur if they discriminate.

Everyday ETHICS

A VERBAL AGREEMENT

Is a verbal agreement enforceable?

LAWN WORK Your neighbor went on vacation for a month and asked that you mow the lawn each week while he was away. You both verbally agreed on a price for your labor when he stopped by your house to drop off the keys to his house. When your neighbor returned, he told you he was going to give you only half the amount he had verbally agreed to because he thought that the original price was too high.

What Would You Do? How do you respond to your neighbor?

DISCUSS IT   In most places, a verbal agreement is legally binding, which means your neighbor owes you the amount promised. You may talk to your neighbor or get a third party involved. With a partner, discuss the possible actions you could take and the consequences of each.

When an agreement is reached, the company signs a *labor contract*, which is a legal agreement specifying wages, work hours, working conditions, benefits, and grievance procedures. The union members must approve the contract before it goes into effect.

There are nearly 16 million union members in the United States representing many different professions, from janitors to teachers to professional baseball players. If you join a union, you will have to pay an initiation fee and regular dues. This money supports the work of the union.

Before you join a union, consider these factors: membership cost; track record, or what the union has done for its workers in the past; and membership benefits, such as health care and pension plans.

Unemployment Insurance and Family Leave

State laws provide for unemployment insurance, which offers financial and other help to workers who lose their jobs. For example, Ben Dyal worked for five years as a sales representative for a sporting goods company. When his company suddenly went out of business, Ben had trouble finding a new job. "I had to eat," he said. "So I went to the local government office and filed for unemployment." Soon he was receiving weekly unemployment checks. Unemployment offices also help people find new jobs.

Sometimes accidents, illnesses, or family responsibilities make it temporarily difficult for people to work. In such cases, workers need to know that they will not lose their jobs. To meet this need, Congress passed the Family and Medical Leave Act in 1993. This law guarantees employees at companies with more than 50 employees up to 12 weeks of leave for personal medical care or to care for a family member, such as a spouse or a child.

As You Read

Summarize What are the benefits of unions for union members?

U **Universal Access**

Interpersonal Learners Have students talk with a family member or friend who is or was a union member. Ask students to inquire about union procedures. Questions might include: Does the union represent workers of a particular occupation? Has the union ever called a strike? How frequently does the union negotiate with employers? Have students present their findings to the class in a three-to five-minute oral report.

As You Read

Union members benefit from having their wages, benefits, and working conditions negotiated by experienced union leaders.

C **Critical Thinking**

Analyze Explain to students that, depending on the state, unemployment insurance is often funded, at least partly, by taxes that employees must pay. Ask: Do you think it is fair to pay taxes for another person to receive unemployment benefits? (Students may not think paying this tax is fair if it benefits someone else; encourage them to think of this tax as insurance if *they* ever become unemployed.)

Everyday ETHICS

What Would You Do? Answer Students might suggest reminding the neighbor that he verbally agreed to the higher amount, and should honor it.

DISCUSS IT   Some students might suggest taking the issue to small claims court. Others might question whether it is worth going to court over a relatively small amount of money. Students may conclude this experience will be a lesson to avoid more costly experiences in the future.

TEACH (cont.)

C Critical Thinking

Analyze Ask students to describe the importance of laws that discourage employment discrimination. Have them explain what they think might happen without these regulations. (Students might point out that without these regulations, workers can be fired, abused, or exploited for any number of reasons, including their age and their nationality.)

N C L B Activity correlated to Mathematics standards.

Math In Action

The state minimum wage is $2.90 ($5.22 = 1.8x; $5.22 ÷ 1.8 = $2.90).

ASSESS

Review Key Terms
Have students write sentences using each key term.

Online Study Tools
Have students go to the OLC through **glencoe.com** to:
- Download **Podcast** study tools.
- Download free **Study-to-Go** content to their PDAs or cell phones.

Resources

ExamView Assessment Suite CD allows you to print out ready-made unit and chapter tests complete with answer keys. You can also create customized tests.

Math In Action

Minimum Wage
In the restaurant where Fran works, servers are paid $5.22 an hour before tips. If this amount is actually 180 percent of the state minimum wage, what is the minimum wage?

Starting Hint: Use the variable x to represent the state minimum wage so that you can set up an equation to solve: $5.22 = 1.8x$.

@ For more math practice, go to this book's OLC through **glencoe.com**.

Laws about Immigrant Workers

Noncitizens who are living in our country without authorization from the government are called *illegal immigrants*. The Immigration Reform and Control Act of 1990 was designed to combat illegal immigration. Employers must make sure that all new employees have proper working papers and identification. Businesses can face fines if they break immigration laws, and workers who are in the United States illegally can be deported. Many states have their own laws regarding illegal immigration, and immigration reform is an issue that is constantly being addressed by federal and local lawmakers.

Laws about Discrimination

Under laws passed by Congress, it is illegal for employers to engage in **discrimination**—unequal treatment based on such factors as age, disability status, race, national origin, religion, or gender.

Major Antidiscrimination Laws
The following state and federal laws help to guarantee that every employee has a legal right to fair treatment in the workplace:

- The **Civil Rights Act of 1964** bans discrimination in employment based on race, color, religion, gender, or national origin. As **Figure 12.1** on page 269 shows, the percentage of minorities in the workforce is increasing.

Creative Business Practices

ATLANTA BRAVES   Diversity Training

During spring training, the Atlanta Braves organization includes a full-day training seminar in diversity. Because of the diversity among American athletes, as well as the increasing number of international baseball players and games, diversity training can help players better understand each other and their managers and coaches.

The Atlanta Braves' diversity training is specifically tailored to the needs and real-life situations of the athletes. Players are encouraged to share their personal experiences with discrimination and stereotypes, especially within the organization. Hearing each others' problems and concerns helps players relate on a personal level and be more accommodating to others.

CRITICAL THINKING How can employees benefit from diversity training?

@ **Connect to the Real World** To learn more about the Atlanta Braves, visit their Web site via the link on this book's Online Learning Center through **glencoe.com**.

Creative Business Practices

CRITICAL THINKING ANSWER By receiving diversity training, employees can recognize any prejudices they may have toward other groups of people, and learn to understand one another better and be more respectful of each other's differences. This will help them work more effectively as a team.

Figure 12.1 CHANGES IN EMPLOYMENT IN THE CIVILIAN WORKFORCE

RACE

Source: U.S. Census

| A CHANGING DEMOGRAPHIC | According to this graph, minorities make up an increasing percentage of the U.S. civilian workforce. *How do you think these percentages will change over the next two decades?* |

Section 12.1

RETEACH

Discussion Starter

Major Antidiscrimination Laws Tell students in alternating rows to close their eyes. Then have one row of students stand and walk to a corner of the room with assistance from students in the next row. Alternate these actions until all students have both needed and provided visual aid.

Ask students how much easier it was to reach their destination with help. Ask students how much the government should do to help people with disabilities gain employment and maintain their independence.

Resources

📁 **Student Activity Workbook** Assign the Chapter 12 activities in the Student Activity Workbook.

- The **Age Discrimination Act of 1967** makes it illegal to discriminate against people over 40.
- The **Rehabilitation Act of 1973** and the **Americans with Disabilities Act of 1990** protect the rights of individuals with disabilities, which are long-lasting impairments of the body and the mind that limit major life activities. Types of major life activities include caring for yourself, walking, reading, learning, and working. These two acts make sure that employers provide aids such as wheelchair ramps and other job accommodations so that disabled workers can do their jobs.

Courts recognize some exceptions to the antidiscrimination laws. Employers may hire only people with certain qualifications if those qualifications are necessary for a particular job. For example, actors may need to be a certain age or gender for a particular role.

Many schools and government agencies practice affirmative action. **Affirmative action** is a policy that aims to increase the number of people who represent traditionally underrepresented groups in a field or a workplace. Traditionally underrepresented groups may include people of color, women, and those with disabilities.

Equal Opportunity for Women and Men

Women have had fewer career choices than men in the past. Today, both men and women can choose any career they wish. Did you ever wonder how being a male or a female might affect your career?

Consider the story of Kate Frye, who worked as a laborer with a landscaping company. One day a male coworker mentioned his salary. Kate was surprised to learn that he was getting paid $3 an hour

Chapter 12 Workplace Legal Matters **269**

EXTEND THE FIGURE **Figure 12.1**

Caption Answer The percentage of minorities in the civilian workforce will continue to rise.

Discussion Lead a discussion by asking students if they think businesses should set aside a certain number of jobs for minority applicants.

(Some students might agree with affirmative action plans that aim to increase work opportunities for minorities. Other students might point out that jobs should always go to the most qualified applicants.)

ASSESS

After You Read

Have students complete the Section 12.1 After You Read section review.

Online Study Tools

Have students go to the OLC through **glencoe.com** to:

- Take the Section 12.1 **Practice Test.**
- Download **Podcast** study tools.
- Download free **Study-to-Go** content to their PDAs or cell phones.

CLOSE

Culminating Activity

Cooperative Learning Have groups of students choose one of the laws discussed in this section and create posters, providing examples of how the law is applied, and illustrating the law with cut-outs from magazines or online resources.

NCLB Activity correlated to Mathematics standards.

Career ✓ Checklist

To Protect Your Legal Interests:

✓ Know your workplace rights.

✓ Voice any legal concerns immediately.

✓ Do not support illegal or inappropriate workplace practices.

✓ Investigate all of your options before considering legal action.

---

more than she was—for doing the same job with the same amount of experience. Kate was a victim of discrimination. The **Equal Pay Act of 1963** requires equal pay for equal work. It gave Kate the right to ask her employer for better pay.

Sexual Harassment Any unwelcome behavior of a sexual nature is referred to as **sexual harassment**. Such behavior may include jokes, gestures, repeated or threatening requests for dates, and unwanted touching. Both males and females can be the victims of sexual harassment.

What should you do if you think you are the victim of sexual harassment? Here are some suggestions:

- Immediately tell the person to stop. Be clear and direct.
- Write down what happened, noting the date, time, and place. Include the names of any witnesses and comments about how the harassment affected your work.
- Inform a trusted supervisor or human resources of the incident and follow up.
- If the issue is not resolved within your company, you can get help from your local human rights office or the office of the U.S. Equal Employment Opportunity Commission.

Section 12.1 After You Read

Review Key Concepts

1. Name one labor law and explain its purpose.
2. Identify two antidiscrimination laws and explain how they protect workers.
3. Explain an effective way to handle this situation: You have refused many times to go on a date with your boss. Your review is coming up, and your boss has told you that if you do not agree to the date, you will not receive a positive review.

Practice Academic Skills

 Mathematics

4. Minimum wage varies from one state to another. If the minimum wage in Colorado is \$5.15 and the minimum wage in California is \$6.75, what percentage of California's minimum wage would Colorado's minimum wage be? Round to the nearest whole percent.

 CONCEPT Dividing Decimals To divide decimals, move the decimal point in the divisor until it is no longer a decimal and move the decimal point in the dividend the same number of places.
Step 1: First, set up a division problem with the divisor and the dividend. Move the decimal point two places to the right in both numbers.
Step 2: Divide until you reach the thousandths place. Your answer will be a decimal that you can write as a percent.

 For math help, go to the Math Appendix located at the back of this book.

Section 12.1 After You Read

Review Key Concepts

1. Students might mention the Fair Labor Standards Act, which set the minimum wage and established the 40-hour workweek and child labor laws. This law protects employees from exploitation and abuse from employers.

2. Two examples of antidiscrimination laws are the Civil Rights Act of 1964, which bans discrimination in employment based on race, color, religion, gender, or national origins; and the Age Discrimination Act of 1967, which makes it illegal to discriminate against people over 40.

3. One way to handle the situation is to tell the person to stop, write down the details of the incident, and tell a supervisor.

Practice Academic Skills

4. Colorado's minimum wage is 76 percent of California's (\$5.15 ÷ \$6.75 ≈ 0.76 or 76%).

You and the Legal System

Reading Guide

Before You Read

Preview Read the Key Concepts for this section. In one or two sentences, predict what you think the section will be about.

Read to Learn

- The difference between civil law and criminal law
- Examples of civil law cases and how they are resolved
- How to find and evaluate legal services

 ### Main Idea

An understanding of legal procedures and services will help you to resolve work-related conflicts.

Key Concepts

- Legal System Basics
- Legal Services

Key Terms

- ◈ civil law
- ◈ summons
- ◈ criminal law
- ◈ felony
- ◈ misdemeanor
- ◈ contingency fee

Academic Vocabulary

You will find these words in your reading and on your tests. Use the academic vocabulary glossary to look up their definitions if necessary.

- ■ procedures
- ■ contract

Graphic Organizer

As you read, note the different ways you can resolve a legal dispute and describe each. You can use a chart like the one shown to organize your information.

Ways to Resolve Legal Disputes	Description

 Log On Go to this book's Online Learning Center through **glencoe.com** for an online version of this graphic organizer.

Academic Standards •

NCLB

English Language Arts

- Read texts to acquire new information. (NCTE 1)
- Use different writing process elements to communicate effectively. (NCTE 5)
- Use information resources to gather information and create and communicate knowledge. (NCTE 8)

Reading Guide

Reading Guide

Before You Read

In Section 12.1, students read about laws in the workplace. Lead a discussion about why employees should know about the legal system even though labor laws should protect them. (Many disputes, including workplace matters, are not clear-cut or easily resolved. Therefore, employees should understand how disputes go from the workplace to the courtroom.)

 ### Develop Concepts

Main Idea Discuss the main idea with students. Ask students to brainstorm situations in which they might need the services of an attorney. (Situations might include an auto accident or discrimination at work.)

Bell Ringer Activity

You and the Legal System

Ask students to describe instances in which they or their families have experienced disagreements with others. How was the disagreement handled? Did the parties seek the advice of a third party? What final course of action was chosen? Use this discussion to introduce the legal system.

 ### Resources

⊙ Interactive Chalkboard

The Interactive Chalkboard CD provides visual teaching aids for this section.

@ Online Learning Center

The OLC through **glencoe.com** features chapter vocabulary, chapter summaries, and other study materials.

Preteaching

Have students look up the meaning of the key terms and use them in a sentence.

Graphic Organizer

Tell students to go to the OLC through **glencoe.com** for a printable graphic organizer. (Graphic organizers should show the five ways to solve a legal dispute as discussed in this section.)

NCLB connects academic correlations to book content.

271

TEACH

Discussion Starter

Legal System Basics Have students respond to this situation: You and a friend agree to trim a neighbor's tree, rake the leaves, sow grass seed, and fertilize the lawn for $100. When you complete the job, the neighbor claims that you did not spend enough time on the yard and only pays you $50. How could you settle this dispute? Ask volunteers to share their answers. Use this discussion to introduce civil law.

R **Reading Strategy**

Conduct Research Have students research the United States Supreme Court and write a fact sheet that includes information such as when it was established and how many justices it has. (The Supreme Court was established in 1789 with six justices; today the court has nine justices who are appointed for life.)

Resources

TeacherWorks™ Plus The TeacherWorks software includes customizable built-in lesson plans and links to printable program resources.

Vocabulary
You can find definitions in the **Key Terms** glossary and **Academic Vocabulary** glossary at the back of this book.

Legal System Basics

The Pledge of Allegiance ends with the words "with liberty and justice for all." In Section 12.1, you learned how labor laws strive to make these words a reality in the workplace. Job-related conflicts do arise, however, and sometimes laws are violated. The legal system provides a set of **procedures** for resolving such conflicts. In court, lawyers, judges, and sometimes jurors make decisions about disputes, or disagreements, between employers and employees. It is important for you to learn some basic facts about our legal system and how it affects you.

Civil Law

Many court cases involve **civil law**, which is law that applies to conflicts between private parties concerning rights and obligations. Divorce, breach of **contract**, and personal injury cases fall into this category. Companies and employees may become involved in civil law disputes.

Here is an example of a work-related civil law case: Michael, an autoworker, was physically searched by his company's security guards, who suspected him of stealing. No stolen goods were found, and Michael's shoulder was bruised during the search. The company was found guilty of deliberate injury.

The legal process starts when a person files an official complaint with the court. The person bringing the charge is the *plaintiff*. The person charged is the *defendant*. The court clerk delivers a **summons**, or an order to appear in court at a specific place and time, to the accused party. This person or company then files an answer.

Small Claims Court

For some legal cases, small claims court is an effective, low-cost solution. *Small claims court* handles minor disputes and small claims on debts. It does not require lawyers. Rules vary by state, but in general, small claims court procedures are less complicated than those of other courts. There is usually a monetary limit on cases heard in small claims court.

CIVIL LAW A civil case does not involve criminal charges. The plaintiff in this civil case is a worker who was injured because of improper workplace conditions. *Can you think of other examples of civil cases?*

 Extend the Photo

Caption Answer Other civil cases might involve auto accidents, personal injury cases, disputes regarding property, disputes involving defective merchandise, divorce, and custody battles.

Discussion Ask two or three volunteers to think of a disagreement they had with a friend or relative and imagine it as a civil case that went to trial. After the cases have been described, ask the class to render a "verdict" in each case.

The 21st Century Workplace

Make E-Mail Work for You

Using e-mail effectively is a valuable job skill. It is a fast and easy way to share ideas and documents and to have conversations with many people at once without having to set up an in-person meeting. Here are some tips for using e-mail on the job:

N C L B

- Be brief and clear. Remember that many people receive over 100 e-mails a day.
- Read the full message you have received before replying. Answer all the points in the message.
- Always reread your message before sending.
- Use a polite and respectful tone, even if the other person does not.
- Reply to e-mails from coworkers and customers as quickly and thoroughly as you can.
- Do not write anything you would not want everyone in your company to see.

CRITICAL THINKING

Why is using e-mail effectively a valuable job skill? What are some ways to use e-mail at work?

In Your Community

Send an e-mail to a member of your local government asking a question. When you receive a response, write an evaluation of both your e-mail and the response you received according to the bulleted tips.

> **@ Extend Your Learning** Many employers have written policies explaining appropriate e-mail procedures. For links to Web sites about e-mail, go to this book's OLC through **glencoe.com**.

Settlements

Most civil cases are resolved before they get to court. The parties to a dispute often come to a settlement, which is a mutual agreement that does not assign blame to either party. A settlement may take the form of a monetary award or a correction of the situation that caused the complaint. To avoid the expense and time of a courtroom trial, many states require that parties to a civil case try to settle out of court.

These are some ways you may settle conflicts out of court:

- **Follow complaint procedures.** If your company has complaint procedures, you may settle your dispute by discussing it with your employer.

R

- **File a formal complaint.** Many states require workers to file a formal complaint with the Equal Employment Opportunity Commission or a similar agency. Sometimes such agencies can settle disputes between employees and management.
- **Mediation.** Mediation is a process in which you and your opponent present the case to a neutral third party, who helps you talk to each other and reach a compromise.
- **Arbitration.** Union disputes are often resolved through arbitration, in which both parties present evidence to an arbitrator, who issues a written decision.

You will learn more about conflict resolution in Chapter 13.

As You Read

Explain What are some ways to settle conflicts out of court?

TEACH (cont.)

R Reading Strategy

Conduct Research Have students research the Equal Employment Opportunity Commission and write two or three paragraphs describing when it was formed, its purpose, and the effect it has had on labor practices. (The EEOC was created as part of the Civil Rights Act of 1964 to give employees who believe they have suffered discrimination a forum for their complaint. The EEOC helps to enforce equal employment opportunities and has helped make the workplace more open to women and minorities.)

As You Read

Conflicts can be settled out of court by following complaint procedures, filing a formal complaint, mediation, and arbitration.

ASSESS

Review Key Terms

Have students write sentences using each key term.

Online Study Tools

Have students go to the OLC through **glencoe.com** to:

- Download **Podcast** study tools.
- Download free **Study-to-Go** content to their PDAs or cell phones.

N C L B Activity correlated to English Language Arts standards.

The 21st Century Workplace

CRITICAL THINKING ANSWER Using e-mail effectively is an easy way to communicate with others, especially coworkers or clients outside the location in which you are working.

In Your Community Evaluate student e-mails for clarity and for a polite and respectful tone.

RETEACH

Discussion Starter

Legal Services Ask students to brainstorm situations in which they might need the services of an attorney. (Situations might include an auto accident, a case of sexual harassment, or discrimination at work.)

✓ Reading Check

COMPARE A misdemeanor is a less serious crime than a felony.

Resources

📂 **Student Activity Workbook** Assign the Chapter 12 activities in the Student Activity Workbook.

▶ **MEDIATION** Many workplace disputes are resolved through mediation, a process in which a third party works to resolve the conflict. *Why do you think many companies prefer mediation to going to court?*

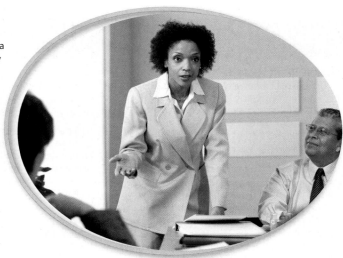

Criminal Law

Civil law covers most workplace disputes. Sometimes, however, an incident on a job site may bring criminal charges and fall under criminal law. Under **criminal law**, the government brings an indictment, or list of criminal charges, against a person or a business. A serious crime punishable by imprisonment or death, such as fraud, murder, or rape, is called a **felony**. A less serious crime, such as shoplifting or striking another worker, is called a **misdemeanor**.

✓ Reading Check **EXPLAIN** What is a misdemeanor?

Legal Services

If your legal problem cannot be settled or brought to small claims court, your next step should be to contact a lawyer. Laws and legal procedures are very complex. Arguing a case in court is best done by an expert. Although hiring a lawyer can be expensive, having a lawyer will probably produce more effective results.

Finding a Lawyer

You want to be sure that the lawyer who takes your case specializes in, or knows, the law the affects it. To start your search, try the following:

- Use your phone book or search online for legal referral services. A local bar association is a good place to begin.
- Ask friends and family members if they can recommend a lawyer.
- If you are a member of a group or prepaid legal plan through your job or other organization, contact this service. Such services may assist with legal advice and costs.

▶▶ *Extend the Photo*

Caption Answer In addition to wanting to avoid court fees and to arrive at a speedier resolution, companies would likely want to avoid negative publicity from a court case.

Discussion Ask students if they have ever been involved in mediation. Remind them that if a parent has had to step in to settle a problem between siblings, that is a form of mediation.

Once you have a list of possible lawyers, interview them to determine who would best represent you. These questions may help you decide:

- What is your specialty and what type of experience do you have?
- What do you estimate your fee will be?
- How long will my case take?
- Will I be regularly updated?
- Would handling my case create a potential conflict with another client?
- Do you have malpractice insurance?
- Do you have a document that explains the legal steps we will take?

Lawyers' Fees

Lawyers generally charge an hourly rate or a flat fee based on how much work they expect to do for you. In addition, some lawyers work for a **contingency fee**, which is payment that is a percentage of any money that you win in the lawsuit. Make sure you understand the fee system and projected costs before hiring anyone.

Low-cost legal assistance in civil cases may be available from The Legal Aid Society or other organizations. If you are charged in a criminal case, the office of the local public defender can provide free legal representation.

No matter where you go for legal advice, be prepared for the meeting: bring documents, records, and names of witnesses. Do not expect your lawyer to do all the work, particularly if you are receiving free or low-cost legal aid. Ask how you can be involved and what you can do to help your case. Remember, too, that legal proceedings can take a very long time—months or even years.

HOT JOBS!

Mediator

A mediator, or conflict resolution associate, helps opposing parties come to agreements without resorting to lawsuits. Such facilitators must be effective communicators who are able to work with people who may be upset or angry, whether in person or on the telephone. Requirements include communication skills, personal skills, and knowledge of the legal system. Mediators are typically employed by public courts of justice; are interested in community service; and can be members of their state's bar.

Section 12.2 After You Read

Review Key Concepts

1. Give an example of a workplace situation that could lead to a civil case and a workplace situation that could lead to a criminal case.
2. Identify two possible ways to resolve a civil law case.
3. List two questions you would ask when deciding whether to hire a lawyer to represent you.

Practice Academic Skills

English Language Arts

4. Write a maximum 500-word e-mail to a friend explaining why it is best to resolve a civil case out of court rather than through a trial.

Social Studies

5. Use library and Internet resources to research the history of small claims court in the United States, and write a brief report on your findings.

@ Check your answers at this book's OLC through **glencoe.com**.

glencoe.com

Section 12.2 After You Read

Review Key Concepts

1. Possible answers: A dispute over age discrimination might lead to a civil case; a disagreement that ended in a physical fight in which a worker was injured might lead to a criminal case.
2. Students might mention following complaint procedures, filing a formal complaint, mediation, and arbitration.
3. Possible questions: What kind of experience do you have with this type of case? What is your fee?

Practice Academic Skills

4. In their e-mails, students might point out that allowing a case to go to trial will cost more time and money.
5. Reports should show research into the history of small claims court in the United States.

ASSESS

After You Read
Have students complete the Section 12.2 After You Read section review.

Online Study Tools
Have students go to the OLC through **glencoe.com** to:

- Take the Section 12.2 **Practice Test**.
- Download **Podcast** study tools.
- Download free **Study-to-Go** content to their PDAs or cell phones.

STUDY TO GO

Resources

ExamView Assessment Suite CD allows you to print out ready-made unit and chapter tests complete with answer keys. You can also create customized tests.

CLOSE

Culminating Activity
Analyze a Trial Have students work in pairs to research a recent (within the past year) trial. The trial can be a local, national, civil, or criminal case. Have students answer the following questions in two-page reports: Is it a civil or a criminal trial? Who are the parties involved? What was the dispute or charges? What was the verdict?

N C L B | Activity correlated to English Language Arts standards.

FOCUS

Discussion Starter
Law, Public Safety, Corrections, and Security Have students brainstorm different careers and jobs that can be found in this career cluster. (Careers may include security guard, lawyer, legal assistant, and judge.)

TEACH

W Writing Support
Independent Practice
Conduct Research Have students research the American Bar Association and describe the organization and its purpose in a one-page report. (The ABA sets academic standards for law schools and formulates legal codes and ethical codes for the profession.)

R Reading Strategy
Research Words and Word Origins Have students research and find the term "bar" as it applies to law and to use the Internet and other resources to find the etymology, or history, of the term as used in that context. Next, tell students that many terms in law in the United States are derived from Medieval Latin. Have students research and provide definitions for one or more commonly used legal terms, such as *pro bono*, *affidavit*, and *habeas corpus*. (Answers will vary depending on the terms chosen. For example, *pro bono* refers to legal work donated for the public good; an *affidavit* is a sworn statement in writing, often made under oath; and *habeas corpus* refers to documents issued to bring a party before a court or judge.)

CAREER SPOTLIGHT

Career Cluster: Law, Public Safety, Corrections, and Security

John Arai Mitchell
Business Law Attorney

Q: Describe your job.
A: There are two parts to my job. First, I advise clients on legal issues that affect their businesses. I help them take steps necessary to achieve their goals, like starting a business or negotiating a contract. Second, I represent my clients in commercial disputes, often involving contracts or intellectual property. Over the years, my clients have included pop culture magazines, high-tech companies, artists, clothing companies, global financial institutions, and a professional football team.

Q: Describe a typical workday.
A: One of the reasons I enjoy being an attorney is that no two days are ever the same. Some days I spend the entire time in the library or in my office researching legal issues and drafting documents to submit to a judge. I may be in court, arguing a motion or in trial. On other days, I may meet with someone who wants to do business with a client. It's not uncommon to find me at the airport, traveling to a hearing or a meeting.

Q: What skills are most important to you in your job?
A: Reading comprehension, writing, and logic and reasoning. As with any job, a good sense of humor and the ability to keep things in perspective are also useful.

Q: What academic skills and lifelong learning skills are helpful in preparing for your career?
A: The most important academic skills are reading, writing, and research. It helps to have natural curiosity and a desire to learn. Like the world around us, laws are constantly evolving. A successful lawyer must stay abreast of those changes.

Q: What is your key to success?
A: The ability to listen. The quality of legal advice an attorney provides depends on how well he or she understands the client's concerns or problems.

Q: What training and preparation do you recommend for students?
A: With few exceptions, to become a lawyer, you must graduate from a four-year college and attend a law school accredited by the American Bar Association. Generally, after three years of law school, you receive a juris doctor and are eligible to take the bar examination in your state. If you pass the bar exam, you can become a licensed attorney in that state.

W
R

Q: What are some ways you recommend students prepare for this career?
A: A rigorous academic schedule that develops strong reading, writing, and analytical skills.

Q: What do you like most about your work?
A: I like learning new things, whether it is the details of a client's business or an unfamiliar area of the law. I like helping my clients, all of whom I consider good friends. I like that I can help people who need legal advice but cannot afford it, so I frequently represent indigent clients in pro bono cases. Even though the day-to-day practice of law can be difficult, it makes for a rewarding professional life.

 For more about Career Clusters, go to this book's OLC through **glencoe.com**.

NO CHILD LEFT BEHIND

NCLB

Teaching Tip

The NCLB Act emphasizes reading skills. Encouraging students to find the definitions of words from context can improve their vocabularies and their ability to figure out the meaning of unfamiliar words. For example, ask a question that can be answered by context and have students check their definitions with a dictionary.

Sample Question According to this interview, a juris doctor is:

a. a client

b. a medical doctor

c. a degree that you receive after attending law school

d. a professor

(Answer: c)

CAREER FACTS

- **Education or Training** To practice law in the courts of any state or other jurisdiction, a person must be licensed or admitted to its bar. To qualify for the bar examination in most states, an applicant usually must earn a college degree and graduate from a law school accredited by the American Bar Association (ABA) or the proper State authorities.

- **Academic Skills Required** English Language Arts, Mathematics, Social Studies, World Languages

- **Technology Needed** Some lawyers supplement conventional law libraries sources with computer sources, such as the Internet and legal databases. Many lawyers use computers to organize and index material.

- **Aptitudes, Abilities, and Skills** Prospective lawyers should develop proficiency in writing and speaking, reading, researching, analyzing, and thinking logically. Courses in English, foreign languages, public speaking, government,

philosophy, history, economics, mathematics, and computer science, among others, are useful.

Workplace Safety Lawyers can work long, stressful hours, and should also be mindful of ergonomics and strain caused by repetitive tasks.

Career Outlook Employment of lawyers is expected to grow about as fast as average over the next ten years, primarily as a result of growth in the population and in the general level of business activities. Job growth will also result from increasing demand for legal services in such areas as health care, intellectual property, venture capital, energy, elder, antitrust, and environmental law.

Career Path Lawyers can become partners or start their own firms. They can also use their knowledge and skills in positions outside the legal industry.

Academic Skills Required to Complete Tasks

Tasks	English Language Arts	Mathematics	Social Studies	World Languages
Advise clients on legal matters	★		★	
Represent clients	★		★	
Research legal issues	★	★	★	★
Draft documents	★		★	
Keep up to date on legal changes	★		★	

NCLB This chart relates academic skills such as English Language Arts, Mathematics, Science, Social Studies, and World Languages to specific tasks that are performed for the job featured in the Career Spotlight feature.

Critical Thinking

Why might states have their own bar exams for prospective attorneys?

Critical Thinking

States might have their own bar exams to ensure that lawyers and other workers in the legal profession are familiar with local and state laws that may vary from state to state.

CAREER SPOTLIGHT

ASSESS

Make Connections Tell students that the Law, Public Safety, Security, and Corrections career cluster contains a number of professions that inspire works of art and entertainment such as television shows and movies. Tell students that some individuals often end up being consultants on or participating in works of art that document or fictionalize their profession. Ask students to research the jobs in this career cluster and to name popular TV shows, movies, comic books, or novels that feature one of the professions featured in this career cluster. Have students research the education and training requirements for these jobs and discuss their findings informally in class.

CLOSE

Culminating Activity

Lifelong Learning and Career Clusters Point out to students that the individual profiled in this career spotlight stresses the need for excellent communication skills for his particular career in the Law, Public Safety, Security, and Corrections career cluster. Ask students what other specific skills or abilities might be useful in the following professions: firefighter, police detective, prison guard in a minimum-security prison, and judge. (Answers may include: Firefighter: the ability to work as a member of a team; detective: problem-solving skills; prison guard: the ability to be diplomatic; judge: the ability to be fair and impartial)

Key Terms and Academic Vocabulary Review

1. Students should use each of the key terms and academic vocabulary terms in a complete sentence. A sample answer might read: "The nation's first *minimum wage* was only $0.40 an hour."

Review Key Concepts

2. Students might mention two of the following FLSA laws: minimum wage laws, the 40-hour workweek, and child labor laws, which set a minimum age of 16 for most nonagricultural jobs. Labor laws protect employees from unfair treatment on the job.

3. The Civil Rights Act of 1964 bans employment discrimination based on race, ethnicity, religion, or gender. The Age Discrimination Act of 1967 makes it illegal to discriminate against people over 40 in hiring, promoting, or discharging employees. The Rehabilitation Act of 1973 and the Americans with Disabilities Act of 1990 protect rights of individuals with disabilities.

4. Immediately tell the person to stop. Write down what happened. Inform a trusted supervisor. Get help from your local human rights office or the office of the U.S. Equal Employment Opportunity Commission.

5. Civil law applies to conflicts between private parties concerning rights and obligations. Criminal law will either be a felony or misdemeanor and involves the government filing criminal charges against someone.

6. Civil law cases include divorce, custody battles, personal injury cases, or civil law cases that involve disputes with employers. These cases may be resolved in small claims court, through settlements, or in a civil court.

7. Find a lawyer through the phone book, by asking friends or family members for referrals, or by contacting a lawyer referral service. Evaluate a potential lawyer by asking questions such as: What type of experience do you have? What is your specialty and what do you estimate your fee will be? How long will my case take? Will I be regularly updated? Would handling my case create a potential conflict with another client? Do you have malpractice insurance? Do you have a document that explains the legal steps we will take?

CHAPTER SUMMARY

Section 12.1

Labor laws help to ensure fair treatment for all employees in the workplace. The Fair Labor Standards Act established the minimum wage, the 40-hour workweek, and child labor law. Workers have the right to form or join labor unions, which negotiate with employers for better working conditions, salaries, and other benefits. The Family and Medical Leave Act guarantees up to 12 weeks a year for personal medical care or to care for a family member. Antidiscrimination laws protect workers from job discrimination based on race, national origin, religion, age, gender, and disability. Both genders have the right to a work environment free from sexual harassment.

Section 12.2

The legal system provides a set of procedures for resolving conflicts. Civil law applies to conflicts between private parties concerning rights and obligations. Small claims court is a low-cost alternative to a court trial. Ways to resolve a civil dispute without going to trial include mediation and arbitration. Criminal law involves criminal charges, which are brought by the government. More serious criminal offenses are felonies, and less serious offenses are misdemeanors. If you need to go to court, you should consult a lawyer. Before hiring a lawyer, ask about the lawyer's specialty and fees, and how you can help with the work for your case.

Key Terms and Academic Vocabulary Review

1. Use each of these key terms and academic vocabulary words in a sentence.

Key Terms
- minimum wage (p. 265)
- compensatory time (p. 265)
- collective bargaining (p. 266)
- discrimination (p. 268)
- affirmative action (p. 269)
- sexual harassment (p. 270)
- civil law (p. 272)
- summons (p. 272)
- criminal law (p. 274)
- felony (p. 274)
- misdemeanor (p. 274)
- contingency fee (p. 275)

Academic Vocabulary
- federal (p. 265)
- procedures (p. 272)
- contract (p. 272)

Review Key Concepts

2. **Name** two labor laws and explain how they protect workers.
3. **Identify** the main antidiscrimination laws and explain their purpose.
4. **Describe** effective strategies for handling sexual harassment.
5. **Explain** the difference between civil law and criminal law.
6. **Describe** an example of a civil law case and explain how it might be resolved.
7. **Explain** how to find and evaluate legal services.

Critical Thinking

8. **Analyze** Why are antidiscrimination laws important? How do they affect you?
9. **Evaluate** How might sexual harassment interfere with a person's career advancement?

Critical Thinking

8. Students might point out that antidiscrimination laws are important, because anyone can be potentially discriminated against on the basis of gender, race, nationality, etc.

9. The stress of sexual harassment can negatively impact a worker's job performance. A person who is being sexually harassed by a manager or supervisor may also feel his or her job is threatened.

Real-World Skills and Applications

Critical Thinking Skills

10. Problem Solving Working in a group of three, come up with an example of a dispute that would require arbitration. Decide who will be the arbitrator, and have the other two group members defend opposite sides of the dispute. After listening to both arguments, the arbitrator should make a judgment in favor of one side, explaining his or her reasons. Then switch roles until all group members have had a chance to be the arbitrator.

Information and Media Literacy Skills

11. Using Research Tools Labor laws have played a major role in U.S. history and culture. Research one federal or state law that has affected one aspect of the world of work—such as hours, wages, child labor, diversity, unions, safety, benefits, or the environment. Prepare a two- to three-minute oral report for the class on conditions before the law and how conditions changed after the law was passed.

Technology Applications

12. Using a Word-Processing Program Locate and read several articles on sexual harassment in the workplace. Use a word-processing program to design and create a written policy or poster for a specific business that can help to ensure a work environment free of sexual harassment.

13. **Finding Legal Services** Imagine that you were working on a temporary basis for a company when you injured your shoulder in a job-related accident. You asked the company to help pay your medical bills and give you time off of work, but they refused. You decided you should seek legal help. Using the procedure for finding a lawyer outlined in the chapter, create a list of lawyers you might ask for advice. Write a list of questions that you will use to interview each lawyer. Pair with another student to ask one another the questions, and record the answers in a two-page document.

14. **Mediation**

Situation While on an errand for his company, Jack was in an accident that destroyed his car. Jack thinks the company is financially responsible for the damages. His employer refuses to pay.

Activity You will play the role of mediator between Jack and his employer. Listen as both sides explain their positions. Remember that you are to remain neutral as you help both parties talk to each other and reach a compromise.

Evaluation You will be evaluated on how well you meet the following performance indicators:

- Listen attentively to both people.
- Ask questions and lead the discussion objectively.
- Help the parties reach a settlement that they both agree is fair.

 ACTIVE LEARNING

13. Questions might include any of the following. What kind of experience do you have representing employees who have been injured on the job? Do you or does your firm represent my employer in any way? What are my options? How much will it cost? What are my chances of winning? What might I recover? How long will it take? What should I expect?

ROLE PLAY

14. Effective mediators should listen carefully and behave objectively throughout the activity. Mediators should also ask questions and make comments that help the two opponents come to a compromise.

Real-World Skills and Applications

10. Encourage students to alternate roles so all students get to role play both a disputing party and an arbitrator. Have students discuss whether they found it difficult to listen to both sides impartially and whether they found it difficult to make a decision.

11. Presentations will vary depending on the labor law chosen. Presentations should explain the conditions before the law and how conditions changed after the law. For example, students who choose to prepare a report about child labor laws might point out that children sometimes worked up to 60 hours a week before the laws were established. Now, because of the law, the minimum age for most workers is 16.

12. Policies and posters should clearly define sexual harassment and set clear guidelines so employees know to avoid potential actions that could be construed as sexual harassment, and what employees should do if they feel they are being sexually harassed.

Academic Skills in the Workplace

15. Reports should clearly state the facts of the case and both sides of the dispute. Students should strive for accuracy in detailing the facts by including correctly spelled proper names, accurate dates, and any other information particular to the case.

16. About 285 (9.5 × 30 = 285) days have passed since the patent application was mailed.

17. Posters might show exercises such as walking, playing a sport, jogging, dancing, biking, swimming, and martial arts.

18. In their oral reports, students should identify the country they have chosen to research and summarize employment opportunities in the country's legal system. Presentations should use visual aids such as graphs or pictures to show information about education and licensing requirements and opportunities students might pursue.

Academic Skills in the Workplace

 English Language Arts

15. Practice Expository Writing Much legal writing is expository writing, which informs readers about a particular subject. To practice expository writing, find a court case or workplace dispute you find interesting. You can research cases in the newspapers, in journals, or on the Internet or arrange a visit to a state or federal courthouse and sit in on a trial. Report the facts of the case in a one-page example of expository writing. Be sure to present both sides of the dispute or case and to check all facts that relate to the case such as the names of the parties involved.

 Mathematics

16. Calculate Time It has been about nine and a half months since you sent in all of the necessary paperwork to apply for a new patent. About how many days has it been?

CONCEPT **Increments of Time** Weeks always have seven days, and there are usually four weeks in a month. Months have varying numbers of days, from 28 to 31. Typically, however, 30 is used as an average to represent the number of days in a month.

Starting Hint Set up an equation to figure out how many days are in 9.5 months, and solve: $9.5 \times 30 = x$

 Science

17. Exercising Modern health research has shown that exercise is good for the heart. It also helps the brain by increasing blood flow there and in all other parts of the body. People who keep up a good exercise plan tend to be able to think more clearly and to be injured less in the workplace. What are some different exercises you can do during the week to keep your heart and brain in good health? Create a poster displaying one or more exercises.

Social Studies

18. Research International Legal Careers Imagine that you are interested in working in the legal field in another country. Choose a country, and use library and Internet sources to research the types of legal careers available in that country and any requirements, including education and licensing. Use presentation software or other visual aids to create a five-minute oral report on the results of your research.

STANDARDIZED TEST PRACTICE

ESSAY

Directions Use a separate sheet of paper to write a one-page response to the following question.

> **Test-Taking Tip** Before answering an essay question, think about what you want to say. Write down a few notes to help you organize your thoughts. Number your thoughts in the order you will write about them.

1. Explain the difference between a civil case and a criminal case. Then describe one workplace situation that could lead to the filing of civil case and one workplace situation that could lead to the filing of a criminal case.

For more Standardized Test Practice, go to the OLC *glencoe.com.*

STANDARDIZED TEST PRACTICE

Answer
1. Essays should clearly detail the facts of the two workplace actions that could lead to civil and criminal cases.

Test-Taking Strategies
The best practice for essay and short-answer test questions is frequent writing assignments with an emphasis on clarity, concision, and correct grammar and spelling. Many students find it difficult to begin an essay if they cannot think of an opening sentence. Encourage students to create an outline, clarify their position on the topic, and then begin the essay with a strong statement of their position.

Writing Skills Practice

19. Creating an Argument Legal arguments can support a point of view of a particular law. An argument expresses your point of view about an idea or subject. Your point of view must be supported by facts and information.

Practice Find a brief article in a news source about a company policy you think your company should adopt. This may be a policy addressing a legal issue, such as diversity training. Write a one-page argument that expresses your opinion that your company should adopt a similar policy. Follow the steps below when writing your argument:

- Identify your main point. Write your topic sentence from this main point.
- As you read, identify facts that support your main point. Make notes or highlight the details that support your main point.
- Review your notes. Keep those that you want to use. Delete those you do not want to use.
- Write a draft. State your main point and support it with details that help to develop your argument.
- Edit and finalize your argument.

Net Connection

20. Research Law Careers Go online to research job requirements, necessary education and training, and career outlook for career options in the field of law.

@ Log On Go to this book's Online Learning Center through **glencoe.com** to find a link to a career Web site. Find four career possibilities in the legal field. Write a one-page summary of your findings.

Reading Connection
@ Go to this book's Online Learning Center through **glencoe.com** for a list of reading suggestions.

Personal Academic and Career Portfolio

Legal Resources

At some point in your career, you may be involved in a legal dispute. Adding information to your **Personal Academic and Career Portfolio** about your legal options and how to find legal advice will help you find the best solution to your conflict.

Make a list of the ways to resolve a legal dispute, including those that involve the courts and those that do not. Then perform research using the procedures outlined in the chapter to determine the legal services and settlement services available in your area. For each service you find, note the name of the service and contact information.

The following guidelines will help you create an effective guide to legal resources for your portfolio:

- Create a list of ways to resolve a legal dispute, including those that involve the courts and those that do not.
- Research using the phone book, the Internet, and other resources to find the legal services and settlement services, such as mediators and arbitrators, in your area. Note the contact information for each.
- Add a file to your portfolio, label it *Legal Resources*, and add this information to it.
- You may check periodically to see if new services are available or if the information is up-to-date.

@ Portfolio Help Go to the *Succeeding in the World of Work* OLC through **glencoe.com** for help developing your portfolio.

Writing Skills Practice

19. One-page arguments should contain a specific company policy and the students' opinion about whether the policy should be implemented at their company. Students should use facts to support the opinion they stated in their topic sentence.

Net Connection

20. Students should use the Internet to find examples of career options in the law field and provide information about the education and training and outlook for workers who want to enter that field.

Resources

ExamView Assessment Suite CD allows you to print out ready-made unit and chapter tests complete with answer keys. You can also create customized tests.

WorkKeys

WorkKeys® is a job skills assessment program. For information on leveled assessment for Interpersonal Skills (Teamwork), go to the WorkKeys link on this book's OLC through **glencoe.com**.

Personal Academic and Career Portfolio

Adding Legal Information

As students make decisions about careers, they will likely focus on areas of work that have specific legal matters. For example, workers in the medical field must keep up-to-date on legislation that affects health insurance and Medicare laws, as well as drug prescription approvals by the Food and Drug Administration. Have students collect articles from newspapers, journals, periodicals, or online sources that detail legislation or recent legal matters that affect careers in their field, and add have them add relevant articles to their **Personal Academic and Career Portfolio**.

Unit 4 Thematic Project

FOCUS

Discussion Starter

Ask students if they know anyone who has been injured on the job or faced health problems because of their work, and what caused the problem. As a class, brainstorm further on-the-job injuries and illnesses that workers may face and what could cause each. (Students may mention stress, insomnia, MSDs, allergies, respiratory disease, burns or cuts, skin conditions, sprains, strains, or breaks, hearing loss, heat stress, chemical exposure, or workplace violence.)

STEP **1**

Evaluate Your Skills and Resources

Have students go to the *Succeeding in the World of Work* OLC through **glencoe.com** for a graphic organizer they can use to organize the skills, tools, and resources they will use to complete the project.

TEACH

C Critical Thinking

Ask students to brainstorm specific circumstances and situations that might make a worker more likely to make a mistake on the job and cause an accident. (Accidents are more likely when workers are fatigued, feel overconfident, have poor safety habits, lack sufficient training or experience, are under stress, or face distractions or interruptions. Confusing displays or controls on equipment, overwork, and lack of strong safety messages from management can also promote accidents.)

282

Ensuring a Safe, Healthy Career

You know that government, employers, and employees share responsibility for creating and maintaining safe workplaces. You also know that some jobs are riskier than others, and that being informed about the health and safety risks of various careers can help you not only to make an informed career choice, but also to stay healthy on the job. In this project, you will research the potential health and safety risks of a career that interests you and develop an action plan to minimize each of those risks.

Project Assignment

- Choose three potential health or safety risks that can affect workers in your desired career field.
- Gather data about on-the-job or other workplace-related injuries and illnesses in this career field by consulting the Bureau of Labor Statistics, employers and employees in your desired field, the Occupational Safety and Health Administration (OSHA), and other library, Internet, and real-world resources.
- Research ways to minimize the three chosen health and safety risks and create an action plan to handle each of those risks.
- Use presentation software to demonstrate your research and suggestions.

Lifelong Learning Connection

Lifelong learning concepts found in this project include:
- Interpersonal communication skills
- Technology skills
- Your career plan and career path

STEP **1** Evaluate Your Skills and Resources

To complete this project, you will need to do research in several different ways. You will need access to the Internet to consult government statistics and other health and safety data. You will also need to talk to employers and employees in your chosen career field to gather information about common workplace hazards, and you will need access to presentation software to format and present your data and conclusions.

Skills you will need to complete the Unit Thematic Project include:

Academic Skills reading, writing, mathematics, social studies

Transferable Skills communication, research, problem-solving, and decision-making skills

Technology Skills presentation software and Internet skills

@ Resources Organizer To find a graphic organizer you can use to determine the skills, tools, and resources you will need for this project, go to this book's Online Learning Center through **glencoe.com**.

glencoe.com

SPOTLIGHT ON TECHNOLOGY

Ergonomic Technology in the Workplace

Because many workers perform the same activities over and over again all day, they sometimes develop musculoskeletal disorders (MSDs), particularly those caused by repetitive stress. The science of ergonomics sprang up in direct response to this problem. Ergonomics focuses on designing and arranging people's workspaces and equipment to make tasks more efficient and to prevent MSDs. Ask students to research innovative ways that companies are using advances in ergonomics to improve worker health and efficiency. (Examples will vary from low-tech adaptations such as anti-fatigue matting in factories to analytical techniques such as motion analysis to software tools that provide rest break reminders.)

STEP 2 Preview a Real-World Company Profile

Company profiles can help you understand the specific industry issues that real-world companies face and can show you how some companies manage these issues. This can help you develop criteria to evaluate the health and safety practices of companies where you might want to work.

Real-World Company: REI

Recreational Equipment, Inc. (REI) was founded as a cooperative in 1938 by a group of 23 mountaineers. Today, REI is the country's largest cooperative, dedicated to inspiring, educating, and outfitting its customer-members for a lifetime of outdoor adventure. REI operates nearly 90 stores nationwide, two online stores, and an outdoor adventure travel company. With more than 2.8 million active members and more than 7,500 employees, the Washington state cooperative is a respected supplier of specialty outdoor gear and clothing and a socially responsible retailer with a commitment to community involvement and environmental action.

David Jayo manages REI's corporate giving programs, which include outdoor gear grants, community grants, and service projects. These programs help the company support local communities and further the work of nonprofit organizations dedicated to conservation and helping people enjoy the outdoors. Jayo uses his skills in program delivery, strategic planning, budgeting, and operations to help him manage the programs.

Real-World Company: REI

Aspects of Industry	Company Facts
Planning	The company has six core values—authenticity, quality, service, respect, integrity, and balance—that guide business decisions and customer service.
Management	REI's culture is team-centered. Managers are accessible and welcome input from employees, vendors, customers, and other stakeholders.
Finance	REI distributes about 85 percent of annual profits to each of its customer-members in the form of a refund.
Technical and Production Skills	Workers at this customer-centered company need communication and service skills as well as knowledge of outdoor sports.
Underlying Principles of Technology	The company seeks out cutting-edge technology for its products—from digital hiking maps to biomechanically engineered snowshoes.
Labor Issues	REI employees benefit recieve performance-based pay, health and wellness programs, a profit sharing plan, tuition assistance, and more.
Health, Safety, and Environmental Issues	REI is focused on being a role model throughout the outdoor industry with its environmental and fair labor standards.
Community Issues	REI supports environmental stewardship efforts. Stores work with nonprofit partners to bring outdoor recreation opportunities to young people.

283

Developing Industry Partners

Build a Service Learning Program

A service-learning program can help your students in many ways. Such a program can help students feel a sense of connection to community, build leadership skills, and learn appropriate work attitudes and practices, such as responsibility, initiative, and self-management. Service learning can also help students recognize their ability to make meaningful contributions to others, which boosts their self-esteem. Just as important, service learning programs foster positive attitudes toward local schools and students.

TEACH (cont.)

STEP 2

Preview a Real-World Company Profile

Ask students what valuable information managers of a company, such as REI, could learn from the input of their employees, vendors, and customers? (Managers could learn about programs, products, and services that are working well, that need improvement, or that should be discontinued. They could also get ideas for new trends, markets, technologies, products, and services, and for better ways to do things.)

W Writing Support
Guided Practice
Aspects of Industry

Remind students that managers plan, organize, and direct an organization's resources—people, money, supplies and equipment, and information. Ask students to work in pairs to brainstorm the skills necessary to be a good manager. (Students should mention skills in interpersonal relationships, communication, delegating, finance, strategic planning, organization, and time management, among others.)

U Universal Access
Naturalistic Learners

Naturalistic learners excel at finding and observing patterns and at organizing data. Ask such learners to keep a journal for one week that records safety and health practices—both good and bad—that they observe at school, home, and in workplace environments such as local stores and businesses. At the end of the week, have students summarize what they learned and offer recommendations for improving any unsafe practices they may have noted.

283

TEACH (cont.)

STEP 3

Research Procedures

Have students go to the *Succeeding in the World of Work* OLC through **glencoe.com** for a graphic organizer they can use to organize the results of their research.

STEP 4

Connect to Community

Ask students how they think an employer's health, safety, and environmental practices could affect not only its employees, but also members of the surrounding community. (Employers' practices affect the environmental quality of the surrounding area as well as the physical and mental health of workers and their families, which has an impact on overall community wellness.) Ask students to make a list of ways they could help enhance safety and protect the environment in their local communities. (Students may mention maintaining or improving a park, helping to reduce pollution and promote recycling, or participating in emergency preparedness drills, CPR courses, or a Neighborhood Watch program.)

STEP 5

Report Your Findings

Give students these tips on crafting their presentations:

- Structure each slide as a series of short sentences or bullet points.
- Present one main point per slide, with relevant supporting evidence.
- Be concise. Include only major points and keywords in your slides.
- Format citations according to the *MLA Style Manual* or another accepted standard.

284

STEP 3 Research Procedures

Follow these steps to compose an effective presentation:

1. Before you begin to write and create your presentation, conduct sufficient research. Use current sources and a variety of resources. Contact people who work in your chosen field; their comments will add a valuable human perspective.
2. Create a "Works Cited" section of your presentation to document all of your resources and explain where you found the data and information.
3. Develop a general outline for your presentation. Devote special attention to key elements, including the introduction and conclusion.
4. Create a separate section for each of your three action plans.

@ Resources Organizer To find a graphic organizer you can use to organize your research, go to this book's OLC through **glencoe.com**.

STEP 4 Connect to Community

Get Local Arrange to visit a local business and to speak to the person in charge of health and safety programs. Ask about common causes of accidents, illnesses, and injuries at the company and how the company and employees work together to reduce these occurrences. Ask to see any safety signs or posters that the employer is required by law to hang in the workplace.

Take the Next Step Interview a worker in your community who has experienced an on-the-job or workplace-related injury or illness. Ask that worker to describe the incident and its cause and to give suggestions on how other workers could protect themselves from a similar occurrence. What suggestions and guidance would the worker give to a new employee starting out to help him or her stay safe and healthy on the job?

STEP 5 Report Your Findings

Your final product for this project should include a presentation with at least 15 slides that identify three current health and safety risks in your chosen field, as well as strategies for reducing or overcoming these hazards. Your presentation should also include a section on "Works Cited."

Helpful Hints When preparing your presentation, do the following:

- Pay special attention to your introduction. Start with interesting information to get the attention of your audience. You can use surprising statistics, humor, testimonials, or a vibrant slide.
- Follow an organized outline. Clearly introduce each new topic.
- Memorize enough of your presentation so that you can work from an outline.
- Design slides that summarize key information. Fill in details and transitions orally.

Developing Community Involvement

Assist Those in Need

Work with social service agencies to identify a local community center or home for senior citizens or people with disabilities. Speak to administrators and identify projects that students could safely perform at the facility, such as raking leaves, painting the lobby, gardening, organizing the library or common room, and cleaning. There may be organizations or individual volunteers in your area that already organize such services and that would be glad to receive students' assistance.

- Limit yourself to a few basic colors and fonts to avoid visual clutter. Do not use too many patterns or photos.
- Make sure you know how to give a slide-show using the presentation software.
- Practice your presentation in front of family members or fellow students.
- Make eye contact with everyone in the room and speak slowly and clearly.
- Conclude by restating and summarizing your main points.

STEP 6 Presentation and Evaluation

Your performance will be evaluated based on:
- depth of research
- organization of research
- accuracy and coherence of information presented
- quality of sources and "Works Cited"

Personal Academic and Career Portfolio

Print out a copy of your presentation to include in your **Personal Academic and Career Portfolio**. Include an electronic copy in your digital portfolio. You can refer to the data in the presentation as you make your career choice and use the presentation to showcase your software and safety-awareness skills to potential employers.

- mechanics—neatness and presentation, including spelling
- quality of delivery and slides
- demonstrated understanding of health and safety risks
- Creativity of action plans proposed

@ **Evaluation Rubric** To find a rubric you can use to evaluate your project, go to this book's OLC through **glencoe.com**.

BusinessWeek Connection

Understanding All Aspects of Industry: Management

Understanding all aspects of an industry can help you prepare to succeed in a career in that industry. Management is the way a company uses its employees, equipment, and money to accomplish its goals. Managers set policies and help to plan the company's direction. They make sure that projects are done on time and on budget, and they hire, mentor, and fire employees. Most large companies have a hierarchy of managers, from the CEO down to individual department managers.

Small companies may have only one manager. At all companies, effective managers are leaders, communicators, decision makers, and problem solvers.

@ Go to this book's Online Learning Center through **glencoe.com** to find a *BusinessWeek* article titled "Keep Franchising or Go Indie?" Read the article and consider the benefits and drawbacks of being part of a franchise. Use a word-processing program to create a one-page summary of the article. Add this summary to your **Personal Academic and Career Portfolio**.

ASSESS

STEP 6

Presentation and Evaluation

Rubric Encourage students go to the *Succeeding in the World of Work* OLC through **glencoe.com** for a rubric they can use to evaluate their project. Encourage students to use the rubric as a content checklist when researching safety and health issues and compiling their research into an effective presentation.

CLOSE

Culminating Activity

Safety Leadership In this Unit Thematic Project, students applied the Unit topic to their own lives by researching and analyzing safety and health risks in a career that interests them. Divide students into small groups and ask them to imagine that they are responsible for safety programs at a large company in an industry of their choosing. Ask them to create a safety plan to keep workplace conditions safe, provide ongoing training and high-quality safety equipment for workers, and encourage workers to report unsafe conditions. Have groups present their recommendations to the class. (Recommendations will vary but may include frequent safety meetings and inspections, creating a clear chain of command, empowering workers to take charge of their own safety, presenting safety awards, retraining workers frequently, and communicating the importance of safety.)

BusinessWeek Connection

All Aspects of Industry: Management

Explain to students that there are many different management styles, as well as blends of these styles. For example, directing managers make most important decisions themselves and give strong directions. Discussing managers encourage two-way communication and teamwork, while delegating managers let their employees manage themselves and make their own decisions. Ask students to write a one-page essay weighing the pros and cons of these styles, or of other styles they discover through their own research, and explaining the style(s) they would use if they were a manager. (Essays and opinions will vary, but students should understand that different management styles may be called for in different situations. For example, the directing style may be effective in a crisis, while the delegating style may be effective when dealing with highly competent staff.)

Chapter	Chapter Objectives
CHAPTER 13 Interpersonal Relationships at Work	• **Identify** personal traits and interpersonal skills that will make you an effective coworker. • **Describe** steps to self-improvement. • **Summarize** the rules of workplace etiquette. • **Describe** the process of conflict resolution. • **Explain** diversity and describe effective ways to work with a diverse group of people.
CHAPTER 14 Teamwork and Leadership	• **Identify** the benefits of teamwork for team members and businesses. • **Explain** how to organize and manage an effective team. • **Describe** how to be a good team member. • **Define** total quality management and explain how it affects workers. • **Explain** the characteristics of effective leaders and name four leadership styles. • **Summarize** the procedure for leading a formal meeting.
CHAPTER 15 Professional Communication Skills	• **Identify** ways to improve your speaking skills. • **Describe** good speaking habits and explain their importance in the workplace. • **Explain** how active listening and note taking can help you listen. • **Summarize** strategies for improving your writing skills. • **Identify** common forms of business writing and the style appropriate to each. • **Explain** reading skills such as skimming and previewing.
CHAPTER 16 Thinking Skills on the Job	• **Apply** the seven-step decision-making process on the job. • **Evaluate** your alternatives. • **Prioritize** your work. • **Identify** the six basic steps of the problem-solving process. • **Describe** how to generate, choose, and implement solutions to problems. • **Evaluate** solutions.
CHAPTER 17 Technology in the Workplace	• **Explain** how technology is transforming the workplace. • **Identify** the skills needed to work in a technological environment. • **Name** computer programs commonly used in business and explain their use. • **Describe** business uses of the Internet. • **Describe** copyright and other laws that affect how we use technology.
CHAPTER 18 Time and Information Management	• **Explain** how to prioritize your work. • **Create** a schedule that will help you accomplish tasks on time. • **Identify** strategies for managing your time effectively. • **Describe** strategies for organizing your work and your work area. • **Describe** how to develop and maintain a system for organizing information.

Understanding Brackets, Letters, and Ability Levels in the Teacher Wraparound Edition

Brackets Brackets on the reduced student edition page correspond to teaching strategies and activities in the Teacher Wraparound Edition. As you teach the lesson, the brackets show you exactly where to use the teaching strategies and activities.

Letters The letters on the reduced student edition page identify the type of strategy or activity. See the key below to learn about the different types of strategies and activities.

Ability Levels Teaching Strategies that appear throughout the chapters have been identified by one of three codes to give you an idea of their suitability for students of varying learning styles and abilities.

Resources Key program resources are listed in each chapter. Icons indicate the format of resources.

KEY TO LETTERS

R **Reading Strategy** activities help you teach reading skills and vocabulary.

C **Critical Thinking** strategies help students apply and extend what they have learned.

S **Skill Practice** strategies help students practice historical analysis and geographical skills.

W **Writing Support** activities provide writing opportunities to help students comprehend the text.

D **Develop Concepts** activities use various strategies to help teachers gauge and plan for students' concept development.

U **Universal Access** activities provide differentiated instruction for English language learners, and suggestions for teaching various types of learners. *These activities may or may not have brackets.*

NCLB **No Child Left Behind** activities help students practice and improve their abilities in academic subjects.

KEY TO ABILITY LEVELS

L1 Strategies should be within the ability range of all students. Often full class participation is required.

L2 Strategies are for average to above-average students or for small groups. Some teacher direction is necessary.

L3 Strategies are designed for students able and willing to work independently. Minimal teacher direction is necessary.

KEY TO RESOURCE ICONS

📁 Print Material

💿 CD-ROM

🖱 Internet

TeacherWorks™
All-In-One Planner and Resource Center

Teacher Wraparound Edition

For the Unit:
Unit Thematic Project Student Rubrics
Unit Test
Unit Connecting Activities Projects

For the Chapter:
Chapter Resources
Program Resources
Additional Print and Media Resources
Lesson Plans
Chapter Summaries, Key Terms, and
Academic Vocabulary *(English and Spanish)*

Graphic Organizers
Reading Activities
Chapter Self-Checks *(English and Spanish)*
Internet Activities
School-to-Career Connections
Work-Based Learning Projects
Personal and Academic Career Portfolio Student Rubrics

Student Activity Workbook with Academic Integration

Strategies for Students with Special Needs

Career Plan Project Workbook

 Link to the **Succeeding in the World of Work** Online **Learning Center with Podcasts** through **glencoe.com**.

Unit Overview
Introduce the Unit

Introduce the unit by describing the main concepts of each chapter in the unit.

Unit 5 focuses on the interpersonal skills, thinking and technology skills, and self-management skills that students will need to succeed in their careers.

Chapter 13 helps students develop the skills to build and maintain strong interpersonal relationships.

Chapter 14 describes effective teamwork and leadership traits.

Chapter 15 introduces students to the skills involved in the four components of communication.

Chapter 16 helps students make wise decisions and solve problems creatively by following the steps in the decision-making and problem-solving processes.

Chapter 17 describes the importance of technology in today's workplace.

Chapter 18 discusses effective methods for managing one's time and work. Students learn to create and follow an effective schedule and how to organize physical and electronic files.

OUT OF TIME?

If class time is too short to cover all of the chapters in this unit, have students:
- Write down the key terms and their definitions.
- Read the chapter summaries at the beginning of each chapter review.
- Go to the *Succeeding in the World of Work* Online Learning Center (OLC) through **glencoe.com** to download free Study-to-Go content to their PDAs or cell phones.

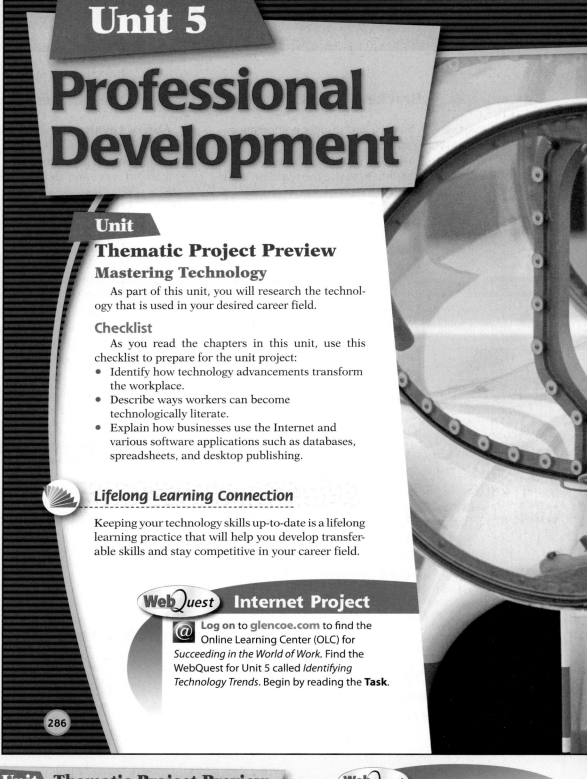

Unit 5
Professional Development

Unit
Thematic Project Preview
Mastering Technology

As part of this unit, you will research the technology that is used in your desired career field.

Checklist

As you read the chapters in this unit, use this checklist to prepare for the unit project:
- Identify how technology advancements transform the workplace.
- Describe ways workers can become technologically literate.
- Explain how businesses use the Internet and various software applications such as databases, spreadsheets, and desktop publishing.

Lifelong Learning Connection

Keeping your technology skills up-to-date is a lifelong learning practice that will help you develop transferable skills and stay competitive in your career field.

WebQuest Internet Project

@ **Log on** to **glencoe.com** to find the Online Learning Center (OLC) for *Succeeding in the World of Work*. Find the WebQuest for Unit 5 called *Identifying Technology Trends*. Begin by reading the **Task**.

286

Unit Thematic Project Preview

Tell students that as part of this unit, they will investigate how technology impacts a career field that interests them. They will research the most frequently used technologies in their field, from software to machinery, and discover the cutting-edge technology tools that are transforming the field. They will then profile three of these technologies and then use one of them to create their own original product.

WebQuest

For WebQuest teaching suggestions and rubrics, go to the Teacher Center of this book's Online Learning Center (OLC) through **glencoe.com**.

A HIGH-TECH WORLD
Willingness to learn new technology
is essential. *What have you done today
that has involved technology?*

(287)

Build Background
Ask students these questions
to activate prior knowledge:

Chapter 13
*How can self-awareness help
you get along with others?*
(by making you aware of
your strengths as well as
weaknesses you can work to
improve.)

What is a stereotype? (an
oversimplified and distorted
belief about a person or
group)

Chapter 14
*Why are teams often more pro-
ductive than workers working
individually?* (Teams can pool
ideas, share skills, and find
efficient ways to collaborate
on tasks.)

*What traits make a good
leader?* (courage, decisiveness, empathy, honesty,
imagination, integrity, tenac-
ity, vision, and other positive
qualities)

Chapter 15
What is customer relations?
(the use of communication
skills to meet the needs of
customers)

*What are common types of
written business documents?*
(business letters, memos,
e-mails, faxes, and reports)

Chapter 16
*Why is evaluating the results
of a solution considered part
of the problem-solving process?* (because you may need
to find a new solution and
because evaluating results
helps you solve problems better in the future)

Chapter 17
*How do businesses use the
Internet?* (as a research tool
and to communicate with
customers, to buy and sell,
to advertise, and to recruit
employees)

Chapter 18
*Why is it important to orga-
nize your files?* (to keep from
losing important information
and to make retrieval easy)

Extend the Photo

Caption Answer Students may mention
checking e-mail or using the Internet, driving
or taking a train or bus, using an ATM machine
or credit card, or similar examples.

Discussion Tell students that being computer
literate means being comfortable with using
computer hardware and software, including
operating systems and applications. It also
means knowing what to do when something
goes wrong. Ask students to rate their own
computer literacy and to share ideas about
how they could improve it. (Students' computer
skills will vary, but all students can benefit from
computer classes, online or in-person tutorials,
and hands-on practice.)

Chapter Resources Planning Guide with Activities and Features

Section	Features	Activities
Section 13.1 **Your Personal Traits at Work**	Real-World Connection (p. 292) 21st Century Workplace (p. 293) Creative Business Practices (p. 294) Hot Jobs! (p. 294) Tech Savvy (p. 295)	Before You Read (p. 290) Graphic Organizer (p. 290) As You Read (p. 292) After You Read (p. 295)
Section 13.2 **Applying Interpersonal Skills**	Career Checklist (p. 297) Everyday Ethics (p. 298) Science in Action (p. 301)	Before You Read (p. 296) Graphic Organizer (p. 296) After You Read (p. 301)

NCLB Activities, information, and skills practice will help your students attain No Child Left Behind proficiency. Students will improve their abilities in the following academic standards areas:

Academic Standards Correlations

Discipline	Standard	Feature/Activity
English Language Arts	**NCTE 1** Read texts to acquire new information.	Creative Business Practices (p. 294) Hot Jobs! (p. 294) Tech Savvy (p. 295)
	NCTE 4 Use written language to communicate effectively.	After You Read (p. 295) Writing Skills Practice (p. 307) Everyday Ethics (p. 298) Academic Skills in the Workplace (p. 306)
	NCTE 8 Use information resources to gather information and create and communicate knowledge.	Real-World Connection (p. 292)
	NCTE 9 Develop an understanding of diversity in language use across cultures.	21st Century Workplace (p. 293)
Mathematics	**Number and Operation:** Understand meanings of operations and how they relate to one another	After You Read (p. 301) Academic Skills in the Workplace (p. 306)
Science	**Unifying Concepts and Processes:** Constancy, change, and measurement	Science in Action (p. 301)
	Earth and Space Science: Energy in the earth system; Geochemical cycles	Academic Skills in the Workplace (p. 306)

CORRELATIONS The charts show the 21st Century Skills, foundation skills, and workplace competencies that students develop as they work in this chapter.

Foundation Skills and Workplace Competencies Correlation Chart

21st Century Skills

Core Subjects: English | Reading/Language Arts | Math

Learning Skills: Information and Media Literacy | Communication Skills | Critical Thinking and Systems Thinking | Problem Identification, Formulation, and Solution | Creativity and Intellectual Curiosity | Interpersonal and Collaborative Skills | Self-Direction | Accountability and Adaptability | Social Responsibility

21st Century Tools: Communication, Information Processing, and Research Tools | Problem-Solving Tools | Personal Development and Productivity Tools

Foundation Skills

Basic Skills: Reading | Writing | Math | Listening | Speaking

Thinking Skills: Creative Thinking | Decision Making | Problem Solving | Seeing Things in the Mind's Eye | Knowing How to Learn | Reasoning

Personal Qualities: Self-Esteem | Responsibility | Sociability | Self-Management | Integrity/Honesty

Workplace Competencies

Resources: Allocating Time | Allocating Money | Allocating Material and Facility Resources | Allocating Human Resources

Information: Acquiring and Evaluating Information | Organizing and Maintaining Information | Interpreting and Communicating Information | Using Computers to Process Information

Interpersonal Skills: Participating as a Member of a Team | Teaching Others | Serving Clients/Customers | Exercising Leadership | Negotiating to Arrive at a Decision | Working with Cultural Diversity

Systems: Understanding Systems | Monitoring and Correcting Performance | Improving and Designing Systems

Technology: Selecting Technology | Applying Technology to Task | Maintaining and Troubleshooting Technology

Yellow blocks indicate areas covered in the chapter

Chapter Overview
Introduce the Chapter
The goal of this chapter is to help students improve their relationships with others.

Section 13.1 examines personal traits and qualities and provides students with a four-step plan for improving their own personal traits.

Section 13.2 looks at workplace etiquette and provides suggestions for resolving conflict.

Build Background
Explain to students that self-awareness refers to a person's knowledge of his or her personality and individuality. Ask students to brainstorm ways to develop self-awareness. Suggest to students that one way to develop self-awareness is to ask close friends or people who work with them to give suggestions about how they could improve their skills.

 Exploring the Photo

Caption Answer
Coworkers rely on each other to complete tasks and goals, so respect for coworkers is essential for maintaining these necessary working relationships.

Discussion Ask: How else can you work effectively with coworkers? (Students might mention personal traits similar to those discussed in this chapter, including responsibility, self-esteem, sociability, self-management, and integrity and honesty.)

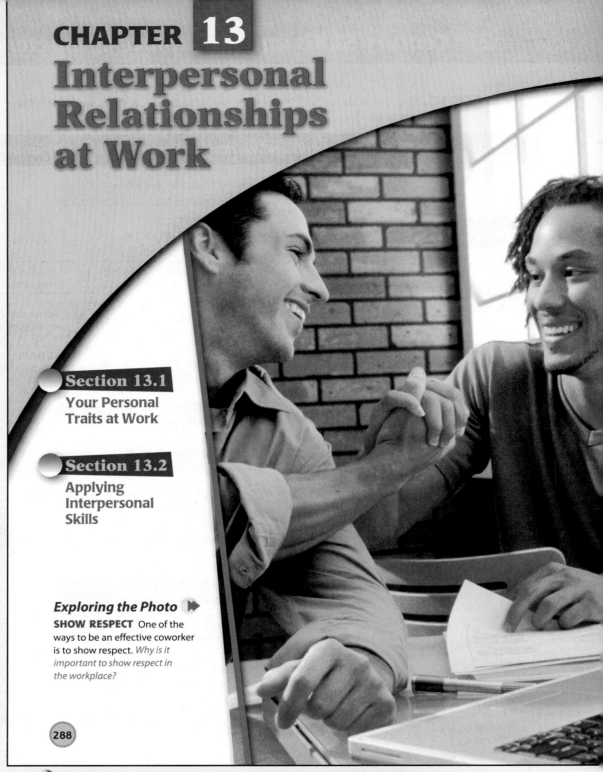

CHAPTER 13
Interpersonal Relationships at Work

Section 13.1
Your Personal Traits at Work

Section 13.2
Applying Interpersonal Skills

Exploring the Photo ▶▶
SHOW RESPECT One of the ways to be an effective coworker is to show respect. *Why is it important to show respect in the workplace?*

288

Classroom Resources

- 📁 Student Edition
- 📁 Teacher Wraparound Edition
- 📁 Student Activity Workbook with Academic Integration
- 📁 Student Activity Workbook with Academic Integration TAE
- 📁 *Fast File,* Unit 5 Resources

- 📁 Inclusion in the Career Education Classroom
- 💿 TeacherWorks™ Plus
- 💿 *ExamView Assessment Suite*
- 💿 Interactive Chalkboard
- 💿 Interactive Student Edition
- 💻 Online Student Edition
- 💻 Online Learning Center (OLC) with Podcasts

Chapter Objectives

After completing this chapter, you will be able to:

- **Identify** personal traits and interpersonal skills that will make you an effective coworker.
- **Describe** steps to self-improvement.
- **Summarize** the rules of workplace etiquette.
- **Describe** the process of conflict resolution.
- **Define** diversity and describe effective ways to work with a diverse group of people.

Writing Activity — Personal Career Notebook

Imagine yourself in the career of your choice. In your notebook, write a list of traits you hope to find in your coworkers. Which of those traits do you have? How will the traits you have help you in your chosen career? What other traits do you need to develop for your career?

Get Motivated! Contact three working adults in your community. Ask them to tell you what traits are the most helpful for them in the workplace. Design a poster that illustrates these traits.

Chapter 13 Interpersonal Relationships at Work **289**

Writing Activity — Personal Career Notebook Answer Guide

Students will likely mention traits similar to those introduced on page 291: responsibility, self-esteem, sociability, self-management, and integrity and honesty. Encourage students to think of examples to support their self-assessment about the traits they already have, and to think of ways to develop the traits they need.

Get Motivated! Posters should combine illustrations or graphics with text to reflect what students learned from working adults about helpful traits in the workplace.

Review the Objectives
Introduce the chapter by reviewing the chapter objectives:

Section 13.1 Objectives
Identify personal traits and interpersonal skills that will make you an effective coworker. (Important personal traits include responsibility, self-esteem, sociability, self-management, and integrity and honesty. Interpersonal skills include respect for others, understanding and empathy, communications skills, and a sense of humor.)

Describe steps to self-improvement. (The steps to self-improvement are: focus on one trait at a time; make a plan and follow it; keep track of your progress; and move on to a new challenge once you feel you have made progress toward your goal.)

Section 13.2 Objectives
Summarize the rules of workplace etiquette. (The basic rules of etiquette that apply to all workplaces are: be courteous, dress appropriately, be punctual, avoid gossip, and respect privacy.)

Describe the process of conflict resolution. (The steps in conflict resolution are: define the problem, suggest a solution, evaluate each solution, think creatively, and compromise. If these steps do not work, seek mediation or arbitration.)

Define diversity and describe effective ways to work with a diverse group of people. (Diversity in the workplace refers to the variety of cultures, religions, ages, genders, and viewpoints that workers encounter on the job. Working effectively with a diverse group of people means respecting differences and avoiding stereotypes.)

Section 13.1

Your Personal Traits at Work

Bell Ringer Activity

Your Personal Traits at Work

Ask students to write the name of one person they enjoy being with or working for. Then ask them to write a list of at least ten adjectives to describe him or her. Have students volunteer to share their lists and write examples on the board.

Resources

 Interactive Chalkboard
The Interactive Chalkboard CD provides visual teaching aids for this section.

@ Online Learning Center
The Online Learning Center (OLC) through **glencoe.com** features chapter vocabulary, chapter summaries, and other study materials.

Preteaching

Have students write a sentence explaining the significance of each of the two key terms.

Graphic Organizer

Tell students to go to the OLC through **glencoe.com** for a printable graphic organizer. (Graphic organizers should show an understanding of personal traits and how students can improve their own traits.)

 NCLB connects academic correlations to book content.

Reading Guide

 Before You Read

Preview Read the Key Concepts. Write one or two sentences predicting what the section will be about.

Read to Learn
- Personal traits and interpersonal skills that will make you an effective coworker
- Steps to self-improvement

D Main Idea
Demonstrating the personal traits and behaviors needed to work well with others will increase your chances of success on the job.

Key Concepts
- Develop Your Personal Traits
- Be an Effective Coworker

Key Terms
◇ tact   ◇ empathize

Academic Vocabulary
You will find these words in your reading and on your tests. Use the academic vocabulary glossary to look up their definitions if necessary.
- develop   - cooperation

Graphic Organizer
As you read, list the personal traits that you want to develop and brainstorm ways in which you can develop those traits. Continue adding to your list after you finish reading. Use a chart like the one shown below to help you organize your thoughts.

Traits	Ways to Develop Traits
Responsibility	• Complete all assigned tasks • Do what you say you will do
Sociability	

@ Log On Go to this book's Online Learning Center through **glencoe.com** for an online version of this graphic organizer.

N C L B
Academic Standards •
English Language Arts
- Read texts to acquire new information. (NCTE 1)
- Use information resources to gather information and create and communicate knowledge. (NCTE 8)
- Develop an understanding of diversity in language use across cultures. (NCTE 9)

Reading Guide

 Before You Read
Point out to students that "self-improvement" does not necessarily mean making improvements to a negative trait. There is always room to improve personal traits.

D Develop Concepts
Main Idea Discuss the main idea with students. Ask: Why do you need to be able to work well with others to achieve career success?

Develop Your Personal Traits

Good relationships at work can help you enjoy your work and do your job more effectively. You can begin to **develop** good relationships at work by assessing your own traits.

Look back at the work you did in Chapter 2 on getting to know yourself. You have already learned about some of the positive traits you have that help you get along with others in the workplace. These traits might include a positive self-concept, friendliness, and the ability to listen to others. Write down traits you already have that help you work well with other people. What traits do you need to develop?

Important Personal Traits

As you learned in earlier chapters, the following skills are important personal qualities to have at school, in social situations, and in the workplace:

R
- **Responsibility,** including dependability and positive motivation
- **Self-Esteem,** including confidence
- **Sociability,** including friendliness, enthusiasm, adaptability, and respect for other workers
- **Self-Management,** including self-control and **tact,** the ability to say and do things in a respectful way
- **Integrity and honesty,** including loyalty and trustworthiness

Most people have a combination of strengths and weaknesses. For instance, you may be honest and dependable, but lack self-esteem or self-management.

Now is the ideal time to work on developing any personal traits or behaviors that need attention. Keep in mind that you strive to improve because your success at work will be an important factor in your sense of overall well-being.

 RESPONSIBILITY
Acting responsibly means doing what is expected of you. *What other personal traits could walking a dog daily help you develop?*

Vocabulary
You can find definitions in the **Key Terms** glossary and **Academic Vocabulary** glossary at the back of this book.

Section 13.1

TEACH

Discussion Starter
Develop Your Personal Traits Ask: How do the personal traits listed on this page help you succeed in school? (One example might be that students need to be responsible in order to complete their school assignments and to get to class on time.)

R **Reading Strategy**
Provide Examples Tell students to write a sentence or two describing how they demonstrate each of the five personal traits on this page in their daily lives. For example, what actions do they take to demonstrate responsibility or to build self-esteem? (Encourage students to be specific and provide examples of how they demonstrate the traits.)

Resources

TeacherWorks™ Plus
The TeacherWorks software includes customizable built-in lesson plans and links to printable program resources.

Extend the Photo

Caption Answer Other traits might include self-management to be patient when a dog misbehaves, and self-esteem to assert control over the dog.

Discussion Ask: What additional traits would a *professional* dog walker need? (Students might mention responsibility to honor dog-walking commitments and sociability to maintain good relationships with clients.)

TEACH *(cont.)*

Discussion Starter

Self-Awareness on the Job Tell students to imagine that a coworker has just said something that made them angry. How would they react? How would their reaction demonstrate responsibility, self-esteem, sociability, self-management, and integrity/honesty? Encourage students to stop and think about these traits *before* they react.

Cooperative Learning
Enrichment

Conduct Research Group students in teams of four. Ask each group to research a recent court case related to the electronic invasion of privacy (for example, computers, e-mail, video recording). Have students prepare visual presentations using the information they find about the case, including how it was resolved.

As You Read

Positive personal traits are essential in communicating with coworkers and working as an effective team member.

✓ Reading Check

ANALYZE One response might be that exercising the skill of self-management will help you maintain a positive attitude and gain the respect of your coworkers.

As You Read

Connect How will your personal traits affect how you relate with your coworkers?

Self-Awareness on the Job

Self-awareness can help you adjust to new work situations. If you are self-aware, you know not only your strengths, but also the traits you need to improve.

Tracy Kagan of Miami, Florida, learned a great deal about her personal traits when she was promoted from restaurant server to assistant manager. While she had been well-liked as a server, Tracy was not popular when she first became assistant manager. In her nervousness, she criticized servers in front of customers.

Fortunately, Tracy's supervisor recognized the problem. She spoke with Tracy about her need to be tactful. Still, changing was not easy. "Whenever I felt pressured, I had to remind myself to be polite," Tracy says. "I made it a habit to take a deep breath when I felt myself getting upset. Then I'd smile."

In time, Tracy developed her self-management skills. Now she enjoys her job and has won back the respect of her coworkers.

✓ Reading Check ANALYZE How might the skill of self-management help you on the job?

Real-World Connection

Election Issues

One of your teachers has suggested that you run for president of the student government. After determining that you would be able to do a good job in this leadership role and still keep up with your courses and other activities, you agree to run. However, you later learn that a good friend is the only other candidate running for president.

Critical Thinking What are some ways to run a successful campaign without attacking your friend? What would the consequences be for the student body if you withdrew from the election, leaving your friend as the sole candidate?

Do Your Own Research Interview a candidate for office or someone who has just been elected to an office. Ask how to keep a campaign focused on the issues and not on the individuals. Write a short essay about why it is important to have a choice of candidates in an election.

Be an Effective Coworker

In most jobs, you will not work alone. You will need to get along with coworkers, supervisors, customers, and colleagues in order to do your job effectively. These four traits are essential for being an effective coworker:

- Respect for others
- Understanding and empathy
- Communication skills
- A sense of humor

Being effective in your job is essential to advancing in your career.

Respect Others

Being respectful in your actions and your words shows others that you value them. Treat all your coworkers with respect, regardless of age, job title, or position. Showing courtesy and tolerating differences are two ways to show respect for others.

Avoid Negative Traits

Some negative traits that keep people from demonstrating respect to others are arrogance, prejudice, and jealousy. Arrogance is the feeling that you are superior to someone else. Remember that each worker has something important to contribute. Prejudice is a negative attitude toward a certain group of people.

Real-World Connection

Critical Thinking Answer By focusing on election issues and not the other candidate's personality, you can run a successful campaign without resorting to personal attacks. If you withdrew from the campaign, you would deprive the student body of a decision-making opportunity.

Do Your Own Research Essays should reflect the student's conversation with a candidate and opinion about the importance of choice in elections.

The 21ˢᵗ Century Workplace

India Inc.

India's educated and skilled workforce, well-developed information technology industry, and stable economy and government have made it a popular country for outsourcing work. Along with English, Hindi is India's most-spoken official language. The language can be traced back to the 7th century, and today it is spoken by more than 437 million people around the world.

NCLB

CRITICAL THINKING _____

Although English is spoken by many people in India, why would it be useful to be able to read or speak a few phrases in Hindi when working in India?

In Your Community

India has the second largest film industry in the world. Research what film festivals, concerts, and other events take place in your community. How could they help you learn about a new culture? Share what you learned with the class.

COMMON HINDI WORDS AND PHRASES	
hello/ goodbye	naamaste
yes	haan
no	naahi
please	kripyaa
thank you	dhanyavaad
good/okay/really?	accha

 Extend Your Learning Hindi is only one of many languages spoken in India. For links to Web sites about the languages of India, go to this book's OLC through **glencoe.com**.

Jealousy can be damaging in the workplace. Jealous workers may view their coworkers as rivals, and **cooperation** can become difficult. A jealous worker may refuse to admit that others deserve praise or promotions.

Remember that respect is a two-way street. In most cases, the more you give, the more you will gain in return. Showing respect for those who are different than you will help you get along.

Understand Others

Understanding others helps you get along and work together. You can develop understanding by showing interest in others.

- Ask your coworkers about their career goals and interests.
- Try to empathize with your coworkers. To **empathize** means to try to see things from another's point of view and to gain an understanding of that person's situation.
- Pay attention to body language. Facial expressions or how a person sits, stands, or moves can express emotions.

Communicate with Others

In communication, how well you listen is as important as what you say. Both listening and speaking well are especially important when you are working as part of a team. If you do not listen well, you will not benefit from being part of the team. Failure to convey information promptly and clearly can disrupt a project. It can make everyone on the team look bad.

TEACH *(cont.)*

C Critical Thinking

Analyze Explain to students that effective communication requires speaking, listening, reading, and writing skills. Ask: How will your ability to communicate affect how you get along with your coworkers? (Effective communicators are more likely to get along and feel they are part of a unified team. Workers with bad communication skills are more likely to confuse and frustrate their coworkers.)

NCLB Activity correlated to English Language Arts standards.

ASSESS

Review Key Terms

Have students write sentences using each key term.

Online Study Tools

Have students go to the OLC through **glencoe.com** to:

- Download **Podcast** study tools.
- Download free **Study-to-Go** content to their PDAs or cell phones.

Resources

 ExamView Assessment Suite **CD** allows you to print out ready-made unit and chapter tests complete with answer keys. You can also create customized tests.

The 21ˢᵗ Century Workplace

CRITICAL THINKING ANSWER When visiting another culture, knowing how to read, speak, and understand phrases of the local languages can enhance your communication with others. It also shows respect for that culture.

In Your Community Students should be able to find events in the area that showcase different cultures. People who attend these events often get an opportunity to see and learn aspects of other cultures, including customs, traditional clothing, and cuisines.

RETEACH

W Writing Activity

Conduct Research Have students visit the library or access the Internet to search for articles and other information on self-improvement. Have students write a one-page summary of their results. Ask volunteers to share their findings in class and discuss which of the resources they found that provided the most useful information.

Resources

Student Activity Workbook Assign the Chapter 13 activities in the Student Activity Workbook.

Creative Business Practices

JPMORGAN CHASE   Networking

The financial services corporation JPMorgan Chase & Co. provides several networking groups for employees. These networking groups also offer employees many advantages. For example, the groups provide support for people of diverse cultures and lifestyles. The groups help employees learn more about coworkers from different backgrounds. The groups also allow senior employees to mentor or advise newer employees and to help employees with professional development.

More than 20,000 employees worldwide are active in at least one of the groups. Some of the networking groups include Administrative Professionals, Asian-Pacific Americans, Cultural Exchange, Employees with Disabilities, Hispanics/Latinos, Native Americans, Women, and Women of Color.

CRITICAL THINKING What would you expect to receive from a networking group within your workplace?

 Connect to the Real World For more information about JPMorgan Chase, visit the company's Web site via the link on this book's OLC through **glencoe.com**.

Do not be reluctant to speak up and ask a coworker or supervisor for help if you need it. Remember that being effective means producing results. A coworker can often provide the guidance you will need to overcome problems and get the job done.

Communicating, however, does not mean talking about your private life. You can be warm and friendly without revealing personal secrets. As you get to know your coworkers, it can be tempting to talk about personal matters. However, it is best to leave personal issues at home and spend time discussing work-related matters.

Keep Smiling

A sense of humor is the ability to see the lighter side of things. It can make it easier to get along with others, can make people feel better about themselves, and can help unite a team. Having a sense of humor means being able to laugh even when the joke is on you.

Improve Your Personal Traits

Find ways to improve your personal traits. One strategy is to keep a journal on how effectively you practice the traits you want to improve. Follow these steps to self-improvement:

- **Focus on one trait at a time.** For example, you might decide that you want to be more responsible, so you will focus on personal responsibility.

W

 HOT JOBS!

Social Investing Associate

Social investing associates help investors invest in businesses whose values align with their own. For example, if you care about the environment, you may want to invest in a company whose business practices recycling. Job requirements for social investors include strong math and finance skills, and awareness of current issues.

Creative Business Practices

CRITICAL THINKING ANSWER Senior members of a networking group can give you helpful advice about your job and career direction. Network members can also share valuable contacts and other helpful industry-related information.

- **Make a plan and follow it.** For example, you might make a list of several chores you could do at home. Make sure you take responsibility for at least one of the chores each day.
- **Keep track of your progress.** For example, check your progress each night by keeping a record of every responsibility you fulfilled that day. Also write notes to yourself about areas in which you might improve. Once a week, ask an observer how you are doing.
- **Move on to a new challenge once you feel you have made progress toward your goal.** Choose another trait on which to focus. For example, you might decide to focus on sociability by reading to students in a local elementary school or by participating in extracurricular activities.

Look back at the list of important personal traits on page 291 and the list of traits essential for being an effective coworker on page 292. In a notebook or journal, write down which traits you think are your strong points and which you would like to improve. Include a plan for improving the traits you want to improve.

TechSavvy

Podcasting

Do you want to learn more about a career from people who work in a specific area? Turn on a computer and listen to or watch a podcast. A podcast is an audio or video file that plays over the Internet. You can listen to a podcast on your computer or any other digital device. Many students and teachers are now writing, recording, and publishing their own podcasts for classroom presentations.

Visit this book's OLC through **glencoe.com** and find the link to learn more about podcasts. Write a two-page radio podcast script that includes information about current events in your school.

Section 13.1

ASSESS

After You Read
Have students complete the Section 13.1 After You Read section review.

Online Study Tools
Have students go to the OLC through **glencoe.com** to:
- Take the Section 13.1 **Practice Test.**
- Download **Podcast** study tools.
- Download free **Study-to-Go** content to their PDAs or cell phones.

CLOSE

Culminating Activity
Help Develop a Positive Attitude Tell students to imagine they are supervisors who have an employee with an attitude problem. Ask: What would you do to help your employee become a more effective worker? Have students write a one-page improvement plan for the employee. (Improvement plans should cite the trait that needs improving and the steps the employee could take to achieve self-improvement.)

Section 13.1 After You Read

Review Key Concepts

1. Give an example of a positive personal trait and explain how it can help you get along with others.
2. Name a personal trait you would like to develop and describe the method you would use to do that.
3. Describe how you would demonstrate respect for a coworker in a job-related situation.

Practice Academic Skills

 English Language Arts

4. You have been chosen to plan a "get to know your coworkers" day in your company. Write a one-page outline that explains what types of activities you have planned for the day.
5. Write a one-page memo that describes two or more suggestions for improving your personal traits.

@ Check your answers at this book's OLC through **glencoe.com**.

Section 13.1 After You Read

Review Key Concepts
1. Students should list one of the five traits from page 291 and give a specific example how it can help them get along with others.
2. Responses should reflect students' understanding of self-improvement.
3. In their descriptions, students should cite a specific example how to show respect for a coworker.

Practice Academic Skills
4. Outlines will vary, but all should be of a workable plan for a one-day celebration of diversity.
5. Memos should reflect an understanding of the steps to self-improvement.

TechSavvy

Podcasting

Answer Scripts should include information about school events. Encourage students to be imaginative in how they present their information, by using different voices or characters, sound effects, or humor to make their podcasts lively.

 Activity correlated to English Language Arts standards.

Section 13.2

FOCUS

Bell Ringer Activity

Applying Interpersonal Skills

Have students list at least ten words that come to mind when they think of the word *etiquette*.

Resources

⊙ **Interactive Chalkboard**
The Interactive Chalkboard CD provides visual teaching aids for this section.

@ **Online Learning Center**
The OLC through **glencoe.com** features chapter vocabulary, chapter summaries, and other study materials.

Preteaching

Read the definitions of the key terms aloud. As you read each definition, ask students to write a sentence using each key term.

Graphic Organizer

Tell students to go to the OLC through **glencoe.com** for a printable graphic organizer. (Graphic organizers should reflect students' understanding of interpersonal skills in the workplace.)

NCLB connects academic correlations to book content.

296

Applying Interpersonal Skills

Reading Guide

Before You Read

Preview Read the Key Terms. Write one or two sentences predicting what the section will be about.

Read to Learn
- The rules of workplace etiquette
- The process of conflict resolution
- What diversity is and how to work with a diverse group of people

D ### Main Idea
Being prepared for common workplace situations will help you to handle them effectively.

Key Concepts
- Workplace Etiquette
- Conflict Resolution
- Diversity in the Workplace

Key Terms
◆ etiquette
◆ conflict resolution
◆ compromise
◆ diversity
◆ stereotype

Academic Vocabulary
You will find these words in your reading and on your tests. Use the academic vocabulary glossary to look up their definitions if necessary.
■ mediation
■ distorted

Graphic Organizer
As you read, make notes on ways to practice good interpersonal skills in the workplace. Continue adding information in your own words after you finish reading. Use a list like the one shown to help organize your information.

Good Workplace Interpersonal Skills
- be courteous
- respect privacy
- practice conflict resolution

@ **Log On** Go to this book's Online Learning Center through **glencoe.com** for an online version of this graphic organizer.

Academic Standards ● ● ● ● ● ● ● ● ● ● ● ● ● ● ● ● ●

English Language Arts
- Read texts to acquire new information. (NCTE 1)

Mathematics
- Understand meanings of operations and how they relate to one another

Science
- Unifying Concepts and Processes: Constancy, change, and measurement

(296) **Unit 5** Professional Development

glencoe.com

Reading Guide

Before You Read
Students may think of the word *etiquette* as an old-fashioned term referring to personal manners and eating habits. Explain to students that it also applies to personal behavior in the workplace.

D ### Develop Concepts
Main Idea Discuss the main idea with students. Ask: what is the difference between etiquette and the personal traits discussed in Section 13.1? (Etiquette refers to how workers behave on the job whereas personal traits influence a worker's job performance. Both are essential to success in the workplace.)

Workplace Etiquette

Etiquette means having good manners in your dealings with people. How do you identify the right behavior for your workplace? Treat people as you would want them to treat you. When in doubt, observe experienced and successful coworkers. How do they conduct themselves at work? What do they do to get along with other people? What kinds of actions or responses do they avoid?

Here are a few basic rules of etiquette that apply to all workplaces:

- **Be courteous.** Greet your coworkers when you come to work, and address people by name whenever you can. Do not interrupt private conversations, and do not talk so loudly that you disturb other people, especially those working near you. Avoid tying up equipment that other people may need to use.
- **Dress appropriately.** Whether or not your job has a dress code, you should wear neat, clean clothes. As a new employee, do not use your wardrobe or hairstyle to attract attention. Let your job performance speak for itself.
- **Be punctual.** Be at work on time, arrive at meetings promptly, and meet your deadlines. If you promise someone that you will call at a certain time, be sure to keep your word.
- **Avoid gossip.** Gossiping wastes valuable work time and can result in the spread of false or hurtful rumors.
- **Respect privacy.** Treat your coworkers' phone calls, faxes, e-mail, and voice mail as you would treat private mail. Do not read or listen to them unless they are addressed to you. If you work in a quiet environment, keep your voice at an appropriate volume.

Career ✓ Checklist

To Be an Effective and Courteous Worker:

✓ Be on time.

✓ Limit personal phone calls and e-mail at work.

✓ Respect others' privacy.

✓ Practice good and positive communication.

✓ Organize your time so that you meet all your deadlines.

 BE COURTEOUS Good workplace etiquette includes dressing appropriately, not reading documents that are not addressed to you, and keeping your voice at an appropriate volume. *In what kinds of workplaces might louder voices be part of the working environment?*

TEACH

Discussion Starter
Workplace Etiquette Lead a class discussion and ask: In what ways do you think good etiquette improves employee relations in the workplace? (Students may point out that using proper etiquette at work and elsewhere minimizes conflict and helps people work together in a positive, professional atmosphere.)

R Reading Strategy
Apply Knowledge Have students work in groups and prepare two-minute presentations demonstrating some form of workplace etiquette. For example, one group may want to demonstrate how to dress appropriately for the workplace by showing magazine or newspaper clippings that illustrate examples of appropriate and inappropriate work attire.

Resources

TeacherWorks™ Plus The TeacherWorks software includes customizable built-in lesson plans and links to printable program resources.

Extend the Photo

Caption Answer Louder voices are commonly found in offices where employees need to make frequent work-related phone calls. Loud voices are often necessary in outdoor workplaces where people need to compete with other outside noises to be heard.

Discussion Explain to students that many employees do not have private offices and often work in partially enclosed cubicles. Ask: What methods can you use to maintain concentration in a hectic workplace? (Students may point out that although they may not be able to control the noise level, they can help their concentration by staying organized and completing one task at a time.)

TEACH (cont.)

C Critical Thinking

Problem Solving Have students comment on this scenario. "Derek often gets to work early and leaves after everyone else. His supervisor seems to only criticize his work. What should Derek do to find out what is wrong?" (Students might suggest that Derek ask his supervisor for a one-on-one meeting where he can get feedback about his job performance. Derek might find that the supervisor thinks he is working extra hours because he is struggling with his job, not because he is taking extra initiative.)

✓ Reading Check

EVALUATE Changing your behavior now can lead to better habits and better relationships with coworkers and supervisors, which in turn can lead to better promotions and job offers in the future.

Everyday ETHICS

INFORMING A SUPERVISOR

When should you tell on others?

TAKING BREAKS You work the late shift at a customer service center where you receive incoming calls from customers about their credit card accounts. The other two workers on your shift are best friends, and they take frequent breaks together and leave you alone to answer all of the calls. You have tried to talk to them, but they have not changed their behavior.

What Would You Do? Should you tell your supervisor about your coworkers' behavior?

DISCUSS IT In teams, brainstorm possible ways you could approach and speak to your coworkers about their frequent breaks, as well as possible ways to approach your supervisor about your coworkers' behavior. Share your responses with the class.

Etiquette and Your Supervisor

You should treat your supervisor with the same proper respect and courtesy you do your coworkers. However, you face the added element of wanting and needing your supervisor's approval. Here are some things you can do to develop and maintain a good working relationship with your supervisor:

- Deal with any criticism from your supervisor in an objective and professional manner. Do not become defensive.
- Show initiative instead of bothering your supervisor with details that do not need approval.
- Whenever you can, offer to help your supervisor.
- If you have a work-related issue, discuss it with your supervisor. Be prepared to suggest your own solution.

✓ Reading Check EVALUATE How could changing your behavior now help you in your future career?

Conflict Resolution

Even when coworkers practice good communication, conflict can still occur. A conflict is a strong disagreement that occurs when people have different needs or ideas. When conflicts arise in the workplace, you will have to decide how to deal with them.

As a worker, you may find yourself involved in a process called **conflict resolution**, a problem-solving strategy for settling disputes and finding solutions that will allow each side to save face and create the least amount of ill feeling. **Figure 13.1** shows the steps in conflict resolution.

Conflict resolution begins with defining the problem. For example, employees may feel that the employer refuses to compensate or reward them for overtime, but still expects them to stay late. Both the employees and the employer need to explain their points of view.

Everyday ETHICS

What Would You Do? Answer Students should carefully consider whether they are overreacting to the behavior of their coworkers. They should consider their objective in speaking to their supervisor. Students should also consider whether they are willing to deal with possible hostility from their coworkers.

DISCUSS IT Students should weigh the possible outcome of talking to their coworkers or supervisor.

After defining the problem, each side suggests a solution to the problem. For example, the employer might suggest providing incentives such as quarterly bonuses or dinner. The employees may state they want to be paid wages for overtime worked.

Next the parties have to evaluate different solutions. Both sides explain what they can or cannot agree with in order to find a solution. Both sides try to reach an agreement. This is the time to think creatively and brainstorm different ways to come up with a solution. Both sides probably will have to **compromise**, which means to give up something.

S Skill Practice
Independent Practice
Acquire and Evaluate Information Have half the class research techniques of mediation and the other half research arbitration. Each group will collect examples from newspapers or magazines. Ask the two groups to discuss their findings in class.

ASSESS

Review Key Terms
Have students write sentences using each key term.

Online Study Tools
Have students go to the OLC through **glencoe.com** to:
• Download **Podcast** study tools.
• Download free **Study-to-Go** content to their PDAs or cell phones.

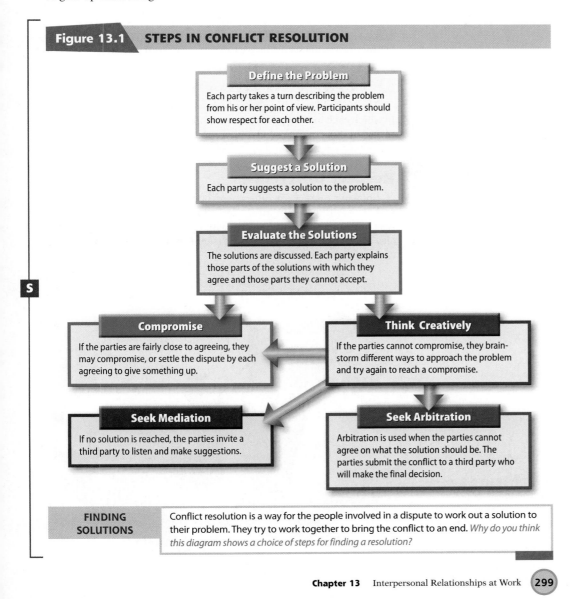

Figure 13.1   STEPS IN CONFLICT RESOLUTION

Define the Problem
Each party takes a turn describing the problem from his or her point of view. Participants should show respect for each other.

Suggest a Solution
Each party suggests a solution to the problem.

Evaluate the Solutions
The solutions are discussed. Each party explains those parts of the solutions with which they agree and those parts they cannot accept.

Compromise
If the parties are fairly close to agreeing, they may compromise, or settle the dispute by each agreeing to give something up.

Think Creatively
If the parties cannot compromise, they brainstorm different ways to approach the problem and try again to reach a compromise.

Seek Mediation
If no solution is reached, the parties invite a third party to listen and make suggestions.

Seek Arbitration
Arbitration is used when the parties cannot agree on what the solution should be. The parties submit the conflict to a third party who will make the final decision.

FINDING SOLUTIONS   Conflict resolution is a way for the people involved in a dispute to work out a solution to their problem. They try to work together to bring the conflict to an end. *Why do you think this diagram shows a choice of steps for finding a resolution?*

Chapter 13   Interpersonal Relationships at Work   **299**

EXTEND THE FIGURE   Figure 13.1

Caption Answer Parties may need to explore more than one approach to resolve their conflict.

Discussion Ask students to give examples of conflicts they have experienced, and have them decide which of the methods might be used to resolve each one.

RETEACH

U Universal Access

Kinesthetic Learners Have students work in groups of three or four to create and present skits on dealing with common diversity issues in the workplace, such as racial issues, physical disability issues, or disparity between men and women. Skits should present a problem and a possible solution.

✓ Reading Check

ANALYZE Careers might include school guidance counselor, psychotherapist, and judge.

Resources

📁 **Student Activity Workbook** Assign the Chapter 13 activities in the Student Activity Workbook.

ASSESS

After You Read

Have students complete the Section 13.2 After You Read section review.

Online Study Tools

Have students go to the OLC through **glencoe.com** to:
- Take the Section 13.2 **Practice Test**.
- Download **Podcast** study tools.
- Download free **Study-to-Go** content to their PDAs or cell phones.

K Vocabulary

You can find definitions in the **Key Terms** glossary and **Academic Vocabulary** glossary at the back of this book.

Sometimes the people involved in conflict resolution cannot reach a solution. They have to seek **mediation**. In mediation, a third party is asked to listen to both sides and try to find a solution. Sometimes even mediation fails and the parties have to seek arbitration. In arbitration, a third party is asked to hear the case, much like in mediation. In arbitration, however, both sides must agree to the solution the third party suggests.

Conflict resolution focuses on the issues, not on the personalities of the people involved. You can prepare yourself for conflict resolution by practicing your communication and problem-solving skills in school and in any disputes you may have with friends.

✓ **Reading Check** **ANALYZE** In what types of careers would conflict-resolution skills be useful?

Diversity in the Workplace

The United States has always been a nation of **diversity**, or variety, in which each individual contributes something special. In most workplaces in this country, many different kinds of people come together for a common purpose—to get a job done and to earn a living.

U Respect Differences

Showing respect for differences in culture, religion, age, gender, and viewpoint can minimize conflict at work. It shows that you are part of a community of workers with common needs and goals. It is also a way to broaden your understanding, and perhaps make some exciting discoveries as well.

 DIVERSITY Seeing each person as an individual can help you work with people of different backgrounds. *What else might help you work in a diverse environment?*

▶▶ *Extend the Photo*

Caption Answer In addition to respecting differences and avoiding stereotypes, students might mention that keeping an open mind will help in working in a diverse workplace.

Discussion Lead a class discussion about how getting along with different people at work can affect other aspects of workers' lives. (By learning to get along with a diverse group of people at work, employees are less likely to be prejudiced in other areas of their lives.)

Overcoming Stereotypes

To succeed in the diverse global workplace, today's workers must look beyond stereotypes. A **stereotype** is an oversimplified and **distorted** belief about a person or group. Negative stereotypes can be harmful.

Many businesses today sponsor diversity training programs to help employees overcome stereotyping in the following areas:

- **Cultural Distinctions** People from different ethnic backgrounds have different customs. What is polite in one culture may be rude in another (such as certain gestures or forms of address). It is important to remember, however, that cultural blunders happen even among those who have the best intentions. Learn by reading and observing, and apologize if you are unintentionally impolite.
- **Gender Distinctions** Effective coworkers have mutual respect for one another regardless of gender. Remember that it is wrong—and illegal—to harass or discriminate against someone because of his or her gender.
- **Generational Distinctions** People of one age group sometimes feel they have little in common with people in other age groups. As a young person, your point of view may differ from that of older people. You can bridge any difference in opinion by listening carefully to the other person's point of view and finding ideas on which you can agree.

By keeping an open mind and treating people fairly, you will pave the way for smooth working relationships based on mutual respect.

Science In Action

Volume

Volume is used to measure the amount of space taken up by a three-dimensional object or substance such as water. A pool has a height of 3 meters, a width of 5 meters, and depth of 3 meters. How many cubic meters of water does the pool hold?

Starting Hint: The volume is measured in cubic meters. Volume = height × width × depth.

@ For more science practice, go to this book's OLC through **glencoe.com**.

Section 13.2 After You Read

Review Key Concepts

1. Describe how you would handle this situation: You just picked up a memo from your boss to another manager detailing the reasons a coworker should be fired.
2. Explain why creative thinking is a big part of the conflict resolution process.
3. Name four behaviors that can help you deal with diversity on the job.

Practice Academic Skills

Mathematics

4. Half of the 40 people in Mara's office are women. If 30% of the women are Latina, how many Latina women work in her office?

   CONCEPT **Multiplying Percents** To multiply percents, first change the percents to decimals. Be sure to place the decimal point in the product correctly.
   Step 1: Multiply the percent of employees who are women (50%) by the percent of the women who are Latina (30%).
   Step 2: Multiply the answer to Step 1 by the total number of employees.

    Math For math help, go to the Math Appendix located at the back of this book.

ASSESS (cont.)

Resources

ExamView Assessment Suite CD allows you to print out ready-made unit and chapter tests complete with answer keys. You can also create customized tests.

NCLB Activity correlated to Science standards.

Science In Action

The pool would hold 45 cubic feet of water (3 × 5 × 3 = 45).

CLOSE

Culminating Activity

Etiquette and Your Supervisor Have students imagine they work in a company's human resources department, and their supervisor has asked them to develop a poster of positive etiquette in the workplace. Have students create a poster with examples of both good etiquette that staff members should adhere to, as well as bad etiquette that should be avoided. (Posters should reflect an understanding of the five etiquette guidelines described in this section.)

NCLB Activity correlated to Mathematics standards.

Section 13.2 After You Read

Review Key Concepts

1. When dealing with this sensitive situation, workers need to exercise respect for the boss's privacy and not read the memo. Furthermore, should avoid gossiping about the matter with coworkers.
2. Conflict resolution requires creative thinking in order to satisfy all parties involved.
3. Respecting differences and overcoming stereotypes will help you deal with diversity.

Practice Academic Skills

4. Six Latina women work in the office (0.5 × 0.3 = 0.15; 0.15 × 40 = 6).

Discussion Starter

Finance Lead a discussion about the various types of careers that can be found in this career cluster. Have students brainstorm various careers and jobs within the career cluster. (Answers will vary but students should show an understanding of the many types of careers that fall within the career cluster.)

**W Writing Support
Independent Practice**

Write a Job Listing Have students imagine they work in a company similar to Nate Rubin's, and they have been assigned to write a job listing for a financial accountant position that has opened up. Tell students to write a 60-word job listing that will be published in the newspaper classified section. Explain to students that they must choose their words carefully in order to include the most important information and not exceed the word limit.

C Critical Thinking

Differentiate Ask: What is the difference between prioritizing and hurrying? Which is most likely to result in work that balances speed and accuracy? Why? (Prioritizing means planning ahead and choosing what needs to be done and in what order. Hurrying generally means rushing to finish a task before a deadline. Prioritizing will likely result in more efficient work, because planning allows for the time needed to finish tasks on time and accurately.)

CAREER SPOTLIGHT   Career Cluster: Finance

Nate Rubin
Financial Accountant

W

Q: Describe your job.
A: I'm a financial accountant for an insurance brokerage firm. I prepare, analyze, and present the various financial statements, supporting schedules, and budgets.

Q: Describe a typical workday.
A: A typical workday begins the night before, when I look at my schedule and to-do list for any urgent items that require immediate attention. I'll start my morning by getting all the urgent items done. Once those tasks are completed, I move onto daily activities, such as monitoring the daily cash flow, scrutinizing and approving (or denying) employee expense reimbursements, and reconciling the cash deposits to our general ledger. It's a little more hectic at the end of the month when, in addition to my daily duties, I'm responsible for reconciling and closing out all the accounts. The financial statements and supporting documents are then generated for presentation.

Q: What skills are most important to you in your job?
A: Proficient computer skills go a long way in making my day easier. Being able to communicate effectively with the staff is another crucial skill.

C

Q: What skills are helpful in preparing for your career?
A: Learn to prioritize. There are only so many hours in a day, and you can only do so much. Figure out what's most important and get that done first. And whether or not you're working on an urgent item, be efficient. As retired UCLA basketball coach John Wooden once said, "Be quick, but don't hurry." There is never enough time to be sure of your decisions—and if you are sure, you're probably too late—but you must always maintain a balance of speed and accuracy.

Q: What is your key to success?
A: Old-fashioned hard work and not taking anything for granted are my keys to success. If you're not working hard, I guarantee there's someone else who is and who's making you look bad in the process. In a corporate environment, it's survival of the fittest.

Q: What training and preparation do you recommend for students?
A: Get used to handling a heavy workload by taking difficult classes that will challenge you. It will make your eventual professional job seem easier. Become proficient in working with computers.

Q: What are some ways you recommend students prepare for this career?
A: Get an internship or part-time job at an accounting firm or in an accounting department. That will help you decide if you like this type of work, its culture, and its environment.

Q: What do you like most about your work?
A: The most rewarding aspect of my job is our accounting department's team dynamic. We have to rely on each other's skills and proficiencies to get our jobs done.

 For more about Career Clusters, go to this book's OLC through **glencoe.com**.

NCLB **NO CHILD LEFT BEHIND**

Teaching Tip

The goals of the NCLB Act include a strong emphasis on reading skills. The use of modeling in your classroom will help students become better at identifying information. For example, ask a question that can be answered by reading the chart on page 303. Verbally identify the elements of the chart that might help the student identify the answer.

Sample Question Which two tasks on the chart do not require social studies skills? (Reviewing drawings to conceptualize a project and estimating a job do not require social studies skills according to the chart.)

- **Education or Training** Most accounting positions require at least a bachelor's degree in accounting or a related field. Beginning accounting and auditing positions in the federal government usually require four years of college or an equivalent combination of education and experience.

- **Academic Skills Required** English Language Arts, Mathematics

- **Technology Needed** Spreadsheet software and accounting and auditing computer software

- **Aptitudes, Abilities, and Skills** It is important to be detail-oriented, able to handle multiple tasks, and have good time management skills. Expertise in specialized areas, such as international business or current legislation is helpful.

- **Workplace Safety** Accountants can work long hours and should pay attention to ergonomics and avoid strain caused by repetitive tasks.

- **Career Outlook** Employment of accountants and auditors is expected to grow faster than average for all occupations over the next ten years. An increase in the number of businesses, changing financial laws and regulations, and increased scrutiny of company finances will drive growth. In addition to openings resulting from growth, the need to replace accountants and auditors who retire or transfer to other occupations will produce numerous job openings.

- **Career Path** Accountants can become CPAs, start their own businesses, or work for the government.

Academic Skills Required to Complete Tasks

Tasks	English Language Arts	Mathematics
Monitor daily cash flow	★	★
Process employee expense reimbursements	★	★
Reconcile deposits to the general ledger		★
Update/generate spreadsheets	★	★
Reconcile and close out accounts		★
Generate and present financial statements		★
Prepare and analyze financial statements	★	★

NCLB

Critical Thinking

How might the growing popularity of accounting software for businesses and consumers affect the accounting field?

ASSESS

Make Connections

Have students research the *Sarbanes-Oxley Act* on the Internet or at the library. Ask: What is this act? How will this act affect the career outlook for workers in the financial accounting field? (As a result of several large-scale corporate financial scandals, Congress implemented the Sarbanes-Oxley Act (SOX), which created legal standards of conduct for publicly held corporations. SOX requires that CEOs, financial officers, accountants, and auditing firms comply with the new regulations and procedures.)

CLOSE

Culminating Activity

Certified Public Accountants Have students research the term CPA. Ask: What are CPAs? What qualifications does an accountant need to be a CPA? (CPA stands for Certified Public Accountant. CPAs are licensed by the states and they must meet certain education requirements and pass a national test.)

NCLB This chart relates academic skills such as English Language Arts, Mathematics, Science, Social Studies, and World Languages to specific tasks that are performed for the job featured in the Career Spotlight feature.

Critical Thinking

Accountants will need to stay abreast of new accounting software and technology in order to effectively serve clients and coworkers who are now relying on software for their day-to-day operations.

Key Terms and Academic Vocabulary Review

1. Students should write complete sentences using each key term. A sample answer might read: "It is important to use *tact* when giving constructive criticism."

Review Key Concepts

2. The following traits and interpersonal skills will help make you an effective coworker: responsibility, self-esteem, sociability, self-management, and integrity and honesty.

3. The steps to self-improvement are to focus on one trait at a time, make a plan and follow it, keep track of your progress, and move on to a new challenge once you feel you have made progress toward your goal.

4. The basic rules of workplace etiquette involve being courteous, dressing appropriately, being punctual, avoiding gossip, and respecting others' privacy.

5. The process of conflict resolution involves defining the problem, suggesting a solution, and evaluating a solution. Often parties must think creatively and compromise. If the parties are unable to resolve their conflict, they will need to seek mediation or arbitration.

CHAPTER SUMMARY

Section 13.1

Getting along with your coworkers is the most important workplace skill to have. Personal traits you may need to develop for the workplace include responsibility, self-esteem, sociability, self-management, integrity and honesty, and self-awareness. To be an effective coworker, you need to respect others, try to understand them, communicate well, and maintain a sense of humor. To improve your personal qualities, work on one trait at a time, devise a plan for working on the trait, check your progress, and then proceed to work on other traits.

Section 13.2

Basic etiquette is the correct behavior in the workplace. Etiquette includes being courteous, dressing appropriately, being punctual, avoiding gossip, and respecting your coworkers' privacy. It also means maintaining a good working relationship with your supervisor. Conflicts will come up in the workplace, and conflict resolution is a way to resolve conflicts. The U.S. workplace is diverse, and workers need to be sensitive to cultural, gender, and generational distinctions.

Key Terms and Academic Vocabulary Review

1. Use each of these key terms and academic vocabulary words in a sentence.

Key Terms
- tact (p. 291)
- empathize (p. 293)
- etiquette (p. 297)
- conflict resolution (p. 298)
- compromise (p. 299)
- diversity (p. 300)
- stereotype (p. 301)

Academic Vocabulary
- develop (p. 291)
- cooperation (p. 293)
- mediation (p. 300)
- distorted (p. 301)

Review Key Concepts

2. **Identify** personal traits and interpersonal skills that will make you an effective coworker.
3. **Describe** steps to self-improvement.
4. **Summarize** the rules of workplace etiquette.
5. **Describe** the process of conflict resolution.
6. **Define** diversity and describe effective ways to work with a diverse group of people.

Critical Thinking

7. **Analyze** How are the personal traits of responsibility and self-management related to one another?
8. **Explain** Why does conflict resolution focus on the problem rather than the personality of the opposing person?

6. Diversity means variety. Working with a diverse group of people means respecting differences in culture, religion, age, gender, and viewpoint. It also means keeping an open mind and treating people fairly. Workers also must overcome stereotypes and, if necessary, seek diversity training programs to help overcome stereotyping of cultural distinctions, gender distinctions, and generational distinctions.

Critical Thinking

7. Responsibility traits and self-management traits involve working on one's own, initiative, and the ability to see a task through to the end.

8. Separating the problem from the personality helps one deal with the conflict as something that can be resolved reasonably. Focusing on personalities may only lead to hurt feelings.

Real-World Skills and Applications

Self-Direction

9. Self-Management Write a one-page paper on why it is important to control emotions in the workplace. Discuss ways in which emotions can be expressed in a positive way and to allow people to work together effectively. Note possible consequences of inappropriate behavior in the workplace. Write about the degree to which you exhibit self-control and take responsibility for your actions.

Technology Applications

10. Using Presentation Software You are in charge of teaching conflict resolution in your company. Using presentation software, write a presentation that you could give to your coworkers. Include the conflict resolution steps you learned in this chapter. Create a potential conflict as an example in your presentation, and discuss how the problem can be resolved.

Interpersonal Skills

11. Working with Diversity Give a two- to three-minute oral report on the ideal workplace that shows respect for diversity. Include how employees can demonstrate respect for individuals with regard to cultural, gender, and generational distinctions.

12. **Cooperative Learning** Organize into groups of four. Discuss the following situation: One of your coworkers had an argument with a supervisor who hates to be wrong about anything. The coworker and supervisor were arguing about a recent news event. The day after the argument, the coworker brought an article to work. The article proved the supervisor was wrong. Discuss what effect the coworker's action will have on the supervisor and on the coworker. Should the coworker have shown more courtesy?

13. **Managing Workplace Distractions**
Situation You work in an office. Because your desk is located near the coffee pot, your coworkers have formed the habit of congregating in front of your work area, and they often try to draw you into their conversations. You would like to be free of the disruption.
Activity In a group, create a skit that models a tactful approach for dealing with the described situation. Be sure to use the conflict resolution steps.
Evaluation You will be evaluated on how well you meet the following performance indicators:
- Present your skit in a mature, convincing manner.
- Model appropriate etiquette.
- Explain why your approach would be effective in a real-life setting.

ACTIVE LEARNING

12. In their responses, students should reflect an understanding that it is sometimes better to not make an issue of showing a supervisor that he or she is wrong.

ROLE PLAY

13. Skits should demonstrate an understanding of interpersonal relations in a workplace, including such traits as respect for others, understanding and empathy, communication skills, and a sense of humor. A method of coping with the situation should be developed and applied in a manner consistent with the real world.

Real-World Skills and Applications

9. Papers will vary, but students should note that the lack of emotional control could lead to hurt feelings, poor working relationships, and even violence. Workers can channel their emotions by learning techniques such as taking a break or taking deep breaths. In their papers, students should also assess their own self-control and sense of responsibility.

10. In their presentations, students should present a specific conflict where two parties strongly disagree. Students should use the steps described in Section 13.2 and in **Figure 13.1** as a reference in detailing how the steps can be used to resolve the conflict.

11. Oral reports should reflect an understanding of, and sensitivity to, diversity. Encourage students to include specific examples based on the concepts of respecting differences and overcoming stereotypes.

Academic Skills in the Workplace

14. Students should include, in clear order, the details of how to use the software. The document might also include tips for beginning computer users, or users who may have difficulty learning new programs.

15. The four sides of the square can be up to five feet long ($\sqrt{25} = 5$).

16. The lava cools at an average hourly rate of 24.4 °C (1,170 °C ÷ 48 hours = 24.4 °C /hour).

17. Bar graphs should reflect accurate age and population information in your state.

Academic Skills in the Workplace

English Language Arts

14. Design a Training Program Imagine that you work in an office that has just acquired new e-mail software. It is a program you know well, and you have been asked to explain the basic functions of the software to your coworkers. Design a document that describes the basic steps of sending and receiving e-mails. Keep in mind that some of your coworkers may have limited knowledge of computers.

Mathematics

15. Calculate Square Roots You are giving a poster presentation at a professional conference. In the guidelines for the conference, you read that the poster can be no more than 25 square feet in size. If you expect your poster to be exactly square, what are the largest dimensions it can have to fit the parameters?

CONCEPT **Squares and Square Roots** The square root of a number is one of two equal factors of the number. The notation $\sqrt{}$ indicates the square root.

Starting Hint Find the square root of 25 in order to determine the largest possible dimensions a square poster can have.

Science

16. Collaborating All around the world, scientists collaborate with one another. For instance, volcanologists often team up with other volcanologists to learn how volcanoes act. In Hawaii, you can still see lava flowing slowly from Mt. Kilauea. Lava is 1,170 °C. Once a thick flow of lava comes to a halt, it can take about two days for the outer part to cool to a crust of rock. What is the average cooling rate of the lava in degrees Celsius per hour?

Starting Hint Divide 1,170°C by 48 hours (2 days) to get the cooling rate.

Social Studies

17. Tracking Diversity Visit the United States Census Bureau Web site to find demographic information about the United States. *Demographics* are statistics that describe a population in terms of personal characteristics. Find the total population of your state. Then use the site to find information on age groups by state. Create a bar graph that shows the following age groups in your state by percent: 18–35, 36–64, and 65 and older.

STANDARDIZED TEST PRACTICE

MULTIPLE CHOICE

Directions Read the question. Then read each answer choice. Choose the best answer choice for the question, and then circle the letter beside the answer choice.

> **Test-Taking Tip** In a multiple-choice test, pay attention to key words in the question and each answer choice. In this question, the key words are *diversity training*. Which answer choice refers specifically to diversity training?

1. Which of the following indicates a need for diversity training in the workplace?

  a. the way technology affects etiquette

  b. a coworker who always shows disrespect for your supervisor

  c. a group of coworkers who tell jokes about older employees

  d. disagreements between employees about supplies in vending machines

STANDARDIZED TEST PRACTICE

Answer
1. c. a group of workers who tell jokes about other employees.

Test-Taking Strategies
Whether your students have a standardized test coming up in a few days or a few weeks, these last-minute test-prep tips and strategies will help students relax and do their best.

Test Format Help your students become familiar with the format of the specific test they are going to take by practicing with test items that imitate the actual test items as closely as possible.

Test Timing Have your students take one or more timed practice tests so that they become comfortable with the test format.

Writing Skills Practice

18. Writing a Persuasive Essay You can use persuasive essays in school whenever you want to tell your views about a subject. You also can write persuasive essays in the workplace when you need to "sell" your views to a manager or coworkers.

 Practice Find a recent article about technology misuse in the workplace. Write a two-page persuasive essay that defends either side of this issue.

Follow these steps to write your essay:

- Use facts to support your viewpoint. Use quotations, factual evidence, and statistics to support your side.
- State the other side. In a sentence or two, explain the opposing point of view. This will answer any questions your reader might have about the subject.
- Write a strong ending. Make sure your ending wraps up everything you want to say.

Net Connection

19. Research Affirmative Action Affirmative action is a controversial policy that seeks to make up for past discrimination. Visit this book's OLC through **glencoe.com** and find the link to the U.S. Department of Labor page on Affirmative Action. Create a fact sheet that covers the purpose of the policy.

@ Log On Research employment Web sites to learn about diversity programs in companies that interest you. Print out any policies and place them in your portfolio for reference.

Reading Connection
Go to this book's Online Learning Center through **glencoe.com** for a list of reading suggestions.

Personal Academic and Career Portfolio

Develop References

Be prepared to supply references when you apply for a job. Create one or more lists of references to include in your **Personal Academic and Career Portfolio**. As you meet and work with new people, you can update and reorganize your lists. You may also create different reference lists for different types of jobs or other applications. For example, you may wish to create a list of academic references when applying for a school. You may wish to create a list of personal references in addition to a list of professional references.

- Develop a list of contacts for references.
- Consider asking current and former teachers, counselors, coaches, club leaders, employers, and internship and volunteer supervisors if they would be willing to act as a reference for you.
- Contact potential references requesting a reference.
- Secure permission from at least five people to use as references.
- Organize your list of references by recording each person's job title, relationship to you, address, phone number, and e-mail address.
- Title each document appropriately and file it in your **Personal Academic and Career Portfolio**.

@ Portfolio Help Go to the *Succeeding in the World of Work* OLC through **glencoe.com** for help you creating your portfolio.

Writing Skills Practice

18. Essays should try to convince the reader to agree with the writer's point of view.

Net Connection

19. Fact sheets should demonstrate a basic understanding of affirmative action policies.

Resources

ExamView Assessment Suite CD allows you to print out ready-made unit and chapter tests complete with answer keys. You can also create customized tests.

WorkKeys

WorkKeys® is a job skills assessment program. For information on leveled assessment for Interpersonal Skills (Teamwork), go to the WorkKeys link on this book's OLC through **glencoe.com**.

Personal Academic and Career Portfolio

Creating a Reference Letter

Once students have created a reference list for their **Personal Academic and Career Portfolios**, they should create a general letter document that they can use to send to potential references. Using word-processing software, students might want to create a letter document that they could use as a template for sending letters to multiple references. Encourage students to personalize each letter so the letter remains sincere. Experienced word-processing users may also use a mail merge feature to send out many letters from one document.

Chapter Resources Planning Guide with Activities and Features

Section	Features	Activities
Section 14.1 **Teamwork and Collaboration**	Math in Action (p. 311) 21st Century Workplace (p. 312) Real-World Connection (p. 313) Creative Business Practices (p. 314) Everyday Ethics (p. 315) Hot Jobs! (p. 316)	Before You Read (p. 310) Graphic Organizer (p. 310) As You Read (p. 315) After You Read (p. 317)
Section 14.2 **Leadership**	Career Checklist (p. 321)	Before You Read (p. 318) Graphic Organizer (p. 318) As You Read (p. 319) After You Read (p. 321)

NCLB Activities, information, and skills practice will help your students attain No Child Left Behind proficiency. Students will improve their abilities in the following academic standards areas:

Academic Standards Correlations

Discipline	Standard	Feature/Activity
English Language Arts	**NCTE 1** Read texts to acquire new information.	Creative Business Practices (p. 314) Hot Jobs! (p. 316)
	NCTE 4 Use written language to communicate effectively.	Writing Skills Practice (p. 327)
	NCTE 12 Use language to accomplish individual purposes.	21st Century Workplace (p. 312) Real-World Connection (p. 313) After You Read (p. 321)
Mathematics	**Number and Operation:** Compute fluently and make reasonable estimates	Math in Action (p. 311)
	Measurement: Apply appropriate techniques, tools, and formulas to determine measurements	After You Read (p. 317)
	Data Analysis and Probability: Develop and evaluate inferences and predictions that are based on data; Understand and apply basic concepts of probability	Academic Skills in the Workplace (p. 326)
Science	**Life Science:** Behavior of organisms	Academic Skills in the Workplace (p. 326)

CORRELATIONS The charts show the 21st Century Skills, foundation skills, and workplace competencies that students develop as they work in this chapter.

Foundation Skills and Workplace Competencies Correlation Chart

21st Century Skills

Core Subjects
- English
- Reading/Language Arts
- Math

Learning Skills
- Information and Media Literacy
- Communication Skills
- Critical Thinking and Systems Thinking
- Problem Identification, Formulation, and Solution
- Creativity and Intellectual Curiosity
- Interpersonal and Collaborative Skills
- Self-Direction
- Accountability and Adaptability
- Social Responsibility

21st Century Tools
- Communication, Information Processing, and Research Tools
- Problem-Solving Tools
- Personal Development and Productivity Tools

Foundation Skills

Basic Skills
- Reading
- Writing
- Math
- Listening
- Speaking

Thinking Skills
- Creative Thinking
- Decision Making
- Problem Solving
- Seeing Things in the Mind's Eye
- Knowing How to Learn
- Reasoning

Personal Qualities
- Self-Esteem
- Responsibility
- Sociability
- Self-Management
- Integrity/Honesty

Workplace Competencies

Resources
- Allocating Time
- Allocating Money
- Allocating Material and Facility Resources
- Allocating Human Resources

Information
- Acquiring and Evaluating Information
- Organizing and Maintaining Information
- Interpreting and Communicating Information
- Using Computers to Process Information

Interpersonal Skills
- Participating as a Member of a Team
- Teaching Others
- Serving Clients/Customers
- Exercising Leadership
- Negotiating to Arrive at a Decision
- Working with Cultural Diversity

Systems
- Understanding Systems
- Monitoring and Correcting Performance
- Improving and Designing Systems

Technology
- Selecting Technology
- Applying Technology to Task
- Maintaining and Troubleshooting Technology

Yellow blocks indicate areas covered in the chapter

Chapter Overview
Introduce the Chapter

This chapter highlights the role of teamwork in the workplace and instructs students to be effective team members and leaders.

Section 14.1 describes types of business teams and the roles that individuals play as team members.

Section 14.2 introduces the qualities that leaders possess and discusses how leadership skills are used in the workplace.

Build Background

Ask students to brainstorm activities, in addition to sports, where teamwork plays a vital role. Encourage them to think of the different "teams" they might be on, such as at home when they do chores with other members of the household, or at school when the class is working together to understand a topic of study.

Exploring the Photo

Caption Answer
Teamwork is essential in many workplaces where team members must rely on each other to achieve common goals.

Discussion Lead a discussion by asking students to give examples of teams that must work together to complete a task or goal.

Teamwork and Leadership

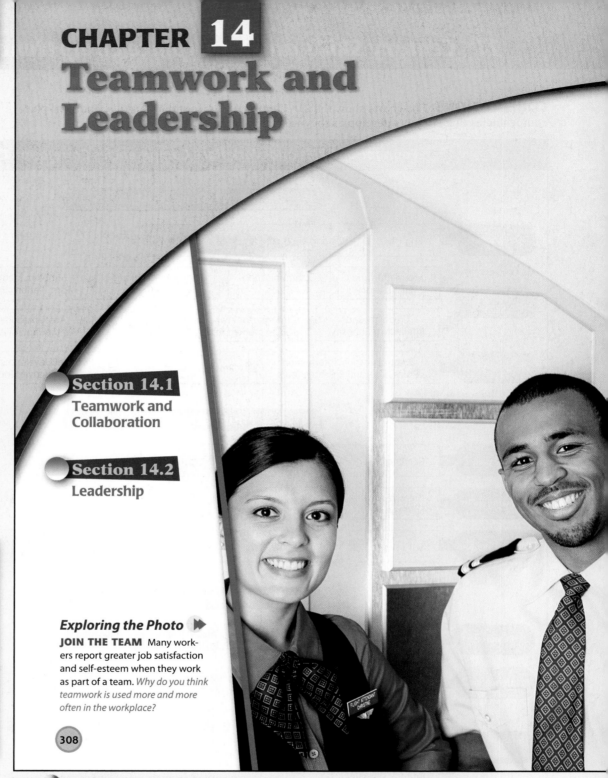

Section 14.1
Teamwork and Collaboration

Section 14.2
Leadership

Exploring the Photo ▶▶
JOIN THE TEAM Many workers report greater job satisfaction and self-esteem when they work as part of a team. *Why do you think teamwork is used more and more often in the workplace?*

308

Classroom Resources

📁 Student Edition
📁 Teacher Wraparound Edition
📁 Student Activity Workbook with Academic Integration
📁 Student Activity Workbook with Academic Integration TAE
📁 *Fast File,* Unit 5 Resources

📁 Inclusion in the Career Education Classroom
💿 TeacherWorks™ Plus
💿 *ExamView Assessment Suite*
💿 Interactive Chalkboard
💿 Interactive Student Edition
💿 Online Student Edition
💿 Online Learning Center (OLC) with Podcasts

Chapter Objectives

After completing this chapter, you will be able to:

- **Identify** the benefits of teamwork for team members and businesses.
- **Explain** how to organize and manage an effective team.
- **Describe** how to be a good team member.
- **Define** total quality management and explain how it affects workers.
- **Explain** the characteristics of effective leaders and name four leadership styles.
- **Summarize** the procedure for leading a formal meeting.

Writing Activity Personal Career Notebook

Think about your recent group activities at school or work. In most situations, are you more comfortable as a leader or a cooperative group member? Why? What qualities do you think a good leader should have? What qualities should team members have in order for the team to work successfully? Use your notebook to record your responses.

Get Motivated! Contact a business or political leader in your community. Ask that person to tell you what qualities a good leader should have. List these qualities in your notebook. Next to the list, note the qualities you possess and those you need to develop.

Chapter 14 Teamwork and Leadership 309

Writing Activity Personal Career Notebook Answer Guide

You may have a general preference for leader or group member, or you might take leadership responsibilities for some projects, and a member role for others. Although "leader" might suggest a more important role than "team member," both leaders and team members are essential to completing group activities.

Get Motivated! Lists will vary but should show an understanding of the information given by the business or political leader. Evaluate lists for clarity and content.

Review the Objectives
Introduce the chapter by reviewing the chapter objectives:

Section 14.1 Objectives
Identify the benefits of teamwork for team members and businesses. (Benefits for team members include greater job satisfaction, improved self-esteem, and better communication. Benefits for businesses include increased employee motivation and morale, improved quality and customer service, and fewer layers of management.)

Explain how to organize and manage an effective team. (Organize and manage a team by setting goals, assigning roles, and communicating regularly.)

Describe how to be a good team member. (Make the team's goals a top priority; listen actively and offer suggestions; follow up on what you have been assigned to do; work to resolve conflicts; and respect and recognize team members' efforts.)

Define total quality management and explain how it affects workers. (Total quality management (TQM) is a theory of management based on continually improving product quality and customer satisfaction.)

Section 14.2 Objectives
Explain the characteristics of effective leaders and name four leadership styles. (Leaders are good communicators, have vision, involve others, are decisive, and have positive attitudes. Leadership styles are directing, coaching, supporting, and delegating.)

Summarize the procedure for leading a formal meeting. (This procedure follows an agenda, which includes reading minutes of previous meeting, and then proceeding to unfinished business and new business.)

Section 14.1

Teamwork and Collaboration

Bell Ringer Activity

Teamwork and Collaboration

Ask students to list at least three ways they practice teamwork at home. Give the example of one family member preparing a meal while another family member sets the table.

Resources

Interactive Chalkboard
The Interactive Chalkboard CD provides visual teaching aids for this section.

@ Online Learning Center
The Online Learning Center (OLC) through **glencoe.com** features chapter vocabulary, chapter summaries, and other study materials.

Reading Guide

Before You Read

Preview Choose a Key Term or Academic Vocabulary word that is new to you. Write it on a piece of paper. When you find it in the text, write down the definition.

Read to Learn
- The benefits of teamwork for team members and businesses
- How to organize and manage an effective team
- How to be a good team member
- What total quality management is, and how it affects workers

Main Idea
D Awareness of workplace trends such as teamwork and total quality management will help you to succeed at work.

Key Concepts
- Teamwork in the Workplace
- Total Quality Management

Key Terms
- ◈ functional team
- ◈ cross-functional team
- ◈ self-directed
- ◈ team planning
- ◈ facilitator
- ◈ total quality management (TQM)

Academic Vocabulary
You will find these words in your reading and on your tests. Use the academic vocabulary glossary to look up their definitions if necessary.
- ■ cooperate
- ■ authority

Graphic Organizer
As you read, list the benefits of teamwork for both employers and employees. Use a chart like the one shown to organize your information.

Benefits of Teamwork	
Employers	**Employees**

 Log On Go to this book's Online Learning Center through **glencoe.com** for an online version of this graphic organizer.

NCLB

Academic Standards •

English Language Arts
- Read texts to acquire new information. (NCTE 1)
- Use language to accomplish individual purposes. (NCTE 12)

Mathematics
- Compute fluently and make reasonable estimates
- Apply appropriate techniques, tools, and formulas to determine measurements

Preteaching
Write the key terms from Section 14.1 on the board. Have students describe how each term relates to teamwork and leadership skills.

Graphic Organizer
Tell students to go to the OLC through **glencoe.com** for a printable graphic organizer. (Graphic organizers should list benefits of teamwork for employers and employees as outlined in this chapter.)

NCLB connects academic correlations to book content.

Reading Guide

Before You Read
Explain to students that they may participate on many teams throughout the day, from a team of family members at home, to a team of classmates completing a project, to a sports team competing for a championship.

D Develop Concepts
Main Idea Ask: Why do you think it is important to be aware of workplace trends? (In order to stay competitive in your field, you need to stay abreast of current workplace trends, such as training issues and the impact of the global economy.)

Teamwork in the Workplace

Have you ever worked in a cooperative learning group at school or played sports with a group? Each of these is an example of a team, a group of people who work together to reach a common goal. Knowing how to work as a team will prepare you for the world of work.

Many businesses rely on teams of employees to **cooperate** to get jobs done. In the past, workers may have focused on just one task. For example, an assembly-line worker may have created the bolts for a door, with little say in how the job was done. Today, workers in jobs from manufacturing to sales are likely to be part of a team. To ensure that their employees are good team workers, some companies offer team-building activities and training.

Benefits of Teamwork

Teamwork is good for business. Teams tend to be more productive than the same number of employees working separately. Greater productivity can lead to greater profits. Other ways companies benefit from teamwork include:
- increased employee motivation
- increased employee morale
- improved product quality
- improved customer service
- fewer layers of management
- improved communication

Math In Action

Work Hours
Your employees are switching from working 5 days a week to 4. In the 5-day schedule, they worked 9 hours a day, including an hour for lunch. If the total hours remain the same, how many hours will employees work daily in the 4-day schedule, including their lunch break?

Starting Hint: First, calculate the hours worked each week.

@ For more math practice, go to this book's OLC through **glencoe.com**.

 COMMUNICATION
Working as a team improves communication among workers. *What are some of the other benefits of teamwork?*

TEACH

Discussion Starter
Teamwork in the Workplace Ask students who play on sports teams to share their thoughts about how teamwork helps them perform better. Discuss reliance on others and how team membership influences their attitude or performance. Then, have students with part-time jobs share their teamwork experiences.

R Reading Strategy
Conduct Research Have each student find and read a current article on teamwork used by a specific business. Tell students to write 100-word summaries describing the business, how it uses teams, and how the teams have helped the company improve its work or profitability.

N C L B Activity correlated to Mathematics standards.

Math In Action

Employees will work 11 hours a day. $[(9 - 1) \times 5 = 40; 40 \div 4 = 10$
$10 + 1 = 11$ hours].

Resources

 TeacherWorks™ Plus
The TeacherWorks software includes customizable built-in lesson plans and links to printable program resources.

Extend the Photo

Caption Answer Possible answers include greater job satisfaction and self-esteem and better morale.

Discussion Lead students in a discussion about why communication is important when working in teams.

TEACH *(cont.)*

R Reading Strategy

Benefits of Teamwork Ask students how they think effective teamwork results in the three benefits listed on this page. As an example, point out that teams that work well together might require fewer layers of management, because team members, through cooperation and communication, are able to get their jobs done efficiently, without the need for extra supervision and guidance.

S Skill Practice

Independent Practice

Problem Solve Tell students to imagine they are members of a functional, self-directed team that packages gift baskets. Each member adds different products. One person consistently puts products in the wrong place and the next team member has to rearrange the products to fit others in the basket. This reduces the team's productivity. Ask students how they would deal with this issue.

N C L B

Activity correlated to English Language Arts standards.

▶ Vocabulary

You can find definitions in the **Key Terms** glossary and **Academic Vocabulary** glossary at the back of this book.

Individual workers also receive the following benefits from being part of a team:

- **Greater Job Satisfaction** Teams often rotate tasks among members. This reduces boredom and allows each team member to develop a variety of skills.
- **Improved Self-Esteem** Team members are usually given the **authority** to help make and carry out decisions. Many team members report that the most satisfying part of their jobs is feeling in charge of their work. Team members must be *self-starters*. They have to work without always being told what to do.
- **Better Communication** By communicating, team members learn about each other's attitudes and ways of thinking. As a result, they get along better and are more accepting of individual differences.

Types of Teams

There are two types of business teams. A **functional team** is a group of people from one department working together to reach a common business goal. For example, one functional team may consist of seven chemists working to improve a cold medicine. A **cross-functional team** is a group of people from two or more departments working together to reach a common business goal. An example of this type of team is a building maintenance supervisor, two bricklayers, and a landscaper developing a plan to landscape company headquarters.

The 21st Century Workplace

Diversity Drives Good Decisions

Did you know that having ethnically diverse coworkers can make you a better decision maker? When we work with people who are different from us, we are less likely to rely on old assumptions that might be wrong. We are also more likely to consider new ideas and points of view.

One recent study discovered that juries with ethnically diverse members thought harder and better about cases than juries whose members were of the same ethnicity. They also got the facts right more often.

Does conflict sometimes go along with diversity? Absolutely. After all, people who are different from us are less likely to "think like us." If others disagree with your opinions, you will need to cite facts and make solid arguments. That is the best basis for smart thinking.

CRITICAL THINKING

Why would someone of a different age, culture, ethnicity, or gender have a different perspective on a job-related decision? Give an example.

In Your Community

Visit a business in your community and interview an employee about how decisions are made in that business. Does a diverse group of workers participate in the decision-making process? Summarize your interview in a one-page report.

@ Extend Your Learning For links to Web sites about diversity and good business, go to this book's OLC through **glencoe.com**.

The 21st Century Workplace

CRITICAL THINKING ANSWER People of different backgrounds have different experiences, frames of reference, skill sets, and ways of approaching decisions and problems. As an example, imagine that you are working on a team that is designing a new restaurant. Working with a diverse group can help you create a concept that appeals to the widest range of possible customers—men, women, families, teenagers, seniors, members of dominant and minority groups, and so on. For example, a father or mother on your team might have ideas for how to make the restaurant appealing to parents with young children.

In Your Community Summaries should reflect student findings on diversity and decision-making.

COMMON GOALS An important part of team planning is establishing common goals. *What might happen if goals are unclear?*

Teams are managed in different ways, too. Some are supervised by managers. Other teams are **self-directed**, which means they are responsible for choosing their own methods of reaching their goals. Self-directed teams work without outside supervision.

Team Planning

Imagine that you and some friends are throwing a party. If each of you does what you think should be done without communicating with one another, the result will be chaos. You may all bring plates, for instance, but no one will bring the cake. If you plan and assign each person a task, however, the party will be a success.

The same is true for team projects at work. If you want the project to succeed, plan before you start. Since you will be working as a team, you should plan as a team. **Team planning** is a process that involves setting goals, assigning roles, and communicating regularly.

Setting Goals

When you plan your career, you set personal career goals. When you work on a team, you must think about group goals. Your company's overall goal, or *mission statement*, is a good place to start.

 Real-World *Connection*

Training Trainers

You are a new technology consultant assigned to system support for a small agricultural supply company. Company employees need training on the new e-mail software that has been installed. The owner plans to pay the software developer to do the training. You know you could save the company thousands of dollars by offering to do the training yourself, but the software company has not officially trained you.

Critical Thinking Should you offer to train the company employees?

Do Your Own Research Research the tutorial help available locally or on the Web for learning the efficient use of e-mail software. Determine the price and length of each course. Check to see if there are any special conditions or training required prior to taking the courses. Write a one-page memo to a supervisor with your training recommendation.

Chapter 14 Teamwork and Leadership 313

TEACH *(cont.)*

Cooperative Learning
Enrichment

Setting Goals Assign students to teams of four or five to plan a class newsletter on career advice. Tell students they have two months to complete this project and they are to set short-, medium-, and long-term goals. Have students compare their completed goals in class.

▶▶ *Extend the Photo*

Caption Answer If a team is working with poorly defined goals, its members will be unsure about the work they need to do, and the goals will be more difficult to achieve.

Discussion Ask: What might be a mission statement, or overall goal, for the employees in this photograph?

Real-World *Connection*

Critical Thinking Answer There is a difference between understanding software for yourself, and being able to explain it to your coworkers. If you have not been properly trained to provide instruction on how to use the new software, you may confuse employees trying to learn the new system. Many software programs have training as part of the licensing requirements. This may mean that one or more persons in a company receive direct training, and they in turn train others. Many systems, however, require no training and employees learn by practice or by taking a course offered by a third party.

Do Your Own Research Memos will vary but should clearly state the price, the length of time to complete each course, and any special conditions or training required prior to using the software.

TEACH (cont.)

C Critical Thinking

Assigning Tasks Effectively
Encourage students to brainstorm a list of reasons team members should divide the workload, and then give an example that demonstrates each reason. (Students might point out that by assigning tasks effectively, team members can work in their strongest areas. For example, a person who is proficient at math would likely excel at tasks involving financial calculations.)

S Skill Practice

Guided Practice
Communicating Effectively Have students work in teams of two and have one member of each pair wait in the hallway while you explain to remaining students that they are to teach a topic of their choice to their partners. Call waiting students back to class and commence the teaching. Have students write one-page reports explaining how successful they were in teaching their partners.

Some mission statements are very brief. For example, the furniture store IKEA's mission is "to create a better way of life for the many." Other mission statements are more detailed. For example ice cream company Ben & Jerry's mission statement consists of three related parts detailing their company, economic, and social goals.

Considering your company's mission will ensure that your goals align with the things the company values and sets as priorities. Keep your company's mission in mind when you begin a project. Then set short-term, medium-term, and long-term project goals. Suppose you work on a team for a sportswear company. Your goals might include the following:

- **Short-Term Goal** Analyze the team's procedure for assembling jackets.
- **Medium-Term Goal** Figure out more efficient procedures.
- **Long-Term Goal** Produce more jackets in less time.

The best way to approach a large project is to break it into smaller tasks. Then assign each task to an individual, and give it a start and end date. A useful tool for doing this is a *tracking schedule*. You can create a tracking schedule with pencil and paper or by using scheduling or spreadsheet software.

Assigning Roles and Duties

Remember the party we talked about earlier? If you had chosen one friend to oversee the process, it would have gone more efficiently.

Creative Business Practices

FedEx
Federal Expre[ss]

FedEx **Environmental Leadership**

FedEx, the world's largest express transportation company, ships to more than 220 countries and territories. This takes time, resources, and fuel. Key FedEx business practices show the company's leadership in environmental business practices for the transportation industry.

One of the ways FedEx can do this is by using FedEx OptiFleet E700 delivery trucks. The vehicles are hybrid standard trucks that reduce smog-causing emissions and use less gas than standard trucks. FedEx also uses envelopes and boxes that are made with recyclable materials. In addition, the inks on the packaging are water-based, which ensures that the ink will not damage the environment and the paper can be recycled. The corporation has received several awards for its leadership in environmental business practices.

CRITICAL THINKING How does FedEx benefit from using hybrid trucks?

@ **Connect to the Real World** For more information about the FedEx, visit the company's Web site via the link on this book's Online Learning Center through **glencoe.com**.

Creative Business Practices

CRITICAL THINKING ANSWER Not only do hybrid vehicles reduce smog emissions, but FedEx also spends less money on gas to fuel the trucks.

Everyday ETHICS

WORK HOURS

Should you ever work "off the clock"?

COVERING FOR A COWORKER You are only allowed to work 18 hours a week because you are 15 years old. Your employer has asked you to work a few hours to cover for a sick coworker "off the clock," which means that the hours will not be recorded. You know that if the violation of the terms of your permit is reported, your employer will have to pay a large fine, and you think you will probably lose your job. However, you also know that the chances of it being reported are small.

What Would You Do? Should you work off the clock? Why or why not?

DISCUSS IT Federal and state laws set strict limits on the hours that young people under the age of 16 may work. Say that you are aware of that, but you still want to help your employer. Are there ways to cover the sick worker's hours without exceeding an 18-hour workweek? With a partner, discuss possible ways to accommodate both your employer and the sick coworker.

Team projects at work also go more smoothly if the team appoints a **facilitator**, who is a member of the team who coordinates the tasks so that the team works efficiently. Self-directed teams often appoint a facilitator.

When assigning roles on a workplace team, it is important to match tasks to abilities. For example, Jason Sedrick works on the landscaping crew at a community zoo. Recently, he was assigned to a self-directed functional team to create a new zoo entrance. The team chose a facilitator with experience in landscape design. Jason knows stonework, so he agreed to handle that part of the job. Other members were assigned roles based on their particular skills.

Communicating

S

Communication is the key to good teamwork. Effective teams communicate regularly to assess progress and address issues. For example, Jason's team meets daily for quick updates. The team meets weekly to evaluate overall progress and take notes summarizing the meeting.

Potential Obstacles

Working in teams is not always easy. These are some common team problems:
- Unclear goals
- Misunderstandings about how much authority the team has and team members have
- Confusion about how to assess the performance of individuals
- Competitiveness among team members

As You Read

Analyze How might communicating help a team overcome problems?

Chapter 14 Teamwork and Leadership **315**

As You Read

Communicating can help troubleshoot problems such as misunderstandings and confusion, and can prevent resentment from team members who sense a lack of recognition.

ASSESS

Review Key Terms
Have students write sentences using each key term.

Online Study Tools
Have students go to the OLC through **glencoe.com** to:
- Download **Podcast** study tools.
- Download free **Study-to-Go** content to their PDAs or cell phones.

Resources

 ExamView Assessment Suite CD allows you to print out ready-made unit and chapter tests complete with answer keys. You can also create customized tests.

Everyday ETHICS

What Would You Do? Answer Student responses should weigh the impact of defying an employer versus that of violating the conditions of the work permit.

DISCUSS IT Answers will vary but one suggestion might be to switch hours so the sick employee takes some of your hours from later in the week, so you can cover his sick time without exceeding your maximum hours for the week.

RETEACH

Discussion Starter

Total Quality Managmenet Explain to students that an important part of the TQM philosophy is that providing high-quality goods or services actually costs less than providing low-quality ones. Ask: Why do you think this is true? (A possible answer is that a low-quailty product might be profitable in the short term, but with continual improvements, long-term profits are more likely to increase.)

✓ Reading Check

ANALYZE Following up is a good practice to ensure that you are completing your assigned task correctly.

U Universal Access

Students with Learning Disabilities Students with attention difficulties may find it easier to concentrate if they are actively involved in learning. Have students take a section of this chapter such as team goal-setting or TQM and teach it to another student. Afterward, discuss whether the students learned better as the teacher or the student.

Resources

📁 **Student Activity Workbook with Academic Integration** Assign the Chapter 14 activities in the Student Activity Workbook.

▶▶ **INSPIRATION** A team member who works hard inspires other team members to do their best. *What are some other qualities of an effective team member?*

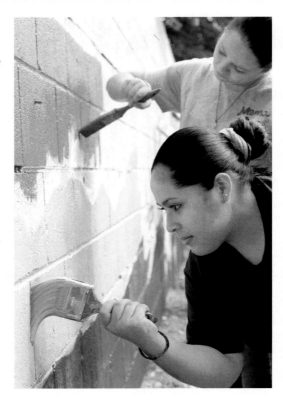

HOT JOBS!

Landscape Architect

Landscape architects are hired by homeowners, private schools, public organizations, shopping malls, zoos, housing developments, and parks to integrate the natural world into the human environment. Almost all architects must work with teams to complete their projects. A bachelor's degree, license, and strong technical skills start most landscape architects on their way.

- Resentment at a lack of individual recognition
- Reduced effort by team members, especially as the size of the team increases

Most obstacles can be overcome if teams define goals clearly, take action promptly, and keep communicating. Talking with the team leader and calling a team meeting are good ways to start solving problems.

Being an Effective Team Member

What makes a person an effective team member? The following are valuable attitudes and actions:

- Make the team's goals your top priority.
- In meetings, listen actively and offer suggestions.
- Follow up on what you have been assigned to do.
- Work to resolve conflicts among team members.
- Respect and recognize the efforts of your team members.
- Try to inspire other employees to get involved and do their best.

✓ Reading Check **ANALYZE** Why is it important that team members follow up on what they are assigned to do?

 Extend the Photo

Caption Answer Good team members also listen actively, follow up on what has been assigned, work to resolve conflicts, and respect and recognize the efforts of their team members.

Discussion Ask: Are the team members in this photograph working together effectively? Why or why not?

Total Quality Management

The team approach in business means that every employee helps to develop and takes responsibility for a company's products and services. A management theory that supports this approach is total quality management. **Total quality management (TQM)** is a theory of management based on continually improving product quality and customer satisfaction. TQM is sometimes referred to as "the quality movement."

In companies that apply TQM, quality comes first at every stage of the business process. It begins with planning and design and carries through to production and distribution. Every worker at every stage is challenged to find ways to improve the quality of the product. Employees are encouraged to find ways their jobs might be done better. The goal is to maximize customer satisfaction.

TQM defines a *customer* as anyone who receives the results of your work. That can mean either a coworker within the company or an outside consumer. This way of defining customers means that the responsibility for providing quality is not limited to the salespeople. It involves each employee all the way down the line.

Section 14.1 After You Read

Review Key Concepts

1. Name two ways teamwork benefits workers and two ways it benefits businesses.
2. Identify one common obstacle to good teamwork, and explain how you would overcome it.
3. List tips for being a good team member that you might give to a new coworker.

Practice Academic Skills

 Mathematics

4. A team from a landscaping design firm is designing a garden for a library. First the team must determine how much fencing is necessary to enclose the garden. The garden is in the form of a right triangle. If the two legs measure 8 yards and 6 yards, how much fencing is needed in all?

   CONCEPT **The Pythagorean Theorem** In a right triangle, the sides adjacent to the right angle are called legs. The side opposite the right angle is the hypotenuse. The Pythagorean Theorem describes the relationship between the legs (a and b) and the hypotenuse (c): $a^2 + b^2 = c^2$.
   Step 1: Determine the length of the hypotenuse by taking the square root of the sum of the lengths of the legs squared.
   Step 2: Add the lengths of all the sides (6, 8, and the length of the hypotenuse) to determine the amount of fencing needed.

    For math help, go to the Math Appendix located at the back of this book.

Section 14.1

ASSESS

After You Read
Have students complete the Section 14.1 After You Read section review.

Online Study Tools
Have students go to the OLC through **glencoe.com** to:
- Take the Section 14.1 **Practice Test.**
- Download **Podcast** study tools.
- Download free **Study-to-Go** content to their PDAs or cell phones.

CLOSE

Culminating Activity
Write a Proposal Have students write a one-page proposal for a team-building exercise that can be used at school.

N C L B Activity correlated to Mathematics standards.

Section 14.1 After You Read

Review Key Concepts
1. Employee benefits include greater job satisfaction, improved self-esteem, and better communication. Business benefits include improved quality, increased employee morale, and fewer layers of management.
2. Students should mention an obstacle detailed on pages 315-316. Teams can overcome obstacles by defining roles clearly, taking prompt action, and communicating effectively.

3. Make the team's goals a top priority; listen actively and offer suggestions; follow up on what you have been assigned to do; work to resolve conflicts; respect and recognize the efforts of team members; and inspire others to get involved and do their best.

Practice Academic Skills
4. Twenty four yards of fencing is needed ($6^2 + 8^2 = 100$; $\sqrt{100} = 10$; $6 + 8 + 10 = 24$).

Leadership

FOCUS

Bell Ringer Activity

Leadership

Ask students to think about group situations in which one person has emerged as the leader even though he or she was not elected or chosen as such. Have students list this person's skills. Ask volunteers to share their lists. Have students explain why they think the personal qualities they mentioned are important to good leaders.

Resources

Interactive Chalkboard
The Interactive Chalkboard CD provides visual teaching aids for this section.

@ **Online Learning Center**
The OLC through **glencoe.com** features chapter vocabulary, chapter summaries, and other study materials.

Preteaching

Read the definitions of the key terms aloud. As you read each definition, ask students to write a sentence using each key term.

Graphic Organizer

Tell students to go to the OLC through **glencoe.com** for a printable graphic organizer. (Graphic organizers should show leadership qualities as discussed in this section.)

 Activity correlated to English Language Arts standards.

Reading Guide

Before You Read

Preview Read the Key Terms and Academic Vocabulary below. In one or two sentences, predict what you think the section will be about.

Read to Learn
- The characteristics of effective leaders and four leadership styles
- The procedure for leading a formal meeting

D Main Idea
Understanding the characteristics of leaders and the procedures they follow will help you to be an effective leader.

Key Concept
- What Is Leadership?

Key Terms
◈ leadership
◈ leadership style
◈ parliamentary procedure

Academic Vocabulary
You will find these words in your reading and on your tests. Use the academic vocabulary glossary to look up their definitions if necessary.
■ interpret
■ process

Graphic Organizer
As you read, list the qualities that make a good leader. Continue adding your own ideas to the list after you finish reading. Use a concept map like the one shown to help organize your information.

@ **Log On** Go to this book's Online Learning Center through **glencoe.com** for an online version of this graphic organizer.

NCLB Academic Standards ·
English Language Arts
- Read texts to acquire new information. (NCTE 1)

Reading Guide

Before You Read
Point out to students that succeeding as a team leader means more than just being "the boss." Ask students to brainstorm effective leadership traits, in addition to authority.

D Develop Concepts
Main Idea Discuss the main idea with students: Ask students if they have ever been called upon to be a leader. As volunteers respond to this question, follow up and ask how they felt about accepting new leadership responsibilities.

What Is Leadership?

What do your favorite teacher, a coach, and the President of the United States all have in common? All are *leaders*. **Leadership** is motivating others to work toward a goal. Leaders guide, direct, and influence people. Businesses also have leaders. How well they lead affects the success of their businesses.

Leadership Qualities

Many leaders share the same qualities:

- **Leaders are good communicators.** Leaders are able to receive information, **interpret** it, and pass it to others effectively. They speak with authority, believe in what they are saying, and project enthusiasm. You can learn more about communication skills in Chapter 15.
- **Leaders have vision.** Leaders have a clear idea of where they want to go and how to get there. For example, a businessperson should see clearly the future he or she wants for the company.
- **Leaders involve others.** Leaders inspire others to work toward their goals. Business leaders help workers to achieve their maximum potential.
- **Leaders are decisive.** Leaders have good judgment and use their knowledge and experience to make wise decisions.
- **Leaders are positive.** Leaders strive for success and often are able to turn failure into success. Many successes are built on past failures.

Do you have some of the qualities of a good leader? Of course, no one is born with all of these qualities. You probably have some of these qualities, though, and you can work to develop others. Learning the attributes of leadership and honing your leadership skills are the first steps toward becoming a leader. **Figure 14.1** on page 320 lists various leadership qualities.

Figure 14.1 on page 320

Vocabulary
You can find definitions in the **Key Terms** glossary and **Academic Vocabulary** glossary at the back of this book.

As You Read
Infer Why do you think the ability to make good decisions might be a leadership quality?

HUMOR Effective leaders get along with others. *How can having a sense of humor help a leader get along with others?*

Teamwork and Leadership **319**

TEACH

Discussion Starter
Leadership Ask students to name people they consider leaders, and write the names on the board. Ask students what the people mentioned have in common. Write the qualities on the board. Then review the list of leadership qualities listed in Figure 14.1 What qualities in the list did students not mention?

R Reading Strategy
Analyze Ask students to respond to this sentence: "Good leaders are born, not made." Have students write 100-word paragraphs telling whether they agree or disagree with the statement, explaining the reasons for their positions, and giving examples that support their positions.

Resources
TeacherWorks™ Plus
The TeacherWorks software includes customizable built-in lesson plans and links to printable program resources.

ASSESS

Review Key Terms
Have students write sentences using each key term.

Online Study Tools
Have students go to the OLC through **glencoe.com** to:
- Download **Podcast** study tools.
- Download free **Study-to-Go** content to their PDAs or cell phones.

Extend the Photo

Caption Answer A sense of humor helps to maintain a positive attitude and to show your coworkers that you are friendly and approachable.

Discussion Explain to students that a sense of humor in the workplace needs to remain professional and free of jokes that may be considered offensive by coworkers.

As You Read
Decision-making skills are essential for leaders because decisions must be made for tasks to be completed and for goals to be achieved.

RETEACH

C **Critical Thinking**

Synthesizing Tell students to imagine that they lead a school club. At the time a club meeting is scheduled to begin, several members keep talking instead of paying attention. Ask students which leadership style they would need to deal with the problem and call the meeting to begin. (The style of leadership would be directing, which calls for a leader to give specific instruction, in this case, to be quiet so a meeting can begin.)

Resources

📂 **Student Activity Workbook with Academic Integration** Assign the Chapter 14 activities in the Student Activity Workbook.

ASSESS

After You Read

Have students complete the Section 14.2 After You Read section review.

Online Study Tools

Have students go to the OLC through **glencoe.com** to:

• Take the Section 14.2 **Practice Test.**
• Download **Podcast** study tools.
• Download free **Study-to-Go** content to their PDAs or cell phones.

Figure 14.1 **LEADERSHIP QUALITIES**

Quality	Definition	Quality	Definition
Accountability	Willingness to take responsibility for one's actions	Imagination	Creativity, ingenuity, resourcefulness
Competitiveness	Drive to succeed	Integrity	Soundness of moral character, sticking to one's values
Courage	Ability to take risks	Loyalty	Faithful commitment, fidelity
Credibility	Trustworthiness	Positive Attitude	Optimistic outlook on life
Decisiveness	Clarity of purpose, determination	Responsibility	Reliability, accountability
Dependability	Stability, consistency	Self-confidence	Belief in one's ability to succeed
Empathy	Identification with and understanding of others	Sense of humor	Ability to see the lighter side of things
Enthusiasm	Eagerness, passion, excitement	Tenacity	Unyielding drive to accomplish one's goals
Honesty	Truthfulness, sincerity	Vision	Clear idea of where one wants to go

LEADERSHIP There are many ways to show leadership. *Which of these qualities would you like to have or to develop?*

Leadership Styles

How you behave when you are in charge of other people is called your **leadership style**. These are the four basic leadership styles:

1. *directing*, or giving others specific instructions and closely supervising tasks
2. *coaching*, which means closely supervising but also explaining decisions and asking for suggestions
3. *supporting*, or sharing decision-making responsibility and encouraging the independent completion of tasks
4. *delegating*, or turning over the responsibility for decision making and completion of tasks to others

Effective leaders change or mix management styles according to the situation. The challenge is to decide which style will work best in a given situation. A directing style may work best with unskilled workers, for instance, and a supporting style may be better for workers with more skills and experience.

Leading a Meeting

As a leader or supervisor, you will probably have to lead meetings. Most business meetings are casual. In other words, they do not

---

EXTEND THE FIGURE **Figure 14.1**

Caption Answer Answers will vary based on students' career goals and personal values. Students should be able to explain why they have chosen particular qualities.

Discussion Have students choose a television character they perceive to be a leader. Then have them identify at least five qualities from this list that they believe the character demonstrates.

follow a strict set of rules. An example of a casual meeting is team members gathering to discuss progress on a project. You may have been involved in casual meetings at school.

Parliamentary Procedure

To keep formal meetings involving many people running smoothly, many organizations follow a **process** with strict rules of order that is known as **parliamentary procedure**. This process was developed in Parliament, England's governing body.

A meeting conducted according to parliamentary procedure follows an *agenda*. This is a list of topics drawn up beforehand that will be discussed at the meeting. The first item on the agenda may be a reading of the *minutes*, a written summary of the last meeting. The agenda will also probably include *unfinished business*, or topics from the last meeting that need more discussion, and *new business*.

Leadership Tips for Supervisors

If you are the supervisor, you will want to know how to work well with others and manage people effectively. Here are some tips:
- Provide enough training, and be a patient teacher.
- Give clear direction.
- Know when to intervene.
- Do not be afraid to admit when you have made a mistake.
- Be consistent in what you say and do.
- Treat workers fairly and equally.
- Be firm when necessary.
- Recognize effort and initiative.
- Congratulate in public; reprimand in private.
- Make sure that workers understand what you expect from them.
- Treat workers the way you would like to be treated.

Career ✓ Checklist

To Build Leadership Skills:

✓ Volunteer to expand your job duties.
✓ Earn the respect of your peers.
✓ Take risks.
✓ Be ready to make mistakes.
✓ Use creativity when solving problems and developing new ideas.

Resources

⊙ **ExamView Assessment Suite** CD allows you to print out ready-made unit and chapter tests complete with answer keys. You can also create customized tests.

CLOSE

Culminating Activity

Exercise Leadership Have students choose a cause for which they would like to raise money; for example, medical research or an environmental issue. Have them create plans for organizing a group to work for their cause. Tell students to write one-page descriptions of the purpose of their group, the specific means they would use to publicize its goals, and the activities they would sponsor to raise money for the cause.

N C L B Activity correlated to English Language Arts standards.

Section 14.2 After You Read

Review Key Concepts

1. Name each of the four leadership styles.
2. Identify the elements of a formal meeting that might help an informal meeting run more smoothly.
3. Define parliamentary procedure.

Practice Academic Skills

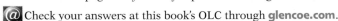
English Language Arts

4. Describe each leadership style in a half-page response.
5. Write a one-page essay on why supervisors need good communication skills.

@ Check your answers at this book's OLC through **glencoe.com**.

glencoe.com

Section 14.2 After You Read

Review Key Concepts
1. The leadership styles are directing, coaching, supporting, and delegating.
2. Even in an informal meeting, an agenda would be helpful, to know ahead of time what will be discussed during the meeting. Discussions of unfinished business and new business would also help team members remember what needs to be discussed so nothing is left out.
3. Parliamentary procedure, developed by England's Parliament, is a formal meeting process with strict rules of order.

Practice Academic Skills
4. Responses should reflect an understanding of the four leadership styles: directing, coaching, supporting, and delegating.
5. Essays will vary but might mention that leaders need to receive information, interpret it, and pass it on to others effectively; speak with authority, believe what they are saying, and speak with enthusiasm.

CAREER SPOTLIGHT
Career Cluster: Architecture and Construction

Discussion Starter

Architecture and Construction Lead a discussion about the various types of careers that can be found in this career cluster. Have students brainstorm various careers and jobs within the career cluster. (Answers will vary but students should show an understanding of the many types of careers that fall within the career cluster.)

W Writing Support
Independent Practice

Conduct Research Use library, Internet, or other resources to research a specific career in the Architecture and Construction career cluster. Write a one-page report on the kinds of work, the skills required, the working conditions, the training and education required, and the career outlook.

C Critical Thinking

Building Experience Ask: Why to you think apprenticeships and internships are common for training workers in many construction occupations? (Apprenticeships are especially valuable in fields such as construction that require hands-on experience to learn trade skills. Construction trades are hands-on occupations requiring knowledge of precise crafts, such as welding, cabinet making, and electrical design, that may take months or years to master.)

Chad Nichols
Construction Manager

Q: Describe your job.
A: I work for a general contractor. My responsibilities include project procurement, estimating, designing, building, and project management.

Q: Describe a typical workday.
A: Daily tasks include pre-bid meetings, job site visits, bid seeking preparation, and sales. A typical day is very fast-paced. I visit job sites, take photos, and usually meet with prospective clients, subcontractors, or suppliers. I also study construction drawings and documents, looking for more efficient ways to complete projects.

Q: What skills are most important to you in your job?
A: General knowledge of construction and construction materials, as well as good communication and math skills. The ability to visualize a project by looking at drawings or blueprints is essential. Financial skills are needed to manage costs.

Q: What skills are helpful in preparing for your career?
A: The abilities to work with people and be organized are important. Writing, math, science, physics, reading, processing information, and critical thinking skills are all very important. Your education will expose you to scheduling, estimating, computer applications, and dynamics, as well as specific things like concrete and asphalt, welding, equipment, concrete formwork and reinforcement, and construction document reading.

Q: What is your key to success?
A: I love what I do and I'm not afraid to try something different. Curiosity about how things work keeps me enthusiastic.

Q: What training and preparation do you recommend for students?
A: I recommend both obtaining a two- or four-year degree in construction management as well as seeking an internship. Working in construction is the most efficient way to gain knowledge of the industry. Taking part in student competitions and contractor-for-a-day programs will complement your training.

Q: What are some ways you recommend students prepare for this career?
A: To compete with those who are more experienced, you need to soak up as much information as possible while a student. This includes working hard in your classes, reading books and industry magazines, and watching engineering and construction programs.

Q: What do you like most about your work?
A: Building the world around us! Construction is a unique industry in its relationship to the earth and to the daily lives of people. My next project could be something that has never been done before, and could have a high impact on the world around me. That excites me.

 For more about Career Clusters, go to this book's OLC through **glencoe.com.**

Teaching Tip

The goals of the NCLB Act include a strong emphasis on reading skills. The use of modeling in your classroom will help students become better at identifying information. For example, ask a question that can be answered by reading the chart on page 323. Verbally identify the elements of the chart that might help the student identify the answer.

Sample Question Which tasks require social studies skills? (Answer: Meeting with prospective clients, working with subcontractors, and visiting and evaluating job sites all require social studies skills.)

- **Education or Training** Those interested in becoming a construction manager need a solid background in building science, business, and management, as well as related work experience in construction. Employers prefer individuals who combine construction industry work experience with an associate degree or a bachelor's degree in construction science, construction management, or civil engineering.

- **Academic Skills Required** English Language Arts, Mathematics, Science, Social Studies

- **Technology Needed** Construction software (project modeling, job costing, estimating, equipment management and accounting); digital photography equipment to take pictures of projects

- **Aptitudes, Abilities, and Skills** Communication and other interpersonal skills; creativity, critical thinking and problem-solving skills; the ability to visualize a finished project

- **Workplace Safety** Construction managers must exercise caution while working at a construction site. There are many safety procedures in place at these sites to protect workers from hazards such as falling debris, live wires, and sparks from equipment.

- **Career Outlook** Employment of construction managers is projected to increase at an average pace for all occupations over the next ten years.

- **Career Path** Construction managers can advance to bigger and more complex projects. Their career path might include work as an engineer, or a landscape or building architect.

N C L B

Academic Skills Required to Complete Tasks

Tasks	English Language Arts	Mathematics	Science	Social Studies
Meet with prospective clients	★	★	★	★
Review drawings to conceptualize a project	★	★	★	
Estimate a job	★	★	★	
Work with subcontractors	★	★	★	★
Visit and evaluate job site	★	★	★	★

Critical Thinking

Why must construction managers be aware of safety regulations?

N C L B This chart relates academic skills such as English Language Arts, Mathematics, Science, Social Studies, and World Languages to specific tasks that are performed for the job featured in the Career Spotlight feature.

Critical Thinking

Construction managers need to know safety regulations because they are responsible not only for the safety of their team members, but also for the safety of the people who will be using the facilities that the construction team builds.

CAREER SPOTLIGHT

ASSESS

Make Connections

Ask students to list specific correlations between academic subjects and workplace tasks. For example, a construction worker would benefit from studying geometry because a construction worker's tasks include reading and understanding blueprints. (Answers will vary but students should show an understanding of how academic skills relate directly to workplace tasks.)

CLOSE

Culminating Activity

Constructing a Career Path Ask students to research a career in landscape or building architecture. What kinds of education and experience would a construction manager need to build a career path to architecture?

Key Terms and Academic Vocabulary Review

1. Students should write complete sentences using each key term correctly. One example might be: "In order for team members to understand their role, proper *team planning* is essential."

Review Key Concepts

2. Employee benefits include greater job satisfaction, improved self-esteem, and better communication. Business benefits include improved quality, increased employee morale, and fewer layers of management.

3. Effective team planning involves setting goals, often based on a mission statement; assigning roles and duties, including a facilitator who coordinates tasks; and communicating regularly to assess the team's progress and to address issues. Teams must also troubleshoot obstacles when they arise and take action promptly.

4. Good team member qualities include making the team's goals your priority; listening actively and offering suggestions in meetings, and communicating with team members outside of meetings; following up on what you have been assigned to do; working to resolve conflicts; and inspiring other employees.

5. Total quality management (TQM) is a theory of management based on continually improving product quality and customer satisfaction. The goal of TQM is to maximize customer satisfaction. Every worker at every stage is challenged to find ways to improve the quality of the product.

6. Leaders are positive, effective communicators, have a

vision, involve others, and make decisions. The four leadership styles are directing, coaching, supporting, and delegating.

7. Parliamentary procedure, used during formal meetings, follows a process of strict rules of order. Meetings follow an agenda with a list of topics drawn up beforehand, as well as a recap of minutes from the last meeting. The agenda normally revisits unfinished business and then proceeds to new business.

Critical Thinking

8. The more people there are on a team, the greater the chance for confusion and miscommunication—and the less responsible each member is likely to feel to the team.

9. Self-directed teams would work well for knowledgeable, experienced employees who can accept the responsibility for choosing their own methods of reaching their goals, and who do not need much supervision.

CHAPTER SUMMARY

Section 14.1

A team is a group of people who work together to reach a common goal. The benefits of teamwork include improved productivity and greater employee job satisfaction. The two basic types of teams are functional teams and cross-functional teams. Teams can be managed or self-directed. Team planning involves setting goals, assigning roles, and communicating regularly. Obstacles to teamwork include unclear goals. Ways to be an effective team member include making the team's goals your top priority. Total quality management (TQM) is a management theory based on continually improving product quality and customer satisfaction.

Section 14.2

Leaders guide, direct, and influence others. Good leaders have good communication skills and vision, involve others, and are positive. Leadership styles, which are the ways of behaving as a leader, include directing, coaching, supporting, and delegating. Leaders often lead meetings, which may be casual or formal. Formal meetings may follow parliamentary procedure, a process that makes meetings run more smoothly. Suggestions for being a good supervisor include giving clear direction and recognizing effort.

Key Terms and Academic Vocabulary Review

1. Use each of these key terms and academic vocabulary words in a sentence.

Key Terms
- functional team (p. 312)
- cross-functional team (p. 312)
- self-directed (p. 313)
- team planning (p. 313)
- facilitator (p. 315)
- total quality management (TQM) (p. 317)
- leadership (p. 319)
- leadership style (p. 320)
- parliamentary procedure (p. 321)

Academic Vocabulary
- cooperate (p. 311)
- authority (p. 312)
- interpret (p. 319)
- process (p. 321)

Review Key Concepts

2. **Identify** the benefits of teamwork for both team members and businesses.
3. **Explain** what team planning involves.
4. **List** two things you can do to be a good team member.
5. **Explain** total quality management.
6. **List** the characteristics of effective leaders and the four leadership styles.
7. **Describe** parliamentary procedure.

Critical Thinking

8. **Evaluate** Why do you think teams that are too large often run into problems?
9. **Analyze** Which leadership style do you think would best suit a group of knowledgeable, experienced employees? Why?

Real-World Skills and Applications

Communication Skills

10. Writing Write a one-page paper that compares the four leadership styles. List and describe one or two characteristics of each leadership style. Suggest situations in which each style might be applied.

Interpersonal Skills

11. Exercising Leadership Valia is a department manager. She is concerned about the morale and behavior of her staff. Employees are often late, show little enthusiasm, and rarely make suggestions or show initiative. What questions should she ask herself about her leadership skills, and what can she do as a leader to address these problems? Write your response as bulleted points.

Technology Applications

12. Creating a Multimedia Presentation Work with three or four other students to create a multimedia presentation on good teamwork. Include information on setting goals, assigning roles and duties, potential obstacles, overcoming obstacles, and communicating effectively. Assign each member of your team a specific task. For example, one student could use word-processing software to gather and outline the information, another could use word-processing software to write the presentation, another could use presentation software or graphic design software to create the graphics or deliver the presentation. Present your multimedia presentation to the class.

13. **Working as a Team** Working in teams of three or four students, develop a list of service businesses, such as restaurants or hair salons. Choose one. Discuss how this business might use teamwork to deliver its service. Identify the tasks that need to be done. Create a one-page flowchart to show the order in which the tasks must be done. Discuss how the failure of any team member can affect the entire process. As a team, write a summary of your discussion.

14. **Collaboration and Planning**
Situation You and three classmates are working as a team to plan your school's prom. Your team must adhere to the budget given by the student council.
Activity Collaborate with your team members to plan the prom and prepare a proposal to submit to the student council. Include a list of the items you will buy and how much each will cost. After you are through, assess your experience in working as a team. List successful strategies that were used. Use the list to complete an "effective team member" profile, which you will add to your **Personal Academic and Career Portfolio**. Share your proposal and effective team member profile with the class.
Evaluation You will be evaluated on how well you meet the following performance indicators:
- Utilize effective teamwork strategies.
- Create an effective team member profile.
- Present a viable and complete proposal.

how she can improve her leadership qualities: communication, vision, involving others, decisiveness, and positivity. For example, she might try to communicate more effectively with her team to determine why morale is low. She might also ensure that her goals for the team are clear and that she is involving her team in achieving those goals.

12. Multimedia presentations should demonstrate good teamwork and include information on setting goals, assigning roles and duties, ways to have regular assessments, and ways to look for potential obstacles.

13. Based on the service businesses they choose, teams should provide flowcharts that list tasks in logical order. Summaries should demonstrate an understanding of how team members depend on each other.

14. Effective teams will demonstrate that they have worked together to make decisions and have assigned various tasks. Furthermore, team proposals and profiles will be detailed and complete.

Real-World Skills and Applications

10. In their papers, students should describe the four leadership styles—directing, coaching, supporting, and delegating, and give real-world examples of how each might be used. For example, students should point out that the directing style involves providing specific instructions and supervising tasks. An example of a leader using the directing style would be a construction crew manager, who will give specific instructions to his crewmembers and then supervise to make sure the work is done efficiently and safely.

11. Questions may include the following: Have I successfully communicated what I expect of my staff? Am I setting a good example with my own behavior? Should I be delegating more responsibility? In order to address these problems, Valia should self-assess and determine

Academic Skills in the Workplace

15. Job descriptions should successfully describe effective team membership and good leadership. The job listings should contain the kind of information students would find in online or newspaper job listings, including the company name, and the titles and departments of the two positions.

16. There are 40,320 possible combinations for groupings of three people (9 × 8 × 7 × 6 × 5 × 4) ÷ (3× 2 × 1) = 40,320).

17. Modern humans cooperate through schools where they teach each other; businesses where employees with different specialties work together to sell a product or service; political groups that support common causes; charities that help those in poverty; hospitals and research labs that help the sick; and firemen and police that save lives and fight crime.

18. Reports will vary depending on the country the student chooses. For example, students who choose to study Japan will discover that Japan is a world leader in TQM, providing high quality with minimal waste and high consumer satisfaction.

Academic Skills in the Workplace

 English Language Arts

15. Write Job Descriptions Write a job description for two new positions in your company. One should summarize the characteristics of an effective team member. The other should summarize the characteristics of a good leader. Give your company a name and identify the titles and the departments of the new positions.

 Mathematics

16. Determine Possible Combinations Employees from XYZ Company are at a team-building retreat. They have been asked to work in groups of three on trust-building exercises. If nine employees are at the retreat, how many possible combinations of three employees are there?

CONCEPT **Permutations and Combinations** Combinations describe possible outcomes in different scenarios. For example, C(10, 5) is the symbol that represents ten (10) things taken five (5) at a time and is calculated as follows: (10 × 9 × 8 × 7 × 6) ÷ (5 × 4 × 3 × 2 × 1).

Starting Hint Given that there are nine (9) people taken three (3) at a time, and order does not matter, you can solve C(9, 3).

 Science

17. Cooperative Behavior Nature is full of cooperative behavior among organisms. Bees in a hive perform specialized functions to keep the hive running well. A pack of wolves works together to bring down its next meal. Humans are also a cooperative species. From society's beginnings to the modern day, humans have cooperated to boost their chances of survival. Brainstorm and list ways modern humans have cooperated to ensure the survival of their species.

 Social Studies

18. Research Quality Assurance You are part of a team that is developing a new quality assurance program for your company. Your job is to research the ways companies here and in one other country ensure the quality of their products. Use library or Internet resources to find information about quality standards or quality assurance. Summarize your findings in a one-page report.

STANDARDIZED TEST PRACTICE

TRUE/FALSE

Directions Read the following paragraph, then read answer the questions that follow.

> **Test-Taking Tip** With true/false questions that rely on information given, read the paragraph very carefully to make sure you understand what it is about. Read the answer choices. Then read the paragraph again before choosing the answer.

What makes a good leader? Good leaders are able to inspire people to do their best. This is true of government leaders and business leaders. Leaders must have a vision for the future and communicate that vision to others.

1. Based on the paragraph above, which of the following statements is true?

   a. Leaders are born, not made.

   b. Leaders need to be good communicators.

   c. Good leaders are needed only in business.

STANDARDIZED TEST PRACTICE

Answer

1. b. Leaders need to be good communicators

Test-Taking Strategies

Whether your students have a standardized test coming up in a few days or a few weeks, these last-minute test-prep tips and strategies will help students relax and do their best.

True/False Questions Read each statement slowly and carefully. If any part of the statement is not accurate, then the entire statement is false. For the statement to be true, every part must be true.

Multiple Choice Questions Read the statement and try to complete it before you look at the choices. If your answer is among the choices, mark it.

Writing Skills Practice

19. Create a Bibliography A bibliography is a list of sources used to find information.

 Practice Research examples of leadership in business. Find at least five sources and create a bibliography of your sources using these steps:

- Record the following information for each source: the full title, author, place of publication, publisher, and date of publication. Also note the page number(s) on which the source appears, and the URL of Internet sources.
- Alphabetize the sources by author last name. Alphabetize sources without authors by title.
- Use this format for books: author last name, author first name, title. Place (city and state of publication): publisher, date of publication.
- Use this format for periodicals: author last name, author first name, name of article, name of newspaper or magazine, volume number or date, place, page numbers of article.
- Follow this order for Internet sources: URL, author name, title, date.

Net Connection

20. Research Team-Building Training Research Web sites to find information about how teams are used in business.

@ Log On Go to this book's OLC through **glencoe.com** to find a link to a Web site providing information about team-building training and activities. Use software to create a table listing the organizations providing the training and the kind of training and activities.

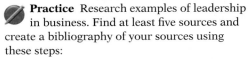

Reading Connection

@ Go to this book's Online Learning Center through **glencoe.com** for a list of reading suggestions.

Personal Academic and Career Portfolio

Teamwork Strategies

The use of teamwork is common in today's global workplace. You may work as part of a team in many different careers. To prepare yourself for working in teams, choose a career of interest and research the importance of teamwork in that career and how it is used. Your research may include library and Internet resources and interviews with people you know or who work in that industry. Write a one-page summary of your findings. Add this information to your **Personal Academic and Career Portfolio**.

The following guidelines will help you:

- Use the keywords "teamwork in business" or "teamwork" and "business" for your library, database, and Internet searches.
- Take notes on the books and articles your find. Be sure to note how to find the book or article again. For example, write down the URL of any Internet sources. Keep a formal bibliography of all your sources.
- Contact people you know or the human resources departments of companies in your field of interest. Ask about the importance of teams and how the teams are used in different jobs within each company.
- Write a one-page summary of the information you find.
- Create a new file in your portfolio and label it *Teamwork*.
- Add your summary to the file. Update it as you learn more about teamwork.

@ Portfolio Help Go to the *Succeeding in the World of Work* OLC through **glencoe.com** for help developing your portfolio.

Writing Skills Practice

19. Bibliographies will vary, but all should contain a list of sources of research materials for leadership; and all entries should conform to proper bibliographic conventions.

Net Connection

20. Tables should reflect research into team-building training activities.

 ### Resources

ExamView Assessment Suite CD allows you to print out ready-made unit and chapter tests complete with answer keys. You can also create customized tests.

WorkKeys

WorkKeys® is a job skills assessment program. For information on leveled assessment for Interpersonal Skills (Teamwork), go to the WorkKeys link on this book's OLC through **glencoe.com**.

Personal Academic and Career Portfolio

Teamwork

Teamwork is one of the most important topics of discussion in today's workplace. Many business magazines and Web sites regularly feature articles with tips and anecdotes about the best ways to maintain teams and be an effective team member. Encourage students to periodically update their **Personal Academic and Career Portfolio** with articles that can help them build their teamwork skills.

Chapter Resources Planning Guide with Activities and Features

Section	Features	Activities
Section 15.1 **Speaking and Listening**	Hot Jobs! (p. 332) 21st Century Workplace (p. 334) Real-World Connection (p. 336) Creative Business Practices (p. 338)	Before You Read (p. 330) Graphic Organizer (p. 330) As You Read (pp. 331, 335) After You Read (p. 339)
Section 15.2 **Reading and Writing**	Tech Savvy (p. 342) Everyday Ethics (p. 345) Science in Action (p. 346) Career Checklist (p. 347)	Before You Read (p. 340) Graphic Organizer (p. 340) As You Read (pp. 341, 345) After You Read (p. 347)

NCLB Activities, information, and skills practice will help your students attain No Child Left Behind proficiency. Students will improve their abilities in the following academic standards areas:

Academic Standards Correlations

Discipline	Standard	Feature/Activity
English Language Arts	**NCTE 4** Use written language to communicate effectively.	21st Century Workplace (p. 334) Real-World Connection (p. 336) After You Read (p. 347)
	NCTE 6 Apply knowledge of language structure and conventions to discuss texts.	Writing Skills Practice (p. 353)
	NCTE 9 Develop an understanding of diversity in language use across cultures.	Hot Jobs! (p. 332)
	NCTE 11 Participate as members of literacy communities.	Tech Savvy (p. 342)
	NCTE 12 Use language to accomplish individual purposes.	Everyday Ethics (p. 345)
Mathematics	**Number and Operation:** Understand meanings of operations and how they relate to one another	After You Read (p. 339)
	Data Analysis and Probability: Formulate questions that can be addressed with data and collect, organize, and display relevant data to answer them	Academic Skills in the Workplace (p. 352)
Science	**Physical Science:** Motions and forces	Science in Action (p. 346)
	Life Science: Biological evolution; Behavior of organisms	Academic Skills in the Workplace (p. 352)

21st Century Skills and Workplace Competencies Correlations

CORRELATIONS The charts show the 21st Century Skills, foundation skills, and workplace competencies that students develop as they work in this chapter.

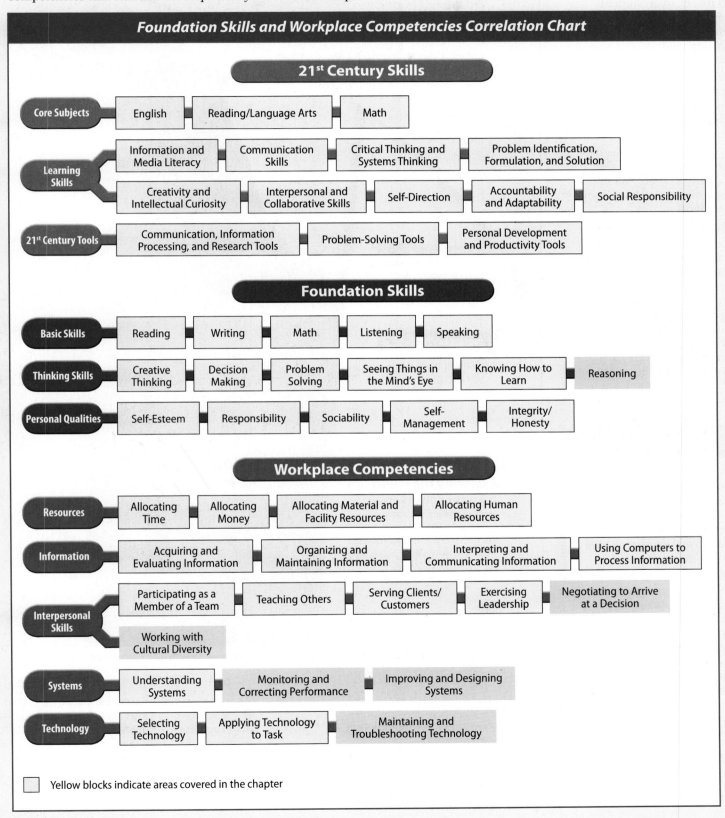

Foundation Skills and Workplace Competencies Correlation Chart

21st Century Skills

Core Subjects: English | Reading/Language Arts | Math

Learning Skills: Information and Media Literacy | Communication Skills | Critical Thinking and Systems Thinking | Problem Identification, Formulation, and Solution | Creativity and Intellectual Curiosity | Interpersonal and Collaborative Skills | Self-Direction | Accountability and Adaptability | Social Responsibility

21st Century Tools: Communication, Information Processing, and Research Tools | Problem-Solving Tools | Personal Development and Productivity Tools

Foundation Skills

Basic Skills: Reading | Writing | Math | Listening | Speaking

Thinking Skills: Creative Thinking | Decision Making | Problem Solving | Seeing Things in the Mind's Eye | Knowing How to Learn | Reasoning

Personal Qualities: Self-Esteem | Responsibility | Sociability | Self-Management | Integrity/Honesty

Workplace Competencies

Resources: Allocating Time | Allocating Money | Allocating Material and Facility Resources | Allocating Human Resources

Information: Acquiring and Evaluating Information | Organizing and Maintaining Information | Interpreting and Communicating Information | Using Computers to Process Information

Interpersonal Skills: Participating as a Member of a Team | Teaching Others | Serving Clients/Customers | Exercising Leadership | Negotiating to Arrive at a Decision | Working with Cultural Diversity

Systems: Understanding Systems | Monitoring and Correcting Performance | Improving and Designing Systems

Technology: Selecting Technology | Applying Technology to Task | Maintaining and Troubleshooting Technology

☐ Yellow blocks indicate areas covered in the chapter

Chapter Overview
Introduce the Chapter
In this chapter, students explore the important roles that speaking, listening, writing, and reading play in career success.

Section 15.1 outlines good speaking and listening habits and emphasizes their connection to relationships and customer service.

Section 15.2 explores the elements of reading and writing and presents guidelines for common forms of business writing.

Build Background
Explain to students that many employers rate communication as the number-one skill they look for in employees. Ask: Why do you think employers value communication skills so highly? Why do you think many employers say it is hard to find job candidates with excellent communication skills?

 Exploring the Photo

Caption Answer You can use language that is meaningful to your audience, make your central points clear, and check with listeners to make sure they have understood you.

Discussion Ask students how they can tell when a speaker is making a central point, rather than a minor or secondary point. (Cues used by many speakers include repetition, slower pace, louder tone, clearer enunciation, or introductory statements such as, "The most important thing to remember is…. ")

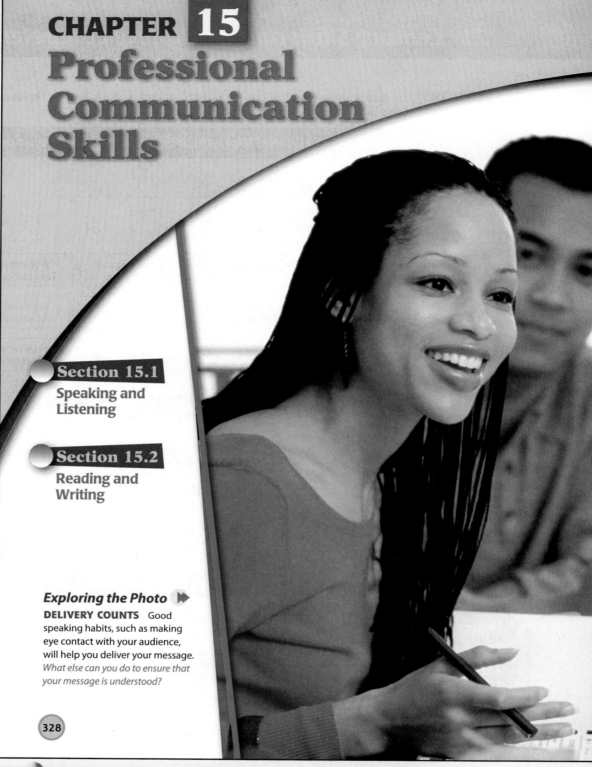

CHAPTER **15**
Professional Communication Skills

● **Section 15.1**
Speaking and Listening

● **Section 15.2**
Reading and Writing

Exploring the Photo ▶▶
DELIVERY COUNTS Good speaking habits, such as making eye contact with your audience, will help you deliver your message. *What else can you do to ensure that your message is understood?*

328

Classroom Resources

- 📁 Student Edition
- 📁 Teacher Wraparound Edition
- 📁 Student Activity Workbook with Academic Integration
- 📁 Student Activity Workbook with Academic Integration TAE
- 📁 *Fast File,* Unit 5 Resources

- 📁 Inclusion in the Career Education Classroom
- 💿 TeacherWorks™ Plus
- 💿 *ExamView Assessment Suite*
- 💿 Interactive Chalkboard
- 💿 Interactive Student Edition
- 🖥 Online Student Edition
- 🖥 Online Learning Center (OLC) with Podcasts

Chapter Objectives

After completing this chapter, you will be able to:

- **Identify** ways to improve your speaking skills.
- **Describe** good speaking habits and explain their importance in the workplace.
- **Explain** how active listening and note taking can help you listen.
- **Summarize** strategies for improving your writing skills.
- **Identify** common forms of business writing and the style appropriate to each.
- **Explain** reading skills such as skimming and previewing.

Writing Activity / Personal Career Notebook

Imagine that at a large state convention, your vocational club is unexpectedly invited to present a five-minute speech. You and the other club members will have only half an hour to prepare. Which task would you choose—to write the speech or to deliver the speech? Why? Write a journal entry describing your responses.

Get Motivated! Think of six occasions over the past week in which you used your communication skills. Assess your performance in each of these situations, recording your thoughts in a journal entry. Include suggestions for improving your skills.

Chapter 15   Professional Communication Skills   **329**

Writing Activity / Personal Career Notebook Answer Guide

Students' responses will vary depending on their self-confidence in their writing and presentation skills. Many people, however, find public speaking stressful.

Get Motivated! Examples might include writing an essay for school, speaking in class, or listening to a friend's concerns. Suggestions might include reading more, practicing various writing forms, and improving spelling and grammar.

Review the Objectives
Introduce the chapter by reviewing the chapter objectives:

Section 15.1 Objectives
Identify ways to improve your speaking skills. (Tailor your words to your purpose, audience, and subject.)

Describe good speaking habits and explain their importance in the workplace. (Good speaking habits include using correct pronunciation, enunciating clearly, and varying one's intonation.)

Explain how active listening and note taking can help you listen. (Active listening helps you extract the full and accurate meaning from what you hear. Note taking helps you pay close attention and remember what you hear.)

Section 15.2 Objectives
Summarize strategies for improving your writing skills. (Strategies for improving writing skills include organizing, paying attention to style, tone, and presentation, checking grammar and spelling, and outlining, free writing, and revising.)

Identify common forms of business writing and the style appropriate to each. (Memos, faxes, e-mail, and business letters all require a polite, businesslike, concise, clear style.)

Explain reading skills such as skimming and previewing. (Skimming is reading quickly through a document to pick out key points. Previewing is reading key parts of a document in order to predict its content.)

Bell Ringer Activity

Speaking and Listening

Ask students to create a chart with two columns, labeled Speaking and Listening. Have students fill in the relevant columns with specific habits or behaviors characteristic of strong speakers and good listeners.

Resources

Interactive Chalkboard
The Interactive Chalkboard CD provides visual teaching aids for this section.

@ Online Learning Center
The Online Learning Center (OLC) through **glencoe.com** features chapter vocabulary, chapter summaries, and other study materials.

Preteaching
Assign key terms to student pairs. Ask them to find the definition of the term in the text and then complete this sentence, using their key term: "_____ is important to speaking and listening well because...."

Graphic Organizer
Tell students to go to the OLC through **glencoe.com** for a printable graphic organizer. (Graphic organizers should mention several of the guidelines given in the text, such as knowing your audience and purpose and noting a speaker's nonverbal signals.)

 NCLB connects academic correlations to book content.

330

Speaking and Listening

Reading Guide

Before You Read

Preview Read the Key Terms and Academic Vocabulary words below. In one or two sentences, predict what you think the section will be about.

Read to Learn
- Ways to improve your speaking skills
- Good speaking habits and their importance in the workplace
- How active listening and note taking can help you listen

D Main Idea
Strong oral communication skills can help you achieve your personal and professional goals.

Key Concepts
- Communication and Relationships
- Speaking: What Is Your Point?
- Become an Active Listener

Key Terms
◇ communication
◇ customer relations
◇ purpose
◇ audience
◇ subject
◇ pronunciation
◇ enunciation
◇ intonation
◇ active listening

Academic Vocabulary
You will find these words in your reading and on your tests. Use the academic vocabulary glossary to look up their definitions if necessary.
- crucial
- cite
- conflicts

Graphic Organizer
As you read, make a list of good speaking and listening skills and habits. Use a chart like the one shown to help organize the information.

SPEAKING	LISTENING
• Enunciate	• Make Eye Contact

 Log On Go to this book's Online Learning Center through **glencoe.com** for an online version of this graphic organizer.

Academic Standards • • • • • • • • • • • • • • • •

English Language Arts
- Develop an understanding of diversity in language use across cultures. (NCTE 9)
- Use language to accomplish individual purposes. (NCTE 12)

Mathematics
- Understand meanings of operations and how they relate to one another

glencoe.com

Reading Guide

Before You Read
Point out to students that, while speaking and listening may seem easy, they are actually among the most difficult skills to master. Explain to students that communicating on the job requires specialized skills, such as handling customer complaints and making presentations.

D Develop Concepts
Main Idea Discuss the main idea with students. Ask: How can strong oral communication skills help you succeed in your personal life as well as at work? (Students should understand that communication is the main way we convey our ideas, resolve conflicts, and make impressions on others.)

Communication and Relationships

The exchange of information between a sender and a receiver is called **communication**. Whatever job you do, you will spend much of your time communicating: speaking, listening, writing, and reading. These communication skills are crucial to your career success. Communication skills help you gain information, solve problems, make decisions, and share ideas.

When we communicate, we do more than just share facts. We reveal a lot about who we are and how we feel about ourselves and others. Our opinions of others are based in large part on their communication style. In fact, all our relationships are built on communication.

Verbal and Nonverbal Signals

We communicate through both verbal and nonverbal signals. Verbal signals are written or spoken words. Nonverbal signals include tone of voice, facial expressions, gestures, postures, and eye contact. Nonverbal signals can convey a much stronger message than verbal signals, especially in emotional situations. Have you ever talked to a person who looked and sounded angry or sad, but said nothing was wrong? The body language probably told you more about that person's real state of mind than words did.

 NONVERBAL SIGNALS COUNT Using positive body language helps you to deliver your message. *What types of body language help you convey a positive message?*

TEACH

Discussion Starter
Communication and Relationships Ask students what we reveal about ourselves through the way we communicate. (We reveal much about our personality, about how we feel about ourselves and others, and possibly about our skills and educational level.)

Reading Strategy
Activating Prior Knowledge Ask students to recall the definition of body language (postures, gestures, and eye contact) and to give examples of body language that might indicate the following emotions: joy, anger, boredom, and sadness. (Examples might include smiling, avoiding eye contact, crossing arms over chest, fidgeting, or slumping in one's chair.)

As You Read
Descriptions might include self-confident and talkative, quiet and reticent, and crisp and decisive.

Resources
TeacherWorks™ Plus The TeacherWorks software includes customizable built-in lesson plans and links to printable program resources.

 Vocabulary
You can find definitions in the **Key Terms** glossary and **Academic Vocabulary** glossary at the back of this book.

 As You Read
Connect How would you describe your communication style? Why?

▶ Extend the Photo

Caption Answer Be aware of your body language and make sure it is supporting—not distracting—from the message you are trying to communicate, and know what messages various postures, gestures, and uses of eye contact can convey.

Discussion Explain to students that good communication is the key ingredient of positive customer relations. Ask students to share their personal experiences with sales or customer service workers. What characterizes good communication with customers? Bad communication? (Good customer communication is alert, respectful, empathetic, and solution-oriented.)

TEACH *(cont.)*

S Skill Practice
Guided Practice

Customer Service Ask students to role-play a conversation between a customer service representative and a customer who is upset about a defective product. The customer service representative should listen to the customer's concerns with interest, clarify all details, and calmly explain what the company can do to remedy the situation.

U Universal Access
Musical Learners Play a selection of songs from a variety of musical styles that include vocals. Have students write down words, images, and emotions that the music inspires. Then ask them what they think the musician's purpose was in "speaking" to the audience in each song. (Purposes might include evoking a feeling, sharing a personal story, or making the audience laugh or want to dance.)

W Writing Support
Analyzing Purpose Ask students to find and read an editorial article in a local or national newspaper. Have them summarize the writer's purpose and analyze whether he or she was effective in communicating this purpose. (Articles will vary; to be effective, writers should provide a clear thesis statement, logical organization, and relevant supporting facts.)

Communication Is the Key to Customer Relations

Because good communication is the basis of good relationships, it is also the key to positive customer relations. **Customer relations** is the use of communication skills to meet the needs of customers and clients.

Customers can be demanding. They choose businesses whose employees listen to their concerns, answer their questions promptly and clearly, and explain the company's actions and policies in clear language. Have you ever dealt with a rude or indifferent worker at a business? If so, you probably came away with a low opinion of that business.

Customer relations skills include speaking, listening, writing, and reading, as well as problem solving and maintaining a calm and positive attitude in challenging situations.

✓ Reading Check **ANALYZE** Why are nonverbal signals an important part of communication?

Speaking: What Is Your Point?

Whether you are speaking to an audience of one or one hundred, you want your listeners to get your point and be receptive to your message. This means that you need to be clear about your purpose, your audience, and your subject. You also need to use good speaking habits.

Know Your Purpose

Every time you speak, you have a **purpose**, an overall reason or goal, that causes you to say what you do. You may want to ask a question, share a thought or feeling, or simply greet someone. Common purposes for speaking include:
- building relationships with customers or clients.
- informing employees of a new policy.
- requesting or giving help or information.
- proposing a new idea or change to a supervisor.

Organize What You Want to Say

Having a clear purpose helps you communicate effectively. Have you ever started to explain something, only to realize that you are not really sure what you are trying to say? Thinking about your purpose ahead of time helps you organize your information and sound clear and confident.

Sometimes you may have more than one purpose. For example, you might need to speak to a customer to resolve a complaint while also using the opportunity to show your supervisor that you can handle important tasks on your own.

HOT JOBS!

ESL Teacher

Students who already speak one or more languages can learn English from specialized English as a Second Language (ESL) teachers. ESL teachers may teach English to people of all ages, both domestically and abroad. Many ESL teachers work in foreign countries so they can gain experience teaching while also learning about cultures.

✓ Reading Check

ANALYZE Nonverbal signals are often as important as words in revealing a speaker's thoughts and feelings. They can support or detract from a speaker's verbal message.

KNOW YOUR AUDIENCE Understanding what your audience knows, believes, and values will help you shape an effective message. *How might the message change if this person were speaking to her coworkers instead of her students?*

After you have determined your purpose, you can use a number of techniques to organize what you want to say:

- Enumeration, or listing key points: "As part of our lawn service, we will cut your grass, weed your garden, and trim your shrubs."
- Generalization followed by examples: "Traffic is getting worse. Last week, it took me two hours to get to work."
- Cause and effect, or telling what happened and why: "Flight 457 will be delayed. Fog is causing low visibility on the runways."
- Compare and contrast, or pointing out similarities and differences: "Our car wash is identical to our competitor's. However, our price is lower than our competitor's price."

Know Your Audience

When you think of an audience, do you imagine people seated at a theater or a stadium? In fact, an **audience** is anyone who receives information. Once you know your purpose in speaking, you need to know your audience. Ask yourself these questions:

- Who are my listeners? Am I speaking to customers, coworkers, supervisors?
- What do they already know about my subject? What do they need to know?
- What are my listeners' beliefs, values, and interests?
- What do they expect from me? Do they expect to be entertained, informed, or persuaded?

Knowing this information helps you create a message that your listeners will hear and accept. If your audience knows little about a topic, for example, you should begin with some background information. If your audience has strong beliefs about a certain issue, you should show respect for those beliefs in order to win their trust.

Chapter 15 Professional Communication Skills **333**

C **Critical Thinking**

Developing Criteria Ask students when they might use each of the four techniques listed here. For example, what subjects or situations would lend themselves to generalization followed by example? To compare and contrast? (Ideas will vary, but enumeration is often used to communicate several items of equal importance; generalization is often used to persuade; cause and effect is used to explain events; and compare and contrast is used to evaluate options.)

R **Reading Strategy**

List Examples Ask students to list various audiences they might speak to during the job search and on the job. (Examples may include contacts and referrals, references, cold-called employers, interviewers, coworkers, customers/clients, supervisors, and subordinates.)

W **Writing Support**
Independent Practice

Knowing Your Audience Ask students to write scripts for two brief oral presentations about their plans for after high school: one to be presented to a group of family and friends and one to be presented to a panel of managers at a job interview. Ask them to describe how the two presentations differ and why. (The presentations should differ in formality of tone, in amount of background information given, and so on.)

 Extend the Photo

Caption Answer The person would speak at a more complex level and assume greater background knowledge on the part of her listeners.

Discussion Ask students to imagine that their boss has asked them to give a presentation about their company's new product to a group of hike leaders from the local environmental club. How could they tailor their presentation to this audience? (Students could demonstrate a respect for their audience's environmentalism and explain how the product is relevant to hiking, outdoor activities, or physical fitness.)

TEACH *(cont.)*

S₁ Skill Practice
Guided Practice

Speak Convincingly Ask students to rewrite these two generalities to make them specific and persuasive: "Most people owe a lot on their credit cards." "Alcohol is linked to crime." (Rewrites might include, "The average American household carries nearly $9,000 in credit card debt" and "About 40 percent of all crimes are committed under the influence of alcohol.")

S₂ Skill Practice
Independent Practice

Pronunciation Ask students to use print or online resources to compile a list of commonly mispronounced words and how to pronounce them correctly. Have students share their lists to compile a class master list. (Words will vary but may include *business, library, nuclear, et cetera, pronunciation, February*, and *probably*, among others.)

NCLB Activity correlated to English Language Arts standards.

The 21ˢᵗ Century Workplace

Ergonomic Recovery

Many workers experience musculoskeletal disorders. To prevent injuries, many employers teach employees how to properly align their computer monitors, keyboards, and chairs. Many manufacturers cover their employees' hand tools in padding to reduce damaging vibrations.

If you believe that your workstation or tools need an ergonomic adjustment, research the tools you use to see how to use them more safely—small adjustments may make a big difference. Meet with your supervisor to bring up your suggestions. Show that you know your audience, purpose, and subject. Recommend adjustments and explain the impact of workplace adjustments on employee health. Show how paying attention to workers' health can benefit everyone.

NCLB

CRITICAL THINKING _____

How can a student benefit from learning the principles of ergonomics?

In Your Community

Choose a place where you work, such as an after-school job, a library workstation, or a home study area. Use print or online information to analyze the ergonomics of this place and make recommendations for improvement.

 Extend Your Learning Ergonomics are important in work, school, and play. For links to Web sites about ergonomics, go to this book's OLC through **glencoe.com**.

Know Your Subject

The **subject** is the main topic or key idea. Whether you are giving a lecture or talking to a customer, make sure you know your subject thoroughly. State your idea clearly, and use specific facts and examples to support what you are saying. Show that you know your subject by speaking clearly and directly. Move logically from point to point as you speak. Reinforce main ideas with vivid examples.

S₁ To show that you know your subject, **cite** solid facts. Compare these statements: "Rainforests are important." "Rainforests are home to over 60 percent of the plant and animal species on Earth." The first statement is a *generality*, or broad statement. The second is a specific fact. Generalities are not very persuasive. Most people are convinced by hard facts or examples.

Use Good Speaking Habits

How you say something is as important as *what* you say. Follow these guidelines whether speaking to someone in person or by telephone.

Use Correct Pronunciation

S₂ Correct pronunciation makes a positive impression. **Pronunciation** is the way a word's vowels and consonants are spoken and how its syllables are stressed. In English, pronunciation often does not reflect spelling. If you are not sure how to pronounce a word, ask a teacher or use an online dictionary that includes sound clips.

Enunciate Clearly

Enunciation is the speaking of each syllable clearly and separately. When you enunciate, you are easier to understand. You also

 334 **Unit 5** Professional Development

glencoe.com

The 21ˢᵗ Century Workplace

CRITICAL THINKING ANSWER Most students spend hours sitting at desks, working at a computer, and reading. They can therefore benefit from learning how to sit properly and how to arrange their workspace and reading posture to prevent injury.

In Your Community Students may mention arranging supplies to avoid awkward reaching, positioning the computer monitor to prevent eyestrain, or adjusting their chairs to fit their frame.

show self-confidence. Avoid nonwords such as *uh* and *um* and "empty" words such as *sort of*, *well*, and *okay* that make you seem uncertain.

Vary Your Intonation

You can send different messages by changing the **intonation**, the rising and falling tone or loudness of your voice. Use a louder pitch to stress key ideas. Varying your intonation helps keep your listeners' interest. Speakers who use a flat tone or who speak at a constant high pitch quickly lose their listeners' attention.

Make Contact with Your Listeners

Make emotional contact with listeners by addressing them by name, making eye contact, and gesturing politely in their direction. As you speak, look for signs from your listeners that your message is being understood. You may need to explain things in a different way. Always ask whether your listeners have questions, opinions, or other feedback. Show that you value their time and input.

Pay Attention to Volume and Speed Try to speak slowly enough to be clear, yet quickly enough to hold interest, and loudly enough to be heard, yet quietly enough to not hurt people's ears. It is difficult to know how you sound to others. Ask a trusted teacher, friend, or coworker for advice. Recording your own speech helps too.

Project a Positive Attitude Focus on solutions instead of problems. Be courteous and attentive, especially when speaking to customers. When speaking in a group, listen to what others say and avoid interrupting them.

Choose Words Wisely Use language that everyone can understand. Avoid slang and clichés, and match your words to the setting. Use your vocabulary to express yourself better, rather than using "big words" just to impress others.

As You Read

Connect Do you use different words when talking to different people? Explain.

🔊 **ANYTIME, ANYWHERE** Cell phones have made it easier to reach coworkers and customers at almost any time of the day or night. *How can you show respect for your listener during a telephone conversation?*

Extend the Photo

Caption Answer Listen actively, be concise, do not interrupt, minimize distractions and background noise.

Discussion Ask students whether it is easier or harder to communicate by phone than in person. (Students should understand that phone conversations lack the element of body language and often suffer from background noise or other distractions.)

As You Read

Most people use different words with different interlocutors and in different situations. For example, many people use informal language and slang with friends and siblings, more formal language with older relatives, and still more formal language with employers.

TEACH *(cont.)*

C Critical Thinking

Evaluating Claims The text states that a speaker should "make emotional contact with listeners." Why should they make emotional contact with listeners even if they are just giving a factual report? (In this context, "emotional contact" refers to engaging listeners' interest and respecting their ideas and opinions. This is a good strategy for any communication.)

S Skill Practice

Independent Practice

Vocabulary Explain to students that having a large vocabulary is a strong indicator of career success. Ask students to list five ways they could improve their vocabulary—both learning new words and practicing using them. (Students might mention reading challenging material, understanding words in context, and using new words in speech or written work.) **L1**

Research Ask students to choose three careers that interest them and, for each, to make a list of job tasks that would require strong speaking skills. (Job tasks will vary but could include participating in meetings, making phone calls to clients, and giving sales presentations.) **L2**

Plan Have students write a paragraph describing their attitude toward speaking in public and honestly evaluating their skills in this area. Have students create a plan to build their public speaking skills over the next six months. (Self-analyses and plans will vary, but students should recognize that practicing public speaking is the best way to build both skills and self-confidence.) **L3**

R Reading Strategy

Predicting Before students read the passage, ask them to predict several guidelines for good phone manners that they might expect to find in the text. (Answers will vary, but may include not putting people on hold for long periods, avoiding eating or chewing gum, and being polite.)

W Writing Support

Independent Practice

Analyzing Explain to students that active listening includes two components—paying close attention and offering appropriate responses. Ask students to write a paragraph describing specific actions they could take to practice and strengthen each skill. (Ideas will vary but might include analyzing speakers' body language, repeating key points, and displaying empathy.)

C Critical Thinking

Questioning Effectively Ask students what they consider an "effective" question. Why are questions that can be answered with a simple "yes" or "no" generally considered ineffective questions? (Generally speaking, effective questions are clear, yield the desired information, and make the hearer want to continue the conversation. Yes/no questions may yield little information or fail to promote dialogue.)

✓ Reading Check

EVALUATE You can show interest in your listeners by making eye contact, asking for feedback, using words they understand, showing respect for their beliefs, values, and interests, and knowing your subject and purpose.

Real-World Connection

Gossip Guide

Four months ago you began working for your local bank. You've been working hard to learn your new job, and today, for the first time, you went to lunch with several coworkers. They talked continually about your boss and other supervisors. You are not sure if the conversation was appropriate.

Critical Thinking How does gossip affect the workplace? Should it be avoided or encouraged?

Do Your Own Research Locate articles from magazines or professional journals about the effect of office gossip. Try to determine the difference between casual conversation, which includes sharing information about coworkers, and gossip. Report your findings in a one-page journal entry.

Use Good Phone Manners

Good speaking habits apply to telephone conversations and voice mail messages as well as to in-person conversations. Good phone skills make you sound professional and are an important part of customer service.

Call when you think the other person is likely to be free to talk. Be aware of differences in time zones when placing calls. Always begin a call or voice mail message by identifying yourself. Give your first and last name, your job title, and the reason for the call. Enunciate by speaking clearly and directly into the mouthpiece. Smiling while you speak can produce a pleasant tone. **R**

If you need to leave a message, make it brief. Clearly state the reason for your call. Give your phone number with area code, slowly and clearly. If the person does not know you well, also spell your name.

If you answer a call for another person, ask, "May I take a message?" Then write a brief, clear message with the date and time, the full name of the caller, his or her phone number, and the purpose of the call. If the caller does not volunteer the purpose of the call, you might ask, "May I note the nature of your call?"

✓ Reading Check

EVALUATE How can you show that you are interested in your listeners?

Become an Active Listener

There is a big difference between hearing and listening. Hearing is an automatic response. Listening is a conscious action. You use your brain to interpret, or make sense of, what you hear.

Active listening is listening and responding with full attention to what is being said. In the world of work, active listening can be your most powerful communication tool. It involves all of the following:

W
- identifying the speaker's purpose
- listening for main ideas
- distinguishing between fact and opinion
- noting the speaker's body language, intonation, speed, and volume
- using your own body language and facial expressions to respond to the speaker—for example, sitting up straight or leaning toward the speaker to show that you are interested
- reacting to the speaker with comments or questions

Active listeners show empathy and concern for the other person's feelings. Try to understand the other person's point of view. For example, how would you feel? How would you want to be treated?

Real-World Connection

Critical Thinking Answer Although some workplace gossip is normal, it can lower morale, spread rumors, and waste time. Gossip should be generally discouraged. Instead, workers should raise their concerns and find ways to solve problems and make the workplace better.

Do Your Own Research Reports should distinguish between friendly conversation and gossip that criticizes or maligns others.

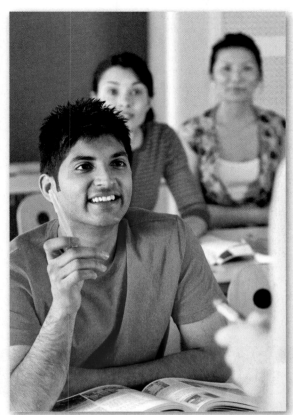

ACTIVE LISTENING
Asking a question shows that you are listening. *How else can you show that you are giving a speaker your full attention?*

When the person is finished speaking, repeat the key points to check that you understood. For example, you might say to an upset client, "Mr. Walker, it must have been extremely frustrating to receive the order two days late, and I understand that you would like to close your account." Then do what you can to correct the problem and to keep the person as a customer. For example, you might say, "What can we do to remedy the situation and keep you as a customer?"

Focus on asking effective questions. Effective questions are clear, ask for specific information, and focus on what is important to the listener. Ineffective questions are vague, confusing, and can be answered with a simple "yes" or "no."

C

Listen Actively to Provide Good Customer Service

R

Active listening is the key to providing good customer service and handling customer complaints. People do not always remember when things go right, but they often remember when things go wrong.

TEACH *(cont.)*

R Reading Strategy
Recalling Ask students to try to recall the definition of customer relations that was presented earlier in the chapter and to list other skills, in addition to active listening, that are key to customer relations. (Customer relations is the use of communication skills to meet the needs of customers and clients. It also includes speaking, writing, reading, problem solving, and maintaining a positive attitude.)

ASSESS

Review Key Terms
Have students write sentences using each key term.

Online Study Tools
Have students go to the OLC through **glencoe.com** to:
- Download **Podcast** study tools.
- Download free **Study-to-Go** content to their PDAs or cell phones.

Resources

ExamView Assessment Suite CD allows you to print out ready-made unit and chapter tests complete with answer keys. You can also create customized tests.

 Extend the Photo

Caption Answer You can demonstrate that you are paying attention by using attentive body language (posture, gestures, and eye contact), repeating key points, and showing empathy.

Discussion Ask students to recall a conversation in which they suspected that the other person was not really listening. How did they know the other person was not paying attention? How did this feel? (Answers will vary but might include feeling hurt, foolish, or irritated.)

RETEACH

W **Writing Support**
Independent Practice

Business Letter Ask students to imagine that a customer visits the clothing store where they work and demands a refund for a shirt he bought one year ago. Ask students to write a script detailing how they could handle the problem diplomatically and show initiative. (Scripts might politely explain the store's return policy, ask about the problem with the shirt, and possibly offer the customer a discount on a newer style.)

C **Critical Thinking**

Synthesizing Ask students what defensiveness is, why it makes communication difficult, and what a speaker could do to help his or her listener feel less defensive. (Defensiveness—hostility caused by a threat to self-esteem—can cause conflicts to escalate or a listener to tune out. A speaker can minimize defensiveness by framing comments as solutions rather than as accusations or criticisms.)

Resources

📂 **Student Activity Workbook** Assign the Chapter 15 activities in the Student Activity Workbook.

Learn your company's policies and procedures for handling customer complaints. Deal with customers politely and professionally by doing the following:

- **Listen Actively** When a customer has a complaint, it is important to give that customer your full attention. Listen carefully to identify the problem and the customer's desired solution. Show the customer that you have listened and understood and will do all you can to solve the problem.
- **Take Notes** Get the facts right by taking notes. Taking notes establishes a written record of the problem and the steps you have taken toward a solution.
- **Show Initiative** Find a creative way to solve the problem. You may not be able to offer the customer exactly what the customer wants, but perhaps you can offer a compromise.
- **Handle Conflicts Diplomatically** Handle **conflicts** calmly. If a customer is angry or confrontational, remember that the customer is upset with the company, not you. Stay calm and do not become defensive or angry.
- **Make Improvements** Complaints are valuable information for a company. They indicate what the company should do to treat its customers better. If you have an idea for reducing complaints and making your company better, share it with your supervisor.

[W]

Creative Business Practices

SOUTHWEST Customer Service

The mission statement of Southwest Airlines includes "dedication to the highest quality of Customer Service." The company's commitment to customer service works—Southwest has had fewer complaints than any other airline. Southwest's many innovations, such as online ticket purchasing, an award-winning customer rewards program, and casual dress for in-flight crews, have been driven by a desire to offer the customer a comfortable, informal, and efficient travel experience.

Southwest's customer service philosophy extends to its own employees. The company was the first domestic airline to establish a profit-sharing plan, which makes employees partial owners of the company. In addition, Southwest employees and family members can receive free tickets to anywhere the airline travels. Low turnover among Southwest's 30,000 employees contributes to the company's success, as loyal and satisfied employees are more likely to know their jobs and their customers well.

CRITICAL THINKING Why might Southwest say they are in the customer service business instead of saying they are in the airline business?

@ **Connect to the Real World** For more information about Southwest Airlines, visit the company's Web site via the link on this book's Online Learning Center through **glencoe.com**.

Creative Business Practices

CRITICAL THINKING ANSWER Southwest says they are in the customer service business in order to reinforce their commitment to service to customers and employees and to distinguish themselves from competing airlines.

Overcome Communication Barriers

C

A communication barrier is a physical or mental factor that makes communication difficult or impossible. Noise, anger, and defensiveness are common communication barriers.

Not listening is another communication barrier. Feelings such as boredom, excitement, or anger can get in the way of listening. Cultural, linguistic, gender, and age differences can also interfere with communication. Take responsibility for delivering your message clearly, especially if your listener is from a different culture or speaks English as a second or foreign language.

Be aware of your feelings and how they affect your listening. When another person is speaking, give your full attention to the speaker. Taking notes can help you focus your attention. Avoid jumping to conclusions or thinking about what you are going to say.

When you are the speaker, remember that delivering a message in an aggressive or angry way can block communication. Your emotions may cause a listener to tune out or become defensive. Avoid name-calling or criticizing. Focus on hearing and being heard rather than on proving that you are "right."

Section 15.1 After You Read

Review Key Concepts

1. Name three things you should know before you speak.
2. List two tips that can help you speak more effectively.
3. Identify the listening skills you would use to respond to this situation: An angry customer calls to complain about a product that was purchased at your shop. Explain why those skills would help.

Practice Academic Skills

 Mathematics

N C L B

4. Elena is going to give a speech at a professional luncheon. Her speech will be accompanied by a slideshow. The presentation time limit is 15 minutes, and Elena figures she will use about 25 slides. What is the average number of seconds she should spend on each slide without going over the time limit?

   CONCEPT **Calculating Average Time** Since a minute has 60 seconds, an hour has 60 minutes, and a day has 24 hours, it is helpful to convert before you divide to calculate an average. To convert minutes to seconds, multiply by 60. Do the same to convert hours to minutes, and to convert days to hours, multiply by 24.
   Step 1: Convert the total number of minutes for the speech (15) to seconds by multiplying by 60.
   Step 2: Divide the answer to Step 1 by the number of slides (25). Be sure to label your final answer with the correct unit of time.

    For math help, go to the Math Appendix located at the back of this book.

ASSESS

After You Read
Have students complete the Section 15.1 After You Read section review.

Online Study Tools
Have students go to the OLC through **glencoe.com** to:
- Take the Section 15.1 **Practice Test.**
- Download **Podcast** study tools.
- Download free **Study-to-Go** content to their PDAs or cell phones.

 STUDY TO GO

CLOSE

Culminating Activity
Communication and Success Ask students to write a paragraph describing how the speaking and listening skills described in this section could help them be impressive job candidates. (Paragraphs will vary, but students should recognize that skills such as listening attentively and conveying messages clearly and confidently can make them effective workers who also earn the respect of others.)

N C L B   Activity correlated to Mathematics standards.

Section 15.1 After You Read

Review Key Concepts
1. Before speaking, you should know your purpose, audience, and subject.
2. Tips for speaking effectively include considering purpose before speaking, organizing your message in an effective way, crafting your message to fit your audience, knowing your subject thoroughly, paying attention to pronunciation, enunciation, tone of voice, volume, and speed, and choosing words appropriate to the situation.
3. Listening skills relevant to this situation include distinguishing between fact and opinion, taking notes, reacting with clarifying questions, showing empathy, and repeating key points. Showing initiative and handling conflicts diplomatically would also be necessary.

Practice Academic Skills
4. Elena should spend an average of 36 seconds per slide (15 × 60 = 900 seconds; 900 ÷ 25 = 36 seconds).

FOCUS

🔔 Bell Ringer Activity

Reading and Writing

Explain to students that writing a business document, such as a résumé or business letter, can be quite different from writing a personal document such as a journal entry, poem, or letter to a friend. Ask: How is business writing different from personal writing?

Resources

💿 Interactive Chalkboard
The Interactive Chalkboard CD provides visual teaching aids for this section.

@ Online Learning Center
The OLC through **glencoe.com** features chapter vocabulary, chapter summaries, and other study materials.

Preteaching

Ask students to skim the chapter to find and define the following: four forms of business correspondence, three writing skills, and five reading skills.

Graphic Organizer

Tell students to go to the OLC through **glencoe.com** for a printable graphic organizer. (Graphic organizers should include prewriting [outlining and free writing], revising, and taking notes.)

 NCLB connects academic correlations to book content.

Reading and Writing

Reading Guide

Before You Read

Preview Read the Key Concepts. Write one or two sentences predicting what the section will be about.

Read to Learn
- Strategies for improving your writing skills
- Common forms of business writing and the style appropriate to each
- How to use reading skills such as skimming and previewing

🄳 Main Idea
You must be able to read and write effectively to succeed in the workplace.

Key Concepts
- Read and Write to Succeed
- Focus on Reading Skills

Key Terms
◆ e-mail
◆ previewing
◆ skimming

Academic Vocabulary
You will find these words in your reading and on your tests. Use the academic vocabulary glossary to look up their definitions if necessary.
- jargon
- infer

Graphic Organizer
As you read, make a list of good writing habits. Assess whether you use these habits, and when you could use them in the future. Use a chart like the one shown to help organize the information.

Good Writing Habit	Do I Use It Now?	When to Use It in the Future
1. Outlining	Only if assigned	Taking notes, making an oral presentation, writing an essay

 Log On Go to this book's Online Learning Center through **glencoe.com** for an online version of this graphic organizer.

Academic Standards •

English Language Arts
- Use written language to communicate effectively. (NCTE 4)
- Apply knowledge of language structure and conventions to discuss texts. (NCTE 6)
- Participate as members of literacy communities. (NCTE 11)

- Use language to accomplish individual purposes. (NCTE 12)

Science
- Physical Science: Motions and forces

Reading Guide

Before You Read

Explain to students that reading and writing are not just one skill, but a collection of skills and abilities that they can build by following the guidelines they will learn in this chapter. For example, they can improve their writing by practicing skills such as outlining and revising.

🄳 Develop Concepts

Main Idea Discuss the main idea with students. Ask: what is "effective" reading? What is "effective" writing? (Effective reading means understanding content and context, retaining what is read, and using it to be productive at work. Effective writing means stating your message in a clear and organized way so that readers can easily grasp the information.)

Read and Write to Succeed

Every job involves writing and reading. Because knowledge workers (workers who work with information and knowledge) are in high demand, your career success will depend on your strong skills in writing and reading.

To speak well, you must define your audience, purpose, and subject. To write well, you must do the same. You must also do the following:

- **Organize** Give your document a clear structure. Use a logical order, such as chronological (time) order or order of importance. Use headers and connecting words such as "however," "therefore," and "by comparison," to guide the reader.

- **Use a Formal but Friendly Tone** Match your *tone*, or manner, to the situation. A businesslike, clear, approachable tone is correct in most business situations. In a letter responding to a customer's request, for example, you would write in a tone that is respectful and polite.

- **Follow Appropriate Style** Use short, simple sentences and direct, comprehensible language. Avoid overused or complicated phrases, slang, and sexist language. For example, instead of saying "every man will make his own choice," write "each person will make an individual choice."

- **Rewrite and Revise** Write your first draft, then revise. Reread and revise again. Reading your writing aloud can help you make sure that there are no awkward words or phrases. If you are unsure of your proofreading skills, ask a colleague or friend to read important documents you have written.

- **Check Spelling and Grammar** Use a dictionary and stylebook, as well as the spell-check tool on a computer program, to check spellings, definitions, and grammatical rules. Carefully proofread your work before sending it out.

- **Pay Attention to Presentation** Present your writing in a professional manner. Use consistent text formatting and spacing throughout, and make sure each page is crisp and unwrinkled. Follow standard formats for different types of business writing, such as reports, memos, letters, and e-mail.

THE READ-ALOUD TEST Reading your writing out loud can help you find mistakes and awkward phrases. *How do you check your writing now? Does your system work?*

As You Read

Connect Do you use different tones when writing for teachers than you do when writing to friends?

341

Section 15.2

TEACH

Discussion Starter

Read and Write to Succeed Ask students to brainstorm different on-the-job activities that involve reading and writing. (Ideas may include reading and writing e-mail and business letters, reading books or manuals to build skills, entering information into a database, and reading or compiling financial information.)

S **Skill Practice**

Independent Practice

Organization Ask students to use print or online sources to create a one-page tip sheet with a variety of ideas for organizing written documents. Ask them to include ideas for sequencing information along with specific formatting ideas and a list of helpful connecting words. (Ideas may include strategies such as enumerating or comparing and contrasting, and formatting ideas such as using a formal outline or presenting ideas as bullet points.)

As You Read

Most students should answer yes. Different audiences and different types of writing assignments call for different styles and tones.

Resources

TeacherWorks™ Plus The TeacherWorks software includes customizable built-in lesson plans and links to printable program resources.

▶ Extend the Photo

Caption Answer Students may not have a system or may mention showing their work to a friend and/or using the grammar- and spell-check features of a word-processing program.

Discussion Mention to students the famous guideline of Strunk and White: "A sentence should contain no unnecessary words, a paragraph no unnecessary sentences." Ask students what they think that means. How can they tell whether their writing has "unnecessary words"? ("Unnecessary words" are words that do not convey added meaning. Every word should add to the writer's point.)

TEACH *(cont.)*

W Writing Support
Guided Practice

Using the Active Voice Ask students to define *active voice* and *passive voice* and to explain why the active voice is generally preferred in English. Ask students to write three pairs of sentences that use the two voices to convey the same basic information. (The active voice is generally preferred because it is more vivid and because it specifies the agent(s) of the action. Sentences will vary but should use the two voices correctly.)

R Reading Strategy

Understanding Words in Context Ask students to guess at the meaning of the word *jargon* based on the context (specialized terminology not accessible to the general reader). Ask: Is there ever a time when it would be appropriate to use jargon? When? (It can be appropriate when writing for readers who use the same jargon and rely on it to communicate precisely.)

S Skill Practice

Time Management Explain to students that it is common for professionals to receive 100 or more e-mails a day. Ask them to write a list of ideas on how they could manage this many e-mails while still getting all their other job tasks done. (Ideas may include setting aside certain times of the day to read and respond to e-mails and organizing e-mails into folders.)

NCLB Activity correlated to English Language Arts standards.

NCLB

TechSavvy

Company Computer

You are the one doing the writing, but does that mean your fax, letter, or e-mail belongs to you? Not at your job. At most jobs, your company owns everything you write—and is responsible for it, too. Businesses have rules about using correspondence to protect both the employees and the company. Follow these basic rules when using a company computer:

- Do not use your company computer to send personal letters, jokes, or photographs. The company could be held liable if someone is offended.
- Use your computer, printer, and fax machine only for company business. If your company states that you may occasionally use the equipment for personal use, respect that rule.
- If you receive an e-mail from a person or company you do not recognize, do not open it. Opening it could launch a computer virus.

@ Visit **glencoe.com** and find the link to learn more about proper use of e-mail at work. Write a list of *dos* and *don'ts* for using e-mail in the workplace.

Vocabulary

You can find definitions in the **Key Terms** glossary and **Academic Vocabulary** glossary at the back of this book.

Write Clearly and Concisely

The most important rule of business writing is to *be clear*. Say things in the clearest and simplest way possible. If your writing is not clear, stop and ask yourself what you are trying to say. You may discover that you do not know. Clarify your message, then start again.

Write in the active voice. For example, write, "Our team won the annual sales trophy," not "The sales trophy was awarded to our team." Be specific. For example, write, "Thirty-five customers cancelled their subscriptions because of the article on the mayor," rather than, "Our last issue wasn't that popular." Choose words your target audience will understand. Replace slang or **jargon** with words that are clear.

W
R

Master Business Correspondence

To write effectively on the job, you also need to master the basic formats of written business correspondence: memos, faxes, e-mail, and business letters.

A *memo*, short for *memorandum*, is an internal company document that announces important information. For example, you might need to write a memo to announce an upcoming meeting or a policy change. A *fax*, short for *facsimile*, is a document that is sent by computer or over phone lines. Business faxes should always have a cover sheet that says what the fax contains and how many pages are in the fax.

E-mail, or electronic mail, is a message sent over the Internet. Many businesses use e-mail to conduct their day-to-day business communication.

S

A business letter is an official printed letter that communicates especially important information, such as a job offer or legal announcement.

Ingredients of Business Communication

Memos, faxes, e-mail messages, and business letters look different but have similar parts. They all include:

- the name and contact information of the sender
- the date
- the names of the recipients, and anyone who is copied on the communication
- a brief statement of the subject
- optional attachments or enclosures

When you write a business e-mail, letter, or fax, you should also include a greeting, such as "Dear Ms. Alvarado:" and a complimentary close, such as "Sincerely yours." Put your title and contact information below your name, and print the letter on company letterhead.

TechSavvy

Company Computer

Answer Answers will vary but should mention dos such as being polite and respectful, writing concisely, and responding within a reasonable timeframe, and don'ts such as writing in all capital letters or sending gossip or huge attachments.

When writing business letters, use a formal, polite tone. Create a business letter like the one in **Figure 15.1** and place it in your **Personal and Academic Career Portfolio** to use as an example.

State Your Purpose, Then Provide Supporting Details

Whether you are writing a memo, fax, e-mail, or business letter, it is important to be brief and to the point. State a clear purpose in the subject line and in the first sentence, then provide supporting details. When you write an e-mail message, type the topic in the subject line of the message. When you write a memo, fax, or business letter, write the topic on a separate line following the word *Subject:* or *Re:*, which is short for "Regarding." If you are including an attachment, explain what it is and why you are sending it.

S

C

W

Personal Academic and Career Portfolio

Go to the chapter review to find guidelines for creating your own **Personal Academic and Career Portfolio**.

Figure 15.1 **BUSINESS LETTER**

Java Joe's Coffee Supply
....

510 Market Street   Chicago, IL 60647
Phone: (312) 555-0144   E-Mail: n.brown@javajj.com
Fax: (312) 555-0142   Web: www.javajj.com

March 24, 20--

Mr. Dexter Reed
Timbuktu Coffee Emporium
1700 Park Boulevard
Indianapolis, IN 46233

Dear Mr. Reed:

Thank you for contacting our billing department yesterday about the overdue payment notice we sent on March 3 for order #45-200-A. I have located the check for $540.95 you remitted to us on January 31 and credited the amount to your account.

I sincerely apologize for this error and for the mistaken overdue notice. We thank you for your business and look forward to a continued relationship with Timbuktu Coffee Emporium.

Sincerely,

Natalie M. Brown

Natalie M. Brown
Accounting Manager

cc: Akiko Fukiyama, Sales Manager

BUSINESS CORRESPONDENCE Many companies use e-mail for their day-to-day correspondence and reserve business letters for important matters that need a permanent or more fomal record. *In what instances might you send a formal letter during your job search?*

TEACH (cont.)

S **Skill Practice**
Independent Practice
E-mail Ask students to imagine that they are responding to a job posting by e-mailing their résumé and list of references. Have students write a short cover letter in e-mail format to accompany the attachments. (Cover letters should begin with a clear statement of purpose and should have a clear subject line and an explanation of the attachments.)

C **Critical Thinking**
Identifying the Main Point Ask students to identify the topic and purpose of the letter in **Figure 15.1**. Ask: Do you think the topic and purpose are clear? Why or why not? (The topic of this letter is a billing error. The purpose is to apologize and to explain how the error has been corrected.)

W **Writing Support**
Independent Practice
Writing a Business Letter Have students choose a local issue that is important to them and write a letter to an elected official expressing their beliefs and asking the official to take action on the issue. Ask students to mail their letters and share any responses. (Letters should have a clear topic and purpose and should follow the standard business letter format shown here.)

EXTEND THE FIGURE **Figure 15.1**

Caption Answer Formal letters sent during the job search include the cover letter sent with a résumé and the thank-you letter sent after a job interview.

Discussion Ask students why they think this writer chose to create a printed business letter rather than send an e-mail. (This letter concerns a billing error, making it important enough to merit a printed letter. The writer also had a printed enclosure [the coupon] to send to the customer.)

W **Writing Support**
Independent Practice
Writing Diplomatically
Have students imagine that they work in a store's customer service department. A customer writes an angry e-mail stating that the refrigerator he bought there is defective and that he will never shop there again. Ask students to write the customer an e-mail responding to his charges and trying to retain him as a customer. (E-mails should take the customer's complaint seriously and should be polite, professional, and error-free.)

C **Critical Thinking**
Comparing and Contrasting
Point out to students that the e-mail in **Figure 15.2** has a greeting and complimentary close, just like a more formal business letter. Ask: Is it necessary to use these formal elements in an e-mail? Why or why not? (Many people neglect to use a greeting or close in e-mail, but students should understand that these elements are important to e-mail etiquette at most workplaces.)

Use E-Mail Effectively

E-mail is the least formal of written business communication. Resist the temptation to be too casual, however. Be brief, professional, and friendly, as shown in the e-mail in **Figure 15.2**. Try to focus on one subject per e-mail. If an e-mail is long or rambling, people may stop reading.

Use the *to:* field for the e-mail addresses of the people you are addressing directly. Use the *cc:* field to "copy" people who may need the information. You may need to copy your supervisor or coworkers. If you are not sure whether your supervisor needs to follow your e-mail correspondence, ask. Always check your e-mail for spelling, grammar, and meaning, and always be courteous and professional.

Figure 15.2   BUSINESS E-MAIL

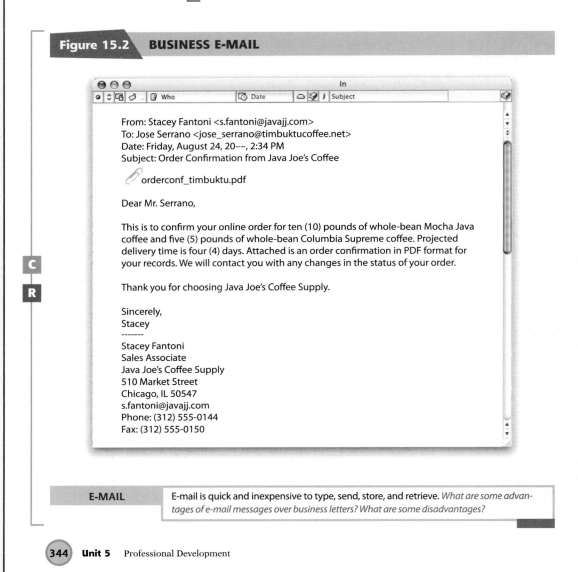

E-MAIL   E-mail is quick and inexpensive to type, send, store, and retrieve. *What are some advantages of e-mail messages over business letters? What are some disadvantages?*

EXTEND THE FIGURE   Figure 15.2

Caption Answer E-mail can be accessed from almost anywhere, and it is quicker and more convenient to send and receive than printed letters. E-mail cannot transmit printed enclosures or the writer's original signature. Some people may not have access to e-mail or may be displeased with the large volume of e-mail they receive.

Discussion Ask students if they have received e-mails with official business from a school or company (such as a bank or insurance company). Did they like or dislike conducting business via e-mail? Why? (Opinions will vary. Students who are comfortable with e-mail may find it convenient.)

Everyday ETHICS

ETHICS AND E-MAIL

Should you read an e-mail that is not addressed to you?

E-MAIL TO THE BOSS You work as an assistant in a small advertising agency. One day, you go into your boss's office to leave a report on her desk. With a quick glance at her computer monitor, you notice that her e-mail program is open and that your name is in the subject line of an unopened e-mail from the owner of the company.

You know your boss is in a meeting at a client's office, so there is no chance she will see you at her computer.

What Would You Do? Will you read the e-mail?

DISCUSS IT Since you are the subject of the e-mail, do you have the right to read it? In teams of two or more, discuss the possible consequences of reading the e-mail.

Prewriting

Prewriting includes everything you do before you actually start your document: researching your topic, making an outline or a cluster map, brainstorming, and talking to people to gather information. Prewriting exercises help you organize your material and narrow your focus. It helps you present clear, organized ideas, and saves you time and energy when you actually start writing.

- *Outlining* helps you organize your ideas and is a great way to begin a writing project or structure notes. First write down your major points or ideas in a numbered list. Then write supporting ideas or subtopics under each major point. Use your outline to check that your ideas flow in a logical order. You may need to rearrange, combine, or delete elements of the outline.
- *Free writing* is simply writing everything that comes to mind about a topic, in any order. Free writing helps you get your ideas flowing and is especially helpful if you find yourself stuck or unsure of where to start.

Revising

A first draft is your first attempt at a written document. A good writer reviews and rewrites text. Rephrase sentences that are repetitive or unclear. Cut unnecessary words and paragraphs, and make sure your ideas flow in a logical order.

Taking Notes

Taking notes helps you remember facts and keeps your attention focused. When you take notes, both your mind and your hands are involved in listening. Here is how to take good notes:

- Do not try to write down everything a speaker says. Instead, focus on key words and main ideas. Jot down summaries in your own words.

As You Read
Extend When might you use free writing at work or in school?

TEACH *(cont.)*

S Skill Practice
Independent Practice
Research Ask students to list and define several different types of prewriting exercises and explain when each might be appropriate. (Exercises might include making a list, journal writing, brainstorming, clustering, diagramming, doing research, writing a list of questions, even sketching or consulting a quotation dictionary.)

As You Read
Free writing can be used to get started on a challenging writing assignment, to help clarify your thoughts on a topic, or to practice and gain fluency with writing.

ASSESS

Review Key Terms
Have students write sentences using each key term.

Online Study Tools
Have students go to the OLC through **glencoe.com** to:
- Download **Podcast** study tools.
- Download free **Study-to-Go** content to their PDAs or cell phones.

Everyday ETHICS

What Would You Do? Answer Students should recognize that reading someone else's mail—whether electronic or paper—is considered an invasion of privacy.

DISCUSS IT The consequences of reading the e-mail could include disciplinary action or even firing. The content of the e-mail may be of little importance or may be something you would have learned later anyway.

RETEACH

S Skill Practice
Independent Practice

Previewing Ask students to choose a book or magazine article on communication skills, to preview it, and to write a two- to three-sentence description of its topic and purpose. Ask students whether, based on their preview, they think the text is worth reading in full.

✓ Reading Check

SUMMARIZE Memos, faxes, e-mail, and business letters have the same basic elements but have different purposes—memos are primarily for internal correspondence, faxes are for quick transmission of printed documents, e-mail is for speedy, day-to-day correspondence, and business letters are for more important communications or those that need a printed record.

R Reading Strategy

Reading Critically Ask students what criteria they can use to tell whether a statement is a fact or an opinion. (Students can evaluate statements by analyzing whether the author's assertions are provable, by scrutinizing evidence the author uses to support his or her statements, and by checking other sources.)

Resources

📁 **Student Activity Workbook** Assign the Chapter 15 activities in the Student Activity Workbook.

N C L B Activity correlated to Science standards.

Science In Action

Weight

Units of scientific measurement have special terminology. For example, the weight of an object is measured in a unit called Newtons (N), which is equal to the mass of an object (in kilograms) times the acceleration of gravity. The acceleration of gravity on Earth is 9.8 meters per second squared (9.8 m/s^2). How much would a 500 kilogram statue weigh?

Starting Hint: weight = mass $\times$ acceleration of gravity

@ For more science practice, go to this book's OLC through **glencoe.com**.

- Use bulleted lists, asterisks, and arrows to show relationships among ideas.
- Note any questions you have or actions you need to take.
- Review your notes to be sure you understand concepts or instructions.
- If necessary, make additions and clarifications to your notes immediately after you finish taking them.
- If you cannot take written notes, make mental notes of the main points.

✓ **Reading Check** **SUMMARIZE** Compare and contrast four common formats of business correspondence.

Focus on Reading Skills

You are likely to spend as much time reading as writing on the job. Name or list in your journal some of the reading skills you have used in social studies, science, and English classes. You will use all of these skills in your job as you acquire, evaluate, and interpret information.

Why is reading important in your career? You will use reading skills to skim help-wanted ads and evaluate whether they are right for you. You will use reading skills to correctly fill out job applications and proofread your résumé and cover letter. You will use reading skills on the job to read and respond to memos, faxes, e-mail, business letters, instructions, and reports, and to reread your own writing before you send or present it to others.

Previewing

Previewing means reading key parts of a written work that help you predict its content. To preview, look at book and chapter titles, headings, photos and photo captions, and key terms. Previewing prepares you for what you will read and helps you retain and understand what you have read.

Skimming

Skimming means reading quickly through a book or a document to pick out key points. To skim, look at the first sentences of paragraphs, as well as key terms and phrases. Skimming is helpful when you need a general idea of what is in a written work but do not have time to read it fully.

Taking Notes

Taking notes is a reading skill as well as a writing skill. Writing down main ideas, useful quotes, questions, new vocabulary, and your own summaries of information helps you understand and recall what you read. Note taking can be especially helpful when you are reading technical information, or when you are preparing for a meeting at work.

Science In Action

The statue would weigh 4900 N
(weight = (500 kg)(9.8 m/s^2) = 4900).

Monitoring Comprehension

To be an effective reader, you also need to check your own comprehension. Stop at the end of every section or page and assess what you have just learned. Restate the main concepts in your own words. If you have trouble remembering or describing what you have read, reread and review. You may need to read a passage two or three times in order to fully understand it.

Critical Reading

Like critical thinking, critical reading involves analyzing, thinking clearly, and evaluating. Think critically about what you read and distinguish between facts and opinions. A fact is a truth that can be proven. An opinion is a belief or preference and cannot be proven, even if it is based on facts. As you read, ask yourself:

R
- Is this a fact or an opinion?
- Do I agree with the author? Why or why not?
- What have I experienced that can help me relate to this passage?
- What can I **infer** from this passage that is not stated directly?

Different kinds of texts require different kinds of reading. A textbook, for example, contains mostly facts. An editorial in a newspaper contains mostly opinions. Use different reading strategies to get the most out of each kind of text.

Career ✓ Checklist

To Show a Professional Attitude:

✓ Speak clearly.
✓ Listen attentively.
✓ Take accurate notes.
✓ Address coworkers and customers with respect.
✓ Check written communication for errors.

Section 15.2 After You Read

Review Key Concepts

1. You have been asked to write a report summarizing your company's achievements over the past year. Describe one way you might organize the material in the report.
2. Give an example of a business situation in which it would be appropriate to use each of the following: e-mail, a letter, and a memo.
3. Identify which reading skill, previewing or skimming, you would use to find your schedule in a list of all employees' schedules. Explain your answer.

Practice Academic Skills

 English Language Arts

N C L B

4. Toni is checking her supervisor Jun's voice mail messages. There is one call, recorded at 2:10 P.M. on February 7: "Hi, Jun. Sam Jennings here. I need to know if you want me to order that special card stock we talked about. If you let me know by the end of the day, I can still get you the discount rate. I'll be here until six o'clock. I'm at 555-0136. Thanks." Using this information, write a professional phone message for Jun from Toni.
5. List and define six specific reading and writing skills, such as previewing and outlining, that can help you strengthen your communication skills. Give a specific example of how you might use each of these six skills in a job that interests you.

@ Check your answers at this book's OLC through **glencoe.com**.

Section 15.2 After You Read

Review Key Concepts

1. Possible answers include chronological order, order of importance, or by department within the company.
2. E-mail could be used to ask a colleague to send the latest sales figures. A letter might be used to thank an important new client for switching to your firm. A memo might be used to announce that the office is closing early the day before Thanksgiving.
3. Because you are looking to pick out specific information, you would use skimming.

Practice Academic Skills

4. Possible message to Jun: Sam Jennings called at 2:10 P.M. on February 7. His number is 555-0136. Please return his call by 6:00 P.M. to get discount rate on the card stock.
5. Lists should include six of the reading and writing strategies explained in this section and examples of how they might be used in a specific job.

ASSESS

Review Key Terms
Have students complete the Section 15.2 After You Read section review.

Online Study Tools
Have students go to the OLC through **glencoe.com** to:

- Take the Section 15.2 **Practice Test**.
- Download **Podcast** study tools.
- Download free **Study-to-Go** content to their PDAs or cell phones. STUDY TO GO

Resources

ExamView Assessment Suite CD allows you to print out ready-made unit and chapter tests complete with answer keys. You can also create customized tests.

CLOSE

Culminating Activity
Business Writing Ask students to write a paragraph describing how the format and style of business writing are different from—or similar to—the format and style of writing they have done in school. Do they think that school has prepared them for being effective writers on the job?

N C L B Activity correlated to English Language Arts standards.

CAREER SPOTLIGHT

FOCUS

Discussion Starter

Education and Training
Ask students to find in the text what Jorge Gonzalez says about the education needed for a teaching career. Ask students to brainstorm other jobs in education and training that would require a postgraduate degree. Ask: Why do many careers in education and training require advanced education? (Students may mention college teacher, instructional designer, counselor, school psychologist, principal or administrator, or speech-language pathologist.)

TEACH

W Writing Support
Independent Practice

Interview Ask students to interview three workers in a career field that interests them about a "typical day" on the job. Ask students to summarize their results and state whether they would prefer a varied workday or a more consistent one. (Results and opinions will vary, but many jobs have some degree of variety and unpredictability.)

C Critical Thinking

Thinking Independently
Ask students what they think Gonzalez means about not running schools "like businesses." Do students agree or disagree with his point of view? Why? (Gonzalez may be referring to concepts of efficiency, profit, and quality control of a "product." Students may agree that students are all different and should not be treated like products from an assembly line.)

348

CAREER SPOTLIGHT

Career Cluster: Education and Training

**Jorge Gonzalez
High School Spanish Teacher**

Q: Describe your job.
A: I am a high school Spanish teacher.

Q: Describe a typical workday.
A: My typical workday consists of teaching six periods of a seven-period day. That's where the "typical" ends. Sometimes the teaching day is filled with lectures, student-directed activities, or a mixture of both. Currently my Spanish 4 students are teaching fourth graders at other schools in our district. I observe them during this quarter-long project. After the school day is over, I grade papers, develop lesson plans, and create tests, quizzes, and worksheets.

Q: What skills are most important to you in your job?
A: In order to get the point across without confusion, verbal and communication skills are most important. In order to show your students empathy, you must be people-oriented and remember what it felt like to be a student. Many businesspeople in our communities often say that schools should be run like businesses. To this, I say emphatically, "No!" Our "products" are people, not cars, computers, or soft drinks. Therefore, we must show much more compassion than is shown on the corporate level.

Q: What academic skills and lifelong learning skills are helpful in preparing for your career?
A: Empathy and compassion for humankind. Also, know the subjects that you will teach as well as humanly possible.

Q: What is your key to success?
A: I think there are two keys to success: Know your subject well and treat your students with respect and dignity.

Following these two edicts has helped me enjoy a successful teaching career.

Q: What are some disadvantages of your career?
A: The obvious disadvantage to teaching is a low salary. But if a person is aware of this disadvantage at the beginning, then the financial incentive is not something you expect.

Q: What training and preparation do you recommend for students?
A: A four-year college degree is required, but a master's degree is even better. In fact, in my state, all new teachers must have a master's degree within 10 years of graduating from college.

Q: What are some ways you recommend students prepare for this career?
A: I tutored in high school and college. Peer tutoring is the single best training for becoming a good teacher.

Q: What do you like most about your work?
A: The aspect I enjoy the most is working with young people. I believe they keep me young at heart.

 For more about Career Clusters, go to this book's OLC through **glencoe.com**.

N C L B — NO CHILD LEFT BEHIND

Teaching Tip

NCLB defines reading as a collection of five skills: phonemic awareness, phonics, fluency, vocabulary, and comprehension. Vocabulary words are learned best in context (rather than as items on a list). Call on students to deduce the meanings of unfamiliar words by analyzing their context and structure.

Sample Question Choose a key vocabulary term, such as *enunciation*, and ask them what experiences or words (such as *announce* or *pronunciation*) it reminds them of. Ask students to role-play to describe behaviors that are part of enunciation.

- **Education or Training** All states require public school teachers to be licensed. Licensure is not required for teachers in private schools in most states. All states require general education teachers to have a bachelor's degree and to have completed an approved teacher-training program with a prescribed number of subject and education credits, as well as supervised practice teaching. A number of states require that teachers obtain a master's degree in education within a specified period after they begin teaching.

- **Academic Skills Required** English Language Arts, Mathematics, Social Studies

- **Technology Needed** Computers; knowledge of any custom software used to teach a particular subject; Web design software to communicate with students and parents.

- **Aptitudes, Abilities, and Skills** Communication and other interpersonal skills, creativity, critical thinking, listening, and problem-solving skills

- **Workplace Safety** Teachers may experience stress in dealing with large classes, heavy workloads, or poor facilities. Constant standing and walking, particularly on hard surfaces, can cause foot physical strain such as foot and joint problems.

- **Career Outlook** Jobs for K-12 teachers are expected to grow as fast as average over the next ten years.

- **Career Path** With additional preparation, teachers may move into positions as school librarians, media or reading specialists, instructional coordinators, or guidance counselors. Teachers may also become administrators or supervisors.

Academic Skills Required to Complete Tasks

Tasks	English Language Arts	Mathematics	Social Studies
Prepare lessons	★		★
Lecture students	★		★
Discipline students	★		★
Grade tests	★	★	
Observe and grade student presentations	★	★	★

NCLB

Critical Thinking

Why do teachers need to have both good speaking and writing skills?

NCLB This chart relates academic skills such as English Language Arts, Mathematics, Science, Social Studies, and World Languages to specific tasks that are performed for the job featured in the Career Spotlight feature.

Critical Thinking

Teachers need good speaking skills to explain information clearly to a variety of students. They need good writing skills to give students clear written feedback and to model good writing skills.

ASSESS

Make Connections

Ask students to think about teachers that they admire or whose classes they have enjoyed. What skills did those teachers have? What subject areas—including English Language Arts, Mathematics, Science, and Social Studies— do they think helped equip the teacher(s) with those skills? (Answers will vary, but students should understand that English Language Arts and Social Studies help equip teachers with skills in communicating and in helping students put the material in context.)

CLOSE

Culminating Activity

Communication and Career Clusters Remind students of the statement at the beginning of this chapter: "Whatever job you do, you will spend much of your time communicating." Ask students to list jobs that interest them and to research specific tasks in those jobs that involve speaking, listening, reading, and writing. How much of their day would they spend using these skills? (Jobs and tasks will vary but may include some of the job scenarios mentioned in the chapter.)

Key Terms and Academic Vocabulary Review

1. Students should use each of the key terms and academic vocabulary terms in a complete sentence. A sample answer might read: "Speakers can use *intonation*, or raising and lowering the tone of their voice, to help hold an audience's interest."

Review Key Concepts

2. Before speaking, hone your message by tailoring your words to your purpose, audience, and subject. Enunciate, pay attention to tone, volume, and speed, and establish an emotional connection to listeners.

3. Good speaking habits include using correct pronunciation, enunciating clearly, varying one's intonation, speaking at a pleasant volume and speed, projecting a positive attitude, and choosing words appropriate to the purpose, audience, and subject.

4. Active listening helps you listen because the skills involved—such as paying attention to body language and asking clarifying questions—help you extract the full and accurate meaning from what you hear. Note taking helps you pay close attention and remember what you hear.

5. Strategies for improving writing skills include outlining, free writing, and revising. Organizing written material clearly, using an appropriate tone and style, proofreading, checking spelling and grammar, and paying attention to presentation are also important writing skills.

6. Common forms of business writing include memos, faxes, e-mail, and business letters. E-mail requires a slightly less formal style,

---

CHAPTER SUMMARY

Section 15.1

Communication is the exchange of information between a sender and a receiver. Communication skills such as speaking, listening, writing, and reading are crucial to career success. Before you speak, consider your purpose, audience, and subject, and organize what you plan to say. When you speak, enunciate clearly and vary your intonation. Active listening involves paying attention to the speaker's words and body language and providing responses to check understanding. Help to prevent communication breakdown by considering the other person's point of view.

Section 15.2

Writing requires some of the same skills as speaking. You need to know your audience, purpose, and subject. You must also be clear, direct, and organized. Rewrite and revise, check your spelling and grammar, and pay attention to presentation. Common formats for business writing include memos, faxes, e-mail, and letters. Prewriting, revising, and taking notes are important writing skills. Good reading skills, including previewing, skimming, monitoring comprehension, and critical reading, are necessary for any type of job.

Key Terms and Academic Vocabulary Review

1. Use each of these key terms and academic vocabulary words in a sentence.

Key Terms
- communication (p. 331)
- customer relations (p. 332)
- purpose (p. 332)
- audience (p. 333)
- subject (p. 334)
- pronunciation (p. 334)
- enunciation (p. 334)
- intonation (p. 335)
- active listening (p. 336)
- e-mail (p. 342)
- previewing (p. 346)
- skimming (p. 346)

Academic Vocabulary
- crucial (p. 331)
- cite (p. 334)
- conflicts (p. 338)
- jargon (p. 342)
- infer (p. 347)

Review Key Concepts

2. Identify ways to improve your speaking skills.
3. Describe good speaking habits and explain their importance in the workplace.
4. Explain how active listening and note taking can help you listen.
5. Summarize strategies for improving your writing skills.
6. Identify common forms of business writing and the style appropriate to each.
7. Explain reading skills such as skimming and previewing.

Critical Thinking

8. Extend Imagine that you are a customer service representative. An angry customer calls to complain about a billing error. Write two scenarios, one which demonstrates negative customer relations, and another which demonstrates positive customer relations.
9. Analyze Why is asking questions a part of active listening? Give an example of an effective question—one that promotes understanding—and an example of an ineffective question.

---

but a polite, businesslike, concise, clear style is appropriate to all four forms.

7. Skimming is reading quickly through a document to pick out key points. Previewing is reading key parts of a document in order to predict its content. Other reading skills include taking notes, monitoring comprehension, and critical reading (such as distinguishing between fact and opinion).

Critical Thinking

8. Scenarios will vary, but indifference, rudeness, failure to listen, and lack of empathy make for poor customer service. Attentiveness, politeness, active listening, and empathy make for positive customer relations.

9. Active listening includes not only receiving information, but also responding to what has been said in order to check comprehension,

Real-World Skills and Applications

Interpersonal and Collaborative Skills

10. Listening Actively Practice active listening during a conversation with a classmate, friend, or family member. Pay close attention to body language, intonation, speed, and volume, and try to understand the message. React to the speaker with body language and with comments or questions that show you have understood. After the conversation, write a paragraph describing the experience. Did active listening feel "different"? If so, how? Did it contribute to a positive interaction? If so, how? If not, why not?

Communication Skills

11. Writing a Business Letter Find the name and address of a local business in a career cluster that interests you. Write a one-page business letter to the human resources manager or hiring manager. Introduce yourself, describe your qualifications and academic skills, and ask whether the company has any current openings for a worker with your skills. Print the letter, proofread and revise, and print again. Fold the letter neatly in thirds and place it in a typed business envelope.

Technology Applications

12. Writing Effective E-Mail You are the office manager of an accounting firm. Write an e-mail to inform employees that the office will close at 2:00 P.M. on the day before Thanksgiving and to remind employees to submit time cards before the holiday closing. Make sure the subject line and first sentence of the e-mail state your purpose clearly.

13. **Researching Customer Service** Visit a business near you that depends on individual customers to stay in business (for example, a restaurant). Ask the manager about the customer service philosophy of the business, what kinds of customer complaints the business receives, how the business handles these complaints, and how it uses them to improve the service it offers. In your journal, analyze whether you think the company provides good customer service and handles complaints well, and why.

14. **Give a Presentation**
Situation You have mastered a new software program at work and must give a presentation in which you teach your colleagues how to use it.
Activity Choose a software program you know well. Prepare a presentation that will help your coworkers understand that software, including how, when, and why to use it. Then create a role-playing exercise in which you give the presentation to a small group, including your supervisor. Use visual aids, such as a poster or presentation software, and clear instructions to help your audience understand the software.
Evaluation You will be evaluated based on how well you meet the following performance indicators:
- Organization of ideas
- Preparation of presentation
- Quality of delivery, including pace, pronunciation, enunciation, intonation, and eye contact

Chapter 15 Professional Communication Skills **351**

12. The e-mail should include the standard elements (name and contact information of sender, date, names of recipients, subject line, and reference to any attachments) and should be direct and professional, with correct grammar and spelling.

 ACTIVE LEARNING

13. Journal entries will vary. Most businesses realize the importance of customer service. However, businesses differ in their specific policies, in their complaint-handling process, and in the degree to which they implement customer feedback.

ROLE PLAY

14. Students should demonstrate, through clear speech and variety in tone and pace, that they understand how to speak in front of a group, how to tailor their message to a specific audience, and how to present information in an organized way.

show empathy, and demonstrate that the listener has paid attention.

Real-World Skills and Applications

10. Students will probably report that active listening feels different—perhaps it made them more self-aware or helped them perceive elements of the message that they would otherwise have missed. Students should understand that active listening promotes relationships by enhancing successful communication.

11. Letters should follow the standard format shown in **Figure 15.1** and should be concise, professional, and polite. Students may need assistance in developing proofreading skills such as reviewing formatting elements, checking punctuation and sentence structure, and looking up words to verify correct spelling and usage.

Academic Skills in the Workplace

15. Differences and recommendations will vary but may include different levels of proficiency in English, different communication styles (such as different degrees of courtesy, assertiveness, or conflict-handling skills), different expectations of a company's responsibilities toward a customer, and different preferences in products and services. Recommendations should focus on understanding and accommodating differences.

16. Drawings should resemble the figure below.

Company Expenditures

- Employee Salaries
- Rent
- Utilities
- Maintenance
- Miscellaneous

17. Students should understand that communication is not just about transmitting factual information. Communication is a "social glue" that helps build and maintain harmonious social relationships (as well as relationships of hierarchy and power). Using empathy and striving to understand others' points of view helps build relationships based on mutual respect.

Academic Skills in the Workplace

English Language Arts

15. Providing Customer Service When you provide customer service, you will deal with people of different linguistic and cultural backgrounds. Use the library and other resources to make a list of at least five cultural or linguistic differences that might affect your ability to provide good customer service. For example, what might happen if the customer speaks limited English? For each cultural or linguistic difference you identify, make one recommendation that could help an employee provide excellent customer service.

Mathematics

16. Presenting Data You have been asked to create a chart for a presentation on your company's budget expenditures. The company spent its budget in the following way: 65% employee salaries, 15% rent for office space, 10% utilities expenses, 8% maintenance expenses, and 2% miscellaneous expenses. Use a compass and ruler or computer software to create a pie chart to represent these data.

CONCEPT **Pie Charts** A pie chart illustrates data as pieces of the whole. Pie charts are useful because they show how data relate to each other. The size of a pie piece corresponds to the percentage of the whole one datum represents.

Starting Hint Draw a circle and divide it into the number of percentages listed.

Science

17. Evolution of Human Behavior Research on the human brain reveals some amazing insights into the social nature of human beings. One of the leading theories in brain research is that the higher order thinking area of our brain, the frontal lobes, evolved out of the success of early humans communicating and talking with each other. This development helped humans picture what other humans were thinking or feeling, which in turn helped them to work together to survive in a harsh environment. How can you use your ability to picture other people's thoughts and feelings to improve communication and cooperation? Brainstorm ideas and create a one-page list.

STANDARDIZED TEST PRACTICE

READING COMPREHENSION

Directions Read the following passage, then answer the question that follows.

English has thousands of words borrowed from French—think of *beauty, honest,* and *forest,* for example. Yet most of our basic, everyday English vocabulary is actually much more similar to German than to French. Compare English *house* and German *Haus* or English *finger* and German *Finger.* In fact, English is much more closely related to German than it is to French. They are both members of the Germanic language family.

1. According to this passage, why does English have many words that are similar to German?

> **Test-Taking Tip** Read the passage carefully, underlining key statements as you go. Answer the questions based *only* on what you just read in the passage, not based on your previous knowledge.

For more Standardized Test Practice, go to the OLC *glencoe.com.*

STANDARDIZED TEST PRACTICE

Answer
1. English and German are in the same language family.

Test-Taking Strategies
Most students do better if they read the passage before looking at the questions. If a question is too tough, students should eliminate the answers they know are wrong and then guess from the remaining choices.

Test Format Reading comprehension questions assess students' ability to extract complete and accurate information from a passage, to distinguish fact from opinion, and to determine the main point or purpose. Students should practice these strategies on a regular basis. Remind students to answer reading comprehension questions based only on what is in the text, not on opinions or prior knowledge.

Writing Skills Practice

18. Writing a Journalistic Article Journalists must prepare and ask effective questions and take good notes to gather needed information.

 Practice Choose a recent news event in your town or school. Write a brief (three-paragraph) journalistic article about the event by following these steps.

- Choose an interviewee who is knowledgeable about the event and arrange a brief interview.
- Write questions that answer the "who, what, when, where, why, and how" of the event. Start each question with one of these question words. Evaluate each question to make sure that it is clear and effective.
- Conduct the interview. Take notes as the interviewee speaks. Get at least one word-for-word quotation to use in your article.
- Write the article. In the first paragraph, answer the "who, what, when, where, why, and how" of the story. In the second paragraph, give background details and use the quote from your interviewee. In the third, explain the effect of the event on your town or school.

Net Connection

19. Reading Strategies Choose two reading strategies and list them on an index card. Practice these strategies over the course of a week, using the index card as a memory aid.

 Log On Go to this book's OLC through **glencoe.com** and find the links to information about reading strategies that can help you understand and retain the information you read. Create a table listing the four strategies you find most helpful and why.

Reading Connection

Go to this book's Online Learning Center through **glencoe.com** for a list of reading suggestions.

Personal Academic and Career Portfolio

Developing Professional Communication Skills

Having good communication skills does more that just land you a good job. It helps you express yourself and understand others. Find a professional who works in the career cluster that interests you. Ask how he or she uses communication skills on the job. Ask for advice on specific ways to improve your skills. After the interview, assess your interviewee's speaking skills. What can you learn from him or her?

The following guidelines will help you organize and add the results of your research to your portfolio:

- Create a new section for your portfolio, using a divider for hard copy material and a computer folder for electronic files.
- Label the section *Communication Skills*.
- You may wish to create subsections or subfolders with names such as *Reading Strategies* and *Active Listening Checklist*.
- Add the section to your table of contents.
- Add the following: an honest assessment of your current communication skills, a list of speaking, listening, reading, and writing strategies you think might help you improve your skills, and feedback from friends, teachers, family members, and interviewers on your communication style and skills.
- Update your Portfolio as you gain experience with on-the-job communication.

 Portfolio Help Go to the *Succeeding in the World of Work* OLC through **glencoe.com** for help developing your portfolio.

Writing Skills Practice

18. Articles should begin with a concise statement of the "who, what, when, where, why, and how" of the story and should demonstrate that students have conducted an effective interview using the question words listed here. Quotes selected for inclusion in the article should illuminate the central point of the story.

Net Connection

19. Tables should include four reading strategies found on the Internet and reasons why they are helpful. For example, students might choose summarizing as a strategy, and point out that detailing key words and phrases helps students understand and remember what they have read.

Resources

⊛ **ExamView Assessment Suite CD** allows you to print out ready-made unit and chapter tests complete with answer keys. You can also create customized tests.

WorkKeys

WorkKeys® is a job skills assessment program. For information on leveled assessment for Communication Skills (Business Writing; Listening; Reading for Information; and Writing), go to the WorkKeys link on this book's OLC through **glencoe.com**.

Personal Academic and Career Portfolio

Maintaining a Portfolio

Explain to students that the **Personal Academic and Career Portfolio** is a way to communicate their job skills to employers. Remind them that presentation counts. Just as effective word choice and correct grammar and spelling count in a cover letter, so do neatness, organization, and careful selection of content count in a portfolio. Work with students to devise basic templates or designs that they can use for many of the elements of their portfolio, such as divider tabs, headers, and titles. Ask them to review and revise elements of their portfolio that could be presented more professionally.

Chapter Resources Planning Guide with Activities and Features

Section	Features	Activities
Section 16.1 Making Decisions in the Workplace	Creative Business Practices (p. 358) 21st Century Workplace (p. 359) Math in Action (p. 361)	Before You Read (p. 356) Graphic Organizer (p. 356) As You Read (p. 357) After You Read (p. 361)
Section 16.2 Workplace Problem Solving	Career Checklist (p. 363) Real-World Connection (p. 365) Everyday Ethics (p. 366) Hot Jobs! (p. 367)	Before You Read (p. 362) Graphic Organizer (p. 362) As You Read (p. 364) After You Read (p. 367)

NCLB Activities, information, and skills practice will help your students attain No Child Left Behind proficiency. Students will improve their abilities in the following academic standards areas:

Academic Standards Correlations

Discipline	Standard	Feature/Activity
English Language Arts	**NCTE 1** Read texts to acquire new information.	Creative Business Practices (p. 358) Hot Jobs! (p. 367)
	NCTE 4 Use written language to communicate effectively.	Writing Skills Practice (p. 373)
	NCTE 7 Conduct research and gather, evaluate, and synthesize data to communicate discoveries.	Real-World Connection (p. 365)
	NCTE 8 Use information resources to gather information and create and communicate knowledge.	21st Century Workplace (p. 359)
	NCTE 12 Use language to accomplish individual purposes.	After You Read (p. 361)
Mathematics	**Problem Solving:** Solve problems that arise in mathematics and in other contexts	Math in Action (p. 361)
	Algebra: Represent and analyze mathematical situations and structures using algebraic symbols	After You Read (p. 367)
	Number and Operation: Understand numbers, ways of representing numbers, relationships among numbers, and number systems	Academic Skills in the Workplace (p. 372)
Science	**Physical Science:** Motions and forces	Academic Skills in the Workplace (p. 372)

CORRELATIONS The charts show the 21st Century Skills, foundation skills, and workplace competencies that students develop as they work in this chapter.

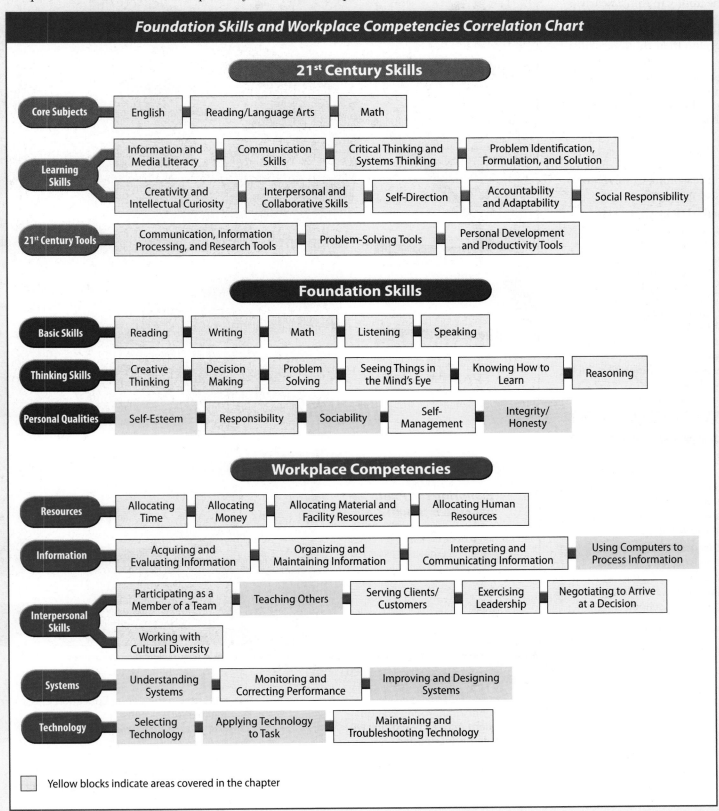

Foundation Skills and Workplace Competencies Correlation Chart

21st Century Skills

Core Subjects: English | Reading/Language Arts | Math

Learning Skills: Information and Media Literacy | Communication Skills | Critical Thinking and Systems Thinking | Problem Identification, Formulation, and Solution | Creativity and Intellectual Curiosity | Interpersonal and Collaborative Skills | Self-Direction | Accountability and Adaptability | Social Responsibility

21st Century Tools: Communication, Information Processing, and Research Tools | Problem-Solving Tools | Personal Development and Productivity Tools

Foundation Skills

Basic Skills: Reading | Writing | Math | Listening | Speaking

Thinking Skills: Creative Thinking | Decision Making | Problem Solving | Seeing Things in the Mind's Eye | Knowing How to Learn | Reasoning

Personal Qualities: Self-Esteem | Responsibility | Sociability | Self-Management | Integrity/Honesty

Workplace Competencies

Resources: Allocating Time | Allocating Money | Allocating Material and Facility Resources | Allocating Human Resources

Information: Acquiring and Evaluating Information | Organizing and Maintaining Information | Interpreting and Communicating Information | Using Computers to Process Information

Interpersonal Skills: Participating as a Member of a Team | Teaching Others | Serving Clients/Customers | Exercising Leadership | Negotiating to Arrive at a Decision | Working with Cultural Diversity

Systems: Understanding Systems | Monitoring and Correcting Performance | Improving and Designing Systems

Technology: Selecting Technology | Applying Technology to Task | Maintaining and Troubleshooting Technology

Yellow blocks indicate areas covered in the chapter

CHAPTER 16
Thinking Skills on the Job

Chapter Overview

Introduce the Chapter

The ability to think clearly is a skill prized by employers; this chapter helps students develop their thinking skills.

Section 16.1 focuses on the decision-making process and ways to use it to clarify thoughts and evaluate possible solutions.

Section 16.2 describes the problem-solving process and ways to use creative thinking and reasoning to solve workplace problems.

Build Background

Ask students why they think it would be useful in the workplace to learn and apply the seven-step decision-making process and the six-step problem-solving process. (Students might point out that workplace decisions and problems often require more than quick "yes" or "no" decisions or "quick fixes" to problems.)

Exploring the Photo

Caption Answer
Students might answer that the abilities to answer questions and solve problems are essential thinking skills in the workplace.

Discussion Lead a discussion by asking students what kinds of thinking skills they use to complete group projects at school.

CHAPTER 16
Thinking Skills on the Job

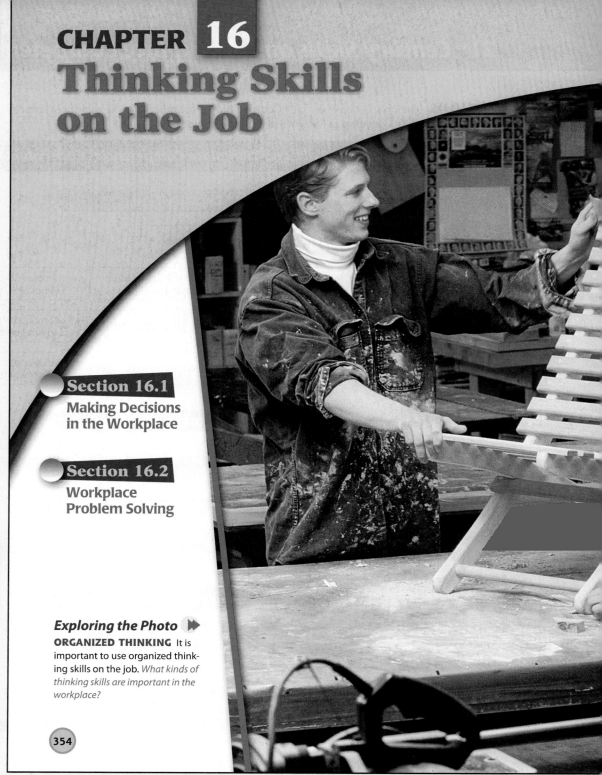

● **Section 16.1**
Making Decisions in the Workplace

● **Section 16.2**
Workplace Problem Solving

Exploring the Photo ▶
ORGANIZED THINKING It is important to use organized thinking skills on the job. *What kinds of thinking skills are important in the workplace?*

(354)

Classroom Resources

📁 Student Edition
📁 Teacher Wraparound Edition
📁 Student Activity Workbook with Academic Integration
📁 Student Activity Workbook with Academic Integration TAE
📁 *Fast File,* Unit 5 Resources

📁 Inclusion in the Career Education Classroom
💿 TeacherWorks™ Plus
💿 *ExamView Assessment Suite*
💿 Interactive Chalkboard
💿 Interactive Student Edition
🖥 Online Student Edition
🖥 Online Learning Center (OLC) with Podcasts

Chapter Objectives

After completing this chapter, you will be able to:

- **Apply** the seven-step decision-making process on the job.
- **Evaluate** your alternatives.
- **Prioritize** your work.
- **Identify** the six basic steps of the problem-solving process.
- **Describe** how to generate, choose, and implement solutions to problems.
- **Evaluate** solutions.

Writing Activity / Personal Career Notebook

Think of a difficult situation you faced recently, either at school or at work. What was the problem? How did you solve it? If you could go back now and deal with the situation again, what would you do this time? Write your experiences and ideas in a one-page journal entry.

Get Motivated! Contact a working adult in your community. Ask that person to tell you how problems are solved at his or her workplace. Write a one-page summary of what you learn from the conversation.

Writing Activity / Personal Career Notebook Answer Guide

Journal entries should include a specific problem and how the student solved it. Encourage students to think about what methods they used to solve the problem. For instance, did they take steps to solve the problem, or just make a quick decision or action?

Get Motivated! One-page summaries should include information the student received from a worker's experience with problem solving.

Review the Objectives

Introduce the chapter by reviewing the chapter objectives:

Section 16.1 Objectives

Apply the seven-step decision-making process on the job. (The seven steps of the decision-making process are define your needs or wants; analyze your resources; identify your choices; gather information; evaluate your choices; make a decision; and plan how to reach your goal.)

Evaluate your alternatives. (Evaluate alternatives by evaluating and predicting possible consequences.)

Prioritize your work. (Prioritize work by completing tasks from first to last, or from most important to least important.)

Section 16.2 Objectives

Identify the six basic steps of the problem-solving process. (The six basic steps are identify and clarify the problem; generate alternative solutions, use creative thinking and logical reasoning; evaluate the probable consequences of the solutions; decide on the best solution; implement the solution; and evaluate the results.)

Describe how to generate, choose, and implement solutions to problems. (To generate solutions, think creatively by recording ideas as they come to you, use graphic organizers to associate groups of ideas, create a model, use an analogy, question assumptions, and brainstorm possible solutions. To choose a solution, stay calm, focus on the problem, and decide on a solution. Implement the solution by explaining the solution to coworkers and putting it into action.)

Evaluate solutions. (Evaluate solutions by looking at both its benefits and its drawbacks. Identify any drawbacks or new problems, and correct them.)

Making Decisions in the Workplace

Bell Ringer Activity

Making Decisions in the Workplace

Have students write down two activities they would like to do this weekend, and have them circle the activity they would most like to do. Have them write the factors that influenced their choice (for example, money, family responsibilities, and other commitments). Ask students whether they made their decisions abruptly or methodically.

Resources

Interactive Chalkboard
The Interactive Chalkboard CD provides visual teaching aids for this section.

@ **Online Learning Center**
The Online Learning Center (OLC) through **glencoe.com** features chapter vocabulary, chapter summaries, and other study materials.

Preteaching

Read the definitions of the key terms aloud. As you read each definition, ask students to write a sentence using each key term.

Graphic Organizer

Tell students to go to the OLC through **glencoe.com** for a printable graphic organizer. (Graphic organizers should list the steps in the decision-making process.)

N C L B **NCLB** connects academic correlations to book content.

356

Reading Guide

Before You Read

Preview Look at the photos and figure in this section and read their captions. Write one or two sentences predicting what the section will be about.

Read to Learn
- How to apply the seven-step decision-making process on the job
- How to evaluate your alternatives
- Ways to prioritize your work

D ### Main Idea
The ability to make good decisions is an indispensable skill that will help you in both your personal and professional life.

Key Concept
- Effective Decision Making

Key Terms
◇ criteria
◇ consequence
◇ procrastinate
◇ prioritize

Academic Vocabulary
You will find these words in your reading and on your tests. Use the academic vocabulary glossary to look up their definitions if necessary.
- significant
- criterion

Graphic Organizer
As you read, use a two-column chart like the one below to list the steps in the decision-making process. Add notes that help you organize the information about the steps.

The Decision-Making Process	
Steps in the Decision-Making Process	**Notes**
1.	
2.	
3.	
4.	
5.	
6.	
7.	

 Log On Go to this book's Online Learning Center through **glencoe.com** for an online version of this graphic organizer.

Academic Standards

N C L B

English Language Arts
- Read texts to acquire new information. (NCTE 1)
- Use information resources to gather information and create and communicate knowledge. (NCTE 8)
- Use language to accomplish individual purposes. (NCTE 12)

Reading Guide

Before You Read
Point out to students that they have likely already used parts of the seven-step decision-making process when making their own decisions. As you go through the steps, ask students to give examples of how they have used each step to make a decision.

D ### Develop Concepts
Main Idea Ask students to write 100-word paragraphs describing why making a career decision is difficult and how a formal process can help them make well-informed decisions. (Career decisions can be difficult because they affect how you live. A formal decision-making process helps you consider alternatives and consequences.)

Effective Decision Making

You make hundreds of decisions every day. In the world of work, you will want to make the best decisions possible, both everyday decisions and **significant** long-term decisions.

The Decision-Making Process

As you learned in Chapter 2, decision making is following a logical series of steps to identify and evaluate possibilities and arrive at a workable choice. Whether you are buying new shoes or facing a big on-the-job decision, the steps are basically the same. What decisions have you made recently that followed the decision-making process?

S
1. Define your needs or wants.
2. Analyze your resources.
3. Identify your choices.
4. Gather information.
5. Evaluate your choices.
6. Make a decision.
7. Plan how to reach your goal.

Step 1: Define Your Needs or Wants

Once you know what you need or want in order to meet your job responsibilities, you have completed the first step of the decision-making process. Having a strong grasp of your purpose will help you clarify the decision you need to make.

Read how Maria Delfino uses the decision-making process at her job. Maria works at a large music store. Her duties include making sure that the display racks are kept filled with the latest CDs. When she discovers an empty rack, she faces a decision. First she identifies her needs and wants. She needs to keep the rack filled, and she needs a new supply of CDs. She wants to fulfill her responsibility and to do a good job as well.

As You Read

Summarize What is the first step of the decision-making process?

 ANALYZING YOUR RESOURCES The second step of the decision-making process involves analyzing your resources. *What resources do you see pictured here?*

TEACH

Discussion Starter

Effective Decision Making Ask students to list the major decisions they will be making over the next few years. (Decisions might include buying a car, renting an apartment, choosing a college, and deciding on a job.)

S **Skill Practice**

Guided Practice

Applying Procedures Discuss each step in the decision-making process by having students decide what they will do after high school. Have students suppose that they are considering continuing their education. Giving examples of each step, guide students through the decision-making process. Have students write answers to each of the steps.

As You Read

The first step in the decision-making process is to define your needs and wants.

 Resources

⊙ **TeacherWorks™ Plus** The TeacherWorks software includes customizable built-in lesson plans and links to printable program resources.

 Extend the Photo

Caption Answer Blueprints, information, facilities, and people are being used.

Discussion Ask students to share their experiences from their part-time jobs when they had to pull additional resources to finish a task.

357

Identifying Cost Factors In the text, Maria faces a decision about filling the CD display rack. Ask students to identify the cost factor that Maria needs to consider when analyzing her resources. (The cost factor is the order for CDs that she might decide to make from the distributor.)

S **Skill Practice**
Guided Practice

Identifying Choices Give students this scenario: Anne's employer has just told her that she will work every weeknight from now on. Anne is worried that she will not have time to study. Ask students: What are Anne's choices? (Students might mention that she has the choice to stay at the job and work the hours or quit the job and look for a new one.)

▶ Vocabulary

You can find definitions in the **Key Terms** glossary and **Academic Vocabulary** glossary at the back of this book.

Step 2: Analyze Your Resources

R Can you make something out of nothing? Of course not. You need resources, which are the things required to get a job done. In the world of work, the most basic resources are time, money, material, information, facilities, and people. Job resources that cost money are called *cost factors*.

At the music store, Maria moves on to the second step of the decision-making process by finding out what resources she has. She checks in the stockroom, and finds that the CD she needs is out of stock. She knows, however, that new supplies—additional resources—are available from a distributor.

Step 3: Identify Your Choices

S What do you do when different choices all seem like good ones? Smart decision makers use criteria. **Criteria** are standards of judgment for comparing and evaluating choices. **Criterion** is the singular form of criteria.

As you learn more about a workplace, you will learn not only how but also why certain decisions are made. In other words, you will learn what criteria are important, including product quality, customer satisfaction, safety, efficiency, and economic factors.

Creative Business Practices

TOYOTA   **Agricultural Education**

Toyota Motor Corporation has made diversity one of its top ten business strategies. The automobile company even supports diversity programs outside the auto industry.

For example, the corporation is involved with the National FFA (Future Farmers of America) Foundation. The money goes to support an ongoing project that helps students become aware of careers in agriculture. Targeted students are those from diverse cultural backgrounds who have not yet participated in agricultural education. Students involved in the program have the opportunity to learn about careers in agriculture, including the food, fiber, and natural resource industries.

The program, which is offered in three San Antonio, Texas, schools, is a partnership with Toyota Motors, the national FFA, Texas A&M University College Station, and MANRRS (Minorities in Agriculture, Natural Resources and Related Sciences).

CRITICAL THINKING Why would a non-agricultural company fund a project to encourage diversity in agricultural education?

@ **Connect to the Real World** For more information about Toyota, visit the company's Web site through the link on this book's Online Learning Center through **glencoe.com**.

Creative Business Practices

CRITICAL THINKING ANSWER Student answers should show an understanding that companies such as Toyota give money to causes that promote their corporate strategies, such as diversity. Doing so is part of being a good corporate citizen. Student answers on how it benefit might be that students of diverse cultural backgrounds will bring their own culture's foods or ways of producing foods to the marketplace, which provides more choices.

The 21st Century Workplace

Soft Skills Make Strong Employees

Employers need and reward workers with soft skills. Soft skills are about getting along with other people—communicating with them, respecting their point of view, adapting to changes they bring, and working out conflicts with them. Which employee would you promote: a likeable employee who offered positive solutions to problems in the workplace, or a difficult employee who avoided problems, blamed others, or simply complained without offering any new ideas?

Types of soft skills include courtesy and respect, communication (speaking, writing, listening, and reading), teamwork, flexibility, work ethic, self-confidence, problem solving, and leadership. Strong soft skills come easily to some people, but most of us have to work at it. Of 1,420 employers surveyed recently, more than half offered their employees training in specific soft skills, such as customer service and conflict resolution. If a company you work for offers training in soft skills,

sign up! If it does not, investigate low-cost courses at your local community college.

CRITICAL THINKING _____

How might employers help their employees develop soft skills?

In Your Community

As a class, come up with a list of politicians, businesspeople, and others in the media. Discuss the positive soft skills each person in the list has and write these next to that person's name. Use the Internet and other resources to find local classes that may help young people develop those skills.

 Extend Your Learning For links to Web sites about how soft skills can make you a better worker, go to this book's OLC through **glencoe.com**.

Maria knows that the store values keeping its display racks filled. However, another criterion, the chain of command, also is important. The chain of command helps employees know from whom they should take orders and to whom they should report. You begin with your team leader or your immediate supervisor. Next on the chain of command is your supervisor's manager or a more senior manager. In Maria's case, she should first go to her supervisor. If her supervisor is absent, she could then go to the store manager.

Maria identifies her three choices. She can (a) order the CDs immediately, (b) inform her supervisor that the CD is out of stock, or (c) do nothing about the CDs and wait for someone else to notice and handle the situation.

Step 4: Gather Information

Sometimes you simply do not have enough information to make a good decision. What is the solution? Get the information you need by asking questions.

Maria knows how to place orders. However, she does not have the authority to do so and does not know the number of CDs to order. Her next move is to ask a coworker for more information. Steven, an assistant who has been on the job for about six months, advises Maria to inform her supervisor of the situation.

The 21st Century Workplace

CRITICAL THINKING ANSWER Managers can create a positive work climate by modeling strong soft skills—respecting employees, being open and communicative, and tackling problems in a proactive way. Employers might also hold workshops or seminars where employees learn specific strategies for handling conflict and improving communication and then practice using these strategies through role-play.

In Your Community Students will mention various soft skills, including courtesy and respect, communication, teamwork, flexibility, work ethics, self-confidence, problem solving and leadership.

TEACH *(cont.)*

C Critical Thinking

Asking Questions What might a supervisor think of a worker who never asks questions? Why do you think people are sometimes hesitant to ask questions? (A supervisor might think that the worker does not care about doing the best job or does not understand the job well enough to know what questions to ask or when to ask them. People might be hesitant to ask questions if they think they should already know the answer, are embarrassed or too shy to ask, or want to appear more knowledgeable than they are.)

ASSESS

Review Key Terms
Have students write sentences using each key term.

Online Study Tools
Have students go to the OLC through **glencoe.com** to:
• Download **Podcast** study tools.
• Download free **Study-to-Go** content to their PDAs or cell phones.

Resources

ExamView Assessment Suite CD allows you to print out ready-made unit and chapter tests complete with answer keys. You can also create customized tests.

 Activity correlated to English Language Arts standards.

359

RETEACH

S Skill Practice
Independent Practice

Improve Prioritizing Skills
Ask students to list all the things they planned to do last weekend but did not have time or forgot to do. Have them write a paragraph, explaining how they could prioritize to make sure they did everything they wanted and needed to do. **L1**

Identify Career Priorities
Have students write 100-word entries for their career journals describing the priorities they will need to consider when making career decisions. (In their entries, students should describe how they can use logic, importance and feasibility, and time to help them prioritize and make important career decisions.) **L2**

Set Priorities Tell students to imagine it is Wednesday. They have band practice on Thursday, a math test on Friday, and household chores this week. Have students write three paragraphs describing how they would prioritize their activities for the next three days. (In their responses, students should assess logic, importance and feasibility, and time.) **L3**

Resources

📂 **Student Activity Workbook** Assign the Chapter 16 activities in the Student Activity Workbook.

Figure 16.1   PRIORITIZING

WHERE DO YOU START? When deciding what to do first in the workplace, take these factors into account: logic, importance and feasibility, and time.
How do you prioritize school assignments and activities?

▶▶ **LOGIC** Sometimes it is only logical to complete one task before going on to the next one. For example, a housepainter paints the ceiling of a room first, because any paint splatters that get on the walls will be covered when the walls are painted.

◀◀ **IMPORTANCE AND FEASIBILITY** If two tasks are equally important, start with the one that you know you can complete. Ask a supervisor for guidance if you are unsure about the importance of a task.

▶▶ **TIME** Sometimes it is best to finish short tasks before beginning more time-consuming tasks. For example, it might be easiest to answer several e-mails before returning a call to a customer who needs extensive advice.

360   **Unit 5**   Professional Development

EXTEND THE FIGURE   Figure 16.1

Caption Answer Students might mention completing tasks first that are due first or starting with an assignment or project they know they can finish.

Discussion Ask students what priorities they follow when they get up and get dressed for school each morning. Do they follow those same priorities on weekend mornings?

Step 5: Evaluate Your Choices

Every decision you make will have a **consequence**, which is an effect or outcome. Evaluating alternatives usually means understanding and predicting possible consequences.

- What are the risks and rewards involved in this decision?
- How does this decision directly affect me? How will I be judged?
- What effect will this decision have on my team or department?
- What effect will this decision have on my company?

Maria thinks about the consequences of the three choices she faces. If she orders the CDs herself, she may be praised for her initiative. However, she may also be reprimanded for breaking the chain of command. If she informs the supervisor, she will be following the store's standard procedure. If she waits and does nothing, she may be accused of not doing her job properly.

Step 6: Make a Decision

After you have evaluated your choices, make your decision. Avoid procrastinating. To **procrastinate** is to put off deciding or doing something. Maria does not procrastinate. She decides to follow the store's standard procedure: inform her supervisor.

Step 7: Plan How to Reach Your Goal

Once you have made a decision, you can put your decision into action. Prioritize the tasks to be done. To **prioritize** means to order things from first to last or from most important to least important. **Figure 16.1** shows different factors you can use to help you prioritize.

Maria prioritizes her tasks. She first informs her supervisor, who praises her attentiveness and places the order. Second, she rearranges the display to make it look appealing until the new supply arrives. Lastly, she checks the other new titles to make sure the situation does not happen again. Maria will reach both her short-term goal (to fill the display) and her long-term goal (to be responsible).

Math In Action

Dimensions

Khaled designed a 18" by 12" poster for a job fair. Half of the poster is occupied by text and one fourth of the poster is taken up by the poster title. How many square inches are left for the figures?

Starting Hint: Calculate the percentage of the poster that remains using fractions, and then find the total square inches left by multiplying length and width.

@ For more math practice, go to this book's OLC through **glencoe.com**.

Section 16.1 After You Read

Review Key Concepts

1. Explain how you would apply the seven-step decision-making process in deciding which computer your school should purchase for a computer lab.
2. Identify the criteria you might use to evaluate different computers.
3. Explain one method of prioritizing your work.

Practice Academic Skills

English Language Arts

4. Write two paragraphs that describe how your personality affects your problem-solving and decision-making skills.

@ Check your answers at this book's OLC through **glencoe.com**.

glencoe.com

Chapter 16   Thinking Skills on the Job   **361**

Section 16.1

ASSESS

After You Read

Have students complete the Section 16.1 After You Read section review.

Online Study Tools

Have students go to the OLC through **glencoe.com** to:

- Take the Section 16.1 **Practice Test.**
- Download **Podcast** study tools.
- Download free **Study-to-Go** content to their PDAs or cell phones.

CLOSE

Culminating Activity

Cooperative Learning Divide the class into seven groups. Assign each group one of the steps in the decision-making process. Have each group create posters or flip charts to present their step to the class. Have them give examples illustrating the actions a person might take at that step in the process.

NCLB Activity correlated to Mathematics Standards.

Math In Action

Twenty five percent of the poster remains (100 percent − 50 percent − 25 percent = 25 percent). Fifty four square inches would remain (18" × 12" = 216 total square inches; 216 × 0.25 = 54 square inches).

NCLB Activity correlated to English Language Arts Standards.

Section 16.1 After You Read

1. 1. Define what you will be using the computer for. 2. Figure out how much money can be spent. 3. Identify the computers that can be bought with the money. 4. Gather information about the different computer models. 5. Compare the different computers and their features. 6. Decide which is the best computer to buy. 7. Figure out how to make the purchase.

2. Criteria for choosing a computer might include assessing its features, including the amount of memory and size of the monitor; the quality of the brand; and how the computer is rated according to consumer reviews.

3. One method of prioritizing your work would be to complete tasks in order of importance from most to least important.

Practice Academic Skills

4. In their paragraphs, students might point out how their values affect their decision-making skills.

361

Section 16.2

FOCUS

Bell Ringer Activity

Workplace Problem Solving

Ask students to mention instances when they have had trouble using a specific item, for example, a tool, a game, or an electronic device. Ask how they would improve the product. As you introduce each step in the problem-solving process, use one of the items students mentioned to illustrate the step.

Resources

Interactive Chalkboard
The Interactive Chalkboard CD provides visual teaching aids for this section.

@ Online Learning Center
The OLC through **glencoe.com** features chapter vocabulary, chapter summaries, and other study materials.

Preteaching

Ask students to skim the chapter to find and define the following: *analogy, assumptions,* and *brainstorming.*

Graphic Organizer

Tell students to go to the OLC through **glencoe.com** for a printable graphic organizer. (Graphic organizers should include the steps in the problem-solving process.)

NCLB connects academic correlations to book content.

Workplace Problem Solving

Reading Guide

Before You Read

Preview Choose a Key Term or Academic Vocabulary word that is new to you. Write it on a piece of paper. When you find it in the text, write down the definition.

Read to Learn
- How to identify and apply the six basic steps of the problem-solving process
- How to generate, choose, and implement solutions to problems
- How to evaluate your solutions

D Main Idea
Problem-solving skills will help you face challenges in both your personal and professional life.

Key Concept
- Troubleshooting Workplace Problems

Key Terms
- analogy
- assumptions
- brainstorming

Academic Vocabulary
You will find this word in your reading and on your tests. Use the academic vocabulary glossary to look up its definition if necessary.
- expose

Graphic Organizer
As you read, list the steps in the problem-solving process. Use a chart like the one below to help you organize the information.

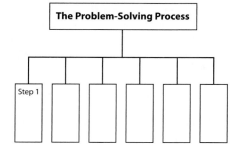

The Problem-Solving Process

Step 1

@ Log On Go to this book's Online Learning Center through **glencoe.com** for an online version of this graphic organizer.

Academic Standards · · · · · · · · · · · · · · · · ·

English Language Arts
- Read texts to acquire new information. (NCTE 1)
- Conduct research and gather, evaluate, and synthesize data to communicate discoveries. (NCTE 7)

Mathematics
- Represent and analyze mathematical situations and structures using algebraic symbols

---

Reading Guide

Before You Read
Point out to students that both simple and complex problems can usually be solved with creative thinking and logical reasoning.

D Develop Concepts
Main Idea Ask students to write 100-word paragraphs about why they think some people seem to accomplish so much more than others. Have them also include ways that show how creative problem-solving skills help people be more productive.

Troubleshooting Workplace Problems

Imagine that you work in a clothing store and a customer wants a certain sweater in blue. You have the sweater in brown and green, but not in blue. You have a problem that needs to be solved in order to help the customer. What would you do?

Understanding the Problem-Solving Process

Learning how to solve problems will help you in school and with your future job. Follow these six steps for solving problems:

1. Identify and clarify the problem.
2. Generate alternative solutions, using creative thinking and logical reasoning.
3. Evaluate the probable consequences of the solutions.
4. Decide on the best solution.
5. Implement the solution.
6. Evaluate the results.

Step 1: Identify and Clarify the Problem

When an obstacle stands between you and something you need or want, you have a problem. The wise move is to see the problem clearly for what it is—a situation that needs a solution.

Assemble all the information you can about the problem. Ask specific questions, stay as objective as possible, and make sure your information sources are reliable.

 ASK QUESTIONS
Asking questions can help clarify a problem. *What are some problem-solving strategies you use?*

Career ✓ Checklist

To Be an Efficient Worker:

✓ Ask questions to clarify problems and job responsibilities.
✓ Prioritize your tasks.
✓ Avoid procrastinating.
✓ Communicate with fellow employees to solve problems.
✓ Evaluate all possible alternatives and solutions.

Section 16.2

TEACH

Discussion Starter

Troubleshooting Workplace Problems Ask students to write a short paragraph describing how being able to apply a problem-solving process will be useful in their careers. (Students might point out that employers look for workers who can solve a problem themselves rather than waiting for someone else to do it.)

R Reading Strategy

Identifying the Problem Ask students if they have ever thought they solved a problem only to find that it was not the one they started out to solve. Write student responses on the board. Ask how they might have used Step 1 in the problem-solving process to approach the problems written on the board.

Resources

Interactive Chalkboard The Interactive Chalkboard CD provides visual teaching aids for this section.

⏩ Extend the Photo

Caption Answer When students mention the problem-solving strategies they use, encourage them to identify how their strategies relate to those in the six-step problem-solving process.

Discussion Lead a discussion by asking students how following a problem-solving process might help them relieve anxiety they suffer over a problem. (By following an organized process, students can divide their problems into manageable steps, so they will not be overwhelmed by the problem as a whole.)

TEACH *(cont.)*

R Reading Strategy

Identify Explain to students that identifying the real sources of a problem can sometimes be troublesome. Writing a statement describing the problem can help, as can discussing the problem with others. For example, tell students to imagine that the school's band needs new uniforms. Ask them to describe the problem. Write their descriptions on the board. (Some students may point out why the new uniforms are needed. The real problem is how to raise the money to pay for the uniforms.)

S₁ Skill Practice

Exercising Leadership Tell students to think about their experiences at home, on the job, or in extracurricular activities. When is it appropriate for them to take action on their own? When should they seek the opinions of others? When should they take matters to the entire group?

C Critical Thinking

Speaking with Others Ask students why speaking about their plans to others can help them clarify their thinking. (Putting plans into words, rather than just having thoughts in your mind, allows others to help you see things you may not have considered.)

Vocabulary

You can find definitions in the **Key Terms** glossary and **Academic Vocabulary** glossary at the back of this book.

R Lewis is an assistant at Avery's, a local hardware store. One day, Mr. Avery, the owner, tells Lewis that business has been slow. He asks Lewis to think about possible solutions to the problem. To clarify the problem, Lewis makes this list of questions:

- Are fewer people coming in?
- Are customers spending less money?
- Do people want a different selection of goods?
- Do people expect lower prices?
- What products do other local hardware stores offer?

By asking their regular customers these questions, Lewis and Mr. Avery clarify the problem: People are buying fewer of certain kinds of items, especially tools, because the selection is better at a new home supply store that recently opened nearby.

Step 2: Generate Alternative Solutions

S₁ When you are working alone to solve a problem, strive to think creatively. For instance, try to approach the problem from a different point of view. Seeing a situation from a new perspective can help you identify new solutions.

Here are a few strategies for creative thinking:

- If an idea comes to you, record it right away.
- Use graphic organizers such as spider maps and clustering to associate groups of ideas.
- Create a model, picture, or symbol to represent the problem. Revealing the "shape" of a problem can **expose** a solution.
- Use an **analogy**, a seeming similarity between two things that are otherwise dissimilar, to suggest a solution. For example: "This problem is like a game of basketball. We need to pass our product from one member of the team to another more quickly."
- Question **assumptions**, which are beliefs you take for granted, and beware of unspoken assumptions. For example, you might ask: "Are we assuming that all our customers are men? What about creating advertising aimed at women?"

C In problem solving, it helps to have more than one person involved because different people have different experiences. **Brainstorming** is a problem-solving technique that involves the spontaneous creation of ideas. Brainstorming can be done alone or in a group. As you brainstorm, try to think of as many solutions as possible, no matter how impossible some might seem. Do not evaluate or judge those ideas right away. If you judge your ideas as you create them, you will disturb the flow of your thoughts and hinder your mind from thinking creatively. There is no disadvantage to creating a long list of possible solutions. After all, multiple solutions increase your chances of finding a successful solution. **S₂**

When you plan to participate in a brainstorming session, it is a good idea to get organized before you start. Identify the problem that you want to solve, and select a group member to be in charge of recording all of the ideas produced in the session. Make sure that

As You Read

Evaluate How does brainstorming help when solving problems?

As You Read

Brainstorming entails having sudden, unexpected ideas that may not have occurred to you before.

◀ **GROUP CREATIVITY**
Brainstorming can result in a variety of creative solutions to a problem. *Why is brainstorming a good problem-solving strategy for a team?*

everyone in the group feels comfortable sharing his or her ideas. If some members of the group are new or shy, having everyone introduce themselves may help to promote a friendly atmosphere in the group.

Mr. Avery, Lewis, and Kim, another assistant, brainstorm one afternoon. Each proposes ideas, such as having a sale, lowering prices, putting up a new sign, and expanding the selection.

Step 3: Evaluate the Possible Results of the Solutions

After you have come up with some possible solutions, you need to evaluate how well each one will actually solve the problem.

List the specific results, both positive and negative, that may follow each possible solution. Which one best meets your short-term and long-term goals? What impact will the solutions have on you, on your team or department, and on your customers or clients? When you have answered these questions, you are ready to decide on one solution.

The problem-solving team at Avery's now looks at consequences, or results of the different possible solutions. Mr. Avery cannot afford to lower prices or to put up a big sign. Expanding the selection of all the items in the store is impractical because Avery's does not have the space.

Real-World Connection

Being Tactful

Your supervisor continually writes memos with grammatical and spelling mistakes. Other members of the team make fun of these memos and rarely take them seriously. The company's mission statement emphasizes a commitment to quality assurance. Today's memo addresses "quality assurance in all aspects of business" and is riddled with errors.

Critical Thinking What are some tactful, non-threatening ways that you could improve the quality of your supervisor's memos?

Do Your Own Research Research the most common mistakes that people make in written communications. Locate a list of basic proofreading symbols and make a copy of them. Use these symbols to proofread another student's work.

NCLB

TEACH (cont.)

S₂ Skill Practice
Brainstorming Solutions Have pairs of students discuss how to handle the following scenario: Bradley's boss has told him to watch for an important UPS package containing material needed for a client presentation the next day. At 2:00 P.M., the package has not arrived. Ask students to brainstorm possible solutions to this problem. (Possible solutions might be to call the sender to make sure the package was sent, then to get the tracking number, and then to call UPS or go online to the UPS Web site to track the package.)

ASSESS

Review Key Terms
Have students write sentences using each key term.

Online Study Tools
Have students go to the OLC through **glencoe.com** to:
* Download **Podcast** study tools.
* Download free **Study-to-Go** content to their PDAs or cell phones.

NCLB Activity correlated to English Language Arts standards.

Extend the Photo

Caption Answer The more people who brainstorm, the more ideas will be generated.

Discussion Lead students in a brainstorming session by choosing a subject, such as a new name for a local sports team, and allowing students to brainstorm possibilities.

Real-World Connection

Critical Thinking Answer Answers may include asking the supervisor to proofread your own memos to broach the subject, or volunteering to proofread for the supervisor. Students should be aware that everything they and their coworkers do at work reflects the standards of the company.

Do Your Own Research Students should find a set of standard proofreading marks.

C Critical Thinking

Covering the Bases Explain to students that prioritizing steps and communicating your plan to others are keys to making a solution work. Ask: What do you think are the advantages of presenting all the steps of a plan at a group meeting? (Presentation at a meeting demands that the steps will be well thought out and correctly ordered. Participants at the meeting may be able to point out corrections or additional necessary topics.)

U Universal Access

Visual/Spatial Learners Have visual learners prepare a bulletin board display illustrating the six steps in the problem-solving process. They might show a problematic work situation, possible solutions, and the consequences of each alternative.

Resources

📁 **Student Activity Workbook** Assign the Chapter 16 activities in the Student Activity Workbook.

Everyday ETHICS

MANAGING EXPECTATIONS

How do you manage others' expectations?

MAKING PROMISES You work at an automobile repair shop, and your boss just told a customer that her car would be ready by 4:00 P.M. today. It is now noon; you have not had lunch, and your boss promised last week that you could leave at 2:00 P.M. for an important doctor's appointment. Even if you worked through lunch, you would not have the car ready by 2:00 P.M. You do not want to disappoint the customer, but this is not the first time your boss has put you in this position.

What Would You Do? How will you respond if your boss asks you to stay at the shop and repair the car?

DISCUSS IT At times, you may have personal obligations that can only be taken care of during the workday. With a partner, discuss possible ways to address the situation with your boss, as well as solutions that would allow you to have a lunch break and still have the car repaired by 2 P.M.

Step 4: Decide on the Best Solution

When you choose a solution, remember that you are choosing the best one under the circumstances. Few solutions are perfect, and occasionally time pressure forces you to choose when you are not quite ready. Stay calm, focus on the problem, and decide.

You may have doubts when choosing a solution. However, using the problem-solving process should allow you to feel confident that you have addressed the matter at hand in a mature, responsible manner.

Gain reassurance by reminding yourself or your team members that you have approached the problem objectively and from all angles. Keep in mind that it is natural to feel doubt or anxiety when confronted with making an important decision. Feeling this way shows that you care and that you are probably not the sort of person who would make a rash decision under any circumstances.

Making decisions and solving tough problems can empower you, and make you feel good about yourself. Most employees enjoy the rewarding feeling they experience when they have made a challenging decision, even though the problem may have caused some frustration.

Lewis, Kim, and Mr. Avery decide that the best solution is similar to what Kim said about "different kinds of hammers." They will increase the selection of certain items, such as hammers, and specialize in tools. Although the team at Avery's is not completely sure that they have made the best decision, they know that they have weighed the evidence carefully. Now they are ready to move on to the next step of the problem-solving process.

Step 5: Put the Solution into Action

C

You may need to explain your solution to coworkers in order to put it into action. Identify the exact steps that everyone needs to follow. Then move ahead.

Everyday ETHICS

What Would You Do? Answer Answers will vary. Students should take into account their personal needs, the needs of the customer, and their boss's needs. Although it is important to maintain customer satisfaction, an unhappy (or unhealthy) worker will be less productive in the long run.

DISCUSS IT Students might suggest coming in before normal work hours to make up the time, or asking a coworker to fill in.

Mr. Avery takes action. He stops offering certain items, such as house paint, to make room for a greater selection of tools. He orders and stocks the new items, sets up new displays, and advertises in the local newspaper.

Step 6: Evaluate the Results

To evaluate a solution, look at both its benefits and its drawbacks. Be as objective in evaluating a solution as you were in identifying the problem. If your solution is working, you should be able to see benefits for yourself, your team, and your customers or clients. If the solution has drawbacks or creates new problems, identify the drawbacks and problems, and correct them. On-the-job problem solving is a continuous process.

Finally, ask yourself what you have learned. Apply what you learn to new situations to prevent similar problems from happening again. At Avery's, the greatest drawback is eliminating best-selling house paint to make room for new tools. However, tool sales are increasing, so the benefits outweigh the drawbacks.

HOT JOBS!

Industrial Designer

Industrial designers work with inventors, concept designers, and engineers to design and fabricate a variety of products and solve problems with existing products. Everything from high-tech electronics to low-tech household items needs someone to create functional and efficient designs for duplication and sale.

Section 16.2 After You Read

Review Key Concepts

1. Name the six steps of the problem-solving process. Describe one.
2. Generate two possible solutions to this problem: Your boss has scheduled you to work the day of a family event you must attend.
3. Explain this saying: "The only really bad decisions are the ones you don't learn from."

Practice Academic Skills

Mathematics

4. Dan is analyzing the demographics of a community. He finds that there are about 25,000 people over 50 in the area. If this group represents about 8% of the population, calculate the total population.

   CONCEPT **Variables and Expressions** A variable is a place holder for a changing value. Any letter, such as x, can be used as a variable. Expressions such as $x + 2$ and $4x$ are algebraic expressions because they represent sums and/or products of variables and numbers.
   Step 1: Change the percent (8%) to a decimal. Use the decimal to create an algebraic expression where x represents the total population.
   Step 2: Write an equation and solve for x by isolating x on one side of the equation.

   Math For math help, go to the Math Appendix located at the back of this book.

Section 16.2 After You Read

Review Key Concepts

1. The six steps are identify the problem; generate alternative solutions; evaluate possible consequences of the solutions; decide on the best solution; implement the solution; and evaluate the results. Students should choose one step and explain it.
2. Students might suggest asking for ways to make up for the work that would be missed if the event was attended. Another solution might be to leave a little early and get to the event a little late.
3. It is important to evaluate decisions, good or bad, to recognize and learn from the drawbacks or new problems they present.

Practice Academic Skills

4. The population is 312,500 people. (.08x = 25,000; x = 312,500).

ASSESS

Review Key Terms
Have students complete the Section 16.2 After You Read section review.

Online Study Tools
Have students go to the OLC through **glencoe.com** to:
- Take the Section 16.2 **Practice Test**.
- Download **Podcast** study tools.
- Download free **Study-to-Go** content to their PDAs or cell phones.

Resources

ExamView Assessment Suite CD allows you to print out ready-made unit and chapter tests complete with answer keys. You can also create customized tests.

CLOSE

Culminating Activity
Applying the Problem-Solving Process Have students identify a problem in your school, perhaps overcrowding, or the need for additional computer labs. Tell students to use the problem-solving process and write responses at each step. Have students share their problems and solutions in the class.

NCLB Activity correlated to Mathematics standards.

Discussion Starter

Science, Technology, Engineering, and Mathematics Lead a discussion about the different types of careers that can be found in this career cluster. Have students brainstorm different careers and jobs within the career cluster. (Answers should show an understanding of the many types of careers that fall within the career cluster.)

W Writing Support
Independent Practice

Conduct Research Dean stresses the importance of 3-D modeling and 3-D modeling computer software. Have students use the Internet to research 3-D modeling programs. Have them create a chart that compares at least two programs and their basic features, system requirements, prices, and whether the programs are intended for professional designers or for hobbyists.

C Critical Thinking

Draw Conclusions Dean mentions that he found that most employers valued work experience, not just education when hiring engineers. Why do think this is?

CAREER SPOTLIGHT

Career Cluster: Science, Technology, Engineering, and Mathematics

Dean Clodfelder
Electrical Engineer

Q: Describe your job.
A: I'm an electrical components engineer for a car manufacturer. I research and design electric components for vehicles, such as buttons, switches, radios, meters, navigation systems, and rear entertainment systems.

Q: Describe a typical workday.
A: I have a desk job where I use a 3-D modeling program to design parts. My parts and other parts can all be assembled using our computers to build a virtual car in 3-D space. I also calculate cost and weight, and make engineering drawings for the suppliers that will produce actual working components from our designs.

Q: What skills are most important to you in your job?
A: 3-D modeling skills are most important. I also need knowledge of plastic molding processes and manufacturing processes in order to understand what designs are possible to produce. Math is an important skill in engineering for measurements, formulas, and cost calculations.

Q: What is your key to success?
A: My key to success with any job is to have fun doing it. Enjoying your job makes your work experience more rewarding for you and your coworkers. Success seems to come easier when you are doing what you enjoy.

Q: What training and preparation do you recommend for students?
A: A bachelor's degree in engineering is a good start. When searching for a job, I found most employers were looking for work experience, not just a high grade-point average or a master's degree. The best training I had came from co-op work experiences while in college.

Q: What are some ways you recommend students prepare for this career?
A: The best way to prepare for an engineering career is to get your feet wet. Many schools have co-op or intern programs with companies so students can learn what the workplace is like, explore specific jobs, and get a chance to practice what they are learning in school in the real world. This also is a great way to gain the work experience that employers are looking for on your resume.

Q: What academic skills and lifelong learning skills are helpful in preparing for your career?
A: One of the most important skills I learned in college is how to work effectively in a team. Learning how to be an effective leader, dividing the workload according to the strengths of the members, and working together efficiently are very helpful skills.

Q: What do you like most about your work?
A: Seeing the finished product is the best part of my work. Along the way, it's fun to see computer models and receive prototype parts from suppliers, but nothing is quite like seeing your parts in a brand-new car and realizing that it is the result of your hard work.

> For more about Career Clusters, go to this book's OLC through **glencoe.com**.

N C L B NO CHILD LEFT BEHIND

Teaching Tip

NCLB puts a strong emphasis on mathematical skills. Students should understand that skills in calculating and mathematical reasoning are necessary not only for jobs in science and engineering, but also for careers in the arts and other fields. Encourage students to become comfortable with numbers by modeling the performance of mental calculations and by calling on them to perform impromptu calculations.

Sample Question Imagine the company you work for asked you to research costs for modeling software. The software you found will cost the company $200, minus a 25 percent corporate discount. How much will the software cost? (Answer: $150)

- **Education or Training** A bachelor's degree in engineering is required for almost all entry-level engineering jobs. College graduates with degrees in physical science or mathematics occasionally qualify for some engineering jobs, especially in special areas in high demand.

- **Academic Skills Required** English Language Arts, Mathematics, Science

- **Technology Needed** Computers and 3-D modeling software, an understanding of the electrical components you are designing (for example, radios, navigation systems, and other broadcast and communication systems).

- **Aptitudes, Abilities, and Skills** Creative, inquisitive, analytical, detail-oriented, able to work effectively in a team

- **Workplace Safety** Like other workers who spend long periods in front of a computer, electrical engineers are susceptible to eyestrain, back discomfort, and hand and wrist problems such as carpal tunnel syndrome or cumulative trauma disorder.

- **Career Outlook** Overall, electrical engineering employment is expected to grow about as fast as average for all occupations over the next ten years.

- **Career Path** Electrical engineers may choose to specialize in areas such as communications, signal processing, and control systems or have a specialty within one of these areas, such as industrial robot control systems or aviation electronics, for example. Engineers may advance to become technical specialists or to supervise a staff or team of engineers and technicians. Some may become engineering managers or enter other managerial or sales positions.

Academic Skills Required to Complete Tasks

Tasks	English Language Arts	Mathematics	Science
Meet with team to review progress of a project	★	★	★
Review specific requirements of a design job		★	★
Design an electrical component using 3-D modeling software	★	★	★
Research the design of existing electrical components	★	★	★
Calculate cost and weight of a product		★	★

NCLB

Critical Thinking

Why do electrical engineers need excellent computer skills?

NCLB This chart relates academic skills such as English Language Arts, Mathematics, Science, Social Studies, and World Languages to specific tasks that are performed for the job featured in the Career Spotlight feature.

Critical Thinking

Electrical engineers need excellent computer skills in order to use 3-D modeling software.

CAREER SPOTLIGHT

ASSESS

Make Connections

Have students research electrical engineering job opportunities and report on the types of jobs available in your area. Have students cite specific job opportunities they find and any information included in the job listing, including educational and experience requirements. (Answers will vary, but students should use their research skills in locating and describing job offers.)

CLOSE

Culminating Activity

Setting Goals Have students write two short-term goals, two medium-term goals, and one long-term goal that they could give someone who wanted to pursue electrical engineering as a career. (Examples of two short-term goals might be to research the educational requirements to become an engineer, and to ask for an informational interview with an electrical engineer. Two medium-term goals might be to take math and science classes while in high school, and then to choose a college that offers a major in electrical engineering. One long-term goal would be to decide what kind of engineering career to pursue.)

Key Terms and Academic Vocabulary Review

1. Students should use each of the key terms and academic vocabulary terms in a complete sentence. A sample answer might read: "*Brainstorming* is helpful when trying to generate new ideas."

Review Key Concepts

2. The seven steps of the decision-making process are define your needs or wants; analyze your resources; identify your choices; gather information; evaluate your choices; make a decision; and plan how to reach your goal.

3. Evaluating alternatives usually means understanding and predicting possible consequences. Ask: What are the risks involved in this decision? Are the rewards worth it? How does the decision directly affect me? How will I be judged? What effect will this decision have on my team or department? What effect will this decision have on my company?

4. To prioritize, order your tasks from first to last or from most to least important.

5. The six basic steps of the problem-solving process are identify and clarify the problem; generate alternative solutions, using creative thinking and logical reasoning; evaluate the probable consequences of the solutions; decide on the best solution; implement the solution; and evaluate the results.

6. Think creatively for solutions, try putting yourself in others' shoes, and brainstorm with others; evaluate the consequences of each solution; decide on the best solution; and then implement the solution by taking action.

CHAPTER SUMMARY

Section 16.1

The seven steps in the decision-making process are to define your needs or wants, analyze your resources, identify your choices, gather information, evaluate your choices, make a decision, and plan how to reach your goal. To determine which decisions are yours to make, follow the chain of command, and know your responsibilities. Collect information and use criteria to compare and evaluate possible choices. Evaluate the possible consequences of alternative decisions. Think about what is most important to act on first, and then create a plan of action. When you are ready to decide, do not procrastinate. Prioritize tasks to be performed in order to create a plan of action.

Section 16.2

The six basic steps in problem solving are to identify and clarify the problem, generate alternative solutions, evaluate probable consequences, decide on the best solution, implement the solution, and evaluate the results. Gather the facts, and then evaluate the information. Make a list of questions to help clarify the problem. Generate alternative solutions with creative thinking strategies such as using a cluster diagram, inventing a model, brainstorming with others, or using analogies. Choose the best solution under the circumstances, and prioritize the steps you need to take. Evaluate the results and look at both the benefits and drawbacks of a solution.

Key Terms and Academic Vocabulary Review

1. Use each of these key terms and academic vocabulary words in a sentence.

Key Terms
- criteria (p. 358)
- consequence (p. 361)
- procrastinate (p. 361)
- prioritize (p. 361)
- analogy (p. 364)
- assumptions (p. 364)
- brainstorming (p. 364)

Academic Vocabulary
- significant (p. 357)
- criterion (p. 358)
- expose (p. 364)

Review Key Concepts

2. **List** the seven steps of the decision-making process.
3. **Explain** how to evaluate your alternatives.
4. **Explain** how to prioritize your work.
5. **List** the six basic steps of the problem-solving process.
6. **Explain** how to generate, choose, and implement solutions to problems.
7. **Explain** how to evaluate solutions.

Critical Thinking

8. **Analyze** Explain in your own words what the following statement says about procrastination: *Do not put off until tomorrow what you can do today*.
9. **Identify** Identify a job or work-related goal, such as repairing a bicycle or building a house. Prioritize at least five tasks that would lead to that goal.

7. Evaluate solutions by looking at both the benefits and drawbacks, remaining objective, and asking yourself what you have learned.

Critical Thinking

8. Possible answer: If you are ready to put a decision into action, do so now.

9. Possible answer for repairing a bicycle: determine what's broken, assemble the parts and tools, remove the broken part, order or buy the new part, and install the new part.

Real-World Skills and Applications

Communication Skills

10. Providing Solutions Choose a problem facing your school or community, and present a solution to the class. Use a verbal or written form, such as an advertisement, a poster, or a song with lyrics, to show how you came up with a solution using the six problem-solving steps in this chapter.

Research Skills

11. Acquiring and Evaluating Information Imagine that you plan to open an ice-cream shop, video arcade, or other business in your community. Create a one-page questionnaire designed to gather the information you need about the products and services that would attract your classmates. Make your questions as specific as possible, and distribute the questionnaire to at least 20 students. Evaluate the responses, and write a report describing how your shop will meet customers' demands. Summarize the questionnaire responses in a chart, table, or graph.

Technology Applications

12. Creating a Spreadsheet You are in charge of buying seeds for 12 different farms. You must record the types of seeds needed, such as soybeans, wheat, corn, or barley. You also need to know when the seeds were ordered, when they were received, and to which farm the seeds are to be shipped. Use spreadsheet software to create a document that can list and categorize all the information.

13. **Sharing Information** Team up with a classmate and take turns telling each other about your part-time job or a job you do at home. Describe how you spend your time on the job, what materials you use, and what you like and dislike about the job. Explain ways you manage personal and material resources to achieve your goals on the job. Also tell your partner what you hope to gain from your experience with this job.

14. **Brainstorm Fundraising Ideas**

Situation Your soccer team has been invited to play in a week-long tournament in Europe. You and your teammates really want to go on the trip; however, your school does not have enough money. Your principal says that the team will have to raise all of the funds necessary to finance the trip. Your coach has estimated that the team will need about $25,000 to pay for travel, accommodations, and other expenses. The team has six months to raise the money.

Activity In groups of four, brainstorm to create an extensive list of fundraising ideas to present to the principal. Then choose the best ideas, and design a plan for raising the necessary amount of money. When you have finished, present your ideas to the class.

Evaluation You will be evaluated based on how well you meet the following performance indicators:
- Conduct a productive brainstorming session.
- Choose realistic and creative ideas to formulate a fundraising plan.
- Present your plan effectively.

14. Students should effectively address the problem of raising money for the team trip by working through the steps in the problem-solving and/or decision-making processes. Students should present complete and thoughtful solutions to the class.

Real-World Skills and Applications

10. Students should clearly outline the solution, including as many details as possible.

11. Reports should demonstrate a direct connection between shop features and data supplied.

12. Spreadsheets will vary depending on the type of seed chosen, but all should show 12 farms, seeds, and shipping dates.

13. Partners should describe how they spend their time on the job, materials they use, and likes and dislikes about the job, ways they manage personal and material resources to achieve their goals, and what they hope to gain from their experience.

Academic Skills in the Workplace

15. Stories will vary, but all should be about a time when the student had to use problem-solving skills at a job or at home. Stories should give details about the people, place, and events, and describe the student's feelings about the prob-lem and the other people involved in the story. Also the story should give details of the solution and how the student arrived at the solution. The last paragraph should explain what the student learned from the process.

16. The more profitable option would be to stay in the cur-rent location and not move [($12,000 × 1.15) − ($10,000 × 1.10) = $2,800 (*the more profitable option); ($12,000 × 1.10) − ($10,000 × 1.05) = $2,700].

17. The outgoing angle would be 45 degrees.

Academic Skills in the Workplace

English Language Arts

15. Practice Narrative Writing Write a two-page story about a time you had to use problem-solving skills while working at a part-time job or on a job at home. Give details about the people, place, and events so your reader will get a clear picture of your feelings about the problem and every-one and everything involved. Explain the problem, the solution, and how you arrived at the solution. In the last paragraph, explain what you learned from the process.

Mathematics

16. Weighing Options Paul is investigat-ing different ways to improve sales at the retail store that he runs. Right now, the monthly costs to run the store are $10,000, and the monthly revenue is $12,000. If he changes the location of the store, the costs will go up by 10%, but the revenue should go up by 15%. If he spends more on adver-tising, the costs will go up by 5%, and the revenue should go up by 10%. Which is the more profitable option?

CONCEPT Understanding Percent Increase To calculate effect of a percent increase, multiply by a decimal greater than one. For example, to calculate a 20% increase on 10, multiply by 1.2. That is, multiply by 1 or 100% plus the percent increase, 0.2 or 20%.

Starting Hint Multiply the numbers for each option by the percent increase: $10,000 × 1.10; $12,000 × 1.15; $10,000 × 1.05; and $12,000 × 1.10. Subtract the increased cost for each option by the corresponding increased total revenue. Choose the option that gives the higher revenue.

Science

17. Light and Reflection Computer ani-mation specialists must often solve real world problems. For instance, they need to know how light reflects off of objects. They do this by using physics equations such as the Law of Reflection. The Law of Reflec-tion states that the incoming angle of light will be equal to the outgoing angle of light, when it reflects off a flat mirror, or shiny substance. If a beam of light came had an incoming angle of 45 degrees, what would the outgoing angle be?

Starting Hint Remember that incoming angle = outgoing angle.

STANDARDIZED TEST PRACTICE

SHORT ANSWER

Directions Write two or three sentences which answer each question.

> **Test-Taking Tip** Put as much information into your answer as possible. Use easy-to-read, short sentences that define key words. Also give an example that explains your answer.

1. How would it benefit you to use the seven-step decision-making process on the job?

2. What are some ways to generate alternative solutions to problems?

For more Standardized Test Practice, go to the OLC glencoe.com.

 ## STANDARDIZED TEST PRACTICE

Answer
Students should write complete sentences that use several details to support their answers to the questions.

Test-Taking Strategy
The best practice for essay and short-answer test questions is frequent writing assignments with an emphasis on clarity, concision, and correct grammar and spelling. Many students find it difficult to begin an essay if they can-not think of an opening sentence. Encour-age students to create an outline, clarify their position on the topic, and then begin the essay with a strong statement of their position.

Writing Skills Practice

18. Create a Brochure A brochure is a mixture of visual and print information about a topic. In business, a brochure might provide information about company products.

 Practice Research a career you find interesting, and then create a three-panel brochure that gives information about jobs in that career.

- Use software or art materials to design your brochure.
- Choose art and text for the front of the brochure.
- Identify the main details about the career on the first panel.
- Identify the different jobs within this career on the second panel.
- Identify skills needed for this career on the third panel.
- Add design, clip art, or photos on the inside panels of the brochure.

Net Connection

19. Assess Critical Thinking Skills Many psychologists have designed tests to measure critical thinking skills. Locate examples of such tests. Take one of the tests that you find, and think about your results. In a one-page journal entry, record your strengths and weaknesses in terms of critical thinking.

@ Log On Go to this book's OLC through **glencoe.com** to find Web sites that suggest methods for improving critical thinking skills. Pay special attention to any advice that addresses your weaknesses. Use a word-processing program to summarize the advice you find and present it in a one-page essay.

Reading Connection

@ Go to this book's Online Learning Center through **glencoe.com** for a list of reading suggestions.

Personal Academic and Career Portfolio

Real-World Problem Solving

You can use your **Personal Academic and Career Portfolio** to keep information on different companies in which you are interested in working. Start by contacting someone in the human resources department of a company, or a supervisor who is in charge of managing and hiring employees. Ask about common human resources problems at the company and how these problems are resolved. Ask for specific examples.

Use the following guidelines to help you.
- Title a folder with the company's name.
- Write a list of questions to ask the human resources person.
- Use the phone book or Internet to obtain the phone number of the company.
- Ask for someone in the human resources department.
- Introduce yourself and explain your assignment.
- Arrange a time for a phone or in-person meeting.
- Be sure to be on time for your meeting.
- Make notes during your conversation.
- After the conversation, expand your notes, and then place them into the folder.
- Write a thank-you note to the human resources person who helped you.
- Refer to the folder whenever you want to review information on problem solving in the workplace.

@ Portfolio Help Go to the *Succeeding in the World of Work* OLC through **glencoe.com** for help developing your portfolio.

Writing Skills Practice

18. Brochures will vary, but all should include information about the students' chosen career and jobs within that career.

Net Connection

19. Journal entries will vary, but should reflect critical thinking about the student's strengths and weaknesses.

Resources

ExamView Assessment Suite CD allows you to print out ready-made unit and chapter tests complete with answer keys. You can also create customized tests.

WorkKeys

WorkKeys® is a job skills assessment program. For information on leveled assessment for Problem-Solving Skills (Applied Mathematics; Applied Technology; Locating Information; and Observation), go to the WorkKeys link on this book's OLC **glencoe.com**.

Personal Academic and Career Portfolio

Maintaining a Portfolio

Explain to students that decision-making and problem-solving skills are essential skills that most employers require. Encourage students to keep their **Personal Academic and Career Portfolio** stocked with newspaper, magazine, and online articles about the strategies businesses use to make effective decisions and solve problems. As students make career decisions, they can focus their article search and collect articles related to skill-building in their career area.

Chapter Resources Planning Guide with Activities and Features

Section	Features	Activities
Section 17.1 Technology Basics	Everyday Ethics (p. 378) 21st Century Workplace (p. 380) Career Checklist (p. 383)	Before You Read (p. 376) Graphic Organizer (p. 376) As You Read (pp. 378, 382) After You Read (p. 383)
Section 17.2 Computer Applications	Real-World Connection (p. 385) Hot Jobs! (p. 387) Creative Business Practices (p. 388) Science in Action (p. 389) Tech Savvy (p. 391)	Before You Read (p. 384) Graphic Organizer (p. 384) As You Read (p. 390) After You Read (p. 391)

NCLB Activities, information, and skills practice will help your students attain No Child Left Behind proficiency. Students will improve their abilities in the following academic standards areas:

Academic Standards Correlations

Discipline	Standard	Feature/Activity
English Language Arts	**NCTE 1** Read texts to acquire new information.	Hot Jobs! (p. 387) Creative Business Practices (p. 388)
	NCTE 4 Use written language to communicate effectively.	After You Read (p. 383) Writing Skills Practice (p. 397)
	NCTE 7 Conduct research and gather, evaluate, and synthesize data to communicate discoveries.	Real-World Connection (p. 385)
	NCTE 8 Use information resources to gather information and create and communicate knowledge.	Tech Savvy (p. 391)
	NCTE 9 Develop an understanding of diversity in language use across cultures.	21st Century Workplace (p. 380)
Mathematics	**Data Analysis and Probability:** Formulate questions that can be addressed with data and collect, organize and display relevant data to answer them	After You Read (p. 391)
	Number and Operation: Understand numbers, ways of representing numbers, relationships among numbers, and number systems	Academic Skills in the Workplace (p. 396)
Science	**Science in Personal and Social Perspectives:** Population growth	Science in Action (p. 389)
	Science as Inquiry: Abilities necessary to do scientific inquiry	Academic Skills in the Workplace (p. 396)

21st Century Skills and Workplace Competencies Correlations

CORRELATIONS The charts show the 21st Century Skills, foundation skills, and workplace competencies that students develop as they work in this chapter.

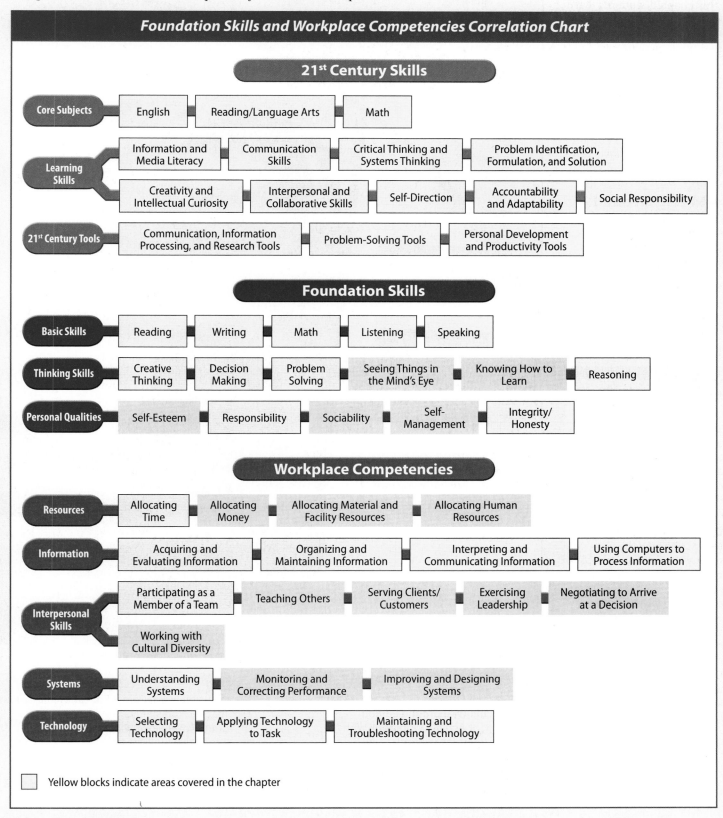

Foundation Skills and Workplace Competencies Correlation Chart

21st Century Skills

Core Subjects
- English
- Reading/Language Arts
- Math

Learning Skills
- Information and Media Literacy
- Communication Skills
- Critical Thinking and Systems Thinking
- Problem Identification, Formulation, and Solution
- Creativity and Intellectual Curiosity
- Interpersonal and Collaborative Skills
- Self-Direction
- Accountability and Adaptability
- Social Responsibility

21st Century Tools
- Communication, Information Processing, and Research Tools
- Problem-Solving Tools
- Personal Development and Productivity Tools

Foundation Skills

Basic Skills
- Reading
- Writing
- Math
- Listening
- Speaking

Thinking Skills
- Creative Thinking
- Decision Making
- Problem Solving
- Seeing Things in the Mind's Eye
- Knowing How to Learn
- Reasoning

Personal Qualities
- Self-Esteem
- Responsibility
- Sociability
- Self-Management
- Integrity/Honesty

Workplace Competencies

Resources
- Allocating Time
- Allocating Money
- Allocating Material and Facility Resources
- Allocating Human Resources

Information
- Acquiring and Evaluating Information
- Organizing and Maintaining Information
- Interpreting and Communicating Information
- Using Computers to Process Information

Interpersonal Skills
- Participating as a Member of a Team
- Teaching Others
- Serving Clients/Customers
- Exercising Leadership
- Negotiating to Arrive at a Decision
- Working with Cultural Diversity

Systems
- Understanding Systems
- Monitoring and Correcting Performance
- Improving and Designing Systems

Technology
- Selecting Technology
- Applying Technology to Task
- Maintaining and Troubleshooting Technology

☐ Yellow blocks indicate areas covered in the chapter

Chapter Overview
Introduce the Chapter

In this chapter, students learn about the importance of technology and the skills needed for technological literacy.

Section 17.1 defines technology and explores its effects on today's workers and workplace.

Section 17.2 focuses on business uses of software and the Internet, as well as how copyright and other laws affect the way we use technology.

Build Background

Ask students to spend three to four minutes brainstorming ideas and feelings they associate with the word *technology*. Ask students to share their responses. Discuss students' associations, particularly their feelings about technology (such as curiosity, fear, enthusiasm, and so on).

▶ Exploring the Photo

Caption Answer
Students may mention using computer programs to write assignments, using a calculator to check their computations, and using the Internet to e-mail and do research.

Discussion Ask students to describe how the technology shown in the photo might help this worker do his job faster or more efficiently, and why. (Answers will vary, but students should mention that technology tools can aid communication and help workers multitask—note that the worker is talking on a headset while referring to his computer.)

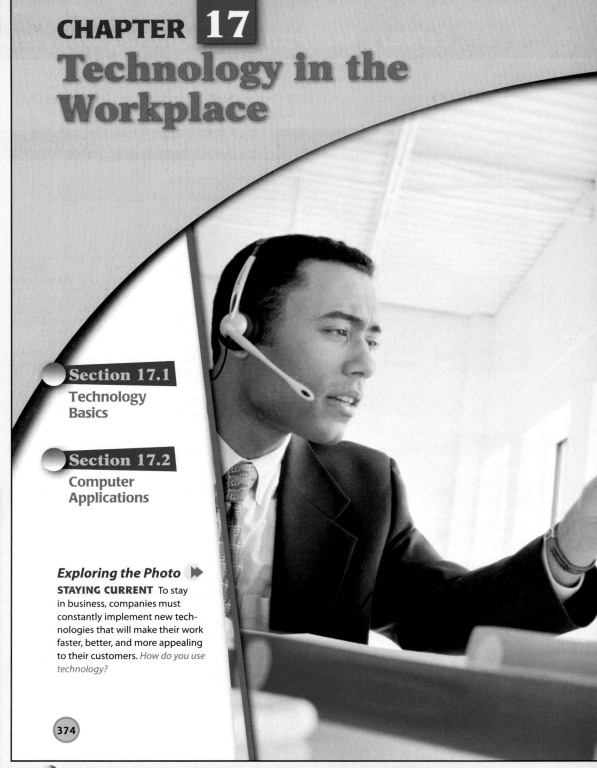

CHAPTER 17
Technology in the Workplace

● Section 17.1
Technology Basics

● Section 17.2
Computer Applications

Exploring the Photo ▶
STAYING CURRENT To stay in business, companies must constantly implement new technologies that will make their work faster, better, and more appealing to their customers. *How do you use technology?*

(374)

Classroom Resources

- Student Edition
- Teacher Wraparound Edition
- Student Activity Workbook with Academic Integration
- Student Activity Workbook with Academic Integration TAE
- *Fast File,* Unit 5 Resources

- Inclusion in the Career Education Classroom
- TeacherWorks™ Plus
- *ExamView Assessment Suite*
- Interactive Chalkboard
- Interactive Student Edition
- Online Student Edition
- Online Learning Center (OLC) with Podcasts

Review the Objectives

Introduce the chapter
by reviewing the chapter
objectives:

Section 17.1 Objectives

Explain how technology is
transforming the workplace.
(By promoting new employ-
ment patterns, globalization,
inclusion, distance learning,
specialization, and the need
for lifelong learning.)

Identify the skills needed
to work in a technological
environment. (Using computers to process information,
selecting and using technology for specific tasks, and
maintaining and trouble-
shooting technology.)

Section 17.2 Objectives

Name computer programs
commonly used in business
and explain their uses. (Word-
processing, database, presentation, desktop-publishing,
spreadsheet, telecommunications, and Internet software.)

Describe business uses of the
Internet. (Communication,
e-commerce, advertising, customer service, research, and
recruiting.)

Describe copyright and
other laws that affect how we
use technology. (Copyright,
online privacy, spam, and
identity theft.)

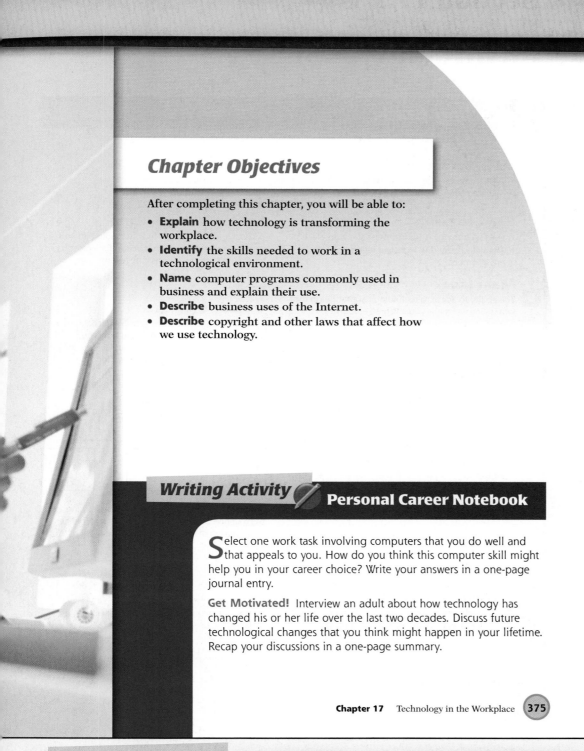

Chapter Objectives

After completing this chapter, you will be able to:

- **Explain** how technology is transforming the workplace.
- **Identify** the skills needed to work in a technological environment.
- **Name** computer programs commonly used in business and explain their use.
- **Describe** business uses of the Internet.
- **Describe** copyright and other laws that affect how we use technology.

Writing Activity — Personal Career Notebook

Select one work task involving computers that you do well and that appeals to you. How do you think this computer skill might help you in your career choice? Write your answers in a one-page journal entry.

Get Motivated! Interview an adult about how technology has changed his or her life over the last two decades. Discuss future technological changes that you think might happen in your lifetime. Recap your discussions in a one-page summary.

Chapter 17 Technology in the Workplace (375)

Writing Activity — Personal Career Notebook Answer Guide

Students' skills may vary, but might range from basic skills such as keyboarding to more advanced skills such as graphic design or HTML coding. Students should understand that even basic technology skills can help them in their careers—and can serve as stepping stones to more advanced technology skills.

Get Motivated! Students might mention that computers will continue to become smaller, more ubiquitous, and more powerful, that electronic communication will continue to increase, or that new technologies will emerge to counter some of our current problems, such as global warming or energy shortages.

Section 17.1

Technology Basics

Bell Ringer Activity

Technology Basics

Ask students what they think makes someone skilled at working with technology—whether it's computers, machinery, or other tools.

Resources

🔘 **Interactive Chalkboard**

The Interactive Chalkboard CD provides visual teaching aids for every section.

@ Online Learning Center

The Online Learning Center (OLC) through **glencoe.com** features chapter vocabulary, chapter summaries, and other study materials.

Preteaching

Ask students to predict the meanings of *technology, information technology,* and *assistive technology*. Then have students look up the terms in the text and compare the given definitions to their guesses.

Graphic Organizer

Tell students to go to the OLC through **glencoe.com** for a printable graphic organizer. (Graphic organizers should include three of the following: new employment patterns, greater mobility, globalization, inclusion, distance learning, lifelong learning.)

 NCLB connects academic correlations to book content.

Reading Guide

Before You Read

Preview Choose a Key Term or Academic Vocabulary word that is new to you. Write it on a piece of paper. When you find it in the text, write down the definition.

Read to Learn
• How technology is transforming the workplace
• The skills needed to work in a technological environment

Main Idea
The ability to adapt to technological changes in the workplace will make you a valued employee.

Key Concepts
• Technology Is All Around Us
• Hardware and Software Basics
• Information Technology Is Changing the Way We Work
• Technological Literacy and Career Success

Key Terms
◇ technology
◇ information technology
◇ computer
◇ laptop
◇ globalization
◇ assistive technology

Academic Vocabulary
You will find these words in your reading and on your tests. Use the academic vocabulary glossary to look up their definitions if necessary.
■ fundamental
■ shift

Graphic Organizer
As you read, describe three workplace changes created by technological change and how you can adapt to these changes. Use a chart like the one shown to help organize the information.

 Log On Go to this book's Online Learning Center through **glencoe.com** for an online version of this graphic organizer.

Academic Standards •

English Language Arts
• Read texts to acquire new information. (NCTE 1)
• Use written language to communicate effectively. (NCTE 4)

• Develop an understanding of diversity in language use across cultures. (NCTE 9)

Reading Guide

Before You Read
Explain to students that technology skills include more than knowing how to use computer programs. Technology skills also include an understanding of what technology is and how it is affecting our lives—from where we shop to how we learn to how we manage our careers.

D Develop Concepts
Main Idea Discuss the main idea with students. Ask: What would happen to an employee who had excellent technical training but found it difficult to adapt to new ways of doing things? (Answers will vary, but students should understand that, because technology changes rapidly, flexibility and adaptability are vital skills in today's workplace.)

◀◀ **THE HIGH-TECH WORKPLACE** Computers are used extensively in engineering, science, and related fields. *How might computer simulations be used in designing new automobiles or aircraft?*

TEACH

Discussion Starter
Technology Is All Around Us Ask students to name examples of technology tools they use or see in their everyday lives. (Answers may include cars, computers, cell phones, television and radio, the Internet, traffic lights, cash registers, motorized wheelchairs, or iPods.)

R **Reading Strategy**
Making Connections Ask students to think of different technologies they have used or heard about that have faded from use and to name tools that have superceded these old tools. (Examples may include typewriters giving way to word-processing software, telegraphs being replaced by e-mail, horse-drawn carriages being replaced by [hybrid] cars, or mimeograph machines being replaced by photocopiers.)

✓ Reading Check
SUMMARIZE An information society is one in which creating and distributing knowledge and information (as opposed to farming, manufacturing, etc.) is the primary economic activity.

Resources

🔹 **TeacherWorks™ Plus**
The TeacherWorks software includes customizable built-in lesson plans and links to printable program resources.

Technology Is All Around Us

No matter what career you choose, you will use technology. **Technology** is the application of technical processes and knowledge to meet people's wants and needs. All the tools, machines, and equipment you use at school or at your job are different forms of technology.

Humans have been inventing new tools for thousands of years, from the wheel to the printing press to the computer. Today, however, technology is changing faster than ever before. Tools that were sophisticated and cutting-edge just a few years ago, such as cell phones with e-mail capability, are commonplace today.

To succeed at your job, you need to be able to understand, learn, and work with technology. Of course, no one can master every technology. You need to focus on the technologies in the career field that interests you. You also need to develop the personal qualities that will help you succeed in a rapidly changing high-tech workplace.

We Are an Information Society

North America is quickly becoming an information society. In an information society, creating and distributing knowledge and information—text, pictures, sound, video—is the main economic activity. That is why, when we talk about technology, we usually mean **information technology**, which is all the tools used to create, store, exchange, and use information.

The **fundamental** tool of information technology is the computer. A **computer** is an electronic machine that accepts, processes, and retrieves information. The most common computers are personal computers (PCs), small computers made for a single person to use. Desktop computers, laptop or notebook computers, and handheld or pocket computers are three different types of PCs.

◀ Vocabulary
You can find definitions in the **Key Terms** glossary and **Academic Vocabulary** glossary at the back of this book.

✓ Reading Check **SUMMARIZE** What is an information society?

Chapter 17 Technology in the Workplace **377**

▶▶ *Extend the Photo*

Caption Answer Computer simulations are used in designing automobiles, aircraft, and other complex products to test the efficiency, usability, and structural integrity of different design options.

Discussion Ask students how computers are used in other career clusters, such as education and training, finance, or health science.

(Answers might include online learning and educational Web sites, spreadsheet programs and financial record-keeping, and computerized diagnostics and electronic medical records.)

TEACH *(cont.)*

**S Skill Practice
Independent Practice**

Sketch Hardware Ask students to sketch a computer hardware system complete with several peripherals, and to label the name and function of each. (Peripherals might include a monitor, keyboard, mouse, external hard drive, DVD burner, scanner, and printer.) **L1**

Compare Computers Ask students to research the prices and features of several models of scanners, printers, or computer monitors and to create a chart comparing and contrasting the features and prices of the different models. (Charts will vary but should compare the models across relevant and consistent criteria.) **L2**

Research Microprocessors Ask students to research what a microprocessor does, what it is made of, and how it works, and to summarize the information in a paragraph or diagram. (Microprocessors are electronic circuits made of silicon. They are usually squares or rectangles no more than a few inches to a side. The switches within a microprocessor "talk" to one another to execute software functions.) **L3**

As You Read

Hardware is the physical pieces of a computer and its associated equipment, whereas software is instructions that enable the hardware to perform useful functions.

Everyday **ETHICS**

BORROWING

What is the difference between borrowing and stealing?

USING SOFTWARE You are starting your own business and need several types of software, including digital imaging software and Web design software, to create a Web site. Your new PC came with a software bundle that only included an OS, word-processing software, and a Web browser. A friend from your old job has offered to lend you the CDs for a suite of Web design software that would cost you over $1,200. You are tempted to "borrow" the software to create the Web site.

What Would You Do? Will you take your friend up on his offer? What are some alternatives?

DISCUSS IT With a partner, discuss why some software cannot be legally copied and why some programs are so expensive. Do you think the cost is worth the benefits?

Hardware and Software Basics

A computer is made up of two basic ingredients: hardware and software. *Hardware* refers to the physical parts of a computer system, including the microprocessor, monitor, keyboard, mouse, and disk drive. Hardware also includes *peripherals,* which are pieces of equipment such as a printer or scanner that you connect to the computer **S** for specific functions.

The microprocessor, also known as the CPU (central processing unit), is the brain of the computer. Today, cash registers, cell phones, ATMs, and even toys contain microprocessors. Computers differ in the speed of their microprocessors, as well as in the amount of memory they contain. Computers use memory to perform tasks. More memory and a faster microprocessor make for a more powerful computer.

Operating Systems and Applications

As You Read

Compare What is the difference between hardware and software?

Your computer's microprocessor needs instructions, called software, in order to run. *Software* refers to codes that tell a computer what tasks to perform.

All computers need software called an operating system. An operating system (OS) is a program that controls the computer's operation, including how the hardware and software work together. Microsoft® Windows and Mac OS are popular operating systems. Both of these programs use windows, areas of the computer screen that you can control separately. Windows let you work on several files or programs at once.

Computers also use software called applications. Applications are software programs that can perform a wide range of tasks, from budgeting to making phone calls. You will learn more about common computer applications in Section 17.2.

Everyday **ETHICS**

What Would You Do? Answer Students should understand that using software they have not paid for and to which they do not have a license is illegal and considered stealing. Alternatives include buying a limited or trial version of the software or using the friend's computer.

DISCUSS IT Software is covered by copyright because it is the expression of a person's intellectual work and effort, just like a book, song, or movie. Some students may feel that software companies charge too much for their products, but they should understand that computer programs often require the work of hundreds or thousands of programmers, engineers, and designers.

Information Technology Is Changing the Way We Work

R

Information technology is not only changing *how* we work—it is changing what we do and where we do it. Important effects of information technology include new work patterns, globalization, and a greater need for lifelong learning.

New Work Patterns, New Workplaces

C

Technology is redefining what it means to be an employee. In the past, many workers spent their entire career working for just one or two employers. Today's information culture, however, has caused a dramatic **shift** in the employer-employee relationship. For example, many companies now choose to hire workers on a temporary or contractual basis. Workers may change jobs seven or eight times during their career—or more.

Workers are also physically distributed, or spread about, in many places. Many employees, for example, work at home, on the road, or at the local office of a company that has offices in multiple geographic locations.

Laptops and Wireless Networking

S

The laptop is a major contributor to the telecommuting trend. A **laptop** is a folding, notebook-sized computer with a built-in monitor and keyboard. It can also be called a notebook computer. Laptops, along with other portable data devices such as cell phones, and PDAs (personal digital assistants), allow workers to work almost anywhere.

Wireless networking also makes it easy to work away from a permanent office. Using a wireless card, workers can connect to the Internet and to their company network wherever there is a wireless access point.

 LAPTOPS Business travelers often use laptop computers to make the most of their travel time. *How else might laptops be used in today's workplace?*

Extend the Photo

Caption Answer Today's laptops are powerful enough to handle all the functions of a standard desktop computer, with the added bonus of being lightweight and portable for telecommuting and other work away from the office.

Discussion Ask students whether they would enjoy a job that requires a lot of travel. What are the advantages of traveling on business? The disadvantages? (Advantages include having new experiences, meeting new coworkers and clients, and seeing new places. Disadvantages include time away from family and friends, fatigue, and occasional unpaid transit time.)

TEACH (cont.)

R Reading Strategy

Predicting Ask students to predict what changes this section will mention. Ask: how do you think computers have changed the way people work and learn? How have they changed the skills workers need to succeed throughout their careers? (Ideas will vary, but students may guess that computers have led to economic changes such as globalization as well as changes in the skills needed by workers.)

C Critical Thinking

Making Inferences Ask students whether the shift in the employer-employee relationship is a positive or a negative development for employees. Is extra freedom worth a loss in security? Why or why not? (Students may like the idea of being able to change jobs as their careers develop or may find the idea of temporary or contract work daunting.)

S Skill Practice
Independent Practice

Research Ask students to visit a local computer store, consult the Web site of a computer retailer, or browse the ads in a computer magazine. Have them find out differences between laptop and desktop computers in size, features, and price. (Today's laptops come in a wide range of sizes; larger models have most of the same features as desktop computers but often cost more.)

R Reading Strategy

Identifying Root Words Ask students to identify the roots in the word *globalization*. (*Global* refers to the globe, or world; *-ization* refers to a process, as in *sterilization* or *colonization*.)

C Critical Thinking

Connecting to Financial Literacy Ask students to imagine that they own a small manufacturing company. How might globalization benefit them financially? How might it hurt them? (Globalization could benefit small companies by opening up access to foreign markets; it can hurt them by making it hard to compete with larger companies that have lower labor or product costs.)

W Writing Support

Problem and Solution Ask students to write a paragraph defining the problem that assistive technology solves and giving specific examples of how it solves that problem. (The problem is the exclusion of people with disabilities from the workforce; solutions include software that reads aloud to help people with limited vision.)

N C L B Activity correlated to English Language Arts standards.

Globalization of the Workplace

Globalization is the trend toward a single global market that crosses national borders. Globalization involves an increased trade in goods, services, labor, and capital from country to country. Modern electronic communication is driving globalization.

Globalization has greatly affected the job market in the United States. Many large corporations have downsized, or reduced, their American operations and moved operations to countries overseas where labor costs are lower. North American companies also face increased competition from companies in other countries. Today, large companies plan their products and services, from movies to frying pans, with an eye to the global marketplace.

Greater Inclusion in the Workplace

Computer technology is helping more people participate in today's workplace. People with special physical or mental needs, such as hearing or mobility impairments, now have tools that help them function better at work. These tools are called **assistive technology**. For example, joysticks and special keyboards help people with limited mobility. Screen readers read text out loud for people with vision or reading impairments. More and more computer programs have built-in assistive features.

The 21st Century Workplace

From Russia with Love

Russia, the largest country in the world, has attracted many foreign investors since the former Union of Soviet Socialist Republics (USSR) collapsed in 1991. At that time Russia, along with the other countries of the former USSR, formed a federation called the Commonwealth of Independent States (CIS). Despite ongoing political instability, the CIS is now a huge and growing market. Numerous languages are spoken there, but Russian is spoken by more people than any other. Most speakers of the other CIS languages, such as Ukrainian, also speak Russian.

CRITICAL THINKING

How might a shift in government economic systems or policies affect the languages students learn in school?

In Your Community

Many communities in the U.S. have sister cities in other countries. Sister cities set up student exchanges, artistic dialogues, and commercial ventures. Find out if your hometown or a city near you has a sister city abroad. If so, research and describe it. If not, write a proposal to another city describing the benefits of a sister city partnership and detailing what your community has to offer.

COMMON RUSSIAN WORDS AND PHRASES	
hello	privyét
goodbye	do svidániya
see you later	poká
yes	da
no	nyet

@ Extend Your Learning What are some languages of the CIS? For links to Web sites about languages in this region, go to **glencoe.com**.

The 21st Century Workplace

CRITICAL THINKING ANSWER
Governments often dictate the foreign languages that their citizens must learn in school. Hence, a change in government policy—such as closer political relations with the English-speaking world—could lead to a change in language policy as well.

In Your Community Existing sister cities will vary. Proposals may list benefits such as greater mutual tolerance and understanding, increased trade and cultural exchanges, student exchange programs, and more.

Accessibility is so important that today's hardware and software makers have a new goal: universal design. Universal design is the design and production of products that are easy to use for everyone, including people with special needs.

Distance Learning

Information technology also drives the popularity of distance learning. *Distance learning* refers to education in which the teacher and the student are not together in a physical location such as a classroom. This type of learning is also called distance education. Today, most distance education takes place over the Internet. These virtual learning environments can stand alone or be part of a traditional classroom. You visit the class Web site for notes and assignments and communicate with teachers and classmates by e-mail, online message boards, or instant messaging. You can earn a high school diploma, a postsecondary degree, or even a graduate degree by distance learning.

Distance education brings new learning opportunities to students with special needs, as well as to adults who work full-time or do not have a school nearby.

Specialization and Lifelong Learning

Because technology is so vast, more and more workers are specializing, or choosing specific areas of focus. Auto mechanics, for example, often specialize in repairing certain brands of cars. Health care workers often specialize in using certain medical equipment, just as graphic designers use specialized software programs to design, create, and produce content in printed, electronic, or multimedia formats. Even within a single field, there is a great deal of technology to master. To succeed in a world of rapidly changing technology, all employees must also participate in *lifelong learning*, which is learning and developing their skills over the course of their lives.

The increased importance of information technology also means that knowledge workers are in high demand. Knowledge workers are specialists who are paid for what they know rather than for what they can physically do. Computer programmers, engineers, teachers, and lawyers are examples of knowledge workers.

✓ Reading Check DESCRIBE How is information technology changing the workplace?

🌲 SPECIALIZATION
Specialization is one result of technology use in the workplace. *What do you think is the purpose of the specialized technology in this photograph?*

TEACH *(cont.)*

**S Skill Practice
Independent Practice**
Universal Design Ask students to describe one or two features of a computer program or other tool that they think could be improved through universal design, and to outline a solution that would made the tool better. (Possible answer: a computer program might be redesigned with larger icons or menu items that are easier to understand.)

✓ Reading Check

DESCRIBE Information technology enables new employment patterns and greater worker mobility, by promoting globalization, greater inclusion, distance learning, and specialization, and by making lifelong learning more important.

ASSESS

Review Key Terms
Have students write sentences using each key term.

Online Study Tools
Have students go to the OLC through **glencoe.com** to:
- Download **Podcast** study tools.
- Download free **Study-to-Go** content to their PDAs or cell phones.

Resources

ExamView Assessment Suite CD allows you to print out ready-made unit and chapter tests complete with answer keys. You can also create customized tests.

▶ Extend the Photo

Caption Answer Students may deduce that the purpose of the specialized technology, the RFID scanner, is to scan the barcode that contains information about the product to which it is attached.

Discussion Ask students how bar code scanners might save store owners time and money.

(Bar code scanners make it quick and easy for cashiers to ring up merchandise at the correct price, and they eliminate the need to apply physical price tags. When linked to a product database, bar code scanners also help keep track of inventory and sales.)

RETEACH

U Universal Access

Bodily/Kinesthetic Learners Have students demonstrate physical skills that could aid them in the careers that interest them. For example, a computer programmer needs keyboarding skills and an auto mechanic needs skill with hand tools. Have each student explain the skill, why it is important, and how they could build it further.

C Critical Thinking

Showing Initiative Ask students how workers can find out what new technologies and knowledge areas they should explore in order to stay current in their careers. (Workers can network with others in their career area, read trade magazines, keep up with technology news, browse local course offerings, and look at requirements listed in job openings in their career area.)

Resources

📁 **Student Activity Workbook** Assign the Chapter 17 activities in the Student Activity Workbook.

TECHNOLOGICAL LITERACY Changes in technology often require new workplace skills. *What technological literacy skills do you have? Which skills do you need to build?*

Technological Literacy and Career Success

How can you prepare for a career in the technological workplace? You need to build your *technological literacy*, which is your knowledge about technology and your ability to use it effectively. To be technologically literate, you need to know how to use computers to process information. You also need to know how to select the right technology in a given work situation, use the technology to accomplish your task, and maintain and troubleshoot the tools you use at your job.

To be technologically literate, you also need to understand the role of technology in our society, as well as its risks and benefits. This means thinking about *why* we use technology, not just about *how* we use it. It also means responding rationally to legal and ethical dilemmas caused by technology.

As You Read

Connect Are you technologically literate? Explain.

Skills for Technological Literacy

How can you improve your technological literacy? One obvious way is to use technology, read about it, and learn new tools, such as new machinery and computer software. Work on building these qualities as well:

- **Curiosity** Cultivate the desire to learn new things and to understand how tools work.
- **Reasoning** Strive to think logically and to solve problems based on solid evidence.
- **Problem-Solving Skills** Learn enough about the technology you use so that you can prevent breakdowns and troubleshoot basic problems yourself.
- **Flexibility** Expect to learn and adapt to new technologies and new ways of doing things throughout your career.
- **Creativity** Be smart with technology—think of new ways it can save you time and help you work more efficiently.

Extend the Photo

Caption Answer Self-assessments will vary. Target skills may include knowing how to choose the right software program for a given task or maintaining technology tools.

Discussion Ask students to guess at what the woman in this photograph is doing and what skills she would need to do her job effectively.

(This woman is looking at text, numbers, and an image generated by the imaging machine in the background. She needs to know how to use this console to operate the machine, and she must quickly synthesize complex information to make an accurate diagnosis, all while dealing compassionately with her human patient.)

Maintaining and Troubleshooting Technology

Like all systems, computers and other technologies sometimes break down. Learn to maintain and troubleshoot the hardware and software you use by attending training sessions and workshops whenever possible. Learn how to keep your equipment working properly, and when to call a specialist for repairs or technical support.

Learn to use the "Help" menu found in most software programs. You can also consult the help forums found on most software manufacturers' Web sites. Save your work frequently, and back up your work on external media such as a CD-R, DVD, or a thumb drive, a small storage drive that is the size of a piece of gum. Many companies will back up any information automatically.

Building New Skills for a New Workplace

Employers value workers who continue to build their technology skills. At your job, do not learn just enough of a program to get by. Read books or take courses. Ask questions to learn more about new and upcoming workplace technology. Use the software's built-in tutorials and help functions to learn new functions and faster ways of doing things, or sign up for online courses that use distance learning technology.

Mala Kovak, an office manager for a construction company, was asked to provide monthly project status reports in memo form. She took the assignment a step further and learned how to link her memos to detailed budget tables kept for all projects. Her method saved a time-consuming step. When Mala showed her new process to her boss, he offered Mala a bonus—and eventually a promotion.

Career Checklist

When Using Technology in the Workplace:

✓ Ask questions about how to use new technology.

✓ Ask for assistance when equipment is not working properly.

✓ Learn your company's policy on using technology for personal matters.

✓ Look for opportunities to update your technological skills.

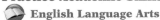

Section 17.1 After You Read

Review Key Concepts

1. Name three ways technology is changing the workplace.
2. Explain how globalization might affect you as a worker.
3. Define *technological literacy* and tell its importance in the workplace.

Practice Academic Skills

English Language Arts

4. All businesses have files and records. Write two paragraphs comparing traditional paper filing systems to computerized record-keeping systems. What do you see as the advantages and disadvantages of each? Why?

5. Imagine that you are a graphic artist setting up a home office. What computer equipment—including an operating system, application software, computer hardware, and peripherals—do you need? If you do not know, how can you find out? How do you research computer models, prices, and features? Create a list of items you need and another list of resources you would use to answer these questions.

NCLB

@ Check your answers at this book's OLC through **glencoe.com**.

glencoe.com

ASSESS

After You Read

Have students complete the Section 17.1 After You Read section review.

Online Study Tools

Have students go to the OLC through **glencoe.com** to:

- Take the Section 17.1 **Practice Test**.
- Download **Podcast** study tools.
- Download free **Study-to-Go** content to their PDAs or cell phones.

CLOSE

Culminating Activity

Technology and Career Success Ask students to write a learning plan that includes five specific actions they can take to learn more about technology and develop the skills and personal qualities needed for technological literacy. (Plans will vary but might include doing online research, asking for tips from people who are technologically literate, taking computer classes, or practicing software applications in the school's computer lab.)

NCLB Activity correlated to English Language Arts standards.

Section 17.1 After You Read

Review Key Concepts

1. Answers might include globalization, inclusion, and lifelong learning.
2. Answers may cite increased contact with coworkers, clients, customers, vendors, and others from other countries.
3. Technological literacy is knowledge about technology and the ability to use it effectively. It is crucial in the workplace because employers look for workers who can quickly adapt to new technologies.

Practice Academic Skills

4. In their comparisons, students might point out that electronic files are quick and easy to retrieve and paper files are long lasting and do not depend on technology.

5. Lists should reflect an understanding of how to research the technology a graphic artist would need and how to research different computers and their prices and features.

Section 17.2

FOCUS

Section 17.2

Computer Applications

Bell Ringer Activity

Computer Applications

Ask students to brainstorm a list of the different functions of computer software—such as sending and receiving e-mail, surfing the Internet, writing reports, adding numbers, and so on—and to label each function as work, personal, or both.

Resources

Interactive Chalkboard
The Interactive Chalkboard CD provides visual teaching aids for every section.

@ Online Learning Center
The OLC through **glencoe.com** features chapter vocabulary, chapter summaries, and other study materials.

Preteaching
Assign key terms to student pairs. Ask pairs to define their term and list five jobs or careers in which this application or concept would be important.

Graphic Organizer
Tell students to go to the OLC through **glencoe.com** for a printable graphic organizer. (Graphic organizers should include details about the five major types of software mentioned in this section.)

NCLB
NCLB connects academic correlations to book content.

Reading Guide

Before You Read

Preview Read the Key Concepts. Write one or two sentences predicting what the section will be about.

Read to Learn
- Computer programs commonly used in business and how to use them
- How businesses use the Internet
- How copyright and other laws affect the way we use technology

D Main Idea
Knowing the common business applications of computer technology will help you succeed at work.

Key Concepts
- Software Is a Powerful Work Tool
- The Internet

Key Terms
◆ word processing
◆ database
◆ presentation software
◆ desktop publishing
◆ spreadsheet
◆ e-commerce
◆ copyright

Academic Vocabulary
You will find these words in your reading and on your tests. Use the academic vocabulary glossary to look up their definitions if necessary.
- archives
- author

Graphic Organizer
Use a chart like the one shown to help organize information about software types and their uses. After you are done reading, research and add the names of specific software products in each category.

Application	Uses	Product Examples
Word-processing software	Create, spell-check, and format printed documents	Microsoft Word, AppleWorks

Log On Go to this book's Online Learning Center through **glencoe.com** for an online version of this graphic organizer.

NCLB
Academic Standards •

English Language Arts
- Conduct research and gather, evaluate, and synthesize data to communicate discoveries. (NCTE 7)
- Use information resources to gather information and create and communicate knowledge. (NCTE 8)

Mathematics
- Formulate questions that can be addressed with data and collect, organize, and display relevant data to answer them

Science
- Science as Inquiry: Abilities necessary to do scientific inquiry

Reading Guide

Before You Read
Explain to students that, in the field of computers, *applications* means specific computer programs. Tell students that, while there are hundreds and even thousands of specific computer applications, this section focuses on the core business applications that most employees are expected to master.

D Develop Concepts
Main Idea Ask students to describe several tasks for which businesses are likely to need software applications. (Tasks include sending and receiving e-mail, building Web sites, writing and publishing reports, managing accounting and payroll, and so on.)

Software Is a Powerful Work Tool

U Balancing a budget, controlling a manufacturing robot, creating a Web site—computer applications let you use a computer for an almost unlimited range of tasks.

Most computer software applications use icons and menus to let you make choices. An icon is a small picture that you click on to take an action. For example, many programs let you click on an icon of a printer to print your document. A menu is a list of options. For example, many programs have a "File" menu that gives you the choice to open, close, or save a file.

Business Software Basics

The most common types of software used in the business workplace are word-processing, database, presentation, desktop publishing, spreadsheet, and telecommunications software.

Word-Processing Software

S Using software that creates text-based documents is called **word processing**. Word-processing software allows you to add, move, and format text easily, as well as check spelling and grammar. Businesses use word-processing software for memos, faxes, reports, and other printed documents.

Database Software

A **database** is an organized collection of information stored on a computer. Database programs allow you to enter and save records, and then search, sort, and update the records. Warehouses and retail stores, for example, use database programs to keep track of inventory. Libraries uses databases to catalog their collections and let patrons search for books.

Presentation Software

Presentation software allows you to combine text, audio, video, graphics, and Web links into a slide show to accompany an oral presentation. You can present your slide show directly on your computer or project it onto a wall or screen. Slideshow presentations are common at business meetings, conferences, and sales presentations.

Desktop Publishing Software

Desktop publishing is using a personal computer and printer to create documents that look as if they were produced by a professional printer. You can use desktop publishing to create printed brochures,

Real-World Connection

Managing an E-Commerce Site

Your company's financial office has decided that all expenses must be cut by 10 percent. The company is about to hire five new employees to handle the redesign of your complex 2,000-page e-commerce Web site. Your manager is hoping that the company can save money by outsourcing this project to an outside firm. She asks you to write a report describing and assessing the pros and cons of her plan.

Critical Thinking What are the pros and cons of outsourcing work on a company Web site? Why?

Do Your Own Research Use e-mail to contact three Web design firms. Ask what services they offer and how much they would charge to design and build a 20-page Web site from scratch. Create a table that compares the companies' costs and services.

Real-World Connection

Critical Thinking Answer Pros of outsourcing might include obtaining expertise not available in-house, getting fresh ideas, and not needing to hire new staff. Cons might include the up-front expense, the risk involved in hiring someone who does not know the company, and the problem of how to maintain the site once it is built.

Do Your Own Research Services and fees vary by geographic area and the technical complexity of the project. Graphics-heavy or database-driven sites, for example, will cost more.

TEACH

Discussion Starter

Software Is a Powerful Work Tool Ask students to describe specific software that they know how to use or that they would like to learn and to share what they can accomplish with this software. (Answers might include creating and editing text, images, video, or audio, accessing the Internet, and sharing files electronically.)

U Universal Access

Gifted Learners Encourage students to explore a wide range of computer applications by signing up for any computer training available at your school, engaging in independent practice activities that build their computer skills, and speaking to successful professionals about how software is used in the workplace.

S Skill Practice

Independent Practice

Report Ask students to use the "Help" menu on a word-processing program of their choice or to consult the Web site of the program's manufacturer to find out what advanced features besides basic text editing the program offers. Have them word-process their findings. (Today's word-processing programs offer hundreds of features including change-tracking functions, version control, and tools to create outlines, forms, templates, and Web pages.)

Resources

⊙ **TeacherWorks™ Plus** The TeacherWorks software includes customizable built-in lesson plans and links to printable program resources.

TEACH *(cont.)*

S Skill Practice
Independent Practice
Calculate Have students use a spreadsheet program to create a bar graph. Ask them to create columns listing the high and low local temperatures for the past seven days and then to use the program's chart function to generate a bar graph of the data. (Graphs should have fourteen bars, seven in one shade, color, or pattern for the week's lows and seven in another shade, color, or pattern for the week's highs. Encourage students to experiment with formatting options.)

C Critical Thinking
Thinking Visually Ask students which of the two presentations of data in **Figure 17.1** they find easier to read—the numbers in the cells or the graph. Ask them to explain their opinion. (Students may say that they find the graph easier to read than the data in the cells because it transforms the data into an easily graspable visual representation.)

newsletters, invitations, logos, business cards, greeting cards, calendars, and more.

Desktop publishers use a variety of applications to design these documents. Digital imaging software lets you change the size, format, and appearance of digital photographs and artwork. Drawing programs let you create vector-based graphics—artwork that you can scale up or down to any size, from a business card to a billboard. Page layout programs let you format text and graphics into documents with a nearly unlimited number of pages. Desktop publishing programs can also be used for Web publishing, or creating content for the Internet.

Spreadsheet Software
A **spreadsheet** program is computer software that arranges or "spreads" data, usually numbers, into rows and columns. Spreadsheet programs perform calculations, such as creating sums and averages. Spreadsheets are useful for organizing statistics and financial records, for making graphs, charts, and tables, for making complex calculations, and for calculating what might happen in different scenarios. **Figure 17.1** shows an example of a spreadsheet.

Figure 17.1   SPREADSHEETS

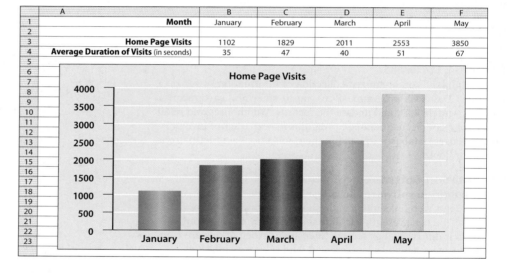

FACTS AND FIGURES Spreadsheets are useful for accounting, budgeting, scheduling, and for creating charts. Each box on the spreadsheet is called a *cell*. When you use a *formula*, changing a number in one cell automatically causes adjustments in other cells. *How might you use a spreadsheet to maintain and update a schedule?*

EXTEND THE FIGURE   Figure 17.1

Caption Answer One example would be to organize the rows as days of the week and the columns as hours of each day. The cells that correspond to the day and time could be used to add appointments, deadlines, and other activities.

Discussion Ask students to define *formula* in the context of a spreadsheet and to give examples of formulas that they might use in a spreadsheet program. (A formula is a set of calculations or transformations that tells the software what to do with a set of data. Useful formulas within spreadsheet programs include averaging, summing, and converting numbers to percentages. Formulas can also be used to format text entries.)

Telecommunications Software

Telecommunications is sending information—voice, text, pictures, video—from one location to another. The most common type of telecommunications software is voice mail, a system of storing and retrieving phone messages. You may also use telecommunications software to participate in a teleconference or webcast or to send or receive text or photos over a cell phone, a PDA, or another wireless device.

The Internet

The Internet is a vast network of computer networks used to share information across the world. The World Wide Web is the part of the Internet that contains multimedia and hyperlinks. You can access the Web with a Web browser, a computer program that lets you view the text, images, sounds, and video provided by a Web site. A Web site is a collection of linked, related Web pages with the same root URL, such as **glencoe.com**. **Figure 17.2** defines key Internet and Web terms.

HOT JOBS!

Web Developer

Web developers use computer languages such as XML and Java™ to build Web sites. They often work with Web designers, Web producers, and writers to combine text, graphics, and photos into appealing, usable designs. They also test the sites they build on different browsers and on computers running different operating systems.

Figure 17.2	INTERNET TERMS
browser	An application that lets you view Web pages.
cookies	Files sent to your hard drive by a Web site that contain information about the choices you have made while visiting that site.
domain Name	The identifying name of a Web site. Example: **glencoe.com**.
download	To transfer or copy a file from the Internet to your computer.
FAQ	Frequently Asked Questions, a list of answers to common questions about a topic.
HTTP	HyperText Transfer Protocol, the method that your browser uses to communicate with a Web server. Usually the first part of a URL.
link (or hyperlink)	A colored or underlined word, phrase, or image in a document that takes you to another Web address when you click on it.
IP address	Internet Protocol address, a unique string of four numbers assigned to every piece of hardware on a network. Example: 12.163.148.180.
ISP	Internet Service Provider, a company that provides Internet access.
PDF	Portable Document Format, a type of file that looks the same on any computer. Web sites often offer PDF downloads for printable documents.
podcasting	Audio or visual broadcasting using the Internet.
search engine	Software that finds Web pages based on keywords.
upload	To transfer or copy a file from your computer to the Internet.
URL	Uniform Resource Locator; an Internet address. Pronounced U-R-L or "earl." Example: **http://www.glencoe.com**.
BE WEB WISE	Employers look for job candidates who are Internet-savvy and Web-savvy. *What links on a Web site can you click on to learn more about the organization running the site?*

Section 17.2

TEACH (cont.)

W Writing Strategy

Diagram Ask students to visit three or four Web sites and look at the elements on each site's home page. Then ask them to use word-processing, page layout, or drawing software to diagram how they would lay out their home page if they were building their own Web site. (Most sites have their name and a graphic at top left, left or top navigation bar(s) with links to areas within the site, text and images in the center, and a copyright notice at bottom. Many sites include links in their navigation bars to "home," "about us," and "contact us.")

C Critical Thinking

Applying Prior Knowledge Ask students to find the definition of *search engine* in **Figure 17.2**. Then ask: When you type a keyword into a search engine, how do you know which of the results is likely to have the most reliable information? (Many search engine users assume that the first result is the best. However, students should look at the title, description, and URL of each result and then judge which ones are most likely to contain unbiased and complete information.)

EXTEND THE FIGURE — Figure 17.2

Caption Answer Links such as *About Us, Company Info,* and *FAQs (Frequently Asked Questions)* will help you learn more about the organization.

Discussion Ask students how they could demonstrate to an employer that they are Web-savvy. (Students could create a digital portfolio, design a personal Web site with an online résumé, and include a list of specific computer skills on their résumé.)

TEACH (cont.)

S Skill Practice

Independent Practice

Research Resources Ask students to compile a list of reliable Web-based research resources with the titles and URLs of at least two Web sites in each of the following categories: dictionaries, encyclopedias, news sources, health and medicine, and science and mathematics. (Resources will vary but should be weighted toward nonprofit or government sites.) **L1**

Web Marketing Ask students to imagine that they are creating a Web site to market themselves to potential employers. What information would they include? What colors and images would they use to create their "brand identity"? Why? (Ideas will vary based on students' personalities, career interests, and design preferences.) **L2**

E-mail Ask students to research different e-mail services—computer applications sold for a fee, free Web-based e-mail services, or both—and to create a chart comparing their costs and features. (Common e-mail programs include Microsoft Outlook, Novell Groupwise, and Eudora. Popular Web-based e-mail services include Yahoo! Mail and Gmail. Web-based e-mail services are generally free, although they offer fewer features than desktop e-mail applications.) **L3**

▶ **Vocabulary**
You can find definitions in the **Key Terms** glossary and **Academic Vocabulary** glossary at the back of this book.

Uses of the Internet

The Internet is a communication tool, an advertising medium, an information resource, a meeting place, and more. The Internet is a cost-effective tool for businesses to:

- **Communicate** The Internet is the communication vehicle for e-mail. Businesses also use FTP (file-transfer protocol) sites to house documents that are too large to e-mail and maintain intranets, which are internal organization Web sites used to share information with staff.
- **Buy and Sell E-commerce** is the buying and selling of goods and services on the Internet. Online sales now account for a majority of many companies' revenues.
- **Advertise** A Web site is both an information resource and a marketing tool. A well-designed Web site gives an organization a memorable identity and promotes its products and services.
- **Provide Customer Service** Companies save money by referring callers to their Web sites to look up information themselves. Many companies, such as banks and utilities, also let customers check their accounts and pay bills online.
- **Conduct Research** Online dictionaries, encyclopedias, government records, and newspaper **archives** provide easy access to reliable information. Many businesses subscribe to online databases that offer data in specific fields, such as law or scientific research.
- **Recruit Employees** Online job listings now outnumber printed ones. Companies often place job ads both on their own Web sites and on career Web sites.

Creative Business Practices

DELL **Building Loyalty Through Donations**

Dell Computers doesn't just sell PCs—it also gives them away. Dell supplies free computers to Operation Homelink, a nonprofit organization that gives refurbished computers to U.S. troops serving overseas and to their families back home. Parents and spouses of servicepeople are eligible for the program, which aims to keep military families connected by e-mail. Dell also provides computers to other nonprofit organizations as part of the company's mission to make computers available to all.

CRITICAL THINKING Why is supporting Operation Homelink a good business strategy for Dell?

@ Connect to the Real World For more information about Dell or Operation Homelink, visit the Web sites via the link on this book's Online Learning Center through **glencoe.com**.

388 **Unit 5** Professional Development

glencoe.com

Creative Business Practices

CRITICAL THINKING ANSWER Supporting a nonprofit organization like Operation Homelink is a good business strategy for Dell because it builds brand loyalty among participants in the program and generates positive publicity for the company for relatively minimal cost.

Legal and Ethical Issues of the Internet

To use the Internet legally and ethically, it is important to understand copyright law and to learn how to protect your privacy, deal with unwanted e-mail, and minimize the risk of identity theft.

Copyright and Intellectual Property

Music, text, images, and videos are easy to download from the Internet. Both ethics and the law, however, require that you give credit to others when you use their intellectual property.

Copyright law exists to help people protect what they create. **Copyright** is the legal right of the **author** or other creator of a work to control the reproduction and use of their works and ideas. Permission is usually required to use copyrighted material. Most original work, including software, music, video, and text, is covered by copyright, even if it does not have a copyright symbol. Only the copyright holder has the right to make or distribute copies, perform or display the work, or adapt or translate it, or to authorize you to do any of these things.

Copyright law protects all written works, whether or not they have been formally published. Even information you have created on your computer is protected. Copying text or software without permission is against the law. It is also unfair to the person who worked hard to create the original.

If you want to use someone else's words or images in your school work, always cite the source. This means giving credit to the creator and describing the exact place where you found the information. Paraphrasing someone's words is not a violation of copyright. Using their exact words without quotation marks and a source, however, is a violation of copyright.

Get to know enough about copyright law to protect yourself. If you are not sure whether or not you need to ask permission, always do so—just to be safe.

Online Privacy

Did you know that you are not really anonymous when you use the Internet? You leave "electronic footprints" every time you go online. For example, your ISP can determine what you search for online and what Web sites you visit. At work, your employer may also monitor your company e-mail and Web use.

Most Web sites collect the IP address of your computer and track the links you click. They also deposit "cookies," which are small files that contain information about your computer activities, such as your user ID and your preferences. Web sites use this information to find out what people like and to make your online experience smoother.

However, privacy advocates are concerned by how difficult it is to control personal information on the Internet. For example, the Internet makes it easy for marketers to collect and share information about you, such as your buying habits, finances, residential history, and even medical conditions.

Science In Action

Statistics: Range

Statisticians look for patterns within data. One of the things they must report is the range of their data. The *range* is the lowest data point and the highest data point recorded. Name the range of this data set of city populations: [100; 400; 5,000; 55,000; 900; 100,000; 200; 40,000; 30,000; 5,000,000].

Starting Hint: Organize the data in order from highest to lowest quantity.

@ For more science practice, go to this book's OLC through **glencoe.com**.

Science In Action

The range of city populations is 100 to 5,000,000.

TEACH (cont.)

C Critical Thinking

Drawing Inferences Ask students why they think the government makes copyright laws. How does society as a whole benefit from copyright protections? (Copyright protection is intended to encourage innovation in science, business, and the arts by ensuring that creators and inventors enjoy the profits of their work.)

W Writing Support

Paraphrasing Ask students to locate an article about copyright in a print or online encyclopedia and to briefly paraphrase the article, taking care not to use the author's exact words. Ask students to turn in a copy of the original along with their paraphrase. (Paraphrases should capture important terminology and concepts from the original without copying entire sentences or phrases.)

ASSESS

Review Key Terms

Have students write sentences using each key term.

Online Study Tools

Have students go to the OLC through **glencoe.com** to:

- Download **Podcast** study tools.
- Download free **Study-to-Go** content to their PDAs or cell phones.

NCLB Activity correlated to Science standards.

RETEACH

S Skill Practice

Independent Practice

Explain Ask students to research what makes a Web site secure. How can a shopper or online banker know whether a site is safe to use? (Secure Web areas begin with the prefix *https*—the *s* stands for *secure* and indicates that the site uses encryption, or scrambling, to protect data. Sites should also use a technology called "SSL" that ensures safe transmission of data.)

As You Read

Passwords often protect sensitive information, including financial records, confidential work documents, and so on. Hackers can use software that guesses thousands of passwords until it finds the right one. Secure passwords are more resistant to such break-ins.

ASSESS

Review Key Terms

Have students complete the Section 17.2 After You Read section review.

Online Study Tools

Have students go to the OLC through **glencoe.com** to:

- Take the Section 17.2 **Practice Test.**
- Download **Podcast** study tools.
- Download free **Study-to-Go** content to their PDAs or cell phones.

As You Read

Extend Why is it important to have passwords that are not easily guessed?

How can you tell what a Web site knows about you? Read its privacy policy, a statement about what types of information the site gathers and what the site does with it. Never give out sensitive information over e-mail or an unsecured Web site. Currently there are few laws protecting online privacy, so know your rights and keep your information secure.

Identity Theft

The amount of information on the Internet has made identity theft easier. *Identity theft* is using a person's personal information to steal money or credit. Identity thieves can use personal information such as your Social Security number, driver's license number, or credit card number to apply for credit cards or access your accounts. Identity thieves can get this information by intercepting wireless connections, tricking you into providing the information for them, hacking into databases, or simply stealing your mail or your computer.

Protect your identity by keeping your passwords, your financial records, and your Social Security and driver's license numbers safe. Only enter personal information on Web sites that are certified to be secure, and always check your financial statements. If you suspect someone has used your account, cancel the account, place a fraud alert on your credit report, and file a complaint with the Federal Trade Commission.

▶ PROTECT YOUR ELECTRONIC IDENTITY Protect yourself from identity theft by keeping your paper and electronic records secure. *What can you do if you suspect that you are the victim of identity theft?*

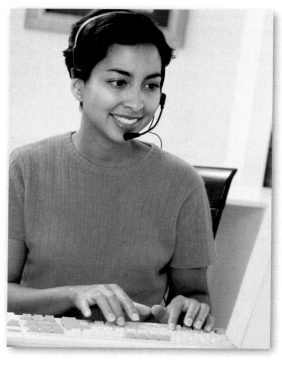

▶ Extend the Photo

Caption Answer If you suspect you are the victim of identity theft, you should cancel the accounts that were used, and place a fraud alert on your credit report through the three credit bureaus, TransUnion, Experian, and Equifax. File a complaint with the Federal Trade Commission.

Discussion Ask if any students know of a family member or friend who has been the victim of identity theft. Ask volunteers who respond to discuss how the victim realized he or she had been the victim of identity theft, and if and how it has been resolved.

Handling Spam

Spam is unsolicited e-mail. Spam often tries to sell you something or trick you into giving financial information. Spam may also contain computer viruses or *spyware*, software that secretly monitors your activities.

Federal law requires senders of commercial e-mail to let you opt out of receiving more e-mail from that company. Few spammers obey this law. Most spammers send anonymously, from fake e-mail addresses.

To protect yourself against spam, only give your e-mail address to people you know well. Do not post your e-mail address on the Web, where spammers can find it. Use spam filters in your e-mail programs to screen out unwanted e-mail. You can also buy or download programs that detect and uninstall spyware. Do not open e-mail unless you know the sender, and never reply to spam or click on links within a spam e-mail.

TechSavvy

Going High-Tech with Wi-Fi

Wi-fi is wireless networking, or connecting computer to computer without wires. You can go wireless by installing a wireless card into your PC. These cards use radio signals to "talk" to wireless routers, which are connected to the Internet via a cable modem or a DSL (digital subscriber line) modem. Wireless hotspots, the areas covered by a wireless router, are springing up everywhere. Hotspots in airports and other public places let you connect for free or for a fee.

@ Visit this book's OLC through **glencoe.com** and find the link to learn more about wireless networking. Make a list of questions you want to ask about wi-fi, then visit a computer store to have an employee answer your questions.

Section 17.2 After You Read

Review Key Concepts

1. Identify the type of computer program you would use to keep track of sales in a skateboard shop and produce a sales report.
2. Describe e-commerce.
3. Give an example of a copyrighted work you might find on the Internet, and explain how copyright law protects the creator of the work.

Practice Academic Skills

Mathematics

4. Ahra set up a spreadsheet for her company's finances. For each month, she has information about earnings and expenditures. Create a monthly spreadsheet to display this data that includes an equation for total cash flow.

    CONCEPT **Spreadsheets** Spreadsheets are basically tables, with rows and columns, used to display information. Computer spreadsheet programs can perform operations automatically when you input an equation into the row or column in question.
    Step 1: Consider which data categories should go in the columns and rows.
    Step 2: Create an equation for total cash flow using earnings and expenditures. Create another line for this data as well.

     For math help, go to the Math Appendix located at the back of this book.

Resources

⊙ **ExamView Assessment Suite CD** allows you to print out ready-made unit and chapter tests complete with answer keys. You can also create customized tests.

CLOSE

Culminating Activity
Software in the Workplace Have students create a chart with three columns: computer applications they already know well, computer applications they would like to learn better, and specific ways they can build their software knowledge.

TechSavvy

Going High-Tech with Wi-Fi

Answer Questions may include: How does wireless networking work? How much does it cost? What hardware and software is required? How do I maintain and troubleshoot it?

N C L B Activity correlated to Mathematics standards.

Section 17.2 After You Read

Review Key Concepts

1. A spreadsheet program would be a good choice for keeping track of sales figures because it allows you to calculate totals and trends and transform figures into graphs and charts.
2. E-commerce is the buying and selling of goods and services on the Internet.
3. Copyrighted works include images, text, music, videos, and software.

Copyright law protects the creator by forbidding others to copy, reuse, distribute, or alter the work, or claim it as their own.

Practice Academic Skills

4. Equation for total cash flow:
Total Cash Flow = Earnings – Expenditures
Spreadsheets should resemble this example.

	Jan.	Feb.
Earnings		
Expenditures		
Total		

Discussion Starter

Information Technology
Ask students to brainstorm different job functions involved with information technology—including tasks related to designing, building, maintaining, troubleshooting, hardware, software, Web sites, and multimedia. (Students may mention writing software, designing and coding Web pages, setting up computer networks, providing technical support, and repairing computers.)

W Writing Support
Independent Practice

Citing Sources Point out to students Daza's comment that "the Internet is always changing." Ask them to research ways that the Internet is currently changing and to write a paragraph—quoting specific sources—summarizing current trends in Internet use or Web technology. (Reports may cite trends such as social networking, blogging, content-on-demand, free online courseware, mobile Web, or the shift to broadband.)

C Critical Thinking

Making Inferences Ask students what qualities they think would help an independent businessman or contractor like Daza stay focused and on schedule. (Daza mentions a good work ethic, attention to detail, and pride in his work. Students may also mention time-management skills, self-discipline, interest in one's work, and motivation to succeed on one's own.)

392

CAREER SPOTLIGHT

Career Cluster: Information Technology

Herden Daza
Online Investigator

Q: Describe your job.
A: Using a computer and high-speed access to the Internet, I browse through peer-to-peer networks in search of music and movie piracy. I report my findings to the copyright holders.

Q: Describe a typical workday.
A: I get in at around 9 A.M., fire up the two Web browsers and some peer-to-peer applications, and start searching through a list of Web sites and networks for suspicious activity. Mainly I look for the illegal downloading of mainstream musical artists and movies. I may also answer a few e-mails from clients. Then I take a lunch break, do more searching, and go home.

Q: What skills are most important to you in your job?
A: Being both computer-savvy and able to utilize intensive Internet research methods allows me to be effective in this line of work. Communicating accurately and succinctly is another important skill, especially when I correspond with clients via e-mail. You'd be surprised how many people can't express themselves well.

Q: What academic skills and lifelong learning skills are helpful in preparing for your career?
A: Strong reading and writing skills are very useful, as well as some foreign language training for the international projects. Having patience, focus, and a good work ethic also helps me stay productive during my lengthy hours behind the desk and on the Web.

Q: What is your key to success?
A: My attention to detail and my ability to adapt have served me very well. Because the Internet is always changing, you need to able to adjust to it.

Q: What are some disadvantages of your career?
A: High-profile client jobs can require extra hours. For example, we may look for Internet users downloading a feature film or highly anticipated album before its official release.

Q: What training and preparation do you recommend for students?
A: Study a foreign language or three! It can only make you more valuable to your employer. More importantly, get as much working experience as you can outside of the classroom environment, because the sooner one becomes acclimated to the world of work, the sooner one can begin to succeed in it.

Q: What are some ways you recommend students prepare for this career?
A: To prepare for a career in this industry, you must be very familiar with the Internet (both its content and the delivery of the content) and research methods. Also, one should learn how to convey one's thoughts in a professional and succinct manner.

Q: What do you like most about your work?
A: I like knowing that everything I do directly affects how people use the Internet.

 For more about Career Clusters, go to this book's OLC through **glencoe.com**.

NCLB NO CHILD LEFT BEHIND

Teaching Tip

To help students meet the NCLB Act's goal of mastering computer technologies, include technology components in assignments where possible:

• Incorporate software tasks into writing assignments. For example, specify that students must spell- and grammar-check their documents or format them to certain specifications.

• Help students evaluate the information they find online by asking them to cite and describe the online sources they use for research assignments.

Sample Question: Ask students to make a list of criteria to use to evaluate whether the information on a specific Web site is reliable.

- **Education or Training** There are no formal education requirements for most online investigator jobs, although many investigators have college degrees. The ability to use computers and the Internet is a job requirement.

- **Academic Skills Required** English Language Arts, Mathematics, Science, Social Studies, World Languages

- **Technology Needed** Online investigators require high-speed access to the Internet as well as a computer and the ability to use current software.

- **Aptitudes, Abilities, and Skills** Most employers look for individuals with advanced Web and research skills and who possess ingenuity, persistence, and assertiveness. Investigators must be able to present the facts in a concise, organized manner.

- **Workplace Safety** Online investigators can work long hours, and should also pay attention to ergonomics and prevent muscle strain caused by repetitive tasks.

- **Career Outlook** Employment of detectives and investigators is expected to grow faster than the average for all occupations over the next ten years. The increase in criminal activity on the Internet, such as identity theft, spamming, e-mail harassment, and illegal downloading of copyrighted materials will increase the demand for online investigators.

- **Career Path** Online investigators may become consultants or form their own companies.

Academic Skills Required to Complete Tasks

Tasks	English Language Arts	Mathematics	Science	Social Studies	World Languages
Set up and maintain computer workstation	★	★	★		
Review/prepare list of sites	★	★		★	
Monitor Internet for clients	★		★		★
Monitor Internet for foreign clients	★			★	★
Customer service	★				★
Write reports	★			★	★
Keep up with Internet trends	★			★	

Critical Thinking

Can an online investigator go too far and invade an Internet user's privacy?

NCLB This chart relates academic skills such as English Language Arts, Mathematics, Science, Social Studies, and World Languages to specific tasks that are performed for the job featured in the Career Spotlight feature.

Critical Thinking

It is possible for any investigator to accidentally infringe on a user's privacy. However, students may argue that people forfeit their right to privacy when they commit illegal acts.

ASSESS

Make Connections

Ask students to describe how strong skills in English Language Arts would help them use the software applications discussed in Section 17.2, such as word-processing and presentation software. (Reading skills are essential to understand instructions and process information quickly, while writing skills are needed to create organized, error-free documents using the software.)

CLOSE

Culminating Activity

Technology and Career Clusters Ask students to choose a career cluster that interests them and to research and describe how workers in this cluster might use computer applications. For example, doctors and nurses in the health science career cluster might use a database program to keep track of patients' medical records or a Web browser to read online medical journals. (Students' descriptions will vary but should be based on reliable career information.)

Key Terms and Academic Vocabulary Review

1. Students should use each of the key terms and academic vocabulary terms in a complete sentence. A sample answer might read: "A *database* lets you search, sort, and update records, such as people's names and addresses or the products stored in a warehouse."

Review Key Concepts

2. Technology is changing the workplace by enabling new employment patterns and greater worker mobility, by promoting globalization, greater inclusion, distance learning, and specialization, and by making lifelong learning and technological literacy more important.

3. Skills needed to work in a technological environment include knowing how to use computers to process information, how to select the right technology in a given work situation, how to use the technology to accomplish specific tasks, and how to maintain and troubleshoot technology tools.

4. Common computer programs used in business include word-processing, database, presentation, desktop-publishing, spreadsheet, and telecommunications software, as well as Web browsers.

5. Businesses use the Internet for multiple purposes, including communicating and sharing information, buying and selling goods and services, advertising, providing customer service, conducting research, and recruiting employees.

6. Copyright is legal protection for the creator of a work that makes it illegal for anyone but the copyright holder to copy, change, or otherwise use or distribute a work. As more and more personal

---

CHAPTER SUMMARY

Section 17.1

Technology is a big part of the workplace. Computers are the main tool of information technology. A computer is made up of hardware and software. The two main types of software are operating systems and application software. Information technology has made the workforce more mobile and has contributed to globalization, to the greater inclusion of workers with disabilities, the rise of online learning, and the need for lifelong learning. Today, career success requires technological literacy, which is knowledge about technology and the ability to use it.

Section 17.2

Word-processing software creates text-based documents. Spreadsheet programs organize and calculate numbers. Database programs store and organize records. Presentation software creates presentations. Desktop publishing software lets you create printed documents. Telecommunications software enhances communication. The Internet is a network of computer networks and is the home of the World Wide Web. It offers quick communication and access to information, and enables e-commerce. Legal issues raised by the Internet include copyright protection, online privacy, identity theft, and spam.

Key Terms and Academic Vocabulary Review

1. Use each of these key terms and academic vocabulary words in a sentence.

Key Terms
- technology (p. 377)
- information technology (p. 377)
- computer (p. 377)
- laptop (p. 379)
- globalization (p. 380)
- assistive technology (p. 380)
- word processing (p. 385)
- database (p. 385)
- presentation software (p. 385)
- desktop publishing (p. 385)
- spreadsheet (p. 386)
- e-commerce (p. 388)
- copyright (p. 389)

Academic Vocabulary
- fundamental (p. 377)
- shift (p. 379)
- archives (p. 388)
- author (p. 389)

Review Key Concepts

2. Explain how technology is transforming the workplace.
3. Identify the skills needed to work in a technological environment.
4. Name computer programs commonly used in business and explain their use.
5. Describe business uses of the Internet.
6. Describe copyright and other laws that affect how we use technology.

Critical Thinking

7. Evaluate A coworker is preparing to desktop-publish an essay about environmental hazards in industry. She plans to state that the work is her own, even though the essay appeared recently in a magazine. This is illegal, but is it also unethical? Why or why not?
8. Predict What transferable technology skills do you think could help you succeed in any career you decide to pursue? Why?

---

data is collected and shared, online privacy is a growing issue. Spam is illegal but common "junk" e-mail. Identity theft is the illegal use of others' personal information for financial gain.

Critical Thinking

7. Students should recognize that publishing another person's work as one's own is unethical because it takes credit from the original creator of the work and because it deceives readers into believing that the work is original. It is also unethical in this specific case because it may wrongly cause supervisors to believe that the work is the intellectual property of the company.

8. Important transferable technology skills include using computer hardware and peripherals, using icons and menus to use operating systems and computer applications, selecting and troubleshooting technology, and knowing how to seek out and learn new information about technology.

Real-World Skills and Applications

Accountability and Social Responsibility

9. Understanding Copyright Visit the Web sites of two organizations that take a public position on copyright and file-sharing. Read what the organizations believe about file-sharing and copyright. Compare and contrast two organizations' positions in a graphic organizer. Present your graphic organizer to the class and share what you have learned about the issue of intellectual property.

Self-Management Skills

10. Creating a Lifelong Learning Plan Choose a career field that interests you. Research and list the technology knowledge and skills required for an entry-level job in that field. Then research and list the technology skills and knowledge that would help you succeed as a leader in that career field.

Create a lifelong learning plan that lists different ways you can develop that knowledge and skill over the course of your career. Brainstorm and include as many creative ways to develop your skills as you can.

Technology Applications

11. Understanding Technology and Productivity Choose one of the following technologies: automated phone systems, online learning, computer aided drafting (CAD), e-commerce, social networking, assistive technology, blogging, or online banking. Define the technology and describe how people use it. Use the Web and other resources to research how the tool has affected productivity at home, at school, and on the job. Does it save time or money, bring people together, or improve the quality of people's lives? Use word-processing software to create a one-page summary of your research.

12. **Understanding Globalization** Find a large company that has a location close to your home. You might choose a retailer, a bank, a manufacturer, or another type of company. Interview a manager at the company and ask about how the company is involved in the global economy. For example, does the company buy or sell products overseas? Summarize your findings in a one-page report.

13. **Asking for Help**
Situation You were recently hired to work as a marketing assistant at a large corporation. Even though you were honest about your lack of technological expertise during the interview process, your supervisor has been assigning you tasks that are far beyond your skill level. You are afraid that you will be perceived as incompetent if you speak up, but at the same time, you feel overwhelmed by some of the assignments you have been given.
Activity Role-play a situation in which you express your concerns to your new supervisor. Plan how you will present your side of the situation, and make sure to present a reasonable solution to the problem at hand.
Evaluation You will be evaluated based on how well you meet the following performance indicators:
- Present workplace problems in a mature, cooperative manner.
- Pose reasonable solutions to improve your work situation.

Chapter 17 Technology in the Workplace **395**

---

11. Students' research will vary based on the technology chosen. Example: computer-aided drafting (CAD) has moved the focus of design in architecture, design, and engineering from the drafting table to the computer, has allowed designers to more quickly and accurately develop and test designs, and may also contribute to the safety, reliability, and structural integrity of products such as bridges, airplanes, and so on.

ACTIVE LEARNING

12. Students' reports should reflect the fact that almost every business is involved in the global economy in some way—whether by buying parts overseas, hiring immigrant workers or outsourcing labor, facing competition from international competitors, or retooling products and services to appeal to consumers in foreign markets or of varied cultural backgrounds.

ROLE PLAY

13. Role plays should be assessed based on how well the student presents the issue to his or her supervisor and on the quality of the solutions proposed. A possible script might read, "As I mentioned in our initial interview, I am still building skills in many design applications. I appreciate the confidence you show by giving me new design assignments, but on the Smith Project I felt that my work would have been much more professional if I had more advanced skills in Illustrator. The local community college is offering a 12-week course in Illustrator on Friday afternoons that I would like to attend. Is that something the company might be able to cover?"

Real-World Skills and Applications

9. Graphic organizers should reflect the fact that organizations that represent creators, such as the Recording Industry Association of America (RIAA), the Motion Picture Association of America (MPAA), and the Association of American University Presses, believe in strict copyright protections and controls on file-sharing. Other organizations, such as the American Library Association, the Electronic Frontier Foundation, and Google, believe in a greater balance of power between copyright holders and users that allows for the freer distribution of information.

10. Students' lists will vary; some careers require much more advanced technology skills at the entry level than do others. However, students should recognize that leaders in career fields must know much more about all relevant technologies than entry-level workers.

Academic Skills in the Workplace

14. Students should mention some or all of the following: communication, distribution, and digital design in communications and the arts; product design and testing, automated manufacturing, basic research, and computer modeling in engineering, industry, and science; diagnostic technology, computerized record-keeping, biometrics, and computerized training in health and human services; and e-commerce, international communication, online marketing in business and marketing. Examples of specific technologies include Microsoft® Word, MRI machines, and Web-publishing tools such as Flash or Dreamweaver.

15. The total population of both countries is 1,371 million, or 1.371 billion (1,306 million + 65 million = 1,371 million or 1.371 billion).

16. Ten computers would be affected the first round (10 × 1 = 10); 100 computers would be affected after the second round (10 × 10 = 100).

17. Research and timelines will vary based on the career field chosen. A student interested in medicine might mention the shift from paper to computerized medical records and from in-person to online communication between patients and health providers, as well as the development of computerized diagnostic tools and other new medical technologies. Students should understand that many fields that were once not heavily dependent on technology now require even entry-level workers to be technologically literate.

Academic Skills in the Workplace

English Language Arts

14. Creating a Report Use the Internet to research how technology is used in these four career areas: communications and the arts; engineering, industry, and science; health and human services; and business and marketing. List three primary uses of technology in each of these career areas. Then name and define a specific type of technology related to each of the three uses. List the URLs you used as the sources.

Mathematics

15. Representing Large Numbers Scott wants to create an Internet ad for China and Thailand and must calculate the combined population of the two countries. If China has 1.306 billion people, and Thailand has 65 million, what is the total population?

CONCEPT **Adding Large Numbers** When you add larger numbers, make sure that they are expressed in the same form.

Starting Hint Express the number for China's population, *1.306 billion,* as 1,306 million, and then add. Remember that one billion is the same as one thousand million.

Science

16. Using Powers of 10 One computer virus infects a computer's e-mail system and sends itself to every e-mail contact in that computer's e-mail address book. If each computer it infects afterward has an average of 10 e-mail addresses in its address book, the number of computers infected in each round would follow this pattern: 10N, where N = round of spreading. How many computers would be infected after the second round?

Social Studies

17. Research Technological Change Choose a career field that interests you. Research how technology has changed in that field over the last ten years and what technology tools are the industry standard and how these have changed over the last decade. Also find out how the importance and reach of technology has changed in the field, and how the technology skills needed to advance in that career field have changed. Then develop a timeline covering the last ten years depicting change in the career field you chose.

STANDARDIZED TEST PRACTICE

TRUE/FALSE QUESTIONS

Directions Read each statement. On the blank line, write "T" if the statement is true, "F" if the statement is false.

Test-Taking Tip Make sure you understand the full statement. All parts of a statement must be correct for the statement to be true. Statements that contain extreme words, such as *all, none, never,* or *always,* or that have unsupported opinions, are often false.

____ **1.** Technological change contributes to globalization.

____ **2.** Spam is unsolicited e-mail that tries to sell you something or spread viruses.

____ **3.** Your online passwords should be easy for anyone to figure out.

For more Standardized Test Practice, go to the OLC *glencoe.com.*

STANDARDIZED TEST PRACTICE

Answers
1. T
2. T
3. F

Test-Taking Strategies
Whether your students have a standardized test coming up in a few days or a few weeks, this test-prep tip will help them to relax and do their best.

True/False True/false tests tend to have more true statements than false ones. True/false statements are usually straightforward, so encourage students not to waste time looking for hidden meanings or "trick" statements. If a statement seems obviously true, it probably is!

Writing Skills Practice

18. Writing Instructions Good instructions transform complex tasks into a clear series of steps. Good instructions are so important that most hardware and software firms hire specialists, known as technical writers, to write their instruction manuals.

Practice Choose a computer program or other technology tool you know well. Write a one-page instruction sheet to help a novice do a specific task. For example, you might explain how to upload an image to a Web site.

- Begin by breaking the task down into steps.
- Write one sentence describing each step. Make sure that each sentence is clear and easy to follow.
- Check that your steps are listed in the correct order.
- Review your instructions by following them yourself—you may spot something you missed, or steps that are unclear.

Net Connection

19. Interview a Freelancer Arrange an interview with a person who works as a freelancer or who telecommutes. Ask this person about advantages and disadvantages of this work arrangement. Share your findings with the class, and describe how you think the trend toward telecommuting might affect your career.

@ Log On Search the Internet for freelance or contractual job opportunities in a field that interests you. Go to **glencoe.com** for links to help you with this activity. In a one-page summary, list three jobs that you find especially appealing and explain why.

Reading Connection

@ Go to this book's Online Learning Center through **glencoe.com** for a list of reading suggestions.

Personal Academic and Career Portfolio

Showcasing Technology Skills

The best way to show an employer what you know about technology is by creating a portfolio showing what you can do with it! As you research the career field that interests you, pay special attention to the hardware, software, and other technology tools that are current in the field. Then, practice using the tools to enhance your portfolio.

The following guidelines will help you organize and add the results of your research and your growing skills to your portfolio:

- Create a new section for your portfolio and label the section *Technology Skills.*
- You may wish to create subsections with names such as *Software, Hardware,* or *Programming Languages.*
- Add the following: a list of hardware and software with which you are familiar, along with portfolio pieces that show your mastery of these tools; a list of current technology for the career field that interests you; and an action plan to improve your technology skills that lists when, where, and how you will develop your skills. You could also include a list of print or online resources, such as technology magazines or Web sites that provide reliable information and reviews of current computer technology. You could also include a glossary of technology terms.
- Update your Portfolio as you gain more experience.

@ Portfolio Help Go to the *Succeeding in the World of Work* OLC through **glencoe.com** for help developing your portfolio.

Writing Skills Practice

18. Instructions should be clear, correctly sequenced, grammatically correct, and free of jargon, with specific calls to action using imperative verbs. Instructions should be clear to a person who has never performed the task before. Examples: 1) Turn on your computer. 2) Launch the program by double-clicking the program's icon on your computer desktop. 3) After the program opens, create a new file by holding down the "Ctrl" key and the letter *n* at the same time.

Net Connection

19. Summaries should include three jobs and explanations of why they are appealing.

Resources

⊙ ExamView Assessment Suite CD allows you to print out ready-made unit and chapter tests complete with answer keys. You can also create customized tests.

WorkKeys

WorkKeys® is a job skills assessment program. For information on leveled assessment for Problem-Solving Skills (Applied Mathematics; Applied Technology; Locating Information; and Observation), go to the WorkKeys link on this book's OLC through **glencoe.com**.

Personal Academic and Career Portfolio

Maintaining a Portfolio

Students who are comfortable with technology may wish to format their **Personal Academic and Career Portfolios** entirely in digital form. They may choose examples of their best work to format as PDFs or as Web pages, which they can attach to e-mailed job applications or, ideally, upload to a Web site of their own. They can also upload examples of work created in various standard software programs, such as Microsoft® Word and Excel. Encourage students to format their résumés in various electronic formats, including PDF and HTML. Most word-processors allow users to create files for the Web (with the extension .html or .htm) without extensive knowledge of HTML code.

Chapter Resources Planning Guide with Activities and Features

Section	Features	Activities
Section 18.1 **Manage Your Time**	Math in Action (p. 401) Everyday Ethics (p. 402) 21st Century Workplace (p. 404) Career Checklist (p. 405)	Before You Read (p. 400) Graphic Organizer (p. 400) As You Read (p. 402) After You Read (p. 405)
Section 18.2 **Organize Your Work**	Real-World Connection (p. 408) Creative Business Practices (p. 408) Hot Jobs! (p. 409)	Before You Read (p. 406) Graphic Organizer (p. 406) As You Read (p. 407) After You Read (p. 409)

NCLB Activities, information, and skills practice will help your students attain No Child Left Behind proficiency. Students will improve their abilities in the following academic standards areas:

Academic Standards Correlations

Discipline	Standard	Feature/Activity
English Language Arts	**NCTE 1** Read texts to acquire new information.	Everyday Ethics (p. 402) Creative Business Practices (p. 408) Hot Jobs! (p. 409)
	NCTE 9 Develop an understanding of diversity in language use across cultures.	21st Century Workplace (p. 404)
	NCTE 12 Use language to accomplish individual purposes.	Real-World Connection (p. 408) Writing Skills Practice (p. 415)
Mathematics	**Problem Solving:** Solve problems that arise in mathematics and in other contexts	Math in Action (p. 401)
	Algebra: Represent and analyze mathematical situations and structures using algebraic symbols	After You Read (p. 405)
	Data Analysis and Probability: Formulate questions that can be addressed with data and collect, organize, and display relevant data to answer them	Academic Skills in the Workplace (p. 414)
Science	**Science as Inquiry:** Abilities necessary to do scientific inquiry	Academic Skills in the Workplace (p. 414)

21st Century Skills and Workplace Competencies Correlations

CORRELATIONS The charts show the 21st Century Skills, foundation skills, and workplace competencies that students develop as they work in this chapter.

Foundation Skills and Workplace Competencies Correlation Chart

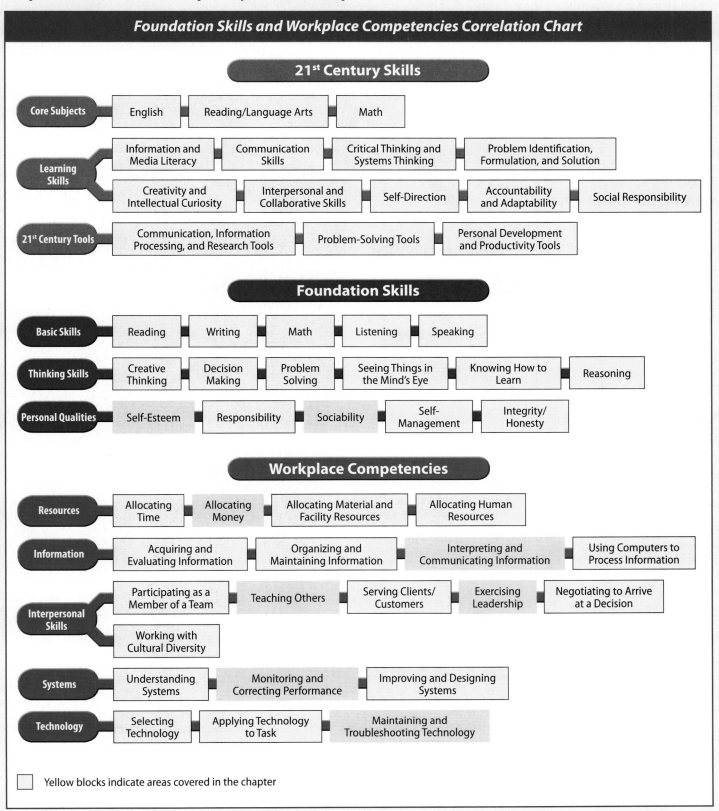

21st Century Skills

Core Subjects: English | Reading/Language Arts | Math

Learning Skills: Information and Media Literacy | Communication Skills | Critical Thinking and Systems Thinking | Problem Identification, Formulation, and Solution | Creativity and Intellectual Curiosity | Interpersonal and Collaborative Skills | Self-Direction | Accountability and Adaptability | Social Responsibility

21st Century Tools: Communication, Information Processing, and Research Tools | Problem-Solving Tools | Personal Development and Productivity Tools

Foundation Skills

Basic Skills: Reading | Writing | Math | Listening | Speaking

Thinking Skills: Creative Thinking | Decision Making | Problem Solving | Seeing Things in the Mind's Eye | Knowing How to Learn | Reasoning

Personal Qualities: Self-Esteem | Responsibility | Sociability | Self-Management | Integrity/Honesty

Workplace Competencies

Resources: Allocating Time | Allocating Money | Allocating Material and Facility Resources | Allocating Human Resources

Information: Acquiring and Evaluating Information | Organizing and Maintaining Information | Interpreting and Communicating Information | Using Computers to Process Information

Interpersonal Skills: Participating as a Member of a Team | Teaching Others | Serving Clients/Customers | Exercising Leadership | Negotiating to Arrive at a Decision | Working with Cultural Diversity

Systems: Understanding Systems | Monitoring and Correcting Performance | Improving and Designing Systems

Technology: Selecting Technology | Applying Technology to Task | Maintaining and Troubleshooting Technology

Yellow blocks indicate areas covered in the chapter

CHAPTER 18

Introduce the Chapter

Chapter 18 informs students of techniques that can help them make the best use of their time and knowledge.

Section 18.1 introduces time-management skills and helps students learn to use their time wisely.

Section 18.2 focuses on how to organize information and make decisions about which documents are important to keep and for how long.

Build Background

Ask students what they think is meant by "using time wisely." Ask them to give examples of occasions when it is important to use time wisely. (Students should point out that using time wisely means to use it effectively or efficiently. It would be important to use time wisely when taking a timed test, meeting a project deadline, or following a recipe.)

▶ Exploring the Photo

Caption Answer Time management would be essential for underwater divers, because they need to be aware of how much time they can spend underwater with the amount of oxygen they have in their tanks.

Discussion Lead a discussion by asking how students have managed their time today. (Answers will vary, but most students need to manage their time in order to get to school on time and to get from class to class on time.)

CHAPTER 18
Time and Information Management

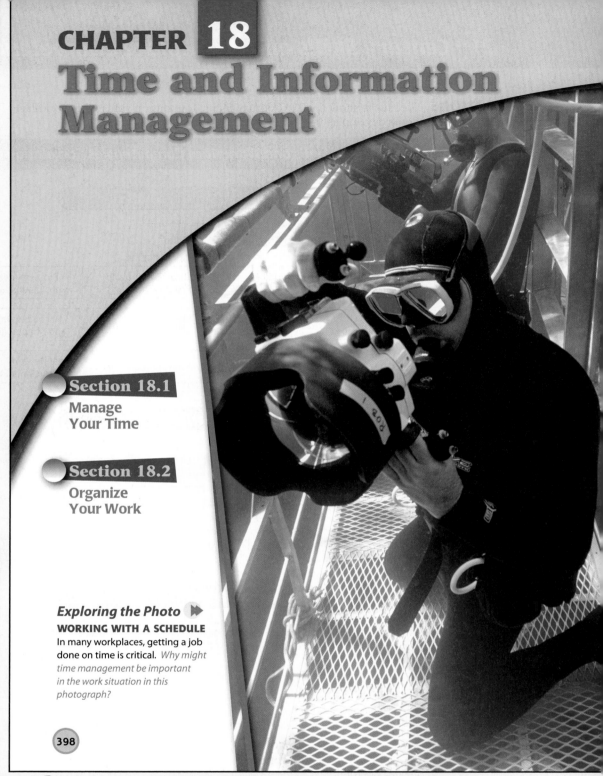

● Section 18.1
Manage Your Time

● Section 18.2
Organize Your Work

Exploring the Photo ▶▶
WORKING WITH A SCHEDULE
In many workplaces, getting a job done on time is critical. *Why might time management be important in the work situation in this photograph?*

398

📖 Classroom Resources

- 📁 Student Edition
- 📁 Teacher Wraparound Edition
- 📁 Student Activity Workbook with Academic Integration
- 📁 Student Activity Workbook with Academic Integration TAE
- 📁 *Fast File*, Unit 5 Resources

- 📁 Inclusion in the Career Education Classroom
- ⚙ TeacherWorks™ Plus
- ⚙ *ExamView Assessment Suite*
- ⚙ Interactive Chalkboard
- ⚙ Interactive Student Edition
- 🖊 Online Student Edition
- 🖊 Online Learning Center (OLC) with Podcasts

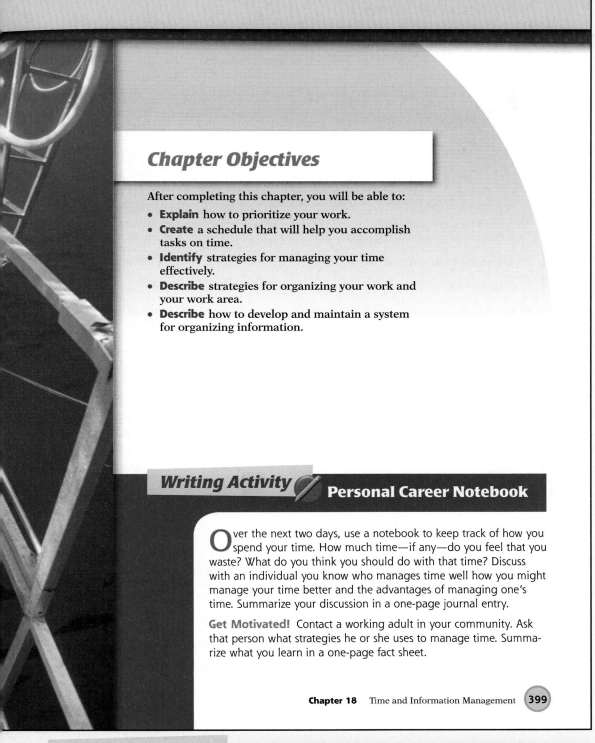

Chapter Objectives

After completing this chapter, you will be able to:

- **Explain** how to prioritize your work.
- **Create** a schedule that will help you accomplish tasks on time.
- **Identify** strategies for managing your time effectively.
- **Describe** strategies for organizing your work and your work area.
- **Describe** how to develop and maintain a system for organizing information.

Writing Activity — Personal Career Notebook

O ver the next two days, use a notebook to keep track of how you spend your time. How much time—if any—do you feel that you waste? What do you think you should do with that time? Discuss with an individual you know who manages time well how you might manage your time better and the advantages of managing one's time. Summarize your discussion in a one-page journal entry.

Get Motivated! Contact a working adult in your community. Ask that person what strategies he or she uses to manage time. Summarize what you learn in a one-page fact sheet.

Chapter 18 Time and Information Management **399**

Writing Activity — Personal Career Notebook Answer Guide

In their journal entries, students should discuss if and how they waste their time, and what time-management suggestions they received from the person with whom they spoke.

Get Motivated! Fact sheets should include time-management strategies given by a working adult.

Review the Objectives
Introduce the chapter by reviewing the chapter objectives:

Section 18.1 Objectives
Explain how to prioritize your work. (Prioritize by deciding the order of importance of different tasks.)

Create a schedule that will help you accomplish tasks on time. (Create a schedule by assigning each task a particular time, noting when it will start and end. Many people use a calendar, day planner, computer planning software, or a personal digital assistant to schedule.)

Identify strategies for managing your time effectively. (Use your downtime to get ahead on a job or improve your skills; avoid procrastination; be flexible; look for ways to combine tasks; make the best of telephone time; use other people's time well by limiting discussions to work-related matters; write down issues to address before speaking to coworkers; and be mindful of your supervisor's time.)

Section 18.2 Objectives
Describe strategies for organizing your work and your work area. (Organize your work area by using the near-far rule; put similar things together; decide how you are going to store the items that you use; take time occasionally to put your work area back in order.)

Describe how to develop and maintain a system for organizing information. (Establish importance of information; set up a file system; and manage electronic information.)

Manage Your Time

Bell Ringer Activity

Manage Your Time

Have students list at least five habits they have that prevent them from getting things done on time (for example, spending too much time on the telephone). Then ask students how they could eliminate some of the things that waste their time. Use this discussion to introduce the time-management process.

Resources

Interactive Chalkboard
The Interactive Chalkboard CD provides visual teaching aids for this section.

Online Learning Center
The Online Learning Center (OLC) through **glencoe.com** features chapter vocabulary, chapter summaries, and other study materials.

Preteaching

Write the key terms from this section on the board. Have students describe how each term relates to using time efficiently.

Graphic Organizer

Tell students to go to the OLC through **glencoe.com** for a printable graphic organizer. (Graphic organizers should list the five steps in the time-management process.)

NCLB connects academic correlations to book content.

Reading Guide

Before You Read

Preview Read the Key Concepts. Write one or two sentences predicting what the section will be about.

Read to Learn

- How to prioritize your work
- How to create a schedule that will help you accomplish tasks on time
- Strategies for managing your time effectively

D **Main Idea**
Knowing how to prioritize tasks and manage your time will help you complete your work and achieve your goals.

Key Concepts

- The Time-Management Process
- Other Tips for Managing Time

Key Terms

- timeline
- schedule
- downtime

Academic Vocabulary

You will find these words in your reading and on your tests. Use the academic vocabulary glossary to look up their definitions if necessary.

- estimate
- indicate

Graphic Organizer

As you read, list the steps in the time-management process. Use a chart like the one shown to help organize your information.

The Time-Management Process
1.
2.
3.
4.
5.

 Log On Go to this book's Online Learning Center through **glencoe.com** for an online version of this graphic organizer.

NCLB
Academic Standards •

English Language Arts
- Read texts to acquire new information. (NCTE 1)
- Develop an understanding of diversity in language use across cultures. (NCTE 9)

Mathematics
- Solve problems that arise in mathematics and in other contexts
- Represent and analyze mathematical situations and structures using algebraic symbols

Reading Guide

Before You Read

Explain to students that they already plan their weekdays around their school schedule. Ask if they schedule how to use free time outside of class. Ask what kinds of activities might go on such a schedule.

D **Develop Concepts**
Main Idea Discuss the main idea with students. Ask: Have you ever been told that you are wasting your time? What do you think was meant by such a comment?

The Time-Management Process

Does time often get away from you? Do you put off studying and then stay up late to get ready for an exam? In today's fast-paced workplace, time can be hard to manage, and the consequences of missing a deadline can be serious. On the job, how well you manage your time affects not just you, but other people, too—your coworkers and your employer. If you miss a deadline, your company may lose money or business. The best way to prepare yourself to get a task done on time is to learn to manage your time.

Think of time management as making choices. When you have work to do, you have to decide which task to do first. If you have just a few tasks, the decision is easy. If you have many tasks, though, the time-management process can help you use your time more effectively. These are the steps of the time-management process:

1. List all your projects, appointments, and other tasks.
2. Break big projects into smaller tasks or steps.
3. Prioritize the tasks.
4. Estimate the time needed to complete each task.
5. Create a schedule for your tasks.

Make a List

R

To choose, you must know your choices, so first make a task list. Write down every project, appointment, or task you have. List those due today and those due in the days and weeks ahead. Next to each, write the date or time it must be completed.

Math In Action

Calculate Time
It takes Jen 38 minutes to prepare one of the gift boxes she sends to her clients during the holidays. How many hours will she spend preparing 30 boxes?

Starting Hint: Before you calculate *hours*, determine *minutes*.

 For more math practice, go to this book's OLC through **glencoe.com**.

 DEADLINES In the workplace, your work always affects others. *What might happen to your coworkers if your work is not completed on time?*

TEACH

Discussion Starter
The Time-Management Process Write these descriptions on the board: *work on several projects at the same time; like to plan what to do but have trouble carrying out plans; can't make decisions about what to do first; everything must be perfect, even if it is late;* and *work on projects only at the last minute.* Have students choose one of the above types that best describe their approach, and ask volunteers to explain why they fit that type.

R Reading Strategy
Making Written Lists Take a quick survey and ask how many students make "mental lists" but do not make written lists. Ask how a written list can be more effective than a mental one. (Students might point out that it is easier to forget things from a mental list. Written lists also help when making choices about what needs to be done first.)

NCLB Activity correlated to Mathematics standards.

Math In Action

Jen will spend 19 hours preparing the boxes (38 minutes × 30 boxes = 1,140 minutes; 1,140 minutes ÷ 60 minutes in an hour = 19 hours).

Resources

 TeacherWorks™ Plus
The TeacherWorks software includes customizable built-in lesson plans and links to printable program resources.

401

Extend the Photo

Caption Answer Answers may include the following: Not completing your work can also affect the tasks of your coworkers. Their work might also be late. They might not be as successful as they would otherwise be. They might not receive the raises or promotions that usually result from success at work.

Discussion Invite a local business manager who regularly evaluates employees on how they manage their time to speak to the class about employers' attitudes toward the use of time.

TEACH (cont.)

C Critical Thinking

Managing Time Tell students to imagine they have been assigned a major report that is due in two weeks. Ask how they could break the project into small steps. Students might want to consider steps such as finding ideas, reading and research, writing, revising, desktop publishing, and proofreading.

S Skill Practice

Prioritizing Tasks Tell students that it is often easy to feel overwhelmed by everything they need or want to do. Have students prioritize three short-term goals (to be met within the next two to three weeks) and three medium-term goals (covering the next two to three months). Have students rank their goals in order of importance. Ask: Are any medium-term goals dependent upon their meeting a short-term goal?

As You Read

It might be easier to estimate how long it will take to complete smaller steps, which will help you manage your time on the larger project.

Everyday ETHICS

WHOSE MISTAKE?

Do you share responsibility for a coworker's errors?

BILLING ERRORS You work in a doctor's office. When you are not helping patients, you and the other office assistants process bills to send to insurance companies. One of your colleagues works well with the patients, but makes many billing mistakes. You have spoken to her about her mistakes, but she said it does not matter because the doctor makes a lot of money.

What Would You Do? Will you talk to the doctor about your colleague? Should you be held responsible for her mistakes? Why or why not?

DISCUSS IT In the workplace, if you and your colleagues share a task, you may be held responsible for any mistakes that are made. Discuss with a partner ways to resolve this problem and the possible consequences of each.

As You Read

Explain How might breaking a large project into steps help you manage your time?

Break Big Projects into Small Steps

Look at the major projects on your list. The best way to handle large projects is to break them into steps. Then treat each step as a separate task.

If you were an assistant manager at a restaurant and were asked to hire a new waiter, for instance, you might break the job into the following steps: (1) Place classified ads, (2) Schedule and conduct interviews, and (3) Meet with the manager to make hiring decisions.

One strategy that may help you break a job into steps is to imagine yourself working through the job. Note each task you see yourself doing. This process is called *visualization*.

Prioritize Your Tasks

If your task list is long, do not worry. You do not have to do everything at once. Successful time management means doing the most important things now and saving the less important tasks for later. You have to prioritize your tasks, which means to order them from first to last or from most to least important.

The following guidelines may help you prioritize your tasks:

- Assign numbers or letters to tasks according to their importance. For example, an important task might be assigned the letter A or the number 1, while a less important task might be assigned the letter B or the number 2.
- Remember that your most important job is the one you were hired to do. If you are a salesperson, for instance, your main task is to sell.
- Do not forget the final tasks on a job, such as cleaning up or filing a report.
- If you are part of a team, divide tasks among team members.

Everyday ETHICS

What Would You Do? Answer Students should consider the number of mistakes made by the other employee, their position, and the doctor's possible office policies regarding such matters.

DISCUSS IT One possibility would be to politely point out the mistakes to your colleague and ask how you can help her avoid making mistakes in the future. Another possibility would be to assess your and your colleague's strengths, and break tasks down into smaller steps, in which your colleague can complete steps she does well.

Estimate Time

The next step is to **estimate** how long each task will take. If you have done the job before, base your estimate on past experience. If not, ask your supervisor or someone with experience how long it should take. If a job depends on other people, be sure to allow for their time.

Create a Schedule

Finally, you need to fit the tasks into a timeframe. One helpful tool is a **timeline**, a chart that shows the order in which events occur. To complete a timeline for a project, you begin with today and end with the date the project is due, then you plot the tasks along the line in the order they must be done. A timeline helps you to see the big picture.

Another important tool for managing time is a **schedule**, which is a list or chart that shows when tasks must be completed. To create a schedule, you assign each task a particular time, noting when it will start and end. You must be sure that all the tasks for a project are done in the correct order and that they are all completed by the project deadline. **Figure 18.1** gives an example of a schedule. A schedule helps you to see what you need to do at a particular time.

◤ Vocabulary

You can find definitions in the **Key Terms** glossary and **Academic Vocabulary** glossary at the back of this book.

Figure 18.1   **A DAILY SCHEDULE**

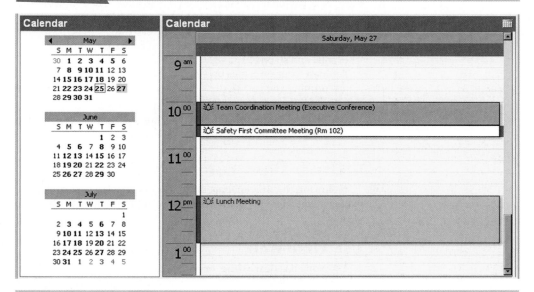

TO DO TODAY   A schedule shows what you have to do over a given period of time. *Why is it important to keep your schedule up-to-date?*

TEACH *(cont.)*

Discussion Starter

Set Up a Schedule Ask students whether they think ahead to the next few days in order to decide what they need to do, or if they wait until something demands their time and then do it.

ⓢ Skill Practice
Guided Practice

Allocating Time Have students create schedules for the weekend, including errands, recreational activities, study time, work, and household responsibilities. Then have them create timelines that show when and how long they will do each item.

ASSESS

Review Key Terms

Have students write sentences using each key term.

Online Study Tools

Have students go to the OLC through **glencoe.com** to:

- Download **Podcast** study tools.
- Download free **Study-to-Go** content to their PDAs or cell phones.

Resources

ExamView Assessment Suite CD allows you to print out ready-made unit and chapter tests complete with answer keys. You can also create customized tests.

EXTEND THE FIGURE   **Figure 18.1**

Caption Answer Schedules should be kept up-to-date in order to adjust priorities or the timeline.

Discussion Ask: What are the benefits of keeping a schedule on your computer instead of in a day planner? What might be the drawbacks?

RETEACH

Discussion Starter

Use Time Well Have students keep a log for the next three days and record the amount of time they spend socializing on the telephone, surfing the Net, and watching television. Discuss whether there were things they had planned to do but could not find the time for. What are other ways they waste time?

W Writing Practice
Independent Practice

Conduct Interviews Have students interview three people—parents, friends, neighbors, or relatives—and ask what types of time-management techniques they use on their jobs. Have students write three paragraphs that include information about the jobs, time-management strategies, and the benefits of the strategies for the people who are interviewed.

Resources

📁 **Student Activity Workbook** Assign the Chapter 18 activities in the Student Activity Workbook.

N C L B Activity correlated to English Language Arts standards.

The 21ˢᵗ Century Workplace

N C L B

Portuguese Beyond Portugal

Portuguese is the official language of Brazil, the largest country in South America. It is also an official language of Portugal, Mozambique, Angola, Macao, and East Timor.

The Portuguese spoken in Portugal differs from the Portuguese spoken in Brazil and Africa. For example, the word *apelido* means "first name" in Portugal, but "nickname" in Brazil. Portuguese is closely related to Spanish, so if you know Spanish, you may be able to understand simple sentences in Portuguese.

CRITICAL THINKING _____

Do you think understanding Spanish would make it easier or more difficult to learn Portuguese?

In Your Community

Find two people in your community whose native language is not English. Interview them about the greatest challenge they encountered while learning English.

COMMON BRAZILIAN PORTUGUESE WORDS AND PHRASES	
hello	alo, oi
goodbye (informal)	tchau
yes	sim
no	não
please	por favor

@ Extend Your Learning Some English words, such as *molasses* and *cobra*, come from Portuguese. Words borrowed from another language are called *loanwords*. For links to Web sites about loanwords, go to this book's OLC through **glencoe.com**.

Many people use a calendar, day planner, computer planning software, or a personal digital assistant to schedule. The following tips will help you create an effective schedule:

- Schedule difficult tasks for times of the day when you perform best.
- Color code your schedule. Use different colors for homework, events, and so on.
- **Indicate** your priorities on your schedule. This will help if you are running late.
- Check off tasks as you complete them.

For your schedule to be useful, you must keep it current. Take a few minutes every morning to update it and plan.

Other Tips for Managing Time

W Following the time-management process is part of effective time management. Here are some other strategies for making the best use of time.

Use Time Well

Everyone has **downtime**, or occasional periods when no tasks are scheduled. Use your downtime to get ahead on a job or improve your skills. Avoid procrastination, or putting off what you need to do. If a job has to be done, start right away. Be flexible. If something happens to disrupt your schedule, move on to something else on your schedule. Look for ways to combine tasks.

 404 **Unit 5** Professional Development glencoe.com

The 21ˢᵗ Century Workplace

CRITICAL THINKING ANSWER Knowing Spanish could help you learn Portuguese because the two related languages share a great deal of vocabulary, as well as many grammatical forms and sounds. However, the very similarity of the two languages could also become confusing. It might be difficult to remember which of two similar words belongs to which language, for example.

In Your Community In their interviews, students should identify the native languages of the people they have interviewed, and they should specify the challenges they encountered when learning English.

Make the best use of telephone time: Before calling, list all of the questions that you would like to be answered. Set a time limit for your phone calls, and stick to business. Set aside a time each day for calls. If someone is unavailable, give a time when you will call back. You could also consider using e-mail rather than calling.

Use Other People's Time Well

When you work with other people, be aware of how you use their time. Limit your discussions and phone calls to work-related matters. If you have downtime, do not start personal conversations. Before you speak with busy coworkers, write down the issues you need to address. At meetings, ask only relevant questions.

Be especially mindful of your supervisor's time. When you are assigned a task, listen carefully. Ask questions if you do not understand. Then you will not have to interrupt your supervisor later to ask questions or to ask for help.

Career ✓ **Checklist**

To Delegate Effectively:

✓ Be clear when assigning responsibilities. Put tasks in writing.

✓ Be available to answer any questions.

✓ Remember that it is your responsibility to ensure that the job gets done.

✓ Delegate or assign tasks respectfully.

✓ Give your coworkers ownership and trust them.

Section 18.1 After You Read

Review Key Concepts

1. Describe how you would prioritize these tasks if you were a shoe-store salesperson: Give a customer change, return a call from a supplier, and read a business magazine. Explain your answer.
2. Identify the steps involved in setting up a schedule.
3. Describe the strategies you would use to manage your time in this situation: Your two supervisors have both given you projects due on the same day.

Practice Academic Skills

 Mathematics

4. Francine would like to work no more than 40 hours a week, and she expects 20% of her salary to go to taxes. Create an inequality that represents the possible hourly wages that Francine should look for in order to end up with weekly take-home pay of $600 or more.

   CONCEPT **Solving Inequalities** When solving an inequality, perform the same operations on either side of the inequality for it to remain valid. For example, if you add 5 to one side of the equation, you must add 5 to the other side.

   Step 1: Using the variable x to represent the hourly wage, write an inequality to solve the problem. The total take-home pay ($600) will be on one side and before-tax income (40 hours multiplied by the hourly wage, x) subtracted by taxes on that income ($0.2 \times 40x$) on the other.

   Step 2: Solve the inequality, making sure to represent the answer as an inequality as well.

    For math help, go to the Math Appendix located at the back of this book.

ASSESS

After You Read
Have students complete the Section 18.1 After You Read section review.

Online Study Tools
Have students go to the OLC through **glencoe.com** to:

- Take the Section 18.1 **Practice Test**.
- Download **Podcast** study tools.
- Download free **Study-to-Go** content to their PDAs or cell phones.

CLOSE

Culminating Activity
Sharing Tips Have students write 500-word articles for the school newspaper giving time-management tips to their fellow students. Tell students to include an appropriate headline and topic sentence. Evaluate articles for correct grammar and punctuation. Articles should include strategies mentioned in this section.

NCLB Activity correlated to Mathematics standards.

Section 18.1 After You Read

Review Key Concepts

1. Students should point out that the salesperson should give the customer change first, because a salesperson's primary responsibility is helping customers. The salesperson should return the call to the supplier second, because the magazine article can be read during downtime.
2. To set up a schedule, schedule difficult tasks for the time of the day when you perform your best; color code your schedule; indicate your priorities on the schedule; and check off tasks as you complete them.
3. Students might mention prioritizing tasks by importance; making a task list for each project; and deciding which project is most important to finish that day, and which could be finished the next day.

Practice Academic Skills

4. Francine would need to earn $18.75 per hour ($600 \leq 40x - (0.2 \times 40x)$; $600 \leq 40x - 8x$; $600 \leq 32x$; $18.75 \leq x$).

FOCUS

Bell Ringer Activity

Organize Your Work

Ask students to visualize their work or study space at home. What do they see? How many would say their study areas are neat, messy, or somewhere in between?

Resources

Interactive Chalkboard
The Interactive Chalkboard CD provides visual teaching aids for this section.

Online Learning Center
The OLC through **glencoe.com** features chapter vocabulary, chapter summaries, and other study materials.

Preteaching
Ask students to guess at how a subdirectory is different from a directory. As they read the section, have students check their guesses against the text.

Graphic Organizer
Tell students to go to the OLC through **glencoe.com** for a printable graphic organizer. (Graphic organizers should list ways to organize work areas and information.)

NCLB connects academic correlations to book content.

406

Organize Your Work

Reading Guide

Before You Read

Preview Choose a Key Term or Academic Vocabulary word that is new to you. Write it on a piece of paper. When you find it in the text, write down the definition.

Read to Learn
- Strategies for organizing your work and your work area
- How to develop and maintain a system for organizing information

Main Idea
Strong organizational skills will enable you to work more efficiently and to be more productive.

Key Concepts
- Organize the Work Area
- Organize Information

Key Terms
◆ access
◆ directory
◆ subdirectories

Academic Vocabulary
You will find this word in your reading and on your tests. Use the academic vocabulary glossary to look up its definition if necessary.
■ logical

Graphic Organizer
As you read, list ways to organize your work area and information. Continue adding your own ideas to the list after you have finished reading. Use a chart like the one shown to help organize your information.

Ways to Organize Your Work	
Your Work Area	**Your Information**
1.	1.
2.	2.

Log On Go to this book's Online Learning Center through **glencoe.com** for an online version of this graphic organizer.

Academic Standards ·
English Language Arts
- Read texts to acquire new information. (NCTE 1)
- Use language to accomplish individual purposes. (NCTE 12)

Reading Guide

Before You Read
Ask students how they organize their paper and electronic files. (Some students will mention keeping both paper and electronic files in file folders and electronic folders. Others may answer that they do not have any particular organizational system.)

D Develop Concepts
The Main Idea Ask: Why do you think it is important to develop a system for organizing information? (Answers will vary. Explain to students that most jobs require workers to retrieve, use, and share important information with other employees, which makes organizational skills imperative.)

406

Organize the Work Area

You have learned strategies for using your time effectively. What else can you do to work faster and better? You can organize the things in your work area. No matter how skilled you are at your job, you can work more efficiently if you can find the tools or materials you need quickly.

Put Everything in Its Place

One rule for organizing a work area is the *near-far rule*. This means that you should place the things you use most often near you and those you use seldom farther away. For example, plumbers often carry a toolbox. The toolbox contains the tools of the trade they use most frequently. The tools they seldom use they keep in the truck.

A second guideline is to put similar things together. Keep files, supplies, and tools used for one type of job together.

Decide how you are going to store the items you use. You might use boxes, drawers, or files. Be sure to label your storage containers. If you have lots of boxes or files, alphabetize them, group them by content, or organize them in some other way. Doing this will enable you to find things easily.

Neatness Counts

Neatness can also save you time. Take time occasionally to put your work area back in order. Return tools to their correct places. Tidy and reorganize your desk. This way, you will not have to spend time searching for things.

 As You Read

Explain What are the advantages of organizing your work space?

✓ **Reading Check** **IDENTIFY** What are some strategies for organizing your work space?

 GET ORGANIZED
Organizing your work space will help you work more efficiently. *What items might this person use frequently?*

TEACH

Discussion Starter
Organize the Work Area
Have students imagine that their boss, who is on an international phone call, asks them for the plans for a new office the company is building for the client on the phone. Ask: How would neatness enable students to quickly locate the plans?

As You Read
You can use your time more effectively if your work space is organized.

✓ **Reading Check**
IDENTIFY Keep things you use frequently nearby; keep similar things together; label storage containers and decide how you are going to store them.

Resources
TeacherWorks™ Plus
The TeacherWorks software includes customizable built-in lesson plans and links to printable program resources.

ASSESS

Review Key Terms
Have students write sentences using each key term.

Online Study Tools
Have students go to the OLC through **glencoe.com** to:
- Download **Podcast** study tools.
- Download free **Study-to-Go** content to their PDAs or cell phones.

Extend the Photo

Caption Answer This woman most likely uses her cell phone, calculator, and computer most frequently.

Discussion Ask students how they can make study areas at home more efficient.

407

RETEACH

S Skill Practice

Independent Practice

Allocating Material and Facility Resources Tell students to keep track of how much time they spend looking for things for a one-week period. Have each determine a system he or she could use to be more efficient about storing and organizing books, keys, and other possessions. Have students write a report summarizing their findings from keeping track of what they looked for, and detailing how their new organizational system will help them be more efficient.

Resources

📁 **Student Activity Workbook** Assign the Chapter 18 activities in the Student Activity Workbook.

 Real-World *Connection*

Critical Thinking Answer Workers who show up late often cause problems for themselves and for other members of their work team. Team members will cover for a coworker on occasion, but often will not tolerate long-term negligence of work responsibilities that cause other team members more work. Negligence is often easily observed by supervisors when the same work is continually not done. The weak team member will often lose their job.

Do Your Own Research In their reports, students might mention that both students and workers are subject to discipline for tardiness.

 Real-World *Connection*

Tardiness

You routinely arrive early for your job. One of your coworkers usually shows up just ahead of the boss, and then leaves early. She always says she arrived earlier than she did. As a result, work is left unfinished, which gives you and your other coworkers more to do.

Critical Thinking What should you and your coworkers do?

Do Your Own Research Research the tardiness policies of one or two companies as well as your school's tardiness policy. Write a one-page report comparing the school and company tardiness policies. What is the purpose of these policies? What are the consequences of tardiness under each policy?

Organize Information

If you handle a lot of information, you should organize it. Otherwise, it will lose its usefulness. A good library, for example, contains vast amounts of information. It is only useful, however, if the information is organized so that you can access it. To **access** means find and use.

Establish Importance

The first step in managing information is to establish its importance. Is this something you or someone else needs to know or act on? Is it something you may need later? If you answer these questions with a "no," you may discard the information.

If the information is important, do something with it immediately. If possible, avoid putting the information in a *pending file*, or holding file, because then you will have to spend time working on or accessing it more than once.

Set Up a File System

If you might need to refer to a paper document later, file it. Put your documents in file folders, then group the folders in hanging files. Following these guidelines will help you set up a file system:

- Categorize information. You might organize documents by customers or projects.
- Label each file and hanging folder.

Creative Business Practices

GOLDMAN SACHS   **Healthy Employees**

85

The global banking and investment firm of Goldman Sachs Group wants its employees to have healthy, well-balanced lives. To help employees do that, the firm began the Wellness Exchange. The Wellness Exchange ensures that established health centers, child-care facilities, medical staff, physical therapists, and fitness and wellness centers are available near or within the buildings where employees work. The Wellness Exchange program is part of the firm's strategy to attract and keep the best employees.

CRITICAL THINKING   How might this program help Goldman Sachs attract good clients?

 Connect to the Real World For more information about Goldman Sachs, visit the company's Web site via the link on this book's Online Learning Center through **glencoe.com**.

Creative Business Practices

CRITICAL THINKING ANSWER Not only does the Wellness Exchange generate good public relations for Goldman Sachs, but clients might also be more likely to gravitate towards the company, because they would benefit from working with a company that has healthy and well-adjusted employees who are more likely to perform well.

- Avoid putting each document in a separate file. Group documents by type.
- Avoid large files. Separate documents by subtopics.
- Color-code folders or labels. For example, use green for one project and blue for another.
- File on a regular basis. Try to file papers the day you receive them.
- Review your files regularly and discard those you do not need.

Manage Electronic Information

Much essential information enters offices as computer files and e-mail. Managing electronic information is as great a challenge as managing paper documents.

Many of the rules for managing paper documents also apply to managing electronic files. Do not clutter your files with information you do not need. Make a separate directory for each category of information. A **directory** is a computer file that contains many files on a broad topic, such as a project.

Do not let directories get too full; create new subdirectories. **Subdirectories** are smaller groupings of files within a directory. For example, you may have a directory for XYZ Company. You might create subdirectories for orders and correspondence.

Name your computer files carefully. Select logical, descriptive names that you will be able to remember in six months. It is also helpful to keep a written record or hard copy of file names.

To ensure that you do not lose the information stored on your computer, you should back it up, or make a copy of it, regularly. You can back up information onto CDs, DVDs, and other hardware. Information you might want to copy may include contact information and important files such as your **Personal Academic and Career Portfolio**.

HOT JOBS!

Epidemiologist

Epidemiologists study and track illnesses and epidemics within specific populations. They use statistics, math, science, and medicine to identify and prevent the further spread of disease. An epidemiologist may work within a single hospital or travel around the world.

Section 18.2 After You Read

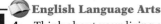

Review Key Concepts

1. Describe the near-far rule and explain how it can help you be a more productive worker.
2. List three tips for setting up a system for organizing information.
3. Explain why it is important to back up your computer files.

Practice Academic Skills

English Language Arts

4. Think about your living space. Is it organized? Can you find things easily? Write a one-page journal entry about how you could better organize and design your living space.

@ Check your answers at this book's OLC through **glencoe.com**.

ASSESS

After You Read
Have students complete the Section 18.2 After You Read section review.

Online Study Tools
Have students go to the OLC through **glencoe.com** to:
- Take the Section 18.2 **Practice Test**.
- Download **Podcast** study tools.
- Download free **Study-to-Go** content to their PDAs or cell phones.

Resources

 ExamView Assessment Suite CD allows you to print out ready-made unit and chapter tests complete with answer keys. You can also create customized tests.

CLOSE

Culminating Activity
Organizing the Personal Academic and Career Portfolio Have students create charts showing how they are organizing their career-related materials in their **Personal Academic and Career Portfolio**. For example, students might have a folder for letters responding to job ads, and others for materials describing specific careers. Tell students to draw a folder representing each topic, then list beneath it the types of documents they file in that folder. Have students share their charts in class.

 Activity correlated to English Language Arts standards.

Section 18.2 After You Read

Review Key Concepts
1. Using the near-far rule means placing things you use most often near you and those you use seldom farther away. Using this rule saves time getting the things you use most often.
2. Establish the importance of the information; set up a file system; and manage electronic information.
3. Back up computer files to prevent stored information from being lost.

Practice Academic Skills
4. In their journal entries, students should describe their current living space and provide specific examples from this section of how they could better organize the space.

CAREER SPOTLIGHT

FOCUS

Discussion Starter

Health Science Lead a discussion about the various types of careers that can be found in this career cluster. Have students brainstorm different careers and jobs within the career cluster. (Answers will vary but should show an understanding of the many types of careers that fall within the Health Science career cluster.)

TEACH

W Writing Support
Independent Practice

Design a Poster Kanthi points out that she must follow safety guidelines while operating the equipment she uses. Have students go online and research radioactive safety requirements and create a poster that would show other employees how to maintain a safe workplace using these safety measures.

C Critical Thinking

Health and Technology
Why is it important for a nuclear medicine technologist to learn about new procedures, machines, and techniques? (Answers will vary but should reflect an understanding that a goal of both science and technology is to look for ways to better understand how each field can be advanced through research and development.)

CAREER SPOTLIGHT

Career Cluster: Health Science

Kanthi Murali
Nuclear Medicine Technologist

Q: Describe your job.
A: I'm a nuclear medicine technologist for a hospital. I perform diagnostic tests on patients using imaging equipment.

Q: Describe a typical workday.
A: I meet with patients to carefully explain test procedures and answer any questions they may have. I prepare radioactive chemical compounds that will be used in a test, and administer that compound to the patient. During testing, I usually operate special equipment that scans the patient's body and takes images of areas being tested. I am always very careful to follow strict safety guidelines so as not to expose others and myself to radioactive materials. I carefully record test results and sometimes discuss those results with physicians and others in my department. Sometimes my work involves research; looking for abnormalities or ways in which radioactive materials react within the body.

Q: What skills are most important to you in your job?
A: Listening skills are important in order to understand the needs of my patients. The desire to care for and help others, compassion and patience, and the ability to pay close attention to detail are also important.

Q: What academic skills and lifelong learning skills are helpful in preparing for your career?
A: Students should have a special love of math, physics, anatomy, and physiology. They should have a constant thirst for learning about new procedures, machines, techniques, and ways of finding abnormalities.

Q: What is your key to success?
A: I love knowing that what I do can make a difference in someone's life. I also enjoy learning and like to be challenged every day.

Q: What training and preparation do you recommend for students?
A: Students should visit a hospital and spend time with a nuclear medicine technologist before committing to this profession. A bachelor of science degree with special training in nuclear medicine is preferable.

Q: What are some ways you recommend students prepare for this career?
A: Do well in high school science classes. Be curious about medicine and what advances might lie ahead. Search the Internet for recent developments in nuclear medicine.

Q: What do you like most about your work?
A: Every day I look forward to doing something different and new. Every case is different. Because I receive different assignments each day, I am constantly challenged. Technology changes and new treatments are continually developed for diseases. I enjoy the ability to help those who are sick, and to make a difference in their lives.

 For more about Career Clusters, go to this book's OLC through **glencoe.com**.

N C L B NO CHILD LEFT BEHIND

Teaching Tip

The goals of the NCLB Act include a strong emphasis on reading comprehension. After students have carefully read the Career Spotlight, ask the following question.

Sample Question What three recommendations does Kanthi make for students who want to pursue a career in nuclear medicine? (Do well in science classes; be curious about medicine and advances; and search the Internet for recent developments.)

410

Education or Training An associate or bachelor's degree in science, with special certification in nuclear medicine is preferred. One-year certificate programs are available for health professionals who already possess an associate degree but who wish to specialize in nuclear medicine.

Academic Skills Required English Language Arts, Mathematics, Science, Social Studies

Technology Needed You must be able to work with computers and complex equipment, such as MRI (magnetic resonance imaging) machines, scanners, cameras, and other imaging equipment.

Aptitudes, Abilities, and Skills Problem-solving and critical-thinking skills, communication and other interpersonal skills, sensitivity to the needs of patients, attention to detail, ability to follow instructions and the ability to work as part of a team. Mechanical ability and manual dexterity are needed to operate complex equipment.

Workplace Safety Maintaining good physical strength is important because technologists are on their feet much of the day and may need to lift or turn patients. Although radiation exposure is possible, it is kept to a minimum by the use of protective devices and by following strict radiation safety guidelines. Technologists wear badges that measure radiation levels.

Career Outlook Employment of nuclear medicine technologists is expected to grow faster than the average for all occupations over the next ten years.

Career Path Technologists may advance to supervisory roles. Some technologists specialize in a particular area of medicine, while others may leave patient care to work in research laboratories, to teach, to work for medical equipment manufacturing firms, or to become radiation safety officers.

ASSESS

Make Connections
Kanthi mentions that listening skills are important for understanding patients' needs. In what other ways would listening skills be important for a nuclear medicine technologist? (Kanthi also needs good listening (and English language) skills when discussing results with physicians and others in her department. She would also need to listen carefully when learning about new safety requirements and other procedures.)

CLOSE

Culminating Activity
Lifelong Learning and Career Clusters This Career Spotlight mentions that health professionals with an associate degree who want to specialize in nuclear medicine can enroll in a one-year certificate program. Have students research one such program and write a 250-word paragraph summarizing the program, its requirements, and cost.

Academic Skills Required to Complete Tasks

Tasks	English Language Arts	Mathematics	Science	Social Studies
Prepare radioactive chemical compounds		★	★	
Explain test procedures to patients	★	★	★	★
Administer compounds		★	★	
Operate technology to create diagnostic images		★	★	
Keep records of patients' results	★	★	★	★

NCLB

Critical Thinking
Why must nuclear medicine technologists monitor the levels of radiation to which they are exposed?

NCLB This chart relates academic skills such as English Language Arts, Mathematics, Science, Social Studies, and World Languages to specific tasks that are performed for the job featured in the Career Spotlight feature.

Critical Thinking
Nuclear medicine technologists must monitor radiation levels because high exposure to certain types of radiation can be harmful to humans.

Key Terms and Academic Vocabulary Review

1. Students should write complete sentences using each term correctly. A sample sentence might read "I keep a *schedule* to help me remember the appointments and meetings I need to attend."

Review Key Concepts

2. Prioritize tasks by deciding the order of importance for different tasks. This may be accomplished by assigning letters or numbers to tasks according to their importance. Also remember that the most important task is the one you were hired to do. Do not forget final tasks, such as cleaning up or filing a report, and if you are part of a team, divide tasks among team members.

3. The time-management process helps you use time effectively. This process involves making a task list, breaking large projects into smaller steps, and prioritizing each task. Additional time-management tips include color coding your schedule; transferring priorities from your task list to your schedule; and checking off tasks as you complete them.

4. Two additional tips for managing time well are to use downtime well, and to use other people's time well.

5. Strategies for organizing the work area include putting everything in its place; storing frequently used things close at hand and seldom used things farther away; and putting similar things together. If you store things in boxes, label them and alphabetize them or group them by content.

6. Organizing paper documents and organizing electronic information

both involve using a filing system. Keep only important information and set up a filing system: categorize information; label each file and hanging folder; group documents by type; divide massive files by subdividing them by subtopics; color code folders or labels; file on a regular basis; sort files ever so often; get rid of files; at the end of each day, leave your desk free of stray papers; store documents on your computer, but be sure to back up files.

CHAPTER SUMMARY

Section 18.1

The time-management process can help you use time effectively. First, make a task list. Second, break large projects into smaller steps. Next, prioritize each task. Then decide how long each task will take to complete. Finally, set up and mantain a schedule. Other time-saving strategies include making good use of downtime, avoiding procrastination, and being flexible when something interrupts your plans. In the workplace, you should also be aware of how you use other people's time. Discuss only work-related matters and listen to assignments carefully.

Section 18.2

Organizing your work area will help you work efficiently. Use the near-far rule and place things you use often near you and those you use seldom farther away. Place similar things together. To organize information, create a file system and review documents to determine their importance and discard those you do not need. Tips for creating a file system include creating folders and labels. Many of the rules for managing paper documents apply to managing electronic information. You must regularly back up electronic files to prevent the loss of important information.

Key Terms and Academic Vocabulary Review

1. Use each of these key terms and academic vocabulary words in a sentence.

Key Terms
- timeline (p. 403)
- schedule (p. 403)
- downtime (p. 404)
- access (p. 408)
- directory (p. 409)
- subdirectories (p. 409)

Academic Vocabulary
- estimate (p. 403)
- indicate (p. 404)
- logical (p. 409)

Review Key Concepts

2. **Explain** how to prioritize your work.
3. **Describe** the time-management process.
4. **Identify** two strategies other than the time-management process for managing your time effectively.
5. **Describe** strategies for organizing your work area.
6. **Compare** the process of organizing paper documents and the process of organizing electronic information.

Critical Thinking

7. **Explain** In managing your time, why should your emphasis be on getting the most important things done rather than on getting everything done?
8. **Analyze** In what ways might a disorganized work area waste time?

Critical Thinking

7. You should emphasize getting the most important things done because you may not have time to finish all of your tasks. Getting the most important things done helps ensure that you finish these tasks without hurrying and possibly creating errors.

8. If the work area is disorganized, you won't know where to find the tools, materials, and other items you need.

Real-World Skills and Applications

Allocating Time

9. Creating a Task List You have been asked to plan your company's annual employee picnic. To start, you must break the assignment into manageable parts. Think of all the things you have to do to prepare for the picnic. Create a task list and prioritize the tasks. Then create a timeline showing how you will complete the tasks in time for the picnic.

Information Literacy

10. Organizing and Maintaining Information Documents on the following topics have arrived on your desk: revised employee insurance policy, company holidays for next year, winter hours for the company gym, vacation policy, flu shots covered under your health plan, how to file for health insurance coverage, New Year's Day work schedule, and an information sheet on gym membership. Create a chart showing how you would organize the documents in files and folders. Assign each document to a file and folder. Name each file and folder.

Technology Applications

11. Creating Directories List two jobs that interest you. On a computer, use the operating system's file manager to create two new directories or folders for these jobs. Title the directories with the job names. Inside each, create three subdirectories. You might create subdirectories for education or training needed, pay, advancement, or benefits. Title the subdirectories. Create a flow chart showing the organization of the directories and subdirectories.

---

12. **Managing Your Time** With a partner, brainstorm different ways to manage your time effectively. List the different strategies. Then research using library resources or the Internet to find information about time management. If searching the Internet, use the key words *time management* and *productivity*. Create a list of the time-management tips you find. Share your lists with the class.

---

13. **Improving Efficiency**

Situation At work you frequently communicate with business clients across the country. To save travel time and expenses, you often participate in conference calls. These calls are essential, but they consume a large part of your day. You need to make your conference calls more efficient so that you have more time to work on other tasks.

Activity Role-play a conference call in which you address a job-related matter with a business client. To make the conference call as productive as possible, use the time-saving strategies and tips for making telephone calls discussed in the chapter.

Evaluation You will be evaluated based on how well you meet the following performance indicators:

- Utilize time-saving strategies to make a conference call efficient.
- Effectively and politely handle matters with client(s).
- Present a realistic, well-developed conference call.

---

the gym hours and gym information documents.

11. Students should create two separate directories for the two different jobs. Directories should be titled and contain subdirectories, which should also be titled. Students should also create flowcharts that accurately show how their two directories and the subdirectories are organized.

12. Partners should first brainstorm and make a list of ways to manage time efficiently. They should then create list of time-management tips they found through research. When sharing their lists with the class, students might compare what they brainstormed with what they found when they researched.

ROLE PLAY

13. Students should design a role-play activity in which they present a realistic and efficient conference call in a professional, rehearsed manner.

Real-World Skills and Applications

9. Task lists might be prioritized in the following order: Decide on the date and time, choose and arrange for the location, select the menu, oversee food preparation, line up entertainment, make alternate plans for bad weather, and set up on the day of the event. In their timelines, students should demonstrate an understanding that certain tasks, such as deciding on a date and time, need to be done well in advance of other tasks, such as setting up on the day of the event.

10. Students should file documents with similar topics together and avoid setting up files containing only one document. For example, a *Health* folder can be created for the insurance policy, flu shot, and health insurance coverage documents; a *Holiday/Vacation* folder can be created to file the holiday and vacation policy documents, and the New Year's Day work schedule; and a *Gym* file can be created to hold

Academic Skills in the Workplace

14. He should postpone the meeting with the distributor; deal with the mail, e-mail, and faxes tomorrow; delegate authority to experienced salespeople for completing the inventory, choosing the sale items, and providing the camcorder training; and cancel lunch with his sister.

15. Choosing names from the phone book is the best option.

16. Reports should show research on the subject of time management in the global workplace.

Academic Skills in the Workplace

English Language Arts

14. Create an Outline Outlining is a way to organize information. When you outline a topic, you create a structure for what you are going to write. You might use a numbering system or bullets to identify subtopics. Use library and Internet sources to research ways to manage information in the workplace, including information in paper documents and on the computer. Write a one-page outline of the information you find.

Mathematics

15. Select Data Randomly For a project that analyzes how people in the workplace manage their time, you are planning to conduct interviews with members of the community. To be sure that your data sample is as unbiased as possible, you want to randomize your choice of interviewees. Would it be better to select interview subjects from the directory of the local professional organization, talk to people at a workplace nearby, or pick names out of the phone book?

CONCEPT) Randomization Randomizing data prevents bias from influencing the results. To randomize data, select a sampling method that involves no prior information about the group being sampled.

Starting Hint Eliminate any group that defines a specific population—for example, selecting interview subjects from only a high school group would mean that your data would not represent the age range, education levels, or other characteristics of the community.

Social Studies

16. Research Time Management Across Cultures People in different cultures have different ways of understanding and using time. This can be a challenge for businesses doing business in the global workplace. Research cultural perceptions of time management and productivity in a country other than the United States using library and Internet resources. Summarize your findings in a one-page report.

STANDARDIZED TEST PRACTICE

MULTIPLE CHOICE

Directions Choose the phrase that best completes the following statement.

1. According to this chapter, the *near-far rule* is:

> **Test-Taking Tip** In a multiple-choice test, the answers should be specific and precise. Read the questions first, then read all the answer choices before you choose. Eliminate answers that you know are incorrect.

a. Place items you use often far from you and items you use seldom near you.

b. Place paper documents in files and files in folders.

c. Place items you use often near you and items you use seldom far from you.

d. Label the storage containers you place documents in with names you can remember.

For more Standardized Test Practice, go to the OLC @ glencoe.com.

STANDARDIZED TEST PRACTICE

Answer

1. c. place items you use often near you and items you use seldom far from you.

Test-Taking Strategies
Whether your students have a standardized test coming up in a few days or a few weeks, these last-minute test-prep tips and strategies will help students relax and do their best.

Test Timing Have your students take one or more timed practice tests so that they become comfortable with the test format.

Multiple-Choice Tests Tell students to read directions to multiple-choice tests carefully. Usually only one answer is required; however, sometimes more than one answer may be possible or necessary.

Writing Skills Practice

17. Write a Descriptive Essay A descriptive essay uses details to describe a person, place, or thing. Writing descriptive essays develops your awareness of your surroundings and your creative thinking skills.

 Practice Write a one-page essay describing your ideal work space. Follow these steps when writing your essay:

- Visualize the work space. Where are you? What are you doing? What tools are you using? How is the space organized?
- Use active verbs to describe the scene and create the mood. For example, if you wish to be a musician on a stage, you might use a phrase such as *the audience applauded loudly*.
- Use all your senses to describe the scene as well as you can.
- Edit your essay. Are all the words spelled correctly? Does each sentence make sense and add to the essay?
- Write a final draft, and then exchange essays with another student to learn about each other's ideal work space.

Net Connection

18. Research Planning Tools Develop a task list of all of your obligations, social events, and school assignments for the next month. Use a calendar to create a schedule for the month.

 Log On Go to this book's OLC through **glencoe.com** to find different planning tool options that can help you schedule. Choose one. Conduct research on the Internet to determine details about and the prices charged for this tool. Summarize your findings in a bulleted list.

Reading Connection
Go to this book's Online Learning Center through **glencoe.com** for a list of reading suggestions.

glencoe.com

Personal Academic and Career Portfolio

Time Management

In the workplace, you will be expected to perform given assignments in a certain timeframe. To prepare yourself for completing tasks on time, write a self-evaluation of your time-management skills. Ask yourself, do I procrastinate? Do I meet deadlines easily or do I scramble to get tasks done on time? Do I use any time-management tools? Then write a plan to improve your time-management skills. Include specific strategies you will use and how you will keep track of your schedule. Add both your self-evaluation and your time-management plan documents to your portfolio. Use the following guidelines:

- To write a self-evaluation: Write a list of questions about your time-management skills. Answer each one honestly. Give examples.
- To write a plan to improve: Read your self-evaluation. Identify areas that need improvement. Write a plan that addresses each area with a specific strategy for improvement.
- Add a folder to your portfolio. Title the folder *Time Management*. Add these documents to the folder.
- Choose one item from your improvement plan and begin doing it today.
- Return to this folder every week and start applying another self-improvement strategy until you have started them all.

 Portfolio Help Go to the *Succeeding in the World of Work* OLC through **glencoe.com** for help developing your portfolio.

Writing Skills Practice

17. Descriptive essays will vary, but all should describe the student's ideal work space.

Net Connection

18. Students should create a calendar that reflects their school duties, social engagements, and other relevant obligations for one month. After investigating organizational tools, students should select resources appropriate for their needs, and conduct research to find out the prices, features, and availability of such items.

 Resources

ExamView Assessment Suite CD allows you to print out ready-made unit and chapter tests complete with answer keys. You can also create customized tests.

WorkKeys

WorkKeys® is a job skills assessment program. For information on leveled assessment for Problem-Solving Skills (Applied Mathematics; Applied Technology; Locating Information; and Observation), go to the WorkKeys link on this book's OLC through **glencoe.com**.

Personal Academic and Career Portfolio

Maintaining a Portfolio

As students compile papers, articles, and other materials for their **Personal Academic and Career Portfolio**, they might want to create a second filing system for storing older materials they are not currently using. By using the electronic and paper storage systems outlined in Section 18.2, students can maintain as much material as they want.

Unit 5
Thematic Project

FOCUS

Discussion Starter
Ask students to name one form of technology they know how to use and to describe how they learned it. Did they learn by trial and error, though instruction, or by some other method? Which learning method do they think works best for them? Why? (Students' ideas will vary. Many people benefit from a combination of organized instruction, which provides fundamentals and a guide to best practices, and independent practice.)

STEP 1

Evaluate Your Skills and Resources
Have students go to the *Succeeding in the World of Work* OLC through **glencoe.com** for a graphic organizer they can use to organize the skills, tools, and resources they will use to complete the project.

TEACH

C Critical Thinking
Remind students that technology includes not only software programs, but also other tools, many of them computer-based, that help to extend human capability and make work more efficient. Ask students to brainstorm different kinds of technology used in fields such as agriculture, manufacturing, transportation, entertainment, health science, and public safety. (Students may mention farm tools and machinery, manufacturing robots, automated assembly line processes, audio and video recording equipment, digital animation, X-rays and MRI machines, and tasers.)

416

Mastering Technology

You have learned that in today's global workplace, being a skilled, responsible worker—a professional—requires many different skills. You need interpersonal, teamwork, and leadership skills; communication, decision-making, and problem-solving skills; and organization, time-management, and technology skills. In this project, you will build and enhance your technology skills by learning about the technology used in your desired career field and by using that technology to create your own creative project.

Project Assignment

- Research the kinds of technology used in your career field using a variety of resources, including newspapers, magazines, and trade journals, the Internet, and personal interviews with workers in your chosen field. Consider specific computer programs as well as other kinds of technology such as tools and machinery.
- Identify the three most important kinds of technology in your field. Write a three-page report that describes all three, assesses your ability to use each, and outlines a realistic plan for learning each.
- Choose one of the three technologies and use it to create a product that showcases your skills.

Lifelong Learning Connection

Lifelong learning concepts found in this project include:
- technology skills
- setting goals and making decisions
- your career plan and career path

STEP 1 Evaluate Your Skills and Resources

To complete this assignment, you will need access to the Internet and print resources. You will also need to talk to local employers and employees in your career field. To prepare your report, you will need access to a word-processing program. To complete your project, you will also need access to a workplace technology of your choice.

Skills you may need to complete the Unit Thematic Project include:
Academic Skills reading, writing, social studies
Transferable Skills communication, research, problem-solving, and decision-making skills
Technology Skills word-processing and Internet skills

@ Resources Organizer To find a graphic organizer you can use to determine the skills, tools, and resources you will need for this project, go to this book's Online Learning Center through **glencoe.com.**

glencoe.com

SPOTLIGHT ON TECHNOLOGY

Technology Breakthroughs
New technologies often develop out of basic research in mathematics and the sciences. For example, a software engineer named Tim Berners-Lee developed the hyperlink—the foundation of what we today know as the World Wide Web—to share information among researchers at a European lab for particle physics. Teenagers are inventing, too. Past winners of the Siemens Competition, for example, have created new building blocks for molecules, taught computers to recognize parts of speech, and converted the energy of ocean waves into electricity. Ask students to list the steps they would take to invent a new technology or product. (Identify a need or problem; brainstorm a solution and evaluate existing competition; make and test a prototype; build and patent the invention.)

STEP 2 Preview a Real-World Company Profile

Researching companies whose workers use technology on the job can help you understand what skills and education you will need to succeed in a high-tech job market. The company featured below is known for its innovative use of Web technology.

Real-World Company: Metacritic

Jason Dietz noticed that there was an abundance of reviews for movies, TV, books, music, and video games, but none of it was organized. Along with two friends, he turned the idea into a Web site, Metacritic.com. The popular site collates, summarizes, and averages critics' reviews and ratings about various entertainment releases, providing entertainment consumers with the big picture of how entertainment products are being viewed by both critics and other consumers.

The company was eventually bought by CNET Networks, a media company that delivers interactive content over the Web. Dietz' current tasks include managing music and TV content and serving as a liason between Metacritic and programmers and database developers. Dietz' previous experience as a business major and a law school graduate came in handy when he and his partners were developing a business plan and negotiating the sale, but he developed most of his technology and production skills studying other Web sites and experimenting on his own.

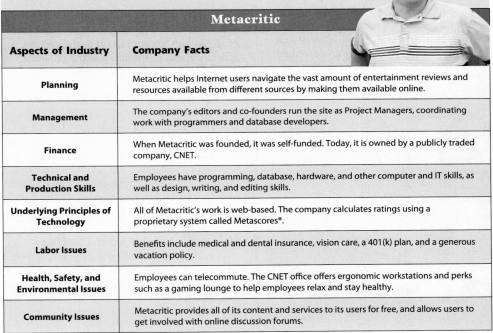

Metacritic	
Aspects of Industry	**Company Facts**
Planning	Metacritic helps Internet users navigate the vast amount of entertainment reviews and resources available from different sources by making them available online.
Management	The company's editors and co-founders run the site as Project Managers, coordinating work with programmers and database developers.
Finance	When Metacritic was founded, it was self-funded. Today, it is owned by a publicly traded company, CNET.
Technical and Production Skills	Employees have programming, database, hardware, and other computer and IT skills, as well as design, writing, and editing skills.
Underlying Principles of Technology	All of Metacritic's work is web-based. The company calculates ratings using a proprietary system called Metascores®.
Labor Issues	Benefits include medical and dental insurance, vision care, a 401(k) plan, and a generous vacation policy.
Health, Safety, and Environmental Issues	Employees can telecommute. The CNET office offers ergonomic workstations and perks such as a gaming lounge to help employees relax and stay healthy.
Community Issues	Metacritic provides all of its content and services to its users for free, and allows users to get involved with online discussion forums.

417

Developing Industry Partners

Recognize Partners

Offering your partners in business and industry as much recognition as possible can greatly contribute to the success and longevity of a school-business partnership. Here are a few suggestions to provide such recognition:

- Ask students to write school newspaper articles about local partners.
- Invite coverage from local media, such as newspapers and TV.
- Send memos or newsletters to parents about your business partners.
- Ask students to write thank-you notes and progress reports or to create banners or posters acknowledging the support of those businesses.

TEACH (cont.)

STEP 2

Preview a Real-World Company Profile

Tell students that many businesses work for years to make a profit before they become successful. For example, Metacritic's founders worked for six years without pay before their site was bought by CNET. Ask students whether they would be willing to see little financial profit for years in order to build a business that they believed would ultimately be successful. (Students' opinions will vary. Some students may enjoy the challenge of working hard and investing in their future success, while others may feel that they would prefer a path of less risk.)

W Writing Support

Independent Practice
Aspects of Industry

Explain to students that underlying principles of technology includes knowledge of technology, technology trends, the reasons to use particular technologies, and the foundations of technology. Ask students to imagine that they are in charge of deciding whether or not to implement a new software system at their company. What factors would they consider, and why? Ask students to write two paragraphs answering these questions and describing their decision-making process. (Opinions will vary but should consider costs versus benefits, efficiency, retraining time and cost, and company infrastructure. Students should follow an organized decision-making process such as the one outlined in Chapter 16.)

Unit 5 Thematic Project

TEACH (cont.)

STEP 3

Research Procedures
Have students go to the *Succeeding in the World of Work* OLC through **glencoe.com** for a graphic organizer they can use to organize the results of their research.

STEP 4

Connect to Community
Ask students whether they use computer technology to participate in online or virtual communities. How would they describe their online community? Why do they enjoy participating in it? What does their online community offer them that they do not find in their "real" lives?

Ask students how technology can improve the quality of life in their real-life neighborhood and community. (Technology can be used to provide job training, to improve public transportation, to clean up the environment, to fight crime, to make communication easier, and more.)

STEP 5

Report Your Findings
Give students these tips on creating their technology product:

- Choose a topic relevant to the technology. For example, use a spreadsheet program to organize financial information.
- If a certain technology is not readily accessible, document your knowledge of it instead.
- Pay attention to presentation.
- Demonstrate mastery by using complex or advanced features of the technology.

418

Unit 5 — Thematic Project

STEP 3 Research Procedures
Choose the career field that most interests you and follow the steps listed below:

1. Perform research on current technologies and emerging technology trends using a variety of electronic and print resources.
2. Compile information on the leading technologies in your career field. Focus on technologies and tools that are the industry standard or that are growing in importance. Name and describe each technology, note its specific uses, identify who uses it and when, and describe how to learn the technology (on the job, at school, by independent study, and so on).
3. Interview at least two or three workers in your chosen career field to verify your findings, to find out how technology is changing in specific companies in the industry, and to learn more about how to master the technologies you have selected.
4. Summarize what you have learned in a three-page report. Name and describe

each technology, explain who uses it and why, and draw up a realistic action plan to guide you in learning each technology.

5. Use one of the technologies you have profiled to create a product that showcases your skills in that technology. For example, you might create a database of your contacts using a database program, or present documentation that shows your ability to use computerized diagnostics to troubleshoot a car with engine problems.

@ Resources Organizer To find a graphic organizer you can use to organize your research, go to this book's OLC through **glencoe.com**.

STEP 4 Connect to Community
Get Local Arrange to visit a local business in your career area and to speak to a manager about the uses of technology at the business. What software programs, tools, or other forms of technology are important to the success, efficiency, and profitability of the business, and why? Summarize your findings in a one-page report.

Take the Next Step Talk to one or two workers at the same business and ask them how they learned the technology skills they need to do their jobs. Also ask what additional technology skills would help them to do their work more efficiently. Finally, ask for recommendations about what students can do right now to start building relevant skills for their careers.

STEP 5 Report Your Findings
Your final project should include a three-page report explaining the technology used in your desired career and an original product created using that technology.

Developing Community Involvement

Create a Student Discussion Forum

Work with a community newspaper, community college, trade school, or other organization to hold a student discussion evening. Solicit topics of concern from area high school and junior college students through the Internet, the local newspaper, or school surveys and fliers. Work with a student committee to choose a moderator and introductory speaker and to create a plan for the evening. Make sure to include topics relevant to career success, such as education and changing technology. Invite the school newspaper and local media to cover the event.

Helpful Hints Consider these technology tips:

- When researching technology used in your desired field, use current sources.
- Verify information you find in print and online resources by interviewing workers in your chosen career field.
- Be creative in thinking of ways to master various technology tools. Can you learn them at school, on the job, in a club, or on your own?
- Design something that you would be proud to present to a prospective employer as part of a portfolio.
- When you've finished your project, identify other technologies that you would like to learn. Set goals for learning how to use all the technology relevant to your field.

STEP 6 Presentation and Evaluation

Your report will be evaluated based on:
- depth of research

Personal Academic and Career Portfolio

Print out a copy of your report and add it to your **Personal Academic and Career Portfolio**. Also add documentation of your technology project, either as a printout, a computer file, or a poster with photographs and captions. You can use the report and project as a model for continuing to investigate new technologies throughout your career.

- presentation and neatness
- grammar and mechanics

Your product will be evaluated based on:
- evidence of mastery
- choice of relevant technology
- presentation and creativity

@ **Evaluation Rubric** To find a rubric you can use to evaluate your project, go to this book's OLC through glencoe.com.

BusinessWeek Connection

Understanding All Aspects of Industry: Underlying Principles of Technology

Understanding all aspects of industry can help you prepare to succeed in a career in that industry. Underlying principles of technology means the specific technology tools used in the workplace, as well as the reasons they are used and the concepts of mathematics, science, and economics that make the tools possible. To be successful, businesses must think intelligently about what technologies to use and how often to upgrade them. Businesses

that fall behind may lose customers to more tech-savvy competitors.

@ Go to this book's Online Learning Center through glencoe.com to find a *BusinessWeek* article titled "Small Businesses Ignore IT at Their Peril." Read the article and identify how technology affects even the smallest businesses. Use a word-processing program to create a one-page summary of the article. Add this summary to your **Personal Academic and Career Portfolio**.

ASSESS

STEP 6

Presentation and Evaluation
Rubric Encourage students go to the *Succeeding in the World of Work* OLC through glencoe.com for a rubric they can use to evaluate their project. Encourage students to use the rubric as a content checklist when researching technologies and technology training options for their project.

CLOSE

Culminating Activity
Sharing Information about Technology In this activity, students applied the Unit topic to their own lives by discovering what technologies they need to master in order to succeed in their chosen career field. Have students who chose similar career fields work in pairs or small groups to share how and why they chose their three technologies, what research resources they used, and how they developed their training plans for each technology. Ask students to discuss how their projects differ and to talk about how their perceptions of the nature of workplace technology may have changed during the course of the Unit Thematic Project. (Encourage students to learn from the experiences and research of their classmates. Through this project, all students should have developed a more realistic and complete understanding of the role of technology in their chosen field.)

BusinessWeek Connection

All Aspects of Industry: Underlying Principles of Technology

Tell students that successful businesses have to do more than adapt to changing technology—they have to anticipate change before it happens. Apple Computer, for example, turned its declining business around with the iPod, the first easy-to-use portable digital music player. Divide the class

into teams and ask each team to create and sketch an idea for a new computer-based device. Ask groups to share their ideas, then have the whole class choose the most promising idea. (Encourage students to be creative but practical. Ideas might include a solar-powered car or computer, a medical robot, or an electronic book that mimics a real book.)

Chapter	Chapter Objectives

CHAPTER 19
Economics and
the Consumer

- **Define** a free-enterprise system and describe producers, consumers, and the marketplace.
- **Explain** why prices go up and down.
- **List** three factors used to measure the health of the economy.
- **Explain** how to make wise shopping decisions.
- **Identify** common types of consumer fraud and ways to protect yourself as a consumer.

CHAPTER 20
Managing Your
Money

- **Identify** the steps to take to prepare a budget.
- **Explain** how to keep records effectively.
- **Describe** strategies that will help you stay within your budget.
- **Name** personal changes that can affect your financial situation.
- **Describe** ways to adapt to changes in the economy.
- **List** sources of help for financial problems.

CHAPTER 21
Banking and
Credit

- **Identify** common ways to save money.
- **Identify** different types of retirement plans.
- **Explain** how to select, manage, and reconcile a checking account.
- **Define** *credit* and name the different types of credit.
- **State** the advantages and disadvantages of using credit.
- **Explain** how to compare credit costs.

CHAPTER 22
Understanding
Insurance

- **Define** common insurance terms.
- **List** ways to lower insurance costs.
- **Explain** the importance of owning home insurance.
- **Describe** the basic types of property, health, and life insurance coverage.
- **Explain** the difference between group and individual health insurance plans.

CHAPTER 23
Taxes and
Social Security

- **Describe** the U.S. tax system and the services it finances.
- **Explain** how to complete a federal tax return.
- **Describe** how the Social Security system works.
- **Identify** Social Security benefits and state social insurance benefits.
- **Describe** the challenges facing the Social Security system today.

Understanding Brackets, Letters, and Ability Levels in the Teacher Wraparound Edition

Brackets Brackets on the reduced student edition page correspond to teaching strategies and activities in the Teacher Wraparound Edition. As you teach the lesson, the brackets show you exactly where to use the teaching strategies and activities.

Letters The letters on the reduced student edition page identify the type of strategy or activity. See the key below to learn about the different types of strategies and activities.

Ability Levels Teaching Strategies that appear throughout the chapters have been identified by one of three codes to give you an idea of their suitability for students of varying learning styles and abilities.

Resources Key program resources are listed in each chapter. Icons indicate the format of resources.

KEY TO LETTERS

R **Reading Strategy** activities help you teach reading skills and vocabulary.

C **Critical Thinking** strategies help students apply and extend what they have learned.

S **Skill Practice** strategies help students practice historical analysis and geographical skills.

W **Writing Support** activities provide writing opportunities to help students comprehend the text.

D **Develop Concepts** activities use various strategies to help teachers gauge and plan for students' concept development.

U **Universal Access** activities provide differentiated instruction for English language learners, and suggestions for teaching various types of learners. *These activities may or may not have brackets.*

NCLB **No Child Left Behind** activities help students practice and improve their abilities in academic subjects.

KEY TO ABILITY LEVELS

L1 Strategies should be within the ability range of all students. Often full class participation is required.

L2 Strategies are for average to above-average students or for small groups. Some teacher direction is necessary.

L3 Strategies are designed for students able and willing to work independently. Minimal teacher direction is necessary.

KEY TO RESOURCE ICONS

📁 Print Material

💿 CD-ROM

🌐 Internet

TeacherWorks™
All-In-One Planner and Resource Center

Teacher Wraparound Edition

For the Unit:
 Unit Thematic Project Student Rubrics
 Unit Test
 Unit Connecting Activities Projects

For the Chapter:
 Chapter Resources
 Program Resources
 Additional Print and Media Resources
 Lesson Plans
 Chapter Summaries, Key Terms, and
  Academic Vocabulary *(English and Spanish)*

 Graphic Organizers
 Reading Activities
 Chapter Self-Checks *(English and Spanish)*
 Internet Activities
 School-to-Career Connections
 Work-Based Learning Projects
 Personal and Academic Career Portfolio Student Rubrics

Student Activity Workbook with Academic Integration

Strategies for Students with Special Needs

Career Plan Project Workbook

 Link to the ***Succeeding in the World of Work* Online Learning Center with Podcasts** through **glencoe.com**.

Unit Overview
Introduce the Unit
Introduce the unit by describing the main concepts of each chapter in the unit.

Unit 6 introduces students to the many skills involved in financial literacy, including budgeting, making wise buying decisions, saving money, using credit, and understanding insurance and the tax system.

Chapter 19 describes the free enterprise system and the characteristics of the marketplace. Students learn how to be smart shoppers and avoid scams and fraud.

Chapter 20 explains how to create, follow, and fine-tune a budget and how to keep financial records. Students also learn how to assume financial responsibility and cope with economic downturns.

Chapter 21 covers the basics of the banking and credit systems.

Chapter 22 describes how insurance policies work and gives students an overview of the various types of insurance they may need.

Chapter 23 introduces students to our tax system and Social Security system.

OUT OF TIME?

If class time is too short to cover all of the chapters in this unit, have students:
- Write down the key terms and their definitions.
- Read the chapter summaries at the beginning of each chapter review.
- Go to the *Succeeding in the World of Work* Online Learning Center (OLC) through glencoe.com to download free Study-to-Go content to their PDAs or cell phones.

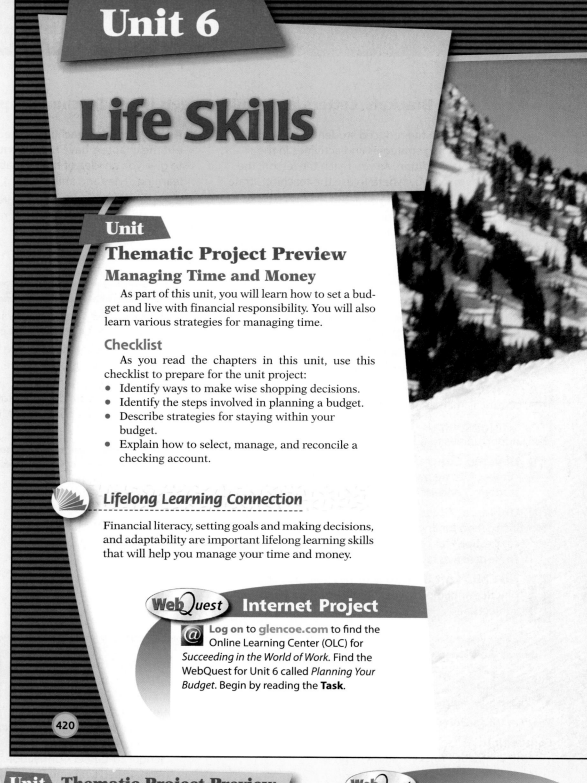

Unit 6

Life Skills

Unit
Thematic Project Preview
Managing Time and Money

As part of this unit, you will learn how to set a budget and live with financial responsibility. You will also learn various strategies for managing time.

Checklist

As you read the chapters in this unit, use this checklist to prepare for the unit project:
- Identify ways to make wise shopping decisions.
- Identify the steps involved in planning a budget.
- Describe strategies for staying within your budget.
- Explain how to select, manage, and reconcile a checking account.

Lifelong Learning Connection

Financial literacy, setting goals and making decisions, and adaptability are important lifelong learning skills that will help you manage your time and money.

WebQuest Internet Project

@ **Log on** to **glencoe.com** to find the Online Learning Center (OLC) for *Succeeding in the World of Work*. Find the WebQuest for Unit 6 called *Planning Your Budget*. Begin by reading the **Task**.

420

Unit Thematic Project Preview

Tell students that as part of this unit, they will plan how they want to spend their time and money as working adults. They will conduct research to determine their likely expenses and their likely income based on the salary of an entry-level worker in their field. They will then set up a realistic and comprehensive monthly budget. They will also itemize and prioritize their activities to set up a monthly schedule.

WebQuest

For WebQuest teaching suggestions and rubrics, go to the Teacher Center of this book's Online Learning Center (OLC) through **glencoe.com**.

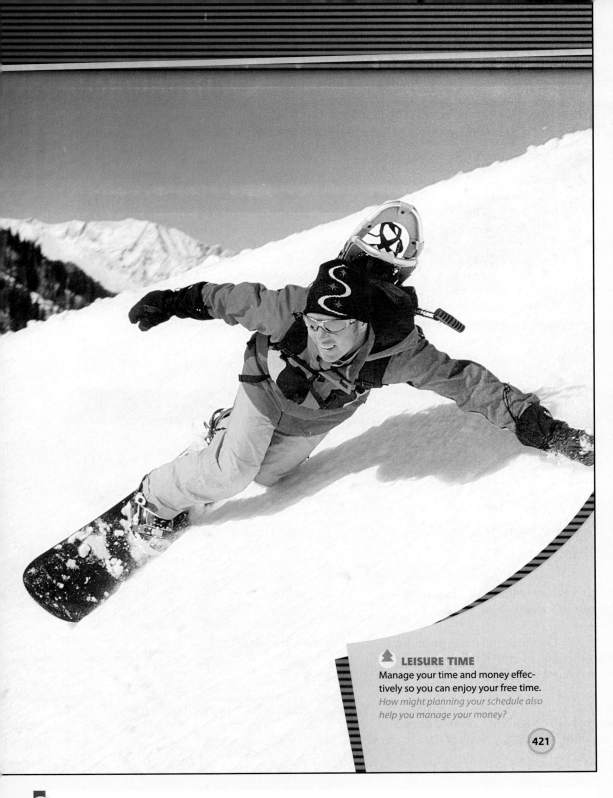

🌲 **LEISURE TIME**

Manage your time and money effectively so you can enjoy your free time.

How might planning your schedule also help you manage your money?

421

Build Background

Ask students these questions to activate prior knowledge:

Chapter 19
What are some factors that affect the prices you pay for goods and services? (supply and demand, production costs, competition, and the state of the economy)

What do smart shoppers do before they buy? (Compare prices and features, check quality, wait for sales, browse discount and second-hand stores, and look for deals online.)

Chapter 20
What is a budget? (a plan for saving and spending money based on your income and expenses)

Why is important to keep detailed financial records? (to keep track of income and expenses, to check for errors, to pay bills on time, and to prepare tax returns)

Chapter 21
When should you start saving for retirement? (when you receive your first paycheck)

What is credit? (money a person can use before having to reimburse, or pay back, the lender)

Chapter 22
How can you find out whether insurance is worth the cost? (Weigh risks and benefits. Find out the premiums and deductibles and scrutinize what is and is not covered.)

Chapter 23
What are taxes? (payments to support the government and pay for government services such as education, roads, and the military)

What is Social Security? (a program that provides income and health benefits to retired and disabled workers)

 Extend the Photo

Caption Answer Many activities cost money. By prioritizing and planning your activities, you can reserve your time and money for those that mean the most to you.

Discussion Tell students that most full-time employees in the United States receive two or three weeks of paid vacation time per year. Ask students what they would do with that time and how they would pay for a vacation. Are vacations a priority for them? Would they save up in order to have money to travel? Why or why not? (Students' priorities will vary, but they should understand that most people benefit greatly from taking a break from work and having a change of scene, and that a vacation need not be expensive or exotic to be enjoyable.)

Chapter Resources Planning Guide with Activities and Features

Section	Features	Activities
Section 19.1 Economic Systems	Hot Jobs! (p. 427) Creative Business Practices (p. 428) Real-World Connection (p. 429) Tech Savvy (p. 430)	Before You Read (p. 424) Graphic Organizer (p. 424) As You Read (p. 428) After You Read (p. 430)
Section 19.2 You, the Consumer	Everyday Ethics (p. 433) Science in Action (p. 433) 21st Century Workplace (p. 434) Career Checklist (p. 435)	Before You Read (p. 431) Graphic Organizer (p. 431) As You Read (p. 432) After You Read (p. 435)

NCLB Activities, information, and skills practice will help your students attain No Child Left Behind proficiency. Students will improve their abilities in the following academic standards areas:

Academic Standards Correlations

Discipline	Standard	Feature/Activity
English Language Arts	**NCTE 1** Read texts to acquire new information.	Hot Jobs! (p. 427) Creative Business Practices (p. 428) Career Checklist (p. 435)
	NCTE 4 Use written language to communicate effectively.	Real-World Connection (p. 429) After You Read (p. 435) Writing Skills Practice (p. 441)
	NCTE 5 Use different writing process elements to communicate effectively.	Tech Savvy (p. 430) 21st Century Workplace (p. 434)
Mathematics	**Number and Operation:** Understand numbers, ways of representing numbers, relationships among numbers, and number systems	After You Read (p. 430)
	Data Analysis and Probability: Formulate questions that can be addressed with data and collect, organize, and display relevant data to answer them	Academic Skills in the Workplace (p. 440)
Science	**Life Science:** Behavior of organisms	Science in Action (p. 433)
	Science as Inquiry: Abilities necessary to do scientific inquiry	Academic Skills in the Workplace (p. 440)

CORRELATIONS The charts show the 21st Century Skills, foundation skills, and workplace competencies that students develop as they work in this chapter.

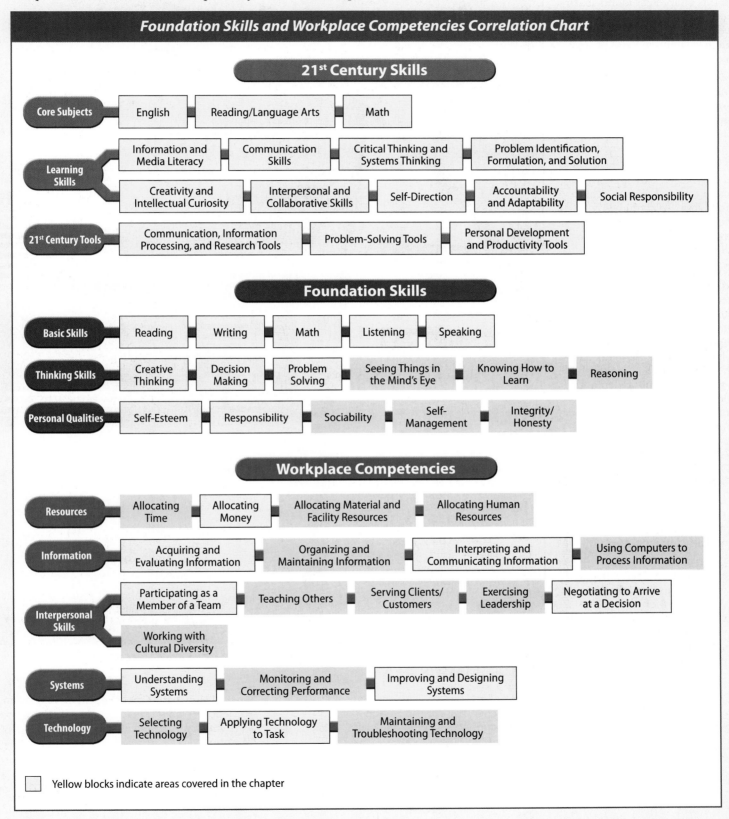

Foundation Skills and Workplace Competencies Correlation Chart

21st Century Skills

Core Subjects
English | Reading/Language Arts | Math

Learning Skills
Information and Media Literacy | Communication Skills | Critical Thinking and Systems Thinking | Problem Identification, Formulation, and Solution
Creativity and Intellectual Curiosity | Interpersonal and Collaborative Skills | Self-Direction | Accountability and Adaptability | Social Responsibility

21st Century Tools
Communication, Information Processing, and Research Tools | Problem-Solving Tools | Personal Development and Productivity Tools

Foundation Skills

Basic Skills
Reading | Writing | Math | Listening | Speaking

Thinking Skills
Creative Thinking | Decision Making | Problem Solving | Seeing Things in the Mind's Eye | Knowing How to Learn | Reasoning

Personal Qualities
Self-Esteem | Responsibility | Sociability | Self-Management | Integrity/Honesty

Workplace Competencies

Resources
Allocating Time | Allocating Money | Allocating Material and Facility Resources | Allocating Human Resources

Information
Acquiring and Evaluating Information | Organizing and Maintaining Information | Interpreting and Communicating Information | Using Computers to Process Information

Interpersonal Skills
Participating as a Member of a Team | Teaching Others | Serving Clients/Customers | Exercising Leadership | Negotiating to Arrive at a Decision
Working with Cultural Diversity

Systems
Understanding Systems | Monitoring and Correcting Performance | Improving and Designing Systems

Technology
Selecting Technology | Applying Technology to Task | Maintaining and Troubleshooting Technology

Yellow blocks indicate areas covered in the chapter

Chapter Overview
Introduce the Chapter
In this chapter, students learn how the economy works, as well as consumer tips to help them save money and protect themselves from fraud.

Section 19.1 explains the free enterprise system, the relationship between producers and consumers, the marketplace in which goods and services are sold, and how the economy is measured.

Section 19.2 explains how to make smart shopping decisions, how to avoid being a victim of consumer fraud, and how various groups protect consumers.

Build Background
Ask volunteers to give descriptions of how they perceive the way the economy functions in the United States. Then ask students what they think happens to the availability and price of a good when public demand for it skyrockets. Discuss how someone could avoid getting ripped off in this situation.

▶ Exploring the Photo

Caption Answer Answers may include price, availability of a product or service, and a customer's needs.

Discussion Have students think about the economic relationships that take place when they shop at a mall or shopping center. Who is the customer? (you) Who is the seller? (a store or vendor) How can the seller also be a customer? (In many cases, the seller must purchase the item so they can resell it.)

CHAPTER **19**
Economics and the Consumer

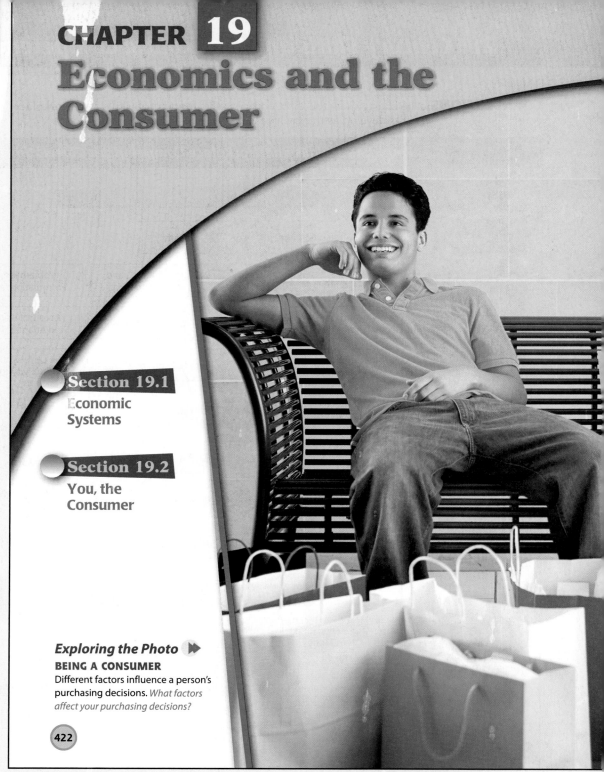

● **Section 19.1**
Economic Systems

● **Section 19.2**
You, the Consumer

Exploring the Photo ▶▶
BEING A CONSUMER
Different factors influence a person's purchasing decisions. *What factors affect your purchasing decisions?*

Classroom Resources

- ▢ Student Edition
- ▢ Teacher Wraparound Edition
- ▢ Student Activity Workbook with Academic Integration
- ▢ Student Activity Workbook with Academic Integration TAE
- ▢ *Fast File,* Unit 6 Resources

- ▢ Inclusion in the Career Education Classroom
- ◉ TeacherWorks™ Plus
- ◉ *ExamView Assessment Suite*
- ◉ Interactive Chalkboard
- ◉ Interactive Student Edition
- ◈ Online Student Edition
- ◈ Online Learning Center (OLC) with Podcasts

Chapter Objectives

After completing this chapter, you will be able to:

- **Define** a free enterprise system and describe producers, consumers, and the marketplace.
- **Explain** why prices go up and down.
- **List** three factors used to measure the health of the economy.
- **Explain** how to make wise shopping decisions.
- **Identify** common types of consumer fraud and ways to protect yourself as a consumer.

Writing Activity

Personal Career Notebook

In your journal, list your last five purchases or purchases that you wish to make. Next, list two factors that influenced or influence your purchasing decisions. On the basis of this list, how would you describe yourself as a consumer?

Get Motivated! Select a local government agency that protects consumers, such as the city health inspector or the building inspector. Interview an agency representative, and learn what kinds of consumer protection are provided. Speculate on how you would be affected if the agency did not exist. Discuss your conclusions with the class.

Chapter 19 Economics and the Consumer **423**

Review the Objectives

Introduce the chapter by reviewing the chapter objectives:

Section 19.1 Objectives

Define a free-enterprise system and describe producers, consumers, and the marketplace. (In a free enterprise system, individuals or businesses may buy, sell, and set prices with little government interference. Producers are companies or individuals who make goods or services. Consumers buy and use goods and services. The marketplace is anywhere goods or services are sold.)

Explain why prices go up and down. (Prices go up and down with changes in supply and demand, when production costs change, or with changes in competition among businesses offering similar products or services.)

List three factors used to measure the health of the economy. (Gross Domestic Product, Consumer Price Index, and unemployment rate)

Section 19.2 Objectives

Explain how to make wise shopping decisions. (Buy well-made items, buy at a time when prices are cheaper, shop at discount and warehouse stores, use coupons and discounts, buy used items if they appear to be reliable, and shop online for convenience and savings.)

Identify common types of consumer fraud and ways to protect yourself as a consumer. (Types of consumer fraud include bait and switch, phony prize notifications, repair fraud, and computer fraud. Protect yourself by never giving personal financial information if you did not place the call, never sending money to any unknown business or organization without checking its legitimacy.)

Writing Activity

Personal Career Notebook Answer Guide

Purchases will likely include goods with relatively low costs, such as a meal, a beverage, an MP3 download, or a tank of gasoline. Have students think about the reasoning that went into choosing the products and services they purchased. Did they compare prices between competitors? Did they look for a sale or discount? Tell students that smart consumers know ways to save money over the course of many small purchases and save a significant amount of money over time.

Get Motivated! Reports should demonstrate an understanding of the information given by the representative. Evaluate reports for clarity, length, and content.

Section 19.1

Economic Systems

FOCUS

Bell Ringer Activity

Economic Systems

Ask volunteers to give definitions of the word *choice*. Next, have them brainstorm a list of the economic choices that we can make in the United States. Tell them that the free-enterprise system is one that allows them to make economic choices.

Resources

Interactive Chalkboard
The Interactive Chalkboard CD provides visual teaching aids for this section.

@ Online Learning Center
The Online Learning Center (OLC) through **glencoe.com** features chapter vocabulary, chapter summaries, and other study materials.

Preteaching

Read the definitions of the key terms aloud. As you read each definition, ask students to write a sentence using each key term.

Graphic Organizer

Tell students to go to the OLC through **glencoe.com** for a printable graphic organizer. (Graphic organizers should demonstrate an understanding of how economic changes might affect consumers.)

NCLB connects academic correlations to book content.

Reading Guide

Before You Read

Preview Read the Key Concepts. Write one or two sentences predicting what the section will be about.

Read to Learn
- How to define a free enterprise system and describe producers, consumers, and the marketplace
- Why prices go up and down
- Three factors used to measure the health of the economy

D Main Idea
Understanding how the economy works will make you an informed consumer and producer.

Key Concepts
- What Is an Economic System?
- The Free-Enterprise System

Key Terms
- economics
- economic system
- free enterprise
- consumers
- producers
- marketplace
- gross domestic product (GDP)
- inflation

Academic Vocabulary
You will find these words in your reading and on your tests. Use the academic vocabulary glossary to look up their definitions if necessary.
- regulation
- fluctuate
- indicators

Graphic Organizer
As you read, list types of economic changes and explain how each of those changes might affect consumers. Use a chart like the one shown to help organize your information.

Economic Changes	How Economic Changes Might Affect Consumers

 Log On Go to this book's Online Learning Center through **glencoe.com** for an online version of this graphic organizer.

Academic Standards • • • • • • • • • • • • • • • • • •

N C L B

English Language Arts
- Read texts to acquire new information. (NCTE 1)
- Use written language to communicate effectively. (NCTE 4)

Mathematics
- Understand numbers, ways of representing numbers, relationships among numbers, and number systems

---

Reading Guide

Before You Read
Tell students that other countries have ways of producing, distributing, and selling products and services that are different from the United States. In some countries, the government controls most or all of these functions. In others, the system is much like the U.S., but the government may impose price controls on certain goods to keep prices reasonable for consumers.

D Develop Concepts
Main Idea Discuss the main idea with students. Ask students to brainstorm ways people come to "understand" the economy. (Answers may include taking classes, being a consumer, working at a business, helping run a business, and reading economics books and journals.)

What Is an Economic System?

How are prices set? What causes prices to drop, rise, or stay the same? How does this system of buying and selling goods and services work? How does it affect you?

These questions have to do with economics. **Economics** is the study of how people produce, distribute, and consume goods and services. Production is the process of creating goods or services. Distribution is the act of transporting and selling goods and services. Consumption is the purchase and use of goods and services. The way people participate in these activities depends on the economic system of the country in which they live. An **economic system** is the way a country utilizes the production, distribution, and consumption of goods and services.

✓ **Reading Check** **CONNECT** What types of goods or services have you used in the past week?

The Free-Enterprise System

The economic system that is used in the United States is known as the free-enterprise system. **Free enterprise** means that individuals or businesses may buy, sell, and set prices with little government interference. The government does have a role in our economic system, however. For instance, the government is responsible for law enforcement, education, roads, mail, safety standards, **regulation** of industries, and consumer protection. **Consumers** are the people who buy and use goods and services. For example, when you buy a sandwich or a CD, you are a consumer. **Producers** are companies or individuals who make goods or provide services.

 CHANGING ROLES
Most people are both consumers and producers, although usually not at the same time. *Who are the consumers in this photograph? Who are the producers? How do you know?*

Vocabulary
You can find definitions in the **Key Terms** glossary and **Academic Vocabulary** glossary at the back of this book.

Section 19.1

TEACH

Discussion Starter
What Is an Economic System? Have students imagine that they have a dog-walking business. Ask students how their place in the economic system is different than it is when they go shopping for clothes at the mall. (When you are dog-walking, you create a service by starting your business and sell it by doing the work and being paid. When you buy clothes, you purchase by paying for them and consume by wearing them.)

R Reading Strategy
Activating Prior Knowledge Tell students that the free-enterprise system functions in large part through individuals and businesses exercising free choice in deciding how products and services are produced and consumed. Ask students what factors might affect their personal economic choices. (Students might point out that people make economic choices based on how much money they have to spend.)

✓ Reading Check

CONNECT Answers will vary. Take a volunteer's example of a good he or she has used and have students speculate on how it was produced, distributed, and consumed.

Resources

 TeacherWorks™ Plus
The TeacherWorks software includes customizable built-in lesson plans and links to printable program resources.

▶▶ Extend the Photo

Caption Answer The service being sold is a musical performance. The consumers are the audience members who have paid for tickets. The producers are the band members giving the performance.

Discussion Ask students to discuss other producer-consumer relationships that are connected to the concert shown in the photo. For example, the concessions company that sells food and beverages is a producer, as are the taxi and limousine drivers who transport concertgoers to the venue. Tell students that in any situation where money is exchanged for a good or service, there is a consumer and a producer.

425

S **Skill Practice**

Guided Practice

Find Context Tell students to read the business section of the local newspaper, a national business newspaper such as *The Wall Street Journal*, or a business magazine such as *BusinessWeek*. Have them clip, print out, or photocopy at least three articles and circle terms and concepts they studied in this section. Then have them discuss how these terms and concepts relate to the pattern of the economy as shown in **Figure 19.1**. (Articles should show the relationship between people and business and industry in a free-enterprise economy.)

Cooperative Learning

Enrichment

Investigate Have students work in small groups to investigate a particular category of consumer goods, such as a type of car or appliance. Have them review issues of *Consumer Reports* and Web sites and other periodicals that rate goods. Have each group present its findings to the class and recommend a particular brand. (Presentations will vary but should show understanding of what motivates consumers.)

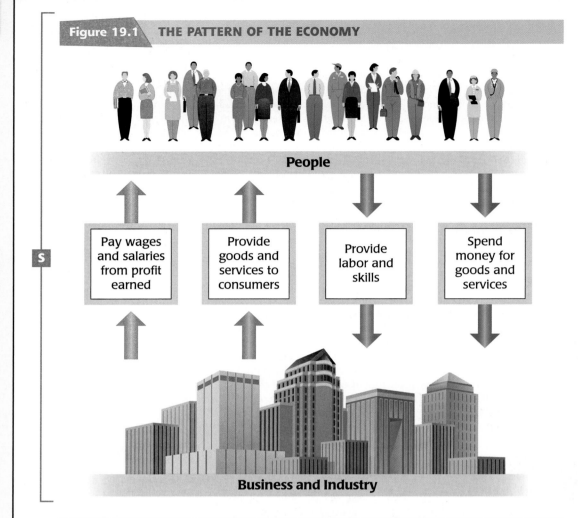

Figure 19.1   THE PATTERN OF THE ECONOMY

People

| Pay wages and salaries from profit earned | Provide goods and services to consumers | Provide labor and skills | Spend money for goods and services |

Business and Industry

FREE ENTERPRISE This figure shows how the money you spend goes into businesses and comes back to you as a worker. It also shows how your skills help produce goods and services that consumers like you need and want. *How does the freedom of choice of a free enterprise system affect these processes?*

Consumers and Producers

If you mow lawns or cut hair, you are a producer of a service. If you make T-shirts or grow tomatoes, you are a producer of goods. Producers often use materials and equipment to make their goods. For example, someone who produces T-shirts might use cloth, thread, and a sewing machine. **Figure 19.1** shows the flow of economic activity between producers and consumers.

EXTEND THE FIGURE   Figure 19.1

Caption Answer In our free-enterprise system, you can choose where you work and what work you do. You can also choose how you spend money on goods and services.

Discussion Ask students what they think happens when consumers lack money to spend on the goods and services marketed by the producers. (Economic activity decreases and a recession may occur. See page 454 for more information about recessions.)

Producers try to make goods or provide services that consumers will want to buy. A producer's main purpose is to make a net profit, which is the amount of money that remains after all expenses have been subtracted.

Once goods and services are produced, individuals or other businesses consume, or buy and use, them. You become a consumer when you purchase a T-shirt or get a haircut. Consumer purchases, wants, and needs impact the cost and supply of goods and services. Producers and consumers accomplish their aims by going to the marketplace.

What Is the Marketplace?

A **marketplace** is anywhere that goods and services are sold. Sometimes producer and consumer are actually in the same physical location, such as when you get your hair cut. Producers and consumers can also be geographically far apart. For example, you might buy a computer that was produced in another country. The Internet creates a virtual marketplace for the buying and selling of goods.

To reach consumers and promote the purchasing of their products, producers must *market* their goods and services. Marketing is the process of getting products to consumers. It includes pricing, packaging, shipping, advertising, and selling.

Price Fluctuations

In a free-enterprise system, prices **fluctuate**, or go up and down, because of three main factors:

- **Supply and Demand** Supply is the amount of goods and services available for purchase by consumers. Demand is the amount of goods and services that consumers are willing and able to purchase. When supply is greater than demand, prices fall. When demand is greater than the supply, prices rise. Demand can also refer to a specific quantity of a good or service that consumers are willing and able to purchase. For example, a consumer may be willing to purchase one gallon of milk for $1.00, but that same consumer may not be willing to purchase only one-half gallon of milk for $1.25.
- **Production Costs** These are the combined costs of material and labor to make a good or service. Because businesses must make a profit, they must sell their goods or services for more than it costs to produce them.
- **Competition** When different businesses provide similar products or services, they are in competition. When there is a lot of competition, prices for a good or service tend to be lower. When there is little or no competition for a good or service, prices tend to be higher. Competition is one factor that can encourage businesses to improve the quality of their products or offer new products or services to attract consumers.

 MARKETPLACES Not all markets have physical locations like this one. *What are some examples of marketplaces without physical locations?*

HOT JOBS!

Natural Pest Control Worker

You can remove household pests without using harmful chemicals. Natural pest control workers use a number of strategies that include eliminating water and food sources, filling cracks and other points of entry, and using traps, baits, and sticky tape. Real-world problem-solving skills are a must for this job.

S Skill Practice
Guided Practice

Marketing Divide students into teams and have them decide on a product or service to offer to classmates. Tell teams to discuss all aspects of making the product available and set a price, taking into account the costs they'll incur in getting their product to market. (Answers should present plausible explanations for how prices might be affected. For example, a company that employs minimum-wage workers would have to raise prices because labor costs were affected by an increase in the minimum wage. A company that sells flower baskets might lower their prices because oversupply led to a lower wholesale price for roses.)

U Universal Access
English Language Learners Find and supply translations as needed for the phrase supply and demand. For example, the Spanish translation is *oferta y demanda*. Use these translations to help describe the concept of supply and demand in your discussion.

▶ Extend the Photo

Caption Answer Possible answers include an online music store and a mail-order catalogue.

Discussion Ask students how Internet shopping might affect local malls and other stores. (Business could decrease as consumers buy through online shopping services, or an innovative business owner could find a way to sell his or her products online as well as in physical stores.)

TEACH *(cont.)*

Discussion Starter

Measuring the Economy
Ask students how they think the business cycle might affect their future career choices. For example, what are the opportunities when business is in an expansion phase versus a contraction phrase? (When the economy expands, businesses add employees and there are more career opportunities across a wider range of job fields. When the economy contracts, employment is reduced and there is greater competition for fewer jobs across a narrower range of job fields.)

As You Read

Answers will vary but the main reasons are differences in overhead (the general cost of running a business) and overall store volume (amount of total goods sold). Students may cite Wal-Mart as a store that offers the lowest prices on a variety of goods. This is due in part to Wal-Mart's being able to make up for a lower per-unit profit by selling a high volume of goods.

Resources

ExamView Assessment Suite CD allows you to print out ready-made unit and chapter tests complete with answer keys. You can also create customized tests.

As You Read

Analyze Why might different stores offer the same product for different prices?

In addition to prices going up and down, the economy itself fluctuates. A period in which the economy is growing is called expansion, and a period in which the economy is declining in growth is called recession. The movement between these two stages is the business cycle.

Measuring the Economy

Fluctuations in the economy help determine wages, spending behavior, and production. Economic **indicators** measure the performance and direction of the economy each year. The government uses the information on the growth and health of the economy to determine economic policy.

Gross Domestic Product

Gross domestic product (GDP) is the value of all goods and services produced by a country in a given time period. The GDP is the main indicator of the size and condition of an economy. GDP enables governments to compare the growth or decline of business activity in an economy.

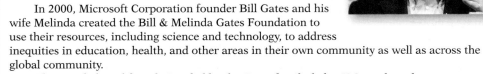

Creative Business Practices

MICROSOFT   **Community Philanthropy**

In 2000, Microsoft Corporation founder Bill Gates and his wife Melinda created the Bill & Melinda Gates Foundation to use their resources, including science and technology, to address inequities in education, health, and other areas in their own community as well as across the global community.

The Seattle-based foundation, led by the Gates family, helps U.S. students by supporting school districts, communities, and organizations that are working to improve public education. The foundation has helped to fund more than 1,500 schools, and has provided scholarships to students from diverse backgrounds. In addition, working with partners, the foundation works to maintain Internet availablity at all public libraries. The foundation also has special programs for residents of the state of Washington, where Microsoft is located, as well as the neighboring state of Oregon.

While the foundation's main area of focus in the United States is to contribute to improvements in education, it also works to improve the conditions that can contribute to learning in areas around the world—especially health. The Foundation's broader goal is to improve the lives of all individuals to reduce poverty and advance health in the global community. For example, the foundation's Global Health program is heavily invested in health products and services such as health workers, health research, and vaccine development and distribution.

CRITICAL THINKING How can health or economic conditions affect education?

 Connect to the Real World For more information about the Bill & Melinda Gates Foundation, visit the link on this book's Online Learning Center through **glencoe.com**.

Creative Business Practices

CRITICAL THINKING ANSWER Educational conditions are closely related to economic conditions. For example, in a good economy there is more tax revenue available to public schools, and donors have more available resources for philanthropic programs. Corporations are more likely to fund grants and scholarships. Conversely, in difficult economic times more costs tend to be passed on to students as public funding shrinks. The quality of pediatric health also affects education. When children enjoy a healthy standard of living and are properly immunized, they are better equipped to learn and less likely to miss school due to illness.

Consumer Price Index

The Consumer Price Index, or CPI, is a collection of data that measures changes in the prices of consumer goods and services. It is based on a monthly survey conducted by the Bureau of Labor Statistics. The survey tracks price changes for about 90,000 items in 364 categories, including food, clothing, shelter, fuel, and medical services. In addition, there is a regional report of price changes for regions around the country.

By showing increases or decreases in the cost of living, the CPI also measures inflation. **Inflation** is a rise in the price of goods and services that results in a decrease in the purchasing power of money. For example, if gasoline prices rise sharply but worker wages stay about the same, it becomes difficult for consumers to buy as much gasoline as they were able to buy before the price of gasoline increased. Because of this, inflation can cause the *standard of living,* which is a measure of the quality of life based on the amount of goods and services a person can purchase, declines. Inflation affects the business cycle and can contribute to unemployment.

C Controlling inflation is one of a government's major goals. When inflation starts to go up, many governments raise interest rates to reduce everyone's ability to borrow money. The result is a slowdown in economic growth, which helps to bring inflation down.

 CONSUMERS IN ACTION Shopping is a favorite activity for many people. *How can you prepare before a shopping trip so that you will not spend more than you should?*

 Real-World Connection

Affordable Style

Your friend Myra dresses in the latest fashions and always tells you about the bargains she gets. You like to wear many of the same labels as Myra, but you nearly always pay full price for your purchases.

Critical Thinking How can you dress fashionably on a budget?

Do Your Own Research Hunting for fashion bargains can be a fun hobby and need not wreck your budget. Check your local newspapers and look for clearance sales. Compare the prices in outlet stores with the cost of similar items in department stores. Make notes about the selection and styles available at both. List at least three advantages of shopping in each type of store.

 ### Extend the Photo

Caption Answer Make a list of what you need, check which stores are having sales, and calculate how much you can spend without exceeding your budget.

Discussion Ask: What effect would inflation have on your shopping activities?

 Real-World Connection

Critical Thinking Answer Survey your closet and decide how you can update your wardrobe with a few well-selected new pieces. Sign up to receive e-mails from your favorite stores so you will know when they are having sales.

Do Your Own Research Encourage students to use the Internet to compare department stores with outlet stores. Online shopping does not require transportation, and online stores often offer discounts.

 ## Section 19.1

ASSESS

Review Key Terms
Have students write sentences using each key term.

Online Study Tools
Have students go to the OLC through **glencoe.com** to:

- Download **Podcast** study tools.
- Download free **Study-to-Go** content to their PDAs or cell phones.

 Resources

📁 **Student Activity Workbook** Assign the Chapter 19 activities in the Student Activity Workbook.

RETEACH

C **Critical Thinking**
Making Inferences Tell students that many college students take out loans to pay for tuition, books, and living expenses. Ask students if the cost of borrowing money for college increases if inflation goes up and the government decides to act to reduce borrowing, and why. (Yes, because the government will increase interest rates. Higher interest rates lead to higher loan costs.)

ASSESS

After You Read
Have students complete the Section 19.1 After You Read section review.

429

Online Study Tools

Have students go to the OLC through **glencoe.com** to:

- Take the Section 19.1 **Practice Test**.
- Download **Podcast** study tools.
- Download free **Study-to-Go** content to their PDAs or cell phones.

TechSavvy

Barcode Standards

Answer Stories should reflect an understanding of barcodes.

CLOSE

Culminating Activity

Estimate Costs Divide students into groups and have each group select a business they want to start with funds of $100,000. Have groups research costs such as equipment, rent for office space, and wages for the number of employees they will need. Have each group summarize their findings in a one-page report.

N C L B Activity correlated to Mathematics standards.

TechSavvy

Barcodes

Barcodes are used by many types of businesses. A barcode is a series of short lines that contain coded information such as price, the country where the object was made, the number of the product, or other information. The barcode can also record when the product was sold so that the company knows when to order more.

Even NASA uses barcodes. Heat tiles on the space shuttle need to be replaced after each flight. Each tile has a barcode so that it can be replaced by the correct type of tile.

@ Visit this book's OLC through glencoe.com and find the link to learn more about barcodes. Write a one-page creative story about how barcodes might be used in the workplace.

Unemployment

A third economic indicator is the unemployment rate. The unemployment rate is a statistic that identifies the percentage of the labor force that is without work but is actively seeking employment. Low unemployment is a sign that the economy is doing well because most people are working, earning wages, and consuming goods and services.

Higher unemployment rates increase the chances of an economic slowdown. The unemployed and their dependents will experience a decreased standard of living. In times of high unemployment, consumer spending decreases. At the same time, businesses must pay more for unemployment insurance, which provides assistance to unemployed workers. The government must also spend more to provide money for unemployment benefits and increased use of social services for those without jobs.

Section 19.1 After You Read

Review Key Concepts

1. Explain the role of producers and consumers in a free-enterprise system.
2. List three factors that affect whether prices go up or down.
3. Name three indicators used to measure the health of the economy. Explain one.

Practice Academic Skills

 Mathematics

4. In one year, the U.S. GDP was estimated at $11,734,000 million. If the GDP of the entire world was about $40,895,000 million, estimate how much the rest of the world's GDP is without the U.S. by rounding to the nearest one trillion.

CONCEPT **Using Large Numbers** In our number system, the lowest whole number place value is the ones, next come the tens and the hundreds. The next set of three place values is called the thousands, and then there are the millions, the billions, and the trillions.

Step 1: Think about which digits are in the trillions place. If these numbers represent millions, then 1 would represent one million, 1,000 would be one billion, and 1,000,000 would be one trillion. Find the right place value and round.

Step 2: Subtract the numbers you rounded in Step 1 and label your answer with the appropriate units.

 For math help, go to the Math Appendix located at the back of this book.

Section 19.1 After You Read

Review Key Concepts

1. In a free-enterprise system, consumers are people who buy and use goods and services. Producers are companies or individuals who make goods or provide services and whose goal is to make a profit. Producers and consumers use the marketplace to interact.

2. Supply and demand, production costs, competition.

3. Prices are affected by the gross domestic product (GDP), the Consumer Price Index (CPI), and the unemployment rate.

Practice Academic Skills

4. The rest of the world's GDP is 29 trillion, or 29,000,000 million (40,895,000 million rounds to 41,000,000 million; 11,734,000 million rounds to 12,000,000 million; 41,000,000 million − 12,000,000 = 29,000,000 million)

You, the Consumer

Reading Guide

Before You Read

Preview Read the Key Concepts. Write one or two sentences predicting what the section will be about.

Read to Learn
- How to make wise shopping decisions
- Common types of consumer fraud and ways to protect yourself as a consumer

D

Main Idea
Wise consumer habits will enable you to save money and protect yourself from deceptive practices.

Key Concepts
- Smart Shopping
- Be a Smart Consumer

Key Terms
◇ warranty
◇ consumer fraud
◇ bait and switch

Academic Vocabulary
You will find this word in your reading and on your tests. Use the academic vocabulary glossary to look up its definition if necessary.
■ fraudulent

Graphic Organizer
As you read, list and describe common types of consumer fraud. Use a chart like the one shown to record your information.

Types of Fraud	Description
1.	
2.	
3.	

 Log On Go to this book's Online Learning Center through **glencoe.com** for an online version of this graphic organizer.

Academic Standards •

N C L B

English Language Arts
- Read texts to acquire new information. (NCTE 1)
- Use written language to communicate effectively. (NCTE 4)
- Use different writing process elements to communicate effectively. (NCTE 5)

Science
- Life Science: Behavior of organisms

Bell Ringer Activity

You, the Consumer
Write these headings on the board: *Item, Place of Purchase, Reasons for Buying*. Have students complete each category with their last three purchases. Tell students to think about these purchases and decide if they used smart shopping strategies.

 Resources

 Interactive Chalkboard
The Interactive Chalkboard CD provides visual teaching aids for this section.

@ Online Learning Center
The OLC through **glencoe.com** features chapter vocabulary, chapter summaries, and other study materials.

Preteaching
Tell students that *bait and switch* is a fraudulent business practice. Have them break the phrase into its individual parts to figure out what it means.

Graphic Organizer
Tell students to go to the OLC through **glencoe.com** for a printable graphic organizer. (Charts should show the types of fraud and descriptions of each.)

 N C L B   **NCLB** connects academic correlations to book content.

Reading Guide

Before You Read
Have volunteers describe a recent shopping experience in which they were smart shoppers or bought something they really didn't want or need because of sales pressure. Afterwards, have students discuss how they could improve their shopping skills.

D Develop Concepts
Main Idea Ask students to share where they have received advice on making smart shopping decisions.

431

TEACH

Discussion Starter

Financial Changes Tell students that if they were looking to buy a car, it is unlikely they would walk into any auto dealership and buy the first car they liked that they could afford. They would research to find a car that is a good value, then shop around for the best price on that particular model. Explain that for everyday items that cost much less, you can save money and buy quality goods and services by employing the same smart shopping tactics.

R Reading Strategy

Using Research Materials Bring to class several ads for identical products (or bring the products themselves)— one name brand and one generic (for example, tissues, laundry soap, paper towels, a food product). Have students compare the unit costs, price, ingredients, and quality of each pair. Discuss which items seem to be the better value, all things considered. Ask students what factors they consider when deciding whether to buy a name brand or generic product.

Resources

TeacherWorks™ Plus The TeacherWorks software includes customizable built-in lesson plans and links to printable program resources.

As You Read

Identify List some ways consumers can be smart shoppers.

Smart Shopping

In a free-enterprise system, individuals as well as businesses make choices about earning and spending money. Making good choices takes skills such as allocating money and evaluating information. Consider how those skills apply to these practical tips:

R

- **Pay attention to quality.** You will save money in the long run by buying well-made items, especially when you expect to keep your purchases for a long time. A high-priced item does not necessarily have better quality. Generic products, or products without brand names, usually have plain packaging and are relatively inexpensive.

- **When possible, plan the timing of your purchases.** You will find more bargains at certain times of the year. Most retailers have end-of-the-season sales. You can also use the law of supply and demand. Instead of rushing out to buy a new CD, wait a few months. By then, the price may have decreased because demand has lessened.

- **Take advantage of discount stores.** Discount and warehouse stores can offer excellent bargains for name brands.

- **Use coupons and special discounts.** Coupons and discounts for products and local retailers can be found in print and online. Some retailers offer discounts for being a member of a group, such as being students or senior citizens.

- **Consider buying used items.** You can save money purchasing used items, such as cars, videogames, or electronics. Used items are usually not returnable, and rarely have a warranty. A **warranty** is a guarantee that a product meets certain standards of quality. Make sure used items work properly by trying them out before you buy them. If you are thinking of buying a used car, have a trusted mechanic check it out before you decide.

- **Explore online options.** Online shopping can be convenient. Use consumer resources to research online shopping before buying online. Not all of the information or companies you will encounter online will be trustworthy.

◀◀ **CAR REPAIRS**
Automobile repairs can be expensive. *Why should you ask for an explanation of the repairs needed?*

 432 **Unit 6** Life Skills

Extend the Photo

Caption Answer Receiving an understandable explanation of needed repairs allows you to research whether the repair cost estimate is too high, get a second opinion from another mechanic, and to improve your understanding of the workings of your automobile so you can be better prepared as a consumer the next time your car needs to be serviced.

Discussion If students in your class drive, ask volunteers to tell about experiences having their automobiles serviced. Ask them if the mechanic provided detailed explanations of needed repairs, and if they felt any pressure to approve of extra repairs that may or may not have been needed.

Everyday ETHICS

CUTTING COSTS

Is it always best to keep workplace costs down?

USED SUPPLIES You work as a construction manager, and your crew has started building an addition on a school. One day, you notice the workers using used wood. When you question them, they say that the owner of the company had the materials sent over because they were cheaper than new ones. You know the construction contract stated that the school's addition would be built with all-new materials.

What Would You Do? How do you respond to the owner's actions? What do you tell your workers?

DISCUSS IT Should you notify the school if the owner refuses to use new materials for the project? In teams, discuss some possible alternatives.

Be a Smart Consumer

Smart consumers protect themselves from being taken advantage of in the marketplace and from consumer fraud. **Consumer fraud** is dishonest business practices used by those who are trying to trick or cheat you.

How can you avoid fraud? First, being aware, informed, and suspicious is often enough not to be caught in a **fraudulent** situation. Remember that if an offer, good, or service sounds too good to be true, it probably is. Here are some common types of consumer fraud:

C

- **Fraudulent Advertising** A **bait and switch** is an illegal sales practice in which a lower-priced item is used to attract customers who are then encouraged to buy a similar product at a higher price. For example, a retailer might advertise a bargain, only to tell customers who arrive that the bargain item is not available.

- **Phony Prize Notifications** "Congratulations! You've just won a prize!" This news may come by mail, e-mail, or phone. To get your prize, all you have to do is send in money or make a small purchase. Some companies ask you to provide a credit card or checking account number for identification. Even cautious consumers can fall for this scam.

- **Repair Fraud** Dishonest mechanics may try to charge you more than the estimated cost of a repair for a machine such as an appliance or automobile. They may replace parts that are not defective. To protect yourself, ask for written estimates and request that mechanics keep the old parts and show them to you. For major repairs, get a second opinion. Ask if there is a warranty on the repairs.

Science In Action

Consumers
Some biological organisms are categorized as consumers. A consumer that eats plants is an *herbivore*, while a consumer that eats animals is a *carnivore*. A consumer that eats both is an *omnivore*. What kind of consumer are you?

Starting Hint: What foods do you eat?

@ For more science practice, go to this book's OLC through **glencoe.com**.

N C L B

TEACH *(cont.)*

C **Critical Thinking**
Making Inferences Give students this scenario: An electronics store is advertising a sale on what it calls a brand-new wide-screen television, but when you go to the store, the salesperson tells you that only the display model is available at the sale price. The same model still in its box costs $150 more. Which fraudulent sales tactic is the store using? (bait and switch)

N C L B Activity correlated to Science standards.

Science In Action

Answers may vary. Most students will say they are omnivores. Vegetarian students are herbivores.

ASSESS

Review Key Terms
Have students write sentences using each key term.

Online Study Tools
Have students go to the OLC through **glencoe.com** to:
- Download **Podcast** study tools.
- Download free **Study-to-Go** content to their PDAs or cell phones.

Everyday ETHICS

What Would You Do? Answer Students should consider their obligation to their employer, their obligation to their client, their obligation to their own personal values, and their personal risk as an employee.

DISCUSS IT Encourage students to envision other ethical considerations that might play a role in your decision. For example, ask: How might your decision be affected if you have a mortgage payment to make on a new house and you know that objecting to the owner's breach of contract could result in your being fired?

RETEACH

S **Skill Practice**
Guided Practice

Write to Advise Have students write a 100-word paragraph advising a friend how to avoid consumer fraud. (Paragraphs should demonstrate understanding of consumer fraud and the methods used by those who commit it.) **L1**

Use Charts Tell students to write down the following: *cough syrup, automobile advertisement, fireworks, parts and labor warranty, bagged spinach, lawnmower.* Have students create a chart with columns for the FTC, CPSC, and FDA. Then have them place the items listed above in the appropriate column according to which agency has authority to regulate a particular item. (FTC: automobile advertisement, parts and labor warranty; CPSC: fireworks, lawnmower; FDA: cough syrup, bagged spinach) **L2**

Apply Technology Ask students how they would use the Internet to investigate a company or business. Assign students to work with a partner and use your school's computer resources to find information on an actual product or business. Have students note the Internet sites they visit and discuss the types of information they find. (Encourage students to find sites that have information that would be useful to consumers. For example, if students research a contractor or other service provider, they should access Web sites for the Better Business Bureau or a state or local contractors' board.) **L3**

N C L B Activity correlated to English Language Arts standards.

434

The 21st Century Workplace

The 24/7 Workplace

N C L B

Breakthroughs in communication technology and transportation have made it easy for many businesses to have customers, clients, and partners from around the globe. As a result, many businesses receive queries or orders at all hours and during every day of the week.

A company which has a worldwide clientele or offices located in different countries and time zones might need to hire workers for multiple shifts—a practice once associated with assembly-line manufacturing. Operating a 24-hour workplace requires rethinking how facilities and equipment are used. For example, different employees may use workstations at different times. In addition, those employees who arrive and leave at nonstandard hours may require different security measures than those who work during "normal" business hours.

CRITICAL THINKING

What are some adjustments that a company might make to handle international business?

In Your Community

Choose a local business and determine ways that the business can profit by selling to international clients, working with global partners, or doing both. Create a presentation with visual aids to share with your class.

@ **Extend Your Learning** Doing business with other countries requires knowledge of international rules and regulations. For links to Web sites about global business, go to this book's OLC through **glencoe.com**.

- **Computer Fraud** Only engage in business online with companies that you trust. Never disclose passwords or personal information unless you know who is asking for it and how it is going to be used. Verify online security or encryption before providing credit card numbers. Be careful about downloading programs or files from sites you do not know. These programs and files could ruin your hard drive, hijack your computer, or secretly collect your private data. Make sure you have installed a virus protection program, and keep it installed.

Many consumer frauds succeed by taking advantage of the consumer's search for a good deal. These tips may prevent you from becoming a victim: First, never give personal financial information over the phone if you did not place the call. Second, do not send money to any unknown business or organization without checking first to be sure it is legitimate. Check with your state or local consumer office or the Better Business Bureau.

Groups That Protect Consumers

S

Suppose you buy an item that breaks the first time you use it. What should you do? First, try to solve the problem by contacting the store where you bought the item or by calling the company that produced it. If this does not work, you might write a letter of complaint. In your letter, be polite but firm. Be sure to save store receipts, and keep records of your communications with the business. As a last resort, you may need to take legal action. However, help is also available from several other sources.

The 21st Century Workplace

CRITICAL THINKING ANSWER Possible adjustments include hiring multilingual employees, presenting seminars by language and culture specialists to help employees understand the customs and business practices in the countries with which the company might have ties, setting up computer programs to easily convert foreign currency amounts into dollars, and giving traveling employees advice on passing through customs stations during international business travel.

In Your Community Presentations will vary, but strategies may include creating a Web site that is open to international customers, moving some production overseas, or entering into business agreements with international partners.

Government Agencies

Specialized federal government agencies enforce consumer protection laws, acting as watchdogs over certain areas of the marketplace.

- The Federal Trade Commission (FTC) enforces rules about labeling, advertising, and warranties. Thanks to the FTC, the labels in your clothes and on other products provide care and safety instructions. This agency also regulates the descriptions of products in ads and commercials to make sure they are accurate. For example, FTC standards state that a warranty must be clearly worded and conveniently placed.
- The Consumer Product Safety Commission (CPSC) helps protect the public against dangerous products. It sets and enforces production safety standards.
- The Food and Drug Administration (FDA) enforces laws about the quality and labeling of food, drugs, and medical devices. It inspects workplaces that produce food and drugs.

Government agencies at the state and local levels also work to protect consumers.

Consumer Groups

Many private groups help consumers by investigating consumer complaints, educating the public on consumer issues, or creating initiatives for consumer legislation. Examples of such initiatives are consumer action programs (CAPs) developed by industry groups, such as The Major Appliance Consumer Action Program (MACAP) for major appliance manufacturers. A well-known consumer group is Consumers Union, which publishes a magazine called *Consumer Reports*. This magazine provides ratings, warnings, and other information about goods and services.

Career ✓ Checklist

To Be an Informed Consumer:

✓ Know consumer rights and laws.
✓ Always compare prices.
✓ Avoid impulse buying.
✓ Remember the difference between wants and needs.
✓ Do not allow yourself to be talked into a purchase you do not want or cannot afford.

Section 19.2 After You Read

Review Key Concepts

1. List five tips that will help make you a smart shopper.
2. Give an example of consumer fraud. Explain what it means.
3. Name two ways to protect yourself against consumer fraud.

Practice Academic Skills

 English Language Arts

4. How do you track your purchases? How might tracking your purchases help you become a smart shopper? Write your responses in a one-page summary.
5. In a one-page essay, explain what consumers can do to protect themselves from consumer fraud.

 Check your answers at this book's OLC through **glencoe.com**.

ASSESS

After You Read

Have students complete the Section 19.2 After You Read section review.

Online Study Tools

Have students go to the OLC through **glencoe.com** to:

- Take the Section 19.2 **Practice Test**.
- Download **Podcast** study tools.
- Download free **Study-to-Go** content to their PDAs or cell phones.

Resources

 ExamView Assessment Suite **CD** allows you to print out ready-made unit and chapter tests complete with answer keys. You can also create customized tests.

CLOSE

Culminating Activity

Insurance and Your Future Have students write 150-word essays describing smart shopping techniques, consumer frauds, and consumer protection offered by government and consumer groups.

N C L B Activity correlated to English Language Arts standards.

Section 19.2 After You Read

Review Key Concepts

1. Pay attention to quality; plan the timing of your purchase; take advantage of discount stores; use coupons and special discounts; and consider buying used items.
2. Possible answer: bait and switch, in which a lower-priced item is used to attract customers who are then encouraged to buy a similar product at a higher price.
3. Never give personal financial information over the phone if you did not place the call; do not send money to an unknown business or organization.

Practice Academic Skills

4. Summaries may include writing a record of all purchases in a notebook, diary, or other type of journal. Tracking purchases allows you to review your choices to see if you made smart shopping decisions.
5. Essays should demonstrate comprehension of the section text.

CAREER SPOTLIGHT

FOCUS

Discussion Starter

FOCUS

Discussion Starter

Agriculture, Food, and Natural Resources Lead a discussion about the different types of careers that can be found in this career cluster. Have students brainstorm different careers and jobs within the career cluster. (Answers will vary but students should show an understanding of the many types of careers that fall within the career cluster.)

TEACH

W **Writing Support**

Independent Practice

Conduct an Interview Have students use the questions in the Career Spotlight to conduct and record an interview with an individual in the featured career cluster. (Answers will vary but should follow the interview format of the Career Spotlight.)

C **Critical Thinking**

Future Technologies and Agriculture Scientists Point out that one of the most important issues facing the United States is energy dependence. Many people believe that finding alternative energy sources to foreign oil is vital to the country's future. Lead a discussion about how future agriculture scientists might help shape future geopolitical events. (Students may note that alternative energy sources are being developed from vegetables. A promising alternative fuel is biodiesel, which is a fuel synthesized from vegetable and sometimes meat waste products. Agriculture scientists work to develop new and improved forms of biodiesel.)

436

Maria Zagala Desagun
Lab Operations Manager

Q: Describe your job.
A: I oversee lab operations, media preparations, greenhouse operations, facility management, and health and safety for a biotech company. We develop plants and plant-based products for a number of diverse industries. Through license-based collaborations and internal product development, we are creating enhanced plants, such as crops for fuel, disease-resistant fruits and vegetables, trees and turf, ornamental flowers, row crops, and plant-based products, such as chemicals, enzymes, nutritional ingredients, personal care ingredients, and pharmaceuticals.

Q: Describe a typical workday.
A: I supervise daily laboratory operations, including lab support services. In addition, I handle facility operations, such as construction, equipment repair, and service agreement, as well as building maintenance. For greenhouse operations, I oversee pest management, maintain temperature control programs, test water quality, check the greenhouse supplies inventory, and maintain the plants on a daily basis. I also keep the company in compliance with local, state, and federal laws by tending to permits, training, hazardous waste disposal, and manifest recordkeeping, inspections, and engineering controls.

Q: What skills are most important to you in your job?
A: I use organizational and communication skills every day. They are necessary to manage the sheer number of tasks and ensure cooperation with coworkers.

Q: What skills are helpful in preparing for your career?
A: Academic skills such as biology and chemistry subject knowledge are very helpful. Laboratory skills, health

and safety knowledge, building construction and maintenance, and greenhouse construction and maintenance are also helpful.

Q: What is your key to success?
A: Having a good attitude is very important, as are determination and diligence.

Q: What training and preparation do you recommend for students?
A: You can't know too much. Learn every skill you can. I have learned laboratory skills, such as tissue culture, sequencing, genotyping, media preparation, transformation using biolistic process, physiological assay screenings, and other skills. These have allowed me to understand the needs of the researchers and help them perform their experiments.

Q: What are some ways you recommend students prepare for this career?
A: Dedication and hard work are the best keys to success. Concentrate on your work and do the best you can. Always conduct research before you start a project and never stop learning.

Q: What do you like most about your work?
A: I like the variety of tasks and the challenges associated with them.

 For more about Career Clusters, go to this book's OLC through **glencoe.com**.

NO CHILD LEFT BEHIND

Teaching Tip

The goals of the NCLB Act include a strong emphasis on reading skills. The use of modeling in your classroom will help students become better at identifying information. For example, ask a question that can be answered by reading the chart on page 437. Verbally identify the elements of the chart that might help the student identify the answer: the stars and the academic skills labels.

Sample Question How many of the tasks on this chart require all four academic skills to complete? (Answer: Two tasks require all four academic skills to complete: manage equipment repair and tend to permits and hazardous waste control.)

Education or Training A bachelor's degree in agricultural science is sufficient for some jobs in applied research or for assisting in basic research, but a master's or doctoral degree is required for advanced research. Degrees in related sciences such as biology, chemistry, or physics or in related engineering specialties also may qualify persons for some agricultural science jobs.

Academic Skills Required English Language Arts, Mathematics, Science, Social Studies

Technology Needed Specialized equipment, such as microscopes and other laboratory equipment. Complex computers and software, such as genomic sequencers, are used to analyze and manipulate genetic material.

Aptitudes, Abilities, and Skills Laboratory personnel need good analytical judgment and the ability to work under pressure.

Workplace Safety Protective masks, gloves, and goggles are often necessary to ensure the safety of laboratory personnel.

Career Outlook Employment of agricultural and foods scientists is expected to grow about as fast as average for all occupations over the next ten years.

Career Path Individuals trained in agricultural and food science can be self-employed, work in the private sector, or work for the government.

ASSESS

Make Connections

Ask students to list specific correlations between academic subjects and workplace tasks. For example, a jeweler might benefit by studying geology, mineralogy, and chemistry because a jeweler's tasks might include heating and mixing liquid metal. An architect must study geometry and physics in order to design structures that balance various forces such as pressure, weight, and gravity. (Answers will vary but students should show an understanding of how academic skills relate directly to workplace tasks.)

CLOSE

Culminating Activity

Lifelong Learning and Career Clusters Encourage students to come up with informal ways that a person might develop skills that would apply to a particular career in Agriculture, Food, and Natural Resources. For example, to learn about pest control and crop rotation, a student might take advantage of the resources provided by organizations such as Future Farmers of America. Another example would be that to learn about keeping organic food fresh without the use of chemicals, a student might join an Internet message group who trade advice and techniques about sustainable agriculture. (Answers will vary but should show evidence of understanding the career as profiled in the Career Spotlight.)

N C L B

Academic Skills Required to Complete Tasks

Tasks	English Language Arts	Mathematics	Science	Social Studies
Supervise lab support operations	★	★	★	
Handle construction and building maintenance	★	★	★	
Manage equipment repair	★	★	★	★
Oversee pest control in greenhouse	★	★	★	
Test water quality in greenhouse		★	★	
Maintain plants in greenhouse		★	★	
Tend to permits and hazardous waste control	★	★	★	★

Critical Thinking

Why is the operations manager crucial to the success of a biotechnology business?

N C L B
This chart relates academic skills such as English Language Arts, Mathematics, Science, Social Studies, and World Languages to specific tasks that are performed for the job featured in the Career Spotlight feature.

Critical Thinking

An operations manager is crucial to any business that uses expensive equipment, maintains strict safety, health, and environmental standards, and employs a large number of people doing specialized work.

CHAPTER **19** Review & Activities

Key Terms and Academic Vocabulary Review

1. Students should write complete sentences using each term correctly. A sample answer might read: "Due to *inflation*, this blouse costs $5 more than it did last year."

Review Key Concepts

2. In a free-enterprise system, individuals or businesses may buy, sell, and set prices with little government interference. Producers are companies or individuals who make goods or provide services. Consumers are people who buy goods or services. The marketplace is anywhere goods or services are sold.

3. Prices go up and down because of supply and demand, changes in production costs, and the level of competition between different businesses selling the same good or service.

4. Three factors used to measure the health of the economy are the gross domestic product (GDP), the Consumer Price Index (CPI), and the unemployment rate.

5. You can make smart shopping decisions by paying attention to quality and buying well-made items that will last for a long time, timing your purchases to avoid buying certain products or services when increased demand has caused prices to rise, shopping at discount and warehouse stores for bargains on name brands, using coupons and special discounts offered in print, online, or for being a member of a group, buying used items that are still in good working order, and using the Internet as both a tool for researching products and services and for convenient, money-saving shopping.

CHAPTER SUMMARY

Section 19.1

The United States has a free enterprise economic system, in which there is limited governmental regulation of the production, buying, and selling of goods and services. The marketplace is the arena where producers and consumers "meet" for buying and selling. Prices may go up or down, depending on supply and demand, production costs, and competition. A period in which the economy is growing is called expansion, and a period in which the economy is declining in growth is called recession. These fluctuations are called the business cycle. The condition of the economy can be measured by the Gross Domestic Product, the Consumer Price Index, and the unemployment rate.

Section 19.2

Smart shopping involves paying attention to quality, timing purchases, taking advantage of discount stores, considering second-hand goods, and exploring online options when possible. There are a number of methods of consumer fraud, including fraudulent advertising, auto repair fraud, and fake prize notifications. Consumers need to be aware of fraud schemes and to be on guard against getting cheated. Government agencies and private consumer groups protect and educate the consumer as well as handle consumer complaints.

Key Terms and Academic Vocabulary Review

1. Use each of these key terms and academic vocabulary words in a sentence.

Key Terms
- economics (p. 425)
- economic system (p. 425)
- free enterprise (p. 425)
- consumers (p. 425)
- producers (p. 425)
- marketplace (p. 427)
- gross domestic product (GDP) (p. 428)
- inflation (p. 429)
- warranty (p. 432)
- consumer fraud (p. 433)
- bait and switch (p. 433)

Academic Vocabulary
- regulation (p. 425)
- fluctuate (p. 427)
- indicators (p. 428)
- fraudulent (p. 433)

Review Key Concepts

2. **Define** a free-enterprise system and describe producers, consumers, and the marketplace.
3. **Explain** why prices go up and down.
4. **List** three factors used to measure the health of the economy.
5. **Explain** how to make wise shopping decisions.
6. **Identify** common types of consumer fraud and ways to protect yourself as a consumer.

Critical Thinking

7. **Compare and Contrast** How would life in the United States be different if our economy had much stricter controls on what types of goods and services could be produced?
8. **Evaluate** Describe a situation in which others might have a negative influence on your shopping choices.

6. Common types of fraud include fraudulent advertising like bait and switch, phony prize notifications, repair fraud, and computer fraud. You can protect yourself by never giving personal financial information over the phone if you did not place the call and not sending money to any unknown business or organization without checking its legitimacy with a consumer office or the Better Business Bureau. You can also use the resources of government agencies and organizations that serve to protect consumers from fraud.

Critical Thinking

7. Answers should note that consumers would have a much smaller range of choices in which products and services they could buy. Stricter controls would also reduce the number of producers, since the means of production would likely be concentrated among those individuals and businesses that already sell the approved goods and services. This would greatly reduce entrepreneurship and incentive for innovation. The lack of competition would cause prices to rise.

Real-World Skills and Applications

Information Literacy Skills

9. Acquiring and Evaluating Information Find the online version of the Consumer Action Handbook developed by the Federal Citizen Information Center. Choose a consumer topic in which you are interested, such as buying a new car, and explore the information provided on the site. Summarize your findings in a one-page report, and explain how the information would be helpful to you as a consumer.

Technology Applications

10. Creating a Spreadsheet Create a spreadsheet that you can use to record price comparisons information for a product you might like to purchase. Include in your spreadsheet specific columns that show comparisons according to brand name,

store, online availability, and any other categories that might apply to this purchase.

Financial Literacy Skills

11. Budgeting for Purchases You are going to attend the school dance. After buying the tickets for yourself and your date, you have $100 left. You had thought you would go out for dessert with friends after the dance, but you also need clothes for the evening and money for gas. Research options and determine how you can stretch your $100 to cover all of your expenses or decide what you will need to cut out. Explain your choices and final estimate for the evening in a one-page plan.

 Log On Go to this book's Online Learning Center through **glencoe.com** for help with financial literacy.

12. **Locating Resources** Use the phone book, the Internet, or library resources to locate various consumer groups and consumer resources in your area. Create a list of these resources and contact two to discover what kind of services or information they offer. Report your findings to the class.

13. **ROLE PLAY** **Stick to Your Budget**

Situation You are a customer at a car dealership, and you are interested in purchasing a new car. You have a limited budget, but the sales representative is determined to sell you an expensive car.

Activity Role-play a situation in which you adhere to your budget when shopping for a new car, despite various persuasive attempts used by the sales representative. Create firm yet polite responses to address the common sales techniques that you expect to encounter in such a situation. Be sure to explain your budget—and the rationale behind it—to the sales representative.

Evaluation You will be evaluated on how well you meet the following performance indicators:

- Use appropriate responses to manage the situation without resorting to anger or frustration, or giving up.
- Demonstrate an understanding of the consumer advice presented in the chapter.

categories that students deem necessary. Evaluate spreadsheets for accuracy and clarity.

11. Student methods of organizing and presenting their school-dance budget may vary but should present realistic figures, a clear explanation for the budget choices made, and demonstrate understanding of the smart shopping tips presented in the chapter material.

ACTIVE LEARNING

12. Answers will depend on the groups or resources chosen, but encourage students to recognize that the services and information offered by consumer groups and consumer resources are valuable tools for making informed consumer decisions.

ROLE PLAY

13. Effective presenters should synthesize the material presented in the chapter in an organized, coherent fashion. They should be able to provide all necessary information about the sales situation to allow the audience to make decisions about why the customer is wise to resist the sales representative's pressure tactics. Evaluate presentations for accuracy, clarity, and creativity. Encourage students with more outgoing personalities to play the part of the representative to lend the role play a greater sense of authenticity.

8. One example might be a salesperson pressuring you to buy a more expensive suit than you can afford.

Real-World Skills and Applications

9. Summaries should show awareness that doing research and taking advantage of available resources helps you make more informed consumer decisions. For example, if a student chooses the section on buying a cell phone, he or she would be advised to find out the area

of the provider's cell coverage, to buy a plan tailored to how often they expect to use the phone, to look into the cost effectiveness of a family-plan option, to make certain that they can cancel a plan without being stuck with a long-term contract, and other information.

10. Spreadsheets should demonstrate that students are able to accurately construct a spreadsheet using computer applications. All spreadsheets should have columns according to brand name, store, online availability, and any other

Academic Skills in the Workplace

14. Posters should demonstrate an understanding of the consumer-protection tips covered in the chapter material. Evaluate posters for accuracy, clarity, and creativity. Encourage students to research consumer tips not covered in the book, or to go into greater detail about how to avoid being the victim of fraudulent business practices. For example, the poster could include information about learning to avoid scams found in "spam" e-mails.

15. Gender, race, and favorite product are examples of categorical data. Age and income are measurement data. To analyze data in order to determine probability, formulate questions that can be addressed with data, then collect, organize, and display relevant data to answer them.

16. Presentations should demonstrate understanding of how producers use the marketplace to market their goods and services to consumers. Presentations should define *sampling* as measuring a subset of the population for statistical purposes and *control groups* as a group in a test setting that closely resembles the test group in demographic terms, but does not use the new product. Evaluate presentations for length, organization, accuracy, and creativity.

Academic Skills in the Workplace

English Language Arts

14. Creative Thinking Imagine that you have taken a job with a consumer protection agency. As part of a team, you are asked to create a poster that provides consumer tips for making good purchases and avoiding consumer fraud. Conduct research to come up with ten tips. Then illustrate each one with drawings or photos. Present your poster to the class.

Mathematics

15. Understanding Data Thomas is analyzing data about the consumer base for a specific company. He has information on consumer age, gender, race, income, geographic location, and favorite product or products. Before he can compute any statistics, he has to decide whether the different variables he is analyzing are categorical data or measurement data.

 Categorical Data and Measurement Data When you analyze data, it is important to know whether it is qualitative or quantitative. *Categorical data* is qualitative and can be split into discrete categories. *Measurement data* or numerical data is quantitative because it is continuous and does not fall into discrete categories.

Starting Hint Since age is continuous, it is measurement data. Gender, on the other hand, falls into two categories, so it is categorical.

Social Studies

16. Sampling and Control Groups Before a new product is brought to the market, marketing professionals often test the market for the product using *sampling* and *control groups*. Using Internet and library resources, find and record the definition of each of these terms as they apply to research and statistics. Next, decide how you might test public reaction to a new product using sampling and/or control groups. Write out your research goals and the steps you would take to reach your goals. Include the materials and the time that you would need to complete this market research. Present this information to the class in a five-minute oral presentation.

STANDARDIZED TEST PRACTICE

TRUE/FALSE QUESTIONS

Directions: Read the following statement and determine whether the statement is true or false.

> **Test-Taking Tip** For true/false questions, look for "clue" words that usually make a statement false. Some of these words are *always, all, only, none,* and *very*. Words such as *usually* and *generally* are often used with true statements.

1. Inflation happens when the prices of goods and services decrease as a result of an increase in the purchasing power of money.

   a. True
   b. False

STANDARDIZED TEST PRACTICE

Answer
1. b. False

Test-Taking Strategies
Whether your students have a standardized test coming up in a few days or a few weeks, these last-minute test-prep tips and strategies will help students relax and do their best.

Test Format Help your students become familiar with the format of the specific test they are going to take by practicing with test items that imitate the actual test items as closely as possible.

Test Timing Have your students take one or more timed practice tests so that they become comfortable with the test format.

Writing Skills Practice

17. Writing Business Letters Business letters between consumers and producers may take the form of complaints or requests for information.

 Practice Prepare a letter either asking for information or complaining about a particular product. Find out who you need to send the letter to and where you need to send it. Next, look up business letter formats on the web or in the library. Follow the format to compose your letter. Follow the steps below as you write your letter:

- Identify the purpose of your letter.
- List the information you need from the company or want to include in the letter.
- Write out a draft of your letter.
- Proofread your letter and be sure to check for correct formatting.

Net Connection

18. Compare Economic Systems Now that you have a basic understanding of the workings of and employment opportunities available in our free-enterprise system, research the economic system, type of government, and job opportunities of a foreign country where you would like to work.

@ Log On Visit this book's OLC through **glencoe.com** to help you find links about the economic system, type of government, and job opportunities for a country other than the United States. Create a Venn diagram comparing and contrasting the economic system, type of government, and job opportunities of this country with those of the United States.

Reading Connection
@ Go to this book's Online Learning Center through **glencoe.com** for a list of reading suggestions.

Personal Academic and Career Portfolio

Creating a Job Application Information Sheet

When you apply for a job, you will probably be asked to fill out an application that will ask for information that may not be on your résumé. For instance, applications often ask for complete addresses and phone numbers of companies where you have worked. It is helpful to have this information close at hand, especially if you need to fill out the application at the job site. In order to save time and reduce stress before your interviews, create a job application information sheet that you can take with you and use as a quick reference. Include the following:

- Your contact information.
- Special skills, including computer and trade skills, foreign languages, typing speed, etc.
- Include your job history, including start and end dates, the individuals to whom you reported, your responsibilities, and contact numbers and addresses.
- Personal reference information, including the number of years you've known your reference and their contact information.
- Awards received and volunteer work.

Create a new section for your portfolio and label the section *Job Application Information Sheet.* Be sure to update your information sheet whenever you have new information to add.

> **@ Portfolio Help** Go to the *Succeeding in the World of Work* OLC through **glencoe.com** for templates you can use to help you create your portfolio.

Writing Skills Practice

17. Business letters will vary according to the type of letter students choose but should adopt a courteous, professional tone, accurately convey the request or complaint, and follow the business letter format and writing steps outlined in the prompt.

Net Connection

18. Venn diagrams will vary but should demonstrate that students have navigated the OLC, found the relevant information, and understand the comparisons and contrasts between the selected country's economic system and that of the United States. Students should be able to connect the information in the diagram with the chapter material.

Resources

@ *ExamView Assessment Suite* CD allows you to print out ready-made unit and chapter tests complete with answer keys. You can also create customized tests.

WorkKeys

WorkKeys® is a job skills assessment program. For information on leveled assessment for Problem-Solving Skills (Applied Mathematics; Applied Technology; Locating Information; and Observation), go to the WorkKeys link on this book's OLC through **glencoe.com**.

Personal Academic and Career Portfolio

Maintaining a Portfolio

Tell students that the Job Application Information Sheet in their **Personal Academic and Career Portfolios** will always be subject to change. As their job experiences, skills, and personal circumstances change, the content on the information sheet should be reviewed and, if necessary, updated. For example, if a student takes a computer course and receives a certificate of competency in using a software program such as Photoshop, the information sheet will need to be updated to reflect this additional skill. Encourage students to review their information sheet periodically to ensure it remains current and effective.

Chapter Resources Planning Guide with Activities and Features

Section	Features	Activities
Section 20.1 **Budgeting**	Everyday Ethics (p. 446) Real-World Connection (p. 448) Math in Action (p. 449) Hot Jobs! (p. 450)	Before You Read (p. 444) Graphic Organizer (p. 444) As You Read (p. 446) After You Read (p. 450)
Section 20.2 **Financial Responsibility**	21st Century Workplace (p. 453) Creative Business Practices (p. 454) Career Checklist (p. 455)	Before You Read (p. 451) Graphic Organizer (p. 451) As You Read (p. 453) After You Read (p. 455)

NCLB Activities, information, and skills practice will help your students attain No Child Left Behind proficiency. Students will improve their abilities in the following academic standards areas:

Academic Standards Correlations

Discipline	Standard	Feature/Activity
English Language Arts	**NCTE 1** Read texts to acquire new information.	Hot Jobs! (p. 450) Creative Business Practices (p. 454)
	NCTE 7 Conduct research and gather, evaluate, and synthesize data to communicate discoveries.	Real-World Connection (p. 448)
	NCTE 9 Develop an understanding of diversity in language use across cultures.	21st Century Workplace (p. 453)
	NCTE 12 Use language to accomplish individual purposes.	After You Read (p. 455) Writing Skills Practice (p. 461)
Mathematics	**Number and Operation:** Compute fluently and make reasonable estimates	Math in Action (p. 449)
	Algebra: Analyze change in various contexts **Geometry:** Use visualization, spatial reasoning, and geometric modeling to solve problems	After You Read (p. 450)
	Data Analysis and Probability: Understand and apply basic concepts of probability	Academic Skills in the Workplace (p. 460)
Science	**Physical Science:** Conservation of energy and increase in disorder	Academic Skills in the Workplace (p. 460)

21st Century Skills and Workplace Competencies Correlations

CORRELATIONS The charts show the 21st Century Skills, foundation skills, and workplace competencies that students develop as they work in this chapter.

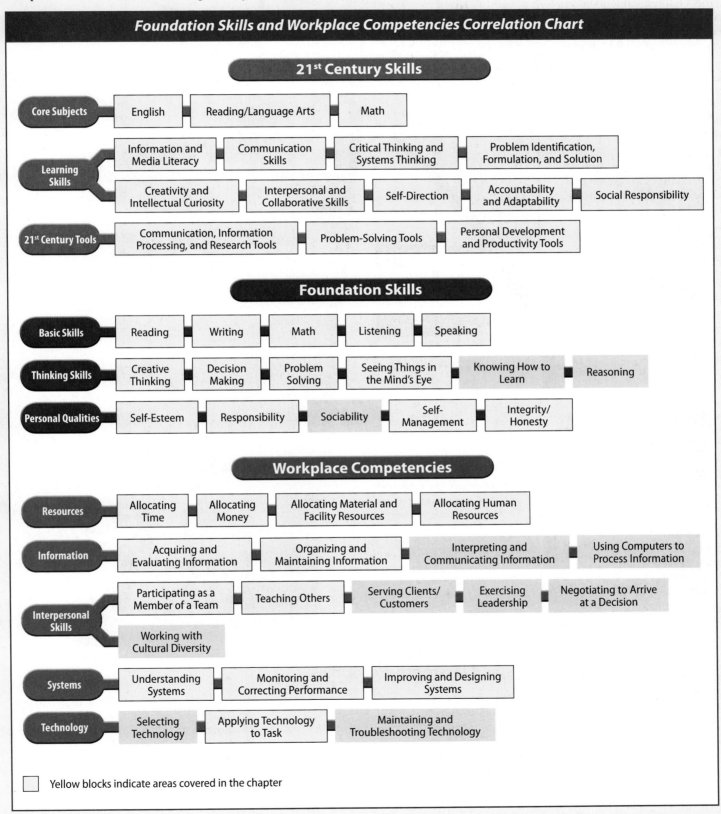

Foundation Skills and Workplace Competencies Correlation Chart

21st Century Skills

Core Subjects
- English
- Reading/Language Arts
- Math

Learning Skills
- Information and Media Literacy
- Communication Skills
- Critical Thinking and Systems Thinking
- Problem Identification, Formulation, and Solution
- Creativity and Intellectual Curiosity
- Interpersonal and Collaborative Skills
- Self-Direction
- Accountability and Adaptability
- Social Responsibility

21st Century Tools
- Communication, Information Processing, and Research Tools
- Problem-Solving Tools
- Personal Development and Productivity Tools

Foundation Skills

Basic Skills
- Reading
- Writing
- Math
- Listening
- Speaking

Thinking Skills
- Creative Thinking
- Decision Making
- Problem Solving
- Seeing Things in the Mind's Eye
- Knowing How to Learn
- Reasoning

Personal Qualities
- Self-Esteem
- Responsibility
- Sociability
- Self-Management
- Integrity/Honesty

Workplace Competencies

Resources
- Allocating Time
- Allocating Money
- Allocating Material and Facility Resources
- Allocating Human Resources

Information
- Acquiring and Evaluating Information
- Organizing and Maintaining Information
- Interpreting and Communicating Information
- Using Computers to Process Information

Interpersonal Skills
- Participating as a Member of a Team
- Teaching Others
- Serving Clients/Customers
- Exercising Leadership
- Negotiating to Arrive at a Decision
- Working with Cultural Diversity

Systems
- Understanding Systems
- Monitoring and Correcting Performance
- Improving and Designing Systems

Technology
- Selecting Technology
- Applying Technology to Task
- Maintaining and Troubleshooting Technology

Yellow blocks indicate areas covered in the chapter

Chapter Overview
Introduce the Chapter

In this chapter, students learn how to prepare a budget, keep effective records, and implement financial planning strategies.

Section 20.1 explains the steps in preparing a budget, keeping records effectively, and strategies to stick to a budget.

Section 20.2 shows how to adjust to personal and economic changes and gives tips for seeking help for financial problems.

Build Background

Ask students to give reasons they should learn how to manage their money now. Then discuss how money management relates to fulfilling short-term and long-term financial goals. Explain that the choices people make can determine whether or not they meet their financial goals.

▶ Exploring the Photo

Caption Answer Other practices including carrying a set amount of cash and keeping track of how money is being spent.

Discussion Have students brainstorm ways to save money when shopping for groceries. For example, depending on the item, generic or in-store brands of certain goods cost less than the same name-brand items. Buying individual components of a salad and making the salad yourself is typically less expensive than buying a bagged, prepared salad.

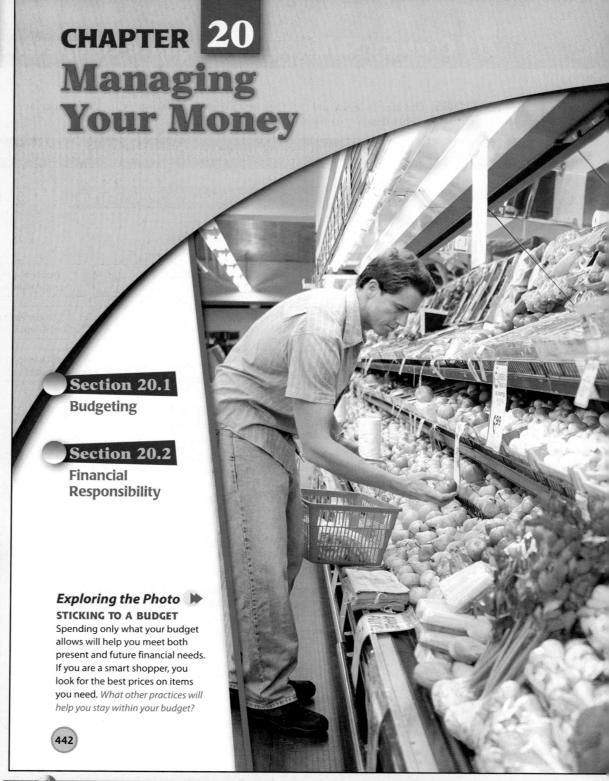

CHAPTER 20
Managing Your Money

● **Section 20.1**
Budgeting

● **Section 20.2**
Financial Responsibility

Exploring the Photo ▶▶
STICKING TO A BUDGET
Spending only what your budget allows will help you meet both present and future financial needs. If you are a smart shopper, you look for the best prices on items you need. *What other practices will help you stay within your budget?*

442

📀 Classroom Resources

📂 Student Edition
📂 Teacher Wraparound Edition
📂 Student Activity Workbook with Academic Integration
📂 Student Activity Workbook with Academic Integration TAE
📂 *Fast File,* Unit 6 Resources

📂 Inclusion in the Career Education Classroom
💿 TeacherWorks™ Plus
💿 *ExamView Assessment Suite*
💿 Interactive Chalkboard
💿 Interactive Student Edition
📝 Online Student Edition
📝 Online Learning Center (OLC) with Podcasts

Chapter Objectives

After completing this chapter, you will be able to:

- **Identify** the steps to take to prepare a budget.
- **Explain** how to keep records effectively.
- **Describe** strategies that will help you stay within your budget.
- **Name** personal changes that can affect your financial situation.
- **Describe** ways to adapt to changes in the economy.
- **List** sources of help for financial problems.

Writing Activity Personal Career Notebook

A budget helps you keep track of your income and expenses. Think about and write down responses to the following questions:
- Should you stick to a budget? Why or why not?
- Should a business stick to a budget? Why or why not?
- Should the government stick to a budget? Why or why not?

Get Motivated! Contact a small business owner or local government official. Ask this person about the importance of budgeting. What strategies does the business or government use to stay within a budget? Under what circumstances might the business or government spend more than the budget allows? Summarize your discussion in a one-page report.

Chapter 20   Managing Your Money   **443**

Writing Activity Personal Career Notebook Answer Guide

Students who follow current events may be aware that governments at a variety of levels, including in the United States, regularly have budget deficits. While a personal budget is extremely small in comparison to that of a government, the principle remains the same: You should take out less than what you bring in. After students have read the chapter, encourage them to brainstorm ways governments reduce their budget deficits.

Get Motivated! Reports will vary but should demonstrate understanding of the information given by the business owner or official. Evaluate reports for clarity, length, and content.

Review the Objectives
Introduce the chapter by reviewing the chapter objectives:

Section 20.1 Objectives
Identify the steps to take to prepare a budget. (Define your short-term, medium-term, and long-term needs and goals, arrange these goals in order of importance, estimate your income and expenses, and use a form to create your budget.)

Explain how to keep records effectively. (Record your daily purchases and keep a well-organized record of your income and expenses.)

Describe strategies that will help you stay within your budget. (Cut back on your expenses, increase your income, carry a limited amount of cash and leave your ATM card at home, shop for discounts, and pay with cash instead of credit.)

Section 20.2 Objectives
Name personal changes that can affect your financial situation. (Personal changes can include changes in family life, such as the birth of a child; professional life, such as receiving a promotion or losing a job; and health, such as having a serious illness.)

Describe ways to adapt to changes in the economy. (Follow the news for signs of economic changes and save money to prepare for these changes, adjust your budget, cut back on unnecessary expenses, and work more hours or find a second job.)

List sources of help for financial problems. (published material, Web sites, schools, government agencies, banks, professionals who offer financial advice, and non-government organizations.)

Section 20.1

Budgeting

Bell Ringer Activity

Budgeting

Tell students to imagine they each have $100 to live on for the next two weeks. Have them list what they will buy and how much they will spend on each item. Remind them that they need to buy a birthday gift for a friend.

Resources

Interactive Chalkboard
The Interactive Chalkboard CD provides visual teaching aids for this section.

@ Online Learning Center
The Online Learning Center (OLC) through **glencoe.com** features chapter vocabulary, chapter summaries, and other study materials.

Preteaching

In this section, the term *flexible expenses* refers to expenses that vary each month. Ask students to write a sentence using the word *flexible* in a way that is similar to how it is used in this section.

Graphic Organizer

Tell students to go to the OLC through **glencoe.com** for a printable graphic organizer. (Graphic organizers should properly note the steps taken to create a budget.)

NCLB connects academic correlations to book content.

Reading Guide

Before You Read

Preview Read the Key Concepts. Write one or two sentences predicting what the section will be about.

Read to Learn
- The steps to take to prepare a budget
- How to keep records effectively
- Strategies that will help you stay within your budget

Main Idea
Developing and staying within a budget will enable you to manage your money effectively.

D Key Concepts
- Managing Your Money
- Following a Budget

Key Terms
- budget
- fixed expenses
- flexible expenses
- record keeping

Academic Vocabulary
You will find these words in your reading and on your tests. Use the academic vocabulary glossary to look up their definitions if necessary.
- allocate
- prioritizing
- exceed

Graphic Organizer
As you read, list the steps involved in preparing a budget. Use a chart like the one shown to help organize your information.

Steps to Create a Budget
1.
2.
3.
4.

 Log On Go to this book's Online Learning Center through **glencoe.com** for an online version of this graphic organizer.

Academic Standards · · · · · · · · · · · · · · · · · ·

N C L B

English Language Arts
- Conduct research and gather, evaluate, and synthesize data to communicate discoveries. (NCTE 7)

Mathematics
- Compute fluently and make reasonable estimates
- Analyze change in various contexts

Reading Guide

Before You Read
Tell students while they may look forward to the independence that is a part of joining the work force, this freedom also brings responsibilities, chief among them being spending and saving money wisely enough to pay for expenses.

D Develop Concepts
Main Idea Discuss the main idea with students. Ask students what they think "staying within a budget" means. (Staying within a budget includes knowing how much money you're making and spending wisely so you have enough to pay for basic needs and other expenses you are obligated to pay.)

Managing Your Money

For many, having a full-time job means financial independence. With independence come financial obligations. For example, you may need to pay rent each month. To be sure you meet your financial obligations, you should write a budget. A **budget** is a plan for saving and spending money based on your income and expenses.

Preparing a Budget

Preparing a budget will help you plan how you save, spend, and use money. A budget always covers a specific time. Most companies make yearly budgets. Most people make their budgets for a month. When you budget, you plan how to **allocate** your money to meet your current needs and achieve your future goals.

Define Your Needs and Goals

Chapters 2 and 5 of this book show you how to define your lifestyle and career goals. Defining your financial needs and goals is a similar process.

Make two lists. Label the first "Short-Term Needs and Goals." On this list, write the things you need or want to spend money on within the next six months. Perhaps you need new glasses or want to buy an MP3 player. Label the second list "Medium-Term and Long-Term Needs and Goals" (medium-term needs and goals can also be called intermediate needs and goals). On this list, put the things you need or want to spend money on in the future, such as paying for career training and education or buying a car.

Next to each item on the lists, assign a target date or time frame. For example, if you need glasses before you start your new job in May, write "May" next to that item. If you buy groceries each week, write "weekly" next to that item.

These lists identify your financial objectives. They are the starting point for your budget.

 SAVING FOR EDUCATION Funding a college education is a common financial goal. *What are some other long-term financial goals?*

Vocabulary

You can find definitions in the **Key Terms** glossary and **Academic Vocabulary** glossary at the back of this book.

 Chapter 20   Managing Your Money   **445**

Discussion Starter

Managing Your Money Ask students to think about their cash flow. Are they finding that they never have enough money to buy the things they need, or that they do not have any money left over for savings? Have students brainstorm why their money might not be spent wisely. (Answers may include eating in restaurants too often, spending money on clothes, CDs, or MP3 downloads, and not having a clear idea of how much money is being spent versus how much is earned through a job or allowance.)

W Writing Support

Explain Have students write a 100- to 150-word paragraph describing how the use of credit can either help or hinder a person trying to prepare a budget. (Paragraphs will vary. Credit helps if it allows a person to buy items needed before a paycheck arrives. Credit hurts if the person cannot pay the balance each month and continually adds more debt.)

Resources

TeacherWorks™ Plus The TeacherWorks software includes customizable built-in lesson plans and links to printable program resources.

Extend the Photo

Caption Answer Answers may include being able to pay for a new car or house, paying for a wedding and honeymoon, and saving enough money for retirement.

Discussion Ask students to discuss how receiving scholarship or grant money can affect a college budget plan. Encourage students to think about ways that money that had been saved for tuition could be used for practical purposes. For example, some of the money could be used to pay for a semester studying abroad, or to pay rent on an off-campus apartment instead of living in dormitories.

TEACH *(cont.)*

S Skill Practice
Guided Practice

Plan Tell students to write down five bills they think they would have to pay in a normal month. Have students use a monthly calendar to mark the dates their bills are due, then have them mark the 1st and 15th as days they will receive paychecks. Ask students to make a plan to meet their financial obligations on time. **L1**

Imagine Tell students to imagine themselves ten years from now. Have them describe their lifestyles in terms of housing, automobile, personal possessions, vacations, and leisure time. Have them write a 100-word paragraph describing what they could do now to reach their future goals? (Explain to students that successful financial management in adult life can be greatly influenced by attitudes and practices developed at a younger age, such as prioritizing and budgeting.) **L2**

Make Choices Have students list five or six things they would like to buy. Then have them divide their list into wants and needs. Explain to students that needs include things that come up unexpectedly and must be resolved immediately, such as repairing one's car in order to get to work. **L3**

As You Read

Sources of income include net earnings, tips, gifts of money, interest earned on bank accounts, and money from the government.

Everyday ETHICS

TAKING TIME OFF

When should you pay back a loan?

PUTTING OFF THE JOB SEARCH You recently graduated from college, and your family has loaned you money to pay your rent until you find a job. Your friend has decided to move in with you, so your living expenses have been cut in half. Because the money from your grandparents will now last twice as long, you are thinking about taking the summer off to travel and looking for a job in the fall.

What Would You Do? Do you think taking the summer off would be wise? Why or why not?

> **DISCUSS IT** What would happen if it took you longer to find a job than you expected? What would your family say about your decision about how to use the money they loaned you? Brainstorm with a partner and discuss the pros and cons of waiting until fall to look for a job.

As You Read

Explain What are some sources of income?

Make Choices

Now you will need to prioritize, or arrange the items in order of importance. **Prioritizing** will help you distinguish between your financial needs and wants and choose how to spend your money. Your needs will probably be a higher priority than your wants.

Estimate Income and Expenses

The next step in developing your budget is to estimate your income and your expenses. Your income is how much money you will have coming in and your expenses are how much will be going out.

If you have a job, your main source of income is likely to be your wages or salary. When you calculate your income, count only your net earnings, which is the amount left after taxes and other deductions have been taken out. Other sources of income include tips, gifts of money, and the interest earned on bank accounts. You may also receive money from the government.

To estimate your expenses, use the lists of needs and goals you already created. Next to each item, assign a cost. For example, if you expect to pay $90 for new glasses, write that amount next to the item. Sometimes people divide expenses into two types. **Fixed expenses** are expenses you have already agreed to pay and that must be paid by a particular date. Rent, health insurance, and car payments are examples of fixed expenses. **Flexible expenses** are expenses that vary each month, such as the costs of food and entertainment.

A good way to estimate income and expenses is to review records of past income and expenses, such as pay stubs, a check register, and bank statements. Be sure to examine your income and expenses over several months. Many expenses (such as car or insurance payments) are paid monthly. Some are paid less often. For planning purposes, divide these kinds of payments into monthly portions. For example, if you pay a car insurance premium every three months, divide the

---

Everyday ETHICS

What Would You Do? Answer One ethical response might be to contact your family and offer to return half of the money you borrowed. Another possible response would be to explain your travel plans to your family and make a mutual agreement on a schedule for repaying the loan.

> **DISCUSS IT** Encourage students to envision complications that might delay finding a job and the consequences of this delay not only on their financial standing, but on their relationship with their family. For example, ask them how they would feel about having to ask to borrow money again, having already made an unwise decision with the previous loan.

payment amount by three and list that amount as a monthly expense. If these amounts are likely to change in the next few months, adjust your amounts to reflect those changes.

Create Your Budget

Now that you have identified and prioritized your financial needs and goals and estimated your income and expenses, it is time to create your budget.

To create your budget, use a standard form such as the form shown in **Figure 20.1**. You can also use budget or spreadsheet software. Transfer your estimated income and expenses to your budget. Your income should be equal to or more than your total expenses. To make this happen, you may need to adjust the amounts in categories such as savings and variable expenses.

Figure 20.1   A BUDGET FORM

MONTHLY BUDGET		
	Estimated	**Actual**
INCOME		
Take-home pay		
Other sources (allowance, gifts, etc.)		
Total Income		
EXPENSES		
Savings		
Savings account		
Emergency fund		
Fixed Expenses		
Rent or mortgage		
Loans and car payments		
Insurance payments		
Credit card payments		
Flexible Expenses		
Food		
Utilities and telephone		
Household supplies		
Medical and dental		
Clothing		
Recreation		
Miscellaneous		
Total Expenses		

PLAN YOUR SPENDING Using a budget form such as this one will help you determine how much you can spend. *How would you use the column at the far right?*

Section 20.1

TEACH *(cont.)*

U Universal Access
Logical/Mathematical Learning Tell students to imagine that they have a life insurance premium of $412 due every three months. Ask them to calculate this premium as a monthly expense. (The monthly amount is $137.33 [$412 ÷ 3].) Tell students that a few months from now, the premium will increase by $27. Ask them to recalculate the premium as a monthly expense. (The recalculated monthly amount is $146.33 [$412 + $27 = $439; $439 ÷ 3].)

C Critical Thinking
Drawing Conclusions Have students imagine that after transferring their estimated income and expenses to their budgets, they find their total income is a little less than their total expenses. Ask students how they can make income equal to or more than expenses on their budget forms. (Either increase the amount in the savings category or decrease the amount in the flexible expenses category.)

EXTEND THE FIGURE   Figure 20.1

Caption Answer You would use it to record actual expenditures and compare them with estimates to determine whether you are sticking to your budget.

Discussion Point out that budgets in which average monthly income is equal to or only slightly higher than average monthly expenses do not allow for significant savings, which is money that is valuable in emergencies or for long-term planning goals. Lead a discussion about which monthly expenses could most easily be lowered without sacrificing one's well being or general happiness.

447

TEACH *(cont.)*

Discussion Starter

Keep Good Records Lead a discussion by asking students what kinds of methods they use to organize their class and study notes. Do they find that when they keep their notes organized, it is easier to study for tests? Ask students to brainstorm various ways they keep notes and how these methods could be effectively adapted for keeping financial records. (Answers may include daily recaps written in notebooks, graphic organizers, computer spreadsheets, file folders, and electronic files.)

✓ Reading Check

IDENTIFY Define your needs and goals, prioritize to help distinguish between needs and wants, estimate income and expenses, and use a form to create your budget.

ASSESS

Review Key Terms
Have students write sentences using each key term.

Online Study Tools
Have students go to the OLC through **glencoe.com** to:

- Download **Podcast** study tools.
- Download free **Study-to-Go** content to their PDAs or cell phones.

Resources

ExamView Assessment Suite CD allows you to print out ready-made unit and chapter tests complete with answer keys. You can also create customized tests.

Real-World Connection

Today's Choices Affect Tomorrow's Goals

You recently inherited enough money from a relative to pay off your college loans. You have a very low interest rate on those loans, so you are considering buying a new car instead.

Critical Thinking How will your decision about using the money affect your short-term and long-term goals?

Do Your Own Research Check with the loan officer of your local bank or use Internet resources to research college loans. Determine if there are penalties for paying off these loans early. Search the Internet to find the depreciation rate of a car you would like to purchase. Write a short report that lists the financial pros and cons of each option.

Notice that in the budget form, there is a category for savings. Saving will enable you to achieve your medium-term and long-term financial goals. Another reason to save is to create an emergency fund, which is money you put aside for needs you may not always be able to anticipate. For example, emergencies, such as a major illness or an accident, can happen to anyone. If you do not have money saved to cover the expenses brought on by these events, they can be financially devastating.

Consider savings a type of expense. If you plan to save the same way you plan to pay your bills, you will be more likely to do it. You can learn about savings options in Chapter 21.

Be realistic when you write your budget. A budget that is too strict will be impossible to follow and will make you resentful. Having a budget does not mean doing without all the things you enjoy. It may mean cutting back, though, and it should get you in the habit of thinking before you spend.

✓ Reading Check IDENTIFY What are the steps involved in preparing a budget?

Following a Budget

No matter how well you prepare your budget, it will not help you unless you follow it. To follow a budget, you must keep track of your expenses and check your expense records against your budget. If your expenses **exceed** the amount allowed, you may need to adjust your budget.

Keep Good Records

Record keeping, which is organizing and maintaining records of your income and spending, is an important part of following a budget. You should choose a way to do this. You might use a notebook to record your daily purchases. Keep all records of income and expenses you receive, such as receipts, bank statements, and pay stubs.

Establish a system for organizing and filing these records regularly. This way, you can easily find your records when you need them. A simple, inexpensive way to organize your records is with an accordion folder or a small filing cabinet. Record-keeping software allows you to keep records on a computer as well as in hard copy.

Check Your Progress

At least once a month, check your financial records against your budget. Review your spending carefully. Do your expenses exceed

---

Real-World Connection

Critical Thinking Answer Answers will vary. For many people, a reliable car is a need because it provides transportation to work. However, the car should be a smart purchase that does not strain a budget or add unnecessary, long-term debt to the already existing college loan debt. The best solution is one that balances the short-term need with the long-term goal of reducing overall debts.

Do Your Own Research Students' reports will vary. Students may find that a brand-new car, especially if a large portion of the price is paid for with a loan, may be an unwise option because of the steep depreciation rate in the first year. They may also find that many college loans have variable rates that can rise over time, increasing the overall debt amount.

your income? Are you spending too much in one area? Remember, your budget is a guide, and it is flexible. You can adjust it as your income, expenses, needs, and wants change.

S If your income does not cover your expenses, you have two choices: You can cut down on your expenses, and you can increase your income.

Cut Down on Your Expenses You can fine-tune your budget by cutting down on your flexible expenses. For example, renting a DVD rather than purchasing it at a retail store, packing your lunch instead of eating at restaurants, and carpooling with a coworker to save money on gas are all examples of ways to reduce flexible expenses.

Increase Your Income Working more hours, finding a second job, or getting a new, better-paying job are ways to increase your income.

It may take a few months to figure out and be able to create a realistic and usable budget. In addition, if you are just starting out on your own and have recently moved into a place of your own, many one-time costs, such as setup costs for utilities or a security deposit, can throw off your monthly expenditures. You might have a short waiting period before getting your first paycheck at a new job, or you might need to make several one-time purchases for household necessities. These things add up quickly and need to be taken into account in your budget. Keep fine-tuning your budget until you have a budget that is flexible and works for you.

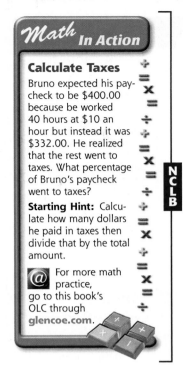

Math **In Action**

Calculate Taxes
Bruno expected his paycheck to be $400.00 because be worked 40 hours at $10 an hour but instead it was $332.00. He realized that the rest went to taxes. What percentage of Bruno's paycheck went to taxes?

Starting Hint: Calculate how many dollars he paid in taxes then divide that by the total amount.

@ For more math practice, go to this book's OLC through **glencoe.com**.

◀◀ **CUTTING BACK**
Cooking meals at home rather than eating out is one way to cut your expenses. *What are some other ways you could cut expenses to stay on budget?*

glencoe.com

RETEACH

S **Skill Practice Guided Practice**

Making Calculations Give small teams of students the following information: They have total weekly expenses of $375, of which $90 are variable expenses. They work 30 hours a week and have a take-home pay of $330 per week. Have teams present a strategy for making total weekly expenses match total weekly income. (Plans will vary but may include one or all of the following strategies: cutting variable expenses, working more hours, asking for and receiving a pay raise, or obtaining a new job that pays a higher hourly wage.)

N C L B Activity correlated to Mathematics standards.

Math **In Action**

The amount that went to taxes is 0.17 or 17 percent ($400 − $332 = $68; $68 ÷ $400 = .17).

Resources

📁 **Student Activity Workbook** Assign the Chapter 20 activities in the Student Activity Workbook.

▶▶ **Extend the Photo**

Caption Answer Answers may include renting videos instead of seeing movies at theaters (or not buying popcorn and soda at theaters), walking or using public transportation instead of driving when practical, using the library to borrow magazines or books instead of purchasing them, and looking for sales and discounts when shopping.

Discussion Have students imagine that after many weeks of cooking meals at home, they are going to a restaurant for a special dinner. Point out that although they are eating out, they can still cut expenses and stay on budget. Lead a discussion about ways to lower a meal check while still enjoying the experience.

ASSESS

After You Read

Have students complete the Section 20.1 After You Read section review.

Online Study Tools

Have students go to the OLC through **glencoe.com** to:

- Take the Section 20.1 **Practice Test**.
- Download **Podcast** study tools.
- Download free **Study-to-Go** content to their PDAs or cell phones.

CLOSE

Culminating Activity

Making the Case for a Budget Tell students to imagine they have a friend who has a good-paying job but is always asking for loans so he can get by until he gets his next paycheck. Have students write a 200-word letter to this friend explaining why he would be able to manage his money better if he prepared a budget and stuck to it. Encourage students to include instructions for the friend to follow in developing his budget.

NCLB Activity correlated to Mathematics standards.

HOT JOBS!

Casting Director

Film, television, print, and advertising production companies hire casting directors to find "talent"—actors, models, or other performers. Job duties can include reading scripts, screening and auditioning applicants, and creating and maintaining a database of potential hires. A casting director needs good interpersonal and organizational skills.

Tips for Staying on Budget

Following a budget requires effort and discipline. It may help to remember that the reason you created a budget was to meet your financial needs and goals.

Here are some other suggestions for staying on budget:

- **Carry a limited amount of cash.** Carry only the cash you need and leave your ATM card or checkbook at home. This can help you prevent impulse buying and get you in the habit of thinking before you buy.
- **Shop smart.** Practice smart shopping strategies such as taking advantage of discounts. This will help you get the best value for your money.
- **Pay with cash.** Paying with cash, rather than taking out a loan or using a credit card, can help you avoid overspending and keep you from paying the high costs of credit. However, be sure to keep track of how you are spending your cash as well.

Section 20.1 After You Read

Review Key Concepts

1. Define *income* and *expenses*. Describe the budgeting step of estimating income and expenses.
2. Explain why good record keeping is important to the budgeting process.
3. Name two strategies that can help you stay within your budget.

Practice Academic Skills

 Mathematics

4. Mario is deciding between two jobs. He wants to analyze how his earnings in each job would change over time. In Job 1, he would start at a salary of $34,000 and receive a $1,000 yearly raise. At Job 2, he would start at $36,000 and receive a $500 yearly raise. To project and analyze the earnings potential of the two jobs, graph both income curves using equations in slope-intercept form.

NCLB

CONCEPT **Slope-Intercept Form** Equations written as $y = mx + b$, where m is the slope and b is the y-intercept, are linear equations in slope-intercept form. You can use the slope-intercept form to graph a line by plotting the y-intercept and using the slope to find another point, then connecting the two.

Step 1: Draw a graph, being sure to label the axes. Create an equation for each income curve using the y-intercepts ($34,000 and $36,000) and the slopes ($1,000 and $500).

Step 2: Plot the y-intercepts for both equations. Put another number into each equation to find two more points, and connect the pairs of points.

 Math For math help, go to the Math Appendix located at the back of this book.

450 **Unit 6** Life Skills

Section 20.1 After You Read

Review Key Concepts

1. *Income* is how much money you have coming in and *expenses* are how much you have going out. Income is estimated by adding together net earnings, tips, gifts of money, interest earned on bank accounts, and any money received from the government. Expenses are divided into *fixed* expenses, which you have agreed to pay and must pay by a particular date, and *flexible* expenses, the amounts of which vary from month to month. You have some control over the amount of your flexible expenses.

2. A sample answer might be that good record keeping allows you to see how well you are sticking to a budget and identify areas that need to be adjusted.

3. Check your financial records against your budget, cut back on expenses, and increase income.

Practice Academic Skills

4. Job 2 has greater earnings potential until the fourth year, when both jobs pay $38,000 salary. After that, Job 1 has greater earnings potential.

Financial Responsibility

Reading Guide

Before You Read

Preview Choose a Key Term or Academic Vocabulary word that is new to you. Write it on a piece of paper. When you find it in the text, write down the definition.

Read to Learn
- How personal changes can affect your financial situation
- Ways to adapt to changes in the economy
- Sources of help for financial problems

Main Idea

D Learning financial planning strategies now will enable you to manage your finances successfully in the future.

Key Concepts
- Financial Changes
- Financial Help

Key Terms
◆ financial responsibility
◆ financial planning

Academic Vocabulary

You will find this word in your reading and on your tests. Use the academic vocabulary glossary to look up its definition if necessary.
■ project

Graphic Organizer

As you read, note the personal and economic changes that can affect your financial situation. Use a chart like the one shown to help organize your information.

Changes that Can Affect Your Financial Situation	
Personal Changes	**Economic Changes**

 Log On Go to this book's Online Learning Center through **glencoe.com** for an online version of this graphic organizer.

Academic Standards •••••••••••••••••••••

English Language Arts
- Read texts to acquire new information. (NCTE 1)
- Develop an understanding of diversity in language use across cultures. (NCTE 9)
- Use language to accomplish individual purposes. (NCTE 12)

 FOCUS

Bell Ringer Activity

Financial Responsibility

Tell students their friend has inherited her grandfather's ranch house and wants to sell it to them for less than market value. However, the real estate market is very slow. Lead a discussion about the pros and cons of making such an investment.

Resources

 Interactive Chalkboard
The Interactive Chalkboard CD provides visual teaching aids for this section.

Online Learning Center
The OLC through **glencoe.com** features chapter vocabulary, chapter summaries, and other study materials.

Preteaching
Read the definitions of the key terms aloud. Tell students that *financial planning* is a component of *financial responsibility*.

Graphic Organizer
Tell students to go to the OLC through **glencoe.com** for a printable graphic organizer. (Charts should show examples of personal and economic changes that can affect a person's financial situation.)

 NCLB connects academic correlations to book content.

Reading Guide

Before You Read
Read the Key Terms and Academic Vocabulary out loud to the class. Ask students to speculate about what the word "project" means in the context of one's future finances. Explain that in this section, the word is a verb with a meaning similar to "anticipate."

D ### Develop Concepts
Main Idea Ask volunteers to give examples of how learning financial planning strategies at a young age is better than waiting until later to learn by trial and error.

Discussion Starter

Financial Changes Ask students to give examples of things for which they are financially responsible now. Then ask them to brainstorm the things for which they will eventually be financially responsible. Write these lists on the board.

R Reading Strategy

Using Words in Context Write the following sentence on the board: *They projected the business costs for the next two years.* Ask students for a definition of *project* in this context. (to estimate for the future)

C Critical Thinking

Contrasting Ask students how not attending college may or may not affect a person's financial planning in contrast to someone who graduates from college owing thousands of dollars in loans. (Long-term expenses may be lower for those who do not attend college due to not owing money for college loans, but long-term income may also be lower due to having fewer lucrative employment prospects.) Point out that it is possible to achieve long-term financial success without attending college, though it may be a more challenging path.

Resources

 TeacherWorks™ Plus
The TeacherWorks software includes customizable built-in lesson plans and links to printable program resources.

◀ **Vocabulary**
You can find definitions in the **Key Terms** glossary and **Academic Vocabulary** glossary at the back of this book.

Financial Changes

As you get older, your **financial responsibility**, which is your accountability in money matters, increases. You may already have more financial responsibility than you had as a child. Maybe you have an allowance or a part-time or full-time job. You may have to help pay for school supplies or help with family purchases. In the future, your level of financial responsibility will increase even more.

How will you handle this additional financial responsibility? What are some factors that might affect your financial situation?

Adjusting to Personal Changes

The key to managing financial responsibility is financial planning. **Financial planning** means developing a strategy to meet present and long-term financial needs. You already learned to prepare and follow a budget. That is part of financial planning. Another part of financial planning is the ability to **project**, or anticipate, changes that might affect your finances and prepare for them.

Changes in your personal life are one type of change that can affect your financial situation. These include changes in your family life, your professional life, and your health. Some changes, such as attending college, may result in increased expenses. Others, such as receiving a promotion, may result in greater income. Increasing independence is another change that will affect your financial situation. What strategies do you use now to adapt to change?

Recognizing these possibilities and learning to adapt will help you to cope when the changes occur. You can also add to your savings regularly.

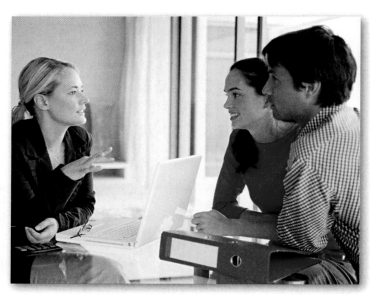

▶▶ **USING AVAILABLE RESOURCES** Most banks will help you with financial planning if you run into difficulties. *How might a bank be able to help you if you were to lose your job?*

▶▶ *Extend the Photo*

Caption Answer Banks can offer personal loans or personal lines of credit to help get through a period without income, though students should understand that this is not "free money" and has to be repaid with interest over time. Most banks offer free financial advice to members, and some host seminars on dealing with financial changes.

Discussion Have students imagine they have lost their job and have rent and bills to pay while they try to find a new position. They have about $2,000 in savings, but they are reluctant to use it now because the money is being saved for a new car. Their bank offers personal loans. Lead a discussion on whether it's best to spend savings or take out a loan.

The 21ˢᵗ Century Workplace

Yes, You Do Know Greek

The English language has borrowed thousands of words from the Greek language. Because the ancient Greeks influenced our culture in the areas of politics and culture, many political and cultural terms, such as *democracy, drama,* and *athletics,* come from Greek *roots* or content words. Some English speakers have created new English words by combining ancient Greek words. For example, a scientist invented the word *photography* in 1839 by joining the Greek roots *photo* ("light") and *graph* ("writing" or "drawing").

CRITICAL THINKING _____

The Greek language that was spoken 3,500 to 2,500 years ago is very different from the Greek language that is spoken in Greece today. Why do you think languages change over time?

In Your Community

In ancient Greek democracy, political participation was limited to upper-class adult males. How and when did *democracy,* or rule by the people, change to include participation by women and members of all economic classes? Ask a social studies teacher to help you research this topic. Share your thoughts with the class in an informal discussion.

@ **Extend Your Learning** Learning Greek roots can help you figure out the meanings of many words you encounter in your reading. For links to Web sites with information about Greek roots, go to this book's OLC through **glencoe.com**.

Adjusting to Economic Changes

Changes in the nation and the world also can affect your finances. Natural disasters, war, changes in technology, the outsourcing of jobs to other countries, and increased energy costs are just a few examples of events that can affect the economy. As also discussed in Chapter 19, economic changes can affect your personal financial situation.

As You Read

Explain How can world and national events affect your financial situation?

Inflation and Recession

S You may need to adjust your budget to reflect changes in the economy. When economic conditions are good, prices tend to rise. This general increase in prices is called *inflation.* During times of inflation, your dollars will buy less than they did before.

As long as wages rise with prices, you will still be able to purchase items and pay your bills. If prices go up but wages do not, however, you may have a difficult time staying on budget.

Here are some tips for coping with inflation:

- **Be prepared.** Following reliable news sources will help you anticipate economic changes. Be prepared for how these changes will affect you.
- **Adjust your budget.** Your budget should reflect your financial situation.
- **Cut back on unnecessary expenses.** These might include eating out and entertainment.
- **Work more hours or look for a second job.** This will increase your income.
- **Be a smart shopper.** Use smart shopping strategies such as taking advantage of sales.

glencoe.com

The 21ˢᵗ Century Workplace

CRITICAL THINKING ANSWER The Greek language has changed greatly over thousands of years due to the development of distinct dialects in different regions of the Greek empire and the mixture of dialects as a result of migration. Migration has a large impact on the development of a language. For example, isolation from Great Britain and the emergence of new American dialects led to the differences between American English and British English that are apparent today.

In Your Community Encourage students to share their research and thoughts. Political participation by women and members of all economic classes is a relatively recent trend in history.

TEACH *(cont.)*

S Skill Practice
Guided Practice

Research Tell students that the opposite of inflation is *deflation,* a sustained, falling general level of prices. Ask students to research and write a 150-word paragraph about whether deflation is good for the economy. (Paragraphs should indicate that deflation has a negative effect on the economy. Students may initially think deflation is a good condition because of increased purchasing power brought by lower prices, but their research should show that deflation also discourages business investment and depresses wages.)

As You Read

World and national events can lead to periods of inflation and recession.

N C L B Activity correlated to English Language Arts standards.

ASSESS

Review Key Terms

Have students write sentences using each key term.

Online Study Tools

Have students go to the OLC through **glencoe.com** to:

- Download **Podcast** study tools.
- Download free **Study-to-Go** content to their PDAs or cell phones.

453

RETEACH

R Reading Strategy

Using Research Materials
Have students perform research in the library or on the Internet to write a 150-word overview of a period of recession in the U.S. during the past 30 years. Encourage students to note the length of the recession, whether the recession was regional, national, or worldwide, and what caused it. (Reports should cover a real event and demonstrate comprehension of the causes of recession.)

✓ Reading Check

IDENTIFY You can prepare for a period of inflation by following reliable news sources to anticipate economic changes and saving money.

Resources

📁 **Student Activity Workbook** Assign students the Chapter 20 activities in the Student Activity Workbook.

ASSESS

After You Read

Have students complete the Section 20.2 After You Read section review.

Online Study Tools

Have students go to the OLC through **glencoe.com** to:

- Take the Section 20.2 **Practice Test**.
- Download **Podcast** study tools.
- Download free **Study-to-Go** content to their PDAs or cell phones.

454

Creative Business Practices

APPLE   **Recycling Electronics**

Did you know that you can recycle not just bottles, papers, and plastic, but also computers? Apple Computer, Inc. practices this kind of recycling through its take-back program. When you purchase a new Apple computer, the company will take back your Apple product free of charge. You may even receive a discount for participating. Apple breaks down and recycles the different materials according to their use. For example, batteries are removed from the computers or iPods and sent to recycling facilities. This program has resulted in more than 7,100 tons of material from returned products being kept out of landfills ever since the program was initiated in the 1990s.

CRITICAL THINKING Why is Apple Computer's take-back program a smart business strategy?

@ **Connect to the Real World** For more information about Apple Computer's take-back program, visit the company's Web site via the link on this book's Online Learning Center through **glencoe.com**.

R When businesses produce more goods than consumers can purchase, or when businesses are no longer able to sell their goods and services, the result is a recession. A *recession* occurs when the economy does not grow for six months or more. Recessions may be local (as when a major employer in an area may go out of business or move to a different location), national, or even global.

During a recession, businesses often lose income and may lay off workers. This increases unemployment. If the situation worsens, as more people become unemployed, the recession could become a depression. During a normal business cycle, however, the economy recovers and individuals are able to get their finances back on track.

The tips for handling inflation on page 453 will also help you during a recession. In addition, you can do the following:

- Create an emergency savings fund and use it if necessary.
- If you lose your job, seek and accept job placement help from the government, public and private organizations, and people within your network. You may have to adjust your career plans.
- Talk to your creditors (people or institutions from whom you have received loans) about your financial situation if you are having difficulty making payments. Most financial institutions have programs to help during periods of financial difficulty.
- Explore the possibility of relocating to another area that offers greater career potential.

✓ **Reading Check** **IDENTIFY** How can you financially prepare for a period of inflation?

Creative Business Practices

CRITICAL THINKING ANSWER Apple's take-back program is a smart business strategy for several reasons. It encourages ecologically-minded Apple customers to return to Apple to upgrade their computer equipment because they know Apple will take care of recycling the materials. The program creates positive public relations for Apple, making the company a more attractive option for consumers looking to buy a new computer or accessory. Also, in many states businesses can receive a corporate tax credit if they recycle a certain amount of materials. This tax credit can reduce or even cancel out the expense of the recycling program to the business.

Financial Help

If you run into trouble managing your finances, help is available. Some suggestions are:

- **Published Material** Books, magazines, and newspapers offer advice about money management. Newspapers and business magazines often have columns devoted to the topic.
- **Online Sources** Internet Web sites provide information, useful statistics, and practical advice on money management. To find them, use search words such as *money management* and *personal finance*.
- **Schools** Many continuing education institutions and community colleges offer money management classes. Teachers and counselors may suggest additional resources.
- **Government Agencies** Free or inexpensive booklets providing financial information are available from government agencies. You can find these at local libraries, federal and county offices, and government Web sites.
- **Banks** Many banks offer free financial advice to their customers. Some even hold seminars on money management.
- **Professionals** Lawyers, accountants, financial planners, and credit counselors also provide financial advice. You may have to pay for their services, however.
- **Nongovernment Organizations** Many nongovernmental organizations give financial assistance, most of it topic-specific. For instance, a nongovernmental organization that focuses on health care for people with financial difficulties could advise about low-cost health-care options.

Career ✓ Checklist

To Manage Your Money:

✓ Create a budget, and stick to it!

✓ Keep track of your expenses.

✓ Avoid unnecessary costs.

✓ Consider the financial effects of any career decision.

✓ Seek help if you are having financial difficulties.

Section 20.2 After You Read

Review Key Concepts

1. Name one change in your personal life and explain how it might affect your financial situation.
2. Identify two steps you could take to cope with inflation.
3. Choose two of the sources listed to help you manage your money, and explain how you might use them now.

Practice Academic Skills

 English Language Arts

4. Name two economic changes that might affect you financially and explain how these changes might affect your financial security. What can you do to prepare for and to handle these changes? Write your responses in a one-page essay.
5. Describe a situation in which you might seek financial help. What steps would you take to get the help you need? Write a one-page summary.

@ Check your answers at this book's OLC through **glencoe.com**.

 Resources

ExamView Assessment Suite CD allows you to print out ready-made unit and chapter tests complete with answer keys. You can also create customized tests.

CLOSE

Culminating Activity

Insurance and Your Future Ask students to write a 200-word paragraph describing the actions they would take to cope with a recession that leads to their being unemployed for three months. Tell them they have rent and bills to pay, and only $500 in savings. (Paragraphs should demonstrate comprehension of ways to successfully manage one's finances.)

 Activity correlated to English Language Arts standards.

Section 20.2 After You Read

Review Key Concepts

1. One example might be a job promotion that increases a salary. Explanations should demonstrate the effect of life changes on income and expenses.
2. Answers may include being prepared for an inflationary period by following reliable news sources and adjusting your budget.

3. One possible answer would be to use the bank to learn about the interest that can be earned with a savings account.

Practice Academic Skills

4. Essays should demonstrate an understanding of topics such as being prepared for changes, adjusting one's budget, recognizing spending habits, working with creditors during difficult financial periods, and using available professional resources for help in managing money.
5. Student essays will vary but should demonstrate comprehension of the various sources of financial help.

FOCUS

Discussion Starter

Business, Management, and Administration Lead a discussion about the different types of careers that can be found in this career cluster. Have students brainstorm different careers and jobs within the career cluster. (Answers will vary but students should show an understanding of the many types of careers that fall within the career cluster.)

TEACH

W **Writing Support**

Independent Practice

Conduct an Interview Have students use the questions in the Career Spotlight to conduct and record an interview with an individual in the featured career cluster. (Answers should follow the interview format of the Career Spotlight.)

C **Critical Thinking**

Organization and Human Resources Point out that a human resources coordinator must be responsible for a great deal of paperwork. Ask students to identify how this requirement relates to preparing and maintaining a budget. Lead a discussion about how learning to be organized now can pay off in a career. (A human resources coordinator must keep track of a large number of files, forms, and records. It is vital that these items be kept in an organized filing system for easy access. The use of computer spreadsheets also plays a large role in a coordinator's duties.)

CAREER SPOTLIGHT

Career Cluster: Business, Management, and Administration

Nicole Ellison
Corporate Human Resources Coordinator

Q: Describe your job.
A: I support our organization in all areas of human resources. This includes coordinating employee activities; administering employee records; ensuring compliance with employment laws and regulations; handling employee complaints and grievances; and administering compensation, benefits, performance, and other programs.

Q: Describe a typical workday.
A: No two days are alike, but typically the first thing I do is check my e-mail and voice mail, which sets the pace for the day. Depending on what comes up or the time of year, I could be performing a new-hire orientation, interviewing candidates, or administering open enrollment for insurance.

Q: What skills are most important to you in your job?
A: Professionalism in every sense of the word is highly important in my job. You need to be personable and able to think and act strategically. It is also important to have strong language and communication skills. Creativity is vital because each person is different. What works for one may not work for another, so you have to find a creative way of handling situations.

Q: What academic skills and lifelong learning skills are helpful in preparing for your career?
A: Communication skills, mathematics, and reading.

Q: What is your key to success?
A: There are four things that have been key to my success: knowing my industry, knowing laws and regulations, knowing our competition, and knowing our workforce. My positive attitude has also aided my success. Attitude is everything; it determines what kind of day you are going to have.

Q: What training and preparation do you recommend for students?
A: I would definitely recommend at least a four-year degree in human resources, with additional Professional Human Resource or Senior Professional Human Resource certification. It is also helpful to build relationships with professors and other students. I trained as a nontraditional student (one who attended college at night), and a lot of times my best resources were other students.

Q: What are some ways you recommend students prepare for this career?
A: Read, read, read. It is important to keep up with changing legislation because this often affects HR either directly or indirectly.

Q: What do you like most about your work?
A: I love the creativity. I love stepping outside of the box and finding new ways of handling situations, and administering benefits and processes.

 For more about Career Clusters, go to this book's OLC through **glencoe.com**.

NO CHILD LEFT BEHIND

Teaching Tip

The goals of the NCLB Act include a strong emphasis on reading skills. The use of modeling in your classroom will help students become better at identifying information. For example, ask a question that can be answered by reading the chart on page 457. Verbally identify the elements of the chart that might help the student identify the answer: the stars and the academic skills labels.

Sample Question How many of the tasks on this chart require three academic skills to complete? (Three tasks require three academic skills to complete: recruit job candidates, train new hires, and coordinate company activities.)

- **Education or Training** A bachelor's degree in one of the following is recommended: personnel; human resources; labor relations; human resources administration or management, training and development; or compensation and benefits. In addition, Professional Human Resource or Senior Professional Human Resource certification is helpful.

- **Academic Skills Required** English Language Arts, Mathematics, Social Studies

- **Technology Needed** Computers and specialty software related to the company and employee benefits, digital photography.

- **Aptitudes, Abilities, and Skills** Communication and organization skills, problem solving and critical thinking skills, attention to detail, the ability to multitask, creativity.

Workplace Safety Human resources workers typically work at a desk and should pay attention to strain from repetitive tasks.

Career Outlook Overall employment of human resources, training, and labor relations managers and specialists is expected to grow faster than average for all occupations over the next ten years.

Career Path Human resource careers can begin in assistant capacity and work up to management or specializations in labor relations, arbitration, and mediation. They also may specialize in training and development, recruitment, and placement. Related positions include counselors, education administrators, public relations specialists, lawyers, psychologists, and social and human service workers.

Academic Skills Required to Complete Tasks

Tasks	English Language Arts	Mathematics	Social Studies
Ensure employer compliance	★		★
Recruit job candidates	★	★	★
Train new hires	★	★	★
Manage employee benefits	★	★	
Coordinate company activities	★	★	★

Critical Thinking

Why should a Human Resources Administrator be aware of changes in workplace legislation?

NCLB This chart relates academic skills such as English Language Arts, Mathematics, Science, Social Studies, and World Languages to specific tasks that are performed for the job in the Career Spotlight feature.

Critical Thinking

Knowledge of changes in workplace legislation is important because a human resources administrator is responsible for both informing employees of their workplace rights and for ensuring that a company complies with any changes in laws pertaining to the workplace.

CAREER SPOTLIGHT

ASSESS

Make Connections

Ask students to list specific correlations between academic subjects and workplace tasks. For example, a bookkeeper might benefit from studying mathematics, computer education, and accounting because a bookkeeper's tasks would include adding figures, using spreadsheets, and maintaining payroll. (Answers should reflect an understanding of how academic skills relate directly to workplace tasks.)

CLOSE

Culminating Activity

Lifelong Learning and Career Clusters Encourage students to suggest informal ways that a person might develop skills that would apply to a particular career in Business, Management, and Administration. For example, in order to create identification cards that both clearly identify a corporate employee and allow the employee to get through a security checkpoint at a corporate office, a human resources professional could study digital photo printing techniques and research ways to create laminated, security-encoded identification cards.

Key Terms and Academic Vocabulary Review

1. Students should write complete sentences using each key term correctly. A sample answer might read: "Without good *record keeping* of all of your expenses, it's hard to figure out what kinds of expenses should be cut to save money."

Review Key Concepts

2. Define needs and goals, which help identify your financial objectives; prioritize, or arrange in order, your list of needs and goals so you can figure out how to spend your money; estimate income, so you know how much money you will have over a period of time; estimate expenses, so you know how much money you expect to spend and see if it is less or more than your income; and write a budget, using a standard form, so you can keep track of your income and expenses.

3. Record keeping is important to budgeting because it helps keep your budget organized and helps you identify specific kinds of spending so that you can easily change your spending habits if you are over budget. Some strategies include recording purchases in a notebook, keeping all records of income and expenses and filing them, and using record-keeping software.

4. Three strategies that will help you stay within your budget are to carry a limited amount of cash and leave your ATM card or checkbook at home to prevent impulse buying, to shop smart by taking advantage of discounts and sales, and to pay with cash instead of credit to avoid overspending and paying interest.

458

CHAPTER SUMMARY

Section 20.1

A budget will help you meet your current financial needs and achieve your future financial goals. To create a budget, you first define and prioritize your financial needs and goals. Next, you estimate your income and expenses. When you write your budget, use a standard budget form. Be sure to include savings as a budget item. To follow a budget, track your expenses and regularly check your expenses against your budget. If your expenses exceed your budget, you can increase your income or cut back on expenses. Tips for staying on a budget include paying with cash and shopping smart.

Section 20.2

The key to managing financial responsibility is financial planning. One aspect of financial planning is being prepared for changes that may affect your financial situation. Personal changes, such as the birth of a child or the loss of a job, and economic changes can affect your personal financial situation. To handle economic changes such as inflation and recession, you may need to cut back on expenses and increase your income. Help for financial problems is available from publications, Web sites, schools, government agencies, and other resources.

Key Terms and Academic Vocabulary Review

1. Use each of these key terms and academic vocabulary words in a sentence.

Key Terms
- budget (p. 445)
- fixed expenses (p. 446)
- flexible expenses (p. 446)
- record keeping (p. 448)
- financial responsibility (p. 452)
- financial planning (p. 452)

Academic Vocabulary
- allocate (p. 445)
- prioritizing (p. 446)
- exceed (p. 448)
- project (p. 452)

Review Key Concepts

2. **List** the steps necessary to prepare a budget. Explain the importance of one.
3. **Explain** why record keeping is important to budgeting and describe one strategy for keeping good records.
4. **Describe** three different strategies that will help you stay within your budget.
5. **List** three personal changes that could affect your finances.
6. **Describe** two ways that you can adapt to changes in the economy.
7. **List** four sources of help for financial problems and describe the kind of information or help you would receive from each.

Critical Thinking

8. **Analyze** When you prepare a budget, why is it important to be honest with yourself when estimating your income and expenses?
9. **Explain** Describe the effects inflation and recession can have on personal financial situations.

---

5. Three personal changes that could affect your finances are changes in your family life, changes in your professional life, and changes in your health.

6. Ways to adapt to changes in the economy include checking reliable news sources to anticipate economic changes, saving extra money in anticipation of changes so you can have an emergency fund, adjusting your budget to reflect the changes instead of continuing pre-change spending habits, cutting back on unnecessary expenses in order to save money,

increasing income by changing jobs or taking on more hours at a current job, and being a smart shopper by taking advantage of sales and discounts.

7. Sources of financial help include published material such as books, magazines, and newspapers, which offer advice about money management; online sources, which provide information, statistics, and advice about money management; schools, which may offer money management classes and additional resources; government agencies, which publish booklets

Real-World Skills and Applications

Information Literacy

10. Organizing and Maintaining Information Assume that you live at home and go to school, have a part-time job, make payments on a car, pay for your own phone, and volunteer at a hospital. Write a paragraph explaining how you will organize and label your record-keeping files.

Collaborative Skills

11. Researching Financial Resources Team up with one or more classmates. Create a list of situations in which you might need financial help. Review the resources for dealing with financial problems listed in the chapter. Assign each team member a different type of resource. For instance, one might look at only print publications. Have each team member locate two sources of information and note the kind of information available, who or what organization provides the information, and how others can access this information. Create a 15-minute presentation that includes visual aids and present it to the class.

Technology Applications

12. Creating a Spreadsheet Budget Form Using spreadsheet software, create a budget form that you can use to prepare a monthly budget. Refer to the standard budget form shown in **Figure 20.1** on page 447 for a guide. List the categories shown and any additional expenses you think are necessary. Be sure to include one column for budgeted expenses and another column for actual expenses. You can add this form to your **Personal Academic and Career Portfolio** and update it regularly.

13. **Brainstorming and Sharing Information** Take a few minutes to brainstorm ways to stay within your budget. Team up with a classmate and share your ideas. Create a list that includes all of your ideas. Report your ideas to the class.

14. ROLE PLAY **Financial Responsibility**
Situation You have just graduated from college, and you want to rent an apartment. However, you have not established any credit, so few landlords are willing to rent to you. You need to convince a landlord that you are financially responsible.
Activity Role-play a conversation in which you convince a landlord to rent an apartment to you. Offer specific reasons why you are a good prospective tenant by describing your monthly budget and previous situations in which you have demonstrated financial responsibility.
Evaluation You will be evaluated based on how well you meet the following performance indicators:
- Offer sound and appropriate evidence of financial responsibility.
- Demonstrate preparation and poise.

Chapter 20   Managing Your Money   **459**

containing financial information; banks, many of which offer free financial advice and seminars to customers; professionals such as lawyers, accountants, financial planners, and credit counselors, who offer advice both for free and for a price; and nongovernment organizations, many of which give financial assistance and advice about money matters.

Critical Thinking

8. Answers should note that an effective budget depends on accurate, honest estimates of income and expenses. If unrealistic estimates are plugged into a budget, sticking to the budget will be difficult, likely cause resentment, and may cause you to stop following the budget altogether. Unrealistic expenses are usually the culprit; if you underestimate how much money you spend in a normal week or month, trying to stick to that spending goal may prove an unreasonable burden. Income projections can also be unrealistic, especially for those who earn money through tips or commissions.

9. Answers should show that inflation causes prices to rise, and that if wages do not rise at the same level as inflation, then you would need to adjust your budget to reflect the lower purchasing power of your money. Students should explain that when the economy does not grow for at least six months, a recession is occurring and businesses often lose income and lay off workers, which has a negative effect on personal finances.

Real-World Skills and Applications

10. Paragraphs should demonstrate an understanding of the different methods used for recording income and expenses and organizing and filing these records. Students should separate records of income (net pay from job) from bills (car payment, phone bill, possible school expenses).

11. Student presentations should demonstrate understanding of the variety of sources of financial help and the specific help offered by each source. Evaluate presentations for accuracy, clarity, and creativity.

12. Student budgets should demonstrate understanding of the component parts of a budget form.

13. Effective presenters should demonstrate how the methods of staying within a budget translates to their personal lives. Evaluate presentations for clarity, accuracy, and creativity.

ROLE PLAY

14. Effective presentations should synthesize the material presented in the chapter in an organized, coherent fashion. Evaluate presentations for accuracy, clarity, and creativity.

Academic Skills in the Workplace

15. Essays should demonstrate an understanding of the principles of financial planning. For example, the essay should explain that it is not enough to simply create a budget if a person does not anticipate and prepare for changes, both personal and economic, that could impact his or her finances.

16. The probability that both Paul's salary and benefits will increase is 0.125 or one-eighth ($\frac{1}{2} \times \frac{1}{4} = \frac{1}{8}$ or 0.125 or 12.5%).

17. Answers will vary but should include material from the chapter, including creating a reliable budget and sticking to it, keeping an organized file of records, living within one's means, anticipating and adjusting for periods of inflation and recession, and seeking professional assistance for financial problems.

18. Summaries should demonstrate comprehension of the different types of financial help covered on page 455. Since in this case the company is offering financial counseling to its employees, one possibility is to pay a financial planner to present a seminar to all employees, or to offer personal meetings as practical, depending on the number of employees. Another possible strategy is to compile financial tips and make them available on the company intranet for employees to peruse at a convenient time.

Academic Skills in the Workplace

English Language Arts

15. Practice Expository Writing Write a two-page expository essay about financial planning. Assume that the reader of the essay has no prior information about the subject. Begin with a clear thesis statement and address the following questions: Why is planning important to achieving future goals? How can the kind of planning you learned about in this chapter help you now and in the future?

Mathematics

16. Calculate Probabilities Paul's boss told him that there is a 50% probability that his salary will increase next year and a 25% probability that his bonus will increase. What is the probability that both will increase?

CONCEPT **Probability of a Compound Event** To calculate the probability that two independent events will both occur, multiply their probabilities.

Starting Hint To make the problem easier, convert the percents into fractions, so 50% becomes $\frac{1}{2}$, and 25% becomes $\frac{1}{4}$. Now multiply and represent your answer as either a fraction or a decimal.

Science

17. Entropy Entropy is a concept in physics that signifies the amount of disorder in a system. Think of a house. Over time, boards will rot, and eventually, the house will fall down if the entropy is not held back with maintenance. The concept of entropy also applies to financial management. Sometimes individuals' spending habits are highly disordered. They buy things they cannot afford and make no plans to pay off their debts. These poor financial habits can result in instability. What are some things you can do to avoid disorder in your finances? Write a two-paragraph response.

Social Studies

18. Financial Counseling You work for a company that plans to cut all salaries. To help employees adjust, the company wants to offer financial counseling. Research resources that could be used in such a program. What do these resources offer? How can the company help their employees access these resources? Using a word-processing program, write a one-page summary of your findings.

STANDARDIZED TEST PRACTICE

TIMED WRITING

Directions Read the following prompt and respond in a two-page essay:

> **Test-Taking Tip** Use the essay prompt as a basis for your thesis statement to help you focus your essay and ensure that you address the essay prompt. For example, you might say "Honesty and integrity are important character traits when managing money because . . . ."

Define honesty and integrity and explain why they are important character traits when managing money. Illustrate your points with examples and details.

STANDARDIZED TEST PRACTICE

Answer
Essays should be two pages in length, clearly written with a topic or thesis statement, and should conform to English language rules of grammar and composition.

Test-Taking Strategies
Whether your students have a standardized test coming up in a few days or a few weeks, this test-prep tip will help students relax and do their best.

Test Format Help your students become familiar with the format of the specific test they are going to take by practicing with test items that imitate the actual test items as closely as possible.

Writing Skills Practice

19. Develop a Proposal Proposals are plans that explain how you are going to complete a project or fix a problem.

 Practice Think of a potential financial problem. Use a word-processing program to create a proposal for resolving the situation.

- State the purpose of your proposal. What is the situation or problem? What specific steps can be taken to fix it?
- Organize your proposal into four sections: project description, materials needed, deadlines and procedures, and outcomes. In the project description, explain your main points. Materials should include all the resources you will need. Deadlines and procedures should outline what you will do and when. Outcomes should explain the expected results.
- Review your proposal, checking for all necessary components.

Net Connection

20. Financial Planning Contact a bank or other organization that helps people with financial planning. Interview a representative about financial tips for graduating high school students. Present this information to the class.

@ **Log On** Go to this book's OLC through **glencoe.com** to find links about financial planning. Choose one and take notes on the advice given. In a one-page essay, compare your notes with the information you received from the representative.

Reading Connection
@ Go to this book's Online Learning Center through **glencoe.com** for a list of reading suggestions.

Personal Academic and Career Portfolio

Creating a Budget

When you have a full-time job, you may have to support yourself and others. This means providing for all necessary wants and needs. Creating a budget will help you to meet those financial obligations and to provide for your future financial needs. Write a budget to fit your present financial circumstances and add it to your **Personal Academic and Career Portfolio**. Check your records against your budget regularly to see how well you are staying within your budget. This will help you to develop good money management habits.

These guidelines will help you prepare your budget:

- Follow the steps outlined in the chapter to create a budget: 1) Define your financial needs and goals. 2) Prioritize your list. 3) Estimate your income and expenses. 4) Use a standard budget form to create your budget.
- Be sure to include savings in your budget.
- Add a folder or computer directory to your portfolio. Title the folder or directory *Budget*. Add your budget.
- Develop a system to organize your financial records.
- At least once each month, check your financial records against your budget. Make adjustments if necessary.
- Use these same guidelines to create budgets for different lengths of time.

 Portfolio Help Go to the *Succeeding in the World of Work* OLC through **glencoe.com** for help developing your portfolio.

Writing Skills Practice

19. Proposals should accurately convey the concepts taught in the chapter and follow the format outlined in the instructions. For example, if the problem is "Need to pay off $3,000 credit card in debt," the proposal should include step-by-step plans for creating a budget that will result in the debt being paid off by a particular deadline. Encourage students to be creative and to make full use of the word-processing program they use.

Net Connection

20. Presentations should provide evidence of the meeting with the representative, including that person's name, employer, and title. Students should be able to connect statements by the representative with material covered in Chapter 20.

Resources

ExamView Assessment Suite CD allows you to print out ready-made unit and chapter tests complete with answer keys. You can also create customized tests.

WorkKeys

WorkKeys® is a job skills assessment program. For information on leveled assessment for Problem-Solving Skills (Applied Mathematics; Applied Technology; Locating Information; and Observation), go to the WorkKeys link on this book's OLC through **glencoe.com**.

Personal Academic and Career Portfolio

Maintaining a Portfolio

Tell students that the Budget in their **Personal Academic and Career Portfolios** will always be subject to change. As their income, spending habits, and personal circumstances change, the figures in their budget should be reviewed and, if necessary, updated. For example, if a student graduates from college and begins paying off loans, his or her budget will need to be updated to reflect this expense. Encourage students to review their budget periodically to ensure it remains current and effective.

Chapter Resources Planning Guide with Activities and Features

Section	Features	Activities
Section 21.1 **Saving and Investing**	Everyday Ethics (p. 466)	Before You Read (p. 464) Graphic Organizer (p. 464) As You Read (pp. 465, 466) After You Read (p. 467)
Section 21.2 **Checking Accounts and Credit**	Science in Action (p. 469) 21st Century Workplace (p. 471) Tech Savvy (p. 472) Hot Jobs! (p. 473) Creative Business Practices (p. 473) Real-World Connection (p. 474) Career Checklist (p. 475)	Before You Read (p. 468) Graphic Organizer (p. 468) As You Read (p. 470) After You Read (p. 475)

NCLB Activities, information, and skills practice will help your students attain No Child Left Behind proficiency. Students will improve their abilities in the following academic standards areas:

Academic Standards Correlations

Discipline	Standard	Feature/Activity
English Language Arts	**NCTE 1** Read texts to acquire new information.	Everyday Ethics (p. 466) Hot Jobs! (p. 473) Creative Business Practices (p. 473)
	NCTE 7 Conduct research and gather, evaluate, and synthesize data to communicate discoveries.	Tech Savvy (p. 472) Real-World Connection (p. 474)
	NCTE 9 Develop an understanding of diversity in language use across cultures.	21st Century Workplace (p. 471)
	NCTE 12 Use language to accomplish individual purposes.	Everyday Ethics (p. 466) Writing Skills Practice (p. 481)
Mathematics	**Number and Operation:** Understand meanings of operations and how they relate to one another	After You Read (p. 467)
	Data Analysis and Probability: Select and use appropriate statistical methods to analyze data	Academic Skills in the Workplace (p. 480)
Science	**Unifying Concepts and Processes:** Constancy, change, and measurement	Science in Action (p. 469)
	Science as Inquiry: Abilities necessary to do scientific inquiry	Academic Skills in the Workplace (p. 480)

CORRELATIONS The charts show the 21st Century Skills, foundation skills, and workplace competencies that students develop as they work in this chapter.

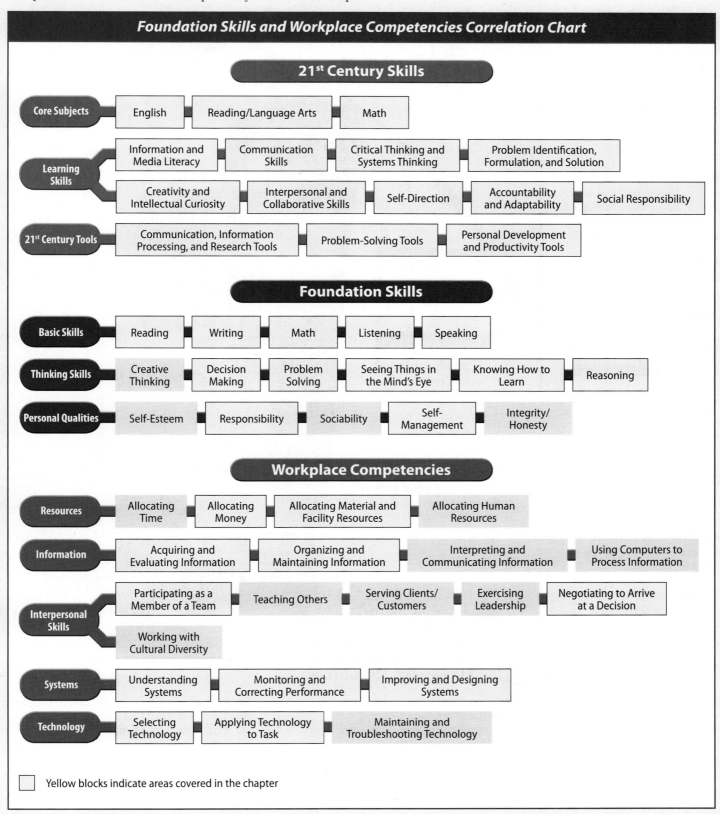

Foundation Skills and Workplace Competencies Correlation Chart

21st Century Skills

Core Subjects: English | Reading/Language Arts | Math

Learning Skills: Information and Media Literacy | Communication Skills | Critical Thinking and Systems Thinking | Problem Identification, Formulation, and Solution | Creativity and Intellectual Curiosity | Interpersonal and Collaborative Skills | Self-Direction | Accountability and Adaptability | Social Responsibility

21st Century Tools: Communication, Information Processing, and Research Tools | Problem-Solving Tools | Personal Development and Productivity Tools

Foundation Skills

Basic Skills: Reading | Writing | Math | Listening | Speaking

Thinking Skills: Creative Thinking | Decision Making | Problem Solving | Seeing Things in the Mind's Eye | Knowing How to Learn | Reasoning

Personal Qualities: Self-Esteem | Responsibility | Sociability | Self-Management | Integrity/Honesty

Workplace Competencies

Resources: Allocating Time | Allocating Money | Allocating Material and Facility Resources | Allocating Human Resources

Information: Acquiring and Evaluating Information | Organizing and Maintaining Information | Interpreting and Communicating Information | Using Computers to Process Information

Interpersonal Skills: Participating as a Member of a Team | Teaching Others | Serving Clients/Customers | Exercising Leadership | Negotiating to Arrive at a Decision | Working with Cultural Diversity

Systems: Understanding Systems | Monitoring and Correcting Performance | Improving and Designing Systems

Technology: Selecting Technology | Applying Technology to Task | Maintaining and Troubleshooting Technology

Yellow blocks indicate areas covered in the chapter

Chapter Overview
Introduce the Chapter

In this chapter, students learn about banking and how banks can help them manage money.

Section 21.1 compares different types of savings plans.

Section 21.2 teaches students how to use a checking account and online banking services and describes types and costs of credit.

Build Background

Poll the class to find out how many students have savings or checking accounts. Then ask for volunteers to describe a recent visit to a bank and the kinds of services they sought or received. Explain that banks offer many ways to help you save money and build wealth.

 Exploring the Photo

Caption Answer Answers may include savings accounts, savings bonds, 401(k) plan, individual retirement account (IRA), and others.

Discussion Ask students to discuss why it is important to understand how banks function and to learn how to perform personal banking tasks. (Answers will vary. Using the services of the bank and performing banking tasks are basic practices in business and your personal life.)

CHAPTER 21
Banking and Credit

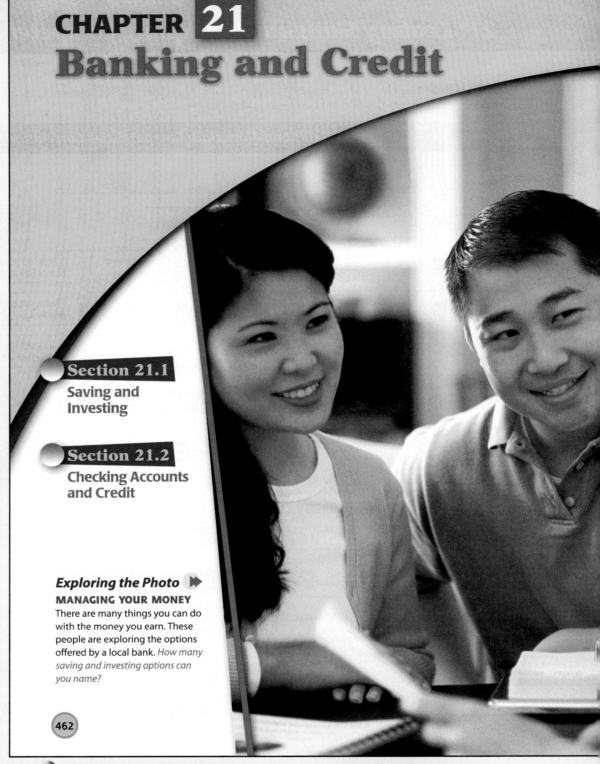

Section 21.1
Saving and Investing

Section 21.2
Checking Accounts and Credit

Exploring the Photo ▶▶
MANAGING YOUR MONEY
There are many things you can do with the money you earn. These people are exploring the options offered by a local bank. *How many saving and investing options can you name?*

462

Classroom Resources

- Student Edition
- Teacher Wraparound Edition
- Student Activity Workbook with Academic Integration
- Student Activity Workbook with Academic Integration TAE
- *Fast File,* Unit 6 Resources

- Inclusion in the Career Education Classroom
- TeacherWorks™ Plus
- *ExamView Assessment Suite*
- Interactive Chalkboard
- Interactive Student Edition
- Online Student Edition
- Online Learning Center (OLC) with Podcasts

Chapter Objectives

After completing this chapter, you will be able to:

- **Identify** common ways to save money.
- **Identify** different types of retirement plans.
- **Explain** how to select, manage, and reconcile a checking account.
- **Define** *credit* and name the different types of credit.
- **State** the advantages and disadvantages of using credit.
- **Explain** how to compare credit costs.

Writing Activity / Personal Career Notebook

Though you do not yet have a full-time job, your first credit card just arrived in the mail. It is preapproved, which means that you can start using it immediately. Will you open the account? Record your responses in a one-page journal entry.

Get Motivated! Interview a loan officer or investment counselor at your local bank. Discuss the person's job responsibilities. Ask what advice a young person needs in a first full-time job about saving, investing, and credit. Summarize your discussion in a one-page journal entry.

Writing Activity / Personal Career Notebook Answer Guide

Credit card companies are targeting teenagers in increasing numbers, sometimes even before they graduate from high school. Many uninformed teens are vulnerable to accumulating adult-sized debt before they enter adulthood. Tell students to think seriously before they write about the lure and potential danger of "free money" that is not actually free.

Get Motivated! Journal entries will vary but should demonstrate understanding of the information given by the bank employee. Evaluate entries for clarity, length, and content.

Review the Objectives
Introduce the chapter by reviewing the chapter objectives:

Section 21.1 Objectives
Identify common ways to save money. (deposit money in an interest-bearing savings account; buy government savings bonds; deposit money in a money market account; and invest money in a certificate deposit.)

Identify different types of retirement plans. (Plans include defined-benefit and defined-contribution pension plans; 401(k) plans; and individual retirement accounts.)

Section 21.2 Objectives
Explain how to select, manage, and reconcile a checking account. (Select a type of checking account according to the minimum balance required, fees charged, and interest earned. Manage a checking account by recording each transaction in the check register, keeping track of the amount in the account, and endorsing and depositing checks you receive. Reconcile a checking account by checking the items on your bank statement against your check register.)

Define *credit* and name the different types of credit. (Credit is money you can use now and must pay back later. Types of credit include loans, such as installment and secured loans, and credit cards.)

State the advantages and disadvantages of using credit. (Advantages include not having to carry a lot of cash, having money available for emergencies, and building a credit history. Disadvantages include paying annual fees and finance charges and the risk of accumulating debt.)

Explain how to compare credit costs. (Compare credit by comparing interest rates and loan periods.)

Section 21.1

FOCUS

Bell Ringer Activity

Saving and Investing

Ask students to discuss reasons they should save $2,000 they earned from a summer job instead of spending it. Have volunteers share lists of ways they could invest the money to make sure it grows.

Resources

Interactive Chalkboard
The Interactive Chalkboard CD provides visual teaching aids for this section.

Online Learning Center
The Online Learning Center (OLC) through **glencoe.com** features chapter vocabulary, chapter summaries, and other study materials.

Preteaching

In mathematics a *dividend* is a number that is to be divided by a divisor. In banking a *dividend* is a share of the profits of a fund or organization.

Graphic Organizer

Tell students to go to the OLC through **glencoe.com** for a printable graphic organizer. (Tables should properly note the different types and characteristics of savings and investment accounts.)

NCLB connects academic correlations to book content.

Saving and Investing

Reading Guide

Before You Read
Preview Choose a Key Term or Academic Vocabulary word that is new to you. Write it on a piece of paper. When you find it in the text, write down the definition.

Read to Learn
- Common ways to save money
- How to distinguish among different types of retirement plans

Main Idea
Saving and investing your money effectively will help you to achieve financial security.

Key Concept
- Ways to Save and Invest

Key Terms
◈ deposit
◈ withdrawal
◈ balance
◈ interest
◈ dividend
◈ certificate of deposit (CD)
◈ 401(k) plan
◈ individual retirement account (IRA)
◈ Keogh plan
◈ simplified employee pension (SEP)

Academic Vocabulary
You will find these words in your reading and on your tests. Use the academic vocabulary glossary to look up their definitions if necessary.
■ accrued
■ redeem

Graphic Organizer
As you read, list the different types of savings and investment accounts and note the characteristics of each. Use a table like the one shown to help organize your information.

Types of Accounts	Characteristics

 Log On Go to this book's Online Learning Center through **glencoe.com** for an online version of this graphic organizer.

Academic Standards •

NCLB

English Language Arts
- Read texts to acquire new information. (NCTE 1)
- Use language to accomplish individual purposes. (NCTE 12)

Mathematics
- Understand meanings of operations and how they relate to one another

Reading Guide

Before You Read
Lead a discussion about the value of saving and planning ahead for future financial needs. Tell students that in this section, they'll learn about various ways of saving and how to evaluate the best plan for their needs.

D Develop Concepts
Main Idea Discuss the main idea with students. Ask students what they think "financial security" means. (Answers will vary but may include being able to pay expenses without going into debt, having money to send kids to college, and being able to retire with enough money to live comfortably.)

Ways to Save and Invest

In this section, you will learn about the different saving and investment options that will help you to provide for your financial future.

Savings Accounts

Most people begin saving by opening a savings account at a financial institution such as a bank, a savings and loan association, or a credit union. A *credit union* is a bank for people that are part of the same organization.

Before you choose a bank, find out what fees you will have to pay. Some accounts charge a maintenance fee or a fee for some deposits and withdrawals. A **deposit** is money that you put into your account. A **withdrawal** is money that you take from your account.

There are two basic types of savings accounts. With a *passbook account*, you record your transactions in a booklet. With a *statement account*, the institution sends you a computerized statement of your transactions. With either type of account, you deposit money and the institution pays you interest on the **balance**, the amount of money in your account. **Interest** is a sum of money that is paid for the use of another's money. It is usually expressed as a percentage of the amount deposited. Normally, the interest on an interest-bearing savings account is *compounded*. That is, it is based on the amount of money you deposit plus the interest that has **accrued** on your deposit.

The Federal Deposit Insurance Corporation (FDIC) insures deposits in most banks and savings associations up to a set amount, currently $100,000. Before you open an account, you should determine whether your deposit will be FDIC-insured. If it is not, you risk losing the amount you have deposited.

 PLANNING FOR THE FUTURE People today are living longer, healthier lives than they did in the past. *How might a longer lifespan affect your saving and investment decisions?*

Chapter 21 Banking and Credit **465**

Section 21.1

 Vocabulary

You can find definitions in the **Key Terms** glossary and **Academic Vocabulary** glossary at the back of this book.

 As You Read

Explain Why might you want your deposit to be insured by the FDIC?

TEACH

Discussion Starter
Ways to Save and Invest
Tell students to assume they save $500 a year for five years and invest it in an interest-bearing account at a 5 percent return. Using a calculator, multiply $500 times 1.05 for the first year. Add $500, then multiply that amount by 1.05 for the second year. Continue this process for the third through fifth years. The total will be $2,900.96. Point out to students that they would have earned $400.96 on the $2,500 saved over the years. Discuss with students the impact of saving even larger amounts or investing it for higher returns.

As You Read
If a bank holding your money goes out of business and your deposit is not FDIC-insured, you risk losing all of your money.

Resources

TeacherWorks™ Plus
The TeacherWorks software includes customizable built-in lesson plans and links to printable program resources.

ASSESS

Review Key Terms
Have students use each key term in a sentence.

Online Study Tools
Have students go to the OLC through **glencoe.com** to:
- Download **Podcast** study tools.
- Download free **Study-to-Go** content to their PDAs or cell phones.

465

 Extend the Photo

Caption Answer A longer lifespan would mean workers will probably enjoy more years of retirement, and therefore should start saving for retirement earlier.

Discussion Have students research the current life span for males and females in the United States. What has been the trend over the past several decades?

Resources

ExamView Assessment Suite CD allows you to print out ready-made unit and chapter tests complete with answer keys. You can also create customized tests.

RETEACH

S **Skill Practice**
Guided Practice

Survey Have students survey their friends and families asking how many save money regularly, and how they invest their money. Students should ask questions such as: What are your reasons for saving? Why did you choose that form of saving? Have students share their findings in class. (Student findings will vary but should show an understanding of incentives for saving and forms of saving.)

As You Read

Money market accounts require a higher minimum balance, are pooled with other deposits and invested, pays a dividend, and have a higher interest rate.

Resources

Student Activity Workbook Assign the Chapter 21 activities in the Student Activity Workbook.

466

Everyday ETHICS

FINANCIAL DECISIONS

What factors should you consider when making financial decisions?

IT'S YOUR MONEY Your sister, who works at a bank, gave you money as a gift for your high-school graduation. She wants you to use the money she gave you to open a savings account at the bank where she is employed as she receives a bonus for each new account that she brings to the bank. However, you did some research and found that another bank offers a better savings interest rate.

What Would You Do? Will you open an account at your sister's employer or at the other bank?

DISCUSS IT In teams, discuss why financial decisions that can affect others can be among the most difficult decisions to make.

As You Read

Compare How does a money market account differ from a regular savings account?

Investments

Investments are financial products you can purchase to make your assets grow. Here are three relatively low-risk investment options:

- **Savings Bonds** When you buy a government savings bond, you lend money to the government. You purchase a bond for a portion of the face value, the amount printed on the bond. Each year the bond grows in value until it reaches the face value amount. You can then **redeem** it, or cash it in, for that amount.
- **Money Market Accounts** Money market accounts are savings accounts offered by banks that require a high minimum balance. The money you deposit is pooled with other deposits and invested. You receive a **dividend**, a share of the profits of a fund or organization. The interest rate on a money market account is higher than the rate for a regular savings account.
- **Certificates of Deposit** A **certificate of deposit (CD)** is a type of investment in which you deposit an amount of money for a fixed amount of time at a stated interest rate. The longer the investment period, the higher the interest rate will be.

Retirement Plans

It is wise to start saving money for retirement as soon as possible. The following are some retirement plan options.

Pension Plans

A *pension plan* is a retirement plan funded, at least in part, by an employer or union. The following are common types of pension plan:
- In a *defined-benefit plan*, your company pays you a fixed amount at retirement.
- In a *defined-contribution plan*, or a profit-sharing plan, your employer contributes a set amount to the plan each year. The amount you receive at retirement depends on the amount in the fund.

Everyday ETHICS

What Would You Do? Answer The ethical dilemma is in choosing between loyalty to a family member and what appears to be a smarter financial decision. However, one ethical option is to tell your sister about your dilemma and asking her what else her bank might offer, such as fewer fees or a more favorable minimum balance, over the other bank.

DISCUSS IT Students might cite peer pressure from others as a reason such decisions can be difficult to make.

A **401(k) plan** is a retirement plan in which you put a portion of your salary into the plan. Employers may match this contribution up to a specific amount or percentage of your salary. The funds in 401(k) plans are invested by your employer. The money you accumulate in a 401(k) plan is *tax-deferred*, meaning that you do not pay taxes on it until you withdraw it.

Individual Retirement Accounts

Even if you have a pension plan, you can still contribute to an **individual retirement account (IRA)**, a personal retirement account into which you can put a limited amount of money each year. Earnings are tax-deferred. One disadvantage of an IRA is that you must pay a penalty if you withdraw money before the age of 59½.

Some investors prefer *Roth IRAs* to traditional IRAs. Contributions to Roth IRAs are not tax-deductible, but earnings are tax-free.

Plans for the Self-Employed If you work for yourself, a Keogh plan or simplified employee pension plan may be the best retirement plan for you. Both have the tax-deferment advantage of an IRA.

- With a **Keogh plan**, you can invest 100 percent of your earnings, up to a set amount, each year for retirement. The rules for establishing a Keogh plan are complicated. You should consult an accountant before setting up this type of plan.
- A **simplified employee pension (SEP)** is a retirement plan with tax advantages for individuals that is simpler to arrange than a Keogh plan. A SEP allows you to set aside as much as 25 percent of your yearly earnings up to a set limit.

Section 21.1 After You Read

Review Key Concepts

1. List and define three types of investments that can help you save money.
2. Contrast a defined-benefit retirement plan with a defined-contribution plan.
3. List retirement plan options for a person who is self-employed.

Practice Academic Skills

 Mathematics

4. Yasmin has $5,000. She can open either a passbook savings account at a 2% interest rate or a money market account at a 4% interest rate. How much more will she make with the money market account?

   CONCEPT **Subtracting Percentages** To subtract percentages, either leave them in percent form or convert them to decimals.
   Step 1: Subtract the rate for the passbook account from the rate for the money market account. Convert the answer to decimal form.
   Step 2: Multiply the Step 1 answer by the total amount invested ($5,000).

   Math For math help, go to the Math Appendix located at the back of this book.

Section 21.1 After You Read

Review Key Concepts

1. Savings accounts are accounts through which a financial institution pays you interest on the money you have deposited. Investments are financial products you purchase to make your assets grow; these can include savings bonds, money market accounts, and certificates of deposit (CD). Retirement plans allow you to put money away to withdraw after you retire; these can include pension plans, 401(k) plans, and individual retirement accounts (IRA).
2. In a defined-benefit plan, a company pays a fixed amount at retirement, while in a defined-contribution plan, the employer contributes a set amount each year, to be paid out at retirement.
3. Retirement plan options for the self-employed include a Keogh plan and a simplified employee pension (SEP).

Practice Academic Skills

4. Yasmin can make $100 more a year with a money market account ([$5,000 × .04] − [$5,000 × .02]).

ASSESS

After You Read
Have students complete the Section 21.1 After You Read section review.

Online Study Tools
Have students go to the OLC through **glencoe.com** to:
- Take the Section 21.1 **Practice Test**.
- Download **Podcast** study tools.
- Download free **Study-to-Go** content to their PDAs or cell phones.

CLOSE

Culminating Activity
Creating Your Own Savings Plan Have students draw a chart with three columns: savings accounts, investments, retirement plans. Create rows showing the different accounts and plans available within these categories. Then have students write a 200-word paragraph detailing a savings plan that combines elements from each column.

NCLB Activity correlated to Mathematics standards.

467

Checking Accounts and Credit

Reading Guide

Before You Read

Preview Choose a Key Concept that is new to you. Write it on a piece of paper. When you find it in the text, write one or two sentences explaining the concept.

Read to Learn

- How to select, manage, and reconcile a checking account
- How to define *credit* and name the different types of credit
- The advantages and disadvantages of using credit
- How to compare credit costs

Main Idea

D Managing your checking account and your credit successfully will give you greater control over your finances.

Key Concepts

- Forms of Payment
- Understanding Credit

Key Terms

- check register
- endorse
- reconcile
- electronic funds transfer (EFT)
- online banking
- credit
- down payment
- finance charge
- annual percentage rate (APR)
- debt
- credit bureau

Academic Vocabulary

You will find these words in your reading and on your tests. Use the academic vocabulary glossary to look up their definitions if necessary.

- transfer
- encryption

Graphic Organizer

As you read, note the different forms of payment discussed and the pros and cons of each. Use a chart like the one shown to help organize your information.

Forms of Payment	Pros	Cons
Checks		
Credit		

Log On Go to this book's Online Learning Center through **glencoe.com** for an online version of this graphic organizer.

Academic Standards •

English Language Arts
- Conduct research and gather, evaluate, and synthesize data to communicate discoveries. (NCTE 7)
- Develop an understanding of diversity in language use across cultures. (NCTE 9)

Science
- Unifying Concepts and Processes: Constancy, change, and measurement

---

Bell Ringer Activity

Checking Accounts and Credit

Discuss the types of checking accounts available and how students can open one. Obtain copies of documents needed to open a checking account at a local bank and make transparencies of them. Then demonstrate how to complete the documents.

Resources

Interactive Chalkboard
The Interactive Chalkboard CD provides visual teaching aids for this section.

@ Online Learning Center
The OLC through **glencoe.com** features chapter vocabulary, chapter summaries, and other study materials.

Preteaching

Endorsing a check is similar to endorsing, or approving, a favorite product or a person's work—that is, you sign the check to show that you are approving its deposit or cashing.

Graphic Organizer

Tell students to go to the OLC through **glencoe.com** for a printable graphic organizer. (Charts should list relevant information about the pros and cons of checks and credit.)

NCLB connects academic correlations to book content.

468

Reading Guide

Before You Read

Read the Key Terms and Academic Vocabulary out loud to the class. Ask students how many of these terms and words they have heard used on television and radio or by their parents or guardians, or seen in print advertisements for banks. Have students speculate which words and terms are used in discussing checking accounts, which are used in discussing credit, and which might apply to both areas.

D Develop Concepts

Main Idea Ask students to share their ideas of how they could successfully manage their checking account and credit.

Forms of Payment

Keeping your money in a bank savings account allows you to keep it safe for the future. You can also use a different account, called a checking account, to pay bills and make purchases.

Checking Accounts

A *check* is a written document that authorizes the transfer of money from a bank account to a person or business. The money to pay a check is drawn from a *checking account*, a bank account designed to hold funds for a short period of time.

You open a checking account with a bank by putting money into the account. To make a deposit, you fill out a deposit slip. Deposit slips come with your checks and are available in banks. You can write checks up to the amount of your balance, which is the total sum of money in your account.

Checks are a convenient way to pay bills or make purchases. They are safer than cash and often less costly than credit. They also provide a simple method of record keeping.

Types of Checking Accounts

Checking accounts differ by the minimum balance required, the fees charged, and the interest earned. A *regular checking account* often requires no minimum balance. However, it may earn little or no interest, and you may be charged a fee for maintaining it. This fee may be a flat monthly rate or a charge for each check you write.

A *NOW account* (Negotiable Order of Withdrawal account) pays interest on your deposits, but you must keep a minimum balance in the account, usually $1,000. A *Super-NOW account* is similar to a NOW account except that the interest rate and minimum balance required are both higher.

 PAYMENT
When you purchase an item, the cashier may ask you how you wish to pay: cash, check, or charge. *What are the advantages and disadvantages of paying with cash?*

glencoe.com

Chapter 21 Banking and Credit **469**

Science In Action

Electrical Energy
Electrical energy can be measured in units called *watts*. Utility companies charge for the amount of kilowatts used. If a machine uses 20 kilowatts of energy, how many watts does the machine use?

Starting Hint: *Kilo* means 1,000.

@ For more science practice, go to this book's OLC through **glencoe.com**.

Section 21.2

TEACH

Discussion Starter
Paying for Purchases Poll students to see how many have a checking account. Have them write a 100-word paragraph explaining why they need or do not need to have a checking account at this point in their lives. (Paragraphs may include keeping track of how they spend and receive money, having an ATM card instead of needing to use a credit card or carry cash, and learning how to be responsible with money.)

R Reading Strategy
Comparing-Contrasting Ask students to list similarities and differences between cash and checks. (Similar: Cash and checks both represent ways of using money to pay for something. Different: Checks authorize a transfer of money from a bank account while cash pays for something directly; checks provide a simpler method of record keeping.) Tell students that accountants and bookkeepers consider checks to be a form of cash.

N C L B | Activity correlated to Science standards.

Science In Action

The machine uses 20,000 watts of energy (20 × 1,000).

Resources

ExamView Assessment Suite CD allows you to print out ready-made unit and chapter tests complete with answer keys. You can also create customized tests.

469

▶▶ *Extend the Photo*

Caption Answer Advantages: You are less likely to accrue debt if you carry a set amount of cash when you go shopping; nearly all stores and businesses accept cash payments. Disadvantages: You need to withdraw cash from the bank in order to spend your money; carrying cash is less secure than carrying credit cards or a checkbook.

Discussion Have students imagine that they are shopping at the mall and see a popular new video game system on sale, but at a price that would take two months' pay from their part-time job to pay off. They have a credit card, but it has a high interest rate. Discuss the pros and cons of using the credit card to buy the system.

TEACH *(cont.)*

C Critical Thinking

Making Inferences Have students look at the "Memo" section of the check shown in **Figure 21.1**. Ask students whether they think writing information in the space provided is as important as filling out the rest of the parts of the check. (The Memo is not as important; filling it in is optional for the person writing the check.) Ask students why it might be useful to fill in the purpose of the check in the Memo section. (Filling in the Memo section is often useful for record-keeping purposes.)

W Writing Support

Writing Support Ask students to write a 50-word paragraph explaining how keeping their check registers accurate and up-to-date would help them with their budgets. (In their paragraphs, students might point out that the register would allow them to compare actual expenses with a budget.)

As You Read

Check each transaction in the bank statement against the check register to make sure the two records agree. Fix any mistakes in your record, and contact the bank if you find any mistakes on the statement.

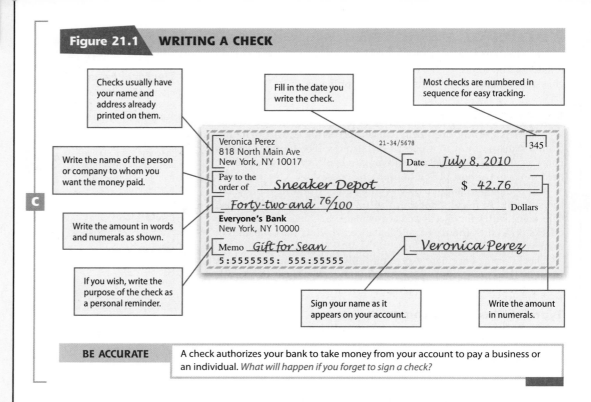

Figure 21.1   WRITING A CHECK

Checks usually have your name and address already printed on them.

Fill in the date you write the check.

Most checks are numbered in sequence for easy tracking.

Write the name of the person or company to whom you want the money paid.

Write the amount in words and numerals as shown.

If you wish, write the purpose of the check as a personal reminder.

Sign your name as it appears on your account.

Write the amount in numerals.

> Veronica Perez
> 818 North Main Ave
> New York, NY 10017   21-34/5678   345
> Date *July 8, 2010*
> Pay to the order of *Sneaker Depot* $ *42.76*
> *Forty-two and ⁷⁶/₁₀₀* _____ Dollars
> Everyone's Bank
> New York, NY 10000
> Memo *Gift for Sean*   *Veronica Perez*
> 5:5555555: 555:55555

BE ACCURATE   A check authorizes your bank to take money from your account to pay a business or an individual. *What will happen if you forget to sign a check?*

Managing Your Checking Account

When you have a checking account, you must keep track of the amount of money that is in it. This ensures that the balance will be sufficient to pay the checks you write or the withdrawals you make.

When you write a check, be sure to fill it out completely and accurately. **Figure 21.1** shows you how to do this. Record any checks you write or the withdrawals you make in your **check register**, a record of your checking account transactions. Subtract the amount of the check from the balance immediately, making sure when you do that there is enough money in the account to cover the check.

Knowing how much money you have in your account keeps you from overdrawing your account. When you write a check that you cannot pay, the check is returned to the bank. This is called *bouncing a check*. You must pay large fees when you overdraw your account or bounce a check. The bank may also return the checks to the businesses that submitted them for payment, and the businesses may charge you an additional fee.

When you receive a check, you should take the check to your bank to deposit it or cash it. To complete either transaction, you must endorse the check. To **endorse** the check means to sign your name on the back of the check in order to obtain the amount that is represented on the face of the check. If you deposit the check, you should

As You Read

Explain How do you reconcile your bank statement with your check register?

EXTEND THE FIGURE   Figure 21.1

Caption Answer Answers will vary but should say that the check is not valid unless it is signed. The check will have to be returned to you, and your payment may end up being late, leading to possible late fees and damage to your credit score.

Discussion Ask students to brainstorm about the checking account of the future, which may be entirely electronic. (Possible ideas might include electronic check registers built into personal digital assistants or PDAs, or credit-card size computers for portable banking.)

record the transaction in your check register so that you have an accurate record of your balance.

Each month, the bank will send you a statement of your account. You should record any fees and interest in your check register. Then reconcile the statement with your check register. To **reconcile** items means to make them agree. Check each transaction in the statement against the check register to make sure the two records agree. Fix any mistakes in your records. If you find a mistake in the bank records, contact the bank.

Electronic Banking Services

Today's banks offer many electronic services. **Electronic funds transfer (EFT)** is the transfer of money from one bank account to another by electronic means. Examples of EFT include transferring money from your savings account to your checking account, using a debit card, and having direct deposit of payroll checks or other sources of income, such as an income tax refund.

C

Debit Cards A *debit card* or check card is a card that you can use to withdraw money directly from your checking account. It can also be called an ATM card. This kind of card has a password and is good for making everyday purchases. You can also use debit cards at an ATM (automatic teller machine) to withdraw or deposit money. Keep your password in a safe place, and never keep it with your card. Do not spend more with a debit card than you have in your account. You will overdraw your account.

▶Vocabulary
You can find definitions in the **Key Terms** glossary and **Academic Vocabulary** glossary at the back of this book.

The 21ˢᵗ Century Workplace

NCLB

Answer in Arabic

Arabic has emerged as an important language to learn for the 21ˢᵗ century. People who want jobs in the Middle East, home to many lucrative businesses, as well as those looking for government work in the United States or Europe, will benefit from studying Arabic. Though only 15 percent of the Muslim world speaks Arabic, it is the official language of many nations because Arabic is the written language of the Koran, the sacred text of the religion of Islam.

CRITICAL THINKING _____

How might learning a language help a person better understand a region's culture?

In Your Community

Music and poetry are interesting ways to learn a different language and culture. Using available resources, research an Arabic song or poem. Present

your selection to the class, giving details such as the artist and genre, and explaining what it reveals about the culture.

COMMON ARABIC WORDS AND PHRASES	
hello	marhaba
goodbye	poka
yes	aiwa
no	la

@ Extend Your Learning Arabic is the sixth most-spoken language in the world. For links to Web sites about Arabic, go to this book's OLC through **glencoe.com**.

C Critical Thinking
Making Inferences Tell students that they are buying groceries and planning to use their debit card to pay for them. However, when they run their card through the card reader, the transaction is rejected. Ask students for a reason why, other than mechanical or computer network failure, the transaction was not allowed to go through. (Answers may vary; the most likely reason is that the purchase overdrew the account.) Tell students that a debit card is not a credit card, and that responsible use involves keeping track of the balance in their checking account.

NCLB Activity correlated to English Language Arts standards.

The 21ˢᵗ Century Workplace

CRITICAL THINKING ANSWER Answers will vary. Learning a language opens up many opportunities for understanding a region's culture. Being able to read newspapers, understand television, radio, and movies, and have conversations that are in another language reduces isolation and increases understanding between you and those who speak that language. If you can speak the language of a region in which

you are traveling, you may be invited into social interactions that would be otherwise impossible.

In Your Community Encourage students to provide translations of the song or poem they researched. Lead a discussion about how their research affected their impressions of the Arabic-speaking world.

S Skill Practice

Independent Practice

Calculate Have students complete this problem. Roberto had a beginning checking account balance of $433.27. He wrote the following checks: $127.44, $15.95, $79.34, and $59.55. He then deposited a paycheck in the amount of $327.50 and withdrew $20 in cash. Now what is Roberto's new checkbook balance? ($458.49: $433.27 − $127.44 − $15.95 − $79.34 − $59.55 + $327.50 − $20.00) **L1**

Interview Invite a representative from a local computer store to demonstrate checking account software. Have the speaker compare manual and electronic methods for recording checks. Prior to the class visit, have students prepare questions. **L2**

Research Have students research local utility companies that participate in online bill payment programs. Have them write a 100-word paragraph that answers the following question: How does online bill payment save money for the company? Have students share their research with the class. (Online bill payment programs save companies such expenses as paper, postage, and the labor involved in preparing and processing paper bills. Since online bill payment deducts money at regularly scheduled intervals, it reduces late payments caused by customers forgetting to pay their bills, saving money that would be spent in collecting delinquent accounts.) **L3**

TechSavvy

Online Money Transfers

Have you or a family member bought an item through an Internet auction house? If so, you may have used an online money transfer service such as PayPal to pay for it. Developed to enable fast, safe transactions over the Internet, the PayPal system establishes an account into which a buyer deposits money to purchase an item. The money can be deposited by using a credit or debit card. The money is then transferred to the merchant without revealing the buyer's financial information, providing added security for the buyer.

@ Visit this book's OLC through **glencoe.com** and find the link to learn more about PayPal and other online purchase options. Write one or two paragraphs explaining how and why these payment options differ from traditional credit card accounts.

Direct Deposit Many employers offer direct deposit as a payment option. *Direct deposit* is the electronic **transfer** of payment from a company or organization to an employee's bank account.

If you choose payment by direct deposit, your employer will give you a voided check, called an *advice of debit*, instead of a paycheck. An advice of debit is a standard paycheck that has been voided and labeled "non-negotiable." In your check register, enter the amount indicated on your advice of debit as if it were a "regular" paycheck.

Online Banking

Online banking allows you to manage your money from a computer with Internet access. You can use this service to transfer money between accounts, access your statement, and pay bills. Most banks offer online banking at no extra charge. Online banking is convenient and saves time and paperwork.

In the past, some people were reluctant to use online banking because they feared that their financial information was not secure. Today, online banking is much safer, although the risk of identity theft still exists. Most of the institutions that offer online banking services have instituted a wide range of security precautions to minimize that risk.

For instance, when you bank online, you are assigned a special ID and password to protect your account from unauthorized use. Banks also use computer **encryption**, firewalls, and other means to protect customers' personal and financial information.

S

✓ **Reading Check** **COMPARE** How does online banking differ from traditional banking?

Understanding Credit

At times, you may need more money than you have on hand. One way to obtain money is through credit. **Credit** is money you can use now and must pay back later.

Types of Credit

Common types of credit include loans and credit cards. People often get loans for school or to purchase large items, such as cars and homes. You must complete an application, available through the financial institution, and be approved to receive a loan.

Most loans are *installment loans*, in which you receive the money as a lump sum and pay it back in regular payments called *installments*.

✓ **Reading Check**

COMPARE Online banking differs in that it allows the customer much more control over banking functions, reducing the need for large bank branches and extra tellers.

TechSavvy

Online Money Transfers

Answer Paragraphs should reflect an understanding of online money transfers. Evaluate paragraphs for the type of information provided about online purchase options, the reasoning provided for student explanations, and the clarity of their writing.

You may have to pay an application fee, which is an amount of money charged to apply for the loan. For large purchases, you may have to make a **down payment**, which is an amount of money, usually a percentage of the total payment, paid at the time of the purchase.

Secured loans are guaranteed by *collateral*, an asset such as the borrower's home or car. If the borrower defaults on the loan—that is, fails to pay it—the lender can take the collateral.

Credit cards are another form of credit. A *credit card* is a small plastic card issued by a bank or other financial institution that allows the cardholder to purchase goods or services at any business that accepts the card.

You must apply for a credit card. If your application is approved, the lender issues you a card showing your name and account number. Usually you are given a *credit limit*, which is a maximum amount you can charge against your account. When you use a credit card, you agree to the terms stated in the credit card agreement. These terms, such as the interest rate you will pay and the repayment schedule, differ depending on the institution.

Many businesses, such as retail stores, offer consumers charge accounts. A charge account is similar to a credit card account, except that it can be used to buy goods or services only from the company issuing the credit.

Making installment payments such as loan payments and credit card payments on time is an effective way to build a good credit history.

HOT JOBS!

Art Curator

Curators are experts at examining, cataloguing, and even appraising (determining the financial value of) artistic works. Curators typically specialize in an era, genre, or geographic area, but should have a broad knowledge of major artists and artistic trends.

Section 21.2

TEACH *(cont.)*

C Critical Thinking
Making Inferences Ask students how they think a credit card company makes a profit. (Credit card companies make a profit primarily from the interest paid by cardholders.) Explain that interest is calculated each month and that the percentage is higher on credit cards than on other forms of consumer credit.

ASSESS

Review Key Terms
Have students write sentences using each key term.

Online Study Tools
Have students go to the OLC through **glencoe.com** to:
- Download **Podcast** study tools.
- Download free **Study-to-Go** content to their PDAs or cell phones.

Creative Business Practices

UAW **Helping Employees with Personal Problems**

The International Union, United Automobile, Aerospace and Agricultural Implement Workers of America (UAW) is one of the largest unions in North America. Since 1935, the UAW has helped members gain higher wages and better employee benefits.

One of those benefits is a group of programs called employee assistance programs, which help employees with personal problems that might interfere with or affect their jobs. For example, if employees are having problems with stress or illness, they can ask for help through the employee assistance program. Help usually is offered through third parties and is provided free of charge or covered through health insurance.

CRITICAL THINKING How could a person's work performance be affected by his or her personal life? Give an example.

 Connect to the Real World To learn more about the UAW and employee assistance programs, visit the UAW's Web site via the link on this book's Online Learning Center at **glencoe.com**.

Creative Business Practices

CRITICAL THINKING ANSWER A person's job performance is influenced by how he or she views their personal life. Family problems, health issues, and personal troubles can have a negative impact at work, leading to diminished performance and contributing to low morale among staff. Another common problem for employees is finding the right balance between their job and their personal life, as stressful work environments sometimes lead to a feeling of stress outside of work. Many companies try to help by offering flexible work hours, alternative schedules, and paid vacations, as well as offering confidential counseling for employees who seek it.

Section 21.2

 Real-World *Connection*

Critical Thinking Answer
Sam should shop around and get prices from several dealers to determine the best price. He should also research the deal offered by Best Automotive to find out the interest rate once the payments start.

Do Your Own Research
Tables will vary but should demonstrate understanding of loans and interest rates.

Resources

📁 **Student Activity Workbook** Assign the Chapter 21 activities in the Student Activity Workbook.

ASSESS

After You Read
Have students complete the Section 21.2 After You Read section review.

Online Study Tools
Have students go to the OLC through **glencoe.com** to:

- Take the Section 21.2 **Practice Test**.
- Download **Podcast** study tools.
- Download free **Study-to-Go** content to their PDAs or cell phones.

 Real-World *Connection*

Credit Offers

Sam Lu saw a Best Automotive car ad that promised "no payments for a year!" He talked to his dad about buying the car. Mr. Lu asked Sam what the interest would be once the payments started and if the car has advertised for the same price elsewhere. Sam did not know the answers to these questions. Mr. Lu suggested that Sam save up the money to buy a car instead of buying one on credit.

Critical Thinking What should Sam do before deciding to buy the car from Best Automotive?

Do Your Own Research Contact several car dealerships or savings institutions and check interest rates and loan amounts for car loans. Create a table that summarizes this information.

Advantages and Disadvantages of Credit

Buying on credit is easy and convenient. You do not have to carry a lot of cash. You can also use credit cards for emergencies.

However, credit cards have disadvantages. The costs of credit can be very high, and the methods of calculating the costs of credit vary from company to company. Common costs include annual fees and finance charges. An annual fee is a yearly charge for the use of the card. A **finance charge** is a fee based on the amount of money you owe and the interest charged on the credit. Finance charges commonly amount to 1.5 percent of your balance per month, or 18 percent per year. The Federal Truth in Lending Act requires lenders to state the cost of the interest as an **annual percentage rate (APR)**, which is the yearly cost of the loan, expressed as a percentage. An APR allows you to compare the costs of credit charged by different lenders. You will pay a lot of interest if you have a card with a high APR.

Some credit cards have a *grace period*, which is a time during which interest is not charged. If you pay the entire amount by the due date, you may avoid interest or other finance charges.

The second disadvantage of credit is that you may accumulate too much debt. **Debt** is the state of owing money. When you are in debt, you owe the amount you have borrowed plus interest, which is the amount you must pay to borrow the money.

▶ **IMPULSE BUY**
It can be tempting to use a credit card to buy expensive items on the spur of the moment. *How could you prevent yourself from overusing credit?*

 474 **Unit 6** Life Skills

 Extend the Photo

Caption Answer Answers will vary. One method to prevent overusing credit is to treat credit purchases like cash. Every time you use your credit card, record the purchase in your check register and subtract the money from your checking account balance. When you receive the credit card statement, pay the credit card amount in full, making sure the amount of the statement matches the total of the individual charges in your check register. Do not record the credit card payment in your check register; the individual charges have already been recorded.

Discussion Ask students to consider the potential problems of starting college or an entry-level job while carrying a large amount of credit card debt.

If you have too much debt, you may not be able to make your payments on time. You may also have to pay a large amount of interest to your credit card company. If you have a secured loan, you risk losing your collateral. Your credit rating may also go down.

Credit Reports

Before lending you money, lenders often take your personal information, such as your name, address, and Social Security number, and obtain a credit report from one or more credit bureaus. A **credit bureau** is an agency that collects information on how promptly individuals and businesses pay their bills and repay their loans and debts. A credit bureau can provide a credit report showing your credit history and a numerical rating called your *credit rating*. Lenders use these to decide how likely you are to repay a loan. A good credit rating can ensure that your receive a loan or a lower interest rate. A poor credit history or credit rating may mean that you will be denied the loan or have to pay a loan back at a higher interest rate.

Make a habit of checking your credit rating regularly. By law, you may request a credit report at no cost every twelve months. You can do this by contacting a credit reporting agency. Report any errors to the credit bureau promptly.

Use Credit Wisely

To use credit wisely: 1) Shop around for the best credit offer. 2) Use credit only when necessary. 3) If you have a problem repaying your debt, seek help through organizations such as American Consumer Credit Counseling and the Consumer Credit Counseling Service.

Career ✔ Checklist

To Establish Good Financial Habits:

✓ Establish a set of savings goals and create a plan to help you reach them.

✓ Avoid banks that have high fees and APRs.

✓ Save for large purchases instead of relying on credit.

✓ Know your financial rights.

Section 21.2 After You Read

Review Key Concepts

1. Describe the steps involved in keeping track of your checking account.
2. Name a type of credit and describe a situation in which you might use it.
3. Explain the advantages and disadvantages of using credit.

Practice Academic Skills

 English Language Arts

4. What are your long-term financial goals, such as paying for college, buying a home, or saving for retirement? Explain how you plan to achieve those goals. What kind of financial tools (accounts, investments, credit) will help you achieve your goals? Write your responses in a one-page essay.
5. Describe the different types of credit. What are some potential advantages and disadvantages associated with using credit? How would you avoid these disadvantages and problems if you had your own credit account? Write your response in a one-page essay.

N C L B

@ Check your answers at this book's OLC through **glencoe.com**.

glencoe.com

Chapter 21 Banking and Credit (475)

ASSESS (cont.)

Resources

⊙ **ExamView Assessment Suite CD** allows you to print out ready-made unit and chapter tests complete with answer keys. You can also create customized tests.

CLOSE

Culminating Activity

Credit Card Debt in the United States Ask students to research and write a 200-word paragraph on personal credit card debt in the United States. Encourage students to answer these questions: Has credit card debt increased in recent years? Why? (Credit card debt has increased in the U.S. as companies have been more willing to extend credit—and higher credit limits—to individuals who in an earlier era would not have qualified for credit cards. There are roughly 1.2 billion credit cards in use in the U.S. According to research, a typical credit card purchase costs 112 percent more than if cash were used.)

N C L B Activity correlated to English Language Arts standards.

Section 21.2 After You Read

Review Key Concepts

1. Fill out your checks completely and accurately and record them in your check register, endorse and deposit any checks you receive, and reconcile your bank statement with your check register.
2. Possible answer: Credit. You get a credit card to build a credit history, have a convenient way to pay for items, and have a source for emergency funds.
3. Advantages include not having to carry a lot of cash and building a credit history. Disadvantages include paying annual fees and finance charges and the risk of accumulating debt.

Practice Academic Skills

4. Possible goals include saving money in interest-bearing accounts, buying certificates of deposit or investing in an IRA, making responsible use of credit cards in order to build good credit, and using that credit to secure loans for college and buying a home.
5. Student essays will vary but should demonstrate an understanding of the different types of credit (loans and credit cards), the positive and negative outcomes of using credit, and possible strategies for responsible use of credit.

Discussion Starter

Arts, Audio/Video Technology, and Communications Lead a discussion about the different types of careers that can be found in this career cluster. (Answers will vary but students should show an understanding of the many types of careers that fall within the career cluster.)

TEACH

W Writing Support
Independent Practice

Conduct an Interview Have students use the questions in the Career Spotlight to conduct and record an interview with an individual in this career cluster. (Interviews should follow the question-and-answer format of the Career Spotlight.)

C Critical Thinking

Abilities and Broadcast Journalism Have students list the personal abilities and traits they might need for a career as a broadcast journalist and news anchor. (Abilities and traits include a dedication to accuracy, a knack for persistence, initiative, poise, resourcefulness, and a good memory.)

CAREER SPOTLIGHT

Career Cluster: Arts, Audio/Video Technology, and Communications

**Lee Ann Kim
Television News Anchor and Reporter**

Q: Describe your job.
A: As a news anchor, I read the news. As a reporter, I find stories, go out in the field and convince people to let me interview them on camera, and put together a decent story to tell our viewers each night. There is more money in anchoring, but my heart is in the storytelling.

Q: Describe a typical workday.
A: There really is none. We're constantly "on," looking for the next story, developing sources, following up on investigations, and waiting for the next breaking news event.

Q: What skills are most important to you in your job?
A: You have to be a curious person. If you don't like meeting people, forget about it. It's also a very competitive business where you want to get information before the other stations, the newspaper, and the Internet. You need good communication skills. And because this is an audiovisual medium, you have to be physically presentable and have a decent voice.

Q: What is your key to success?
A: Being a kind and honest person. I think what sets me apart is that I'm compassionate when I report, and I come from a cultural background that makes me more sensitive to ethnic issues. Also, it helps in my region, San Diego, if you know how to speak Spanish.

Q: What training and preparation do you recommend for students?
A: Get an internship at a news station in your sophomore or junior year of college. If you want to be in news, read the newspaper and watch broadcast news! Also, there are many organizations that provide scholarships, training, and mentoring opportunities.

Q: What are some ways you recommend students prepare for this career?
A: High school courses in English, journalism, and social studies provide a good foundation for college programs. Useful college courses include English, sociology, political science, economics, history, and psychology. Courses in computer science, business, and speech are useful as well. Find someone in the business you admire and get that individual to be your mentor. Know who the top people in the industry are, find out how they got into the business, and network as much as you can.

Q: What academic skills and lifelong learning skills are helpful in preparing for your career?
A: Communication is the key: taking good notes and sharing information. That sounds easy, but try to tell someone's life story in 90 seconds. Critical thinking is a must in this industry, and so is being able to stand out creatively. It also helps to have some knowledge of political science, law, and economics.

Q: What do you like most about your work?
A: I love how each day has a different story and a different challenge. Also, television is such a powerful medium; it's a privilege to be part of an industry that shapes the way the world thinks.

 For more about Career Clusters, go to this book's OLC through **glencoe.com**.

NCLB NO CHILD LEFT BEHIND

Teaching Tip

The goals of the NCLB Act include a strong emphasis on reading skills. The use of modeling in your classroom will help students become better at identifying information. For example, ask a question that can be answered by reading the chart on page 477. Verbally identify the elements of the chart that might help the student identify the answer: the stars and the academic skills labels.

Sample Question What are tasks that require skills in both English language arts and social studies? (Answer: Anchor news program, develop sources, interview subjects, research and report stories, and mentor aspiring journalists.)

- **Education or Training** Most employers prefer a bachelor's degree in journalism or communications, but some hire graduates with other majors. They look for experience at school newspapers or broadcasting stations, and internships with news organizations.

- **Academic Skills Required** English Language Arts, Social Studies

- **Technology Needed** Reporters typically need good research and word-processing skills and the ability to use specific technology, such as recording devices. Broadcast journalists must also master broadcasting technology such as DAT recorders, microphones, cameras, and editing software.

- **Aptitudes, Abilities, and Skills** Reporters should be dedicated to providing accurate and impartial news. A nose for news, persistence, initiative, poise, resourcefulness, a good memory, and physical stamina are important, as is the emotional stability to deal with pressing deadlines, irregular hours, and dangerous assignments.

- **Workplace Safety** Covering some events, such as natural or human-made disasters, can be dangerous.

- **Career Outlook** Employment of news analysts, reporters, and correspondents is expected to grow more slowly than average for all occupations over the next ten years. Consolidation should continue in the publishing and broadcasting industries.

- **Career Path** Reporters can become anchors or create other news-related programs.

Academic Skills Required to Complete Tasks

Tasks	English Language Arts	Social Studies
Develop sources	★	★
Interview subjects	★	★
Research and report stories	★	★
Anchor news program	★	★
Mentor aspiring journalists	★	★

NCLB

Critical Thinking

How might knowledge of social studies help a journalist anchor a news program?

NCLB This chart relates academic skills such as English Language Arts, Mathematics, Science, Social Studies, and World Languages to specific tasks that are performed for the job in the Career Spotlight feature.

Critical Thinking

Answers will vary. Knowledge of social studies is very important for anchoring a news program because a credible anchor has working knowledge of local, national, and world politics, understands how governments function, and has excellent knowledge of geography.

CAREER SPOTLIGHT

ASSESS

Make Connections

Ask students to list specific correlations between academic subjects and workplace tasks. For example, a jeweler might benefit by studying geology, mineralogy, and chemistry because a jeweler's tasks might include heating and mixing liquid metal. An architect must study geometry and physics in order to design structures that balance various forces such as pressure, weight, and gravity. (Answers will vary but students should show an understanding of how academic skills relate directly to workplace tasks.)

CLOSE

Culminating Activity

Lifelong Learning and Career Clusters Encourage students to come up with informal ways that a person might develop skills that would apply to a particular career in Arts, Audio/Video Technology, and Communications. For example, digital animators, who create moving images using computer software, take their inspiration from "concept artists" who create drawings or pictures of art using traditional media such as oils, charcoal, and sculpture. Another example would be that broadcast journalists might keep an online blog to practice their writing skills. Have students volunteer to share their ideas in class. (Answers will vary but should show evidence of understanding the career as profiled in the Career Spotlight.)

Key Terms and Academic Vocabulary Review

1. Students should write complete sentences using each term correctly. A sample answer might read: "After I withdrew $40 at the ATM, my *balance* was $152.16."

Review Key Concepts

2. The common methods of saving money include opening a savings account, into which money is deposited and accrues interest, an amount of money that is paid for the use of another's money; buying investments, which are financial products used to make money grow and can include savings bonds, money market accounts, and certificates of deposit (CD); and entering into a retirement plan such as a pension, a 401(k), an individual retirement account (IRA), a Keogh plan, or a simplified employee pension (SEP), all of which involve putting away money for investment purposes to be withdrawn after retirement.

3. Answers will vary according to the plans selected. Plans should compare the characteristics of two of the following: pension (defined benefit or defined contribution), 401(k), individual retirement account (IRA), Keogh plan, or a simplified employee pension (SEP).

4. You can manage a checking account by filling out your checks completely and accurately and recording your checks and other withdrawals in your check register, promptly endorsing and depositing any checks you receive, and reconciling your bank statement with your check register.

5. A charge account is similar to a credit card except that it is offered by a specific business and can be used to

478

CHAPTER SUMMARY

Section 21.1

An interest-bearing savings account with compounded interest is a good way to save for the future. A money market account pays a higher interest but requires a higher balance. Other ways to save and invest include savings bonds and certificates of deposit. You should start saving for your retirement right away. Types of retirement plans include 401(k) plans and individual retirement accounts (IRAs). Tax-deferred retirement plan options for the self-employed include Keogh plans and simplified employee pension (SEP) plans.

Section 21.2

A check withdraws money from a checking account. If you have a checking account, you must manage it to be sure you have enough money to pay for checks and withdrawals. Each month you should reconcile your check register with the bank statement. Other banking services include electronic funds transfer and online banking. Credit allows you to buy something now and pay later. Forms of credit include loans and credit cards. Advantages include convenience and the ability to make large purchases. Disadvantages include high costs and debt.

Key Terms and Academic Vocabulary Review

1. Use each of these key terms and academic vocabulary words in a sentence.

Key Terms
- deposit (p. 465)
- withdrawal (p. 465)
- balance (p. 465)
- interest (p. 465)
- dividend (p. 466)
- certificate of deposit (CD) (p. 466)
- 401(k) plan (p. 467)
- individual retirement account (IRA) (p. 467)

- Keogh plan (p. 467)
- simplified employee pension (SEP) (p. 467)
- check register (p. 470)
- endorse (p. 470)
- reconcile (p. 471)
- electronic funds transfer (EFT) (p. 471)
- online banking (p. 472)
- credit (p. 472)
- down payment (p. 473)

- finance charge (p. 474)
- annual percentage rate (APR) (p. 474)
- debt (p. 474)
- credit bureau (p. 475)

Academic Vocabulary
- accrued (p. 465)
- redeem (p. 466)
- transfer (p. 472)
- encryption (p. 472)

Review Key Concepts

2. **List** the common methods of saving money. Describe one.
3. **Compare** the characteristics of two types of retirement plans.
4. **Explain** how to manage a checking account.
5. **Explain** the difference between a credit card and a charge account.
6. **Describe** the advantages and disadvantages of using credit.
7. **Explain** how to compare credit costs.

Critical Thinking

8. **Evaluate** What factors might help you choose between a safe investment with a low interest rate and a riskier investment with a higher interest rate?
9. **Analyze** If you had $1,000 to save or invest, what kind or kinds of accounts would you choose for your money? Why?

buy goods and services only from the company issuing the credit.

6. Advantages of credit include not having to carry a lot of cash, having cash available for emergencies, and being able to build a good credit history through responsible use of credit. Disadvantages include the high cost of credit, including annual fees and finance charges (expressed as an annual percentage rate [APR], and the risk of falling into debt, the state of owing the money you have borrowed plus interest.

7. You can compare credit costs by looking at the annual percentage rate (APR) offered, whether the creditor offers a grace period, and whether there are any annual fees.

Critical Thinking

8. Answers should demonstrate comprehension of credit, loans, and interest rates. All investors have to decide for themselves whether a particular investment is worth the risk, but factors that could influence their decision include whether they can make the high monthly payments caused by the higher interest rate,

Real-World Skills and Applications

Problem-Solving Skills

10. Managing Credit Imagine that you earn a good salary but you have allowed the balances on several credit cards to get too high. Write a plan that includes at least two actions you might take to begin solving your problem. Explain how you would implement your plan in a one-page summary.

Technology Applications

11. Research Online Banking Visit local banks or research online to discover the various transactions that can be conducted through online banking at two or more banks. Using spreadsheet software, create a chart summarizing this information. Note any fees charged for these transactions.

Financial Literacy Skills

12. Research Savings and Investment Options Team up with one or more classmates to research various savings and investment options. Research online or visit several banks for information and brochures. Create a three-panel printed or electronic brochure describing these options and where they are available. Be sure to describe the advantages and disadvantages of each type of investment option. Present your findings and your brochure to class.

@ Log On Go to this book's Online Learning Center through **glencoe.com** for help with financial literacy.

13. **Interviewing for Information** Brainstorm questions you have about opening a checking, savings, or other type of account. Write down the questions. Visit a local bank and ask to speak to someone about opening an account. Ask your questions. Be sure to record the answers. Summarize your findings in a one-page report. Bring the report to class and share your findings with other students.

14. **Credit Counseling**
Situation Your friend recently got her first job and has just dropped by to tell you how well she is doing. You soon find out that she is close to her limit on one credit card and is not sure how to use her check register.
Activity Role-play a conversation in which you explain to your friend the basics of managing her finances. Explain why she should not spend more than she makes and how she should handle her checking account.
Evaluation You will be evaluated based on how well you meet the following performance indicators:
- Offer accurate and useful information about spending and money management habits.
- Present your advice in a constructive and friendly manner.
- Correctly answer any questions your friend may have.

least two banks and relevant information about online transactions.

12. Student methods of organizing and presenting their brochures may vary. Encourage students to find examples of the types of savings and investing options covered in the chapter and to show the different interest rates offered by banks. Tell students that it is important to use similar methods when trying to decide what investment options to pursue in real life.

ACTIVE LEARNING

13. Reports will vary. Tell students that doing research, asking questions, and getting as much information as possible is advantageous when making important financial decisions.

ROLE PLAY

14. Effective role plays should demonstrate understanding of how to manage a checking account and the advantages or disadvantages of having a credit card, and be able to provide all necessary information about these subjects to allow the audience to make decisions regarding responsible credit management. Evaluate presentations for accuracy, clarity, and creativity.

whether it's worth risking possible damage to their credit score by making the investment with a greater possibility of failure, and whether the potential payoff of the riskier investment is great enough to be worth the risk.

9. Answers should demonstrate comprehension of savings accounts, investments, and retirement plans.

Real-World Skills and Applications

10. Summaries should demonstrate understanding of the risk of going into credit card debt. The most effective plans involve a combination of eliminating or drastically reducing credit card use and cutting other expenses in order to increase available income to make larger credit card payments. Another possibility, not covered in the chapter text, is to consolidate credit card debt by transferring the high-interest accounts to a card with a lower annual percentage rate.

11. Spreadsheets should demonstrate that students are able to accurately construct a spreadsheet using computer applications. All spreadsheets should include the names of at

Academic Skills in the Workplace

15. Essays should explain the levels of credit scores, the variety of accounts used in a credit report, and how creditors will offer favorable interest rates to loan applicants with high credit scores and less favorable rates (or deny loans altogether) to applicants with low credit scores or insufficient credit history.

16. Account A will pay $10 more a year in interest than Account B ($1,000 × .05 = $50; $1,000 × .04 = $40; $50 − $40 = $10) the first year. The difference in interest paid in subsequent years can be calculated by using the equation I = Prt for each account, then subtracting Account B's result from Account A's result.

17. The median value of the houses is $500,000. Explain to students that when there is an even number of values to analyze, the median can be found by adding together the two middle values and dividing the result by 2.

18. Letters will vary but should demonstrate comprehension of the various retirement plans and benefits covered in the chapter. A possible scenario is to find parallels between the retirement options in another country and the kinds commonly found in the U.S., such as pension plans, individual retirement accounts, and Keogh plans.

Academic Skills in the Workplace

 English Language Arts

15. Using Citations Research information about credit bureaus and credit reports. What kind of information is included on credit reports? What do the scores mean? How do creditors use credit scores? Summarize your findings in a one-page report, citing the sources of your information.

 Mathematics

16. Comparing Simple Interest Rates Mia has $1,000 in savings and wants to deposit her money in the savings account that will pay the most annual interest. She is choosing between two accounts: Account A pays 5% and Account B pays 4%. Which account will pay more interest? How much more will it pay each year?

 Calculating Interest Simple interest is determined by multiplying the interest rate by the principal times the amount of time the amount is deposited.

Starting Hint The formula for calculating simple interest is as follows: I = Prt, Where P = principal, r = annual rate of interest, and t = number of years invested.

 Science

17. Analyze Data Sets To make sense of data, economists use statistical analysis. One of the tools used in statistical analysis is the median. To find the median, arrange a set of data in ascending order. The median is the middle number in the group. When there is an even number of items in the data set, the median is the average of the middle two numbers. If you want to borrow money from a bank to buy a house, it might be helpful to know the median price of houses in the area. Identify the median value of the following houses: $400,000, $450,000, $500,000, $550,000, $600,000.

 Social Studies

18. Compare Retirement Plans Juan is considering moving to another country to take a job. He is concerned about his financial security during retirement. Research how people in one other country plan for retirement. Does the government provide any retirement benefits? What options do workers have? Write a one-page letter to Juan summarizing your findings.

STANDARDIZED TEST PRACTICE

TIMED WRITING

Directions Read the writing prompt and respond in a full essay.

Test-Taking Tip When writing an essay test response, it is important to take a few moments to plan. Read the question several times and underline key words or phrases. Key words or phrases tell you what you have to do. For example, "explain how you made your choice" is a key phrase in the question above.

Prompt: High school students are faced with many choices upon graduation. Some choose to go to college, while some choose technical schools or apprenticeships. Write an essay explaining what you will do after high school and how it will affect your finances. Be sure to explain how you made your choice, the events or people who influenced your choice, and the impact your choice will have on your finances. Support your explanations with details and examples.

For more Standardized Test Practice, go to the OLC **glencoe.com.**

STANDARDIZED TEST PRACTICE

Answer

Essays should address all questions in the prompt and should be checked for grammar, clarity, and content.

Test-Taking Strategies

Whether your students have a standardized test coming up in a few days or a few weeks, these last-minute test-prep tips and strategies will help students relax and do their best.

Test Format Help your students become familiar with the format of the specific test they are going to take by practicing with test items that imitate the actual test items as closely as possible.

Test Timing Have your students take one or more timed practice tests so that they become comfortable with the test format.

Writing Skills Practice

19. Organize an Expository Essay Organizing an essay before you begin writing will help you to focus on the main point.

 Practice Develop an outline for an essay about good money management. Be sure to discuss how saving, investing, and payment options affect money management.

Follow the steps below when organizing your essay:

- **Introduction** Introduce your topic: What are you writing about? Who is your audience? Why are you addressing this audience?
- **Body** Each subtopic, or point, in the body, should support your main topic. The aspects of good money management, for instance, could be your main points. Details and examples help a reader to understand what you are trying to say.
- **Conclusion** Summarize the main points of your essay. Does your reasoning lead to a conclusion?

Net Connection

20. Choose a Credit Card Compare the advantages and disadvantages of five credit cards. Take into account fees, APR, and other factors. Use spreadsheet software to create a chart comparing the cards and write a paragraph telling which would be best for you and why.

 Log On Visit this book's OLC through **glencoe.com** for links to help you investigate at least three options for repairing a bad credit rating. Write a paragraph explaining how each works and the effect it would have on your credit rating.

Reading Connection

Go to this book's Online Learning Center through **glencoe.com** for a list of reading suggestions.

glencoe.com

Personal Academic and Career Portfolio

Credit Management Checklist

When you have a regular salary, your purchasing power will increase, but so will your financial responsibilities. Like most people, you may purchase some very expensive items, such as a car and a house, with credit. Making timely payments on your credit accounts will save you money by helping you to avoid high interest payments and fees. It will also safeguard your good credit rating and ensure your ability to borrow in the future. To help you manage your credit, create a credit management checklist and add it to your **Personal Academic and Career Portfolio**.

The following guidelines will help you practice good credit management:

- List all the tips for good credit management listed in the chapter, such as comparing APRs before opening an account and checking your credit rating regularly. Add your own tips if you wish.
- Organize the list by category, for instance, credit card accounts and credit reports.
- Before each item, add a line or box for checking.
- Add a folder to your portfolio and label it *Credit Management*.
- Make several copies of the checklist and add them to the folder.
- On a regular basis, use a copy of the checklist to check to see how well you are managing your credit.

 Portfolio Help Go to the *Succeeding in the World of Work* OLC through **glencoe.com** for help developing your portfolio.

Writing Skills Practice

19. Outlines should show how students would organize an essay about money management. Outlines should clearly define how the student would write the introduction, body, and conclusion.

Net Connection

20. Charts will vary but should demonstrate that students fully understand the concepts of credit and how credit cards work. Students should name the credit card companies and the specific offers of a particular card. Tell them to take into account any fees or special offers associated with using a card (such as frequent flyer miles) when making their assessments.

Resources

ExamView Assessment Suite CD allows you to print out ready-made unit and chapter tests complete with answer keys. You can also create customized tests.

WorkKeys

WorkKeys® is a job skills assessment program. For information on leveled assessment for Communication Skills (Business Writing; Listening; Reading for Information; and Writing), go to the WorkKeys link on this book's OLC through **glencoe.com**.

Personal Academic and Career Portfolio

Maintaining a Portfolio

Tell students that the Credit Management Checklist in their **Personal Academic and Career Portfolios** will always be a work in progress. As their circumstances, purchases, and investments change, there will periodically be a need to open credit accounts. For example, if they need to purchase an automobile, they will need to update their checklist to reflect this purchase. Tell students it is advisable to order copies of their credit report annually. Copies of these reports can be placed in the credit folder. Encourage students to review their checklist periodically to ensure it remains current and effective.

Chapter Resources Planning Guide with Activities and Features

Section	Features	Activities
Section 22.1 **Insurance Basics**	Creative Business Practices (p. 486) Real-World Connection (p. 487) Career Checklist (p. 488)	Before You Read (p. 484) Graphic Organizer (p. 484) As You Read (p. 485) After You Read (p. 488)
Section 22.2 **Property, Health, and Life Insurance**	Math in Action (p. 492) 21st Century Workplace (p. 492) Everyday Ethics (p. 494) Hot Jobs! (p. 495)	Before You Read (p. 489) Graphic Organizer (p. 489) As You Read (p. 490) After You Read (p. 495)

NCLB Activities, information, and skills practice will help your students attain No Child Left Behind proficiency. Students will improve their abilities in the following academic standards areas:

Academic Standards Correlations

Discipline	Standard	Feature/Activity
English Language Arts	**NCTE 1** Read texts to acquire new information.	Creative Business Practices (p. 486) Hot Jobs! (p. 495)
	NCTE 7 Conduct research and gather, evaluate, and synthesize data to communicate discoveries.	Real-World Connection (p. 487)
	NCTE 9 Develop an understanding of diversity in language use across cultures.	21st Century Workplace (p. 492)
	NCTE 12 Use language to accomplish individual purposes.	Everyday Ethics (p. 494) After You Read (p. 495)
Mathematics	**Number and Operation:** Understand meanings of operations and how they relate to one another	After You Read (p. 488) Academic Skills in the Workplace (p. 500)
	Problem Solving: Solve problems that arise in mathematics and in other contexts	Math in Action (p. 492)

21ˢᵗ Century Skills and Workplace Competencies Correlations

CORRELATIONS The charts show the 21ˢᵗ Century Skills, foundation skills, and workplace competencies that students develop as they work in this chapter.

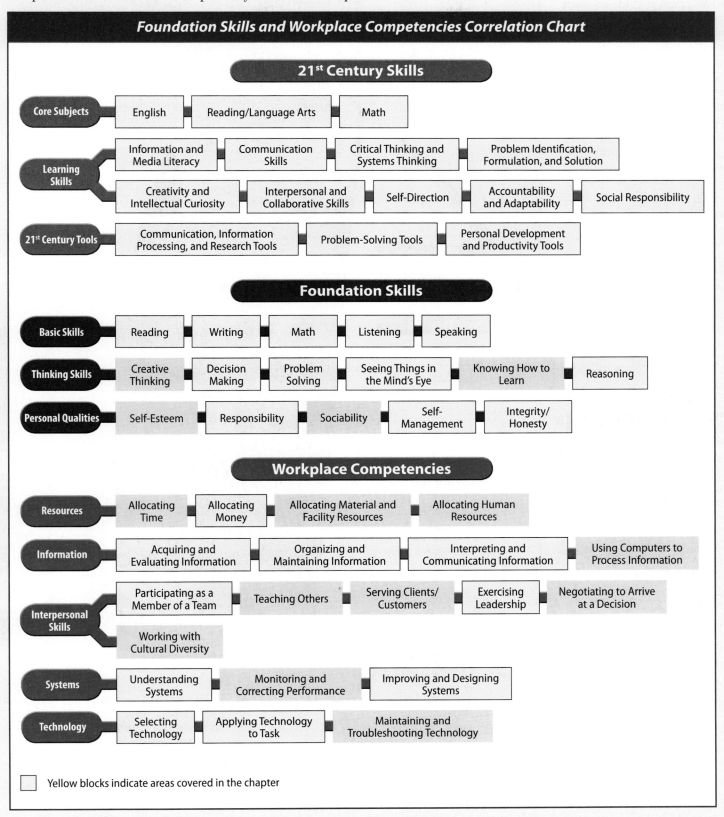

Foundation Skills and Workplace Competencies Correlation Chart

21ˢᵗ Century Skills

Core Subjects: English | Reading/Language Arts | Math

Learning Skills: Information and Media Literacy | Communication Skills | Critical Thinking and Systems Thinking | Problem Identification, Formulation, and Solution | Creativity and Intellectual Curiosity | Interpersonal and Collaborative Skills | Self-Direction | Accountability and Adaptability | Social Responsibility

21ˢᵗ Century Tools: Communication, Information Processing, and Research Tools | Problem-Solving Tools | Personal Development and Productivity Tools

Foundation Skills

Basic Skills: Reading | Writing | Math | Listening | Speaking

Thinking Skills: Creative Thinking | Decision Making | Problem Solving | Seeing Things in the Mind's Eye | Knowing How to Learn | Reasoning

Personal Qualities: Self-Esteem | Responsibility | Sociability | Self-Management | Integrity/Honesty

Workplace Competencies

Resources: Allocating Time | Allocating Money | Allocating Material and Facility Resources | Allocating Human Resources

Information: Acquiring and Evaluating Information | Organizing and Maintaining Information | Interpreting and Communicating Information | Using Computers to Process Information

Interpersonal Skills: Participating as a Member of a Team | Teaching Others | Serving Clients/Customers | Exercising Leadership | Negotiating to Arrive at a Decision | Working with Cultural Diversity

Systems: Understanding Systems | Monitoring and Correcting Performance | Improving and Designing Systems

Technology: Selecting Technology | Applying Technology to Task | Maintaining and Troubleshooting Technology

Yellow blocks indicate areas covered in the chapter

482B

Chapter Overview
Introduce the Chapter

In this chapter, students learn about insurance policies, such as home, auto, health, and life insurance.

Section 22.1 introduces insurance basics such as policies, coverage, beneficiaries, and deductibles, as well as kinds of insurance.

Section 22.2 explains home and automobile insurance, health insurance plans and coverage, and disability and life insurance.

Build Background

Tell students that insurance is a common part of adult life. Ask volunteers to describe instances when family members purchased insurance and the type of insurance they purchased. Point out that some students may already be covered by an automobile policy, or included in a life insurance policy.

▶ Exploring the Photo

Caption Answer Losses covered include damage to cars and payment of medical bills in the case of an accident, and the theft of a car or its contents. Insurance is mandatory so people can afford the risks of driving.

Discussion Ask students how they would be able to pay for thousands of dollars in vehicle damage. Tell them that insurance reduces everyone's risk.

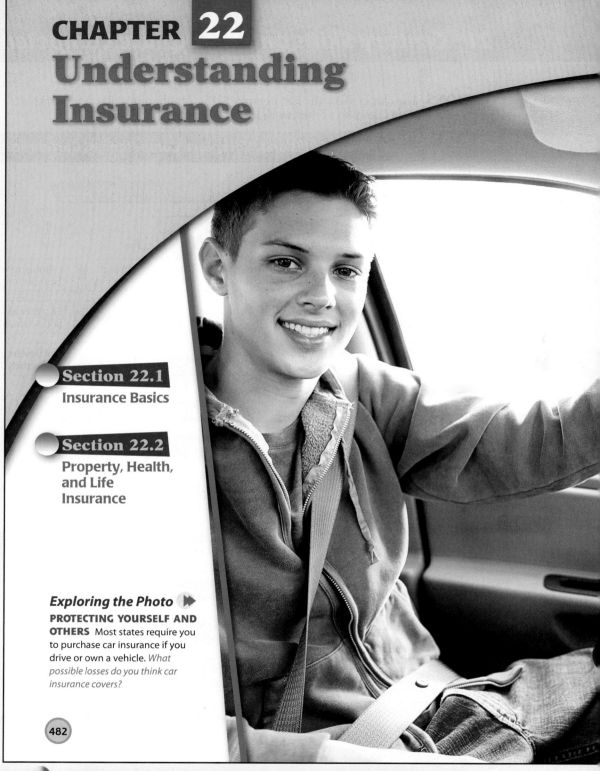

CHAPTER **22**
Understanding Insurance

● **Section 22.1**
Insurance Basics

● **Section 22.2**
Property, Health, and Life Insurance

Exploring the Photo ▶▶
PROTECTING YOURSELF AND OTHERS Most states require you to purchase car insurance if you drive or own a vehicle. *What possible losses do you think car insurance covers?*

Classroom Resources

- 📁 Student Edition
- 📁 Teacher Wraparound Edition
- 📁 Student Activity Workbook with Academic Integration
- 📁 Student Activity Workbook with Academic Integration TAE
- 📁 *Fast File,* Unit 6 Resources

- 📁 Inclusion in the Career Education Classroom
- 💿 TeacherWorks™ Plus
- 💿 *ExamView Assessment Suite*
- 💿 Interactive Chalkboard
- 💿 Interactive Student Edition
- 💻 Online Student Edition
- 💻 Online Learning Center (OLC) with Podcasts

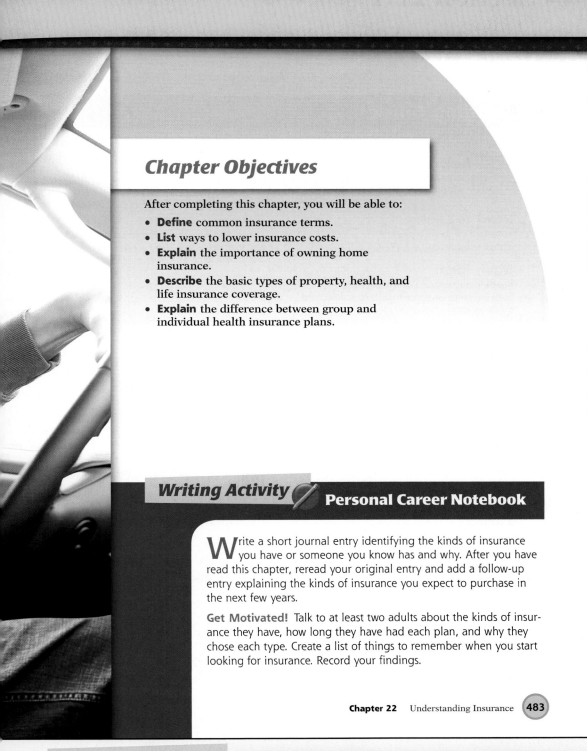

Chapter Objectives

After completing this chapter, you will be able to:

- **Define** common insurance terms.
- **List** ways to lower insurance costs.
- **Explain** the importance of owning home insurance.
- **Describe** the basic types of property, health, and life insurance coverage.
- **Explain** the difference between group and individual health insurance plans.

Writing Activity — Personal Career Notebook

Write a short journal entry identifying the kinds of insurance you have or someone you know has and why. After you have read this chapter, reread your original entry and add a follow-up entry explaining the kinds of insurance you expect to purchase in the next few years.

Get Motivated! Talk to at least two adults about the kinds of insurance they have, how long they have had each plan, and why they chose each type. Create a list of things to remember when you start looking for insurance. Record your findings.

Chapter 22   Understanding Insurance   **483**

Writing Activity — Personal Career Notebook Answer Guide

Many students, particularly those who drive their own vehicles, have some familiarity with automobile insurance. Other initial notebook entries may identify health insurance. After students have read the chapter and completed their follow-up entries, ask for volunteers to describe the type of insurance they expect to buy, and the kinds of coverage they think is appropriate.

Get Motivated! Lists should show an understanding of the information provided by the adults. Evaluate lists for clarity, length, and content.

Review the Objectives
Introduce the chapter by reviewing the chapter objectives:

Section 22.1 Objectives
Define common insurance terms. (*Insurance* is a product that protects you against the risk of loss, an *insurance policy* is a legal contract between the insured and the insurance company, a *premium* is the amount of money paid for insurance, a *deductible* is an amount you pay out of pocket before the insurance company pays for anything, and a *claim* is a formal written request to an insurance company to pay for a loss.)

List ways to lower insurance costs. (Shop around to find the best coverage, look for discounts, increase your deductible, limit your claims, and do not overinsure.)

Section 22.2 Objectives
Explain the importance of owning home insurance. (Home insurance is necessary to avoid financial hardship in the event of damage to a home or its contents.)

Describe the basic types of property, health, and life insurance coverage. (The most common property insurance protects homes; possessions not covered by home insurance; and automobiles. Health insurance allows you to afford health care and can be purchased individually or as part of a group; medical services are bought through fee-for-service, managed care, and preferred provider plans.)

Explain the difference between group and individual health insurance plans. (Group plans spread risk over a large number of people, which helps keep individual costs down. Individual plans are available but are more expensive.)

Insurance Basics

Section 22.1

FOCUS

Bell Ringer Activity

Insurance Basics

Ask students to make a list of five personal possessions they imagine have been destroyed. Make three columns on the board: "Can afford to replace"; "Too expensive to replace"; "Priceless." Have volunteers write the names of items in the appropriate columns.

Resources

Interactive Chalkboard
The Interactive Chalkboard CD provides visual teaching aids for this section.

Online Learning Center
The Online Learning Center (OLC) through **glencoe.com** features chapter vocabulary, chapter summaries, and other study materials.

Preteaching

In this section, the key term *premium* refers to the amount of money paid for insurance. Ask students to write a sentence using another definition of *premium*.

Graphic Organizer

Tell students to go to the OLC through **glencoe.com** for a printable graphic organizer. (Graphic organizers should properly note the terms used in insurance and their definitions.)

NCLB connects academic correlations to book content.

484

Reading Guide

Before You Read
Preview Read the Key Concepts. Write one or two sentences predicting what the section will be about.

Read to Learn
- Common insurance terms
- How to lower insurance costs

Main Idea
Knowing the language of insurance and ways to keep insurance costs down will help you find and purchase appropriate coverage.

Key Concepts
- What Is Insurance?
- Kinds of Insurance

Key Terms
 insurance
- insurance policy
- premium
- deductible
- claim

Academic Vocabulary
You will find this word in your reading and on your tests. Use the academic vocabulary glossary to look up its definition if necessary.
- statistics

Graphic Organizer
As you read, note the main terms used in insurance and their definitions. Use a concept web like the one shown to help organize your information.

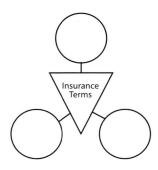

Log On Go to this book's Online Learning Center through **glencoe.com** for an online version of this graphic organizer.

Academic Standards • • • • • • • • • • • • • • • •

English Language Arts
- Conduct research and gather, evaluate, and synthesize data to communicate discoveries. (NCTE 7)
- Use language to accomplish individual purposes. (NCTE 12)

Mathematics
- Understand meanings of operations and how they relate to one another

---

Reading Guide

Before You Read
Tell the class that there are different kinds of insurance for different needs. Explain that an important part of financial planning is being able to understand insurance, the kinds of insurance available, and how to avoid being underinsured or overinsured.

D Develop Concepts
Main Idea Ask students how purchasing insurance is similar to hunting for bargains on material goods. (Just as bargain hunters do research to search out the best deals, learning about insurance and how to keep costs down will help you get what you want for the best price.)

What Is Insurance?

Suppose someone backed into your car, or you broke your leg skateboarding and required surgery. These kinds of unexpected events can be very costly. How would you pay for the repairs or the surgery?

Insurance is a financial product that protects you against the risk of loss. If you experience or cause a loss that is covered by your insurance, the insurance company will help to pay for the loss. Insurance helps people pay expenses they could not afford on their own. Without insurance, most people would not be able to afford the risks of owning a car or home, or participating in sports that have a high risk of injury.

How does insurance work? A basic insurance concept is that by buying insurance, you share the potential costs of sharing individual losses among many people. When you buy insurance, you pay the insurance company an amount that is less than the amount you would pay for your loss. For example, you might pay $500 a year for $100,000 worth of automobile insurance. The insurance company pools the money paid by all individuals who purchase insurance. It then uses those funds to pay for individual losses.

Common Insurance Terms

To understand the basics of insurance, you must learn a few insurance terms. This will help you shop for insurance and understand what you have purchased.

Insurance Policy

An **insurance policy** is a legal contract between the insured, or purchaser of a policy, and the insurance company. The policy defines the terms of your agreement with the insurance company. It explains:

R

- **Insurance Coverage** This refers to the losses for which the insurance company agrees to pay. The amount of coverage is the actual dollar amount that will be paid by the insurance company in the event of a loss.

 COVERAGE Different insurance policies cover different things. *Why is it important to understand both what a policy covers and what it does not cover?*

TEACH

Discussion Starter

What Is Insurance? Ask students to estimate the amount of money they think the whole class would need to contribute to pay for medical expenses for a single student who had an emergency appendectomy. Explain that insurance works by pooling money from the many to pay for the few.

R Reading Strategy

Understanding Words in Context Tell students that "coverage" is a dollar amount the insurance company pays out in the case of loss. Ask students if they can think of a common phrase using the root word "cover" that describes what insurance does for the insured. (Answers may vary but should be a variation on "It has them covered.")

As You Read

The purpose of insurance is to help people pay for losses that they could not afford on their own.

Resources

TeacherWorks™ Plus The TeacherWorks software includes customizable built-in lesson plans and links to printable program resources.

As You Read

Explain What is the purpose of insurance?

Extend the Photo

Caption Answer Answers may include that knowing what a policy covers ensures that you have the insurance you need, and that you do not buy unnecessary insurance, which helps keep your costs down.

Discussion Ask students to discuss the extent of damage typical in a "fender bender" accident and what repairs might be paid for by an automobile insurance policy. Encourage students to think about advancements in automobile technology that can reduce damage and injuries in such accidents as well as driver behaviors that reduce accident risk.

TEACH (cont.)

S Skill Practice

Guided Practice

Read Distribute copies of a sample insurance policy and have each student carefully read it. Encourage questions about what the students have read. **L1**

Explain Have each student write a 200-word paragraph explaining why making regular premium payments for adequate insurance shows responsibility. **L2**

Use Organizers Ask students to make a graphic organizer listing the types of insurance needed at different stages in life. (Organizers should show that different types of insurance fit different needs.) **L3**

ASSESS

Review Key Terms

Have students write sentences using each key term.

Online Study Tools

Have students go to the OLC through **glencoe.com** to:

- Download **Podcast** study tools.
- Download free **Study-to-Go** content to their PDAs or cell phones.

Resources

ExamView Assessment Suite CD allows you to print out ready-made unit and chapter tests complete with answer keys. You can also create customized tests.

486

▶ Vocabulary

You can find definitions in the **Key Terms** glossary and **Academic Vocabulary** glossary at the back of this book.

- **Exclusions** These are losses that are not covered by the policy.
- **Conditions** These are the specific conditions under which payment will be made.
- **The Cost of the Insurance** It is the policyholder's responsibility to understand the coverage and exclusions of his or her policy.

When buying insurance, read your insurance policy carefully. Ask questions about any unclear information before signing the contract.

Benefit and Beneficiary

Money paid by an insurance company for a loss is called a *benefit*. In many cases, the benefit is paid to the *beneficiary*, the person named to receive the benefit.

Premiums

The amount of money a policyholder pays for insurance is known as the **premium**. You can usually pay your premium in installments: monthly, quarterly, biannually (twice a year), or annually (once a year).

S The premium you are charged is directly related to your potential for loss. The insurance industry uses **statistics** to predict potential losses. If you belong to a group with a statistically higher risk for loss, you will pay a higher premium. For example, young drivers are charged higher premiums because there is a greater chance that they will have a car accident.

Creative Business Practices

SYLVAN LEARNING CENTERS

Offering Online Benefits

Sylvan Learning Centers provides personalized tutoring services to students of all ages and skill levels in centers that are located throughout North America as well as online.

For employees, Sylvan offers information online about company benefits, such as health insurance and retirement accounts. Sylvan employees can access information about their benefits through the company's in-house Web site, which is called an intranet. They can learn the current details of their benefit plans, update their information, and view recent activities, such as doctor visits. The online access gives employees control over their benefit plans. It also helps Sylvan lower the costs of managing the program.

CRITICAL THINKING How do you think online access to benefits information affects employees' relationships with human resources ?

 Connect to the Real World For more information about Sylvan Learning Centers, visit the company's Web site via the link on this book's Online Learning Center through **glencoe.com**.

 486 **Unit 6** Life Skills

Creative Business Practices

CRITICAL THINKING ANSWER Answers will vary. Having online access to benefits can lead to employees being better informed about their choices, but it can also lead to more questions. Human resources personnel need to be knowledgable about benefits plans so they can help employees make good decisions about which plans to select. Human resources personnel also need to know how to navigate the company's intranet so that they can assist with technical questions.

Other factors besides age affect your potential for loss and your premium. Examples of such factors include your driving record (for automobile insurance), your health habits (for health and life insurance), and your geographic location (for homeowners insurance).

Deductibles

When you buy many types of insurance, you agree to pay a deductible. This amount is often described as "out of pocket." A **deductible** is the set amount that you pay out of pocket before the insurance company pays anything. For example, suppose you break your car's front windshield. The cost to replace the windshield is $400, and your deductible is $250. You must pay $250 out of pocket before the insurance company pays its portion of the remaining $150.

By agreeing to pay a higher deductible, you decrease the insurance company's potential for loss and lower your premium. For example, if you increase your deductible from $250 to $1000, you may lower your premium by 25 percent. Before you do that, though, be sure that you will be able to pay the higher deductible in the event of a loss.

Claim

A **claim** is a formal written request to an insurance company to pay for a loss. A claim can be made by the policyholder or by someone whose loss has been caused by the policyholder. One common example of this is a car accident in which one driver is at fault. The insurance company of the driver at fault may be responsible for any losses caused by the accident.

✓ **Reading Check** CONTRAST How does an exclusion differ from a condition?

Kinds of Insurance

You can purchase insurance for virtually anything. Insurance is commonly bought to cover homes, cars, health, and life. You can also purchase disability insurance, which protects against the loss of income due to an illness or accident, and insurance for specific possessions, such as jewelry, boats, musical instruments, or computers.

Government Insurance Programs

These programs are supported by federal and state government to help provide coverage if you lose your job (unemployment insurance), are injured while on the job (workers' compensation), or qualify for health coverage (Medicare and Medicaid). You can learn more about some of these programs in Chapter 23 of this book.

Real-World Connection

Safe or Sorry

You and your roommate are preparing to move into your first apartment. You have mostly secondhand furniture, but you have new computers, an entertainment system, and all of your new professional clothes. Renters insurance will cost an additional monthly fee. You would like to purchase it, but your roommate thinks it is a useless expense.

Critical Thinking Is renters insurance necessary? Is it worth paying the entire premium yourself?

Do Your Own Research Research the cost of renters insurance from several insurance companies. Check to see if it would cover the items listed above. Ask about discounts for fire extinguishers and smoke detectors in your apartment. Write a one-page journal entry and explain why you would or would not purchase renters insurance.

Real-World Connection

Critical Thinking Answer Students should recognize that anyone who owns valuable possessions needs to have financial protection in case of fire, theft, or natural disaster.

Do Your Own Research Students' answers will vary, depending on the companies researched. Renters insurance usually does not cover computers, which may be insured separately. Most insurance companies offer discounts for safety measures such as fire extinguishers.

RETEACH

U **Universal Access**
Verbal/Linguistic Learning
Ask students to find the clue in the root of the word "deductible" that describes what a deductible does. (The deductible "deducts," or takes away, a set amount before the insurance company pays anything. The deducted amount is paid by the policyholder.)

C **Critical Thinking**
Differentiating A deductible requires a policyholder to share the risk of loss. Ask students why or why not opting for the lowest possible deductible is a good idea. (If the deductible is high, the premium amount is lower; if the deductible is low, the premium amount is higher. A policyholder must find the right balance between being able to pay a certain amount out of pocket and being able to afford the premium amount.)

Resources

📁 **Student Activity Workbook** Assign the Chapter 22 activities in the Student Activity Workbook.

✓ **Reading Check**

CONTRAST Conditions refer to specific conditions under which payment will be made, while exclusions are losses that are not covered on the policy agreement.

ASSESS

After You Read
Have students complete the Section 22.1 After You Read section review.

Online Study Tools
Have students go to the OLC through **glencoe.com** to:
- Take the Section 22.1 **Practice Test**.
- Download **Podcast** study tools.
- Download free **Study-to-Go** content to their PDAs or cell phones.

CLOSE

Culminating Activity
Policies and Budgets Tell students they are buying an insurance policy for a new house and that they have the choice of a $500 deductible and $150 monthly premium or a $1,000 deductible and $100 monthly premium. Have students write a 150-word paragraph describing the pros and cons of each choice. Tell students that a realistic assessment of a personal budget is crucial when determining what kind of insurance to buy.

N C L B Activity correlated to Mathematics standards.

Career ✓ Checklist

When Buying Insurance:
- ✓ Research different insurance providers.
- ✓ Be sure you understand all deductibles and coverage involved in your plan.
- ✓ Keep all documents and receipts relating to insurance policies and claims.
- ✓ Be careful not to allow any lapse in insurance coverage.

Saving on the Cost of Insurance
You should purchase insurance the way you would make any other significant purchase. Practice smart shopping. These additional tips will help you save on insurance:

- **Shop around.** Research online or contact several insurance companies and discuss coverage options, costs, claims handling, and services.
- **Look for discounts.** Insurance companies often offer a discount if you purchase more than one policy, such as both car and renters insurance. Discounts may also be available for specific protective measures. Examples include security systems, safety features, and proximity to a fire station or fire hydrant for property insurance; and a gym membership for health insurance.
- **Increase your deductible.** This will lower your premium.
- **Limit your claims.** Making frequent claims can cause your premium to increase or your policy to be cancelled.
- **Do not overinsure.** To avoid overpaying, purchase only the coverage you need.

Section 22.1 After You Read

Review Key Concepts
1. Explain the difference between an insurance premium and a deductible.
2. Imagine that you are creating a new budget for the coming year. Describe three ways to save money on your insurance costs.
3. List some reasons that insurance companies might charge some customers higher premiums. What can you do to avoid these higher costs?

Practice Academic Skills
 Mathematics

4. Manuel currently pays $550 for car insurance twice a year. When he turns 21, his payments will decrease by 10%. After that, if he takes a safe driving course, he will pay $80 less each year. How much will he pay each year after both these reductions?

   CONCEPT **Decreasing by a Percent** Instead of multiplying a number by the percent it will decrease and subtracting the result from the original number, calculate by subtracting the percent decrease from 100% and multiplying.

   Step 1: Subtract the percent decrease (10%) from 100%. Multiply the new percent by the insurance payment ($550). Make sure to multiply this amount by two to figure out the amount he will pay per year.

   Step 2: Subtract the other insurance ($80) decrease from the answer to Step 1.

    For math help, go to the Math Appendix located at the back of this book.

 N C L B

488 **Unit 6** Life Skills

Section 22.1 After You Read

Review Key Concepts
1. A premium is the amount of money paid for insurance; a deductible is the amount paid out of pocket by the policyholder before the insurance company pays a claim.
2. A sample answer might be to know what kind of insurance you want; to contact different insurance agencies and learn about coverage, costs, and deductibles; and to buy the right amount of coverage, with a higher deductible to lower premium costs.
3. A sample answer might be that insurance companies charge higher premiums to people they think are more likely to file a claim, so you can lower your costs by being a safe driver, not smoking, and being in overall good health.

Practice Academic Skills
4. Manuel will pay $910 each year (100% − 10% = 90%; $550 × 90% = $495; $495 × 2 = $990; $990 − $80 = $910).

Property, Health, and Life Insurance

Reading Guide

Before You Read

Preview Choose a Key Term or Academic Vocabulary term that is new to you. Write it on a piece of paper. When you find it in the text, write down the definition.

Read to Learn

- Why it is important to own home insurance
- The basic types of property, health, and life insurance coverage
- How to distinguish between group and individual health insurance plans

Main Idea
D
Basic knowledge of how insurance works, what you need, and why you need it will help protect you.

Key Concept
- Types of Insurance

Key Terms
◇ liability insurance
◇ collision insurance
◇ comprehensive insurance
◇ coinsurance
◇ major medical coverage
◇ term life insurance
◇ face value
◇ cash-value life insurance
◇ whole life insurance

Academic Vocabulary

You will find these words in your reading and on your tests. Use the academic vocabulary glossary to look up their definitions if necessary.

■ supplemental
■ require

Graphic Organizer

As you read, list the different types of insurance and note important information about each. Use a chart like the one shown to help organize your information.

Types of Insurance	Notes
1.	
2.	
3.	
4.	

 Log On Go to this book's Online Learning Center through **glencoe.com** for an online version of this graphic organizer.

Academic Standards ● ● ● ● ● ● ● ● ● ● ● ● ● ● ● ●

English Language Arts
- Develop an understanding of diversity in language use across cultures. (NCTE 9)
- Use language to accomplish individual purposes. (NCTE 12)

Mathematics
- Solve problems that arise in mathematics and in other contexts

---

Reading Guide

Before You Read

Read the Key Terms aloud to the class. Ask students to speculate about what the words and phrases *liability*, *comprehensive*, *term life*, *face value*, *cash value*, and *whole life* mean in an insurance context. Explain that when used as part of an insurance term, these words and phrases have a specific meaning.

D Develop Concepts

Main Idea Ask volunteers to give an example of a situation in which having property, health, or life insurance can protect a person and his or her family.

 Bell Ringer Activity

Property, Health, and Life Insurance

Tell students to imagine that they have won a brand new sports car. Explain that though the car is free, they still have to buy automobile insurance. Lead a discussion about what coverage they need to buy and factors that might affect their premium.

Resources

◉ **Interactive Chalkboard**
The Interactive Chalkboard CD provides visual teaching aids for this section.

@ **Online Learning Center**
The OLC through **glencoe.com** features chapter vocabulary, chapter summaries, and other study materials.

Preteaching
Read the definitions of the key terms aloud. Tell students that many of these terms refer to individual parts of a complete insurance policy.

Graphic Organizer
Tell students to go to the OLC through **glencoe.com** for a printable graphic organizer. (Organizer lists should show the different types of insurance and relevant information about each.)

 NCLB connects academic correlations to book content.

489

TEACH

Discussion Starter

Types of Insurance Ask students to take a few minutes to write down the different types of insurance of which they are aware. If any students drive, ask them to share with the class their experiences of having automobile insurance.

As You Read

Supplemental insurance is useful to protect valuable items that are not covered by a homeowners insurance policy.

C Critical Thinking

Making Inferences Tell students a renter is looking to purchase a renters insurance policy. The house is 100 years old, made of wood, lacks smoke detectors, and is next to a river. Ask students how the insurance company might view the situation. (The cost of insurance will most likely be higher because of these factors.)

Resources

TeacherWorks™ Plus
The TeacherWorks software includes customizable built-in lesson plans and links to printable program resources.

Types of Insurance

What kinds of insurance will you need? Some types of insurance, such as liability insurance for your car, are required by law. Whether you purchase other types of insurance depends on your needs and what you can afford. People commonly insure against losses that would cause financial hardship, such as homes, cars, health, and life.

Home Insurance

A homeowners insurance policy usually covers the house, the house's contents, loss of use (such as motel and dining expenses incurred when your dwelling is damaged), and liability (damage to someone or someone's property). This type of policy provides coverage for damage caused by fire, storm (except flood), theft, and liability. **Supplemental** insurance is available to cover losses not covered by the homeowners policy (for example, expensive jewelry, computers, and losses caused by flood or earthquake).

Renters insurance covers losses to a rental unit. It is similar to homeowners insurance, except that it does not cover damage to the building, which is insured by the owner.

The cost of a homeowners or renters policy depends on factors such as building construction (brick, wood, or vinyl), location and age of the home, closeness to a fire hydrant, and security or fire alarm system.

If you file a claim, your insurance company will require you to complete a form that details your losses. For this reason, it is critical that you have an inventory of your possessions, such as the inventory shown in **Figure 22.1** on page 491. Many insurance companies recommend that you photograph or make a video recording of your possessions yearly and store those records safely outside your home.

As You Read

Analyze Why might you purchase supplemental homeowners insurance?

PROTECTING YOUR POSSESSIONS Renters insurance covers the contents of the rental unit and liability, or injury to another or another's property. *Why might renters insurance not cover damage to the building?*

▶ Extend the Photo

Caption Answer Answers should show an understanding that damage to the building would be covered by the building owner's property insurance policy.

Discussion Ask students what they might do if they were renters and owned a large amount of antique china and other fragile kitchen items. Encourage students to consider the valuable possessions they may have in the first years when they live on their own and are living in a rental property, and why having renters insurance might be important to them.

Figure 22.1 INVENTORY OF PERSONAL PROPERTY

Item	Purchase Price	Date of Purchase	Model/ Serial Number	Item	Purchase Price	Date of Purchase	Model/ Serial Number
Electronic Items				Collections			
TV				CDs			
DVD player							
Jewelry				Tools			
Watch							
Furniture				Business Items			
Musical Instruments				Kitchen Items			
Clothing				Other Valuables			

KEEPING RECORDS Keeping an inventory of your possessions will help you in the event of a claim. *Why should you update your inventory regularly?*

Automobile Insurance

Automobiles can be involved in many types of losses, such as theft or accidents. An accident can damage vehicles and other property, and can cause injuries to vehicle occupants and others. Most people could not afford to take the risk of driving without automobile insurance. To ensure a minimum level of protection, many states **require** drivers to purchase liability insurance.

These are the primary types of automobile coverage:

- **Liability Insurance** **Liability insurance** covers damage or injury caused by you to another person or another person's property.
- **Medical Payments Insurance** This insurance pays the medical expenses for you or any passengers injured in your car, no matter who is at fault for the accident.
- **Collision Insurance** **Collision insurance** covers the cost of repairing damage to your car caused by an accident. This type of insurance is usually required when you take out a car loan.
- **Comprehensive Insurance** **Comprehensive insurance** covers damage to your car that is not caused by a collision. Theft, fire, and damage by a falling tree are covered under this type of insurance, which may be required when you take out a car loan.

Chapter 22 Understanding Insurance **491**

Section 22.2

TEACH *(cont.)*

R Reading Strategy

Using Research Materials Have students perform research in the library or on the Internet to determine which states require drivers to purchase liability insurance. Lead a discussion about the risks drivers in states that do not require liability insurance take by not having such coverage. Point out that in these states drivers have extra incentive to purchase uninsured/underinsured motorist insurance.

C Critical Thinking

Drawing Conclusions Ask students which driver's liability insurance covers damages if more than one car is involved in an accident. (The insurance of the driver who was at fault.) Tell students that without liability coverage, you could be responsible for hundreds of thousands of dollars in claims by others.

EXTEND THE FIGURE **Figure 22.1**

Caption Answer Answers will vary. It is advisable to update your inventory annually because a lot of turnover in one's possessions can take place in a single year. For example, one might acquire a new bicycle, television, or video game console, and sell other possessions. It is also important that copies of the inventory be kept somewhere other than the home or rental in case of fire or natural disaster.

Discussion Ask students to think about the many homeowners and renters who lost most or all of their possessions during Hurricane Katrina and the ensuing floods in 2005. Lead a discussion about the importance of insurance and a possessions inventory to those who suffered catastrophic damages.

TEACH (cont.)

W Writing Support

Drawing Conclusions Have students write a 100-word paragraph outlining reasons why they think some states have a no-fault system of auto insurance. (An insurance company in a no-fault system pays for losses regardless of blame for an accident. The main reason the no-fault system exists is to limit the ability of and incentive for accident victims to sue drivers who are to blame for injury crashes. This kind of litigation is viewed by many as leading to a logjammed court system and excessive jury awards.)

C Critical Thinking

Applying Prior Knowledge Have students answer these questions about their own health care: Do you wait until you're ill to seek health care, or do you get regular checkups? Do you want to be able to choose your own health-care providers, even if it costs more money to have this choice? Would you prefer to go to a clinic and perhaps see a different doctor each time, or would you prefer to see one doctor only? Explain that in choosing a health care plan, one has many choices, but what they choose has an influence on how much gets paid out of pocket.

NCLB Activity correlated to Mathematics standards.

Math In Action

Calculate Costs

Roberto pays $900 in home insurance annually, $375 in car insurance semiannually, and $225 in health insurance monthly. What percentage of his $54,375 yearly salary goes to insurance?

Starting Hint: Total the insurance, then divide to find the percentage.

@ For more math practice, go to this book's OLC through **glencoe.com.**

- **Uninsured/Underinsured Motorist Insurance** This insurance provides coverage for damage or injury to you and your occupants caused by a driver with little or no liability insurance.

Some states have a *no-fault system* of auto insurance. This means that your insurance company pays for your losses, no matter who is to blame for the accident.

Buying Automobile Insurance

Many factors affect your auto insurance premium. These include your age, gender, and credit rating; where you live; the type and age of vehicle; and how many miles you drive the car annually.

In addition to the savings tips listed in Section 22.1, the following may help you to save on your auto insurance: good grades (some companies offer a discount for students who maintain above a "B" average); a good driving record; driver education classes; and safety features such as airbags, antilock brakes, and antitheft devices.

Health Insurance

Health care costs are rising. Some expect the total cost of health care in the United States to double within the next ten years. Few people can afford good health care without health insurance. Because the cost of health insurance is also increasing, it is important to shop wisely and choose a plan that fits both your needs and your budget.

Types of Plans

Health insurance plans vary by how you purchase health insurance and how you receive medical services. The type of plan you choose will affect your cost and your ability to choose medical providers.

The 21st Century Workplace

Swahili: An African Common Language

Swahili is the most widely spoken language in eastern Africa. Only five million people, mostly members of the Swahili ethnic group, speak Swahili as their native language. However, ten times that number speak Swahili as a second language. For that reason, Swahili is often known as an African *lingua franca*, or common language. Swahili is the official language of Tanzania and Kenya. Trade along the eastern African coast has also spread Swahili to countries in southeastern Africa such as Zambia, Malawi, and South Africa.

Like many other African languages, Swahili has a complicated system of prefixes in its grammar. For example, Swahili speakers add the prefix *ki-* to nouns that refer to languages. Thus they call their language not *Swahili,* but *Kiswahili.*

CRITICAL THINKING

Why might east African people who do not speak Swahili as their native language need to learn it?

In Your Community

Find someone in your community who speaks more than one language fluently. Ask them if they use different languages in different situations (such as at school, at home, and at social events) and why. Share your findings with the class.

@ **Extend Your Learning** For links to Web sites about Swahili, go to this book's OLC through **glencoe.com.**

Math In Action

Eight percent or 0.08 goes to insurance
900 + (2 × $375) + (12 × $225) = $4,350.00; $4,350.00 ÷ $54,375 = 0.08

The 21st Century Workplace

CRITICAL THINKING ANSWER Thousands of languages are spoken in Africa, and not all are mutually intelligible. In order to be understood at school, in the military, or in business dealings, a person who speaks another African language at home needs to learn the common language of the area.

Unlike in North America, in Africa speaking more than one language is the norm.

In Your Community Encourage students to share the findings of their discussions with multilingual community members.

You can purchase health insurance through a group plan or an individual plan. Most people in the United States belong to group plans through their employers or organizations such as trade associations.

- **Group Plans** Group plans keep costs down by spreading the risk over a large number of people. If your employer offers insurance, you may be asked to pay part of the premium.
- **Individual Plans** People not enrolled in a group plan can buy insurance coverage through an individual plan.

The two main ways to receive medical services are through a fee-for-service plan or a managed care plan.

- **Fee-for-Service** Fee-for-service plans allow you to choose a hospital and physician. These plans require you to pay an insurance premium, deductible, and coinsurance. Once the deductible is met, you must pay **coinsurance**, which is a percentage of the medical expenses you are required to pay. This may be 20 percent or more. The primary benefit of fee-for-service plans is choice of provider, but these plans may be more costly.
- **Managed Care** This type of plan offers the most comprehensive coverage for the lowest cost. It keeps costs down through preventative care and early detection. The *health maintenance organization (HMO)* is the most common form of managed care. With an HMO, you choose a primary physician, who manages all your medical care. There is no deductible. Each visit to a network physician or prescription requires a *copayment*, a fixed amount charged for each service. For example, a doctor visit may cost you $15. The main advantage of managed care is the low cost. Disadvantages include a limited choice of physicians and the need to be referred to a specialist by your primary physician.
- **Other Plans** A number of other plans combine features of fee-for-service and managed care. *Preferred provider organizations (PPOs)* offer some of the low-cost advantages of HMOs while allowing more freedom of choice of doctors. With a PPO you often pay higher costs than you would with an HMO. You can choose any provider, but your cost is lower if you choose a provider from a preselected list.

Types of Coverage

One type of health insurance is **major medical coverage**, which is a type of insurance that covers most hospital and medical expenses. These may include the costs of doctor visits, hospital care, preventative care, and prescription drugs. Health coverage not provided by major medical insurance, such as vision and dental insurance, can be purchased separately.

▼ CHOOSING HEALTH CARE Health care plans that allow you to choose your provider are more expensive than those that do not. *Are you willing to pay more to choose?*

Chapter 22 Understanding Insurance **493**

TEACH *(cont.)*

S Skill Practice
Guided Practice

Read Have each student find and read an article about managed health care. Tell students to find answers to these questions: What is managed care? What does managed care mean for consumers in terms of accessibility and quality of health care? Have students share their findings in class. (Findings should demonstrate an understanding of how managed care works and the advantages and disadvantages of this type of plan.) **L1**

Decide Ask students to decide how important it is to them to have an employer offer and partially pay for a group health insurance plan. Ask whether they would turn down a job offer that did not include insurance. (Students should consider the potential costs of paying for an individual health care plan, the risks of not having health insurance, and whether the job offer is attractive enough to consider an option other than a group health insurance plan.) **L2**

Using Charts Have students make charts listing local providers for three categories of health insurance: health maintenance organizations, preferred provider organizations, and major medical coverage. Have them list the major features of each program in their charts. (Charts should show an accurate listing of providers and major features of each program.) **L3**

Extend the Photo

Caption Answer Some students may have a particular provider with whom they feel comfortable and would be willing to pay more to see. Other students may like the freedom of being able to go straight to a specialist instead of having to be referred by the primary doctor.

Discussion Tell students that their new job offers a choice of an HMO or a PPO, but that a physician they have seen and trusted for years is not on the list of available HMO physicians. They can still see their favored physician, but only if they choose the PPO, which is a more expensive plan. Have volunteers explain why or why not they would choose the PPO.

ASSESS

Review Key Terms
Have students write sentences using each key term.

Online Study Tools
Have students go to the OLC through **glencoe.com** to:
- Download **Podcast** study tools.
- Download free **Study-to-Go** content to their PDAs or cell phones.

RETEACH

W Writing Support
Writing Persuasively The text tells you that disability insurance and life insurance provide coverage for unexpected events. Have students write a 200-word paragraph in which they try to convince new parents, about 25 years old, to purchase disability and life insurance policies despite living on a tight budget. (Paragraphs may include warnings that although the new parents are young and healthy and that it seems the money could be better spent on something else, they never know what might happen and that it's better to be safe than sorry when their child's welfare is at stake.)

Resources

 Student Activity Workbook Assign the Chapter 22 activities in the Student Activity Workbook.

Everyday ETHICS

REPORTING ACCIDENTS

What should you do after a car accident?

FENDER BENDER Last week, you were delivering pizza for your job in the company van and someone rear-ended you. The van was not damaged, but you took the other driver's insurance information and gave it to your supervisor just in case. The supervisor told you that he was not going to report the accident because then the insurance would go up and the owner would be upset because his insurance rates would increase. However, your neck has been hurting since the accident, so you are thinking of telling the owner to see how you should handle your medical expenses.

What Would You Do? What could you tell the supervisor about your injury? If your supervisor does nothing, what are your other options? Will you go above your supervisor to talk to the owner?

> **DISCUSS IT** Whose responsibility is it to deal with the accident? What could the supervisor have done? What could the owner do? Discuss the possible outcomes of different choices with a partner.

Buying Health Insurance
When purchasing health insurance, look for a plan that offers the protection you need at a cost you can afford. In addition to the tips listed in Section 22.1, the following will help you save on health insurance:
- **Look for discounts.** Most companies offer discounts for healthy habits, such as joining a gym or not smoking.
- **Buy the insurance you need.** If you purchase the least expensive coverage, it may not cover necessary expenses, such as doctor visits and prescription drugs. You will have to pay for these out of pocket.

Disability Insurance
Suppose that you are sick, injured, or have a medical condition that prevents you from working either temporarily or permanently. How will you pay your bills and expenses? Disability insurance pays you a percentage of your salary during the period of time in which you are unable to work. Short-term disability insurance covers you for only a few months. Long-term disability can help you cover your expenses for a longer amount of time.

Life Insurance
Life insurance provides your dependents, such as a spouse and children, with money when you die. Your employer may offer life insurance. If this does not provide enough coverage, you may need to purchase an individual policy.

Everyday ETHICS

What Would You Do? Answer One ethical response might be to reveal your neck pain to the supervisor to give him a chance to reconsider his previous action and report the accident to the owner. If he refuses, then it would be advisable to talk to the owner.

> **DISCUSS IT** Encourage students to envision complications that might arise that would play a role in your decision. For example, ask: What would you do if your supervisor suggested he would cut your hours if you reported the accident?

Types of Life Insurance

The two basic types are term life insurance and cash-value life insurance.

Term Life Insurance Term life insurance provides protection for your dependents in the event of your death for a set number of years. If you should die during that time, your beneficiary will receive the face value, which is the amount of money stated in the policy. For example, if you purchase a $250,000 policy, your beneficiary will receive that amount. Though the premium increases as you get older, term life insurance is less costly than cash-value insurance.

Cash-Value Life Insurance Cash-value life insurance is part insurance and part investment. You can borrow money against the total amount of premiums paid on a cash-value policy. Whole life insurance is a type of cash-value life insurance that provides protection throughout your life as long as the premiums are paid. The premium amount is fixed for life.

Buying Life Insurance

Consider these questions before buying life insurance:
- **Do you need life insurance?** If someone depends on you for your earning power, you should have life insurance. If not, you may not need the insurance.
- **How much life insurance do you need?** This depends on your age, whether you have dependents, and how much debt you will leave behind in the event of your death.

HOT JOBS!

Adventure Travel Organizer

These specialized travel agents book transportation and accommodations for clients who want a more challenging travel experience, such as white-water rafting on the Colorado River or hang gliding in the Andes. Familiarity with geography, current events, global politics and climate, and local customs and locations are essential for this exciting career.

Section 22.2 After You Read

Review Key Concepts

1. Why is it important for homeowners to purchase homeowners insurance?
2. List five types of automobile insurance, three types of health insurance, and two types of life insurance. Define one from each group.
3. Explain the difference between group health insurance plans and individual health insurance plans.

Practice Academic Skills

 English Language Arts

4. What kinds of life changes might cause you to choose certain types of insurance? Write a two-paragraph response.
5. You need to purchase auto insurance but have only a limited amount of money to spend on the premium. What should you consider when comparing different policy options? What types of coverage would be most important to you? How might you reduce costs while still making sure you have the coverage you need? Write your responses in a one-page essay.

@ Check your answers at this book's OLC through **glencoe.com**.

ASSESS

After You Read

Have students complete the Section 22.2 After You Read section review.

Online Study Tools

Have students go to the OLC through **glencoe.com** to:
- Take the Section 22.2 **Practice Test**.
- Download **Podcast** study tools.
- Download free **Study-to-Go** content to their PDAs or cell phones.

Resources

ExamView Assessment Suite CD allows you to print out ready-made unit and chapter tests complete with answer keys. You can also create customized tests.

CLOSE

Culminating Activity

Insurance and Your Future Ask students to write a one-paragraph description about how their study of this section has changed or informed their ideas about the kinds of insurance available and how insurance may factor into their future plans.

Activity correlated to English Language Arts standards.

Section 22.2 After You Read

Review Key Concepts

1. Home insurance protects a homeowner from financial hardship if their property is damaged or destroyed.
2. Answers should show an understanding of the different types of insurance explained in this section.
3. Group plans spread the risk over a large number of people, keeping costs down; individual plans are for a single person and are more expensive.

Practice Academic Skills

4. Student essays may include the following: buying a new car; moving into a new apartment; buying a house; getting married; having children; taking a job involving physical labor.
5. In their essays, students should base their considerations on the types of automobile coverage discussed in this section.

CAREER
SPOTLIGHT

FOCUS

Discussion Starter

Hospitality and Tourism
Lead a discussion about the different types of careers that can be found in this career cluster. Have students brainstorm different careers and jobs within the career cluster. (Answers will vary but students should show an understanding of the many types of careers that fall within the career cluster.)

TEACH

W Writing Support
Independent Practice

Conduct an Interview Have students use the questions in the Career Spotlight to conduct and record an interview with an individual in the featured career cluster. (Answers will vary but should follow the interview format of the Career Spotlight.)

C Critical Thinking

Commitment to Running a Business Have students list the physical, financial, and time commitments necessary to starting and maintaining a restaurant. Then ask them to discuss the advantages and disadvantages to running your own restaurant as opposed to working in a restaurant owned by another person. (Answers will vary. The potential for profit, and the sense of satisfaction that comes with it, is far greater for the owner of a restaurant than an employee. However, starting and maintaining a business requires a great deal of self-sacrifice and financial risk.)

Career Cluster: Hospitality and Tourism

Fritz Krimmer
Restaurant Owner
and Manager

Q: Describe your job.
A: I am the owner, operator, and manager of a pizza restaurant.

Q: Describe a typical workday.
A: I arrive about an hour before my scheduled time. First I ring out and balance the register from the previous day. Then I check inventory and order needed items. I oversee all preparatory work and verify that all rooms are properly cleaned. If we will be shorthanded, I call for backup help. I also hire and train new employees, and when necessary will let an employee go. Throughout the day, I make sure food is being made correctly and on time. After the lunch hour, I prepare the restaurant and kitchen for the dinner rush. I pay bills, calculate payroll, and make weekly work schedules.

Q: What skills are most important to you in your job?
A: Leadership skills, communication skills, and excellent customer service skills are essential. Working well under pressure is important, as is the ability to use common sense in order to solve problems.

Q: What academic skills and lifelong learning skills are helpful in preparing for your career?
A: Math, communication and listening skills, and lots of confidence

Q: What is your key to success?
A: I am willing to put forth the time and effort needed to be successful. It is important to me to serve my customers a superior and consistent product.

Q: What are some disadvantages of your career?
A: The main one is the time it takes away from doing things with my family

and other things that I would rather be enjoying. Unfortunately, being on call 24/7 means juggling my personal life with my job.

Q: What training and preparation do you recommend for students?
A: I worked in the industry for two years while attending high school, and at the age of 19, I had the opportunity to purchase my first restaurant. The training and preparation for me was provided by hands-on experience. I would recommend getting an entry-level position at a restaurant and working your way up.

Q: What are some ways you recommend students prepare for this career?
A: Because I purchased the restaurant at age 19, I learned many things by trial and error. If I had had the opportunity, I would have earned a business management degree, including courses in accounting and marketing. Working for someone else in the industry provides the practical experience needed to be successful.

Q: What do you like most about your work?
A: Being a leader and satisfying my customers provides a sense of accomplishment that I have built a successful business.

 For more about Career Clusters, go to this book's OLC through **glencoe.com**.

N C L B NO CHILD LEFT BEHIND

Teaching Tip

The goals of the NCLB Act include a strong emphasis on reading skills. The use of modeling in your classroom will help students become better at identifying information. For example, ask a question that can be answered by reading the chart on page 497. Verbally identify the elements of the chart that might

help the student identify the answer: the stars and the academic skills labels.

Sample Question How many of the tasks on this chart require only one academic skill to complete? (One task requires one academic skill to complete: balance daily receipts.)

Education or Training Experience in the food services industry is essential training for a restaurant manager or owner. Many food service management companies and national or regional restaurant chains recruit management trainees from two- and four-year college hospitality management programs, which require internships and real-life experience to graduate.

Academic Skills Required English Language Arts, Mathematics, Science, Social Studies

Technology Needed Computers and appropriate software for payroll, inventory, budgeting, and other business management activities. Some restaurants may use special technology for food preparation.

Aptitudes, Abilities, and Skills Customer service, organizational skills, personnel management, accounting skills, leadership

Workplace Safety Restaurant owners/managers may experience the typical minor injuries of other restaurant workers, such as muscle aches, cuts, or burns. They might endure physical strain from moving equipment, receiving and storing daily supplies from vendors, or making minor repairs to furniture or equipment.

Career Outlook Employment of food service managers is expected to grow at an average pace over the next ten years.

Career Path Restaurant managers typically advance to larger establishments or regional management positions within restaurant chains. Some may open their own food service establishments. Related positions in the hospitality field include lodging managers and gaming managers.

Academic Skills Required to Complete Tasks

Tasks	English Language Arts	Mathematics	Science	Social Studies
Balance daily receipts		★		
Check inventory, place orders	★	★		
Food preparation		★	★	
Manage staff	★			★
Customer service	★			★
Prepare work schedule and payroll	★	★		

N C L B

Critical Thinking

What types of classes could you take to prepare you for a career as a restaurant owner?

N C L B This chart relates academic skills such as English Language Arts, Mathematics, Science, Social Studies, and World Languages to specific tasks that are performed for the job in the Career Spotlight feature.

Critical Thinking

Classes that can prepare you for a career as a restaurant owner include statistics, world languages, business education courses, home economics, biology, and social studies.

CAREER SPOTLIGHT

ASSESS

Make Connections
Ask students to list specific correlations between academic subjects and workplace tasks. For example, an archaeologist might study world history and chemistry in order to understand both the historical significance of his or her findings and the scientific processes that might reveal the age of artifacts. (Answers will vary but students should show an understanding of how academic skills relate directly to workplace tasks.)

CLOSE

Culminating Activity
Lifelong Learning and Career Clusters Encourage students to come up with informal ways that an aspiring hotel or restaurant owner might develop skills that would apply to a particular career in Hospitality and Tourism. For example, in order to work with both staff and clientele who are from places all over the world, an aspiring hotel owner might join foreign language conversation groups in their community in order to learn basic phrases that could be useful in a tourism setting. Another example would be that an aspiring restaurant owner would make a point of meeting the owner or manager of every restaurant at which he or she dines in order to ask questions about the industry and receive guidance that they could apply later when they have their own business.

Key Terms and Academic Vocabulary Review

1. Students should write complete sentences using each key term correctly. A sample answer might read: "A *deductible* is the set amount that the policyholder pays out of pocket before the insurance company pays for anything."

Review Key Concepts

2. An insurance policy is a legal contract that defines the terms of your agreement with the company. A premium is the amount of money a policyholder pays for insurance. A deductible is the set amount paid out of pocket before the insurance company pays for anything. A claim is a formal written request to an insurance company to pay for a loss. Student explanations will differ; one must understand these terms to be able to make smart decisions when buying insurance.

3. Ways to lower your insurance costs include comparing prices, taking protective measures, increasing your deductible, limiting your claims, and not overinsuring.

4. Restoring a damaged or destroyed home often costs more than what most people can pay out of pocket. Home insurance protects a homeowner from financial hardship if their property is damaged or destroyed.

5. Answers should reflect an understanding of the types of insurance covered in this chapter.

6. A group plan keeps cost down by spreading risk over a large group of people and, in many cases, having members pay part of the premium; an individual plan is for a single person and typically costs more.

CHAPTER SUMMARY

Section 22.1

Insurance protects you against the risk of loss. An insurance policy is a contract between the insured and the insurance company. A policy explains your insurance coverage, or the losses for which the insurance company will pay, and the exclusions, losses that are not covered. Insurance costs include the premium, the amount paid for a policy. The deductible is the portion of a loss you pay for out of pocket. You can hold down your insurance costs by shopping around, looking for discounts, increasing your deductible, limiting your claims, and purchasing only the insurance you need.

Section 22.2

People commonly purchase property, health, and life insurance. Homeowners and renters insurance covers the home, the contents of the home, and liability. Types of automobile insurance include liability, medical payments, collision, comprehensive, and uninsured/underinsured motorist coverage. Fee-for-service health insurance plans allow you to choose your provider, while managed care health plans offer the most comprehensive coverage. Disability insurance pays you when you are unable to work. Common types of life insurance include term life, cash-value, and whole life insurance.

Key Terms and Academic Vocabulary Review

1. Use each of these key terms and academic vocabulary words in a sentence.

Key Terms
- insurance (p. 485)
- insurance policy (p. 485)
- premium (p. 486)
- deductible (p. 487)
- claim (p. 487)
- liability insurance (p. 491)
- collision insurance (p. 491)
- comprehensive insurance (p. 491)
- coinsurance (p. 493)
- major medical coverage (p. 493)
- term life insurance (p. 495)
- face value (p. 495)
- cash-value life insurance (p. 495)
- whole life insurance (p. 495)

Academic Vocabulary
- statistics (p. 486)
- supplemental (p. 490)
- require (p. 491)

Review Key Concepts

2. **Define** four common insurance terms and explain how understanding these terms will help you choose an insurance policy.
3. **List** three strategies that can lower your insurance costs.
4. **Explain** the importance of owning home insurance.
5. **Define** the basic types of home, automobile, health, and life insurance coverage.
6. **Compare and contrast** group and individual health insurance plans.

Critical Thinking

7. **Analyze** Why do you think most insurance policies require a deductible?
8. **Evaluate** Which type of auto insurance coverage do you think is most important?

Critical Thinking

7. Answers should show an understanding of how deductibles work and the inverse relationship between premium amounts and deductible levels. Deductibles help keep the cost of insurance down by passing on some of the insurance company's expense to customers who file claims. This expense also reduces policyholders' likelihood to file claims, which also reduces overall costs.

8. Answers may note that the most important auto coverage is the kind that is required either by law (as liability coverage is in many states) or, if one has a car loan, the lender (such as collision coverage). Others may note that liability insurance is important because it protects against getting sued if you cause an accident, comprehensive insurance protects you from damage not caused by a collision, and uninsured/underinsured motorist insurance protects you from damage caused by uninsured drivers.

Real-World Skills and Applications

Acquiring and Evaluating Information

9. Researching Safety Features Research on the relationship between lower auto insurance rates and automobile safety and security features. Research both existing safety features as well as information on the development of future safety and security features. Prepare a list of both existing and future features, with a brief description of each.

Financial Literacy

10. Choosing a Health Plan You recently started a job at a new company. The company offers group medical coverage and gives you a choice between an HMO and a PPO plan. You like the flexibility of the PPO plan. You would be able to stay with your current doctor and would not need a referral to see a specialist. If you choose the PPO plan, you will have to contribute $60 per paycheck. The HMO plan will cost only $15 per paycheck. Create a list of the pros and cons for each plan and explain which would be a better choice for you.

 Log On Go to this book's OLC through **glencoe.com** for help with choosing a health plan.

Technology Applications

11. Creating a Presentation Team up with one or more classmates. You are a sales team for an insurance company and have to create a presentation for your latest products (insurance plans). Choose a type of insurance and use presentation software to develop a presentation explaining the importance of this type of insurance, the different types of coverage, and how much the plan might cost.

12. **Conducting a Phone Interview** Contact an insurance company and find out what kinds of coverage they offer for a particular type of insurance. Ask what factors might affect your insurance premiums. Summarize your findings and report them to the class in a brief oral presentation. Include the name and number of the company and the name of the person with whom you spoke.

13. **The Need for Insurance**
Situation Your best friend just bought a car from his uncle and came to take you for a ride. While you are talking, your friend tells you that he does not plan to buy car insurance. He says that if he gets into an accident while uninsured, the other driver's insurance will pay for everything as long as it is not his fault. In the meantime, he will save money.
Activity Role-play a conversation in which you explain to your friend that, while he may be technically right, he is missing the main point about car insurance—and he may be behaving illegally.
Evaluation You will be evaluated based on how well you meet the following performance indicators:
- Accurately explain how different types of auto insurance work.
- Effectively inform your friend of the safety risks he is taking.
- Correctly answer any questions your friend may have.

 ACTIVE LEARNING

12. Student presentations will vary but should demonstrate comprehension of the insurance terms and concepts covered in the chapter. Encourage students who may be considering purchasing insurance (such as automobile insurance, if they drive or plan to drive) to be thorough in real-world insurance inquiries.

ROLE PLAY

13. Effective presenters should demonstrate familiarity with the different types of automobile coverage and the legal ramifications of not carrying auto insurance. Evaluate role plays for clarity, accuracy, and creativity.

Real-World Skills and Applications

9. Student lists should show safety features that are designed to protect drivers from injury and reduce collision damage to automobiles. When injury and death rates in accidents are reduced, insurance companies pay out less money in claims and are able to pass their savings along to customers in the form of lower premiums.

10. Lists should demonstrate comprehension of the differences between the HMO and PPO plans. One way to decide is by adding annual costs of each plan and determining if the PPO plan is within your budget. While the PPO plan may seem more attractive for its flexibility, a responsible action is to choose a plan that you are able to afford.

11. Student presentations should demonstrate an understanding of all the aspects of coverage for the type of insurance selected and display realistic costs of coverage. Encourage students to take advantage of the possibilities offered by presentation software. Evaluate presentations for clarity and creativity.

Academic Skills in the Workplace

14. Letters should demonstrate an understanding of prescription drug coverage and HMO and PPO plans. For example, if the prescription drug coverage has been removed and the plan has been changed to HMO, then the premium should be lower. Since the premium has not been lowered, it is reasonable to assume there has been a mistake.

15. The rate without benefits is the more profitable option (with benefits $2,900 [$14.50 × 50 × 4]; without benefits $2,950 [($15.50 × 50 × 4) − $150]).

16. Summaries should demonstrate comprehension of the different types of automobile coverage and proof of research on Mexican automobile insurance. U.S. auto insurance policies are invalid in Mexico and drivers can be jailed for not carrying liability coverage, even if they are not at fault for an accident and no one is injured. U.S. citizens planning to drive their own car in Mexico are urged to purchase at least $100,000 worth of Civil Liability Insurance, coverage that is required by Mexican law.

500

Academic Skills in the Workplace

English Language Arts

14. Practice Business Letter Writing You recently received a letter from your health insurance company confirming your choice to eliminate your prescription drug coverage and change from a preferred provider (PPO) plan to an HMO plan. However, you never requested these changes to your coverage and your premium has not changed. Draft a one-page business letter to your insurance company calling their attention to this mistake and requesting that it be fixed.

Mathematics

15. Compare Health Care Costs During a job interview, a prospective employer tells you that you have the option of being paid $14.50 an hour with health benefits or $15.50 without health benefits. Getting health insurance on your own would cost you $150 a month. If you were to work 50 hours per week, which option would be more profitable over a month?

CONCEPT **Calculating Income** To calculate income, multiply the rate by the number of hours by the length of the time you are analyzing. Subtract any additional expenses that you are analyzing.

Starting Hint Determine how much you would make with health benefits by multiplying the hourly rate ($14.50) by the number of hours per week (50) by the number of weeks in a month (4). Then, do the same for the rate without benefits ($15.50 × 50) and subtract the amount you would have to pay for outside insurance ($150). Compare and choose the more lucrative option.

Social Studies

16. Research Insurance Requirements Kai is a supervisor for an electronics company located in North Carolina. The company wants him to spend a year training new supervisors in its plant in Monterey, Mexico. Kai will use his own car while he lives in Mexico. Research using the Internet and other sources to determine insurance requirements for using a car that is registered and insured in the United States in Mexico. Write a paragraph summarizing your findings.

STANDARDIZED TEST PRACTICE

MULTIPLE CHOICE

Directions Read the following question. Read the answer choices and choose the best answer.

Test-Taking Tip In a multiple-choice test, be sure to read all answers, paying attention to the words like *correct* and *best*. If you are asked to choose the *best* answer, there may be more than one *correct* answer from which to choose.

1. One way to lower your insurance costs is to _____.

  a. raise your risk
  b. lower your deductible
  c. raise your premium
  d. raise your deductible

For more Standardized Test Practice, go to the OLC glencoe.com.

STANDARDIZED TEST PRACTICE

Answer
1. d. raise your deductible

Test-Taking Strategies
Whether your students have a standardized test coming up in a few days or a few weeks, these last-minute test-prep tips and strategies will help students relax and do their best.

Test Format Help your students become familiar with the format of the specific test they are going to take by practicing with test items that imitate the actual test items as closely as possible.

Test Timing Have your students take one or more timed practice tests so that they become comfortable with the test format.

Writing Skills Practice

17. Organizing Ideas When organizing ideas by order of importance, present your most convincing evidence first, to capture the reader's attention, or last, so that it remains in the reader's mind. The rest of your ideas should follow from or build up to your most important idea.

 Practice Write an outline for an essay presenting the reasons for purchasing automobile insurance. Follow the steps below.

- Identify your topic and brainstorm ideas to discuss in your essay.
- Research to find supporting evidence.
- Decide which idea is the most important and develop a thesis statement.
- Organize your thesis, ideas, and evidence into an outline.

Net Connection

18. Compare Plans Contact the human resources departments of at least two companies, and find out what health insurance plans they offer their employees. Find out the type of plan, how much each employee must pay each month, and how long one has to work at the company to qualify for the plan. Summarize your findings in a brief essay.

@ **Log On** Go to this book's OLC through **glencoe.com** to find links giving detailed information about HMO and PPO plans. What are their advantages and disadvantages? What factors might influence your choice? Use a word-processing program to write a paragraph detailing which plan you would choose and why.

 Reading Connection

@ Go to this book's Online Learning Center through **glencoe.com** for a list of reading suggestions.

Personal Academic and Career Portfolio

Create an Insurance Checklist

To protect yourself against loss, you should purchase insurance. To help you keep track of your insurance needs and purchase the insurance you need, create an insurance checklist and add it to your **Personal Academic and Career Portfolio**.

The following guidelines will help you create your insurance checklist:

- Using spreadsheet or word-processing software, create a grid or table for each type of insurance you learned about in this chapter: home, automobile, health, disability, and life.
- In each table, create columns with the following names: *Types of Coverage, Advantages/Disadvantages, Reasons to Buy, Do I Need?,* and *Date Reviewed.*
- Complete as much of the tables as you can, using the information provided in the chapter.
- Create a new folder in your portfolio. Label it *Insurance*.
- Print or copy several copies of your checklists and place them in the folder.
- Use a set of these checklists to assess your current insurance needs. Be sure to date each checklist.
- At least once a year, use your checklists to re-examine your insurance needs and help you purchase insurance if necessary.

@ **Portfolio Help** Go to the *Succeeding in the World of Work* OLC through **glencoe.com** for help developing your portfolio.

Writing Skills Practice

17. Essay outlines should concisely and accurately demonstrate comprehension of the different types of automobile coverage and the reasons for purchasing auto insurance. Encourage students to attach a copy of research and notes that show development of their thesis, ideas, and evidence.

Net Connection

18. Essays will vary but should briefly and coherently present the types of plans, worker contributions, and enrollment requirements of each company. For their paragraphs, students should demonstrate comprehension of HMO and PPO plans in presenting their arguments and should be able to identify the differences in terms of costs and freedom of choice in selecting physicians and specialists.

Resources

◆ *ExamView Assessment Suite* **CD** allows you to print out ready-made unit and chapter tests complete with answer keys. You can also create customized tests.

WorkKeys

WorkKeys® is a job skills assessment program. For information on leveled assessment for Communication Skills (Business Writing; Listening; Reading for Information; and Writing), go to the WorkKeys link on this book's OLC through **glencoe.com**.

Personal Academic and Career Portfolio

Maintaining a Portfolio

Tell students that the insurance checklist in their **Personal Academic and Career Portfolios** will always be subject to change. As their circumstances, interests, and lifestyles change, students should review and update the content of their checklist. For example, if a student acquires an automobile, he or she will need to update their checklist and use it to purchase auto insurance. Encourage students to review their checklist annually to ensure it remains current.

Chapter Resources Planning Guide with Activities and Features

Section	Features	Activities
Section 23.1 **All About Taxes**	Creative Business Practices (p. 506) Everyday Ethics (p. 508) Science in Action (p. 508) Hot Jobs! (p. 509) Tech Savvy (p. 513) Real-World Connection (p. 514) Career Checklist (p. 515)	Before You Read (p. 504) Graphic Organizer (p. 504) As You Read (p. 505) After You Read (p. 515)
Section 23.2 **Social Security**	21st Century Workplace (p. 518)	Before You Read (p. 516) Graphic Organizer (p. 516) As You Read (pp. 518, 519) After You Read (p. 519)

NCLB Activities, information, and skills practice will help your students attain No Child Left Behind proficiency. Students will improve their abilities in the following academic standards areas:

Academic Standards Correlations

Discipline	Standard	Feature/Activity
English Language Arts	**NCTE 3** Apply strategies to interpret and evaluate texts.	Creative Business Practices (p. 506) Everyday Ethics (p. 508) Tech Savvy (p. 513) After You Read (p. 515) 21st Century Workplace (p. 518)
	NCTE 8 Use information resources to gather information and create and communicate knowledge.	Real-World Connection (p. 514)
Mathematics	**Number and Operation:** Compute fluently and make reasonable estimates	After You Read (p. 519) Academic Skills in the Workplace (p. 524)
Science	**Unifying Concepts and Processes:** Constancy, change, and measurement	Science in Action (p. 508)
	Earth and Space Science: Origin and evolution of the universe	Academic Skills in the Workplace (p. 524)

CORRELATIONS The charts show the 21st Century Skills, foundation skills, and workplace competencies that students develop as they work in this chapter.

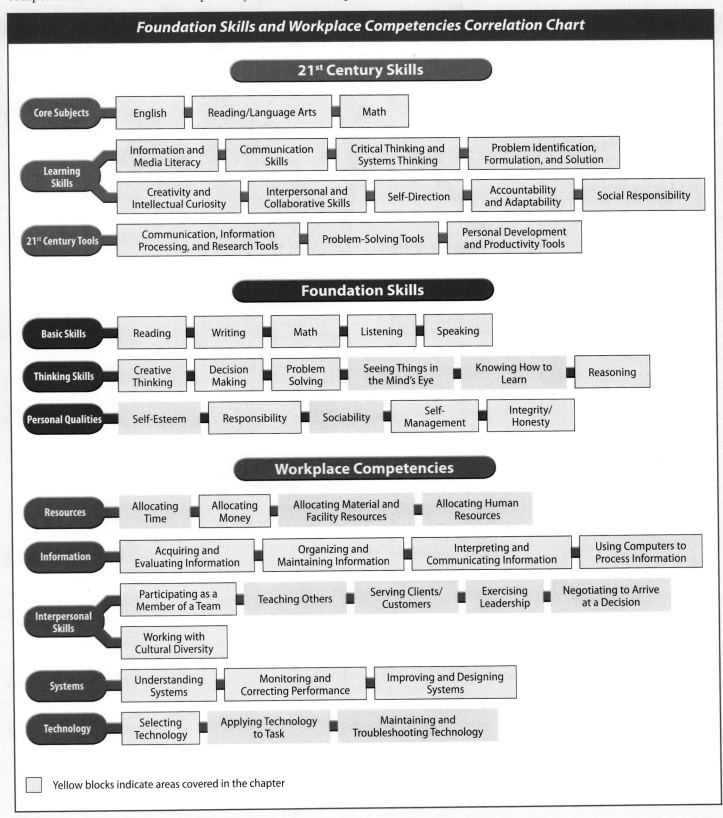

Foundation Skills and Workplace Competencies Correlation Chart

21st Century Skills

Core Subjects
- English
- Reading/Language Arts
- Math

Learning Skills
- Information and Media Literacy
- Communication Skills
- Critical Thinking and Systems Thinking
- Problem Identification, Formulation, and Solution
- Creativity and Intellectual Curiosity
- Interpersonal and Collaborative Skills
- Self-Direction
- Accountability and Adaptability
- Social Responsibility

21st Century Tools
- Communication, Information Processing, and Research Tools
- Problem-Solving Tools
- Personal Development and Productivity Tools

Foundation Skills

Basic Skills
- Reading
- Writing
- Math
- Listening
- Speaking

Thinking Skills
- Creative Thinking
- Decision Making
- Problem Solving
- Seeing Things in the Mind's Eye
- Knowing How to Learn
- Reasoning

Personal Qualities
- Self-Esteem
- Responsibility
- Sociability
- Self-Management
- Integrity/Honesty

Workplace Competencies

Resources
- Allocating Time
- Allocating Money
- Allocating Material and Facility Resources
- Allocating Human Resources

Information
- Acquiring and Evaluating Information
- Organizing and Maintaining Information
- Interpreting and Communicating Information
- Using Computers to Process Information

Interpersonal Skills
- Participating as a Member of a Team
- Teaching Others
- Serving Clients/Customers
- Exercising Leadership
- Negotiating to Arrive at a Decision
- Working with Cultural Diversity

Systems
- Understanding Systems
- Monitoring and Correcting Performance
- Improving and Designing Systems

Technology
- Selecting Technology
- Applying Technology to Task
- Maintaining and Troubleshooting Technology

Yellow blocks indicate areas covered in the chapter

Chapter Overview
Introduce the Chapter
Chapter 23 explains the tax system, procedures for filing a federal tax return, and the Social Security program.

Section 23.1 focuses on the taxes paid to federal, state, and local governments.

Section 23.2 highlights the Social Security program.

Build Background
Have students preview the chapter, looking at the pictures, reading captions, and noting content headings. Ask students to describe what they expect to learn in this chapter.

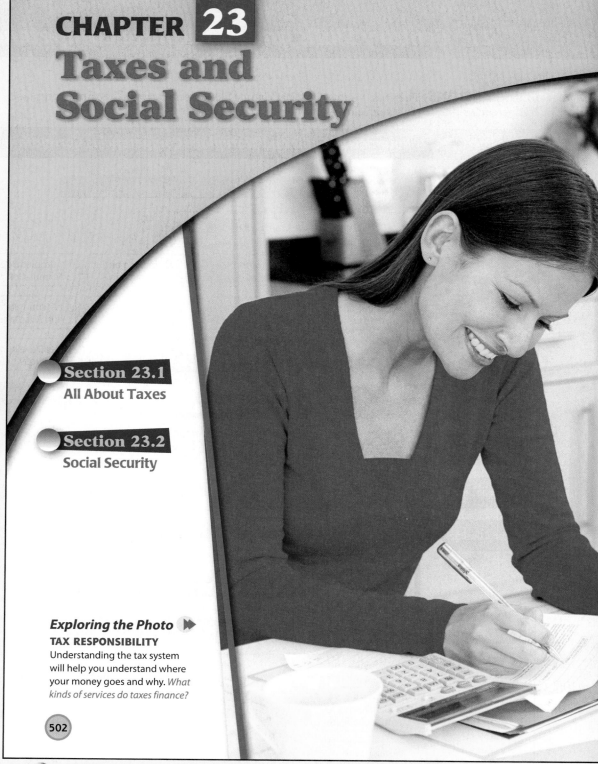

Taxes and Social Security

Section 23.1
All About Taxes

Section 23.2
Social Security

Exploring the Photo ▶
TAX RESPONSIBILITY
Understanding the tax system will help you understand where your money goes and why. *What kinds of services do taxes finance?*

502

▶ Exploring the Photo

Caption Answer
Students might mention paying for government operations and services, including paying officials and employees as well as maintaining roads, running public schools, and operating police and fire stations.

Discussion Inform students that certain states have no sales tax for back-to-school shopping. Ask them why a state might do this. (Students may suggest that it keeps shoppers from doing business in a neighboring state with lower sales tax.)

Classroom Resources

📂 Student Edition
📂 Teacher Wraparound Edition
📂 Student Activity Workbook with Academic Integration
📂 Student Activity Workbook with Academic Integration TAE
📂 *Fast File,* Unit 6 Resources

📂 Inclusion in the Career Education Classroom
💿 TeacherWorks™ Plus
💿 *ExamView Assessment Suite*
💿 Interactive Chalkboard
💿 Interactive Student Edition
💽 Online Student Edition
💽 Online Learning Center (OLC) with Podcasts

Chapter Objectives

After completing this chapter, you will be able to:

- **Describe** the U.S. tax system and the services it finances.
- **Explain** how to complete a federal tax return.
- **Describe** how the Social Security system works.
- **Identify** Social Security benefits and state social insurance benefits.
- **Describe** the challenges facing the Social Security system today.

Writing Activity Personal Career Notebook

Research the recent changes in Social Security that will affect your Social Security benefits by the time you retire. Write your findings in a one-page journal entry. Consider whether or not you would like to work until your retirement age. Add your thoughts to your journal entry.

Get Motivated! Talk to several adults who have recently retired or who are considering retiring. How have they prepared for leaving the workforce? How much will they rely on Social Security? Have their experiences changed the way you think about your retirement? Record your answers.

Chapter 23 Taxes and Social Security **503**

Writing Activity Personal Career Notebook Answer Guide

After students write journal entries about the state of Social Security, ask them to share their findings. Most will agree that workers should supplement Social Security benefits with their own retirement plans.

Get Motivated! Interviews will vary, but workers who have recently retired or are considering retiring may suggest 401(k), IRA, or other methods of saving money for their retirement.

Review the Objectives
Introduce the chapter by reviewing the chapter objectives.

Section 23.1 Objectives
Describe the U.S. tax system and the services it finances. (Taxes are payments that you make to support the government and to pay for government services, such as education, defense, transportation, and safety.)

Explain how to complete a federal tax return. (Completing a 1040EZ tax form entails adding one's total income, subtracting standard deduction and personal exemptions, and using the tax table to find out how much tax is due.)

Section 23.2 Objectives
Describe how the Social Security system works. (Workers and employers pay the Social Security payroll tax and benefits, which are used to help disabled and retired people.)

Identify Social Security benefits and state social insurance benefits. (Benefits are given for disabled workers, families who survive a worker who dies, retirees, and people who need hospitalization or other medical care.)

Describe the challenges facing the Social Security system today. (People are living longer, receiving more benefits, and retiring earlier, while there are fewer workers that are contributing to the system.)

FOCUS

Bell Ringer Activity

All About Taxes

Ask students what they think about taxes. Are they positive or negative? Why should we pay taxes?

Resources

 Interactive Chalkboard
The Interactive Chalkboard CD provides visual teaching aids for this section.

@ Online Learning Center
The Online Learning Center (OLC) through **glencoe.com** features chapter vocabulary, chapter summaries, and other study materials.

Preteaching

Assign key terms to student pairs. Have the pairs find the words in context, define them, and then present their words and definitions to the class.

Graphic Organizer

Tell students to go to the OLC through **glencoe.com** for a printable graphic organizer. (Facts needed to fill out an income tax return include your total income from working and other sources, your standard deduction and personal exemption, and other exemptions.)

NCLB connects academic correlations to book content.

504

All About Taxes

Reading Guide

Before You Read

Preview Read the Key Concepts. Write one or two sentences predicting what the section will be about.

Read to Learn
- How the tax system works
- How to complete a federal tax return

D Main Idea
Taxes are money paid to support the government and government services.

Key Concepts
- What Are Taxes?
- Federal Income Tax Returns

Key Terms
◆ withhold
◆ Form W-4
◆ Form W-2
◆ Internal Revenue Service (IRS)
◆ income tax return
◆ deduction
◆ exemption

Academic Vocabulary
You will find these words in your reading and on your tests. Use the academic vocabulary glossary to look up their definitions if necessary.
■ percentage
■ contribute

Graphic Organizer
As you read, use a graphic organizer like this to list the facts you need to know in order to fill out your income tax return.

my income	Facts I Need to Know	

@ Log On Go to this book's Online Learning Center through **glencoe.com** for an online version of this graphic organizer.

Academic Standards · · · · · · · · · · · · · · · · · ·

N C L B

English Language Arts
- Apply strategies to interpret and evaluate texts. (NCTE 3)
- Use information resources to gather information and create and communicate knowledge. (NCTE 8)

Science
- Unifying Concepts and Processes: Constancy, change, and measurement

---

Reading Guide

Before You Read
Suggest to the class that taxes are necessary to run a government, and that it is every citizen's responsibility to pay them. Explain that services such as a fire department, police department, public schools, and other services require financing.

D Develop Concepts
Main Idea Ask students whether citizens should pay taxes for things they don't agree with. For example, should tax dollars of citizens who disapprove of space exploration go toward supporting NASA? (Explain that tax laws are often a subject of debate. Introduce the idea of social responsibility and the importance of doing what is best for the good of all.)

What Are Taxes?

Taxes are payments that you make to support the government and to pay for government services. A tax system is a legal system for assessing and collecting taxes. The basis of the U.S. tax system is that we all should **contribute** our fair share of taxes.

Most people believe a fair tax system has certain features:
- Everyone who is able to pay should pay his or her fair share.
- Tax laws should be clear and simple.
- Taxes should be collected at a convenient time when most people are able to pay.
- A tax system should be flexible. The government may find it necessary to adjust the tax system to bring in more or less money.

Some citizens believe that higher income earners should pay a higher percentage of tax; others believe that the tax rate should be the same for all. Some object to paying for services they do not use, and others do not agree with how the government spends the money.

Voters elect representatives at every level of government. There are three levels of government: federal, state, and local. The federal government runs the country as a whole. State governments manage the 50 states. Local governments govern counties, cities, and towns. All three levels of government need money to operate, and you must pay taxes to all three.

Lawmakers decide what taxes you must pay, and how your tax money is spent. It is the responsibility of citizens to vote for officials

As You Read

Analyze What would be the pros and cons of having all taxpayers pay the same amount in taxes?

 GOVERNMENT SERVICES Taxes pay for government services such as the military. *Where else do your tax dollars go?*

Chapter 23 Taxes and Social Security **505**

Section 23.1

TEACH

Discussion Starter
What Are Taxes? Have students brainstorm the various kinds of taxes we have; list them on the board. (Types of taxes include income, sales, and taxes charged on items such as cigarettes, alcohol, and telephones.) Then ask students if people should pay whatever is requested or try to minimize their taxes. Have them justify their answers.

R Reading Strategy
Vizualize Have students read the paragraph about the three levels of government: federal, state, and local. As a class, make a table with the three levels as the headers. In one row, write what each level manages or oversees. In another row, write who elects respresentatives. In the final row, write how money is raised for each level of government.

As You Read

Pros would include having a simpler procedure to follow. Cons would include people who make less money paying a large percentage of their earnings and people who make more money paying a small percentage of their earnings.

Resources

 TeacherWorks™ Plus
The TeacherWorks software includes customizable built-in lesson plans and links to printable program resources.

 Extend the Photo

Caption Answer Tax money goes to public schools, libraries, roadways, mass transit, airports, law enforcement, fire protection, hospitals, postal services, and government officials and operations.

Discussion Ask students the benefits of having public services provided by private or government agencies. (Benefits of private agencies include less burden on the government and more competition for jobs. Benefits of government agencies include the interests of the public taking precedent over profits.)

TEACH *(cont.)*

 Critical Thinking

Taxation Without Representation Prior to the American Revolution, James Otis, a colonist from Massachusetts, reportedly said, "Taxation without representation is tyranny." Have students write a paragraph explaining what Otis meant and its relevance today. (Paragraphs will vary, but students should note that citizens have a right to determine how their tax money is spent by the government.)

 Skill Practice

Communicate Divide students into small groups. Have all groups review the section entitled "How Are Your Tax Dollars Spent?" Then either assign or allow groups to select a service organization in your area that receives tax money. Have each group interview the organization's personnel to learn how the organization spends its tax money. Tell each group to prepare a five- to ten-minute presentation.

 Critical Thinking

Making Connections Tell students that there is always a conflict between increased government services and lower taxes—the more services, the higher the taxes. Ask students to explain in an essay why the government cannot increase services and lower taxes at the same time.

---

who best represent their beliefs. As a citizen or legal resident of the United States of America, you have a responsibility to pay your share of the cost of running this country.

How Are Your Tax Dollars Spent?

Tax revenue provides the money that federal, state, and local governments need to operate and provide services. The federal government's revenue comes primarily from income taxes. State and local governments usually use income tax, property tax, sales tax, and user fees to generate revenue.

Each year, federal, state, and local governments take in billions of dollars in taxes. Where does this money go? Here is just a partial list of services paid for in full, or in part, by your tax dollars:

- education, including public schools and libraries
- military, homeland security, and national defense
- transportation, ranging from roadways and mass transit to dams, bridges, and airports
- safety, including law enforcement and fire protection
- health, ranging from hospitals to food preparation oversight
- postal services
- administration, including the government officials and offices to implement policy

---

Creative Business Practices

INTUIT   **Grading the Bosses**

The bosses at Intuit, Inc. want to know what their employees think. The makers of financial software, including Quicken and TurboTax, Intuit has been called the number one "Most Admired Software Company" by *Fortune* magazine. One reason to admire the software company, in addition to its annual revenues of about $2 billion, is its willingness to listen to what employees have to say.

Part of the company's commitment to its employees is an annual survey where employees get to sound off on important issues, such as how they are included in the team, how their contributions are recognized, and how well their managers maintain a positive work environment. By recognizing the importance of all its employees, Intuit has maintained a competitive edge not just in offering useful products, but also in attracting the most talented workers.

CRITICAL THINKING How do managers benefit from hearing what their employees have to say?

@ **Connect to the Real World** To read more about Intuit, visit the company's Web site via the link on this book's Online Learning Center through **glencoe.com**.

Creative Business Practices

CRITICAL THINKING ANSWER Students may suggest that managers can benefit from their employees' hands-on knowledge of everyday situations in the workplace. For the employees, such involvement results in a feeling of empowerment, by having a voice and being listened to.

Figure 23.1 SAMPLE PAY STUB

MICHAELS, ALYSSA C.
0987426143

(STATEMENT OF EARNINGS AND DEDUCTIONS. DETACH AND RETAIN FOR YOUR RECORDS. NON-NEGOTIABLE)

DESCRIPTION	RATE	HOURS	EARNINGS	YEAR TO DATE
Regular Earnings	54 00	380 50	2 280 05	

	TAXES/DEDUCTIONS	YEAR TO DATE
FEDERAL	23 03	138 18
STATE	4 29	25 74
FICA (SOCIAL SECURITY)	7 20	43 20
MEDICARE	5 45	32 70

	EARNINGS	TAXES	DEDUCTIONS	NET PAY	PAY PERIOD	WARRANT NO	AMT OF WARRANT
CURRENT	380 00	39 97	0	340 53	BEGIN 03-19	22072196	338 90
YEAR TO DATE	2,280 00	239 82	0	2,040 23	END 04-02		

NET PAY   Net pay, sometimes called take-home pay, is the amount that remains after various deductions such as taxes. *How much did the employer withhold from this paycheck?*

Types of Taxes

There are many kinds of taxes. The following are common ones.

Income Taxes You pay income tax on your income, or the money you make. This income may come from working or from other sources, such as the interest your bank pays you on your savings. Income taxes are the federal government's main source of money.

Income tax is calculated as a **percentage** of the taxable income you earn. Your taxable income is your income after you subtract certain permitted amounts. At the present time, the federal income tax ranges from 10 percent to 35 percent. In general, the greater your taxable income, the higher the rate of income tax you must pay. Your employer will withhold taxes from your income. To **withhold** tax means to deduct money from your paychecks to pay income tax due on your wages.

In most states, people also pay state income tax. Many cities also have income taxes.

Social Security Taxes Workers pay Social Security taxes so that they can receive benefits when they retire. Employers withhold money from paychecks to pay Social Security taxes, just as they do for income taxes. Your paycheck stub may show the money withheld for Social Security taxes in a row labeled "FICA," which stands for Federal Insurance Contributions Act. **Figure 23.1** shows a sample pay stub that includes income tax deductions and deductions for FICA (Social Security). Like income taxes, Social Security taxes

Vocabulary

You can find definitions in the **Key Terms** glossary and **Academic Vocabulary** glossary at the back of this book.

Chapter 23   Taxes and Social Security   **507**

R Reading Strategy

Income Taxes Ask students how many of them worked last year; ask those students how many of them filed income tax returns. Ask students if they know who must file and discuss the issue with them. (People who must file are residents of the U.S., whose income is above a certain amount, which is based on your filing status and other factors such as your age.)

S Skill Practice
Guided Practice

Listening Have students interview five or six people and ask them about their top four financial concerns (for example, saving for a child's education), ranking concerns one to four, one being the most important. Have students compare their findings in class. **L1**

Learning How to Learn Have each student talk to a financial planner or a tax accountant. Tell students to ask about the three most common mistakes people make when preparing their tax returns, sharing what they learn in class. How can students avoid these mistakes when filing their own tax returns? **L2**

Reasoning Divide the class into groups of three or four. Then have each group discuss the benefits derived from taxes paid to various branches of government. Have groups list each government level and the corresponding benefits. **L3**

EXTEND THE FIGURE   Figure 23.1

Caption Answer The employer withheld $39.97.

Discussion Ask students, if you are preparing a monthly budget, should you plan on using your gross pay or your net pay? Why? (You should use your net pay because it is the amount of money you will actually have on hand.)

TEACH *(cont.)*

S Skill Practice
Guided Practice

Creative Thinking Although many people see the need for taxes, they don't like paying them. Assign students to groups of four or five and have each group design and write an ad that will encourage people to pay taxes. Have each group display its ad. **L1**

Interpreting and Communicating Information Have students research, possibly on the Internet, their state legislature's current slate of bills and find out whether any pending legislation affects taxes. Have students write a one-page summary of their findings. **L2**

Working with Cultural Diversity Working in pairs, tell students to imagine that one of them is a foreigner; have that student ask questions about the U.S. system of taxation and the other explain the various taxes that are deducted from an employee's earnings and the reason for such deductions. **L3**

N C L B Activity correlated to Science standards.

Science In Action

The surface area of the panel would be 150 square meters (30 m × 5 m = 150).

Everyday ETHICS

REPORTING EARNINGS

Can you avoid paying taxes?

UNDER THE TABLE You have a full-time job, but you also help out at your friend's hair salon sometimes. She pays you cash, and you calculated that you earned almost $2,000 by working at her salon last year. She did not take taxes out of your pay. Your friend mentions that because she paid you in cash, there is no way for the IRS to trace the money. She says that you should not report the extra income on your tax return.

What Would You Do? Will you report the earnings? Why or why not?

DISCUSS IT The IRS also requires employers to report the income they pay to employees. How might a decision to report your salon earnings affect your friend?

Science In Action

N C L B

Surface Area

You are designing a solar panel for your roof to reduce your local energy taxes. The more surface area a panel has, the more energy it can collect from the sun. Your roof is 30m long and 5m wide. What should the surface area of the panel be?

Starting Hint: surface area = length × width

@ For more science practice, go to this book's OLC through **glencoe.com**.

---

are calculated as a percentage of the money you earn. You will read more about Social Security in Section 23.2.

Sales Taxes When you purchase something, the salesperson may add sales tax to the price of what you are purchasing. This tax goes to the state or local government. Almost every state has a sales tax. Sales tax is calculated as a percentage of the price of an item. The state sales tax rate varies from state to state and currently ranges from 2 percent to 7.25 percent. In addition to state taxes, local sales taxes may also be added to the cost of items you purchase.

User Fees These taxes are collected only from people who use a particular service. User fees are often applied to licenses and building permits, and at sports arenas, museums, and zoos. User fees can also be collected as tolls when you drive on certain roads and bridges. The money collected through user fees provides the main source of revenue for the service.

Property Taxes The main source of money for many local governments is property taxes. These taxes are based on the value of property, such as land and buildings.

S

Paycheck Tax Withholding

Taxes withheld from a paycheck can include federal, state, and city income taxes and payroll taxes. State and local income tax rates vary, but these rates are generally lower than the federal rates. The Social Security tax and the Medicare tax make up the payroll taxes. Social Security taxes or FICA provide benefits for workers who retire or become disabled, as well as for their dependents. Medicare taxes provide medical benefits for eligible people when they reach retirement age. You will learn more about Medicare benefts in Section 23.2.

Everyday ETHICS

What Would You Do? Answer Answers will vary, but most students will agree that reporting your friend will get her in trouble with the IRS. She will probably have to pay back taxes as well as be audited for further infractions.

DISCUSS IT Ask students what harm there is in being paid "under the table" and not paying taxes. (Answers will vary, but may involve civic duty and fairness to other businesses in the trade.)

When you begin a job, you will be asked by your employer to complete a form called a W-4. The **Form W-4** is a form that tells your employer how much money to withhold for taxes from your paycheck. Some people who are self-employed must withhold their own tax money and make quarterly (four times a year) tax payments based on estimates from what they paid the prior year. Others, such as students, can be exempt from paying taxes because they earn less than the federal minimum income requirement.

Completing a W-4 form is easy:

- Fill in your name, address, Social Security number, and marital status.
- Determine the number of allowances, or deductions, you are claiming. The more allowances you claim, the less federal tax is withheld.
- Indicate whether you are exempt, or do not have to pay tax.
- Sign and date the form.

See **Figure 23.2** on page 510 for an example of a W-4. It is important that you set aside the proper amount of income tax so that you can avoid an unexpected tax bill during tax time.

Wage and Tax Statement (W-2)

Each January your employer will send you a Form W-2 Wage and Tax statement. Your **Form W-2** is a form that states how much money you earned and how much your employer withheld for taxes. See **Figure 23.3** on page 511 for an example of a Form W-2. The information on the W-2 is needed to prepare your federal and state tax returns by the April 15 due date. Failure to complete your income tax return by the due date, making false statements, or underreporting your income can result in fines and criminal penalties.

✓ Reading Check) **IDENTIFY** What are three common types of taxes other than income taxes?

▶▶ YOUR TAXES AT WORK
Local services, such as fire and police protection, are paid for primarily through local taxes. *What other services does your community provide?*

Chapter 23 Taxes and Social Security (509)

HOT JOBS!

Personal Chef

Personal chefs typically have culinary degrees, and they can provide personalized dishes or cook in their clients' kitchens. Besides cooking, personal chefs need to be able to use their math skills to estimate costs and amounts of ingredients, and manage time and tax records for multiple projects.

R Reading Strategy
Read About Tax Filing
Have each student read an article describing how to determine the amount of salary to withhold for federal taxes. Tell students to take notes and be prepared to discuss what they read in class.

U Universal Access
Students with Visual Impairments Because visually impaired students usually rely on taped lectures rather than written notes when studying, think carefully about what you say in class. "This (pointing) plus that (pointing) equals 11," will mean nothing. However, "four plus seven equals 11," is clear.

▶ Extend the Photo

Caption Answer Answers will vary, but may include schools, libraries, public transportation, mass transit, hospitals, and defense.

Discussion Inform students that elections are held to determine how public money is spent by the government. Ask students, if most people don't vote, is this fair? (Answers will vary, but most students should agree that those with the right to vote, should vote.)

TEACH (cont.)

S Skill Practice

Filling Out Forms Obtain blank copies of Form W-4 and have students practice filling them out. Most students should have Social Security numbers; if a student does not, obtain the forms needed to apply for a Social Security number and have him or her fill it out. Discuss with students the requirements to apply for a number. (He or she must be a citizen or a legal resident of the U.S.)

Figure 23.2 **FORM W-4**

Form W-4 (2006)

Purpose. Complete Form W-4 so that your employer can withhold the correct federal income tax from your pay. Because your tax situation may change, you may want to refigure your withholding each year.

Exemption from withholding. If you are exempt, complete only lines 1, 2, 3, 4, and 7 and sign the form to validate it. Your exemption for 2006 expires February 16, 2007. See Pub. 505, Tax Withholding and Estimated Tax.

Note. You cannot claim exemption from withholding if (a) your income exceeds $850 and includes more than $300 of unearned income (for example, interest and dividends) and (b) another person can claim you as a dependent on their tax return.

Basic instructions. If you are not exempt, complete the **Personal Allowances Worksheet** below. The worksheets on page 2 adjust your withholding allowances based on itemized deductions, certain credits, adjustments to income, or two-

earner/two-job situations. Complete all worksheets that apply. However, you may claim fewer (or zero) allowances.

Head of household. Generally, you may claim head of household filing status on your tax return only if you are unmarried and pay more than 50% of the costs of keeping up a home for yourself and your dependent(s) or other qualifying individuals. See line **E** below.

Tax credits. You can take projected tax credits into account in figuring your allowable number of withholding allowances. Credits for child or dependent care expenses and the child tax credit may be claimed using the **Personal Allowances Worksheet** below. See Pub. 919, How Do I Adjust My Tax Withholding, for information on converting your other credits into withholding allowances.

Nonwage income. If you have a large amount of nonwage income, such as interest or dividends, consider making estimated tax payments using Form 1040-ES, Estimated Tax for Individuals. Otherwise, you may owe additional tax.

Two earners/two jobs. If you have a working spouse or more than one job, figure the total number of allowances you are entitled to claim on all jobs using worksheets from only one Form W-4. Your withholding usually will be most accurate when all allowances are claimed on the Form W-4 for the highest paying job and zero allowances are claimed on the others.

Nonresident alien. If you are a nonresident alien, see the Instructions for Form 8233 before completing this Form W-4.

Check your withholding. After your Form W-4 takes effect, use Pub. 919 to see how the dollar amount you are having withheld compares to your projected total tax for 2006. See Pub. 919, especially if your earnings exceed $130,000 (Single) or $180,000 (Married).

Recent name change? If your name on line 1 differs from that shown on your social security card, call 1-800-772-1213 to initiate a name change and obtain a social security card showing your correct name.

Personal Allowances Worksheet (Keep for your records.)

A Enter "1" for **yourself** if no one else can claim you as a dependent . . . . **A** _____

B Enter "1" if: {
 • You are single and have only one job; or
 • You are married, have only one job, and your spouse does not work; or
 • Your wages from a second job or your spouse's wages (or the total of both) are $1,000 or less. } . . **B** _____

C Enter "1" for your **spouse.** But, you may choose to enter "-0-" if you are married and have either a working spouse or more than one job. (Entering "-0-" may help you avoid having too little tax withheld.) . . . . . **C** _____

D Enter number of **dependents** (other than your spouse or yourself) you will claim on your tax return . . . . . . **D** _____

E Enter "1" if you will file as **head of household** on your tax return (see conditions under **Head of household** above) . **E** _____

F Enter "1" if you have at least $1,500 of **child or dependent care expenses** for which you plan to claim a credit . . **F** _____
 (**Note.** Do **not** include child support payments. See **Pub. 503,** Child and Dependent Care Expenses, for details.)

G **Child Tax Credit** (including additional child tax credit):
 • If your total income will be less than $55,000 ($82,000 if married), enter "2" for each eligible child.
 • If your total income will be between $55,000 and $84,000 ($82,000 and $119,000 if married), enter "1" for each eligible child plus "1" **additional** if you have four or more eligible children. . . . . **G** _____

H Add lines A through G and enter total here. (**Note.** This may be different from the number of exemptions you claim on your tax return.) ▶ **H** _____

For accuracy, complete all worksheets that apply.	{	• If you plan to **itemize or claim adjustments to income** and want to reduce your withholding, see the **Deductions and Adjustments Worksheet** on page 2.
		• If you have **more than one job** or are **married and you and your spouse both work** and the combined earnings from all jobs exceed $35,000 ($25,000 if married) see the **Two-Earner/Two-Job Worksheet** on page 2 to avoid having too little tax withheld.
		• If **neither** of the above situations applies, **stop here** and enter the number from line H on line 5 of Form W-4 below.

- - - - - - - - - - - - - - - - - - **Cut here and give Form W-4 to your employer. Keep the top part for your records.** - - - - - - - - - - - - - - - - - -

Form W-4
Department of the Treasury
Internal Revenue Service

Employee's Withholding Allowance Certificate
▶ **Whether you are entitled to claim a certain number of allowances or exemption from withholding is subject to review by the IRS. Your employer may be required to send a copy of this form to the IRS.**

OMB No. 1545-0074

2006

1 Type or print your first name and middle initial.	Last name		2 Your social security number
Linda B.	*Thompson*		*123 : 45 : 6789*

Home address (number and street or rural route)
33 Gable Lane

3 ☒ Single ☐ Married ☐ Married, but withhold at higher Single rate.
Note. If married, but legally separated, or spouse is a nonresident alien, check the "Single" box.

City or town, state, and ZIP code
Brownsville, MD 01234

4 **If your last name differs from that shown on your social security card, check here. You must call 1-800-772-1213 for a new card.** ▶ ☐

5 Total number of allowances you are claiming (from line **H** above **or** from the applicable worksheet on page 2) **5** *0*

6 Additional amount, if any, you want withheld from each paycheck . . . . **6** $

7 I claim exemption from withholding for 2006, and I certify that I meet **both** of the following conditions for exemption.
 • Last year I had a right to a refund of **all** federal income tax withheld because I had **no** tax liability **and**
 • This year I expect a refund of **all** federal income tax withheld because I expect to have **no** tax liability.
 If you meet both conditions, write "Exempt" here . . . . . ▶ **7**

Under penalties of perjury, I declare that I have examined this certificate and to the best of my knowledge and belief, it is true, correct, and complete.

Employee's signature
(Form is not valid unless you sign it.) ▶ *Linda B. Thompson* Date ▶ *10/18/2009*

8 Employer's name and address (Employer: Complete lines 8 and 10 only if sending to the IRS.)	9 Office code (optional)	10 Employer identification number (EIN)

For Privacy Act and Paperwork Reduction Act Notice, see page 2. Cat. No. 10220Q Form **W-4** (2006)

WITHHOLDING All employees must fill out a Form W-4. *Why is it important to complete this form accurately?*

EXTEND THE FIGURE **Figure 23.2**

Caption Answer The employer uses the information on Form W-4 to determine how much money to withhold for taxes.

Discussion Ask students how often they should fill out a new W-4 or what events might require a change in their withholding accounts? (Examples include when they change employers, when they marry, or have children.)

Figure 23.3 **FORM W-2**

Section 23.1

a Control number	22222		OMB No. 1545-0008		

b Employer identification number (EIN) 09-X1X2X3X		1 Wages, tips, other compensation 12175	2 Federal income tax withheld 921.42

c Employer's name, address, and ZIP code	3 Social security wages 12175	4 Social security tax withheld 240.53
ABC Painting Co., Inc.	5 Medicare wages and tips 12175	6 Medicare tax withheld 69.96
563 Sagebrush Lane	7 Social security tips	8 Allocated tips
Brownsville, MD 01234		

d Employee's social security number 123-45-6789	9 Advance EIC payment	10 Dependent care benefits

e Employee's first name and initial	Last name	Suff.	11 Nonqualified plans	12a
Linda B.	Thompson		13 Statutory employee ☐ Retirement plan ☐ Third-party sick pay ☐	12b
33 Gable Lane			14 Other	12c
Brownsville, MD 01234				12d

f Employee's address and ZIP code					

15 State Employer's state ID number MD 11- X1X2X3X	16 State wages, tips, etc. 12175	17 State income tax 436	18 Local wages, tips, etc. 12175	19 Local income tax 148	20 Locality name Brownsville

Form **W-2** Wage and Tax Statement

2006

Department of the Treasury—Internal Revenue Service

Copy 1—For State, City, or Local Tax Department

WAGE AND TAX STATEMENT	Your employer will send you a Form W-2 in January. *What information on this form will help you prepare your income tax return?*

Federal Income Tax Returns

The **Internal Revenue Service (IRS)** is the government agency that collects federal taxes and oversees the federal tax system. To determine your federal income tax, you must complete and file an **income tax return**, a form that shows how much income you received from working and other sources, and how much tax you must pay. If you are single and earn more than a certain amount, you must file a tax return each year. If your employer withheld more money from your paychecks than you owe, you will receive a tax refund. If your employer did not withhold enough money, you will have to pay the difference.

There are three basic tax forms: 1040EZ, 1040A, and 1040. Form 1040EZ is the simplest form to complete, and is often used by single people and married couples earning less than $100,000 without dependents. A dependent is someone whom you support financially, such as a child or other qualifying family member. **Figure 23.4** on page 512 shows Form 1040EZ.

Chapter 23 Taxes and Social Security **511**

TEACH (cont.)

W **Writing Support**
Interview and Summarize Have students who work interview their employers to learn more about the process for completing payroll and tax forms. Tell students who do not work to choose a local company and interview someone in the accounting department. Have students ask how the company keeps track of payroll and tax data, when it sends taxes to the government, and when it prepares tax forms for employees. Have students write summaries of their findings for class discussion.

C **Critical Thinking**
From Simple to Complicated Ask: Why would single people and married couples who earn less than $100,000 without dependents use a simpler tax form than those who earn more money and have dependents. (Workers who earn more money or have larger families will have more factors to consider when determining the amount of taxes owed.)

EXTEND THE FIGURE Figure 23.3

Caption Answer Form W-2 states how much money you earned and how much was taken out of your taxes.

Discussion Ask students who work what they should do if they have not received a Form W-2 from their employers by the end of January? (Telephone or e-mail the employer's payroll department to report the missing form and ask for another copy to be sent immediately.)

TEACH *(cont.)*

S Skill Practice

Filling Out Forms Obtain blank copies of Form 1040EZ for each student to fill out. Those who have part-time jobs may want to use their own information; others could use the current minimum wage, a 20-hour work week during the school year, and 40 hours during the summer weeks. Have students use your state's income tax rate and a federal withholding rate of 15 percent. Work through these calculations prior to the activity.

W Writing Support

Write Directions Have students write a step-by-step description of how to fill out a Form 1040EZ, citing line numbers in the form when describing where to write specific information.

U Universal Access

Intrapersonal Learning If students are having difficulty with Form 1040EZ, have them work in pairs. Tell each pair to create a taxpayer, providing name, age, job, and one or more bank accounts earning interest.

Figure 23.4   **FORM 1040EZ**

Department of the Treasury—Internal Revenue Service

Form 1040EZ

Income Tax Return for Single and Joint Filers With No Dependents (99) **2005**

OMB No. 1545-0074

Label (See page 11.) Use the IRS label. Otherwise, please print or type.

Your first name and initial: *Linda B.*   Last name: *Thompson*

If a joint return, spouse's first name and initial   Last name

Your social security number: 123 45 6789

Spouse's social security number

Home address (number and street). If you have a P.O. box, see page 11.   Apt. no.

33 Gable Lane

You **must** enter your SSN(s) above.

City, town or post office, state, and ZIP code. If you have a foreign address, see page 11.

Brownsville, MD 01234

Checking a box below will not change your tax or refund.

Presidential Election Campaign (page 12) ▶

Check here if you, or your spouse if a joint return, want $3 to go to this fund? ... ▶ ☐ **You**   ☐ **Spouse**

Income
Attach Form(s) W-2 here. Enclose, but do not attach, any payment.

1. Wages, salaries, and tips. This should be shown in box 1 of your Form(s) W-2. Attach your Form(s) W-2. → **1** *12175*

2. Taxable interest. If the total is over $1,500, you cannot use Form 1040EZ. → **2** *70*

3. Unemployment compensation and Alaska Permanent Fund dividends (see page 13). → **3**

4. Add lines 1, 2, and 3. This is your **adjusted gross income**. → **4** *12245*

5. If someone can claim you (or your spouse if a joint return) as a dependent, check the applicable box(es) below and enter the amount from the worksheet on back.
   ☐ **You**   ☐ **Spouse**
   If someone cannot claim you (or your spouse if a joint return), enter $8,200 if **single**; $16,400 if **married filing jointly**. See back for explanation. → **5** *3900*

6. Subtract line 5 from line 4. If line 5 is larger than line 4, enter -0-. This is your **taxable income**. ▶ **6** *8345*

Payments and tax

7. Federal income tax withheld from box 2 of your Form(s) W-2. → **7** *921*

8a. **Earned income credit (EIC).** → **8a**

  b. Nontaxable combat pay election. **8b**

9. Add lines 7 and 8a. These are your **total payments.** ▶ **9** *921*

10. **Tax.** Use the amount on **line 6 above** to find your tax in the tax table on pages 24–32 of the booklet. Then, enter the tax from the table on this line. → **10** *945*

Refund
Have it directly deposited! See page 18 and fill in 11b, 11c, and 11d.

11a. If line 9 is larger than line 10, subtract line 10 from line 9. This is your **refund.** ▶ **11a**

  ▶ b. Routing number   ▶ c. Type: ☐ Checking ☐ Savings

  ▶ d. Account number

Amount you owe

12. If line 10 is larger than line 9, subtract line 9 from line 10. This is the **amount you owe.** For details on how to pay, see page 19. ▶ **12** *24*

Third party designee

Do you want to allow another person to discuss this return with the IRS (see page 19)? ☐ **Yes.** Complete the following. ☐**No**

Designee's name ▶   Phone no. ▶ ( )   Personal identification number (PIN)

Sign here
Joint return? See page 11. Keep a copy for your records.

Under penalties of perjury, I declare that I have examined this return, and to the best of my knowledge and belief, it is true, correct, and accurately lists all amounts and sources of income I received during the tax year. Declaration of preparer (other than the taxpayer) is based on all information of which the preparer has any knowledge.

Your signature: *Linda B. Thompson*   Date: *2/14/09*   Your occupation: *Construction Manager*   Daytime phone number ( )

Spouse's signature. If a joint return, **both** must sign.   Date   Spouse's occupation

Paid preparer's use only

Preparer's signature ▶   Date   Check if self-employed ☐   Preparer's SSN or PTIN

Firm's name (or yours if self-employed), address, and ZIP code ▶   EIN   Phone no. ( )

For Disclosure, Privacy Act, and Paperwork Reduction Act Notice, see page 23.   Cat. No. 11329W   Form **1040EZ** (2005)

TAX RETURN   Many young taxpayers can use Form 1040EZ for at least the first few years after entering the world of work and filing returns. *What form do you need to attach to Form 1040EZ?*

EXTEND THE FIGURE   **Figure 23.4**

Caption Answer Form W-2 needs to be attached to Form 1040EZ.

Discussion Ask students what would happen if they had a savings account that earned $480 in interest last year? (They could not use Form 1040EZ since interest income for this form is limited to $400.)

You can probably file Form 1040EZ if you meet the following qualifications.

- You are single and earned less than $50,000 during the year, or you are married and earned, with your spouse, less than $100,000 in the year. Check each year with the IRS about the current maximum earnings.
- You had no other income, such as taxable interest or dividends, that amounted to more than $400.
- You are not claiming an exemption for being over 65 or for being blind.
- You have no dependents.

S Check with the IRS for additional requirements for using Form 1040EZ. Completing this form involves several basic steps:

- Add up your total income from working and from other sources.
- Subtract your standard deduction and personal exemption.
- **Figure 23.5** shows part of a tax table. By comparing this amount with the taxes withheld on your Form W-2, you will see if you owe more taxes or are entitled to a refund.

TechSavvy

File Your Taxes Online

The IRS allows you to file online. This is called e-filing, or electronic filing. The IRS Web site gives you step-by-step directions on how to e-file.

First, you need certain information. The IRS Web site even gives you a list of the information you will need. Next, follow the directions on the site. If you need help, look under tax experts. The IRS provides experts to answer any questions you might have, and the help is free. Tax preparation and e-filing service companies have formed partnerships with the IRS to help you. All you have to do is log onto the Web site and ask for help.

 Visit this book's OLC through **glencoe.com** and find the link to learn more about how to file your taxes online. Read the information about how to file your taxes electronically, and create an outline of the information.

Figure 23.5 ▸ TAX TABLE

If Form 1040EZ, line 6, is—		And you are—		If Form 1040EZ, line 6, is—		And you are—		If Form 1040EZ, line 6, is—		And you are—		If Form 1040EZ, line 6, is—		And you are—	
At least	But less than	Single	Married filing jointly	At least	But less than	Single	Married filing jointly	At least	But less than	Single	Married filing jointly	At least	But less than	Single	Married filing jointly
		Your tax is—				Your tax is—				Your tax is—				Your tax is—	
9,000				**12,000**				**15,000**				**18,000**			
9,000	9,050	989	903	12,000	12,050	1,439	1,203	15,000	15,050	1,889	1,524	18,000	18,050	2,339	1,974
9,050	9,100	996	908	12,050	12,100	1,446	1,208	15,050	15,100	1,896	1,531	18,050	18,100	2,346	1,981
9,100	9,150	1,004	913	12,100	12,150	1,454	1,213	15,100	15,150	1,904	1,539	18,100	18,150	2,354	1,989
9,150	9,200	1,011	918	12,150	12,200	1,461	1,218	15,150	15,200	1,911	1,546	18,150	18,200	2,361	1,996
9,200	9,250	1,019	923	12,200	12,250	1,469	1,223	15,200	15,250	1,919	1,554	18,200	18,250	2,369	2,004
9,250	9,300	1,026	928	12,250	12,300	1,476	1,228	15,250	15,300	1,926	1,561	18,250	18,300	2,376	2,011
9,300	9,350	1,034	933	12,300	12,350	1,484	1,233	15,300	15,350	1,934	1,569	18,300	18,350	2,384	2,019
9,350	9,400	1,041	938	12,350	12,400	1,491	1,238	15,350	15,400	1,941	1,576	18,350	18,400	2,391	2,026
9,400	9,450	1,049	943	12,400	12,450	1,499	1,243	15,400	15,450	1,949	1,584	18,400	18,450	2,399	2,034
9,450	9,500	1,056	948	12,450	12,500	1,506	1,248	15,450	15,500	1,956	1,591	18,450	18,500	2,406	2,041
9,500	9,550	1,064	953	12,500	12,550	1,514	1,253	15,500	15,550	1,964	1,599	18,500	18,550	2,414	2,049
9,550	9,600	1,071	958	12,550	12,600	1,521	1,258	15,550	15,600	1,971	1,606	18,550	18,600	2,421	2,056
9,600	9,650	1,079	963	12,600	12,650	1,529	1,263	15,600	15,650	1,979	1,614	18,600	18,650	2,429	2,064
9,650	9,700	1,086	968	12,650	12,700	1,536	1,268	15,650	15,700	1,986	1,621	18,650	18,700	2,436	2,071
9,700	9,750	1,094	973	12,700	12,750	1,544	1,273	15,700	15,750	1,994	1,629	18,700	18,750	2,444	2,079
9,750	9,800	1,101	978	12,750	12,800	1,551	1,278	15,750	15,800	2,001	1,636	18,750	18,800	2,451	2,086
9,800	9,850	1,109	983	12,800	12,850	1,559	1,283	15,800	15,850	2,009	1,644	18,800	18,850	2,459	2,094
9,850	9,900	1,116	988	12,850	12,900	1,566	1,288	15,850	15,900	2,016	1,651	18,850	18,900	2,466	2,101
9,900	9,950	1,124	993	12,900	12,950	1,574	1,293	15,900	15,950	2,024	1,659	18,900	18,950	2,474	2,109
9,950	10,000	1,131	998	12,950	13,000	1,581	1,298	15,950	16,000	2,031	1,666	18,950	19,000	2,481	2,116

TAXES OWED To use a tax table, find the line that corresponds to your taxable income. Then find the column that corresponds to your status. Your tax is the amount shown where the income line and status column meet. *If you are single and your taxable income is $12,200, how much tax will you owe?*

TEACH (cont.)

S Skill Practice

Interviewing Have students visit the IRS Web site and research the services and types of assistance the IRS gives people in filling out their tax returns. Have students share their findings in class.

ASSESS

Review Key Terms

Have students write sentences using each key term.

Online Study Tools

Have students go to the OLC through **glencoe.com** to:

- Download **Podcast** study tools.
- Download free **Study-to-Go** content to their PDAs or cell phones.

Resources

ExamView Assessment Suite **CD** allows you to print out ready-made unit and chapter tests complete with answer keys. You can also create customized tests.

EXTEND THE FIGURE   Figure 23.5

Caption Answer You would owe $1,469.

Discussion Obtain a larger tax table or several pages of tax tables for the current tax year. Give students examples of different taxable incomes and have them find the tax amount for each.

RETEACH

R Reading Support

Minimize Taxes Have students find and read an article on how to reduce their taxable income, taking notes and deciding at what point in their lives the advice might be useful. Then have the class compare articles and notes. Have students file useful articles in their **Personal Academic and Career Portfolio**.

C Critical Thinking

Consider a Flat Tax Ask students whether a flat tax rate with no exemptions or deductions would make it easier to fill out a tax return. Also have them think about the advantages and disadvantages of a flat rate. Debate their findings as a class.

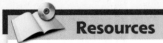

Real-World *Connection*

Critical Thinking Answer Answers will vary, but most students should agree that it is an effective way of saving and earning money, especially if one is just starting out in the world of work.

Do Your Own Research Graphs should show that starting at a younger age is more profitable than starting later on.

Resources

📁 **Student Activity Workbook** Assign the Chapter 23 activities in the Student Activity Workbook.

514

Real-World *Connection*

401 "K"nowledge

You have just gotten your first professional job and you are eligible to participate in the company's 401(k) retirement plan. You are years away from retirement, and there are many things that you want to buy with the money that would otherwise be contributed. But unless you make the minimum contribution, the company will not be providing any funds for a retirement plan for you.

Critical Thinking Should you participate in the 401(k) plan?

Do Your Own Research Find out what a 401(k) retirement plan is by asking a Certified Public Accountant (CPA) or someone from a bank. Find out the kinds of savings plans that are available to a young person just starting out in a professional job and the advantages of each type. Make a graph of how much money you will have at different points in your life (such as 35, 50, and 65 years old) if you save the minimum each month in a typical plan.

 FILE ONLINE Filing your income tax returns online can save you time, help avoid handwriting problems, and make it harder to misplace the form. *How else can you save time when filing your tax returns?*

The government provides a number of ways to reduce your taxable income. A **deduction** is a qualifying expense that you are allowed to subtract from your income; the standard deduction was $5,000 in a recent year. If you have children or other dependents or itemized deductions, such as home mortgage interest, gifts to charity, and job expenses, you would use either the 1040A or 1040 tax forms. An **exemption** is a fixed amount of money that is excused from taxes. Recently, each taxpayer could claim a $3,200 personal exemption.

How Do You File a Return?

You have several options to get the proper tax forms. You can access the Internal Revenue Service Web site and download forms, instructions, and even electronically file your income tax return. You can also call the IRS or pick up forms, instructions, and helpful publications at many public libraries and post offices. If you use professional tax services, they will provide the forms.

Along with the proper tax form, you will need to gather the necessary information, including your Form W-2 and records of any other earnings, such as statements of interest from your bank. If you have filed a tax return before, have a copy of your previous return on hand for reference.

▶ **Extend the Photo**

Caption Answer Answers will vary, but may include gathering receipts and necessary forms beforehand and filing early, so that it would be easier to get assistance if needed.

Discussion Ask students why the U.S. government encourages citizen to file electronically. (It saves money on postage, is easier to archive, and can be easier to check.)

You can choose to complete the tax form yourself, hire a tax professional or accountant, or log onto a tax preparation Web site that walks you through the tax return process. The IRS provides a toll-free number in case you have specific questions or need assistance.

Take your time completing the forms. Read all instructions carefully, and get help if you need it. Be sure to provide all the required information, and double-check your math.

Your completed tax return must be electronically sent or mailed to the regional Internal Revenue Service center by April 15 to avoid penalties. Keep a photocopy of the completed tax return for your records.

The lower your taxable income, the less tax is due. Many people try to reduce the amount of income they report. Putting money into a 401(k) retirement fund or IRA, or donating to a charitable organization are legal ways to reduce your taxable income. Some taxpayers resort to illegal methods such as fraud or tax evasion to reduce their taxable income.

The most common form of tax evasion is not declaring income in the annual tax return. To deter illegal tax reporting, the IRS performs random audits. During an audit, the IRS requires a business or individual to prove that the information on a tax return is accurate. Failure to report income, or falsifying information can lead to fines and possible criminal charges.

Career ✓ Checklist

When Paying Taxes:

✓ Understand what you claim on your tax forms and why.

✓ Review your pay stubs to make sure that you are being taxed correctly.

✓ Keep copies of all tax returns and related documents.

✓ Don't be afraid to ask for tax help.

Section 23.1

ASSESS

After You Read
Have students complete the Section 23.1 After You Read section review.

Online Study Tools
Have students go to the OLC through **glencoe.com** to:
- Take the Section 23.1 **Practice Test**.
- Download **Podcast** study tools.
- Download free **Study-to-Go** content to their PDAs or cell phones.

CLOSE

Culminating Activity
Tax Systems Divide students into two groups. Have one group create a bulletin board display of the U.S. tax system, including taxes for all three levels of government, clipping newspaper or magazine photos to illustrate. Have the second group create a display explaining the federal tax return and giving instructions for how to complete it. Have students obtain copies of necessary tax forms from the local library.

N C L B Activity correlated to English Language standards.

Section 23.1 After You Read

Review Key Concepts

1. List five characteristics of an effective tax system. Why are these features desirable?
2. How does the amount of money you earn and the amount withheld determine whether you owe income tax?
3. What documents are necessary for you to have in order to file your tax return?

Practice Academic Skills

English Language Arts

4. Doing your own taxes can be a fun challenge, like completing a crossword or sudoku puzzle. However, many taxes can be complicated. Write a paragraph describing whether you would prefer to file your own taxes or hire a tax professional to do it for you. Explain your opinion.
5. Different states have different sales and income tax rates. Would you rather have a higher state sales tax rate or a higher state income tax rate? Write a paragraph, giving reasons for your answer.

N C L B

@ Check your answers at this book's OLC through **glencoe.com**.

Section 23.1 After You Read

Review Key Concepts

1. Characteristics include able citizens paying their fair share, clear and simple rules, collection at a convenient time, flexibility, and higher income earners paying a higher percentage of tax. Reasons include fairness and realism.
2. The amount of money you earn determines the amount of taxes you owe. If the amount of money withheld is less than what you owe, additional payment is due.
3. Form W-2 and statements of interest from your bank.

Practice Academic Skills

4. In their paragraphs, students might suggest that paying a professional will ensure that the taxes are filed properly and that all possible benefits are taken advantage of.
5. Answers will vary, but might depend on one's income or how much he or she shops locally.

Social Security

FOCUS

Bell Ringer Activity

Social Security

Ask how many students know their Social Security number. Then ask if they know how the number is used and what is the purpose of Social Security.

Resources

 Interactive Chalkboard
The Interactive Chalkboard CD provides visual teaching aids for this section.

@ Online Learning Center
The OLC through **glencoe.com** features chapter vocabulary, chapter summaries, and other study materials.

Preteaching
Read the definition of the key terms aloud. Ask students to write a sentence using each key term.

Graphic Organizer
Tell students to go to the OLC through **glencoe.com** for a printable graphic organizer. (Graphic organizers should list benefits provided by the Social Security system.)

NCLB connects academic correlations to book content.

Reading Guide

Before You Read

Preview Write one or two sentences about what you know about Social Security and then compare your predictions with what you read in the section.

Read to Learn
- How the Social Security system works
- How to identify four Social Security program benefits and two state social insurance benefits
- The challenges facing the Social Security system today

D ### Main Idea
Understanding issues facing Social Security will help you plan for your future.

Key Concept
- What Is Social Security?

Key Terms
◆ Social Security
◆ work credits
◆ Medicare

Academic Vocabulary
You will find this word in your reading and on your tests. Use the academic vocabulary glossary to look up its definition if necessary.
■ obtained

Graphic Organizer
As you read, use a graphic organizer like the one shown to list the benefits that Social Security provides.

(Taxes)

roads
_____
_____
_____
_____

 Log On Go to this book's Online Learning Center through **glencoe.com** for an online version of this graphic organizer.

NCLB **Academic Standards** ● ● ● ● ● ● ● ● ● ● ● ● ● ● ● ● ● ●
English Language Arts
- Apply strategies to interpret and evaluate texts. (NCTE 3)
- Use information resources to gather information and create and communicate knowledge. (NCTE 8)

Mathematics
- Compute fluently and make reasonable estimates

Reading Guide

Before You Read
Have students share their predictions in class. Inform them the Social Security system was designed to help workers in their life of retirement. Suggest that it is not a replacement for retirement planning or individual savings.

D ### Develop Concepts
Main Idea Ask students if they have ever saved for costs that they expect to face in the future. What strategies did they use to save money?

What Is Social Security?

Social Security is a federal government program that helps individuals who are disabled or retired people and their families. For example, if a worker becomes disabled, Social Security will help his or her family cope with the loss of income.

Your Social Security Number

Your parent or guardian probably **obtained** a Social Security number for you when you were very young. This is your permanent identification number. The government uses it to keep track of your contributions and work history. All workers need a Social Security number, and your employer will ask you for it when you start.

Your Social Security number is confidential. Be careful about sharing your number with anyone who asks for it. Someone illegally using your Social Security number and assuming your identity can cause a lot of problems.

Identity theft is one of the fastest-growing crimes in America. When a dishonest person has your Social Security number, that person can use it to obtain other personal information about you. Identity thieves can use your number to apply for credit in your name. Then they use the credit cards and do not pay the bills. You do not find out that someone is using your number until you are turned down for credit, or you begin to get calls from unknown creditors demanding payment for items you never bought.

Social Security and Taxes

The Social Security payroll tax paid by workers and their employers pays for Social Security benefits. Employers deduct Social Security tax from your paycheck. Your employer matches your contribution. If you are self-employed, you must pay both the employee's and employer's

 HELPING OLDER AMERICANS Medicare is a Social Security health service. *Who pays for Medicare? How?*

Section 23.2

TEACH

Discussion Starter
What Is Social Security?
Ask students why they should pay Social Security taxes if there is a chance the benefits will decrease by the time they retire.

S Skill Practice
Individual Practice
Writing Have students research the benefits of Social Security and prepare one-page brochures that explain the benefits. **L1**

Learning How to Learn Have students explore the difference between Social Security and an annuity. Tell them to create a table showing typical amounts available at age 65 under each system. (An annuity depends on amounts paid into it. Social Security guarantees a minimum and is not directly tied to the amounts paid in.) **L2**

Integrity/Honesty Have students choose a state senator or representative to research. Tell students to review campaign literature and obtain the person's voting record regarding Social Security. Does the voting record match campaign promises? Discuss findings in class. **L3**

Resources

TeacherWorks™ Plus The TeacherWorks software includes customizable built-in lesson plans and links to printable program resources.

 Extend the Photo

Caption Answer Medicare, like other Social Security benefits, is funded by income taxes.

Discussion Have students research the current Social Security and Medicare tax rates. Tell students who work to calculate the amount of money they pay toward Medicare each month. Have students who do not work use the current minimum wage and a 20-hour workweek to calculate the same.

As You Read

By raising the age for receiving full benefits, the Social Security system would accrue more money for every year the age limit is extended.

ASSESS

Review Key Terms
Have students write sentences using each key term.

Online Study Tools
Have students go to the OLC through **glencoe.com** to:
- Download **Podcast** study tools.
- Download free **Study-to-Go** content to their PDAs or cell phones.

STUDY TO GO

RETEACH

W Writing Support
Survey Says

Write a Report Have each student interview at least five people and ask what benefits they get in return for paying taxes. Have students write their results in a one-page paper to share with the class.

N C L B Activity correlated to English Language Arts standards.

Resources

📂 **Student Activity Workbook** Assign the Chapter 23 activities in the Student Activity Workbook.

The 21st Century Workplace

N C L B

Freelance for All
Freelancing takes self-motivation as well as time management, money management, and networking skills, as well as any additional skills required by specific employers.

A key benefit of freelancing is flexibility. Freelancers can choose to work as much as they want and for whom they want. If working with the client in person isn't necessary, a freelancer can work at home or at night; anything goes, as long as deadlines are met.

CRITICAL THINKING
What are some reasons behind the increasing popularity of freelance work?

In Your Community
Find a local temp agency that lists jobs for freelancers. Use information from their ads or Web site to determine why a freelancer might choose to find work through such an agency.

@ **Extend Your Learning** Freelance work has different tax requirements than other kinds of employment. For more information about freelance work, go to this book's OLC through **glencoe.com**.

---

share of the tax. Your contributions to Social Security provide protection for you and your family. The amount of Social Security tax paid, and the number of years worked, directly influence your Social Security benefits. Each year, a copy of your W-2 Wage and Tax Statement is sent to Social Security to record your earnings and work credit. It is critical that your Social Security number is correct on your W-2 and employer pay forms.

Becoming Eligible for Benefits
Work credits are measurements of how long you have worked and the amount of your earnings. You must earn a certain number of work credits to be eligible for Social Security benefits. You earn work credits for the amount of time you work and pay Social Security taxes.

Types of Benefits
There are many different kinds of Social Security benefits. Some are for eligible people of any age.

Disability benefits Disability benefits are paid to disabled workers who cannot work because of a physical or mental condition. The amount of the benefit is based on the worker's average earnings and number of work credits.

Survivors' benefits Survivors' benefits are paid to the family of a worker who dies. The amount paid is based on the person's age at the time of death.

Retirement benefits Retirement benefits are paid to workers who retire. Up to a certain amount, the higher your average yearly earnings, the higher your benefits. The retirement age for reduced benefits is now 62. The retirement age for full benefits is now 65 or 66. Because life expectancies are increasing in length, the age requirement will gradually rise to 67 by 2027. You must work at least ten years to be eligible for retirement benefits.

As You Read
Discuss How would Social Security benefit by gradually raising the age for receiving full retirement benefits to 67?

The 21st Century Workplace

CRITICAL THINKING ANSWER Answers will vary, but may include flexible schedule, home-office technology, and freedom to pick and choose projects.

In Your Community Findings will vary, but may include agencies that specialize in certain types of work, such as technology, medical, or the arts.

Medical benefits Medical benefits help with medical costs for individuals with low incomes and limited resources. *Medicaid* is a joint federal and state program that covers certain individuals. **Medicare** is a federal health insurance program that provides medical benefits for people 65 years or older, certain individuals with disabilities, and individuals with a certain type of kidney disease.

As You Read

Analyze What can you do to influence the decisions that are made about Social Security?

Social Security's Future

The Social Security taxes you pay provide benefits for workers who have already retired. When it is your turn to retire, younger workers will pay the taxes to fund your retirement.

Social Security is an important issue these days. People are living longer, so they receive more benefits, and many are retiring earlier so they pay less into the system. At the same time, the birthrate is declining. This means that there will be fewer young workers around to support retired people in the future. The situation will worsen as the large number of workers now in their 40s and 50s reach retirement age. Before long, the money being paid out will exceed the amount coming in.

There are many proposed solutions to this problem. Some would increase taxes. Others would cut benefits. The government is making decisions about Social Security every day. You can play a part in making these changes by participating in your government and by staying informed about the issue.

Section 23.2 After You Read

Review Key Concepts

1. Why is it important to build up work credits?
2. Why is the program discussed in this section called Social Security?
3. Who is responsible for changing Social Security?

Practice Academic Skills

Mathematics

4. Mike makes $10/hour for regular hours and $15/hour for overtime. He worked 67.5 regular hours and 22.25 overtime hours this month. About 18% of his salary goes to taxes. Use rounding to estimate his net pay.

CONCEPT **Rounding and Estimation** When rounding numbers, look at the digit to the right of the place to which you are rounding. If the digit is 5 or greater, round down. If the digit is less than 5, round up.

Step 1: Round Mike's hours (67.5 and 22.25) to the nearest ten. Multiply the rounded numbers by the corresponding rates per hour.

Step 2: Add the two numbers together and multiply by the tax rate (18%) rounded to the nearest ten percent. Finally, subtract the taxes to find the estimated total income.

 For math help, go to the Math Appendix located at the back of this book.

After You Read
Have students complete the Section 23.2 After You Read section review.

Online Study Tools
Have students go to the OLC through **glencoe.com** to:

- Take the Section 23.2 **Practice Test**.
- Download **Podcast** study tools.
- Download free **Study-to-Go** content to their PDAs or cell phones.

Resources

ExamView Assessment Suite CD allows you to print out ready-made unit and chapter tests complete with answer keys. You can also create customized tests.

CLOSE

Culminating Activity
Content Have students create a flyer describing Social Security benefits.

NCLB Activity correlated to Mathematics standards.

Section 23.2 After You Read

Review Key Concepts

1. You must earn a certain number of work credits to be eligible for Social Security benefits.
2. Social Security helps certain contributing members of society to be secure in times of loss of income.
3. Voters are responsible for changing Social Security.

Practice Academic Skills

4. $10 × 70 + $15 × 22 = $700 + $330 = $1030; $1030 × .2 = $206; $1030 − $206 = $824.

CAREER SPOTLIGHT
Career Cluster: Hospitality and Tourism

FOCUS

Discussion Starter

Human Services Lead a discussion about the different types of careers that can be found in this career cluster. Have students brainstorm different careers and jobs within the career cluster. (Answers will vary but students should show an understanding of the many types of careers that fall within the career cluster.)

TEACH

C Critical Thinking

Realize Your Goals Ask students what is most important for a kitchen worker: Satisfying customers, satisfying the chef, or satisfying one's self. (Answers will vary, but most students will suggest a combination of the three.)

W Writing Support

Independent Practice

Prioritize and List Tell students that reviewing one's workload and prioritizing projects can be applied to any job or even daily tasks as a student. Have them prioritize and list their tasks for one week. (Lists will vary, but some students might find it useful to reconsider their lists at the end of the school day, after homework has been assigned.)

Linda Tang
Assistant Pastry Chef

Q: Describe your job.
A: I cook pastries and desserts for a major hotel chain.

Q: Describe a typical workday.
A: After punching in, the first thing I do is review the day's workload, which includes banquet events and a prep list. Then I prioritize projects and plan my day accordingly. If I start working at 4 A.M., I'll bake breakfast foods and set up for the restaurant, room service, and banquet events. After that, I'll prepare the restaurant's lunch and dinner dessert line before prepping the line for the following day. If I start at 8 A.M., I focus more on serving the day's parties and the production of product. We make everything from breakfast pastries and afternoon brownies to chocolate mousse cake with an espresso center, crunch hazelnut, and *dulce de leche* ice cream.

Q: What skills are most important to you in your job?
A: Speed, organization, and efficiency are very important if you are to execute recipes correctly and quickly. In the kitchen, you need every edge possible to make the dishes, please customers, and appease the chef.

Q: What academic skills and lifelong learning skills are helpful in preparing for your career?
A: A high school diploma will do, but I attended a two-year culinary school program that covered everything you'd ever want to know about preparing food. In terms of personal strengths that are helpful in my career, anyone who aspires to be a chef in a professional kitchen will need emotional resilience. As you pursue your dreams, criticism will be thrown at you from all directions.

Q: What is your key to success?
A: I am very determined and stubborn, and I will not let obstacles get in the way of my dreams.

Q: What are some disadvantages to your career?
A: Disadvantages include low wages, a male-dominated environment, and an autocratic management system, which, fortunately, is slowly changing.

Q: What training and preparation do you recommend for students?
A: Students should get a job in a professional kitchen to get a taste of what the culture is really like before applying to a culinary school. Life does not seem so nurturing when you're caught between a hot stove and a chef who needs to satisfy paying customers.

Q: What are some ways you recommend students prepare for this career?
A: Get a real-world kitchen job before spending thousands of dollars for lessons from chef instructors.

Q: What do you like most about your work?
A: I like the instant gratification. I can literally taste my success or choke on my failures. Plus, the hospitality industry attracts such colorful people. There's no shortage of fun, camaraderie, or community when life is good.

 For more about Career Clusters, go to this book's OLC through **glencoe.com**.

NO CHILD LEFT BEHIND

Teaching Tip

To help achieve some of the goals of the NCLB Act, you might try a shared writing exercise in which you act as the scribe while students dictate their answers. Have students look over the Career Spotlight to answer your questions.

Sample Question: What education did Linda receive in addition to high school? (Record students' answers on the board. Encourage them to modify their answers as they see their words in writing.)

Education or Training A high school diploma is not required for beginning jobs, but it is recommended for those planning a career as a cook or chef. Some chefs and cooks may start their training in high school or post-high school vocational programs. Others may receive formal training through independent cooking schools, professional culinary institutes, or two or four year college degree programs in hospitality or culinary arts.

Academic Skills Required English Language Arts, Mathematics, Science, World Languages

Technology Needed Chefs and cooks use a variety of pots, pans, cutlery, and other equipment, including ovens, broilers, grills, slicers, grinders, and blenders.

Aptitudes, Abilities, and Skills The ability to work well as part of a team, a keen sense of taste and smell, the ability to accurately calculate and measure volume, amount, and time, the ability to understand the chemical processes involved in baking, and working efficiently to turn out meals or other food products. Personal cleanliness is essential.

Workplace Safety Workers must withstand the pressure and strain of standing for hours at a time, lifting heavy pots and kettles, and working near hot ovens and grills. Job hazards include slips and falls, cuts, and burns.

Career Outlook Job openings are expected to be plentiful in the food-service industry over the next ten years; many of these jobs are filled by entry-level workers who later transfer to different occupations or industries.

Career Path Bake desserts for other restaurants, open catering business, open restaurant.

Academic Skills Required to Complete Tasks

Tasks	English Language Arts	Mathematics	Science	World Languages
Learn and invent recipes and techniques	★	★	★	★
Prepare for restaurant, room service, and banquets	★	★	★	
Prepare for lunch and dinner desserts	★	★	★	
Bake lunch and dinner desserts	★	★	★	
Communicate with event teams and clients	★	★	★	★

N C L B

Critical Thinking

What non-culinary skills would a pastry chef need to open his or her own shop?

NCLB This chart relates academic skills such as English Language Arts, Mathematics, Science, Social Studies, and World Languages to specific tasks that are performed for the job featured in the Career Spotlight feature.

Critical Thinking

Food workers who want to open their own shop will require business and mathematics skills to maintain the finances. They will also need marketing savvy as well as language skills to communicate with employees, customers, and health officials.

CAREER SPOTLIGHT

ASSESS

Make Connections
Ask students to list specific correlations between academic subjects and workplace tasks in a food-service job. For example, a manager must use math skills to estimate and maintain food, cleaning, and paper supplies on a daily basis. (Lists will vary according to jobs chosen. Examples may include chefs using math to measure amounts of ingredients, science to know what temperatures and pans are required by certain cooking processes, or health to develop nutritious dishes.)

CLOSE

Culminating Activity
Lifelong Learning and Career Clusters Remind students that food preparation skills are also useful for people outside of the hospitality and tourism career cluster. Ask them to create posters showing how non-food industry workers can benefit from learning about preparing food. (Posters will vary but should include being able to buy and prepare a variety of healthy foods.)

Key Terms and Academic Vocabulary Review

1. Students should use each of the key terms and academic vocabulary terms in a sentence. A sample answer might read: "When Pablo didn't receive his *Form W-2* from his employer by February, he requested a copy so he could file his taxes on time."

Review Key Concepts

2. The tax system is a legal system for assessing and collecting taxes. Taxes are payments that people must make to support federal, state, and local governments, which distribute the funds to pay for services such as public schools, libraries, the military, transportation, law enforcement, postal services, and government administration.

3. To file a return, get the proper tax forms and gather necessary information, including Form W-2, records of other earnings, and a copy of the previous year's return. Decide whether to hire a tax professional to complete the tax form. Read all tax form instructions carefully and get help if needed. Be sure to provide all the required information and double-check the math. Send the tax return electronically or by mail by April 15 to avoid penalties. Keep and file a photocopy.

4. Social Security is a federal government program that helps disabled and retired people. The money for benefits comes from Social Security taxes paid by workers and employers.

5. Social security benefits include disability benefits, survivors' benefits, retirement benefits, and health insurance benefits. State

---

CHAPTER SUMMARY

Section 23.1

Taxes are payments that people must make to support federal, state, and local governments. A good tax system should be fair, simple, convenient, stable, and flexible. Tax dollars pay for a wide range of services, such as education, transportation, and military services. Common taxes include income taxes, Social Security taxes, sales taxes, user fees, and property taxes. Your income tax return shows how much income you received and how much tax you owe. Form W-4 tells your employer how much tax to withhold, and Form W-2 shows how much you earned.

Section 23.2

Social Security is a federal government program that helps disabled and retired people and their families. The money for Social Security benefits comes chiefly from Social Security taxes paid by workers and employers. The government uses your Social Security number to keep track of your contributions and work history. Social Security benefits include disability benefits, survivors' benefits, retirement benefits, and health insurance benefits. The Social Security system must change to keep the amount of money being paid out from exceeding the amount coming in.

Key Terms and Academic Vocabulary Review

1. Use each of these key terms and academic vocabulary words in a sentence.

Key Terms
- withhold (p. 507)
- Form W-4 (p. 509)
- Form W-2 (p. 509)
- Internal Revenue Service (IRS) (p. 511)

- income tax return (p. 511)
- deduction (p. 514)
- exemption (p. 514)
- Social Security (p. 517)
- work credits (p. 518)
- Medicare (p. 519)

Academic Vocabulary
- contribute (p. 505)
- percentage (p. 507)
- obtained (p. 517)

Review Key Concepts

2. **Describe** the U.S. tax system and the services it finances.
3. **Explain** how to complete a federal tax return.
4. **Describe** how the Social Security system works.
5. **Identify** Social Security benefits and state social insurance benefits.
6. **Describe** the challenges facing the Social Security system today.

Critical Thinking

7. **Analyze** How does voting give all citizens a voice in deciding how their government spends tax dollars?
8. **Connect** Your employer has recorded the wrong Social Security number for you. Why is it important to correct the error?

---

social insurance benefits include Medicare and unemployment.

6. The Social Security system must be changed to keep the amount of money being paid out from exceeding the amount of money coming in.

Critical Thinking

7. Voters elect representatives at every level of government: federal, state, and local. These elected lawmakers decide what taxes must be paid, and how tax money is spent. Voting gives citizens an opportunity to elect lawmakers who represent their beliefs.

8. If your employer has recorded the wrong Social Security number for you, you will not be receiving the work credits you deserve.

Real-World Skills and Applications

Information Skills

9. Acquiring and Evaluating Information It is time to file an income tax return. However, you are not sure which form to complete or how to complete it. In a two-paragraph report, describe and compare two ways of finding answers to your questions.

Technology Applications

10. Human Resources Software Imagine you work in the human resources department of your employer. You have been asked to help run a workshop for new employees. Part of the workshop will focus on taxes and tax-preparation software. Research tax-preparation software in the library, via the Internet, or by speaking with taxpayers who have used such programs. Are there any that you would recommend? Create a spreadsheet that shows comparisons among the software programs and their features.

Financial Literacy

11. Planning Retirement If Social Security money runs out before you retire, how can you plan for retirement? Fortunately there are retirement funds that you can manage yourself, such as 401 (k) and individual retirement accounts (IRAs). Go to a bank's Web site to research the retirement plans it offers and summarize your findings in a one-page report.

@ Log On Go to this book's Online Learning Center through **glencoe.com** for help with financial literacy.

12. **Learn About State Income Tax** Learn about your state's income tax. Visit the Web site of the income tax office for your state. Find out how much income tax your state collected last year. Then find out how your state spent this money. Make a pie chart to show how your state spent income tax revenue last year.

13. **Make Your Case**
Situation You are a member of a nonprofit organization dedicated to the reform of the Social Security system. You have set up a meeting with a senator from your state to convince him or her of your views.
Activity Role-play a conversation in which you describe your organization's position on Social Security, explaining how you feel the system should be reformed. Use your knowledge of both the tax system and the Social Security system to defend your organization's opinions.
Evaluation You will be evaluated based on how well you meet the following performance indicators:
- Defend your position by accurately using the realities of the tax and Social Security systems.
- Point out the flaws in the current system and the advantages offered by your proposal.
- Correctly answer any questions your senator may have.

 ACTIVE LEARNING

12. Pie charts will vary, but the sections should reflect the percentages and add up to roughly 100. Inform students that pie charts are an excellent way to compare sizes of parts of a whole in a visual manner.

 ROLE PLAY

13. Students should present their arguments for Social Security reform by citing its problems, pointing out its flaws, and suggesting improvements. Students should organize their presentations accordingly, and be prepared to answer questions.

Real-World Skills and Applications

9. In their paragraphs, students might choose to compare among such information sources as the IRS toll-free phone number, the IRS Web site, accounting software, a professional tax service, and books about tax returns.

10. Tables will vary, but should compare various tax-preparation software packages. Aspects may include price, computer requirements, and special features.

11. Retirement plans will vary, but should emphasize the importance of personal savings as well as the benefits of starting sooner than later.

Academic Skills in the Workplace

14. Students' ads will vary, but may promise a fair price, speedy service, and quality work. The information should specifically mention income tax returns, and can recommend customers bring their Form W-2 for fastest service.

15. $50,000 × 0.2 = $10,000. Frank expects to pay $25,000, much more than what he likely owes.

16. It would take four years because it is four light years away.

17. Reports will vary, but should include details such as age of retirement, how benefits are funded, and how they compare to retirement in the United States.

Academic Skills in the Workplace

English Language Arts

14. Writing an Advertisement You have been asked to design a new advertisement for your local newspaper that shows young adults how to prepare their own tax returns with Form 1040EZ. What kinds of information would you include to attract new customers and to explain your service? Use key terms from the chapter in your ad.

Mathematics

15. Understanding Taxes Your coworker, Frank, is worried. Usually about 20% of his salary is withheld for taxes, but this year, only about $10,000 was withheld. He figures that he will owe about $15,000 more. You and Frank earn about the same amount, about $51,220. Judge the accuracy of Frank's calculations. Is he unnecessarily worried?

CONCEPT Judging Reasonableness When solving an equation, you can judge the reasonableness of your answer by using estimation. Round the numbers in the equation and make a quick estimate of the answer to determine what a reasonable answer might be.

Starting Hint Round your salary to $50,000 and multiply by 0.2, then determine if that number is about the same as the amount Frank expects to pay ($10,000 + $15,000).

Science

16. Calculating Light Years Many U.S. scientific programs are funded by taxes. One taxpayer-funded project was the Hubble Space Telescope. With this telescope, astronomers could see objects millions of light years away. A light-year is the distance light travels in one year. The speed of light is approximately 3×10^8 meters/second (m/s), or 300,000,000 m/s. The nearest galaxy to our Milky Way galaxy is the Andromeda galaxy. It is about 4 light years away. Calculate approximately how many years would it take for light to travel from the earth to the Andromeda galaxy.

Social Studies

17. Research Retirement Benefits Choose a country other than the United States and research its retirement benefits. Does the country offer retirement benefits to citizens over a certain age? Are these benefits funded by income taxes? If not, how are they funded? Compare and contrast those retirement benefits with those of the United States. Explain your findings in a five-minute oral report.

STANDARDIZED TEST PRACTICE

MULTIPLE CHOICE

Directions Read the following question, then choose the appropriate answer.

Test-Taking Tip Look for negative words such as *not* and *no* in multiple choice questions. These words can be easily missed but can change the entire meaning of a sentence.

1. Which of the following is not a characteristic of a good tax system?

(a) Everyone pays his or her fair share.
(b) Tax rules are clear and simple.
(c) Taxes are collected at the beginning of each year.

STANDARDIZED TEST PRACTICE

Answer
1. c. Taxes are collected at the beginning of each year.

Test-Taking Strategies
Whether your students have a standardized test coming up in a few days or a few weeks, these last-minute test-prep tips and strategies will them to relax and do their best.

Pick the Best Answer Tell students that when more than one answer may seems correct, pick the one that is more correct.

Fill in the Bubble Tell students that neatness counts on automated tests. Tell them to fill in answers carefully.

Writing Skills Practice

18. Writing a Persuasive Letter What if your local elected officials proposed tax cuts that would affect some of the programs at your school? The cuts might mean losing some of the elective subjects at your school, such as art, band, and auto mechanics. What is your position on this issue?

 Practice Write a letter to an elected official stating and supporting your position.

- Research and identify the person to whom you would address your letter.
- Identify the programs at your school that would be affected by these proposed cuts.
- Develop persuasive arguments and details that support your position.
- Edit and proofread your draft.

Net Connection

19. Social Security Debate Research the current Social Security debate in Congress by reading recent articles from major newspapers. Contact your state representatives in Congress and ask their positions on the issue. Based on this issue, would you vote for your current representatives? Use a word-processing program to write your opinions in a brief essay.

 Log On Go to this book's OLC through **glencoe.com** to research two or more different party positions on Social Security. What does each party say? With whom do you agree? Write a one-page response.

 Reading Connection

Go to this book's Online Learning Center through **glencoe.com** for a list of reading suggestions.

Personal Academic and Career Portfolio

Fill out Form W-4

When you begin a new job, your employer will ask you to fill out Form W-4 so they can withhold the correct amount of income tax from your pay.

Use the following guidelines to prepare a Form W-4 for your portfolio.

- Visit the Web site for the IRS. Find the section called "Fill-In Form W-4." Find this form by searching in Forms and Publications for "W-4."
- Fill out the form online. Print it out, and then sign and date it.
- Highlight the sections that are likely to change when you change your job. For instance, if you have two part-time jobs rather than just one job, you may decide to declare a different number of exemptions for each one.
- Create a new section for your portfolio and label the section *Form W-4*.
- Add the section to your table of contents.
- Place it in your **Personal Academic and Career Portfolio**.
- Be sure to check with the IRS to make sure you are using the most recent Form W-4. Many government forms are updated each year.
- Recalculate your withholding whenever your employment tax situation changes.
- Recalculate and review your withholding if your dependent or marital information changes.

 Portfolio Help Go to the *Succeeding in the World of Work* OLC through **glencoe.com** for help developing your portfolio.

Writing Skills Practice

18. Opinions will vary, but letters should identify a local official, list school programs that are affected by tax cuts, and provide a strong, well-organized argument why they should be kept or eliminated. Compositions should be checked for grammar, spelling, and effective organization.

Net Connection

19. Answers will vary, but students should grasp the challenges faced by Social Security and local state representatives' positions on the issue. Their essays should defend or criticize the representatives and their stands.

Resources

ExamView Assessment Suite CD allows you to print out ready-made unit and chapter tests complete with answer keys. You can also create customized tests.

WorkKeys

WorkKeys® is a job skills assessment program. For information on leveled assessment for Communication Skills (Business Writing; Listening; Reading for Information; and Writing), go to the WorkKeys link on this book's OLC through **glencoe.com**.

Personal Academic and Career Portfolio

Adding Tax Information

Tell students that their **Personal Academic and Career Portfolios** will always be a work in progress. They will have to be aware of changes in Form W-4 and tax laws in general, as well as the changes in the way they will change their filing if they become married and have dependents. Encourage students to review their portfolios regularly to ensure that they remain current.

Unit 6
Thematic Project

FOCUS

Discussion Starter

Give students the following list of financial choices: owning my own home; driving a nice car; obtaining a high-quality education; enjoying entertainment, dining, and vacations; and saving for the future. Give students a few minutes to list these choices in the order of their importance to them. Then ask students to share their lists with the class and explain how they chose their priorities.

STEP 1

Evaluate Your Skills and Resources

Have students go to the *Succeeding in the World of Work* OLC through **glencoe.com** for a graphic organizer they can use to organize the skills, tools, and resources they will use to complete the project.

TEACH

S Skill Practice

Ask students to keep a log of all purchases they make during the course of their work on this Unit Thematic Project. The log should include all goods and services, from clothing and transportation to entertainment to food and snacks. Ask students to include the amount of each purchase and what prompted the purchase, then total all expenses and write a paragraph analyzing whether they think they spent their money wisely, and why. (Logs will vary, but analyses should identify at least one or two areas for possible improvement.)

Managing Time and Money

You have learned that managing time and managing money are important life skills that can help you at home and in the workplace. You know that being a smart consumer, budgeting wisely, and understanding taxes, banking, and insurance can benefit you both as a worker and as an individual. In this project, you will consider your career and lifestyle goals and create both a monthly schedule and a monthly budget to determine your financial situation and manage your resources.

Project Assignment

- Research the time demands of the career that most interests you right now.
- Make a list of all the activities that you want or need to pursue outside work. Talk to working adults to fill in activities you may have missed.
- Use this information to create a schedule for one month that includes time spent working, as well as time for all your other commitments and activities.
- Research the average pay in the career that interests you. What is the average monthly pay, after taxes, of an entry-level worker with the educational level you hope to attain?
- Research the average cost of living in your area. How much will you have to spend on rent, food, transportation, and all other expenses? Ask others about expenses you may not have anticipated.
- Use this information to draw up a realistic and comprehensive monthly budget.

STEP 1 Evaluate Your Skills and Resources

To complete this assignment, you must have access to the Internet as well as books, magazines, and other media. You will also need to interview workers and other adults in your area about their typical expenses and activities. To draw up your schedule and budget, you will need access to spreadsheet and calendar software.

Skills you may need to complete the Unit Thematic Project include:

Academic Skills reading, writing, mathematics, social studies

Transferable Skills communication, research, problem-solving, and decision-making skills

Technology Skills presentation and word-processing skills

 Resources Organizer To find a graphic organizer you can use to determine the skills, tools, and resources you will need for this project, go to this book's Online Learning Center through **glencoe.com**.

Lifelong Learning Connection

Lifelong learning concepts found in this project include:
- self-assessment
- setting goals and making decisions
- financial literacy
- adaptability

SPOTLIGHT ON TECHNOLOGY

Information Management

With more and more information stored on and generated by computers, information management—the field devoted to storing, organizing, retrieving, and analyzing data—has grown exponentially. Ask students to research information management. Why does information need to be "managed"? What software and other technology tools do information managers use

to do their jobs? (Information needs to be managed so that an organization can know what information to collect, how and where to store it, how to retrieve it when needed, how to analyze it to make it meaningful, and how to handle legal challenges. Information managers use tools such as databases, Web servers, data warehousing, and security systems to prevent break-ins.)

STEP 2 Preview a Real-World Company Profile

Both companies and individual workers have to manage their time and money wisely in order to succeed. Companies use planning and management to create and meet goals and schedules. The company featured below succeeds by hiring workers with strong technology and production skills.

Real-World Company: Belkin

Belkin was started in 1983 by two guys hand-assembling computer cables in a garage. Since then, the privately-held business has grown into a global leader in connectivity products, including cables, wireless accessories, and networking solutions. With offices in California, Indiana, and New York as well as Australia, New Zealand, Singapore, China, and the U.K., the company records over $1 billion in sales annually.

Before Ken Mori was hired by Belkin, he worked for a design firm that had a contract with the company. It made sense for Belkin to hire someone they knew and trusted. As a senior industrial designer, Mori is involved in all phases of product design, including user research, initial conceptualization, engineering, marketing, and manufacturing. Since working at Belkin, he has expanded his CAD skills and gained experience in the latest rapid proto-typing machines. These technology skills help the company create products that succeed in an industry in which swift time-to-market is essential.

Belkin

Aspects of Industry	Company Facts
Planning	Belkin focuses on innovation. It develops ideas for new products by observing how people perform their daily activities.
Management	Products are designed by specialized teams. Employees are rewarded for individual initiative.
Finance	Belkin's founder started the company with his own money, and it is still privately financed.
Technical and Production Skills	Employees need skills in design, engineering, drawing, 3-D modeling, project management, marketing, and sales.
Underlying Principles of Technology	The company keeps up with cutting-edge technologies, from HDTV and iPods to wireless Bluetooth devices.
Labor Issues	Employee benefits include medical and dental insurance and 401(k) plans.
Health, Safety, and Environmental Issues	Only those trained to use hand and power tools are able to use the workshop and the tools. Facilities are OSHA compliant and checked on a regular basis.
Community Issues	Money is donated to local causes, and employees are encouraged to give presentations to students and to participate in charitable efforts such as Habitat for Humanity.

527

Developing Industry Partners

Harness the Power of the Web

Does your school or town have its own Web site? Get involved! Create a Web page or multi-page site for your school-to-work program that links all of your program's participants and potential participants provides a forum for sharing news. You can use the Web to identify employers, find new mentors, share information about student-learners, and let the rest of your community know what's going on in your school-to-work program. Set up your own blog on the site or on a free third-party blogging site to provide a forum for participants to share their experiences.

TEACH (cont.)

STEP 2

Preview a Real-World Company Profile
Tell students that many professionals, such as the industrial designer profiled here, have two appealing career options: working as a full-time employee or being self-employed as a consultant or contractor. Ask students what they see as the pros and cons of each option. Ask: Which option would you choose? Why? (Pros of being self-employed include control over one's schedule and the opportunity to work for more than one client; cons include an unpredictable workload and a lack of benefits such as health insurance. Having a full-time corporate job offers less flexibility but provides opportunities for decision-making and advancement.)

R Reading Strategy
Guided Practice

Conduct Research Remind students that understanding aspects of industry can aid their transition to employment in the rapidly changing global workplace and help them connect their academic coursework to the world of work. Ask students to use print and online resources, as well as telephone or e-mail interviews, to research a product they use to find out where and how it is made. What workers contribute to the creation of the product, from raw materials to final product? Ask students to summarize their findings for the class. (Reports will vary. Students should become aware of the wide array of skills and worker roles required to build even the simplest product.)

TEACH (cont.)

STEP 3

Research Procedures
Have students go to the *Succeeding in the World of Work* OLC through **glencoe.com** for a graphic organizer they can use to organize the results of their research.

STEP 4

Connect to Community
Ask students to assess the availability and price of transportation and fresh, healthy food in their neighborhood. Is public transportation convenient and affordable? If not, is carpooling an option? Are supermarkets, produce markets, or farmer's markets conveniently located? If not, where can students go to get healthy food? (Transportation and availability of healthy food vary widely by location. Encourage students to find creative solutions to transportation costs and to include in their schedule and budget the time and money necessary to eat healthfully.) Ask students whether they think it is important to set aside time in their schedules to participate in community activities. Why or why not?

STEP 5

Report Your Findings
Give students these tips on drawing up their budget:
- Make sure your budget includes *everything* you spend money on.
- Include at least $50 a month for savings.
- Remember that some expenses, such as utilities, vary from month to month.
- Do not make a budget so tight that it is impossible to keep.

528

STEP 3 Research Procedures

Conduct research on the salary and work hours of various careers in your chosen career field. Choose a career that interests you and perform the following steps to learn how it will affect your time and financial resources:

1. Find out the typical number of hours you will have to work in the career of your choice. How many hours are in a typical workweek? Is overtime, night, or weekend work required or offered? How flexible is your schedule likely to be? Consider whether you will work overtime if given the option.
2. Talk to workers in your career field to verify your research. For example, ask whether most entry-level workers work the about same number of hours.
3. Make a list of all the activities you will do in a month. Estimate how long each will take.
4. Find out the typical salary for an entry-level worker in your chosen career and to calculate your take-home pay (pay after taxes).
5. List and estimate all the expenses you will have in a month.

6. Talk to workers in your career field to verify your research. For example, you could ask whether having certain technology skills or educational achievements might boost your salary.

@ Resources Organizer To find a graphic organizer you can use to organize your research, go to this book's OLC through **glencoe.com**.

STEP 4 Connect to Community

Get Local Determine the expenses of living in your current neighborhood. Ask friends and relatives and use the Internet to determine costs such as housing, insurance, and food. Compare the costs of living in various neighborhoods and explain which ones are most affordable given your budget.

Take the Next Step Talk to at least two older adult residents in your neighborhood and ask how costs of living have changed over the past 5, 10, and 20 years.

STEP 5 Report Your Findings

Your final products for this project should include a detailed schedule and budget for one month of your adult working life.
- Use spreadsheet software to create a two-column budget listing and categorizing income and expenses for one month. Use the sum function in the software to verify that income and expenses are equal. Include one paragraph summarizing the sources of your information.
- Use scheduling or calendar software, or the chart function in a word-processing program, to create a detailed, day-by-day schedule for one month. Include one paragraph summarizing the sources of your information.

Developing Community Involvement

Share Health Information

Work with a hospital, nonprofit clinic, or other health organization in your area to develop a health education series for teens at your school. Ask students to brainstorm health topics of interest to them, such as mental health, reproductive health, disease prevention, smoking cessation, and so on.

Then invite speakers to come to the school to discuss the topics. Also, ask students to form teams to research and create educational displays or Web pages about each health topic. Have teams work with a research mentor, such as doctor or nurse, from the community.

Helpful Hints When anticipating how to budget your time, consider how much time you will need to devote to the following activities:
- work (including commute)
- grocery shopping and other errands
- cleaning
- paying bills
- exercising and staying healthy
- recreation/entertainment
- socializing with friends
- spending time with family
- education

When developing your monthly budget, think of how much money you will need to reserve for the following expenses:
- transportation
- rent/mortgage and utilities
- groceries and eating out
- clothing and laundry
- recreation/entertainment
- health care and hygiene
- insurance
- education
- savings

Personal Academic and Career Portfolio

Format and print out a copy of your budget and schedule to include in your **Personal Academic and Career Portfolio**. You can use the budget as a model to help you manage your financial resources. You can use the schedule as a model to help you manage your time.

STEP 6 Presentation and Evaluation

Your budget and schedule will be evaluated based on:
- depth of planning and research
- presentation and neatness
- accuracy of data

@ **Evaluation Rubric** To find a rubric you can use to evaluate your project, go to this book's OLC through **glencoe.com**.

BusinessWeek ◄ Connection

Understanding All Aspects of Industry: Technical and Production Skills

Understanding all aspects of an industry can help you prepare to succeed in a career in that industry. Technical and production skills are the knowledge and know-how required to do the full range of tasks at a job. They include not only job-specific skills, such as programming a robot, sterilizing surgical instruments, or using an air drill, but also academic skills, such as reading, writing, mathematics, social studies, and science. In fact, academic skills are the foundation for all job-specific skills.

@ Go to this book's Online Learning Center through **glencoe.com** to find a *BusinessWeek* article titled "Mother Nature's Design Workshop." Read the article and identify the ways the scientists profiled in the article use their academic skills to develop new technologies. Use a word-processing program to create a one-page summary of the article. Add this summary to your **Personal Academic and Career Portfolio**.

BusinessWeek ◄ Connection

All Aspects of Industry: Technical and Production Skills

Ask students to imagine that they are starting an athletic shoe company. Ask students to work in teams to make a list of all the skills they will need and all the tasks they must do in order to get their first shoe made. For example, they will need design skills to design the shoes and machine skills to make the prototype, and they will need to buy raw materials and set up assembly-line equipment to fabricate the shoes. (Students should list skills relating to organization, management, planning, design, technology, production, procurement, and marketing. Tasks should include designing the shoe, building and testing prototypes, hiring and training employees, and setting up a rational production process.)

STEP 6

Presentation and Evaluation

Rubric Encourage students go to the *Succeeding in the World of Work* OLC through **glencoe.com** for a rubric they can use to evaluate their project. Encourage students to use the rubric as a content checklist when listing the items that should be included in their budgets and schedules.

CLOSE

Culminating Activity

Schedule and Budget Feedback In this project, students applied the Unit topic to their own lives by drawing up a realistic monthly budget and schedule. Have students work in pairs to present and discuss their budgets and schedules and to share feedback on whether they seem complete and realistic. Encourage students to share the reasoning and decision-making process behind their budgets and schedules. Have each student list at least two useful observations made by their partners. (Discussions and observations may vary, but encourage students to be open to feedback, as well as tactful and noncritical in their observations. Encourage students to use this activity as a reality check to verify whether their budgets and schedules are realistic.)

Chapter	Chapter Objectives
CHAPTER 24 Adapting to Change	• **Describe** ways to prepare for the future. • **Identify** qualities, skills, and behaviors that often lead to promotions. • **Explain** why workers may change jobs. • **Describe** strategies for changing jobs. • **Explain** how to handle a job loss.
CHAPTER 25 Balancing Work and Personal Life	• **Explain** how to choose a place to live and set up a household. • **Describe** how to organize your living space and establish good housekeeping habits. • **Identify** ways to balance your work and personal life. • **Name** some company policies that help employees balance work and family life. • **Explain** your role as a citizen and identify ways to participate in the community.

Understanding Brackets, Letters, and Ability Levels in the Teacher Wraparound Edition

Brackets Brackets on the reduced student edition page correspond to teaching strategies and activities in the Teacher Wraparound Edition. As you teach the lesson, the brackets show you exactly where to use the teaching strategies and activities.

Letters The letters on the reduced student edition page identify the type of strategy or activity. See the key below to learn about the different types of strategies and activities.

Ability Levels Teaching Strategies that appear throughout the chapters have been identified by one of three codes to give you an idea of their suitability for students of varying learning styles and abilities.

Resources Key program resources are listed in each chapter. Icons indicate the format of resources.

KEY TO LETTERS

R **Reading Strategy** activities help you teach reading skills and vocabulary.

C **Critical Thinking** strategies help students apply and extend what they have learned.

S **Skill Practice** strategies help students practice historical analysis and geographical skills.

W **Writing Support** activities provide writing opportunities to help students comprehend the text.

D **Develop Concepts** activities use various strategies to help teachers gauge and plan for students' concept development.

U **Universal Access** activities provide differentiated instruction for English language learners, and suggestions for teaching various types of learners. *These activities may or may not have brackets.*

NCLB **No Child Left Behind** activities help students practice and improve their abilities in academic subjects.

KEY TO ABILITY LEVELS

L1 Strategies should be within the ability range of all students. Often full class participation is required.

L2 Strategies are for average to above-average students or for small groups. Some teacher direction is necessary.

L3 Strategies are designed for students able and willing to work independently. Minimal teacher direction is necessary.

KEY TO RESOURCE ICONS

📁 Print Material

💿 CD-ROM

🖐 Internet

All-In-One Planner and Resource Center

Teacher Wraparound Edition

For the Unit:
  Unit Thematic Project Student Rubrics
  Unit Test
  Unit Connecting Activities Projects

For the Chapter:
  Chapter Resources
  Program Resources
  Additional Print and Media Resources
  Lesson Plans
  Chapter Summaries, Key Terms, and
    Academic Vocabulary *(English and Spanish)*

Graphic Organizers
Reading Activities
Chapter Self-Checks *(English and Spanish)*
Internet Activities
School-to-Career Connections
Work-Based Learning Projects
Personal and Academic Career Portfolio Student Rubrics

Student Activity Workbook with Academic Integration

Strategies for Students with Special Needs

Career Plan Project Workbook

 Link to the *Succeeding in the World of Work* **Online Learning Center with Podcasts** through **glencoe.com**.

Unit Overview
Introduce the Unit

Introduce the unit by describing the main concepts of each chapter in the unit.

Unit 7 equips students with the information they need to transition to independence. Students learn how to think about and balance adult responsibilities in a way that will provide a lasting feeling of satisfaction and achievement.

Chapter 24 explains how students can actively manage their careers. Students learn the importance of lifelong learning, identify the skills necessary for raises and promotions, and master strategies for handling job changes and layoffs.

Chapter 25 helps students make the important personal decisions that come with independence. Students learn how to choose rental property and how to handle necessary household tasks. They also learn how to balance their various life roles in order to devote appropriate time to work, family, friends, community involvement, and other goals.

▦▦·▦▦ OUT OF TIME?

If class time is too short to cover all of the chapters in this unit, have students:
- Write down the key terms and their definitions.
- Read the chapter summaries at the beginning of each chapter review.
- Go to the *Succeeding in the World of Work* Online Learning Center (OLC) through **glencoe.com** to download free Study-to-Go content to their PDAs or cell phones.

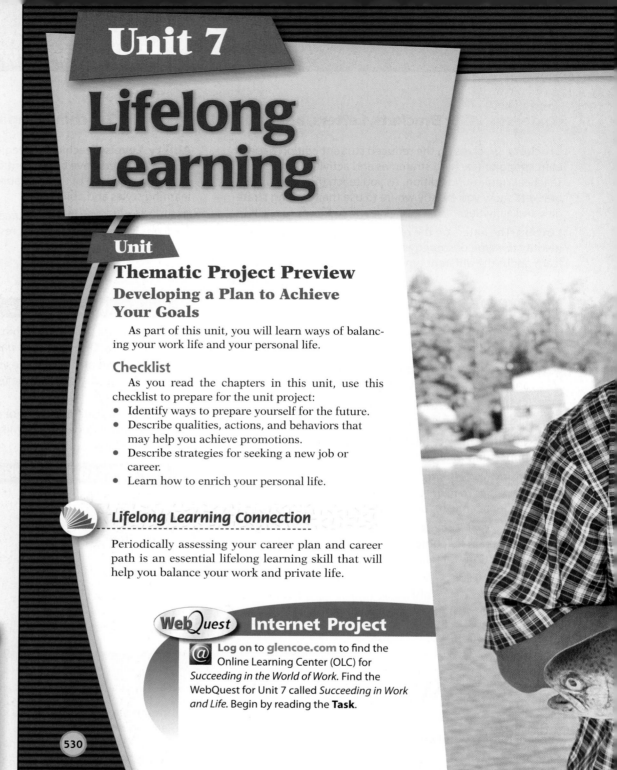

Unit 7
Lifelong Learning

Unit
Thematic Project Preview
Developing a Plan to Achieve Your Goals

As part of this unit, you will learn ways of balancing your work life and your personal life.

Checklist

As you read the chapters in this unit, use this checklist to prepare for the unit project:
- Identify ways to prepare yourself for the future.
- Describe qualities, actions, and behaviors that may help you achieve promotions.
- Describe strategies for seeking a new job or career.
- Learn how to enrich your personal life.

Lifelong Learning Connection

Periodically assessing your career plan and career path is an essential lifelong learning skill that will help you balance your work and private life.

WebQuest Internet Project

@ Log on to **glencoe.com** to find the Online Learning Center (OLC) for *Succeeding in the World of Work*. Find the WebQuest for Unit 7 called *Succeeding in Work and Life*. Begin by reading the **Task**.

530

Unit Thematic Project Preview

Tell students that as part of this unit, they will create a ten-year timeline that describes their ultimate career goal, as well as the education and training goals and other short- and medium-term goals they will need to accomplish along the way. They will also identify and chart other important goals, such as financial, personal, and family goals, to create a roadmap for success.

WebQuest

For WebQuest teaching suggestions and rubrics, go to the Teacher Center of this book's Online Learning Center (OLC) through **glencoe.com**.

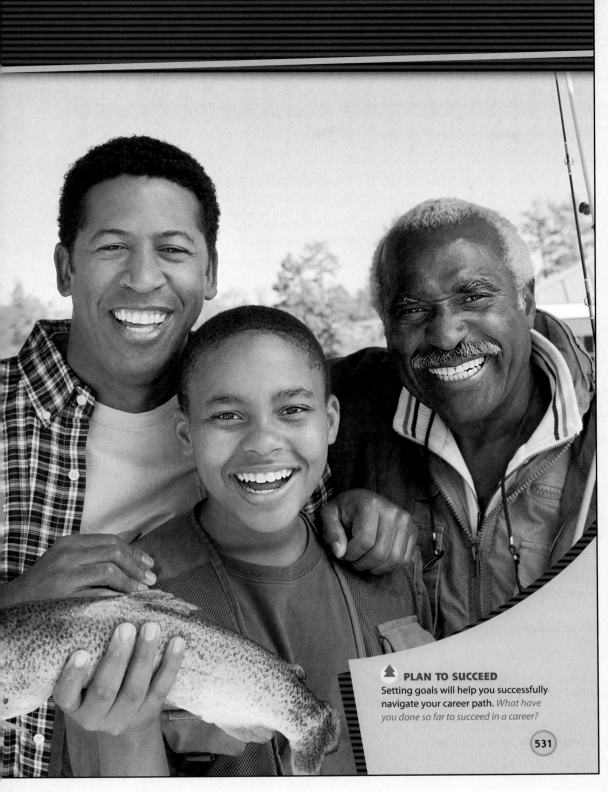

PLAN TO SUCCEED
Setting goals will help you successfully navigate your career path. *What have you done so far to succeed in a career?*

(531)

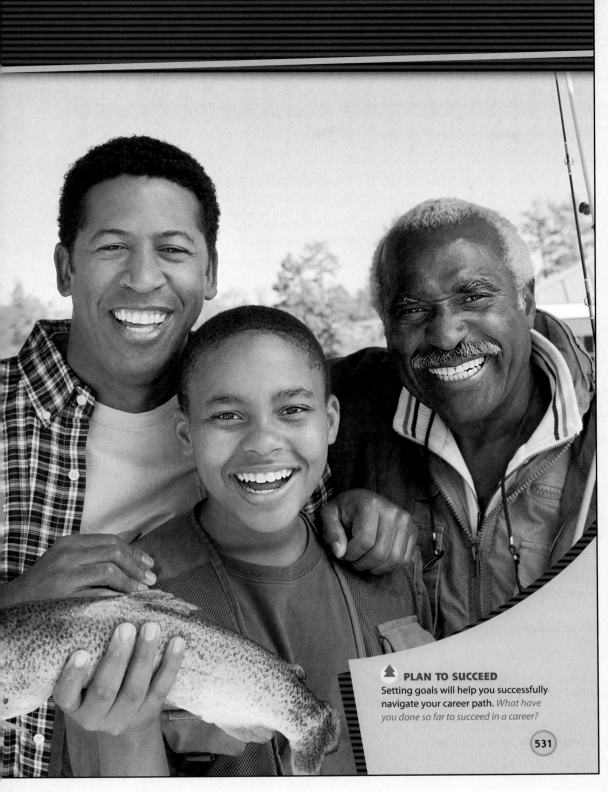

PLAN TO SUCCEED
Setting goals will help you successfully navigate your career path. *What have you done so far to succeed in a career?*

(531)

Build Background
Ask students these questions to activate prior knowledge:

Chapter 24
What is downsizing? (the elimination of jobs in a company to promote efficiency or cut costs)

How can you be a lifelong learner at your job? (Take advantage of education and training offered by your employer, learn new skills, and take on new tasks wherever possible.)

What skills and qualities do employers look for when giving promotions and raises? (seniority, knowledge and competence, willingness to learn, initiative, perseverance, cooperativeness, thinking skills, adaptability, and solid education and training)

Is it ever acceptable to decline a promotion? (Yes, if you offer specific reasons and remain open to future growth.)

Chapter 25
What should you consider before deciding whether to live independently? (Weigh the positive aspects of being independent against the costs and responsibilities of being on your own.)

What expenses must renters pay, in addition to rent? (When moving in, new renters must pay a security deposit and sometimes other deposits, such as a pet deposit. Renters must also pay for utilities, such as water, gas, and electricity.)

How are your roles in life— such as worker, friend, and family member—related? (Each role gives you a sense of pride and accomplishment that enhances your ability to fulfill your other roles.)

What is your main responsibility as a citizen? (to be informed and vote)

 Extend the Photo

Caption Answer Answers will vary, but students should understand that all of the education, training, and experience they have collected so far in life, at school, and on the job has been part of their career preparation.

Discussion Remind students that, throughout this book, they have read about the importance of setting goals. Ask: Do you feel confident that you can reach the goals you set? Why or why not? How can you become more confident about your ability to reach your goals? (Students may feel that they want to improve their ability to set realistic goals, to stay motivated, or to overcome stumbling blocks. Remind students that setting and achieving goals becomes easier with practice and that trial and error is part of the process.)

Chapter Resources Planning Guide with Activities and Features

Section	Features	Activities
Section 24.1 **Managing Your Career**	Everyday Ethics (p. 536) Math in Action (p. 537) Real-World Connection (p. 538) 21st Century Workplace (p. 538)	Before You Read (p. 534) Graphic Organizer (p. 534) As You Read (p. 535) After You Read (p. 539)
Section 24.2 **Changing Jobs or Careers**	Creative Business Practices (p. 541) Hot Jobs! (p. 543) Career Checklist (p. 545)	Before You Read (p. 540) Graphic Organizer (p. 540) As You Read (p. 541) After You Read (p. 545)

NCLB Activities, information, and skills practice will help your students attain No Child Left Behind proficiency. Students will improve their abilities in the following academic standards areas:

Academic Standards Correlations

Discipline	Standard	Feature/Activity
English Language Arts	**NCTE 1** Read texts to acquire new information.	Creative Business Practices (p. 541) Hot Jobs! (p. 543)
	NCTE 4 Use written language to communicate effectively.	21st Century Workplace (p. 538) After You Read (p. 545) Writing Skills Practice (p. 551)
	NCTE 5 Use different writing process elements to communicate effectively.	Real-World Connection (p. 538)
	NCTE 12 Use language to accomplish individual purposes.	Creative Business Practices (p. 541)
Mathematics	**Number and Operation:** Understand meanings of operations and how they relate to one another	Math in Action (p. 537)
	Problem Solving: Apply and adapt a variety of appropriate strategies to solve problems	After You Read (p. 539)
	Algebra: Understand patterns, relations, and functions	Academic Skills in the Workplace (p. 550)
Science	**Life Science:** Biological evolution	Academic Skills in the Workplace (p. 550)

21st Century Skills and Workplace Competencies Correlations

CORRELATIONS The charts show the 21st Century Skills, foundation skills, and workplace competencies that students develop as they work in this chapter.

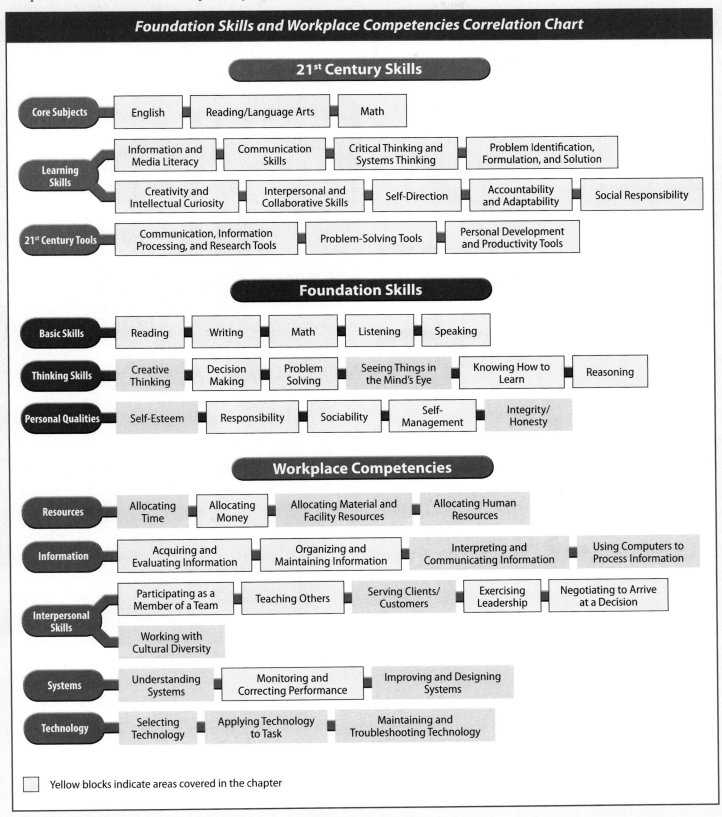

Foundation Skills and Workplace Competencies Correlation Chart

21st Century Skills

Core Subjects
- English
- Reading/Language Arts
- Math

Learning Skills
- Information and Media Literacy
- Communication Skills
- Critical Thinking and Systems Thinking
- Problem Identification, Formulation, and Solution
- Creativity and Intellectual Curiosity
- Interpersonal and Collaborative Skills
- Self-Direction
- Accountability and Adaptability
- Social Responsibility

21st Century Tools
- Communication, Information Processing, and Research Tools
- Problem-Solving Tools
- Personal Development and Productivity Tools

Foundation Skills

Basic Skills
- Reading
- Writing
- Math
- Listening
- Speaking

Thinking Skills
- Creative Thinking
- Decision Making
- Problem Solving
- Seeing Things in the Mind's Eye
- Knowing How to Learn
- Reasoning

Personal Qualities
- Self-Esteem
- Responsibility
- Sociability
- Self-Management
- Integrity/Honesty

Workplace Competencies

Resources
- Allocating Time
- Allocating Money
- Allocating Material and Facility Resources
- Allocating Human Resources

Information
- Acquiring and Evaluating Information
- Organizing and Maintaining Information
- Interpreting and Communicating Information
- Using Computers to Process Information

Interpersonal Skills
- Participating as a Member of a Team
- Teaching Others
- Serving Clients/Customers
- Exercising Leadership
- Negotiating to Arrive at a Decision
- Working with Cultural Diversity

Systems
- Understanding Systems
- Monitoring and Correcting Performance
- Improving and Designing Systems

Technology
- Selecting Technology
- Applying Technology to Task
- Maintaining and Troubleshooting Technology

Yellow blocks indicate areas covered in the chapter

CHAPTER **24**
Adapting to Change

Chapter Overview
Introduce the Chapter

In this chapter, students learn how to manage their careers by developing their skills and preparing for career changes.

Section 24.1 focuses on life-long learning and the skills required for career advancement and promotions.

Section 24.2 helps students evaluate whether and when to change jobs or switch careers.

Build Background

Explain to students that most people find change stressful. Ask students to brainstorm ways that a major change—such as leaving school, starting a new job, or moving—could have both positive and negative consequences. (Positive consequences include having exciting new experiences, attaining goals, and meeting new people; negative consequences include feeling uncertain or out of place, and losing contact with friends.)

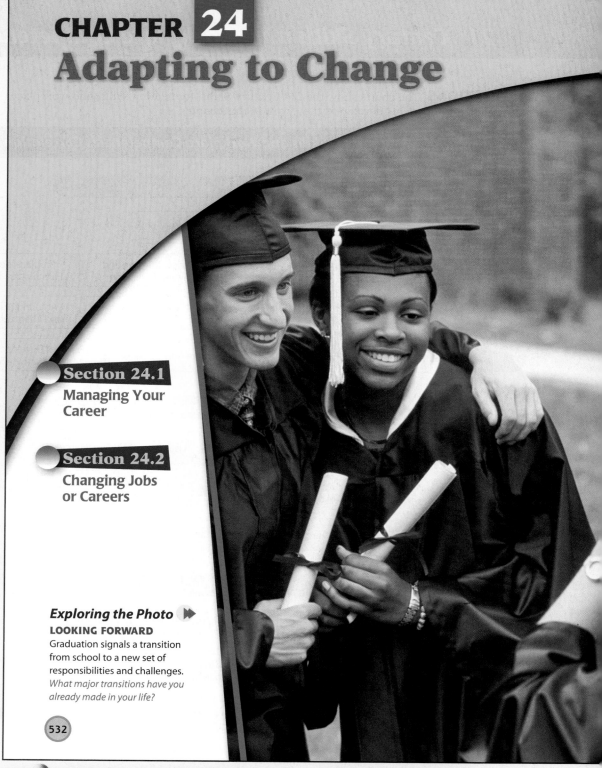

● **Section 24.1**
Managing Your Career

● **Section 24.2**
Changing Jobs or Careers

▶ Exploring the Photo

Caption Answer
Students may mention beginning high school, entering the workforce, or adapting to a move or family change.

Discussion Explain to students that some people see changes as setbacks and others see them as opportunities. Why are some changes bad and others good—does it depend more on the person's attitude or more on the specific change? (Both factors are important. However, a person with a positive attitude may be able to transform even a negative change into an opportunity for learning and personal growth.)

Exploring the Photo ▶▶
LOOKING FORWARD
Graduation signals a transition from school to a new set of responsibilities and challenges. *What major transitions have you already made in your life?*

532

Classroom Resources

- 📁 Student Edition
- 📁 Teacher Wraparound Edition
- 📁 Student Activity Workbook with Academic Integration
- 📁 Student Activity Workbook with Academic Integration TAE
- 📁 *Fast File,* Unit 7 Resources

- 📁 Inclusion in the Career Education Classroom
- 💿 TeacherWorks™ Plus
- 💿 *ExamView Assessment Suite*
- 💿 Interactive Chalkboard
- 💿 Interactive Student Edition
- 🖳 Online Student Edition
- 🖳 Online Learning Center (OLC) with Podcasts

Chapter Objectives

After completing this chapter, you will be able to:

- **Describe** ways to prepare for the future.
- **Identify** qualities, skills, and behaviors that often lead to promotions.
- **Explain** why workers may change jobs.
- **Describe** strategies for changing jobs.
- **Explain** how to handle a job loss.

Writing Activity Personal Career Notebook

The end of high school is a time of transition and change. Do you have a transition plan, or a list of goals you want to achieve after high school? You will need to answer some important questions as you make your plan. Will you continue your education? Will you work full-time or part-time? Will you live at home, on your own, or with help? Write a one-page journal entry describing a possible transition plan.

Get Motivated! Interview someone who has graduated from college and is now working at his or her first job since graduation. Ask how the person felt about that first change after graduation. Are there any similarities between this person's feelings and your own? Summarize the interview in a one-page response.

Chapter 24 Adapting to Change **533**

Review the Objectives
Introduce the chapter by reviewing the chapter objectives:

Section 24.1 Objectives
Describe ways to prepare for the future. (Anticipating change, developing skills, choosing a career that is growing, and learning how to change jobs and careers effectively and to cope with job loss.)

Identify qualities, skills, and behaviors that often lead to promotions. (Seniority, competence, willingness to learn, initiative, perseverance, cooperativeness, thinking skills, adaptability, and education.)

Section 24.2 Objectives
Explain why workers may change jobs. (Because they are not happy in their current job, because they are not growing personally or professionally, because they want a new direction, or because the job is terminated.)

Describe strategies for changing jobs. (Finding a similar job at another organization, switching to a new job within the same organization, or starting over.)

Explain how to handle a job loss. (Dealing with your emotions, assessing available benefits and services, budgeting, and looking for a new job.)

Writing Activity Personal Career Notebook Answer Guide

Students should be honest about their plans (or lack of plans) as they end high school. They should be realistic about the costs of living on their own and should understand that some form of education or training after high school can help them attain their career goals.

Get Motivated! Students should recognize some similarities in the transition from college to the workforce and their own transition out of high school. They may feel less confident than college graduates, who have trained for two or more years in a specific career field.

Managing Your Career

Reading Guide

FOCUS

Bell Ringer Activity

Managing Your Career

Ask students to write down a job they might like to have in ten or fifteen years. Ask them to list various other jobs that they might hold on the way to that career goal.

Resources

Interactive Chalkboard
The Interactive Chalkboard CD provides visual teaching aids for this section.

@ Online Learning Center
The Online Learning Center (OLC) through **glencoe.com** features chapter vocabulary, chapter summaries, and other study materials.

Preteaching

Ask students to find the definitions of the key terms in the text and to fill in the following sentence for each: "_____ relates to managing my career because_____."

Graphic Organizer

Tell students to go to the OLC through **glencoe.com** for a printable graphic organizer. (Graphic organizers will vary but should list skills and abilities that are valuable to employers.)

NCLB connects academic correlations to book content.

534

Reading Guide

Before You Read

Preview Review the Key Concepts and Read to Learn. Write one or two sentences describing what you want to learn from reading the section.

Read to Learn
- Ways to prepare for the future
- Qualities, skills, and behaviors that often lead to workplace promotions.

D Main Idea
Preparing for changes in your career will help you adapt well when the changes come.

Key Concepts
- Preparing for the Future
- Growing in Your Job

Key Terms
- downsizing
- promotion
- seniority
- perseverance

Academic Vocabulary
You will find this word in your reading and on your tests. Use the academic vocabulary glossary to look up its definition if necessary.
- significant

Graphic Organizer
Being able to explain how your skills and abilities make you a strong employee can be key to obtaining a job or a promotion. Brainstorm your skills and abilities and develop explanations that show how these skills and abilities make you a strong choice for an employer. Use a chart like the one below to organize your information.

Skills and Abilities	Why Do These Skills and Abilities Make You a Strong Employee?

 Log On Go to this book's Online Learning Center through **glencoe.com** for an online version of this graphic organizer.

Academic Standards • • • • • • • • • • • • • • • •

English Language Arts
- Use written language to communicate effectively. (NCTE 4)
- Use different writing process elements to communicate effectively. (NCTE 5)

Mathematics
- Understand meanings of operations and how they relate to one another
- Apply and adapt a variety of appropriate strategies to solve problems

NCLB

Reading Guide

Before You Read

Explain to students that this section describes the "qualities, skills, and behaviors" that lead to promotions and career success. Emphasize that workers can take charge of their careers by developing the skills and qualities that employers want and by performing professionally on the job.

D Develop Concepts

Main Idea Discuss the idea of change with students. Ask: What changes in your work life might you plan? What are some changes that might come unplanned? (Planned changes may include changing jobs, returning to school, or starting a family; unplanned changes may include a layoff or promotion, or a family change requiring a move.)

Preparing for the Future

Think back over the last two years. How have you changed? In the years ahead, changes will continue to occur. Your skills and interests will keep expanding in new directions. New career possibilities will emerge. The world of work will change, too. Changes at work may open even more doors. Can you predict these changes? No. You can, however, prepare yourself to respond to them.

You may know people who took jobs when they were young and stayed with the same company for their entire working lives. Forty years ago, that was a typical employment history. Today it is not. As you learned in the first chapter of this book, the average American will have more than eight different jobs by the age of 32. People can expect to change employers several times before they retire.

Today's workplace is changing quickly. Jobs that once employed many are less **significant** to the economy than they once were. Many companies have gone through **downsizing**, which is the elimination of jobs in a company to promote efficiency or to cut costs. Some people may lose their jobs through downsizing, other jobs are changed. When positions are eliminated, individual workers may acquire more work and additional responsibilities.

Keeping Up

Fortunately, the company you may work for wants to meet the changing demands of today's workplace at least as much as you do. To help workers, many of today's companies invest heavily in employee training and education. At your job, make use of all opportunities to keep your skills and knowledge up-to-date. In other words, become a *lifelong learner*.

Vocabulary
You can find definitions in the **Key Terms** glossary and **Academic Vocabulary** glossary at the back of this book.

As You Read
Explain Why is it important to keep your skills and knowledge up-to-date?

 SKILL EXPECTATIONS
Today, employees perform complicated tasks requiring advanced skills. *How has this change benefited workers?*

Chapter 24 Adapting to Change **535**

Section 24.1

TEACH

Discussion Starter
Preparing for the Future
Ask students to share how they see the future. Do they see themselves as figuring it out as they go along, or do they believe it is important to prepare? (Opinions will vary, but students should understand that preparing for the future is more likely to yield a satisfying outcome.)

R Reading Strategy
Activating Prior Knowledge
Ask students whether they know any adults who have worked at the same company for ten years or more. If so, are these workers happy with their jobs? Have their careers grown? Why or why not? (Answers will vary; some workers stay at a company because they enjoy the work, while others stay because they are afraid of change or of the unknown.)

As You Read
Keeping your skills and knowledge up-to-date enables you to meet the changing demands of today's workplace.

Resources

TeacherWorks™ Plus
The TeacherWorks software includes customizable built-in lesson plans and links to printable program resources.

Extend the Photo

Caption Answer Mastering more complex skills makes a worker's job more interesting. It also makes a worker more valuable, and hence better able to obtain a raise or promotion or to find work with a different company.

Discussion Ask students how they feel about the fact that today's workers need more skills than in the past. Are they happy to have the opportunity to learn and do more, or are they afraid that their skills may not be adequate for today's workplace? (Students' reactions will vary. Emphasize the positive to students by pointing out that today's workers have more opportunities than ever to take charge of their own careers.)

U Universal Access

English Language Learners
Students who do not speak English as their native language face ongoing challenges in improving their reading, writing, and speaking skills. Emphasize that improving communication skills is an important part of lifelong learning. Encourage all students to develop competency in at least one other language.

W Writing Support

Developing an Argument
Ask students to imagine that they work at a small company without a formal training program. Have them write a letter to their managers explaining the benefits of continuing training and listing some specific courses or programs they could attend to build their skills. (Letters should cite enhanced job skills in areas such as technology or leadership. Courses and training programs are offered at local community and trade colleges, private institutions, and online.)

S Skill Practice

Independent Practice
Interview Ask students to interview an experienced professional in a career field that interests them and ask how he or she keeps current as the field grows and changes. Have students summarize the interview in two paragraphs. (Interviewees may indicate that they read books and articles, take classes, participate in on-the-job training, and so on.)

✓ Reading Check

ANALYZE Lifelong learning opportunities might include attending training sessions or taking courses at a community college.

536

Everyday ETHICS

EVALUATING LOYALTY

What is loyalty?

SHOPPING AROUND You have worked as an assistant to the elderly owner of a small eyeglass shop for several years. You have become friends with the owner, helping him with tasks around his house and even inviting him to your family's home for holidays. Because he has no children, the owner says he will leave the shop to you when he passes away. Yesterday, the manager of a new eyeglass shop offered you a position that pays double your current salary. You told him you would get back to him soon.

What Would You Do? Is it unethical for you to take the job that pays better?

DISCUSS IT You may feel you have an ethical obligation to stay with the shop owner since he has offered to pass the business along to you. Would a sense of obligation affect your decision to accept the other job offer? Why or why not? In teams of three or four, discuss possible actions you could take.

The competitive global market puts added demands on workers. Businesses want to maintain their competitive advantages. These companies require workers with state-of-the-art knowledge and skills.

U Since no one can predict with certainty what new technology will appear, you should develop solid reading, writing, math, speaking, and listening skills. These skills will give you the basic tools for understanding new technology.

W When new technology appears in your workplace, get involved right away. Volunteer for training sessions or tasks that will give you hands-on training. Take technology courses at community colleges and vocational and technical centers. Many companies offer paid tuition for employees who want to take courses in areas related to their jobs. What else can you do to become a lifelong learner?

✓ Reading Check **ANALYZE** What are some ways to be a lifelong learner?

Growing in Your Job

S Continuing to update and improve your skills and knowledge will make you valuable to your employer. It may also help you earn a promotion. A **promotion** is a job advancement to a position of greater responsibility and authority. Promotions will offer new challenges. Promotions often bring increased income as well.

Who Gets Promoted?

The people who earn promotions are the people who have shown their supervisors that they can handle additional responsibility and authority. What qualities and behaviors do employers look for?

Everyday ETHICS

What Would You Do? Answer It is not unethical to take a job that pays better. Unless you have made promises to your current employer, it is wise to take a job in which you are more highly compensated—as long as you discuss the decision in advance with your current employer. However, it is also important to remember that owning your own store might lead to greater financial rewards later.

DISCUSS IT Most people in this situation would feel some sense of obligation. One good approach would be to talk to the elderly owner and explain the situation. He might offer a higher salary, bring you on as a partner, or suggest another solution.

- **Seniority** is the position or prestige you achieve by working for an employer for a sustained length of time. Greater seniority is usually thought of as indicating greater experience and dependability.
- **Knowledge and Competence** Most employers want workers who know how to do their jobs, even if the new job requires different skills. Employers also look for workers who go a step beyond this—workers who excel. These employees are likely to do well in jobs with more responsibility.
- **Willingness to Learn** Employers promote workers who show they want to increase their knowledge and skills.
- **Initiative** You will probably advance in your career if you make it clear to your supervisor that advancement is an important goal for you. A good time to talk about career goals is during your performance evaluation. Avoid giving the impression that you want to get out of your current job, however. Emphasize that you want more responsibility and challenge.
- **Perseverance** is the quality of finishing what you start. Employers want to know that you will see a job through to completion. Potential employers are especially interested in workers who can overcome obstacles to complete challenging tasks and goals.
- **Cooperativeness** When you have more responsibility, you will have to cooperate with more people. Employers want people who can get along well with others.
- **Thinking Skills** Employers promote people who can think through situations and solve problems.

🔺 **JOB GROWTH** The ability to cooperate and work well with others can help earn you a promotion—and the respect of your coworkers. *Why might employers promote individuals who work well with others?*

glencoe.com

Chapter 24 Adapting to Change **537**
Image Source RF/Getty Images

Math In Action

Salaries
An investment company offers a 35% higher salary to people with an MBA. If the salary for a person without an MBA is $45,000, what is the salary for someone with an MBA?

Starting Hint: Multiply the salary by 100 percent plus the increase: $45,000 × 1.35 = **?**

@ For more math practice, go to this book's OLC through **glencoe.com**.

TEACH (cont.)

S Skill Practice
Independent Practice
Interview Ask students to interview two adults who work full-time. Ask them to describe how they or their coworkers excel at their jobs. What makes the difference between just doing a job and "going a step beyond"? Ask students to summarize and give a brief presentation. (Interviewees may mention hard work, positive attitude, keeping skills current, team spirit, initiative, and leadership.) **L3**

Math In Action

The salary would be $45,000 × 1.35 = $60,750.

ASSESS

Review Key Terms
Have students write sentences using each key term.

Online Study Tools
Have students go to the OLC through **glencoe.com** to:
- Download **Podcast** study tools.
- Download free **Study-to-Go** content to their PDAs or cell phones.

Resources

 ExamView Assessment Suite CD allows you to print out ready-made unit and chapter tests complete with answer keys. You can also create customized tests.

▶▶ **Extend the Photo**

Caption Answer Working well with others helps workers communicate well, be effective team members, lead others, and build morale.

Discussion Workers without advanced skills often earn little more than minimum wage. Ask students to calculate how much a full-time worker would earn per year at a minimum wage of $5.50 per hour. Ask: Would you be willing to work for minimum wage? If not, what can you do to ensure that you have the skills to land a higher-paying job? (Developing specialized skills in a growing career field through education and training can help guarantee that students will earn better than minimum wage.)

RETEACH

C Critical Thinking

Predicting Ask students to imagine that they are offered a "promotion" to paid supervisor of their class, in charge of giving directions and supervising performance. What would the benefits and drawbacks of such a promotion be? How might it change their relationships with their classmates? (Benefits would include greater income and a feeling of accomplishment; drawbacks might include the resentment of former classmates and the stress of new responsibilities.)

Real-World Connection

Critical Thinking Answer You might ask the owner if he or she is interested in hearing your experiences, or suggest ways to retain key best-selling products while implementing the changes. You might also engage a loyal customer in conversation within earshot of the owner.

Do Your Own Research Surveys will vary but may include general questions such as, "I shop at Smith's Variety because _____," as well as specific ones such as "The most important thing to me is a) price; b) service; c) location; d) cleanliness; or e) other: _____."

Resources

📁 **Student Activity Workbook** Assign the Chapter 24 activities in the Student Activity Workbook.

N C L B Activity correlated to English Language Arts standards.

538

Real-World Connection

Market Analysis

The store where you work has been sold. The new owner wants to change all the displays and begin offering new merchandise. You know that many loyal customers come to the store to buy certain items that they cannot find elsewhere.

Critical Thinking How can you convince the new owner to meet customer needs?

Do Your Own Research Investigate surveys that show customer preferences. Develop a ten-question survey that will help to determine the merchandise needs of customers in a small, locally owned variety store.

- **Adaptability** Employers want workers who can adapt to new situations and a changing business.
- **Education and Training** Employers promote people who have the training needed for the new job.

Handling Your New Responsibilities

Being promoted to another job may change your work life in many ways. You will have more responsibilities. A promotion might also mean that you will supervise others. You will be responsible for both your own work and the work of others. Look at Chapter 14 of this book to remind yourself of the qualities of a good supervisor.

Be aware that as a supervisor your relationships with your former coworkers will probably change. You will be the boss. You must oversee their work and give direction. You will set goals for them and review their performance. Being a supervisor can affect your relationships with the people you supervise. Be sure you are prepared for all of these changes.

C

The 21st Century Workplace

Work and Home: A Balancing Act

When you enter the workforce, you will probably spend more than 40 hours a week at your job. Will that leave you enough time to care for yourself and your family? When you are home, will work pressures drain the energy you need for your personal life?

There is good news. More employers now offer workers the flexibility they need to balance work and personal life. Some workers telecommute from home one or two days a week. Others have flexible work schedules that allow them to pick their kids up from school, for example. Some companies provide on-site child care, assistance in finding elder care, and time off to care for a new child. Some offer full benefits to part-time workers.

Helping employees achieve a work/life balance is a good business strategy, even though it costs money. Companies that support employees' work/life balance win their employees' loyalty. They also gain reputations as great places to work, which can attract the best-qualified job candidates.

CRITICAL THINKING _____

Consider this statement from Work and Family—Allies or Enemies? *by Stewart D. Friedman and Jeffrey H. Greenhaus:* "Having a life is not so much an issue of time as it is a matter of managing the psychological interweaving of work and family." *What do you think this statement means? Do you agree or disagree? Why?*

In Your Community

Interview a business owner in your community about how to help employees achieve a good work/life balance. Interview employees about how the employer's efforts have improved their lives.

@ Extend Your Learning For links to Web sites that give tips on how to balance work and home, go to this book's OLC through **glencoe.com**.

The 21st Century Workplace

CRITICAL THINKING ANSWER This statement emphasizes that work and family both make demands on your attention, thought, and energy, and that it can be difficult to balance the amount of these resources that you give to each area of your life.

In Your Community Employers' programs will vary; smaller employers may offer greater flexibility, while larger employers may offer larger-scale programs such as child care. Employers will also differ in their degree of interest in their employees' outside lives.

Declining a Promotion

Being offered a promotion shows you have earned your employer's trust and appreciation. However, not every promotion is right for you. Perhaps the promotion requires too many personal sacrifices. For example, you might be asked to relocate or to take on responsibilities for which you are unprepared. You may know that you cannot handle the tasks involved in the new position.

It is okay to decline a promotion. Just because you are not ready for more responsibility now does not mean you will not be ready later. Most employers will respect your judgment. Avoid closing the door on future offers, however. Even if this promotion is not right, the next one might be. Let your supervisor know your specific reasons for declining a promotion. Leave your supervisor with the impression that you like your work and want to be considered for future promotions.

Section 24.1 After You Read

Review Key Concepts

1. Explain how lifelong learning can help you prepare for career and job changes.
2. Name three qualities, skills, or behaviors that can help you get promoted.
3. List the advantages and disadvantages of accepting a promotion.

Practice Academic Skills

 Mathematics

4. Igor is interested in getting an MBA (Master's in Business Administration) degree, but he can only do so by taking night classes since he has a full-time job. He has to complete 36 credits in all, and he can take only 3 credits per quarter. Since there are four quarters in a year, how long will it take?

CONCEPT Understanding Word Problems When a word problem involves multiple steps, it is helpful to outline the information before you solve it. Make a list of the information you already have and the information you are investigating, then decide how to use the information to solve the problem.

Step 1: Make a list of the information you already have: the total number of credits needed (36), the number of credits per quarter (3), and the number of quarters per year (4). Now list the piece of information you are looking for: the time needed to complete the degree.

Step 2: Start working with the information to see what you come up with: 3 credits per quarter × 4 quarters per year = 12 credits per year. Is 36 divisible by 12? Solve.

 For math help, go to the Math Appendix located at the back of this book.

NCLB *(side tab)*

Section 24.1 After You Read

Review Key Concepts

1. Lifelong learning enhances existing skills and develops new ones. It therefore helps you excel at your current job and get raises and promotions. Having top-notch skills also makes it easier to find a new job if you move or are laid off.
2. Students should mention three of the following: experience on the job (seniority), knowledge and competence, willingness to learn, initiative/ambition, perseverance, cooperativeness/interpersonal skills, thinking skills, adaptability, and appropriate education.
3. Pros of accepting a promotion include higher salary, new challenges and responsibilities, and the chance to build new skills and make more decisions. Cons include changed relationships with coworkers, possible longer hours or increased workload, and leadership tasks that may be stressful at first, such as evaluating others' work.

Practice Academic Skills

4. Igor will need three years to complete 36 courses (3 credits/quarter × 4 quarters/year = 12; 36 ÷ 12 = 3 years).

539

Section 24.1 ASSESS

After You Read
Have students complete the Section 24.1 After You Read section review.

Online Study Tools
Have students go to the OLC through **glencoe.com** to:

- Take the Section 24.1 **Practice Test**.
- Download **Podcast** study tools.
- Download free **Study-to-Go** content to their PDAs or cell phones.

CLOSE

Culminating Activity
Behavior and Career Success Ask students to write a 200-word advice column for others of their age group that uses information from this section—as well as prior knowledge and their own ideas—to explain what workers can do to excel at their jobs, earn promotions, and feel good about the work they do each day.

 Activity correlated to Mathematics standards.

Section 24.2

FOCUS

Bell Ringer Activity

Changing Jobs or Careers

Ask students to brainstorm a list of reasons someone might change not just jobs but careers, and to list the pros and cons of taking this major step. (Reasons may include a desire to grow personally and financially, or dissatisfaction with one's current career. Pros include new opportunities and personal growth; cons include risk and uncertainty.)

Resources

◉ Interactive Chalkboard

The Interactive Chalkboard CD provides visual teaching aids for this section.

@ Online Learning Center

The OLC through **glencoe.com** features chapter vocabulary, chapter summaries, and other study materials.

Preteaching

Ask students to find the definition of the key term in the text.

Graphic Organizer

Tell students to go to the OLC through **glencoe.com** for a printable graphic organizer. (Graphic organizers should include factors such as personal growth and job loss, and strategies such as using experience to make good choices.)

NCLB connects academic correlations to book content.

540

Changing Jobs or Careers

Reading Guide

Before You Read

Preview Look at the photos and figure in this section and read their captions. Write one or two sentences predicting what you will learn as you read.

Read to Learn
- Why workers may change jobs
- Strategies for changing jobs
- How to handle a job loss

D Main Idea

Learning effective strategies for making job and career changes will help to ensure that those transitions go smoothly.

Key Concepts
- Changing Your Job
- Dealing with Job Loss

Key Term
◈ notice

Academic Vocabulary

You will find these words in your reading and on your tests. Use the academic vocabulary glossary to look up their definitions if necessary.
- signal
- valid

Graphic Organizer

As you read, list different reasons why people might leave their jobs. Brainstorm strategies for finding a new job for each of these reasons. Use a chart like the one below to organize your information.

Reasons for Leaving a Job	Strategies for Finding a New Job

 Log On Go to this book's Online Learning Center through **glencoe.com** for an online version of this graphic organizer.

NCLB

Academic Standards •
English Language Arts
- Read texts to acquire new information. (NCTE 1)
- Use written language to communicate effectively. (NCTE 4)
- Use language to accomplish individual purposes. (NCTE 12)

Reading Guide

Before You Read

Explain to students that, even though the career decision they make now is important, they may change careers as they change and discover new interests. Being open to change and new opportunities can help them lead a satisfying life.

D Develop Concepts

Main Idea Discuss the main idea with students. Ask: Why is it a good idea to prepare for job change or job loss even if everything is going well at your current job? (Changes may come suddenly and unexpectedly. Also, becoming comfortable with the idea of change makes it easier to initiate positive change when necessary.)

Changing Your Job

As you know, you are likely to change employers several times during your work career. Sometimes you may choose the change because you want to seek new opportunities. At other times, the change may be forced on you by events beyond your control.

Why Change Jobs

Changing your job should never be a decision that you make lightly. Before making a change, you should analyze what is missing from your current job and what you want from a new one. Always make sure you have thought through the change carefully.

You Are Not Happy

When you are unhappy at work, a job change may be one solution. **Figure 24.1** on page 542 is a checklist of signs that may **signal** that you are not happy at your job. Use the checklist to evaluate your job situation regularly.

Before giving up on your job, consider whether there might be a way to stay and solve the problem or issue that is contributing to your unhappiness. If you decide to stay, set work goals for yourself. What do you want to achieve in your job—a pay raise, a promotion, new responsibilities or challenges? How long will you give yourself to reach your goals?

As You Read

Connect Why do you think some people change jobs often?

Creative Business Practices

RED HAT   **Web-Based Performance Reviews**

North Carolina's Red Hat, Inc. distributes a version of the Linux computer operating system and develops and manages other Internet-based technology, such as secure Web servers. It is only natural that Red Hat would have Web-based employee performance appraisals. Employees enter goals and regularly record their progress in an online performance management system. Managers log on to monitor employee goals and performance.

Because managers and employees update the system frequently, performance is tracked consistently. This makes formal yearly performance reviews more comprehensive, because managers evaluate employees based on their documented progress.

The Web-based performance management system also benefits the Red Hat company, because executives can easily see if the company is on track to meet its goals.

CRITICAL THINKING   How can a performance appraisal make employees more productive?

 Connect to the Real World   To read more about Red Hat, visit the company's Web site via the link on this book's Online Learning Center through **glencoe.com**.

---

glencoe.com   **Chapter 24**   Adapting to Change   **541**

Section 24.2

TEACH

Discussion Starter
Changing Your Job? Ask: What might be exciting about changing jobs? What might be stressful or scary? (Changing jobs involves meeting new people, learning new things, and possibly receiving better pay or more responsibilities, but it can be stressful to say goodbye to familiar people and surroundings and to launch out into the unknown.)

W Writing Support
Goals and Objectives Ask students to imagine that they are the assistant to the owner of a chain of clothing stores. They are unhappy in their job because they do mostly office tasks and are not learning about the fashion business. Ask students to write two goals they could set for themselves and two measurable, time-specific objectives for each. (One goal might be to learn more about fashion marketing; related objectives could include taking a marketing course, helping to research a marketing plan, or designing a store display.)

As You Read
Some people might change jobs often because they are unsure of their career path, or because they have unrealistic expectations of what they should be getting from their job experiences.

Resources

TeacherWorks™ Plus
The TeacherWorks software includes customizable built-in lesson plans and links to printable program resources.

Creative Business Practices

CRITICAL THINKING ANSWER Answers will vary, but students may say that frequently performing self-assessments and routinely keeping track of performance can help employees be more productive by maintaining their focus on their goals and giving them tools to rate their progress.

541

TEACH *(cont.)*

C Critical Thinking

Analyzing Ask students why they think coworkers' behavior (ignoring or becoming upset) is on the list in **Figure 24.1**. How might coworkers' behavior be a "sign of trouble"? (Conflict with coworkers may not be your fault, but it might be a sign that you are not the right fit for the job or organization. Conflict can also make a job unpleasant and stressful.)

S Skill Practice
Guided Practice

List Ask students to imagine that they are dissatisfied with their jobs and want to switch careers. How could they find out what career might be a better match? Have students work in pairs to brainstorm ideas and present them to the class. (Asking trusted colleagues, friends, and family members for advice, doing research on other career fields, conducting informational interviews, taking self-assessments, and seeking career counseling are ways to explore careers at any life stage.)

R Reading Strategy

Determining Meaning by Context Ask students to guess at the definitions of *downsizing* and *restructuring* by looking at their context in this paragraph and by taking the words apart into their two parts. (*Downsizing* means to size down, or shrink, a company's workforce by cutting jobs. *Restructuring* means to give a company a new structure, or organization, which also frequently results in job cuts.)

Figure 24.1   SIGNS OF TROUBLE

C

☐ *Is the company I work for downsizing?*
☐ *Do my coworkers ignore me or leave me out?*
☐ *Do I feel that I'm wasting my time?*
☐ *Do I find myself daydreaming about other opportunities?*
☐ *Do I feel I have outgrown my job?*
☐ *Do I feel as though I don't have a future with the company or a chance for advancement?*

EVALUATE   Answering *yes* to any of these questions may indicate that you should change jobs. *How might you solve a work problem if you planned to stay at your job?*

You Want to Grow

S   It is possible to outgrow your job. Perhaps you feel unfulfilled and unchallenged. Perhaps you have discovered that what you are doing is not really what you want to do. In these cases, a job change may be what you need.

Your Job Is Terminated

R   There are times, of course, when a job change is forced on you. Downsizing, corporate restructuring, and global economic factors have created a working world in which change is constant.

You *can* prepare for an unexpected job loss. Stay alert to signs of trouble. These include signals that your supervisor is displeased with your work or that the company is not doing well. Read news about your industry to detect industry trends.

Making the Change

When you decide to make a career or job change, you must put your decision-making skills to work. First, define your needs or wants.

Focus Your Search

Consider where you want to look for a new job. Here are three possible ways to focus your search.

 542   **Unit 7**   Lifelong Learning

EXTEND THE FIGURE   Figure 24.1

Caption Answer Ways to solve a work problem include speaking with manager(s) or coworker(s) to resolve specific causes of dissatisfaction; setting and pursuing specific goals; asking for more responsibility; and evaluating one's own attitude.

Discussion Ask students what they would do if they had a job they liked that offered no chance for advancement. Would they stay in the job, or would they take the risk of moving to a new company? (Students' ideas will vary. Liking one's job is an excellent reason to stay; however, after a few years it may be necessary to move on to avoid feelings of boredom or frustration.)

Same Job, New Company If you like what you are doing, explore similar positions with other companies. You already know you have the right skills for the job. A different company, however, may offer better opportunities.

New Job, New Company What if you have the right skills for your job but you really do not like it? That happened to Lisa Von Drasek. She was working in book sales when a layoff forced her to rethink her career goals. She suddenly realized she did not feel fulfilled in her career. She wanted a job that would allow her to make a difference in the world. When a friend suggested library school, Lisa was skeptical. After talking with several librarians, however, she signed up for a master's program in library science.

Today Lisa is a children's librarian at the Brooklyn Public Library. Every day, she helps young people discover the world of books. "The kids run up to my desk," she says. "I make a difference."

Starting Over A third possibility is to turn a hobby or interest into a career. Geoffrey Macon had spent 17 years in the banking industry. When downsizing cost him his job, he turned his career in a different direction. Geoffrey had always had a passionate interest in cycling. He became an entrepreneur, opening his own bike shop.

What Is Different This Time Around?

In this book, you have been introduced to many job search strategies. These strategies are just as useful when you are finding a new job or changing your career. You will still need to research jobs, apply for jobs, and succeed in interviews. In addition, consider the following points:

- Because you have been out in the world of work, you have more experience. What are your skills? Which tasks have you enjoyed the most?
- Consider how you can use proven skills in new ways. Suppose you have been a receptionist. Your telephone skills could be used in marketing. Your ability to remain in control when all the telephone lines are flashing could be valuable in retail sales.

▶▶ MAKING WORK ENJOYABLE This entrepreneur has turned a personal interest into a way of making a living. *Which of your interests might you turn into a business?*

HOT JOBS!

Information Retriever

With a world of information at their fingertips, Internet users can be overwhelmed by the simplest search. Using alternative banks of information, including databases such as Lexis-Nexis and libraries consisting of audiovisual and print records, information retrievers compile and analyze information.

TEACH *(cont.)*

S Skill Practice

Independent Practice

Interview Ask students to interview a working professional who has changed jobs at least once and to ask how he or she went about finding the new job(s). Ask students to write a paragraph summarizing what they learned.

W Writing Support

Business Plan Ask students to use real-world business plans (described in Chapter 4) as models to write an outline for their own original business plan. (Business plans should describe the product/service, location, employees, organization, marking plan, competition, financing, and other relevant factors.)

ASSESS

Review Key Terms

Have students write sentences using each key term.

Online Study Tools

Have students go to the OLC through **glencoe.com** to:

- Download **Podcast** study tools.
- Download free **Study-to-Go** content to their PDAs or cell phones.

STUDY TO GO

 Extend the Photo

Caption Answer Encourage students to see how almost any interest—from sports to music to animals—could inspire the idea for a business.

Discussion Ask students how they take steps toward opening their own business without leaving the security of a full-time job. (Students should understand that many steps are involved in starting one's own business. Before quitting an existing job, aspiring entrepreneurs should do research, write a business plan, practice their skills with weekend projects or freelance work, and so on.)

RETEACH

S Skill Practice
Independent Practice

List Have students list at least five people they have met or talked to before who might be able to help them find job openings, and what they might say to them if they were looking for a new job. (Contacts should be people with knowledge of and connections in the job market. Students should be polite but should honestly state that they are looking for job leads.)

✓ **Reading Check**

SUMMARIZE Three ways to approach a job change are to look for the same or similar type of job at a new organization; to look for a new type of job at the same organization; or to start over in a new direction.

Resources

📂 **Student Activity Workbook** Assign the Chapter 24 activities in the Student Activity Workbook.

ASSESS

After You Read
Have students complete the Section 24.2 After You Read section review.

Online Study Tools
Have students go to the OLC through **glencoe.com** to:
- Take the Section 24.2 **Practice Test**.
- Download **Podcast** study tools.
- Download free **Study-to-Go** content to their PDAs or cell phones.

544

▶ Vocabulary
You can find definitions in the **Key Terms** glossary and **Academic Vocabulary** glossary at the back of this book.

S

- List jobs or careers that you might like. What are the pros and cons of each? How can your skills and interests be applied to them?
- Network. You have probably built up a network of contacts at your current job. Use these contacts to explore new directions.
- Try to arrange your interviews so that you do not miss work.
- Do not burn your bridges with your present employer. You do not want to lose your current job until you have landed a new one. Besides, you never know when your old contacts will once again be valuable to you.
- When you have found a new job, give proper notice to your current employer. **Notice** is an official written statement that you are leaving the company. Most people prepare a formal letter of resignation. Businesses usually have a policy stating how long they expect employees to work after giving notice.
- Do not tell coworkers about your job hunt. Inform coworkers about the new job *after* you have given notice.
- Stay motivated at work. People will remember if you do not do your job well during your last two weeks. Leave a good impression.
- Let people outside the company know what is happening. Tell clients or other business contacts that you are leaving. Do not criticize the company, however, no matter how disappointed or angry you feel. Doing so could cost you a future job.

✓ **Reading Check** **SUMMARIZE** What are three possible ways of focusing a new job search?

 A NEW JOB A job loss can be an opportunity for positive change. *How can you prepare for job loss?*

Dealing with Job Loss

Most people are laid off or have their jobs terminated at least once during their working careers. It is almost always a difficult experience. If it happens to you, you may feel depressed, embarrassed, resentful, angry, afraid, or discouraged.

These are **valid** emotions, and you should not be ashamed of feeling them. However, do not let them overwhelm you. Try to remain positive. Look on the event as an opportunity to start over. Perhaps, you may be able to do what you have always wanted. You may even be able to earn a better income than you did before. Here are some things you should do if you get laid off:

 544 **Unit 7** Lifelong Learning

▶ Extend the Photo

Caption Answer Prepare for job loss by building your employability skills, keeping your résumé and contacts current, and being on guard for danger signs.

Discussion Explain to students that when companies look for managers, they often consider candidates from companies in completely different fields. For example, in 2006 Ford hired a new CEO who was the head of Boeing's aircraft division. Why would a company think that an airplane expert could run a car company? (Transferable skills—such as communication and management skills—are so important that employers are often willing to hire someone with these skills even if he or she comes from a totally different business.)

- **Ask Questions** Your first response to the news of the job loss may be a powerful negative emotion such as anger or sadness. As soon as you have your emotions under control, talk with your supervisor. Ask about job-search services available through your employer, severance pay (money that may be offered to employees who are dismissed), funds from profit-sharing or pension plans, payment for unused vacation time, and terms for extension of your health insurance coverage.

- **Review Your Budget** Next, review your financial situation. Figure out how much money you have to live on. Then prepare a budget to be sure you can still pay for the things you must have. Find ways to cut back on your expenses.

- **Apply for Benefits** In most cases, workers who lose their jobs can get unemployment benefits. These checks will help you get by until you find your next job. Every state has its own guidelines for applying for unemployment compensation. Most states require official documentation of your termination.

- **Look for a New Job** Update and improve your résumé. Remember that it should be brief and to the point. Ask several people to read it over, and consider having it printed professionally. Use every strategy you can think of in your job search. These include networking, contacting employment agencies, using job search Web sites, and reading the classified ads.

- **Seize the Opportunity** Stay positive as you go for interviews. A job loss can be a good opportunity to find a better job or to follow your dreams.

A job loss can put your career and your job security in your own hands. That can be to your advantage if you maintain a positive self-concept and use your self-management skills.

Career ✓ Checklist

When Changing Careers:
- ✓ Keep your long-term goals in mind.
- ✓ Remember that many successful individuals make career changes.
- ✓ Never fear moving on to a more challenging job.
- ✓ View change as a positive way to learn more about yourself and your interests.

Section 24.2 After You Read

Review Key Concepts
1. List three signs that should tell you it is time to look for another job.
2. Explain why seniority could lead to a promotion.
3. Describe the steps you would take if you lost your job.

Practice Academic Skills

 English Language Arts

4. Landing a new job can be a difficult task. However, once you are working at a new job, what strategies would you use to keep it? What would you do to ensure that you were considered a valued employee? How would you show your boss that you would be a good choice for a promotion? Write a one-page response using details and examples.

N C L B

@ Check your answers at this book's OLC through **glencoe.com**.

Resources

ExamView Assessment Suite CD allows you to print out ready-made unit and chapter tests complete with answer keys. You can also create customized tests.

CLOSE

Culminating Activity

Dealing with Change Ask students to write a paragraph describing their feelings about change and assessing their ability to cope with major changes. Do they enjoy change or find it unsettling or scary? How would they feel if they lost their job and had to find a new one? (Most people are challenged by change. Students should recognize that the best approach is to accept what is beyond their control and to focus on solutions.)

N C L B Activity correlated to English Language Arts standards.

Section 24.2 After You Read

Review Key Concepts
1. Warning signs that it is time to look for a new job include extreme stress over your current job; a feeling that you are wasting your time; conflicts with or exclusion by coworkers; dreading going to work; and lack of advancement or growth potential.
2. Working for an employer for a sustained amount of time often results in increased experience and improved skills and knowledge, which employers look for when they promote workers.
3. Steps to follow after a job loss include coping with emotions, reviewing your budget, applying for benefits, and looking for a new job.

Practice Academic Skills
4. Keeping a job requires many of the same skills and qualities as landing a job—working hard, building knowledge and skills, showing perseverance, ambition, and initiative, solving problems in creative ways, showing a positive attitude, and getting along with others and earning their respect.

CAREER SPOTLIGHT

Career Cluster: Information Technology

FOCUS

Discussion Starter
Information Technology
Lead a discussion about the various careers relating to the Internet and World Wide Web. For example, what kinds of workers might be needed to build a large Web site? (Web developers, programmers, designers, multimedia artists, writers and editors, marketers, quality assurance testers, network administrators.)

TEACH

W Writing Support
Independent Practice
Interview Ask students to interview someone who works in information technology. Have them ask the questions in the Career Spotlight and inquire about the outlook for computer careers in their geographic area. (Answers will vary but should follow the interview format of the Career Spotlight.)

C Critical Thinking
Creativity and Computers
Thomson says that most of his job is coding (programming) rather than art or design. Ask students why he nonetheless advises them to "concentrate on your creative skills"? (Creativity is necessary not only in art and design, but also in developing solutions to problems and coming up with new ideas.)

Ben Thompson
Web Developer

Q: Describe your job.
A: I enhance existing Web sites and develop new ones by translating graphic designs into a Web format. I work closely with other developers, Web designers, editors, marketers, and copywriters.

Q: Describe a typical workday.
A: I start with a review of current tasks, anything from creating one small component to several different pages for multiple Web sites. I might make minor updates to pages, develop full-blown Web sites, or set up e-mail blasts. I meet with clients in order to fully understand the requirements and specifications of a project, then develop a plan. Next, actual coding and development begins. Development is usually a combination of designing and programming. A typical day consists of gathering requirements, designing, developing, and testing.

Q: What skills are most important to you in your job?
A: Creativity, critical thinking, and problem solving are the most vital skills.

Q: What is your key to success?
A: Staying current on new technologies by knowing a little bit about everything. As a Web developer, you create Web sites and applications that are compliant across many different platforms using many different computer languages.

Q: What training and preparation do you recommend for students?
A: Start learning today! You don't want to be left behind, so it's important to start learning about current technology in order to have a better understanding of the newest trends. Be sure to concentrate on your creative skills as well as your problem-solving and programming skills.

Q: What are some ways you recommend students prepare for this career?
A: Get a solid understanding of the fundamentals of programming and design. If classes aren't available, there are a number of books, both in-depth and reference, that will quickly get you on your way to creating your first Web site. Surf the Internet. With the growing number of blogs, newsgroups, message boards and Web sites, it's very easy to find online tutorials and advice that can help you get started.

Q: What skills are helpful in preparing for your career?
A: Math, problem solving, critical thinking, communication, and teamwork are all essential. It's also important to be able to communicate clearly with your client in order to fully understand and meet their requirements.

Q: What do you like most about your work?
A: Diversity and creativity are what I enjoy most about Web development. The Internet is constantly growing and expanding. As technology continues to drive change, new Web sites pop up every day and existing Web sites require upgrades and constant maintenance. It's a nice sense of job security knowing that there's always work to be done.

 For more about Career Clusters, go to this book's OLC through **glencoe.com**.

NO CHILD LEFT BEHIND

Teaching Tip
In career and life skills courses, one way to help students meet the NCLB goal of proficiency with technology is to create activities in which students use technology tools and resources to manage and communicate personal and career information, such as budgets, schedules, contact lists, and correspondence and research about careers.

Sample Question Ask students to use spreadsheet software or the scheduling feature of an e-mail program to create an electronic schedule for the next week that includes their class schedule, to-do items, and deadlines for homework assignments.

- **Education or Training:** A bachelor's degree is necessary for many jobs in this field; however, some jobs may require only a two-year degree. Relevant work experience is important. For more technically complex jobs, persons with graduate degrees are preferred. Because technological advances occur so rapidly in this field, continuous training is needed.

- **Academic Skills Required** English Language Arts, Mathematics, Science, Social Studies

- **Technology Needed** Computers and computer-specific technical knowledge; knowledge of any custom software and database systems in use by the client; knowledge of photo, graphics, and Web-editing software.

- **Aptitudes, Abilities, and Skills** Communication and other interpersonal skills, art and graphic design skills, creativity, critical thinking, and problem-solving skills

- **Workplace Safety** Like other workers who spend long periods in front of a computer terminal typing on a keyboard, Web developers are susceptible to eyestrain, back discomfort, and hand and wrist problems such as carpal tunnel syndrome or cumulative trauma disorder.

- **Career Outlook** Jobs as Web developers and specialty computer scientists are expected to grow much faster than average over the next ten years.

- **Career Path** Web developers work on a specific part, or every aspect of, day-to-day creation and design of a Web site. Related jobs include webmasters, network systems and data communication analysts, data administrators, telecommunication analysts, theorists, researchers, and inventors.

ASSESS

Make Connections
Ask students to look at the HTML code that drives a Web page. Tell them to access a Web page in a Web browser and then use the "View Source" tool to see the code. What personal qualities and academic skills do they think would be required to write code like this? Why? (Patience, attention to detail, logic, problem-solving skills, and the ability to follow instructions and troubleshoot errors are necessary to write computer code.)

CLOSE

Culminating Activity
Change and Career Clusters Within every career cluster, some jobs are growing faster than others. Ask students to choose the career cluster that interests them and to report on which jobs or job areas are growing and which are shrinking or growing less quickly, and why. For example, the demand for software engineers is growing much more rapidly than the demand for workers in computer factories, due to globalization and increased efficiency. (Reports will vary by career cluster but should be based on reliable data such as that in the *Occupational Outlook Handbook*.)

NCLB

Academic Skills Required to Complete Tasks

Tasks	English Language Arts	Mathematics	Science	Social Studies
Meet with clients	★	★		★
Problem-solve on current projects	★	★	★	
Create code		★	★	
Graphic design work		★	★	
Test the results of work		★	★	

Critical Thinking

Do you think being a good "team player" is important in the field of Web development? Why or why not?

NCLB This chart relates academic skills such as English Language Arts, Mathematics, Science, Social Studies, and World Languages to specific tasks that are performed for the job featured in the Career Spotlight feature.

Critical Thinking

A Web site requires the work and input of a whole range of workers, from writers to graphic artists. It is therefore crucial to respect others' work and ideas, and to get along with coworkers of different skills and backgrounds.

Key Terms and Academic Vocabulary Review

1. Students should use each of the key terms and academic vocabulary terms in a sentence. A sample answer might read: "One's interests, abilities, and lifestyle goals are *significant* factors in the choice of a career."

Review Key Concepts

2. Planning for the future, anticipating change, and being a lifelong learner are important ways to prepare for the future. You can control your own career and job security by choosing a career that is growing, by spending the time to find a job that is the right match, by changing jobs and careers when necessary, by excelling at your job, and by learning to deal effectively with job loss.

3. Skills, qualities, and behaviors that lead to promotions include experience on the job (seniority), knowledge and competence, willingness to learn, initiative/ambition, perseverance, cooperativeness/interpersonal skills, thinking skills, adaptability, and appropriate education.

4. Workers may change jobs because they are not happy or well-suited to their current job, because they are not growing in their current job, because they want a new direction, because the job is terminated, or for other personal reasons.

5. Strategies for changing jobs include finding a similar type of job at a new organization, finding a new job within the same organization, or starting over by choosing a new career or starting a new business.

6. Handle a job loss by dealing with the mixed and powerful emotions that may follow, assessing what funds,

benefits, or services may be available to help you, preparing a budget to get through the crisis, and looking for a new job.

Critical Thinking

7. Tracking employment trends helps you manage your career because it shows you which industries and career areas are growing and which are shrinking, which skills are in increasing demand, and which technologies are growing in importance. This helps you decide which

CHAPTER SUMMARY

Section 24.1

You can prepare for the future by managing your own career. Many businesses are downsizing, or eliminating jobs to cut costs. Some employees lose their jobs, and others gain new responsibilities. Businesses help employees meet the demands of the workplace by offering training and sometimes paying for education. Employers look for many different qualities and behaviors when selecting employees to promote, including competence, willingness to learn, initiative, and adaptability. Getting a promotion may change your relationships with coworkers. If a promotion is not right for you, decline it. Keep your options open, however. Let your employer know you are open to future offers.

Section 24.2

You may choose to change jobs for a number of reasons, including unhappiness in your job, the desire to grow, or termination of your job. Focus your job search. You might look for a job like the one you have but with a different company. You might look for a job that will use your current skills but in a different field. You might look for a job that involves a hobby or personal interest. If you lose your job, first find out what your former employer is offering to you at termination. Then assess your financial situation, and arrange for unemployment benefits. Update and improve your résumé.

Key Terms and Academic Vocabulary Review

1. Use each of these key terms and academic vocabulary words in a sentence.

Key Terms
- downsizing (p. 535)
- promotion (p. 536)
- seniority (p. 537)
- perseverance (p. 537)
- notice (p. 544)

Academic Vocabulary
- significant (p. 535)
- signal (p. 541)
- valid (p. 544)

Review Key Concepts

2. Describe ways to prepare for the future, explaining how your career and your job security are in your hands.
3. Identify qualities, skills, and behaviors that often lead to promotions.
4. Explain why workers may change jobs.
5. Describe strategies for changing jobs.
6. Explain how to handle a job loss.

Critical Thinking

7. Explain How can tracking employment trends help you manage your own career?
8. Evaluate Imagine that you find a new job, and you know that you will never want to work for your former employer again. Why is it still a good policy not to criticize your former employer?

skills to build, which industries to choose or avoid, and which career areas to select.

8. Employers do not like to hire employees who are bitter toward or critical of past employers. You may also need references from your former employer, and you may cross paths with former coworkers in future jobs.

Real-World Skills and Applications

Monitoring and Correcting Performance

9. Creating an Employee Evaluation Imagine you work for a growing electronics company. Your boss has asked you to create an employee evaluation that can be used to assess your coworkers' performance. Use the Internet to research employee evaluations. Then write a one-page evaluation that your boss could use to give employees feedback on their performance in your company.

Technology Applications

10. Creating a Résumé Use the résumé wizard in your word-processing program to develop a résumé describing your work and volunteer experiences and skills. Include clear descriptions of accomplishments. Your résumé should be detailed enough to give an employer a clear picture of what kind of worker you are.

Interpersonal Skills

11. Exercising Leadership You supervise a coworker who is also a good friend. She has begun coming to work late, leaving early, and not performing as well on the job as before. When you talk with her, she says: "What's the big deal? I thought you were my friend. You sure have changed since you became a boss." In a few paragraphs, explain how you would handle the situation, including what you would say to your friend. Then team up with a classmate. Role-play your response with you as the supervisor and your classmate as the friend. Also, role-play your classmate's response. Discuss the pros and cons of both scenarios.

12. **Brainstorming for Interviews** Take a few moments to brainstorm how you would explain to a potential employer why you chose to leave your last job. Team up with a classmate and share your answers. Discuss why you think the explanations would or would not convince the employer that you left for good reasons. Share your responses with the class.

13. **Declining a Promotion**
Situation You work as a senior accountant at a large advertising firm. You have worked hard and have done a good job for your employer over the past five years. The president of the company is impressed with your job performance and would like to make you the company's controller. Although you are flattered by the offer, you are happy with your current position and do not want the added responsibility of being in charge of the company's finances.
Activity With a partner, role-play a situation in which you refuse the president's promotion. Show a good way and a poor way to decline a promotion. Present your role plays to the class.
Evaluation You will be evaluated based on how well you meet the following performance indicators:
- Present valid, positive reasons for declining the offer of a promotion.
- Conduct yourself maturely and professionally during your conversation with your employer.

---

emphasize that the conflict is not personal and that he or she is also concerned about the friend's advancement and job security at the company.

ACTIVE LEARNING

12. Reasons for leaving jobs vary. However, employers are more likely to be comfortable with reasons that show a desire for growth such as, "I am ready for more responsibility," "I would like to focus more on _____, which your company specializes in," or "Because I realized that I would be a better match for a job in _____" than with negative reasons such as "The pay was too low," "It was boring," or "I didn't like my boss."

ROLE PLAY

13. Role plays should depict a mature, reasonable and courteous decline of a job promotion, as well as a poor approach to declining a promotion (disrespectful, confused, or abrupt). Students should exhibit preparation and poise in presenting both role-play activities to the class.

Real-World Skills and Applications

9. Effective employee evaluations describe employees' work over a given time period, assess its quality, and compare it against goals set in the previous year's evaluation or laid out in the employee's job description. Effective evaluations should also list goals for the coming year and outline specific steps employees should take to improve their work or skills.

10. Résumés should focus on the positive and be concise, organized, and well-written. Encourage students to follow the guidelines discussed in Chapter 6.

11. The new boss might explain to the coworker and friend that because her position has changed, she is now responsible for overseeing employees' work, and that it would not be fair to hold her friends to different standards than she does other employees. He or she might also

Academic Skills in the Workplace

14. Letters should follow the format and guidelines presented for cover letters in Chapter 6. Letters should make a strong case for why the writer is changing careers, should reflect knowledge of the addressee's industry and company, and should demonstrate how skills developed in the old career are relevant to the new one.

15. Natalia's salary would increase 40 percent if she takes the new job ($50,400 ÷ $36,000 = 1.4 or 140%; 140% − 100% = 40%).

16. Like organisms adapting to their changing environment, workers must adapt to the changing workplace. This means keeping up with economic and industry news to learn which careers and jobs are growing and shrinking; proactively planning job or career changes to take advantage of new interests and opportunities; learning new technologies; and developing transferable skills that will be useful in any job or industry.

Academic Skills in the Workplace

 English Language Arts

14. Writing a Letter of Introduction

You have decided to change careers and are sending out letters and résumés to potential employers. Develop a letter introducing yourself, explaining your interest in this particular employer, describing your strongest skills with examples and one of your accomplishments. The letter should be no more than one page, and typed and formatted as a formal business letter. Remember, employers do not have a lot of time to sift through résumés, so the letter should be short and interesting and should leave the reader wanting to learn more about you.

 Mathematics

15. Increasing Salary

Natalia currently makes $36,000 per year. She discovers that she is qualified for a job that pays $50,400 per year. If she were to get this new job, what would her percent increase in salary be?

CONCEPT **Percent Increase** To calculate percent increase, you can divide, but remember that an increase is only the part greater than 1.

Starting Hint Divide the new salary by the current one: $50,400 ÷ $36,000. Remember, this is the new salary's percent of the current one. To figure out the percent increase only, subtract 1.0 (100%).

 Science

16. Evolution

Evolution explains how organisms adapt to an environment over time. Those with genetic traits that help them to survive and produce offspring are more likely to have their traits represented in the next generation. Those with traits that are not fit for the environment do not survive or produce offspring. Therefore, those traits diminish or disappear in the next generations. The economy is also an ever-changing environment to which people must adapt by developing new knowledge and learning new skills. Sometimes there can be major changes, where whole industries that were once useful are no longer as useful or simply disappear. On the other hand, with change, there are always opportunities to develop new businesses and skills. What are some ways you can adapt to changes in the world of work?

STANDARDIZED TEST PRACTICE

TIMED WRITING

Directions Read the following prompt and write a full essay using details and examples to illustrate your points.

> **Test-Taking Tip** Plan out your essay before you begin writing. Jot down the main points or details you want to focus on in the margins of your test. Refer to these points frequently as you write. This will help you remain focused.

Prompt: Employers are often looking for people who are natural leaders to become the leaders (supervisor and managers) within their company. Write an essay describing a person you know who is a natural leader. Vividly describe this person's abilities and accomplishments using examples and details. Your reader should feel as if they know this person after reading your essay.

STANDARDIZED TEST PRACTICE

Answer

Answers will vary but should give details—such as a description of the person's personality, speech, or sense of humor—that bring the figure to life.

Test-Taking Strategies

Whether your students have a standardized test coming up in a few days or a few weeks, this test-prep tip will help students relax and do their best.

Test Format Introduce students to standard essay formats, such as the five-paragraph essay (introduction, three supporting paragraphs, and conclusion), the one-paragraph short answer, and the three-paragraph essay (short introduction, longer body paragraph, and short conclusion).

Writing Skills Practice

17. Essay Introductions An essay introduction can encourage readers to continue reading further.

Practice Develop or revise an introduction for the standardized test practice essay prompt. Include a thesis statement. Follow the steps below to develop an introduction:

- Identify your topic and develop interest. Attract your reader's interest by defining an important term, starting with a story or interesting quote, asking a challenging or thought-provoking question, or making a dramatic statement.
- Identify the main points you plan to cover. Give your reader a taste of what you are going talk about in the body of your essay.
- State your thesis. The reader should know your opinion on your subject after reading your introduction. In this case, it would be why you think a particular person is a natural leader.

Net Connection

18. Conduct an Interview Talk to a person who was laid off or downsized at some point. Ask the person about matters relevant to his or her loss of employment, including warning signs and severance pay. Ask your interviewee about strategies that he or she used to survive financially. Record your findings in your journal.

 Log On Visit this book's OLC through **glencoe.com** for links to help you research the economic factors that trigger companies to lay off workers or downsize. List actions that some major corporations take to ease the blow of downsizing.

 Reading Connection

Go to this book's Online Learning Center through **glencoe.com** for a list of reading suggestions.

Personal Academic and Career Portfolio

Creating a Technology Skills Chart

Much of the competition in today's job market is driven by employees who have experience using computers and other technology. Many kinds of jobs and careers also require proficiency using job-specific technology. As you grow in your job and gain new experience, you should keep track of any new technology or technology applications you learn to use.

Knowing your technology experience will help you when you ask for a promotion or plan to change jobs.

Make a spreadsheet or chart of the technology you know how to use.

- Make a chart with three columns.
- In the first column, list the name of the technology.
- In the second column, give the definition of the technology, and write a brief description of how you use the technology in your job.
- In the third column, explain how much experience you have with the technology. You could also list any formal training you have had with the technology.
- Create a new section for your portfolio, using a divider for a hard copy of your spreadsheet.
- Add the section to your table of contents.
- Update your portfolio as you gain more technology experience.

 Portfolio Help Go to the *Succeeding in the World of Work* OLC through **glencoe.com** for help developing your portfolio.

Writing Skills Practice

17. Introductions should include a strong statement of opinion about why the subject is a natural leader and list (without details) a few reasons why. The first sentence should grab the reader's attention.

Net Connection

18. Interviewees' experiences may vary. Many people are taken by surprise by layoffs; others may know well in advance that they will lose their jobs, or may sense that layoffs are impending but believe that their job will be safe. Financial strategies for coping with layoffs will also vary, but might include relying on emergency savings, taking loans, dramatically reducing expenses, or taking part-time work.

Resources

ExamView Assessment Suite CD allows you to print out ready-made unit and chapter tests complete with answer keys. You can also create customized tests.

WorkKeys

WorkKeys® is a job skills assessment program. For information on leveled assessment for Problem-Solving Skills (Applied Mathematics; Applied Technology; Locating Information; and Observation), go to the WorkKeys link on this book's OLC through **glencoe.com**.

Personal Academic and Career Portfolio

Maintaining a Portfolio

Remind students that employers are looking for workers who can prove that they have the skills to hit the ground running in a new job. This is where the portfolio comes in. Tell students that their **Personal Academic and Career Portfolios** should include at least three types of technology information: research about technology trends and issues relevant to their desired career field; detailed descriptions of technology tools they have mastered (such as the Technology Skills Chart outlined here); and examples of their best work in technology, such as a spreadsheet, a database, a brochure, or a Web page or site.

Chapter Resources Planning Guide with Activities and Features

Section	Features	Activities
Section 25.1 Setting Up Your Own Household	Everyday Ethics (p. 556) Tech Savvy (p. 558)	Before You Read (p. 554) Graphic Organizer (p. 554) As You Read (p. 555) After You Read (p. 559)
Section 25.2 Work, Family, and Community	Real-World Connection (p. 563) Science in Action (p. 564) Career Checklist (p. 565) Creative Business Practices (p. 565) 21st Century Workplace (p. 566)	Before You Read (p. 560) Graphic Organizer (p. 560) As You Read (p. 562) After You Read (p. 567)

NCLB Activities, information, and skills practice will help your students attain No Child Left Behind proficiency. Students will improve their abilities in the following academic standards areas:

Academic Standards Correlations

Discipline	Standard	Feature/Activity
English Language Arts	**NCTE 1** Read texts to acquire new information.	Everyday Ethics (p. 556) Creative Business Practices (p. 565)
	NCTE 4 Use written language to communicate effectively.	Tech Savvy (p. 558) After You Read (p. 567)
	NCTE 8 Use information resources to gather information and create and communicate knowledge.	Real-World Connection (p. 563) Writing Skills Practice (p. 573)
	NCTE 9 Develop an understanding of diversity in language use across cultures.	21st Century Workplace (p. 566)
Mathematics	**Number and Operation:** Compute fluently and make reasonable estimates	After You Read (p. 559)
	Number and Operation: Understand meanings of operations and how they relate to one another **Problem Solving:** Build new mathematical knowledge through problem solving	Academic Skills in the Workplace (p. 572)
Science	**Physical Science:** Motions and forces	Science in Action (p. 564)
	Life Science: Life cycles of organisms	Academic Skills in the Workplace (p. 572)

CORRELATIONS The charts show the 21st Century Skills, foundation skills, and workplace competencies that students develop as they work in this chapter.

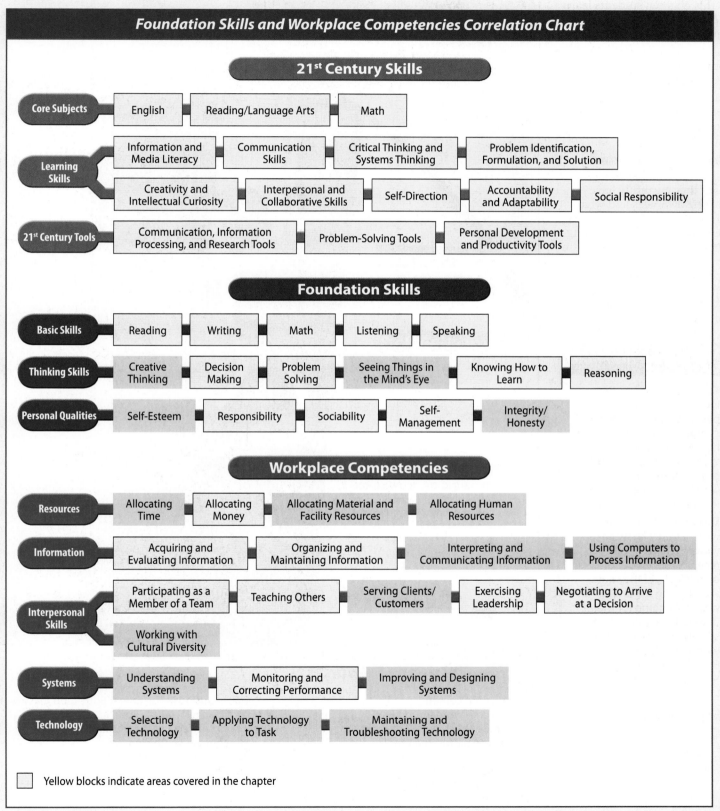

Foundation Skills and Workplace Competencies Correlation Chart

21st Century Skills

Core Subjects
- English
- Reading/Language Arts
- Math

Learning Skills
- Information and Media Literacy
- Communication Skills
- Critical Thinking and Systems Thinking
- Problem Identification, Formulation, and Solution
- Creativity and Intellectual Curiosity
- Interpersonal and Collaborative Skills
- Self-Direction
- Accountability and Adaptability
- Social Responsibility

21st Century Tools
- Communication, Information Processing, and Research Tools
- Problem-Solving Tools
- Personal Development and Productivity Tools

Foundation Skills

Basic Skills
- Reading
- Writing
- Math
- Listening
- Speaking

Thinking Skills
- Creative Thinking
- Decision Making
- Problem Solving
- Seeing Things in the Mind's Eye
- Knowing How to Learn
- Reasoning

Personal Qualities
- Self-Esteem
- Responsibility
- Sociability
- Self-Management
- Integrity/Honesty

Workplace Competencies

Resources
- Allocating Time
- Allocating Money
- Allocating Material and Facility Resources
- Allocating Human Resources

Information
- Acquiring and Evaluating Information
- Organizing and Maintaining Information
- Interpreting and Communicating Information
- Using Computers to Process Information

Interpersonal Skills
- Participating as a Member of a Team
- Teaching Others
- Serving Clients/Customers
- Exercising Leadership
- Negotiating to Arrive at a Decision
- Working with Cultural Diversity

Systems
- Understanding Systems
- Monitoring and Correcting Performance
- Improving and Designing Systems

Technology
- Selecting Technology
- Applying Technology to Task
- Maintaining and Troubleshooting Technology

☐ Yellow blocks indicate areas covered in the chapter

Chapter Overview
Introduce the Chapter
In this chapter, students learn the basics of living an independent and balanced life.

Section 25.1 explores the steps involved in finding and setting up one's own home.

Section 25.2 encourages students to find ways to balance work, family, and community life.

Build Background
Ask students what roles and tasks they currently have in their own lives and what strategies they use to balance their time and energy among them. (Students may mention school, job, family, friends, and extracurricular activities, and strategies such as prioritizing, scheduling, and making compromises.)

 Exploring the Photo

Caption Answer Being independent is exciting because it means being in charge of your life and your home. Leaving home and the familiar environment of school and entering the workforce may also be challenging and lonely at times.

Discussion Ask students whether they know any young people who have recently moved out on their own. What did they enjoy about going it alone? What was challenging for them? (Students may have friends, siblings, or other relatives who live independently. Balancing freedom with financial pressures is likely to be a common theme.)

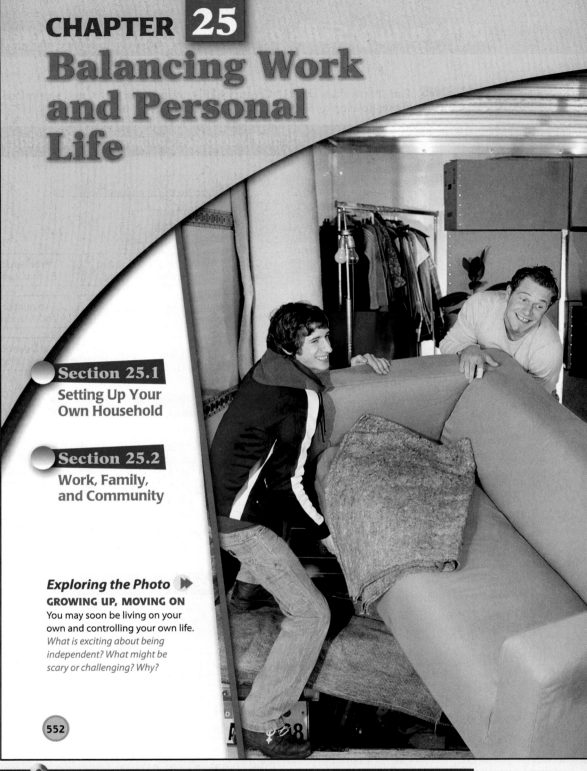

CHAPTER 25

Balancing Work and Personal Life

Section 25.1
Setting Up Your Own Household

Section 25.2
Work, Family, and Community

Exploring the Photo ▶▶
GROWING UP, MOVING ON
You may soon be living on your own and controlling your own life. *What is exciting about being independent? What might be scary or challenging? Why?*

552

Classroom Resources

- 📁 Student Edition
- 📁 Teacher Wraparound Edition
- 📁 Student Activity Workbook with Academic Integration
- 📁 Student Activity Workbook with Academic Integration TAE
- 📁 *Fast File,* Unit 7 Resources

- 📁 Inclusion in the Career Education Classroom
- 💿 TeacherWorks™ Plus
- 💿 *ExamView Assessment Suite*
- 💿 Interactive Chalkboard
- 💿 Interactive Student Edition
- 🖱 Online Student Edition
- 🖱 Online Learning Center (OLC) with Podcasts

Chapter Objectives

After completing this chapter, you will be able to:

- **Explain** how to choose a place to live and set up a household.
- **Describe** how to organize your living space and establish good housekeeping habits.
- **Identify** ways to balance your work and personal life.
- **Name** some company policies that help employees balance work and family life.
- **Explain** your role as a citizen and identify ways to participate in the community.

Writing Activity / Personal Career Notebook

You may soon be living on your own. What are the most exciting and interesting aspects of this change? Which aspects do you expect to find most difficult? Why? Write a one-page journal entry describing your ideas and feelings.

Get Motivated! Talk to several adults about their experiences when they first lived on their own. How did they manage the change? Do their experiences change your feelings and ideas about living on your own? Record what you learned in a journal entry.

Chapter 25 Balancing Work and Personal Life **553**

Review the Objectives
Introduce the chapter by reviewing the chapter objectives:

Section 25.1 Objectives
Explain how to choose a place to live and set up a household. (Create a budget, research and evaluate rentals, have utilities connected, arrange for your mail to be forwarded, and obtain furniture and essentials.)

Describe how to organize your living space and establish good housekeeping habits. (Measure available space and note the position of windows and outlets. Establish a schedule for necessary household tasks.)

Section 25.2 Objectives
Identify ways to balance your work and personal life. (Prioritize roles, make compromises, uphold commitments, and take advantage of work-life benefits.)

Name some company policies that help employees balance work and family life. (Flextime and telecommuting, on-site child care, paid or unpaid leave, life skills training, and education assistance.)

Explain your role as a citizen and identify ways to participate in the community. (Be informed, vote, and volunteer.)

Writing Activity / Personal Career Notebook Answer Guide

Students should be realistic about the psychological and financial challenges of independence. They may be excited about having their own space, managing their own schedule, and feeling a sense of pride in supporting themselves.

Get Motivated! Experiences may include challenges such as making ends meet, as well as exciting experiences such as making new friends and enjoying a new sense of freedom.

Setting Up Your Own Household

 Bell Ringer Activity

Setting Up Your Own Household

Ask students to work in pairs to brainstorm all the ingredients of a household—from dishes to telephone service—and to rank each as "necessary," "optional at first," or "luxury." (Lists will vary, but students should be realistic about what is a necessity and what is a luxury.)

 Resources

Interactive Chalkboard
The Interactive Chalkboard CD provides visual teaching aids for this section.

@ Online Learning Center
The Online Learning Center (OLC) through **glencoe.com** features chapter vocabulary, chapter summaries, and other study materials.

Preteaching

Ask students to define the key terms and explain how each term relates to the theme of setting up a household.

Graphic Organizer

Tell students to go to the OLC through **glencoe.com** for a printable graphic organizer. (Graphic organizers should mention basics such as looking for rentals and assembling furniture and supplies.)

NCLB connects academic correlations to book content.

Reading Guide

Before You Read

Preview Choose a Key Term or Academic Vocabulary word that is new to you. Write it on a piece of paper. When you find it in the text, write down the definition.

Read to Learn
- How to choose a place to live and set up a household
- How to organize your living space
- How to establish good housekeeping habits

D ### Main Idea
Choosing, organizing, and maintaining your living space are important life skills.

Key Concepts
- Building an Independent Life
- Settling In

Key Terms
◇ life stage
◇ utilities
◇ commute
◇ security deposit

Academic Vocabulary
You will find this word in your reading and on your tests. Use the academic vocabulary glossary to look up its definition if necessary.
■ compatible

Graphic Organizer
As you read, write notes about what you need to do to set up your own household. Use a checklist like the one shown to help organize the information.

To Do to Create My Own Place
- Create a monthly budget ☑
-
-

 Log On Go to this book's Online Learning Center through **glencoe.com** for an online version of this graphic organizer.

NCLB ### Academic Standards • • • • • • • • • • • • • • • •

English Language Arts
- Read texts to acquire new information. (NCTE 1)
- Use written language to communicate effectively. (NCTE 4)

Mathematics
- Compute fluently and make reasonable estimates

Reading Guide

Before You Read

Tell students that they have many living options once they enter the workforce. They may choose to continue to live at home, to live alone, or to live with one or more roommates, among other options. Each has advantages and disadvantages, which this chapter will describe.

D ### Develop Concepts

Main Idea Discuss the main idea with students. Ask: What is home, besides a place to sleep and eat? What does a person's home symbolize? (Some students may feel that a home is an expression of one's identity, personality, and values.)

Building an Independent Life

As you plan your future, it is important to think about your personal life, too. For most people, landing your first full-time job is part of entering a new life stage. A **life stage** is a period in your physical and emotional journey through life. After infancy and childhood, most people pass through the following life stages:

- *Adolescence* is a stage of transition between childhood and adulthood. During adolescence, you work to find your own identity and to decide what kind of person you want to be. Adolescence can end at age 18, or later.
- *Early adulthood* is a time to get established. This is when you start your career and build relationships, often with a life partner. We may be in this stage until we are in our 30s or 40s.
- *Middle adulthood* is a phase of focus on work and family. Success comes from feeling in charge of your life and on track toward your long-term goals. Middle adulthood can last until the 50s or early 70s, when it gives way to later adulthood.

Beginning your career is one big step from adolescence into early adulthood. Creating your own home is another. This is one of the most exciting steps you will ever take.

A Place of Your Own

You may believe you are ready to move into a place of your own. Before you decide, weigh the advantages and disadvantages of living at home.

Living with family or guardians is usually much less expensive than living independently. Even if you pay room and board, this will still probably be less expensive than renting an apartment. You may also save money on furniture, food, and laundry. On the negative side, living at home means you will not be able to make all your own decisions, and you may wish you had more privacy.

What are the advantages and disadvantages of having your own place? Being more independent is one advantage. The challenge of being on your own, the enjoyment of fixing up your own place, and a sense of pride and responsibility are important advantages, too.

What are some disadvantages of having your own home? You will have to pay the monthly rent on time each month. You may need to adjust to being alone more, or you may need to spend time finding a **compatible** roommate.

Look for a roommate who shares your preferences on important matters—noise or quiet, late nights or early mornings, hip-hop or classical. Prevent disagreements by talking honestly before you move in. Make sure you both know what costs you will face and how you will share them.

As You Read

Connect How have you grown and changed physically, emotionally, and intellectually over the past five years?

 CHOOSING WISELY

When you become independent, you will need to budget wisely to make ends meet. *What can you do if you cannot afford a place where you would feel comfortable and safe?*

TEACH

Discussion Starter

Building an Independent Life Ask students to explain the difference between *adolescent* and *adult*. How will they know when they are adults and no longer adolescents? (Students may cite emotional maturity, financial independence, taking responsibility for one's own decisions, and other factors.)

C Critical Thinking

Analyzing Self Ask students if they have figured out what kind of person they want to be—what values are most important to them and what main goals they want to pursue. (Students' ideas will vary; encourage them to think about the basic values discussed in Chapter 2.)

R Reading Strategy

Activating Prior Knowledge Ask students how they define independence. (Independence may look different for each student, but common elements include earning money, making one's own decisions, and taking responsibility for one's own life.)

As You Read

Students may cite changes such as growing physically, developing emotional maturity, and developing stronger thinking skills.

 Resources

TeacherWorks™ Plus The TeacherWorks software includes customizable built-in lesson plans and links to printable program resources.

Extend the Photo

Caption Answer Possibilities include living with a roommate or staying at home to save money for a more suitable apartment in the future.

Discussion Ask students to think of some ways they could make themselves and their homes safer when living alone. (Students may mention using or installing security features such as locks and window bars, getting to know neighbors, being aware of crime spots in the neighborhood, and alerting police to any suspicious activity.)

C₁ Critical Thinking

Connecting to Financial Literacy Most financial advisors recommend spending no more than 30 percent of one's net income on rent or mortgage. Ask students to calculate how much they would need to earn (after taxes) to afford the average one-bedroom apartment in their local area.

C₂ Critical Thinking

Evaluating Ask: How can you evaluate whether a neighborhood is safe? (Check the local crime statistics, ask residents of the neighborhood, talk to officers at the local police station, or visit the neighborhood at night to check for suspicious activity.)

S Skill Practice

Independent Practice

Apply Technology Ask students to use the Internet to find three local listings for one-bedroom apartments in a neighborhood where they would like to live, then to compare features and price, and describe which is the best value. (Students should compare rentals along criteria such as location, amenities, square footage, rent and fees, and so on.)

Everyday ETHICS

YOU AND YOUR LANDLORD

What can happen when a tenant disobeys a landlord?

PET PEEVE You and a friend recently found an apartment together and are moving in this weekend. When you first moved in, the landlord asked you if youhad any pets, and you signed a lease saying you did not. But now, your roommate has decided to keep her cat. You thought the cat was staying at her parents' house, but she said she would miss him too much. She says that he's a quiet cat and the landlord will never know he's there.

What Would You Do? What do you tell your roommate?

DISCUSS IT If the landlord needs to enter your apartment to repair anything, he might see the cat. What might the landlord do? Discuss the options with a partner.

▶ Vocabulary

You can find definitions in the **Key Terms** glossary and **Academic Vocabulary** glossary at the back of this book.

Budget, Research, Decide

Before you decide where to live, prepare a budget. Estimate how much it will cost each month to live on your own or with a roommate. Use your budget to help you identify places you can afford.

Budget not only for the monthly rent, but also related costs, such as utilities. **Utilities** are services for your home that can include electricity, heat, sanitation, and water. Utility costs vary widely. Some utilities may be included in your monthly rent—look in the advertisement or ask the landlord to be sure. You may also need to pay for telephone and Internet service.

You should also consider how long it will take you to commute to work.

Find the Right Place for You

You can find vacant rentals online, in your local newspaper, and by looking for "For Rent" signs in neighborhoods that you like. As you look for a home, ask yourself these questions:

- Is the neighborhood safe?
- Is it close to public transportation? Is it close to my friends and family?
- Is it near places I go frequently, such as a park, a gym, and the grocery store?
- How far will I have to commute? To **commute** means to travel to get to a job or place of work.

Remember one of the most important elements you have learned about decision making: As a first step, gather all the information you can. Before deciding on a place to live, inspect it thoroughly. **Figure 25.1** is a useful checklist of things to look for. Use it to compare places and to choose the one that is best for you.

Everyday ETHICS

What Would You Do? Answer Students should tell the roommate that having the cat at the apartment is too great a risk and that it was unfair to move in under false pretenses. The roommate could also keep the cat at her parents' house for the time being and visit it there.

DISCUSS IT The landlord could ask the tenants to correct the situation or move immediately. Violating a lease can lead to eviction and the loss of any deposits.

Before You Move In: Leases and Deposits

When you rent a property, you will probably need to fill out a rental application. The manager or owner will check your financial history to see whether you will be a good tenant. If you are approved, you will then sign a rental agreement or a lease that explains the responsibilities of the owner and of the *tenant*, or renter. For example, the rental agreement or lease should state which repairs and maintenance jobs are the landlord's responsibility and which are yours. The lease should say whether or not pets are allowed. The lease should also specify the monthly rent and the due date, and whether there is a penalty for late payment.

S

Figure 25.1   RENTAL PROPERTY CHECKLIST

W

MY CHECKLIST	
Inside Areas	
Hallways and Common Areas	**Storage**
❑ Halls and stairways are clean	❑ Enough room for clothing and linens
❑ Elevator or stairs are safe and well lit	❑ Place to store bicycle or other large items
The Apartment	**Windows and Screens**
❑ Clean and sanitary	❑ Windows close tightly and work smoothly
❑ Working smoke alarms	❑ Window have locks or bars, if needed
❑ Enough space for me and my roommates	❑ Window screens in good condition
Kitchen	**Doors and Exits**
❑ Appliances work and are modern	❑ Doors sturdy and secure
❑ Cabinet doors and drawers work	❑ Working dead bolts
❑ Faucets and sink in good condition	❑ Clearly accessible fire exit
Bathroom	**Laundry**
❑ Faucets, sink, toilet, and shower/bath in good condition	❑ Washers and dryers in the building
❑ Good water pressure	❑ Washers and dryers in a nearby facility
Outside Areas	
Neighborhood	**Safety**
❑ Safe	❑ Convenient and safe parking
❑ Convenient to school and work	❑ Parking space included in rent

BEFORE YOU RENT Make copies of this checklist, and complete them as you visit different rental properties. *Which items on this checklist are most important to you? Why?*

S **Skill Practice**
Guided Practice
Summarizing Ask students to find three sample rental agreements or leases and create an outline summarizing their common elements. (Outlines should include such key elements as rent and fees, names of approved occupant(s), payment due date, and tenants' rights and responsibilities.)

W **Writing Practice**
Narrative Writing Ask students to use the list in **Figure 25.1** to write a narrative describing everything they will do when visiting and evaluating a rental property. (Students should write a structured narrative in the future tense explaining each step of what they will assess in the rental.)

ASSESS

Review Key Terms
Have students write sentences using each key term.

Online Study Tools
Have students go to the OLC through **glencoe.com** to:
- Download **Podcast** study tools.
- Download free **Study-to-Go** content to their PDAs or cell phones.

Resources

ExamView Assessment Suite CD allows you to print out ready-made unit and chapter tests complete with answer keys. You can also create customized tests.

EXTEND THE FIGURE   **Figure 25.1**

Caption Answer Choices will vary but should be justified in terms of safety, sanitation, convenience, or money savings.

Discussion Explain to students that when they rent property, they can call the manager or landlord to report maintenance issues such as plumbing problems or broken locks.

Ask students to work in pairs to role-play reporting a maintenance issue to a manager. (Students playing the renter should be polite yet assertive. Referring to the terms of the lease and the legal responsibilities of the landlord are effective strategies.)

RETEACH

C Critical Thinking

Ask students to list possible disadvantages of paying bills online. (Answers may include not receiving bills because of infrequent Internet access or fraud from identity theft.)

S Skill Practice

Independent Practice

Make a Grocery List Ask students to research recipes to plan five nights of dinners. Have students use the ingredients required in the recipes to compile a grocery list sorted by type. (Lists should include a wide variety of foods and be grouped by categories such as produce, meat, dairy, canned or dried goods, cereals, etc.)

Resources

📂 **Student Activity Workbook** Assign the Chapter 25 activities in the Student Activity Workbook.

ASSESS

After You Read

Have students complete the Section 25.1 After You Read section review.

Online Study Tools

Have students go to the OLC through **glencoe.com** to:

- Take the Section 25.1 **Practice Test**.
- Download **Podcast** study tools.
- Download free **Study-to-Go** content to their PDAs or cell phones.

TechSavvy

Pay Your Bills Online

Paying bills on time helps you build a solid credit record and avoid hefty late fees. You can pay bills the old-fashioned way by writing and sending paper checks, but today you can also schedule automatic debits from your bank account or credit card or pay bills online. With automatic debit, the company takes money from your account each month to cover your bill. With online bill paying, you visit a Web site and decide which bills to pay and when. Most banks offer free or low-cost online bill pay with your checking account. Many companies also let you pay your bills directly via their individual Web sites, even if you do not have online banking. You can also sign up for e-mail reminders that help keep you on schedule.

@ Visit this book's OLC through **glencoe.com** and find the link to learn more about online banking. Write step-by-step directions on how to set up an account to pay a bill online.

When you sign your lease, you will probably need to pay a **security deposit**, money you pay to cover any damage you might cause to the property. A security deposit is often equal to one or two months' rent. The security deposit should be returned to you when you move out if the property is in good condition.

✓ **Reading Check** **SUMMARIZE** What skills do you need in order to find a suitable place to live? Why?

Settling In

As soon as you have signed your agreement call your utility companies to have services turned on. Make sure to find out whether you need to pay a deposit and when you will get the deposit back.

Have your mail forwarded to your new address by filling out a change-of-address form at the post office or on the U.S. Postal Service Web site. Give your new address and phone number to family, friends, and business contacts as well.

Create a Comfortable Home

Now it is time to measure the rooms and begin deciding where your furniture will go. Plan a comfortable furniture arrangement. Create an environment that feels relaxing to you. For example, you may want to create a quiet area for a desk or computer, or a comfortable space to read. If you need new furniture, measure your living space first to see how much room you have. Resale stores, thrift stores, and online marketplaces are good places to find well-priced furniture.

Measure doorways and check corners to make sure that you will be able to lift large pieces of furniture into your new place. Note the placement of outlets, phone jacks, and cable for the television. Do not put furniture above or in front of hot or cold air vents. Avoid placing electronic equipment in front of windows; this protects it from theft, as well as from wear and tear caused by temperature changes.

Establish Good Housekeeping Habits

Save time, money, and stress by establishing good housekeeping habits when you move in. Develop a system for paying bills on time. Paying your monthly bills builds a good credit record. It also saves a lot of money on late fees and credit card finance charges.

Set aside time each week for housecleaning. If you live with a roommate, agree on who will do what chores—and when. A checklist of tasks, such as doing laundry, washing dishes, vacuuming, and cleaning the bathroom, can help keep you on track.

✓ **Reading Check**

SUMMARIZE Budgeting, research, and decision-making skills are key to finding a suitable place to live.

TechSavvy

Pay Your Bills Online

Answer Steps vary depending on the type of bill-paying service chosen—a bank's Web site, a company's or utility's online payment system, or a third-party bill-paying site.

Develop good habits. Save money and conserve resources by recycling, minimizing trash, and being frugal with resources such as water, light, and heat. Buy energy-efficient appliances and turn off lights and faucets.

Learn to cook healthful meals. This will keep you healthy and save money, too. Eating out often costs much more than cooking at home. Most food bought at restaurants also has more fat and salt than food you cook yourself with fresh vegetables, grains, and protein. Make grocery shopping easy by keeping a running list of groceries and household items you need to buy.

 FRIENDLY SUPPORT
Although moving is hard work, it can be fun. *What are some advantages in getting friends to help with your move?*

CLOSE

Culminating Activity

Becoming Independent Ask students to list the decisions their parents or guardians now make for them that they will have to make for themselves once they are on their own. (Lists will vary but should include both large decisions, such as how to budget one's time and money, and smaller ones, such as what groceries and household items to buy.)

 Extend the Photo

Caption Answer
Getting friends to help you move can save you money on moving costs, make the process more fun, and provide emotional support during a potentially stressful time.

Discussion Ask students how they would find potential roommates and how they would evaluate them for compatibility. (Students could advertise online, use a roommate-finding service, or ask friends and relatives. Students should set priorities and draw up a list of issues to discuss with potential roommates.)

Section 25.1 After You Read

Review Key Concepts

1. Explain what a life stage is and list three life stages.
2. List the utilities and services you would have to contact when setting up your own place.
3. Name one housekeeping task and describe the schedule you would establish to accomplish it.

Practice Academic Skills

 Mathematics

4. Jean and Alex are looking for a new house in a neighborhood in a specific school system. One house they looked at is on the market for $346,113 and another one they looked at costs $272,895. Use front-end estimation to make a quick estimate of the difference in housing costs.

CONCEPT **Front-End Estimation** To make a quick estimate of the sum or difference between two numbers, you can use front-end estimation. Just add or subtract the digits of the two highest place values, and replace the other place values with zero. This will give you an estimate of the solution to a problem.
Step 1: Front estimate both numbers in the problem ($346,113 to $340,000 and $272,895 to $270,000).
Step 2: Now subtract using the new numbers.

 For math help, go to the Math Appendix located at the back of this book.

NCLB Activity correlated to Mathematics standards.

Section 25.1 After You Read

Review Key Concepts

1. A life stage is a period in one's physical and emotional journey through life. The three life stages defined in the text are adolescence, early adulthood, and middle adulthood.
2. Basic utilities include gas, water, electricity, and (if needed) trash service. Related services include telephone service, Internet service, newspaper delivery, and possibly cable television.

3. Students should name a basic household task such as laundry, vacuuming and mopping, or grocery shopping, and describe when and how often (such as weekly or twice weekly) they would do that task.

Practice Academic Skills

4. The estimated difference is $70,000 ($346,113 rounds down to $340,000 and $272,895 rounds down to $270,000; $340,000 − $270,000 = $70,000).

Section 25.2

Bell Ringer Activity

Work, Family, and Community

Ask students to explain whether and how they participate in their community now, and to explain whether and how they would like to participate in their community when they become independent.

Resources

🔘 **Interactive Chalkboard**
The Interactive Chalkboard CD provides visual teaching aids for every section.

@ **Online Learning Center**
The OLC through **glencoe.com** features chapter vocabulary, chapter summaries, and other study materials.

Preteaching

Ask students to define the four key terms and to explain to which life roles *leisure, vote,* and *register* correspond.

Graphic Organizer

Tell students to go to the OLC through **glencoe.com** for a printable graphic organizer. (Graphic organizers will vary but should list roles such as worker, friend, family member, and individual.)

NCLB connects academic correlations to book content.

Work, Family, and Community

Before You Read

Preview Read the Key Concepts. Write one or two sentences predicting what the section will be about.

Read to Learn
- Ways to balance your roles in work and personal life
- Company policies that help employees balance work and family life
- Your role as a citizen and ways to participate in the community

D
Main Idea
Learning to balance the demands of work, home, and community will help you to live a rich and rewarding life.

Key Concepts
- Find Happiness in Balance
- Work-Life Benefits on the Job
- Your Role as a Citizen

Key Terms
◇ role   ◇ vote
◇ leisure   ◇ register

Academic Vocabulary
You will find these words in your reading and on your tests. Use the academic vocabulary glossary to look up their definitions if necessary.
■ competent
■ differentiate

Graphic Organizer
As you read, create a diagram depicting your roles in life. Use a chart like the one shown to help organize the information. Add as many ovals as you need to describe all your roles.

@ **Log On** Go to this book's Online Learning Center through **glencoe.com** for an online version of this graphic organizer.

N C L B

Academic Standards ●
English Language Arts
- Read texts to acquire new information. (NCTE 1)
- Use written language to communicate effectively. (NCTE 4)
- Use information resources to gather information and create and communicate knowledge. (NCTE 8)

- Develop an understanding of diversity in language use across cultures. (NCTE 9)

Science
- Physical Science: Light, heat, electricity, and magnetism

Before You Read

Remind students that, while work is an important part of life, it is not all of life. Ask: What are some basic human needs that work can fulfill? What are some needs it cannot fulfill? (Work pays for life's necessities and can create a feeling of self-worth and accomplishment, but it cannot fulfill the need for close relationships, family, and community involvement.)

D ## Develop Concepts
Main Idea Discuss the main idea with students. Ask: What does a "rewarding life" mean to you? (Ideas may include having friends and family, being financially successful, and feeling proud of one's accomplishments.)

Find Happiness in Balance

Your job will probably take up a lot of your time and energy. In a happy life, however, work is just one part. You need to balance work with personal and family needs.

You will have many roles in your life. A **role** is a set of responsibilities toward yourself and other people in a specific area of your life. What roles will you play when you are out on your own? Will you be an employee, a supervisor, a friend, a spouse, a volunteer, a citizen, a pet owner, or a parent? You may have all these roles in your life, and more. Your roles will change as you grow and develop.

Each of your roles gives you a sense of pride and identity that makes you stronger and happier. Knowing which life roles are most important to you will help you make a solid career decision.

Your Role as a Worker

Work is more than what you do to earn a living. It is also part of your identity. Your role as a worker can give you a feeling of pride and accomplishment that carries over to the other parts of your life. Feeling **competent** at your job helps you feel competent in the rest of your life. And of course, working at a job also provides the money you need to support a family and pursue your other goals.

Your Role as a Friend

Friends are people who share thoughts and feelings and provide companionship and support. Being a friend and having connections with other people make it easier to deal with the problems that are sometimes a part of life.

 YOUR MANY ROLES
Balancing work with friends, family, and leisure is an important part of leading a happy life. *How might having a strong social life make you a better worker?*

Vocabulary
You can find definitions in the **Key Terms** glossary and **Academic Vocabulary** glossary at the back of this book.

TEACH

Discussion Starter
Find Happiness in Balance
Ask students to think of people they know who seem happy or content in their lives. Do they have a balance between work and the rest of their lives? If so, how do they achieve that balance? (Ideas will vary, but students may say that people they know who are happy devote time to friendships, family, and personal interests, as well as work.)

R Reading Strategy
Explain Ask students to list their current roles and to indicate how each contributes to their sense of identity. (Roles will vary, but students should show how each of their roles contributes to how they see and feel about themselves.)

Resources

TeacherWorks™ Plus
The TeacherWorks software includes customizable built-in lesson plans and links to printable program resources.

Extend the Photo

Caption Answer A strong social life can create a sense of emotional well-being that carries over to work.

Discussion Explain to students that the adults in our lives are important models for us as we learn how to balance roles. Ask students to share how the adults they know balance work with friends, family, and leisure. What can they learn from these adults? What might they want to do differently in their own lives?

TEACH (cont.)

U Universal Access

Visual/Spatial Learners
Ask students to use colors, shapes, abstract or representational forms, and collage elements such as photographs and small three-dimensional objects to depict people, things, or situations that evoke a sense of belonging. Ask advanced students to create their project using an image-editing or drawing program.

C Critical Thinking

Evaluating Ask students why they think it would be important to have friends outside of work. What are some plusses and minuses of having coworkers who are also friends? (For many people, it is easier to relax and get away from the pressures of work with friends they have met elsewhere than at work. Being friends with coworkers makes work more pleasant, but may also make it difficult to get away from work during leisure hours.)

As You Read

Students' roles (or responsibilities) will vary, but students should recognize that their school, family, and personal responsibilities affect the way they spend their time, energy, and money.

► **FAMILY ROLE** Families come in all shapes and sizes. *How might your career goals change if you became a parent? Why?*

C Having friends outside of work is an important part of your work-life balance. Join a group that participates in activities you love. Get involved with an organization that interests you, such as an environmental association, arts group, or charity. Sign up for a sports league. Join a book group at a local bookstore. Take up a hobby or enroll in evening classes at a local community college.

As You Read

Connect How do your current life roles influence your lifestyle?

Your Role as a Family Member

Your family consists of relatives or other people who give you a sense of belonging and being loved. What does your ideal family look like? You probably do not know yet, and that is fine.

Finding time for both work and family is one of life's biggest challenges. This is especially true if you decide to have children. Most people find having children the most rewarding experience of their lives. Children have many needs, of course. They need to be fed, clothed, bathed, taken to activities, and helped with homework. Most importantly, they need to be loved, and love takes time and energy.

Think about how your career can support the family role you want. For example, do you need flexible hours to care for children or elders? Make smart career choices that will allow you to create the family life you want.

Your Role as an Individual

You have another important role, too—your role as you. Set time aside every day to care for yourself by resting, eating well, exercising, and doing things that you enjoy. Make time for **leisure**, activities you do to enjoy yourself and feel good about your life. Read, take courses, and do other things that build your sense of identity and self-esteem.

► **Extend the Photo**

Caption Answer Your career goals may change if you become a parent because you may wish to have a career that allows you to balance your work life with the time you spend with your family. Having a child may also increase your motivation to work hard and succeed financially in order to financially support your family and your family's goals.

Discussion Ask students to brainstorm ways becoming a parent through birth or adoption might change other aspects of their life.

Balance Your Roles

To stay healthy, meet your goals and responsibilities, and avoid stress, you need to balance your life roles. Everyone is different, so you need to design a balance that works for you. Decide on your priorities, then be realistic and willing to compromise when necessary. **Differentiate** between what you really want and what you can live without. Live up to your commitments, but also recognize your human limits.

Adapt to Your Changing Life Roles

Different life roles lead to different lifestyles, or ways of spending time, energy, and money. For example, individuals who must travel to see their families may spend more money on leisure activities than those whose families live nearby. If being an employee is your most important role, you may have more money, but less time to be a friend or family member. Your life roles change over time, and so will your lifestyle.

Balance Career Success with Life Goals

As you change in body and mind, your motivations and goals will also change. This will affect your career and your career goals. For example, imagine that you want to spend more time volunteering or taking care of a young child or sick relative. You may have to spend less time at work, which might make it harder to get a raise or a promotion. You will need to decide whether this is a good compromise for you.

Your needs and wants will change with time too. Take stock of where your life is going and whether your lifestyle is consistent with your goals.

STAY ACTIVE Everyone needs time to play in order to remain mentally and physically healthy. *Why is it important to make time for physical activities?*

Real-World Connection

Budget Balance

You will be graduating in a few months, and you're working at a job that you like very much. You want to find your own apartment and begin to live independently. You know that you will have to save money now to make that happen, but your friends want to shop and eat at expensive stores and restaurants.

Critical Thinking How can you help your friends understand and respect your goals?

Do Your Own Research Research the cost of apartments, utilities, and other living expenses. Check with a relocation service in your area that may provide valuable information about the cost of living in your community. Develop a realistic budget that includes savings and recreation as categories.

TEACH (cont.)

S Skill Practice
Independent Practice
Interview Ask students to interview three working adults about their roles. Students should ask the interviewees to rank the roles of worker, family member, friend, individual, volunteer, community member, and citizen in order of importance in their lives and to explain their choice. Have students share their findings. (Students should see from this exercise that people balance their roles in different ways.)

C Critical Thinking
Predicting Ask students to predict how the following events would change their lifestyles: a major illness in the family; a major promotion at work. (Helping an ill family member, or assuming a job with major responsibility would greatly influence how a person spends his or her time, energy, and money.)

W Writing Support
Narrative Writing Ask students to imagine that they are writing a short speech for their tenth high school reunion. Ask students to write 150 words about how their lifestyle, career, and roles have changed over the past decade. (Speeches should demonstrate an understanding of the fact that goals, roles, and lifestyle choices change as one grows and develops.)

Real-World Connection

Critical Thinking Answer Students should explain to their friends that becoming independent is very important to them right now. Students might reassure their friends that they still want to spend time together and suggest less costly activities.

Do Your Own Research Encourage students to cut nonessential expenses and to avoid borrowing and credit card debt.

Extend the Photo

Caption Answer Physical activities help a person recharge physically and mentally, fight illness, and stay fit.

Discussion Ask students to describe any adults they know who make exercise a regular part of their schedule. How do the adults fit the physical activity in with their other responsibilities? (Students may mention setting aside time each day or other strategies.)

TEACH (cont.)

S Skill Practice
Independent Practice

Weigh Pros and Cons Ask students to imagine that they need to leave work by 4:30 P.M. each day to pick up their children from day care. They are offered a high-paying job that requires them to stay until 6:00 P.M. Would they take the job? Why or why not? (Some students may say that they would stick to their previous commitment, while others may say that the extra money is a good reason to make a schedule change.) **L1**

Compromise Ask students to work in pairs to brainstorm issues that have to be negotiated and compromises that have to be struck when both members of a couple have a career. (Couples might need to negotiate tasks and schedules for shared responsibilities. They might also need to compromise on time spent at work and on time and money spent on other activities.) **L2**

Role-Play Ask students to imagine that they have a personal commitment that requires them to leave at a certain time each day. Ask them to role-play the part of the job interview where they explain this commitment to a possible employer and ask whether this could be accommodated. (Students should be polite but self-confident in explaining their commitment and should present it in terms that highlight their positive qualities to the employer.) **L3**

N C L B Activity correlated to Science standards.

Science In Action

Refraction

Light bends when it moves from one medium to another, such as from air to water. This phenomenon is called *refraction*. To demonstrate, fill a glass with water. Put a pencil in the water, look at it from the side and from the top, and describe what you see.

Starting Hint: The same phenomenon will occur at any water-to-air interface.

@ For more science practice, go to this book's OLC through **glencoe.com**.

N C L B

Work-Life Benefits on the Job

The American family is changing. Today, most single people and family members who are also caregivers work full-time. More and more employers are recognizing this and helping workers balance their life roles. Employers know that employees who are under less stress are more loyal and more productive.

As you look for jobs, evaluate what you will need from your job to achieve a solid work-life balance. For example, imagine that you are an individual who needs to leave work at the same time each day to fulfill an important role, such as picking your children up from school or attending night classes. Look for a job that will allow you to keep these commitments. Explain your commitments and ask the employer about any accommodations you might need *before* you take the job. If the employer says no, you will need to think about whether the job is right for you. **S**

Benefits vary widely, even from job to job within a company. Some common work-life benefits to look for, however, are:

- **Flextime and Telecommuting** Flexible work hours and opportunities to work at home help you create a schedule that is best for you and your family.
- **On-Site Child Care** Some employers provide child care for a reasonable fee. Bringing your children to work is often easier than taking them elsewhere, and you can visit them during breaks or lunch.

▶ SAFE AND SECURE On-site child care centers are one of the most popular employee benefits for working parents. *How do such child care centers help parents concentrate on their jobs?*

Science In Action

Students will see the pencil appear to bend at the interface between the water and air. The same phenomenon will occur at any water-to-air interface.

▶ Extend the Photo

Caption Answer On-site child care gives parents peace of mind and saves them transportation time.

Discussion Ask students whether they think companies should subsidize child care expenses. (Opinions will vary. Some students may feel that employers are wise to provide benefits that increase employee job satisfaction.)

- **Paid and Unpaid Leave** Most companies allow employees to take time off for important family events, such as the birth of a baby or an illness in the family.
- **Life Skills Training** Many companies offer training in skills that help you at work and at home, such as communication, conflict resolution, time management, and financial planning.
- **Education Assistance** Your company may help you pay for training or courses that teach you new skills and help you reach your career goals.

✓ **Reading Check** SYNTHESIZE Why are more employers offering work-life benefits?

Career ✓ Checklist

To Balance Work and Personal Life:

✓ Make time for your personal interests and hobbies.

✓ Maintain a positive outlook and healthy self-esteem.

✓ Challenge yourself.

✓ Maintain your **Personal and Academic and Career Portfolio** to chart your growth.

Your Role as a Citizen

There is another important role that most adults have in our society: the role of citizen. As you move into the world of work and get your own place to live, your responsibilities as a citizen will grow. You will be a working adult, a taxpayer, and a voter.

Be Informed and Vote

Staying informed is the responsibility of every citizen. Read the newspaper and follow radio, television, and Internet news reports. Talk to your neighbors to learn what they think about issues. Learn

Creative Business Practices

JOHNSON & JOHNSON

Helping Balance Work and Home Life

The global pharmaceutical company Johnson & Johnson offers a range of work-life benefits to make its employees' lives easier. Its Work & Family leave program, for example, allows full-time employees to take up to a full year to care for a family member or themselves. The company has six company-sponsored day-care centers that offer full-time care to employees' children and their grand-children. It also offers flextime, allows employees to work from home when appropriate, and runs a corporate wellness program designed to help employees get fit and stay healthy. Johnson & Johnson also provides referral programs to help employees take care of life decisions, such as buying a new home or car or finding care for elderly family members.

CRITICAL THINKING Work-life benefits can cost companies millions of dollars each year. Do you think these benefits are worth the investment? Why or why not?

 Connect to the Real World To read more about Johnson & Johnson, visit the company's Web site via the link on this book's Online Learning Center through **glencoe.com**.

TEACH (cont.)

W Writing Support

Defining Ask students to write a 50-word definition of a "good citizen." What makes a person an asset to his or her society and community? (Students may mention behaviors such as voting, being informed, following the law, and giving to the community.)

✓ **Reading Check**

SYNTHESIZE More employers are recognizing that work-life benefits can boost employees' loyalty and job performance, especially as more and more parents both work full-time.

ASSESS

Review Key Terms
Have students write sentences using each key term.

Online Study Tools
Have students go to the OLC through **glencoe.com** to:
- Download **Podcast** study tools.
- Download free **Study-to-Go** content to their PDAs or cell phones.

STUDY TO GO

Creative Business Practices

CRITICAL THINKING ANSWER Some students may feel that such benefits are too expensive or provide no financial or other benefits to companies, while other students may feel that employers have a social responsibility to provide such benefits or that increased employee productivity, performance, and loyalty is worth the investment.

Section 25.2

RETEACH

 C **Critical Thinking**

Connecting to the Community Ask students to list volunteer opportunities that could help them build skills in their chosen careers. (Lists will vary by interest area. For example, a student interested in computers could volunteer in the computer lab at a community center.)

 NCLB Activity correlated to English Language Arts standards.

Resources

📁 **Student Activity Workbook** Assign the Chapter 25 activities in the Student Activity Workbook.

ASSESS

After You Read
Have students complete the Section 25.2 After You Read section review.

Online Study Tools
Have students go to the OLC through **glencoe.com** to:
- Take the Section 25.2 **Practice Test**.
- Download **Podcast** study tools.
- Download free **Study-to-Go** content to their PDAs or cell phones.

Resources

💿 **ExamView Assessment Suite CD** allows you to print out ready-made unit and chapter tests complete with answer keys. You can also create customized tests.

566

The 21st Century Workplace

Parlez-Vous Français?

French is second only to English as a worldwide language of business and diplomacy. Millions of people learn French as a second language in Europe, Africa, North America, the Caribbean, and elsewhere. Having a grasp of French will make you an attractive candidate to employers who work with French-speaking customers. It is also a huge asset if you are interested in a career that requires knowledge of European history, culture, politics, or science.

CRITICAL THINKING _____
In Europe, many people are multilingual, speaking three or more languages fluently. Why might multilingualism be more common in Europe than it is in the United States?

In Your Community
Survey three high schools near you, including your own, to find out how many students learn French and how many learn other languages. Create a chart of your results.

COMMON FRENCH WORDS AND PHRASES	
hi/bye (informal hello)	salut
hello/good morning	bonjour
good evening	bonsoir
goodbye	au revoir
yes	oui
no	non
thank you	merci
you're welcome (informal)	de rien
you're welcome (formal)	je vous en prie

@ Extend Your Learning French is an official language of more than 25 countries. For links to Web sites about the French language, go to this book's OLC through **glencoe.com**.

---

where your tax money goes. Then put your knowledge to work by voting. To **vote** is to choose leaders or decide on initiatives. You vote by filling out a ballot at your local polling place on special election days. Voting is your most important obligation as a citizen. Your vote helps decide who our leaders will be and what our laws will be.

Before you can vote, you must be at least 18 years old and register to vote. To **register** to vote means to officially sign up as a qualified voter. Methods for registering vary from place to place. To find out how it is done in your area, call or visit the Web site of the League of Women Voters, your county election commission, or the county registrar's office.

Your Role as a Volunteer

Volunteering in your community is another way to create a successful life balance. Volunteer work helps you widen your circle of friends, learn new skills, and make your community a better place to live.

C How can you get involved? Think of the activities you enjoy and the concerns that are important to you. Whether you are interested in mentoring a child, restoring old buildings, reading to the elderly, or coaching basketball, you have got a lot to give. Call the organizations that promote those activities and ask if they offer volunteer opportunities. Talk to people, ask questions, and attend meetings. For example, you could attend a community meeting to meet your neighbors and get to know their concerns.

The 21st Century Workplace

CRITICAL THINKING ANSWER Many countries in Europe have two, three, or more official languages that are taught in school. Close geographic, cultural, and economic ties among the members of the European Union also ensure that Europeans have more frequent and sustained contact with speakers of other languages than Americans do.

In Your Community Results will vary. Spanish is the most widely taught language in most areas, followed by French and German. Courses in Asian languages such as Chinese, Japanese, and Korean are now being offered in an increasing number of schools.

566

USE YOUR VOTE
To cast an informed vote, research the candidates and issues. *Does your vote matter in an election in which thousands or millions of people vote? Explain.*

CLOSE

Culminating Activity

Balance and Career Success Ask students to write an essay summarizing how they define success in life and describing the role of career achievement in this success. (Students' essays should recognize that career success, while extremely important, is only one of several important parts of overall success in life.)

Volunteering is also a great way to stay informed on local and national issues that are important to you. It makes you a more aware citizen and a better informed voter. The more you are involved with your community—and with friends, family, work, and yourself—the happier and more successful you will be, in any career you choose.

Section 25.2 After You Read

Review Key Concepts

1. Explain the importance of balancing your work and personal life. Name one thing you could do to achieve that balance.
2. Give an example of a family-friendly company policy, and explain how it benefits both employee and employer.
3. Describe what you must do in order to vote.

Practice Academic Skills

 English Language Arts

4. List and describe your current roles in the following areas: personal life, leisure, community, school, family, and work. Describe how these roles are connected and analyze how well you balance them in your life.

Social Studies

5. Imagine that you and a roommate have just rented an apartment together. The only furniture you have is bedroom furniture. You each have $500 to contribute toward furnishing the new apartment with furniture, linens, and kitchen and bathroom necessities. Make a list of items you need. Then research to find the best prices on those items. List which items you will buy new, which you will buy used, and which you will wait to buy until you have saved more money. Also list the items you can do without, and explain why.

@ Check your answers at this book's OLC through **glencoe.com**.

Extend the Photo

Caption Answer Yes. Some elections are decided by very tight margins. Additionally, every vote cast sends a message to politicians and other decision makers.

Discussion Ask students to list effective ways to obtain information about political candidates and issues.

Activity correlated to English Language Arts standards.

Section 25.2 After You Read

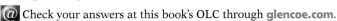

Review Key Concepts
1. Balancing work and personal life is important to avoid burnout in any one area, and to create a strong sense of self-esteem and identity. Strategies include prioritizing, sticking to a fixed work schedule, and setting aside time for other activities.
2. One example would be child care assistance. Such programs help employees reduce stress, solve personal problems, and grow in their careers; they help employers by promoting employee loyalty and productivity, and by attracting top job candidates.
3. A potential voter (who is 18 or over and an American citizen) must first register, or officially sign up, to vote.

Practice Academic Skills
4. Students' roles and strategies for balance will vary. Students should understand that feelings of pride and success in one role can carry over to other life roles.
5. Students' lists should include basic items such as a bed, cleaning supplies, and dishware. Most items can be bought used, although students may prefer to buy linens and other more personal items new.

567

CAREER SPOTLIGHT

FOCUS

Discussion Starter

Transportation, Distribution, and Logistics Explain to students that workers in this career cluster help move goods and people. Ask students to brainstorm all the different jobs involved in moving people and in moving products from factory to store. (Students may mention pilots and drivers, flight attendants, air traffic controllers, warehouse workers, truck drivers and dispatchers, shipping, receiving, and stock clerks, wholesalers, and store managers.)

TEACH

W Writing Support Independent Practice

Interview Ask students to ask three adults who work full-time to explain and give examples of how they use communication and organization skills on the job. Have students summarize their findings. (Interviewees may mention communicating with managers, coworkers, and customers and managing tasks, deadlines, and schedules.)

C Critical Thinking

Analyzing Statements Torrez mentions the importance of follow-through. Ask students to evaluate the saying (attributed to Woody Allen) "Eighty percent of success is showing up." What does this mean? Do they agree or disagree? (The statement means that reaching a goal requires steady, hard work. Students should acknowledge that having luck or a good idea is no guarantee of success.)

568

CAREER SPOTLIGHT

Career Cluster: Transportation, Distribution, and Logistics

Juliette Torrez
Publications Wholesaler

Q: Describe your job.
A: I work for a small company that publishes and sells art books, graphic novels, toys, and literature to independent specialty stores and boutiques. We also sell directly to customers online.

Q: Describe a typical workday.
A: In the morning, I catch up on daily correspondence, find out what the new arrivals are in the warehouse, and place orders for out-of-stock items. Then I'll either place telephone calls or make and send mailers to our customers to follow up on orders or let them know what we have to offer. Some days, I research upcoming and potential titles from catalogs, the Internet , and customer recommendations. We carry everything from obscure magazines to bestsellers.

Q: What skills are most important to you in your job?
A: Communication and organization are very important. So is the desire to be part of a small company's team. That means picking up the slack if someone is out sick, or working weekends if we're exhibiting at a convention.

Q: What academic skills and lifelong learning skills are helpful in preparing for your career?
A: I'm grateful to those teachers who instilled in me a love of reading and ideas. Now books and art surround me.

Q: What is your key to success?
A: Treat people with respect and value their time and effort. That includes people you disagree with. You can learn a lot from people who don't share the same tastes or experiences.

Q: What training and preparation do you recommend for students?
A: Develop an appreciation for art and writing. Constantly create. Don't be afraid to fail. Be open to ideas. So many of the publications and materials that we distribute started off as someone's kooky idea but successfully became a book, a magazine, or an art object. So many people have let opportunities slip through their hands by not following through. Follow through! Believe in yourself and your work!

Q: What are some ways you recommend students prepare for this career?
A: Work with others to create spaces where art can happen or form a writing circle where everyone makes their own 'zine. Then give your collective a name and take your work on tour. On the road or in the community, you'll meet others and find mentors. You can also be an intern or volunteer at businesses that are interesting to you. More often than not, they will result in a paid job or at least a great reference.

Q: What do you like most about your work?
A: The people I talk to are fascinating! The storeowners, buyers, publishers, artists, and writers all have dreams and aspirations that are inspiring to me.

 For more about Career Clusters, go to this book's OLC through **glencoe.com**.

NO CHILD LEFT BEHIND

Teaching Tip

The No Child Left Behind Act mandates testing to assess school performance. Help students prepare for and succeed on standardized tests by discussing test content and format and by explaining the rationale for the tests and the importance of the skills they assess. Help students become reflective about their own performance by sharing and discussing rubrics for evaluation of assignments throughout the school year.

Sample Question Ask students to write a paragraph describing an adult they know who balances several life roles. Share the criteria for evaluation of the assignment and discuss how those criteria relate to skills the students must build in order to succeed in their careers.

- **Education or Training** Although some workers need a college degree, most jobs in the wholesale trade can be entered without education beyond high school.

- **Academic Skills Required** English Language Arts, Mathematics, Social Studies, World Languages

- **Technology Needed** Operation of inventory management databases, online purchasing systems, or electronic data interchange systems.

- **Aptitudes, Abilities, and Skills** Sales associates will need proficiency in English, mathematics, and marketing. World languages skills can help with international products and distribution.

- **Workplace Safety** Working conditions and physical demands of wholesale trade jobs vary greatly. Moving stock and heavy equipment can be physically strenuous. Workers in some automated warehouses use computer-controlled storage and retrieval systems that further reduce labor requirements.

Career Outlook Over the next ten years, wage and salary employment in wholesale trade is projected to grow by 8 percent, versus 14 percent growth for all industries combined.

Career Path Wholesale trade firms often emphasize promotion from within, especially in the numerous small businesses in the industry. Even some of the largest firms have top executives who began in warehouse positions.

Academic Skills Required to Complete Tasks

Tasks	English Language Arts	Mathematics	Social Studies	World Languages
Customer service	★	★	★	★
Order/re-order books for inventory	★	★		★
Research potential inventory	★		★	★
Learn products	★		★	
Create mailers	★	★		
Sell books to customers	★	★	★	★
Exhibit at conventions	★	★	★	★

NCLB

Critical Thinking

How can an independent book wholesaler compete against larger bookstores?

NCLB

This chart relates academic skills such as English Language Arts, Mathematics, Science, Social Studies, and World Languages to specific tasks that are performed for the job featured in the Career Spotlight feature.

Critical Thinking

An independent bookseller might be able to compete with larger bookstores by offering more personalized customer service and by offering local, hand-selected, or unusual products that the larger bookstores do not carry.

CAREER SPOTLIGHT

ASSESS

Make Connections

Ask students why they think customer service requires the full range of academic skills, as shown in this chart, and to give examples. (English Language Arts is crucial for writing and speaking clearly; Mathematics is necessary for managing sales and account details; Social Studies helps with understanding other cultures and points of view; and World Languages assists in communicating with international customers.)

CLOSE

Culminating Activity

Balance and Career Clusters Point out to students that Torrez has achieved a balance in her career between working with people, with distribution processes and technology, and with art and literature. Ask students to describe various interests and skills they would like to use in their careers and to envision a job that might let them combine some or all of these interests and skills. (Ideas will vary; a student who enjoys sports, art, and working with children might envision being an art teacher and coaching soccer, while a student who enjoys working with machinery and talking with others might envision a job managing a machine shop or being a parts salesperson.)

CHAPTER **25** Review & Activities

Key Terms and Academic Vocabulary Review

1. Students should use each of the key terms and academic vocabulary terms in a sentence. A sample answer might read: "Time needed to *commute*, or travel back and forth to work, is an important factor to consider in choosing a place to live."

Review Key Concepts

2. First, weigh pros and cons of living independently. Then create a budget, research and evaluate rental properties, and choose a compatible roommate. Have utilities and other necessary services connected, arrange for your mail to be forwarded, and buy or borrow necessary furniture and household essentials.

3. Organize your living space in a way that is practical and comfortable. Measure your available space and note the position of windows and outlets in order to arrange your furniture and appliances. Establish a schedule and convenient method for paying bills, cleaning, shopping, and doing other necessary household tasks.

4. Strategies for balancing work and personal life include prioritizing your roles, making compromises, upholding commitments, and taking advantage of any work-life benefits offered by your employer.

5. Company policies that help employees with the work-life balance include flextime and telecommuting, on-site child care, paid or unpaid leave to take care of personal or family events, life skills training, and education assistance.

6. The citizen's central role is to be informed and vote. Volunteering is a great way to participate in the

CHAPTER SUMMARY

Section 25.1

As you enter the life stage of early adulthood, you will begin to develop your independence. Setting up your own household is a major step toward independence. Before moving out, prepare a budget and consider the advantages and disadvantages of having your own place. Choose a location that is safe and convenient and that fits your needs. Before you sign a rental agreement or lease, be sure you understand all the costs and responsibilities involved. Plan how your furniture will fit in your apartment, and establish good housekeeping habits.

Section 25.2

In your life you will balance many different roles. Success in one role, such as worker, helps you build success in other roles, such as family member. Balancing work and personal needs is key to achieving a happy life. Today, more and more employers are helping workers achieve balance by offering benefits such as flexible work schedules and on-site child care. You also have a role as a citizen. Staying informed, voting, and volunteering helps you and your community.

Key Terms and Academic Vocabulary Review

1. Use each of these key terms and academic vocabulary words in a sentence.

Key Terms
- life stage (p. 555)
- utilities (p. 556)
- commute (p. 556)
- security deposit (p. 558)
- role (p. 561)

- leisure (p. 562)
- vote (p. 566)
- register (p. 566)

Academic Vocabulary
- compatible (p. 555)
- competent (p. 561)
- differentiate (p. 563)

Review Key Concepts

2. Explain how to choose a place to live and set up a household.
3. Describe how to organize your living space and establish good housekeeping habits.
4. Identify ways to balance your work and personal life.
5. Name some company policies that help employees balance work and family life.
6. Explain your role as a citizen and identify ways to participate in the community.

Critical Thinking

7. Reflect Think back over the past five years. How have your goals and motivations changed, and why? How have these changes affected your career development?
8. Synthesize How can work contribute to a happy and productive life? How can it contribute to a happy and productive family environment?

community, get to know others, and share skills and talents.

Critical Thinking

7. Responses will vary; students may have achieved developed greater independence and self-awareness, developed an idea of who they would like to be in the future, and begun to think about career and family goals. Such changes may have affected their career development plans by helping them understand what jobs would match their skills, interests, and life goals.

8. Work can give a person a sense of purpose, accomplishment, and pride that carries over into other areas of life. People who feel good about themselves are better able to deal with stress and give more to their families.

Real-World Skills and Applications

Information Literacy Skills and Social Responsibility

9. Becoming Informed Imagine that a proposition is on the ballot for the next election. The proposition calls for a special tax to support state parks. What are three sources of information you might use to form your decision about how to vote on this issue? How could you evaluate each source to determine if it is accurate and unbiased? Write a one-paragraph response to each question and share the sources of information you found with the class.

Critical Thinking and Self-Direction

10. Assessing Life Roles and Lifestyle What life roles are most important to you? Brainstorm all possible life roles that might be important to you, then list them in order

of importance. In a one-page summary, describe how you think your chosen life roles will affect your future lifestyle and your career goals.

Technology Applications

11. Creating a Budget Imagine that your take-home pay is $1,800 per month. You have a monthly car payment of $200. Your car insurance is $850 every six months. Estimate additional expenses for food, rent and utilities, clothes, gas and repairs for your car, laundry, and so on. Base your estimates on your actual spending habits and the cost of living in your area. Use a spreadsheet program to draw up a monthly budget. Use a formula to add up your monthly expenses and see how much is left over each month for other expenses or savings.

12. **Survey Work-Life Benefits** What benefits do today's employers offer their employees? Contact the human resources departments of two large employers in your town or city. Ask what benefits each company offers its employees to help them balance work and personal responsibilities. Also ask what benefits the company is considering offering in the future. Compare and contrast the two companies' benefits in a one-page summary.

13. **Balancing Work and Personal Life**
Situation You have been independent for a few years now. A younger friend of yours has just graduated from college and started a new job. He has confided to you that he is feeling overwhelmed by his professional responsibilities. He wants to do a good job but does not want to sacrifice his personal life and free time.
Activity Role-play a conversation with your friend in which you explain how to balance conflicting priorities. Explain to him how he can determine his priorities and what strategies he can use to live the balanced life he desires.
Evaluation You will be evaluated based on how well you meet the following performance indicators:
- Understand the conflicting motivators in your friend's situation.
- Present creative strategies for balancing professional and personal demands.
- Answer any questions that your friend may have.

 ACTIVE LEARNING

12. Benefits vary widely from company to company but are likely to include some of the common programs described on page 565.

ROLE PLAY

13. Role-play activities should demonstrate a clear understanding of the need for balance between work and non-work life, as well as of strategies for achieving such balance. Students should be well prepared and demonstrate a realistic understanding of the dilemma presented.

Real-World Skills and Applications

9. Voters have the civic duty to choose candidates and decide ballot measures. They need to know the facts and understand the issues at stake in order to make these important decisions responsibly.

10. Lists should contain life roles that students find important. Students should also summarize how they prioritized their lists and how they think their life roles would affect their future lifestyle and career goals.

11. Students' take-home pay after car payments and insurance is less than $1,500. Depending on food, gas, health care and other expenses, many students are likely to have $700 or less for rent and utilities each month. Encourage students to include savings as well as periodic expenses, such as parking, haircuts, gifts, and so on in their budgets.

Academic Skills in the Workplace

14. Students are likely to be in the life stage of adolescence, with some perhaps entering into early adulthood. Students are probably continuing to mature physically and to develop emotional maturity, self-awareness, and skills in critical thinking and decision making. For most students, the coming life stage will bring new responsibilities and challenges, such as entering the workforce and living independently.

15. Hector will donate a total of $437.50 this year ($100 + $100 + $75 + $75 = $350 $350 × 1.25 = $437.50).

16. Students' conclusions should be based on accurate data about a variety of factors that affect a worker's family life and lifestyle, such as schedule, rate of on-the-job injuries and illnesses, stress level, and time spent traveling or otherwise away from home. Some high-paying careers may provide good financial support for family and lifestyle goals, but may also entail long hours and high stress, while some more modestly compensated careers may offer a better work-life balance.

17. Relevant questions include: Do you have a regular income? What hours do you work? When do you go to bed and get up? Do you smoke? Do you watch TV/listen to music? If so, how much and what kind? Do you have or want a pet? How often do you have friends over to visit? What kind of housekeeper are you? How long do you want to share a place?

Academic Skills in the Workplace

English Language Arts

14. Understanding Life Stages Review the life stages described on page 555. Describe which stage you are in now and what physical, emotional, and intellectual changes you are experiencing. Then describe what changes you experienced in your previous life stage and what changes you might experience in the life stage that will come next.

Mathematics

15. Making Donations Hector is making donations to his favorite charities. He would like to give 25% more this year than he did last year. Last year he gave $100 to an organization that helps schools in low-income areas, $100 to fund HIV research, $75 to an environmental organization, and $75 to his local radio station. How much will he donate in total this year?

CONCEPT **Solving Problems Efficiently**
There is usually more than one way to solve a problem. Often one way is quicker than another. Not only will the quicker way save you time, but it may involve fewer calculations and fewer chances to make a mistake.

Starting Hint Instead of multiplying each value donated by 125% and adding, which involves five separate calculations, you can add up the values and then multiply the total by 125%, making only two calculations.

Social Studies

16. Researching Effects of Careers Choose three careers that interest you and research how these careers affect the family life and lifestyle of the people who pursue them. Look at a variety of factors, including cost and length of training, hours worked per week, income, job satisfaction, social status, and health and environmental risks (such as stress and risk of injury). Assess your results. Do some careers offer a healthier work-life balance than others? Why or why not?

Science

17. Conducting a Survey Create a list of 12 questions you could use to interview potential roommates to see whether they are compatible. For each question, explain briefly why this information is important for you to know before you make your choice.

STANDARDIZED TEST PRACTICE

MATH WORD PROBLEMS

Directions Read the word problem and possible answers. Then choose the correct answer.

Test-Taking Tip Solve a word problem in two steps. First, translate the words into an equation of numbers and variables. Then solve each equation in order to get the correct answer.

1. You are getting ready to move out of your first apartment. Your landlord is deducting 32% of your security deposit for carpet cleaning and minor repairs. Your check will amount to $578. What was the original amount of your security deposit?

a. $800   **c.** $850
b. $610   **d.** $393

STANDARDIZED TEST PRACTICE

Answer
c. $850.00

Test-Taking Strategies
When test time is short, students can often benefit from using educated guesses to answer word problems. For example, students know that $578 is *less* than the original security deposit. They can therefore quickly eliminate choice d. They also know that $578 is about a third less than the original deposit, which can help them eliminate choice b. Now they can work backwards from choices a. and c. by multiplying each one by .68 to see which is the correct answer.

Writing Skills Practice

18. Writing the Personal Essay A personal essay is a nonfiction article that discusses a topic from the author's personal point of view.

 Practice Write a five-paragraph essay that presents your opinion on the importance of balancing different roles, such as worker, family member, community member, citizen, parent, etc.

- Start by deciding on your point of view. Is it important to have a balance among different life roles? If so, why? If not, why not?
- Begin with an introductory paragraph that contains a topic sentence stating your point of view, and three pieces of evidence that support your point of view.
- Write one short paragraph describing each piece of evidence.
- Finish with a concluding paragraph that summarizes your argument and describes why you think your evidence proved your case.

Net Connection

19. Finding an Apartment Make a list of ten things you would look for in an apartment. Use the Web to locate three apartments for rent in your area. Ask the landlords specific questions to find out which apartment would be best for you. Choose the apartment that you like best and use a word-processing program to write a short paragraph explaining your choice.

Log On Visit at least two Web sites that list apartments for rent. Visit this book's OLC through **glencoe.com** for links that may help. Choose at least two apartments that would suit you and follow up on each to find out more.

 Reading Connection

Go to this book's Online Learning Center through **glencoe.com** for a list of reading suggestions.

Personal Academic and Career Portfolio

Planning Your Career— and Beyond

Thinking about what you want from life as a whole can help you choose a career that not only interests you but also meets your needs for balance outside of work. Create a snapshot of your future life by writing down your lifestyle goals and the life roles you would like to play in the future. Also write down goals you have for getting involved in your community and your vision of yourself as an informed citizen.

The following guidelines will help you organize and add the results of your research to your portfolio:

- Create a new section for your portfolio labeled *Life Goals and Balance*.
- You may wish to create subsections or subfolders with names such as *Life Roles* and *Community*.
- Add the following: your lifestyle goals; the life roles that are important to you; the ways you do (or can begin to) stay informed about important news in your community, state, and country; a record of volunteer work you do or have done; and a list of careers that you believe would fit well with your lifestyle goals. You may also want to add at least one profile of a working professional whose lifestyle and life goals you admire.
- Update your Portfolio as you learn more about careers—and yourself.

Portfolio Help Go to the *Succeeding in the World of Work* OLC through **glencoe.com** for help developing your portfolio.

Writing Skills Practice

18. Essays should be clearly written and should follow the five-paragraph format outlined here. Essays may adopt any point of view, as long as that point of view is well articulated and defended with accurate facts and statistics, relevant examples or stories from their personal lives, or other supporting evidence.

Net Connection

19. Paragraphs should include details about the apartments students have chosen and their explanations for their choices.

Resources

ExamView Assessment Suite CD allows you to print out ready-made unit and chapter tests complete with answer keys. You can also create customized tests.

WorkKeys

WorkKeys® is a job skills assessment program. For information on leveled assessment for Interpersonal Skills (Teamwork), go to the WorkKeys link on this book's OLC through **glencoe.com**.

Personal Academic and Career Portfolio

Maintaining a Portfolio

This chapter emphasizes that people's roles, lifestyles, motivations, and goals all change with time and experience. Explain to students that their **Personal Academic and Career Portfolios** are a great way to keep track of those changes. Students may want to create new versions of their portfolios each year, deciding what to keep and what to modify or discard depending on how their goals and sense of self have changed. For example, students may discover new skills and interests, or may decide to eliminate some previous career possibilities from consideration. Encourage students to keep the past versions of their portfolios and to look at them from time to time, to see how they have changed, and to retrace the decision-making path that led them to where they currently are.

FOCUS

Discussion Starter

Give students two or three minutes to complete the following sentence: "The most difficult part of career planning is _____, because _____." Ask students to read their sentences aloud. As a class, discuss students' ideas and share solutions that can make the difficult aspects of career planning more manageable.

STEP 1

Evaluate Your Skills and Resources

Have students go to the *Succeeding in the World of Work* OLC through **glencoe.com** for a graphic organizer they can use to organize the skills, tools, and resources they will use to complete the project.

TEACH

W Writing Support

Independent Practice

Summarize Ask students to describe the steps they have already taken toward preparing for the specific career that interests them. Ask students to summarize all the steps they have taken, such as coursework or class projects at school, after-school activities, jobs or internships, or independent research and exploratory interviews. Ask students to summarize which of these steps have proven most effective and helpful so far, and why. (Summaries will vary, but students should understand that every step they take to prepare for a successful career can serve as a valuable learning experience, even if it does not seem to pay off right away.)

574

Developing a Plan to Achieve Your Goals

You know that career success is up to you. You have learned that change is certain throughout your career and that adapting to and anticipating change can help you succeed and meet your goals. You have also learned that career success is one part of success in life, and that setting goals and priorities can help you find happiness and balance. In this project, you will create a timeline that describes your major goals for the next ten years and create a plan to reach them.

Project Assignment

- Revisit your career plan, and redesign or refine it using everything you have learned throughout the units of *Succeeding in the World of Work*.
- Present your plan as a ten-year timeline, including your personal and financial goals, such as buying a house, along with your career goals.
- For each major goal, include that goal's related short-term goals and medium-term or intermediate goals.
- Conduct research to determine a realistic time frame and sequence for accomplishing each goal.
- Present your timeline to the class.

Lifelong Learning Connection

Lifelong learning concepts found in this project include:
- self-assessment
- setting goals and making decisions
- your career plan and career path
- adaptability

 574 **Unit 7** Lifelong Learning

glencoe.com

STEP 1 Evaluate Your Skills and Resources

To complete this project, you will need to consult school counselors, library reference materials, the Internet, workers in your desired field, companies where you might gain employment, real estate agents, financial advisors, and anyone else with knowledge that can be of use. The more extensive your research, the more realistic and useful your timeline will be.

Skills you may need to complete the Unit Thematic Project include:

Academic Skills reading, writing, mathematics, social studies

Transferable Skills communication, research, problem-solving, and decision-making skills

Technology Skills presentation software, word-processing, and Internet skills

@ Resources Organizer To find a graphic organizer you can use to determine the skills, tools, and resources you will need for this project, go to this book's Online Learning Center through **glencoe.com**.

SPOTLIGHT ON TECHNOLOGY

Cutting-Edge Jobs

Have students create a list of technology-related jobs or job functions that exist today but did not exist ten or twenty years ago. Then ask students to brainstorm technology-based jobs that might exist in another ten or twenty years. Ask students to explain whether they would be interested in having a job on the cutting edge of technology. Why or why not? (Examples of current jobs include video game developer, database administrator, or Web designer. New jobs might include bioinformatician, e-book author, nanotechnologist, or computational linguist. Students may like or dislike the intellectual challenge and fast pace of change in a technology career.)

STEP 2 Preview a Real-World Company Profile

For most people, a job is more than a paycheck. Most people want to work for a company that acts with integrity and that pays attention to issues of health, safety, and the environment. Companies that have socially responsible policies, such as the one featured below, can inspire employee loyalty.

Real-World Company: Lovecraft Biofuels

Lainey Johns never expected that she would work in a garage. But when her friend bought a car from Lovecraft Biofuels, Johns noticed that the company was busy. Although she was not an expert in engines or alternative fuels, she believed in the company and wanted to help. On a typical day, Johns might juggle helping customers, assisting mechanics, and answering phones.

Lovecraft Biofuels is a business that converts cars with diesel engines so that they can run on new or waste vegetable oil. The business also sells conversion parts and cars that have been converted. Most are Mercedes-Benz models from the 1980s.

To promote the clean-burning fuel, the company also sells vegetable oil and helps drivers set up their own vegetable oil distribution. Other processes that use new fuels are being developed as well. Johns and all employees must keep up with such developments.

Because Lovecraft is a small company that has been growing quickly every year, every worker is prepared to do whatever is necessary; job descriptions are flexible and evolving every day.

Lovecraft Biofuels

Aspects of Industry	Company Facts
Planning	Lovecraft Biofuels started with one service station and an ambitious plan to create a network of private and community fueling stations across the West.
Management	The founder makes many of the decisions, but the business is run as a cooperative in which everyone has a say.
Finance	The founder began the business as a hobby, then teamed up with a partner to open his first service station. Fueling stations are funded by membership dues and sales.
Technical and Production Skills	Mechanics at Lovecraft need specialized skills in working with car engines and exhaust systems.
Underlying Principles of Technology	The company installs a special filtering and heating system that allows standard diesel engines to run on nontoxic oils.
Labor Issues	Lovecraft is a startup company experiencing rapid growth. Workers are expected to be flexible and put in their strongest effort.
Health, Safety, and Environmental Issues	The company follows all safety precautions in its auto shop. Its technology cleans up the air by reducing smog-forming emissions.
Community Issues	The company conducts educational efforts in the media and is working to establish a membership-based network of vegetable oil fueling stations.

575

Developing Industry Partners

Find Government Partners

As you establish contact with local employers through your school-to-work program, don't forget the government. Local government agencies, as well as representatives of state and federal agencies and offices, may be eager to participate by providing job shadowing, mentoring, and volunteer opportunities or even paid part-time employment for students. Government workers may also be willing to visit the school to discuss careers in public administration or to set up field trips to help students better understand the work of their local government.

TEACH (cont.)

STEP 2

Preview a Real-World Company Profile

Point out to students that the founder of Lovecraft Biofuels turned his commitment to the environment into a career. Remind students of the core values discussed in Chapter 2—responsibility, relationships, compassion, courage, achievement, and recognition. Ask students to brainstorm other values that are important to them. Then ask how they might express these values in their careers. (Students' values and career ideas will vary. Encourage students to be creative in finding ways to express their values. Values can be expressed both in the specific careers students choose and in the way they approach their jobs every day.)

W Writing Support Guided Practice

Profiling Local Businesses
Remind students that understanding aspects of industry can aid their transition to employment in the rapidly changing global workplace and help them connect their academic coursework to the world of work. Ask students to work in pairs to create a profile of a local business modeled on the one shown here. Ask pairs to write two to three sentences summarizing the company's approach to each of the eight aspects of industry and to present their profiles to the class. Ask students to explain what they particularly like (and dislike) about the company. (Students' profiles should reflect thorough research and an accurate understanding of the eight aspects of industry.)

Unit 7 Thematic Project

STEP 3

Research Procedures

Have students go to the *Succeeding in the World of Work* OLC through **glencoe.com** for a graphic organizer they can use to organize the results of their research.

STEP 4

Connect to Community

Ask students how much they know about the career paths of working adults close to them, such as family members, neighbors, and others in their community. Do they know what career path the adults followed? Do they know how they chose or ended up in their current jobs? (Answers may vary. Many students may not know or have thought about how the adults who are close to them selected their careers. Encourage students to talk to the adults in their community to learn lessons about career preparation and success.) Ask students whether they know any adults who make it a priority to be informed and to vote. How do the adults stay informed? Where and when do they vote?

STEP 5

Report Your Findings

Give students these tips on creating their career timelines:

- Include short-term goals that you can begin working on right now.
- Make sure that your short-term, medium-term, and long-term goals are aligned.
- Be realistic about the amount of time required to achieve each goal.
- Color-code goals for different life areas, such as career, finances, and family.

576

STEP 3 Research Procedures

Follow the steps listed below to create your timeline:

1. Review the career profile you created in the Unit 1 Thematic Project. Make any necessary modifications.
2. Identify your career goal. Do research using online, print, and in-person resources to figure out the steps you will need to take to reach this goal. Include education and training as well as jobs, internships, or volunteer positions you may need to hold along the way toward achieving your ultimate career goal. Make sure to include short-term goals that you can begin to accomplish right away.
3. Identify personal goals for the next ten years that are related to your roles in life. Include goals related to family, friends, personal achievement, finances, community involvement, and any other areas that are important to you. Do research using online, print, and in-person resources to

figure out the steps you will need to take to reach each goal. Make sure to include short-term goals that you can begin to accomplish right away.

4. Assign a tentative date for accomplishing each long-term and medium-term or intermediate goal, then list all your goals in time order.

@ Resources Organizer To find a graphic organizer you can use to organize your research, go to this book's OLC through **glencoe.com**.

STEP 4 Connect to Community

Get Local Ask local friends or relatives how they have changed their career and personal goals through the years. How has the community changed, and how have those changes affected their plans? What tips or suggestions do they have for you?

Take the Next Step Create a list of things that will change over the next decades and how they might affect your plans. Consider items such as changes in technology, culture, the economy, and the environment. What are some major changes that could cause you to change your personal or career goals?

STEP 5 Report Your Findings

Your product for this project should include a poster that features your timeline and explains your personal and career goals. Finally, you will give an oral presentation to the class.

- Use graphic design, word-processing, or desktop publishing software to create a timeline that presents your goals in time order and uses colors or other graphical devices to visually indicate which long-term goals relate to which medium-term or intermediate goals.

Developing Community Involvement

Improve Local Recycling Programs

Work with students to introduce or improve recycling services at a local facility such as a school, apartment or industrial complex, or park or community center. Ask students to form teams focusing on specific materials, such as green waste, plastics, glass, metal, electronics, and construction waste. Have students research the existing recycling programs at the chosen facility and then contact local companies that process recyclables and ask how businesses can improve their recycling programs. Teams should use what they learn to create recommendations for improving the facility's recycling efforts.

- Create an oral presentation that describes your timeline and your process for creating it, highlights your long-term goals, and explains how each medium-term or intermediate goal gets you closer to your ultimate goals.

Helpful Hints Try some of the following approaches to help craft your timeline and set your goals for the future:
- Talk to an adult whom you respect. Ask this person how he or she arrived at his or her current station in life.
- Ask your school guidance counselor for referrals to workers in your desired career field.
- Consider taking a formal career interest or aptitude test.
- Focus on gaining appropriate training and education as your first goal.

STEP 6 Presentation and Evaluation

Your timeline will be evaluated based on:

Personal Academic and Career Portfolio

Print out or create a copy of your timeline to include in your **Personal Academic and Career Portfolio**. You can use this timeline as a roadmap to achieving your goals, and you can adjust it as you develop new goals and as you adapt to changes in the workplace and in your personal life.

- development of comprehensive, realistic short-term, medium-term, and long-term goals based on thorough research
- creativity, thoughtfulness, and neatness of timeline
- quality of presentation

Evaluation Rubric To find a rubric you can use to evaluate your project, go to this book's OLC through **glencoe.com**.

BusinessWeek Connection

Understanding All Aspects of Industry: Health, Safety, and Environmental Issues

Understanding all aspects of industry can help you prepare to succeed in a career in that industry. Responsible businesses keep their workers, their communities, and the planet healthy and safe by following all safety, health, and environmental laws and regulations. Businesses that are responsive and attentive to consumer and worker health and safety issues and concerns can retain goodwill in the job market and in the marketplace. For

example, more and more businesses are also developing products to appeal specifically to environmentally conscious consumers.

Go to this book's Online Learning Center through **glencoe.com** to find a *BusinessWeek* article titled "Chinese Will Pay More for Green PCs." Read the article and identify actions a business can take to minimize its effect on the environment. Use a word-processing program to create a one-page summary of the article. Add this summary to your **Personal Academic and Career Portfolio**.

ASSESS

STEP 6
Presentation and Evaluation
Rubric Encourage students go to the *Succeeding in the World of Work* OLC through **glencoe.com** for a rubric they can use to evaluate their project. Encourage students to use the rubric as a content checklist when setting goals and creating a timeline.

CLOSE
Culminating Activity
Future Plans In this project, students applied the Unit topic to their own lives by creating a roadmap to their personal and professional goals. Ask students to work in pairs to create timelines detailing their goals and anticipated activities for the first year after leaving school. Will they work, attend school, or both? How will they support themselves? What do they hope to accomplish during this year? How will they continue their career development? Ask students to discuss how their vision for this year may have changed during the course of the Unit Thematic Project. (Students' plans will vary, but all students should understand that planning is essential to career success and that setting and achieving specific goals can help them take charge of their lives and achieve independence and a feeling of accomplishment.)

BusinessWeek Connection

All Aspects of Industry: Environmental Issues

Ask students if they are willing to spend more for environmentally friendly products than for conventional ones. Have them consider items such as organic produce, nontoxic cleaning agents, clothing made from natural fibers, or vehicles that run on biodiesel or hybrid technology. How

could a business convince them to spend extra money for these products? (Students may suggest that businesses could emphasize the benefits and quality of their products, make them trendy by having celebrities endorse the products, or educate consumers about the health and ecological consequences of toxic or wasteful production processes.)

Agriculture, Food, and Natural Resources

Architecture and Construction

Arts, Audio/Video Technology, and Communications

Business, Management, and Administration

What Is the Career Clusters Appendix?

The Career Clusters Appendix provides you and the students with additional information about career clusters. On these pages, you will find a basic introduction to the career clusters concepts of pathways, knowledge, and skills. Pages 578–585 provide a more detailed look at each of the 16 career clusters and at each individual cluster's pathways.

For more information about the 16 career clusters, visit the career clusters through the *Succeeding in the World of Work* Online Learning Center through **glencoe.com**.

What Are Career Clusters?

Career clusters are groups of similar occupations and industries. By studying career clusters, you and the students can explore the range of careers available in today's 21st century global workplace. Career clusters were developed by the Office of Vocational and Adult Education (OVAE) of the U.S. Department of Education to provide an organized, engaging way to help students identify their career interests and plan their careers.

Career clusters are organized by industry and occupation. Each cluster covers a fundamental part of the economy, such as farming, forestry, and mining; banking and insurance; or policing, corrections, law, and security. Industries produce goods and services, and occupations require workers to have specific job skills and knowledge. Most occupations fall in one cluster, but some careers may fall within two different career clusters. For example, a child psychologist is part of both the Human Services career cluster and the Health Science career cluster. Workers in this career must use their medical training to provide services to people.

Career clusters provide students with a meaningful context through which they can learn about a group of occupations. Each cluster contains a variety of jobs that will appeal to students of widely varying interests. These clusters provide links between what students learn in the classroom and the knowledge and skills that they will need in for success both in school and in the world of work.

The career clusters are:
- Agriculture, Food, and Natural Resources
- Architecture and Construction
- Arts, Audio/Video Technology, and Communications

- Business, Management, and Administration
- Education and Training
- Finance
- Government and Public Administration
- Health Science
- Hospitality and Tourism
- Human Services
- Information Technology
- Law, Public Safety, Corrections, and Security
- Manufacturing
- Marketing, Sales, and Service
- Science, Technology, Engineering, and Mathematics
- Transportation, Distribution, and Logistics

Why 16 Clusters?

To be useful, career clusters must strike a balance between the general and the specific. They must be specific enough to have a foundation of knowledge and skills, but broad enough to expose students to a variety of job possibilities, from hands-on entry-level work to professional and managerial work that requires extensive training and/or experience.

Many states have developed their own career cluster framework, though many use fewer than 16 clusters. The advantage of teaching 16 clusters is that students get a broader picture of the range of jobs in each individual career cluster. For example, many states combine manufacturing, construction, and transportation careers in a single cluster, because these industries are alike in some ways; many entry-level jobs, for instance, involve manual labor and do not require extensive postsecondary training or education. However, workers in these three industries do very different things. Welding a car frame, building a wooden roof, and driving a truck all require technical skills, but they are unlikely to appeal equally to the same students. The 16 career clusters take into account that meaningful career planning will engage students' interests, aptitudes, personality, and values, in addition to their technical and job-specific skills. The OVAE has separated manufacturing, construction, and transportation into three clusters: Architecture and Construction; Manufacturing; and Transportation, Distribution, and Logistics.

Education and Training

Finance

Government and Public Administration

Health Science

Hospitality and Tourism

Human Services

Information Technology

Law, Public Safety, Corrections, and Security

By learning career information in an industry-wide context, students can make real connections about the meaning and purpose of potential careers. For example, by studying the Architecture and Construction career cluster, they can learn not only about the technical tasks involved in building a roof, but also how and why structures are designed, planned, and built, and how they might play a part in this process.

What Are Career Pathways?

To bring the variety of occupations in a career cluster into focus, each of the 16 career clusters is divided into a number of career pathways. A career pathway is an area of occupational interest and concentration within a particular career cluster. Each pathway contains a group of careers that require similar academic skills, technical skills, education, training, or certification. For example, within the Finance career cluster, jobs in the business financial management pathway require excellent analytical skills, math skills, and communication skills. These jobs also require a knowledge of business financial and accounting laws and practices. Career pathways can help students identify routes they can take from secondary school to further training and education, including two-year schools, four-year schools, vocational schools, graduate schools, and the workplace. They help students select the education and training appropriate for their career goals.

To develop definitive knowledge and skill standards for each career pathway, the OVAE worked with an umbrella organization of states, the States' Career Clusters. This organization has created cluster-specific committees of secondary and postsecondary educators, industry and labor representatives, trade and professional associations, and government agencies. These committees and other organizations work to develop knowledge and skill statements for each of the career clusters.

Why Use Career Clusters?

Modern educators are calling for a more integrated approach to career education, one that replaces the emphasis on isolated technical skills with an integrated curriculum that develops the high-level transferable skills that today's workers need to succeed. Using career clusters provides a framework for this kind of career education by offering real-world context and by challenging students to apply critical thinking and analysis to their career planning.

Some educators go a step further and advocate reorganizing high school curricula around individual career clusters, like career academies. In this model, high schools would be much like career academies, in which real-world experience and career preparation are used to reinforce academic skills. Students can build their foundation skills through the application of academics to real-world scenarios from a selected career cluster.

Even comprehensive high schools with traditional curricula can benefit by incorporating career clusters into career education. Study of career clusters expands students' career awareness by providing opportunities for them to:

- understand the importance of academic success to future career success
- make connections among occupations, among career pathways in a cluster, and among different career clusters
- understand the variations in knowledge and skills needed for careers within a cluster
- understand basic skills, or the skills that are needed for all careers in all clusters
- learn about the education and training options within each career cluster and career pathway
- explore emerging and rapidly growing careers
- build self-awareness and understand the importance of personal interests, aptitudes, and skills in choosing a career, and
- develop workplace readiness skills, such as responsibility, teamwork skills, and technology skills.

For teachers and other educators, career clusters can be used to:
- design instructional units and activities to demonstrate the connection between academic skills and careers
- provide a real-life context from the real world of work to reinforce the importance of academic success to success in the workplace
- provide a springboard for students' independent career exploration, research, and decision making
- develop experiential activities in conjunction with business and industry partners. These activities may include visits to work sites, job shadowing, service learning, and in-school work-related activities.

Manufacturing

Marketing, Sales, and Service

Science, Technology, Engineering, and Mathematics

Transportation, Distribution, and Logistics

Career Clusters Appendix

Go to the *Succeeding in the World of Work* OLC through **glencoe.com** for more information about the 16 career clusters.

 ## Agriculture, Food, and Natural Resources

There are seven pathways in the agriculture, food, and natural resources career cluster.

- **Food products and processing systems** is preparing food for sale.
- **Plant systems** is plant and soil science, gardening, and forestry.
- **Animal systems** is work with large and small animals, wildlife, and research animals.
- **Power, structural, and technical systems** is work with energy and computer systems.
- **Natural resource systems** is work with nature such as logging, parks, mining, and fishing.
- **Environmental service systems** is checking water and air quality and handling waste.
- **Agribusiness systems** is sales, service, management, and entrepreneurship related to agriculture.

Architecture and Construction

There are three pathways in the architecture and construction career cluster.

- **Design and pre-construction** is planning structures, such as roads and houses.
- **Construction** is building all the parts of structures.
- **Maintenance and operations** is doing repairs and making sure structures work as they should.

Arts, Audio/Video Technology, and Communications

There are six pathways in the arts, audio/video technology, and communications career cluster.

- **Audio and video technology and film** is making, selling, installing, and repairing audio and video equipment and presenting sound, video, and data.
- **Journalism and broadcasting** is bringing people news and entertainment through radio, television and movies.
- **Performing arts** are theater, music, and dance.
- **Printing technology** is printing books, newspapers, and other printed material.
- **Telecommunications** is working with communications and computer equipment.
- **Visual arts** are painting, drawing, sculpting, photography, and animation.

Business, Management, and Administration

There are six pathways in the business, management, and administration career cluster.

- **Management** is making decisions and planning.
- **Business financial management and accounting** is doing accounting and finance to help make businesses successful.
- **Human resources** is hiring and training employees, and helping them to be productive.
- **Business analysis** is finding solutions for business problems and making businesses work.
- **Marketing** is managing products and services and deciding which goods and services people will want to buy.
- **Administration and information support** is using technology to do administrative work such as running an office.

Education and Training

There are three pathways in the education and training career cluster.

- **Teaching and training** is showing people how to learn a subject or a skill.
- **Professional support services** provide counseling and assistance to people seeking education and training.
- **Administration and administrative support** manage the day-to-day activities and goals of schools and other educational and training facilities.

Finance

There are four pathways in the finance career cluster.

- **Financial and investment planning** is providing advice about money and what to do with it.
- **Business financial management** is creating accounting systems used to make financial decisions for businesses.
- **Banking and related services** provide banks, loans, and credit services.
- **Insurance services** provide financial protection from loss.

Government and Public Administration

There are seven pathways in the government and public administration career cluster.

- **Governance** is creating and enforcing laws and public policies.
- **National security** is being a member of the armed forces and protecting our country.
- **Foreign service** workers represent the interests of our country to other nations.
- **Planning** is making goals and plans for how to use land and resources.
- **Revenue and taxation** is collecting and monitoring taxes from citizens and businesses.
- **Regulation** makes sure that industries, utilities, buildings, the environment, and technology are properly used, maintained, and protected.
- **Public management and administration** is running agencies or companies that deal with public resources, such as a city or utility.

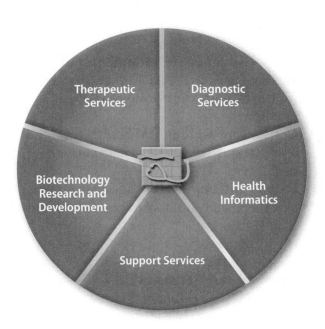

Health Science

There are five pathways in the health science career cluster.

- **Therapeutic services** maintain and improve health over time by providing care, treatment, counseling, and health information.
- **Diagnostic services** detect, diagnose, and treat medical conditions.
- **Health informatics** includes health care administration as well as the collecting and managing patient and health care information and technology.
- **Support services** provide an environment for health care delivery.
- **Biotechnology research and development** involves studying, discovering and creating health conditions, treatments, information and services.

Hospitality and Tourism

There are four pathways in the hospitality and tourism career cluster.

- **Restaurant and food and beverage services** provide places and services where customers can eat and drink.
- **Lodging** is all the services involved in providing a place to live for one or several days.
- **Recreation, amusements, and attractions** are services on location for leisure activities such as sports, festivals, or amusement rides.
- **Travel and tourism** employees develop and manage places, guides, and services for travelers.

Human Services

There are five pathways in the human services career cluster.

- **Early childhood development and services** is all the services that provide for the care and nurturing of young children.
- **Counseling and mental health services** assist people with issues, decisions, and problems.
- **Family and community services** provide assistance and care for human beings and their social needs, such as financial or family counseling, employment training, and disabled-access services.
- **Personal care services** deal with physical and emotional well-being. These services can include hairstylists, dentists, dance teachers, and funeral attendants.
- **Consumer services** help people make decisions about their finances and their purchases.

Information Technology

There are four pathways in the information technology career cluster.

- **Interactive media** deals with digital media such as the World Wide Web, DVDs, and CD-ROMs.
- **Programming and software development** is designing and maintaining computer operating systems and software.
- **Network systems** deal with the maintenance of computer networks.
- **Information support and services** deal with creating, maintaining, and providing technical assistance for computer systems.

Law, Public Safety, Corrections, and Security

There are five pathways in the law, public safety, corrections, and security career cluster.

- **Correction services** workers manage and help individuals who are in or have been in corrections facilities such as jail.
- **Emergency and fire management services** protect the public in case of fires and other emergencies.
- **Security and protective services** work to protect public and private property such as museums or businesses.
- **Law enforcement services** maintain public order and protect lives and property.
- **Legal services** assist individuals or businesses in seeking legal help in civil or criminal matters.

Manufacturing

There are six pathways in the manufacturing career cluster.

- **Production** is making or assembling parts or products.
- **Manufacturing production process development** is designing products and manufacturing processes.
- **Maintenance, installation, and repair** is maintaining equipment.
- **Quality assurance** is making sure things are done and made correctly.
- **Logistics and inventory control** is keeping track of and moving manufacturing products and materials.
- **Health, safety, and environmental assurance** is making sure that the workplace is safe.

 # Marketing, Sales, and Service

There are seven pathways in the marketing, sales, and service career cluster.

- **Management and entrepreneurship** is forming and running businesses.
- **Professional sales and marketing** is developing and promoting products for sale.
- **Buying and merchandising** is the service of getting products to the customer.
- **Marketing communications and promotion** is getting information out to the public about a good or service.
- **Marketing information management and research** is understanding people's needs and wants and developing products for them.
- **Distribution and logistics** is moving and keeping track of products and materials.
- **E-marketing** is using electronic tools such as e-mail for marketing.

Science, Technology, Engineering, and Mathematics

There are two pathways in the science, technology, engineering, and mathematics career cluster.

- **Science and mathematics** is using science and math skills to perform research, create products, and solve problems.
- **Engineering and technology** is using and applying scientific principles and processes in the real world.

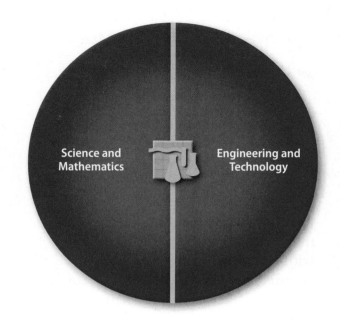

Science and Mathematics

Engineering and Technology

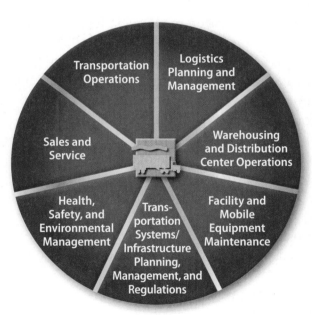

Transportation Operations

Logistics Planning and Management

Sales and Service

Warehousing and Distribution Center Operations

Health, Safety, and Environmental Management

Transportation Systems/ Infrastructure Planning, Management, and Regulations

Facility and Mobile Equipment Maintenance

Transportation, Distribution, and Logistics

There are seven pathways in the transportation, distribution, and logistics career cluster.

- **Transportation operations** is getting things and people safely from one place to another.
- **Logistics planning and management** is distributing and transporting materials.
- **Warehousing and distribution center operations** keep track of and manage cargo.
- **Facility and mobile equipment maintenance** is making sure transportation vehicles are working and functional.
- **Transportation systems/infrastructure planning, management, and regulations** is managing and designing public transportation.
- **Health, safety, and environmental management** is handling and planning for risks.
- **Sales and service** is marketing and selling transportation services.

Number and Operations

▶ *Understand numbers, ways of representing numbers, relationships among numbers, and number systems*

Fraction, Decimal, and Percent

A percent is a ratio that compares a number to 100. To write a percent as a fraction, drop the percent sign, and use the number as the numerator in a fraction with a denominator of 100. Simplify, if possible. For example, $76\% = \frac{76}{100}$, or $\frac{19}{25}$. To write a fraction as a percent, convert it to an equivalent fraction with a denominator of 100. For example, $\frac{3}{4} = \frac{75}{100}$, or 75%. A fraction can be expressed as a percent by first converting the fraction to a decimal (divide the numerator by the denominator) and then converting the decimal to a percent by moving the decimal point two places to the right.

Comparing Numbers on a Number Line

In order to compare and understand the relationship between real numbers in various forms, it is helpful to use a number line. The zero point on a number line is called the origin; the points to the left of the origin are negative, and those to the right are positive. The number line below shows how numbers in fraction, decimal, percent, and integer form can be compared.

Percents Greater Than 100 and Less Than 1

Percents greater than 100% represent values greater than 1. For example, if the weight of an object is 250% of another, it is 2.5, or $2\frac{1}{2}$, times the weight.

Percents less than 1 represent values less than $\frac{1}{100}$. In other words, 0.1% is one tenth of one percent, which can also be represented in decimal form as 0.001, or in fraction form as $\frac{1}{1,000}$. Similarly, 0.01% is one hundredth of one percent or 0.0001 or $\frac{1}{10,000}$.

Ratio, Rate, and Proportion

A ratio is a comparison of two numbers using division. If a basketball player makes 8 out of 10 free throws, the ratio is written as 8 to 10, 8:10, or $\frac{8}{10}$. Ratios are usually written in simplest form. In simplest form, the ratio "8 out of 10" is 4 to 5, 4:5, or $\frac{4}{5}$. A rate is a ratio of two measurements having different kinds of units—cups per gallon, or miles per hour, for example. When a rate is simplified so that it has a denominator of 1, it is called a unit rate. An example of a unit rate is 9 miles per hour. A proportion is an equation stating that two ratios are equal. $\frac{3}{18} = \frac{13}{78}$ is an example of a proportion. The cross products of a proportion are also equal. $\frac{3}{18} = \frac{13}{78}$ and $3 \times 78 = 18 \times 13$.

Representing Large and Small Numbers

In order to represent large and small numbers, it is important to understand the number system. Our number system is based on 10, and the value of each place is 10 times the value of the place to its right.

The value of a digit is the product of a digit and its place value. For instance, in the number 6,400, the 6 has a value of six thousands and the 4 has a value of four hundreds. A place value chart can help you read numbers. In the chart, each group of three digits is called a period. Commas separate the periods: the ones period, the thousands period, the millions period, and so on. Values to the right of the ones period are decimals. By understanding place value you can write very large numbers like 5 billion and more, and very small numbers that are less than 1, such as one tenth.

Scientific Notation
When dealing with very large numbers like 1,500,000, or very small numbers like 0.000015, it is helpful to keep track of their value by writing the numbers in scientific notation. Powers of 10 with positive exponents are used with a decimal between 1 and 10 to express large numbers. The exponent represents the number of places the decimal point is moved to the right. So, 528,000 is written in scientific notation as 5.28×10^5. Powers of 10 with negative exponents are used with a decimal between 1 and 10 to express small numbers. The exponent represents the number of places the decimal point is moved to the left. The number 0.00047 is expressed as 4.7×10^{-4}.

Factor, Multiple, and Prime Factorization
Two or more numbers that are multiplied to form a product are called factors. Divisibility rules can be used to determine whether 2, 3, 4, 5, 6, 8, 9, or 10 are factors of a given number. Multiples are the products of a given number and various integers.

For example, 8 is a multiple of 4 because $4 \times 2 = 8$. A prime number is a whole number that has exactly two factors: 1 and itself. A composite number is a whole number that has more than two factors. Zero and 1 are neither prime nor composite. A composite number can be expressed as the product of its prime factors. The prime factorization of 40 is $2 \times 2 \times 2 \times 5$, or $2^3 \times 5$. The numbers 2 and 5 are prime numbers.

Integers
A negative number is a number less than zero. Negative numbers like −8, positive numbers like +6, and zero are members of the set of integers. Integers can be represented as points on a number line. A set of integers can be written {..., −3, −2, −1, 0, 1, 2, 3, ...} where ... means "continues indefinitely."

Real, Rational, and Irrational Numbers
The real number system is made up of the sets of rational and irrational numbers. Rational numbers are numbers that can be written in the form a/b where a and b are integers and $b \neq 0$. Examples are 0.45, $\frac{1}{2}$, and $\sqrt{36}$. Irrational numbers are non-repeating, non-terminating decimals. Examples are $\sqrt{71}$, π, and 0.020020002....

Complex and Imaginary Numbers
A complex number is a mathematical expression with a real number element and an imaginary number element. Imaginary numbers are multiples of i, the "imaginary" square root of −1. Complex numbers are represented by $a + bi$, where a and b are real numbers and i represents the imaginary element. When a quadratic

equation does not have a real number solution, the solution can be represented by a complex number. Like real numbers, complex numbers can be added, subtracted, multiplied, and divided.

Vectors and Matrices

A matrix is a set of numbers or elements arranged in rows and columns to form a rectangle. The number of rows is represented by m and the number of columns is represented by n. To describe the number of rows and columns in a matrix, list the number of rows first using the format $m \times n$. Matrix A below is a 3×3 matrix because it has 3 rows and 3 columns. To name an element of a matrix, the letter i is used to denote the row and j is used to denote the column, and the element is labeled in the form $a_{i,j}$. In matrix A below, $a_{3,2}$ is 4.

$$\text{Matrix A} = \begin{pmatrix} 1 & 3 & 5 \\ 0 & 6 & 8 \\ 3 & 4 & 5 \end{pmatrix}$$

A vector is a matrix with only one column or row of elements. A transposed column vector, or a column vector turned on its side, is a row vector. In the example below, row vector b' is the transpose of column vector b.

$$b = \begin{pmatrix} 1 \\ 2 \\ 3 \\ 4 \end{pmatrix}$$

$$b' = \begin{pmatrix} 1 & 2 & 3 & 4 \end{pmatrix}$$

▶ Understand meanings of operations and how they relate to one another

Properties of Addition and Multiplication

Properties are statements that are true for any numbers. For example, $3 + 8$ is the same as $8 + 3$ because each expression equals 11. This illustrates the Commutative Property of Addition. Likewise, $3 \times 8 = 8 \times 3$ illustrates the Commutative Property of Multiplication.

When evaluating expressions, it is often helpful to group or associate the numbers. The Associative Property says that the way in which numbers are grouped when added or multiplied does not change the sum or product. The following properties are also true:

- **Additive Identity Property:** When 0 is added to any number, the sum is the number.

- **Multiplicative Identity Property:** When any number is multiplied by 1, the product is the number.

- **Multiplicative Property of Zero:** When any number is multiplied by 0, the product is 0.

Rational Numbers

A number that can be written as a fraction is called a rational number. Terminating and repeating decimals are rational numbers because both can be written as fractions.

Decimals that are neither terminating nor repeating are called irrational numbers because they cannot be written as fractions. Terminating decimals can be converted to fractions by placing the number (without the decimal point) in the numerator. Count the number of places to the right of the decimal point, and in the denominator, place a 1 followed by a number of zeros equal to the number of places that you counted. The fraction can then be reduced to simplest form.

Writing a Fraction as a Decimal

Any fraction $\frac{a}{b}$, where $b \neq 0$, can be written as a decimal by dividing the numerator by the denominator. So, $\frac{a}{b} = a \div b$. If the division ends, or terminates, when the remainder is zero, the decimal is a terminating decimal. Not all fractions can be written as terminating decimals. Some have a repeating decimal. A bar indicates that the decimal repeats forever. For example, the fraction $\frac{4}{9}$ can be converted to a repeating decimal, $0.\overline{4}$

Adding and Subtracting Like Fractions

Fractions with the same denominator are called like fractions. To add like fractions, add the numerators and write the sum over the denominator. To add mixed numbers with like fractions, add the whole numbers and fractions separately, adding the numerators of the fractions, then simplifying if necessary. The rule for subtracting fractions with like denominators is similar to the rule for adding. The numerators can be subtracted and the difference written over the denominator. Mixed numbers are written as improper fractions before subtracting. These same rules apply to adding or subtracting like algebraic fractions. A fraction that contains one or more variables in the numerator or denominator is called an algebraic fraction.

Adding and Subtracting Unlike Fractions

Fractions with different denominators are called unlike fractions. The least common multiple of the denominators is used to rename the fractions with a common denominator. After a common denominator is found, the numerators can then be added or subtracted. To add mixed numbers with unlike fractions, rename the mixed numbers as improper fractions. Then find a common denominator, add the numerators, and simplify the answer.

Multiplying Rational Numbers

To multiply fractions, multiply the numerators and multiply the denominators. If the numerators and denominators have common factors, they can be simplified before multiplication. If the fractions have different signs, then the product will be negative. Mixed numbers can be multiplied in the same manner, after first renaming them as improper fractions. Algebraic fractions may be multiplied using the same method described above.

Dividing Rational Numbers

To divide a number by a rational number (a fraction, for example), multiply the first number by the multiplicative inverse of the second. Two numbers whose product is 1 are called multiplicative inverses, or reciprocals. $\frac{7}{4} \times \frac{4}{7} = 1$. When dividing by a mixed number, first rename it as an improper fraction, and then multiply by its multiplicative inverse. This process of multiplying by a number's reciprocal can also be used when dividing algebraic fractions.

Adding Integers

To add integers with the same sign, add their absolute values. The sum then takes the same sign as the addends. The equation $-5 + (-2) = -7$ is an example of adding two integers with the same sign. To add integers with different signs, subtract their absolute values. The sum takes the same sign as the addend with the greater absolute value.

Subtracting Integers

The rules for adding integers are extended to the subtraction of integers. To subtract an integer, add its additive inverse. For example, to find the difference $2 - 5$, add the additive inverse of 5 to 2: $2 + (-5) = -3$. The rule for subtracting integers can be used to solve real-world problems and to evaluate algebraic expressions.

Additive Inverse Property

Two numbers with the same absolute value but different signs are called opposites. For example, -4 and 4 are opposites. An integer and its opposite are also called additive inverses. The Additive Inverse Property says that the sum of any number and its additive inverse is

zero. The Commutative, Associative, and Identity Properties also apply to integers. These properties help when adding more than two integers.

Absolute Value

In mathematics, when two integers on a number line are on opposite sides of zero, and they are the same distance from zero, they have the same absolute value. The symbol for absolute value is two vertical bars on either side of the number. For example, $|-5| = 5$.

Multiplying Integers

Since multiplication is repeated addition, $3(-7)$ means that -7 is used as an addend 3 times. By the Commutative Property of Multiplication, $3(-7) = -7(3)$. The product of two integers with different signs is always negative. The product of two integers with the same sign is always positive.

Dividing Integers

The quotient of two integers can be found by dividing the numbers using their absolute values. The quotient of two integers with the same sign is positive, and the quotient of two integers with a different sign is negative. $-12 \div (-4) = 3$ and $12 \div (-4) = -3$. The division of integers is used in statistics to find the average, or mean, of a set of data. When finding the mean of a set of numbers, find the sum of the numbers, and then divide by the number in the set.

Adding and Multiplying Vectors and Matrices

In order to add two matrices together, they must have the same number of rows and columns. In matrix addition, the corresponding elements are added to each other. In other words $(a + b)_{ij} = a_{ij} + b_{ij}$. For example,

$$\begin{pmatrix} 1 & 2 \\ 2 & 1 \end{pmatrix} + \begin{pmatrix} 3 & 6 \\ 0 & 1 \end{pmatrix} = \begin{pmatrix} 1+3 & 2+6 \\ 2+0 & 1+1 \end{pmatrix} = \begin{pmatrix} 4 & 8 \\ 2 & 2 \end{pmatrix}$$

Matrix multiplication requires that the number of elements in each row in the first matrix is equal to the number of elements in each column in the second. The elements of the first row of the first matrix are multiplied by the corresponding elements of the first column of the second matrix and then added together to get the first element of the product matrix. To get the second element, the elements in the first row of the first matrix are multiplied by the corresponding elements in the second column of the second matrix then added, and so on, until every row of the first matrix is multiplied by every column of the second. See the example below.

$$\begin{pmatrix} 1 & 2 \\ 3 & 4 \end{pmatrix} \times \begin{pmatrix} 3 & 6 \\ 0 & 1 \end{pmatrix} = \begin{pmatrix} (1\times3)+(2\times0) & (1\times6)+(2\times1) \\ (3\times3)+(4\times0) & (3\times6)+(4\times1) \end{pmatrix} = \begin{pmatrix} 3 & 8 \\ 9 & 22 \end{pmatrix}$$

Vector addition and multiplication are performed in the same way, but there is only one column and one row.

Permutations and Combinations

Permutations and combinations are used to determine the number of possible outcomes in different situations. An arrangement, listing, or pattern in which order is important is called a permutation. The symbol P(6, 3) represents the number of permutations of 6 things taken 3 at a time. For P(6, 3), there are $6 \times 5 \times 4$ or 120 possible outcomes. An arrangement or listing where order is not important is called a combination. The symbol C(10, 5) represents the number of combinations of 10 things taken 5 at a time. For C(10, 5),

there are $(10 \times 9 \times 8 \times 7 \times 6) \div (5 \times 4 \times 3 \times 2 \times 1)$ or 252 possible outcomes.

Powers and Exponents

An expression such as $3 \times 3 \times 3 \times 3$ can be written as a power. A power has two parts, a base and an exponent. $3 \times 3 \times 3 \times 3 = 3^4$. The base is the number that is multiplied (3). The exponent tells how many times the base is used as a factor (4 times). Numbers and variables can be written using exponents. For example, $8 \times 8 \times 8 \times m \times m \times m \times m \times m$ can be expressed $8^3 m^5$. Exponents also can be used with place value to express numbers in expanded form. Using this method, 1,462 can be written as $(1 \times 10^3) + (4 \times 10^2) + (6 \times 10^1) + (2 \times 10^0)$.

Squares and Square Roots

The square root of a number is one of two equal factors of a number. Every positive number has both a positive and a negative square root. For example, since $8 \times 8 = 64$, 8 is a square root of 64. Since $(-8) \times (-8) = 64$, -8 is also a square root of 64. The notation $\sqrt{}$ indicates the positive square root, $-\sqrt{}$ indicates the negative square root, and $\pm\sqrt{}$ indicates both square roots. For example, $\sqrt{81} = 9$, $-\sqrt{49} = -7$, and $\pm\sqrt{4} = \pm2$. The square root of a negative number is an imaginary number because any two factors of a negative number must have different signs, and are therefore not equivalent.

Logarithm

A logarithm is the inverse of exponentiation. The logarithm of a number x in base b is equal to the number n. Therefore, $b^n = x$ and $\log_b x = n$. For example, $\log_4(64) = 3$ because $4^3 = 64$. The most commonly used bases for logarithms are 10, the common logarithm; 2, the binary logarithm;

and the constant e, the natural logarithm (also called $ln(x)$ instead of $\log_e(x)$). Below is a list of some of the rules of logarithms that are important to understand if you are going to use them.

$$\log_b(xy) = \log_b(x) + \log_b(y)$$
$$\log_b(x/y) = \log_b(x) - \log_b(y)$$
$$\log_b(1/x) = -\log_b(x)$$
$$\log_b(x)y = y\log_b(x)$$

▶ Compute fluently and make reasonable estimates

Estimation by Rounding
When rounding numbers, look at the digit to the right of the place to which you are rounding. If the digit is 5 or greater, round up. If it is less than 5, round down. For example, to round 65,137 to the nearest hundred, look at the number in the tens place. Since 3 is less than 5, round down to 65,100. To round the same number to the nearest ten thousandth, look at the number in the thousandths place. Since it is 5, round up to 70,000.

Finding Equivalent Ratios
Equivalent ratios have the same meaning. Just like finding equivalent fractions, to find an equivalent ratio, multiply or divide both sides by the same number. For example, you can multiply 7 by both sides of the ratio 6:8 to get 42:56. Instead, you can also divide both sides of the same ratio by 2 to get 3:4. Find the simplest form of a ratio

by dividing to find equivalent ratios until you can't go any further without going into decimals. So, 160:240 in simplest form is 2:3. To write a ratio in the form 1:n, divide both sides by the left-hand number. In other words, to change 8:20 to 1:n, divide both sides by 8 to get 1:2.5.

Front-End Estimation
Front-end estimation can be used to quickly estimate sums and differences before adding or subtracting. To use this technique, add or subtract just the digits of the two highest place values, and replace the other place values with zero. This will give you an estimation of the solution of a problem. For example, 93,471 − 22,825 can be changed to 93,000 − 22,000 or 71,000. This estimate can be compared to your final answer to judge its correctness.

Judging Reasonableness
When solving an equation, it is important to check your work by considering how reasonable your answer is. For example, consider the equation $9\frac{3}{4} \times 4\frac{1}{3}$. Since $9\frac{3}{4}$ is between 9 and 10 and $4\frac{1}{3}$ is between 4 and 5, only values that are between 9 × 4 or 36 and 10 × 5 or 50 will be reasonable. You can also use front-end estimation, or you can round and estimate a reasonable answer. In the equation 73 × 25, you can round and solve to estimate a reasonable answer to be near 70 × 30 or 2,100.

Algebra

▶ *Understand patterns, relations, and functions*

Relation

A relation is a generalization comparing sets of ordered pairs for an equation or inequality such as $x = y + 1$ or $x > y$. The first element in each pair, the x values, forms the domain. The second element in each pair, the y values, forms the range.

Function

A function is a special relation in which each member of the domain is paired with exactly one member in the range. Functions may be represented using ordered pairs, tables, or graphs. One way to determine whether a relation is a function is to use the vertical line test. Using an object to represent a vertical line, move the object from left to right across the graph. If, for each value of x in the domain, the object passes through no more than one point on the graph, then the graph represents a function.

Linear and Nonlinear Functions

Linear functions have graphs that are straight lines. These graphs represent constant rates of change. In other words, the slope between any two pairs of points on the graph is the same. Nonlinear functions do not have constant rates of change. The slope changes along these graphs. Therefore, the graphs of nonlinear functions are *not* straight lines. Graphs of curves represent nonlinear functions. The equation for a linear function can be written in the form $y = mx + b$, where m represents the constant rate of change, or the slope. Therefore, you can determine whether a function is linear by looking at the equation. For example, the equation $y = \frac{3}{x}$ is nonlinear because x is in the denominator and the equation cannot be written in the form $y = mx + b$. A nonlinear function does not increase or decrease at a constant rate. You can check this by using a table and finding the increase or decrease in y for each regular increase in x. For example, if for each increase in x by 2, y does not increase or decrease the same amount each time, the function is nonlinear.

Linear Equations in Two Variables

In a linear equation with two variables, such as $y = x - 3$, the variables appear in separate terms and neither variable contains an exponent other than 1. The graphs of all linear equations are straight lines. All points on a line are solutions of the equation that is graphed.

Quadratic and Cubic Functions

A quadratic function is a polynomial equation of the second degree, generally expressed as $ax^2 + bx + c = 0$, where a, b, and c are real numbers and a is not equal to zero. Similarly, a cubic function is a polynomial equation of the third degree, usually expressed as $ax^3 + bx^2 + cx + d = 0$. Quadratic functions can be graphed using an equation or a table of values. For example, to graph $y = 3x^2 + 1$, substitute the values -1, -0.5, 0, 0.5, and 1 for x to yield the point coordinates $(-1, 4)$, $(-0.5, 1.75)$, $(0, 1)$, $(0.5, 1.75)$, and $(1, 4)$. Plot these points on a coordinate grid and connect the points in the form of a parabola. Cubic functions also can be graphed by making a table of values. The points of a cubic function from a curve. There is one point at which the curve changes from opening upward to opening downward, or vice versa, called the point of inflection.

Slope
Slope is the ratio of the rise, or vertical change, to the run, or horizontal change of a line: slope = rise/run. Slope (m) is the same for any two points on a straight line and can be found by using the coordinates of any two points on the line:

$$m = \frac{y_2 - y_1}{x_2 - x_1}, \text{ where } x_2 \neq x_1.$$

Asymptotes
An asymptote is a straight line that a curve approaches but never actually meets or crosses. Theoretically, the asymptote meets the curve at infinity. For example, in the function $f(x) = \frac{1}{x}$, two asymptotes are being approached: the line $y = 0$ and $x = 0$. See the graph of the function below.

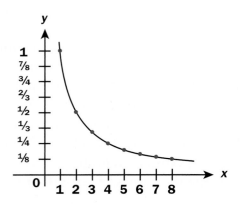

▶ Represent and analyze mathematical situations and structures using algebraic symbols

Variables and Expressions
Algebra is a language of symbols. A variable is a placeholder for a changing value. Any letter, such as x, can be used as a variable. Expressions such as $x + 2$ and $4x$ are algebraic expressions because they represent sums and/or products of variables and numbers. Usually, mathematicians avoid the use of i and e for variables because they have other mathematical meanings ($i = \sqrt{-1}$ and e is used with natural logarithms). To evaluate an algebraic expression, replace the variable or variables with known values, and then solve using order of operations. Translate verbal phrases into algebraic expressions by first defining a variable: choose a variable and a quantity for the variable to represent. In this way, algebraic expressions can be used to represent real-world situations.

Constant and Coefficient
A constant is a fixed value unlike a variable, which can change. Constants are usually represented by numbers, but they can also be represented by symbols. For example, π is a symbolic representation of the value 3.1415.... A coefficient is a constant by which a variable or other object is multiplied. For example, in the expression $7x^2 + 5x + 9$, the coefficient of x^2 is 7 and the coefficient of x is 5. The number 9 is a constant and not a coefficient.

Monomial and Polynomial
A monomial is a number, a variable, or a product of numbers and/or variables such as 3×4. An algebraic expression that

contains one or more monomials is called a polynomial. In a polynomial, there are no terms with variables in the denominator and no terms with variables under a radical sign. Polynomials can be classified by the number of terms contained in the expression. Therefore, a polynomial with two terms is called a binomial $(z^2 - 1)$, and a polynomial with three terms is called a trinomial $(2y^3 + 4y^2 - y)$. Polynomials also can be classified by their degrees. The degree of a monomial is the sum of the exponents of its variables. The degree of a nonzero constant such as 6 or 10 is 0. The constant 0 has no degree. For example, the monomial $4b^5c^2$ had a degree of 7. The degree of a polynomial is the same as that of the term with the greatest degree. For example, the polynomial $3x^4 - 2y^3 + 4y^2 - y$ has a degree of 4.

Equation

An equation is a mathematical sentence that states that two expressions are equal. The two expressions in an equation are always separated by an equal sign. When solving for a variable in an equation, you must perform the same operations on both sides of the equation in order for the mathematical sentence to remain true.

Solving Equations with Variables

To solve equations with variables on both sides, use the Addition or Subtraction Property of Equality to write an equivalent equation with the variables on the same side. For example, to solve $5x - 8 = 3x$, subtract $3x$ from each side to get $2x - 8 = 0$. Then add 8 to each side to get $2x = 8$. Finally, divide each side by 2 to find that $x = 4$.

Solving Equations with Grouping Symbols

Equations often contain grouping symbols such as parentheses or brackets. The first step in solving these equations is to use the Distributive Property to remove the grouping symbols. For example $5(x + 2) = 25$ can be changed to $5x + 10 = 25$, and then solved to find that $x = 3$.

Some equations have no solution. That is, there is no value of the variable that results in a true sentence. For such an equation, the solution set is called the null or empty set, and is represented by the symbol $\varnothing$ or {}. Other equations may have every number as the solution. An equation that is true for every value of the variable is called the identity.

Inequality

A mathematical sentence that contains the symbols < (less than), > (greater than), ≤ (less than or equal to), or ≥ (greater than or equal to) is called an inequality. For example, the statement that it is legal to drive 55 miles per hour or slower on a stretch of the highway can be shown by the sentence $s \le 55$. Inequalities with variables are called open sentences. When a variable is replaced with a number, the inequality may be true or false.

Solving Inequalities

Solving an inequality means finding values for the variable that make the inequality true. Just as with equations, when you add or subtract the same number from each side of an inequality, the inequality remains true. For example, if you add 5 to each side of the inequality $3x < 6$, the resulting inequality $3x + 5 < 11$ is also true. Adding or subtracting the same number from each side of an inequality does not affect the inequality sign. When multiplying or dividing each side of an inequality by the same positive number, the inequality remains true. In such cases, the inequality symbol does not change. When multiplying or dividing each side of an inequality by a negative number, the inequality symbol must be reversed. For example, when dividing each side of the inequality $-4x \geq -8$ by -2, the inequality sign must be changed to $\leq$ for the resulting inequality, $2x \leq 4$, to be true. Since the solutions to an inequality include all rational numbers satisfying it, inequalities have an infinite number of solutions.

Representing Inequalities on a Number Line

The solutions of inequalities can be graphed on a number line. For example, if the solution of an inequality is $x < 5$, start an arrow at 5 on the number line, and continue the arrow to the left to show all values less than 5 as the solution. Put an open circle at 5 to show that the point 5 is *not* included in the graph. Use a closed circle when graphing solutions that are greater than or equal to, or less than or equal to, a number.

Order of Operations

Solving a problem may involve using more than one operation. The answer can depend on the order in which you do the operations. To make sure that there is just one answer to a series of computations, mathematicians have agreed upon an order in which to do the operations. First simplify within the parentheses, and then evaluate any exponents. Then multiply and divide from left to right, and finally add and subtract from left to right.

Parametric Equations

Given an equation with more than one unknown, a statistician can draw conclusions about those unknown quantities through the use of parameters, independent variables that the statistician already knows something about. For example, you can find the velocity of an object if you make some assumptions about distance and time parameters.

Recursive Equations

In recursive equations, every value is determined by the previous value. You must first plug an initial value into the equation to get the first value, and then you can use the first value to determine the next one, and so on. For example, in order to determine what the population of pigeons will be in New York City in three years, you can use an equation with the birth, death, immigration, and emigration rates of the birds. Input the current population size into the equation to determine next year's population size, then repeat until you have calculated the value for which you are looking.

▶ *Use mathematical models to represent and understand quantitative relationships*

Solving Systems of Equations

Two or more equations together are called a system of equations. A system of equations can have one solution, no solution, or infinitely many solutions. One method for solving a system of equations is to graph the equations on the same coordinate plane. The coordinates of the point where the graphs intersect is the solution. In other words, the solution of a system is the ordered pair that is a solution of all equations. A more accurate way to solve a system of two equations is by using a method called substitution. Write both equations in terms of y. Replace y in the first equation with the right side of the second equation. Check the solution by graphing. You can solve a system of three equations using matrix algebra.

Graphing Inequalities

To graph an inequality, first graph the related equation, which is the boundary. All points in the shaded region are solutions of the inequality. If an inequality contains the symbol $\leq$ or $\geq$, then use a solid line to indicate that the boundary is included in the graph. If an inequality contains the symbol $<$ or $>$, then use a dashed line to indicate that the boundary is not included in the graph.

▶ *Analyze change in various contexts*

Rate of Change

A change in one quantity with respect to another quantity is called the rate of change. Rates of change can be described using slope:

$$\text{slope} = \frac{\text{change in } y}{\text{change in } x}.$$

You can find rates of change from an equation, a table, or a graph. A special type of linear equation that describes rate of change is called a direct variation. The graph of a direct variation always passes through the origin and represents a proportional situation. In the equation $y = kx$, k is called the constant of variation. It is the slope, or rate of change. As x increases in value, y increases or decreases at a constant rate k, or y varies directly with x. Another way to say this is that y is directly proportional to x. The direct variation $y = kx$ also can be written as $k = \frac{y}{x}$. In this form, you can see that the ratio of y to x is the same for any corresponding values of y and x.

Slope-Intercept Form

Equations written as $y = mx + b$, where m is the slope and b is the y-intercept, are linear equations in slope-intercept form. For example, the graph of $y = 5x - 6$ is a line that has a slope of 5 and crosses the y-axis at $(0, -6)$. Sometimes you must first write an equation in slope-intercept form before finding the slope and y-intercept. For example, the equation $2x + 3y = 15$ can be expressed in slope-intercept form by subtracting $2x$ from each side and then dividing by 3: $y = -\frac{2}{3}x + 5$, revealing a slope of $-\frac{2}{3}$ and a y-intercept of 5. You can use the slope-intercept form of an equation to graph a line easily. Graph the y-intercept and use the slope to find another point on the line, then connect the two points with a line.

Geometry

▶ *Analyze characteristics and properties of two- and three-dimensional geometric shapes and develop mathematical arguments about geometric relationships*

Angles

Two rays that have the same endpoint form an angle. The common endpoint is called the vertex, and the two rays that make up the angle are called the sides of the angle. The most common unit of measure for angles is the degree. Protractors can be used to measure angles or to draw an angle of a given measure. Angles can be classified by their degree measure. Acute angles have measures less than 90° but greater than 0°. Obtuse angles have measures greater than 90° but less than 180°. Right angles have measures of 90°.

Triangles

A triangle is a figure formed by three line segments that intersect only at their endpoints. The sum of the measures of the angles of a triangle is 180°. Triangles can be classified by their angles. An acute triangle contains all acute angles. An obtuse triangle has one obtuse angle. A right triangle has one right angle. Triangles can also be classified by their sides. A scalene triangle has no congruent sides. An isosceles triangle has at least two congruent sides. In an equilateral triangle all sides are congruent.

Quadrilaterals

A quadrilateral is a closed figure with four sides and four vertices. The segments of a quadrilateral intersect only at their endpoints. Quadrilaterals can be separated into two triangles. Since the sum of the interior angles of all triangles totals 180°, the measures of the interior angles of a quadrilateral equal 360°. Quadrilaterals are classified according to their characteristics, and include trapezoids, parallelograms, rectangles, squares, and rhombuses.

Two-Dimensional Figures

A two-dimensional figure exists within a plane and has only the dimensions of length and width. Examples of two-dimensional figures include circles and polygons. Polygons are figures that have three or more angles, including triangles, quadrilaterals, pentagons, hexagons, and many more. The sum of the angles of any polygon totals at least 180° (triangle), and each additional side adds 180° to the measure of the first three angles. The sum of the angles of a quadrilateral, for example, is 360°. The sum of the angles of a pentagon is 540°.

Three-Dimensional Figures

A plane is a two-dimensional flat surface that extends in all directions. Intersecting planes can form the edges and vertices of three-dimensional figures or solids. A polyhedron is a solid with flat surfaces that are polygons. Polyhedrons are composed of faces, edges, and vertices and are differentiated by their shape and by their number of bases. Skew lines are lines that lie in different planes. They are neither intersecting nor parallel.

Congruence

Figures that have the same size and shape are congruent. The parts of congruent triangles that match are called corresponding parts. Congruence statements are used to identify corresponding parts of congruent triangles. When writing a congruence statement, the letters must be written so that corresponding vertices appear in the same order. Corresponding parts can be used to find the measures of angles and sides in a figure that is congruent to a figure with known measures.

Similarity

If two figures have the same shape but not the same size they are called similar figures. For example, the triangles below are similar, so angles A, B, and C have the same measurements as angles D, E, and F, respectively. However, segments AB, BC, and CA do not have the same measurements as segments DE, EF, and FD, but the measures of the sides are proportional.

For example, $\dfrac{\overline{AB}}{\overline{DE}} = \dfrac{\overline{BC}}{\overline{EF}} = \dfrac{\overline{CA}}{\overline{FD}}$.

Solid figures are considered to be similar if they have the same shape and their corresponding linear measures are proportional. As with two-dimensional figures, they can be tested for similarity by comparing corresponding measures. If the compared ratios are proportional, then the figures are similar solids. Missing measures of similar solids can also be determined by using proportions.

The Pythagorean Theorem

The sides that are adjacent to a right angle are called legs. The side opposite the right angle is the hypotenuse.

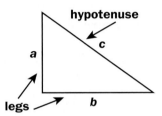

The Pythagorean Theorem describes the relationship between the lengths of the legs a and b and the hypotenuse c. It states that if a triangle is a right triangle, then the square of the length of the hypotenuse is equal to the sum of the squares of the lengths of the legs. In symbols, $c^2 = a^2 + b^2$.

Sine, Cosine, and Tangent Ratios

Trigonometry is the study of the properties of triangles. A trigonometric ratio is a ratio of the lengths of two sides of a right triangle. The most common trigonometric ratios are the sine, cosine, and tangent ratios. These ratios are abbreviated as *sin*, *cos*, and *tan*, respectively.

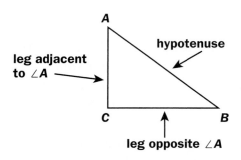

If ∠A is an acute angle of a right triangle, then

$$\sin \angle A = \frac{\text{measure of leg opposite } \angle A}{\text{measure of hypotenuse}},$$

$$\cos \angle A = \frac{\text{measure of leg adjacent to } \angle A}{\text{measure of hypotenuse}}, \text{ and}$$

$$\tan \angle A = \frac{\text{measure of leg opposite } \angle A}{\text{measure of leg adjacent to } \angle A}.$$

▶ *Specify locations and describe spatial relationships using coordinate geometry and other representational systems*

Polygons
A polygon is a simple, closed figure formed by three or more line segments. The line segments meet only at their endpoints. The points of intersection are called vertices, and the line segments are called sides. Polygons are classified by the number if sides they have. The diagonals of a polygon divide the polygon into triangles. The number of triangles formed is two less than the number of sides. To find the sum of the measures of the interior angles of any polygon, multiply the number of triangles within the polygon by 180.

That is, if *n* equals the number of sides, then $(n - 2)$ 180 gives the sum of the measures of the polygon's interior angles.

Cartesian Coordinates
In the Cartesian coordinate system, the *y*-axis extends above and below the origin and the *x*-axis extends to the right and left of the origin, which is the point at which the *x*- and *y*-axes intersect. Numbers below and to the left of the origin are negative. A point graphed on the coordinate grid is said to have an *x*-coordinate and a *y*-coordinate. For example, the point (1,–2) has as its *x*-coordinate the number 1, and has as its *y*-coordinate the number –2. This point is graphed by locating the position on the grid that is 1 unit to the right of the origin and 2 units below the origin.

The *x*-axis and the *y*-axis separate the coordinate plane into four regions, called quadrants. The axes and points located on the axes themselves are not located in any of the quadrants. The quadrants are labeled I to IV, starting in the upper right and proceeding counterclockwise. In quadrant I, both coordinates are positive. In quadrant II, the *x*-coordinate is negative and the *y*-coordinate is positive. In quadrant III, both coordinates are negative. In quadrant IV, the *x*-coordinate is positive and the *y*-coordinate is negative. A coordinate graph can be used to show algebraic relationships among numbers.

▶ *Apply transformations and use symmetry to analyze mathematical situations*

Similar Triangles and Indirect Measurement
Triangles that have the same shape but not necessarily the same dimensions are called similar triangles. Similar triangles have corresponding angles and corresponding

sides. Arcs are used to show congruent angles. If two triangles are similar, then the corresponding angles have the same measure, and the corresponding sides are proportional. Therefore, to determine the measures of the sides of similar triangles when some measures are known, proportions can be used.

Transformations

A transformation is a movement of a geometric figure. There are several types of transformations. In a translation, also called a slide, a figure is slid from one position to another without turning it. Every point of the original figure is moved the same distance and in the same direction. In a reflection, also called a flip, a figure is flipped over a line to form a mirror image. Every point of the original figure has a corresponding point on the other side of the line of symmetry. In a rotation, also called a turn, a figure is turned around a fixed point. A figure may be rotated 90° clockwise, 90° counterclockwise, or 180°. A dilation transforms each line to a parallel line whose length is a fixed multiple of the length of the original line to create a similar figure that will be either larger or smaller.

▶ *Use visualizations, spatial reasoning, and geometric modeling to solve problems*

Two-Dimensional Representations of Three-Dimensional Objects

Three-dimensional objects can be represented in a two-dimensional drawing in order to more easily determine properties such as surface area and volume. When you look at the triangular prism, you can see the orientation of its three dimensions, length, width, and height. Using

the drawing and the formulas for surface area and volume, you can easily calculate these properties.

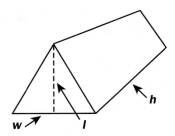

Another way to represent a three-dimensional object in a two-dimensional plane is by using a net, which is the unfolded representation. Imagine cutting the vertices of a box until it is flat then drawing an outline of it. That's a net. Most objects have more than one net, but any one can be measured to determine surface area. Below is a cube and one of its nets.

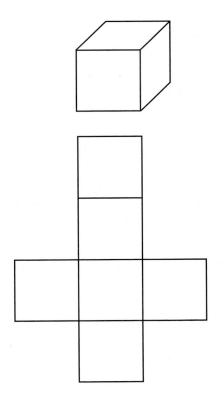

Measurement

▶ Understand measurable attributes of objects and the units, systems, and processes of measurement

Customary System

The customary system is the system of weights and measures used in the United States. The main units of weight are ounces, pounds (1 equal to 16 ounces), and tons (1 equal to 2,000 pounds). Length is typically measured in inches, feet (1 equal to 12 inches), yards (1 equal to 3 feet), and miles (1 equal to 5,280 feet), while area is measured in square feet and acres (1 equal to 43,560 square feet). Liquid is measured in cups, pints (1 equal to 2 cups), quarts (1 equal to 2 pints), and gallons (1 equal to 4 quarts). Finally, temperature is measured in degrees Fahrenheit.

Metric System

The metric system is a decimal system of weights and measurements in which the prefixes of the words for the units of measure indicate the relationships between the different measurements. In this system, the main units of weight, or mass, are grams and kilograms. Length is measured in millimeters, centimeters, meters, and kilometers, and the units of area are square millimeters, centimeters, meters, and kilometers. Liquid is typically measured in milliliters and liters, while temperature is in degrees Celsius.

Selecting Units of Measure

When measuring something, it is important to select the appropriate type and size of unit. For example, in the United States it would be appropriate when describing someone's height to use feet and inches. These units of height or length are good to use because they are in the customary system, and they are of appropriate size. In the customary system, use inches, feet, and miles for lengths and perimeters; square inches, feet, and miles for area and surface area; and cups, pints, quarts, gallons or cubic inches and feet (and less commonly miles) for volume. In the metric system use millimeters, centimeters, meters, and kilometers for lengths and perimeters; square units millimeters, centimeters, meters, and kilometers for area and surface area; and milliliters and liters for volume. Finally, always use degrees to measure angles.

▶ Apply appropriate techniques, tools, and formulas to determine measurements

Precision and Significant Digits

The precision of measurement is the exactness to which a measurement is made. Precision depends on the smallest unit of measure being used, or the precision unit. One way to record a measure is to estimate to the nearest precision unit. A more precise method is to include all of the digits that are actually measured, plus one estimated digit. The digits recorded, called significant digits, indicate the precision of the measurement. There are special rules for determining significant digits. If a number contains a decimal point, the number of significant digits is found by counting from left to right, starting with the first nonzero digit. If the number does not contain a decimal point, the number of significant digits is found by counting the digits from left to right, starting with the first digit and ending with the last nonzero digit.

Surface Area

The amount of material needed to cover the surface of a figure is called the surface area. It can be calculated by finding the area of each face and adding them together. To find the surface area of a rectangular prism, for example, the formula $S = 2lw + 2lh + 2wh$ applies. A cylinder, on the other hand, may be unrolled to reveal two circles and a rectangle. Its surface area can be determined by finding the area of the two circles, $2\pi r^2$, and adding it to the area of the rectangle, $2\pi rh$ (the length of the rectangle is the circumference of one of the circles), or $S = 2\pi r^2 + 2\pi rh$. The surface area of a pyramid is measured in a slightly different way because the sides of a pyramid are triangles that intersect at the vertex. These sides are called lateral faces and the height of each is called the slant height. The sum of their areas is the lateral area of a pyramid. The surface area of a square pyramid is the lateral area $\frac{1}{2}bh$ (area of a lateral face) times 4 (number of lateral faces), plus the area of the base. The surface area of a cone is the area of its circular base (πr^2) plus its lateral area (πrl, where l is the slant height).

Volume

Volume is the measure of space occupied by a solid region. To find the volume of a prism, the area of the base is multiplied by the measure of the height, $V = Bh$.

A solid containing several prisms can be broken down into its component prisms. Then the volume of each component can be found and the volumes added. The volume of a cylinder can be determined by finding the area of its circular base, πr^2, and then multiplying by the height of the cylinder. A pyramid has one-third the volume of a prism with the same base and height. To find the volume of a pyramid, multiply the area of the base by the pyramid's height, and then divide by 3. Simply stated, the formula for the volume of a pyramid is $V = \frac{1}{3}bh$. A cone is a three-dimensional figure with one circular base and a curved surface connecting the base and the vertex. The volume of a cone is one-third the volume of a cylinder with the same base area and height. Like a pyramid, the formula for the volume of a cone is $V = \frac{1}{3}bh$. More specifically, the formula is $V = \frac{1}{3}\pi r^2 h$.

Upper and Lower Bounds

Upper and lower bounds have to do with the accuracy of a measurement. When a measurement is given, the degree of accuracy is also stated to tell you what the upper and lower bounds of the measurement are. The upper bound is the largest possible value that a measurement could have had before being rounded down, and the lower bound is the lowest possible value it could have had before being rounded up.

Data Analysis and Probability

▶ *Formulate questions that can be addressed with data and collect, organize, and display relevant data to answer them*

Histograms

A histogram displays numerical data that have been organized into equal intervals using bars that have the same width and no space between them. While a histogram does not give exact data points, its shape shows the distribution of the data. Histograms also can be used to compare data.

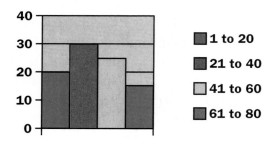

- 1 to 20
- 21 to 40
- 41 to 60
- 61 to 80

Box-and-Whisker Plot

A box-and-whisker plot displays the measures of central tendency and variation. A box is drawn around the quartile values, and whiskers extend from each quartile to the extreme data points. To make a box plot for a set of data, draw a number line that covers the range of data. Find the median, the extremes, and the upper and lower quartiles. Mark these points on the number line with bullets, then draw a box and the whiskers. The length of a whisker or box shows whether the values of the data in that part are concentrated or spread out.

Scatter Plots

A scatter plot is a graph that shows the relationship between two sets of data. In a scatter plot, two sets of data are graphed as ordered pairs on a coordinate system. Two sets of data can have a positive correlation (as *x* increases, *y* increases), a negative correlation (as *x* increases, *y* decreases), or no correlation (no obvious pattern is shown). Scatter plots can be used to spot trends, draw conclusions, and make predictions about data.

Perfect Positive Correlation

Randomization

The idea of randomization is a very important principle of statistics and the design of experiments. Data must be selected randomly to prevent bias from influencing the results. For example, you want to know the average income of people in your town but you can only use a sample of 100 individuals to make determinations about everyone. If you select 100 individuals who are all doctors, you will have a biased sample. However, if you chose a random sample of 100 people out of the phone book, you are much more likely to accurately represent average income in the town.

Statistics and Parameters

Statistics is a science that involves collecting, analyzing, and presenting data. The data can be collected in various ways—for example through a census or by making physical measurements. The data can then be analyzed by creating summary statistics, which have to do with the distribution of the data sample, including the mean, range, and standard error. They can also be illustrated in tables and graphs, like box-plots, scatter plots, and histograms. The presentation of the data typically involves describing the strength or validity of the data and what they show. For example, an analysis of ancestry of people in a city might tell you something about immigration patterns, unless the data set is very small or biased in some way, in which case it is not likely to be very accurate or useful.

Categorical and Measurement Data

When analyzing data, it is important to understand if the data is qualitative or quantitative. Categorical data is qualitative and measurement, or numerical, data is quantitative. Categorical data describes a quality of something and can be placed into different categories. For example, if you are analyzing the number of students in different grades in a school, each grade is a category. On the other hand, measurement data is continuous, like height, weight, or any other measurable variable. Measurement data can be converted into categorical data if you decide to group the data. Using height as an example, you can group the continuous data set into categories like under 5 feet, 5 feet to 5 feet 5 inches, over 5 feet five inches to 6 feet, and so on.

Univariate and Bivariate Data

In data analysis, a researcher can analyze one variable at a time or look at how multiple variables behave together. Univariate data involves only one variable, for example height in humans. You can measure the height in a population of people then plot the results in a histogram to look at how height is distributed in humans. To summarize univariate data, you can use statistics like the mean, mode, median, range, and standard deviation, which is a measure of variation. When looking at more than one variable at once, you use multivariate data. Bivariate data involves two variables. For example, you can look at height and age in humans together by gathering information on both variables from individuals in a population. You can then plot both variables in a scatter plot, look at how the variables behave in relation to each other, and create an equation that represents the relationship, also called a regression. These equations could help answer questions such as, for example, does height increase with age in humans?

▶ Select and use appropriate statistical methods to analyze data

Measures of Central Tendency

When you have a list of numerical data, it is often helpful to use one or more numbers to represent the whole set. These numbers are called measures of central tendency. Three measures of central tendency are mean, median, and mode. The mean is the sum of the data divided by the number of items in the data set. The median is the middle number of the ordered data (or the mean of the two middle numbers). The mode is the number or numbers that occur most often. These measures of central tendency allow data to be analyzed and better understood.

Measures of Spread

In statistics, measures of spread or variation are used to describe how data are distributed. The range of a set of data is the difference between the greatest and the least values of the data set. The quartiles are the values that divide the data into four equal parts. The median of data separates the set in half. Similarly, the median of the lower half of a set of data is the lower quartile. The median of the upper half of a set of data is the upper quartile. The interquartile range is the difference between the upper quartile and the lower quartile.

Line of Best Fit

When real-life data are collected, the points graphed usually do not form a straight line, but they may approximate a linear relationship. A line of best fit is a line that lies very close to most of the data points. It can be used to predict data. You also can use the equation of the best-fit line to make predictions.

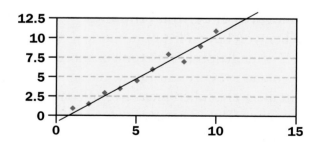

Stem and Leaf Plots

In a stem and leaf plot, numerical data are listed in ascending or descending order. The greatest place value of the data is used for the stems. The next greatest place value forms the leaves. For example,

if the least number in a set of data is 8 and the greatest number is 95, draw a vertical line and write the stems from 0 to 9 to the left of the line. Write the leaves from to the right of the line, with the corresponding stem. Next, rearrange the leaves so they are ordered from least to greatest. Then include a key or explanation, such as 1|3 = 13. Notice that the stem-and-leaf plot below is like a histogram turned on its side.

0|8
1|3 6
2|5 6 9
3|0 2 7 8
4|0 1 4 7 9
5|1 4 5 8
6|1 3 7
7|5 8
8|2 6
9|5

Key: **1|3 = 13**

▶ *Develop and evaluate inferences and predictions that are based on data*

Sampling Distribution

The sampling distribution of a population is the distribution that would result if you could take an infinite number of samples from the population, average each, and then average the averages. The more normal the distribution of the population, that is, how closely the distribution follows a bell curve, the more likely the sampling distribution will also follow a normal distribution. Furthermore, the larger the sample, the more likely it will accurately represent the entire population. For instance, you are more likely to gain more representative results from a population of 1,000 with a sample of 100 than with a sample of 2.

Validity

In statistics, validity refers to acquiring results that accurately reflect that which is being measured. In other words, it is important when performing statistical analyses, to ensure that the data are valid in that the sample being analyzed represents the population to the best extent possible. Randomization of data and using appropriate sample sizes are two important aspects of making valid inferences about a population.

▶ Understand and apply basic concepts of probability

Complementary, Mutually Exclusive Events

To understand probability theory, it is important to know if two events are mutually exclusive, or complementary: the occurrence of one event automatically implies the non-occurrence of the other. That is, two complementary events cannot both occur. If you roll a pair of dice, the event of rolling 6 and rolling doubles have an outcome in common (3, 3), so they are not mutually exclusive. If you roll (3, 3), you also roll doubles. However, the events of rolling a 9 and rolling doubles are mutually exclusive because they have no outcomes in common. If you roll a 9, you will not also roll doubles.

Independent and Dependent Events

Determining the probability of a series of events requires that you know whether the events are independent or dependent. An independent event has no influence on the occurrence of subsequent events, whereas, a dependent event does influence subsequent events. The chances that a woman's first child will be a girl are $\frac{1}{2}$, and the chances that her second child will be a girl are also $\frac{1}{2}$ because the two events are independent of each other. However, if there are 7 red marbles in a bag of 15 marbles, the chances that the first marble you pick will be red are $\frac{7}{15}$ and if you indeed pick a red marble and remove it, you have reduced the chances of picking another red marble to $\frac{6}{14}$.

Sample Space

The sample space is the group of all possible outcomes for an event. For example, if you are tossing a single six-sided die, the sample space is {1, 2, 3, 4, 5, 6}. Similarly, you can determine the sample space for the possible outcomes of two events. If you are going to toss a coin twice, the sample space is {(heads, heads), (heads, tails), (tails, heads), (tails, tails)}.

Computing the Probability of a Compound Event

If two events are independent, the outcome of one event does not influence the outcome of the second. For example, if a bag contains 2 blue and 3 red marbles, then the probability of selecting a blue marble, replacing it, and then selecting a red marble is $P(A) \times P(B) = \frac{2}{5} \times \frac{3}{5}$ or $\frac{6}{25}$.

If two events are dependent, the outcome of one event affects the outcome of the second. For example, if a bag contains 2 blue and 3 red marbles, then the probability of selecting a blue and then a red marble without replacing the first marble is $P(A) \times P(B \text{ following } A) = \frac{2}{5} \times \frac{3}{4}$ or $\frac{3}{10}$. Two events that cannot happen at the same time are mutually exclusive. For example, when you roll two number cubes, you cannot roll a sum that is both 5 and even. So, $P(A \text{ or } B) = \frac{4}{36} + \frac{18}{36}$ or $\frac{11}{18}$.

Academic Vocabulary Glossary

A

accrue Accumulate or be added periodically (p. 465)

accurate Free from error, especially as the result of care (p. 139)

affect Produce an effect upon (p. 31)

allocate Assign to a specific purpose or to particular persons or things (p. 445)

anticipate Look forward to or be prepared for (p. 156)

appropriate Especially suitable or compatible (p. 187)

archive A repository or collection, especially of information (p. 388)

author One who originates or creates (p. 389)

authority The power to influence or command thought, opinion, or behavior (p. 312)

C

cite Quote by way of example, authority, or proof (p. 334)

clarity The quality or state of being clear (p. 232)

community A body of persons of common and especially professional interests scattered through a larger society (p. 211)

compatible Capable of existing together in harmony (p. 555)

competent Having the capacity to function or develop in a particular way (p. 561)

conduct A mode or standard of personal behavior (p. 211)

conflict Disagreement, dispute, or the competitive or opposing action of incompatibles (p. 338)

contract A binding agreement between two or more persons or parties (p. 272)

contribute Play a significant part in bringing about an end or result (p. 505)

cooperate Act or work with another or others (p. 311)

cooperation The act of working together for a common benefit (p. 293)

criterion A standard on which a judgment or decision may be based; the singular form of criteria (p. 358)

crucial Of extreme importance (p. 331)

culture The set of values, conventions, or social practices associated with a particular field, activity, or societal characteristic (p. 214)

D

decline A decrease or the state of decreasing (p. 72)

determine Settle or decide by choice of alternatives or possibilities (p. 10)

develop Make active or promote the growth of (p. 291)

differentiate Mark or show a difference in or between (p. 563)

distort Twist out of the true meaning or proportion (p. 301)

E

economic Of, relating to, or based on the production, distribution, and consumption of goods and services (p. 15)

encryption The conversion of something (such as a message) into a code (p. 472)

enterprise A project or undertaking that is especially difficult, complicated, or risky (p. 83)

environment The circumstances, objects, or conditions by which one is surrounded (p. 10)

establish Put on a firm basis or into a favorable position (p. 166)

estimate Determine roughly the size, extent, or nature of (p. 403)

examine Inquire into carefully (p. 36)

exceed Be greater than or beyond a set limit (p. 448)

expose Make known (p. 364)

F

factor Something that actively contributes to the production of a result (p. 103)

federal Of, or relating to, the central government (p. 265)

fluctuate Rise and fall (p. 427)

fraudulent Intentional falsehood, deceit, or perversion of truth in order to induce another to part with something of value or to surrender a legal right (p. 433)

fundamental Basic (p. 377)

G

gene The functional unit of inheritance controlling the transmission and expression of one or more traits (p. 243)

I

incentive Something that incites or has a tendency to incite to determination or action (p. 192)

index Categorized list of documents (p. 62)

indicate Point out or point to (p. 404)

indicators Any of a group of statistical values (such as level of employment) that taken together give a view or indication of a particular thing (such as the health of the economy) (p. 428)

infer Derive as a conclusion from facts or premises (p. 347)

intermediate Being or occurring at the middle place, stage, or degree between extremes (p. 107)

interpret Explain or tell the meaning of (p. 319)

J

jargon The technical terminology or characteristic idiom of a special activity or group (p. 342)

L

logical Capable of reasoning or of using reason in an orderly cogent fashion (p. 409)

Academic Vocabulary Glossary

M

mediation Intervention between conflicting parties to promote reconciliation, settlement, or compromise (p. 300)

mental Of or relating to the mind (p. 243)

minimize Reduce or keep to a minimum (p. 155)

O

obtain Gain or attain, usually by planned action or effort (p. 517)

P

perceive Attain awareness or understanding of (p. 225)

percentage A part of a whole expressed in hundredths (p. 507)

potential Existing in possibility (p. 71)

prioritizing List or rate (as projects or goals) in order of importance (p. 446)

procedure A particular way of accomplishing something or of acting (p. 272)

process A series of actions or operations leading to an end (p. 321)

project Plan, figure, or estimate for the future (p. 452)

proprietor A person who has the legal right or exclusive title to something (p. 90)

pursue Employ measures to obtain or accomplish something (p. 105)

Q

qualification A quality or skill that fits a person (p. 131)

R

receptive Open and responsive to ideas, impressions, or suggestions (p. 225)

redeem Get back or win back (p. 466)

regulation Being under the control of law or constituted authority (p. 425)

relate Show or establish logical or causal connection between (p. 137)

require Demand as necessary or essential (p. 491)

revise Look over again in order to correct or improve (p. 249)

S

sequence Order of succession (p. 32)

shift Change the place, position, or direction of (p. 379)

signal To communicate or indicate by something (as a sound, gesture, or object) that conveys notice or warning (p. 541)

significant Having or likely to have influence or effect (p. 535)

simultaneously Existing or occurring at the same time (p. 165)

source A thing or person that provides information (p. 59)

specific Applying to, characterized by, or distinguishing something particular, special, or unique (p. 7)

statistics A quantity that is computed from a sample (p. 486)

strategy A careful plan or method (p. 185)

structure Coherent form or organization (p. 205)

supplemental Something that completes or makes an addition (p. 490)

terminate Bring something, such as a job, to an end (p. 195)

trait A distinguishing quality (as of personal character) (p. 84)

transfer Convey from one person, place, or situation to another (p. 472)

valid Meaningful or justifiable (p. 544)

violate Break a law or go against an order (p. 252)

visualize Form a mental visual image (p. 69)

vocation An occupation or career (p. 113)

Academic Vocabulary Glossary

Key Terms Glossary

A

ability A skill you have already developed (p. 40)

access Find and use (p. 408)

active listening Listening and responding with full attention to what is being said (p. 336)

addiction A physical or psychological need for a substance (p. 244)

affirmative action A policy that aims to increase the number of people who represent traditionally underrepresented groups in a field or a workplace (p. 269)

analogy A seeming similarity between one thing and another thing that are otherwise dissimilar (p. 364)

annual percentage rate (APR) The yearly cost of a loan, expressed as a percentage (p. 474)

apprentice Someone who learns how to do a job through hands-on experience under the guidance of a skilled worker (p. 113)

aptitude A potential for learning a certain skill (p. 40)

arrogance Overbearing behavior marked by excessive self-importance (p. 228)

assertive Being direct, honest, and polite (p. 228)

assistive technology Tools used to help people with special physical or mental needs (p. 380)

assumptions Beliefs you take for granted (p. 364)

attitude Your basic outlook on life and your way of looking at people and the world (p. 225)

audience Anyone who receives information (p. 333)

B

bait and switch An illegal sales practice in which a lower-priced item is used to attract customers who are then encouraged to buy a similar product at a higher price (p. 433)

balance The amount of money in your account (p. 465)

benefits Employment extras, which may include health insurance, paid vacation and holiday time, and retirement plans (p. 71)

body language The gestures, posture, and eye contact you use to send messages (p. 159)

brainstorming A problem-solving technique that involves the spontaneous creation of ideas (p. 364)

budget A plan for saving and spending money based on your income and expenses (p. 445)

C

career A series of related jobs built on a foundation of interest, knowledge, training, and experience (p. 9)

career clusters Groups of related occupations (p. 59)

career pathways Routes that lead to a particular career (p. 70)

cash-value life insurance Borrowing money against the total amount of premiums paid on a cash-value policy (p. 495)

certificate of deposit (CD) A type of investment in which you deposit an amount of money for a fixed amount of time at a stated interest rate (p. 466)

check register A record of your checking account transactions (p. 470)

civil law Law that applies to conflicts between private parties concerning rights and obligations (p. 272)

claim A formal request to an insurance company to pay for a loss (p. 487)

coinsurance A percentage of medical expenses that you are required to pay (p. 493)

collective bargaining A process through which unions use the power of their numbers (the workers in the union) to negotiate for such things as wages, benefits, pensions, and working conditions (p. 266)

collision insurance Covers the cost of repairing damage to your car caused by an accident (p. 491)

commission Earnings based on how much a person sells (p. 192)

communication The exchange of information between a sender and a receiver (p. 331)

commute Travel to get to work (p. 556)

company culture The behavior, attitudes, values, and habits of the employees and owners that are unique to each company (p. 186)

compensatory time Time off from work rather than money for working overtime (p. 265)

comprehensive insurance Insurance that covers damage to your car that is not caused by a collision (p. 491)

compromise A solution to an argument in which both sides give up something (p. 299)

computer An electronic machine that accepts, processes, and retrieves information (p. 377)

confidentiality Not talking about company business with other people (p. 213)

conflict resolution A problem-solving strategy for settling disputes and finding solutions that will allow each side to save face and create the least amount of ill feeling (p. 298)

consequence An effect or outcome (p. 361)

constructive criticism Criticism presented in a way that can help you learn and grow (p. 231)

consumer fraud Dishonest business practices used by those who are trying to trick or cheat you (p. 433)

consumers The people who buy and use goods and services. (p. 425)

contact list A list of people you know who might be helpful in your job search (p. 131)

contingency fee Payment that is a percentage of any money that you win in a lawsuit (p. 275)

continuing education Formal courses of study designed for adult students (p. 114)

cooperative program An arrangement in which local businesses team up with schools, hiring students to perform jobs that use knowledge and skills taught in their school classes (p. 65)

cooperativeness A willingness to work well with others to reach a common goal (p. 205)

copyright The legal right of authors or other creators of works to control the reproduction and use of their works and ideas (p. 389)

corporation A business, chartered by a state, that legally operates apart from the owner(s) (p. 90)

cover letter A one-page letter telling an employer who you are and why you are sending your résumé (p. 144)

credit Money you can use now and must pay back later (p. 472)

credit bureau An agency that collects information on how promptly people and businesses pay their bills (p. 475)

criminal law The form of law in which the government brings an indictment, or list of criminal charges, against a person or a business (p. 274)

criteria Standards of judgment for comparing and evaluating choices (p. 358)

cross-functional team A group of people from two or more departments working together to reach a common business goal (p. 312)

customer relations The use of communication skills to meet the needs of customers and clients (p. 332)

 D

data Information, knowledge, ideas, facts, words, symbols, figures, and statistics (p. 39)

database An organized collection of information stored on a computer (p. 385)

debt The state of owing money (p. 474)

decision-making process A series of steps that can help you identify and evaluate possibilities and make a good choice (p. 31)

deductible The set amount that you pay out of pocket before the insurance company pays anything (p. 487)

deduction A qualifying expense that you are allowed to subtract from your income for tax purposes (p. 514)

defensive Closed to other people's opinions about you or your actions (p. 231)

deposit Money that you put into your account (p. 465)

depression A severe ongoing sadness and hopelessness that makes it difficult to go about your daily life (p. 246)

desktop publishing Using a personal computer and printer to create documents that look as if they were printed by a professional printer (p. 385)

directory A computer file that contains many files on a broad topic, such as a project (p. 409)

discrimination Unequal treatment based on such factors as age, disability status, race, national origin, religion, or gender (p. 268)

diversity Variety (p. 300)

dividend The share of the profits of a fund or organization (p. 466)

down payment An amount of money, usually a percentage of the total payment, paid at the time of the purchase (p. 473)

downsizing The elimination of jobs in a company to promote efficiency or to cut costs (p. 535)

downtime Occasional periods when no tasks are scheduled (p. 404)

E

e-commerce The buying and selling of goods and services on the Internet (p. 388)

economic system The way a country utilizes the production, distribution, and consumption of goods and services (p. 425)

economics The study of how people produce, distribute, and consume goods and services (p. 425)

economy The ways in which a group produces, distributes, and consumes its goods and services (p. 15)

electronic funds transfer (EFT) The transfer of money from one bank account to another by electronic means (p. 471)

e-mail Electronic mail, a message sent over the Internet (p. 342)

emergency action plan A plan that describes what you should do to ensure your safety if a workplace emergency occurs (p. 253)

empathize Seeing things from the point of view of others and gaining an understanding of their situation (p. 293)

endorse Sign your name on the back of a check in order to obtain the amount that is represented on the face of the check (p. 470)

enthusiasm Eager interest (p. 226)

entrepreneur Someone who organizes and then runs a business (p. 83)

enunciation The speaking of each syllable clearly and separately (p. 334)

Environmental Protection Agency (EPA) The arm of the federal government that enforces environmental laws (p. 252)

ergonomics The science of designing the workplace to fit the worker (p. 250)

ethics The principles of conduct that govern a group or society (p. 211)

etiquette Having good manners in your dealings with people (p. 297)

evaluation Comparing and contrasting sets of data to rank them and determine the best choice (p. 103)

exempt employees Workers who earn a salary (p. 192)

exemption A fixed amount of money that is excused from taxes (p. 514)

exploratory interview A short, informal talk with someone who works in a career that appeals to you (p. 63)

face value The amount of money stated in the policy that your beneficiary will receive (p. 495)

facilitator A team member who coordinates the tasks so that the team works efficiently (p. 315)

felony A serious crime punishable by imprisonment or death, such as fraud, murder, or rape (p. 274)

finance charge A fee based on the amount of money you owe and the interest charged on the credit (p. 474)

financial planning Developing a strategy to meet present and long-term financial needs (p. 452)

financial responsibility Accountability in money matters (p. 452)

first aid Emergency care for an injured person (p. 255)

fixed expenses Expenses you have already agreed to pay and that must be paid by a particular date (p. 446)

flexible expenses Expenses that vary each month, such as the costs of food and entertainment (p. 446)

flextime A workplace practice in which workers construct their work schedules to suit their lives (p. 69)

Form W-2 A form that states how much money you earned, and how much was taken out for taxes (p. 509)

Form W-4 A form that tells your employer how much money to withhold for taxes from your paycheck (p. 509)

401(k) plan A retirement plan in which you put a portion of your salary into the plan (p. 467)

franchise The legal right to sell a company's goods and services in a particular area (p. 88)

free enterprise System in which individuals or businesses that may buy, sell, and set prices with little government interference (p. 425)

functional team A group of people from one department working together to reach a common business goal (p. 312)

global economy The ways in which the world's economies are linked (p. 15)

globalization The trend toward a single global market that crosses national borders (p. 380)

goodwill The loyalty of existing customers (p. 88)

Key Terms Glossary

gossip Saying negative things about people behind their backs (p. 232)

gross domestic product (GDP) The value of all goods and services produced by a country in a given time period (p. 428)

gross profit The difference between the cost of goods and their selling price (p. 91)

income statement A summary of a business's income and expenses during a specific period, such as a month, a quarter, or a year (p. 91)

income tax return A form that shows how much income you received from working and other sources, and how much tax you must pay (p. 511)

individual career plan A course of action for planning your career (p.107)

individual retirement account (IRA) A personal retirement account into which you can put a limited amount of money each year (p. 467)

inflation A rise in the price of goods and services that results in a decrease in the purchasing power of money (p. 429)

information technology The tools used to create, store, exchange, and use information (p. 377)

initiative Doing what needs to be done without being told (p. 206)

insurance A financial product that protects you against the risk of loss (p. 485)

insurance policy A legal contract between the insured, or purchaser of a policy, and the insurance company (p. 485)

interest An amount of money that is paid for the use of another's money (p. 465)

interests The things you like to do (p. 7)

Internal Revenue Service (IRS) The government agency that collects federal taxes and oversees the federal tax system (p. 511)

Internet A worldwide public system of computer networks (p. 134)

internship A short-term job or work project that usually requires formal commitment (p. 66)

interview A meeting between an employer and a job applicant to discuss possible employment (p. 155)

intonation The rising and falling tone or loudness of your voice (p. 335)

job Work that people do for pay (p. 9)

job application A form that asks questions about a job applicant's skills, work experience, education, and interests (p. 139)

job lead Information about a job opening (p. 131)

job market The demand for particular jobs (p. 15)

job shadowing Following a worker on the job for a few days (p. 65)

K

Keogh plan A investment plan where you can invest 100 percent of your earnings, up to a set amount, each year for retirement (p. 467)

L

laptop A folding, notebook-sized computer with a built-in monitor and keyboard (p. 379)

layoff A job loss that results from a business decision (p. 195)

leadership Motivating others to work toward a goal (p. 319)

leadership style How you behave when you are in charge of other people (p. 320)

learning styles The different ways that people naturally think and learn (p. 43)

lease A contract to use something for a specified period of time (p. 88)

leisure Activities you do to enjoy yourself and feel good about your life (p. 562)

liability insurance Insurance that covers damage or injury caused by you to another person or another person's property (p. 491)

life stage A period in your physical and emotional journey through life (p. 555)

lifelong learning Continuing to learn more about new technologies, new practices, and new ideas throughout your life (p. 21)

lifestyle The way you use your time, energy, and resources (p. 10)

lifestyle goals The ways you want to spend your time, energy, and resources in the future (p. 36)

M

major medical coverage A type of insurance that covers most hospital and medical expenses (p. 493)

market outlook The potential for future sales (p. 88)

marketplace Anywhere that goods and services are sold (p. 427)

Medicare A federal health insurance program that provides medical benefits for people 65 years or older, certain individuals with disabilities, and individuals with a certain type of kidney disease (p. 519)

mentor An informal teacher or guide who helps new employees adjust to their new workplace (p. 188)

minimum wage The lowest hourly wage that an employer can legally pay for a worker's services (p. 265)

misdemeanor A less serious crime, such as shoplifting or striking another worker (p. 274)

musculoskeletal disorders (MSDs) Ailments of the muscles, joints, nerves, tendons, ligaments, or spinal discs caused by forceful or repeated motions (p. 251)

MyPyramid A guideline created by the U.S. Department of Health and Human Services to show us the nutrients and other things we need for good health (p. 243)

Key Terms Glossary

net profit The amount left after operating expenses are subtracted from the gross profit (p. 91)

networking Communicating with people you know or can get to know to share information and advice about jobs (p. 131)

nonexempt employees Workers who are normally paid an hourly wage and are entitled to earn overtime (p. 192)

notice An official written statement that you are leaving a company (p. 544)

nutrients The substances in food that the body needs to produce energy and stay healthy (p. 243)

occupation The type of work you do (p. 9)

Occupational Safety and Health Administration (OSHA) The branch of the U.S. Department of Labor that sets job safety standards and inspects job sites (p. 249)

online banking Allows you to manage your money from a computer with Internet access (p. 472)

online learning Computer-based training that uses interactive technologies such as computers, CD-ROMs, and digital television (p. 111)

on-the-job training On-site instruction in how to perform a particular job (p. 112)

operating expenses The costs of doing business, such as the costs of manufacturing and selling the product (p. 91)

orientation A program that introduces you to the company's policies, procedures, values, and benefits (p. 187)

outsourcing When businesses hire other companies or individuals to produce their services or goods (p. 17)

overtime Pay received for working more than 40 hours in a week (p. 192)

parliamentary procedure A process to keep formal meetings running smoothly (p. 321)

partnership A legal arrangement in which two or more people share ownership (p. 90)

pension plan A savings plan for retirement (p. 193)

performance bonuses Bonuses that reward workers for high performance (p. 192)

performance review A meeting between you and your supervisor to evaluate how well you are doing your job (p. 194)

perseverance The quality of finishing what you start (p. 537)

Personal Academic and Career Profile A collection of documents and projects that can help you achieve the career and lifestyle you want (p. 9)

personal career profile A chart in which you can arrange side by side what you have learned about yourself and what you have learned about a career possibility (p. 104)

personal fact sheet A list of all the information about yourself that you will need for a job application form (p. 139)

personality Your unique combination of attitudes, behaviors, and characteristics (p. 42)

prejudice A negative attitude toward a person or group (p. 214)

premium The amount of money a policyholder pays for insurance (p. 486)

presentation software Software that allows you to combine text, audio, video, graphics, and Web links into a slide show (p. 385)

previewing Reading key parts of a written work that help you predict its content (p. 346)

prioritize To order the tasks to be done from first to last or from most to least important (p. 361)

probation The initial period of employment, during which your employer will monitor you closely to evaluate whether you are suited to the job (p. 194)

problem solving Using thinking skills to suggest a solution (p. 166)

procrastinate To put off deciding or doing something (p. 361)

producers Companies or individuals who make goods or provide services (p. 425)

professionalism The ability to handle problems, criticism, and pressure gracefully and maturely (p. 230)

profit-sharing plan Workers receive a share of the company's profits (p. 192)

promotion A job advancement to a position of greater responsibility and authority (p. 536)

pronunciation The way a word's vowels and consonants are spoken and its syllables are stressed (p. 334)

purpose An overall goal or reason, that causes you to say what you do (p. 332)

reconcile To make transactions and the registry of your checkbook agree (p. 471)

record keeping Organizing and maintaining records of your income and spending (p. 448)

references People who will recommend you to an employer (p. 139)

referral A recommendation from a contact who is part of your network (p. 132)

register To officially sign up as a qualified voter (p. 566)

resources Things that can be used for help and support (p. 103)

responsibility The willingness to accept an obligation and to be accountable for an action or situation (p. 207)

résumé A brief summary of your personal information, education, skills, work experience, activities, and interests (p. 140)

revenue Income from sales (p. 91)

role A set of responsibilities toward yourself and other people in a specific area of your life (p. 561)

role-playing A situation in which you are asked to play a role in an invented situation and are evaluated on the skills you display (p. 166)

S

salary A fixed amount of pay for a certain period of time, usually a month or a year (p. 192)

schedule A list or chart that shows when tasks must be completed (p. 403)

school-to-work programs Bring schools and local businesses together to give students the opportunity to gain work experience and training (p. 133)

security deposit Money you pay to cover any damage you might cause to a rental property (p. 558)

sedentary Requiring much sitting or not physically active (p. 245)

self-concept The way you see yourself (p. 42)

self-directed Responsible for choosing one's own methods of reaching one's goals (p. 313)

self-esteem Recognition and regard for yourself and your abilities (p. 226)

self-management Being able to manage your own behavior to get the results you want (p. 208)

seniority The position or prestige you achieve by working for an employer for a sustained length of time (p. 537)

service learning Programs that connect academic work with community service, allowing students to explore issues discussed in the classroom through personal experiences and community work (p. 66)

sexual harassment Any unwelcome behavior of a sexual nature (p. 270)

simplified employee pension (SEP) A retirement plan with tax advantages for individuals that is simpler to arrange than a Keogh plan (p. 467)

skills The things you know how to do (p. 7)

skimming Reading quickly through a book or a document to pick out key points (p. 346)

sleep hygiene The practice of following good sleep habits to sleep soundly and be alert during the day (p. 245)

Social Security A federal government program that helps disabled and retired people (p. 517)

Social Security number A unique number issued by the federal government that is required for all workers (p. 137)

sole proprietorship A business completely owned by one person (p. 90)

spreadsheet Computer software that arranges or "spreads" data, usually numbers, into rows and columns (p. 386)

standard English The form of writing and speaking you have learned in school (p. 138)

start-up costs The expenses involved in going into business (p. 87)

stereotype An oversimplified and distorted belief about a person or group (p. 301)

stress Mental or physical tension that is the body's natural response to conflict (p. 166)

subdirectories Smaller groupings of files within a directory (p. 409)

subject The main topic or key idea (p. 334)

summons An order to the accused party to appear in court at a specific place and time (p. 272)

 T

tact The ability to say and do things in a respectful way (p. 291)

team An organized group that has a common goal (p. 17)

team planning Setting goals, assigning roles, and communicating regularly within the team (p. 313)

technology The application of technical processes and knowledge to meet people's wants and needs (p. 377)

telecommute Work from home or an office center using a computer, fax (facsimile), and telephone to perform jobs (p. 17)

temp job A temporary job (p. 134)

temp work Short-term employment; also temporary work (p. 65)

temp-to-hire job A temporary job that becomes a permanent job after a period of evaluation by the potential employer (p. 134)

term life insurance A form of insurance that provides protection for a set number of years for your dependents in the event of your death (p. 495)

timeline A chart that shows the order in which events occur (p. 403)

total quality management (TQM) A theory of management based on continually improving product quality and customer satisfaction (p. 317)

trade school A privately run institution that trains students for a particular profession (p. 113)

transferable skills Skills that you can use in many different situations (p. 7)

 U

utilities Services for your home that can include electricity, heat, sanitation, and water (p. 556)

 V

values Your beliefs and principles. (p. 37)

vocational-technical center A school that offers a variety of skills-oriented programs, such as courses in automotive or computer technology (p. 113)

vote Choose leaders or decide on initiatives (p. 566)

wage A fixed amount of money paid to a worker for a set amount of time spent working (p. 192)

warranty A guarantee that a product meets certain standards of quality (p. 432)

whole life insurance A type of cash-value life insurance that provides protection throughout your life as long as the premiums are paid (p. 495)

withdrawal Money that you take from your account (p. 465)

withhold To deduct money from your paychecks to pay income tax due on your wages (p. 507)

word processing Using any software that creates text-based documents (p. 385)

work credits Measurements of how long you have worked and the amount of your earnings (p. 518)

work environment Your physical and social surroundings at work (p. 69)

work permit A document that shows you are allowed to work in the United States (p. 138)

workers' compensation An insurance program that provides financial help to cover lost wages and medical expenses for employees who are injured on the job (p. 249)

A

ability/habilidad Destreza que ya has desarrollado

access/tener acceso a Hallar y usar información

active listening/escucha activa Implica escuchar con suma atención y responder a lo que se dice

addiction/adicción Necesidad física o sicológica de una sustancia

affirmative action/acción afirmativa Política que pretende incrementar el número de personas que representa a grupos con tradicionalmente poca representación en un campo o sitio de trabajo

analogy/analogía Aparente similaridad entre dos cosas que son en cierta forma desiguales

annual percentage rate (APR)/tasa de porcentaje anual Costo anual del préstamo, expresada como un porcentaje

apprentice/aprendiz Alguien que aprende cómo hacer un trabajo por medio de experiencia directa bajo la guía de un trabajador calificado

aptitude/aptitud Potencial para aprender determinadas destrezas

arrogance/arrogancia Comportamiento autoritario caracterizado por excesiva autoimportancia

assertive/afirmativo Directo, honesto, y cortés

assistive technology/tecnología asistencial Instrumentos para ayudar a personas con necesidades físicas o mentales especiales a desenvolverse mejor en un trabajo

assumptions/suposiciones Creencias que damos por sentado, por hechos reales

attitude/actitud Tu visión básica de la vida y tu manera de ver a la gente y el mundo

audience/audiencia Cualquiera persona que recibe información

B

bait and switch/(táctica de) enganche y cambio Práctica ilegal de ventas en la que un artículo más barato es usado para atraer a los clientes antes de ser después estimulados a comprar un producto similar a más alto precio

balance/saldo Cantidad de dinero que hay en tu cuenta

benefits/beneficios Suplementos en un empleo, que pueden incluir seguros de salud, vacaciones pagas y días festivos, y planes de retiro

body language/lenguaje corporal Gestos, postura, y contacto visual que usas al expresarte

brainstorm/análisis creativo Técnica de resolución de problemas que implica la creación espontánea de ideas

budget/presupuesto Plan para ahorrar y gastar el dinero basado en tus ingresos y gastos

C

career/carrera Serie de trabajos
u ocupaciones relacionados
cimentados sobre una base de interés,
conocimiento, entrenamiento y
experiencia

career clusters/ramas ocupacionales
Grupos de ocupaciones relacionadas

career pathways/senderos ocupacionales
Rutas que te conducen a una carrera
en particular

**cash-value life insurance/seguro de vida
de valor efectivo** Tomar prestado
dinero contra la suma total de primas
pagadas en una póliza de este tipo

**certificate of deposit (CD)/certificado de
depósito** Tipo de inversión en la que
depositas una suma de dinero por un
tiempo determinado fijo a una cierta
tasa de interés

check register/registro de cheques Cédula
o libro donde llevas la cuenta de tus
transacciones de cheques

civil law/derecho civil Ley que se aplica a
conflictos entre individuos referentes
a derechos y obligaciones

claim/demanda Reclamación formal
ante una compañía de seguro para que
pague por una pérdida

coinsurance/coaseguro Porcentaje de los
gastos médicos que se requiere que
pagues

collective bargaining/regateo colectivo
Proceso mediante el cual las uniones
usan el poder de sus números
(trabajadores en la unión) para
discutir con la administración de una
compañía aspectos como sueldos,
beneficios, pensiones, y condiciones
de trabajo

collision insurance/seguro para choques
Póliza que cubre el costo de reparar
los daños causados a tu auto a causa
de un accidente

commission/comisión Pago basado en
cuánto una persona vende

communication/comunicación
Intercambio de información entre
alguien que la envía y otro que la
recibe

commute/viajar Utilizar medios de
transporte público para asistir a un
empleo o centro laboral

company culture/cultura corporativa
Comportamiento, actitudes, valores
y hábitos de los empleados y
propietarios que son únicos en cada
compañía

compensatory time/tiempo compensatorio
Tiempo libre del trabajo en lugar de
pagar dinero por trabajar tiempo
suplementario

comprehensive insurance/seguro general
Seguro que cubre daños a tu carro no
causados por un choque

compromise/compromiso Ceder dos
partes en algo para llegar a un
acuerdo

computer/computadora Máquina electrónica que acepta, procesa y recobra información

confidentiality/confidencialidad No hablar sobre los asuntos de una compañía con otras personas

conflict resolution/resolución de conflictos Estrategia para solucionar disputas y hallar soluciones que le permitan a las dos partes no quedar mal, así como minimizar la mala sangre entre éstas

consequence/consecuencia Efecto o resultado (de una decisión o acción, etc)

constructive criticism/crítica constructiva Crítica presentada de forma que pueda ayudarte a aprender y mejorar, crecer

consumer fraud/fraude al consumidor Prácticas deshonestas de negocios usadas para tratar de engañarte o estafarte

consumers/consumidores La gente que compra y usa bienes y servicios

contact list/lista de contactos Lista de personas conocidas que pudieran ser útiles en tu búsqueda de un empleo

contingency fee/tarifa de contingencia Pago a un abogado de un porcentaje del dinero que ganas en un proceso judicial

continuing education/educación continua Cursos formales de estudio concebidos para estudiantes adultos

cooperative program/programa cooperativo Acuerdo por medio del cual negocios locales se asocian con escuelas, reclutando a estudiantes para realizar trabajos que utilizan conocimientos y destrezas enseñados en clases

cooperativeness/cooperatividad Voluntad para trabajar con los demás para alcanzar una meta común

copyright/derechos de autor o propiedad intelectual Derecho legal de un autor u otro creador de un trabajo para controlar la reproducción y el uso de sus obras e ideas

corporation/corporación Negocio fundado a nivel estatal que opera legalmente e independientemente de su(s) propietario(s)

cover letter/carta de presentación Carta breve que te presenta a un empleador y explica por qué le estás enviando tu curriculum vitae (résumé)

credit/crédito Dinero que puedes usar ahora y tienes que pagar después

credit bureau/buró de crédito Agencia que colecta información sobre cuán a tiempo individuos y negocios pagan sus deudas

criminal law/derecho penal Tipo de ley por la cual el gobierno presenta una acusación, o lista de cargos criminales, contra una persona o un negocio

criteria/criterios Normas de juicio para comparar y evaluar opciones y/o preferencias

cross-functional team/equipo funcional cruzado Grupo de gente de dos o más departamentos que trabajan juntos para alcanzar una meta laboral común

customer relations/relaciones con los clientes Uso de las destrezas comunicativas para satisfacer las necesidades de los clientes

data/datos Información, conocimiento, ideas, hechos, palabras, símbolos, cifras y estadísticas

database/base de datos Colección organizada de información almacenada en una computadora

debt/deuda El hecho de deber dinero

decision-making process/proceso de toma de decisión Serie de pasos que te pueden ayudar a identificar y evaluar las posibilidades para tomar una buena decisión

deductible/deducible Cantidad establecida que pagas antes que la compañía de seguro pague nada

deduction/deducción Gasto calificado que se te permite sustraer de tus ingresos

defensive/defensivo Cerrado a las opiniones de los demás sobre ti o tus acciones

deposit/depósito Dinero que pones en una cuenta

depression/depresión Amargura y desesperanza severa y sostenida que hace difícil proseguir la vida diaria

desktop publishing/autoedición Uso de una computadora personal y de una impresora para crear documentos que lucen como si hubieran sido producidos en una imprenta profesional

directory/directorio Archivo de una computadora que contiene muchos archivos sobre un tema amplio y determinado, como en un proyecto

discrimination/discriminación Tratamiento desigual basado en factores tales como la edad, la situación de deshabilitación, la raza, la nacionalidad, la religión o el género

diversity/diversidad Variedad

dividend/dividendo Acción o cuota de las ganancias de un capital u organización

down payment/anticipo, pago inicial Suma de dinero, generalmente un porcentaje del pago total, que se paga en el momento de la compra

downsizing/recorte (de personal) Eliminación de empleos en una compañía para promover la eficiencia o reducir los costos

downtime/tiempo muerto Períodos ocasionales en que no hay tareas programadas

e-commerce/comercio electrónico Compra y venta de bienes y servicios en el Internet

economic system/sistema económico Forma en que un país utiliza la producción, la distribución y el consumo de bienes y servicios

economics/economía El estudio de cómo la gente produce, distribuye, y consume bienes y servicios

economy/economía Forma en que un grupo produce, distribuye y consume sus bienes y servicios

electronic funds transfer (EFT)/ transferencia electrónica de fondos Traspaso de dinero de una cuenta bancaria a otra por medios electrónicos

e-mail/correo electrónico Mensaje enviado por medio del Internet

emergency action plan/plan de emergencia Plan que describe lo que debes hacer para garantizar tu seguridad si ocurre una emergencia en el sitio de trabajo

empathize/ponerse en el lugar de alguien Tratar de ver las cosas desde el punto de vista de otra persona y lograr comprender su situación

endorse/endosar Firmar tu nombre detrás de un cheque para recibir la cantidad estipulada en el frente del mismo

enthusiasm/entusiasmo Mostrar gran interés

entrepreneur/empresario Persona que organiza y dirige un negocio

enunciation/enunciación Dicción clara y separada de cada sílaba

Environmental Protection Agency (EPA)/Agencia de Protección del Medio Ambiente Rama del gobierno federal que hace cumplir las leyes medioambientales

ergonomics/ergonomía Ciencia de diseñar un sitio de trabajo adecuado para el trabajador

ethics/ética Principios de conducta que gobierna a un grupo o sociedad

etiquette/etiqueta Mostrar buenos ademanes al tratar a la gente

evaluation/evaluación Comparación y contraste de datos e información para clasificarlos y determinar la mejor opción

exempt employees/empleados exentos Trabajadores que ganan un salario

exemption/exención Suma fija de dinero que es excusada de impuestos

exploratory interview/entrevista exploratoria Conversación corta, informal con alguien que trabaja en una carrera que te resulta atractiva

face value/valor nominal Suma de dinero declarada en la póliza que recibirá tu beneficiario

facilitator/facilitador Miembro del equipo que coordina las tareas para que el equipo trabaje eficazmente

felony/felonía Un crimen serio castigable con encarcelamiento o la muerte, como fraude, asesinato, o violación sexual

finance charge/cargo financiero Tarifa basada en la cantidad de dinero que debes y el interés que te cobran por el crédito

financial planning/planeamiento financiero Desarrollar una estrategia para satisfacer las necesidades financieras actuales y a largo plazo

financial responsibility/responsabilidad financiera Tus obligaciones en asuntos monetarios

first aid/primeros auxilios Cuidado de emergencia a una persona lesionada

fixed expenses/gastos fijos Gastos que ya has acordado pagar y que deben ser pagados para una fecha determinada

flexible expenses/gastos flexibles Gastos que varían todos los meses, como el costo de la comida y el entretenimiento

flextime/tiempo flexible Práctica laboral por medio de la cual los trabajadores conforman horarios de trabajo adaptados a sus vidas

Form W-2/Formulario W-2 Formulario que indica cuánto ganaste y cuánto te retuvieron por razones de impuestos

Form W-4/Formulario W-4 Formulario que le dice a tu empleador cuánto dinero de tu salario debe retener por razones de impuestos

401(k) plan/plan 401(k) Plan de retiro en el cual depositas una porción de tu salario

franchise/sucursal Derecho legal para vender los bienes y servicios de una compañía en un área en particular

free enterprise/libre empresa Cuando individuos o negocios pueden comprar, vender, y establecer precios con escasa interferencia del gobierno

functional team/equipo funcional Grupo de gente de un departamento que trabaja junta para alcanzar una meta laboral común

global economy/economía global Forma en que están acopladas las economías mundiales

globalization/globalización Tendencia hacia un mercado global único que trasciende las fronteras nacionales

goodwill/clientela fiel Lealtad de los actuales clientes de un negocio que es uno de sus activos más valiosos

gossip/chismorreo Decir cosas malas de la gente por detrás de sus espaldas

gross domestic product (GDP)/producto bruto interno Valor de todos los bienes y servicios producidos por un país en un período de tiempo dado

gross profit/ganancias brutas Diferencia entre el costo de los bienes y su precio de venta

I

income statement/declaración de impuestos Sumario de las ganancias y gastos de un negocio durante un tiempo específico, como un mes, un trimestre, o un año

income tax return/declaración de ganancias Formulario que muestra cuántos ingresos recibiste por trabajar y otras fuentes, y cuántos impuestos tienes que pagar

individual career plan/plan ocupacional individual Línea de acción para planear tu carrera

individual retirement account (IRA)/cuenta de retiro individual "IRA" Cuenta de retiro personal en la cual puedes depositar una suma limitada de dinero todos los años

inflation/inflación Incremento en el precio de bienes y servicios que resulta en una disminución del poder de compra del dinero

information technology/tecnología de la información Instrumentos de trabajo usados para crear, archivar, intercambiar y usar información

initiative/iniciativa Hacer lo que sea necesario sin que haya que decírtelo

insurance/seguro Producto que te protege contra el riesgo de alguna pérdida

insurance policy/póliza de seguro Contrato legal entre el asegurado, o comprador de una póliza, y la compañía de seguro

interest/interés Suma de dinero que se paga por usar el dinero de otro/s

interests/intereses Lo que te gusta hacer

Internal Revenue Service (IRS)/(Ministerio de) Hacienda Agencia gubernamental que colecta impuestos federales y supervisa el sistema federal de impuestos

Internet/Internet Sistema público mundial de redes de computadoras

internship/puesto de interno Proyecto de empleo o trabajo a corto plazo que usualmente requiere un compromiso

interview/entrevista Reunión entre un empleador y un solicitante de trabajo para discutir la posibilidad de ser empleado

intonation/entonación Forma en que sube y baja el tono y la sonoridad de la voz

 J

job/empleo Trabajo que haces por un pago

job application/formulario de empleo Hoja en la que hacen preguntas sobre las destrezas, la experiencia laboral, la educación y los intereses de un solicitante de trabajo

job lead/pista de empleo Información sobre un trabajo que está disponible

job market/mercado laboral Demanda de determinados empleos

job shadowing/hacer sombra en un empleo Seguir los pasos de un trabajador en su empleo por varios días

Keogh plan/plan "Keogh" Inversión de un 100% de tus ingresos todos los años, hasta una cantidad predeterminada, para tu retiro

laptop/laptop, computadora portátil Computadora plegable tamaño cuaderno con monitor y teclado incorporados

layoff/cesantía Pérdida de un empleo como resultado de la decisión de un negocio

leadership/liderazgo Consiste en motivar a otros a trabajar para alcanzar una meta

leadership style/estilo dirigente (de un líder) Cómo actúas cuando estás a cargo de otras personas

learning styles/estilos de aprendizaje Diferentes formas en que la gente piensa y aprende naturalmente

lease/arrendamiento Contrato para usar algo por un período de tiempo determinado

leisure/ocio Actividades que realizas para divertirte tú mismo/a para sentirte a gusto sobre tu vida

liability insurance/seguro contra terceros Seguro que cubre heridas a otra persona, o daños a la propiedad de otra persona, causados par ti

life stage/etapa de (la) vida Período de tu viaje físico y emocional por la vida

lifelong learning/aprendizaje de por vida Continuar aprendiendo más acerca de nuevas tecnologías, nuevas prácticas, y nuevas ideas a través de tu vida

lifestyle/estilo de vida Forma en que usas tu tiempo, energía, y recursos

lifestyle goals/metas del estilo de vida Forma en que quieres emplear tu tiempo, energía y recursos en el futuro

major medical coverage/cobertura médica global Tipo de seguro que cubre la mayor parte de los hospitales y gastos médicos

market outlook/perspectiva mercantil Potencial para futuras ventas

marketplace/mercado Cualquier sitio donde se venden bienes y servicios

Medicare/"Medicare" Programa federal de seguro de la salud que proporciona beneficios médicos a gente de 65 años de edad o más, a ciertos individuos con deshabilidades, y a individuos con cierto tipo de enfermedad renal

mentor/mentor Maestro o guía informal que ayuda a los nuevos empleados a ajustarse a su nuevo sitio de trabajo

minimum wage/sueldo mínimo El sueldo por horas más bajo que paga un empleador por los servicios de un trabajador

misdemeanor/infracción, delito menor Un crimen menos serio, como robar en una tienda o pegarle a otro trabajador

musculoskeletal disorders (MSDs)/ trastornos osteomusculares Aquejos en los músculos, las articulaciones, los nervios, los tendones, los ligamentos, o las vértebras causados por movimientos forzados o repetidos

MyPyramid/MiPirámide Guía creada por el Departamento Norteamericano de Salud y Servicios Humanos para mostrarnos los nutrimentos y otras cosas que necesitamos para mantener una buena salud

net profit/ganancias netas Cantidad de dinero que queda después que los gastos operacionales son deducidos de las ganancias brutas

networking/conexiones Comunicación con personas conocidas o que conoces para compartir información y consejos sobre empleos

nonexempt employees/empleados no- exentos Trabajadores a los que se les paga normalmente un sueldo por horas y que tienen derecho a recibir tiempo suplementario

notice/aviso Declaración oficial escrita para informarle a una compañía que vas a dejarla

nutrients/nutrimentos Sustancias en las comidas que necesita el cuerpo para producir energía y mantenerse saludable

occupation/ocupación Tipo de trabajo que haces

Occupational Safety and Health Administration (OSHA)/Administración de la Salud y la Seguridad Ocupacional Rama del Departamento Norteamericano del Trabajo que establece y hace cumplir las normas de seguridad laboral e inspecciona los sitios de trabajo

online banking/transacciones bancarias en línea Administrar tu dinero desde una computadora con acceso al Internet

online learning/aprender en línea Entrenamiento computarizado que usa tecnología interactiva, como computadoras, CD-ROMs, y televisión digital

on-the-job training/entrenamiento laboral Instrucción práctica en un sitio sobre cómo realizar un trabajo determinado

operating expenses/gastos operacionales Costos de mantener un negocio, como los costos de fabricación y venta de un producto

orientation/orientación Programa que te presenta las normas, procedimientos, valores y beneficios de una compañía

outsourcing/subcontratar Cuando los negocios contratan a otras compañías o individuos para producir sus servicios o bienes

overtime/tiempo suplementario Pago recibido por trabajar más de 40 horas por semana

parliamentary procedure/procedimiento parlamentario Reglas estrictas del orden que siguen muchas organizaciones

partnership/consorcio Acuerdo legal por el cual dos o más personas comparten propiedad

pension plan/plan de pensiones Plan de ahorros para el retiro

performance bonuses/bonos de rendimiento Bonos para premiar a los trabajadores que obtienen altos niveles de desempeño

performance review/revisión de rendimiento Reunión entre tú y tu supervisor para evaluar cuán bien estás haciendo tu trabajo

perseverance/perseverancia Cualidad de terminar lo que empiezas

Personal Academic and Career Portfolio/ Cartera Académica y Ocupacional Personal Colección de documentos y proyectos que pueden ayudarte a lograr la carrera y el estilo de vida que quieres

personal career profile/perfil ocupacional de una persona Gráfica en la que comparas lo que has aprendido sobre ti mismo/a y lo que has aprendido sobre una posibilidad ocupacional en particular

personal fact sheet/hoja de datos personales Lista de toda la información sobre tu persona que necesitarás para llenar un formulario de empleo

personality/personalidad Tu combinación única de actitudes, comportamientos y características

prejudice/prejuicio Actitud negativa hacia una persona o un grupo

premium/prima Suma de dinero que paga un asegurado por una póliza de seguro

presentation software/programas computarizados de presentación Programa que permite combinar texto, audio, video, gráficas, y conexiones del "Web" en una demostración de diapositivas para acompañar una presentación oral

previewing/previsualizar Leer partes esenciales de un trabajo escrito para ayudar a predecir su contenido

prioritize/priorizar Ordenar las tareas que debemos hacer de primera a última o de más a menos importante

probation/a prueba Período inicial de empleo durante el cual tu patrón te controlará de cerca para evaluar si eres la persona adecuada para ese trabajo

problem solving/solución de problemas Uso de destrezas mentales para sugerir una solución

procrastinate/procrastinar (aplazar) Diferir al tomar una decisión o hacer algo uno

producers/productores Compañías o individuos que producen bienes o proveen servicios

professionalism/profesionalismo Habilidad para enfrentar problemas, críticas, y presión con distinción y madurez

profit-sharing plan/plan de participación en las ganancias Cuando los trabajadores reciben una parte de los ingresos de una compañía

promotion/promoción Avance en un empleo a una posición de mayor responsabilidad y autoridad

pronunciation/pronunciación Forma en que se dicen las vocales y consonantes de una palabra y cómo son acentuadas las sílabas

purpose/propósito Razón o meta global que tiene una persona cuando habla

R

reconcile/conciliar Hacer que coincidan las transacciones y/en tu libro de cheques

record keeping/registros Organización y mantenimiento de datos sobre tus ingresos y gastos

references/referencias Personas que te recomendarán a un empleador

referral/recomendación Alabanza que te da un contacto que forma parte de tus conexiones

register/registrarse Anotarse oficialmente como votante calificado

resources/recursos Cosas que pueden ser utilizadas como ayuda y apoyo

responsibility/responsabilidad Voluntad de aceptar una obligación y de ser responsable por una acción o situación

résumé/"curriculum vitae" Breve sumario de la información personal, educación, destrezas, experiencia laboral, actividades e intereses de un solicitante de empleo

revenue/ingresos Entradas, ganancias por motivo de ventas

role/papel Conjunto de responsabilidades para contigo mismo y para con otra gente en un área específica de tu vida

role-playing/jugar un papel Cuando se te pide que desempeñes un papel en una situación inventada y eres evaluado/a según las destrezas que demuestres

S

salary/salario Cantidad fija de pago recibida por un cierto período de tiempo, usualmente un mes o un año

schedule /horario Lista o gráfico que muestra cuándo tienen que ser completadas ciertas labores

school-to-work programs/programa escolar-laboral Programa que reúne a escuelas y negocios locales para darles a los estudiantes la oportunidad de recibir entrenamiento y experiencia laboral muy valiosos

security deposit/depósito de garantía Dinero que pagas para cubrir cualquier daño que puedas causarle a la propiedad

sedentary/sedentario Que permanece sentado mucho tiempo o no está físicamente activo

self-concept/concepto propio Forma en que te ves tú mismo/a

self-directed / autodirigido Responsable de escoger sus propios métodos para alcanzar sus metas

self-esteem/autoestimación Ser capaz de dirigir tu propia conducta con vistas a obtener los resultados que deseas

self-management/autogestión Hacer todo lo que sea necesario para edificar la carrera que quieres

seniority/senioridad Posición de prestigio que consigues al trabajar para un empleador por un período ininterrumpido de tiempo

service learning/aprendizaje práctico Programa que combina el trabajo académico con servicios comunitarios, permitiéndole a los estudiantes explorar asuntos claves discutidos en la sala de clases por medio de experiencias personales y trabajo comunitario

sexual harassment/hostigamiento sexual Cualquier comportamiento desagradable de naturaleza sexual

simplified employee pension (SEP)/pensión simplificada del empleado Plan de retiro individual con ventajas fiscales, más simple de planear que un plan Keogh

skills/destrezas Lo que sabes hacer

skimming/ojear Leer rápidamente a través de un libro o documento para hacer resaltar sus puntos claves

sleep hygiene/higiene del sueño Práctica de seguir buenos hábitos para dormir y poder hacerlo profundamente y así poder mantenerte alerta durante el día

Social Security/Seguro Social Programa del gobierno federal que ayuda a los deshabilitados y a personas retiradas y a sus familias

Social Security number/número del Seguro Social Número exclusivo de nueve cifras emitido por el gobierno federal que es requerido para todos los trabajadores

sole proprietorship/propiedad única Negocio que pertenece completamente a una sola persona

spreadsheet/hoja electrónica de cálculo Programa de computadoras que ordena o expande datos, usualmente números, en filas y columnas

standard English/inglés corriente Tipo de inglés regular que enseñan en las escuelas

start-up costs/costos iniciales Gastos relacionados con empezar un negocio

stereotype/estereotipo Creencia simplista y distorsionada acerca de una persona o grupo

stress/estrés Tensión mental o física como respuesta natural del cuerpo ante un conflicto

subdirectories/subdirectorios Agrupación menor de archivos dentro de un directorio

subject/asunto Tópico principal o idea clave

summons/citación Orden para personarse en la corte en un lugar y a una hora específicos

tact/tacto La habilidad de decir y hacer las cosas de una manera respetuosa

team/equipo Grupo organizado con una meta común

team planning/planeamiento de equipo Incluye establecer metas, designar responsabilidades, y comunicarse regularmente

technology/tecnología Aplicación de procesos y conocimientos técnicos para satisfacer los deseos y necesidades de la gente

telecommute/teletrabajo Trabajar desde la casa o en un centro de oficinas, usando tecnología como computadoras, facsímil (fax), teléfonos celulares, y teléfonos para realizar un trabajo

temp job/empleo temporal Empleo que no es permanente

temp work/trabajo temporal Empleo a corto plazo; también empleo temporal

temp-to-hire job/empleo temporal-a-contratado Empleo temporal que se convierte en empleo permanente tras un período evaluativo del empleador potencial

term life insurance/seguro de vida a plazo fijo Forma de seguro que proporciona protección por un número determinado de años para tus familiares dependientes en caso que mueras

timeline/cuadro horario Gráfico que muestra el orden en que ocurren los acontecimientos

total quality management (TQM)/gerencia total de calidad Teoría administrativa basada en mejorar continuamente la calidad de los productos y la satisfacción de los clientes

trade school/escuela de oficios Institución privada que entrena a sus estudiantes para una profesión específica

transferable skills/destrezas transferibles Destrezas que puedes usar en muchas situaciones diferentes

utilities/utilidades Servicios para tu casa que pueden incluir la electricidad, la calefacción, el saneamiento, y el agua

values/valores Tus creencias y principios

vocational-technical center/centro técnico-vocacional Escuela que ofrece una variedad de programas orientados de destrezas, como cursos en tecnología automotriz o de computadoras

vote/voto Escoger a los líderes o decidir sobre qué iniciativas tomar

wage/sueldo Cantidad fija de dinero que se le paga a un trabajador por un determinado tiempo de trabajo efectivo

warranty/garantía Aval de que un producto cumple con ciertas normas de calidad

whole life insurance/seguro de por vida Tipo de seguro de valor efectivo que proporciona protección de por vida mientras que las primas sigan siendo pagadas

withdrawal/retiro de fondos Dinero que sacas de una cuenta

withhold/retener Deducir dinero de tu salario para cubrir impuestos a las ganancias que debes de tu paga

word processing/tratamiento de texto Programa de computadoras que crea documentos basados esencialmente en texto

work credits/créditos laborales Medidas de cuánto tiempo has trabajado y cuánto has ganado, cuáles han sido tus ingresos

work environment/ambiente laboral Tu entorno físico y social en el trabajo

work permit/permiso de trabajo Documento que muestra que te está permitido trabajar en los Estados Unidos

workers' compensation/compensación laboral Programa de seguros que provee ayuda financiera para ayudar a cubrir sueldos perdidos y gastos médicos de empleados que se lesionan en el trabajo

Index

Index

Index

Index

Photo Credits and Figure Sources

Cover Photography Credits: Shown clockwise left to right: Bill Frymire/Masterfile; Michael Malyszko/Getty Images; Jack Hollingsworth/Photodisc Green (RF)/Getty Images; John Lund/Drew Kelly/Blend Images (RF)/Getty Images; Holger Winkler/zefa/Corbis

Photography Credits: 2-3 Paul Barton/Corbis; **4-5** Lucidio Studio, Inc./Alamy; **7** Adrian Sherratt / Alamy; **8** J A Giordano/Corbis/SABA; **10** Royalty-free/Getty Images; **15** Henry Westheim Photography / Alamy; **16** G. Baden/zefa/Corbis; **v, 18**(c) David Sanger Photography/Alamy; **18**(t) Royalty-free/Corbis; **v, 18**(b) The Image Bank/Getty Images; **21** Ronnie Kaufman/Corbis; **28-29** Royalty-free/Age Fotostock; **31** Royalty-free/Corbis; **33** David Young Wolff/PhotoEdit; **36** The Image Bank/Getty Images; **38** Royalty-free/Alamy; **40** Peter Beck/Corbis; **54-55** Blend Images/SuperStock RF; **vi, 56-57** E. Klawitter/Corbis; **59** Erik Dreyer/Getty Images; **62** Blend Images/Alamy; **64** Andreas Altwein/DPA/Corbis; **65** Gabe Palmer/Corbis; **69** Jaume Gual/Age Fotostock; **73** Royalty-free/Age Fotostock; **80-81** Royalty-free/Getty Images; **84** The Image Bank/Getty Images; **87** Royalty-free/Corbis; **88** Scott Wilson/Getty Images; **89**(tl) Bob Schatz/International Stock; **100-101** ICIMAGE/Alamy; **103** Jon Feingersh/Masterfile; **107** Big Cheese Photo/SuperStock; **109**(bc) LWA-Dann Tardif/Corbis; **110**(t) Stockbyte/SuperStock; **110**(c) G. Braden/zefa/Corbis; **110**(b) Masterfile; **112** Getty Images; **124** Phil Boorman/Getty Images; **vii, 126-127** Age Fotostock RF; **128-129** Royalty-free/Age Fotostock; **131** Taxi/Getty Images; **133** Royalty-free/Age Fotostock; **134** Royalty-free/Getty Images; **137** Stone/Getty Images; **152-153** Royalty-free/Alamy; **155** Royalty-free/Corbis; **157** Royalty-free/Alamy; **159**(t) Royalty-free/Getty Images; **160**(t) Royalty-free/SuperStock; **160**(c) Royalty-free/Getty Images; **160**(b) Royalty-free/Getty Images; **163** Royalty-free/Alamy; **167** Kwame Zikomo/SuperStock; **178** Veer/Royalty-free; **180-181** BananaStock RF/Jupiter Images; **182-183** Royalty-free/SuperStock; **vii, 185** Royalty-free/Getty Images; **186** Jack Sullivan/Alamy; **193** Royalty-free/Corbis; **202-203** Antonio Mo/Getty Images; **205** Royalty-free/Getty Images; **207** Kevin Foy/Alamy; **208** Jolanda Cats & Hans/Corbis; **215** Taxi/Getty Images; **222-223** Chuch Savage/Corbis; **225** Veer RF; **227** Royalty-free/Age Fotostock; **230** Visions of America, LLC/Alamy; **233** Masterfile; **240-241** Royalty-free/Getty Images; **245** Royalty-free/Alamy; **246** ImageState/Alamy; **249** Holger Winkler/zefa/Corbis; **251** Ryan McVay/Photodisc Green RF/Getty Images; **253** Najiah Feanny/Corbis; **262-263** Paul A. Souders/Corbis; **265** Bonnie Kamin/PhotoEdit; **266** Royalty-free/Alamy; **268** Gary Cameron/Reuters/Corbis; **272** Royalty-free/Alamy; **274** Royalty-free/Corbis; **ix, 284** Blend Images RF/Jupiter Images; **286-287** Masterfile/Royalty-free; **288-289** Paul Barton/Corbis; **291** Alex Mares-Manton/Getty Images; **294** Rick Gomez/Masterfile; **297** Royalty-free/Corbis; **300** Royalty-free/Alamy; **308-309** Masterfile/Royalty-free; **311** Banana-Stock/SuperStock; **313** Kevin Dodge/Corbis; **314** Manfred Bauman/Age Fotostock; **316** Jim West/Alamy; **x, 319** Jon Feingersh/Masterfile; **328-329** Ariel Skelley/Corbis; **xi, 331, 333** Yellow Dog Productions/Getty Images; Pixtal/SuperStock RF; **335** Stockbyte/SuperStock RF; **337** Corbis Royalty-free; **338** Tim Boyle/Getty Images News; **341** David Young Wolff/Getty Images; **354-355** Tom Stewart/Corbis; **357** Stuart Pearce/Age Fotostock; **358** Bob Daemmrich/PhotoEdit; **360**(t) Corbis Royalty-free; **360**(c) Bonnie Kamin/PhotoEdit; **360**(b) Jose Luis Pelaez/Blend Images RF/Getty Images; **363** Masterfile Royalty-free (RF); **365** Digital Vision Ltd./SuperStock RF; **374-375** Jim Craigmyle/Corbis; **377** Michael Rosenfeld/Getty Images; **379** Simon Marcus/Corbis; **381** David Young Wolff/PhotoEdit; **382** Steve McAlister/Getty Images; **388** Stefan/Zaklin/Getty Images; **390** Ariel Skelley/Corbis; **xii, 398** Jeff Rotman/Getty Images; **401** Gabe Palmer/Corbis; **408** Chris Hondros/Getty Images; **418** Peter M. Fisher/Corbis; **420-421** Mike Chew/Corbis; **422-423** Corbis Royalty-free; **425** Tim Mosenfelder/Getty Images; **427** Owen Franken/Corbis; **428** Reuters/Corbis; **429** Peter M. Fisher/Corbis; **432** Anna Lundgren/SuperStock; **442-443** eStock/Royalty-free; **445** Digital Vision Ltd./SuperStock RF; **449** Stockbyte/SuperStock RF; **452** Masterfile Royalty-free (RF); **454** Jerzy Dabrowski/Corbis; **462-463** Ariel Skelley/Corbis; **465** Stephen Beaudet/zefa/Corbis; **xiii, 469** Masterfile Royalty-free; **473** Bettmann/Corbis; **474** Ed Lallo/Index Stock; **xiv, 482-483** Stockbyte/SuperStock RF; **485** Stewart Cohen/Blend Images RF/Getty Images; **486** Stockbyte RF/SuperStock; **490** Digital Vision Ltd./SuperStock RF; **493** Michael A. Keller/zefa/Corbis; **502-503** Masterfile Royalty-free; **505** Mike Powell/Getty Images; **506** Bill Aron/PhotoEdit; **509** Corbis/Royalty-free; **514** Artifacts Images/Photodisc Red RF/Getty Images; **517** Jose Luis Pelaez/Getty Images; **52** Yang Liu/Corbis; **528** Royalty-free/Corbis; **530-531** Age Fotostock RF; **532-533** Charles Gupton/Corbis; **535** Ed Lallo/Index Stock; **537** Image Source RF/Getty Images; **541** Anton Vengo/SuperStock; **543** Jose Luis Pelaez/Corbis; **544** Bahar Yurukoglu/zefa/Corbis; **552-553** Alexander Walter/Photodisc Red RF/Getty Images; **xv, 555** David Young Wolff/PhotoEdit; **559** Stockbyte/SuperStock RF; **561** Will Hart/PhotoEdit; **562** Manchan/Getty Images RF; **563** Brand X/SuperStock RF; **564** Ed Bock/Corbis; **565** David Young Wolff/PhotoEdit; **567** Royalty-free/Corbis; **576** Jon Feingersh/zefa/Corbis.

Figure Sources: Figure 1.1, American Consumer Spending (11): Consumer Expenditures Survey; **Figure 9.1,** Commonly Observed Unethical Behavior (211): Ethics Resource Center (ERC); **Figure 11.1,** MyPyramid (243): http://www.MyPyramid.gov, United States Department of Agriculture (USDA); **Figure 12.1,** Changes in Employment in the Civilian Workforce (269): U.S. Census Bureau, 2000 and U.S. Department of Labor, Bureau of Labor Statistics, 2006.

MEREDITH COLLEGE

0 1234 0117207 7

DATE DUE

GAYLORD			PRINTED IN U.S.A.